The New Book of

POPULAR SCIENCE

The New Book of POPULAR SCIENCE

1

Astronomy

Space Science

Mathematics

Past and Future

Index

GROLIER

An imprint of

SCHOLASTIC

Library of Congress Cataloging-in-Publication Data

The new book of popular science.
        p. cm.
    Includes bibliographical references and index.
    ISBN 0–7172–1225–4 (set)
        1. Science—Encyclopedias, Juvenile. 2. Technology—
Encyclopedias, Juvenile. 3. Medicine—Encyclopedias, Juvenile.
4. Science—Popular works. 5. Technology—Popular works.
6. Medicine, Popular. I. Scholastic Library Publishing.

Q163.N55 2006
503—dc22
                                                2005029898

CONTRIBUTORS

BENJAMIN F. ABELL, M.S., *Professor of Meteorology and Aviation Sciences, Parks College of St. Louis University, Cahokia, Illinois*

DARRYL ABRIOLA, Ph.D., *Medical writer*

ELISABETH ACHELIS, *Former President, World Calendar Association, Inc.*

JOHN G. ALBRIGHT, Ph.D., *Former Chairman, Department of Physics, University of Rhode Island*

JOANNE M. ALEXANDROVICH, Ph.D., *Professor, University of South Indiana, Evansville, Indiana*

FIKRI ALICAN, M.D., *Assistant Professor of Surgery, The University of Mississippi Medical Center, Jackson*

KENNETH ANDERSON, *Science writer*

LAURA ANDERSSON, Ph.D., *Department of Chemistry, Vassar College*

STANLEY W. ANGRIST, Ph.D., *Department of Mechanical Engineering, Carnegie-Mellon University*

ELIAS M. AWAD, M.B.A., M.A., *Associate Professor, Graduate School of Business, DePaul University*

S. HOWARD BARTLEY, Ph.D., *Professor of Psychology, Michigan State University*

J. FREMONT BATEMAN, M.D., *Former Superintendent, Columbus State Hospital, Columbus, Ohio*

W. W. BAUER, M.D., *Former consultant in health education; former Director, Department of Health Education, American Medical Association*

LOUISE BAXTER, Ph.D., *Department of Biological Sciences, Central Washington University, Ellensburg, Washington*

CHARLES BEICHMAN, Ph.D., *Astronomer, Department of Astrophysics, California Institute of Technology*

LYMAN BENSON, *Professor Emeritus of Botany, Pomona College; author, Cacti of the United States and Canada*

SUE BERKMAN, *Freelance writer specializing in medicine*

M. H. BERRY, M.S., *Chairman, Division of Science and Mathematics, and Professor of Botany, West Liberty State College*

CHRISTOPHER J. BISE, Ph.D., *Assistant Professor of Mining Engineering, College of Earth & Mineral Sciences, Pennsylvania State University*

JAMES A. BLACKMAN, M.D., M.P.H., *Professor of Pediatrics, University of Virginia; Director of Research, Kluge Children's Rehabilitation Center, Charlottesville, VA*

WILLIAM BLAIR, Ph.D., *Astronomer and research scientist, Department of Physics and Astronomy, Johns Hopkins University, Baltimore*

NICHOLAS T. BOBROVNIKOV, Ph.D., *Professor Emeritus, Astronomy, Ohio State University; former Director, Perkins Observatory*

BART J. BOK, Ph.D., *Chairman, Astronomy Department, University of Arizona*

YVONNE BONNAFOUS, *Science writer*

BARBARA BRANCA, *Science writer*

FRANKLYN M. BRANLEY, Ph.D., *Astronomer, American Museum of Natural History—Hayden Planetarium*

DEBBIE BRONK, Ph.D., *Assistant Professor, University of Georgia, Department of Marine Sciences*

JEFF BRUNE, M.S., *Science writer and former editor,* Discover *magazine*

BRYAN H. BUNCH, *President, Scientific Publishing, Inc.*

ALAN C. BURTON, Ph.D., *Professor of Biophysics, The University of Western Ontario Faculty of Medicine*

CHARLES F. CALEY, Pharm.D., BCPP, *Associate Clinical Professor, University of Connecticut, Storrs, and Burlingame Research Center Institute of Living, Hartford, CT*

ANTHONY J. CASTAGNO, M.A., *President, The Rowe Group*

JANE CHESNUTT, *Editor, Environmental Information Center*

CLYDE M. CHRISTENSEN, Ph.D., *Professor of Plant Pathology, University of Minnesota*

JAMES E. CHURCHILL, JR., *Freelance writer*

DANIEL M. COHEN, Ph.D., *Laboratory Director, Ichthyological Laboratory, Bureau of Commercial Fisheries, U.S. Fish and Wildlife Service*

DEBORAH M. COLLIER, *Technical Information Specialist, Centers for Disease Control and Prevention*

JOSEPH G. COWLEY, *Research Institute of America*

WILLIAM J. CROMIE, *Executive Director, Council for the Advancement of Science Writing*

F. JOE CROSSWHITE, Ph.D., *Associate Professor of Mathematics Education, Ohio State University*

BRUCE DAVIES, *Account Executive, Michael Bobrin Public Relations/Advertising*

GODE DAVIS, *Freelance writer*

JERRY DENNIS, *Freelance writer; author:* The Living Great Lakes, It's Raining Frogs and Fishes, *and* From a Wooden Canoe

GERARD De VAUCOULEURS, Ph.D., *Professor, Department of Astronomy, University of Texas*

JOSEPH DeVITO, *Freelance writer based in East Rockaway, New York*

HERBERT S. DIAMOND, M.D., *Chairman, Department of Medicine, Western Pennsylvania Hospital, Pittsburgh*

DAVID DOOLING, *Research Associate, Essex Corporation; former science editor,* The Huntsville " (Alabama)" Times

ROY DUBISCH, Ph.D., *Professor, Department of Mathematics, University of Washington*

BETH DWORETZKY, M.S., *Research Analyst, Woods Hole, Massachusetts*

GUIDE TO
THE NEW BOOK OF POPULAR SCIENCE

The middle- to high-school years have always been a period of tremendous discovery for students. This can prove particularly so in the sciences, where deepening understanding opens up a whole new world of wonder—from the physics that holds our universe together to the dynamics of our own bodies, our place in the larger biosphere, and the very elements that make us what we are. Too often, however, the reverse proves true, when plodding texts and bewildering content kill interest in the sciences instead of kindling it.

This is where *The New Book of Popular Science* steps in. Authored by many of North America's leading science writers, the articles in the set's six volumes engage and entertain without sacrificing the depth of understanding needed to keep pace in the 21st century—be it as a college-bound student or as any other responsible citizen of the world. No dreary listing of facts and theorems, every crafted article addresses satisfactorily the most relevant question of all: "How does this information affect me?" Written in clear, jargon-free language, the hundreds of articles in this set also stand ready as quick reference for the interested and curious of all ages and backgrounds.

This engaging, readily understood approach taken by *The New Book of Popular Science* does not come at the cost of the latest in scientific thinking. As writers continually update and rewrite the 14 sections that build this set, they do so under the close supervision and review of scientists at North America's leading universities, each with an eye to educating students in the vital basics of his or her field of interest.

As a result, the arrangement of articles in each section provides a logical, step-by-step presentation of subject matter in specific fields of scientific study. At the same time, each article constitutes a unit in itself—a well-rounded introduction to a particular topic. Subheads within each article give readers a concise overview of content, with related topics of special interest set in inviting, colorful sidebars. Throughout the text, metric equivalents accompany standard measurements, helping readers to solidify their association between the units of everyday life and the International System of Units employed by scientists worldwide.

As a simple, cursory look through these volumes will reveal, vivid illustrations have become a more prominent feature of *The New Book of Popular Science* than ever before, with more than one-third of the set devoted to descriptive art and photography, nearly all pieces in full color. The grandeur of an iceberg, the violence of a volcano, the power of an earthquake, the terror of a tsunami—all spring to life through vivid photography. Complex concepts in chemistry and physics become simple, and the human body discloses its astounding organization in clear, eye-catching diagrams. Electron micrographs of viruses and bacteria and underwater photographs of newly discovered deep-sea habitats promise to take readers to barely imagined realms. Throughout, the illustrations complement adjoining text to explain, expand, and beautify the reader's experience. Especially popular with librarians, teachers, and students are the set's many contemporary articles on careers in the sciences, with comprehensive descriptions of both the history and future of each field, as well as clear outlines of 21st-century educational requirements and job opportunities. For readers wishing to delve still deeper into specific subjects, the editors have provided Selected Readings, placed at the end of each volume, with recommended books and accompanying evaluations. Wrapping up each volume, an alphabetical index to the full set enables quick reference to specific topics, keywords, and notable scientists.

ASTRONOMY and SPACE SCIENCE   Vol. 1

From the Big Bang to the International Space Station, the Astronomy and Space Science section takes the reader on a tour of the universe and humankind's heroic efforts to study and explore it. The section opens with one of the set's most popular career overviews, "Astronomers and Their Science." Next, we examine the latest equipment and methods applied to study the heavens today, from the Hubble Space Telescope to the Very Large Array radio telescope in New Mexico. We then begin in-depth study of our solar system and its Sun, planets, moons, comets, asteroids, and meteors. Moving out, deeper into space, we encounter the stars and galaxies, their exotic supernovas and black holes, quasars, and brown dwarfs. Finally comes the space program, manned and unmanned—where we have been and where we are going. The section concludes with the search for life on other planets.

MATHEMATICS   Vol. 1

The 17 articles of the Mathematics section provide a thorough grounding in the many applications of numerical calculation being used today. First comes an overview of all of mathematics, its most famous practitioners, and the field's career opportunities. The focus then turns to numerals—the symbols we use to represent numbers—and the many systems employed before the Arabic notation system became the standard. Subsequent articles explore, in turn, the basic mathematical operations known as arithmetic; algebra's substitution of numbers by letters; geometry's study of shapes, both plane (two-dimensional) and solid (in three dimensions); trigonometry (triangle measurement); analytical geometry (expression of geometric figures in algebraic terms); and non-Euclidean geometry. The section wraps up with articles on applied mathematics—namely, the fields of statistics, probability, game theory, calculus, set theory, binary numerals, and accounting.

PAST and FUTURE   Vol. 1

What has come before and what awaits us: these are the topics that concern the new Past and Future section. The first article offers an in-depth examination of archaeology, the study of the human past through the analysis of the material remains that peoples and societies leave behind. The section then narrows its focus, examining the methods and discoveries of the ancient astronomers, and their influence on our perceptions of time, with special emphasis on the evolution of the calendar. Then we delve even further back with an examination of paleontology—the study of fossils—and a fascinating survey of prehistoric animals. Finally, we fast-forward to what tomorrow may hold in the dynamic "Science Fiction," and the always fascinating "Forensic Science."

EARTH SCIENCES   Vol. 2

Awesome forces shape our world—forces that build mountains, drive hurricanes, and shake land and water. Earth scientists study these powerful forces, as well as the gentler but no less intractable phenomena of changing tides, tumbling snowflakes, and rippling auroras. The Earth Sciences section presents the diverse marvels of Earth, sky, and sea in a logical sequence that begins with the birth of our planet and the formation of its interior and crust. We explore the planet's tectonic plates and related agents of geologic change—earthquakes, volcanoes, erosion, and glaciers. Also examined are the dynamic landforms of mountains, plateaus, rivers, lakes, caves, and many others. Next comes the atmosphere and the forces of wind, lightning, hurricanes, tornadoes, clouds, and precipitation. We enter the oceans to explore their mysterious currents, unfathomable depths, and today's unprecedented deep-sea discoveries. Throughout this section, articles about geologists, meteorologists, oceanographers, geographers, and other Earth scientists invite us to share the history and diversity of their fields and future opportunities for Earth scientists in training.

ENERGY   Vol. 2

From water mills and windmills to nuclear reactors and geothermal energy, the story of civilization is also the story of humankind's quest for new and more-powerful sources of energy. The Energy section opens with an overview of how energy is generated, captured, and harnessed, how the quantity of this useful energy has skyrocketed over the centuries, and how scientists predict our energy needs will change in the future. Next, the section focuses on the production of the most technologically useful of all energy forms—electricity. Subsequent articles delve deeper into our most important sources of energy, from fossil fuels—petroleum, natural gas, and coal—to the ever-controversial nuclear energy. Other articles examine hydroelectricity, solar power, and geothermal energy. The section concludes with a comprehensive survey of the alternative-energy sources that promise to play an increasingly important role in the 21st century and beyond.

ENVIRONMENTAL SCIENCES   Vol. 2

What kind of planet will we pass to future generations? What must we understand in our efforts to wisely steward the only home humankind has ever known? The Environmental Sciences section begins with an overview of conservation, the science of environmental protection, and the sustainable use of natural resources. Subsequent articles guide the reader through the ways water and wind shape our world and toward an understanding of the unsurpassed importance of our planet's water supply. Today, of course, humans have themselves become a major force for environmental change, sometimes for the worse. Consequently, the Environmental Sciences section delves deeply into the threats of ground, water, and air pollution, including the serious phenomenon of acid rain. The final third of Environmental Sciences presents an informed look at some of the most pressing issues facing present and future generations: climate change, waste disposal, and the preservation of endangered species and the wild habitats required for their survival.

CHEMISTRY   Vol. 3

A grain of sand, a drop of water, a living cell—all things living and nonliving ultimately reduce down to one or more of 92 naturally occurring chemical elements. The Chemistry section opens with an overview of chemists at work, past and present, that illustrates how these scientists have shaped modern life and will, in great measure, influence our future. From this introduction, the 21 articles of the Chemistry section build logically from the study of matter to our evolving understanding of that basic unit of all matter—the atom. Subsequent articles take readers on a tour of the chemical elements and their families, the nature of chemical bonds, and the formulas and equations used to describe them and their powerful reactions. Readers will likewise explore the different states of matter—solid, liquid, and gas—and the unique qualities of acids, bases, and salts. After a thorough grounding in the forces behind oxidation, reduction, and electrochemistry, the section introduces the vital subdisciplines of organic chemistry, biochemistry, nuclear chemistry, and analytical chemistry. The Chemistry section wraps up with a highly practical overview of laboratory techniques and measurement.

PHYSICS

In the words of physicist Richard Feynman, "Nature is a great chess game being played by gods, which we are privileged to watch." The rules of that game, Feynman liked to explain, make up the science of physics. The 27 articles of the Physics section investigate the forces that relate energy and matter, beginning with an overview of physicists and their science. The section also profiles the two physicists who largely defined classical and modern physics with their revolutionary theories—Isaac Newton and Albert Einstein. Other articles explore the nature of electricity, its relationship to magnetism and electromagnetic radiation, and the aesthetic phenomena of sound, optics, and color. Delving into the strange world of atomic physics, readers also examine elementary particles, quarks, radioisotopes, and quantum theory. The section concludes with an overview of the futuristic field of superconductors.

BIOLOGY

What is life . . . and how do we study it, exploit it, and protect it on the enduring biosphere we call Earth? The Biology section takes readers through an overview of life on our planet, then focuses on the realm of viruses (Are they alive?), microbiology, and the classification of living things. After a solid grounding in genetics and heredity, readers explore the structure, dynamics, and division of individual cells, then expand their understanding of the reproduction and embryology of multicellular organisms such as ourselves. Not to be neglected is life's anticlimax, as described in "Aging, Death, and Decomposition." The section then moves on to the life science of ecology, with special focus on populations and communities, ecosystems, biomes, and the biosphere. The section closes with evolutionary biology and a practical "handbook" on experimental biology and guide to safe laboratory techniques.

PLANT LIFE

The Plant Life section explores the solar-powered "green machines" that imbue our planet with oxygen, food, and beauty. Considering the basic question "What Is a Plant?," readers gain an understanding of the fundamental process of photosynthesis before touring the realm of photosynthetic organisms, from the Kingdom Monera to the more-familiar true plants. A separate article introduces the "plantlike" kingdom of fungi. Following an overview of botanical classification, individual articles introduce the major phyla, from mosses through flowering plants. Readers broaden their understanding of the plant world with articles on plant succession and communities, as well as an intriguing exploration of plant behavior and some of the plant kingdom's more unusual species, including carnivorous plants. Throughout this section, articles on botanists, foresters, horticulturists, and agronomists invite students to explore career opportunities in these and other related fields.

ANIMAL LIFE

From protists to prehistoric animals, the 48 articles of the Animal Life section begin our exploration of the mind-boggling diversity of life that constitutes the Kingdoms Protista and Animalia. The section opens with an overview of zoologists and their science, before answering the fundamental questions of what distinguishes the life-forms we call "animal" and what determines their behavior. The important subdivisions within this large section include the invertebrates, with special emphasis on insects, the most numerous and prolific animals on Earth. Readers also explore the primitive chordates before moving on to the world of fishes—jawless, cartilaginous, and bony. An overview of herpetologists and herpetology opens a subsection on amphibians and reptiles. "Ornithologists and their Science" introduces 10 articles on birds. Wrapping up the Animal Life section is a piece on veterinary science, followed by an in-depth examination of places people go to view animals—"Zoos, Aquariums, and Wildlife Parks"—and concluding with a fond look at the animals most closely associated with humans: "Pets."

MAMMALS   Vol. 5

Picking up where Volume 4 left off, the Mammals section explores the powerful, fragile, beautiful, terrible, graceful, and often cunning class of animals that includes our own species. After opening with an overview of the Class Mammalia, the section focuses sequentially on the 20 orders within this fascinating group, from the strange egg-laying monotremes and pouched marsupials through the diverse primates. The Order Carnivora receives special attention with featured articles on the families of dog, cat, weasel, and the civets, mongooses, and hyenas. The often-domesticated ungulates—the horses; rhino; pigs and hippos; camels and llamas; deer; giraffes; antelope; and the closely related bison, buffalo, and oxen—each receive individual treatment. Finally, "Primates" takes an intriguing look at our closest cousins.

HUMAN SCIENCES   Vol. 5

The species *Homo sapiens* warrants its own section of 17 articles that span the study of human evolution, anatomy, health, nutrition, medicine, and the brave new world of bionics, or artificial body parts. The Human Sciences section opens with a discussion of what distinguishes our species from all others, then turns to a structural overview and in-depth analysis of the human body and its systems, with additional articles focusing on human heredity, reproduction, and birth. A large medical subsection explores nutrition; exercise and fitness; sleep; physical, mental, and learning disorders; new and emerging medical technologies; and the workaday worlds of physicians and nurses. The section concludes with an overview of alternative medicine as an increasingly popular avenue of healing.

TECHNOLOGY   Vol. 6

The expanded volume covering technology first presents a sweeping overview of the advance of technology across the ages, from the chiseling of the first Stone Age ax to the genetic engineering of new life-forms. From this introduction, the volume opens its first subsection—Construction and Engineering—by exploring the fundamental human activity of shelter-building. The Agriculture subsection explores the modern farm, the rapidly advancing science of agricultural genetics, modern-day food processing, and "aquaculture," or fishing and fish farming. The eight articles making up the Transportation subsection explore the means by which we move our goods and ourselves from place to place. Materials and Manufacturing encompasses the technologies of metalworking, factories, robots and automation, and the chemical industry, with special emphasis on plastics, polymers, ceramics, fiber optics, and other modern materials. Communication comes alive with articles tracing the invention and development of such innovations as the telephone, television, cellular technology, and the Internet—precisely those technologies that have shrunk our world into a single global community. The Communication unit concludes with a "how-to" article on science projects and fairs, and an in-depth survey of science education. Finally, the volume explores nanotechnology, lasers, particle accelerators, computers, and other high-tech tools used by scientists conducting research on the edge of tomorrow.

VOLUME 1

Contents

What Is Science?   1 – 7

Astronomy and Space Science   8 – 325

Mathematics   326 – 459

Past and Future   460 – 516

Index

WHAT IS SCIENCE?

Science is knowledge, and knowledge is power, declared the philosopher Francis Bacon more than 350 years ago. Science, by definition, is also much more. Knowledge becomes *scientific* only when someone finds relationships and meaning in the facts. A typical telephone book, for example, contains more than 100,000 pieces of information. But all that information doesn't make it a science book.

To put it another way, science attempts to make sense of the world around us by combining observed facts with reasoning. We see this clearly in the process known as the scientific method. The scientific method begins with observation. Next, the scientist develops a reasonable explanation for the observed facts. Finally, the scientist must rigorously test his or her proposed explanation.

Imagine, for example, that you discover a new kind of bird. Let's also say that you see it feeding on a particular kind of flower and only that kind of flower. You might then conclude, "Bird X feeds only on the blossoms of Plant Y."

But this observation does not constitute a scientific result. In fact, what you have is an idea, or *hypothesis*, which needs testing. To do so, you must design an appropriate investigation or experiment. Your investigation might involve observing greater numbers of these newly discovered birds. You would also want to observe them in different loca-

tions, at various times of the day, and even in different seasons. In the process, you would collect an abundance of information, or data, to check against your hypothesis. Does your original conclusion hold true? (Does Bird X feed only on Plant Y?) Only after following all of these steps of observation, reasoning, and testing, does an idea become "scientific."

SCIENCE EVOLVES

Another important quality of science is that of progress. With further study, answers that at first appeared simple often turn out to be complicated. You might discover, for example, that Bird X feeds only on the flowers of Plant Y, except when it is caring for its young. At that time,

For some, the majesty of science becomes a reality at monumental exhibitions in great urban centers. For others, bird-watching by a secluded pond on a quiet afternoon is all that it takes.

enabled people to predict the coming and going of seasons according to calendars. They also made a simple model of the universe that placed our own planet at the center, with the Sun and all the stars orbiting it.

It took hundreds of years of observation and scientific reasoning to reveal the more complex model of the universe that astronomers hold today. Earth, we now know, does not stand at the center of the universe, or even at the center of our solar system. In reality, our planet and many others orbit around the Sun, which itself is just one of billions of stars in the galaxy we call the Milky Way, one of countless galaxies in a vastly larger universe. Moreover, modern-day astronomers realize that they have barely begun to fathom the mysteries of our universe, which brings us to another essential quality of science. Science, by its nature, remains "unfinished business." There is always something more—indeed, much more—to learn.

Weighing oneself yields an objective result—no personal beliefs, opinions, or tastes influence the outcome. Similarly, scientists have known for years that the results of a valid experiment should be the same for anyone performing the same experiment using the identical procedure.

it instinctively seeks out the pollen of Plant Z, which it carries back to the nest to feed its young. This continued observation of Bird X has revealed new and potentially important information about this species.

While scientific knowledge often builds upon itself in this way, at times scientific investigation disproves previously held ideas. A great example of this can be seen in astronomy, one of the oldest fields of science. Thousands of years ago, humans began noticing that stars and constellations (groups of stars) rose above the horizon a bit earlier each night, before "traveling" across the sky at a steady rate. Eventually, they realized that after about 365 days, every star and constellation was back in the same place in the sky at the same time of night. From these observations, early skywatchers developed scientific ideas about our universe and how it operated. They developed the concept of a "year," which

SCIENCE IS OBJECTIVE

Science, together with art, religion, and philosophy, have been called the four major achievements of the human mind. What distinguishes science from these other major fields of study?

In a word: objectivity. Science depends on objective methods and produces objective results. By objective, we mean something that does not depend on personal beliefs, opinions, or tastes. A recipe, for example, is a set of objective instructions because it does not depend on the cook's personal preferences. Anyone following the recipe should produce the same result. Contrast this with a half dozen cooks each creating a soup according to his or her tastes.

Similarly, a well-designed scientific experiment produces the same result no matter where, when, or by whom it is performed (so long as it is consistently performed in the correct manner). Scientific results must likewise be objective. That is, they should appear the same to any reasonable person.

Art, by contrast, expresses personal feelings and produces results unique to each artist. Moreover, people judge the value of art subjectively. What is beautiful to one person may be unappealing to another. Religion is another subjective pursuit: it involves deeply held beliefs and highly personal ideas about the world around us. Furthermore, religious beliefs, by their nature, rely more on "faith" in the unseen than objective examination and testing. Philosophy, like science, calls for careful reasoning. But like religion and art, philosophy centers on individual beliefs and expresses the philosopher's personal perspectives about the world.

What science, philosophy, art, and religion all share is an attempt to give "meaning" to the world around us. Each field pursues this goal in different ways and with different results. Yet they do not necessarily contradict one another. Indeed, many of the world's greatest scientists have been great philosophers, artists, or religious scholars.

Scientists need data to formulate theories. Monitoring devices used to track birds and other animals can provide the scientist with an enormous amount of information.

And yet all good scientists—past and present, in every field of study—share common principles and methods of investigation. Above all, perhaps, successful scientists must know how to ask meaningful questions. This may be what sets the scientifically minded person apart from those who take the workings of the world "for granted." Good scientists continually question how things happen and why things take the forms that they do. Indeed, virtually all scientific inventions—from the first telescope to modern-day electron microscopes—stem from the scientist's desire and need to look farther, closer, deeper, and in different ways than previously possible.

THE MAJOR FIELDS OF SCIENCE

Astronomy. The oldest of all the sciences may be astronomy. No doubt, humans have been gazing at the stars since prehistoric times. The methodical study of star movements began

THE MANY METHODS OF SCIENCE

The term "scientific method" refers to a specific set of steps for developing and testing a scientific idea. But it would be misleading to say there is just one way to advance scientific knowledge. Different fields of science use different techniques, from the chemist analyzing a compound with a gas chromatograph in the laboratory to the medical researcher interviewing patients in a hospital. Scientific techniques also change over time. Compare, for example, ancient astronomers whose only instrument was the naked eye with modern astronomers armed with space-based telescopes that capture not only the visible light of heavenly objects, but also their electromagnetic emanations.

Computers have revolutionized science. Using computer simulation, scientists can ascertain the performance of a spacesuit under a variety of conditions—and without a human subject.

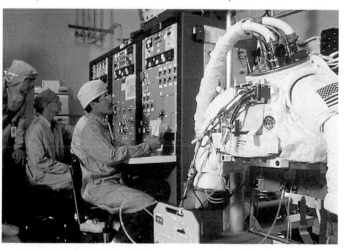

Careers in Scientific Research

For many people, the term "scientist" brings to mind the picture of someone in a white lab coat bending over a microscope or other high-tech laboratory device. Certainly, many scientists pursue their research in this manner. Others can be found climbing mountains, diving into oceans, braving sub-freezing polar temperatures, slashing their way through dense jungle, or pursuing their research in urban hospitals, at suburban office parks, or on rural farms. Indeed, scientists can be found in almost every work setting imaginable. But wherever they pursue their research, scientists bring similar qualities and goals to their work.

The first is a driving curiosity about the subject of their research, be it a star, flower, rock, or disease. It is fair to say that most successful research scientists spent their childhood asking lots of questions. A research scientist must likewise be able to be objective—that is, interested in uncovering the facts regardless of whether they fit with his or her preconceived ideas. Finally, add accuracy and diligence to the qualities a research scientist must have to succeed.

Today, virtually all scientific researchers have one or more college degrees in their chosen field of study. In preparing for college, students interested in a research career should take as many science courses as they can during middle school and high school. A student with a strong interest in a particular field may choose to emphasize courses in that area. But all science students need a basic foundation of mathematics, biology, chemistry, and physics. Familiarity and skill

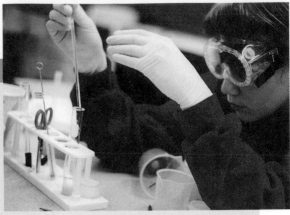

Laboratory courses emphasize the scientific techniques and procedures that students must know in order to find a research position in their chosen field.

with computers have likewise become vitally important to scientific studies.

Generally speaking, a bachelor of science degree (four years of college) qualifies a graduate to work as an entry-level researcher or technologist, assisting more-experienced scientists. Most career researchers combine such entry-level work with two to five years of graduate training in their particular field of interest. Gaining entry to a respected graduate program in science tends to be highly competitive, and acceptance is just the beginning of years of demanding work.

At one time, most research scientists worked for universities or government-sponsored research institutions. Today, just as many are employed in private industry, where they help produce the newest medicines and develop commercial and industrial products. Scientists also work for world-health and wildlife conservation organizations, for which they lend their scientific expertise to the betterment of humankind and the natural world on which it depends.

---

some 6,000 years ago in the Middle East. Over the next 1,000 years, astronomers there charted the cycles of hundreds of stars as well as the movements of our Sun and Moon. Around 3000 B.C., the Egyptians used this knowledge to develop the first calendars and simple clocks. Modern astronomy includes not only observation of the heavens, but also the investigation of the physical forces that form and move stars, planets, moons, and the like. Astronomy, then, is

the study of the physical laws, motions, materials, origins, and fate of all celestial bodies.

Space Science. The much newer field of space science goes beyond simply observing the heavens to physically exploring them. Space science is the stuff of rockets, satellites, space probes, and space ships. It began in the 1940s, when scientists rocket-launched the first scientific measuring devices into the upper atmosphere and beyond. Next came Sputnik, the first

Even seemingly mundane topics come up for scientific discussion and experimentation. A knowledge of the physical properties of sand, for example, might ultimately give a sand sculptor the winning edge in a contest.

study of Earth's solid materials—from sand and rocks to mountains and entire continents. It is also the study of the dynamic processes that shape these materials, from the violence of volcanoes and earthquakes to the slow, carving power of streams and glaciers. Atmospheric science is the study of the envelope of gas that surrounds our planet. It deals with the familiar phenomena of weather and climate as well as the chemistry, physical qualities, and dynamic processes of the atmosphere. Oceanography includes the study and exploration of the vast seas that cover nearly three-fourths of our planet's surface—their chemical and physical qualities, their unique forms of life, and the geological features of the ocean floor.

humanmade satellite (an object that orbits a planet), in 1957. By the start of the 21st century, space science had taken humans to the Moon and back and sent unmanned probes to the outer reaches of our solar system. In the future, space science may even enable contact with extraterrestrial forms of life unimaginable to us today.

Mathematics. Mathematics is the science of quantity, size, and shape. It is the study of numbers, the relationships between them, and the mental operations performed with them and on them. Mathematics is also a logical method for organizing and interpreting information and analyzing and communicating ideas. Importantly, we use mathematics in all other fields of science, as well as the parts of our lives not necessarily considered "scientific" (balancing our budget, telling time, even drawing pictures and diagrams). Mathematics has also given us computers, which operate wholly on the basis of mathematical principles.

Earth Sciences. The Earth sciences include geology, atmospheric science, and oceanography. Geology encompasses the

Energy. From water mills and windmills to nuclear reactors and geothermal energy, the story of civilization is also the story of humanity's quest for new and more-powerful sources of

Science has its controversies. The ability of scientists to manipulate human cells—not to mention strands of DNA—has both fascinated and alarmed a public uncertain of the outcome.

energy. Many fields of science—including geology, chemistry, and engineering—come to bear on our need to generate, capture, and harness useful energy. The study of energy also includes the science of predicting how our energy needs will change in the future.

Environmental Sciences. Environmental science is the study of our planet's living systems and the ways that we, as humans, affect them. It includes conservation, environmental protection, and the wise use of natural resources.

A scientific laboratory need not be enclosed in a building. An unusual plant on a remote island might best be studied in its natural environment.

It addresses such pressing issues as pollution, global warming, and the protection of endangered species and habitats.

Chemistry. A grain of sand, a drop of water, a living cell—all things living and nonliving ultimately reduce down to one or more of the 92 chemical elements that occur naturally. The science of chemistry is the study of the physical properties and energetic forces of these elements and the many complex substances that they form. It is also the story of the three states of matter—solid, liquid, and gas—and their unique qualities.

Physics. The science of physics explores the forces that relate energy and matter, including electricity, magnetism, sound, optics, and color. Delving into the weird world of subatomic phenomena, modern-day physicists have also discovered an unimaginable "zoo" of elementary particles (bosons, leptons, and mesons, to name a few), quarks (up, down, top, bottom, strange, and charmed), and radioactive isotopes.

Biology. What is life, and how do we study it, exploit it, and protect it on the enduring biosphere we call Earth? Biology, the science of life, encompasses everything from the study of cells (the basic units of life) to the study of ecosystems (entire communities of interrelated organisms). Its many specialties include the study of animals (zoology), plants (botany), microscopic life (microbiology), and inherited traits (genetics). Biologists likewise study the development of new traits and entire species (evolution), as well as the crucial relationships

An enduring goal of technology has been to design machines that will relieve humans of arduous labor. A more specialized goal has been to design machines that look— and think—like humans. Robotics, although having advanced greatly in recent years, still has a long way to go before true learning by a robot becomes a reality.

Examining a larger-than-life model of the human heart can be an illuminating experience for students and other nonscientists. For the scientist, much more is learned by studying the underlying series of chemical reactions that, although occurring at a subatomic level, play an essential role in keeping the heart pumping and the blood circulating.

between different species and their environments (ecology).

Plant Life. One of the largest of the biological sciences, botany explores the solar powered "green machines" that imbue our planet with oxygen, food, and beauty. Fields classified within botany include horticulture, agronomy, and forestry—the sciences of growing plants for human use. Some specialized botanists study the "plantlike" kingdoms of mushrooms and molds (the Kingdom Fungi) or photosynthetic microbes (the Kingdom Monera).

Animal Life. What is an animal? Early *zoologists*, or animal scientists, studied everything that could move and eat—the two qualities they used to distinguish animals from plants. Today, zoologists use a somewhat more sophisticated definition, defining animals as multicellular organisms that feed on other organisms or their remains. Animal research can look at anatomy, physiology (body function), behavior, classification (the relatedness of species), even the medical needs of animals (veterinary medicine). Still other animal scientists choose to study the mysterious, microscopic world of the animal-like microorganisms known as protists.

Human Sciences. Understandably, no species holds more interest to scientists than *Homo sapiens.* For thousands of years, researchers have been studying the human body, alive and dead, in sickness and in health. Scientists can describe, in detail, the structure of a single blood cell, as well as the architecture of the human brain. The applied use of this knowledge is the rapidly advancing science of medicine.

Technology. Technology is the science of invention. Toolmaking, construction, agriculture, mining, manufacturing, communication, and transportation all fall under the gigantic umbrella of this field. Humankind's oldest technologies—stone tools, the wheel, and the domestication of animals—came from what we would now consider uneducated minds. Modern technology, by contrast, is almost always a product of advanced knowledge in one or more scientific fields.

SCIENCE AND SOCIETY

The drive to gather information and understand our world has always distinguished humans from other life on our planet. The principles and methods of science have proven themselves especially powerful in this endeavor. Indeed, much of what we call "modern life" stems from humanity's ever-expanding scientific knowledge. The alarm clock that wakes you in the morning, the bus that transports you to school, the books and papers you read, the electric lights by which you read, and even the computers to which you log on—all come to you thanks to centuries of scientific progress. So do the life-saving drugs and agricultural methods that have raised the quality of life for billions of people around the world.

It must likewise be said that science has given us the ability to destroy life on a scale once unimaginable. Perhaps the greatest scientific challenge of all lies in our future—the challenge of ensuring that science is always harnessed for the greater good of all.

ASTRONOMY and SPACE SCIENCE

For most of us, daily life rarely extends beyond the terrestrial realm. Fortunately, there exists the science of astronomy, which compels us to look skyward, to the stars and beyond. To help us in this endeavor, scientists have fashioned celestial globes (above), which show the configuration of the constellations and their relationship to Earth. Yet to appear on any celestial globe are the positions of planets outside our solar system, some of which (like the artist's depiction at left) may meet the conditions for supporting life as we know it.

10–17	Astronomers and Their Science
18–23	The Origin of the Universe
24–36	The Night Sky and Constellations
37–44	The Big Scopes
45–52	Eyes in the Sky
53–54	Invisible Astronomy
55–57	Radio Astronomy
58–59	X-Ray Astronomy
60–64	Infrared and Ultraviolet Astronomy
65–72	Planetariums
73–79	The Solar System
80–93	The Sun
94–98	Mercury
99–102	Venus
103–112	Earth
113–126	Moon
127–132	Mars
133–138	Jupiter
139–146	Saturn
147–150	Uranus
151–155	Neptune
156–157	Pluto
158–166	Comets
167–169	Asteroids
170–174	Meteors and Meteorites
175–180	Eclipses
181–189	The Milky Way
190–196	The Stars
197–203	Collapsed and Failed Stars
204–214	Black Holes
215–217	Quasars and Energetic Galaxies
218–223	Interstellar Space
224–231	Cosmic Rays
232–237	Space Scientists and Their Science
238–257	Manned Space Programs
258–263	The Future of the Space Program
264–269	Space Stations
270–279	Dressing for Space
280–289	Astronauts in Training
290–301	Space Probes
302–315	Space Satellites
316–325	The Search for Extraterrestrial Life

ASTRONOMERS AND THEIR SCIENCE

by Dennis L. Mammana

For millennia, the question has been debated: Are we alone in the universe? And if not, just where are the warm, moist worlds on which other life-forms have arisen and evolved?

It was against just such a backdrop that astronomers Michel Mayor and Didier Queloz of the Geneva Observatory in Switzerland began their search for planetary systems beyond our solar system. Their idea was to monitor the movements of nearby Sunlike stars to see if any "wobbled." This, they argued, would suggest that these stars were accompanied by planets too small and dim to see, yet massive enough to tug gravitationally on their parent star.

In 1995, Mayor and Queloz announced that they had discovered a planet in orbit around the star 51 Pegasi some 42 light-years away. This

Today's astronomer's view of outer space is augmented by such advanced technology as the radio telescope, which detects and interprets radio-frequency electromagnetic radiation from sources beyond Earth.

world, with less than half the mass of Jupiter, circled its star in only 4.2 days. While many questions remain about the nature of this planet—if indeed it is one—many astronomers cite this event as the first detection of an extrasolar world. And since that historic day, researchers from around the world have found more than 11 dozen stars that show evidence of being accompanied by their own planetary systems.

Mayor and Queloz are just two of thousands of men and women around the world who dedicate their lives to the search for the most-profound secrets of the cosmos. They work in the exciting field called *astronomy*—one in which new technology helps them make discoveries at a furious pace.

WHAT IS ASTRONOMY?

The word *astronomy* comes from the Greek *astron*, meaning "star," and *nomos*, meaning "law." Astronomy, then, is the study of the physical laws, composition, motions, origins, and deaths of all celestial bodies. Because the science encompasses such a vast array of subjects, most astronomers prefer to concentrate on a particular specialty. Some study the planets, others the Sun, the origin and evolution of stars and star clusters, or the birth of galaxies.

There are two principal types of astronomers. Observational astronomers work with telescopes on the ground or in space to answer questions or test theories. Theorists use complex computer models to understand or explain the physical processes reported by observational astronomers, or to suggest new projects for them.

Astronomy is different from most sciences in that researchers cannot directly interact with the objects they study. Except for an occasional Moon rock or meteorite, all celestial bodies are completely out of reach. In other words, astronomers cannot dissect, weigh, touch, or smell celestial bodies. The only way scientists can learn about them is by observing the light they emit or reflect and by monitoring their positions and movements.

EARLY ASTRONOMY

It was under the clear, dark skies of the Middle East that the first true astronomers began their work about 6,000 years ago. From towering ziggurats, early Babylonian sky watchers carefully charted the movements of the heavens. Their purpose was not to learn the mechanisms by which the universe worked; they sought, instead, the will and wisdom of the gods in the stars and the planets.

For millennia, the heavens have intrigued inquisitive minds. Aristotle (below left) brought the ideas of many earlier thinkers into one coherent model. Galileo (below), using telescopes that he built himself (center), made numerous discoveries about the Moon and planets.

By about 3000 B.C., the cycles of the Moon and other bodies in the heavens were well known. Around this time, the Egyptians were learning how to use the stars to predict the annual flooding of the Nile, to develop an accurate calendar and timekeeping system, to plan and build temples and pyramids, and to develop an early form of mathematics.

As this ancient Egyptian culture was reaching its peak, the early Greeks also began watching the heavens and charting the movements of the Sun, Moon, and planets. They used these discoveries to regulate their daily activities, much as the Egyptians had done. But rather than using the stars to decipher the "will of the gods," the ancient Greeks believed that the universe was understandable because it had internal order—rules that it must obey.

Perhaps the first of all true astronomers was the ancient Greek philosopher/scientist known as Thales, who developed a method of building theoretical models to explain the structure and behavior of nature, much as we do today. And he constantly sought confirmation of his ideas through analogies with more-familiar events.

Many Greek philosophers pondered the cosmos over the centuries, but the one who had the most impact on the burgeoning science of astronomy was Aristotle (384–322 B.C.). This great thinker melded the numerous ideas of his predecessors into a single conceptual model of nature—a kind of

grand unified theory that explained the workings of the entire known universe as had never before been achieved.

Centuries later, the Roman Catholic Church incorporated Aristotle's ideas into its doctrine. Among its tenets was the belief that Earth and humans were the center of all that exists—a belief that would continue for centuries.

For many centuries, astronomy research stagnated. Then, in the 16th century, Polish astronomer Nicolaus Copernicus made the momentous announcement that Earth was merely one of the planets orbiting the Sun, challenging Aristotle's view of an Earth-centered universe. German mathematician Johannes Kepler later calculated the motions of the planets—including Earth—and discovered physical laws that define their orbital properties exactly.

In 1609, the Italian scientist Galileo Galilei heard about a new Dutch optical invention called the telescope, which, when aimed toward distant objects, magnified them. Galileo built a telescope of his own and used it to gaze at the heavens. He discovered many things, including the cratered surface of the Moon, the constantly moving moons of Jupiter, the phases of Venus, and the countless stars that make up the wispy light of the Milky Way. Galileo, in one stroke of scientific genius, overturned the ideas of Aristotle once and for all, and opened the door to the true science of astronomy as we now know it.

ASTRONOMY TODAY

Modern astronomy seeks to answer some of the most fundamental and profound questions ever facing humans: How did the universe begin? How were Earth and its planetary family born? Where did life come from? And what is the ultimate fate of the universe?

These age-old problems are now tackled daily by some 6,000 astronomers throughout the United States, and thousands more in other countries. They use an arsenal of electronic equipment, computers, and optical devices. But the most important tool of all is the telescope.

Noted U.S. astronomer Edwin P. Hubble (above) demonstrated the existence of galaxies outside our own and established that the universe is expanding. In recognition of Hubble's many contributions to astronomy, NASA named its orbiting "eyes in the sky" the Hubble Space Telescope (right), which was launched in 1990.

Careers in Astronomy

People often think of an astronomer as someone who spends every night gazing through a telescope at the mysteries of the universe. This image may have been accurate in the past, but in this age of modern electronic imaging devices, astronomers very seldom peer intently through telescopes anymore.

Today, most astronomers hold positions at colleges and universities, where they combine teaching, writing, and research. Astronomers can be theorists, creating complex computer models of astrophysical phenomena; they can work with spacecraft journeying to distant planets and moons; they can teach; they can work in a planetarium or science museum; or they can use their skills in jobs in private industry or the government. And, of course, there are thousands of "amateur" astronomers—folks who simply like to look up at the night sky as a hobby.

Professional research astronomers must be observant and able to make sense of what they see. They must be good at mathematics, and they must be analytical, logical, capable of sound reasoning, and computer literate. They must also have the patience and determination to stick with a problem until it is solved—a process that sometimes takes years, or perhaps even decades. Astronomers—like all scientists—also must be able to communicate their ideas clearly, both verbally and in writing.

There is a severe shortage of jobs for astronomers in the United States, with little improvement likely in the near future. This means that only the very best are selected.

Modern students of astronomy are likely to spend more time attempting to master a complex virtual-reality program (above) than they are on bringing an optical telescope into focus.

Students interested in astronomy should take courses in physics, math, computing, and all other sciences. Studying subjects in areas outside the sciences is also important.

About 100 universities offer coursework in astronomy, and students can obtain degrees ranging from a bachelor of science to master's degrees and doctorates. After all coursework has been completed, continuing education is often required to gain greater proficiency. In all, it may take 12 to 15 years of education and training to achieve a solid position as a professional astronomer.

Becoming a professional astronomer requires much hard work, the job market is tight, and the financial gains are limited. Astronomy is, nevertheless, one of the most exciting and rewarding careers imaginable.

Telescopes are essentially buckets for harvesting faint flickers of starlight. The larger the mirror or lens used for collecting starlight, the greater the telescope's ability to detect faint objects. Telescope size has rapidly increased over the course of the past century.

Two of the world's largest optical telescopes—the Keck telescopes on Mauna Kea, Hawaii—are both 33 feet (10 meters) in diameter. Each massive instrument consists of seg- mented mirrors that are tiled together to form one gigantic mirror. Enormous radio telescopes—the largest, in Arecibo, Puerto Rico, measures 100 feet (30 meters) in diameter—are essentially immense dishes made of steel. These huge "eyes" and "ears" can detect radiation from objects invisible to the human eye.

One method modern astronomers use to obtain information about a distant light source is called spectroscopy. A spectrograph dissects

Not all astronomers are professional scientists. Many are average people who do it just because they enjoy it. These amateur astronomers gaze at the sky just for fun.

One might think that an "amateur" astronomer is one who is not as good at what he or she does as a professional. Fortunately, that notion simply is not true.

Some amateur astronomers invest heavily in advanced equipment, which they carry with them around the world in search of prime vantage points for observing solar eclipses and other astronomical phenomena.

The word "amateur" derives from the Latin word for "to love." Amateur astronomers are people who study the universe because they love it—not because it's their job. In many cases, amateurs are just as dedicated and knowledgeable about astronomy as are their professional counterparts.

Amateur astronomers come in all ages, sizes, social classes, races, and professions. The one thing they all share is that, when their regular job is finished for the day, they head outdoors to study the sky.

Just about every large city in the world—and many small ones, too—have organizations for amateur astronomers. Many are associated with science museums or planetariums, others with colleges or universities. Some amateur-astronomy clubs have a "dark-sky" observing site, far from the lights of a city, where members gather for meetings and to observe the sky together.

An especially important activity of amateur-astronomy clubs is the assistance they lend to educating the public and school-children about the wonders of the heavens. Often clubs will sponsor events in which members take telescopes to schools or museums so people can peer at the sky—sometimes for the first time in their lives! Members also work with museums, planetariums, libraries, and universities to share with the public their love and enthusiasm for their hobby.

Since there are many more amateur astronomers than there are professionals, amateurs can make an important contribution to our knowledge of the universe. For example, amateurs spend great amounts of time searching for exploding stars, called supernovas. They count meteors, they map the Moon and planets of our solar system, and they take splendid photographs of the nighttime sky.

Some amateurs regularly observe variable stars—those stars that change their brightnesses over time. By studying them, amateurs help professionals understand the workings of these strange objects.

Others wait for the Moon or a planet to pass in front of a bright star, and measure the exact time that this occurs. By observing these "occultations," amateur astronomers can help the professionals learn more about the Moon's size and its exact orbit.

One of the amateur activities that receives the most attention is that of "comet hunting." Hundreds of amateurs around the world engage in a friendly competition to scour the skies in search of new comets. Someone who finds a comet has his or her name attached to it for eternity. Some can become rather famous for their finds—including Alan Hale and Thomas Bopp, amateur astronomers who independently discovered the comet now named in their honor.

Not all amateur astronomy activities take place at night, however. Many amateurs equipped with telescopes and safe filters study our nearest star: the Sun. They watch for changing solar activity, such as the number of sunspots, and regularly report these to research organizations.

Another fun daytime activity of amateurs is to travel around the world to watch and photograph total solar eclipses. In this way, they can not only experience this re-

For most amateurs, minimal equipment is needed to observe an eclipse (above) or otherwise pursue their hobby. For some, the experience of observation is enough to spark an enduring interest in astronomy.

markable astronomical event, but can meet and work with other amateurs.

Much of the work of amateur astronomers is conducted through telescopes that they build themselves. Often, they create inventive or inexpensive techniques to capture light from the universe. They are proud to show their handiwork at amateur-astronomy conferences around the world, teach classes on how to pursue their hobby, and publish articles and photographs of their work. And all because they love the sky.

Astronomers (above) wear special glasses to view a three-dimensional map of the surface of Venus. Astronomers were intimately involved in every step of the creation of the map, including the design of the space probe that initially observed the Venusian topography.

starlight into its component colors—its spectrum. When analyzed and decoded, a spectrum reveals the temperature, chemical composition, rate of rotation, magnetic fields, and other physical characteristics of the light source. It can even be used to tell how fast an object is moving toward or away from Earth. Such data help astronomers to assemble a three-dimensional view of the way stars and galaxies are distributed across space.

SPACE ASTRONOMY

Until recently, astronomers have been working almost blindly. That is because the universe emits a whole palette of radiation, from radio waves to visible radiation to X rays, most of which is blocked by our planet's atmosphere. Trying to understand the universe by looking only at the visible spectrum is like trying to assemble a jigsaw puzzle by putting together only the pieces that are of one particular color.

Today, rockets launch specially designed telescopes above Earth's atmosphere to gain a clear, unobstructed view of the entire electromagnetic spectrum. These spaceborne instruments have revealed a remarkably different universe in infrared, ultraviolet, X-ray, and gamma-ray light. When combined, this radiation produces a clearer, more complete, and undistorted picture of the universe.

The Hubble Space Telescope (HST), launched by the National Aeronautics and Space Administration (NASA) in 1990, is the greatest space observatory to date. It reveals celestial objects with 10 times greater clarity than can be achieved by even the largest ground-based instruments. Through its findings, the Hubble Space Telescope has completely revolutionized what for decades had been some of the prevailing concepts of the universe.

PLANETARY SCIENCE

Scientists who study the planets and their moons, asteroids, comets, and other objects of our solar system once held exclusive claim to the title "astronomer." This subdivision of astronomy is now referred to as planetary science, and its practitioners work in fields as diverse as geology, meteorology, physics, chemistry, oceanography, volcanology, and biology, which they then apply to astronomy.

Even engineers contribute to planetary science, since distant celestial bodies are now studied by robot spacecraft that either orbit around or land on them. These robots carry extremely sophisticated packages of electronic hardware, optical instrumentation, and highly advanced computers to perform research far from the watchful eyes of Earthbound scientists.

WHAT HAVE WE LEARNED?

While astronomy is the oldest of all sciences, it is only within the past century that we have gained most of our insights into the workings of the cosmos. We have discovered that we live on a tiny world that is accompanied by others left behind from the formation of the Sun about 4.6 billion years ago. Except for being Earth's parent star, the Sun is a relatively unremarkable celestial body that lies in the outer regions of the rather large galaxy known as the Milky Way.

We've found that the stars that shine in our nighttime sky are suns much like our own. Some are hotter and some are cooler; some are larger and some are smaller, but all are colossal thermonuclear furnaces that pump out light and energy at a prodigious rate.

And, as suns in their own right, the stars are home to their very own planets and plane-

tary systems. In the decade since they first discovered them, astronomers have counted more than 150 planets in orbit around nearby stars. Most seem to be large, massive gas giants—worlds like Jupiter or Saturn—although researchers believe that small, Earthlike worlds are also out there in tremendous numbers.

At least 150 billion stars populate the spiral galaxy we inhabit—the Milky Way—along with countless tons of gas and dust astronomers see as nebulous clouds. It is in these clouds that astronomers have recently found the birthplaces of new stars and planetary systems.

In addition to mature stars and the birthplaces of stars, astronomers have found stars at various stages of the death process. These phenomena come in the form of exploding stars known as supernovas, and as the nearly burned-out cinders of once-brilliant suns known as white dwarfs. And they have found stellar corpses now emitting powerful radiation in bizarre ways—neutron stars, pulsars, and the oddest of all—the black holes.

The Milky Way is part of a cluster of galaxies we know as the Local Group, which itself is one of probably millions or billions of other such clusters. On the largest scale, the structure of the universe resembles that of a great sponge, where long filamentary clusters of galaxies form the fabric in the sponge, and mysterious, as-yet-unidentified dark voids in space are the holes.

We have also learned that the universe is not the static and eternal place that astronomers believed it to be only a century ago; rather, it is active, dynamic, and ever-changing. Galaxies collide, black holes devour matter, stars are born of interstellar debris, and stars die in unbelievably violent explosions.

We know that human beings are made of the very chemical elements forged in the hearts of ancient stars that have been blown into space during their violent death throes, only to combine again elsewhere in the galaxy. And the evolution of life on our planet may have been influenced by cosmic catastrophes—including an asteroid's collision with Earth, radiation from a nearby supernova, or changes in the Sun's brightness—and similar events may occur again in the future.

We have learned that everything that exists—the very fabric of space and time itself—

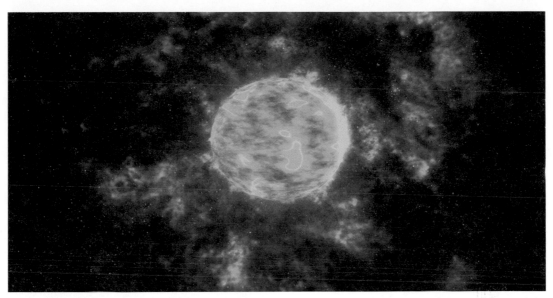

Technology has all but revolutionized the work of the astronomer. Advanced imagery techniques can be used, for example, to simulate the events leading up to the collapse of a massive star. One such digital scenario depicts a dying star as enshrouded by eerie swirling wisps of gas and debris, a stage preceding a gamma-ray burst.

was apparently formed in the spectacular event known as the Big Bang: an incredible explosion that occurred between 13 billion and 15 billion years ago. Scientists have further discovered that the expansion of the universe may not be slowing down because of gravitation, but instead accelerating. This is, without a doubt, one of the most puzzling of all discoveries in the history of astronomy, and scientists will certainly be debating it for decades to come.

THE FUTURE OF ASTRONOMY

Through the ages, the study of our cosmos has immeasurably influenced our view of life here on Earth—and elsewhere. Entire civilizations have been developed around celestial principles; our calendar and timekeeping system are measured by the movements of Earth and Sun; our religions and philosophies are based on where we believe we fit into the grand universe; architectural wonders such as the pyramids and the monuments of Stonehenge were constructed from accurate measurements of stellar, solar, and lunar positions; agriculture and hunting owe their successes over the ages to the use of seasonal and lunar cycles; writers, artists, poets, and composers have always been inspired by a starlit or moonlit night; and much of the tech-

nology we enjoy today comes from astronomers and space scientists who dared to dream far beyond the capabilities of their time.

No longer does a single astronomer work at a telescope making individual discoveries about the universe. Today, teams of astronomers from around the world work together to build powerful new equipment and probe the many mysteries of the cosmos.

At the beginning of the 21st century, scientists and engineers are constructing, designing, or planning a number of high-tech tools for the astronomer. These include nine optical or infrared telescopes with diameters up to 3,900 inches (100 meters) across, four radio telescopes, 20 space observatories, three gravitational wave telescopes, 15 high-energy particle observatories, and five cosmic-ray telescopes, at a cost totaling more than $20 billion.

In addition, space scientists are building or planning at least three dozen additional missions involving Earth-orbiting satellites and interplanetary or interstellar probes.

All their efforts are focused on answering many profound questions: Where did the universe come from, and where is it going? How did our world come to be? Is there a way to travel to other stars and planetary systems? Are we alone in the universe?

Some scientists theorize that our universe began with the so-called Big Bang—a titanic explosion that created energy, matter, space, and time.

THE ORIGIN OF THE UNIVERSE

by David Fishman

How and when did the universe begin? No other scientific question is more fundamental or provokes such spirited debate among researchers. After all, no one was around when the universe began, so who can say what really happened? The best that scientists can do is work out the most foolproof theory, backed up by observations of the universe. The trouble is, so far, no one has come up with an absolutely indisputable explanation of how the cosmos came to be.

THE BIG BANG

Since the early part of the 1900s, one explanation of the origin and fate of the universe, the Big Bang theory, has dominated the discussion. Proponents of the Big Bang maintain that, between 13 billion and 15 billion years ago, all the matter and energy in the known cosmos was crammed into a tiny, compact point. In fact, according to this theory, matter and energy back then were the same thing, and it was impossible to distinguish one from the other.

Adherents of the Big Bang believe that this small but incredibly dense point of primitive matter/energy exploded. Within seconds the fireball ejected matter/energy at velocities approaching the speed of light. At some later time—maybe seconds later, maybe years later—energy and matter began to split apart and become separate entities. All of the different elements in the universe today developed from what spewed out of this original explosion.

Big Bang theorists claim that all of the galaxies, stars, and planets still retain the explosive motion of the moment of creation and are moving away from each other at great speed. This supposition came from an unusual finding about our neighboring galaxies. In 1929 astronomer Edwin Hubble, working at the Mount Wilson Observatory in California, announced that all of the galaxies he had observed were receding from us, and from each other, at speeds of up to several thousand miles per second.

The Redshift

To clock the speeds of these galaxies, Hubble took advantage of the Doppler effect. This phenomenon occurs when a source of waves, such as light or sound, is moving with respect to an observer or listener. If the source of sound or light is moving toward you, you perceive the waves as rising in frequency: sound becomes higher in pitch, whereas light becomes shifted toward the blue end of the visible spectrum. If the source is moving away from you, the waves drop in frequency: sound becomes lower in pitch, and light tends to shift toward the red end of the spectrum. You may have noticed the Doppler effect when you listen to an ambulance siren: the sound rises in pitch as the vehicle approaches, and falls in pitch as the vehicle races away.

To examine the light from the galaxies, Hubble used a spectroscope, a device that analyzes the different frequencies present in light. He discovered that the light from galaxies far off in space was shifted down toward the red end of the spectrum. Where in the sky each galaxy lay didn't matter— all were redshifted. Hubble explained this shift by concluding that the galaxies were in motion, whizzing away from the Earth. The greater the redshift, Hubble assumed, the greater the galaxy's speed.

Some galaxies showed just a slight redshift. But light from others was shifted far past red into the infrared, even down into microwaves. Fainter, more distant galaxies seemed to have the greatest red shifts, meaning they were traveling fastest of all.

An Expanding Universe

So if all the galaxies are moving away from the Earth, does that mean Earth is at the center of the universe? The very vortex of the Big Bang? At first glance, it would seem so. But astrophysicists use a clever analogy to explain why it isn't. Imagine the universe as a cake full of raisins sitting in an oven. As the cake is baked and rises, it expands. The raisins inside begin to spread apart from each other. If you could select one raisin from which to look at the others, you'd notice that they were all moving away from your special raisin. It wouldn't matter which raisin you picked, because all the raisins are getting farther apart from each other as the cake expands. What's more, the raisins farthest away would be moving away the fastest, because there'd be more cake to expand between your raisin and these distant ones.

The American astronomer Edwin Hubble (below) was a pioneer in extragalactic astronomy. In 1925, he composed the classification scheme for the structure of the galaxies that is still used today.

The Observatories of the Carnegie Institution of Washington

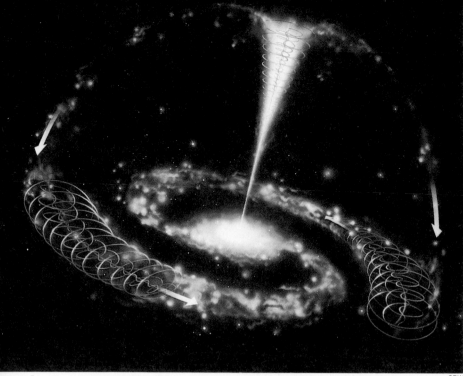

Plasma, the predominant form of matter in the universe, is made of electrically charged particles subject to both gravity and electromagnetism. Some theorists unhappy with the Big Bang theory believe that the many-stranded electromagnetic currents thought to permeate plasmas may be strong enough to supplant gravity as the primary force for sculpting the cosmos.

SRW

That's how it is with the universe, say Big Bang theorists. Since the Big Bang explosion, they reason, the universe has been expanding. Space itself is expanding, just as the cake expanded between the raisins in their analogy. No matter whether you're looking from Earth or from an alien planet billions of miles away, all other galaxies are moving away from you as space expands. Galaxies farther from you move faster away from you, because there's more space expanding between you and those galaxies. That's how Big Bang theorists explain why light from the more distant galaxies is shifted farther to the red end of the spectrum. In fact, most astronomers now use this rule, known as Hubble's law, to measure the distance of an object from Earth—the bigger the redshift, the more distant the object.

In 1965 two scientists made a blockbuster discovery that solidified the Big Bang theory. Arno Penzias and Robert Wilson of Bell Telephone Laboratories detected faint microwave radiation that came from all points of the sky. They and other physicists theorized that they were seeing the afterglow from the Big Bang's explosion. Since the Big Bang affected the entire universe at the same moment in time, the afterglow should permeate the entire universe and could be detected no matter what direction you looked. This afterglow is called the cosmic background radiation. Its wavelength and uniformity fit nicely with other astronomers' mathematical calculations about the Big Bang.

How Lumpy Do You Like Your Universe?

The Big Bang model is not uniformly accepted, however. One problem with the theory is that it predicts a smooth universe. That is, the distribution of matter, on a large scale, should be roughly the same wherever you look. No place in the universe should be unduly lumpy.

But in 2001, astronomers announced the discovery of a group of galaxies and quasars that fills more than 125 million million cubic light-years of space, and is presently the largest structure in the universe. Instead of an even distribution of matter, the universe seems to contain great empty spaces punctuated by densely packed streaks of matter.

Big Bang proponents maintain that their theory is not flawed. They argue that gravity from huge, undetected objects in space (clouds of cold, dark matter we can't see with telescopes, or so-called cosmic strings) attracts matter into clumps. Other astronomers, still reluctant to believe in invisible objects just to solve an inexplicable

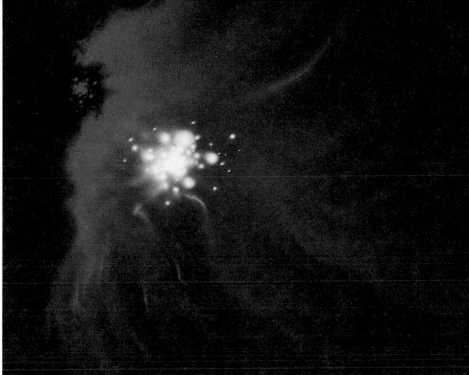

In the artist's conception at right, huge nebulas containing glowing gas and interstellar debris are spawning new stars.

SRW

problem, continue to question fundamental aspects of the Big Bang theory.

In spite of its problems, the Big Bang is still considered by most astronomers to be the best theory we have. As with any scientific hypothesis, however, more observation and experimentation are needed to determine its credibility. Advances ranging from more-sensitive telescopes to experiments in physics should add more fuel to the cosmological debate during the coming decades.

THE STEADY STATE THEORY

But the Big Bang is not the only proposed theory concerning our universe's origin. In the 1940s a competing hypothesis arose, called the Steady State theory. Some astronomers turned to this idea simply because, at the time, there wasn't enough information to test the Big Bang. British astrophysicist Fred Hoyle and others argued that the universe was not only uniform in space—an idea called the cosmological principle—but also unchanging in time, a concept called the perfect cosmological principle. This theory didn't depend on a specific event like the Big Bang. Under the Steady State theory, stars and galaxies may change, but on the whole the universe has always looked the way it does now, and it always will.

The Big Bang predicts that as galaxies recede from one another, space becomes progressively emptier. The Steady State theorists admit that the universe is expanding, but predict that new matter continually comes to life in the spaces between the receding galaxies. Astronomers propose that this new material is made up of atoms of hydrogen, which slowly coalesce in open space to form new stars.

Naturally, continuous creation of matter from empty space has met with criticism. How can you get something from nothing? The idea violates a fundamental law of physics: the conservation of matter. According to this law, matter can neither be created nor destroyed, but only converted into other forms of matter, or into energy. But skeptical astronomers have found it hard to directly disprove the continuous creation of matter, because the amount of matter formed under the Steady State theory is so very tiny: about one atom every billion years for every several cubic feet of space.

The Steady State theory fails, however, in one important way. If matter is continuously created everywhere, then the average age of stars in any section of the

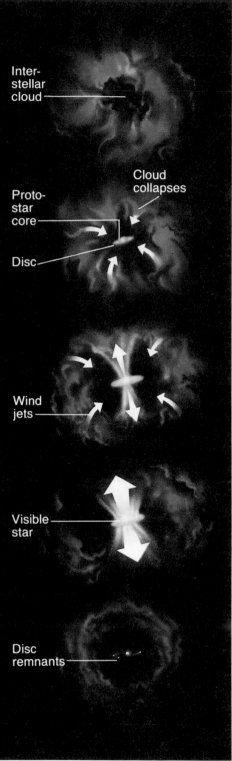

Inter-stellar cloud

Cloud collapses

Proto-star core

Disc

Wind jets

Visible star

Disc remnants

SRW

A STAR IS BORN

After the primordial explosion of the Big Bang, matter was dispersed in every direction.

1. *Within a galaxy, a cloud forms that is 3 trillion miles wide.*

2. *The denser inner regions begin to collapse, a core is formed, and rotating gases create a disc.*

3. *As the collapse continues, the core grows, and wind jets carry mass outward.*

4. *Winds expand, blowing the cloud away to reveal an infant star inside the disc.*

5. *Remnants of the disc are shaped by gravity to create planets surrounding the star.*

universe should be the same. But astronomers have found that not to be true.

Astronomers can figure out how old a galaxy or star is by measuring its distance from Earth. The farther away from Earth an object is, the longer it has taken light from the object to travel across space and reach Earth. That means that the most distant objects we can see are also the oldest.

For example, take quasars, the small points of light that give off enormous amounts of radio energy (see also page 215). Because the light from quasars is shifted so far to the red end of the spectrum, astronomers use Hubble's law to calculate that these powerhouses lie at a great distance from Earth, and hence are very old. But quasars exist only at these great distances— none are found nearer. If the Steady State theory were true, there ought to be both young and old quasars. Since astronomers haven't found quasars that formed recently, they conclude the universe must have changed over time. The discovery of quasars has put the Steady State theory on unsteady ground.

THE PLASMA UNIVERSE AND LITTLE BANGS

Not happy with either the Big Bang or the Steady State theory? A minority of astronomers are formulating other views of the creation of the universe. One model comes from the mind of Nobel laureate Hannes Alfvén, a Swedish plasma physicist. Called the Plasma Universe, his model starts by noting that 99 percent of the observable universe (including the stars) is made of plasma. Plasma, an ionized gas that conducts electricity, is sometimes called the fourth state of matter. This theory states that the Big Bang never happened, and that the universe is crisscrossed by gigantic electric currents and huge magnetic fields.

Under this view the universe has existed forever, chiefly under the influence of an electromagnetic force. Such a universe has no distinct beginning and no predictable end. In the Plasma Universe, galaxies come together slowly over a much greater

Quasars (as in the above artist's conception) only exist at very great distances, and are thus very old. If the Steady State theory were viable, then both young and old quasars would exist.

time span than in the Big Bang theory, perhaps taking as long as 100 billion years.

Little of the evidence for the Plasma Universe comes from direct observations of the sky. Instead, it comes from laboratory experiments. Computer simulations of plasmas subjected to high-energy fields reveal patterns that look like simulated galaxies. Using actual electromagnetic fields in the laboratory, researchers have also been able to replicate the plasma patterns seen in galaxies. While still a minority view, the Plasma Universe is gaining favor with younger, more laboratory-minded astronomers who value hard empirical evidence over mathematical proofs.

Meanwhile, another group of astronomers is developing a steady-state theory that actually conforms to astronomical observations. Like its predecessor, this steady-state theory proposes a universe with no beginning and no end. Rather, matter is continuously created via a succession of "Little Bangs," perhaps associated with mysterious quasars. In this new theory, galaxies would form at a rate determined by the pace at which the universe expands. These theorists can even account for the cosmic background radiation: they maintain that the microwaves are actually coming from a cloud of tiny iron particles—and are not the residual effects of some primordial explosion.

THE END OF THE UNIVERSE

Will the universe continue expanding? Will it just stop or even begin to contract? The answer depends on the amount of mass that the universe contains. If the universe's mass exceeds a certain crucial value, then gravity should eventually stop everything from flying away from everything else.

With enough mass, the universe will eventually succumb to the overpowering force of gravity and collapse again into a single point—a theory often called the Big Crunch. But without enough mass, the universe will continue to expand. As of 2005, most scientists believe that the latter hypothesis appears the most likely.

In 1998, astronomers found an even more remarkable puzzle: the universe seems to be accelerating while expanding, as if being pulled by some kind of "antigravity" force. Other astronomers have since corroborated this finding using a variety of methods, and have all but confirmed the existence of this mysterious "dark energy."

THE NIGHT SKY AND CONSTELLATIONS

Before the dawn of history, people peering up into the night sky began seeing designs in the grouping of stars. One saw a crab, its body and legs sketched in stars. Another saw a great hunter, his belt studded in stars, and his outstretched arm culminating in a starry club. Yet another saw a winged horse. And so, through the ages, the stars became divided into fanciful groups, or constellations, of which there

are now 88. These constellations fill the entire sky, with no overlapping or empty spaces between them. Every visible star belongs in one of them.

Many of the constellations are located in what may be the most dramatic starry structure in the night sky: the rich, luminous band of stars called the Milky Way. We now realize that when we look at the Milky Way, we are in fact peering into the center of our own galaxy. Our Sun is a rather average-size star located on a spiral arm of this galaxy, about three-quarters of the way out from the galactic center.

Some stars have individual names in addition to their constellation name. Sirius and Aldebaran are two well-known examples. Other stars are designated simply by letters of the Greek alphabet followed by the Latin name of the constellation.

In most cases, though not all, the brightest star in a constellation is the alpha of that group, the next brightest is beta, the next gamma, and so on, down through the Greek alphabet. For example, Sirius, the brightest star in the constellation Canis Major (the Greater Dog), is also known as Alpha Canis Majoris.

We cannot, however, tell how intrinsically bright a star is just by looking at it. A brilliant star that is far away may seem much fainter than a less brilliant, but closer one. The astronomer refers to the brightness of a star as it appears to us as its "apparent magnitude" or, simply, its *magnitude*. A first-magnitude star looks about 2.5 times as bright as a second-magnitude star, which in turn is about 2.5 times as bright as one of third magnitude, and so on. The few stars brighter than first magnitude are given minus magnitudes.

With a simple telescope, we can not only see the stars—which shine with the energy of their own nuclear-powered furnaces —but also our own planet's moon, most of our solar system's planets, and several of their moons. Planets and moons shine with the reflected light of the Sun.

On a crystal-clear night far from city lights, a person may be able to see some 2,000 stars with the unaided eye. But remember: at any one time, one sees less than half the sky. The remaining portions are visible from other parts of the world, or during different seasons of the year.

READING A SKY MAP

The Northern Constellations

Map 1 shows the main northern constellations that are visible year-round and throughout the night north of 40 degrees north latitude (which passes through Philadelphia; Columbus, Ohio; and just south of the northern California border). To use *Map 1,* find the approximate date in the outer circle. If you are observing on November 15, for instance, and facing north, hold the map so that the middle of the section labeled November is at the top. You may find it helpful to hold the map over your head as you face north. Those constellations at the bottom of the map (such as Ursa Major) will now be close to the northern horizon, and those at the top of the map (such as Cassiopeia) will now be higher in the sky than Polaris, the star that almost exactly marks the north pole—the central point of the northern heavens.

Your meridian—the imaginary line running from the north point of your horizon, through a point directly overhead, to the south point of your horizon—will then run exactly from the top of the map to the bottom. The stars on that line will be on your meridian about 9:00 P.M. standard time.

The circle of numbers within the outer rim of the chart marks hours. The numbers tell you how far east or west a star is in the sky, and will help you find the stars that will be on your meridian later or earlier in the evening. Since *Map 1* reflects the position of stars at 9:00 P.M., the hour marked 0 actually reflects 9:00 P.M. So if you want to locate stars at, say, 11:00 P.M., turn the map counterclockwise from the position for 9:00 P.M. (marked by the 0 hour), through two hours. The top of the map will then be about halfway between the hours 2 and 3. Again, the stars at the bottom of the map will be near the northern horizon; and those at the top, above the pole. If you want to observe at 7:00 P.M. on the same night, simply turn the map two hours in a clockwise direction.

Perhaps the most familiar star group in the northern sky is the Big Dipper, which is part of the constellation Ursa Major, or the Greater Bear. You can easily find the Big Dipper at the bottom of *Map 1,* clearly outlined by its seven bright stars. If you imagine a line passing through the two brightest stars on the front edge of the Dipper's bowl, and then extend that line

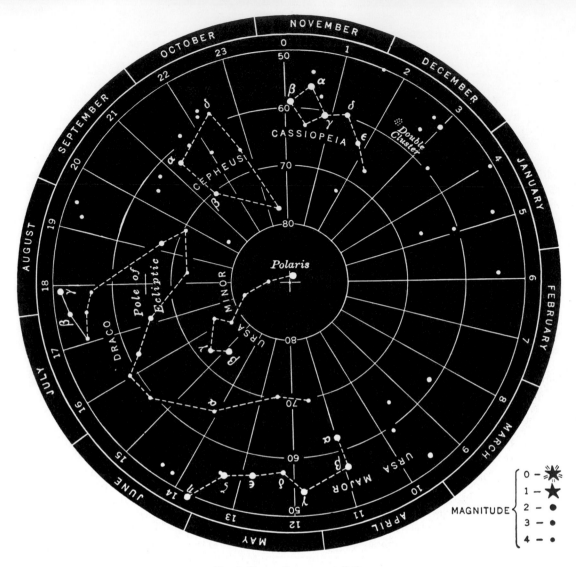

Map 1. The northern constellations.

straight up (above the bowl), you will find the bright polestar Polaris.

Polaris lies approximately over the Earth's North Pole and is the central point around which the stars of the Northern Hemisphere turn in a counterclockwise direction. You can always use Polaris like a compass, to find the north. Polaris is also the star forming the end of the handle of the Little Dipper. The Little Dipper, in turn, belongs to the constellation Ursa Minor, the Lesser Bear. Polaris also marks the midpoint in the sky between Ursa Major (the Big Dipper) and the constellation Cassiopeia, the Lady in the Chair. You will recognize Cassiopeia best as a huge *W* or *M*. Next to Cassiopeia is Cepheus, the

King. This constellation is not as easy to see as the other groups, although, with care, you can make out its figure, almost like a tent or a building with a steeple. The long, winding constellation between Cepheus and the Big Dipper is Draco, the Dragon. His head is formed by a V-shaped group of stars about halfway around the sky between Cassiopeia and the Dipper's bowl. The end of his tail is marked by faint stars.

The Southern Constellations

Those viewing the sky from below the equator will see the constellations in *Map 2*. The south celestial pole is at the center of the cross in the middle of the diagram, but there is no bright star to mark it con-

From *Astronomy* by Robert H. Baker, 8th ed., D. Van Nostrand Co., Inc.

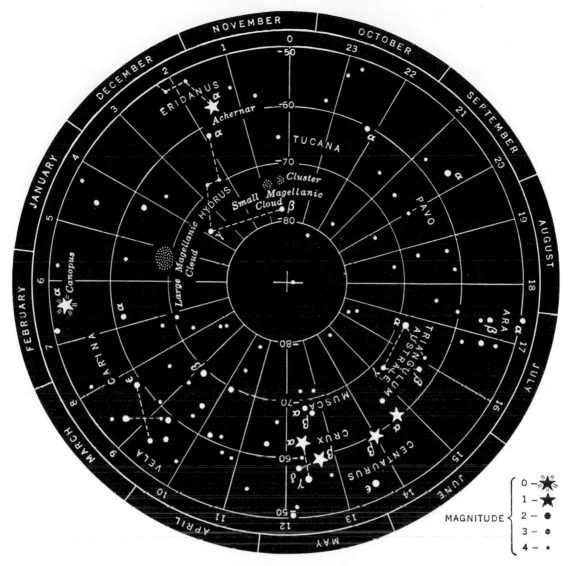

Map 2. The southern constellations.

veniently for navigators on the southern seas or in the skies. There is a guide to the south celestial pole, however: the constellation Crux, the Southern Cross. The longer axis of the Cross points almost directly to the south pole of the heavens.

The two bright stars Alpha and Beta Centauri point to the top of the Southern Cross—the star Gamma Crucis. Proxima Centauri, a faint neighbor of Alpha Centauri, is considered the nearest star to Earth, aside from the Sun. Proxima Centauri lies about 25 trillion miles (40 trillion kilometers) away. Alpha Centauri, a double star, is likely the third-nearest star to Earth. Nearby the Southern Cross is a famous dark nebula, the Coalsack. The Magellanic Clouds ap-

pear as hazy objects to the unaided eye. A telescope reveals, however, that they are actually spectacular masses of stars, nebulas, and star clusters.

Around the first of December, at the end of the constellation Eridanus, the star Achernar is seen above the South Pole. It is the one brilliant object in that long stream of stars. It forms, roughly, a right-angle triangle with the two Magellanic Clouds.

Canopus, second only to Sirius among the stars in brightness, is in the constellation Carina, the Keel. This constellation was once part of the big constellation Argo Navis, the Ship Argo, which in modern times has been broken up into several smaller constellations.

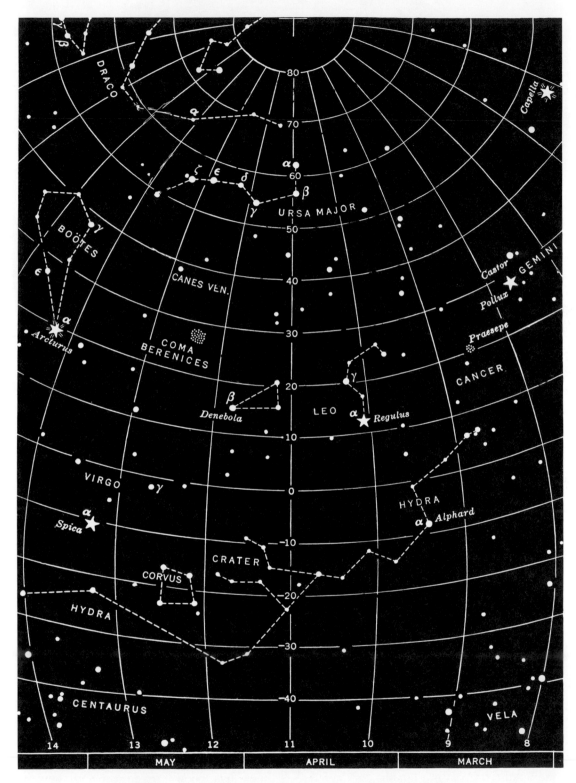

Map 3. The spring constellations, as seen from the middle northern latitudes.

Reading the Seasonal Maps

The four seasonal star maps reproduced in this book show the heavens as they appear from middle northern latitudes in spring, summer, fall, and winter, respectively. In using the maps, remember that each night, any given star passes by the same place in the heavens about four minutes earlier than it did the night before. This makes a difference of about two hours a month. For instance, a star that rises at 10:00 P.M. tonight will rise about 8:00 P.M. a month from now.

Choose the map for the season in which you are viewing the sky. If you are viewing in the middle of a season—say, April, using the spring map (*Map 3*)—the stars along the meridian of the map (the middle line that runs from top to bottom) will appear along the meridian of your night sky (the imaginary line running from south to north, directly over your head). If you are viewing later in the season—say, in May —look farther to the left of the meridian on your map to find the stars along the sky's meridian. If you are viewing earlier in the season, look farther to the right of the meridian on the map.

Remember that the star maps show constellations in their positions at 9:00 P.M. If you are viewing later in the evening, look farther to the left on your map. If you are viewing earlier in the night, look farther to the right. Also, don't forget to hold the map over your head, with the top of the map (where the plus sign indicating Polaris is located) pointed north. Or imagine that the maps in the book are mirror images of the sky. Otherwise, the discussions of east and west will be confusing.

SPRING SKIES

Use *Map 3* to find the Big Dipper, and continue the curve of its handle away from the bowl to locate the bright star Arcturus, in the constellation Boötes, the Herdsman. Arcturus is one of the first bright stars that appears over the eastern horizon in the bright spring evenings.

Going back to the Big Dipper, again continue the curve of the handle to Arctu-

rus and on down to the next-brightest star, Spica, in the constellation Virgo, the Maiden. Virgo is one of the 12 constellations of the zodiac, the narrow belt in the sky through which the planets, the Sun, and the Moon appear to move.

Near the southern horizon is the small, four-sided constellation Corvus, the Crow, which precedes Spica into the sky; its top stars point to Spica. To the west of Arcturus is a splendid star cluster known as Coma Berenices—the Hair of Berenice.

Once again, go back to the Big Dipper as a guide group. Extend the line of the pointer stars (the last two stars that form the cup of the dipper) backward, away from the pole, and they will lead you to Leo, the Lion, another constellation of the zodiac. The part of the Lion to the west resembles a sickle. The other conspicuous group of stars in Leo is a right-angle triangle, to the east of the sickle. Denebola, or Beta, marks the tip of the Lion's tail; and Regulus, or Little King, marks the Lion's heart, at the end of the sickle's handle.

To the west of Leo is Cancer, the Crab, also in the zodiac. It is not a well-defined constellation, but if you look out of the corner of your eye, you will be able to make out, on a clear night, the faint star cluster Praesepe, sometimes called the Beehive. Stretching across the southern sky south of Virgo and Leo is the long, faint figure of Hydra, the Sea Serpent. The head is composed of five stars south of Praesepe.

SUMMER SKIES

On *Map 4*, find the bright star Arcturus within the constellation Boötes. Just to the east of Boötes is the beautiful crown of stars called Corona Borealis, the Northern Crown. Its brightest star is Alphecca, sometimes known as Gemma, the gem in the crown. All the other stars of the group are of fourth magnitude.

Look carefully, just south of Corona Borealis, for an *X* made up of five faint stars. It is the head of Serpens, the Serpent. This constellation is closely associated with the large, clearly defined figure of Ophiuchus, the Serpent Bearer of Greek legend.

Another group of stars, one to the east of Ophiuchus, is also called Serpens. The group containing the head is known as Serpens Caput (head). The other is Serpens Cauda (tail). By including the triangle of stars to the west of Ophiuchus, imagine this constellation forming one long serpent stretching across the figure of the Serpent Bearer.

One of the most striking constellations in the heavens is Scorpius, the Scorpion, visible in the summer just above the southern horizon. To some people, it looks a bit like a fishhook. Antares, the brightest star in the constellation, marks the heart of the Scorpion. To the west of Scorpius is Libra, the Scales, another zodiacal constellation.

To the east of Scorpius is Sagittarius, the Archer, yet another constellation of the zodiac. Some stargazers see in this constellation a teakettle, or a little dipper. Through it runs the brightest part of the Milky Way.

To the east of Corona Borealis is the H-shaped figure of Hercules. The Alpha of this constellation, Ras Algethi, is very close to Ras Alhague, the Alpha of Ophiuchus. Between the Zeta and Eta stars is one of the most beautiful star clusters in the whole sky. It can just barely be glimpsed with the unaided eye.

Following Hercules over the northeastern horizon comes Lyra, the Lyre, a small but extremely beautiful constellation, composed of a parallelogram and a triangle joined together. The outstanding star of this group is Vega, which is brighter than first magnitude. It is the brightest star that we can see in northern latitudes in the summertime, and the third-brightest star in the whole sky. The northernmost star of the triangle of which Vega forms part is Epsilon Lyrae; it is a famous double-double star, which may be possible to make out with the unaided eye.

To the east of Lyra is Cygnus, the Swan. It is often called the Northern Cross, though the stars that form the cross are only some of those that make up the Swan. The star at the Swan's tail is Deneb, which forms the top of the Cross.

In the Milky Way, not very far from the foot of the Northern Cross, is a first-magnitude star that is the central one of three. The bright star is Altair in the constellation Aquila, the Eagle; the two stars that flank it are much fainter.

AUTUMN SKIES

Use *Map 5* to find Altair and its companion stars in Aquila. Using them as pointers to the south, find the rather faint but large group of stars that comprises the zodiacal constellation Capricorn, the Sea Goat. Actually, the constellation looks like a tricorn hat upside down.

Between Capricorn and Cygnus are two small, inconspicuous groups called Delphinus, the Dolphin, or Job's Coffin, and Sagitta, the Arrow. East of these groups is Pegasus, the Winged Horse, best known for a conspicuous square of stars. The star Alpheratz, in the northeast corner of "The Square," forms part of both Pegasus and the constellation Andromeda, the Chained Lady.

Stretching from the Square's northeastern corner, you will see an almost-straight line of three fairly bright stars—Alpha, Beta, and Gamma Andromeda. Almost directly above Beta, which is called Mirach, it is possible to make out with the unaided eye a faint, elongated patch of light. This is the Great Nebula in Andromeda—a galaxy of thousands of millions of stars very much like our own Milky Way galaxy. By extending the imaginary line connecting the three stars of Andromeda, you can follow it to Algenib, the Alpha of the constellation Perseus, the Champion.

Perseus is in the part of the sky from which a famous meteor shower—the Perseids—appears around the 10th to the 12th of August. The Beta of Perseus—Algol—is one of the most fascinating stars that the amateur astronomer can watch. For almost exactly two days and 11 hours, Algol shines steadily as a star of 2.3 magnitude. Then, in a period of about five hours, it decreases to magnitude 3.5. In a second period of five hours, it regains its former brilliance and once more remains at that brightness for about 59 hours. This startling change is due to the fact that Algol consists of two stars

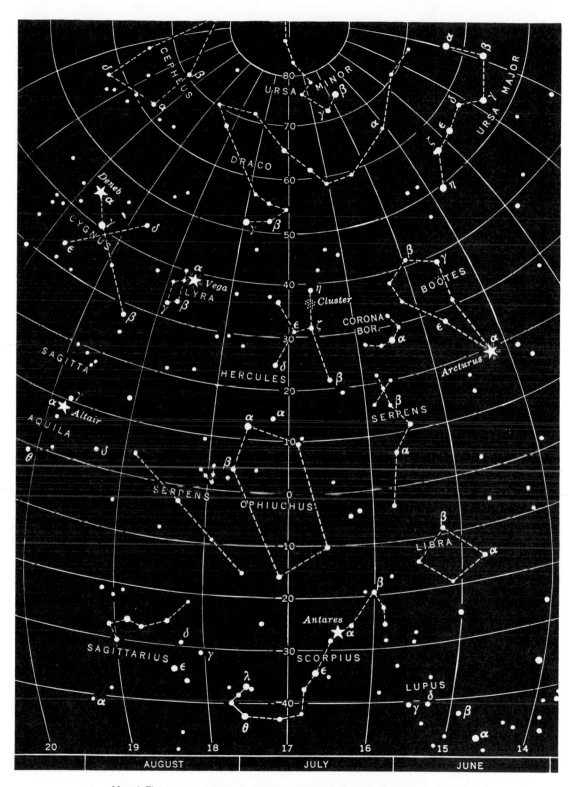

Map 4. *The summer constellations, as seen from the middle northern latitudes.*

revolving around their common center of gravity, with the edge of the system turned toward Earth. One star is much brighter than the other. When the fainter star comes between us and the brighter component, Algol seems to be dimmed.

Directly below the Great Square of Pegasus is a circle of stars that marks the Western Fish, also called the Circlet, in the long, ribbonlike constellation Pisces, the Fishes. To the east of Pisces is the constellation Aries, the Ram. To the west, there is a veritable cascade of stars—the constellation Aquarius, the Water Carrier, in the zodiac. None of the stars of Aquarius is bright. Below Aquarius and close to the southern horizon is the bright star Fomalhaut in Piscis Austrinus, the Southern Fish.

WINTER SKIES

There is no more superb celestial sight than the sky of winter, illustrated in the winter constellations map. One of the most splendid of all the constellations is Orion, the giant Hunter of the heavens. To find the rectangular figure of Orion, first look for his right shoulder (he is facing you). It is marked by the first-magnitude star Betelgeuse, a gigantic red sun hundreds of times as large as our own Sun. Rigel, a gorgeous blue-white star, marks Orion's left foot. Dividing Orion's rectangle in two are the three stars of the belt, from which hangs the Hunter's sword. The top star of the belt, Delta, is almost exactly on the celestial equator. One of the most interesting objects in this constellation is the great gaseous nebula—M42—that surrounds the middle star of the sword. You can barely glimpse it with the unaided eye.

South of Aries, we find the head of the constellation Cetus, the Whale. The head is made up of five stars. Cetus has a remarkable long-period variable star Mira, known as the Wonderful. When Mira is at its most brilliant, it is usually about magnitude 3.5. At its faintest, it is about ninth magnitude, far below the level required for naked-eye viewing. Mira cycles through these changing magnitudes over a period that averages about 330 days.

Northwest of Orion, we come upon the first-magnitude star Aldebaran, which represents the eye of Taurus, the Bull, a constellation of the zodiac. The face of the Bull is a V-shaped group of stars—an open star cluster called the Hyades. Taurus boasts another, even more beautiful, open cluster of stars, the Pleiades, to the northwest of the Bull's face. The Pleiades mark the shoulder of the Bull. (Only the forepart of the Bull is represented.) With the unaided eye, most people can make out six of the Pleiades. Beta Tauri, known as El Nath, "that which butts," marks the tip of the left horn. It also belongs to the five-sided constellation Auriga, the Charioteer. Its brightest star is Capella, the She-goat. Near Capella is a small triangle of three stars representing Capella's kids, a very good guide group to help you make sure you have actually found Capella.

By extending the line of Orion's belt to the southeast, we discover Sirius, the Dog Star, and the brightest star in the entire sky. It is in the constellation Canis Major, the Greater Dog. Forming an almost equilateral triangle with Betelgeuse and Sirius is Procyon, another first-magnitude star, in Canis Minor, the Lesser Dog. At Orion's left foot, Rigel, the long, meandering constellation Eridanus, the River, begins. Most of its stars are faint.

Gemini, the Twins, a zodiacal constellation, is easily recognized by its two parallel lines of stars, with Pollux (Beta) at the northern head of one line, and Castor (Alpha) at the northern end of the other. The constellation can be located by drawing a line from Rigel, in Orion, through Betelgeuse and as far again beyond.

THE CELESTIAL SPHERE

Just as geographers draw reference lines of latitude and longitude on models of Earth, astronomers have developed a celestial sphere with reference lines that can be used to locate heavenly bodies. Earth is the center of this imaginary celestial sphere (see diagram on page 36).

Astronomers generally use the "equatorial system" to establish reference lines around the celestial sphere. Using this refer-

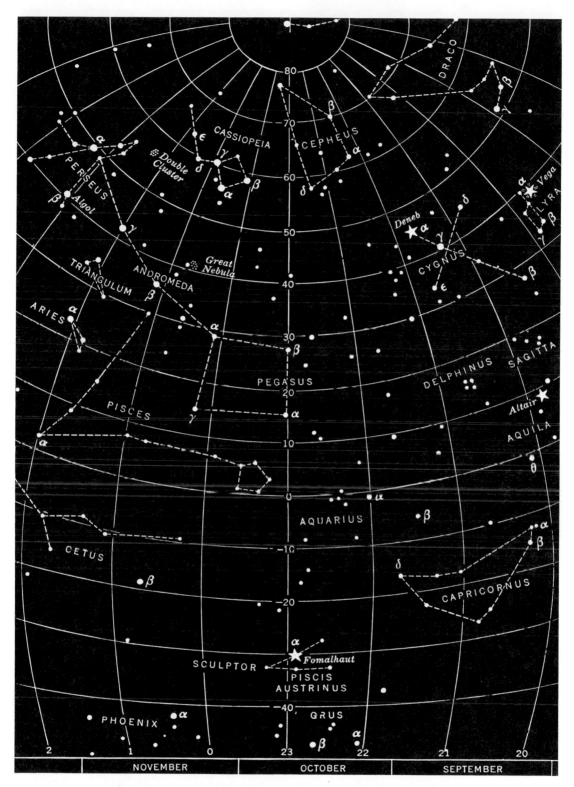

Map 5. The autumn constellations, as seen from the middle northern latitudes.

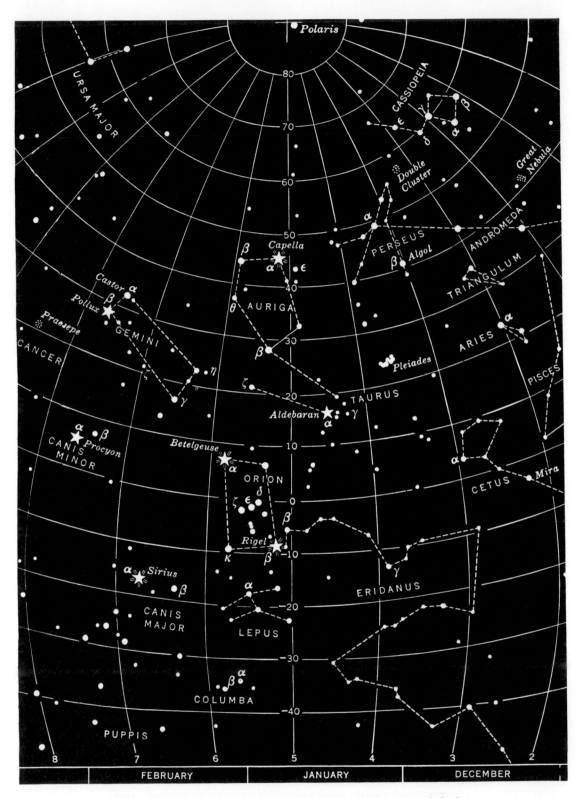

Map 6. The winter constellations, as seen from the middle northern latitudes.

The 88 Official Constellations

Latin Name	English Name
Andromeda	Chained Lady
Antlia	[Air] Pump
Apus	Bird of Paradise
Aquarius	Water Carrier
Aquila	Eagle
Ara	Altar
Aries	Ram
Auriga	Charioteer
Boötes	Herdsman
Caelum	Graving Tool (Chisel)
Camelopardalis	Giraffe
Cancer	Crab
Canes Venatici	Hunting Dogs (Greyhounds)
Canis Major	Greater Dog
Canis Minor	Lesser Dog
Capricornus	Sea Goat
Carina	Keel (of former Argo)
Cassiopeia	Lady in the Chair
Centaurus	Centaur
Cepheus	the King
Cetus	Whale
Chamaeleon	Chameleon
Circinus	Pair of Compasses
Columba	[Noah's] Dove
Coma Berenices	Hair of Berenice
Corona Australis	Southern Crown
Corona Borealis	Northern Crown
Corvus	Crow
Crater	Cup
Crux	Southern Cross
Cygnus	Swan
Delphinus	Dolphin
Dorado	Swordfish
Draco	Dragon
Equuleus	Colt
Eridanus	River
Fornax	Furnace
Gemini	Twins
Grus	Crane (a bird)
Hercules	Strong Man
Horologium	Clock
Hydra	Sea Serpent
Hydrus	Water Snake
Indus	Indian

Latin Name	English Name
Lacerta	Lizard
Leo	Lion
Leo Minor	Smaller Lion
Lepus	Hare
Libra	Scales
Lupus	Wolf
Lynx	Lynx
Lyra	Harp
Mensa	Table
Microscopium	Microscope
Monoceros	Unicorn
Musca	Fly
Norma	Rule
Octans	Octant
Ophiuchus	Serpent Bearer
Orion	Hunter
Pavo	Peacock
Pegasus	Winged Horse
Perseus	Champion
Phoenix	Phoenix (a mythical bird)
Pictor	Painter's Easel
Pisces	Fishes
Piscis Austrinus	Southern Fish
Puppis	Stern (of former Argo)
Pyxis	Mariner's Compass
Reticulum	Net
Sagitta	Arrow
Sagittarius	Archer
Scorpius	Scorpion
Sculptor	Sculptor's Apparatus
Scutum	Shield [of Sobieski]
Serpens	Serpent
Sextans	Sextant
Taurus	Bull
Telescopium	Telescope
Triangulum	Triangle
Triangulum Australe	Southern Triangle
Tucana	Toucan (a bird)
Ursa Major	Greater Bear
Ursa Minor	Lesser Bear
Vela	Sails (of former Argo)
Virgo	Maiden
Volans	Flying Fish
Vulpecula	Little Fox

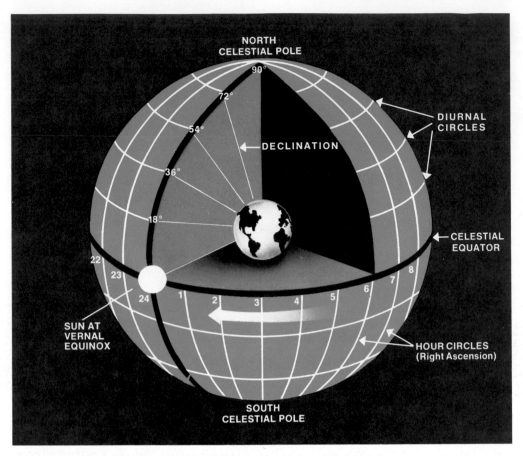

A celestial sphere uses reference lines similar to a geographer's lines of latitude and longitude to map the position of celestial bodies in relation to Earth. A star's east-west position, known as its right ascension, is similar to lines of longitude, while a star's north-south position, its declination, is akin to lines of latitude.

ence system, you can find your way through the most complicated of star maps.

In the equatorial system, it is helpful to imagine a pole running through Earth's axis and extending through the North and South Poles—out into space till it touches our imaginary celestial sphere.

At one end of our imaginary pole is the north celestial pole, and at the other is the south celestial pole. Equidistant between the celestial poles is the imaginary line known as the celestial equator, dividing the heavens into the Northern and Southern Hemispheres.

Lines of declination—somewhat akin to the geographer's latitude lines—divide the sphere between the equator and the poles. Declination is given in degrees, minutes, and seconds, north or south of the celestial equator. A star that is 10 degrees

north of the celestial equator is given a declination of +10 degrees; one 10 degrees to the south, –10 degrees.

Running through the celestial poles and at right angles to the celestial equator are 24 hour circles. Remembering that the circumference of any circle is 360 degrees, we know that each of our 24 "hours" contains 15 degrees. Each degree contains 60 minutes (60´), and each minute contains 60 seconds (60´). We use these lines to designate a star's east-west position, referred to by astronomers as its R.A., for hours of right ascension.

A star's right ascension is always measured eastward from the vernal equinox (one of the two places where the celestial equator crosses the annual path of the Sun across the sky) to the place where the star's hour circle crosses the celestial equator.

THE BIG SCOPES

by Dennis Meredith

Since Galileo first peered through his modest telescope to view the craters of the Moon in 1609, humans have strived for ever-larger telescopes to study the heavens. Galileo's telescope stunned scientists by showing that the Moon was no heavenly, perfect object made of an otherworldly "aether," but a craggy body as imperfect as Earth.

Could Galileo have imagined the gargantuan instruments of today—telescopes weighing as much as whales, with mirrors dozens of feet across? Like his handheld tube, today's big scopes have yielded startling new images of the exotic objects that populate the universe.

The telescopes with which we are most familiar are optical telescopes, which gather light. The world's largest optical telescope, the Very Large Telescope (VLT) at the Paranal Observatory, in Chile, uses four 27 foot (8.2 meter) mirrors that, together, act as a telescope 646 inches (16.4 meters) across. Powerful optical telescopes are basically "light buckets." That is, they gather and focus as much light as possible from a distant planet, star, or galaxy. The larger the light-collecting surface—a curved mirror or lens—the more light can be gathered, and hence the more information scientists can extract from it.

But light isn't the only kind of radiation from which astronomers can gather information. The biggest telescopes on Earth pick up radio waves from distant objects. Others collect X rays, and ultraviolet and infrared light. Some float in orbit clear of Earth's atmosphere, which absorbs and distorts many radiation wavelengths (see also page 45). Each of these types of radiation describes a different aspect of the object that emits the radiation: how bright it is, what it's made of, how warm it is, how energetic it is, and so on.

The powerful telescopes housed in today's observatories bear little resemblance to the primitive telescope first used by Galileo in 1609. Yet the telescopes from both eras have expanded our horizons immeasurably.

HOW OPTICAL TELESCOPES WORK

There are three general types of optical telescopes: refracting telescopes, or refractors; reflecting telescopes, or reflectors; and telescopes that combine features of both types.

A refracting telescope is a long tube. At one end sits a large convex lens. This lens, called the *objective*, is the part of the telescope that gathers light from a celestial object. The lens bends, or refracts, the light rays. This refraction brings the incoming light rays to a focus, to produce a sharp image. The image is then magnified and

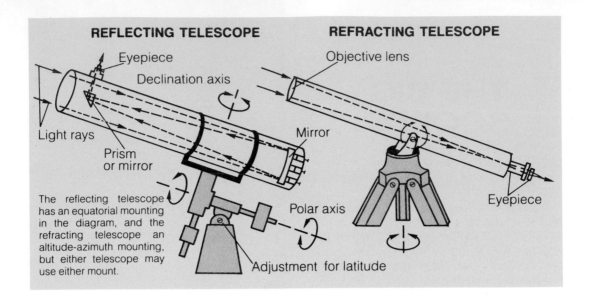

REFLECTING TELESCOPE

Eyepiece

Declination axis

Light rays

Prism or mirror

The reflecting telescope has an equatorial mounting in the diagram, and the refracting telescope an altitude-azimuth mounting, but either telescope may use either mount.

Mirror

Polar axis

Adjustment for latitude

REFRACTING TELESCOPE

Objective lens

Eyepiece

viewed through another lens device known as an eyepiece, which is at the opposite end of the telescope tube from the lens.

Reflecting telescopes have a more complex design. In these telescopes, the objective is a glass mirror with a curved surface shaped like the headlamp of an automobile. This is known as a parabolic mirror. The mirror gathers and focuses incoming light rays to a point in front of the mirror, called the prime focus. A second mirror, near the prime focus, relays the light beam elsewhere, to a place convenient for the observer. Several different mirror arrangements can accomplish this.

For example, a flat mirror, set at a 45-degree angle to the telescope tube, is used to move the focus to a spot just outside the tube. This arrangement is known as *Newtonian focus*, because 17th-century mathematician-astronomer Isaac Newton first developed it. Newtonian focus is popular in small reflecting telescopes used by amateur astronomers.

In another design a curved mirror intercepts the light beam from the main mirror. The curved mirror sends the beam back through a hole in the main mirror so that it comes to a focus behind that mirror. This arrangement, called *Cassegrain focus*, is what most professional astronomers use in their reflecting telescopes.

A similar arrangement is the *coudé focus*, whereby light is also bounced from a small mirror back toward the primary mirror. However, before it reaches the pri-

mary mirror, the light is reflected out one side of the lower end of the telescope. With a coudé-focus telescope, instruments at its focus need not shift as the telescope tracks objects.

Besides refractors and reflectors, there are the combination telescopes, which use both mirrors and lenses. Such telescopes can achieve a wide field of view or make a large-scale image in a short distance.

In a combination telescope, light passes through a weak refracting lens called a corrector plate. The light then strikes a spherical mirror and comes to a focus. Unlike parabolic mirrors, spherical mirrors do not bring all of the light to the same focus. That is why the corrector plate is used—to correct this unwanted condition.

The common caricature of an astronomer squinting into the eyepiece of a telescope is really not accurate. Most astronomers use television monitors to see what is being viewed through the telescope. The scopes are guided automatically, and the data they gather are likewise recorded automatically by sophisticated instruments.

Optical telescopes may contain arrays of electronic sensors, called charge-coupled devices, to capture the images of stars and galaxies. Computers immediately transform these images into data to be displayed and analyzed. Similarly, astronomers can train optical telescopes on the faint infrared, or heat, emanations from celestial objects such as warm dust clouds. They use infrared detectors supercooled for maximum sensitivity. However, photographic plates still work for such purposes as broad surveys of the sky, which produce catalogs of stars and galaxies. The combination telescopes, with their wide field of view, capture such images on photographic plates.

ALL DONE WITH MIRRORS

The very first telescopes, like Galileo's, were simple magnifying lenses. But astronomers quickly recognized the advantages of mirrors. Mirrors can be supported at the back as well as at the sides, making larger systems easier to design. Also, the mirror glass need not be perfect except at its reflecting surface, since light does not pass through it. In a lens, by contrast, the glass must be free of faults all the way through.

The earliest large reflectors had mirrors made, not of glass, but a metal called speculum, a nickel compound that polished up to a nice shine. Speculum tarnished easily, however, and it was a nuisance to take the telescope apart every few weeks for repolishing. In addition, the speculum expanded and contracted when the temperature changed, producing distorted images. Therefore, these telescopes fell into disfavor. Until the craft of making large mirrors developed further, very large reflectors could only be built in astronomers' dreams.

Meanwhile, a major problem in early refracting telescopes was that the lens broke up the image into different colors. A lens bends light of different colors at different angles, resulting in a *chromatic aberration*. In the late 1600s, astronomers learned how to combine two or more lenses to correct for chromatic aberration. Refractors became the most commonly built telescopes over the next two centuries. The largest refracting telescope is the 40-inch (102-centimeter) telescope at Yerkes Observatory in Wisconsin, in use since the 1890s. Larger lenses have never been built, because huge pieces of glass bend under their own weight.

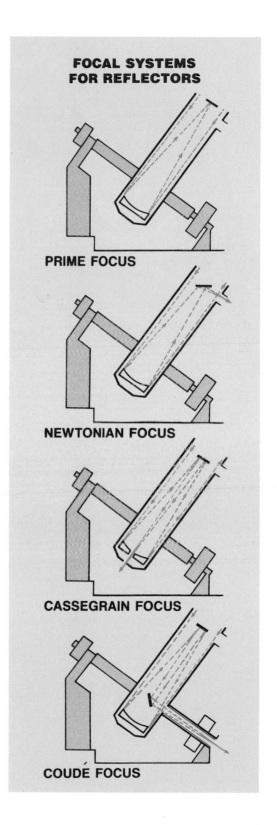

FOCAL SYSTEMS FOR REFLECTORS

PRIME FOCUS

NEWTONIAN FOCUS

CASSEGRAIN FOCUS

COUDÉ FOCUS

Palomar Observatory

George Ellery Hale helped develop many of the world's largest telescopes, but the 16-foot refracting telescope at Mount Palomar, California, was his crowning achievement. Conceived in 1928 and operational in 1949, Hale's Telescope weighs 500 tons, and was the largest astronomical telescope in the world for nearly 50 years.

Smithsonian Institution

But the discovery of more-suitable materials for giant mirrors permitted scientists to build larger and larger reflecting telescopes in the 20th century. For reflectors to perform well, their mirrors must expand and contract as little as possible in response to temperature changes. Instead of glass and metal, astronomers found that mirrors made of Pyrex and quartz are well suited. Today, materials are available that scarcely change at all with temperature. None of the great modern reflecting telescopes has a mirror made of common glass.

THE BIGGEST AND BEST

George Ellery Hale, the noted mastermind behind some of the largest telescopes ever built, expressed astronomers' urge to build ever-larger telescopes when he wrote in 1928: "Starlight is falling on every square mile of Earth's surface and the best we

A replica of the telescope used by Galileo to discover lunar mountains, the starry nature of the Milky Way, and previously unnoted Jovian moons.

can do is to gather up and concentrate the rays that strike an area 100 inches [254 centimeters] in diameter?" The giant of Hale's day was the Mount Wilson Telescope near Los Angeles, but Hale yearned for a telescope twice as big.

Hale's dream came true in 1948, in the form of the monster telescope at the California Institute of Technology's (Caltech's) Palomar Observatory near San Diego. The Hale Telescope's 16-foot (5-meter), 14.5-ton (13-metric-ton) mirror made it the world's premier optical telescope for several decades.

In 1976, astronomers in the then Soviet Union opened an even larger telescope toward the sky. With a solid glass mirror 236 inches (6 meters) in diameter, this telescope seemed to offer unprecedented potential for observations of distant objects in the universe. Unfortunately, the telescope suffered from optical and structural problems because of its enormous weight. A mirror that large tends to sag out of shape and warp as the telescope moves to follow an object across the sky. But in 1992, the frontiers of

telescope building expanded again with the completion of the 33-foot (10-meter) Keck Telescope, located on Mauna Kea in Hawaii, by Caltech and the University of California. A second, identical telescope—Keck II—became operational in 1996, and, together, they now represent the two largest telescopes in the world.

Instead of one mirror, each Keck Telescope contains 36 individual lightweight hexagonal mirrors, each weighing about 880 pounds (400 kilograms). These fit together to form the 33-foot (10-meter) main mirror. Each segment rests on a computer-controlled piston that constantly adjusts the segment while the telescope is in use.

At the University of Arizona, engineers have taken another approach to building larger, lighter telescope mirrors. They are casting giant mirrors inside a spinning furnace. The centrifugal force pressing evenly against a slab of molten glass will cause it to flow outward, naturally forming the concave surface of a telescope mirror without the need for extensive grinding and polishing. To stand up to grinding, most giant mirrors

The Pic du Midi Observatory stands 8,600 feet above sea level in the French Pyrenees. The rarified air at that altitude allows for better imaging of stars and galaxies.

are lightweight and hollowed out on the bottom. Astronomers at the University of Arizona have used the technique to build mirrors up to 28 feet (8.5 meters) in diameter.

Building a single giant collecting surface is only one way to increase a telescope's ability. For example, the Large Binocular Telescope (LBT) on Mt. Graham, in Arizona, is made of two twin 27.6-foot (8.4-meter)-diameter mirrors that are capable of detecting as much light as a single telescope 468 inches (12 meters) across.

RADIO TELESCOPES

Ground-based optical telescopes can capture infrared, visible, and some wavelengths of ultraviolet light from outer space. Astronomers also build gigantic radio telescopes to gather radio waves from a wide assortment of cosmic objects.

Just as reflecting telescopes use large parabolic mirrors to collect light from the heavens and concentrate it, so radio telescopes do the same with radio waves from celestial objects. But because radio wavelengths are far longer than those of light, the surfaces of radio dishes need not be as precise. Typically, the surfaces of radio-telescope dishes are made of perforated metal or wire mesh, which reflects radio waves just as glass reflects light. These metal reflectors focus the radio signals at a point above the dish, where other antennas capture the signals and send them to sensitive detectors housed nearby.

The world's largest radio telescope is Cornell University's Arecibo radio/radar dish in Puerto Rico. Its 105-foot (32-meter)-diameter collecting surface covers more than 18.5 acres (7.5 hectares). Nestled in the natural bowl of a small valley, the dish consists of some 39,000 aluminum panels. Such a gigantic telescope provides incredible sensitivity, which astronomers need because radio waves from space are not very powerful. All the radio energy ever collected by radio telescopes on Earth is equal to the energy released when only a few raindrops hit the ground!

Cornell's Arecibo dish can also be employed as a radar telescope, sending out powerful radio pulses that bounce off such objects as moons, asteroids, and planets in

The Sun rises over the Very Large Array (VLA) radio telescope near Socorro, New Mexico. Consisting of 27 movable dishes arranged in a Y-shaped configuration, the VLA has a resolution equivalent to that of a single dish about 20 miles in diameter.

The 13,800-foot summit of Mauna Kea, Hawaii, is home to the world's two largest optical telescopes. One of these, the Keck I Observatory (foreground), uses a segmented reflecting mirror. Behind and to its right lie the smaller NASA Infrared Telescope Facility and the Canada-France-Hawaii Telescope.

our immediate celestial neighborhood. The radar-reflection data can be used by astronomers to map these objects and determine their composition.

Because radio waves have such long wavelengths, radio astronomers rely on enormous collecting surfaces like Arecibo's dish for resolving power, the ability to focus fine detail. To match the resolving power of an optical telescope, however, a telescope working at a radio wavelength of 20 inches (50 centimeters) would need a collecting surface 1 million times as wide. This could amount to a width of 3,100 miles (5,000 kilometers), clearly an impractical feat any way you look at it.

But astronomers have found a way to work around this problem. Two radio telescopes placed far apart but connected by a cable can act in concert. The overall effect is that of a telescope as wide as the distance between the two receivers. Of course, the two smaller telescopes do not collect as much radio energy as would a single enormous radio telescope—they are unable to pick out weak radio signals from small or distant objects.

One such multiple-telescope system is the Very Large Array in New Mexico. This collection of 27 giant radio dishes, each 82 feet (25 meters) across, stands on a Y-shaped set of railroad tracks with arms about 13 miles (21 kilometers) long. The 213-ton (190-metric-ton) dishes roll into various arrangements along the tracks for different observations. When the radio dishes are moved farthest apart, they have the greatest resolving power. When they are bunched closest together, they sacrifice some of their resolving power, but they are able to detect fainter radio signals.

Another array of radio telescopes, the Very Long Baseline Array (VLBA), consists of 10 telescopes spread out across the United States—from the U.S. Virgin Islands to Hawaii—for increased resolving power. Their combined operation yields our most detailed maps of distant galaxies.

TELESCOPES AND RESOLVING POWER

A telescope's resolving power depends largely on the wavelength of the incoming radiation it is being used to view. Light, radio waves, and X rays are all part of the electromagnetic spectrum. They exist in the form of electromagnetic waves, and these waves have different lengths.

All other things being equal, a telescope working to collect visible light, whose wavelength is about 5,000 angstroms (one angstrom equals 0.00000001 centimeter), has twice as much resolving power as that same telescope does when it is attempting to collect infrared waves, at the longer wavelength of 10,000 angstroms. In other words, telescopes can focus the shorter wavelengths of light twice as well as they can concentrate the longer ones.

Opticians have to polish a telescope's mirror, its "light-ray collector," to an accuracy of one-eighth the wavelength at which the telescope is to operate. So a telescope

---

TELESCOPES IN MOTION

Few telescopes stand rigidly in one position. To be effective, these instruments must turn to follow celestial objects as those objects travel across the sky. Most of the movement we observe is due to the fact that Earth is rotating on its axis. As Earth rotates from west to east, celestial objects appear to rise in the east and move westward.

The earliest telescopes were simply moved by hand. For a long while thereafter, telescopes were driven by weights, the same mechanism used by cuckoo clocks. Today almost all telescopes have motor drives controlled by electronic systems. Many have automatic devices, and some use computers. Today's telescopes are very carefully balanced on their mountings so that they can move smoothly and with little force.

The world's largest telescope, the 18.5-acre (7.5-hectare) Arecibo radio/radar telescope, however, is rigidly fixed in place. To collect radio signals from objects that are not directly above the dish, radio astronomers adjust the angle of the receiver above the dish, so that it "sees" one side of the dish or another, thereby collecting signals coming in at an angle.

---

being operated at 200,000 angstroms—the far infrared—need be only 1/40th as precisely polished as a telescope that collects visible light at 5,000 angstroms.

The resolving power of a telescope also depends on the width of its collecting surface, or aperture. Thus the aperture of a telescope operating at 10,000 angstroms must be twice as wide as that of a telescope operating at 5,000 angstroms if it is to have the same resolving power.

A combination of many telescopic images provides enhanced resolution, allowing astronomers to view the "wobble" of a distant star—a sure sign of an orbiting planetary body. Most of the "extrasolar" worlds found to date have been gas giants larger than Jupiter, but scientists have also detected a handful of more "Earthlike" planets. In 2005, astronomers announced the discovery of a rocky world perhaps eight times larger than Earth, about 15 light-years distant.

Of course, the resolving power of even the largest ground-based optical telescopes is limited by Earth's atmosphere. The same air turbulence that causes stars to seem as though they twinkle also bedevils astronomers trying to make the finest possible images of stars or galaxies.

Astronomers try to get above this turbulence by building their observatories on high mountaintops. Such high-altitude locations also reduce absorption of infrared radiation by water vapor in the air and cut down on "light pollution" from cities. Astronomers are even contemplating building optical and radio telescopes on the Moon, where such hindrances as atmospheric distortion, light pollution, and radio interference are completely nonexistent.

Although ground-based astronomers cannot entirely eliminate atmospheric distortion, in the future they may be able to reduce it enormously by using "smart mirrors" in a technology called adaptive optics. These systems use computer links to automatically sense and correct distortions by subtly changing the mirrors' shapes. Such advanced optics may allow astronomers to come close to achieving on Earth the resolution of telescopes orbiting high above the planet's atmosphere.

As the number of telescopes launched into orbit has expanded, so too has our ability to make in-space repairs.

EYES IN THE SKY

by Dennis Meredith

Peering into a velvet-black night sky teeming with crystalline stars, you may think that our atmosphere is a crystal-clear window to the universe. But to astronomers seeking to capture and analyze cosmic images, the atmosphere is a frustrating, ever-shifting veil.

The same atmospheric turbulence that makes stars twinkle on even the clearest night prevents scientists from capturing high-resolution pictures of cosmic bodies. Earthbound astronomers also have to contend with clouds, storms, atmospheric dust, and the glow of city lights. Their vision is spoiled by the interfering shine of the Moon at night and the Sun in the daytime. Even in the depths of a moonless night, the faint "airglow" of the atoms and molecules in the upper atmosphere adds an unwelcome glare to observations.

Even if all this reflected glow were to suddenly vanish, the molecules of the atmosphere would still pose a barrier, because they absorb many kinds of radiation from the heavens. To understand this, imagine if you could tune your eyes to individual wavelengths of light. The heavens would change drastically in appearance as you proceeded through the spectrum from our Earthbound vantage point.

If you began at the longest wavelengths—radio waves—the heavens would appear bright, because those waves easily penetrate the atmosphere. Then, as you adjusted your eyes to perceive shorter-wavelength "microwaves," the stars would

High-altitude balloons, while still unable to surmount our distorting atmosphere, are used for observing the heavens in regions where the atmosphere is relatively thin. This balloon, launched by Caltech, will be sent to float 100,000 feet over Australia.

© Roger Ressmeyer/Starlight

entirely disappear behind the atmosphere's veil. The sky would remain dark through most of the infrared wavelengths, as there are only a few wavelengths of infrared radiation that can penetrate the atmosphere to reach the ground.

As we tune our eyes through the visible wavelengths, the stars would suddenly burst forth again, only to disappear through most of the ultraviolet and all X-ray and gamma-ray regions.

So you see, from the surface of our planet, we can view only a tiny fraction of the immense panoply of radiation from the cosmos. Yet astronomers know that every wavelength carries an immense amount of information about the stars and other celestial objects.

Realizing their blindness, astronomers have long tried to overcome the atmospheric veil. In the 1920s and 1930s, they tried—largely unsuccessfully—to detect ultraviolet radiation from the ground by moving their instruments to the far northern latitudes, where they believed the ultraviolet-absorbing ozone layer was relatively thin. They also carried their instruments into the atmosphere high above Earth's surface in manned balloons.

But it was not until 1946, with the use of captured German V-2 rockets, that the dreamed-of era of space-based astronomy

finally began. The V-2s and other rockets allowed astronomers to throw instruments above the atmosphere, where they began mapping X rays and ultraviolet rays from the Sun.

High-altitude balloons and sounding rockets are still useful for space astronomy. While balloons cannot surmount the atmosphere entirely, they do offer long observing times in regions where the atmosphere is relatively thin. High-altitude aircraft are likewise useful for viewing the heavens through the thin upper atmosphere. Astronomers use them to aid the study of certain infrared wavelengths.

Sounding rockets, which can thrust well above the atmosphere, remain there only for a few minutes before plunging back to Earth. Astronomers knew they would have to surmount the atmosphere for considerable amounts of time to study the heavens thoroughly.

The most important breakthrough for space astronomy came on October 4, 1957, when the U.S.S.R. launched the first Earth-orbiting satellite, Sputnik. Astronomers quickly seized on the idea of orbiting telescopes. From the late 1950s onward, the size and sophistication of astronomy satellites has steadily risen.

Astronomers have begun to build a variety of space-based telescopes that can

Space-based telescopes typically collect light from a distant star or planet and convert it into radio signals. These signals are relayed via satellite and ground stations until they reach the command center.

In April 1990, after years of precision design and engineering on the ground, the Hubble Space Telescope was launched into orbit. Its five light-detecting instruments made it the first orbiting telescope to operate in the visible part of the spectrum.

close the gaps in our vision of stellar radiation. The centerpiece of this enterprising effort is the National Aeronautics and Space Administration's (NASA's) "Great Observatory Program," an ambitious plan that has deployed into orbit the 95-inch (2.4-meter)-diameter optical Hubble Space Telescope in 1990 and the Chandra X-Ray Observatory in 1999. In 2003, these giants were joined by the final component of the Great Observatories program: the infrared Spitzer Space Telescope. The Compton Gamma Ray Observatory (CGRO), launched in 1991, was brought down in 2000.

Now let us survey the past, present, and future of space-based astronomy by proceeding through the electromagnetic spectrum, from the longest wavelengths to the shortest, from radio and microwaves through infrared, visible, ultraviolet, X rays, and gamma rays.

RADIO ASTRONOMY IN SPACE

While radio waves penetrate the atmosphere with little distortion, space-based radio telescopes would still have an edge on Earthbound instruments. One important advantage is that the gigantic dishes needed for radio astronomy could maintain their shape much more precisely and consistently in the microgravity of Earth's orbit. Radio

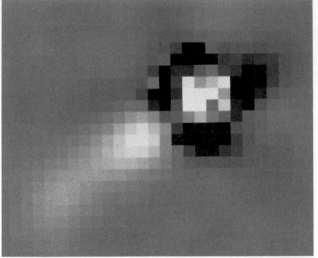

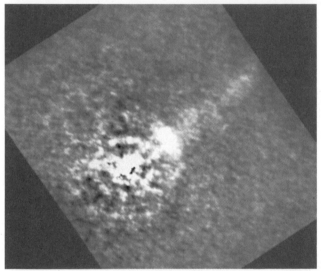

astronomers using the technique of Very Long Baseline Interferometry (VLBI) would also find space useful—not for its lack of atmosphere, but for its immense roominess. VLBI is a technique of observing the same object with widely separated radio telescopes and then combining the data. The resulting power is virtually equivalent to what astronomers would get from one immense dish spanning the distance separating these individual telescopes. By launching a radio telescope into orbit, astronomers can combine its orbital observations with those of Earth-based telescopes thousands of miles away. This will triple the resolution, or sharpness, of images of radio-emitting objects such as quasars and certain energetic galaxies.

While no true radio telescope has yet been launched in space, the Cosmic Background Explorer (COBE), launched in November 1989, enabled astronomers to study radiation in wavelengths that are nearly as "long" as radio waves, such as microwaves and long-infrared radiation. During its four-year mission, COBE studied the exceedingly faint radiation left over from the Big Bang, the theoretical explosion that many scientists believe gave birth to our universe. These echoes of the Big Bang may be 100 million times fainter than the electromagnetic radiation emitted by a birthday candle. This radiation would have begun as gamma rays that would have been stretched out into longer wavelengths over billions of years by the expansion of our universe.

INFRARED ASTRONOMY IN SPACE

Infrared radiation is emitted by such warm objects as distant galaxies undergoing extensive star birth, supernovas, and interstellar clouds of gas and dust that also give birth to new stars. Astronomers have long

Space-based telescopes have expanded our knowledge of the heavenly horizons enormously. From a ground-based telescope (top), the phenomenon of plasma jets ejected from distant galaxies is hardly visible. The Hubble (center) produces the clearest image to date of these jets. From the Hubble images, artists are able to conceptualize what the jets would look like close up (bottom).

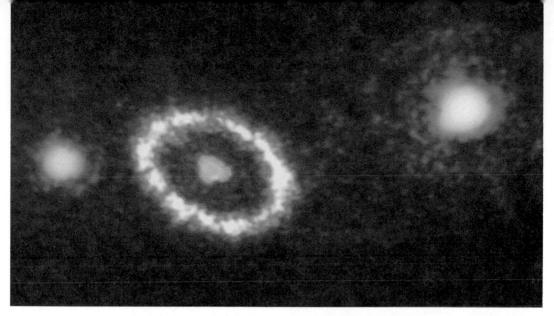

When aimed at the remnant of Supernova 1987A, which exploded in February 1987, the Hubble discovered a ring of stellar debris that is about 1.3 light-years across and has a temperature exceeding 20,000° F.

used ground-based optical telescopes fitted with special infrared detectors to peek at certain wavelengths of infrared radiation that can slip through our atmosphere. Then, in 1983, the 10-month flight of the Infrared Astronomical Satellite (IRAS) added an immense wealth of infrared data to astronomy's store. With supercold sensors cooled by liquid helium, IRAS successfully mapped the entire sky at infrared wavelengths. As a result, it discovered 250,000 new sources of infrared radiation, including some 10,000 new galaxies that cannot be seen at visible wavelengths.

Following IRAS was the infrared-sensitive Spitzer Space Telescope (formerly known as SIRTF—the Space Infrared Telescope Facility), which was launched in 2003. Spitzer is 1,000 times more sensitive to infrared radiation than are the most powerful Earth-based telescopes, and as much as 1 million times more sensitive than IRAS. Also, unlike IRAS, which could only scan the sky, the Spitzer Space Telescope has the ability to focus on specific objects in space.

VISIBLE ASTRONOMY IN SPACE

The most famous—some would say infamous—of all orbiting telescopes is undoubtedly the 11.5-ton (10.4-metric-ton) Hubble Space Telescope (HST), carried aloft by the space shuttle on April 12, 1990.

The HST is the first orbiting telescope to operate in the visible part of the spectrum. Its telescope is actually composed of six light-detecting instruments that can capture optical, infrared, and ultraviolet light reflected from its 94.5-inch (240-centimeter) primary mirror. These include the Wide Field/Planetary Camera 2 (WF/PC2), HST's chief instrument. In a wide-field mode, this camera captures images of large, faint objects, such as galaxies, galactic clusters, and quasars. In its small-aperture mode, the WF/PC2 camera can focus on individual bright objects, such as planets.

Among HST's other instruments is the Advanced Camera for Surveys (ACS), a system capable of taking photographs on three separate channels. HST is also equipped with three Fine Guidance Sensors (FGS). They help the telescope lock on to a target object as the spacecraft continues to orbit Earth, as well as to take extremely accurate measurements of the positions of stars. HST's final two instruments are the Near-Infrared Camera and Multi-Object Spectrometer (NICMOS) and the Space Telescope Imaging Spectrograph (STIS).

Shortly after HST's launch, astronomers discovered that the manufacturers of its main mirror had polished its shape too flatly. Ideally, the mirror's concave surface should be shaped such that all incoming light is focused at a single point, producing

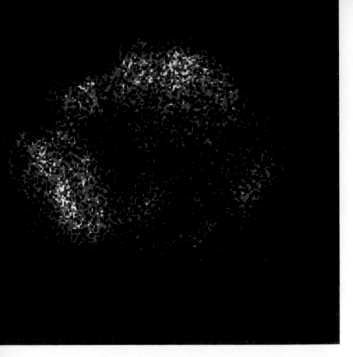

An X-ray image of the supernova remnant Cas A, which exploded in A.D. 1670. This image was taken by ROSAT, a joint satellite project of Germany, the United Kingdom, and the United States.

a sharp image. But the mistake in polishing had produced a flaw, called a "spherical aberration," that caused light striking the edge of the primary mirror to focus at a different point than light striking near the center of the image. The result was fuzzy, out-of-focus pictures.

The size of the error—the edges of the mirror seemed to be about 2 micrometers (millionths of a meter) lower than they should be—was surprisingly large given that the mirror was ground to an astonishing overall precision of better than one-hundredth of a micrometer.

Investigators determined that the problem occurred when a measuring rod was inserted backward in an optical device used to guide grinding of the mirror. This rod was vital to properly spacing the mirrors and a lens in a device known as a reflective null corrector. By shining a laser light through this null corrector and onto HST's mirror, technicians would test the mirror's curvature. But with the measuring rod inserted backward, the null corrector's components were misspaced by about the thickness of a dime. And as a result, the shape of HST's mirror was off by less than the thickness of a sheet of paper.

The investigators also determined that budget restrictions and managerial problems led to incomplete testing by the manufacturer and inadequate supervision by NASA. The space telescope also experienced slight shaking due to expansion and contraction of its solar panels as they passed in and out of Earth's shadow. This shaking further reduced the sharpness of HST's images.

But astronomers needed a fully operational telescope that could perform up to its original specifications. So, in its first servicing mission in December 1993, the robotic arm of the space shuttle *Endeavour* snared the telescope 360 miles (580 kilometers) above the South Pacific Ocean; over the next five days, space-walking astronauts completed a series of critical repairs.

In addition to upgrading electronics, computer components, and camera hardware, the astronauts replaced faulty gyroscopes and solar panels, and were able to improve the Hubble's vision with a set of corrective mirrors known as COSTAR (Corrective Optics Space Telescope Axial Replacement). After boosting the telescope into a slightly higher orbit, the astronauts released the fully repaired telescope back into Earth orbit on December 10, 1993, to once again continue its exploration of the cosmos.

In other regularly scheduled servicing missions during 1997, 1999, and 2002, even more upgrades were successfully added. In the wake of the space shuttle *Columbia* catastrophe in February 2003, all servicing missions to the Hubble Telescope were canceled, leaving the great observatory in danger of "dying" in orbit.

ULTRAVIOLET ASTRONOMY IN SPACE

Perhaps the most widely used space telescope—at any wavelength—was the International Ultraviolet Explorer (IUE). Launched in 1978 as a joint project of NASA, the European Space Agency (ESA), and Great Britain, its 18-inch (46-centimeter) telescope was used by astronomers nearly 24 hours a day in their studies of the short-wavelength, ultraviolet radiation that emanates from stars, planets, galaxies, and quasars throughout the cosmos.

Before the Gamma Ray Observatory was deployed from the shuttle Atlantis *in April 1991, an unexpected space walk was required to manually repair a malfunction in one of the satellite's antennas.*

During its mission, IUE captured more than 104,000 images, including those of virtually every type of astronomical object. Although it was originally designed for a three-year mission, IUE survived for nearly two decades, consistently returning high- and low-resolution images of many astronomical sources. It was finally deactivated in September 1996.

But the first thorough and detailed map of the extreme-ultraviolet and the X-ray regions of the sky was provided by the Roentgen Satellite (ROSAT), launched in June 1990. ROSAT was also an international project, built in Germany and using instruments provided by Great Britain and the United States. Before its mission ended in February 1999, ROSAT had been successfully employed for extensive ultraviolet studies as well as an all-sky X-ray survey.

Two other important space missions for ultraviolet exploration of the cosmos were fairly brief, operating inside the cargo bay of the space shuttle. Astro-1 was carried aboard *Columbia* from December 2 to 11, 1990, and Astro-2 flew aboard *Endeavour* from March 2 to 18, 1995. Each mission used several telescopes, and was able to analyze radiation from a wide variety of objects including black holes, stars in the process of birth and death, distant galaxies, planets, and comets.

Yet another ultraviolet telescope, the Extreme Ultraviolet Explorer (EUVE), operated in Earth-orbit from June 1992 until January 2001, and produced the first comprehensive all-sky survey in extreme-ultraviolet wavelengths.

X-RAY ASTRONOMY IN SPACE

While scientists got their first glimpse of X rays from space long ago, using balloons and sounding rockets, it was not until 1970 that they launched the first X-ray satellite. The Small Astronomy Satellite 1, nicknamed Uhuru (the Swahili term for "freedom"), was not a telescope in the traditional sense of the word. That is, it did not actually capture images of celestial bodies. It just pointed astronomers in the right direction, working in a manner much like a radio antenna, enabling scientists to find the direction of X-ray "transmitters." Uhuru enabled astronomers to revise the number of known X-ray sources from the 30-odd they had detected from the ground to several hundred.

The next major X-ray space telescope was the High Energy Astrophysical Observatory-2 (HERO-2), nicknamed the Einstein Observatory, launched in 1978. HERO-2 could actually form pictures of the celestial objects that emit X rays. During its two-and-one-half-year lifetime, it produced more than 7,000 such images.

As mentioned earlier, ROSAT, in addition to its ultraviolet studies, has produced a complete X-ray survey of the heavens, which revealed some 6,000 images of previously unknown X-ray sources.

In December 1995, the Rossi X-ray Timing Explorer (RXTE) was launched to study how X-ray sources vary in brightness over time periods ranging from microseconds to months.

Over the next decade, the most important orbiting X-ray observatory will be the Chandra X-ray Observatory. Launched into orbit in July 1999, it allows astronomers for the first time to study in great detail thousands of known sources of X rays, such as suspected black holes and exploding stars called supernovas. Chandra's X-ray measurements will also act as a "tracer" to reveal where large amounts of dark matter in the universe may lie. This mysterious dark matter, which produces no radiation of its own, is believed to make up the largest portion of the universe. Yet astronomers have not been able to identify even a fraction of it. By measuring X rays from large observable objects floating in space, scientists can determine if it is the gravity of a significant amount of nearby, unseen dark matter that is holding them in place.

GAMMA-RAY ASTRONOMY IN SPACE

Gamma rays, the highest-energy emanations from the heavens, are produced by the universe's most violent objects: black holes, neutron stars, supernovas, and mysterious "gamma-ray bursters," which suddenly blast forth huge amounts of gamma rays for wholly unknown reasons.

Gamma rays are also the most difficult type of radiation for astronomers to study. At present, they need huge instruments to capture these energetic rays. Like X rays, gamma rays were studied in the 1960s with a series of small satellites and high-altitude balloons. With these instruments, astronomers were only able to glimpse gamma rays in certain wavelengths or study just small sections of the sky.

Astronomers' gamma-ray eyes were fully opened with the April 1991 launch of the Compton Gamma Ray Observatory (CGRO). It carried four instruments, three of which were the size of small cars. To detect gamma rays, these instruments used "scintillators"—crystals, liquids, and other materials that emit brief flashes of light when they are struck by gamma rays. CGRO was able to provide the first detailed gamma-ray map of the sky before being brought down to a fiery end in Earth's atmosphere on June 4, 2000.

THE LASTING NEED FOR GROUND-BASED TELESCOPES

Astronomers do not expect space telescopes to take the place of ground-based observatories. For example, ground-based telescopes can be far larger than those that are launched into space. As a result, these enormous telescopes can gather more light for such critical studies as spectrographic analysis. In spectrographic analysis, instead of imaging the star or other object, the light from it is separated into its different wavelengths to obtain important "fingerprints" that give astronomers details about the object's overall composition.

Also, ground-based telescopes can be more easily repaired and refurbished than can space telescopes, and they do not require expensive backup systems or devices for remote control. In fact, many say that some of the newest ground-based telescopes can approach, and may someday even match, the resolution of space telescopes. Such advancements in ground-level astronomy are due to the continuing development of "adaptive optics," which can automatically adjust the shape of a telescope's mirrors to compensate for atmospheric distortion.

Images from ground-based telescopes can also be improved through optical interferometry. In this process, images of the same object taken through separate telescopes are combined to give the effect of one huge telescope, virtually the size of the distance separating the two instruments.

But most importantly, space- and ground-based telescopes complement each other. For example, when a space telescope discovers a new object by using its high-resolution imaging capability, that information can be relayed to astronomers on the ground, who can use their Earthbound telescopes to better analyze the spectrum of the new object's light qualities.

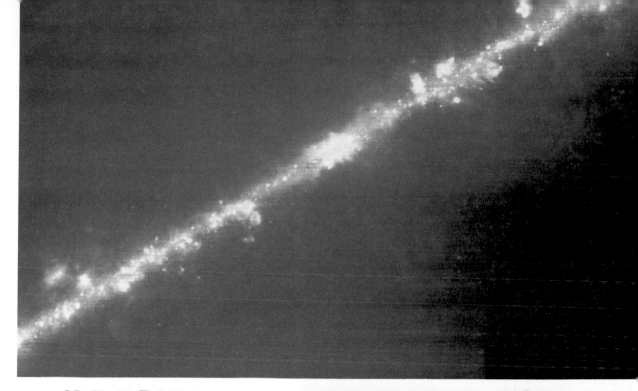

INVISIBLE ASTRONOMY

by William P. Blair

Early astronomers used only the naked eye to view the heavens. Later, observations became more refined with the aid of optical telescopes. But in the last four decades, astronomers have exploited other wavelengths, such as the infrared radiation used to image the Milky Way (above) and the Andromeda Galaxy (right).

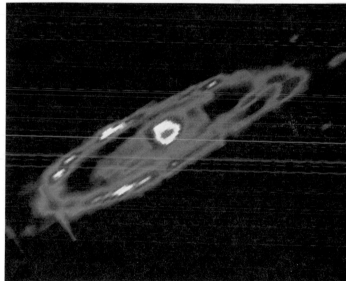

Both photos: JPL/NASA

The field of astronomy has changed dramatically over the past 40 years, and astronomers have changed along with it. Gone is the image of the grizzled astronomer, hunched over with an eye to the telescope, recording notes and measurements in a notebook. Astronomy today is high tech, exploiting every kind of electronic wizardry imaginable.

The tremendous advances in our understanding of the universe are due largely to discoveries made through invisible astronomy, that is, astronomy using wavelengths of light outside the visible spectrum. And with the prospect of new, more powerful and precise instruments and computer technology, these discoveries will continue for years to come.

When optical light is passed through a prism, it breaks up into a rainbow of colors —red, orange, yellow, green, blue, indigo, and violet. Each color represents a different wavelength of light. This optical spectrum is a tiny portion of a much larger range of wavelengths called the "electromagnetic spectrum," which extends outward from both the blue and red portions of the optical spectrum. Hence, the ends of the optical spectrum are not really "ends," but rather limits to what our eyes can detect. Beyond the red limit of the optical spectrum (toward longer wavelengths), one encounters first infrared and then radio light. Beyond the violet limit, one finds ultraviolet, X-ray, and gamma-ray light. There are no "borders" between parts of the spectrum—they are all part of the same continuous spectrum of electromagnetic radiation.

Although these extreme wavelengths of light are invisible to the naked eye, we can build instruments to sense and measure these wavelengths, and computers to transform their signals into information we can see and analyze.

Observations at invisible wavelengths tell us much about our universe that could not be learned from visible astronomy alone. For instance, the center of our Milky Way galaxy is shrouded from view at optical wavelengths by clouds of interstellar gas and dust. Infrared and radio light can penetrate this dust, however, and allow us to see such regions directly. Also, many objects in the universe emit primarily at wavelengths other than optical. Conse-

quently, hot stars, active galaxies, and the exploded remnants of dead stars can be most effectively studied at ultraviolet and X-ray wavelengths. Some of the galaxies discovered using infrared instruments are 1,000 times more luminous than our own galaxy, yet they are undetectable at optical wavelengths!

It is no coincidence that our eyes are sensitive to visible light—visible wavelengths pass through our atmosphere to reach the Earth's surface. But among the invisible wavelengths, only radio waves and a few narrow regions of infrared penetrate the atmosphere. The rest of the electromagnetic spectrum gets blocked by our atmosphere. While this blockage is fortunate for life on Earth, since ultraviolet and X-ray emissions are deadly, the atmosphere's veil does cause some obvious problems for invisible astronomy. Not surprisingly, the vast majority of advances in invisible astronomy have occurred since the advent of the space age and the concurrent technical ability to place instruments above the Earth's atmosphere.

Astronomers can now study the wide variety of celestial bodies using all the wavelengths of the electromagnetic spectrum. (A) Balloons and orbiting satellites have collected X-ray and gamma-ray radiation emitted from the Sun's corona, providing invaluable information about the Sun's structure, density, and temperature. (B) Ultraviolet studies of Mars and other planets have revealed atmospheric compositions and pressures. (C) Observations of all objects using the visible portion of the spectrum remain important to astronomers. (D) Infrared studies of planets such as Mars, as well as the stars, furnish details about their origin. (E) Radar units yield data about distances and rotation rates of celestial bodies. (F) Radio telescopes provide information about pulsars and quasars.

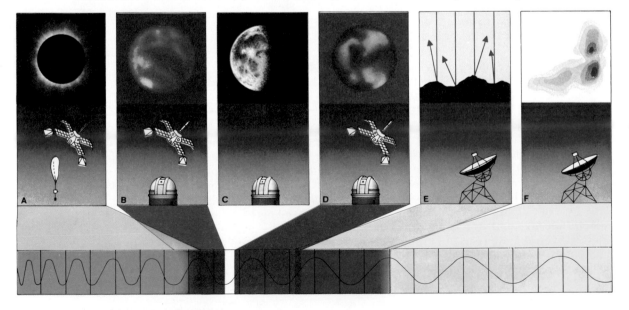

Cornell University Photographs

The radio-radar telescope facility at Arecibo Observatory in Puerto Rico is used to monitor radio emissions from inside and outside our galaxy.

RADIO ASTRONOMY

Radio astronomy was the first part of invisible astronomy to be exploited—largely because a "window" in the Earth's atmosphere allows radio waves from less than an inch to about 98 feet (30 meters) in length to reach the ground. The first cosmic-radio sources were discovered in December 1931 by Karl G. Jansky, an engineer at Bell Telephone Laboratories who was working on the problem of radio static. After eliminating Earthly sources of static, he found that he was still left with a persistent hiss, whose source moved across the sky from east to west. With careful tests, he showed that this source of cosmic-radio noise came from our own galaxy, the Milky Way. In 1936 an American amateur radio operator named Grote Reber built a radio receiver in his backyard in Wheaton, Illinois, and produced the first radio map of the sky at 24-inch (61-centimeter) wave-

lengths. Yet such pioneering work received little attention for years, obscured as it was by the focus on military science during World War II.

In the long run, however, the war greatly advanced radio astronomy. Once peace was achieved, it was a relatively straightforward task to turn military radio receivers upward to investigate the heavens. Early discoveries included radio emissions from the Sun, and radar studies of the Moon and meteors as they entered our atmosphere. Although rather mundane by today's standards, these observations opened the door to much greater discoveries. Ever-larger radio telescopes were built, and a wider range of radio wavelengths was investigated, through the 1950s and early 1960s. Radio emissions at the 8-inch (21-centimeter) wavelength, emanating from interstellar hydrogen, were used to map the

RADIO ASTRONOMY   55

great clouds of gas in our galaxy. Many discrete sources of radio emissions were also found, including the enigmatic quasars—their name an acronym for "quasi-stellar radio sources." Radio astronomy was also responsible for the detection of pulsars—rapidly spinning neutron stars formed in some supernova explosions.

The resolution of a telescope (that is, its ability to see fine spatial detail) is a function of both the wavelength of light being sampled and the diameter of the telescope. At good sites, optical telescopes (which are also limited by turbulence in the atmosphere) achieve angular resolutions of about one second of arc (or 1/3600 of a degree). Because wavelengths of radio light are so much longer than those of optical light, radio observations were intrinsically of lower resolution than optical observations. Hence, astronomers wanting to see faint, distant objects and to improve resolution of closer ones were highly motivated to build very large radio telescopes.

The largest fully steerable radio telescope is the 328-foot (100-meter) dish in Bonn, Germany. Its curved, metallic dish is the size of a football field—yet readily movable. In Arecibo, Puerto Rico, astronomers use a 984-foot (300-meter) radio dish built right into the landscape. Instead of moving the telescope, a radio receiver at the focus of the dish is moved.

INTEROMETRY

One of the revolutions in radio astronomy has been the development of a technique called interferometry, which permits astronomers to combine radio signals from separate telescopes and, by doing so, see much finer detail. At least two radio telescopes are needed for interferometry, and the wider their separation, the higher the resolution achieved. Some information about the objects being observed is lost with this technique, but the more radio telescopes you add to such a network, the

The Very Large Array radio telescope in New Mexico combines radio signals from 27 separate radio dishes arranged in a Y configuration that extends as far as 17 miles.

closer it comes to simulating a single, enormous instrument. The practical use of interferometry is by and large dependent on advanced computer technology, since it requires complex processing systems to combine and coordinate the signals from separate telescopes.

One of the most powerful interferometers today is the Very Large Array of radio telescopes (or VLA) near Socorro, New Mexico. Twenty-seven separate radio dishes, each 82 feet (25 meters) in diameter, are arrayed in one of four alternate Y-shaped configurations for observations. The most extended of these configurations has a diameter of 22 miles (35 kilometers). The VLA's radio antennas can be moved when necessary by placing them on railroad tracks. Socorro's VLA radio telescope produces radio images with a resolution comparable to ground-based optical images. And it has been used by hundreds of astronomers to observe everything from planets to quasars. The VLA has observed some of the largest single structures in the universe—mysterious double plumes of radio emissions that extend outward from the cores of some very active galaxies.

The best resolutions can be obtained by combining signals from radio telescopes separated by thousands of miles, even continents. Such Very Long Baseline Interferometry (VLBI) lacks the full imaging capability of the VLA, but has nonetheless achieved impressive resolutions of certain celestial objects. VLBI measurements are so sensitive that they can be used to detect movements of less than 1 inch (2.5 centimeters) in the Earth's crust between the individual telescopes!

VLBI measurements are accomplished largely by arrangements made among the researchers who control radio telescopes around the world. Radio telescopes dedicated to VLBI measurements now work as the world's largest dedicated, full-time astronomical instrument. Called the Very Long Baseline Array, or VLBA, it includes 10 82-foot (25-meter)-diameter radio telescopes located from Hawaii to the Virgin Islands, and is controlled remotely from the Array Operations Center in Socorro.

Radio and optical astronomy complement each other in the study of the heavens. After radio emissions have been detected from a particular part of the sky, the optical astronomer then knows where to focus his telescope to discern the object and discover more about it. The radio source emitted by Cygnus A led optical astronomers to discover that it was actually a double nebula (above), possibly a collision of two galaxies.

THE FUTURE OF RADIO ASTRONOMY

Although astronomers need not go into space to detect radio light, an orbiting radio telescope could be used in conjunction with ground-based telescopes to obtain even longer baselines and higher resolutions than ever before. An international coalition will be needed to fund and execute such a project, however.

Another reason to pursue radio astronomy from space would be to get away from Earth-based "radio pollution," human-made signals that interfere with radio astronomy in much the same way that "light pollution" plagues optical astronomers. Although specific parts of the radio spectrum are set aside for the sole use of radio astronomy, it is becoming increasingly difficult to find sites where radio telescopes are not affected by television- and radio-station signals. Hence, the idea of putting radio telescopes on the back side of the Moon, away from Earthly interference, is a hot topic among future-minded astronomers.

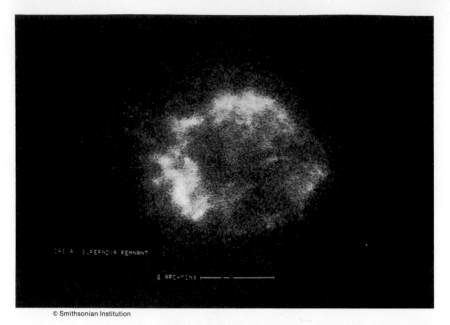

© Smithsonian Institution

X-ray radiation glows in this spectacular image of Cassiopeia A, a supernova remnant of gas and debris that was left when a star exploded. Supernova explosions can continue to emit X rays for hundreds or thousands of years.

X-RAY ASTRONOMY

X-ray light and its high-energy cousin, gamma-ray light, are found at extremely short wavelengths. X rays typically have wavelengths about 4,000 times shorter than those of visible light, or less than a few angstroms (one angstrom is equal to one ten-billionth of a meter). Gamma-ray wavelengths are still smaller by a factor of 100 to 1,000. To put it another way, X-ray wavelengths are roughly the size of atoms, while gamma rays have wavelengths about the size of atomic nuclei. Since wavelengths are inversely proportional to the energy needed to create the light, these emissions come from the most energetic phenomena.

X-ray astronomy provides a very different perspective on our universe. This new way of looking at the skies has brought into focus hot young stars, exploding stars, and neutron stars, as well as active and exploding galaxies, and perhaps even black holes.

EARLY X-RAY ASTRONOMY

As early as the late 1940s, scientists fitted suborbital rockets with crude detectors to monitor X rays coming from the Sun. For nearly 15 years, the Sun was the only object bright enough to be detected in X-ray light. But in 1962, with better X-ray detectors and improved rockets, astronomers discovered an X-ray-emitting object in the constellation Scorpius. This object, dubbed Sco X-1, turned out to be a member of one of the primary classes of X-ray sources: a close binary star where solar material is actually jumping from one star to the other. With the discovery of Sco X-1, X-ray astronomy was born.

In 1970 astronomers launched the first satellite designed to study X-ray emissions. Named Uhuru, this satellite carried a simple scanning device that could tell bright from dark X-ray areas. The early instruments used in X-ray astronomy were like the light meters used by photographers. They could tell whether a patch of the sky was dim or bright in X rays, but they could not take pictures. While Uhuru could map the sky at X-ray wavelengths, it could not really "see." As X-ray-detector technology developed, scientists learned how to convert X rays to visible light. With this great advance, they were able to make X-ray pictures.

THE EINSTEIN AND ROSAT MISSIONS

The first satellite capable of taking X-ray pictures of the sky was launched in 1978. It was named the Einstein X-ray Observatory. The Einstein telescope consisted of a special X-ray grazing-incidence mirror, two X-ray cameras, and two X-ray spectrographs. For nearly two and a half years of operation, this telescope and spacecraft were controlled by onboard computers and radio commands from a ground-based control center. The telescope detected many thousands of X-ray sources, some 1,000 times fainter than any previously observed.

Scientists learned that X-ray emitters include normal stars, young and old; neutron stars and black holes; remnants of supernova explosions; galaxies; quasars; and even clusters of galaxies. Researchers today continue to learn from the data returned by the Einstein satellite.

On June 1, 1990, NASA launched the ROSAT X-ray mission into orbit on a Delta II rocket. ROSAT, built by scientists in Germany, includes instruments built by Great Britain and the United States and was launched by the United States. The ROSAT X-ray mirror was the finest one ever made, and its instruments were upgraded versions of the ones that worked so well on the Einstein satellite. ROSAT performed an all-sky X-ray survey before moving on to studying individual objects. In 1995, the Rossi X-ray Timing Explorer (RXTE) was launched into

Earth's orbit to study how X-ray sources vary over time periods ranging from mere microseconds to several months.

FUTURE OF X-RAY ASTRONOMY

The United States, Japan, and Europe all have active X-ray-astronomy research programs. At the end of the 1990s, the National Aeronautics and Space Administration (NASA) launched a mission called the Chandra X-ray Observatory. It features an enlarged and improved version of the Einstein telescope that provides pictures 10 times sharper of distant X-ray objects. The telescope also covers a wider range of X-ray wavelengths and provides higher-quality X-ray spectra. Chandra represents the X-ray portion of NASA's highly successful Great Observatories program.

In October 2000, NASA scientists launched the High Energy Transient Explorer (HETE-2) to detect and pinpoint gamma rays, the highest known energies of electromagnetic radiation. Although gamma rays had been studied by NASA's Compton Gamma-Ray Observatory (CGRO) before its demise in 2000, little is known about the origin of this high-energy form of radiation.

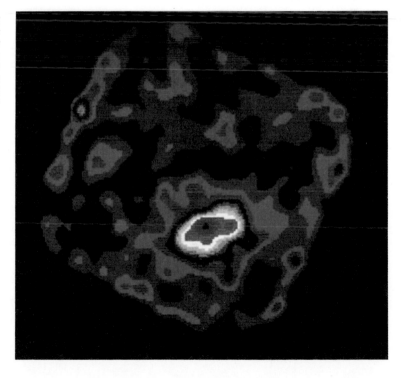

The ROSAT satellite captured this X-ray image of the cluster galaxy Abell 2256. Cluster galaxies are traditionally strong X-ray emitters, due to the tremendously hot gases that are swept out of violently colliding galaxies to accumulate in intergalactic space.

An edge-on view of the galaxy NGC 4565. The reddish area represents infrared light, which passes more easily through obscuring interstellar dust than does visible light.

INFRARED AND ULTRAVIOLET ASTRONOMY

Infrared Astronomy

The infrared wavelengths lie between the optical part of the light spectrum and the radio region. A few small portions of the near-infrared spectrum (those wavelengths closest to optical light) are able to slip through the Earth's atmosphere to where they can be observed directly from the ground. The longer far-infrared wavelengths, however, are completely absorbed by the slightest amount of atmospheric water vapor and gas.

Infrared light, also known as heat radiation, was first measured in an astronomical context by the English astronomer Sir William Herschel in the early 19th century. After breaking the Sun's light into a spectrum, Herschel used a thermometer to measure the temperature of various colors of sunlight, and noticed that he continued to get readings beyond the red end of the visible spectrum.

In the 20th century, astronomers attached electrical devices called thermocouples to optical telescopes to discover that stars appearing red radiate relatively more infrared energy than stars of other colors. In this way, they have also discovered that the planet Jupiter gives off twice as much energy as it receives from the Sun. (This discovery led to the conclusion that the massive planet is producing its own energy by gravitational contraction.)

Since infrared light readily passes through interstellar dust, while optical light gets absorbed, infrared observations have been used to learn much about the dusty regions where stars are being born.

Water vapor, which is the main block to infrared wavelengths, is concentrated in Earth's lower atmosphere. Hence, one need not go all the way out of the atmosphere to observe some parts of the infrared spectrum. Infrared telescopes have been built in very dry and high places and sent aloft aboard special balloons and suborbital sounding rockets. Such technology has enabled astronomers to obtain detailed information on individual sources of infrared light and regions of star formation, but it has not been able to provide a complete infrared survey and map of the heavens.

Refrigerators In Space

In actuality, everything in the universe emits some energy at infrared wavelengths —that is, everything gives off some heat. One of the ramifications of this is that even an Earth-based telescope "glows" at infrared wavelengths, and so can obscure faint infrared signals from objects in space. Astronomers recognized that one solution to this problem would be to place an infrared telescope in space (see also page 45). Besides providing a viewing platform far above the atmosphere, space provides an insulating vacuum. Using liquid helium, an orbiting infrared telescope could be chilled to within a few degrees of absolute zero (–459° F, or –273° C), reducing the instrument's own infrared background radiation and ultimately making the telescope much more sensitive. In addition, an orbiting infrared satellite would at last make it possible to survey the entire sky for radio-wave-emitting objects.

Thus, in cooperation with Great Britain and the Netherlands, the United States launched the Infrared Astronomical Satellite (IRAS) aboard a Delta rocket on January 25, 1983. IRAS was the largest cryogenic (operating at very low temperatures) telescope

ever put into Earth orbit. Its detectors operated at four far-infrared wavelengths, providing a wealth of temperature information on the objects being observed. IRAS was placed in a polar orbit at an altitude of 560 miles (900 kilometers), and was programmed to observe a 2-degree-wide band perpendicular to the line joining the Earth and Sun. Thus, as the Earth slowly moved around the Sun, IRAS slowly built up an infrared map encompassing nearly the entire celestial sphere.

During its 10 months of operation, IRAS provided astronomers with a new view of the universe. This 22-inch (57-centimeter) telescope was 1,000 times more sensitive than any infrared instrument on Earth. It peered through the interstellar dust that obscures our visible view of the center of the Milky Way galaxy, providing for the first time a clear, panoramic view of the center of our own galaxy. Among the discoveries logged by IRAS are a disk of dust around the star Vega, six new comets, very strong infrared emissions from colliding galaxies, and wisps of warm dust (called "infrared cirrus") in almost every direction of space.

The comet IRAS-Araki-Alcock, long invisible to optical telescopes, was discovered using the infrared-sensitive IRAS telescope.

JPL/NASA

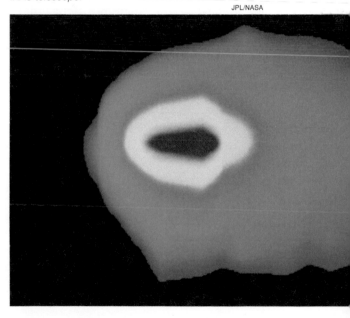

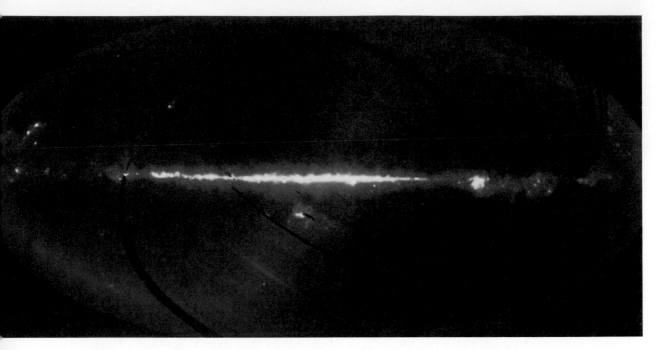

Most of our knowledge of the infrared-emitting objects in our universe is due to the IRAS satellite.

Outside our solar system, IRAS found that Vega, the brightest star in the constellation Lyra, is surrounded by a ring of solid particles 15 billion miles (24 billion kilometers) across—the kind of space debris that may eventually coalesce to form planets around this star. IRAS also peered deep into interstellar clouds of gas and dust to show that star-forming regions—stellar nurseries—are much more prevalent in the universe than previously thought. In all, IRAS cataloged more than 250,000 individual infrared sources and covered more than 98 percent of the sky.

In late 1989, NASA launched an additional refrigerated telescope. The Cosmic Background Explorer (COBE) was designed to survey infrared radiation thought to be the remains of the titanic explosion called the "Big Bang," which is believed to have started the universe's expansion some 13 billion to 15 billion years ago. Hence, COBE looked past the stars, past the galaxies, and past the quasars to the very earliest times in the universe. COBE found that this cosmic background is not uniform in all directions. Its tiny fluctuations might help astronomers explain how galaxies and galaxy clusters actually originated.

The Future of Infrared Astronomy

Scientists will spend many more years studying the infrared data produced by IRAS and COBE. And now, NASA has developed an infrared telescope 1,000 times more sensitive than IRAS. This powerful instrument, the Spitzer Space Telescope—a 34-inch (0.85-meter)-diameter infrared telescope—was launched atop a Delta rocket in August 2003, as the fourth and final element of NASA's highly successful Great Observatories Program.

ULTRAVIOLET ASTRONOMY

Ultraviolet (UV) astronomy encompasses the range of wavelengths from about 50 angstroms up to about 4,000 angstroms. Astronomers find it convenient to subdivide this range into the near UV (3,000 to 4,000 angstroms), the far UV (912 to 3,000 angstroms), and the extreme UV (below 912 angstroms). Near-UV light can penetrate our atmosphere and be observed from Earth's surface. Far- and extreme-UV light does not penetrate the atmosphere, and therefore can only be observed from space.

The wavelength at 912 angstroms is of interest to scientists because, at this wavelength, interstellar hydrogen gas cuts off our "sight" of nearly all objects outside our solar system. Hydrogen, the most abundant element in the universe, effectively absorbs wavelengths for several hundred angstroms short of 912 angstroms, making observations in this range impossible. However, as one moves to shorter wavelengths, hydrogen becomes less effective at absorbing light, and our observations improve. Given this difficulty, relatively little work has been done in the extreme UV.

Early Discoveries in Ultraviolet Astronomy

As with infrared astronomy, astronomers have lofted UV telescopes above the atmosphere by balloon and sounding rockets. But the majority of discoveries in UV astronomy have come by way of true, space-based telescopes. In 1972 the Copernicus satellite was the first to obtain high-resolution images at the short-wavelength limit of the far-UV range. This satellite was

largely restricted to observing the hottest bright stars, and returned a wealth of information about these stars, as well as about interstellar gas.

In the mid-1970s, a satellite called TD-1 performed a survey of the entire sky at four far-UV wavelengths. The satellite cataloged more than 31,000 objects with bright UV emission.

Until recently, the biggest workhorse in UV astronomy was the International Ultraviolet Explorer (IUE), a joint venture of NASA, the European Space Agency (ESA), and Great Britain. Launched in 1978 for a planned three-year mission, IUE survived for nearly 19 years. The IUE telescope was a mere 16 inches (41 centimeters) in diameter, yet its location above the atmosphere and its geosynchronous orbit (above the equator and moving at the same speed as Earth rotates) enabled it to obtain long exposures and observe fairly faint objects. When its mission ended in September 1996, IUE had captured 104,000 individual spectral

The data relayed by the International Ultraviolet Explorer satellite, launched in 1978, provided information on virtually every type of astronomical object.

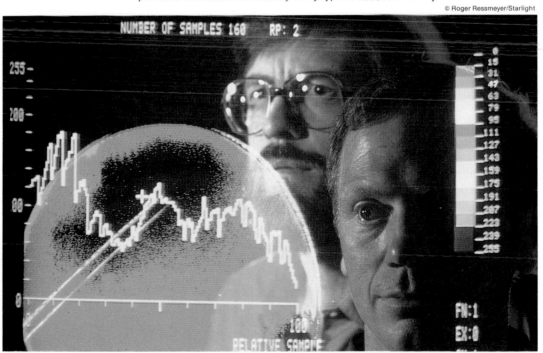

Satellites in orbit far above Earth's obscuring atmosphere, containing telescopes sensitive to the invisible portion of the spectrum, are revealing a universe that, until recently, has been largely inaccessible to astronomers.

exposures. Virtually every class of astronomical object was examined with IUE. And it returned high- and low-resolution images of a wide range of astronomical sources emanating in the far UV.

Of course, IUE was a relatively small telescope. Many years of planning and effort culminated in April 1990 with the launch of the now-famous Hubble Space Telescope, which is equipped with both far-UV and optical telescopes. Hubble is pushing UV investigations to fainter objects and greater distances than ever before possible.

Because of absorption by interstellar hydrogen, relatively little exploration has occurred in the extreme UV region beyond 400 angstroms. In 1990, the X-ray satellite ROSAT carried aloft a Wide Field Camera developed in Great Britain. This camera produced the first all-sky survey at extreme-UV wavelengths. A much more advanced instrument, called the Extreme Ultraviolet

Explorer (EUVE) mission, was launched by NASA in 1992. Until its instruments were officially deactivated in January 2001, EUVE successfully mapped the extreme ultraviolet radiation of the entire sky and probed even deeper into the universe with its "Deep Survey" telescope. EUVE reentered the atmosphere and burned up over central Egypt in January 2002.

The Future of UV Astronomy

Astronomers are now excited about a mission that only recently got under way. The Far Ultraviolet Spectroscopic Explorer, or FUSE, was launched aboard a Delta rocket in June 1999. This satellite produces very high-resolution spectra of objects in the far- and extreme-UV part of the spectrum. FUSE is about 50,000 times more sensitive than the Copernicus satellite that flew in the early 1970s, and is extending high-resolution UV spectroscopy to many more exciting objects.

Courtesy of Audio-Visual Imagineering, Inc.

Planetariums, long renowned for showcasing the heavens, are now used for a variety of entertainment purposes, including spectacular laser light shows.

PLANETARIUMS

by Dennis L. Mammana

The doors open, and a large, circular theater looms before us. As we take our seats and look around, we can feel the excitement build as powerful music rises and darkness falls. The floor slowly drops away. We are now surrounded by stars, more than we've ever seen at one time in our lives. Some are familiar: There's the Big Dipper. Over there is Orion, the Hunter. And there is. . . . Wait. The sky is beginning to change. No, we're moving, drifting up and away from . . . wherever we are in the universe. Planets and asteroids rush by. A strange orange planet rises in front of us, growing ever larger. Suddenly we are immersed in the planet's clouds, a swirling reddish brown haze. Above, we see two suns—one blue and one yellow—engaged in a graceful cosmic dance. We soon forget them, however, as a huge lightning bolt tears through the clouds, literally shaking us to the core with its tremendous blast. Now what?! We reach for something to cover us as rain begins to fall. Is it water sprinkling onto our skin, or some strange, alien chemical?

Obviously, this is no ordinary theater. It is a remarkable multimedia coliseum of illusion, an engulfing experience that can capture our five senses and our imagination and carry us places we thought impossible. This is a modern planetarium.

EARLY PLANETARY MODELS

The fantastic space theaters of today have evolved from a long line of planetariums with a rich history extending back many centuries. The earliest planetariums began as scale models of the sky—though we might hardly recognize them as such.

The ancient Greek astronomer Eratosthenes may have been the first to build a sky model, around 250 B.C. His device, a metal sphere and surrounding rings, moved on two axes. The metal "celestial sphere" moved on one axis, while the rings, which represented the paths of the Sun and other planetary bodies, moved on the other. The device and those like it became known as armillary spheres.

The Greek mathematician and inventor Archimedes built an impressive armillary sphere powered by water. It is said to have been so accurate that it could reproduce eclipses of the Sun and Moon. Another ancestor of the modern planetarium is the celestial globe. This was a sphere on which the positions of the stars and constellations were marked so they could be viewed from the outside.

One other popular model, built in the 1700s, was the *orrery*, named after the British earl of Orrery, for whom it was built. It was notable for showing that the Earth was just one of the solar system's children planets, all of which were mounted on rotating arms surrounding a central sun. Orreries are still popular in science classrooms today, and are sometimes incorporated into a clock that coordinates their movements.

The first planetarium theater was built in 1657 by Andreas Busch. He constructed a large globe into which twelve people could climb. The stars were fixed on the inside of the globe, and the planets moved along a set of internal rings. Visitors could

sit and gaze at the artificial stars and planets as if sitting under a perfectly clear night sky.

Astronomers continued to team with engineers to build such globes right up to the 20th century. Dr. Wallace Atwood of the Chicago Academy of Science built the last of these globes. Fifteen feet (4.5 meters) wide and powered by electricity, it is still on display at the academy.

Scala

Photo Tomsich Rome

These early models of the sky are actually precursors to the modern planetarium. An 18th-century Copernican model (top) shows the Earth, Moon, Venus, and Mercury revolving around the Sun. An armillary sphere (right) is surrounded by metal rings, each mounted on a different axis to represent the paths of the Sun and other celestial bodies across the sky.

THE MODERN PLANETARIUM

For most of us, the word "planetarium" conjures up the image of a domed room with a large, dumbbell-shaped projector, or "bug," in its center. Here is a place where stars, the Moon, and planets can be realistically viewed in the middle of the day.

This modern form of the planetarium was developed in the early 1900s by Drs. Max Wolf of the Heidelberg Observatory and Walter Bauersfeld of the Carl Zeiss Company in Jena, Germany. These men were the first to envision and design a planetarium projector. Their idea, as Bauersfeld described it in 1919, revolutionized our ability to re-create the cosmos: "The great sphere shall be fixed; its inner white surface shall serve as the projection surface for many small projectors which shall be placed in the center of the sphere. The reciprocal positions and motions of the little projectors shall be interconnected by suitable driving gears in such a manner that the little images of the heavenly bodies, thrown upon the fixed hemisphere, shall represent the stars visible to the naked eye, in position and in motion, just as we are accustomed to see them in the natural clear sky."

In August 1923, Bauersfeld demonstrated the first "Zeiss Model I" planetarium projector in a makeshift plaster dome on the roof of the Zeiss factory. It showed in stunning detail the stars, Sun, Moon, and planets as they would normally be visible from Munich. Two months later the projector was installed in the Deutsches Museum, opening to the public on October 21, 1923. "The Wonder of Jena," as it soon became known, captured the public's imagination as no astronomical novelty ever had.

The Zeiss Company soon began constructing more planetarium projectors and developed the dumbbell-shaped projecting instrument. Descendants of these projectors are still seen in many planetariums today. At the center of each end of the dumbbell is a high-powered lamp. Arranged around each lamp are numerous lens systems, each containing a metal slide

Cie generale de physique

The Zeiss projector (above), the mainstay of many modern planetariums, projects images of the stars and planets as they appear at different times during the day or year, in both the northern and southern hemisphere.

of an area of the sky. Tiny holes in the slides represent individual stars and constellations. As light passes through each hole, a point of light—or star—is formed on the dome ceiling. Bigger holes are needed to project brighter stars. Re-creating the brightest stars requires separate projectors equipped with filters to produce each star's correct color. Similar projectors are used to show the images of planets, while still larger projectors create images of the Sun and Moon.

The first such planetarium in the United States was built in 1930 in Chicago. It became known as the Adler Planetarium, and was one of only half a dozen planetariums in the world. The equipment, backup facilities, and staff needed to run these planetariums were tremendously expensive. Only the largest of major-city museums could afford them.

In 1947 Armand Spitz, an amateur astronomer from Philadelphia, designed and built a smaller, simpler, and less expensive planetarium projector. His invention en-

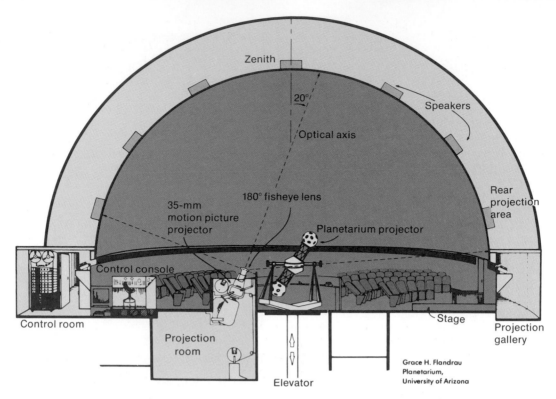

Zenith

20°

Optical axis

Speakers

180° fisheye lens

35-mm
motion picture
projector

Planetarium projector

Rear
projection
area

Control console

Control room

Projection
room

Stage

Elevator

Projection
gallery

Grace H. Flandrau
Planetarium,
University of Arizona

A typical planetarium has a characteristic dome ceiling, a Zeiss projector, a control console for the lecturer, and seats arranged for easy viewing of the ceiling.

In addition to the motions of celestial objects, planetariums often are equipped to project images of outer space, such as this lunar landscape exhibit at New York City's Hayden Planetarium.

Courtesy of the Virginia Living Museum

A show at the Virginia Living Museum captures the vibrant intensity of the Orion nebula, which is composed of gas and dust that reflect the light of nearby stars.

abled many small museums, libraries, and schools to install their own, more economical planetariums.

Since that time, planetariums have been springing up at an average rate of about 30 a year. Today there are nearly 1,400 operating around the world. In addition to the Zeiss and Spitz models, some 165 different types can be found in 64 countries on six continents.

HOW DOES IT ALL WORK?

A planetarium instrument is more than a static projector. It is a complicated machine of optical and mechanical parts that moves the stars, Sun, Moon, and planets across the "heavens." The gear systems that perform the work have been developed through detailed mathematical analysis of the paths of the heavenly bodies. A planetarium projector can show four basic motions: daily motion, annual motion, latitude

motion, and precession, the motion created by the subtle wobbling of our planet on its axis.

The sky's daily motion—the sunrise in the east and the sunset in the west, for example is really a manifestation of the Earth's daily rotation. While it takes 24 hours for the Earth to turn once, most planetarium projectors can perform the same feat in less than a minute. Using this daily motion, the planetarium operator can select any time of day to be shown on the dome.

Annual motion is the movement of the Earth and other planets as they move around the Sun. The planetarium operator can take the audience through a year in less than a minute, and re-create the sky on any day of any given year.

Latitude motion allows the planetarium operator to simulate the changing sky as seen from different latitudes on Earth. This enables the audience to view the heavens as they would appear above the North

The "Space Transporters" program at the Adler Planetarium in Chicago allows visitors to explore the atmosphere and environment of the Sun, Moon, and planets.

Pole, from New York City, Rio de Janeiro, or from virtually any point on the Earth's surface. One trip around our planet can be accomplished in a matter of seconds.

The subtle planetary motion called precession, which changes the celestial north pole in the sky, brings a slightly different array of stars into view over a given point on Earth. This subtle motion takes some 26,000 years to complete one cycle. Yet in the planetarium, audiences can experience the effects of a complete precession cycle in less than a minute.

By moving the projector along its many separate axes, the operator can also turn a planetarium into a space-and-time machine. Not only can it show you what the stars, Sun, Moon, and planets look like from any point on Earth, it can let you view the sky as it was on the night you were born, or how it will appear 50 or 100 years from now. Some planetariums now have the capability of re-creating solar and lunar

eclipses, variable stars such as supernovas, meteors, weather phenomena like racing clouds, and beautiful sunrises and sunsets. All of this is done with remarkable scientific accuracy.

Today all this wizardry can be controlled by a solitary operator, who creates the desired effects with the knobs and buttons on the planetarium console. These professionals usually have training in both astronomy and the operation of electromechanical devices. Thanks to computer technology, operators can even preprogram a show, then just sit back and enjoy it.

And just as the hardware behind the shows has changed to match the times, our concept of a planetarium "show" has changed as well. Live lectures, with an astronomer describing the sky as audiences would normally see it at night, are still an important part of a planetarium's schedule. But the big crowd pleasers are spectacular multimedia extravaganzas.

LASER SHOWS AND SPACE THEATERS

Modern planetariums can create remarkable three-dimensional illusions of space travel. Shows now combine the projection of stars with flashy special effects that whisk the audience into space. Virtually anything real or imagined can be produced in the planetarium. Planetarium devices can take you on a journey across our galaxy, race you across the surface of Mars, or cast you into a black hole.

The shows literally surround an audience with realistic otherworldly landscapes and distant skyscapes. Colorful lasers, rotating planets, swirling clouds, and whizzing spacecraft fill the planetarium dome. Several planetariums are even equipped with special plumbing systems that actually sprinkle audiences with purified water to simulate a rainstorm! All this wizardry is controlled by computers and accompanied by powerful sound tracks. Often the prerecorded voices of movie stars and other well-known narrators guide the audience in their journeys across the universe.

Behind such spectacular illusions lies the hardware that forms the planetarium itself. The dome is often made of sheet aluminum, perforated with tiny holes. These holes, invisible to the casual visitor, make the dome virtually translucent. They also keep air ventilating through the planetarium theater, make the dome lighter, and allow the placement of immense audio speakers, which provide the spectacular sound tracks. Modern planetariums also hide elaborate special effects behind this inner dome. Exploding stars and space-walking astronauts stand invisible until the operator throws a switch.

Still, the planetariums continue to produce new magic tricks that amaze audi-

This unique space exhibit includes three-dimensional scale models of the Sun, planets, and the largest moons of the solar system.

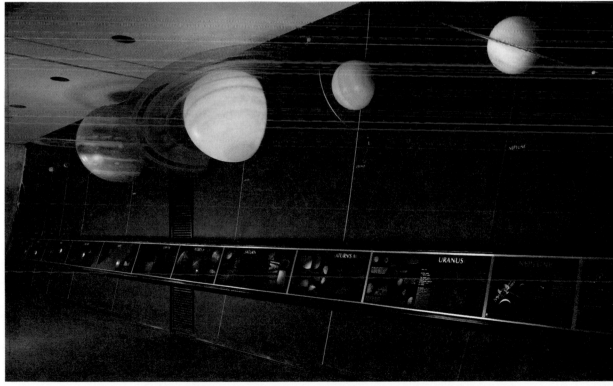

ences. In 1983, a totally new type of planetarium instrument burst onto the scene. Introduced by Evans and Sutherland Computer Corporation of Salt Lake City, Utah, the "Digistar," a computer-graphics-imaging device, projects first-generation computer animation onto the planetarium dome. With this device, it has become possible to move at will within a simulated three-dimensional scene composed of computerized data fields. In other words, audiences can now experience scientifically accurate simulated spaceflights to stars within 1,000 light-years of Earth. With amazing realism, we can watch how our immediate solar neighborhood changes over a given year or over the next million years.

This new technology, along with laser and fiber-optic technology, has even been used to create animated three-dimensional models of everything from atoms and molecules to planets, stars, and entire galaxies. Such instruments may one day entirely replace the electromechanical projectors used in most of today's modern planetariums.

Through the advance of technology, the planetarium, which has long been used to educate the public about astronomy, now serves many functions. It has truly become an awe-inspiring vehicle—not only for recreating space travel or the view of a star-filled night as seen from another world, but also for journeying through history and learning about the evolution of Earth.

OTHER USES FOR PLANETARIUMS

Many modern planetariums also use their domed theaters for spectacular laser light shows, accompanied by rock, jazz, and classical music. They are likewise used for live plays, science-fiction programs, and live concerts performed under the stars and planets and accompanied by special light, sound, and motion effects.

In addition, some planetarium theaters are used to show motion pictures with immense film formats and gigantic, yet crisp, images. IMAX presentations, for example, require "Omnimax" projectors to show 70-mm-wide films across the interior of an entire dome. Smaller theaters may use 35-mm projectors such as the "Cine 360" to create similar wraparound illusions. Such "space theaters" are designed to fill the audience's entire field of vision with images, and so create a three-dimensional illusion of being transported through space and time.

Planetarium theaters have come a long way since the idea was born just a century ago. Today they are visited by hundreds of millions of people around the world, who leave inspired and awed by the wonder and mystery of the universe.

The Adler Planetarium in Chicago opened its doors to the public in May 1930; it was the first-ever modern planetarium operating in the Western Hemisphere.

The inner planets of our solar system—Mercury, Venus, Earth, and Mars (pictured above)—travel in nearly circular orbits around the Sun. The outer planets—Jupiter, Saturn, Uranus, Neptune, and Pluto—have more eccentric orbits.

THE SOLAR SYSTEM

by Ray Villard

Imagine you were on a starship deep within interstellar space, heading toward the solar system where Earth resides. As you approached from tens of billions of miles away, the Sun would appear to grow ever brighter. Eventually you would detect Earth as a faint pinpoint of light. If you observed for long enough, you would notice that Earth follows a wide path around the Sun. You would also see, at various distances from the Sun, eight other objects of various sizes. You might detect that many of these planets are circled by still smaller objects— their moons. In the space between the orbits of two of the planets, Mars and Jupiter, you would see thousands of very small "planets," or asteroids, also revolving around the Sun. You might even spot a few comets, their long, streaming tails slicing across the planetary orbits.

THE SUN

The Sun lies at the very heart of our solar system. It is a typical star, one of the 150 billion in the Milky Way galaxy. Because the Sun is much closer to us than is any other star, it seems many, many times larger than the more distant bodies. Its disk appears about the size of a full Moon.

Compared with the other stars of our galaxy, the Sun is an average-size star. But

All of the planets except tiny Mercury (far left) are somewhat tilted on their axes. Uranus rotates practically on its side (97.9-degree tilt), while Venus (177.4-degree tilt) is nearly upside down. Earth's 23.4-degree tilt is relatively similar to the tilts of Mars (25.2), Saturn (25.3), and Neptune (28.3). Jupiter's tilt measures only 3.1 degrees.

it is giant compared with even the largest planets. Its diameter of 865,278 miles (1.39 million kilometers) is more than 100 times greater than that of Earth. Even though it is of gaseous composition, the Sun weighs more than 300,000 times as much as Earth. Its surface temperature is 9,945° F (5,507° C). At its center, the temperature may reach as high as 25,000,000° F (14,000,000° C)— hot enough to smash atoms and generate energy through a process called nuclear fusion. Each second, the Sun converts 661 billion tons of hydrogen into 657 billion tons of helium. In the process, 4 billion tons of matter are converted to pure energy. This energy initially takes the form of deadly gamma rays, but by the time it bubbles to the surface of the Sun, the energy has been transformed into light, illuminating the planets and nurturing life on Earth.

CHILDREN OF THE SUN

The nine planets, in order of their distance from the Sun, are Mercury, Venus, Earth, Mars, Jupiter, Saturn, Uranus, Neptune, and Pluto. The planets all lie in about the same orbital plane, and they orbit the Sun in the same direction. This suggests that the solar system is a relic of a vast disk of dust and gas that surrounded the Sun as it formed 4.6 billion years ago. In the first few million years after the Sun ignited, major planets, ranging from several thousand to tens of thousands of miles across, formed within this gaseous disk. The largest chunks of leftover debris became trapped in the gravitational fields of the newly formed planets, and began orbiting them as moons.

Gravity pulled the smaller chunks to the surfaces of the planets and moons. Many of the craters that pepper the surfaces of these bodies are relics of this early period of intensive bombardment by interplanetary debris.

The solar system has two types of planets. The tiny rock, or terrestrial, planets all lie close to the Sun, like campers huddled around a bonfire. The immense outer planets—Jupiter, Saturn, Uranus, and Neptune—lie in the colder reaches of the solar system. They consist mostly of liquid and gas. The farthest planet from the Sun, Pluto, though still called a planet, may not be one after all. Recent evidence indicates that it may be the last remaining "fossil" of a population of thousands of "icy dwarf" bodies that once inhabited the solar system. In 2002, astronomers found a previously unknown planetoid, about half the size of Pluto, in the outer reaches of the solar system.

We have used robot spacecraft to fly by, orbit, and even land on, eight of the nine planets of our solar system. Probes have transmitted spectacular close-up pictures of all the planets (except Pluto), and in the process have revolutionized our understanding of how the celestial objects in our solar system evolved. Some of the Moon rocks brought back by the Apollo astronauts were found to be 4.5 billion years old, providing additional evidence that the formation of the planets and moons accompanied that of the Sun.

Moons

A moon is any natural body that orbits a planet. There are more than 140 known moons in our solar system. The majority of them orbit the giant planets Jupiter and Sat-

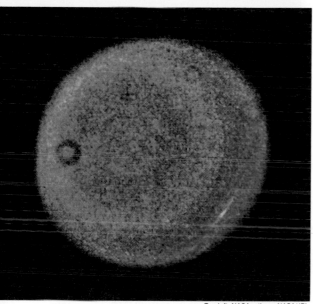

En route to Neptune, Voyager 2 collected data that greatly expanded our knowledge of other outer planets. Passing by Jupiter (above left), the probe identified volcanic eruptions on the Jovian moon Io. At Saturn (above), Voyager 2 determined the composition of Saturn's rings, information that may give clues to their origin. Whizzing by Uranus (left), Voyager 2 made the startling discovery of 10 new moons.

urn, and are little more than huge, airless balls of ice, ranging from hundreds to more than a thousand miles across. One of the largest moons, Saturn's Titan, is so big (3,449 miles, or 5,550 kilometers, in diameter) that it retains its own atmosphere of nitrogen. Mars has some of the smallest moons, a pair called Deimos and Phobos, each no bigger than an asteroid, which indeed they may have been at one time.

Asteroids

In the 18th century, astronomers calculated astrophysical laws that predicted they would find an as-yet-unseen planet between Mars and Jupiter. And they eagerly searched the skies for it. On the night of January 1, 1801, the Italian astronomer Giuseppe Piazzi discovered a small celestial body, which he took to be a planet, in the space between the orbits of Mars and Jupiter. This body, which was later called Ceres, was found to have a diameter of only 623 miles (1,002 kilometers). Over the years, many more small, planetlike bodies were found in the gap between Mars and Jupiter—a region of space dubbed the Asteroid Belt. Today, some 30,000 of these small bodies are discovered every year, and more than 210,000 are known to exist in our solar system. Some even have moons of their own.

These small bodies are now known as minor planets, or asteroids. The orbits of some extend beyond the Mars-Jupiter gap. But their combined mass is only a fraction of Earth's.

Astronomers once thought that asteroids were the fragments of a big planet that once orbited the Sun in a path between Mars and Jupiter and then broke apart for unknown reason. But in recent years, scientists have come to believe that asteroids are probably debris from throughout the solar system that never coalesced to form a planet.

Comets

Comets are among the strangest members of the solar system. Instead of moving as the planets do, in nearly circular orbits in the same direction, comets revolve around the Sun in very elongated ellipses, and from every conceivable direction. Much of the time they are so far away from the Sun that they are invisible even to our largest, most powerful telescopes.

Today, astronomers know that comets are members of the Sun's family. Many "long-period comets" may originate in a vast shell of icy debris called the Oort cloud, 50,000 times farther from the Sun than is Earth. Others, particularly those known as "short-period comets," come from the Kuiper Belt, a region 30 to 50 times farther from the Sun than is Earth. Both of these sources contain trillions of icy comet bodies that are gravitationally bound to the Sun.

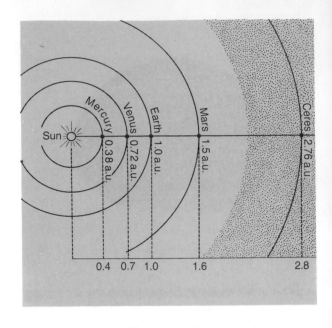

In this photomosaic of the solar system as seen from the Moon, the Earth is backlit by the Sun. The planet just above the Moon is Venus, and at top, from left to right, are the planets Jupiter, Mercury, Mars, and Saturn, replete with rings.

When astronomers first discover a comet, it usually appears as a faint, diffused, fuzzy star, with a dense, starlike center and a veil-like region, known as its *coma*. As the comet approaches the Sun, its coma becomes brighter, as more and more material vaporizes off the surface of the comet's solid, icy nucleus. When they are some 100 million miles (160 million kilometers) from the Sun, some comets begin to show a tail streaming behind them, pointing directly away from the Sun. Comet tails consist of very thin gases that fluoresce, or glow, under sunlight, as well as a fine stream of dust particles. This material is forced away from the Sun by the pressure of sunlight and the solar wind.

Meteors

Comets eventually break up into particles, which are sometimes seen entering Earth's atmosphere as meteors. Meteors—some of which originate in comets, and others as chunks from asteroids, moons, or other planets—range in size from specks the size of a pinhead to huge stones weighing many tons. We become aware of meteors only through the bright light produced when they collide with air molecules in our atmosphere. Most meteors disintegrate once they strike the atmosphere. Those that reach the ground are called meteorites. Most meteorites are fragments of asteroids, but a small number of them may have come from the Moon or Mars.

EARLY IDEAS OF THE SOLAR SYSTEM

The ancient Greek philosophers did not realize that Earth itself is a planet, or wanderer in the heavens (which, incidentally, is what *planet* means). Earth, they thought, hung motionless at the very center of the universe. They believed that each of the five planets they had seen (Mercury, Venus, Mars, Jupiter, and Saturn) were attached to concentric, invisible crystal spheres. The Moon and the Sun were attached to other spheres. These crystalline spheres, set one within the other, revolved around Earth, carrying with them the heavenly bodies. This theory could not explain certain phenomena, however.

For one thing, the planets do not move at an even rate across the sky. At certain times, they move more rapidly than at others. An even greater mystery was the observation that a planet such as Mars occasionally ceases its apparent eastward motion among the stars and reverses itself to head westward for a time. To explain this "retrograde motion" of the planets, early astronomers invented a complicated system of "epicycles." They held that each planet traveled along the circumference of a small circle, the center of which traveled along the circumference of a larger circle. Earth, it was maintained, was at the center of the larger circle.

This model of the universe prevailed for more than 1,000 years. In the first half of the

16th century, however, Polish astronomer Nicolaus Copernicus revived an idea that had been first proposed by the Greek philosopher Aristarchus of Samos—that the Earth and other planets move around the Sun. This system was called the heliocentric theory, since it placed the Sun (*helios*, in Greek) at the center of the universe.

Motions of the Planets

It required a lifetime effort on the part of several great astronomers to prove the Copernician heliocentric system. The 16th-century Danish nobleman Tycho Brahe made a long and accurate series of observations of the planets. Johannes Kepler, a German disciple of Brahe, drew up three laws of planetary motion that still hold true today. Kepler also improved on the Copernician model, which maintained that the planets move in circular orbits around the Sun. This belief led to inaccuracies in predicting planetary positions. Kepler was able to show, instead, that orbits are ellipses, rather than true circles.

While Kepler was refining his theories, Italian inventor and scientist Galileo Galilei used the telescope, a recent Dutch invention, to gather additional evidence support-ing Copernicus' theory. The telescope allowed Galileo to see the phases of Venus, which proved that it orbited the Sun, not Earth. Galileo also saw four tiny moons orbiting the distant planet Jupiter, in perfect accordance with Kepler's laws of motion.

The research of Kepler and Galileo clearly explained the nature of the planets' movements around the Sun, but neither scientist understood the force that governed these movements. This force was first revealed in 1687, when the great English scientist Isaac Newton presented his law of universal gravitation. This law states that every particle of matter in the universe attracts every other particle. This force of gravitation increases with the mass of an object, and depends on the distance between two objects. Newton showed mathematically that this is truly a universal law, since it applies not only to objects upon the Earth, but to heavenly bodies as well. The law of universal gravitation explains why planets, asteroids, and meteors keep orbiting the Sun, which is by far the most massive object in the solar system.

Using the law of universal gravitation, we can now analyze the motions of the planets with great accuracy. We can ac-

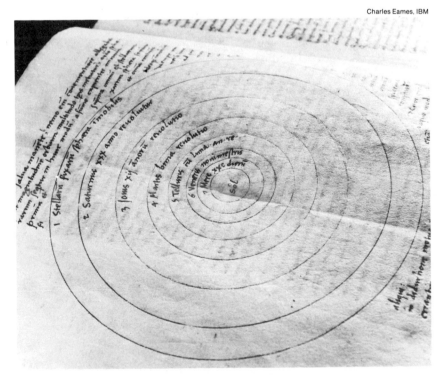

The Polish astronomer Nicolaus Copernicus published this diagram of a Sun-centered, or heliocentric, solar system in 1543. The theory wasn't fully accepted until the late 17th century.

count for the small deviations that arise as one planet affects the orbit of another.

It was the study of such deviations that led directly to the discovery of the planet Neptune. After Uranus had been discovered by Sir William Herschel in 1781, careful studies showed that it did not follow the orbit predicted by the law of universal gravitation. This led young Englishman John Couch Adams and French astronomer Urbain-Jean-Joseph Leverrier to conclude that Uranus was being attracted by another planet even more distant from the Sun. Both men calculated the position in the sky of the unknown planet without ever having seen it. On September 23, 1846, on the basis of Leverrier's calculations, German astronomer Johann Gottfried Galle located Neptune.

Astronomers suspected the existence of Pluto because of the disturbances of motion they had seen in the orbits of Uranus and Neptune. Such deviations suggested that the two planets were being gravitationally tugged by yet another unseen body. Pluto was discovered in 1930 after a year-long detailed search by astronomers at Flagstaff Observatory in Arizona.

In 1978 astronomers discovered that Pluto has at least one moon, which they called Charon. By plotting the moon's six-day orbit, astronomers were able to calculate the mass of Pluto, which turns out to be only 1/500 that of Earth. Pluto's orbit is rather unusual, taking a path some 17 degrees inclined to the plane taken by the other planets. Pluto's orbit is also highly elliptical, so much so that Pluto moves inside Neptune's path for about 20 years out of its 248-year orbit.

Because of Pluto's puny size, its solid icy surface, and its peculiar elongated orbit, many astronomers have begun to debate its status as an actual planet. It may, in actuality, be the largest of a new class of relatively large icy bodies beyond the orbit of Neptune, or maybe even a strange type of comet. In 1999, however, the International Astronomical Union tabled such debate and ruled that, until other evidence becomes available, Pluto will remain classified as the solar system's ninth planet.

Yerkes Observatory

Galileo used the telescope, recently invented in Denmark, to gather information about the motion of the planets. In his records of Jupiter and its moons (above), a sphere represents the planet and an asterisk represents moons.

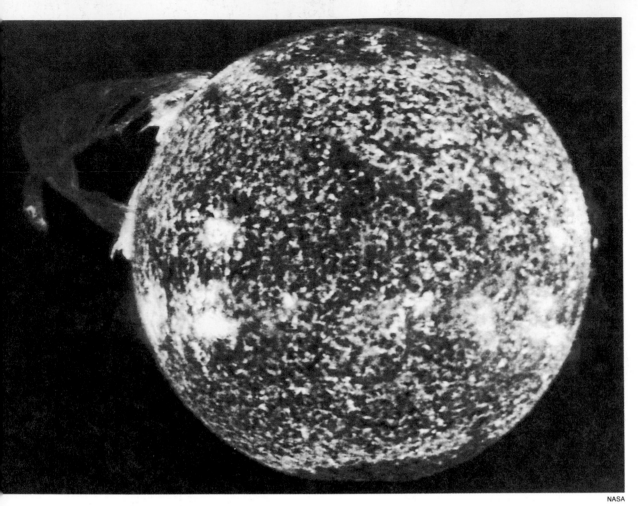

The Sun is the center of our solar system and the star upon which Earth depends for the existence of life.

THE SUN

by Oran R. White

"All the lines were busy, all the screens lit up. Bells sounded, and dashed lines of every color traced across a dozen monitors. An enormous explosion appeared on one console, while measurements of its effects were displayed on others, overprinted with alert notices in bold red letters. A U.S. Air Force duty officer paced back and forth behind civilian technical specialists, and next door a teletype swiftly transmitted an urgent warning to the Soviet Union. From Alaska to Omaha, bases and field posts were reporting to the National Oceanic and Atmospheric Administration (NOAA). I had never seen anything like this, except in space-war movies," recalls astronomer Steve Maran of the American Astronomical Society. "But this was no cinematic attraction or civil-defense drill. This was a storm on the Sun, an electromagnetic maelstrom so fierce that Earth, 93 million miles (150 million kilometers) across space, was being bathed in high-energy radiation."

The date was March 13, 1989, and astronomers were in the midst of documenting and studying the greatest peak of sunspot activity in recorded history. A solar flare thousands of miles across was producing magnetic storms and interference across Earth, knocking out the power of entire cities, scrambling radio and telephone communications, and producing rarely seen and very spectacular aurora borealis displays as far south as Mexico. The Solar Maximum of 1989 would stretch into 1992, wreaking electro-magnetic havoc, not only on Earth, but also in the skies. Increased radiation from the Sun heated and expanded Earth's atmosphere, dragging vital satellites to their premature and fiery deaths. Even the Solar Maximum Mission (Solar Max), a satellite lofted specifically to gather data on the Sun, was pulled into the heated atmosphere, where it disintegrated much earlier than originally planned.

During such solar peaks, occurring every 11 years or so, the Sun—taken for granted perhaps even more than the air we breathe—becomes front-page news. Yet even in the most mundane of times, no other heavenly body comes close to being as important to life on Earth. Not surprisingly, then, people have been observing the Sun for centuries. Today, spacecraft are providing new data about the Sun and how it affects Earth.

PHYSICAL DATA

The Sun is the center around which Earth and the other planets of our solar system revolve. It is a rather ordinary star of average size. Of course, the Sun appears much bigger and brighter to us because it is much closer to Earth than is any other star. It is about 93 million miles (150 million kilometers) away. The next-nearest star, Proxima Centauri, is nearly 25 trillion miles (40 trillion kilometers) away.

Our Sun is only one of about 150 billion stars in our galaxy, the Milky Way. It is located in one of the outer, spiral arms of the Milky Way, about three-quarters of the way from the galactic center.

The Sun is a vast ball of hot, glowing gas, some 865,278 miles (1.39 million kilometers) across—more than 100 times the diameter of Earth. The Sun's mass, however, equals that of 332,946 Earths. This tremendous weight produces a pressure at the center of the Sun of more than 1 million metric tons per square centimeter.

The Sun's gravity is 28 times stronger than that of Earth. So a man weighing 150 pounds (68 kilograms) on Earth would weigh 28 x 150 pounds (28 x 68 kilograms), or 4,200 pounds (1,905 kilograms), *if* he could stand on the surface of the Sun.

In spite of the great mass of the Sun, its average density—the weight of a standard volume of its matter—is only 1.4 times the weight of an equal volume of water. Earth, on the other hand, is 5.5 times denser than water. This low solar density is easy to explain. The center of the Sun, because of the enormous pressure, is more than 100 times denser than water. But much of the Sun beyond the center is composed of gas that is often thinner than Earth's atmosphere. When these densities are averaged together, the general density of the Sun turns out to be surprisingly low.

The Sun is very much like a huge furnace, fired by nuclear, or atomic, energy at its core. Temperatures at the center may be 25,000,000° F (14,000,000° C) or more. At the surface, temperatures are actually much cooler—approximately 9,945° F (5,507° C)—

STRUCTURE OF THE SUN

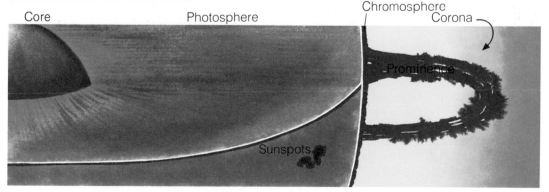

Core   Photosphere   Chromosphere   Corona

Prominence

Sunspots

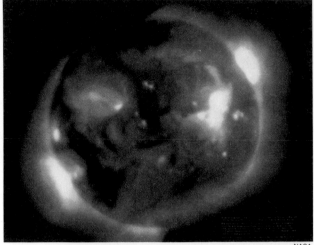

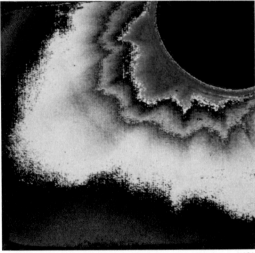

NASA

NASA

This Skylab photo captured the Sun's hot outer layer, or corona (top), which has a temperature of 4,000,000° F. The image above represents the densities of the corona, with the inner blue area being the most dense and the outer yellow area having the least density.

still hot enough to vaporize nearly all substances that exist as solids or liquids on the Earth.

ATMOSPHERE OF THE SUN

The Sun is composed of several distinct regions. It has a two-layer atmosphere. The solar atmosphere extends far upward from the *photosphere*, or solar surface. Consisting mostly of hydrogen gas, the atmosphere is also much less dense than the photosphere.

The lower atmospheric layer is the *chromosphere*, or "sphere of color." It ex-

tends as high as 7,500 miles (12,000 kilometers) above the surface. The upper layer is the *corona*, or "crown." The corona forms a beautiful white halo around the entire Sun, sending long streamers millions of miles out into space.

Normally, the effects of our own atmosphere and the bright glare of the photosphere blot out our view of the solar atmospheres. They become visible during a total eclipse, when the Moon covers the photosphere. Astronomers also study the corona through a special telescope called a coronagraph, which produces an artificial solar eclipse. The corona is also visible to astronauts flying above the Earth's atmosphere.

Temperatures in the corona and the chromosphere vary in a very unexpected manner. The lower part of the chromosphere may be less than 9,000° F (5,000° C), while the temperature rises in the outer reaches of the chromosphere, from 18,000° to 180,000° F (10,000° to 100,700° C). The corona, in turn, is much hotter than the chromosphere. Astronomers have estimated an astounding temperature of 3,600,000° F (2,000,000° C) for the corona's outer reaches.

Why should the corona, which is so far from the source of the Sun's energy, be so much hotter than the photosphere? One explanatory theory holds that strong shock waves, caused by turbulent movements of the photosphere, intensely heat the very thin gases of the corona.

A spectacular activity occurring in the chromosphere is the presence of *prominences*. These huge streamers of glowing gas can reach heights of hundreds of thousands of miles into the overlying corona. They take a great variety of shapes. Prominences are best observed during a solar eclipse or with a coronagraph.

Some prominences are eruptions or explosions, rising quickly and soon fading away. Other types last much longer. Still others seem to originate high in the chromosphere and then rain gas downward toward the Sun. The occurrence and lifetimes of prominences are influenced by solar magnetic fields.

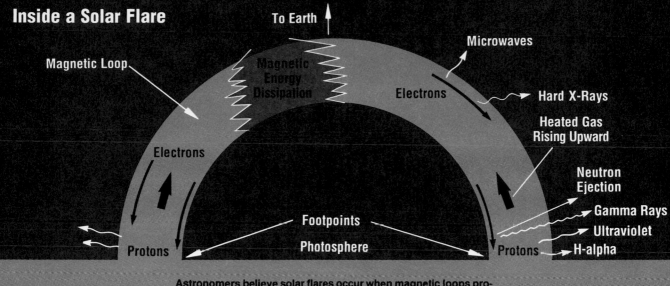

Inside a Solar Flare

To Earth

Microwaves

Magnetic Loop

Magnetic Energy Dissipation

Electrons

Hard X-Rays

Heated Gas Rising Upward

Electrons

Neutron Ejection

Gamma Rays

Ultraviolet

Footpoints

Photosphere

Protons

H-alpha

Protons

Astronomers believe solar flares occur when magnetic loops projecting from the Sun's surface "snap" from the buildup of stresses, accelerating large numbers of electrons and protons. These charged particles spiral along magnetic field lines, emitting electromagnetic radiation and heating the atmosphere at the base of the loop. This heated material then surges up the loop while gas at the "footpoints" emits H-alpha light.

The chromosphere also displays much smaller jets or filaments of gas, called *spicules*. These may result from strong movements of hot chromospheric gas. These gas movements appear in the chromosphere as coarse cells, called supergranulation.

From time to time, the chromosphere is active in other ways. Astronomers often notice hot, bright markings: *plages*, areas of hot brightness, and *flares*, high-energy outbursts of radiation and subatomic particles. These particles sometimes reach the Earth's atmosphere.

SURFACE OF THE SUN

It may seem strange to talk of the "surface" of a wholly gaseous globe. Yet the Sun's surface has a definite border. This layer, called the solar disk, or photosphere, is the deepest visible part of the Sun.

The photosphere is a relatively thin region, some 200 miles (320 kilometers) deep. This is less than 1/2,000 the solar radius.

The photosphere was once thought to be a uniform orb of light. But even in ancient times, observers occasionally saw spots on it. In the early 1600s, Italian scientist Galileo Galilei became the first person to study the Sun and its spots through a telescope. These so-called sunspots are dark, irregular patches. In addition to sunspots, two other main features have been found on the solar surface: bright, irregular areas called *faculae*, or "little torches," and a network of fine cells, the *photospheric granulation*.

Faculae are hot, glowing regions, ranging from tiny, bright marks to huge splotches that have a coarse-grained structure. They resemble the plages in the chromosphere. They often surround sunspot groups, but they may occur alone. Faculae often arise where sunspots later appear, and linger after the sunspots have vanished. Many astronomers consider them to be huge masses of gas that are hotter than the rest of the gaseous solar surface.

Through the telescope, photospheric granulation looks like bright grains of rice. The grains are separated from one another by dark boundaries. A typical grain, or cell, measures about 1,000 miles (1,600 kilometers) across. Astronomers consider the granulation to be photospheric gas in continuous and violent motion because of heat. On film the cells look like boiling fluid bringing up gas from the depths of the Sun.

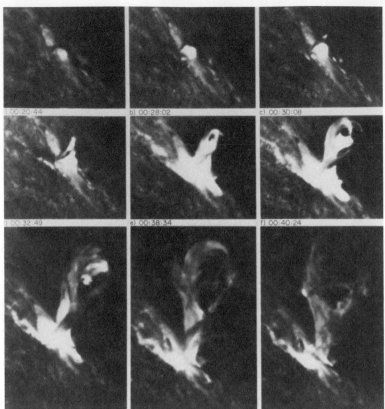

a) 00:20:44   b) 00:28:02   c) 00:30:08

d) 00:32:49   e) 00:38:34   f) 00:40:24

Big Bear Solar Observatory, photo courtesy R. L. Moore

To the naked eye the Sun appears constant. But a telescope reveals that the Sun's atmosphere is wracked by the tremendous explosions of solar flares. These solar flares grow rapidly, with the sequence at left occurring over only 34 minutes. During this time billions of tons of material are ejected from the Sun at speeds approaching 1,000,000 miles per hour.

Sunspots

Sunspots appear dark because, at a mere 7,000° F (4,000° C), they are cooler and less bright than the rest of the photosphere. A typical sunspot has two distinct parts: a dark central region, called the *umbra* ("shadow"), and a lighter surrounding area, the *penumbra* ("almost shadow"). Like the photosphere in general, the umbra shows a granular structure, which suggests the circulation of hot gas. At certain positions near the edge of the Sun, the spots look like depressions, or hollows, in the photosphere.

A single spot may be tens of thousands of miles wide. Its duration may last anywhere from a few days to a few months. Sunspots often develop in pairs, which tend to drift apart slowly. At times, they may form by the hundreds, while at other times, there may be practically no sunspots at all.

Many theories have been advanced to at least partially explain the nature of sunspots. They have been compared to low-pressure areas, tornadoes, or huge whirlwinds in the solar gas. And, in fact, complex movements of gas both into and away from a sunspot have been observed.

More-recent theories hold that sunspots are cool areas produced by reactions between the charged gases of the Sun and solar magnetic fields. That is, a local magnetic field breaks through the surface of the photosphere, producing a spot at that point. This disturbance also affects the solar atmosphere overlying the spot.

Solar Cycle

Sunspots appear and then disappear in a definite 11-year cycle, called the sunspot cycle, or the solar cycle. A sunspot cycle begins with a few small spots at solar latitudes of 30 to 40 degrees north and south of the Sun's equator. With the passage of time, more sunspots of larger size appear. These new spots arise closer and closer to the solar equator, until much of the Sun is covered by dark patches.

The cycle nears its end when spots in the higher solar latitudes begin to vanish. Finally only a few spots are left around the equator. Then the spots of the next cycle start to appear, at 30 to 40 degrees north and south of the solar equator.

Some astronomers have linked the sunspot cycle to a complex circulation of solar gas from the surface of the Sun down and then up again, and from the solar poles to the equator and back. The heat and rotation of the Sun are supposed to produce this effect. This circulation has been compared to that of the Earth's winds and ocean currents.

More-modern sunspot theories make use of new discoveries about magnetic fields. Scientists have found that a hot, electrically charged fluid, such as the solar gas, produces magnetism. As the gas moves, the lines of magnetic force follow. Regular movements of solar gas and its accompanying magnetic fields may cause the sunspot cycle.

Astronomers have discovered that the north and south magnetic poles in the Sun switch polarity in a regular, repeated fashion. These changes take place at the beginning of each sunspot cycle. The result is a magnetic cycle of 22 years, or double the duration of the sunspot cycle. This seems to indicate that the spot cycle is definitely connected with magnetic forces in the Sun, but exactly how is a mystery.

Sunspots are not the only features affected by the solar cycle. During a sunspot maximum, when many spots exist, the entire Sun becomes more active. Prominences are larger and more common. Huge solar flares, with temperatures in the millions of degrees, burst forth.

The corona undergoes changes in shape and brightness during different phases of the solar cycle. Man-made satellites have also photographed a strange feature, known as solar polar caps, in the corona. These coronal caps, centered over the north and south poles of the Sun, are

The solar wind is a continuous stream of high-speed protons and electrons emitted from the Sun's corona. This wind distorts the Earth's magnetic field, producing such observable effects as the auroras in high latitudes.

NASA

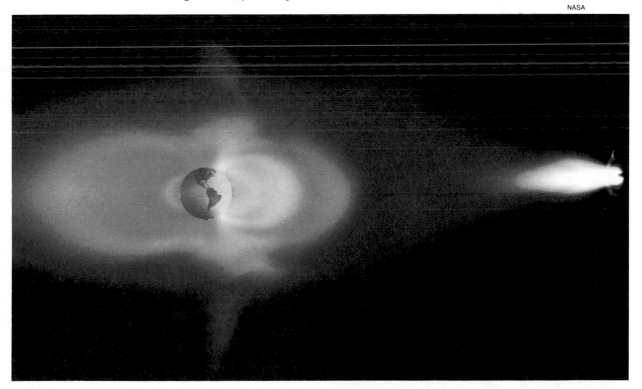

relatively cool masses of gas. At about 1,800,000° F (1,000,000° C), the caps are only about half as hot as the rest of the corona. During a sunspot maximum, the polar caps are very small or absent. During a sunspot minimum, when only a few spots exist, the caps become much larger.

During sunspot maximums, other parts of the corona become about twice as hot as usual—7,200,000° F (4,000,000° C), with the highest temperatures in the regions of solar flares.

The activities associated with sunspot cycles often affect the Earth and its atmosphere. These effects are due in large part to the many electrically charged, high-speed particles, and also to ultraviolet and X rays emitted from the Sun during a solar maximum. Many solar particles are trapped in the Earth's magnetic field and may create magnetic storms on Earth. They can also interfere with compasses, communications, and electrical-power transmission.

To observe an eclipse, the eyes must be protected from the direct rays of the Sun at all times. Since even an instant's glance can cause damage, indirect methods should be used.

INTERIOR OF THE SUN

There is little direct evidence available to scientists concerning the inside of the Sun. Astronomers studying the Sun know mostly about the heat, light, magnetism, and particles that come from the upper layers of the photosphere and solar atmosphere.

There are, however, some clues to the nature of the Sun's interior. Scientists believe that certain atomic particles, called *neutrinos*, reach the Earth directly and very quickly from the core of the Sun. These minute particles have no charge and virtually no mass, but move at the speed of light. Because of these properties, neutrinos easily pass through great thicknesses of matter, making them hard to detect. Nevertheless, scientists have managed to detect and count some of the solar neutrinos by using elaborate laboratory chambers filled with tracer gases. From neutrino research and from what is known about the outer layers of the Sun, scientists have constructed the following theoretical model of the solar interior.

A "nuclear-energy furnace" probably forms the Sun's hot and dense core. It fills a relatively small volume. The intense conditions strip the atoms of their electrons, so they consist only of nuclei.

Circulating currents bring hydrogen—atomic fuel—to the "furnace" and carry away the resulting product: helium. The tremendous energy produced in this way is transferred outward, away from the core. As the energy reaches the Sun's surface, circulating currents of solar gas carry it away.

Like boiling water or hot air shimmering over a fire, the gas of the photosphere rises and falls from the energy. These photospheric movements produce the many phenomena seen at the Sun's surface: granulation, faculae, and spots.

Scientists estimate that it takes several million years for energy at the core of the Sun (with the exception of the rapid neutrinos) to reach the surface. From the solar surface, this energy then radiates in all directions.

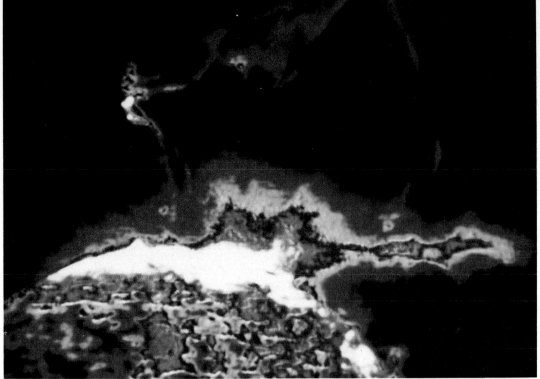

The huge streamers of glowing gas, called the solar prominences, show amazing diversity. Some rise to great heights above the chromosphere, while others originate above the chromosphere and rain down toward the Sun.

ROTATION OF THE SUN

Like the Earth, the Sun spins on its axis, rotating from west to east. But unlike a solid planet, the gaseous Sun spins faster in some places than in others.

Astronomers have several ways to calculate the rate of the Sun's rotation. Sunspots and faculae that last for several weeks or months are carried along as the Sun rotates. So astronomers can track them to measure the speed of solar rotation.

In latitudes where spots and faculae are absent, other methods must be used to measure the Sun's period—the time it takes the Sun to complete one turn on its axis. The spectroscope breaks up ordinary white sunlight into a spectrum. The Sun's spectrum is crossed by many dark lines, which provide clues to solar rotation. When the Sun moves away from an observer, the dark lines shift their positions toward the red end of the spectrum. If the Sun approaches the observer, the lines shift in the opposite direction, toward the violet end of the spectrum. These shifts of the spectrum lines are called the Doppler effect.

As the Sun spins on its axis, one side of the Sun approaches the observer, while, at the same time, the other side moves away. From studying the resulting Doppler effect, astronomers can determine the period of the Sun at any latitude.

Investigators have discovered that the period is shortest at the equator—26.9 days. Rotation becomes slower farther away from the equator. At the north and south poles, the period is 34 days. This difference of nearly 10 days in period between the solar equator and the poles is due to the fact that the Sun is not solid.

CHEMISTRY OF THE SUN

Our knowledge of the chemical elements in the Sun is based mostly on study of the solar spectrum. The Sun's spectrum is covered by many dark lines. These are called *Fraunhofer lines*, after the German physicist Joseph von Fraunhofer. Fraunhofer lines are also known as *absorption lines*. They represent certain colors, or wavelengths, of light absorbed by different elements in the Sun's atmosphere.

The atoms of an element, when hot enough, emit light of certain colors. The atoms also absorb light of these colors, thus producing dark absorption lines. The combination of colors and lines forms a spectrum characteristic of the element. Spectrums of earthly elements have been produced in laboratories and compared with the solar spectrum. In this way, chemists have learned what elements exist in the Sun.

A number of the absorption lines seen in the solar spectrum, however, are caused by certain atoms in the Earth's atmosphere. These atoms absorb some of the sunlight passing through the atmosphere. There are about 6,000 of these so-called *telluric* ("earth") lines. But scientists can easily distinguish telluric from solar lines. For example, telluric lines show no Doppler effect from the Sun's rotation.

Astronomers have learned that most, if not all, of the chemical elements present on Earth also exist in the Sun. Hydrogen is the most common solar element, making up more than 80 percent of the Sun's mass.

Helium is second, at 19 percent. The remaining 1 percent of the solar mass consists mostly of the following important elements, in descending order of concentration: oxygen, magnesium, nitrogen, silicon, carbon, sulfur, iron, sodium, calcium, nickel, and some trace elements.

The Sun is a mixture of gas atoms, atomic nuclei, and still smaller atomic particles. These atomic particles are electrons (negatively charged), protons (positively charged), neutrons (no charge), positrons (positively charged), and neutrinos (no charge).

This entire mass of hot, gaseous solar material is called a *plasma*. The high temperatures make it almost impossible for most chemical compounds to exist in the Sun.

SOLAR RADIATION

The Sun radiates energy at practically all wavelengths. This electromagnetic energy ranges from long radio waves to the shorter microwaves and the infrared, light, ultraviolet, and X rays. We can see only the light waves; the infrared we can sense as heat; the other forms of radiation can be detected only by means of special instruments and films.

There is some question whether the rate of solar radiation is always exactly the same. The amount of light leaving the Sun seems to be steady, or constant. But the quantity of other kinds of radiation emitted by the Sun may depend on the number of sunspots present.

The Sun also sends subatomic particles into space. Particle emission increases sharply during a sunspot maximum, when solar flares are exceptionally strong. Flares release vast numbers of protons, electrons, and atomic nuclei.

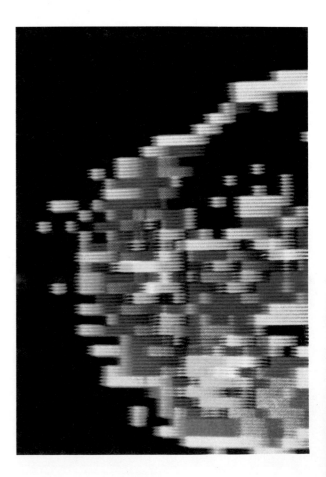

The computerized color display of the Sun's corona at right, in which the north and south poles are black and the hottest regions are white, was obtained by the Orbiting Solar Observatory (far right). The satellite contains a coronagraph, an instrument that creates an artificial eclipse for the express purpose of studying the Sun's corona.

Even during a sunspot minimum, the Sun is always emitting particles. The fine "rain" of particles that passes from the corona toward and around Earth is called the *solar wind*.

Many solar particles do not reach Earth or its atmosphere. They are trapped by Earth's magnetic field and become part of a belt of radiation, called the Van Allen belt, surrounding Earth.

About 30 percent of the solar radiation is screened away from the ground by our atmosphere. It is well that this is so, for some of this radiation is deadly.

Strong solar radiation ionizes many of Earth's higher atmospheric gases, producing electrically charged layers. Many scientists call these layers the ionosphere. The ionosphere shields Earth below from harmful solar radiation. During a solar maximum, the intense solar radiation and particles may disturb this upper atmospheric layer, disrupting long-distance radio communications on Earth. It may also create spectacular and colorful lights in the atmosphere over both polar regions of the planet. These astonishing phenomena are known as the aurora borealis (northern lights) and the aurora australis (southern lights).

ATOMIC ENERGY OF THE SUN

In 1939, German-American physicist Hans Bethe proposed an atomic, or nuclear, explanation of the Sun's energy. What goes on deep in the Sun's interior is probably what happens in a fusion reaction. Four nuclei of hydrogen atoms fuse, or join, to form the nucleus of a helium atom.

Bethe's fusion cycle takes place in six steps, which chiefly involve the element carbon, as well as hydrogen. This complex cycle is thus also called the carbon cycle. The carbon in the Sun is used both in the fusion process and produced during the reactions. The net result is that the number of carbon atoms is not changed. On the other hand, hydrogen is used up.

We now know that the carbon cycle occurs only in extremely hot stars. The Sun is actually very cool compared to other stars, so another reaction plays a more important role: the proton-proton reaction. In this process, solar energy comes from the direct fusion of hydrogen nuclei, or protons, without going through the six-step carbon

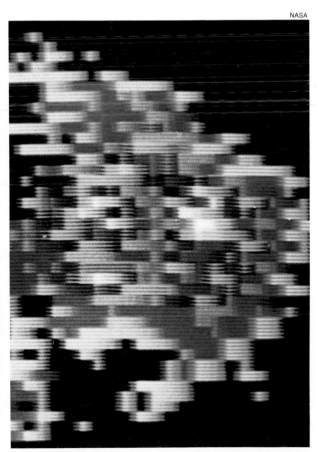

NASA

NASA

cycle. The proton-proton process also consumes hydrogen.

Scientists have calculated that 110 tons (100 metric tons) of hydrogen changing into helium yields more energy than all humans on Earth now use in a single year. At the present rate of solar energy production—about 4.4 million tons (4 million metric tons) of mass or matter turning into pure energy per second—the Sun contains enough hydrogen to remain as bright and hot as it is today for the next 30 billion years, and perhaps longer.

THE SUN'S INFLUENCE ON EARTH

Most of the Earth exists as we know it only because of the Sun's light and heat. The Sun makes all life possible. There would even be no weather without the Sun. The Sun directly or indirectly provides us with energy to light and heat our homes and to power our machines.

Because it is so small and so distant from the Sun, the Earth gets only about ½ billionth of the total solar-energy output. The quantity of solar energy reaching the edge of the Earth's atmosphere equals about 2 calories per square centimeter per minute. A calorie is the quantity of heat needed to raise the temperature of 1 gram of water 1° C. This rate of 2 calories per square centimeter per minute is called the solar constant. About 70 percent of this energy, on the average, reaches the ground. The Earth's atmosphere cuts off the rest.

The Sun provides light and warmth. It provides us with food and oxygen by way of green plants, which use solar energy to create themselves out of carbon dioxide and water. As the plants do this, they release oxygen to the environment.

SOLAR ENERGY

Most fuels are a chemical form of solar energy. Coal, for example, is actually the transformed residue of ancient green plants that lived and died many ages ago and were buried in the rocks. When we burn coal, we release solar energy once stored as chemical energy by green plants in their tissues.

Petroleum, or oil, is similar to coal in this respect.

Hydroelectric plants, which generate electricity from running water, also depend on the Sun. Without the weather cycle, whose energizing force is the Sun's heat, no rain would fall. There would be no running water to move the turbines of hydroelectric-power stations.

Solar energy is used more directly in various ways by humans, but on a very limited scale as yet. Sunlight heats our homes in summertime or year-round in the tropics. Solar heat evaporates seawater in one rather primitive technology used in the salt-making industry.

Solar energy is strong, but it is so scattered that complex systems of mirrors and lenses are needed to collect it for uses demanding more power than in the examples just given. Once concentrated, however, the power of the Sun's heat is fearsome. In a solar furnace, for example, it can melt iron or steel at temperatures of several thousand degrees. Sunlight generates electricity in light-sensitive cells known as solar batteries. They are used most often in space vehicles and satellites to power their equipment. Solar engines usually produce steam for power from water heated by the Sun. The use of these engines is rather limited at present, however.

As the Earth's fuel reserves are used up, we may have to turn more and more to the Sun as our primary source of energy. Efforts are being made to harness the Sun's power for human use. For a discussion of some of these efforts, see the articles in *The New Book of Popular Science* section on Energy.

SOLAR TELESCOPES

Astronomers studying the Sun gain much information on the basic nature of other stars. Remember, however, that astronomers today use elaborate instruments to protect their eyes. One should never look directly at the Sun, either with the naked eye or through an ordinary telescope or binoculars, because the Sun's rays may damage the eyes, causing blindness.

Scientists use spectroscopes to analyze the atmosphere of the Sun and other stars. The spectroscope works by dispersing light or radiation to form a spectrum. Since each chemical element has its own particular spectrum, scientists can compare the spectra produced by a star with known spectral patterns produced in the laboratory.

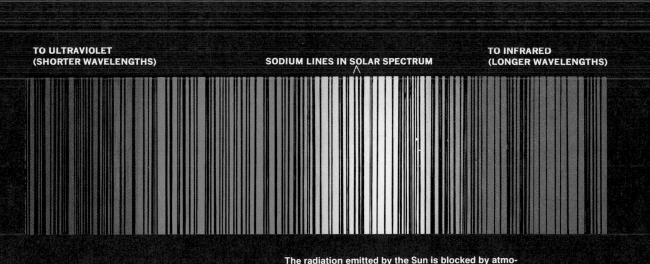

TO ULTRAVIOLET
(SHORTER WAVELENGTHS)

SODIUM LINES IN SOLAR SPECTRUM

TO INFRARED
(LONGER WAVELENGTHS)

The radiation emitted by the Sun is blocked by atmospheric gases. The resulting dark-line, or absorption, spectrum is the exact reverse of a bright-line spectrum. For example, the dark lines in the solar spectrum (above) match the bright-line spectrum of sodium.

The Ulysses spacecraft used Jupiter's gravity to jump into the orbit around the Sun's north and south poles.

Various instruments for observing the Sun have existed for many hundreds of years. Before the invention of the telescope and other modern astronomical devices, people used simple mechanical solar instruments to measure the positions and paths of the Sun.

Most modern solar telescopes are very different from ordinary astronomical telescopes. One kind of solar telescope is called a *tower telescope* because the mirrors and lenses for concentrating sunlight are located atop a tower. A tower telescope projects an enlarged image of the Sun down onto a screen at ground level. Below the tower are instruments such as spectrographs and spectroheliographs that analyze the image.

Another type of solar telescope is the *coronagraph*. It reduces the glare emitted from the solar surface, or photosphere, by means of a polished metal disk and nearly perfect lenses. In this way, astronomers can study the corona, the outermost atmosphere of the Sun, even when there is no total solar eclipse. The coronagraph is usually located on a mountaintop, where the air is thin and dust-free. Special types of radio telescopes, called radioheliographs, are used to detect radio waves, which are normally broadcast by the chromosphere (the lower part of the Sun's atmosphere) and the corona.

PAST AND FUTURE

How long has the Sun been radiating energy? How long can it continue to do so? Scientists are attempting to answer these questions. The Sun certainly has been shining for at least 5 billion years. At its present rate, as stated earlier, it could go on shining for another 30 billion years at least, if not longer.

But has the Sun always been radiating energy at the same rate? Will it continue at the same rate? The answer to the first question is maybe; to the second, probably not.

At present the amount of visible solar radiation, or light, varies only slightly, if at all. Many astronomers think that this has always been the case. Others, however, disagree. They point to the great ice sheets that from time to time have engulfed much of Earth's surface. These, they say, are evidence that the Sun's total radiation may drop off. Even slight decreases would freeze vast areas on Earth.

Some astronomers believe that, as the Sun grows older, it will begin to use up hydrogen at an increasingly faster rate. This would cut its future life span to about 10 billion years. As radiation increases, the Sun will become so hot that our oceans will actually boil away, and most life on Earth will be killed as the planet becomes uninhabitable.

When its hydrogen supply finally gives out, the Sun will shrink into a very small star—a so-called white dwarf. Later it will die out completely.

SATELLITES AND SUN PROBES

Solar instruments are being sent into space aboard small, unmanned astronomical observatories. The craft are placed into orbit far above Earth's distorting atmosphere. The U.S. manned space observatory, *Skylab*, and its Soviet (now Russian) counterpart, *Soyuz*, both conducted solar investigations.

One of the first probes to study the Sun closely is the 815-pound (370-kilogram) Ulysses spacecraft, launched in October 1990 from the cargo bay of the space shuttle *Discovery*. Ulysses (the Roman equivalent of Odysseus, the Greek mythical hero who angered the Sun-god during his long journey home) is a joint effort of the National Aeronautics and Space Administration (NASA) and the European Space Agency (ESA).

Shortly after escaping Earth's gravitational influence, Ulysses became the fastest human-made object in history, reaching a velocity relative to Earth of 112,000 miles (180,000 kilometers) per hour.

It is the first spacecraft aimed at orbiting the Sun perpendicular to the ecliptic plane, the plane where all the planets circle the Sun. Enormous energy was required to boost the spacecraft out of the ecliptic plane, so Ulysses used a gravity-assist maneuver—resulting in a burst of speed from what is popularly referred to as the "slingshot effect." It first traveled outward from the Sun toward Jupiter, and it used Jupiter's gravity to pick up speed as it swung back toward the Sun at an angle that took it under the giant planet's south solar pole.

Ulysses carries nine instruments to study the Sun. Its primary mission is to observe the solar wind emitted from the high latitudes of the Sun's surface. The solar wind is comprised of relatively low-energy protons and electrons forming a hot magnetized gas that continuously streams out from the Sun. Scientists want to learn how the solar wind interacts with the Sun's magnetic field near the poles.

Although the spacecraft travels around the Sun at about twice the distance that Earth does, its unique orbit puts it in a prime position to observe the Sun's magnetic field, or magnetosphere. The most recent solar maximum occurred in 2000 to 2001, during which Ulysses transmitted valuable data about the speeds of solar wind particles and the Sun's changing magnetic fields.

In August 1991, the Yohkoh satellite, an observatory for studying X rays and gamma rays from the Sun, was launched from Kagoshima, Japan. Its four fine-tuned instruments cover a wide energy range of the high energy solar spectrum, and make the Yohkoh satellite a unique and powerful tool for studying the Sun.

Another ambitious solar-observing satellite was launched in 1995. SOHO, the Solar and Heliospheric Observatory, is a spacecraft designed by NASA and ESA to study the relationship between the Sun's environment and Earth's environment better than ever before. In our first uninterrupted view of the Sun, SOHO has found "rivers" of hot plasma flowing beneath the visible face of the Sun; flashes that erupt sporadically over the solar atmosphere—each about the size of Earth; and tens of thousands of magnetic loops that thread upward into the Sun's corona, become twisted, and heat up the surrounding gas to millions of degrees.

Mercury (above, in an artist's conception) reflects light so poorly that its sunlit side is only dimly illuminated.

MERCURY

by Jeffrey Brune

Mercury lies closer to the Sun than do any of the other planets. The smallest planet save Pluto, Mercury is, nonetheless, one of the brightest at certain intervals. Unfortunately, even under the best of conditions, Mercury is difficult to see with the naked eye. Mercury appears in the heavens only at dawn and twilight, a time when even the brightest stars seem dim. Its position near the horizon often causes the planet to be obscured by haze. In fact, through all his years of heavenly observation, the great Polish astronomer Nicolaus Copernicus never once saw Mercury, a strange twist of fate perhaps due to the low, misty region where he lived.

MORNING AND EVENING STAR

Mercury makes a small circuit around the Sun. As a result, it never rises in the morning or sets in the evening much before or after the Sun does. Because it appears sometimes in the east and sometimes in the west, some ancient peoples—including the Egyptians, Hindus, and Greeks—thought of it as two separate heavenly bodies—a morning star and an evening star. The Greeks called the morning star "Apollon," after the god of the Sun. They called their evening star "Hermes," the name of the swift messenger of the gods, because the planet's apparent motion among the stars was so swift. The Greek philosopher Pythagoras, who lived in the 6th century B.C., is thought to be the first to recognize that the morning star and evening star were one and the same heavenly body. That fact was well known to Roman astronomers, who worshiped Hermes under the name of Mercury (or Mercurius, in Latin).

In the Northern Hemisphere, Mercury can be seen with the naked eye for only a few days at dawn in late summer or early autumn, and also at twilight early in the spring. Fortunately, using telescopes, astronomers do not have to confine their observations of the planet to these periods.

When viewed through the telescope, Mercury looks a good deal like the Moon as seen with the naked eye. The telescope reveals that the disk of Mercury has phases like those of our Moon. It increases from a thin crescent to a full disk, and decreases again to a crescent. Then it disappears altogether when the planet is almost directly between the Earth and the Sun. These phases are not visible to the naked eye.

HEAVY, BUT FAST

Mercury is almost perfectly spherical. It has an equatorial diameter of 3,031 miles (4,878 kilometers), almost two-fifths that of the Earth. Mercury is only one-eighteenth as massive as the Earth. Yet its density—the average amount of mass it contains per unit volume—is very similar to that of our planet: 5.43 grams per cubic centimeter for Mercury versus 5.52 grams per cubic centimeter for Earth. In fact, even though Mercury is smaller than Venus or Mars, its density is greater than that of either planet.

If Mercury is so dense for its small size, it must be composed mostly of heavy materials. Scientists think that Mercury is like a Ping-Pong ball filled with heavy cement: it has a very thin, light covering, or crust, and a much thicker and heavier core. Mercury's crust is probably made of light silicate rocks, while most of the planet below the surface is composed of iron, a very heavy metallic element.

At one time in its early history, Mercury probably had a much thicker outer crust. That would mean it had more light rock than it does today, and thus a lower overall density. Astronomers think that, soon after the formation of the solar system, Mercury may have been bombarded by a shower of rocky asteroids. One of these asteroids hit Mercury so hard that it blasted most of the light crust away, leaving the heavy iron core behind.

A mosaic of photos taken by Mariner 10 shows how much the heavily cratered surface of Mercury resembles the surface of the Moon. The largest crater seen here measures 125 miles in diameter.

NASA

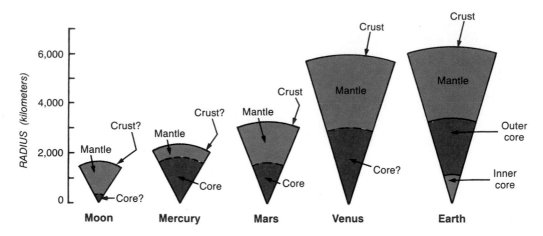

Mercury's size and density suggest that the planet's iron core is unusually large compared to the cores of the Moon and the three other terrestrial planets—Mars, Venus, and the Earth (above). Indeed, Mercury's core may account for 40 percent of the planet's entire volume. Astronomers debate whether or not Mercury has a liquid outer core and, if not, what phenomenon gives rise to the planet's weak magnetic field.

Above: Courtesy of Sky & Telescope magazine; below: NASA/JPL

Mercury has unusual systems of very long cliffs, or scarps, on its surface. The scarp that extends from the upper left to the bottom right of the photo is nearly 200 miles long.

Mercury is, on average, almost 36 million miles (58 million kilometers) from the Sun. At times, however, the planet can be much closer—as close as 29 million miles (47 million kilometers). At other times, Mercury can be as far away as 44 million miles (70 million kilometers). Why does the planet get so up close and personal to the Sun, then so aloof? The path it follows around the Sun is not circular; rather, it is stretched out into an elongated ellipse, with the Sun far from the center. In fact, Mercury's orbit is much more "eccentric" than Earth's or that of any other planet except Pluto.

In keeping with its namesake, the "winged messenger," Mercury is the fastest-moving of all the planets. It whips around the Sun in only 88 days, while the Earth takes 365 days, and lazy Pluto about 248 *years*! The speed at which Mercury moves in its orbital path varies according to its distance from the Sun. When Mercury is farthest from the Sun, it travels at 23 miles (37 kilometers) per second. When it is nearest to the Sun, however, it speeds up to a velocity of 35 miles (56 kilometers) per second—a speed that enables Mercury to escape being sucked into the fiery solar furnace.

Slow-Moving Rotation

While swift in its race around the Sun, Mercury rotates slowly on its axis. The planet takes almost 59 Earth days for one complete rotation.

Mercury's sluggish twirl means that while one hemisphere of the planet faces the scorching Sun for long periods of time, the other side is exposed to the chill of interplanetary space. Surface temperatures on the sunlit side can reach 950° F (510° C); on the dark side, temperatures plummet to −346° F (−210° C).

One would imagine that Mercury's daytime side might be blindingly bright. Actually, the surface remains fairly dim, more like twilight than noon on Earth. This is because Mercury's surface reflects only about 6 percent of the sunlight that hits it. Because Mercury is so near the Sun, however, this has been enough to keep the planet veiled in mystery—until we went for a close look.

MARINER 10 FLYBY

In 1973 the United States launched the space probe Mariner 10 to Mercury. In March 1974, it flew to within 435 miles (700 kilometers) of the planet. The probe then circled the Sun and returned to within about 29,827 miles (48,000 kilometers) in September of that same year. On March 16, 1975, Mariner 10 made its last useful flyby, coming within 125 miles (200 kilometers) of the planet's surface. The wealth of photographs and other data collected by special instruments aboard the space probe revealed much about Mercury.

In the photographs, Mercury can be seen to be covered with hundreds of thousands of impact craters—holes made when space rocks smash into the planet's surface. Some of the craters appear to have been smoothed over by ancient lava flows. This suggests that the planet was volcanically active at one time in its early history. Temperature measurements indicate that Mercury is covered with a fine-grained, porous material. This fine dust, together with the many craters, gives Mercury an appearance much like Earth's Moon. As expected, Mariner 10 revealed not a single Mercurial moon.

Mercury is crisscrossed with long cliffs, or scarps, up to 1.2 miles (1.9 kilometers) high and 930 miles (1,500 kilome-

Mercury's closeness to the Sun has made it difficult to study the planet from Earth. Scientists one day hope to land a spacecraft on Mercury (shown below in an artist's conception) to study the planet more extensively.

© Pamela Lee

ters) long. Scientists think the scarps formed after Mercury's hot early history. As the planet cooled, the surface contracted and formed the scarps.

Scientists were surprised to discover that Mercury has a very thin helium atmosphere. Further research revealed the presence of sodium and oxygen atoms and traces of potassium and hydrogen. The word "atmosphere" may actually be an exaggeration, since Mercury's gases are so sparse—a million billion times less dense than Earth's atmosphere.

Another surprise discovery was a weak magnetic field around Mercury. The existence of this magnetic field suggests that the planet has a hot molten core, perhaps mostly iron and some nickel. (The magnetic field would be generated by a core of molten metal mixed by streams of electrically charged materials.) New evidence, however, shows that Mercury's core may not be molten after all, but cool instead. Scientists used the Very Large Array radio telescope in New Mexico to measure the heat coming off the surface of Mercury. Analysis of the heat waves indicates that the heat is coming not from the core, but only from sunlight that has reflected off Mercury's surface.

So what is responsible for Mercury's magnetic field? It may be the solar wind—the stream of charged particles flowing from the Sun. Scientists are still debating this issue.

Mercury has been the center of another, perhaps more passionate, debate. Naming its major craters, some of which are 50 miles (80 kilometers) in diameter, caused an uproar in the scientific community. The International Astronomical Union (IAU), which decides the names of various geographic features on planets, had planned on naming the craters after birds. But some scientists were outraged at the thought of using bird names on a barren, airless planet.

The late astronomer Carl Sagan wrote to the IAU: "If the present inclination is followed, I suppose we will find other solar system objects sporting the names of fish, minerals, butterflies, spiders, and salamanders. I have nothing whatever against salamanders; but from the perspective of a millennium hence, it will be thought interesting that no features larger than a kilometer or so across have been named after Shakespeare, Dostoevsky, Mozart, Dante, Bach...."

After bitter debate, the IAU settled on names of famous artists, writers, musicians, and other great contributors to the humanities. Major craters on Mercury now hold such distinguished names as Tolstoy, Mark Twain, Bach, Michelangelo, Shakespeare, and Renoir.

MERCURY IN TRANSIT

Since the planet Mercury lies inside Earth's orbit, it can pass directly between our planet and the Sun. Such a passage is known as a *transit*. If Mercury's orbit were in the same plane as that of Earth, there would be three transits of Mercury each year. It would revolve about four times around the Sun in our year, and Earth would revolve only once during the same period of time. However, the orbit of Mercury is inclined by about 7 degrees to the ecliptic—the plane of Earth's orbit around the Sun. Mercury therefore crosses the ecliptic twice every 88 days, but generally not in a line with Earth and the Sun.

A transit of Mercury can take place only when the planet is between Earth and the Sun, and is at the same time crossing the ecliptic. These conditions are satisfied from time to time, but not at any definite intervals. All of Mercury's transits occur in May and November; the most recent occurred on May 7, 2003. The next will come on November 8, 2006.

As the planet makes its transit, the astronomer peering through a telescope can see the tiny black disk creeping across the dazzling solar background. This cannot be called an eclipse, because only an insignificant amount of the Sun's surface is obscured. Carefully observing the transit, astronomers can determine the exact position of Mercury in the heavens, and can also obtain added information about the planet's orbit.

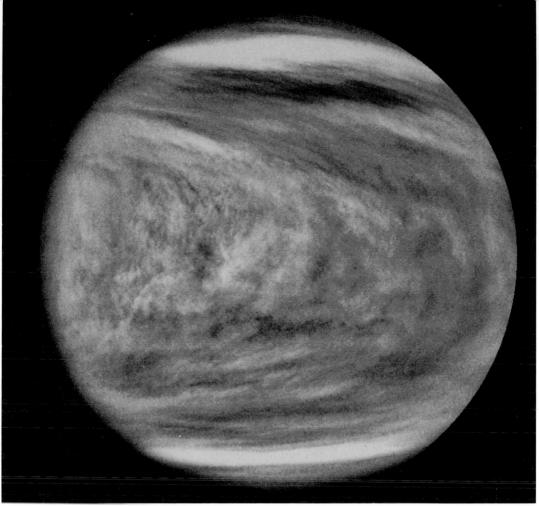

Venus, the planet second from the Sun, Is often called Earth's sister for its similar size and mass. The clouds that shroud the planet reflect enough light to make Venus the second-brightest object (after the Moon) in the night sky.

VENUS

by Jeffrey Brune

The elegant white planet orbiting the Sun between Mercury and Earth is called Venus after the Roman goddess of beauty. Although similar to the Earth in size (with a diameter of about 7,500 miles—12,100 kilometers—compared with Earth's diameter of 7,900 miles—12,750 kilometers) and mass (Venus is a bit more than four-fifths the mass of Earth), the Venusian surface and atmosphere are far different from ours.

Like Mercury, Venus is at times an evening star and at other times a morning star, depending on whether it is to the east or west of the Sun as viewed from the Earth. The planet may rise as much as four hours before the Sun, and may set as much as four hours after it.

Venus revolves around the Sun once every 225 days in an orbit that is very nearly circular. And as it revolves, it slowly rotates about its axis—about once every 243 Earth days, in a direction opposite that of Earth and most other planets.

When Venus is on the far side of the Sun from the Earth, it is quite far indeed. But at its closest, when it is between the Sun and the Earth, it is only some 26 million miles (41,840,000 kilometers) away.

Venus, like Mercury, shows a complete cycle of "phases," or shapes, to an observer on Earth armed with a small telescope or good binoculars. When the planet is at the farthest part of its orbit from the Earth, it appears as a disk. When Venus is between the Sun and the Earth, it is seldom visible. About 35 days before and after this time, it appears as a crescent and is at its brightest—two and one-half times brighter than when it is seen as a disk.

BENEATH THE GODDESS' VEIL

The surface of Venus is obscured by the planet's thick clouds, and so is invisible to optical instruments. For centuries, astronomers could only guess what lay beneath this veil. Some conjured tales of swamps, forests, and strange creatures.

Starting in 1962, the United States and the Soviet Union sent more than 20 probes to the planet for a true view. The U.S. Pioneer-Venus 1 craft and the Soviet Venera 15 and 16 orbiters used radar to pierce the thick clouds and make low-resolution maps of the planet's surface. The mapping revealed mainly rolling upland plains, some lowland plains, and two highland areas. One, called Aphrodite Terra, is about half the size of Africa. The other highland, Ishtar Terra, is about the size of the United States and contains a 7-mile (11-kilometer)-tall mountain named Maxwell Montes.

Other Venera probes actually traveled through the clouds, landed softly on the surface, and transmitted the first color pictures of the planet's surface. Chemical analyses of the Venusian crust, conducted by the probes, showed that it contained basaltic rock similar to that associated on Earth with recent volcanic activity.

The U.S. spacecraft Magellan, launched in May 1989, radar-mapped most of the Venusian surface with far better resolution than previous craft. Magellan sent sharp images of a world strewn with cracks and fissures, rugged mountains, and bizarre "pancake domes" formed by hot lava welling up from beneath the surface.

Magellan also photographed giant craters formed when large hunks of rock from space crashed into the planet. Interestingly, even the smallest craters found on Venus are quite huge—more than 2.5 miles (4 kilometers) in diameter. Only very large hunks of space rock can survive the fiery passage through Venus' thick atmosphere and reach the surface.

Perhaps the biggest surprise from Magellan's pictures was the apparent lack of erosion on Venus. The mountains, craters, and other surface features appear rough and unweathered, almost as if they were newly formed. A major reason for this is that Venus is bone-dry. Water on Earth smooths down surface features. Rivers, for example, gradually change mountains into valleys. But with surface temperatures of 896° F (480° C), Venus is too hot for water. If Venus did have water in its past, it must have quickly evaporated.

Though there appear to be no signs that water ever flowed across Venus' sur-

NASA

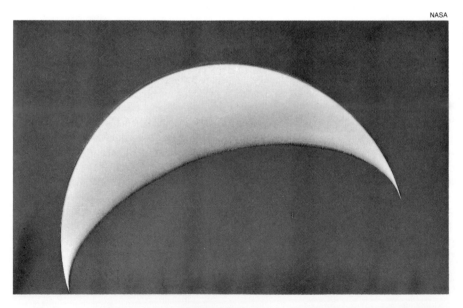

Much like the Moon and the planet Mercury, Venus exhibits an entire cycle of phases. Venus appears brightest when it is at the crescent phase.

The artist's conception above pictures the Magellan space probe after its 1989 deployment from the space shuttle Atlantis, *using radar to map the cloud-shrouded surface of Venus.*

face, Magellan's pictures show long channels cut by rivers of hot lava. Volcanoes must have resurfaced Venus in its recent past, because the planet has far fewer craters than do Mars or the Moon. Scientists suspect that Venus' volcanic face-lift came within the past few hundred million years.

Scientists are also trying to understand the geologic forces responsible for producing the volcanoes, mountain belts, and other surface features of Venus. On Earth the crust is divided into separate moving plates. Their movement, a process known as plate tectonics, is responsible for mountain building, seafloor spreading, and earthquakes. The crust of Venus does not appear to work in this way. Instead, upwellings of hot, light material and downwellings of cooler, denser material may pull and shove the surface crust.

Hot, Dense Atmosphere

About 95 percent of Venus' atmosphere consists of carbon dioxide, with some clouds of sulfuric acid. Traces of oxygen, hydrogen, nitrogen, neon, and ammonia have also been found.

The thick cloak of carbon dioxide is responsible for surface temperatures high enough to melt lead. In a process called the "greenhouse effect," sunlight passes through the thick atmosphere and heats up the planet's surface, which in turn gives off mainly infrared heat rays. But unlike sunlight, the infrared rays cannot penetrate the carbon dioxide of the atmosphere. The rays are thus trapped, and the planet heats up like a giant greenhouse.

Air pressure at the base of Venus' cloud cover is up to 100 times as high as it is at the Earth's surface. This massive pressure is a great obstacle to human exploration. At ground level the atmosphere of Venus is so dense that it is probably very slow-moving. To walk on the surface of the planet would be somewhat like walking through a furnace full of boiling oil—not a very pleasant thought!

In 1986, two Soviet Vega spacecraft dropped weather balloons into the Venusian atmosphere. Floating about 34 miles (55 kilometers) above the planet's surface, the balloons revealed that the planet is buffeted by powerful east-west winds of up to 155 miles (250 kilometers) per hour.

Severe winds and storms probably occur as the air circulates around the planet. One enormous, long-lasting storm, somewhat akin to Jupiter's Great Red Spot, has been observed. This storm, called the Venusian "Eye," is approximately the size of the United States.

The multiprobe Pioneer-Venus 2 found several hundred times more argon and neon in the Venusian atmosphere than is found in Earth's. This has caused astronomers to rethink one theory about the formation of the solar system. According to that theory, Venus would have less of these gases than does Earth.

The unmanned probes indicate that Venus, unlike Earth, has no appreciable magnetic field. As a result, there is no zone of trapped radiation in a magnetosphere, such as surrounds our planet. Venus does have an ionized atmospheric layer, or ionosphere, above its surface, due to the reaction between its atmosphere and the stream of particles and radiation coming from the Sun. This ionosphere, much thinner and lower than Earth's, helps protect Venus' surface from bombardment by fierce solar radiation.

VENUS IN TRANSIT

Because the planet Venus circles the Sun inside the orbit of Earth, it occasionally passes in between our planet and the Sun. During these "transits," Venus can be seen in silhouette against the brilliant face of our solar system's central star.

Such a transit occurred on June 8, 2004, and was the first since 1882. The next one will not occur until 2012.

Images of Venus transmitted from Magellan show a planet of towering mountains and volcanoes. The black lines in the image below are areas that lack radar data.

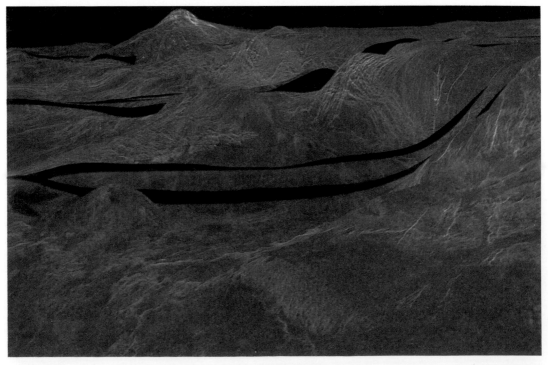

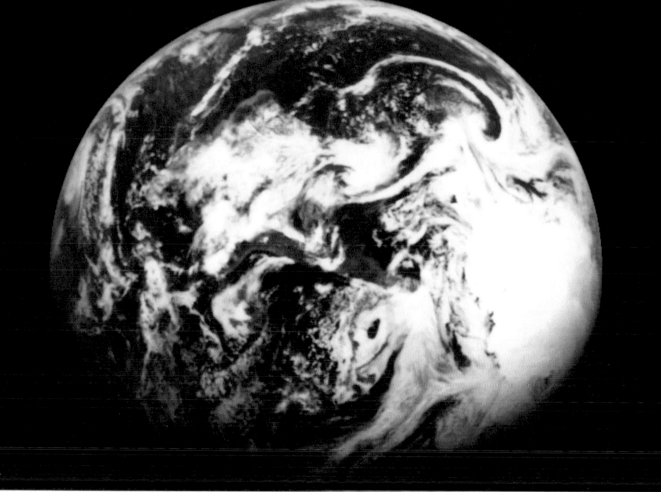

From space, Earth might be called the blue planet, since three-quarters of its surface is covered with water. The white swirls in the photo above are clouds—water vapor that has condensed in the atmosphere.

EARTH

by Franklyn M. Branley

Four planets in the solar system are smaller than the planet Earth. Four are considerably larger. The Earth in terms of mass, therefore, is not an outstanding member of the vast solar family—except, of course, as our home, and the vantage point from which we view the universe.

Astronomers have proposed many explanations of how the Earth and the other planets in our solar system originated. They are little more than ingenious conjectures, however, since they are based on insufficient data. Though we know little about the beginnings of the Earth, we know a great deal about our planet's shape, structure, properties, and motions.

THE SHAPE OF THE EARTH

Photographs of the Earth taken from rockets, satellites, and other spacecraft far above the surface show its distinct curvature, indicating it is nearly round. Before this evidence became available, the roundness of the Earth could be inferred from certain facts. It was known, for example, that as a lunar eclipse advances, the Earth casts a curved shadow on the Moon.

The Earth is not a perfect sphere, but slightly flattened. This shape is probably caused by our planet's force of rotation, which deforms the somewhat plastic Earth into a form that is in balance with the forces of rotation and gravity. The diameter of the Earth is 7,900 miles (12,700 kilometers) from pole to pole, and 7,920 miles (12,750 kilometers) around the equator. Recent measurements also indicate that the Earth is slightly more flattened on the South Pole than on the North Pole, which makes it slightly pear-shaped.

THE EARTH'S MASS AND DENSITY

The mass of an object represents the concentration of matter in it. It is a constant value, as opposed to weight, which is actually a measure of gravity that changes from place to place. Various methods were used to determine Earth's mass. In 1735 mathematician Pierre Bouguer, while in Ecuador, measured the extent to which a plumb line was deflected by the gravitational pull of a mountain, the peak called Chimborazo. Since he could estimate the mass of the mountain, he was able to estimate the mass of the Earth after the deflection was measured.

Today a sensitive instrument called a torsion balance is generally used to determine the Earth's mass. The attraction of a large ball of known mass to a small ball is compared with the attraction of the Earth to the small ball. According to a recent estimate, the mass of the Earth is 6.59×10^{21} tons (5.98×10^{21} metric tons).

To determine the Earth's density, we divide the mass in grams by the volume in cubic centimeters. The volume of the Earth is 1.083×10^{27} cubic centimeters. If we divide 5.98×10^{27} by 1.083×10^{27}, we get approximately 5.5 grams per cubic centimeter as the figure for the density of the Earth. That is, if we mixed together the air, water, and rock of our planet, the mixture would weigh about 5.5 times the same quantity of water. The Earth is the densest of all the planets.

GRAVITY AND MAGNETISM ON EARTH

Gravity and magnetism are still mysterious forces in many respects, and yet we have gathered considerable information about them. In the 17th century, Sir Isaac

Newton clarified our understanding of gravity when he formulated his famous law of gravitation. It states that every particle in the universe attracts every other particle with a force that varies directly as the product of their masses, and inversely as the square of the distance between them. This is the statement of universal gravitation.

The term gravity (or, more accurately, terrestrial gravity) is applied to the gravitational force exerted by the Earth. Gravity is the force that pulls all materials toward the center of the Earth. This force becomes smaller as we move away from the center. You are really measuring the force of gravity every time you weigh yourself. If your weight is 143 pounds (65 kilograms), you are pulled toward the center of the Earth with a force of 143 pounds. Since weight decreases farther from the center, you will weigh slightly less on the top of a mountain than in a deep valley.

In 1600 Sir William Gilbert, an English physician, advanced the idea that the Earth behaves like a huge magnet, with north and south poles. This idea is now universally

SHAPE OF THE EARTH

FLATTENED AT THE POLES

BULGING AT THE EQUATOR

SHAPE EARTH WOULD HAVE IF IT WERE PERFECTLY ROUND

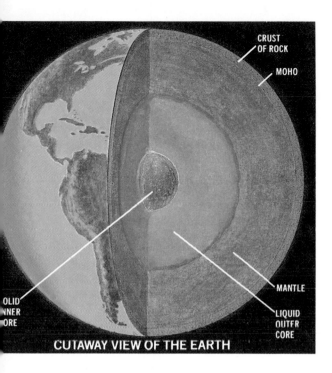

CUTAWAY VIEW OF THE EARTH

CRUST OF ROCK

MOHO

MANTLE

LIQUID OUTER CORE

SOLID INNER CORE

accepted. When you use a compass, the needle falls along the lines of force that run from one magnetic pole to the other. The magnetic poles do not correspond exactly to the geographic poles.

THREE PARTS OF THE EARTH

The Earth is made up of air, water, and solid ground—or, as a scientist would say, the atmosphere, hydrosphere, and lithosphere. The scientific terms are derived from Greek roots: *atmos* means vapor; *hydro*, water; and *lithos*, stone.

The atmosphere. The air surrounding the Earth is composed of about 78 percent nitrogen, 21 percent oxygen, and 1 percent other gases, including water vapor and carbon dioxide. Dust is also present.

The lower layer of the air envelope is the *troposphere*. *Tropos* means "change" in Greek, and the troposphere is the region where great changes take place in the temperature, pressure, and water-vapor content of the air. It is the part of the atmosphere where our weather occurs. Although most atmospheric changes take place relatively close to the Earth, the troposphere extends to an altitude of about 6 miles (10 kilometers). At the outer limit of the troposphere, there is a zone of division between the troposphere and the next sphere, called the *tropopause*.

The next atmospheric layer, extending from 6 to 25 miles (10 to 40 kilometers) above the Earth's surface, is the *stratosphere*. It is the zone of the strange winds known as jet streams—fast-moving currents of air that may reach velocities of 250 miles (400 kilometers) per hour. Temperature in the stratosphere rises from a low of −76° F (−60° C) at an altitude of 6 miles (10 kilometers), to a high of 32° F (0° C) at about 25 miles (40 kilometers).

At this point the stratosphere gives way to the *mesosphere*, which reaches from 25 to 44 miles (40 to about 70 kilometers) above our planet's surface. Temperature in the mesosphere ranges from a high of 32° F (0° C) at 25 miles (40 kilometers) elevation, to a low of −130° F (−90° C) at about 50 miles (80 kilometers) up. The air of the mesosphere is much thinner than that of the stratosphere.

The region of the atmosphere extending from 44 to 250 miles (70 to 400 kilometers) above the Earth is the *thermosphere*, where the air is extremely thin. Because of exposure to radiation from space and the Sun, many of the molecules and atoms are electrically charged, or ionized. Scientists often call these layers the *ionosphere*.

From 250 miles (400 kilometers) altitude and higher is the *exosphere*, the outermost fringe of the atmosphere. The extremely thin gas there consists chiefly of hydrogen. The exosphere eventually merges with the Sun's atmosphere.

In the late 1950s, it was discovered that the Earth is encircled by a large belt of radiation. This belt is now known as the Van Allen radiation belt, after its discoverer, American scientist James A. Van Allen. The belt begins about 400 miles (650 kilometers) above the Earth, and extends out some 25,000 miles (40,000 kilometers) into space. It is made up of charged particles radiated by the Sun and trapped by the Earth's magnetic field.

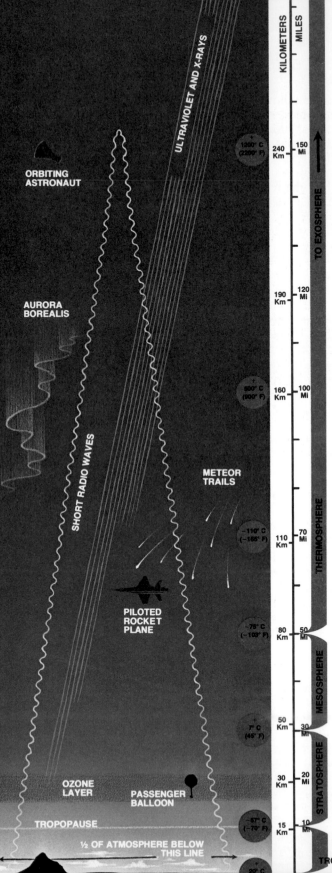

Layers of the atmosphere differ in the way they absorb radiation from the Sun, and thus differ in temperature. The bottom 10 miles of atmosphere—the troposphere —is where all weather takes place. Pollution has led to the formation of holes in the ozone layer.

The hydrosphere. The Earth appears to be the only planet that contains large amounts of liquid water. About three-fourths of the surface is covered by the oceans. These bodies of water, together with large inland lakes, contribute great amounts of water vapor to the air. They play a large part in the atmospheric changes that we call weather.

Of the Earth's surface water, almost 96 percent by weight is made up of hydrogen and oxygen. Sodium, chlorine, and many other elements are also found in oceanic waters. Traces of all the elements would probably be revealed if instruments with enough sensitivity were used.

The plants and animals found in the sea are an immensely valuable resource. They provide us with food, fertilizers, and industrial materials. The ocean is also a vast storehouse of minerals, such as common salt (sodium chloride), magnesium, manganese, gold, iron, copper, uranium, and silver. Some of these, such as salt and magnesium, are obtained from the sea in quantity. Others will no doubt be made available to us as more-efficient methods for extracting them are developed.

The lithosphere. The solid part of the Earth is made up of three types of rock— *igneous*, *sedimentary*, and *metamorphic*— and soil. Soil consists of rock debris combined with organic materials. Igneous rock is derived from the molten, rock-producing matter called *magma*. Sedimentary rock consists principally of rock fragments that have accumulated through untold millennia and have been pressed together. When igneous rock or sedimentary rock becomes altered through changes in temperature and pressure and other forces within the Earth, it gives rise to metamorphic rock.

We do not know for certain just what we would find if we were to dig to the center of our planet. However, Earth scien-

"The Living Earth" (above) is a composite of satellite photos taken over three years. The colors indicate biological activity both on land and in the sea, and thus help to convey the interactive nature of Earth's environments.

tists, gathering evidence from various indirect sources, have developed a more-or-less clear picture of the Earth's interior.

One of these scientists, Keith E. Bullen of the University of Sydney in Australia, has presented the following view: the Earth has a solid outer *mantle* about 1,740 miles (2,800 kilometers) thick. The Earth's crust makes up only a small part of this mantle. It extends only 25 miles (40 kilometers) or so below the Earth's surface. Beneath the mantle is the *core,* with a radius of some 2,200 miles (3,500 kilometers). It is divided into a solid inner core and a molten outer core.

AGE OF THE EARTH

The most-exact method known to science for determining the age of the Earth is based on the study of the radioactivity of certain minerals. In these minerals, one or more chemical elements decay radioactively, that is, their atoms give off very small particles and other radiation. During this process the radioactive elements are changed into other elements. A given element may also have different forms, or *isotopes*, which have different atomic weights. Some of these isotopes may be radioactive and undergo change.

Each radioactive-decay process takes a fixed length of time, regardless of external circumstances, depending on the isotope and its atomic weight. As the element decays, its quantity in the rock or mineral becomes smaller, while the amount of the element it is changing into becomes greater. Knowing the decay times of elements and the proportions of these elements and of their end products, scientists can calculate the age of the rock or mineral.

OUR FRAGILE WORLD: THE MISSION TO PLANET EARTH

When the Apollo astronauts traveled to the Moon, they looked back on Earth and saw a tiny blue-and-white ball floating in space. That view, captured in pictures, conveyed as never before just how fragile our planet really is. We learned that we must take care of it.

But before we can intelligently care for Earth, we must understand its complexities. How do the oceans affect weather? How do our life-styles—driving cars, using electricity, and disposing of garbage—affect the land, sea, and air around us?

As part of its home-observatory program called the Earth Science Enterprise, the National Aeronautics and Space Administration (NASA) is monitoring the overall health of the planet. Throughout the 1990s the agency launched a series of observatory satellites to monitor such things as Earth's ozone levels, changing temperatures, rainforest destruction, volcanic eruptions, ocean currents, ice cover, sea levels, the extent of pollution, ocean life, and the increase in gases that may contribute to the "greenhouse effect." With such information, scientists are able to make more-accurate conclusions about Earth's health. These, in turn, can help all of us make the appropriate changes in our life-styles to save our fragile blue world before it is too late. The following problems, among the most important threats to our environment, continue to be under intense study:

• **The ozone hole**. Ozone is a three-atom molecule of oxygen. Formed high in the atmosphere, it shields life on Earth from the Sun's deadly ultraviolet rays. These rays can cause skin cancer, eye damage, immune deficiencies, and other health problems. The rays can also harm crops and aquatic life.

Ozone is very scarce in the upper atmosphere, making up less than one part per million of the gases there. In 1985 scientists announced that the springtime amounts of ozone over Antarctica had decreased by more than 40 percent between 1977 and 1984. With less ozone in the atmosphere, more harmful ultraviolet radiation reaches Earth's surface. Alarmed, the scientists rushed to find out the causes of the "ozone

There are several radioactive elements, or isotopes, that are commonly used to date ancient objects, including rocks and minerals. These elements are carbon 14 (carbon isotope with atomic weight 14), rubidium 87, potassium 40, strontium 90, and uranium 235 and 238. The quantities of isotopes in a sample are measured by radiation detectors and other methods. The age of a rock may be based on one or more isotopes. However, these methods are not exact—and there may be an uncertainty of as much as several hundred million years, or there may be disagreement in ages measured with different isotopes. The oldest known rock on Earth was formed nearly 4 billion years ago. The planet Earth itself is thought to be about 4.6 billion years old.

hole." One contributing factor was found to be chlorofluorocarbons (CFCs), a class of chemicals used in refrigerators, air conditioners, and other industrial devices. It has been estimated that one CFC molecule can destroy thousands of ozone molecules.

The use of CFCs has now been virtually eliminated and replaced by a variety of other aerosols. Unfortunately, even now that CFCs are no longer used, full recovery of the ozone layer could take decades or even centuries. Indeed, in the early 21st century, scientists reported record levels of ozone depletion over parts of Northern Europe, Antarctica, and the United States. Researchers will continue to monitor ozone levels around the world, using spacecraft, aircraft, and balloons.

• **Global warming.** Without carbon dioxide gas in our atmosphere, our planet would be covered with ice. Like the glass panes of a greenhouse, carbon dioxide allows sunlight to penetrate the atmosphere, and then traps some of the heat produced when sunlight reflects off Earth's surface. But the presence of too much carbon dioxide, such as in the atmosphere of the planet Venus, causes surface temperatures to rise to inferno-like levels.

Human activities, such as the burning of fossil fuels, have caused a substantial increase in carbon dioxide levels and other "greenhouse" gases in the past century. As a result, Earth is gradually getting warmer. According to NASA's Goddard Institute for Space Studies, 1998 was the warmest year on record, followed by 2002. To date, the 1990s were the warmest decade ever, with the 1980s second.

No one really knows what climatic changes, if any, may occur in the future. But if the climate does change, the effects could be devastating. In a worst-case scenario, the polar ice caps would melt, inundating coastal cities. Rainfall patterns may drastically change, causing droughts in some areas and floods in others.

Scientists are using the vantage point of space to study the influence that oceans, ocean life, and land vegetation have on carbon dioxide levels. In the meantime, some nations are already taking steps to reduce consumption of fossil fuels.

• **Rain-forest destruction.** There is no better example of the rich diversity of life on Earth than the countless birds, flowers, monkeys, and insects of the rain forests. Tragically, humans are destroying the world's rain forests and other woodlands at an astonishing rate.

Trees naturally absorb carbon dioxide, a greenhouse gas. Cutting down trees destroys a natural defense against the threat of global warming. Burning trees adds carbon dioxide into the air. Worst of all, by destroying the forests, we destroy the homes of many plants and animals. In Brazil, species have been lost even before they have been identified.

In 1988, astronauts aboard the space shuttle *Discovery* photographed a massive smoke cloud hovering over South America's Amazon River basin (see photo, facing page). The cloud, measuring over three times the size of Texas, was literally and figuratively part of a lush rain forest that had gone up in smoke.

Jeffrey Brune

EARTH'S MOTION

In ancient times and throughout the Middle Ages, many people believed that Earth stood motionless. They explained the succession of day and night and the changing positions of the stars by saying that Earth was still, and that the sky somehow moved around Earth. We have since learned that the apparent daily movement of the stars in the heavens is due to the rotation of the planet about its axis. Earth makes a single complete rotation in exactly 23 hours, 56 minutes, and 4.09 seconds.

One of the best proofs we have of the rotation of our planet is the pendulum experiment first performed in 1851 by a French physicist, Jean-Bernard-Léon Foucault.

He suspended a heavy weight at the end of a steel wire, which was suspended from the dome of the Pantheon, a public building in Paris. A pin attached to the end of the weight rested on a circular ridge of sand. Foucault set the pendulum swinging. The pendulum moved to and fro, in the same plane, and the pin at the end of the weight began to trace lines in the sand. As the pendulum continued to swing, the lines followed different directions. There could be only one explanation. The pendulum did not change direction. Therefore, it must be the ridge of sand that was turning. Since the sand rested on the floor of the Pantheon, and since the Pantheon itself rested on the Earth, Foucault concluded that the Earth itself must be rotating.

The device with which Foucault proved the rotation of the Earth is called the Foucault pendulum. One of these pendulums has been erected in the General Assembly Building of the United Nations in New York City.

The alternation of day and night is due to the rotation of the Earth about its axis. As our planet turns, a given place on its surface will be in sunlight or in darkness, depending upon whether it is facing the Sun or facing the part of the sky on the other side of the Earth from the Sun. The Earth's rotation also causes air currents to be turned toward the right in the Northern Hemisphere, and to the left in the Southern —a phenomenon called the *Coriolis force* (see Volume 2, page 114).

An interesting effect, due to the rotation of the Earth, can be produced by focusing a camera on the North Star and leaving the shutter open for several hours. The stars will appear, not as points, but as curved lines. This is because the Earth, on which the camera rests, has been rotating on its axis.

Yearly Motion

At the same time that it rotates, the Earth revolves about the Sun. It completes a revolution in 365 days, 6 hours, 9 minutes, and 10 seconds, when reckoned relative to the position of the stars in space. This is called a *sidereal* (star) *year*.

The orbit of the Earth around the Sun is an ellipse, with the center of the Sun at one of the two foci. The definition of an ellipse is that it is the path of a point, the sum of whose distances from two fixed points—the foci—is constant. An ellipse can be drawn by the method described below.

Place two pins on a piece of paper resting on a flat surface. Prepare a piece of string more than twice as long as the distance between the two pins, and splice the ends of the string. Place the string around the two pins, and set a pencil in position. Stretching the string to the fullest extent, pass the pencil point over the paper, going around the pins. The figure drawn by the pencil is an ellipse. The pins will represent the two foci, F^1 or F^2. If this ellipse represented the orbit of the Earth around the Sun, the Sun would be at F^1 or F^2. Actually, the ellipse described by the Earth in its movement around the Sun is very nearly a circle.

The distance of the Earth from the Sun will vary according to its position in its elliptical orbit. At *perihelion*—its nearest approach to the Sun—the Earth is some 3 million miles (4.8 million kilometers) closer to the Sun than at *aphelion*, when it is farthest away. According to a commonly accepted figure, the mean distance is 93 million miles (149.6 million kilometers). This is often used as a unit of length—the astronomical unit (A.U.)—by astronomers for measuring large distances. For example, instead of giving the distance of the planets from the Sun in miles or kilometers, an astronomer could give it in A.U. To Mars, for instance, it would be 1.5 A.U.; to Jupiter, 5.2.

As the Earth revolves about the Sun, its axis is tilted at an angle of 23.5 degrees from the perpendicular to the plane of its orbit. As a result the Northern Hemisphere will be tilted toward the Sun in one part of the orbit and away from it in another part, as will the Southern Hemisphere. This accounts for the fact that the days are longer in summer than in winter in the Northern Hemisphere. In the summer months, this hemisphere is tilted toward the Sun. Hence, a given spot on the hemisphere—

The Earth's motions (above) give our planet its days and its years. Every 24 hours, the Earth completes one rotation on its axis, a fact proven by the Foucault pendulum (right) in 1851. Every 365¼ days, the Earth completes one orbit around the Sun.

say, Chicago—will be in sunlight more than it will be in darkness in the course of a single rotation of the Earth. In the winter the Northern Hemisphere is tilted away from the Sun. Hence, Chicago will be in the shadow longer than it will be in sunlight.

The situation will be reversed in the Southern Hemisphere.

The motion of the Earth about the Sun and the tilting of its axis are the principal causes of seasonal changes. As we saw, the Northern Hemisphere is tilted toward the

Sun during its summer months and away from it in the winter months. When it is summer in the Northern Hemisphere, the Sun's rays fall more directly upon the hemisphere, heating it more effectively, and areas in the Northern Hemisphere remain longer in the sunlight than they do in the shadow. For a time, more heat is therefore received from the Sun than can be radiated away. During our winter months, the Sun's rays fall more obliquely upon the surface of the Northern Hemisphere. The more the rays slant, the less effectively they heat the surface of the Earth. Likewise, because the days are shorter than the nights, the heat received from the Sun has more time to radiate away. That is why temperatures are lower during the winter.

The Southern Hemisphere is tilted away from the Sun during the time that the Northern Hemisphere is slanted toward it. Hence, the winter months south of the equator correspond to the summer months north of it. It is winter in January in Chicago, while it is summer in the same month in Buenos Aires.

Our planet moves at an average speed of about 19 miles (30 kilometers) per second along its path around the Sun. Sometimes the Earth moves slower, sometimes faster, in its orbit. It is also traveling through space at a much faster speed as it follows the Sun in its wanderings through the heavens. The Sun revolves around the center of the galaxy called the Milky Way, completing a turn in about 2 million years. As a satellite of the Sun, the Earth takes part in this journey, maintaining a speed estimated at 118 to 168 miles (190 to 270 kilometers) per second.

Wobbly Motion

In addition to the motions that we have just described, the Earth also wobbles, or *precesses*, as an astronomer would say. Precession is due to the combined effects of gravitational attraction and the Earth's rotation. The Moon (and, to a lesser extent, the Sun) is constantly pulling upon the Earth. This effect, combined with the Earth's rotation, causes the axis of our planet to wobble about its center. As it does so, it traces out two cones in space. These cones have their vertexes, or tips, at the Earth's center, and their bases in space above the geographic poles.

We might compare the effect with the spinning of a top at a slant. If we extended the axis of the top, say, to the ceiling of the room in which it is rotating, the axis would describe a cone with its vertex at the point of the top and its base at the ceiling. It would take the top a fraction of a second to complete a single spin. It takes the axis of the Earth about 25,800 years.

Because of precession, different stars become our North Star—the one most directly above the north geographic pole—in the course of the years. Right now, Polaris is the North Star. Alpha Cephei will be nearest the pole in A.D. 7500; Vega, in A.D. 14,000. Eventually the full cycle will be completed, and Polaris will be the North Star again.

Areas A, B, and C receive equal amounts of solar energy on June 21. A's and C's energy is spread over larger areas than is B's energy, which is concentrated over the Tropic of Cancer. B's area is thus the warmest on June 21.

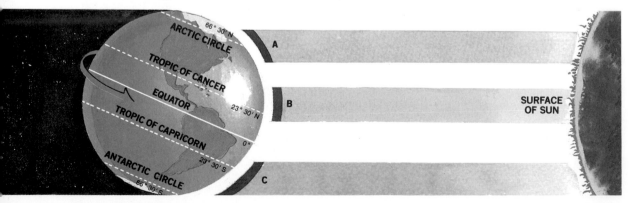

NASA

The Moon, seen in this Apollo photograph, is the only natural satellite of Earth. When astronauts landed on the Moon's surface in 1969, it was the realization of a centuries-old dream.

THE MOON

by Cecelia Payne-Gaposchkin
and Katherine Haramundanis

The Moon, circling Earth under the pull of our planet's gravity, passes across our sky once every 24 hours, exerting its own considerable gravitational pull on all of Earth's oceans and seas. Since the dawn of history, the peoples of the world have used the regularly changing shape of the Moon's face as a calendar. But the Moon remained more an object of legend than of science until 1609, when Galileo first focused his telescope on the details of its surface. He recognized mountains and large, flat, dark areas, which he called *maria*, the Latin word for "seas." Astronomers now know that there is no water on the Moon, although the term is still used.

The light and dark areas we see from Earth are, respectively, the Moon's uplands and its low-lying flat regions. Shadows thrown by some of the Moon's features can be used to estimate their heights. Among the most striking features is the 146-mile (235-kilometer)-wide crater Clavius, its rim surrounded by mountains 3.2 miles (5.2 kilometers) high. Telescopes also reveal bright streaks radiating from some craters. Because these rays do not throw shadows, we know they are not elevated. Other dark, riverlike features, called *rills*, are probably dry cracks cutting through the Moon's surface.

As astronomers built more-powerful telescopes, more lunar details have been noted and mapped. Beginning in the 1960s, artificial satellites and manned spacecraft were launched to pass near the Moon and eventually to land on it. Pictures from these missions revealed the surface in extraordinary detail, even making visible small boulders. Moon probes have provided us with detailed close-up photographs of the far side of the Moon, which is always hidden from an Earthbound observer's view.

ORIGIN AND HISTORY

From the chemistry and structure of lunar samples returned by Apollo astronauts, scientists now believe that the Moon is about 4.6 billion years old—about the same age as Earth. Where the Moon originated, however, is much more puzzling.

The Moon was once believed to be formed from the same dusty material as Earth and other planets. If this were true, its composition would be much more Earth-like than it is. Instead, its chemical makeup appears more like Earth's *surface*—with no dense metallic core. This has led scientists to speculate that the Moon may have originated when a planet-sized body hit Earth billions of years ago.

In this scenario, the crust of the two bodies would have been vaporized by the tremendous impact, and the iron core of the intruder body would have bored through Earth and merged with its core. Earth's atmosphere would have been vaporized and replaced by one of molten rock. From the jolt, our planet would have spun faster.

Over the ages, friction slowed down Earth's rotation rate, and its spin was transferred to the molten rock "atmosphere," which then became a ring around Earth. Eventually, Earth cooled to the solid body it is today, and the ring coalesced into one solid body as well: the Moon.

For years, scientists believed there was no water on or in the Moon. Recently, however, the Clementine and Lunar Prospector missions found evidence of 6 billion tons of water ice hidden in the permanently shadowed regions inside deep craters near the Moon's north and south poles.

The Moon's phases depend on the part of its sunlit side facing Earth. Its apparent shape changes nightly, depending on the positions of the Sun, Earth, and Moon.

THE PHASES OF THE MOON

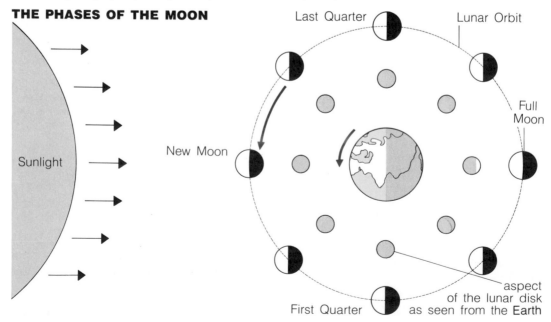

Scientists also found no chemical evidence that living things have ever existed naturally on the Moon. Despite this lack of direct evidence for life, some of the lunar soil did contain minute amounts of amino acids and possibly other related organic compounds, the very building blocks of life.

LUNAR STATISTICS

By measuring the time it takes for a laser beam to reflect off a set of mirrors left on the lunar surface by U.S. astronauts, astronomers can gauge the distance between Earth and the Moon to within less than 1 inch (2.5 centimeters). This distance is not constant, however, as the orbits of Earth and the Moon are elliptical. The yearly average distance is around 240,000 miles (386,000 kilometers). The Moon is slowly pulling away at a rate of about 1.5 inches (4 centimeters) a year.

The Moon's diameter is 2,163 miles (3,480 kilometers), about a quarter of Earth's diameter. Some planets in our solar system have larger moons, but the moons of Earth and Pluto are the largest with respect to the size of their parent planets. In fact, some scientists believe that the Earth-Moon system may actually constitute a double-planet system. The mass of our Moon, as measured by its gravitational effect on Earth, is $1/81$ of Earth's; its volume is a somewhat larger proportion—$1/50$—meaning that the Moon is less dense than our planet. Actually, the Moon is approximately as dense as the rocks on Earth's surface.

BRIGHTNESS OF THE MOON

The Moon produces no light of its own, but shines by reflected light. The percentage of light reflected by the Moon is known as its *albedo*. On average the Moon reflects only 7 percent of the sunlight that falls vertically upon it, with some areas reflecting more light than others. All the light by which we see the Moon comes from the Sun, either directly or after reflection from Earth. As the second-brightest object in the sky, the Moon sends us only two-millionths as much light as the Sun.

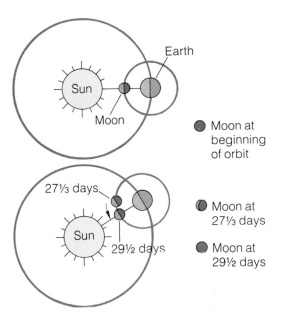

The period in which the Moon completes an orbit around Earth and returns to the same position in the sky is 27¹/₃ days. But because Earth is also moving in its orbit around the Sun in the same direction as the Moon, it takes two more days before the Moon is again between Earth and the Sun. So the interval from one new moon to the next is 29¹/₂ days.

PHASES OF THE MOON

We all have noticed that the Moon's apparent shape changes from night to night, and it runs through a complete cycle in about a month. These shape changes, or phases, are caused by the relationship between the positions of the Moon, Sun, and Earth.

When the Moon is directly in line between the Sun and Earth, the Sun is shining on the far side of the Moon; this phase is referred to as the *new moon*. As the Moon travels around Earth and moves out of the Sun-Earth line, the illuminated part becomes visible to us as a thin crescent, which increases, or waxes, night after night. When the line from Earth to Moon makes an angle of 90 degrees with the line from Earth to Sun, we see half the Moon's face illuminated. This phase is called the *first quarter*. When the Earth, Moon, and Sun are again in line, with Sun and Moon

Lunar craters range in size from 684 miles across (Mare Imbrium) to only inches across.

on opposite sides of the Earth, we see the whole face of the Moon illuminated. This phase is the *full moon*. Thereafter the Moon wanes, and the illuminated surface grows smaller. When the direction from Earth to Moon again makes an angle of 90 degrees with the direction from Earth to Sun, we again see half the Moon's face illuminated in the *last quarter* phase. The crescent continues to wane until new moon is reached again. Between the quarters and new moon, the shape of the illuminated portion of the Moon is called a *crescent*. Between the quarters and full moon, the shape of the illuminated disk is described as *gibbous*—that is, not fully circular.

The line that separates the illuminated and dark portions of the Moon is known as the *terminator*. The crescent moon, whether waxing or waning, has horns, or cusps, which always point away from the Sun. Near the time of new moon, it is often possible to see the whole disk of the Moon faintly illuminated. The light by which we

see this phenomenon is light that has been reflected from the bright surface of the Earth.

Although the illuminated area changes, we always see virtually the same side of the Moon. This is because the Moon is gravitationally locked to the Earth and makes one rotation on its own axis in nearly the same time it takes to make one revolution around the Earth. However, it should not be forgotten that the Sun shines on all its sides in turn.

The Months: Synodic and Sidereal

Astronomers recognize more than one kind of month. The simplest is the *synodic* month, or *lunation*, the interval from one new moon to the next new moon—29½ days. This, however, is not the time taken by the Moon to make one complete orbit around the Earth. The Moon falls behind because the Earth's motion around the Sun carries our planet about 1/12 of the way around its orbit between lunations. The

A unique view of a portion of both the near and far sides of the Moon as captured by the Galileo probe.

true orbit of the Moon, known as the *sidereal* month, is 27⅓ days. Gravitationally locked to the Earth, the Moon rotates on its axis once in a sidereal month.

THE TIDES

Because of its close proximity to the Earth, the Moon's gravity pulls powerfully on our oceans, seas, and lakes, and even upon solid land. The Sun, too, tugs at the planet's waters, but, owing to its greater distance, the effect is much smaller. These forces, working together, are always creating two maximum tidal bulges at diametrically opposite sides of the Earth. These bulges, or high tides, draw water from all points between, creating two areas of low tides along meridians 90 degrees removed from them. As a result, every shoreline experiences two high tides and two low tides each day.

Twice a month the Sun, Moon, and Earth fall into perfect alignment, exerting their gravitational force in a mutual or additive way. At the full moon, the Earth moves between the Sun and the Moon; and at the new moon, the Sun and Moon lie on the same side of the Earth. These higher high tides and lower lows are called *spring tides*.

When the Sun and Moon make an angle of 90 degrees in relation to the Earth, they reduce each other's effect, producing semimonthly *neap tides*, when the difference between high and low is at a minimum. The exact times of high and low tides at a given location vary, however, depending on variations in coastlines, physical barriers such as reefs, strong winds, and even changes in barometric pressure.

ORBIT OF THE MOON

The motion of the Moon is far from simple. Its shape and position relative to the Sun and Earth are continually changing. For these reasons, the part of the

Moon seen from the Earth varies slightly, so that, over a period of time, we can view 59 percent of the Moon's surface from a place of observation on the Earth. Because the changes in the Moon's orbit run in cycles, its visible surface seems to undergo rocking motions, or librations, which bring small areas near the edges of the observable disk into view. Several decades elapse before all possible areas are visible to viewers on Earth.

Eclipses of the Sun and Moon

The relative sizes of the Moon and the Sun—as seen from the Earth—are almost exactly the same. This is an extraordinary coincidence, because the more-distant Sun is about 64 million times the volume of the Moon.

If the orbit of the Earth around the Sun and the orbit of the Moon around the Earth were in exactly the same plane, the Moon would pass directly across the face of the Sun at every new moon, producing a monthly solar eclipse. Similarly, at every full moon, the shadow of the Earth would fall on the Moon, producing a total eclipse of the Moon.

But the Moon's orbit is inclined by about 5 degrees to that of the Earth. This means that the Moon can come in front of the Sun only near the position where the two orbits intersect, points called the *nodes* of the Moon's orbit. When a new moon occurs very near the node, the Moon will pass exactly across the face of the Sun, and there will be a *total eclipse* of the Sun. Farther from the node, the Moon will cover only part of the Sun's face, resulting in a *partial eclipse*. Because neither the Moon's nor the Earth's orbit is circular, the distances from Earth to Moon and Sun are not constant. As these distances vary, so do the apparent sizes of the Sun and Moon. At times the Moon may not cover the entire solar disk, allowing a thin rim of sunlight to be visible around its edge—an *annular eclipse* of the Sun.

An eclipse of the Sun is visible only from the small portion of the Earth on

As the world watched in awe on July 20, 1969, Edwin E. Aldrin, Jr., the second man to step on the Moon, heralded this major accomplishment of space exploration by planting the flag of the United States firmly on the Moon's surface.

A lunar module stands on the cratered surface of the Moon, highlighted by the Sun. The lunar surface consists of a layer of fine particulate material and rock fragments extending down from the surface about one to three yards. The forbidding landscape is never marred by erosion, since the Moon lacks wind, rain, or other weather.

which the Moon's shadow is cast. The shadow moves rapidly across the surface of the Earth, and total eclipses last only a few minutes, as seen from one station.

As for lunar eclipses, they take place when the Moon passes through the Earth's shadow. Therefore, lunar eclipses always occur at the time of a full moon, with partial eclipses seen when the Moon passes partially within the Earth's shadow. Unlike solar eclipses, eclipses of the Moon are seen from every part of the Earth where the Moon would ordinarily be visible at the time (see also page 175).

LUNAR TEMPERATURE

When it is midday on the Moon, with the Sun directly overhead, the temperature reaches 212° F (100° C). At lunar midnight the temperature drops to about −177° F (−116° C). It should also be remembered that the Moon rotates only once in about 27.3 of our Earth days—giving it long periods of daylight and darkness during which it heats and cools.

But the Moon's astounding temperature extremes are due primarily to the lack of atmosphere, which would act as an insulating blanket. You can directly see that the Moon has no atmosphere by watching an *occultation*, that is, the passing of a star behind the Moon. If the Moon had an atmosphere, the star would twinkle and fade gradually, but it always vanishes abruptly, and abruptly reappears at the other edge.

It is not surprising that the Moon has no appreciable atmosphere, because gravity at its surface is only one-sixth that of the Earth's. This is not enough to retain most gases. Small amounts of gas have been seen to exude from certain points on the Moon's surface, but they seem to quickly dissipate into space.

LUNAR GEOGRAPHY

As mentioned earlier, the largest features on the Moon, readily seen with the naked eye, are the dark maria. These flat areas are strewn with small boulders and pocked with craters. We now know that, remarkably, all the maria but one are on the side of the Moon facing the Earth. The largest is Mare Imbrium, about 684 miles (1,100 kilometers) across. It is generally thought that the maria are hardened lavas that flowed in the distant past, perhaps due to the impact of huge extraterrestrial objects or due to some internal processes.

The Moon's surface is also heavily pocked with circular craters. They have clearly raised rims, and some have central peaks. Many craters overlap with each other, and may occur within the maria and on the mountain chains. Some craters appear to be filled with hardened lava, others

to be partially buried in dust flows. In the photographs of the great crater known as Aristarchus, both types of flow may be seen. Aristarchus has a central peak, and its floor seems to be filled with lava. The crater nearby is very shallow and has been nearly obliterated by a dust flow. A number of much smaller, bowl-shaped craters dot the area.

Very large craters are often called "walled plains," because they enclose fairly level surfaces. These walled plains may be light in color, like lunar uplands, or dark, like maria. The crater wall, or rampart, is roughly circular and has often been designated as a circular mountain range. However, the wall is often low in comparison with the surrounding land, and even in comparison with the enclosed surface, or crater floor. The diameters of the largest craters reach more than 185 miles (300 ki-

heavily bombarded by meteoric bodies over a long period of time. This bombardment has most likely produced not only a large percentage of the craters, but also the maria. The great dust splash extending halfway around the Moon from the huge crater Tycho is clear evidence that it is an impact crater. A large impact crater usually has many small impact craters near it, probably formed by the debris thrown out by the original impact. The boulders found near impact craters have a similar origin.

A possible example of a volcanic crater on the Moon is Aristarchus. Many small changes have been recorded near it, and gases may emerge from it on occasion. It has a pronounced central peak and what appears to be a lava-filled floor.

Lunar *rays* are Moon features that extend radially outward from certain craters

The Apollo 17 lunar landing (left) was the last of six manned Moon missions. The data collected from these missions have helped explain mysteries about the Moon that have haunted humanity for centuries. Scientists now conclude, for instance, that most of the Moon's craters (below) were created by meteorites bombarding the lunar surface, while a smaller portion were formed by Earth-style volcanoes.

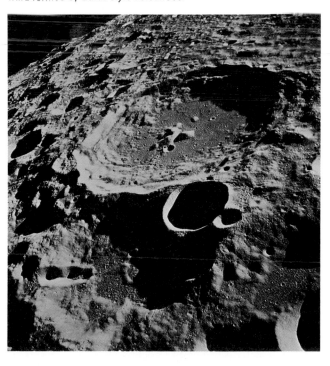

lometers). Some craters, however, are so deep that their bottoms are always in shadow. Still other craters are mere pits in the lunar surface, with little or no raised rim surrounding the central depression.

On the Earth, there are two major types of craters: the volcano and the impact crater. Volcanic craters have steep sides and often a central rise or knob. Crater Lake in Oregon is a good example. Impact craters, such as the Meteor Crater in Arizona and the Chubb Crater in Canada, are shallower relative to their diameters, and do not usually possess central peaks. Impact craters can be very much larger than volcanic craters: the southeastern shore of Hudson Bay may be the remainder of a great impact crater.

Craters similar to Earth types can be recognized on the Moon. There is little doubt that the Moon's surface has been

Astronauts left a variety of instruments on the Moon's surface to collect data. The Laser Ranging Retro-Reflector (left of lunar module) is a set of mirrors that helps astronomers gauge the exact distance between the Earth and the Moon.

such as Tycho and Copernicus. They appear lighter than the surrounding terrain principally because they reflect light better. This is probably because they are made of very finely divided particles. The reflectivity of particles depends largely on their average size, finer particles reflecting light more brilliantly under vertical illumination than do coarse ones.

Rills are narrow, riverlike valleys made visible by shadows cast into them. They may be cracks in the surface, or possibly canyons formed by ash flow from volcanoes. Some are twisted and tortuous, and some are associated with chains of craters. Some of the straight rills seem to be associated with natural settling around the maria. Others may have been furrowed by rolling boulders.

The mountains of the Moon form large, rugged chains principally concentrated around the maria. Their heights can be measured by the length of the shadows they cast. The highest, the Leibniz Mountains, attain a height of 5 miles (7.9 kilometers). Lunar mountains seem to have been thrust up as a result of impact rather than formed by folding of rocks, as has been the case with many mountains on the Earth. A mountainous feature known as the Straight Wall, in Mare Nubium, south of the lunar equator, appears to be a 68-mile (110-kilometer)-long line of cliffs produced by faulting.

Naming Lunar Features

The early astronomers examining the Moon by telescope gave the principal maria chains fanciful Latin names, and many mountain chains were named after well-known European mountains. Since that time, advances in observational techniques have revealed more and more detail, and thousands of features have been named. The International Astronomical Union (IAU) now has the responsibility for assigning names, a task that has been enormously increased by observation of the far side of the Moon. Typically, major craters have been named after astronomers or scientists. Other prominent individuals, such as Jules Verne, a 19th-century author, and Plato, a Greek philosopher, have also been commemorated.

LUNAR EXPLORATION

In the early 20th century, astronomers began to be able to view many never-before-seen details of the lunar surface. These discoveries inspired scientists to seriously consider means for traveling to the Moon. The vivid imaginations of fiction writers, in the meantime, were not idle. Authors such as Jules Verne and H. G. Wells kept popular interest in our solar system alive with their tales of interplanetary and lunar adventures.

Although rockets had been in use for fireworks and as weapons since the 13th century, few individuals ever considered them as a safe or reliable means of travel. But the 20th century saw the fruition of the rocket-ship dream. In the 1920s and the 1930s, the groundwork for rocket-ship technology was laid. During the later 1940s and the 1950s, the Soviet Union and the United States sent rockets aloft to explore the upper atmosphere and near space. They then decided to launch artificial satellites to circle the Earth and later to orbit or land on the Moon.

TO THE MOON AND BACK

In 1957 the Soviet Union launched Sputnik, the first artificial satellite to orbit the Earth. The United States followed suit with Explorer I in early 1958. The Soviet Union then sent unmanned probes to the Moon in its series of Luniks. In 1959 Lunik 2 crashed on the Moon. Later the same year, Lunik 3 circled the Moon and relayed the first pictures of the lunar far side. It was not until 1966 that Lunik 9 made a soft landing on the Moon and sent pictures of the lunar surface back to Earth.

In the meantime, the United States prepared to send unmanned probes to the Moon. Its Ranger series of mooncraft in 1964 and 1965 were designed to crash on the Moon, but before a Ranger would crash, it took thousands of photos of the approaching surface of the Moon. The photographs were transmitted to Earth electronically. Three Ranger craft, 7 through 9, showed details of the lunar surface about 1,000 times greater than could be seen with the best Earth telescopes. Even small craters only 1 or 2 yards across could be seen.

From 1966 to 1967, the United States launched unmanned artificial satellites to orbit the Moon. Known as Lunar Orbiters, five of these vehicles swept close to the Moon's surface and took thousands of photographs, which were then relayed to Earth. These vehicles also took photos of the Earth as seen from the Moon. Another series of unmanned craft were designed and launched with the purpose of soft-landing on the Moon. Known as Surveyors 1 through 7, five of them settled gently on various spots on the Moon to test its surface. They determined that the Moon was safe for landing. They also carried out various tests of the Moon's surface, and excavated some of it for study. Surveyor 5 made a chemical test of lunar rocks by irradiating them with atomic particles and recording how the rocks reacted. In this way, scientists on Earth deduced something of the chemical composition of lunar material. They concluded it was like Earthly basalt, a volcanic rock. The Surveyors showed that the Moon's surface was covered with pulverized rock and larger pieces of stone. The spacecraft also sent many photos of the Moon to Earth, as well as pictures of the Earth as seen from the Moon.

In the 1960s and 1970s, the Soviet Union continued its program of unmanned lunar exploration. Probes circled the Moon or landed on its surface. Luna probes took samples of lunar soil and sent them, by means of rockets, back to Earth for study. Two wheeled vehicles—Lunokhods 1 and 2 —were landed on the Moon. They were driven across the lunar surface by remote control from Earth.

As early as 1961, the United States had decided to land astronauts on the Moon, and soon inaugurated Project Apollo. From late in 1968, a series of Apollo missions sent U.S. astronauts into orbit around the Moon, and, in July of 1969, the first humans landed on the lunar surface. The astronauts brought back many specimens of rock that have added immensely to our knowledge about the Moon. They also took thousands of photographs of the Moon and the Earth, while on the Moon itself and from the Apollo spacecraft. They set up scientific experiments on the lunar surface, the results of which were telemetered to Earth.

On December 7, 1992, the spacecraft Galileo, on its roundabout way toward Jupiter, cruised to within 68,500 miles (110,200 kilometers) of the Moon's north polar region. Its measurements and images suggested that water ice may exist within deep craters on the lunar surface. In July 1999, Lunar Prospector failed to discover definitive evidence when it slammed into a crater on the lunar south pole. To date, the question of whether water exists on the Moon remains unresolved.

Travel on the Moon

The Moon presents many obstacles to travel on or above its surface. Conventional modes of Earth transportation—airplane, automobile, train, and ship—would be very difficult or impossible there. The Moon has no air, so combustion engines—such as gasoline, diesel, steam, and jet engines—cannot operate unless a supply of air or oxygen as well as fuel is provided. The absence of an atmosphere on the Moon also rules out aircraft. Only rockets or nuclear-powered-space vessels would make flight through the lunar skies possible.

Locomotion on the lunar surface in a ground vehicle involves many problems. Motors need to be powered by electricity. The low lunar gravity—one-sixth the gravity at Earth's surface—makes control of the vehicle difficult, so special suspension, steering, and axle systems needed to be designed for the Apollo astronauts.

Traction, or grip, on the soft and yielding lunar dust is difficult to achieve. Engineers knew that air-filled tires would not work—they would simply explode in the Moon's near vacuum of an atmosphere. Treads or tracks, as on a tank, were one solution. But drivers and engineers had learned that wheels with thick, flexible tires offer the best means of locomotion through soft dirt and sand. It was decided that airless tires were the best choice.

Other requirements for a lunar vehicle are lightness and compactness, for easy transport to the Moon; a tough, flexible chassis and axles, for movement over rough lunar ground; an ability to withstand the airlessness and great temperature extremes of the Moon; and enough speed for traveling significant distances in a reasonable time. The vehicle had to have room for at least two astronauts with their equipment, experimental packages, and specimens of lunar rock. Navigational and communication systems were also vital.

The United States incorporated all these features into its first lunar roving vehicle (LRV). On its first mission, the LRV carried two U.S. astronauts on several short journeys of exploration across the Moon's barren but rugged surface.

When the aluminum LRV was unfolded from the lunar module on the Moon's surface, it was 10 feet (3 meters) in length. Each of its four wheels was powered by a one-quarter-horsepower electric motor. Flexible wire-mesh tires provided excellent traction. Power was supplied by electric batteries. Top speed was about 10 miles (16 kilometers) per hour; maximum range, around 40 miles (65 kilometers). The LRV could cross cracks in the ground 24 inches (60 centimeters) wide and move up slopes of 25 degrees. The astronauts steered the LRV with a control stick much like those in airplanes. All four wheels could be turned, for sharp maneuvers.

The vehicle carried two astronauts and their equipment. Computerized navigation instruments told the astronauts where they were. A color-television camera on the LRV relayed views of the Moon to Earth.

The LRV's Earth weight was 440 pounds (200 kilograms); on the Moon, it was somewhat over 75 pounds (34 kilograms). The vehicle was designed to operate even if some of its vital parts broke down, which in fact did happen at first.

EXPERIENCING THE MOON IN PERSON

The Apollo astronauts returned to Earth with vivid descriptions of the lunar world they visited. Its barren, forbidding landscape appears only in shades of gray and the sky is black. Without atmosphere, there can be no

Scientists expect it will not be too long before an astronaut again views the Earth over the lunar horizon.

blue sky and no weather. There can be no sound and no life. In the sunshine the temperature is that of boiling water, but without an atmosphere, a step into the shadow brings one to a temperature far below freezing. There are no beautiful sky colors at sunset and sunrise, and no twilight. Like the blue sky, these Earthly beauties depend on our atmosphere. On the airless Moon, they are absent.

For these reasons a visitor to the Moon needs protection, not only from extremes of temperature and lack of air, but also from the incessant bombardment of cosmic rays and particles, and from the effects of ultraviolet radiation. On the Earth, we are shielded from the deleterious effects of strong solar and cosmic rays by our atmosphere and the Earth's magnetic field. But the lunar explorer has no such natural protection, since the Moon is without an atmosphere and has an extremely weak magnetic field.

Since gravity at the Moon's surface is one-sixth that on the Earth, all weights on the Moon are diminished by a factor of six. A man who weighs 175 pounds (80 kilograms) on Earth weighs about 29 pounds (13 kilograms) on the Moon, and, with the same muscular effort, would be able to jump six times as high or lift six times as great a weight as on Earth. This compensates to some extent for the weight of the equipment that lunar explorers have to carry to protect themselves from the severe conditions. Similarly, the launching of a rocket from the surface of the Moon would require only one-sixth of the thrust required to launch the same rocket from the Earth's surface. This makes the return journey of an astronaut from the Moon and its vicinity easier.

In some cases, this diminished weight works to the disadvantage of the lunar visitor—for instance, when he or she must push a lever or dig with a shovel.

Explorers Confirm Theories

The Moon probes and U.S. Apollo missions have confirmed the existence of at least some lunar features that strongly resemble volcanic features on Earth—domes and lava flows. The question remains whether volcanic activity was ever widespread and important in the geologic history of the Moon. Extensive rock melting was undoubtedly caused by impacts of large meteorites on the lunar surface. Meteorites probably also produced the large craters and the maria, or plains.

Lunar rocks brought back to Earth by the Apollo astronauts generally resemble the Earth rocks known as basalts, which are finely grained, and gabbros, which are coarser-grained. These are dark, dense, chemically related rocks of igneous origin.

Among the youngest of Moon rocks are the mare basalts. These rocks formed from dark lavas that poured out from volcanic structures 3 billion to 3.8 billion years ago to form the floors of many large craters and maria. The rocks also confirm that the Moon has had a long, complex history, beginning about 4.6 billion years ago or even earlier, when the original crust is believed to have solidified.

EARTH AS SEEN FROM THE MOON

A person standing on the Moon sees Earth as a disk two and one-half times the size of the Moon seen from Earth. Because of its high albedo, the surface of Earth has five times as much reflecting power as the surface of the Moon. Also, because of its greater apparent size, the full Earth sends about 30 times as much light to the Moon as the full Moon sends to us. To the lunar explorer, our clouds look brilliantly white, the oceans dark blue, and the continents almost all purplish brown.

Because the Moon and Earth are gravitationally locked, lunar observers do not see Earth rise or set. From the near side of the Moon, Earth is always visible. If explorers venture to the far side of the Moon, they will not see Earth at all.

When the observer on the Moon is at lunar midnight, he or she sees a *full earth*, completely illuminated, unless the Moon is directly in line between the Sun and Earth. In that case, he or she observes an eclipse of Earth by the Moon at the same time as Earth observers see a solar eclipse. When the observer is at lunar midday, and the Sun is directly behind Earth, he or she observes *new earth*. If the Sun is completely eclipsed by Earth, Earth would be seen surrounded by a bright halo caused by the sunlight scattered in Earth's atmosphere. Conditions for such an eclipse are very similar to those for a solar eclipse seen from Earth, but the track of totality on the Moon would be two and one-half times as wide.

IN THE FUTURE . . .

The Moon would make an ideal site for astronomical observatories. Its lack of turbulent atmosphere that blurs faint telescopic images and inclement weather that periodically hinders observations, coupled with its lesser gravity, mean that lunar telescopes could be built larger and see farther than any in existence today.

Some suggest that the Moon would provide an excellent site to study the interplay of the Sun's radiation with Earth, and to learn how that interaction helps control our planet's climate. Others would like to use the Moon to collect sunlight, transform it into other forms of energy, and beam it back to Earth to replace our current need to burn rapidly dwindling fossil fuels. And still others believe that atoms of helium spewed out for centuries by the Sun and captured in the lunar soil could be used to fuel nuclear-power reactors on the Moon.

NASA and commercial enterprises have begun to develop plans for a manned lunar base that would become operational sometime in the 21st century. There, scientists would continue the work begun by astronauts in the 1960s. Such a base might be used as a laboratory to conduct geological and astronomical research; as a manufacturing plant to create from lunar resources rocket fuel and other materials needed for survival; and even as a "transfer station" for much longer trips to Mars and other planets in the solar system.

Of all the planets in our solar system, Mars most closely mimics the life-sustaining conditions on Earth. Scientists are trying to determine if the planet has ever supported life or could do so in the future.

MARS

by Jeffrey Brune

Mars, the fourth planet from the Sun, has long fascinated us. In many ways, Mars is much like Earth, and the apparent similarities between the two planets have raised the possibility that life might exist there. The planet assumes a bricklike color in the night sky, a phenomenon that has led to its nickname—the Red Planet. Mars is named for the Roman god of war.

Except for the Moon, and perhaps Mercury, Mars is the only solid body in the solar system whose surface we can view from Earth with ground telescopes. The planet has been under telescopic observation for over three centuries. Telescopes show Mars as a small disk with red, dark, and white markings. The red areas, which cover nearly three-fourths of the surface, are called *continentes* (Latin for "mainlands"). The dark regions are the *maria* ("seas" in Latin). White polar caps cover the planet's geographic pole.

For many years, astronomers thought Mars to be much like the Earth, with oxygen, water, and polar ice. Somewhat later they realized that Mars is dry, with no large or visible bodies of water at all.

During the late 1800s, some astronomers claimed they saw many fine lines crisscrossing much of the Martian surface. These lines were named *canali*—Italian for "channels" or "grooves." The Italian word can also be translated as "canals" or "waterways." This translation led to the widespread belief that there were intelligent beings on Mars who had built the canals. Perhaps coincidentally, this myth arose shortly after the building of the Suez Canal, when plans were being drawn for constructing the Panama Canal.

A satellite probe traveled within 200 miles of Mars to capture this infrared photo of the Red Planet and one of its orbiting moons, Phobos.

In the 20th century, improved telescopes and cameras revealed that these apparent Martian canals were mere optical illusions. However, the search for life on Mars continued undaunted, as did the quest to understand the planet better.

SOME BASIC STATISTICS

Mars lies about one and one-half times farther from the Sun than does Earth. A good deal smaller than Earth, Mars' equatorial diameter—4,200 miles (6,758 kilometers)—is a little more than half that of our planet. The surface area of Mars is a little more than one-quarter of Earth's; its volume is about one-seventh of our planet's; its mass, 11 percent; and, finally, its density, 71 percent of Earth's.

Due to its greater distance from the Sun, the amount of light and heat that Mars receives is also diminished—less than one-half that received by Earth. As one would expect, Mars is therefore quite a bit colder, with temperatures ranging as low as −305° F (−187° C), enough to freeze carbon dioxide gas into "dry ice." Temperatures rarely rise high enough to melt ordinary ice into water.

The mean distance of Mars from the Sun is about 140 million miles (225 million kilometers), some 48 million miles (78 million kilometers) farther away than is Earth. At the perihelion of its orbit—the nearest point to the Sun—Mars lies about 126 million miles (203 million kilometers) away. At aphelion—the farthest point from the Sun—the distance is about 155 million miles (250 million kilometers). This means that its elliptical orbit is quite eccentric. (The more an ellipse departs from the shape of a circle, the more eccentric it is.)

The distance between Mars and our own planet varies widely. When Mars is in conjunction—that is, on the other side of the Sun from Earth—its distance from us averages 234 million miles (377 million kilometers). When it is in opposition—that is, on the other side of Earth from the Sun—its distance from Earth ranges from about 35 million miles (56 million kilometers) to about 61 million miles (98 million kilometers), depending on the point in the Martian orbit where the opposition occurs.

Mars is in opposition about every 26 months and, at those times, appears largest and brightest to us. The opposition of August 27, 2003, when Mars came as close as

34.6 million miles (55.8 million kilometers) from us, marked the closest approach of the Red Planet in nearly 60,000 years. During this opposition, Mars appeared brighter than everything in the night sky except Venus and the Moon. Its next approach this close will not occur for another three centuries.

Mars completes its orbit around the Sun in 687 of our days, traveling along its path at an average rate of 15 miles (24 kilometers) per second. The orbit is inclined to the ecliptic—the plane of Earth's orbit—by less than 2 degrees, and the planet rotates on its axis. The clear markings on its surface have made it possible to determine the speed of that rotation with great accuracy. The Martian day is 24 hours, 37 minutes, and 23 seconds long—almost the same as an Earth day.

Like Earth, Mars is somewhat flattened at its poles. Its equator is inclined about 25 degrees to the plane of the planet's orbit. In comparison, the inclination of Earth to its orbital plane is 23.5 degrees—only a little less. This tilt accounts for seasonal changes on Earth. In the case of Mars, too, the corresponding tilt brings about changes of season. Since it takes Mars almost twice as long as Earth to complete an orbit around the Sun, each of the Martian seasons is nearly six months in length—that is, almost twice as long as the corresponding season on Earth.

Mars reflects 15 percent of the light received from the Sun. Area for area, the disk of Mars is a better reflector than that of either our Moon or the planet Mercury, but far inferior to that of Venus, owing primarily to the thick clouds that shroud the Venusian surface. Therefore, Mars does not appear as bright as Venus.

A CLEARER PICTURE

Detailed studies of the surface of Mars began with the images provided by Mariner 9 in 1969. An even clearer picture was revealed with the landing of the U.S. space probes Viking 1 and 2. Viking 1 landed on Mars on July 20, 1976. Viking 2 followed,

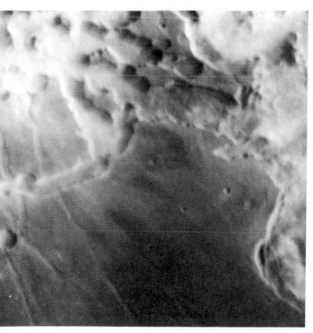

As the Sun rises over Mars, bright clouds of ice crystals rest above the canyons of this high plateau region called the "Labyrinth of the Night."

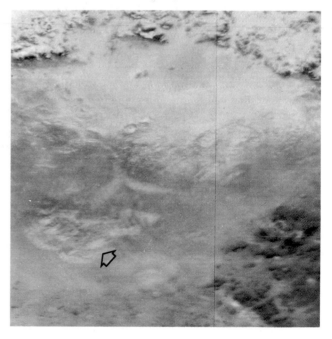

Winds of up to several hundred miles per hour trigger a Martian dust storm (arrow), strong enough to erode terrain structures with a sandblasting effect.

landing 4,600 miles (7,400 kilometers) from the Viking 1 site on September 3 of that year.

These Martian probes revealed that the surface of Mars is very similar but more rugged than the Earth's. There is hardly a land formation on Earth that does not have an equivalent on Mars. Mars has high mountains and plateaus, craters many miles across, broad plains, valleys, steep cliffs, jagged ridges, canyons deeper than the Grand Canyon, sand dunes, long scratches, and faults extending for great distances.

While Earth's crust is made of a number of plates that shift and move, the crust of Mars is believed to be made of a single, very thick plate that hardly budges at all. That may be why Mars has so many giant volcanoes. The largest, Olympus Mons, is taller than any surface feature on Earth. While volcanoes on Earth eventually shift away from their underground source of lava and peter out, Martian volcanoes seem to stay in the same place, continuing to grow ever larger. The absence of moving

plates could also help explain why the seismometer on the Viking 2 lander didn't detect a single tremor in 1,200 hours of testing. On Earth, quakes are caused by plates bumping against each other.

If the Earth were drained of all its water, it would be at least as rugged as Mars. Empty ocean basins would form deep depressions, with long rifts and jagged ridges along their bottoms. Certain Martian cracks and ridges look like those found on the floors of Earth's oceans.

Some scientists think that about 3.5 billion years ago, parts of Mars were covered with an ocean of water, much of which has since evaporated. As evidence, they point to the scarcity of impact craters—large holes formed by falling meteorites—in some regions. While the southern hemisphere of Mars is pockmarked with impact craters, parts of the northern hemisphere have many fewer craters. A deep blanket of water may have covered these northern parts, shielding them from meteorites.

There is other evidence that large amounts of water once existed on Mars.

Lowell Observatory Photo; NASA

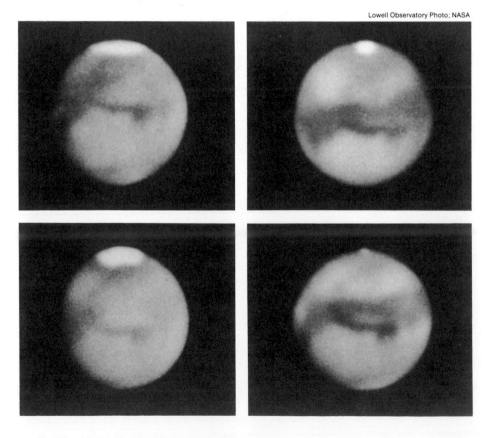

The surface features of Mars change with the seasons. The polar cap expands in winter, sometimes reaching 45 degrees latitude, and then melts away during the Martian spring and summer.

Certain Martian valleys, gullies, and deposits seem as if they were formed by flowing water. Some plateaus are also marked by long grooves and scratches resembling those made by glaciers on Earth.

There may still be lots of water on Mars. Some scientists think the entire planet may have a thick layer of permafrost (permanently frozen water) under its apparently barren surface of dust and rock. Soil samples taken by the Viking probes yielded a good deal of water upon heating. The presence of water is especially exciting to planetary biologists searching for extraterrestrial life. Water would also be extremely useful for human outposts on Mars, serving as a source of drinking water, oxygen for breathing, and hydrogen for rocket fuel.

Past scientific studies show that Martian atmospheric dust and surface rocks contain a wide range of minerals. They resemble Earth rocks chemically, showing that Mars, like Earth, has had a long, complex development. Like Earth, Mars probably has a dense core at its center, which produces a weak magnetic field.

The Viking landers revealed many interesting facts about the chemistry of Mars' soil. As suspected, the soil's rusty red color is due to a high concentration of iron. The soil also contains large amounts of oxygen. Some preliminary Viking tests showed that the soil contained organic compounds—the carbon-based building blocks of life—at a concentration of about one part per million; later tests seemed to contradict this finding.

Some scientists believe that life may exist on Mars, and at first, the meteorite known as ALH84001 seemed to confirm that theory. Discovered in Antarctica in 1984, the 3.9-billion-year-old space rock originated on Mars, and likely arrived on Earth some 15,000 years ago. Initial scientific analysis of the meteorite appeared to reveal microscopic fossil evidence of primitive life, but most other researchers have since dismissed that claim.

On July 4, 1997, the Mars Pathfinder spacecraft landed in an ancient Martian flood plain known to scientists as Ares Vallis. The following day, the lander deployed a robot rover named Sojourner, which imme-

On July 4, 1997, the Mars Pathfinder landed on the Martian surface. The next day, the lander deployed a robot rover named Sojourner, which analyzed the soil and rocks.

diately began performing its chemical analysis of the soil and rocks.

Pathfinder's companion spacecraft, the Mars Global Surveyor (MGS), has been orbiting the planet and providing scientists with images clearer than ever before. These show details on the Martian surface as small as 13 feet (4 meters) across.

While the Mars Climate Orbiter and its accompanying Deep Space 1 and 2 probes never reached their destination, NASA continues to study the Red Planet.

Mars Odyssey now orbits Mars, returning spectacular high-resolution photos of the Red Planet. And twin rovers, "Spirit" and "Opportunity," made headlines in 2004 when they proved that Mars once had liquid water on its surface. Equipped with precision drilling tools and ultrasensitive cameras, the two robotic geologists found mineral deposits that on Earth normally result from prolonged exposure to water.

THE MARTIAN ATMOSPHERE

That Mars is surrounded by air has been known for a long time. What could be explained only as atmospheric hazes, clouds, and dust storms have often been observed. Mars' blanket of air is too thin, however, to sufficiently protect much of its surface from the radiation of space. The atmospheric pressure on Mars is only about 6.1 millibars, much less than the average 1,013 millibars found on Earth.

Whereas Earth's atmosphere is dominated by nitrogen and oxygen, the Martian atmosphere is 95 percent carbon dioxide, with only faint traces of oxygen, nitrogen, and water vapor. Thin clouds—composed perhaps of dust, dry-snow crystals, and frozen water—often form. Clouds rise daily over high elevations. They may come from volcanoes or may simply be condensed atmospheric vapors.

The most spectacular and puzzling features of the Martian atmosphere are the gigantic dust storms that periodically sweep the entire planet. The Mariner 9 probe arrived during the height of such a tempest. Winds averaging about 174 miles (280 kilometers) per hour whip up enormous clouds of dust from the desertlike surface. A storm of this kind may last for weeks or months, during which the planet is one vast dust bowl. By comparison the worst Sahara sandstorm on Earth would seem like a mere breeze.

MOONS OF MARS

Mars has two satellites, or moons. They were discovered in 1877 by the American astronomer Asaph Hall. He named them Deimos and Phobos ("Terror" and "Fear"), after the two mythical sons and attendants of the ancient god Mars.

Both moons are irregular in shape and very small. Deimos, the outer one, measures about 6 to 7 miles (9 to 11 kilometers) in diameter. Phobos, the inner one, measures about 10 to 14 miles (16 to 22 kilometers). Pictures show them to be dark, rocky bodies, pitted with craters. Results from the Soviet Phobos space-probe mission in 1989 support the widely held view that Phobos and Deimos are asteroids that strayed from the nearby asteroid belt, only to be captured by Mars' gravity.

Deimos and Phobos both revolve around the equatorial region of Mars in nearly circular orbits, in the same direction that Mars spins on its axis—west to east. Deimos orbits Mars at an average distance of about 12,000 miles (19,300 kilometers) above the planet's surface. It takes 30 hours and 18 minutes to go once around Mars completely. On Mars, Deimos would be seen to cross the sky from east to west once in about two and one-half Martian days.

Phobos is only some 3,700 miles (6,000 kilometers) above the Martian surface. It orbits the planet once every seven hours and 39 minutes. Because it circles Mars faster than the planet rotates, Phobos is seen there to rise in the west and set in the east. It makes two crossings of the sky in one Martian day.

NASA

Martian atmospheric dust causes scattering and absorption of sunlight, producing the white-to-red-to-blue variation in sky color seen in this image of a sunset taken by the Viking Lander 1.

Jupiter, named for the Roman king of the gods, has a diameter 11 times that of Earth. The Great Red Spot—the vortex of a storm—is Jupiter's foremost feature.

JUPITER

by Jeffrey Brune

Jupiter is the largest planet in our solar system, bigger than many stars, though not as large as our Sun. Jupiter's volume is 1,300 times that of the Earth, with a diameter of 88,770 miles (142,860 kilometers). In comparison the Earth's diameter is less than 8,000 miles (13,000 kilometers)— scarcely $\frac{1}{11}$ of Jupiter's.

Despite its huge bulk, Jupiter spins on its axis much faster than our planet, making one complete turn in slightly under 10 hours. This fact explains why Jupiter is noticeably flattened at its north and south poles, and bulges around its equator. Jupiter's fast spin also draws out the planet's clouds into colorful horizontal bands.

For all its enormous size, however, Jupiter is only 318 times more massive than the Earth and has only a quarter of the density of the Earth. This suggests that Jupiter is made mostly of materials considerably lighter than the rock, soil, and iron that make up our planet. Jupiter is thought to consist mostly of gases—primarily hydrogen, some helium, and traces of methane, water, and ammonia.

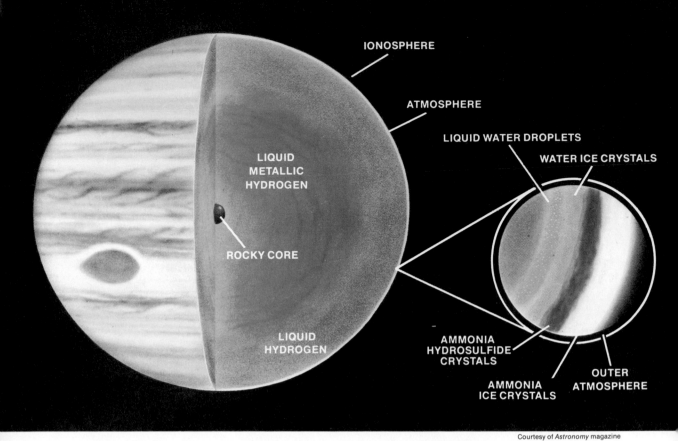

IONOSPHERE

ATMOSPHERE

LIQUID WATER DROPLETS

WATER ICE CRYSTALS

LIQUID METALLIC HYDROGEN

ROCKY CORE

LIQUID HYDROGEN

AMMONIA HYDROSULFIDE CRYSTALS

AMMONIA ICE CRYSTALS

OUTER ATMOSPHERE

A model of Jupiter's interior reveals a small rocky core surrounded primarily by a ball of liquid hydrogen. Jupiter's atmosphere (close-up at right), about 620 miles deep, consists of layers of ammonia, hydrogen sulfide, hydrogen, helium, methane, and water. Despite its huge size, Jupiter is much less dense than Earth.

Jupiter lies between the orbits of Mars and Saturn, at an average distance from the Sun of nearly 484 million miles (779 million kilometers). Because of this vast distance, Jupiter takes nearly 12 years to go once completely around the Sun. At its apogee (closest approach to Earth), Jupiter is about 370 million miles (591 million kilometers) away. At its perigee (farthest point), it is 600 million miles (966 million kilometers) away.

Jupiter's magnetic field, which is the strongest of all the planets' in the solar system, traps charged particles that make up the "solar wind" that flows out continuously from the Sun. These particles produce extremely high radiation levels around the planet. The Pioneer and Voyager probes, which flew past Jupiter, revealed that its magnetic field extends out some 5 million miles (8 million kilometers).

Though Jupiter was previously thought to be ringless, Voyager 1 revealed a relatively thin, gossamer ring surrounding the planet. Some 29,800 miles (48,000 kilometers) above the Jovian cloud tops, the ring is only about 19 miles (30 kilometers) thick and 5,600 miles (9,000 kilometers) wide. It is too faint to be seen from the Earth.

JUPITER'S APPEARANCE

Despite its great distance from us, Jupiter is easily visible to the unaided eye. It is very large, and reflects more than 70 percent of the sunlight falling on it. As a result, among the planets of our solar system, only Venus and Mars appear brighter.

Just a pair of binoculars shows the planet as a disk, sometimes surrounded by four spots of light. These are the four "Galilean satellites," the largest of Jupiter's moons. They were discovered in 1610 by the Italian scientist Galileo Galilei, who was the first to observe Jupiter with a telescope.

Viewed through a large telescope and in the Pioneer photographs, Jupiter is a spectacular sight. Its wide disk is crossed by many bands of color—pastel shades of blue, brown, pink, red, orange, and yellow. These bands—or belts, as astronomers call them—run parallel to Jupiter's equator.

Jupiter's belts, despite changes in their colors and other features from time to time, are mostly permanent. Jupiter's face is also marked by shifting patches and spots, the most obvious of which is the famous Great Red Spot.

PHYSICAL CONDITIONS

Jupiter is thought to be composed of three basic layers: a gaseous outer layer, a liquid middle layer, and a solid core at the center of the planet.

The multicolored belts we see on Jupiter's "face" are actually part of the planet's gaseous outer layer, or atmosphere. These belts are layers of dense clouds, composed of liquid drops and frozen particles. Just how deep the atmosphere and its clouds extend is not certain, but the depth is probably about 620 miles (1,000 kilometers). Scientists are learning more from data gathered in 1995, when the Galileo spacecraft hurled a robotic probe into Jupiter's atmosphere. In addition to gauging the atmosphere's depth, the probe analyzed its chemical makeup, clocked wind speeds, and scanned violent storms for lightning.

As one approaches the interior of the planet, its clouds probably become denser and denser with increasing pressure and eventually assume a liquid form. In Jupiter's middle layer, there may be great oceans of liquefied gas such as hydrogen. This massive ocean may be some 12,400 miles (20,000 kilometers) deep, and can be thought of as Jupiter's "surface."

Beneath the great oceans of liquid gases, the pressure becomes so enormous that the liquid gases turn solid. In this third of Jupiter's layers, scientists suspect there may be a gigantic ball of metallic hydrogen. Within that ball, at the very center of the planet, may be an iron-and-silicate rock mass about the size of Earth.

Because of Jupiter's rapid spin, its great distance from the Sun, and its deep clouds, the planet's weather must be very strange indeed. Yet certain cloud formations in Earth's atmosphere resemble the belts of Jupiter. And Jupiter, like Earth, has great cyclonic storms, or regions of low atmospheric pressure, as well as anticyclonic flows that are accompanied by high pressure.

Jupiter radiates two or three times as much energy as it receives from the Sun. This means that the planet has a great internal source of energy—probably left over from the time when it was first formed. Some astronomers think of Jupiter as a star that simply did not "make it" because of its relatively small mass. That is, its mass was not large enough to produce the intense internal pressures and temperatures needed to set off the nuclear reactions that take place inside a star.

If Jupiter had 84 times more mass than it does, it would have been able to trigger thermonuclear reactions at its core, and it would be a star. Had that been the case, the solar system would have had a binary structure: two stars orbiting each other, with the varying gravitational forces of both stars making it virtually impossible for our current planetary system to have formed.

Voyager 1 captured this image of a volcanic eruption faintly silhouetted on the horizon of Io, one of Jupiter's 16 known moons.

JPL

Jupiter also radiates energy in the form of radio waves, which scientists detect with radio telescopes. The radio waves come from solar-wind particles trapped in belts around Jupiter by the planet's large magnetic field. These radiation belts are thought to produce the strongest radio signals in the solar system.

CHEMICAL COMPOSITION

The substances in Jupiter's atmosphere would probably poison or suffocate most living things found on the Earth. These dangerous substances include the elements hydrogen and helium and the hydrogen-carrying compounds methane, ammonia, and possibly hydrogen sulfide. Jupiter lacks the chief ingredients of the Earth's atmosphere: free oxygen, nitrogen, and carbon dioxide. But the planet probably has water vapor, which constitutes about 1 percent of Earth's atmosphere.

If you somehow could survive breathing Jupiter's atmosphere, you would probably say it stinks—literally. Ammonia is a pungent compound of hydrogen and nitrogen. On Earth, it is produced by the decay of certain proteins. Hydrogen sulfide, another protein-decay product, contains sulfur and smells like rotten eggs.

The other chief constituents of Jupiter's atmosphere—hydrogen, helium, methane, and water—are odorless. Methane is a chemical compound of hydrogen and carbon. It is formed on Earth by the decay of organic matter in the absence of atmospheric oxygen. It is also called marsh gas, because it frequently arises in swamps and bogs.

A color-enhanced view of Jupiter's Great Red Spot, captured by Voyager 1. Believed to be a major storm greater than the size of Earth, the spot has raged for centuries with no signs of a letup.

THE GREAT RED SPOT

In the three centuries that astronomers have been peering at Jupiter through the telescope, they have been puzzled by the planet's Great Red Spot. We now know that it is a swirling storm in the upper atmosphere that is so large it could hold two planets the size of Earth.

Located at 20 degrees latitude in Jupiter's southern hemisphere, the oval Great Red Spot measures about 31,000 miles (50,000 kilometers) at its widest. But its size varies. It also changes hue over periods of many years—from a bright, brick red to an almost invisible pink and then back.

Although the spot maintains more or less the same latitude, it may change its longitudinal position markedly. Also, the Great Red Spot has a speed of rotation around Jupiter's axis averaging a few miles per hour slower than those of the areas close to the spot itself.

Interestingly, the storm that is the Great Red Spot has been raging since before it was first observed nearly 400 years ago. The reason the storm can continue unabated is that Jupiter has no true solid surface to impede its progress and slow it down.

Close-up photographs taken by the Pioneer and Voyager spacecraft show the "pinwheel" structure of the Great Red Spot. It is spinning so rapidly that it displaces the clouds of the south tropical zone. Temperature measurements indicate that the storm rises some 8 miles (13 kilometers) above the surrounding cloud deck.

The photographs also reveal the presence of other, smaller storm centers, such as the Little Red Spot in the northern hemisphere of Jupiter. In fact, the face of Jupiter as a whole is a scene of dramatic weather activity. The grayish white zones are warm, upward-rising weather "cells" that carry heat from the interior of the planet to the surface. The lower, reddish-brown areas are downward-sinking cells.

The Voyager probes have provided a wealth of information about Jupiter's many natural satellites. Europa (top), Jupiter's brightest moon, has an icy crust resembling a cracked eggshell. The mountains and valleys of Ganymede (right) show evidence of continental drift.

MOONS OF JUPITER

Jupiter has 61 known moons, four of which are 1,860 miles (3,000 kilometers) or more in diameter. Other Jovian moons have been reported but not yet confirmed. Some of the small, outer moons may be former asteroids captured by the planet's vast gravitational field. The inner moons are rocky, while the outer ones may be gaseous or made of frozen liquid.

Perhaps Jupiter's most attention-grabbing moon is Io, the most volcanically active

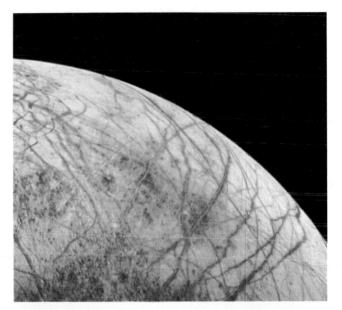

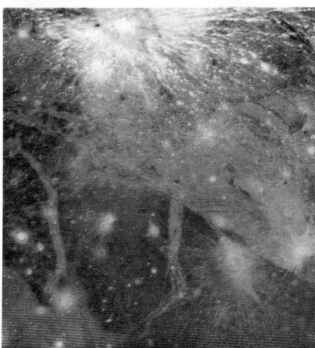

body in the solar system. During Voyager 1's flyby, it photographed Io's gigantic volcanoes spewing sulfurous debris more than 90 miles (145 kilometers) above its surface. The spacecraft's infrared sensor detected enormous hot lava lakes, ranging in temperature from 172° to 199° F (78° to 93° C).

The volcanoes of Io are responsible for producing the largest visible object in the solar system, a huge sodium cloud detected by telescopes from Earth. Besides spewing sulfur, the volcanoes also kick out sodium high above Io's surface. The sodium is then accelerated to more than 155,340 miles (250,000 kilometers) per hour by Jupiter's magnetic field and slung into interplanetary space. The sodium forms a cloud around Jupiter that is 50 times bigger than the Sun.

Europa is Jupiter's brightest moon, partly because of its large size, and partly because it is covered with a highly reflective crust of ice. Its icy crust and the dark, linear features on its surface give Europa the appearance of a giant, cracked egg.

There are few impact craters on Europa, suggesting that its crust is slightly soft. The Jupiter-orbiting Galileo spacecraft has found that beneath the moon's icy crust may lie a subterranean saltwater ocean. Scientists believe that this watery world may closely resemble the aquatic environment beneath Antarctica on Earth.

Ganymede is Jupiter's largest moon. Indeed, it is the largest moon in the solar system. At 3,275 miles (5,270 kilometers) in diameter, Ganymede is even larger than the planets Mercury and Pluto. The Galileo orbiter got a close-up look at this moon, which showed evidence of continental drift, especially in its numerous parallel faults (cracks), which appear similar to those on the Pacific and Atlantic Ocean basins of Earth. Galileo also found a cloud of microscopic dust particles surrounding the moon, probably caused by meteorites slamming into Ganymede's surface.

The moon Callisto, almost as large as Ganymede, has an icy surface, beneath which may lie another deep, salty ocean. The ice is riddled with impact craters from heavy meteorite bombardment long ago. Nothing appears to have happened to Callis-to since its final formation. All its craters appear to be old, rounded, and smooth, rather than jagged and fresh. One of Callisto's most striking features is a bull's-eye formation called Valhalla. This probably formed when the moon was blasted with a large object, producing waves along Callisto's surface that froze in place.

COLLISION WITH A COMET

Between July 16 and 22, 1994, the fragments of a comet designated Shoemaker-Levy 9 (S/L-9) collided with the giant planet Jupiter. The shattered comet was discovered on March 24, 1994, by Eugene and Carolyn Shoemaker of the Lowell Observatory in Flagstaff, Arizona; and David H. Levy, an amateur astronomer from Tucson, Arizona.

Photos taken with the Hubble Telescope showed that the comet's train of nuclei—its "string of pearls," as one astronomer described it—was stretching, changing its length from about half the Earth-Moon distance at the time of its discovery to more than 3 million miles (5 million kilometers) by mid-July.

On the evening of July 16, 1994, a photo of the first impact was released. It showed in the upper atmosphere of Jupiter a "bruise" larger than Earth. And over the following week, many more fragments smashed into the planet.

The Hubble Telescope's Faint Object Spectrograph found evidence in the Jovian atmosphere of sulfur-bearing compounds as well as ammonia, silicon, magnesium, and iron, some of which could have been left behind by the impacting bodies themselves. Hubble's Wide Field Planetary Camera made global maps of Jupiter to track changes in the dark debris caught up in the high-speed winds at Jupiter's cloud tops.

En route to Jupiter, the Galileo spacecraft could see slightly "behind" the giant planet—onto its dark side. From this unique vantage point, Galileo transmitted to Earth images showing sequences of explosive plumes thousands of miles above the Jovian cloud tops, proving the predictions of scientists before the collisions.

Saturn, the sixth planet from the Sun, is distinguished by its magnificent rings. The rings are made up of everything from dust particles to huge boulders.

SATURN

by Jeffrey Brune

For beauty and interest alike, there are few objects in the starry heavens to compare with Saturn. This magnificent planet, the sixth from the Sun, provided an unforgettable spectacle when viewed by the U.S. spacecraft Voyagers 1 and 2, in 1980 and 1981. The Saturnian system also includes numerous rings and at least 18 moons.

Saturn is so far from the center of the solar system that, viewed from its orbit, the Sun would appear as a brilliant pinpoint rather than as a disk. Saturn receives only one-ninetieth of the heat and light that we receive on Earth.

The mean distance of Saturn from the Sun is 887 million miles (1,428,000,000 kilometers), or about 9.5 times the distance of the Earth from the Sun. It completes its orbit once every 29.5 years. Our own planet, the Earth, overtakes it and comes in line between it and the Sun once every 378 days. Saturn is inclined to the ecliptic, the apparent path of the Sun among the stars, by 2.5 degrees. Its orbit, as it revolves around the Sun, is also much more eccentric than that of the Earth.

The distance of Saturn from the Earth varies according to the position of the two planets in their orbits: from 744 million miles (1,197,000,000 kilometers) to 1,027,000,000 miles (1,654,000,000 kilometers)—a variation not sufficient to cause any great difference in the planet's brightness.

SWIFTLY SPINNING EGG

The globe of Saturn is greatly flattened, so that when the planet is in such a position that the plane of its equator passes through the Earth, its profile appears distinctly egg-shaped, or elliptical. The planet's polar diameter is nearly nine-tenths that of its equatorial diameter—67,100 miles (108,000 kilometers) and 74,600 miles (120,000 kilometers), respectively. These dimensions show the vast size of the planet. Its volume is more than 750 times that of the Earth's and its superficial area is over 80 times that of our globe.

The density of Saturn is much lower than that of any other planet and, in fact, only three-quarters that of water. (If Saturn were the size of a tennis ball, it would float in a bucket of water.) The reason Saturn has such a low density is that it is composed largely of gas. There may be liquid beneath its thick atmosphere, and, deeper yet, a small, rocky core. Saturn's flattened shape is due to its mostly gas composition and to its rapid rotation.

Saturn's swift rotation on its axis was first observed in 1794 by English astronomer Sir William Herschel. By timing how long it took Saturn's cloudlike markings to make one complete rotation, Herschel calculated a rotation period of 10 hours and 16 minutes. In 1876 American astronomer Asaph Hall noticed a brilliant white spot on Saturn's equator. Using this spot as a point of departure for his calculations, he found that the equatorial period of rotation was 10 hours and 14 minutes, two minutes less than the period determined by Herschel.

In 1981 radio astronomers using data from Voyagers 1 and 2 were finally able to pin down Saturn's rotation rate to 10 hours, 39 minutes, 24 seconds. The inaccuracies of earlier measurements were due to their being based on the planet's shifting cloud cover.

STORMY WEATHER

Saturn's atmosphere is composed mostly of hydrogen with some helium and traces of methane and ammonia. And this atmosphere, like Jupiter's and Neptune's, is turbulent. Near Saturn's equator, there is a wide band of extremely high winds called a jet stream. Voyager probes clocked clouds traveling in this stream at 1,100 miles (1,770 kilometers) per hour—three times faster than the jet streams on Jupiter.

Scientists don't yet know why Saturn's equatorial winds are so strong or why they happen to blow eastward.

Over the past two centuries, astronomers have observed nearly two dozen "white spots," short-lived storms in the top layers of Saturn's atmosphere. In September 1990, amateur astronomers first detected what was to become one of the largest of these storms. This white spot was first seen near the equator as a relatively small, oval-shaped storm. About a month later, the National Aeronautics and Space Administration (NASA) pointed the Hubble Space Telescope toward Saturn and photographed a monster storm, one that had grown to the size of 10 Earths placed end to end. The huge system of swirling clouds and eddies was called the "Great White Spot," similar to, but much larger than, Jupiter's "Great Red Spot." This storm system probably developed when warm ammonia gas bubbled up from deep within the atmosphere. Once at the top of the cool cloud deck, the ammonia gas crystallized and was swept away by high winds.

The Pioneer 11 probe, which flew past Saturn in 1979, discovered that the ringed planet has a strong magnetic field. The field traps high-energy electrons and protons spewed from the Sun and keeps them in belts around the planet. Saturn's rings absorb and wipe out many of these electrons and protons, making the radiation that surrounds the planet much less intense.

SURROUNDED BY PARTICLES

Saturn is surrounded by a vast swarm of solid objects, ranging in size from dust to car-sized boulders. Each of the particles, composed mostly of ice and frosted rock, follows an individual orbit around the planet. Together, these particles form many rings, some of which are quite complex in structure.

Saturn's rings were long thought to be unique in the solar system. We now know that the other giant planets—Jupiter, Uranus, and Neptune—all have rings, though not nearly as extensive nor as beautiful as Saturn's. Study of Saturn's rings pro-

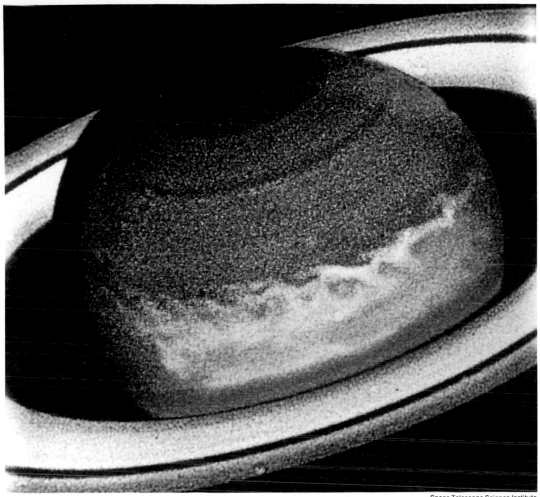

The whitish area above the rings is a great storm on Saturn detected by the Hubble Space Teloscope. The Saturnian storm was large enough to envelop the entire Earth.

ceeded slowly over the centuries and then took a giant step forward with the surprise findings of the Voyager probes.

It was not until the telescope was discovered, in the first decade of the 17th century, that we even had an inkling that the rings existed. When Galileo examined Saturn in 1610 with a telescope that he had made with his own hands, he came to the conclusion that the planet had a triple form. "When I observe Saturn," he wrote to a friend, "the central star appears the largest; two others, one situated to the east, the other to the west, and on a line that does not coincide with the direction of the zodiac, seem to touch it. They are like two servants who help old Saturn on his way and always remain at his side. With a smaller telescope, the star appears lengthened, and of the shape of an olive."

Continuing to watch this strange performance month after month, Galileo was amazed to see Saturn's attendants becoming smaller and smaller, until they finally disappeared altogether. He doubted the evidence of his telescope. "What can I say," he wrote, "of so astonishing a metamorphosis? Are the two small stars consumed like sun spots? Have they vanished and flown away? Has Saturn devoured his own children? Or have the glasses cheated me, and many others to whom I have shown these appearances, with illusions?" Discouraged, he abandoned his quest.

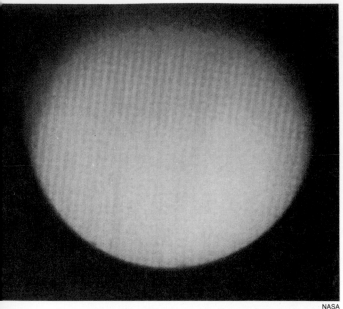

NASA

Titan, Saturn's largest moon, is larger than either Mercury or Pluto. Titan's substantial atmosphere contains molecules necessary for the evolution of life.

NASA

Saturn's moon Iapetus is composed almost entirely of water ice. The Voyager probes detected a large "stain of organic matter" on the moon's surface.

Others, however, watched the planet whenever it was in view, and they gradually established the fact that Saturn's unusual appendages underwent regular changes. They appeared first as bright, straight lines stretching outward on either side of the planet's elliptical disk. For the next seven years, these mysterious lines would expand into two luminous crescents attached to the planet like handles to a dish. For yet the next seven years, the crescents would flatten until they were again lines projecting from Saturn. Finally they would disappear altogether. For as the planet pursues its vast orbit, slanting always in the same direction, its rings, at opposite points in its orbit, appear in an edgewise position to observers on Earth. Between these two edgewise appearances, the north and south faces of the rings are visible in turn, always foreshortened. Each is seen for a period of about 15 years.

In 1655 Dutch mathematician, physicist, and astronomer Christiaan Huygens invented an improved method of grinding lenses. As a result, he was able to construct a powerful telescope that showed details more clearly than any earlier instrument. Using his new telescope, Huygens observed that the rings of Saturn cast shadows on the planet and were separated from

it. From this observation, he deduced the true nature of Galileo's "appendages," which had long puzzled astronomers.

SATURN'S MANY RINGS

The idea that Saturn had rings was accepted in time. Huygens' fellow astronomers, including the renowned Giovanni Domenico Cassini, began to study the rings more carefully. In 1675 Cassini observed a dark band in what was then believed to be the single ring of Saturn. This band divided the ring into two separate rings. The dividing "band," which was really a gap, has since been labeled the Cassini division.

A third ring was observed in 1838 by German astronomer Johann Gottfried Galle. But Galle's report was ignored by his contemporaries. It was not until the ring was observed and reported simultaneously in 1850 by W. C. Bond at Harvard and W. R. Dawes in England that its existence became an accepted fact. In the third ring, there is apparently much less material that can reflect the Sun's light back to us. It has been likened to translucent crepe paper or gauze. As a matter of fact, it is often called the crepe, or gauze, ring.

In 1837 Johann Franz Encke, the director of the Berlin Observatory, saw what he believed to be another division in the outer ring. It was not complete and was not equally distinct at all times. This indistinct and transitory division has been called the Encke division.

In 1969 French astronomer Pierre Guerin discovered a fourth faint ring of Saturn, long undetected because it is so close to the bright globe of the planet. Scientists later found two more rings, for a total of six. Then came the Voyager flybys in 1980 and 1981 and a wealth of new discoveries.

As the Voyager probes approached Saturn, 100 or so ringlets were seen dividing up the major rings. When the rings came between Voyager 2 and a bright star —and when the rings passed in front of a star as seen from Earth in 1989—the probe was able to detect hundreds of thousands of rings. Voyager even found ringlets within the Cassini and Encke divisions, once thought to be empty space. Luckily, scientists didn't follow an early plan that would have sent Voyager through a division; the craft might have collided with one of the boulders that make up the rings.

Ring Dimensions

The major rings of Saturn, going from the outermost to the innermost, are designated by the letters E, F, A, B, C, and D.

The E, or extended, ring lies outside the other major rings and may be as much as 62 miles (100 kilometers) thick.

The F ring has generated much interest —and confusion. Voyager 1 pictures showed a very narrow, wispy ring composed of three ringlets. The ringlets appeared to be braided, perhaps because they were orbiting in different planes. But when Voyager 2 took higher-resolution pictures of the same F ring, it found not three, but five ringlets; and the braids, for the most part, were gone. Perhaps the braiding— when it is seen—is caused by two tiny moons found straddling the F ring. These "shepherd" moons are thought to compress the ring into its narrow path by a kind of gravitational pinching action. Perturbations in the moons' gravity field might somehow cause the ringlets to twist.

Ring A is the second-brightest ring. It is 9,940 miles (16,000 kilometers) wide and has an outside diameter of 170,000 miles (273,000 kilometers). It may be no more than 328 feet (100 meters) thick. In this ring appears the narrow Encke division, containing multiple ringlets. Rings on either side of the division have wavy ripples like those produced in the wake of a speedboat, suggesting the presence of a moon that pushes material away from its orbit. In

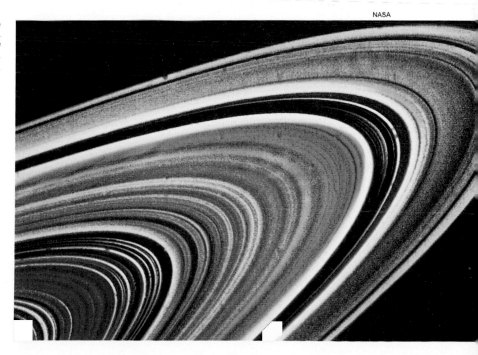

The Voyager 2 space probe discovered that Saturn is actually circled by hundreds of thousands of rings. Saturn's many moons all lie outside the planet's elaborate ring system.

1990, after years of analyzing Voyager pictures, astronomers found this tiny and elusive moon, the 18th confirmed Saturnian satellite, measuring a mere 12 miles (20 kilometers) in diameter.

The Cassini division, which lies between Rings A and B, is about 2,200 miles (3,500 kilometers) wide. As mentioned earlier, astronomers are now certain that it contains a series of ringlets, some tightly packed together.

Ring B is the brightest ring, with a width of 16,156 miles (26,000 kilometers) and an outside diameter of 146,000 miles (235,000 kilometers). Voyager studies revealed that the B ring comprises some 300 ringlets, each of which may be made up of some 20 to 50 subringlets. The biggest surprise involving the B ring, however, was the appearance of "spokes" across it. The spokes move with the ring as spokes do on a bicycle wheel, and are thought to be clouds of dust-size particles raised above the plane of the ring. Meteor collisions might be responsible for producing the spokes, as might lightning-like electrical discharges observed in the B-ring plane.

Ring C is the crepe or gauze ring. It is separated from Ring B by only about 1,000 miles (1,600 kilometers). It is 11,500 miles (18,500 kilometers) wide. Its outside diameter is 121,800 miles (196,000 kilometers). Ring D is the faintest of all. It extends from the surface of Saturn to the inner edge of the C ring.

How Did the Rings Originate?

In 1850, Edouard Roche proved mathematically that the gravitational forces of a planet would tear apart any satellite within a certain distance of it. The gravitational force exerted by one body on another is inversely proportional to the distance between them. As they approach one another, the force becomes greater. Roche calculated that the exact distance at which the force of gravity of a planet would be great enough to tear apart its satellite is 2.44 times the radius of the planet. This distance is now known as Roche's limit.

A line drawn from the center of Saturn to the outside edge of the visible ring system would be approximately 2.35 times the radius of the planet. This places the visible ring system inside Roche's limit. All of the known moons of Saturn are outside Roche's limit. Even the moons first observed by Pioneer and Voyager probes and believed to be closest to the planet are at distances at least 2.55 times the radius of Saturn. Roche's calculations thus delineate a specific region within which satellites do not appear.

So here we have a clue to the origin of the rings. According to one theory, the rings are the remains of "wandering moons" torn apart by the planet's gravitational forces. The fragments of the former satellites now form the material of the rings. There is another, quite similar, theory of the origin of the rings. It holds that when the gases in the vicinity of the planet cooled and formed the various solid balls, or satellites, the gases inside Roche's limit were prevented from combining into satellites by the strong gravitational forces of the planet. Therefore, instead of merging into balls, they cooled as small fragments. These fragments revolve around Saturn separately in the form of the rings. The fact that the bona fide satellites of Saturn are all outside Roche's limit seems to support these interesting theories.

SATURN'S SATELLITES

Titan

Of Saturn's 34 known moons, a few are so recently found that they have not yet received proper names. Titan, as its name suggests, is the largest. Greater in diameter than either Mercury or Pluto, Titan is like a planet in its own right. It is the only moon in the solar system known to have a substantial atmosphere. The Voyager probes found that Titan's atmosphere is composed mainly of nitrogen, the predominant ingredient of Earth's atmosphere.

Titan's atmosphere also has a small percentage of methane, carbon monoxide, acetylene, ethylene, and hydrogen cyanide. The presence of hydrogen cyanide is of particular interest to scientists, for this molecule is believed to be a necessary precursor to the chemical evolution of life. It is doubtful, however, that life as we know it exists on Titan, since the moon's surface temperature is a frigid –292° F (–180° C). Some scientists, though, have suggested that Titan's interior may be hot enough to produce thermal vents at the surface, which would provide vital heat. Scientists hope that further study of Titan may unveil clues about how life began and evolved on Earth.

Astronomers have long desired to penetrate Titan's dense orange shroud and study the mysterious moon in detail. In 1989 and 1990, U.S. researchers bounced radar signals off Titan's surface. The study revealed for the first time that Titan does indeed have liquid on it, although not enough to cover the moon entirely.

NASA's Cassini spacecraft, appropriately named after the 17th-century Italian astronomer, entered orbit around Saturn in mid-2004. Connected to Cassini was the European Space Agency's (ESA's) Huygens probe, which disengaged and ultimately landed on Titan in early 2005. Immediately, Huygens began analyzing the atmosphere, shooting photographs, and even recording sounds. Before permanently losing power, the probe had transmitted to excited Earth-bound scientists data on the moon's chemical composition and landscape. Titan was revealed to be a "flammable world" containing "dirty" ice ridges and seas of liquid methane. Its frigid temperature, at –290° F (–180° C), allows the gas to fall as rain to the soggy surface. But because there is no oxygen present, the abundant pools of methane cannot ignite.

Other Moons of Saturn

Mimas, Tethys, Enceladus, Rhea, and Dione are all nearly perfect spheres. Each appears to be composed almost entirely of frozen water ice.

Mimas and Tethys are perhaps best known for their heavily cratered surfaces. Voyager pictures of Mimas showed an impact scar one-third the moon's diameter, with a central mountain almost as large as Mount Everest on Earth. Halfway around Mimas is a large canyon scientists believe may have been formed by the same impact that

Saturn appears differently from Earth at various times of the year. Sometimes (bottom right), the rings seem to disappear, an illusion that confused early astronomers.

formed the crater. Photographs of Tethys revealed an even larger crater than the one observed on Mimas.

Enceladus, on the other hand, appears much smoother. Some scientists think that in the moon's recent past, slush may have gurgled up, filled in impact craters, and then froze. The moon's icy surface reflects nearly 100 percent of the sunlight that strikes it, making it appear very bright.

Rhea is brownish in color and has a crater-saturated surface. The craters are of different sizes, suggesting to some astronomers that Rhea may have undergone two stages of impact: one series of impacts from the formation of the Saturnian system, and another from debris from the rest of the solar system. Rhea and Dione both have dark, wispy marks on their icy surfaces, suggesting some material leaked from their interiors along fractures in their crusts and later froze.

The Voyager probes also studied the moons Iapetus and Hyperion. The composition of Iapetus was found to be 80 percent ice, with at least half of its surface covered with "a stain of organic material." The moon appears to have a light and dark side, the dark side perhaps resulting from a coating of dust particles.

Hyperion held some surprises. This strange, misshapen moon—about 230 miles by 174 miles by 140 miles (370 kilometers by 280 kilometers by 225 kilometers)—may have been smashed into its irregular shape by a colossal impact with another body. Hyperion tumbles erratically when it passes Titan, as it is tugged by the larger moon's gravity field.

Phoebe, one of Saturn's outermost large moons, orbits the planet in a direction opposite that of the other satellites. For this reason, scientists think Phoebe may be a captured asteroid.

The beauty of Saturn has made it a natural subject for science-fiction artists. Below is a painting of how Saturn might look from the surface of the moon Titan.

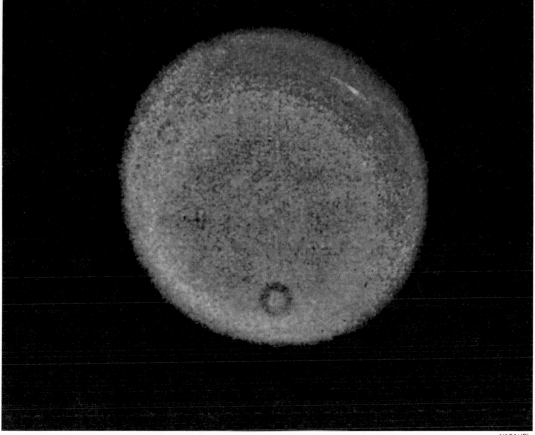

Voyager 2 unveiled much new information about Uranus, including immense clouds in its atmosphere (bright streak near the planet's upper edge above).

URANUS

by Jeffrey Brune

Of all the planets, Uranus may be the most bizarre. The seventh planet from the Sun, Uranus' orbit around the Sun is like a rolling ball instead of a spinning top like the other planets. Its poles, which take turns facing the Sun, receive a great deal more sunlight than its equator, and yet the whole planet has about the same temperature. Its magnetic field is off-center and tipped 60 degrees from its rotational axis.

Tipped on its side, Uranus looks like a bull's-eye, especially with its moons and rings orbiting roughly in the planet's equatorial plane. In 1977 scientists launched the space probe Voyager 2 toward this floating target in space. Most of what we know today about the planet was revealed by Voyager 2.

DISCOVERY

Uranus was not even known to exist until the late 18th century. It was first recognized by German-born English astronomer William Herschel. On the night of March 13, 1781, Herschel was observing the stars in the constellation Gemini with a 7-inch (18-centimeter) reflector telescope he had just made. Suddenly he observed what seemed to be a star shaped like a disk. Herschel was puzzled, since all true stars (with the exception of the Sun) appear as mere points of light, even when viewed with the most powerful telescope. Observing the unknown body night after night, he noted that it changed its position among the stars. He then came to the conclusion that his "moving star" was a comet, a celestial chunk of rock and ice that orbits the Sun.

The supposed comet was carefully followed by astronomers. They noted that it followed an almost circular orbit far beyond the orbit of Saturn, then thought to be the outermost planet. As time went on, they realized that the new body was a planet, and Herschel was hailed as its discoverer.

Herschel named the new planet Georgium Sidus (the Georgian Star), after the reigning monarch, George III. English astronomers called the planet the Georgian Star until about 1850; to others, it was known as Herschel. The name finally given to it—Uranus—was proposed by German astronomer Johann Elert Bode, who pointed out that all the other planets had been named after ancient gods. In Roman mythology, Uranus was the god of the heavens.

THE URANIAN ATMOSPHERE

Uranus can just barely be made out by the naked eye on a clear, moonless night. Through a telescope, it appears as a light blue-green disk. The planet has a diameter of about 31,750 miles (51,100 kilometers) at its equator, about four times that of the Earth. But despite its large size, Uranus is only one-fourth as dense as the Earth.

That's because the planet is made mostly of the light element hydrogen.

The Voyager 2 probe found Uranus' atmosphere to contain 83 percent hydrogen, 15 percent helium, 2 percent methane, and scant amounts of ammonia and water. Beneath the atmosphere lie deep oceans of water, ammonia, and methane. Uranus' temperature rises with increasing depth. The planet probably has a rocky core of iron and silicon.

As Voyager 2 approached Uranus, it found little activity in the planet's atmosphere, certainly nothing like the storms found raging on Jupiter, Saturn, and Neptune. Scientists were rather bored with a featureless planet that stubbornly refused to change in appearance. They called the planet "the fuzzy blue tennis ball."

Just 10 days before Voyager 2's closest approach, however, it found a few small clouds in the upper atmosphere. These clouds were enough to help scientists determine wind speeds on the planet—from 130 to 535 feet (40 to 160 meters) per second. On Earth, jet streams race along at about 160 feet (50 meters) per second.

Despite external differences, Uranus and Neptune have similar internal structures. Both have a rocky core with a mantle of liquid water, methane, and ammonia. Both also have an atmosphere of hydrogen and helium gas.

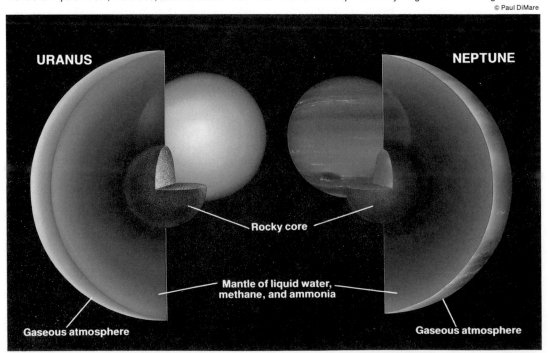

Umbriel is the darkest of the Uranian moons. Astronomers think that Umbriel may contain large amounts of the same carbonaceous material that makes up the rings and the smaller moons.

Titania, the largest moon of Uranus, is about half the size of Earth's moon. Although heavily cratered, Titania's surface has been much modified by geological processes that have occurred since its formation.

THE MOTION OF URANUS

Uranus revolves around the Sun once about every 84 Earth years. A day on Uranus lasts about 17 hours and 14 minutes—the time it takes the planet to make one complete rotation on its axis. As mentioned, the planet rotates on its side; its axis of rotation is tipped about 98 degrees from the vertical, so that it is nearly horizontal to the plane of the planet's orbit around the Sun. Scientists believe that the planet was knocked off-balance by a cosmic collision with a planet-sized space rock or asteroid.

Because it rotates on its side, Uranus has the longest seasons of any planet—each of its seasons lasts about 21 Earth years as different hemispheres take turns facing the Sun. Any given point on the planet is lit up about half the Uranian year. For example, the planet's north pole points toward the Sun and receives almost constant sunlight for about 42 Earth years. For the next 42 years, the north pole is in darkness, while the south pole receives almost constant sunlight during that time.

Because Uranus orbits at an average distance from the Sun of 1.78 billion miles (2.86 billion kilometers), it receives only 1/400th as much sunlight as reaches Earth. Still, with one pole receiving continuous sunlight for half a Uranian year, it should be much warmer than the other pole, which is receiving no sunlight. But Voyager found that Uranus has a uniform temperature of −353° F (−214° C). Some unknown mechanism is apparently spreading out the heat in Uranus' atmosphere.

ENCIRCLED BY RINGS

When Uranus passed in front of a distant star in 1977, astronomers were surprised to see that the planet has at least nine rings. Just before Uranus blocked out the star, it "winked" on and off nine times. On the other side of the planet, at nearly the same distances, the star winked on and off an additional nine times. The astronomers concluded that each wink—before and after Uranus blocked the star—occurred when a ring around the planet blocked the star's light.

During its flyby, Voyager 2 detected two more rings, for a total of 11. The spacecraft also sent back measurements of the rings, which appear remarkably narrow and neat. While the rings are about 155,000 miles (250,000 kilometers) in circumference, most are less than 6 miles (10 kilometers) in width. The exception is the outermost ring, epsilon, which spans 60 miles (100 kilometers).

The particles that make up the rings may be scattered remnants of a moon crumbled by Uranus' gravity or broken up by an impact with a high-speed asteroid. Instead of spreading out, the particles seem to be herded together into close-knit bands by "shepherding" moons, as is the case with Saturn's rings. Voyager 2 discovered two small moons, Cordelia and Ophelia, whose gravity seems to shepherd the particles of Uranus' epsilon ring.

Though dust and tiny particles are common in Jovian and Saturnian rings, they are uncommon in Uranian rings. Radio measurements of the epsilon ring, for example, show that it is composed mostly of ice boulders no smaller than beach balls. It is thought that Uranus' extended hydrogen atmosphere sweeps smaller particles and dust from the ring.

Scientists say that the rings are younger than the planet itself. The rings are thought to be short-lived as well. In time, the boulders in the rings will collide with each other and grind down to dust. As the planet's atmosphere sweeps away the dust, the rings will vanish, appearing again only with the breakup of another moon.

URANIAN MOONS

The 27 Uranian moons are named after characters in the plays of Shakespeare and the poems of Alexander Pope. There are five major moons: Ariel, Umbriel, Titania, Oberon, and Miranda. Voyager 2 discovered

Miranda, the innermost of Uranus' large moons, was not discovered until 1948. Miranda has likely been subjected to meteoric bombardment in its past.

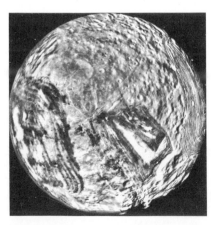

10 minor moons, the largest of which is named Puck, the mischievous sprite in Shakespeare's *A Midsummer Night's Dream*. Craters dot the dark surface of Puck, which is slightly more than 100 miles (160 kilometers) in diameter. Twelve other natural satellites—many classified as irregular moons—have been discovered since 1997 using ground-based telescopes.

Titania, Uranus' largest moon, is about 1,000 miles (1,600 kilometers) in diameter, roughly half the size of Earth's moon. Like Umbriel and Oberon, Titania is heavily cratered, suggesting that it has a long history. Ariel appears to have a geologically younger surface, with many fault valleys. Many of the craters formed in its early history appear to have been erased by extensive flows of icy material. All of the five major moons appear to be composed mainly of water ice and rock, with some ammonia and methane ices as well. The surfaces appear gray and dark, most likely because they contain sooty, carbon-based materials.

With its bizarre collection of terrains, Miranda is probably the most fascinating Uranian moon. In some regions, there are cratered plains. In others, there are canyons some 13 miles (20 kilometers) deep. Miranda is also marked by glacial flows, huge fractures, broad terraces, high cliffs, and grooves that look like claw marks made by some mythical cosmic monster. All these strange features are mixed together in a seemingly haphazard way.

What could have formed such a jumbled mess of geology? Scientists think Miranda was blasted apart as many as five times by meteorites. Each collision cracked the moon into smaller pieces, which later fell back together by the force of gravity.

Voyager 2 was able to zoom in on Miranda's alien landscapes, measure the tidy Uranian rings, and survey the topsy-turvy world of Uranus itself. If one craft revealed so much on just a quick flyby, imagine what could be learned if a craft orbited the planet for a long period of time. Imagine what we may someday learn by hitting the Uranian "bull's-eye," sending a probe plunging past the blue-green veil that covers this bizarre, mysterious planet.

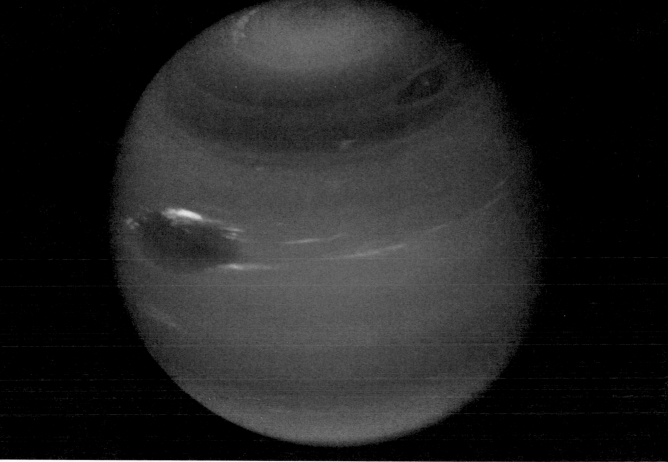
ASP Neptune Kit, William Kaufman & JPL

NEPTUNE

by Jeffrey Brune

Neptune, the eighth planet from the Sun, is named for the Roman god of the sea. The planet's Great Dark Spot (center left, above), an Earth-sized storm system, was just one of the outward signs of Neptune's turbulent atmosphere discovered by Voyager 2 in 1989.

Nearly 2.8 billion miles (4.5 billion kilometers) from the Sun lies a pale blue planet named Neptune. This, the outermost of the giant gas planets, was discovered in 1846. Yet Neptune remained largely a mystery until 1989, when the Voyager 2 probe flew by for a close look.

Voyager revealed that Neptune is alive with activity. In its turbulent atmosphere, a storm the size of Earth rages, with winds fierce enough to make our hurricanes seem like gentle breezes. On Triton, Neptune's largest moon, icy geysers spew forth freezing gas.

Voyager also discovered six new moons orbiting Neptune, giving the planet a known total of eight. Neptune and its moons orbit the Sun very slowly—once in about 165 years. That means the planet has not yet completed a single orbit around the Sun since it was first discovered in 1846! Neptune's elliptical orbit is only slightly eccentric; that is, the Sun lies nearly at its center. The plane of Neptune's equator is inclined by about 29 degrees to the plane of the planet's orbit. It rotates once in about 16 hours. Neptune's equatorial diameter is about 31,000 miles (49,500 kilometers); its volume is large enough to swallow nearly 60 Earths.

INVISIBLE TUG

Neptune might never have been discovered had neighboring Uranus followed its expected orbit. In 1790 French astronomer Jean Baptiste Delambre mapped the orbit of Uranus. For a few years, the ob-

INSIDE AN ICY GIANT

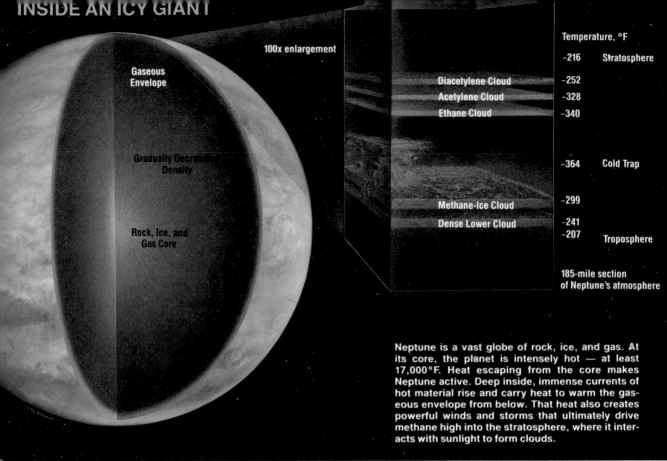

100x enlargement

Gaseous Envelope

Gradually Decreasing Density

Rock, Ice, and Gas Core

Temperature, °F	
−216	Stratosphere
Diacetylene Cloud −252	
Acetylene Cloud −328	
Ethane Cloud −340	
−364	Cold Trap
−299	
Methane-Ice Cloud	
Dense Lower Cloud −241	
−207	Troposphere

185-mile section of Neptune's atmosphere

Neptune is a vast globe of rock, ice, and gas. At its core, the planet is intensely hot — at least 17,000°F. Heat escaping from the core makes Neptune active. Deep inside, immense currents of hot material rise and carry heat to warm the gaseous envelope from below. That heat also creates powerful winds and storms that ultimately drive methane high into the stratosphere, where it interacts with sunlight to form clouds.

© Paul DiMare

served positions of Uranus generally agreed with Delambre's astronomical tables. Over time, however, the discrepancy between the tables and the actual orbit of Uranus increased. Astronomers agreed on the need for revision.

French astronomer Alexis Bouvard undertook this task. His calculations of Uranus' orbit seemed accurate at first, but soon they, too, failed to agree with the planet's actual positions. Bouvard suspected that an undiscovered planet lying beyond the orbit of Uranus must be pulling it away from its calculated course.

On July 3, 1841, John Couch Adams, then an undergraduate at St. John's College, Cambridge, entered the following memorandum in his notebook: "Formed a design, in the beginning of this week, of investigating as soon as possible after taking my degree, the irregularities in the motion of Uranus, which are as yet unaccounted for; in order to find whether they may be attributed to the action of an undiscovered planet beyond it, and if possible thence to determine approximately the elements of its orbit, etc., which would probably lead to its discovery."

By 1845 Adams had completed some ingenious calculations that showed that a heavenly body—probably a planet—beyond the orbit of Uranus was indeed exerting a gravitational tug on the latter planet. The next step was to carefully search the region of the skies in which the undiscovered planet might be found. In September 1845, Adams shared his results with the eminent astronomer Sir George Biddell Airy, and asked him to undertake the search.

For a time, Airy did nothing, perhaps because he was not interested in the request of the unknown Adams. In July 1846, however, Airy asked astronomer James Challis to search for the planet. Challis observed Neptune on August 4, 1846, but he failed to recognize it at the time.

DISCOVERY OF NEPTUNE

In the meantime, French astronomer Urbain-Jean-Joseph Leverrier had calculated the unknown planet's orbit, quite independently of Adams. Leverrier sent a series of three memorandums to the French Academy on this subject—in November 1845 and in June and August 1846. Then he wrote to Johann G. Galle, chief assistant at the Berlin Observatory, enclosing his calculations and urging Galle to look for the planet. The letter reached Galle on September 23, 1846. That same night he turned his telescope toward the quarter of the heavens suggested by Leverrier, and found the planet less than one degree from the place where Leverrier said it would be. Galle's discovery of Neptune was made possible because the Berlin Observatory had just received a new and complete map of the stars in that region of the skies.

There was a good deal of rather unpleasant controversy for a time concerning who would receive credit for Neptune's discovery. It is now generally agreed that Adams and Leverrier deserve equal credit for the abstruse calculations that led to the discovery. To Galle goes the distinction of having been the first to identify the planet in the heavens.

The new planet was named Neptune, after the Roman god of the sea. Its discovery was a fine example of what has been called the "astronomy of the invisible," that is, the detecting of heavenly bodies before they are actually observed in the skies, through the attraction they exert on known bodies.

Since Neptune's discovery, little else was revealed about the mysterious planet until Voyager 2 passed to within 3,000 miles (5,000 kilometers) of it on August 25, 1989.

STORMY BLUE WORLD

Neptune's atmosphere is composed primarily of hydrogen and helium with a dash of methane. It is the methane that gives the planet its lovely blue color. Methane absorbs longer wavelengths of sunlight (near the red end of the visible-light spectrum), and reflects shorter wavelengths (near the blue end of the spectrum).

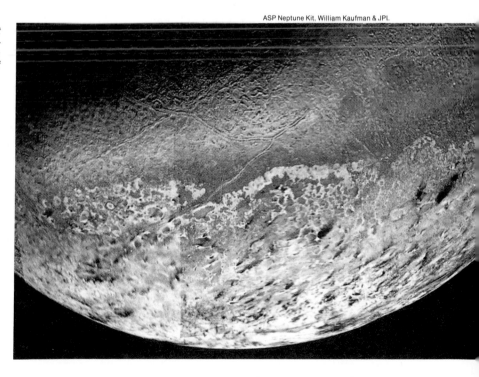

ASP Neptune Kit, William Kaufman & JPL

Triton, Neptune's largest moon, has the unusual distinction of following an orbit in a direction opposite to that of the planet's rotation.

Voyager 2 found Neptune ravaged by furious weather, the most violent area being a phenomenon dubbed the Great Dark Spot, an Earth-sized, pulsating swirl laced with white clouds. This hurricanelike storm lies in the planet's southern hemisphere, spins in a counterclockwise direction, and from time to time spawns smaller dark spots in a trail to the west. In many ways the Great Dark Spot is similar to Jupiter's Great Red Spot, though it changes in size and shape far more often. Near Neptune's south pole is another major spot, shaped like an almond, called Dark Spot 2. It has distinctive white clouds in its center that bubble up from below and spread out.

Though high winds streak the entire planet, the fastest occur near the Great Dark Spot. Here winds blow over 1,500 miles (2,400 kilometers) per hour—the strongest winds measured on any planet, including blustery Saturn. The winds of Neptune push wispy, cirruslike clouds of frozen methane gas around the planet. One particularly prominent cloud whips around the planet so fast that scientists call it "Scooter."

Scientists were surprised that Voyager found Neptune so stormy. On Earth, storms are driven by heat energy from the Sun. But Neptune receives 1,000 times less sunlight than the Earth receives. What's more, three years earlier Voyager found Neptune's planetary neighbor, Uranus, to have relatively little atmospheric activity; cold Uranus was thought to be too far from the warm Sun to have stormy weather. Surely Neptune would be equally as calm as Uranus, if not calmer, given that Neptune is a billion miles (1.6 billion kilometers) farther away from the Sun.

The existence of high winds and hurricanes on Neptune suggested that the planet was getting its heat from a source other than the Sun. But where? Scientists say that Neptune must have an internal heat engine, which probably fuels the planet's storms. As proof, Voyager showed that Neptune enjoys temperatures similar to those of Uranus, even though Uranus is much closer to the Sun. In fact, Neptune, unlike Uranus, emits more heat than it re-

ceives. The heat may come from the intensely high temperatures and pressures of the planet's innermost rocky core.

MAGNETIC FIELD

Voyager 2 confirmed that Neptune has a strong magnetic field. The probe also showed this field to be tilted 47 degrees from the planet's rotation axis. The magnetic field of Uranus has a similar tilt, suggesting that the two planets are magnetic "twins."

Because magnetic fields originate deep within a planet, they reveal much about a planet's interior. Neptune and Uranus are each believed to have a hot, rocky core, surrounded by a huge slushball of water ice, frozen gases, and liquid gases. Covering all that is the atmosphere.

Studies of Neptune's magnetic field allowed scientists to determine more precisely the length of a Neptunian day—how long it takes the planet to complete one rotation. Before Voyager, the best estimate was 18 hours. This was determined by using Earth-based telescopes to track cloud features in the Neptunian atmosphere. The practice, however, can be inaccurate because clouds speed up and slow down with the changing wind. How fast the part of the planet below the cloud layers is moving is best determined by studying the magnetic field generated by the planet's interior. An instrument aboard Voyager measured the pulse of radio waves created by Neptune's magnetic field. From these radio heartbeats, scientists determined that the planet spins once every 16 hours, seven minutes.

RINGS AND MOONS

As astronomers on Earth watched Neptune pass in front of distant stars, those stars sometimes winked out briefly, while other times they did not. On yet another occasion, one telescope captured an image of a star winking out behind Neptune, while, at the same time, a nearby telescope did not. It appeared from these observations that Neptune had partial rings, or "ring arcs," instead of complete rings.

Voyager 2 discovered a system of rings revolving around Neptune. The rings encircle the planet at distances between 17,000 and 24,000 miles.

Voyager 2, however, found at least five rings that go all the way around the planet, although they are extremely thin in some areas and clumpy in others.

Astronomers have long recognized two of Neptune's moons: Triton, discovered in 1846; and Nereid, discovered in 1949. Voyager 2 discovered six, and astronomers using ground-based telescopes recently found five more.

Triton, Neptune's largest and most fascinating moon, orbits in a direction completely opposite to the planet's rotation. Triton's retrograde motion suggests that it did not originate out of Neptune. Some astronomers think that Triton was once a small planet until it passed too close to Neptune. Then Neptune "harpooned" Triton with its strong gravitational pull, keeping the moon close to its side ever since.

After Voyager's flyby of Neptune, the probe took a series of close-up photos of Triton. Ironically, this moon ended up capturing far more scientific attention than did Neptune itself. Scientists had expected Triton to be a cold, drab world. The moon did indeed prove cold at −391° F (−235° C). But it turned out to be far from drab. Voyager 2

revealed an unexpectedly varied and colorful terrain. The frosty white-, blue-, and pink-splotched moon was covered with cliffs and faults and sprinkled with craters. In some areas, dimples and dark spots ringed by whitish bands gave the moon the look of cantaloupe skin. Elsewhere, methane and nitrogen glaciers flowed slowly, icy slush oozed out of fractures, and ice lava formed frozen lakes.

Probably the most intriguing features on Triton are its frequent geyserlike eruptions. It is thought that pressurized nitrogen gas spurts out from beneath Triton's frozen nitrogen surface. This gas spray, or plume, rises vertically about 5 miles (8 kilometers) into the moon's thin nitrogen atmosphere. Each plume creates a cloud composed of dark particles and possibly ice crystals that drifts some 93 miles (150 kilometers) westward. Energy to trigger these ice geysers may originate from solar heat building up in the ice. Another theory is that hot radioactive elements in the moon's core warm and expand the nitrogen gas. When enough pressure builds up, the geyser violently spouts off. What bizarre worlds Voyager 2 revealed at the edge of the solar system!

© Ron Miller

Pluto is the ninth and smallest planet of the solar system. Astronomers think that Pluto (foreground) and its moon Charon may constitute a binary planet system.

PLUTO

by Jeffrey Brune

Mysterious Pluto is the only planet that has not been studied closely by a space probe. Still, what scientists have been able to see using Earth-based telescopes is very odd indeed.

In its corner of the solar system, Pluto is a dwarf amid four giants. It has a solid surface, while those four giants—Jupiter, Saturn, Uranus, and Neptune—are made mostly of gas. Pluto's orbit is the most elongated and tilted of all the planets. And, probably oddest of all, it has a huge moon about half its size. Because Pluto and its moon, Charon, are so similar in size, astronomers consider the pair to be virtually a "double planet."

Pluto is only dimly visible because of its vast distance from the Sun—on average, about 3.7 billion miles (5.9 billion kilometers). Even through a powerful telescope, Pluto appears only as a very faint, yellow-ish point of light. Discovering this dimly lit planet in a background of countless bright stars was indeed a challenge.

DISCOVERY OF PLUTO AND CHARON

The road to Pluto's discovery began with another planet, Uranus, and followed the discovery of Neptune. The quirkiness of the orbit of Uranus led scientists to surmise that the gravity of some other planet was pulling Uranus out of its orbit. That planet turned out to be Neptune. But even taking Neptune's gravity into account, Uranus did not follow the course that astronomers had expected.

A number of astronomers, including Percival Lowell, director of the Lowell Observatory near Flagstaff, Arizona, decided to investigate the matter. In 1915 Lowell published *Memoir on a Trans-Neptunian Planet*, in which he presented his mathematical calculations of a ninth planet's probable position. He believed that it would be found in one of two areas in the sky. The search continued for years.

At last, in February 1930, Clyde W. Tombaugh, an assistant on the Lowell Observatory staff, found what seemed to be the long-sought planet as he studied a series of photographs he had taken. In March of that year, the observatory announced the discovery. The planet was named Pluto, after the Roman god who rules the underworld, because of its position in the distant part of the solar system.

It turns out that Pluto, with a mass only 1/450th that of Earth, is not big enough to distort the orbit of Uranus with the pull of its gravity. This suggests the possibility of another planet beyond Pluto!

The discovery of Pluto's moon came much later. In 1978, James W. Christy of the U.S. Naval Observatory was methodically examining photographic plates to measure Pluto's position throughout its orbit. On one plate, Christy noticed Pluto had a slight bump. Looking at other plates, he noticed the bump moved around the planet. Christy quickly realized he had discovered a moon orbiting Pluto. He named the new moon Charon, after both his wife Charlene ("Char," for short) and the boatman in Greek mythology who ferried souls across the River Styx.

Some astronomers argue that Charon formed from the debris of a massive impact on Pluto. Other scientists suggest that Pluto and its moon—the largest proportionally of any moon to its planet in our solar system—are, in fact, a bi-planetary system. The close proximity of Pluto and Charon results in a unique relationship between the two, in which gravity has slowed their rotations down to the point where they are always revealing the same face to each other—an unusual phenomenon in our solar system.

SMALLEST AND SOMETIMES FARTHEST

With an equatorial diameter of 1,430 miles (2,300 kilometers), Pluto is the smallest of the known planets. Sometimes Pluto orbits closer to the Sun than does Neptune. This was the case from 1979 to 1999.

Pluto's orbit is also the most tilted of all the known planets in the solar system. It is inclined more than 17 degrees to the plane in which Earth revolves around the Sun.

STUDY FROM AFAR

Only twice during Pluto's 248-year trek around the Sun can the orbit of its moon be seen edge-on from Earth. One of those rare chances for study occurred in 1987 through 1988. During that time, Charon appeared to pass completely in front of Pluto, then completely behind it, then in front again, and so on every 3.2 days.

When Charon fell behind Pluto, only the light from the planet reached Earth. Scientists studied the colors in the light and concluded that Pluto's surface is frozen methane. When Charon was in front of Pluto, scientists measured the light from both bodies. They then subtracted Pluto's light to get only the light from Charon. Analysis showed that the moon is covered mostly with frozen water. Pictures taken by the Hubble Space Telescope support these findings. Hubble shows Pluto to be much brighter than its moon: methane ice (Pluto's covering) reflects more sunlight than Charon's water ice.

Twinkling starlight confirmed that Pluto has only a thin atmosphere. In 1988, Pluto passed in front of a star as seen from Earth. Instead of turning on and off like a light switch, the star gradually dimmed as its light passed through the hazy covering surrounding Pluto. Scientists think the heat from the Sun turns Pluto's methane ice into gas, which may occasionally fall as snow.

The Hubble Telescope has produced clear images of Pluto and its moon Charon, and has shown surface detail on Pluto as small as 373 miles (600 kilometers) across. Photographs show what appears to be an ice cap at the planet's north pole, which may be composed of frozen nitrogen, methane, carbon monoxide, and carbon dioxide.

Today, most scientists classify Pluto as an exceptionally large Kuiper object, part of a field of debris in the outer solar system called the Kuiper Belt. In 2005, astronomers announced the discovery of a Kuiper object larger than Pluto, but almost 9 billion miles (14 billion kilometers) from the Sun. Some astronomers hope to have this object, known scientifically as 2003UB313, officially proclaimed the 10th planet.

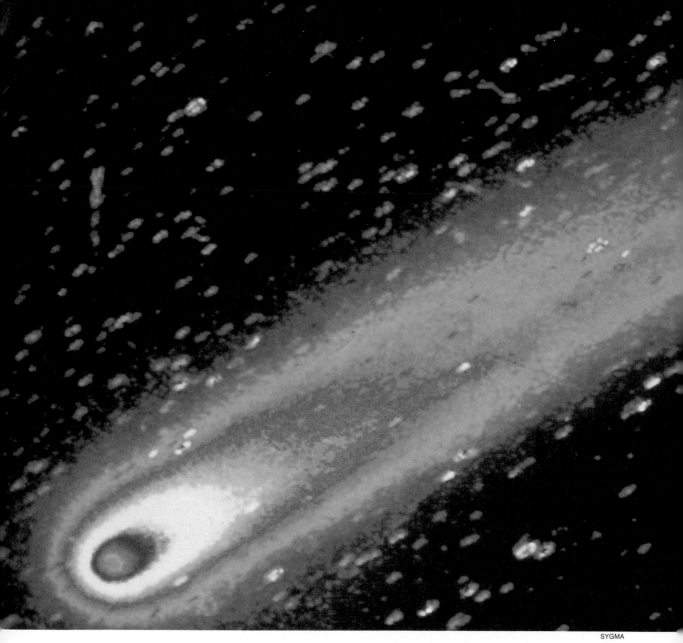

As a comet nears the Sun, its surface glows brightly and a tail forms. The best-known comet, Halley's (above, in a computer-enhanced photo), appears every 86 years.

COMETS

by Dennis L. Mammana

As the ancients gazed at the night skies, they were occasionally startled to see strange celestial objects intruding upon the familiar pattern of stars, Moon, and planets. These mysterious apparitions looked like fuzzy stars with long trains of light, moving from one constellation to another and cutting across the paths of the planets at every conceivable angle. The trains of light suggested a woman's tresses; hence, the celestial intruders came to be known as "long-haired stars," or *komētēs*, the Greek word for "long-haired."

A bright comet was a terrifying spectacle in antiquity. It was thought to foreshadow some dire catastrophe—plague, famine, war, or perhaps the death of a ruler. Today we realize that comets are simply another member of the solar system, and that their coming is no more portentous than the appearance of the first stars at twilight.

HOW COMETS APPEAR

When a particular comet is first discovered, it usually appears as a faint, diffuse body with a dense area near its center. This dense part, which sometimes looks like a tiny star, is known as the *nucleus*. The nebulous, or veil-like, region around it is the *coma*. Nucleus and coma together form the *head* of a comet.

In a certain number of cases, however, a spectacular transformation takes place as the comet approaches the Sun. The coma changes from a diffuse, round mass to sharply defined layers, called *envelopes*. Nebulous matter streams away from the comet's head in the direction opposite to the Sun and forms an immense tail. Most comets of this type have only one tail. A very few have two or more. Some comets occasionally also have forward spikes. As a comet recedes from the Sun, the tail (or tails) can no longer be seen, the coma becomes diffuse again, and, in the great majority of cases, the comet itself disappears from view.

ORIGIN AND STRUCTURE

How do comets originate? According to one theory, they represent celestial building blocks left over after the formation of the planets. According to another, they are remnants of shattered worlds. All this is pure conjecture, as are the various theories that attempt to explain how comets are launched on their journey around the Sun. One theory, proposed by Dutch astronomer J. H. Oort in 1950, holds that there is a vast storehouse of comets—as many as 100 billion, perhaps—in the icy reaches beyond the farthermost planetary orbit. According to Oort's theory, a given comet would normally remain entirely inactive in the "deep freeze" of space unless the passage of a star disturbed it. The comet then would swing into the sphere of gravitational attraction of a major planet and would revolve around the Sun a few hundred or a few thousand times until it disintegrated.

Photographs by the Hubble Telescope provide the first direct evidence that a huge belt of at least 100 million comets is circling the solar system beyond the orbit of Neptune. This ring, called the Kuiper belt, was first suggested in 1951 by Dutch astronomer Gerard P. Kuiper, and appears to be the origin of many comets.

We are on solid ground when we try to analyze the structure and composition of comets. The general belief is that the nucleus consists of a vast number of small, solid bodies held together by mutual attraction. The nuclei of certain comets that have ventured close to Earth have been measured with considerable precision. The tail of the great comet of 1861, for example, stretched across two-thirds of the sky and was bright enough to create shadows on the ground. Yet it had a nucleus less than 100 miles (160 kilometers) in diameter.

As the nucleus of a comet approaches the Sun, the solar heat vaporizes the material on the outer surface of the nucleus. Escaping gases, carrying fine dust with them, diffuse into the coma. They are then swept away by the force of the Sun's radiation to form the tail. The gases and the dust they transport are illuminated partly by reflected sunlight and partly because they absorb ultraviolet light and re-emit it in the form of visible light.

The tail, which flows away from the Sun, increases in breadth as the distance from the head increases. The tail does not form an exact line between the Sun and the comet's head. The greater the distance from the head, the more the gases and dust that make up the tail lag behind. Hence, the tail often has the shape of a curved horn, with its tip at the comet's head.

When the comet turns away from the Sun, the material that formed the tail is swept off into space. In time, comets gradually lose all their substance, unless it can be replenished by dust and by gas molecules swept up in the course of their journeys through space.

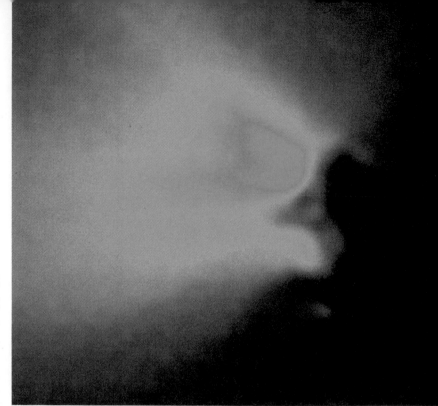

Astronomers think that the green jets in the nucleus of Halley's comet (right) represent the emission of gas and dust from the comet. Until relatively recently, comets were thought to hold supernatural significance. Below, the Bayeux tapestry records the passage of Halley's comet just prior to the Norman conquest of England in 1066.

COMPOSITION

Analysis has revealed that comets contain various gases, including cyanogen (CN), carbon (C_2), carbon monoxide (CO), nitrogen (N_2), hydroxyl (OH), and nitrogen hydride (NH). The presence of such highly poisonous gases as cyanogen and carbon monoxide gave rise to a certain uneasiness in 1910, when Halley's comet passed between the Earth and the Sun. Astronomers had announced that our planet was certain to pass through at least a part of the comet's tail, triggering fears that the Earth's inhabitants would be subjected to gas poi-

soning. After the comet had passed, however, it was realized that such fears were groundless. The gases in the tail did not produce the slightest effect as they swept over the surface of the Earth.

Undoubtedly the Earth has passed through the tails of comets many times, and, as far as we know, without causing any harm to living organisms. The reason is that there are too few molecules in the tails to contaminate the Earth's atmosphere. It has been calculated that the best vacuum obtainable in the laboratory contains millions of times more matter per unit of volume than does the tail of a comet.

Small Amount of Matter

The total amount of matter in a comet, nucleus and all, is so small that it does not exert any significant gravitational pull on planets or moons. Through indirect methods, astronomers have surmised that the entire mass of Halley's comet cannot be more than one one-billionth that of the Earth.

Despite its small mass, however, a comet may be very large. The head of the great comet of 1811 was considerably larger than the Sun! As a rule the head of even a very small comet has a diameter larger than Earth's. The tail may stretch over several hundred million miles.

Every time a comet approaches the Sun, the strong gravitational pull exerted by that huge body subjects the comet to a tremendous strain. As a result, the comet may be broken up into two or more smaller bodies. That is what happened to Biela's comet, which split into two comets in the winter of 1845–1846. These two comets were next observed in 1852, traveling not far apart from each other in what had been Biela's original orbit. They were no longer visible at the predicted returns of 1859 and 1866. On what would have been the next approach of these comets to the Sun—in 1872—a dazzling meteor shower was observed, indicating that the comets had disintegrated. We know that the breathtaking spectacle produced by other meteor showers, including the Perseids each August and the Leonids each November, have been due to the disintegration of comets.

The Dirty-Snowball Theory

In the early 1950s, U.S. astronomer Fred L. Whipple of the Harvard Observatory proposed a novel theory of the nature of comets—the so-called icy-conglomerate, or the "dirty-snowball," theory. Whipple maintained that 70 to 80 percent of the mass of a comet is made up of icy particles consisting of such hydrogen-containing compounds as methane (CH_4), ammonia (NH_3), and water (H_2O). As a comet approaches the Sun, according to Whipple, the ice particles on its outer surface sublimate, or pass directly from the solid to the gaseous state. The resulting gases, together with fine dust particles, form the tail. The remaining 20 to 30 percent of the comet's mass—consisting of compounds of the heavier elements—do not vaporize appreciably. These comparatively heavy compounds are the particles that produce spectacular meteoritic showers when a comet finally disintegrates.

Whipple's dirty-snowball theory was strengthened in 1986 when Soviet spacecraft Vega 1 and 2 flew within 6,000 miles (9,660 kilometers), and the European Space Agency's Giotto craft flew within 376 miles (605 kilometers), of Comet Halley's nucleus. Astronomers found the nucleus to be a very black, potato-shaped object about 10 miles (16 kilometers) long and 5 miles (8 kilometers) wide. According to astronomer Horst Uwe Keller of the Max Planck Institute for Astronomy, the comet's nucleus is "like velvet. As dark as the darkest objects in the solar system." Data from space probes also indicate that the gas and dust from the comet's core are emitted in focused streams.

Even several years after its closest approach to the Sun, astronomers were still watching Halley's from more than 2 billion miles away. The comet is still full of surprises. For instance, although it has reached the coldest, darkest regions of the solar system, Halley's continues to occasionally shoot off jets of gas. The energy source behind the display remains a mystery. The Hubble Space Telescope and large ground-based telescopes continue to help astronomers keep an eye on Halley's.

In January 2004, NASA's aptly named Stardust probe successfully navigated its way through the turbulent cloud of dust and gas emanating from Comet Wild 2. The spacecraft snapped photographs of the comet's nucleus and scooped up a sample of particles for scientists to study when the probe returns to Earth in January 2006. On July 4, 2005, NASA's "Deep Impact" probe transmitted data and images back to scientists as it crashed into Comet Tempel 1. Astronomers are studying this information to learn more about comet composition.

MOTION OF COMETS

The motion of the comets baffled astronomers for a long time. In contrast to the sometimes complex but always reliable movement of the planets, comets emerge into view with a flourish, only to disappear for years on end. They traverse all regions of the sky at various angles to the plane of the solar system. No wonder that, until the late 16th century, comets were thought to be phenomena of Earth's upper atmosphere, like the aurora borealis.

It was not until 1705 that the true nature of cometary motion was established.

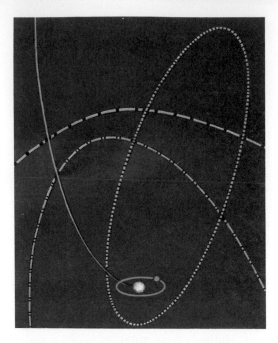

Periodic comets like Halley's follow an elliptical orbit (dotted line) through the heavens. Comets that appear only once follow open curves, either parabolic (dot-and-dash line) or hyperbolic (dashed line). Still others (solid line) disintegrate in the solar system.

In that year, Edmund Halley, a friend of Sir Isaac Newton, applied the law of gravitation to the observations of a number of comets. He found that they traveled in space in accordance with that law. He noted, too, that the comets of 1682, 1607, 1531, and 1456 had moved in much the same way. He came to the conclusion, therefore, that these supposedly different comets were really one and the same body, which reappeared every 75 or 76 years. Halley predicted that the comet would return in 1758, and his prophecy was fulfilled. Halley's comet appeared also in 1835 and in 1910. When it became visible again, early in 1986, spacecraft launched the previous year by the European Space Agency (ESA), the Soviet Union, and Japan rendezvoused with the comet. These spacecraft transmitted close-up pictures of the comet as well as data on its composition and temperature.

Historical investigation revealed that the comet had been observed at every appearance as far back as the year 240 B.C. It should have been visible in 315 B.C. and 391 B.C., but there are no actual records of its appearance in those years. However, the comet of 467 B.C., the first ever recorded, was undoubtedly Halley's comet.

When Halley demonstrated that comets move around the Sun according to the law of gravity, he dispelled forever the idea that they are signs of divine wrath. Since Halley's time the orbits of many comets have been traced. To understand the nature of these orbits, it is necessary to point out that, according to the law of gravitation, comets must move around the Sun in conic sections. A conic section is a curve obtained when a plane cuts through a cone. There are only two such curves that are closed—the circle and the ellipse. A body moving in either one of these curves ultimately returns to the place from which it started. As astronomers would say, the body has a definite period of revolution. The point in a comet's orbit when it's nearest to the Sun is called perihelion. The opposite point in the orbit, farthest from the Sun, is called aphelion.

A comet cannot move in a circle. If it started by tracing a circular path, the gravitational attraction of planets in the solar system would soon distort the comet's path into an ellipse. All periodic, or regularly returning, comets move in elliptical orbits around the Sun.

Other comets move in conic sections that are open curves—parabolas and hyperbolas. A comet moving in one of these curves would travel around the Sun and off into space, never to be seen again.

NAMING COMETS

Astronomers must be able to identify comets in order to calculate their orbits. Each comet, therefore, is distinguished by a special name. This contains the year when a particular appearance was first discovered, and a letter indicating the order of discovery among the comets of that year. But this is only a temporary name. Once the orbit has been computed and the time of perihelion worked out, the same comet is designated by the year of perihelion passage, and a Roman numeral, indicating its order among the comets that have reached perihelion that year.

© SRW

Halley's comet will next appear in the year 2062. Astronomers have fully mapped its orbit around the Sun.

For example, Halley's comet in its last apparition was first called 1909c and then 1910-II. This means that it was the third comet discovered in 1909, and the second comet to pass perihelion in 1910. In the case of more recently sighted comets, the name of the discoverer is added in parentheses. Thus, the bright comet temporarily designated as 1936a is now referred to as 1936-II (Peltier). Thus, it was the first comet discovered in 1936, it was the second comet to pass perihelion in that year, and the discoverer was Peltier.

News of a comet's discovery in the Eastern Hemisphere is immediately sent to the observatory in Copenhagen, Denmark, the international clearinghouse for information of this kind. When the Harvard Observatory receives word of the discovery from Copenhagen, it telegraphs the information to all the observatories in the Western Hemisphere. News of a discovery in the Western Hemisphere is sent to the Harvard Observatory, which then forwards the news to other observatories.

DETERMINING THE COMET'S ORBIT

After a comet is discovered, astronomers begin to measure the apparent position of the comet in reference to known stars. Its position, measured at intervals of a few days, gives the astronomer enough information to calculate a preliminary orbit and to predict the comet's motion in the future. Some of these measurements may be in error, or the comet may be too diffuse to be measured precisely. As a result the first calculation of the orbit is usually somewhat inaccurate. It is amended as further observations become available. When the comet has disappeared from view, all observations are collected, and the definitive or final orbit is computed.

The main difficulty in determining an orbit is that at first we have no idea how distant the comet is. It is presumably "near" the Earth—(that is, within 100 million miles, or 160 million kilometers)—but it appears to be as remote as the stars. It is only when it moves against the background of the constellations that we can begin to calculate its actual distance from the Earth. There is an added complication. The apparent motion of the comet among the constellations is due principally to its real motion around the Sun, but it is also due in part to the motion of the Earth during the interval between observations. The astronomer must disassociate, or separate, the motion of the Earth from that of the comet.

At best, even with modern calculating machines, the computation of the orbit is very tedious, and even the best computers make mistakes. Therefore two computers generally work independently and check their results from time to time. After the orbit has been computed, the *ephemeris* is

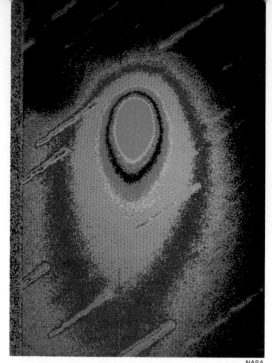

The colors in the computer-enhanced image of Comet Giacobini-Zinner above indicate levels of brightness. Comets are initially named for the year of their discovery; later, they take the names of their discoverers.

set up. An ephemeris is a statement, in the form of a table, of the assigned places of a celestial body for regular intervals.

It may take a long time to work out the definitive orbit. Each observation must be checked, the best-known position for each comparison star must be obtained, and the attraction, or perturbation, by other members of the solar system must be calculated. From all these computations, various quantities are derived, which are called elements of the orbit. One of the elements is the time of perihelion. Another is the distance of perihelion from the Sun, measured in astronomical units. An astronomical unit (abbreviated A.U.), used by astronomers for great distances, equals the distance from the Earth to the Sun, or approximately 93 million miles (149.6 million kilometers).

Short and Long Periods

The time that elapses between two returns of a comet to perihelion is called its period. Some comets move in comparatively small ellipses, so that they come back to perihelion every few years; that is, they are short-period comets. Encke's comet has the shortest known period—about 3.3 years. It was first discovered in 1786, and has since been seen returning to perihelion more than 40 times. None of the short-period comets are bright. Under the best conditions, Encke's comet is barely visible to the naked eye.

If the orbits of a certain group of about 30 short-period comets are plotted, it is seen that all of their aphelia, or positions farthest from the Sun, fall near the orbit of Jupiter. Obviously this giant among the planets exerts an important influence upon these comets. It can be shown mathematically that they were deflected by Jupiter from their original orbits and made to move around the Sun in small ellipses. Therefore, these short-period bodies are called Jupiter's family of comets.

Other planets have also deflected comets in much the same way, and now have their own comet families. Saturn's family is small. It includes the remarkable Comet 1925-II (Schwassmann-Wachmann), which has a period of 16 years and an almost-circular orbit. It was the first comet to be observed in every part of its orbit, from perihelion to aphelion. This strange body is subject to remarkable changes in brightness, the cause of which is unknown. Sometimes it flares up and becomes more than 500 times as bright as it had been a few days previously. Unfortunately, this comet is always so far from both the Earth and Sun that, even at its brightest, a good telescope is necessary to see it at all.

Halley's comet belongs to Neptune's family, which, like Saturn's family, has only a few members. Some of these, including Halley's comet and Comet 1884-I (Pons-Brooks), are quite bright.

For some comets, periods of 100, 200, or 500 years have been calculated. The longer the period, the more uncertain it is. The trouble is that we can observe such comets only in the small part of their orbit near perihelion. In the case of comets with periods of more than a few thousand years, the orbit that can be observed shows exceedingly little curvature. This often makes it impossible to figure out the shape of the orbit or the length of the period. According to Estonian astronomer E. Opik, some of the longer orbits may extend out to the nearest stars, more than 4 light-years away. A light-year is approximately 6 trillion miles (9.6 trillion kilometers).

Most astronomers believe that all comets are periodic, although the periods may be many thousands or even millions of years. It is thought, for example, that Comet 1914-V (Delavan) has a period of 24 million years. It is possible, however, that the orbits of some comets may form an open curve, whose ends can never meet. In such cases the comet may have been traveling in an elliptical orbit when it entered the planetary region of the solar system, and may have been thrown into an orbit forming an open curve because of the gravitational attraction of the major planets.

Collision with a Planet

Since comets move in all directions in the solar system, it is conceivable that one could collide with a planet like Earth. We have already watched this occur when the fractured comet Shoemaker-Levy 9 collided with Jupiter in 1994. What would happen to Earth if this occurred here?

Fortunately, the chances of such an event are very small. Yet in Earth's long history, there must have been a few collisions with comets. In such an event, there would certainly be a brilliant display of meteors as the comet's nucleus disintegrated upon coming in contact with Earth's atmosphere. The larger pieces of the comet's nucleus might cause considerable destruction if they were to fall into a populated region.

APPARENT BRIGHTNESS

As we have observed, the illumination of comets is due, directly or indirectly, to the Sun. The nearer to the Sun a comet is, therefore, the brighter it is. The distance of the comet from the Earth will also naturally affect its apparent brightness. In 1910 Halley's comet appeared brightest not at perihelion, but a month later, about the middle of May, when it came closest to our planet. The brightness of comets is measured by the same scale of apparent magnitudes used to measure the apparent brightness of the stars.

One of the brightest comets ever seen in the skies was that of 1577. It was carefully observed by Tycho Brahe, who then proved that it was not traveling in our atmosphere. This demonstration disproved the old theory that comets are vapors from the surface of the Earth, ignited in the upper atmosphere of our planet.

Only a few truly bright comets have appeared in the 20th century, though there have been many easily visible to the naked eye. We have already mentioned Halley's comet, which appeared in 1910, and again, in less spectacular fashion, in 1986. Comet Skjellerup in 1927 was very bright, but it was almost entirely ignored by the general public because it appeared to be so close to the Sun. Another extremely bright comet was Ikeya-Seki. Discovered by two ama-

Halley's 1986–87 passage disappointed many comet watchers in the Northern Hemisphere. Still, many vivid displays were captured on film, including the photo below of Halley crossing the Arkansas night sky.

© Greg Polus

teur Japanese astronomers, K. Ikeya and T. Seki, in September 1965, it created quite a sensation. After passing within 310,700 miles (500,000 kilometers) of the Sun, the nucleus of the comet broke into three pieces, which then sped back into space.

More than three decades passed before an even more spectacular comet visited Earth's neighborhood. In March 1996, comet Hyakutake sped within 10 million miles (16 million kilometers) of our planet; only a year later, Comet Hale-Bopp became a celestial showpiece for many months.

AMATEURS DISCOVER MANY

Many amateur astronomers actively search for new comets. As a matter of fact, most new comets are discovered by amateurs. A professional astronomer using telescopes follows a rigid program of observation, and, for the most part, studies individual stars or small parts of the sky. Once in a while, a hitherto-unknown comet will come within this field of view, but not often. The amateur who undertakes a deliberate search for a comet by scanning every quarter of the night sky is more likely to make a discovery.

The amateur comet hunter should use a small telescope that has a wide field of view—four or five times the diameter of the Moon—and should work out a definite system of observation. One excellent method is to sweep the sky from east to west and to change the position of the telescope with every sweep so that the new field partially overlaps the old one. The most promising areas to search are the western sky after nightfall, and eastern sky before dawn.

The comet-hunting amateur will find many celestial objects that look like comets. Many of these, however, will prove to be nebulas and globular clusters. The only way to distinguish between such permanent celestial bodies and comets is to memorize the positions of the nebulas and globular clusters or to consult a sky atlas, such as *Norton's*. The real comet will betray its nature by changing its position among the stars within a few hours. Only occasionally will an observer come upon a comet with an unmistakable tail. In most cases the comet will be faint, diffuse, and tailless.

Only a fairly skillful amateur astronomer can search for new comets with any hope of success. The comet hunter must be able to operate a telescope efficiently, must know how to distinguish a comet from a nebula, and must be able to determine with what speed and in what direction the new comet is moving. Besides a certain amount of proficiency in astronomy, an amateur comet hunter must also have a great deal of persistence, and must realize, too, that the best of efforts may be fruitless. Luck plays an important part in every discovery. Even so, there are plenty of encouraging stories.

A comet, reportedly as bright as Halley's, was discovered in the summer of 1986 by a 24-year-old student, Christine Wilson. Wilson, working at a summer job at Mount Palomar Observatory, noticed the comet on a photographic plate. Comet Wilson takes more than 10,000 years to complete an orbit around the Sun.

The champion discoverer of comets was Jean-Louis Pons, who had been a janitor at the Marseilles Observatory. Between the years 1802 and 1827, he discovered 28 comets—more than one a year—with his homemade telescope. American amateur comet hunters W.R. Brooks and E.E. Barnard attained such fame for their discoveries that they ultimately became professional astronomers. Brooks discovered 25 comets between 1883 and 1911, and Barnard found 22 in about the same period.

STILL PROBLEMS TO SOLVE

Much remains to be learned about these frozen relics of our solar system's birth. Where do they come from? Is their chemical and physical makeup the same? How do they behave as they approach the Sun? How many are there? And are comets responsible for the water and life we enjoy here on Earth?

In the coming years and decades, close-up observation of comets from space, and the return of sample materials to Earth, may provide answers to these and the countless other questions that still puzzle scientists.

ASTEROIDS

by Dennis L. Mammana

In the region between the orbits of Mars and Jupiter, a vast number of small celestial bodies known as asteroids, or minor planets, make their home. About 2,000 of these bodies have already been cataloged, and there may be more than 100,000. Some of them have orbits that swing beyond Jupiter, and some come inside the orbit of Mars.

The asteroids were discovered as a result of an apparent flaw in the law astronomers used for estimating the relative distances of the planets from the Sun. This law, formulated by German astronomer Johann Elert Bode in 1772 and known as Bode's law, was based on the fact that as the distance from the Sun increases, the planetary paths are more and more widely separated. Bode claimed that the increasing distances of the planets from the Sun followed a more or less regular ratio. Today we realize that the law is based upon coincidence and, in fact, does not apply at all to the two outermost planets, Neptune and Pluto, which were not known in Bode's day. However, for a number of years after it was proposed, the law was accepted by astronomers.

At first the only flaw in Bode's law was an apparent gap between Mars and Jupiter, one too great to be explained by the law. Astronomers came to the conclusion that another planet, hitherto undiscovered, must lie within this belt. Toward the end of the 18th century, an association of astronomers was formed for the express purpose of hunting for the missing planet. They realized that the object of their search must be very small, or else it would not have been able to escape observation for such a long time.

DISCOVERY OF A "MISSING PLANET"

When Giuseppe Piazzi, an Italian astronomer, announced on January 1, 1801, that he had discovered a new heavenly

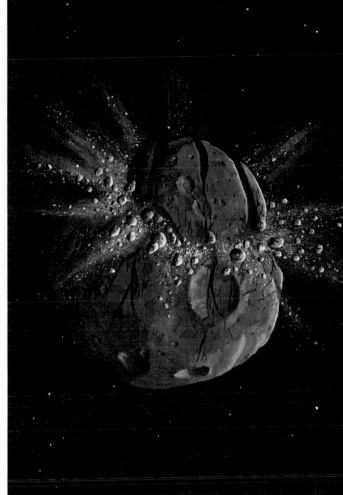

© William K. Hartmann

Astronomers think that asteroids are chunks of cosmic matter that somehow never united to form a planet. A collision of two asteroids creates vast amounts of debris, as suggested in the artist's conception above.

body in the zone between the orbits of Mars and Jupiter, astronomers assumed that this was the planet for which they had been searching. Curiously enough, Piazzi came upon the supposed planet more or less by accident. He was engaged in making a catalog of the fixed stars. He had developed a very exact method for mapping the sky by determining the relative positions of the stars within a given area on a number of successive occasions. If any "star" moved in relation to its neighbors, it was obviously not a star at all, but some other sort of heavenly body, such as a planet or a comet. The moving body would not be included, therefore, in Piazzi's catalog.

Piazzi had already mapped out more than 150 areas of the sky without incident.

However, when he compared four successive observations of the constellation Taurus, he discovered that a certain small star within the constellation had changed its position from one observation to another. The Italian astronomer suspected that the "star" was really a comet. But when Bode heard of its movements, he decided that it was the planet for which so many astronomers had been searching.

Three More "Planets"

Piazzi fell ill before he had time to make many observations of the new heavenly body, and it was lost to view for a time. But word of the discovery had come to Karl Friedrich Gauss, a young mathematician from Göttingen, Germany. Using a new method for determining planetary orbits, Gauss was able to calculate the path of the supposed planet from the few observations made by Piazzi, and, as a result, the new heavenly body was rediscovered in December 1801. It received the name of Ceres, after the Roman goddess of agriculture. Not long after Ceres had been rediscovered in the heavens, astronomers discovered three other "planets"—Pallas (1802), Juno (1804), and Vesta (1807). It was realized by this time that these newly discovered heavenly bodies were too small to rank as full-fledged planets. Rather, they were minor planets, also dubbed asteroids or planetoids.

Ceres, Pallas, Juno, and Vesta are considered the Big Four among the asteroids, the only ones that have definite diameters and that appear as disks through a telescope. Ceres is about 480 miles (770 kilometers) in diameter; Pallas, 304 miles (490 kilometers); Vesta, 240 miles (385 kilometers); and Juno, 118 miles (190 kilometers).

Many More on Film

It was not until 1845 that the fifth asteroid, Astraea, was discovered. Astronomers were finding the search for the comparatively tiny asteroids painstakingly slow and very laborious. But in 1891 a new asteroid-hunting technique was developed by Max Wolf, a German astronomer. He attached a camera to a telescope that was moved by clockwork in such a way that it continually pointed to the same fixed stars. A photographic plate was set in the camera and exposed for a certain period of time. When the plate was developed, the stars in the photograph appeared as white points. If there were any asteroids within the field of the telescope, they would appear as short white lines, because the asteroids would have moved in their orbits during the exposure of the plate. After adopting Wolf's technique, astronomers found so many new asteroids that it became difficult to keep track of them.

On October 29, 1990, the Galileo spacecraft swept within 1,000 miles (1,600 kilometers) of the asteroid 951 Gaspra at a speed of nearly 18,000 miles (29,000 kilometers) per hour, along the way snapping photos and collecting data on the body's composition and physical properties.

This 10-mile (16-kilometer)-long chunk of iron and stone is believed to be a fairly representative asteroid. Hundreds of craters and muted grooves suggest that it was chipped off a larger body some 200 million years ago. "Daytime" temperatures on the body were measured at about 109° F (43° C), and indicate that the asteroid is covered by a "soil" of pulverized rock and dust, though one thinner than the Moon's.

Nearly three years later, Galileo shot a photo of the asteroid 243 Ida and revealed for the first time a natural satellite orbiting the asteroid.

Another close-up view came in 1997, when the NEAR-Shoemaker (Near Earth Asteroid Rendezvous) mission flew within 745 miles (1,200 kilometers) of 253 Mathilde. In 2000, the craft became the first to orbit an asteroid (433 Eros). On February 12, 2001, NEAR-Shoemaker landed on Eros, the first-ever landing on an asteroid.

And in 1998, astronomers may have discovered a new class of asteroid that orbits the Sun completely within the orbit of Earth. The object, designated 1998 DK36, is only about 132 feet (40 meters) across.

VARIED ORBITS

The asteroids cover a wide belt in space. Hidalgo, at its farthest distance from the Sun, approaches the orbit of the planet

Space probes venturing beyond Mars encounter the asteroid belt, where thousands of the tiny bodies orbit the Sun. So far, no probe has collided with an asteroid.

Saturn. Icarus, discovered in 1948, moves in an orbit that passes beyond Mars and then closer to the Sun than the planet Mercury itself—a distance of only 19 million miles (30 million kilometers), which is about half that of Mercury from the Sun. The asteroid Hermes, only about a mile (1.6 kilometers) across, sometimes comes as close as 198,840 miles (320,000 kilometers) to Earth's orbit—closer than the orbit of the Moon. In 1937, Hermes moved to within 500,000 miles (800,000 kilometers) of Earth itself. Evidently, the orbits of the asteroids are highly varied and distorted compared to those of the planets. They may intersect each other, and often lie at high angles to the planes of Earth's path and the paths of the other planets.

CLOSE APPROACHES AND IMPACTS

The asteroids have never been seen to collide with each other or with any of the planets, but undoubtedly they have in the past. At times, some asteroids actually cross Earth's orbit. Perhaps as many as 1,000 asteroids larger than a half mile wide have crossed our planet's path. On January 18, 1999, a brilliant fireball slammed into western Canada, exploding with the energy of more than 2,000 tons of dynamite. A 6-ounce (170-gram) piece of the meteorite was recovered and sent to NASA's Johnson Space Center for analysis.

One of the most famous collisions may have caused the extinction of the dinosaurs some 65 million years ago. Many scientists believe that the subsequent explosion would have completely blanketed Earth with dust, cutting off sunlight for long periods of time and wiping out a significant number of species—including the dinosaurs.

ORIGIN OF THE ASTEROIDS

Astronomers believe that asteroids are chunks of cosmic matter that somehow never finally united to form a planet during the time that the solar system was coming into being. Here, too, the gravitational attraction of Jupiter would be the decisive factor. It would prevent the chunks from drawing together and ultimately forming a single body.

A meteor is matter from outer space that enters the Earth's atmosphere. As gravity pulls it toward Earth, the meteor vaporizes, leaving behind a glowing trail (above). A meteor that survives its plunge to Earth is called a meteorite.

METEORS AND METEORITES

by Ray Villard

From time to time, you might glance into the sky to see a point of light trailed by a fleeting, luminous train as it races against the background of stars. It may be barely visible or as bright as the full Moon. This object is often called a "shooting star."

Actually, what you're watching is not a far-off star in motion, but something quite close to home. A fast-moving body from outer space has penetrated Earth's atmosphere and has become so heated from air resistance that it begins to glow.

The term *meteor* refers to solid bodies that burn up into vapor when they scorch through our atmosphere. If the celestial visitor survives its fiery plunge and reaches the ground, it is called a *meteorite*.

Meteorites provide us with an unusual opportunity to study specimens from outer space. From these specimens we can determine the composition of matter from beyond the Earth and Moon. We can also draw conclusions about the conditions under which this matter originated and evolved, as well as estimate its age.

Scientists believe most meteorites coalesced from the same cloud of dust and minerals that condensed to form all the planets and moons in the solar system. Others are no doubt fragments of shattered asteroids or debris thrown off from comets, moons, or even planets. Radioactive-dating techniques show that most meteorites date back to what is thought to be the beginning of the solar system, 4.6 billion years ago. So meteorites also provide scientists with a cosmic clock by which to estimate the age of our solar system.

METEOR SHOWERS

On a typical clear night, you can see the occasional meteor blazing across the heavens. But meteors also appear in groups at more or less regular intervals. These showers may consist of no more than five meteors in an hour, but may reach as many as 75. On rare, fantastic occasions, the sky may be lit by thousands of meteors per hour. For example, some 35,000 or so meteors fell in one hour during the Leonid meteor shower of November 1833. And before dawn on November 18, 2001, astronomers recorded the best Leonid shower in 35 years, counting as many as 8,000 meteors per hour.

It seems more than coincidence that the timing of meteor showers directly corresponds to the known orbits of certain comets. Astronomers conclude that the showers come from a stream of debris through which Earth passes as a comet shoots by.

Spectacular Impacts

While meteor showers dazzle, meteorite falls can pack a wallop. Many scientists believe that, in 1908, a meteorite exploded over Siberia, Russia, flattening a wide area of forest. Then, in the late 1940s, there were two spectacular meteorite falls. On the morning of February 12, 1947, a solid metallic meteorite fell and shattered as a "shower of iron" in the Ussuri taiga, also in Russia. The pieces created more than 120 large craters. On February 18, 1948, a stony meteorite disintegrated into fragments over Kansas and Nebraska. Its main mass, now known as the Furnas County stone, weighs more than a ton. Before it struck the atmosphere, it probably carried a mass of more than 11 tons.

A few other meteorites come close to the size of the meteorites in the Ussuri and Furnas County incidents. They include a huge, iron-rich meteorite of perhaps 77 tons near Hoba, Namibia, and a 33-ton iron meteorite brought back from Greenland by the American explorer Robert Peary.

Shortly after midnight on February 8, 1969, a 30-ton meteor broke up over the town of Pueblito de Allende in northern Mexico. Thousands of fragments rained out

A huge meteor striking the ground can leave an enormous crater. One such crater, the Canyon Diablo crater in Arizona, also called the Barringer Crater, resulted from a meteor impact more than 50,000 years ago.

American Museum of Natural History

Workers needed a crane to move the 33-ton Anaghitto meteorite into New York's American Museum of Natural History. The meteorite fell in Greenland; had it fallen in a populated area, the meteorite would have caused great damage.

of the sky, the largest weighing nearly 5 tons (4.5 metric tons).

On August 10, 1972, a 54-yard (49-meter)-wide meteor weighing 1 million tons skipped across Earth's atmosphere as a fireball and sped back into space. Had it struck Earth, it would have exploded with the force of an atomic bomb!

Scientists today can spot meteors with radar and estimate how many bombard our planet. Some figure that 110 tons (100 metric tons) of meteorites reach Earth every day. Most of these bodies are too small to see—so tiny that they can pass through the atmosphere without vaporizing. Eventually these particles drift down to the surface, virtually unaltered.

Meteors that actually flash across the night sky range from the size of a sand grain to that of a peanut shell. Visiting less frequently are the larger meteorites, weighing 10 pounds (4.5 kilograms) or more. These don't completely burn up during their atmospheric travel, so that small but recog-

nizable portions reach Earth's surface, occasionally forming meteorite craters.

Statistically speaking, a meteor will probably hit someone in North America once every 180 years. The only such documented case occurred on November 30, 1954, in Sylacauga, Alabama. A 13-pound (6-kilogram) meteorite crashed through the roof of a house and struck Mrs. Hewlett Hodges in her bedroom. She was bruised, but not seriously injured.

A recent "close encounter" with a meteorite occurred on February 18, 1997, when a 0.75-pound (340-gram) stone smashed through the trunk of a car in Neagari, Japan. It had been seen minutes earlier as a bright fireball over the Sea of Japan. Fortunately, no one was injured.

WHAT'S IN A METEORITE?

Meteorite composition generally falls into one of the three following groups: (1) irons, or *siderites*; (2) stones, or *aerolites*; and (3) stony irons, or *siderolites*.

Meteorites are composed of the same elements contained in the solid portion of Earth, but in different relative abundance. Whereas oxygen (49.4 percent), silicon (25.8 percent), aluminum (7.5 percent), and iron (4.7 percent) make up almost 90 percent (by weight) of Earth's crust, these elements show up in differing amounts in the three classes of meteorites.

Irons, or siderites, are about 91 percent iron and 8.5 percent nickel. They also contain cobalt, phosphorus, and minute quantities of other elements. Stones, or aerolites, contain, on the average, 41 percent oxygen, 21 percent silicon, 15.5 percent iron, 14.3 percent magnesium, and smaller percentages of other elements. The aerolites are much less dense than the siderites and break more easily. Consequently, they shatter on their way through the atmosphere and rain down in widely scattered showers of small masses, only a few of which are recovered. People see aerolite falls about 10 times more frequently than siderite meteorites.

Stony irons, or siderolites, show characteristics of both the iron and the stony meteorites. Much less common in collections than either siderites or aerolites, stony irons remain objects of mystery.

What Prizes Inside?

It was once thought that meteorites carry living spores and thus propagate life in different parts of the universe. Today's experts no longer hold this theory. But scientists have found the chemical building blocks of life—amino acids and other organic compounds—in meteorite samples. Over a long period of time, organic compounds could have formed in space, where the elements carbon, hydrogen, nitrogen, and oxygen are known to exist.

Within some meteorites are microscopic "pieces" of other stars, which mixed with meteors when the solar system originally formed. Meteor researchers can recognize these interstellar grains because they contain carbon, nitrogen, and possibly other elements in odd combinations of atomic forms, or isotopes. These combinations are different from those found in the solar system. Supernova explosions could have distributed some of these grains throughout the cosmos. This suggests that the radioactive debris from a nearby exploding star may have "seeded" our very early solar system. Researchers have also found microscopic diamonds within meteorite dust.

PIECES OF PLANETS?

Antarctica is the meteorite continent. There, scientists have found nearly 10,000 meteorites preserved under the ice. A few of these samples appear to be pieces of the planet Mars. Unlike most meteorites, these pieces appear to have once been molten rock that solidified 1.3 billion years ago. The Mars meteorites also have different isotopes than do those found in most other meteorites. The crystalline structure of the Mars meteorites indicates that they underwent a severe compression and shock, as if they'd been smashed with a mighty sledgehammer.

With all this evidence, scientists think that a 7.5-mile (12-kilometer)-wide asteroid crashed into Mars about 200 million years ago. Some of the debris was blasted into space, and, after no more than about 10 million years, a small fraction of that shrapnel fell to Earth. The Martian meteorites contain organic compounds and, some scientists think, evidence of microfossils.

Scientists have also found golf-ball-size meteorites that evidently came from the Moon, no doubt through similar cosmic collisions. These meteorites match exactly the chemical signature of Moon rock samples brought back to Earth by astronauts during the Apollo missions of the late 1960s and early 1970s.

© Roger Ressmeyer

The presence of the element iridium in certain dinosaur deposits has promted Walter Alvarez (at right in photo) and his son Luis to speculate that a giant, iridium-rich meteorite collided with Earth, causing the extinction of dinosaurs and other prehistoric species.

Craters as Calling Cards

A truly gigantic meteorite would probably be virtually destroyed upon striking the Earth's surface. That's because it would be too heavy to slow down as it tore through our atmosphere. Experiments have shown that when a projectile hits a target at high speeds, the projectile and a considerable part of the target are simply blown up, and an explosion crater is formed. Although such a crater would be relatively shallow, its volume would be surprisingly large compared to the size of the projectile that created it.

If a large enough meteorite were to hit Earth, both the meteorite and the chunk of Earth it struck would vaporize almost immediately. The resulting explosion would carve out an enormous crater.

Earth bears scars from at least 130 such impacts. More and more ancient, buried craters are turning up as scientists learn how to recognize them. The best-preserved evidence of such an explosive impact is the Barringer Crater, near Winslow, Arizona. The crater has a circumference of nearly 3 miles (5 kilometers) and is nearly 328 yards

(300 meters) deep. The meteorite that blew out this vast hole had a mass estimated at between 2 million and 8 million tons (1.8 million and 7.2 million metric tons). Evidence indicates that this huge meteorite collided with Earth 50,000 years ago.

In 1908 a mysterious, atom-bomb-type explosion devastated 193 square miles (311 square kilometers) of forest in Siberia. Because there is no large impact crater from the event, the destruction may not have been due to a monster meteor, but perhaps a small comet or asteroid that exploded in the atmosphere.

Death of the Dinosaurs

The dinosaurs dominated Earth for 250 million years. Yet they mysteriously vanished 65 million years ago. A number of competing theories try to explain what happened. One possibility is that a 1-mile (1.6-kilometer)-wide meteorite hit Earth. Such an impact would have destroyed everything within hundreds of miles. More important, the dust raised by the explosion could have severely altered Earth's climate, devastating plant life. Such a disruption in the food chain would have been particularly lethal to larger animals, like dinosaurs.

There is evidence for this catastrophe in the geologic record. About 65 million years ago, a layer of iridium, an element rare on Earth but common in meteors and asteroids, was deposited over the entire world. At the same time, a layer of soot fell, possibly from forest fires. Grains of shocked quartz, the best evidence for a tremendous crash, have also been found at this same geologic layer.

Such an impact should have left behind a huge crater at least 93 miles (150 kilometers) across. But where is it? Experts believe they have found at least three craters dating back 65 million years: a 111-mile (180-kilometer)-diameter ring buried under Mexico's Yucatán Peninsula, a 62-mile (100-kilometer)-diameter multiring impact basin in Siberia, and a 22-mile (35-kilometer) crater near Mason, Iowa. Perhaps all three craters were made simultaneously by pieces of an asteroid or comet that broke apart before hitting Earth.

If a giant meteorite killed the dinosaurs, their extinction likely resulted from the debris hurled into the atmosphere by the force of the impact, debris that ultimately shielded Earth from sunlight.

© Don Davis

A solar eclipse occurs when the Moon, passing between the Earth and the Sun, briefly blocks the Sun's rays. Scientists can then study the solar atmosphere, the only part of the Sun visible during totality.

ECLIPSES

by Dennis L. Mammana

An eclipse of the Sun or Moon is truly an awe-inspiring spectacle. The word "eclipse" comes from the Greek word *ekleipsis*, meaning "forsaking" or "abandonment," indicating how the ancients dreaded this celestial drama. As the Sun or Moon disappeared from view, it seemed indeed to be deserting mankind. Eclipses, like comets, were held to be portents of war, pestilence, the death of princes, or even the end of the world. To this day, certain primitive peoples come to the aid of the Sun or Moon, as it is being eclipsed, with solemn rites and loud entreaties.

We know now that there is a perfectly logical explanation for eclipses—they are caused by the enormous shadows of the Earth and of the Moon. Both of these bodies are opaque. Hence, when they are lit by the Sun, each has a shadow extending out into space, away from the Sun.

The shadow cast by the Earth or Moon has several parts (see *Diagram 1*). There is a region of complete shadow, which is known as the *umbra* (the Latin word for "shadow"). Since both the Earth and the Moon are smaller than the Sun, the umbra of each is conical in shape. It diminishes in diameter as it extends farther out in space until, finally, it comes to a point. No light comes directly from the Sun to any object within the umbra. Surrounding the cone of complete shadow, there is a region of partial shadow, called the *penumbra* (Latin for

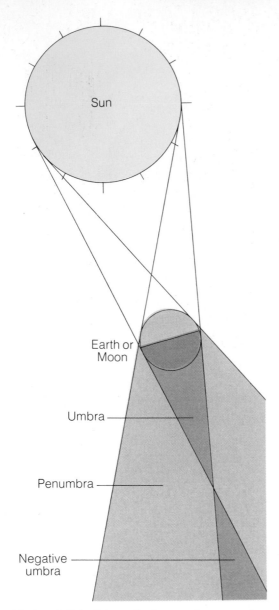

Diagram 1. *Scientists use the terms* umbra, penumbra, *and* negative umbra *to describe the shadows cast by the Earth or by the Moon during an eclipse. The* umbra *is the area of complete shadow, which appears on the Earth as a solar eclipse. The area of partial shadow is called the* penumbra. *The* negative umbra *represents the continuation of the lines that bound the complete shadow.*

LENGTH OF THE SHADOW

It is evident from the diagram that the length of the cone of complete shadow depends on three factors: the diameter of the source of light—the Sun; the diameter of the Earth or Moon; and the distance between the Sun and the Earth or Moon.

It is important to bear in mind that while the diameters of the Sun, Earth, and Moon are constant factors, the distances between the Earth and the Sun and between the Moon and the Sun are variable. For this reason, the umbra of the Earth or of the Moon varies in length. The average length of the Earth's umbra is about 870,000 miles (1,400,000 kilometers); the average length of the Moon's umbra, about 233,000 miles (375,000 kilometers).

When the Earth enters the Moon's shadow, an eclipse of the Sun takes place. A solar eclipse can take place only at the time of new moon, when the Moon is between the Sun and the Earth. A lunar eclipse always takes place at full moon, when the Earth is between the Sun and the Moon (see *Diagram 2*).

There would be an eclipse of the Sun at every new moon, and an eclipse of the Moon at every full moon, if the Moon's orbit were in exactly the same plane as the Earth's orbit around the Sun. However, this is not the case. The Moon's orbit is slightly inclined (about 5 degrees) to that of the Earth (see *Diagram 3*).

The Moon passes through the plane of the Earth's orbit around the Sun twice every month, at points called the *nodes* of the Moon's orbit. Generally, the Moon is at one side or the other of the Earth's orbital plane at new moon or at full moon. If it is not in the plane at new moon, its shadow does not fall upon the Earth, and the Sun is not eclipsed. If the Moon is not in the plane of the Earth's orbit at full moon, it remains outside of the Earth's shadow, and the Moon is not eclipsed. From time to time, the Moon is at full or new moon at about the time when it crosses the plane of the Earth's orbit. When that happens, there is a lunar eclipse at full moon and a solar eclipse at new moon.

"almost a shadow"). Any object within this area receives light from a portion of the Sun. If the lines bounding the conical region of complete shadow are extended outward, as shown in *Diagram 1*, an inverted cone is formed. It is called the *negative umbra* and, as we shall see, it is an important factor in certain eclipses of the Sun.

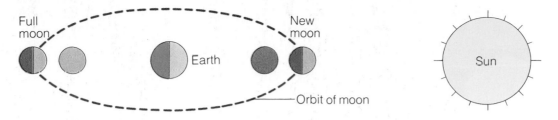

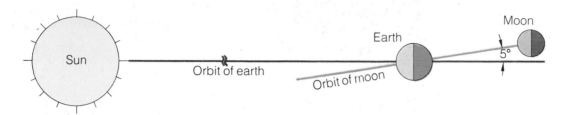

Diagram 2. *Solar eclipses only occur during a new moon, when the Moon is between the Earth and Sun. Lunar eclipses only occur during the full moon, when Earth is between the Sun and Moon.*

Diagram 3. *The plane of the Moon's orbit around the Earth is slightly inclined to the Earth's orbit around the Sun. If the planes were the same, there would be a solar and a lunar eclipse each month.*

ECLIPSES OF THE MOON

For an eclipse of the Moon to take place, then, it must be full and it must be near an orbital node. When the Moon plunges into the cone-shaped area of complete shadow, it is much nearer to the base of the cone than to its tip. The diameter of the cone, where the Moon passes through it, is about two and one-half times the diameter of the Moon.

If the path of the Moon happens to pass through the center of the shadow, the Moon may remain totally eclipsed for about an hour. The shadow may cover part of it for about two hours. A lunar eclipse begins when the Moon enters the penumbra, and ends when it leaves the penumbra. There is little significant darkening, however, until the Moon enters the umbra.

If the path of the Moon takes it near the edge of the umbra shadow, the total phase of its eclipse may last only a few minutes. If the Moon's path is such that only a portion of its disk, and not the whole of it, enters into the conical shadow of the umbra, the eclipse is partial and not total. Sometimes the Moon in its path passes, not through the cone of complete shadow, but through only the penumbra. If this happens, so much light is still received from a portion of the Sun's disk that there will be no marked obscuring of the Moon unless it passes very close to the true shadow. The Moon is usually not altogether lost to view even in the midst of a total eclipse. It shines with a strange, copper-colored glow.

Eclipses of the Moon occur less frequently than solar eclipses. Each year, there are at least two and as many as five solar eclipses. But there are years when there are no lunar eclipses, and only rarely is there more than one. This may seem to run counter to our experience. After all, it seems that more people have seen lunar than solar eclipses. This is because, during a solar eclipse, the Moon's shadow covers only a small part of the Earth's surface. As a result, solar-eclipse enthusiasts may have to travel thousands of miles to stand in the narrow track where the full eclipse is visible. During a lunar eclipse, however, the Earth's shadow covers the entire face of the Moon—so that the eclipse is seen over half the Earth, the half where it is night.

ECLIPSES OF THE SUN

There are three kinds of solar eclipses: *total*, *annular*, and *partial*. We have seen that the average length of the Moon's shadow is about 233,000 miles (375,000 kilometers), and it never extends beyond about 236,000 miles (380,000 kilometers). The average distance of the Earth from the Moon, however, is about 240,000 miles

The Moon gradually moves through the Earth's shadow and reappears (above, left to right), during a total lunar eclipse. Because of light refracted by the Earth's atmosphere, the Moon is never wholly dark, even during totality.

(385,000 kilometers), so that in general the Moon's umbra—its true shadow—is not long enough to reach the Earth. At times, however, the Moon is only about 221,500 miles (356,500 kilometers) from the Earth's surface. The true shadow then falls upon a small part of the Earth's surface, causing a total eclipse of the Sun over an area that never exceeds 168 miles (270 kilometers) in diameter. At other times the Moon may be more than 252,277 miles (406,000 kilometers) from the Earth. If it is then interposed between the Sun and the Earth, its negative umbra will partially obscure a small area of the Earth's surface, causing an annular eclipse of the Sun at that point. In an annular eclipse, the Sun's rim appears as a "ring" of light around the dark Moon. (*Annulus* means "ring" in Latin.)

Around the area where there is a total eclipse or an annular eclipse of the Sun, there is always a much larger area where there is a partial eclipse. This area is in the Moon's penumbra. It generally extends for more than 1,865 miles (3,000 kilometers) of the Earth's surface on each side of the path where the total eclipse can be seen. Sometimes the area of partial eclipse extends nearly 3,100 miles (5,000 kilometers) on each side of the path of totality.

The Moon's shadow passes along this path at great speed—about 1,000 miles (1,700 kilometers) an hour. The longest period of total eclipse, under the most favorable conditions, is about 7.5 minutes.

Few spectacles in the heavens are as startling as a solar eclipse. The approach of a total solar eclipse is particularly impressive and, to some persons, alarming. The sky darkens ominously; birds fly to shelter. Finally the dark shadow of the Moon, like a vast thundercloud, advances with awe-inspiring rapidity from the western horizon and covers the land. Usually, just before the last rays of the Sun are obscured, one can see swiftly moving bands of light and shade, which are probably due to uneven refraction in the atmosphere. Then the day becomes like an eerie night.

As the eclipse approaches totality, the Sun is seen as a very narrow crescent of brilliant light. The crescent then becomes a curved line, and finally breaks off into irregular beads of light known as Baily's beads. The beads are caused by irregularities in the surface of the Moon.

But even at totality, the atmosphere that surrounds the Sun extends so far out in space that it is never completely covered by the Moon. We see the eclipsed Sun surrounded by a beautiful glow. While observing a solar eclipse, remember that the eyes must at all times be protected from the direct rays of the Sun!

SUMMER ECLIPSE OF 1991

One of the most spectacular solar eclipses on record occurred on July 11, 1991. On that day the Moon's 150-mile-(241-kilometer)-wide shadow drifted eastward from Hawaii, across the Pacific Ocean, across Baja California and mainland Mexico, and into Central and South America, before trailing back into space. Astronomers were able to make unprecedented observations of this eclipse from one of the most celebrated observatories—

that on Mauna Kea in Hawaii. An international crew of astronomers trained seven of Mauna Kea's 10 large telescopes on the Sun's corona.

During its trek across the Earth's surface, the Moon's shadow also passed over some of the most popular tourist spots in the world and five Latin American capitals. According to estimates, some 50 million "eclipto-philes" drove, sailed, flew, or hitchhiked to witness this cosmic event. In Mexico City alone (where the total eclipse lasted nearly seven minutes, longer than any until the year 2132), some 17 million people were swept into the eerie darkness of the Moon's shadow—more than had ever before witnessed a single, total solar eclipse in recorded history.

PREDICTING ECLIPSES

Inasmuch as eclipses of both the Sun and the Moon depend upon the regular movements of the Sun, Earth, and Moon, they can be calculated with great accuracy. In the 1880s, for example, Austrian astronomer Theodor Oppolzer published a book called the *Canon of Eclipses*, in which he gave a table of 8,000 solar eclipses and 5,200 lunar eclipses taking place between 1207 B.C. and A.D. 2162. His *Canon* has now been extended to A.D. 2510 and revised with the aid of computers. In the case of solar eclipses, he indicated the areas of the Earth from which the eclipses would be visible.

Our knowledge of when eclipses occurred in the past helps modern historians pinpoint the exact time of a surprising number of important events. Ancient writers who associated eclipses with battles, royal births or deaths, and other occurrences inadvertently provided us with a foolproof method of assigning precise dates (often down to the hour and minute) of many significant occasions.

SERIES OF ECLIPSES

The interval between an eclipse of the Sun or Moon and the next one in a given series is called a *saros*. Each saros is 18

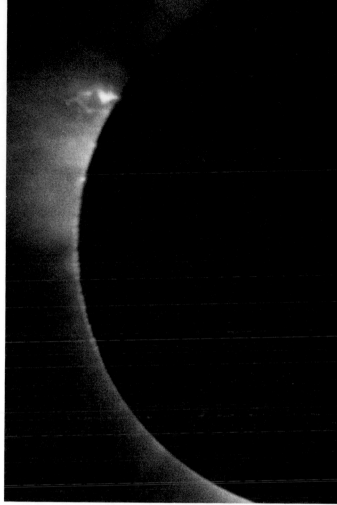

© Alberto Levy

During totality, solar prominences become visible, extending like tongues from the obscured Sun. Prominences dramatically appeared during the sensational total solar eclipse of July 1991 (above).

years and 11⅓ days long (or 18 years and 10⅓ days long if there are five leap years instead of four in a saros). While a given series of solar eclipses may run through 70 saroses and last for 1,250 years, there are only 48 or 49 saroses in the average series of lunar eclipses. A given series of lunar eclipses lasts somewhat under 900 years.

The first eclipse in a series of solar eclipses is partial, the Moon encroaching but slightly on the Sun's disk. At the next eclipse, the Moon obscures a somewhat larger area of the Sun. Each subsequent eclipse becomes more extensive, until there is an annular or total eclipse. Then there follows a succession of partial eclipses, each one obscuring a smaller area of the Sun's disk than the one before.

OPPORTUNITY FOR STUDY

Total solar eclipses offer astronomers exceptional opportunities to study the atmosphere of the Sun; the distribution of its material; the chromosphere, or Sun's inner layer; and the splendor of the corona, or outer layer. Furthermore, only at the time of total eclipse can astronomers photograph celestial objects close to the Sun.

Unfortunately, few total eclipses of the Sun take place in areas where well-equipped astronomical observatories are located—the eclipse of July 1991 being a notable exception. Astronomers must generally undertake expensive expeditions and erect temporary research camps to install costly scientific instruments within the narrow band of shadow where the eclipse can be viewed—usually for a matter of just a few minutes.

The simplest observations made during a total eclipse of the Sun are the precise moments of each "contact." The first contact takes place when the Moon first encroaches on the Sun's disk. In the second contact, the Sun disappears behind the Moon, and the solar corona becomes visible. In the third the Sun's rim is seen again. In the fourth the Moon passes completely off the Sun's disk. If the times of contact are observed at widely separated stations along the path of the eclipse, scientists get detailed information about the Moon's position and motion.

In the period of total eclipse, observers can search for possible undiscovered planets within the orbit of Mercury, the planet closest to the Sun. Thus far, no new planet within the orbit of Mercury has been discovered. The search for hitherto-unknown comets during solar eclipses has been a more rewarding exercise. A number of new comets have been tracked at perihelion—the part of their orbit where they pass closest to the Sun.

On his fourth voyage to the New World, Columbus used his foreknowledge of a lunar eclipse to avoid a conflict with Indians. Modern astronomers have pinpointed the eclipse to February 19, 1504, shortly after 6 P.M.

The New York Public Library Picture Collection

The Milky Way (above, in an artist's conception) is a giant spiral of about 150 billion stars that includes our Sun. Its true shape, size, and nature were not discovered by astronomers until the 20th century.

THE MILKY WAY

by Dennis L. Mammana

The Milky Way, the part of our galaxy visible to the naked eye, is one of the most striking sights in the night skies. It is too faint to be seen in bright moonlight or amid the myriad lights of our large cities, but on moonless nights in the country, the outlines of its cloudy track of light across the heavens are easily discernible. If viewed through a powerful telescope, the Milky Way is unveiled as the combined light of vast numbers of stars; none of these stars can be made out individually without the aid of a telescope.

We know today that when we look at the Milky Way, we are looking into the heart of a vast system of stars that includes our Sun—lying as it does in the system's outer suburbs. In the past, however, the Milky Way was a celestial puzzle. Many explanations were provided in Greek and Roman mythology. Some writers called it the highway of the gods, leading to their abode on Mount Olympus. Others held that it sprang from the ears of corn dropped by the goddess Isis as she fled from a pursuer. Still others believed that the Milky Way marked the original course of the sun god as he sped across the skies in his chariot.

In medieval times, pilgrims associated the Milky Way with their journeys to various sanctuaries. In Germany, for example, it became known as Jakobsstrasse, or James' Road, leading to the shrine of St. James at what is now Santiago de Compos-

Ronald Royer, courtesy of ASTRONOMY magazine

In the southern hemisphere of the Milky Way lies a strikingly large, dark area called the Coalsack. This inky black void, really a mass of obscuring matter, is surrounded by bright stars.

tela, in Spain. In England, it was called the Walsingham Way. It was associated with the pilgrimages to the famous shrine of Walsingham Abbey. The pilgrims of those days did not seriously believe that the Milky Way had anything to do with their travels. Rather, they saw it lying overhead, a misty path in the heavens. Their belief in the universal kinship of all things caused them to find comfort in its presence.

The best time to view the Milky Way is on an autumn or winter evening. It is then highest in the heavens, and therefore its light is least affected by our atmosphere. It is seen to stretch like a vast, ragged semicircle over the skies of the Northern or the Southern Hemisphere. Actually, it traces a rough circle that continues through both hemispheres.

IRREGULAR SHAPE

The path traced by the Milky Way is full of irregularities. It is by no means a simple stream of stars. Its average width is about 20 degrees, but it varies considerably, both in width and in brightness. Even with the naked eye, one can make out something of its irregular detail when the atmosphere is unusually clear and the Moon is new. When viewed under such conditions through a good telescope, the Milky Way is a truly exciting spectacle.

Its general effect has been likened to that of an old, gnarled tree trunk, marked here and there with prominent knots. As details become clearer in a telescopic view, we see that at one point the Milky Way may consist of separate stars scattered irregularly upon a dark background. Elsewhere, there are numerous gorgeous star clusters. In many places the track is engulfed in a nebulous blur in which a great many stars are embedded.

A powerful telescope reveals a great many dark bands in the Milky Way. Sometimes these dark bands are parallel; sometimes they radiate like spokes from a common hub; sometimes they are lined with bright stars. In certain places, they are quite black, as if utterly void of content. In others, they are slightly luminous, as if powdered with small stars.

THE COALSACK AND OTHER APPARENT VOIDS

Large, dark areas occur here and there. The most famous of these is the so-called Coalsack, which is near the constellation called the Southern Cross, visible in the Southern Hemisphere. Just before the Milky Way divides into two branches in the southern constellation Centaurus, it broadens. It becomes studded with a collection of brilliant stars, making it one of the most resplendent areas in its whole course. Right in the center of this host of bright stars, near the four stars that form the Southern Cross, is the inky black cavern known as the Coalsack.

The Coalsack is by no means unique. There are many similar black areas in the Milky Way, though they are generally less clearly defined and less striking in appearance. American astronomer Edward E. Barnard described one of these, in the constellation Sagittarius, as "a most remarkable, small, inky-black hole in a crowded part of the Milky Way, about two minutes in diameter, slightly triangular, with a bright orange star on its north northwesterly border, and a beautiful little star cluster following."

STUDYING THE SYSTEM

The starry band seen extending across the heavens is really part of our own galaxy, or system of stars. Every star that can be seen with the naked eye belongs to this vast system, including our Sun and the other members of our solar system.

An infrared image of the Milky Way produced by NASA's Cosmic Background Explorer (COBE), which collects data about the origin of the universe.

NASA

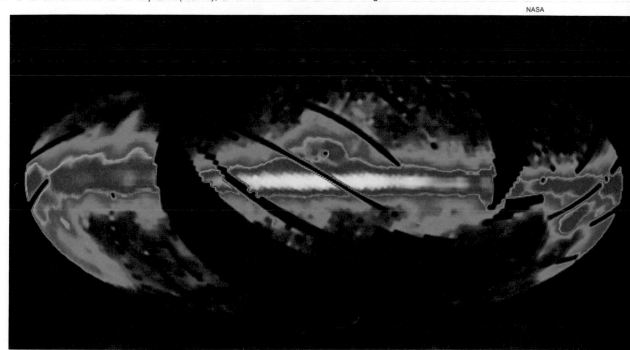

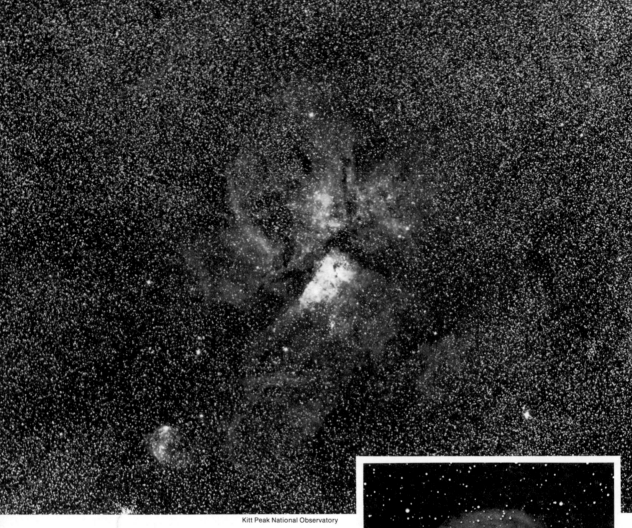

The apparent luminosity of many nebulas, such as the Eta Carinae nebula (above), is actually the reflection of light from neighboring stars. Planetary nebulas, like the Dumbbell nebula in Vulpecula (right), are gaseous envelopes surrounding hot stars.

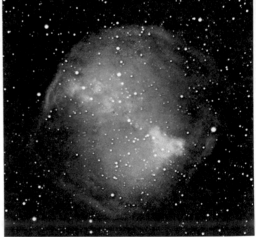

Various methods have been used to solve the mystery of its structure. The eighteenth-century German-English astronomer William Herschel decided to attack the problem by making a survey of the stars. He called his method "star gauging." It consisted of counting all the stars visible in a reflecting telescope that had an 18-inch (45-centimeter) mirror and a field 15 inches (38 centimeters) in diameter.

Dutch astronomer J. C. Kapteyn developed an even more elaborate method for determining the distribution of stars in the heavens. He selected 206 areas distributed uniformly over the whole sky, and he urged astronomers to determine the apparent magnitudes and other data for all the stars in these regions. A number of the great observatories of the world took part in the cooperative venture suggested by Kapteyn. Two outstanding contributions to the program are the Mount Wilson Catalog and the Bergedorfer Spectral-Durchmusterung

(Bergedorfer Spectral Catalog). The latter gives not only the apparent magnitudes of the stars, but also the spectral classes of the stars.

Another way of determining the dimensions and structure of our galaxy is to observe the positions and distances of some of its members, such as the Cepheid variables. We can find the approximate distances of these star groups from the Earth if we know their apparent magnitudes.

The chief difficulty in determining the extent and structure of our galactic system is that the Earth is so deeply embedded in it that a comprehensive idea of the system is impossible to obtain through mere observation. It is almost as if we were required to make a map of New York City, for example, from a vantage point somewhere in a crowded section of the Bronx. However, we do have a clear overall view of a number of other galaxies, such as the magnificent spiral galaxy in Andromeda (a galaxy called Messier 31) and the Whirlpool in Canes Venatici (Messier 51). Our knowledge of these other galaxies, and radio-telescope and infrared astronomy, enable us to draw a number of plausible conclusions about our own galaxy.

A Spiral Galaxy

An analysis of our galactic system by the methods described above indicates that most of the stars it contains are crowded into a sort of wheel with a pronounced hub. When viewed edge on, the wheel and hub look something like the illustration on page 188. Of course, since the Sun, our own star, is located within the wheel, we cannot see the wheel edge on. We infer its shape from viewing other galaxies whose form we can make out and think are similar. Our Sun does not lie anywhere near the center, or hub, of the wheel. It is at a distance of about three-quarters of the way from the center to the outer rim. The wheel as a whole is inclined at an angle of 62 degrees to the plane of the celestial equator.

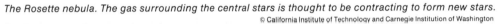

The Rosette nebula. The gas surrounding the central stars is thought to be contracting to form new stars.

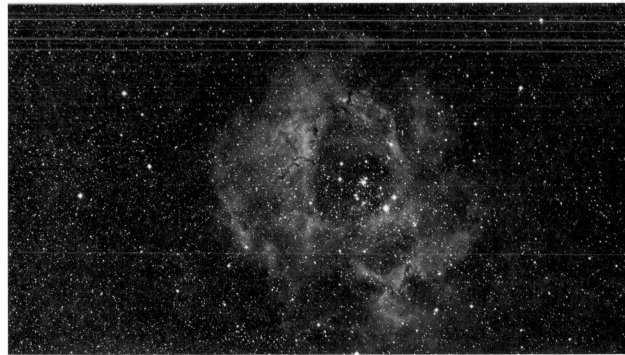

© California Institute of Technology and Carnegie Institution of Washington

The dust near the Pleiades, or "Seven Sisters," star cluster scatters starlight to form nebulas around each of the stars.

The stars that make up the wheel show a distinct spiral pattern. Astronomers therefore classify our galaxy as a spiral galaxy. The spiral arms spring from a nucleus or core at the center of the galactic system. In the spirals are found individual bright stars, star clusters, bright nebulas, and a great deal of obscuring matter. This obscuring matter is made up of dust particles and various gases. The general haze it causes has been detected through the dimming and reddening effects that it produces.

Dark Nebulas

Astronomers have given the name "dark nebulas" to the masses of obscuring matter that have no nearby stars to illuminate them. Some of these dark masses can be seen quite clearly with the naked eye, and have been known to astronomers for a long time. The earlier astronomers thought of them as gaps in the starry firmament. The dark nebulas, or masses of obscuring matter, cut off our view of vast numbers of stars that lie beyond them. To obtain an idea of the form of the galactic system, certain observers have counted the stars in various parts of the sky, and have then made allowances for the obscuring matter and estimated the form of the galaxy.

Obscuring matter is responsible for the large, dark areas such as the Coalsack. It was once thought to be an optical illusion, but this hypothesis never seemed too convincing, since its huge size, its utter darkness, and the similar brightness of the starry edge surrounding it could never be explained. The existence of obscuring matter, now proved, offers a simple explanation of what was once a mystery.

STAR CLUSTERS

The clouds and wisps of illuminated nebulosity mentioned earlier are the bright nebulas, whose atoms have either been excited by the hot stars in the vicinity or reflect the light of nearby stars. It is interesting to note that the most luminous stars are all to be found in the wheel of our galaxy. The so-called galactic clusters are also confined to this area. They are sometimes called "open clusters." They consist of many groups of hot stars, each group consisting of several hundred stars. These stars excite the atoms of dust or gases in their vicinity; hence, they are embedded in bright nebulas. Among the best known of the galactic clusters are the Pleiades, the Hyades, Praesepe (also called the Beehive cluster), and Coma Berenices.

The globular clusters are distributed through a roughly spherical region bisected by the plane of the galaxy. American astronomer Harlow Shapley held that the main aggregation of stars in the galactic system is arranged in the form of a wheel and that this is enclosed in a roughly globular haze of stars—globular clusters and others. Globular clusters differ in many respects from the galactic clusters. For one thing, each one contains hundreds of thousands of stars, or perhaps even millions, compactly and symmetrically grouped. They are comparatively free of gas or dust.

GALACTIC CORE

The core or nucleus of the galactic system is so heavily obscured by clouds of dust and gas that it was not until 1983, when the InfraRed Astronomical Satellite (IRAS) was launched, that astronomers were able to obtain a comprehensive view of its structure. They have since begun to map the heavy concentration of stars in this area. It has been estimated that these stars account for something approaching one-half of the total mass of our galactic system.

Measurements of radio waves, infrared, gamma rays, and X rays over several decades indicate that the core of our galaxy contains a black hole, which scientists have designated Sagittarius A.

In 2000, astronomers, using the telescopes at the giant Keck Observatory in Hawaii, watched stars speed up as they revolved about the galactic core. They were able to locate the exact position of the galactic core—right where Sagittarius A is located—and calculate the black hole's mass to be more than that of 2.6 million Suns.

THE ROTATION OF OUR GALAXY

The entire galactic system is rotating around an axis, which is at right angles to the wheel of stars. Outside the dense nucleus of the galaxy, the speed of rotation decreases, and the period increases with greater distance from the center. Corresponding differences in period and speed can also be noted in the planets that revolve

Our Milky Way galaxy is a member of what astronomers call the Local Group. We now recognize 40 member galaxies of this group spread over a volume nearly 10 million light-years in diameter.

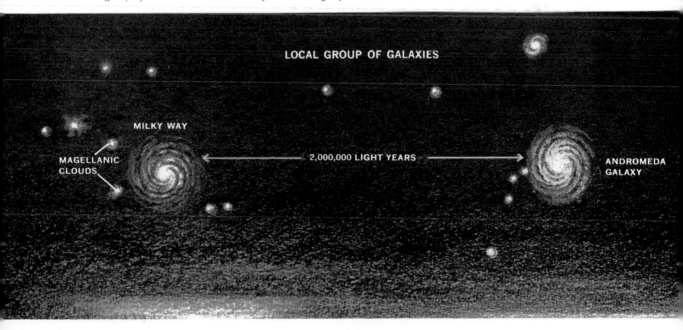

LOCAL GROUP OF GALAXIES

MILKY WAY

MAGELLANIC CLOUDS

2,000,000 LIGHT YEARS

ANDROMEDA GALAXY

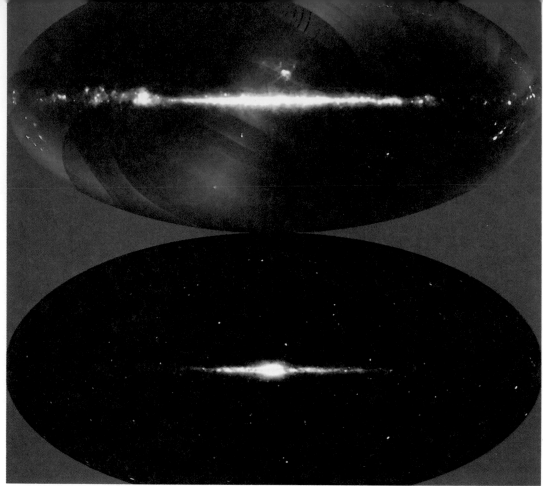

NASA

Our galaxy, when viewed on edge, appears like a wheel and hub, with the Sun lying about 28,000 light-years from the hub (below). NASA's COBE satellite collected data from both the far-infrared wavelengths of our galaxy, capturing radiation from cold dust (top), and from the near-infrared wavelengths (above), showing radiation from the stars. Scientists believe that a black hole may exist at the center of our galaxy.

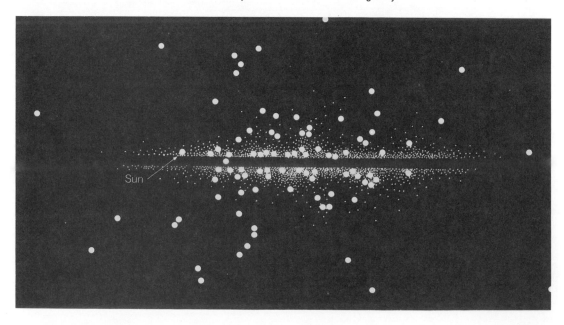

Sun

about the center of our solar system—that is, the Sun. The nearer a planet is to the Sun, the faster it revolves around it, and the shorter the period of revolution. For example, in the case of Mercury, the planet nearest the Sun, the period is only 88 days, compared with the period of 248.43 years of the planet Pluto, whose orbit is farthest from the Sun.

Our solar system orbits the Milky Way's galactic center every 220 million years, which astronomers call one "cosmic year." Obviously, the stars closer to the galactic core travel around its center more rapidly than the Sun does, and eventually overtake and pass it. On the other hand, the stars between the Sun and the outer rim of the wheel revolve around the center of the galactic system more slowly than the Sun does. As a result, they lag farther and farther behind our star in their voyaging.

THE DIMENSIONS OF OUR GALAXY

The foregoing discussion has presented general concepts of the form of our galaxy. Astronomers have also sought to discover its dimensions in space. Recent research based on the study of special types of variable stars (the Cepheid variables) and on the visual, photographic, and spectrographic analysis of globular clusters has revealed how extraordinarily great these dimensions are. This is natural enough when we consider that our own solar system, vast and complex though it is, is an infinitesimally small part of the galactic system. The estimates of the dimensions of our galaxy vary considerably, but even the smallest are almost overpowering when we seek to grasp their significance.

According to one of the more conservative estimates, made by American astronomer Heber D. Curtis, a pulse of light, starting from one edge of the galactic system and traveling at the speed of more than 186,282 miles (299,792 kilometers) per second, would take from 20,000 to 30,000 years to reach the other edge. According to Harlow Shapley, Curtis' estimate, staggering though it may seem to us, is far too modest. To accept Shapley's figures, we must tax our imagination still further. He maintains that it would take about 100,000 years for a pulse of light to travel from one confine of the galaxy to the other. In other words, the diameter of the galactic disk is approximately 100,000 light-years.

In the mid-1970s, astronomers studying the rotational speed of the Milky Way and its speed toward the Great Andromeda Galaxy, some 2 million light-years away, came to a startling conclusion. To account for the motions they observed, the Milky Way must be significantly larger and more massive than they had believed—perhaps as much as five to 10 times greater. But where was all this material? Scientists have speculated that it may consist of "dark matter"—clouds of dark particles, neutrinos, brown dwarfs, unseen planets, even black holes. Astronomers have yet to account for all the suspected missing mass, much less hazard a good guess as to where to look for it.

As remarkably huge as our galaxy is, it is only one of billions of other isolated galactic systems. Each of these "island universes" contains hundreds of billions of stars. The nearest—two irregular galaxies called the Magellanic Clouds—lie at distances of 176,000 and 210,000 light-years, respectively, from Earth, and both orbit the Milky Way galaxy.

THE "EDGE" OF THE UNIVERSE

Whether we shall ever see the "limit" of the universe is extremely doubtful. For if the universe is 12 billion years old, as some scientists believe, our horizon will be limited to a distance of 1 billion light-years from Earth, even if the universe actually extends far beyond that distance. The reason is that the light from galaxies beyond that mark will not have been able to reach us since the beginning of time. The same is true of the radio waves emanating from such galaxies, since light waves and radio waves travel at the same speed—roughly 186,282 miles per second. Such galaxies, therefore, will remain a deep mystery to astronomers, unless some hitherto-unsuspected method of detecting them is discovered at some point in the future.

A star begins life as a dense cloud of gas that condenses and contracts to produce a protostar.

THE STARS

by Charles Beichman

The thousands of millions of stars in the heavens are so far away that, with the exception of our Sun, they are visible only as twinkling points of light. How far away are the stars? What are they made of? What powers them? How old are the stars, and how are they formed? These questions are among the most basic in astronomy. To develop a fundamental understanding of stars, let's first examine a typical star, and the closest one to Earth: our own Sun.

THE SUN AS A STAR

The Sun is a globe of glowing gas. Despite its sharply defined disk, it has no solid surface. Its diameter is about 865,278 miles (1,390,000 kilometers), or 109 times that of Earth. However, the gaseous Sun is less dense than the rocky Earth, and its mass is only 330,000 times as large. The temperature at its surface is about 9,945° F (5,507° C). A new technique called *helioseismology* has enhanced our understanding of the interior of the Sun. Astronomers study the vibrations of the Sun much like geologists, who learn about Earth's depths by measuring the sound waves carried by its rocky interior after an earthquake. A global network of telescopes monitors the Sun around the clock, measuring physical waves roiling across its surface. The intervals between these waves and sets of waves may range from a few minutes to several weeks. The amplitude, or fullness, of these waves gives astronomers much information about the physical conditions deep within the Sun. From such measurements and sophisticated computer models, we now know that the temperature and pressure rise swiftly toward the center of the Sun, reaching values of about 25,000,000° F (14,000,000° C) and 100 billion atmospheres, respectively.

Even though the Sun is millions of miles away, we have also been able to determine its composition using a technique called *spectroscopy*. Every element emits or absorbs specific colors of light; these patterns can be used as fingerprints to identify an element, to determine its abundance, and to determine the temperature and pressure in its surroundings. By measuring the Sun's spectrum, we have learned that the lightest element, hydrogen, is by far the most common, accounting for more than 92 percent of its atoms. The second most abundant element in the Sun, and in the universe as a whole, is the lighter-than-air gas helium. It makes up about 8 percent of the Sun. Roughly speaking, the heavier the element, the less of it exists in the Sun. Certain elements particularly common on Earth—such as carbon, nitrogen, and oxygen—total less than 0.1 percent of the Sun's material.

The basic properties of the Sun are common among all stars. Although all other stars are so distant as to appear only as points of light, astronomers have gained a surprising amount of information about these heavenly bodies by careful observation and the application of physical laws.

DISTANCE TO THE STARS

The apparent brightness of stars belies their true nature. A star may appear bright because it is nearby, or because it is intrinsically luminous. It is impossible to determine the intrinsic brightness of a star unless we also know how far away it is.

Astronomers measure the distances to the closest stars using the same principles of triangulation that a surveyor might use. Suppose we observe a star on a given date and again six months later, when the Earth is on the opposite side of its orbit. The position of the star will be displaced slightly against the background of more-distant stars. The shift in the star's position, called its *parallax*, can be combined with the size of the Earth's orbit to yield the distance to the star.

Unfortunately, even the closest stars are very far away, so that the angles used to calculate their distances are small, a second of arc (1/3600 of a degree) or less. Only the distances to the closest few hundred stars have been determined using the parallax method. The distances to stars farther away must be inferred indirectly.

Once the distance of a star is known, we can calculate its absolute brightness. With all stars compared on a common scale, we see that our Sun is quite ordinary. Some stars are intrinsically a million times brighter; others are a thousand times fainter. The brighter stars are quite rare, while fainter stars are very common and outnumber those like our Sun.

TEMPERATURE, SIZE, AND MASS

The laws of radiation, familiar to blacksmiths and physicists alike, permit us to calculate the temperature and size of a star. Stars, like horseshoes being forged, first glow red-hot, then yellow-hot, then blue-hot, and finally white-hot, as their temperatures increase. Thus, a star's color reveals its temperature. Measurement of the star's temperature and absolute bright-

The shift in a star's position in relation to Earth, known as its parallax, is used to calculate the star's distance.

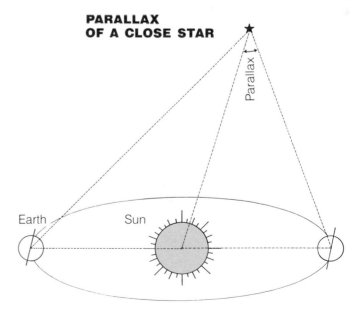

PARALLAX OF A CLOSE STAR

Parallax

Earth   Sun

TEMPERATURES AND DIMENSIONS OF TYPICAL STARS

	STAR	SURFACE TEMPERATURE IN DEGREES C	RADIUS IN SUNS	MASS IN SUNS	DENSITY IN SUNS	ABSOLUTE MAGNITUDE
SUPER-GIANTS	Beta Lyrae	12,000	19.2	9.7	.0014	0.1 ?
	Rigel	11,300	78	20?	.00004	− 7.0
	Deneb	10,200	96	20?	.00002	− 7.0
	Gamma Cygni	4,100	67	20?	.00007	− 5.0
	Betelgeuse	2,700	1000	10?	.0000005	− 5.8
	Antares	2,900	776	20?	.00000004	− 4.0
GIANTS	Capella	4,800	13	2.1	.00096	0.3
	Arcturus	3,800	35	8	.00018	− 0.1 ?
	Aldebaran	2,700	87	4	.000006	− 0.3
	Beta Pegasi	2,000	40	9	.00014	− 1.4
MAIN SEQUENCE STARS	Hadar	21,000	22	25	.0023	− 5.1
	MU-1 Scorpii	20,000	5.2	14.0	.1000	− 5.1
	Sirius A	10,200	1.9	2.3	.335	1.2
	Altair	7,300	1.6	1.7	.415	2.4
	Procyon A	6,800	2.6	1.8	.102	2.1
	Sun	5,900	1.0	1.0	1.0	4.86
	61 Cygni A	2,600	0.7	0.58	1.69	7.65
	Krueger 60	2,800	0.35	0.27	6.30	11.9
	Barnard's Star	2,700	0.15	0.18?	53.3	13.2
WHITE DWARFS	Sirius B	5,000?	0.022	0.99	90,000	11.4
	40 Eridani B	5,000?	0.018	0.41	71,000	11.2
	Van Maanen's Star	5,000?	0.007	0.14?	47,000	14.2

ness establishes its surface area and its diameter. The table above compares the size and other properties of the Sun relative to other stars.

The mass of a star can be determined only by the gravitational effects of one star on another. Since about half of all stars are found in systems where two or more stars orbit one another, we have been able to estimate the masses of many hundreds of stars. The most luminous stars are typically the most massive.

TYPES OF STARS

The properties of stars fall into four distinct categories, or sequences. Most of the stars in the neighborhood of our Sun belong to the *main sequence*, which is a regular series that runs from hot, bright stars down through cool, faint ones. There are many more stars at the faint end of this sequence than at the bright end. For every luminous, massive star, there are millions of faint ones.

Red giants form another distinct group of stars that are cooler, but much larger in radius, than the main-sequence stars. The *supergiants* are even larger and more luminous than giant stars, but are very rare. In contrast, stars called *white dwarfs* are so faint that they are extremely difficult to find, even though they may be more common than stars like our Sun.

SOURCES OF STELLAR ENERGY

The Sun radiates energy at the rate of 3.8×10^{23} kilowatts. Ordinary processes of combustion or gravitational contraction cannot account for the continuous release of so much energy over the 4.6 billion years that the Sun has been shining. Scientists have learned, however, that the energy that streams out of the Sun is due to the fusion of hydrogen atoms into helium atoms.

A variety of similar nuclear reactions play a role in the energy production in stars. While some stars have nuclear reactions involving heavier elements such as

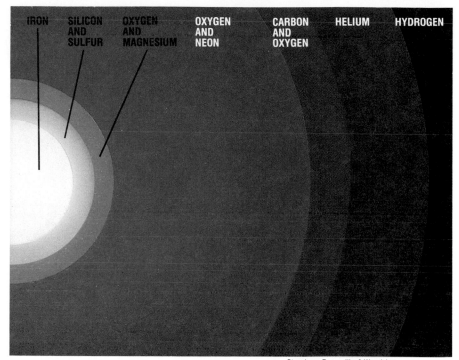

IRON SILICON AND SULFUR OXYGEN AND MAGNESIUM OXYGEN AND NEON CARBON AND OXYGEN HELIUM HYDROGEN

A giant star begins as a sphere of mostly hydrogen atoms. For most of the star's 10-million-year life, the hydrogen atoms fuse to form helium, releasing energy that makes the star shine. In its dying stages, the star builds up layers of other elements. Helium in the core is converted to carbon and oxygen; further conversions produce still heavier elements until at the very end, the core is pure iron. Since iron cannot produce energy, the stellar fires in the core eventually die out.

Stansbury, Ronsaville, & Wood, Inc.

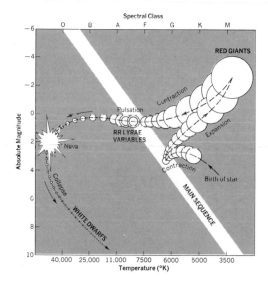

This Hertzsprung-Russell diagram illustrates the changing spectra and magnitude of the various stages of a star's life. When cosmic material condenses to form a star, it falls in the main sequence range. Near the end of its life, a star expands to a red giant, then contracts again, sometimes erupting as a nova. Eventually it becomes a white dwarf and dies.

THE EVOLUTION OF STARS

A star's life is a constant fight between the power of gravity—trying to pull all the star's material toward its center—and various outward forces, which resist that pull. Stars begin their existence as condensations of cool gas within dense clouds of gas. Gravitational forces overpower the weak gas pressure, and the clumps contract into protostars. When the interior of a contracting star reaches the temperature at which the hydrogen-to-helium fusion begins, its contraction is stopped by the resulting internal pressure of the heated gas or the outpouring of radiation.

The star then takes its place on the main sequence. If it is of high mass, it will have already become very hot at the surface, perhaps 90,000° F (50,000° C). A star like the Sun has an initial main-sequence temperature around 9,945° F (5,507° C). The important fact is that the basic characteristics of a star—its temperature, absolute brightness, and lifetime—depend primarily on its original mass.

The lifetimes of stars vary widely. The mass-luminosity law states that a star's luminosity is proportional to nearly the fourth power of its mass. Thus, a main-

carbon and nitrogen, the principle is the same: light elements—such as hydrogen, with an atomic mass of 1—combine into heavier ones—such as helium, with an atomic mass of 4—thus liberating energy.

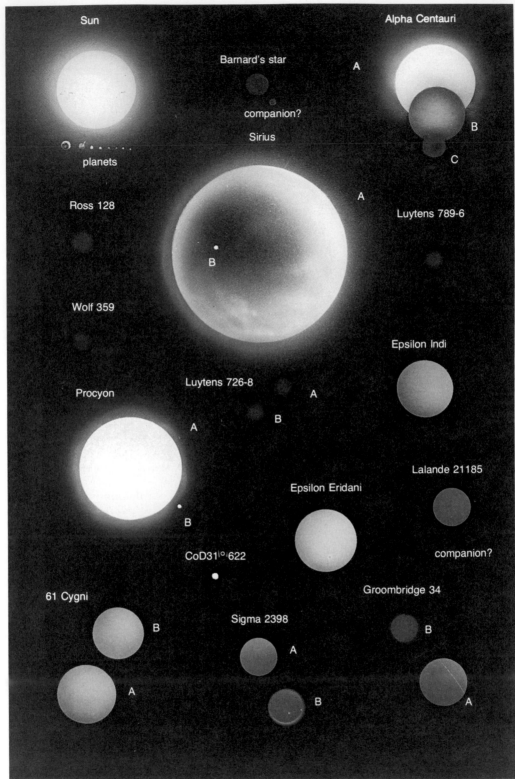

Sun

Alpha Centauri

Barnard's star

A

companion?

B

Sirius

C

planets

Ross 128

A

Luytens 789-6

B

Wolf 359

Epsilon Indi

Procyon

Luytens 726-8

A

B

A

B

Lalande 21185

Epsilon Eridani

companion?

CoD31⁰ 622

Groombridge 34

61 Cygni

B

Sigma 2398

B

A

A

A

B

A

ASTRONOMY magazine painting by Mark Paternostro

Very few stars are completely isolated. Scientists estimate that half of all stars have planetary or stellar companions. The farther away a star is, the harder it is to identify its companions. Pictured above are the relative sizes and spectral differences of our Sun and its closest neighbors.

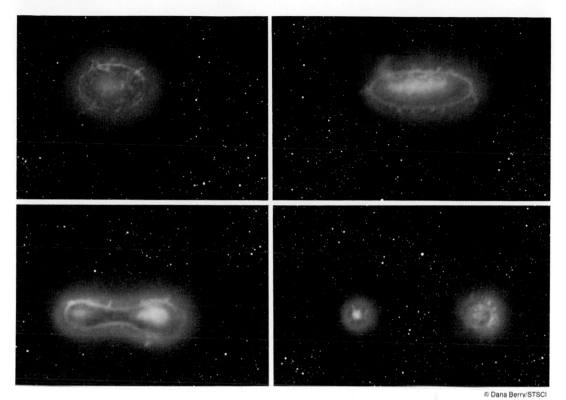

One theory of binary-star origin suggests that gravity causes a star to shrink and increase its rotation speed, as shown in the artist's conception above. Eventually the star, its equator drawn out into an ellipse, assumes a dumbbell shape that finally divides.

sequence star with 10 times the Sun's mass uses up its initial supply of hydrogen about 10,000 times more rapidly than does the Sun. At the Sun's rate of consumption, calculations suggest that its store of hydrogen will last about 11 billion years; about half this interval is already past. The most massive stars known have about 50 times as much mass as the Sun, are about 1 million times more luminous, and will live only 100,000 years.

When a star has used up its available supply of hydrogen, it can no longer generate energy by hydrogen-to-helium reactions. However, the star can release gravitational energy by contracting. As it does so, its internal temperature rises again. And at this higher temperature, the star can use helium as fuel, fusing it into still heavier molecules, such as carbon. It has a new lease on life. A new equilibrium is established, with the star's surface being cooler, but much larger in size. No longer on the main sequence, the star has become what astronomers refer to as a "red giant." After a few million years consuming its remaining fuel as a giant star,

the nuclear-energy resources of the star are almost entirely depleted. What happens next largely depends upon the star's overall mass.

Relatively small stars whose mass is no more than 1.4 times the mass of the Sun will gradually contract and grow fainter and denser. In these stars the pull of gravity is balanced by the pressure of electrons resisting being squeezed too closely together. These stars wind up as *white dwarfs*, which will continue to glow until they can contract no longer. Then they will cease to give off light. More-massive stars suffer a more violent fate, ending their lives in massive explosions called *supernovas*.

IS THE NUMBER OF STARS INFINITE?

How many stars are there? The answer is a complex one, for space is not filled uniformly with stars. The stars that we see with the unaided eye, and most of those that we are able to photograph, are parts of a system of stars known as the Milky Way system—our own galaxy. The Milky Way is actually so enormous that light, speeding at 186,282 miles

(299,792 kilometers) per second, may take as long as 100,000 years to cross from one end of the galaxy to the other. Yet, in spite of this mind-boggling expanse, the Milky Way is indeed finite. It is a flattened, disk-shaped system, whirling like a pinwheel. It consists of a densely populated center wreathed with coiled spiral arms, rich in stars, gas, and dust. It contains about 150 billion stars.

However, there are billions of other galaxies outside of our own—each one containing tens of billions of stars. The collective light of the stars in distant galaxies is observable by telescopes only as a faint blur. The total number of stars is indeed enormous, numbering perhaps more than a trillion million. Yet, as far as we know, the number is finite.

THE EVOLUTION OF THE MILKY WAY

From careful observations, we know that some stars are very young, only a few million years old, while others are much older, perhaps 10 billion to 15 billion years old. Since spectroscopic data show that the oldest stars contain only small quantities of the heavy elements, we believe that the first stars in the Milky Way formed out of the simplest materials in the universe, hydrogen and helium. The carbon, oxygen, silicon, iron, and other elements created within these stars were strewn about the galaxy by stellar winds and by supernova explosions, enriching the interstellar gas out of which subsequent generations of stars have formed. Later stars added still more heavy elements. As this process continued over billions of years, enough heavy elements were eventually manufactured and scattered through space so that stars like our Sun, along with its surrounding planets, and ultimately, all of the living creatures found here on Earth, could come into being.

Although science long ago dismissed the ancient notions that the positions of the planets and stars influence the course of human events, astronomers have nevertheless found a deeper bond between us and the cosmos. The carbon, nitrogen, oxygen and all the other elements necessary for life were processed through the nuclear furnaces within distant stars. Thought of in these terms, we are really only stardust.

A star is born (below, in an artist's conception) when the density of interstellar material is significantly increased and is pulled inward toward the center by gravity. It takes several hundred thousand years to produce a star.

Astronomers believe that stars continuously form, evolve, expand, and, eventually, contract and die out.

COLLAPSED AND FAILED STARS

by Charles Beichman

When a star is born, it is essentially a huge ball of hydrogen atoms mixed with a smattering of other elements. The strong pull of gravity in the star's core creates levels of heat and pressure high enough to cause the hydrogen atoms to fuse, forming helium. These nuclear fusion reactions generate the energy that balances the inward pull of gravity. Eventually, however, the supply of hydrogen atoms runs out. When this happens, the star, depending upon its size, either contracts and dies or violently explodes.

SUPERNOVAS

The explosion of a star, called a supernova, is among the most violent events imaginable. What causes a single star, erupting unexpectedly, to outshine 100 billion ordinary stars, and then disappear?

Novas

The most common—and least violent—stellar eruption is called a *nova*, from the Latin word for "new." Novas are thought to occur in binary systems in which a white-dwarf star orbits a red-giant star. Material from the red giant is pulled by gravity onto the white dwarf. The material slowly accumulates on the white dwarf's surface for years or thousands of years, until the pressure and temperature surge high enough to trigger a sudden outburst of nuclear reactions. The star throws off a shell of incandescent material and, in doing so, increases its brightness a thousandfold. After a few months, the star fades back to its former anonymity. Since many novas recur again and again, astronomers believe that the process does not destroy either star. Nevertheless, one wouldn't want to live too close to such a celestial volcano.

Supernovas

A star comes to the end of its life when the energy thrown off by its nuclear furnace can no longer resist the inward pull of gravity. At this point, stars up to 1.4 times the mass of the Sun contract into white-dwarf stars that cool and slowly fade from view. More-massive stars, however, feel a greater gravitational pull than can be resisted; instead of fading out, they erupt in explosions of unimaginable violence.

Numerous supernovas have been seen in historical times. The "guest star" observed by Chinese astronomers in 1054 created the Crab nebula now visible in the constellation Taurus. European astronomers Tycho Brahe and Johannes Kepler observed supernovas in 1572 and 1604. Rock paintings suggest that American Indians also marveled at one or more of these events. Judging by the frequency of supernovas in our own and other galaxies, we infer that a typical galaxy experiences a supernova explosion about every 100 years. The most recently observed was a bright supernova sighted in a neighboring galaxy in 1987.

When the Center Will Not Hold

With the use of supercomputers, astronomers have developed models that detail the last minutes of a dying star. As nuclear fuel is depleted, the star burns its own nuclear ashes, breeding and then con-

A supernova occurs when a massive star can no longer resist the inward pull of gravity and explodes, increasing the star's brightness by a factor of many billions. Below, photos of the same portion of the sky, taken 13 years apart. The photo on the right shows the emergence of a supernova just below the galaxy at center.

Hale Observatories

NOAO

Supernovas are relatively rare phenomena in terms of human life spans. So astronomers rejoiced when a supernova blazed into view in February 1987 (above).

suming progressively heavier elements such as oxygen, magnesium, sulfur, and silicon. Each element requires higher temperatures and higher pressures to fuse into still heavier elements. But the star is doomed—these nuclear fires can stave off collapse for only a short time. The nuclear furnace eventually converts the star's core into iron, which can neither fuse nor fission to produce additional energy.

Suddenly the final and devastating collapse begins. In an instant the temperature at the core rises billions of degrees, and the iron core breaks up into elementary particles like neutrons, protons, and neutrinos. The collapse ends when the inner core reaches densities characteristic of an atomic nucleus. The sudden rebound, or bounce, of the infalling core sends some of the inner core outward, to crash into the still collapsing outer core. The collision

makes the explosion even more violent. Heavy elements in the outer skin of the star and those created in the blast wave are strewn throughout space at speeds of nearly 1,000 miles (1,600 kilometers) per second. These heavy elements are the final legacy of the dying star, an inheritance for subsequent generations of stars that will ultimately shine in the heavens.

Type I and II Supernovas

Astronomers have observed two types of supernovas. Type I explosions may simply be violent versions of the nova explosions described earlier, in which a companion star dumps material onto a white-dwarf star. In some cases the amount of material falling onto the compact white dwarf may be so great, and the rate of infall so rapid, that the star suddenly exceeds the 1.4 solar masses permissible for white

Yerkes Observatory

Although not in the same league as a supernova, the light output of a nova explosion can still exceed 100,000 suns for several days. In the photo above, the arrow points to the star, now known as Nova Aquilae 1918, as it appeared before the outburst that made it a nova. The facing page photo shows how much brighter the star became after the explosion. Experts estimate that about 40 novas occur a year.

Giraudon/Art Resource

Some astronomers speculate that the fabled star of Bethlehem, which heralded the birth of Jesus Christ (left), may have actually been the magnificent display of a supernova.

dwarfs. The star collapses and explodes. Type I supernovas are mostly found in parts of galaxies where older stars are located.

Type II explosions come from the collapse of a massive star at the end of its short life. Such supernovas are found in the disks and spiral arms of galaxies containing massive, young stars. These stars consume their resources so rapidly that they live for only a few million years before meeting violent deaths.

Supernova Remnants

The blast from a supernova rushes outward into space, sweeping up surrounding material, heating and compressing it. These telltale signs of an explosion, recognized by their peculiar optical, radio, or X-ray patterns, are known as supernova remnants. Astronomers have identified more than 100 remnants of supernovas in the Milky Way alone. Careful examination of the light from supernova remnants shows they are abundant in hydrogen, helium, and heavy ele-

ments. The abundance of these elements in our own solar system has led some to suggest that the blast wave from a nearby supernova explosion triggered the collapse of the cloud of gas that became our Sun.

Our ideas about supernovas were dramatically and unexpectedly confirmed in 1987, when a star exploded in a nearby galaxy, the Large Magellanic Cloud.

In 1994, the Hubble Telescope first obtained remarkable images of a mysterious mirror-imaged pair of rings of glowing gas that surround the site of the stellar explosion Supernova 1987-A. It is believed to be material ejected from the supernova colliding at 9,000 miles per second (or 1/20 the speed of light) with an outer ring of gas that was ejected before the star exploded.

PULSARS

A star is not completely destroyed in a supernova. Some of the core survives, held together by nuclear forces. These cores are known as *neutron stars*. A neutron star is born when a supernova explosion compresses the subatomic particles in a star so tightly that a cube the size of a sugar lump would weigh 100 million tons! Such stars can be as small as 20 miles (32 kilometers) in diameter.

Rapidly spinning neutron stars are often wreathed in strong magnetic fields that give rise to intense, narrow beams of radiation that sweep across the sky like lighthouse beacons. These periodic bursts of radiation were first detected in 1967, when a British graduate student, Jocelyn Bell, and her colleagues detected regular pulses of radio waves sweeping toward Earth every second or so from specific directions in space.

Other astronomers soon explained the signals in terms of a swiftly rotating neutron star, and coined the name *pulsars*. Since that time, some 1,000 pulsars have been found. Their rotation periods range from a few seconds to a few thousandths of a second.

In 1998, astronomers found an entirely new class of neutron stars. These strange objects, with magnetic fields 100 to 1,000 times stronger than those of typical neutron stars, are the most highly magnetized stars in the universe. They are called "magnetars," and they regularly experience such bizarre phenomena as quakes and fractures.

BLACK HOLES

The most massive stars may collapse so completely that not even a neutron star can survive. These dying stars may become black holes—stars so dense that even light cannot escape from their surface. The surface of a black hole containing the mass of

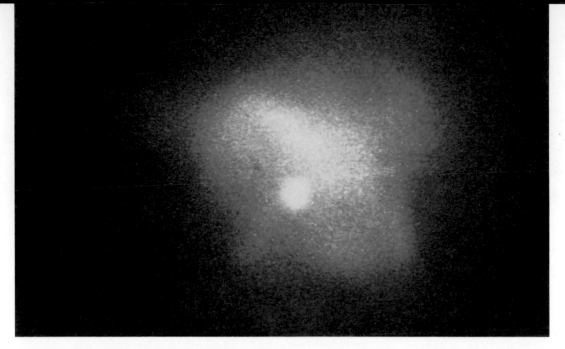

The Crab nebula supernova that exploded in A.D. 1054 contains a stellar remnant known as a pulsar (large white spot, above). Spinning 30 times per second, this pulsar emits regular signals once per revolution.

the Sun would be only 2 miles (3 kilometers) across. The physics of such objects is poorly understood, but it is thought that the X-ray emissions detected from some celestial objects come from material streaming into black holes. As the black hole forcefully sucks material away from nearby stars, this material is heated to millions of degrees, emitting more and more energetic radiation before the gas spirals into oblivion (see also page 212).

BROWN DWARFS

Astronomers reserve the name "star" for an object that is massive enough to convert hydrogen into helium as its primary source of energy. The planet Jupiter, which contains only one-thousandth of the mass of the Sun, may have almost become a star. Even now the planet gives off more energy than it receives from the Sun, as it slowly shrinks and cools, converting gravitational energy into heat radiation.

But Jupiter is not a star, since its central core will never reach the extremes of temperature and pressure necessary for stellar birth. Computer calculations show that a star must be at least 0.08 the mass of our Sun before it will convert hydrogen into helium, and thus begin nuclear fusion. Objects that are smaller than this will never become true stars.

These "failed" stars are known as brown dwarfs. The first brown dwarf was found by astronomers in 1994. Named Gliese 229B, it orbits a small red star about 19 light-years away.

Brown dwarfs may start out being just as hot as the smallest stars, with temperatures about 3,600° F (2,000° C). But lacking an inner fire, brown dwarfs cool. Over tens of millions of years, they may drop to around room temperature! At this level of coolness, they would emit only one-millionth the power of the Sun.

In contrast to any other type of star, brown dwarfs do not even glow red-hot. So it is not surprising that they have remained invisible to telescopes operating in the visible-light spectrum. Astronomers rightly predicted that brown dwarfs would be faint sources of infrared radiation. They may be found orbiting larger stars, just as Jupiter currently orbits our Sun, or floating freely in interstellar space.

The coolest, faintest, hydrogen-burning stars seen so far have masses right around the 0.08 solar-mass cutoff. Astronomers are continuing to search for brown dwarfs throughout our stellar neighborhood, and the number of discoveries is steadily rising.

Brown dwarfs may be an important but so-far-undocumented population within our galaxy. Imagine how distorted a census of a city would be if the census takers ignored all people shorter than 6 feet (1.8 meters) tall! Some astronomers suspect that the current number of known stars in the galaxy will remain seriously underestimated until scientists can detect brown dwarfs.

The greatest evidence of brown dwarfs lies in the estimated mass of our own galaxy. Astronomers estimate this mass much like accountants trying to balance a checking account. On one side of the ledger, astronomers estimate the gravitational pull in a region of space by measuring the motions of nearby stars. On the other side of the ledger, astronomers total up all the mass they can see: stars of all types, plus interstellar gas. But somehow the columns in this ledger do not balance, leaving scientists to speculate about "missing mass."

Judging from the movements of stars, which reflect the gravitational forces acting on them, the galaxy may contain twice as much mass as we can see! Such a conclusion remains controversial, however.

The missing-mass problem also exists on larger scales as well. The motions within many other galaxies demand the existence of 10 times more material than can be bound up by the stars and gases that astronomers have observed.

Brown dwarfs are not the only explanation. Large numbers of subatomic particles might also provide the gravitational tug necessary to keep galaxies spinning properly.

Today, astronomers know of hundreds of brown dwarfs among the nearby stars. They may represent the "missing links" that could help settle the debate over whether brown dwarfs are actually among some of the most numerous objects in the universe.

BLACK HOLES

by Mark Strauss

"Abandon all hope, ye who enter here," would be an appropriate warning for any space traveler foolish enough to approach a black hole. Black holes are proposed by astrophysicists as regions of space where gravity is so strong that the black holes act like stellar vacuum cleaners, sucking in matter and energy from space and allowing nothing, not even light, to escape.

The American physicist John Wheeler coined the term "black hole" in 1969, but, in fact, the theory has been around for much longer. As far back as 1783, English astronomer John Michell suggested that if a star were massive enough, it would have such a strong gravitational field that any light leaving the star would immediately be dragged back to the star's surface.

Michell's theories were largely ignored until 1939, when physicists Robert Oppenheimer and Hartland S. Snyder demonstrated that, based upon Albert Einstein's general theory of relativity, it would be possible for a star to collapse to the point where it would become a black hole.

HOW A STAR AGES

In order to understand how a star could collapse into a black hole, it is first important to understand the life cycle of a star. A star is, essentially, a giant fusion reactor. At the central core of the star, swirling atoms of hydrogen gas collide with one another and merge to form helium. In the process of fusing together, these hydro-

Astronomers propose that when a massive star dies, it collapses to form a black hole (pictured in the artist's conception above). This tiny, dense area has a surface gravity strong enough to suck any nearby light and matter into the hole, never to escape.

gen atoms release a tremendous amount of energy in the form of heat.

At the same time, the star as a whole is continuously struggling against the inward pull of gravity. The inward gravity is from the central core of the star, which is surrounded by a massive envelope of gas. This inward pull is so immense that the star is always on the verge of collapsing under its own weight.

What prevents the star from collapsing? Tremendous internal pressure that is generated by the extreme heat at the star's core, which pushes outward, counterbalancing the inward pull of gravity. In our own Sun, for example, the temperature at the core is about 25,000,000° F (14,000,000° C), generating pressure 100 billion times the air pressure at sea level on Earth.

After thousands of millions of years, however, a star comes to the end of its hydrogen fuel supply. It starts to cool and contract. What happens next will depend entirely on the mass of the star.

Small stars, such as our Sun, will collapse to form objects called *white dwarfs*. About the size of the planet Earth, white dwarfs resist further collapse with internal pressure caused by electrons spinning at near the velocity of light. White dwarfs are very dense objects: 1 cubic inch of white dwarf weighs several tons. But they are considered lightweights when compared to *neutron stars*.

Neutron stars are the evolutionary end products of larger stars—those 1.4 to 2 times as large as the Sun. Electrons cannot resist the greater gravitational collapse of such stars, and are pushed into atomic nuclei, where they combine with protons to form uncharged, tightly packed neutrons. Neutron stars are only a few miles in diameter. They weigh about 1 million tons per cubic centimeter. They can resist further collapse only by invoking the strongest force in nature—appropriately called the "strong force"—the force that binds together an atomic nucleus.

X-ray binary stars are composed of a small, normal star (in orange in the artist's conception below) that orbits around an X-ray-emitting invisible companion—possibly a black hole.

Painting by Steven Simpson, Courtesy Sky & Telescope Magazine

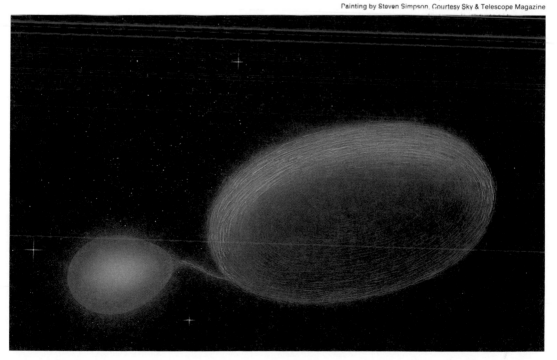

The strong force halts the imploding matter so abruptly—in a tenth of a second—that the collapsed stellar core acts as an explosive charge. The resulting explosion in the star's outer regions is called a *supernova*. Such celestial fireworks, observed by Chinese astronomers in July 1054, produced the Crab nebula, a cloud of gas that still writhes and glows today, 4,000 light-years from Earth.

What happens to a dying star that is more than twice as large as the Sun? Even the strong force cannot halt its in-falling momentum. It collapses completely, beyond the neutron-star stage, to an even smaller, denser object. Back in 1939, Oppenheimer and Snyder calculated that the gravitational field at the surface of such an object would become so strong that even light (traveling at a speed of 186,282 miles—299,792 kilometers—per second) would be unable to escape. According to Einstein's theory of relativity, nothing in the universe can travel faster than light. Therefore, if light cannot escape, neither can anything else. The collapsed star becomes what we call a black hole.

Perhaps the best way to visualize a black hole is to imagine, for a moment, that space is a flat rubber sheet. If you were to drop a steel ball on the sheet, the rubber would curve downward, forming a shallow hole. This, in a nutshell, is how Einstein interpreted gravity. According to Einstein, gravity exists because massive objects bend the fabric of space around them. If, for example, we rolled a small marble across our rubber sheet, it would roll around the top of the hole formed by the steel ball, much in the way that the Earth orbits around the Sun.

Now imagine that we could increase the weight of the steel ball that we dropped on our rubber sheet. As the weight increased, the ball would sag farther and farther downward, creating a deep "gravity" hole. Eventually the rubber would be stretched so tight that the top of the hole would pinch together, closing off from the outside world the region containing the steel ball. Similarly, a collapsed star could eventually become so dense that it would

curve space completely around on itself, isolating it from the rest of the universe.

How far would a star have to collapse before it "disappeared" from the visible universe? Astronomers refer to that critical size as the "event horizon" (otherwise known as the "Schwarzschild radius," named after German physicist Karl Schwarzschild). The event horizon is the outer boundary of a black hole, the exact point at which light rays fail to escape. The horizon acts as a one-way membrane—light and matter can cross the horizon into a black hole, but once inside, the horizon can never be recrossed.

The size of the event horizon is proportional to the mass of the collapsing star. Typically, the event horizon of a star would be on the order of miles. (For example, a star 10 times as massive as our Sun would have a Schwarzschild radius of 18.6 miles—30 kilometers.)

Yet, according to our current knowledge of theoretical physics, once a star starts collapsing, no known force can stop it. It will continue to shrink past its event horizon, smaller and smaller, until it becomes a "singularity"—a mathematical point with zero volume and infinite density. This singularity lies at the very center of a black hole.

EXPLORING A BLACK HOLE

If an astronaut were to attempt to visit a black hole, it would be a one-way trip. Before the astronaut even arrived at the event horizon, he or she would encounter tremendous tidal forces exerted by the black hole. Imagine, for example, that the astronaut is falling feetfirst toward the hole. The gravitational force pulling on the legs would be considerably stronger than the gravitational force pulling on the head. The difference between those two forces would stretch the astronaut like a piece of taffy.

As if that weren't bad enough, every single atom in the astronaut's body would be pulled toward the singularity at the black hole's center. For the astronaut the sensation might be similar to being squeezed by a giant fist.

The Uhuru satellite (right) was the first satellite designed for X-ray astronomy. It found the star Cygnus X-1 (above), a binary system located about 6,000 light-years from Earth. Astronomers believe that Cygnus X-1 may contain a black hole.

After being stretched and squeezed by the black hole's gravitational forces, our intrepid space traveler would resemble a strand of spaghetti, and would likely not be in the mood for any further exploration.

Let's imagine for a moment that we could instead send a robot probe to investigate the black hole, one that could somehow stay intact despite the tremendous tidal forces. For the sake of discussion, we will mount a clock and a light source on the outside of our probe.

If we were watching the robot back on Earth, we would notice a curious phenomenon. The light source mounted on the side of the probe would start to change color. If the light, for instance, started out green, it would turn yellow, and then red as it got closer and closer to the event horizon of the black hole.

This is because light is composed of particles known as *photons*. As the photons move away from the black hole, they expend some of their energy as they try to escape from the hole's tremendous gravitational pull. The closer they are to the event horizon, the more energy they need to pull away.

The energy of a photon is proportional to the frequency of its radiation. As a result, light that loses energy will have a reduced frequency, and therefore a longer wavelength. This effect is known as "gravitational redshift." When light has a long wavelength, it is red in color.

Eventually, as the robot probe moves closer and closer to the event horizon, the light source will seem to disappear from view. The wavelength of the light will have become so long that it can only be detected with infrared and radio telescopes.

Just above the event horizon of the black hole, the wavelength of the light will approach infinity. Theoretically, radiation from the light source would still reach us back on Earth, but by then the wavelengths would be so long that no known scientific instruments would be able to detect them.

Meanwhile, the clock mounted on the side of our robot probe would also be behaving rather oddly. According to Einstein's theory of relativity, time slows down in the presence of a strong gravitational field—at least as viewed by an outside observer. As the probe got nearer and nearer to the black hole, astronomers back on Earth would notice that the clock was ticking more and more slowly.

The clock would continue to slow down, until the probe arrived at the event horizon, at which point the clock would stop altogether. The probe would appear frozen in time, hovering at the brink of the black hole for the rest of eternity.

Relativity predicts, however, that from the perspective of the robot, time would not seem to be affected in any way. The probe would arrive at the event horizon and enter the black hole without the clock slowing down for even an instant. Yet our dutiful robot explorer would have only a fraction of a second to contemplate this peculiar law of nature, at which point it would be pulled toward the center of the black hole, where it would encounter the singularity and be crushed to infinite density.

PROVING THAT BLACK HOLES EXIST

All of this might sound very strange, and, in fact, for many years the majority of astronomers and physicists were reluctant to believe it. (The prominent English astronomer Sir Arthur Eddington even declared

© François Colos

2. Black hole absorbs one of the particles

3. One of the particles emitted into space as "Hawking radiation"

1. A pair of virtual particles is created

English physicist Stephen Hawking theorizes that black holes can emit radiation in the form of subatomic particles that do not obey the traditional laws of physics. These "virtual" particles are created in pairs in outer space, where they collide and annihilate each other. But if a pair of virtual particles is created in the vicinity of a black hole, one particle is sucked into the black hole, while the other particle escapes into space as "Hawking radiation." Over time, as the black hole loses energy, it may shrink, perhaps eventually evaporating with an enormous burst of energy.

H.K. Wimmer

The physical processes that occur when a large star collapses to form a black hole (above) may be the same processes that would be involved in the collapse of the universe.

that there must be "a law of Nature to prevent a star from behaving in this absurd way!") If astronomers were to believe in black holes, they wanted more than just mathematical equations on a blackboard; they wanted hard, physical evidence.

Such evidence became available in 1967, when two British astronomers, Jocelyn Bell and Antony Hewish, discovered objects in space that were emitting regular pulses of radio waves. At first the astronomers thought that they had made contact with an alien civilization in a distant galaxy. They even named the objects "LGMs," for Little Green Men. Eventually, however, astronomers came to the conclusion that the objects were rotating neutron stars, emitting radiation in the form of narrow beams. Like a celestial lighthouse, each time the neutron star spun toward Earth, astronomers could detect a pulse. Hence, these objects were named *pulsars*.

This was the first hard evidence that neutron stars actually exist. If a star

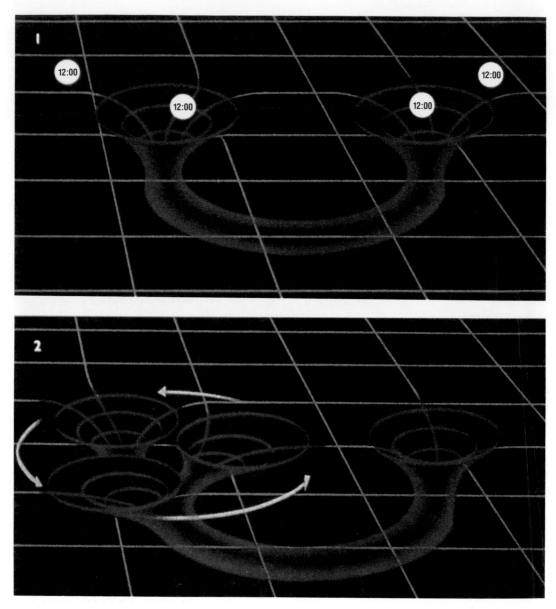

A wormhole is a hypothetical tunnel that could hold the key to time travel. It is envisioned as a black hole that has two "mouths" connected by a "throat." Picture a wormhole where the two mouths lie only one hour apart by spaceship (top). Before time travel can occur, one of the wormhole's "mouths" would have to be accelerated (above) to near the speed of light for one hour (starting at noon, for argument's sake).

could collapse into an object as small as a neutron star, it then seemed reasonable to assume that it could collapse to an even smaller size and become a black hole.

One problem remains. How do you find a black hole? They aren't as accommodating as neutron stars, in that they don't emit easily detectable beams of radiation. In fact, according to conventional theory, black holes don't emit anything at all.

Astronomers saw a way out of this dilemma. Black holes exert an enormous gravitational force on nearby objects. So although scientists can't see a black hole

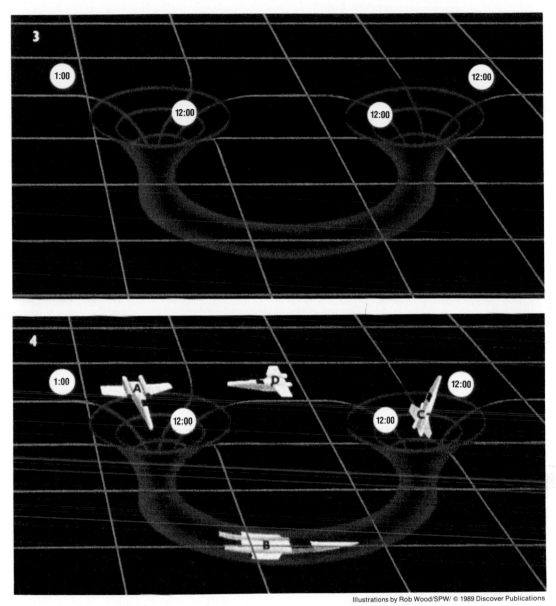

Illustrations by Rob Wood/SPW/ © 1989 Discover Publications

A clock outside the wormhole now reads 1:00 P.M., while clocks inside the wormhole and outside the stationary mouth are still at noon (top). The wormhole is now ripe for time travel. If a spaceship (above) plunges into the accelerated mouth (A), it can speed through the wormhole in an instant (B), emerge from the stationary mouth just seconds after noon (C), and return to the other mouth the long way around (D), in time to see itself going in.

"in the flesh," so to speak, they can observe how it would affect its surrounding environment.

To date, binary-star systems offer the best hope for locating a black hole. Astronomers have detected many such systems, where two stars orbit around one another.

In some cases the astronomers have observed only one visible star, which seemed to be in orbit around an unseen companion. It is possible that the companion might be a star too faint to be seen from Earth. It is also possible, however, that the second object could be a black hole.

If a black hole were part of a binary-star system, its enormous tidal forces would pull gaseous material off the surface of the neighboring star. Like water draining out of a bathtub, the gaseous material would slowly spiral into the black hole, forming a swirling disk of gas around the event horizon, a phenomenon that astronomers refer to as an *accretion disk*.

Within the accretion disk, compression and internal friction would heat the gas to temperatures measured in the millions of degrees. When gas gets this hot, it radiates a tremendous amount of energy in the form of X rays detectable by astronomers.

In 1970, a United States artificial satellite, the Uhuru, was launched off the coast of East Africa. (*Uhuru* is the Swahili word for "freedom.") Its purpose was to detect sources of X rays while above the interference of Earth's atmosphere. Uhuru has found more than 100 stars emanating X-ray pulses. One of the most powerful X-ray sources was Cygnus X-1, located about 8,150 light-years from Earth.

Closer examination of Cygnus X-1 revealed it to be a binary-star system, with a supergiant star orbiting around an unseen companion. By measuring the velocity and the orbital period of the supergiant star, astronomers were able to roughly calculate the mass of the unseen object. The object was estimated to be at least six solar masses (six times the mass of the Sun), far too massive to be either a white dwarf or a neutron star. By 1974, astronomers concluded that Cygnus X-1 must contain a black hole.

In 1997, astronomers found in the core of the active galaxy NGC 6521 what appears to be a warped, dusty disk swirling around a supermassive black hole, giving them the first direct line of sight into the immediate environment of a black hole.

In January 2000, astronomers found what may be the closest black hole to Earth—a mere 1,600 light-years away. Located near the center of the Milky Way in the direction of the constellation Sagittarius, the black hole emits gamma rays continuously rather than in flashes or bursts.

And deep within the core of the distant galaxy NGC 4395, astronomers discovered what may be a new type of mid-mass black hole, weighing perhaps as "little" as 10,000 to 100,000 Suns.

Perhaps the best black-hole candidate yet discovered is a binary-star system that goes by the uninspiring name A0620-00. Like Cygnus X-1, A0620-00 emits intense levels of X-ray radiation. The binary system has a visible orange dwarf star, which orbits around a dark, unseen mass. In the late 1980s, astronomers studied the motions of the orange dwarf and estimated that the star's dark companion was 3.2 times the mass of our Sun.

With a mass that large, the dark object was placed high on the black-hole suspect list. But in order to get a more accurate estimate, astronomers would have to measure the velocity of the dark object. At first that seemed impossible: How can you measure an object that you cannot even see?

The Hubble Telescope has found seemingly conclusive evidence for massive black holes at the cores of many galaxies throughout our universe. One such galaxy, known as M87, is bright enough to see with a small backyard telescope. Others are distant galaxies with highly energetic nuclei. In some of the galaxies, the Hubble Telescope has detected disks of material spiraling inward toward the black hole; in other galaxies, it has found beams of energetic radiation and gaseous knots being ejected at tremendous speeds.

HAWKING RADIATION

English physicist Stephen Hawking suggested that radiation might not only exist in the vicinity of a black hole, but that it actually might be leaking from the hole itself. Energy leaking from a black hole? It sounds impossible. But Hawking says that black holes emit radiation in the form of subatomic particles that do not obey the traditional laws of physics. Such "virtual" particles, as Hawking calls them, can be created in pairs in empty space, only to instantly collide and annihilate each other. If such a pair were to come into being near a black hole, one particle would be sucked in, while the other would escape into space.

As a black hole loses energy, it would also lose a proportionate amount of mass. Hawking's theory suggests that there might come a time when a black hole will lose so much mass that it will no longer be able to curve space around itself. The black hole would cease to be a black hole, and the remaining mass would likely explode outward, with a force equivalent to millions of hydrogen bombs.

But don't look up in the sky expecting to see a fireworks display of exploding black holes. A large black hole lives a very long time. More specifically, it would take trillions upon trillions of years for it to lose enough energy to explode outward. The universe itself has been around for only 20 billion years.

Yet it may be possible that very small black holes, formed in the early days of the universe, might be exploding just about now, releasing energy in the form of gamma rays, equivalent to about 100 million volts of electricity.

Astronomers are now searching the skies for just such bursts of gamma radiation. If found, then astronomers could verify what Stephen Hawking has been saying for the last 20 years. "Black holes ain't so black."

TIME TRAVEL

In 1895 H. G. Wells wrote a book about a device that could carry a man back and forth through time. The book was called *The Time Machine*, and for a century after it was published, the concept of time travel remained a favorite topic among writers of science fiction.

In 1988, however, science fiction moved closer to becoming science fact when American physicist Kip Thorne and his colleagues at the California Institute of Technology (Caltech) published a paper in the prestigious journal *Physical Review Letters*, titled "Wormholes, Time Machines, and the Weak Energy Condition."

Thorne didn't actually publish a blueprint for a do-it-yourself time machine. He speculated that an "arbitrarily advanced civilization" might be able to find a loophole in the laws of physics that would allow individuals to travel through time.

The loophole that Thorne had in mind is what physicists call a "wormhole." A wormhole is similar to a black hole, but with one noteworthy difference. At the bottom of a black hole, there is a singularity, a mathematical point of infinite mass through which nothing can pass.

A wormhole, by contrast, has no bottom. It has two "mouths" connected by a "throat." It is, essentially, a tunnel through space. A space traveler entering one mouth of a wormhole might emerge from the second mouth only a few seconds later, but halfway across the galaxy.

Time travel could leave the realm of science fiction if wormholes are found to really exist. Physicists are worried, however, about the possible ramifications if time travelers are able to tamper with events in either the past or the future.

Einstein's equations predict that wormholes exist, although nobody has ever found one. American physicist John Wheeler has suggested that a good place to look for one would be at a submicroscopic level, where random fluctuations occur in the fabric of space-time. In such an environment, wormholes would spontaneously appear and collapse, giving space a frothy, foam-like appearance.

Kip Thorne suggests that an advanced civilization could pull a wormhole out of this foam, enlarge it, and then move its openings around the universe until the wormhole assumed a desired size, shape, and location. Unfortunately, once such a wormhole was created, it would be highly unstable. If a space traveler entered the wormhole, the throat might instantly pinch shut. Even moving at the speed of light, the space traveler might be unable to reach the other side of the wormhole before it collapsed around him or her.

In order to avoid such a catastrophe, the Caltech physicists recommend that our hypothetical advanced civilization thread the throat of the wormhole with what they call "exotic material." In order to prop open a wormhole a half a mile or so across, the material would have to possess a radial (outward) tension comparable to the pressure at the center of a neutron star. Kip Thorne believes that there is a 50–50 chance that the laws of physics permit such a substance to exist.

Once our "arbitrarily advanced scientists" finished building a safe, traversable wormhole, they would be ready to convert it into a time machine. At this point they would rely upon Albert Einstein's general theory of relativity. According to Einstein, time slows down for a moving object when it is measured by a stationary observer.

This is often illustrated with what is known as the "twin paradox." Imagine that you have twin brothers, named Bill and Ted, each 20 years old. Bill takes off in a spaceship, while Ted stays back on Earth. Bill's destination is a star 25 light-years away. (A light-year is the distance that a beam of light can travel in one year.) His spaceship can attain a speed of 99.9 percent of the speed of light. From Ted's point of view, Bill will be gone for 50 years (25 years to reach the star, plus 25 years to return). However, from Bill's point of view on board the spaceship, the entire trip will last only one year. This effect is known as "time dilation." When Bill returns to Earth, he will be only 21 years old, but his brother Ted will be a 70-year-old man.

Now, instead of two brothers, imagine that we are dealing with two mouths of a wormhole. Our advanced civilization could move one end of the wormhole, perhaps by using a heavy asteroid or a neutron star as a kind of gravitational tugboat. If the mouth of the wormhole were accelerated to a high enough speed and then returned to its original position, it would behave just like our space-traveling twin brother. A clock fixed to the moving mouth would tick more slowly than one at the stationary mouth.

For instance, the clock outside the accelerated mouth might read 12:00 noon, but the clock outside the stationary mouth would read 1:00 P.M. By passing from one mouth to the other, a space traveler could move back and forth through time.

How far could our traveler move through time? That would depend upon how long and how fast the wormhole mouth is accelerated. If the mouth were moved at 99.9 percent of the speed of light for 10 years, the time difference between the two mouths would be nine years and 10 months. Theoretically, if you accelerated a wormhole mouth fast enough and long enough, the time difference between the two mouths could be stretched across several centuries.

There is, however, a limitation to Kip Thorne's time machine. Common sense tells us you cannot travel back to a time before you created the wormhole and accelerated one of the mouths through space. After all, what we're doing is exploiting the relative rate at which time passes under the effects of speed. So, unfortunately, you could not pop back through time to visit the dinosaurs. Unless, of course, you were lucky enough to find a time hole that had already been constructed by an advanced civilization several million years ago.

Courtesy NRAO/AUI

Quasars are very luminous objects; some shine 100 times brighter than the brightest known galaxy.

QUASARS AND ENERGETIC GALAXIES

by Charles Beichman

Normal galaxies consist of stars and various amounts of interstellar gas and dust. Some galaxies are large, containing 100 times the number of stars in our own galaxy, the Milky Way, while some are smaller, containing 100 times fewer stars than our galaxy.

For 100 million light-years in any direction, we see only normal galaxies, tens of thousands of spirals and ellipticals—some large, some small, some isolated, some in clusters—but all consisting of various populations of stars. At still greater distances, however, a few rare galaxies stand out as particularly bright. The luminosity, or total energy output, of such galaxies is 10 to 10,000 times greater than that of a typical galaxy such as our own. These distant objects, at least 100 times rarer than galaxies like the Milky Way, have some sort of additional source of energy that astronomers are still trying to understand. Intriguing possibilities include massive black holes or enormous amounts of star births.

So-called active, or energetic, galaxies are characterized by a compact nucleus that seems to be responsible for most of their tremendous energy output. Astronomers often detect strong radio, infrared, or X-ray emissions emanating from such galaxies. Such a phenomenon is rare around more-typical luminous objects.

Jets of energetic particles traveling at close to the speed of light are often seen

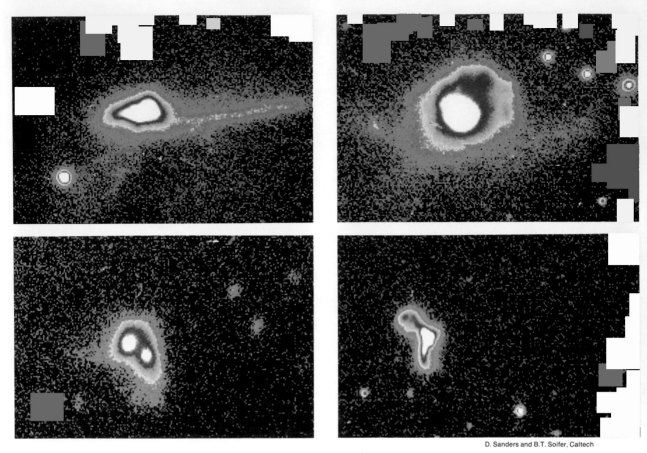

D. Sanders and B.T. Soifer, Caltech

Ultraluminous objects are only found in merging galaxies. The collision and merger processes may be necessary to trigger the huge luminosities. The photos above show galaxies in various stages of merger.

escaping from the nucleus of these galaxies. These particles are often highly ionized atoms being ejected from the galaxy at velocities of thousands of miles per second.

One way to explain many of these characteristics is to suppose that a black hole lies at the center of such an active galaxy. Black holes are thought to be the mysterious end result of stars and collections of stars that have become so massive and compact that no known force can resist the crushing force of their gravity.

A black hole only 4 miles (6 kilometers) across would still have more mass than our Sun. A black hole containing the mass of a billion suns would be no larger than our own solar system! Nothing, not even light, can escape from a black hole. But as gaseous material spirals into the mouth of a black hole, it is compressed and heated to millions of degrees, emitting co-

pious amounts of energy, from X rays to radio waves.

Astronomers have seen the brightness of some active galaxies double in just a few days. Perhaps they were seeing a sudden burst of energy produced when a star falling into a black hole was shredded by the intense gravitational field. Some astronomers even speculate that all galaxies harbor black holes, some of which may occasionally burst into prominence to create an "active" galaxy.

STARBURSTS

Another type of luminous galaxy is the starburst galaxy, so called because most of its excess energy appears to be due to a large number of hot, young stars in the violent process of birth. Such a starburst galaxy may give rise to as many as 100 stars per year. In comparison, a galaxy like our own sees about one star formed per year.

Starburst galaxies are prominent at infrared wavelengths because star formation often occurs within dense clouds of gas and dust, which absorb visible starlight and reradiate the energy as heat. The InfraRed Astronomical Satellite (IRAS) identified more than 50,000 such galaxies. Such rapid star formation may be triggered by a galaxy's collision with another, or by the voracious appetite of a supermassive black hole located within the galactic core.

QUASARS

A "quasi-stellar object," or quasar, represents an extreme type of active galaxy. Quasars, even brighter than active galaxies, are up to 10,000 times more luminous and 1 million times rarer in a given volume of space than galaxies like the Milky Way. Their cores are in constant motion, shooting out plumes of gas at a velocity of several thousand miles per second.

Comparison of the emission lines of the quasar 3C 273 (below) with those of a standard laboratory spectrum reveals that the quasar's lines are shifted to the red end of the spectrum. This indicates that the quasar is receding from Earth at 15 percent of the speed of light.

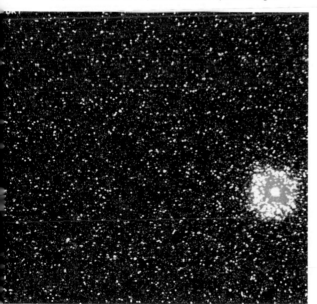

Quasars are so named because, when they were discovered in the 1960s, these apparently compact galaxies were hard to distinguish from individual stars. Now, however, we know that what astronomers are looking at are faint galaxies surrounding bright quasar cores. The same mysterious process that powers active galaxies may supply the even-greater amounts of energy needed to produce quasars.

Since quasars are the brightest beacons in the universe, they can be seen at enormous distances, billions of light-years away. But because light travels at a finite speed, telescopes act like time machines, permitting astronomers to view distant quasars as they once appeared billions of years ago. Thus, we see quasars as they appeared when the universe was new.

As we look deeper into the universe—and thus, farther back in time—the number of quasars increases. Their population seems to have reached a peak around the time when the universe was only 2 billion or 3 billion years old, just a fraction of its current age. What happened in the universe's youth to produce such high-energy objects? Understanding this concept remains one of the primary challenges in astronomy.

PROTOGALAXIES

As we look backward in time through our most powerful telescopes, to a period when the universe was only a few billion years old, we should begin to see galaxies themselves forming out of intergalactic gas. Although such protogalaxies should be intensely powerful, they will probably appear as faint smudges—due to their tremendous distance from Earth.

A number of distant galaxies and galaxy clusters now appear to contain protogalaxies. One of the infrared galaxies discovered with the IRAS satellite appears to be the most luminous object ever found in the universe. It is emitting more than 10,000 times the energy of the Milky Way. This object may be the first galaxy caught in the very process of formation. Astronomers may at last be viewing an entire generation of stars being born before their eyes.

Space Telescope Science Institute

Interstellar space is filled with tiny frozen crystals that condense to form a protostar (above), the first stage in the birth of a new star.

INTERSTELLAR SPACE

by Dennis L. Mammana

Modern astronomers are concerned not only with heavenly bodies of considerable size, such as the stars and the planets; they are also vitally interested in the space between the stars, areas filled with gases, solid particles of matter, and scattered atoms. In the early 20th century, this material was considered merely an obstacle to the study of the distant stars. Astronomers have come to realize, however, that interstellar matter is interesting in its own right. Today it is one of the greatest aids to our understanding of the structure and development of the stars and of the galaxies.

Perhaps as many as 150 billion stars make up the gigantic, flattened pinwheel that is our own Milky Way galaxy, in which the Sun and the planets of the solar system

are located. It is estimated that light, which travels some 186,282 miles (299,792 kilometers) a second, may take as long as 100,000 years to cross the Milky Way. This gives some idea of its immensity. Vast as it is, our galaxy is only one of many. There are others, probably hundreds of millions, in the far reaches of space. Some of them are systems like our own. Others are quite different in shape and size. Interstellar materials are found in almost all of these systems of stars. We are beginning to suspect, too, that such materials also exist in the vast spaces between the different galaxies.

Our first knowledge of interstellar matter came from bright, diffuse nebulas—luminous clouds in the heavens. Perhaps the best known of these is the Great Nebula in

218   **INTERSTELLAR SPACE**

Orion, faintly visible to the naked eye as a greenish blur. Hundreds of other bright nebulas are known; most of them lie within or near the Milky Way. Other galaxies, especially those that are like our own, also contain bright nebulas.

THE NATURE OF NEBULAS

The early observers thought that nebulas like the one in Orion might really consist of faint stars. As more-powerful telescopes were built, astronomers tried to resolve the nebulas—that is, to illuminate individual stars. In certain instances, they were successful. Some of the nebulas proved to be galaxies or smaller star groups. However, a great number of them could not be resolved in this way. When astronomers viewed them even through the most powerful telescopes at their disposal, they could see only finely shredded, cloud-like structures. Late in the 19th century, it was proved through the use of the spectroscope, which measures electromagnetic radiation, that bright nebulas, such as the one in Orion, are not made up of stars, but of enormous balls of gas.

The instrument that enabled astronomers to make this observation—the spectroscope—gives us invaluable information about heavenly bodies by decoding the messages that their celestial light brings to us. White light is made up of all the colors of the rainbow. When the light of a star or of a distant galaxy passes through the spectroscope, the light is broken up into a band of colors—a spectrum. By the position and pattern of the lines of color in this band, we can tell what elements, in the form of incandescent gas, are present in the heavenly body being observed. Each element has its own distinguishing pattern of lines, with its own place in the long band of the electromagnetic spectrum.

A spectrum that shines with definitely separate, or discrete, colors is the earmark of a glowing, tenuous gas. The Great Nebula in Orion has just such a spectrum. Many other bright nebulas have spectra very much like this, and clearly also consist of glowing gas.

Solid Material

Not all the bright nebulas have gaseous spectra, however. The spectrum of the nebulous material that surrounds the Pleiades, a cluster of rather hot stars, resembles those of the bright stars within it. But we would be wrong in concluding that this nebula itself consists of stars. Actually, it is simply reflecting the light of the bright stars near it. We assume that it must contain solid particles. Otherwise, it would not be able to reflect starlight as well as it does. It is probable that the Pleiades nebula contains not only solid particles, but also gases.

We have another way of knowing that solid matter is present in interstellar space. Clouds of particles screen off, or obscure, the light of more-distant stars. Some clouds, like the Coalsack in the southern sky, are opaque and have well-defined edges. Others can be located by the general dimming of the stars behind them and, more important, by the reddening of the starlight that passes through them. If the observed color of a star is redder than astronomers expect it to be, they know that it is screened by a cloud that is absorbing some of the starlight. We can also tell how much of this obscuring material there is. Most of this matter lies in the plane of the Milky Way.

Solid particles are not the only obscuring bodies in the space between the stars. Individual atoms, too, can obscure starlight. Each atom absorbs radiation of the same wavelength as the atom itself emits. The radio telescope is a spectacular tool for discovering the existence of atoms in interstellar space. It detects electromagnetic radiation in the radio frequencies. The wavelength of red light (also a form of electromagnetic radiation), to which the eye is sensitive, is about 0.0000025 inch (0.000065 millimeter). The radio telescope can detect radiation with a wavelength of about 8 inches (200 millimeters). It happens that the atom of hydrogen, the most common substance, emits radiation of about this wavelength. After American physicists built a radio receiver to search for the predicted existence of radiation from hydrogen in the

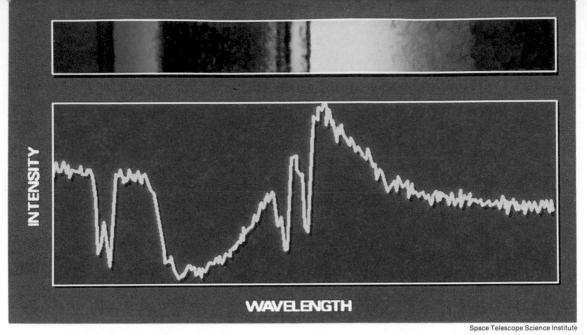

INTENSITY

WAVELENGTH

All elements produce a characteristic spectrum on a spectroscope. Experts analyze the spectra of celestial elements to identify the composition of interstellar space.

sky, they soon succeeded in picking up the signals sent out by interstellar hydrogen. The detection of radiation emitted by hydrogen marked a new era in the history of astronomy.

GLOWING GASES

The bright, gaseous nebulas are found only near stars burning at a temperature greater than about 25,000° F (13,900° C) at the surface. The light of these nebulas shows the colors of the spectrum characteristic of glowing hydrogen, and also helium, carbon, nitrogen, oxygen, sulfur, and other atoms. The Orion nebula contains over 300 atoms per cubic centimeter. Here, again, most of the material is hydrogen.

These atoms glow because they are close to a hot star. The hydrogen and helium atoms in the nebulas absorb extreme ultraviolet light from the star and re-emit it in the form of their particular radiations, or wavelengths. Oxygen, nitrogen, and sulfur atoms give out light after they collide with electrons that have been detached from other atoms—mainly hydrogen atoms—by the high-temperature radiation of the star. If the material had densities comparable to those in stellar atmospheres, collisions with other atoms would, in a short time, rob these atoms of the energy conferred by the

electrons. But the density of the Orion nebula is so low that collisions may not take place for months. Under these conditions the atoms of oxygen, nitrogen, and sulfur will radiate the lines seen in the nebular spectrum, which are called the "forbidden lines." They are forbidden only in the sense that they are suppressed under stellar or laboratory conditions by constant collisions with neighboring atoms.

A fine gaseous haze, much fainter than these conspicuous knots of gas, pervades the Milky Way. Powerful instruments are required to photograph its spectrum, for it is 6,000 times fainter than the Great Nebula in Orion. On the average, this haze contains about one atom per cubic centimeter. The enormous majority are atoms of hydrogen. They shine because of the radiation that falls on them—the very faint light of many distant stars. There is evidence that atoms of oxygen, nitrogen, and sulfur are also present.

In addition to the glowing gases within the Milky Way, astronomers have also observed extremely hot, gaseous clouds that appear to be floating throughout the galaxy. According to Ralph Fiedler of the Naval Research Laboratory in Washington, D.C., these clouds may be responsible for temporary dips detected in the intensity of radio waves emitted by quasars. The Milky

Way may contain as many as 1,000 times more of these clouds than stars do. According to Fiedler, who based his findings on daily radio-wave observations from 1979 to 1985, other celestial clouds are at least 20,000 times wider than the newly discovered clouds. The observed dips are apparently the result of the deflection of radio waves as they pass between Earth and distant celestial objects.

OUTLINING GALAXIES

Interstellar hydrogen and solid particles help us to make out the details of some of the galaxies. These are divided into several types. In the spiral galaxies, huge curving arms are set around a nucleus, which may be spherical or in the form of a straight bar. Our Milky Way is an example of a spiral galaxy. Other galaxies, called irregular, have no marked symmetrical form. Still others, the elliptical galaxies, are distinguished only by their elliptical shape.

When astronomers used the radio telescope to observe the interstellar hydrogen in the faint nebulosity of the Milky Way, they found that the interstellar hydrogen gas outlines the spiral structure of our stellar system. The gas lies most densely in the spiral arms, and thins out between them. The hydrogen is accompanied by absorbing particles, which follow the course of the spiral arms. In the galaxy called the Great Spiral in Andromeda, the spiral arms are found to be studded with bright, gaseous nebulosities and associated with well-marked lanes of obscuring materials.

Yerkes Observatory

The Great Nebula, M42, located 1,500 light years away in the Orion constellation, appears as a faint blur to the naked eye. Powerful telescopes, however, reveal a churning mass of glowing atoms, illuminated by the light of a nearby group of stars.

The chaotic, irregular galaxies are even richer in bright and dark nebulous material than are the spiral galaxies. Even many of the featureless elliptical galaxy systems, which contain few if any solid particles, are pervaded by a very diffuse haze of glowing atoms.

Astronomers have found that several distinct clouds, moving at different speeds, lie between us and many distant stars. Evidence has shown that these separate clouds are associated with different spiral arms of our galaxy. Each is moving at its own speed, and is silhouetted against the light of very distant stars.

The interstellar gases furnish us with enlightening evidence about conditions in space between the stars. For example, in the region of faint, hazy nebulosity, the temperature of a solid particle would be a few degrees above absolute zero, which is $-460°$ F ($-273°$ C).

SMALL CRYSTALS

Interstellar solids must be very finely divided to absorb as much starlight as they do. From studies of the motions of stars, scientists have determined that these solids cannot have a density greater than 0.00000000000000000000000008 grams per cubic centimeter. At a density as low as this, the particles may have diameters of about 0.0000059 inch (0.000015 centimeter). But the size required to account for the observed absorption depends on whether the particles are metallic or not. If they are metallic, they need not be so small. Metallic atoms do not seem to predominate in the universe, however. In the Sun, which is a fairly typical example of cosmic material, there is less than one metallic atom per 6,000 atoms.

The extremely high reflecting power of nebulas—greater than that of snow—sug-

Views of the Milky Way using optical telescopes were long obscured by interstellar dust (below). Scientists, finding that radio waves pass through this dust, used radio telescopes to reveal the Milky Way's spiral structure.

Yerkes Observatory

The Milky Way, shown above in an artist's conception, is a slightly warped, scalloped disk. The elements it contains may be the building blocks from which life develops elsewhere in the universe.

gests that most of the solids in space are tiny frozen crystals of compounds of the most common chemical elements. Perhaps they are substances such as ammonia, methane, and even water, built of the cosmically common atoms of hydrogen, carbon, nitrogen, and oxygen.

Other evidence indicates that the interstellar particles must be elongated crystals, for the light of the distant stars is polarized. This means that the light vibrations tend to be lined up perpendicularly to the light ray. The polarization is associated with interstellar reddening. Spherical particles would not have this effect. Moreover, the particles seem to be lined up more or less parallel in any one region.

There is much controversy as to how these observations should be interpreted. The consensus is that the elongated particles are lined up by magnetic fields in interstellar space. One theory suggests that small, highly magnetic particles are embedded in the icy grains.

STELLAR NURSERIES

Interstellar matter does not serve merely as a space filler, but rather is important in the formation of stars and galaxies. We know that, under the right conditions, an interstellar cloud of gas and dust will condense and assume a spherical shape.

This sphere is a protostar, or early stage, which will eventually lead to the birth of a new star.

While astronomers have long believed that such interstellar clouds were the birthplaces of stars, no one had ever seen the process take place—until recent technology made it possible. The Hubble Telescope is now revealing places where stars are being born, as gales of high-speed particles from young massive stars compress nearby dust and gas until they form into smaller and fainter Sun-like stars not far from their "parent" star.

Radio and infrared telescopes have detected a variety of chemical elements and compounds in space. These substances exist as individual atoms, as molecules, or as parts of molecules. Many of these molecules are biological in nature. That is, they are chemically identical to substances found in or produced by living things on Earth. Among them are hydrogen, water, ammonia, and carbon-containing compounds such as formaldehyde and cyanogen. A number of scientists believe that these interstellar materials may be the building blocks from which life as we know it could develop elsewhere in the universe. Thus, the study of interstellar space, particularly by means of the radio telescope, is extending the science of astronomy into the realm of biology and the origin of life.

Cosmic rays are charged atomic nuclei that bombard the Earth constantly from every direction. Only about 1 percent of the cosmic rays that strike the atmosphere and interact with air molecules make it to the Earth's surface.

COSMIC RAYS

by Volney C. Wilson

Whizzing through our galaxy at all times, in every direction, and at fantastic speeds, are the charged particles that we call cosmic rays. They are really atomic nuclei—that is, atoms stripped of their electrons. Traveling at nearly the velocity of light, some cosmic rays have energies far greater than those produced with powerful atom smashers.

The cosmic rays that fly through outer space are called primary cosmic rays. A thin rain of these particles constantly strikes the upper atmosphere of the Earth. As they enter the upper part of the atmosphere, they collide with atoms of air. The fragments known as secondary cosmic rays result from these collisions.

About 1 percent of these secondary rays penetrate the remaining atmosphere and reach sea level. Roughly 600 rays pass through the human body every minute, day and night. This should not be alarming, though—a wristwatch with a radium-painted face exposes us to the same dose of radiation. Doctors estimate that the dose must be 30 to 300 times greater to produce the increasing rate of mutations that lead to harmful genetic effects on human beings.

If we could harness the energy of all cosmic particles striking sea level over the entire world, it would yield little more power than a modern automobile engine. Cosmic rays will never power our machines, but they do provide nuclear physicists with a natural laboratory for the study of super-high-energy phenomena. They may reveal the secrets of the forces that bind together the particles of matter in atomic nuclei. And they may tell us about the universe beyond our solar system.

DETECTION OF COSMIC RAYS

Cosmic rays made their presence felt long before they were identified. About the beginning of the 20th century, physicists discovered that electroscopes, which determine the electric charge on a body, and ionization chambers, which are used to measure the intensity of radiation, were affected by certain mysterious rays existing in the atmosphere. These rays were far more penetrating than X rays or any other form of radiation known at the time. X rays could be stopped by a lead plate only 0.06 inch (1.6 millimeters) thick; but 3.94 inches (10 centimeters) of lead would absorb only 80 percent of the "new" rays.

The first and most natural assumption was that these penetrating rays issued from some special radioactive material in the Earth's crust and atmosphere. Beginning in 1909, however, enterprising experimenters carried ionization chambers aloft in balloons and found that the rays grew more intense with increasing altitude. Between 1910 and 1914, Victor F. Hess of Austria and Werner Kolhörster of Germany made the first precise measurements, at altitudes up to 29,528 feet (9,000 meters). At this height the rays were 10 times more intense than at sea level. Clearly, the penetrating rays traveled downward through the atmosphere. Hess came to the conclusion that the mysterious rays must have their origin in outer space.

In 1925 a series of experiments by a team of physicists headed by Robert A. Millikan of the California Institute of Technology (Caltech) confirmed Hess' hypothesis. Millikan and his colleagues lowered ionization chambers into two snow-fed lakes at high altitudes in California in order to determine the absorption of the penetrating rays in water, as compared with their absorption in air. Measuring the intensity

of the rays under different depths of water and at different altitudes, they came to the conclusion that the rays must originate outside the atmosphere. In the report of these experiments, the name "cosmic rays" was used for the first time.

In a few years, two newly invented instruments revealed important new facts about cosmic rays, and later became the cosmic-ray physicist's chief tools. In 1927 Russian physicist D. V. Skobeltsyn first adapted the Wilson cloud chamber to the study of the rays. With this instrument the path of an ionizing particle, or ray, is made visible as a trail of water droplets.

In a series of balloon-borne high-altitude experiments, Victor Hess (below) helped prove the existence of cosmic rays, an achievement for which he shared the 1936 Nobel Prize for physics.

To study cosmic rays, Carl D. Anderson (left) used a cloud chamber in which a series of lead plates (below) causes the rays to slow down and split. In the course of his cosmic-ray investigations, Anderson, almost by chance, confirmed the existence of positrons—positively charged electrons. He shared the 1936 Nobel Prize with Hess for his findings.

In 1928 and 1929, Werner Kolhörster and another German, Walther Bothe, devised a research technique using sets of Geiger-Müller counters, devices that detect particles by electrical discharges. By arranging the counters in a straight line and providing them with the proper electrical circuits, one could trace the path of a single cosmic ray.

The bubble chamber, developed in 1952 by Donald Glaser, also proved helpful in the analysis of the rays. In the bubble chamber, a liquid is kept just below the boiling point. The pressure is suddenly lowered, and the liquid becomes superheated. When high-speed charged particles now pass through, their passage will be indicated by a series of bubbles.

These devices helped establish that most of the secondary cosmic rays are high-energy, electrically charged particles.

COSMIC RAYS AND EARTH'S MAGNETIC FIELD

In 1927 Dutch scientist Jacob Clay discovered that primary cosmic rays are affected by the Earth's magnetic field. During a voyage between Amsterdam (in the Netherlands) and Indonesia, he observed that the intensity of cosmic rays drops as one approaches the magnetic equator from higher latitudes. The existence of this "latitude effect" anticipated the 1952 discovery that primary cosmic rays are electrically charged particles.

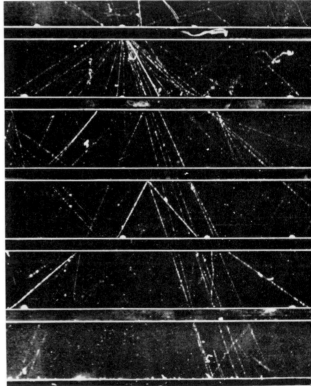

A neutral (uncharged) particle moving in a straight line through a magnetic field is not influenced by the field. However, a charged particle in the same situation will have its path bent into a curve if it moves approximately at right angles to the magnetic lines of force.

Earth's magnetic field is very weak, but it extends for thousands of miles into space. Any charged particle approaching Earth must travel immense distances through the field, and will be appreciably deflected by the curving force. This force is greatest on particles that approach exactly at right angles to the lines of force, and weakest on those that travel parallel with the lines. The bending is more pronounced for slow-moving, or low-momentum, particles than for faster, or high-momentum, ones.

This is illustrated in the diagram on page 228. The dotted lines represent Earth's magnetic lines of force. A, B, C, D, and E are all charged particles approaching Earth with the same momentum or energy. A is only slightly deflected by the field, because it approaches near the pole and thus moves almost parallel with the lines of force. On the other hand, E approaches near the equator, moving exactly at right angles to the lines. The strong curving force on this particle eventually turns it back into the direction from which it came. The paths taken by B, C, and D will depend upon the angle formed by their direction as they approach Earth and the magnetic lines of force. For a particle to penetrate the magnetic field and the atmosphere at the equator (particle F), it would have to start out with many times more momentum than the other particles.

Cosmic-Ray Intensity

If the particles are indeed electrically charged, we should expect many fewer rays to reach Earth's surface at the equator than at the higher latitudes. This was conclusively shown in 1930. In that year, a worldwide survey was begun, under the direction of Arthur H. Compton of the University of Chicago, to determine cosmic-ray intensities at different latitudes and altitudes all over the globe. The 1933 report based on the survey's findings established that, from the geomagnetic latitudes of 50 degrees north (or south) to the equator, cosmic-ray intensity at sea level drops approximately 10 percent. It showed that primary cosmic particles are electrically charged.

Is the charge positive or negative? Manuel S. Vallarta, a Mexican mathematician, calculated in 1933 that a positive particle with low momentum could reach Earth more easily when approaching from the west than from the east. The directions would be reversed for a negative particle. By 1938 experiments proved that the rays falling from the west were definitely more intense than those from the east. This led to the conclusion that the primary cosmic rays are positively charged.

American physicist Scott E. Forbush discovered that cosmic-ray intensities decrease during high sunspot activity. The Sun is continuously throwing out tremendous quantities of protons moving at a speed of about 994 miles (1,600 kilometers) per second. This magnetic particle stream is referred to as the *solar wind*. During periods of sunspot activity, solar wind in the direction of Earth is greatly increased. This in turn increases the strength of the magnetic field near Earth to such an extent as to shield out some of the low-energy cosmic rays. This is called the Forbush effect.

Rockets and artificial satellites have been frequently used to measure cosmic-ray intensity above Earth and analyze the effect of the solar wind upon Earth's magnetic field. Scientists have also discovered "free spirit" atoms, which are electrically neutral and therefore immune to the solar wind. Scientists may be able to predict the arrival times of solar storms based on their studies of these atomic particles.

Cosmic-Ray Showers

In 1932, Italian-born physicist Bruno Rossi showed that if three or more Geiger-Müller counters were spread out horizontally in an irregular pattern, they would sometimes be tripped simultaneously, indicating that showers of particles were traveling together. These showers could be produced as cosmic-ray particles passed through lead or other substances containing heavy atoms. Rossi concluded that each shower was produced from a single cosmic-ray particle as it passed close to the nucleus of a nearby atom. Showers could also be observed taking place in a Wilson cloud chamber that had a lead plate across it. The track of a single cosmic-ray particle is seen entering

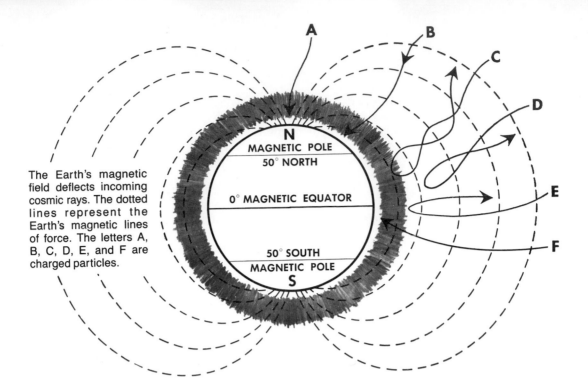

The Earth's magnetic field deflects incoming cosmic rays. The dotted lines represent the Earth's magnetic lines of force. The letters A, B, C, D, E, and F are charged particles.

N
MAGNETIC POLE
50° NORTH

0° MAGNETIC EQUATOR

50° SOUTH
MAGNETIC POLE
S

the chamber. As it passes through the lead plate, the track splits in two. These tracks split again and again, producing a shower of particles.

In the same year in which Rossi revealed the existence of cosmic-ray showers, American Carl D. Anderson discovered a new fundamental particle in cosmic radiation—the positive electron, or *positron*. It appeared in a photograph of a cloud chamber containing a lead plate in a strong magnetic field. Anderson's historic achievement won him a share of the 1936 Nobel Prize in physics.

Cloud-chamber photographs soon showed that each time a shower track split, the two branches were oppositely curved, and an electron and a positron were created. A pair-production theory of cosmic-ray showers was then formulated. It was maintained that the process of shower formation represented the conversion of energy into charged matter and vice versa.

According to the pair-production theory, this is what takes place. As a gamma-ray photon—a fragment of light energy—penetrates the nuclear field of an atom, a portion of its energy is suddenly transformed into a pair of electrons, positive and negative. The remaining energy provides the velocities of the electron and the posi-

tron. Each of the daughter electrons may disappear in its turn, producing another gamma ray, if it is suddenly slowed down in the field of another nucleus. Two gamma rays may produce four electrons; four gamma rays may then arise, then eight electrons, and so on.

In 1938 such cosmic-ray showers were discovered in the atmosphere, up to .21 mile (0.33 kilometer) in diameter and with millions of particles each. The energy of one cosmic-ray particle causing a shower may reach 1 billion GeV (1 GeV equals 1 gigaelectron volt, or 1 billion electron volts). An electron volt is the energy gained by an electron when accelerated by 1 volt of electricity. In contrast, fission of a uranium atom releases only 200 MeV (1 MeV equals 1 million electron volts).

THE PRIMARY COSMIC RAYS

Primary cosmic rays contain 91 percent positive particles, or protons (the nuclei of hydrogen atoms); 8 percent alpha particles, or helium nuclei, with two protons apiece; and 1 percent nuclei of heavier elements, such as lithium (three protons per nucleus), beryllium (four protons), boron (five protons), oxygen (eight protons), and iron (26 protons). These particles are detected by photographic emulsions in high-altitude balloons.

A variety of heavier cosmic-ray nuclei are being discovered. Scientists have learned that moving heavy particles damage mica and plastics, leaving tracks, which, when etched, give an idea of the particles' sizes and charges. One nucleus has been found to contain 109 protons, representing an element more massively charged than uranium, which has 92 protons per nucleus.

Cosmic-ray composition is similar to the known distribution of chemical elements in stars, nebulas, and interstellar dust. Cosmic-ray composition and the distribution of the quantities of elements in the universe show sharp differences in the numbers of atoms having odd and even numbers of protons per nucleus, with a peak in regard to iron. "Even-numbered" nuclei are more common. These facts give a clue to the origin of primary cosmic rays.

TWO COMPONENTS OF SECONDARY COSMIC RAYS

Secondary cosmic rays are composed of two very different classes of particles, which can be separated by a piece of lead about 5 inches (13 centimeters) thick. One component is completely absorbed in this thickness. This soft component consists mainly of electrons, positrons, and gamma-ray photons—the typical particles of a cosmic-ray shower. The intensity of this soft component increases from the top of the atmosphere down to an altitude of about 11 miles (17 kilometers), where it makes up roughly four-fifths of the total radiation. From this altitude downward, the intensity decreases until it makes up only one-quarter of the total at sea level.

The other component passes through 5 inches (13 centimeters) of lead almost unobstructed. It is called the hard, or penetrating, component. It decreases in intensity continuously from the top of the atmosphere down to sea level. Approximately one-half of these rays at sea level can still penetrate 15 inches (38 centimeters) of lead. The difference in the absorp-

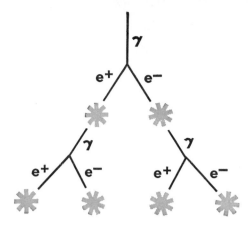

In the pair-production theory of cosmic-ray showers, a gamma ray (indicated by γ) yields a pair of electrons, positive and negative, indicated by e+ and e−, respectively. Each of these electrons may disappear, producing another gamma ray as it does. Each of the gamma rays in turn may yield two electrons. As the process is continued, a cosmic-ray shower is produced.

tion pattern and penetrating power of the two components represented a puzzling problem to physicists for many years.

In 1936 the riddle was finally solved by the teams of C. D. Anderson and S. H. Neddermeyer at the California Institute of Technology (Caltech), and J. C. Street and E. C. Stevenson at Harvard University. Working independently, these teams showed that all the evidence pointed to a new type of fundamental particle, intermediate in mass between the proton and the electron. This was the mesotron, now called the *meson*.

In the meantime, the author of this article (Volney Wilson of the General Electric Company) had been measuring the penetration of cosmic rays below the ground in a copper mine in northern Michigan. He reported that some rays were able to penetrate as much as 1,640 feet (500 meters) of rock. Further investigation showed that these rays were corpuscular, or made up of tiny particles, and that they ionized the rock and lost energy all the way down. Calculations showed that they must be the newly discovered mesons. It is now agreed that mesons make up the bulk of the hard component of secondary cosmic rays. The high energy of mesons accounts for the penetrating power of this component.

The existence of the meson had been predicted by Japanese nuclear physicist Hideki Yukawa in 1935. He also predicted

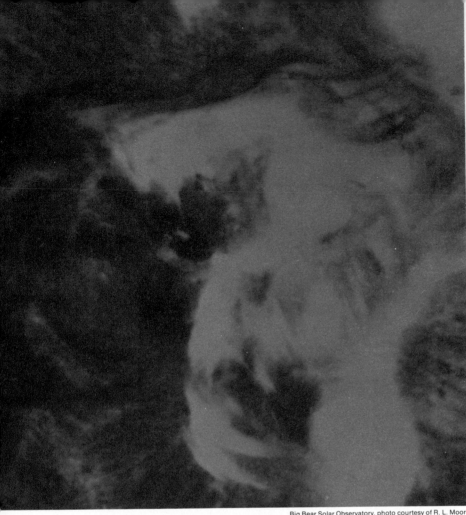

Solar flares (left) and other dramatic outbursts from the Sun's surface may serve as one nearby source of cosmic rays.

Big Bear Solar Observatory, photo courtesy of R. L. Moore

that the meson would be unstable outside the nucleus, decaying with the emission of an electron. In 1940 this decay was actually photographed for the first time in a Wilson cloud chamber.

In 1948 researchers at Berkeley, California, succeeded in producing mesons artificially by bombarding carbon atoms with alpha particles accelerated to 380 MeV. Both positive and negative mesons were produced. Some, known as *pi-mesons*, decay in about 200-millionths of a second into a lighter variety called *mu-mesons*. Mu-mesons live for roughly 2-millionths of a second before they disintegrate into electrons or positrons. In secondary cosmic-rays the heavier pi-mesons are created by tiny "nuclear explosions" in the upper atmosphere, which occur when primary cosmic rays collide with the nuclei of the atoms of the gases that make up the atmosphere. The pi-mesons usually decay immediately into mu-mesons, which live long enough to travel great distances. It is the mu-mesons that form the major component of secondary cosmic rays at sea level.

ORIGIN OF COSMIC RAYS

What is the source of cosmic rays, and how do they acquire their fantastic energies? Some astronomers have long held that the universe was created in a single primordial explosion, and that cosmic rays are tiny remnants of this colossal event. But the presence of heavy nuclei in the primary rays shows that their energies must be acquired gradually. In an explosive process, the larger nuclei would be completely shattered.

Present evidence suggests that most cosmic rays originate and remain largely within our own galaxy. Let us suppose that the distribution of rays observed in our galaxy extends far beyond its borders throughout the universe. We know the average energy of the rays in our region. From this, we can calculate the total energy carried by cosmic rays everywhere. The figure reached would equal the entire mass of the universe if this were converted into energy. Scientists consider such an idea impossible. Moreover, the solar system is constantly rotating along with the rest of our galaxy. If rays are entering the galaxy from the outside, certain complex effects due to the rotation of the galaxy should be visible. None have ever been observed.

At least 90 percent of the cosmic rays originate inside our own galaxy. The maximum lifetime of a cosmic ray is about 2 million years. The known characteristics of cosmic rays suggest they originated in thermonuclear (atomic) explosions in certain kinds of stars.

Old stars rich in iron atoms reach a stage when they just blow up. They then release vast amounts of particles and electromagnetic radiation, including light. These explosions occur by a process called neutron capture. Neutrons—heavy nuclear particles with no charge—can move freely outside the nuclei of atoms. They may, however, be absorbed, or captured, by the nuclei of atoms; this event makes the atoms unstable. The atomic nuclei therefore release energy in the form of alpha particles, protons, neutrons, and radiation of very short wavelengths, especially gamma rays, in a gigantic blast.

An exploding star is called a *supernova*. It is much brighter than an ordinary nova, which does not really explode, but shoots out matter instead. The best-known supernova was the event of A.D. 1054, recorded by Chinese astronomers. The remnant of this nova is the Crab nebula.

At present the Crab nebula is observed to emit radio waves and light that is markedly polarized. That is, the radiation waves vibrate along a single plane or along a few planes, instead of at many angles, as ordinary (unpolarized) radiation does. The polarization means that the Crab nebula's radiation originates from electrons moving at great speeds in strong magnetic fields.

This is called *synchrotron radiation*. A synchrotron is an atom smasher, or accelerator, that speeds up electrons and other particles by means of intense, changing magnetic fields. Polarized electromagnetic radiation is observed to arise from electrons accelerated in a synchrotron.

The Crab nebula, then, may act as a giant cosmic accelerator of particles—or cyclotron—with energies that dwarf those of human-made accelerators. The most powerful human-made accelerator to date reaches only 500 GeV. Some cosmic-ray energies reach an amazing 1 billion GeV!

Within the Crab nebula, astronomers have identified a *pulsar*—a very small and very dense star composed mostly of neutrons, which emits radiation in very short bursts, or pulses. The pulsar itself is part of the exploding star that was seen by Chinese astronomers over 900 years ago. This pulsar may be the chief energy source of the Crab nebula. Not only does it radiate energy, but it ejects large numbers of particles from its surface. These particles are being accelerated in the very strong rotating magnetic field of the pulsar.

Scientists estimate that one to two supernovas occur in our galaxy per century. If they contain pulsars, the energy balances are such that these supernovas could just about produce the observed cosmic rays. Rays with energies of 1 billion GeV or less are trapped in the magnetic field of our Milky Way galaxy. They last an average of about 1 million years before striking an atom and being annihilated in the process.

The extremely few cosmic rays with energies greater than 1 billion GeV may have arrived at the Earth before escaping the galaxy, or may even have come from outside the Milky Way. Observations so far suggest that no more than 10 percent of cosmic rays come from beyond our galaxy.

Using the Energetic Gamma Ray Experiment Telescope (EGRET) on the Earth-orbiting Compton Gamma Ray Observatory in 1991, scientists completed the first all-sky map of celestial gamma-ray emissions, and found that cosmic rays emanate from individual galaxies, some of which are more prolific generators than others.

SPACE SCIENTISTS AND THEIR SCIENCE

by Dennis L. Mammana

On July 4, 1997, space scientist Bridget Landry slept the day away, as she was scheduled to work the night shift at the Jet Propulsion Laboratory (JPL) near Pasadena, California. While she rested, Landry missed all the excitement—not the fireworks, parades, and baseball games that usually mark the Independence Day holiday, but a much more significant event.

On that particular day, a robot spacecraft that Landry had helped to design landed on Mars and began sending photographic images and scientific data back to Earth. Millions of people around the world watched in amazement—both on television and on the Internet—as Pathfinder and its tiny robot sidekick, Sojourner, began their historic mission on the Red Planet. But few of them were more interested

than Landry was, since, in her capacity as deputy uplink systems engineer at the JPL, she had worked with a team of scientists to teach the computers on the ground and on the spacecraft to speak the same language.

Over many months, Pathfinder and Sojourner carried out their mission in nearly flawless fashion, sending to Earth more than 16,000 images, 20 rock and soil analyses, and innumerable measurements of the Martian temperature, air pressure, and winds.

Space scientists focus on rockets, satellites, space probes, and manned space travel, and the scientific investigations that are made possible by them. Thanks to unmanned probes, for instance, space scientists have access to images of Uranus and Neptune (above).

Although Landry missed one of the most exciting moments in the history of space exploration, she and her team had helped to make it all possible. Without them, the spacecraft might have performed just fine, but no one on Earth would have ever known.

WHAT IS SPACE SCIENCE?

Space science is the term applied to those scientific investigations made possible by rockets, satellites, and space probes—either manned or unmanned. In other words, it is the study of all things above our planet, from the middle levels of Earth's atmosphere, about 35 miles (56 kilometers) up, to the very edges of the universe itself, billions of light-years away.

There is much overlap between space science and astronomy. It may be helpful to view astronomy as the science of celestial bodies and their origins, motions, and constitution. Space science can be thought of as the means by which astronomical research is carried out. Thus, some people even view astronomy as being encompassed by space science.

However one defines it, space science is not a new discipline, but an important extension and blend of nearly every science, including—in addition to astronomy—physics, planetary science, optics, geology, biology, geodesy, meteorology, engineering, and chemistry.

EARLY SPACE SCIENCE

When the first U.S. rockets carried scientific equipment high above Earth to measure the upper atmosphere and the Sun in 1946, no one knew that, within little more than a decade, an entirely new field of study would be born.

Between the surprise launch of Sputnik 1 by the Soviet Union in 1957 and the creation of the National Aeronautics and Space Administration (NASA) in 1958, scientific research in Earth's upper atmosphere and in space began to be called "space science." According to NASA historian Homer E. Newell, the first formal use of the phrase was in the pamphlet titled "Introduction to Outer Space," issued on March 26, 1958, by members of President Dwight D. Eisenhower's Science Advisory Committee.

Scientists from such diverse disciplines as atmospheric research and meteorology, solar physics, and, eventually, lunar and planetary science were attracted by the new tools they could apply to their sciences. And as technology improved over the decades, space science took off—not only in the United States, but also around the world.

SPACE SCIENCE TODAY

The primary space-science research organization in the United States today is NASA. Its Office of Space Science (OSS) oversees this work in four main areas: exploring our solar system; studying the relationship between the Sun and Earth; determining the origin of Earth

In 1957, Western space scientists were shocked when the Soviet Union launched Sputnik 1, the first artificial satellite to be placed into Earth orbit.

and other bodies in the universe; and discovering the underlying structure of the universe.

Exploration of the Solar System

One of the most visible areas of scientific research by NASA is the visiting of other worlds by robot spacecraft. In their research, space scientists try to learn how our solar system formed, and if planetary systems are common or rare. They also explore the diverse changes that planets have undergone throughout their histories, including those that distinguish Earth as a planet. The researchers are investigating the processes that led to life on Earth, and whether life

Space science meets fashion design in the laboratory where engineers mix and match space-suit parts (right) to achieve the best fit for a particular astronaut. Inside the Biomass Production Chamber (below), space science meets agriculture, as teams of scientists test a wide range of crops to determine which plants will best produce food, water, and oxygen on long space missions.

began elsewhere in our solar system. And, in preparation for human visits to and colonization of other worlds, scientists hope to discover and catalog natural resources on these other worlds.

The Sun-Earth Connection

Through the relatively new field of space physics, space scientists study the heliosphere (the sphere of influence of the Sun) as one system and explore the dynamics of the Sun and its interactions with Earth, with other planetary bodies, and with interstellar material. Questions they are asking include the following: How are the conditions for life on Earth maintained? How does the solar output vary? How does Earth's magnetic field trap radiation and protect our planet? What knowledge from space can improve the quality of life on Earth?

The Search for the Origin of the Universe

Space scientists follow the 15-billion- to 20-billion-year-long chain of events from the beginning of the universe until the present in search of clues to our cosmic "roots." They address many questions, including the following: How did the first galaxies form? How do stars and planetary systems form? Are there any planets outside our solar system capable of sustaining life? How did life originate on Earth? Is there any kind of life outside our solar system?

The Structure and Evolution of the Universe

In their quest to learn the structure and fate of the universe, space scientists hope to identify dark matter (an as-yet-undetectable form of matter that many scientists believe forms 90 percent of the universe's mass) and learn how it shapes galaxies and clusters of galaxies; find out where and when the chemical elements were made; understand the cycles in which matter, energy, and magnetic fields are exchanged between stars and interstellar gas, and how violent cosmic jets can burst out of them; and measure

Using a fiber spectrograph and other advanced equipment, the researcher above is able to monitor data from 112 galaxies. Space scientists design the programs that allow computers to integrate and analyze such data.

Rocket Scientists

To the nonscientist, rocket science describes a field of study of nearly impossible-to-understand concepts and enormously complex methods. By extension, then, a rocket scientist is a man or woman of profound intelligence, a person possessed of truly deep insights, a visionary of extraordinary proportions. It's no wonder, then, that American English has taken the terms "rocket science" and "rocket scientist" and applied them figuratively to describe, respectively, the most difficult endeavor imaginable and the smartest person imaginable.

One of the first persons to meet the criteria necessary to be designated a "rocket scientist" was Robert Goddard (1882–1945), who, on May 16, 1926, in Roswell, New Mexico, launched the first liquid-fueled rocket to a then-staggering height of 46 feet (14 meters). By the 1930s, Goddard was using gyro-controlled rockets with automatic steering devices that could go as high as 2 miles (3 kilometers). Through the years, rockets became considerably more complex and were launched to even greater heights.

And then, in the autumn of 1957, after many failed attempts of its own, the United States was embarrassed when the Soviet Union launched the first artificial satellite—Sputnik 1—into Earth orbit. One month later, the Soviets launched another satellite—Sputnik 2—that carried a live dog named Laika.

Under mounting pressure, the United States hired German rocket scientist Wernher Von Braun (1912–77) to direct its effort to beat the Soviets into space.

Von Braun had formerly worked to build weapons for Hitler's Third Reich—against his will. And then, in 1945—near the end of World War II—the U.S. government brought him to the United States to help work on the army's guided missiles.

Many postwar Americans had doubts about Von Braun—a former German scientist. But it was under Von Braun's tireless direction that the United States successfully launched its first satellites into space and—less than a dozen years later—landed a man on the Moon and quickly gained unquestioned leadership in space research.

These days, rocket science rarely makes headlines. But, interestingly, the terms "rocket science" and "rocket scientist" remain

Robert Goddard's work with experimental rockets in the 1920s and 1930s laid the foundation for modern rocketry and paved the way for space travel.

very much alive. At some undetermined point, many speakers of everyday American English began applying the terms almost exclusively—and somewhat slangily—in the negative. So now, to say of a task "it's not rocket science" is to minimize its difficulty. To say of a person that "he (or she) is no rocket scientist" is to cast doubt on his (or her) intellect. In a roundabout way, then, we are reminded now and again of the brilliance and achievements of a small group of scientists.

how strong gravity fields operate near black holes and how they affected the early universe.

Some of the greatest recent advances in our knowledge of space science have come from robot spacecraft in orbit around Earth or visiting other celestial bodies. For example, the Near Earth Asteroid Rendezvous (NEAR) mission provided stunning images of the asteroid Mathilde. Images of Jupiter's moon Europa, relayed to Earth by the Galileo probe, suggest the possibility of liquid water beneath the moon's icy surface. The Solar and Heliospheric Observatory (SOHO) and other satellites have peered deeply into the Sun and have studied its effects on Earth. The Compton Gamma Ray Observatory (CGRO) recorded a fountain of antimatter being emitted from the center of our galaxy. The Lunar Prospector has shown the first evidence that there may be water and ice in the craters at the Moon's poles. The Mars Global

Careers in Space Science

There has never been a more exciting time to pursue a career in space science. Experts are always needed in such fields as space medicine, astrophysics, astronomy, earth science, meteorology, atmospheric physics, radar engineering, satellite technology, astronautics, remote sensing, computer

Some young scientists find that they can discover fascinating facets of space science by exploring the enormous number of astronomy-related Web sites.

systems, and many others. One day, space scientists may well travel throughout our solar system—and perhaps even beyond—in their quest for knowledge. Some space scientists have already traveled into Earth orbit aboard the U.S. space shuttle, where they have performed important research high above our planet's atmosphere.

An essential attribute of space scientists is the ability to be observant and make sense of what they see. Mathematical skills, the ability to think analytically and logically, and computer literacy are also fundamental requirements. In addition, space scientists need to be patient and determined, because they must often grapple with difficult problems that take many years to solve. Also important for space scientists is the ability to communicate well—public speaking and writing skills are essential.

To become a mission specialist aboard the space shuttle, a person must first become a scientist, and then an astronaut—not a particularly easy task. A prospective astronaut must have at least a bachelor's degree in engineering, one of the sciences, or mathematics, as well as three years of related professional experience or an advanced degree in a scientific field. Any man or woman in excellent physical condition who has met these basic qualifications can then apply for entry into the rigorous astronaut-training program, but the odds of being selected are exceedingly low. In one recent class, for example, only 20 out of the almost 4,000 applicants were chosen as astronaut candidates.

Whether you work as a space scientist on the ground, in Earth orbit, or, someday, on another world, the competition for jobs is fierce. To qualify for a position in one of the many space-science fields, a person must excel in such courses as physics, math, computing, and all the other sciences. Students should also study a variety of subjects outside the sciences, as a broad general education can be very helpful in getting a rewarding job in this field.

Astronaut testing and training falls under the scope of space science. In one test, astronaut candidates are spun at high speed in a giant centrifuge (above), and their reactions evaluated. Under the watchful eyes of space scientists, shuttle astronauts rehearse planned extravehicular activity in gigantic pools of water (right) long before the mission begins.

Surveyor (MGS), from its orbit around Mars, is mapping the planet's surface topography for use by future missions. And, perhaps the most prolific of all, the Hubble Space Telescope (HST), launched in 1990 and upgraded in 1993, 1997, 1999, and 2002, has relayed to Earth thousands of images that have revealed vast amounts of information about the universe.

SPACE SCIENCE IN THE FUTURE

For all we have learned so far, many fundamental questions about our universe remain.

At this writing, 34 spacecraft and Earth-based missions are in operation, trying to answer some of these questions. The next several decades will witness an exciting succession of increasingly sophisticated telescopes and spacecraft, each designed to gather even more information. These include the recently launched Spitzer Space Telescope (formerly SIRTF), which has up to 10 times the sensitivity of pre-vious infrared observatories; the Relativity Mission (also called Gravity Probe B), whose purpose is to verify Albert Einstein's general theory of relativity; a sample-return mission to Mars; a series of craft launches to the outer planets, including missions to Europa (a moon of Jupiter) and distant Pluto; a Next Generation Space Telescope (NGST); and a Terrestrial Planet Finder (TPF) mission.

Because of the intellect and imaginations of men and women who look up and wonder, and who devise new means of gathering and analyzing data, our understanding of the cosmos is growing at an unprecedented rate. We live at a time that future historians will look back upon as a golden age of discovery, as exciting and significant as when humans first turned their telescopes skyward.

MANNED SPACE PROGRAMS

On the launchpad at Cape Kennedy, a space shuttle is minutes away from liftoff. Inside the shuttle's spacious cabin—which can accommodate up to eight crew members—the mission commander, pilot, and mission and payload specialists are reclining in seats contoured exactly to their bodies. The astronauts listen as the minutes, then seconds, are counted down systematically by a mission controller.

When the count reaches the final 10 seconds, the shuttle's three main engines fire up.

During the few seconds they take to build up to their maximum thrust of 1.1 million pounds (500,000 kilograms), the shuttle is held on the launchpad by immensely strong clamps. Then, when the count reaches zero, the two solid-fuel boosters also ignite, the clamps release their

Perfectly executed space-shuttle liftoffs now seem routine. Nevertheless, sending astronauts safely into space remains a remarkable accomplishment, one built on years of success, failure, innovation, and insight.

grip, and the shuttle shoots skyward at the end of an immense plume of fire, riding on a total force of 7 million pounds (3 million kilograms) of thrust. Inside the crew cabin, all is noise, pressure, and shaking during the eight-and-a-half-minute ride into orbit. The astronauts and mission specialists are hanging on for the ride of their lives.

Travelers on the space shuttle, the current mode of transportation into space for the United States, experience forces that would be familiar to the pathbreaking astronauts who flew in the Mercury, Gemini, and Apollo spacecraft of the 1960s and 1970s. Now, in the 21st century, liftoffs have come to seem almost routine.

All those involved in the space program are well aware of the hazards that accompany space travel. The three lives lost in 1967 when a fire swept through an Apollo command module during a ground test, and the 14 lost with the explosions of the shuttles *Challenger* and *Columbia*, are forever etched in the memories of space travelers. At least four Soviet cosmonauts have also perished over the years.

Yet all these setbacks proved to be only temporary. America continued on its path toward the Moon despite the Apollo disaster. Two years after the *Challenger* explosion, the space-shuttle program resumed with the successful launch of *Discovery*. The U.S. commitment to the space shuttle was renewed in 1991, when the National Aeronautics and Space Administration (NASA) unveiled the shuttle *Endeavour*. Following a two-year hiatus in the wake of the 2003 *Columbia* accident, NASA returned to space with *Discovery* in summer 2005.

Of course, American astronauts can also reflect on the dramatic accomplishments of the space program. In particular, there was the historic landing of two men on the Moon on July 20, 1969. People the entire world over tuned in to watch the first live television images broadcast from the Moon's surface. U.S. President Richard M. Nixon relayed the global mood to the astronauts via telephone from the White House when he said, "For one priceless moment in the whole history of man, all the people on this Earth are truly one."

Astronaut John H. Glenn has made history twice—initially, as the first American to orbit Earth (in 1962, above) and then in 1998, when he became the oldest person to travel to space.

The Moon landing was the culmination of an ancient dream, made real by a space program which, at that time, had existed for barely a decade. Although humans would have gone into space no matter what, the early days of the space program took on a special flavor because of the fierce competition between the United States and the Soviet Union.

THE EARLY DAYS

The idea of traveling in space goes back at least hundreds of years, but practical efforts did not begin until after World War I had ended. In 1919, the American scientist Robert H. Goddard published a paper titled "A Method of Reaching Extreme Altitudes," outlining the basic mathematics of rocketry. Goddard's paper also proposed that a solid-propellant rocket could be launched with enough velocity to reach the Moon, and then signal its arrival to earthbound observers by setting off flash powder.

Today, the thought of astronauts sending up flash-powder flares in order to communicate with Earth seems hopelessly old-fashioned, but when Goddard was developing his design, there was little alternative. Radio transmitters and receivers were large and bulky, with limited range and power. Television was still in the experimental stage.

Of the original Mercury astronauts above, all but one, Donald "Deke" Slayton (far right), made it to space. The others each embarked on solo missions to solve basic problems associated with human spaceflight.

sary power. Although the small Mercury spacecraft was launched by the single-stage Atlas rocket, the larger Gemini and Apollo capsules used launchers with several stages. The powerful space rockets used by the Soviet Union were multistaged.

The early American space capsule was shaped like a cone with the point lopped off. Inside the capsule, the atmosphere consisted of oxygen pumped from tanks. Astronauts sat on a contoured couch, specially constructed according to each one's measurements. Since the nose of the capsule pointed straight upward at the moment of launch, the astronaut had to lie on his back. Pipes connected his space suit to a network of tanks and air pumps. Once in orbit, the astronaut could remove his helmet and breathe the oxygen in the capsule. If anything were to go wrong with the capsule's ventilating and filtering system, the astronaut would replace his helmet, and his space-suit system would take over.

The capsule had an elaborate control system connected to small rocket engines set around the craft. Controls were automatic during the launch. The pilot had the option of either taking control or leaving the craft on automatic. The pilot would take control during crucial maneuvers such as space docking or decelerating the craft out of orbit. A similar control system is used today to position the shuttle for the deployment of satellites and other work in space.

In the early spacecraft, no maneuvers were more vital than those required to bring about safe reentry through Earth's atmosphere. When it was time for reentry, the command pilot would turn his craft around so that it was moving with the blunt end—the base of the cone—foremost. Retro-rockets mounted in the blunt end then fired, slowing the craft. A heat shield, located on the craft's blunt end, absorbed most of the intense heat caused during reentry by friction with Earth's atmosphere.

Until the development of the space shuttle, all U.S. spacecraft landings took place at sea. In preparation for a water landing, the capsule's speed first slowed to a few hundred miles per hour. When the craft was near the target area,

Within the next 40 years, however, the field of electronics advanced in spectacular fashion. Radio and television technologies reached a level where it was possible not only to use them to guide unmanned spacecraft, but also to transmit all sorts of scientific data, including photographs, to ground stations back on Earth.

It was that kind of technology that made it possible for America's then-archrival, the Soviet Union, to launch Sputnik, the world's first artificial satellite, into orbit in 1957. The news came as something of a slap in the face to the United States, which had always imagined itself the world's technological leader. It was also a tremendous propaganda boost for the Soviet Union in its Cold War with the West.

In order to restore America's prestige and close any gaps in technology, President John F. Kennedy, in his State of the Union message to Congress on May 25, 1961, declared that the nation should commit itself to the goal of "landing a man on the Moon and returning him safely to Earth" by the end of the decade.

Our First Manned Rockets

The early rocket researchers figured out one thing quickly: any large spacecraft would have to be launched by multistage rockets. A single-stage rocket would not have the neces-

small parachutes, called drogues, opened for further braking. Finally, when the capsule was about 9,900 feet (3,000 meters) above the target area, larger parachutes opened. The velocity dropped to about 22 miles (35 kilometers) per hour, and the craft "splashed down" into the sea.

Mercury and Vostok

Before the Apollo project, which led to landings on the Moon, the U.S. space program passed through two preliminary stages, Projects Mercury and Gemini. At the same time, the Soviet Union was testing and operating its own projects, Vostok and Voskhod.

Both the Mercury and Vostok projects were designed to explore the concepts of manned spaceflight. Although each country took a different approach, the initial flights of each nation tested the ability to launch a human being in a spacecraft, keep the ship in orbit for a period of time, and then return it safely to Earth at a designated point. Both countries gained valuable information about the design and operation of space vehicles, and observed the reactions of human beings to the space environment. Unfortunately, at this point in space history, the United States and the Soviet Union were competing with each other, and were disinclined to share what they had learned.

In 1961, Soviet cosmonaut Yuri Gagarin became the first person to travel in space; he made a single Earth orbit.

Under Project Mercury, conducted in the United States from 1959 through 1963, a spacecraft carried a single astronaut aloft. The goals of the program were to test the physical reactions of the pilot and to monitor his ability to perform various tasks while weightless. Project Mercury was also designed to solve basic problems of spaceflight, including reentry into Earth's atmosphere.

The Vostok Project, conducted in the Soviet Union from 1958 through 1963, also sent a single voyager—called a cosmonaut—into space with each mission. The program's goals were much the same as Project Mercury's, and the Soviet scientists also collected data about the space operations as it related to zero gravity.

In addition, the Soviets studied the problems associated with space rendezvous and with tracking more than one spacecraft simultaneously.

By contrast with the conical shape of the Mercury capsule, Vostok was a sphere. The cosmonaut sat in the same kind of ejection seat used by jet-fighter pilots. Unlike Mercury astronauts, who landed back on Earth while still in their craft, Vostok cosmonauts ejected before their spaceship landed, and parachuted the final mile or two to Earth.

Yuri Gagarin (Soviet Union) became the first person to travel in space with his single-orbit flight on April 12, 1961. Less than a month later, on May 5, 1961, Alan Shepard (U.S.) entered the history books as the first American in space by flying in a suborbital trajectory—above Earth's atmosphere, but not in orbit. Two months later, Gus Grissom (U.S.) flew a second suborbital flight. Then, on August 6, 1961, Gherman Titov (Soviet Union) completed 17 orbits on a journey that lasted 25.3 hours. The first American to actually orbit Earth was John H. Glenn (U.S.), departing Cape Canaveral on February 20, 1962.

In the next year, three more American astronauts were launched into orbit around Earth. M. Scott Carpenter flew a three-orbit mission, and Walter M. Schirra piloted a six-orbit mission. L. Gordon Cooper orbited 22 times in a little more than 34 hours in 1963 on Project Mercury's last mission.

In this same time period, the Soviet Union took the first steps toward spacecraft rendezvous. In 1962, the Vostoks of Andrian Nikolayev and Pavel Popovich came within 3 miles (5 kilometers) of each other. The following year, Valery Bykovsky flew for nearly five days, and came within 3 miles of a spacecraft carrying Valentina Tereshkova, the first woman to fly in space. The Vostok crafts could not actually rendezvous, however, because they did not have the rocket power to maneuver in space.

Although the Soviet scientists sent up longer flights, they limited the tasks assigned to

Anatomy of a Rocket

Sir Isaac Newton would have loved rockets. Rockets are working models of his famous third law of motion, which states that for every action, there must be an equal and opposite reaction. When a rocket fires, the fuel burns, and combustion gases quickly expand and push out the rear. As the gases thrust downward, the rocket is pushed upward. Although a rocket's motion is virtually independent of the surrounding air, it flies considerably faster in a vacuum where there is no air to resist the rocket's upward motion, or to impede the downward exhaust.

The actual thrust of the rocket depends on only two factors. The first is the quantity of combustion gases produced (which depends on the amount of fuel being burned). The exhaust blast resulting from the combustion leaves the exhaust nozzle, which is shaped in such a way that the gases push against the nozzle as they expand. The second factor is the ejection speed of these gases.

Liquid-fuel technology, by which pumps can control how quickly fuel and oxidizer from two separate tanks mix, was used for the Saturn V rocket (right) that launched American astronauts to the Moon. This achievement evolved from the ingenuity of physicist Robert Goddard and his colleagues, shown above with a test rocket.

Types of Rockets

Currently, scientists divide all rockets into one of two categories: liquid fuel or solid fuel. A liquid-fuel rocket has two tanks—one containing fuel, and the other containing an "oxidizer," which causes combustion when it reacts chemically with the fuel. Typically, the fuel is either alcohol or refined kerosene, and the oxidizer is liquid oxygen. Pumps force the two liquids into a combustion chamber, where they are then ignited and burned.

In a solid-fuel rocket, the "fuel tank" and the "combustion chamber" are one and the same. The fuel tank contains hard, rubbery explosives into which an oxygen-rich chemical has been kneaded during the manufacturing process. To the touch, the fuel feels very much like an automobile tire. It is shaped like a tube with very thick walls and a small central hole. The fuel burns outward from the central hole, which constitutes the combustion chamber. To bring about combustion, a pyrotechnic igniter is triggered. The igniter consists of an electric wire surrounded by a powder charge; when the wire is heated, it sets off the charge.

Liquid-fuel rockets, although more complicated, have one big advantage over solid-fuel rockets: pumps can control how quickly the fuel and oxidizer mix. That's why Saturn V, the rocket that launched men toward the Moon, was liquid-fueled. Today, the National Aeronautics and Space Administration's (NASA's) space-shuttle system relies on solid-fuel boosters simply to add extra thrust to get off Earth's surface. The liquid-fueled main rocket engines of the shuttle do the work once the shuttle is in space.

The Saturn V Rocket

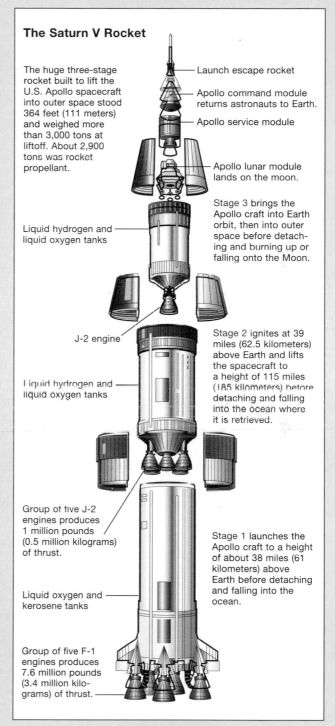

The huge three-stage rocket built to lift the U.S. Apollo spacecraft into outer space stood 364 feet (111 meters) and weighed more than 3,000 tons at liftoff. About 2,900 tons was rocket propellant.

Launch escape rocket

Apollo command module returns astronauts to Earth.

Apollo service module

Apollo lunar module lands on the moon.

Stage 3 brings the Apollo craft into Earth orbit, then into outer space before detaching and burning up or falling onto the Moon.

Liquid hydrogen and liquid oxygen tanks

J-2 engine

Liquid hydrogen and liquid oxygen tanks

Stage 2 ignites at 39 miles (62.5 kilometers) above Earth and lifts the spacecraft to a height of 115 miles (185 kilometers) before detaching and falling into the ocean where it is retrieved.

Group of five J-2 engines produces 1 million pounds (0.5 million kilograms) of thrust.

Liquid oxygen and kerosene tanks

Group of five F-1 engines produces 7.6 million pounds (3.4 million kilograms) of thrust.

Stage 1 launches the Apollo craft to a height of about 38 miles (61 kilometers) above Earth before detaching and falling into the ocean.

Until the introduction of the shuttle, all U.S. space missions ended with an ocean splashdown. In 1971, the Apollo 15 command module arrived home safely—despite the failure of one of its parachutes (above).

Among the most spectacular feats completed during Project Gemini was the "space walk." In this extravehicular activity (EVA), one astronaut floated free of the capsule, tethered by a lifeline known as an umbilical. The lifeline furnished oxygen supplied by the capsule's pumping system and had an electrical system that enabled the spacewalker to talk to the second astronaut inside the capsule.

Meanwhile, the Soviet Union worked on the Voskhod program. In the race to outdo the United States in space accomplishments, the Vostok capsule was modified to hold up to three cosmonauts. Soviet space capsules came down on land, rather than landing in the sea, as U.S. capsules did. Because there was no room for ejection seats in the crowded Voskhod, a system for "soft" landing was developed: a group of small solid-fuel rockets in the base of the Voskhod capsule slowed the reentry speed to less than 3 feet (1 meter) per second.

On October 12, 1964, the *Voskhod 1* carried the first three-person crew into space. During the flight of *Voskhod 2* in March 1965, Alexei Leonov became the first person to walk in space. A few weeks later, the United States launched its first manned Gemini mission. In July 1965, Edward H. White left the relative safety of *Gemini 4* and became the first American to walk outside a spacecraft.

The Soviets did not launch any more manned missions in the Voskhod program. The remaining Gemini flights for the Americans more fully explored the problems of working outside a spacecraft and refined rendezvous and docking techniques in preparation for a landing on the Moon.

cosmonauts. By comparison, the NASA program was conducted such that human beings could function as pilots, engineers, and scientists in space. By early 1964, the visions for both countries included multiperson crews and more-complicated missions. While the Mercury and Vostok programs were still operating, U.S. and Soviet engineers had begun designing a second generation of manned spacecraft.

Gemini and Voskhod

The U.S. program, Project Gemini, ran from 1961 until late 1966. Named for the twins in the zodiac, a Gemini spacecraft could carry two astronauts. These well-trained crews rehearsed the tasks required to land astronauts on the Moon and then return safely to Earth. They also executed genuine maneuvers in orbit, such as taking the craft off-course and guiding it back again. They practiced rendezvous in space, in which two capsules would fly to within several feet of each other. The last Gemini flights of the series went even further, by docking with rocket engines while in orbit.

MEN WALK ON THE MOON

All of these much-publicized adventures were merely dress rehearsals for Project Apollo, the program which would ultimately put astronauts on the Moon. The early Apollo missions, which tested systems in Earth orbit, were launched by the Saturn IB, a two-stage rocket with a thrust of 1,653,467 pounds (750,000 kilograms). Beginning with *Apollo 8*, the first lunar flight, the launch vehicle was the giant Saturn V rocket, a three-stage vehicle 364 feet (111 meters) high, with a takeoff thrust of about 7 million pounds (3 million kilograms).

The Apollo spacecraft consisted of three basic parts: the conical command module, the cylindrical service module, and the lunar module. Additionally, a spacecraft–lunar module adapter attached the Apollo craft to the Saturn V rocket. Each Apollo flight also featured a launch-escape function, which could whisk the astronauts to safety in case of a malfunction during the initial launching stages.

The command module was the control center of the spacecraft. There, three astronauts worked and lived during a mission (except when two of the men were in the lunar module or on the Moon). The service module contained electrical and propulsion systems, as well as most of the spacecraft's oxygen supply. The lunar module, consisting of a descent stage and an ascent stage, was used for the actual exploration of the Moon's surface.

The first manned flights of the Apollo spacecraft were planned for 1967. In January of that year, however, while testing their Apollo vehicle at Cape Kennedy, three astronauts were killed when the capsule caught fire. Uncovered wiring had caused a spark in the pure-oxygen atmosphere. The ensuing investigations and redesign of the vehicle delayed the program for more than a year.

Between 1968 and 1969, several practice Apollo flights took place. Not only did the as-

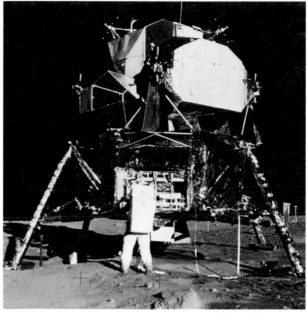

While crewmate Michael Collins stayed aboard the command module Columbia in orbit, the lunar module Eagle separated, transporting Neil Armstrong and Edwin Aldrin to the Moon's surface, where they unloaded scientific experiment packages (above).

tronauts test the flight performance of the craft, but they also scouted ahead for potential lunar landing sites.

On July 16, 1969, *Apollo 11* was launched for the Moon. Four days later, Neil Armstrong and Edwin "Buzz" Aldrin landed on the lunar surface, while Michael Collins remained with the orbiting command ship. For more than two hours, the two Moon walkers collected rocks, photographed the area, and set up scientific experiments. Despite their bulky space suits and portable life-support systems and communication gear, the men moved easily in the low-gravitational field.

In the years that followed, six other Apollo missions took off for the Moon. *Apollo 13,*

Apollo 17's commander Eugene Cernan rides the battery-powered Lunar Roving Vehicle across the Moon's Taurus-Littrow region, where the mission's crew would later conduct geological surveys and collect samples.

Animals in Space

As strange as it may seem from today's perspective, it was not so long ago that scientists did not know if it was possible for a human being to leave Earth's atmosphere and survive in the conditions of outer space. Those researchers who dreamed of space travel knew that there was no air to breathe in orbit, that there was clearly danger to humans from radiation exposure, and that a

that would put animals in space in order to find practical ways to protect humans who would travel beyond Earth's atmosphere. Nearly 15 years passed before any human was sent aloft; meanwhile, animals were the "astronauts" making test flights—and most of them returned to Earth alive. Scientists believed that if an "astro-animal" could survive space travel, humans could survive, too.

Beginning in 1947, researchers launched a number of live organisms into space. On the first flights, fruit flies, as well as seeds and spores, were the test subjects. In 1948, primates followed. One rhesus monkey, Albert 1, even reached an altitude of 38 miles (61 kilometers).

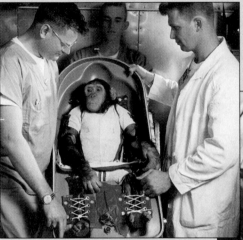

Ham (the chimpanzee) and Laika (the dog) were just two of many animals that, in the 1950s and 1960s, endured the physical effects of spaceflight, and thereby paved the way for safe human space travel.

person's body would be subjected alternately to greatly increased gravitational forces and to weightlessness. Indeed, one question remained foremost in their minds: Was it possible to develop the technology that would allow humans to survive outside of Earth's protective atmosphere?

Since there was no way to duplicate the conditions of outer space on Earth, American and Soviet scientists developed programs

The Soviet Union used mainly canines as experimental subjects. In 1957, the country launched a dog named Laika aboard Sputnik 2. She became the first living creature to actually orbit the Earth. For seven days, Laika ate, barked, and moved about her capsule with no apparent ill effects. At the time, unfortunately, there was no way to return a spacecraft to Earth from orbit, so Laika died in space, but her unprecedented journey sparked great interest. The

launched in 1970, had to return to Earth following an oxygen-tank explosion. The final spacecraft to fly as part of the project, *Apollo 17*, returned to Earth on December 19, 1972.

During Moon landings, astronauts placed several seismometers on the lunar surface. These have enabled scientists to continue to monitor seismic events, both moonquakes and

magnitude of the accomplishment of keeping an animal alive in space for a week received global recognition. Laika's image even appeared on postage stamps.

The United States approached this same challenge, but with a focus on primates. After training more than 60 chimpanzees, the two most alert among them—Ham and Enos—were chosen for flight. In January 1961, strapped inside a Mercury capsule, Ham survived a suborbital flight of 6.6 minutes. This successful flight was the precursor to that of the first American in space, Alan B. Shepard, in May. Six months later, Enos was launched into full Earth orbit to test systems in preparation for John Glenn's mission in February 1962.

Unlike the other animals sent into outer space, whose main task was simply to survive, the chimpanzees were expected to perform simple mechanical tasks. To facilitate these, the spacecraft the chimps rode in were equipped with a reward system. If the animals pulled the correct lever, they received a banana-flavored pellet; for an incorrect lever, they received a mild shock. One chimpanzee pulled levers 7,000 times in 70 minutes—and made fewer mistakes than several human subjects who tried the exercise! The ability to operate mechanical devices in space proved that higher primates—and, more importantly, humans—could effectively function in the microgravity above Earth's atmosphere.

October 1963 brought the first flight of a feline into space. Felix, a black-and-white tomcat, was launched by France in the nose cone of a Veronique rocket. The "astro-cat" rode to a height of 120 miles (193 kilometers) before returning safely to Earth. Ground stations monitored the cat's responses to stimuli through readings from electrodes that had been implanted in his brain.

meteorite impacts. Meanwhile, a laser reflector that the astronauts left on the Moon has allowed scientists to measure the distance between Earth and the Moon to an accuracy of 6 inches (15 centimeters). It has also provided invaluable information on the possible weakening of gravitational forces between the two bodies.

While on the Moon, the astronauts also gathered particles blown out from the Sun. By exposing a sheet of aluminum foil, they collected a small number of these atomic particles, which make up the solar wind. Of great interest to both scientists and the general public was the precious cargo of lunar rocks that arrived with the return of lunar missions. This material included core samples as well as surface rocks and soil. Some were igneous rocks, which suggested that the Moon might once have had volcanic activity. Despite the tremendous success of the Moon-exploration program, space planners soon realized that the Apollo-Saturn system, based upon expendable rocket launchers, was too expensive to continue. Indeed, the four-year Apollo program cost more than $20 billion.

Apollo-Soyuz Test Project

While the United States was concentrating on its Moon program, the Soviets had replaced Voskhod with a much-improved spacecraft, which they named Soyuz. The first manned flight in April 1967 ended in tragedy when the craft's parachute lines became tangled during reentry, causing *Soyuz 1* to crash, killing cosmonaut Vladimir Komarov. Nevertheless, the Soviets carried out many Soyuz missions to investigate the problems of rendezvous and docking in preparation for both a Moon landing of their own and an Earth-orbiting space station.

In July 1975, the Apollo-Soyuz Test Project took place, marking the first time that the United States and the Soviet Union had worked together, and the first time a manned spaceflight was conducted by two nations. The history-making mission was designed to test rendezvous-and-docking-system compatibility for American and Soviet spacecraft, and opened the way for future joint human flights.

For this mission, the United States used an existing Apollo spacecraft with a design nearly identical to the one that had orbited the Moon. The Soviet Union used a Soyuz spacecraft. The docking module was designed and constructed by NASA to serve as an air lock and transfer corridor between the Apollo and the Soyuz.

Both spacecraft were launched on July 15, 1975. The *Soyuz* took off first, followed by

Soyuz spacecraft. It was during a Salyut mission that three cosmonauts died during reentry, when their capsule suddenly lost all its oxygen due to a defective valve.

In 1986, the *Mir* ("Peace") space station, an improved version of the Salyut, was launched. *Mir* was continuously occupied for more than 13 years—from March 1986 to August 1999. An important *Mir* record was set on March 22, 1995, when Valeri Polyakov returned to Earth after enduring a record 438 days aboard the space station.

The United States also put up a space station—*Skylab*—in 1973. Equipped to house a crew of three, *Skylab* carried an array of instruments for studying space, the stars, Earth, and the biological effects of space on astronauts. All told, three separate crews of astronauts occupied *Skylab*. The space station was slated to stay in orbit until 1983, but it entered the atmosphere in 1979 and was destroyed. (For more information about *Mir* and *Skylab*, see the article "Space Stations.")

MEET THE SPACE SHUTTLE

In 1969, President Nixon appointed a NASA task force to find a low-cost alternative to the Saturn rocket, and, in 1972, NASA approved a new design for the space shuttle. Nine years passed before the shuttle first roared into orbit, but today it is the workhorse of the space program. Comparing the shuttle with the Apollo spacecraft is similar to comparing a Porsche to a Model T. The space shuttle can launch satellites, carry a large science laboratory, and repair satellites in orbit or bring them back to Earth. At the completion of a mission, the shuttle reenters Earth's atmosphere and lands on a runway in much the same way as does an airplane.

Originally, NASA engineers envisioned the space shuttle as a spacecraft with two manned

Apollo seven hours later. Approximately 52 hours after the *Soyuz* launch, the American astronauts maneuvered the *Apollo* spacecraft to a point where it was possible to rendezvous and dock with *Soyuz*. The *Apollo* and *Soyuz* crews conducted a variety of experiments over a two-day period. Approximately 43 hours after separation, *Soyuz* returned to Earth, while *Apollo* remained in space six more days.

Apollo's Legacy: Space Stations

Following the fall of the Soviet Union, Russia gradually revealed that it also had had plans to land a man on the Moon in the late 1960s or early 1970s. The Soviet effort was more modest than the Apollo program—two cosmonauts would have flown a modified Soyuz into lunar orbit, with only one actually landing and spending a short time on the Moon's surface. The program was canceled after four consecutive failures of the giant N-1 booster rocket.

Although its Moon program failed, the Soviet Union continued its commitment to a manned space program, and began launching Salyut space stations in 1971. Cosmonauts were transferred to and from the stations using the

stages. The booster craft, about the size of a Boeing 747, would carry the orbiter piggyback until it reached a high enough altitude, at which point the two vehicles would separate. The booster crew would then turn around and fly back to base, while the orbiter would fire its rocket engines and continue into orbit. Ultimately, budget restrictions forced NASA to consider a simpler design. The space shuttle as we know it today consists of three separate elements—the orbiter itself, twin solid-rocket boosters, and an external fuel tank.

The solid-rocket boosters (SRBs) are the largest solid-fuel rockets ever developed for spaceflight. They give the shuttle two minutes of powerful thrust to get it above the thickest layers of Earth's atmosphere, to where the three main engines built into the orbiter can work most efficiently. After the SRBs burn out, they parachute into the ocean for recovery and are later reused. Each booster stands 141 feet (43 meters) high and weighs almost 1,325,000 pounds (600,000 kilograms) when fueled. A single booster provides liftoff thrust of 3,306,935 pounds (1.5 million kilograms) at launch.

The external fuel tank carries liquid hydrogen and oxygen in separate compartments to feed the orbiter's three main rocket engines. The tank's diameter is 28 feet (8.5 meters), its height is 154 feet (47 meters), and its empty weight is 75,000 pounds (34,000 kilograms). The base of the shuttle's launch platform holds boxlike fueling stations for liquid hydrogen and oxygen. Machinery pumps these extraordinarily cold liquids into the rocket's external tanks in the final hours before liftoff.

The only part of the shuttle system that goes into orbit is the orbiter itself. The vehicle is 121 feet (37 meters) long, spans 79 feet (24 meters) across the wingtips, and stands 56 feet (17 meters) tall on its landing gear. The crew cabin, located in the front part of the craft, carries an average of seven people, or up to 10 in special cases. The mission commander and the pilot sit at the forward flight deck, surrounded by far more control lights and pan-

els than found in any Earthbound vehicle. The other crew members—technical and scientific personnel—work on the rear flight deck or inside the payload bay. They are referred to as either mission specialists (NASA astronauts) or payload specialists (noncareer astronauts, usually scientists).

Each orbiter is designed to last for 100 flights. To accomplish this longevity, NASA's engineers had to overcome a major obstacle: damage from the amazingly high temperatures created by friction when the spacecraft reenters Earth's atmosphere.

Their solution was to cover the undersurface of the orbiter with special tiles. The current shuttle design uses 20,548 individually shaped silica-fiber tiles, varying in thickness from 1 inch (25.4 millimeters) to 5 inches (127 millimeters). Each tile is specially shaped to hug the contours of the orbiter, and can withstand temperatures up to 2,300° F (1,260° C). The nose cap and the edges of the wings, which are subjected to the most heat during reentry, are covered with a material that can withstand temperatures up to 3,000° F (1,649° C), a temperature hot enough to melt steel. Engineers use lightweight thermal-insulation blankets woven from silica fibers on parts of the orbiter's upper

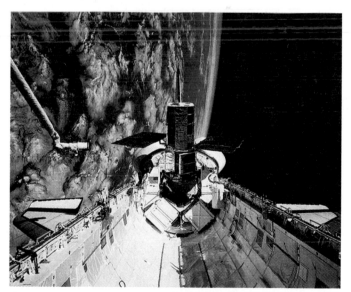

A shuttle crew, ready to begin work on the Solar Maximum Mission observatory, viewed the four-year-old satellite as it awaited repair in the craft's cargo bay. Following its repair and redeployment, the satellite went on to spend another five years capturing images of the Sun.

Launching a few pounds of electronic hardware into space was one thing. But sending a human was something different altogether. Many problems had to be solved before manned spaceflight could be achieved. Among these problems were the physical effects of excessive acceleration, weightlessness, radiation in space, and the reentry into Earth's atmosphere.

Thanks to intensive training, astronaut Scott Parazynski has the confidence to work outside the International *Space Station, anchored to the station's robotic arm solely by a mobile foot restraint.*

Anyone venturing into orbit on a spaceship, scientists calculated, would be subjected to acceleration forces as high as 8 G's, or eight times the force of gravity. Experts already knew that the top limit that a pilot could withstand without passing out was 4 G's. How, then, could future astronauts withstand even greater acceleration?

To test humans' ability to tolerate high acceleration, engineers spun them as fast as possible. A gondola was suspended from the end of a large arm, which in turn was attached to a rotary motor. A volunteer sat in the gondola. As the motor began running, the gondola sped round and round with increasing speed. Volunteers who remained in a sitting position underwent alarming effects. Blood circulation slackened. When blood failed to reach certain vital areas of the brain, the volunteer would lose consciousness. But if he lay on his back with his head slightly raised and the knees slightly bent, the physical effects were not nearly so severe. It became evident that astronauts would have to lie almost supine—or on their backs—during moments of extreme acceleration.

Another concern was how astronauts would be affected by weightlessness. Here on Earth, investigators simulated a state of weightlessness by means of an airplane maneuver. The pilot would first make a shallow dive, then point the nose of the plane upward while throttling back, cutting power to the engine. The plane went through a curve, moving upward at first, then leveling out, and finally pointing downward. From the instant the pilot released the throttle until full-engine power was restored, the plane and everything it contained were weightless. The periods of weightlessness ranged from 25 seconds to about a minute.

During this brief time, people in an experimental chamber in the plane floated about freely. So did all loose objects. Weightlessness produced physiological side effects. It made humans disoriented, dizzy, nauseous, and unable to control their movements. The plane became known as the Vomit Comet, for obvious reasons. These effects varied widely in different individuals. They seemed to be slight in some, overpowering in others.

Clearly, astronauts would have to go through a period of physical conditioning to endure extreme acceleration and weightlessness. To test this idea, researchers put animals through training, and then sent them into orbit. Most animals returned safely to Earth, apparently little worse for their experience. Scientists concluded that well-trained astronauts should

In the weightlessness of space, astronauts quickly notice a decrease in muscle tone. Frequent and vigorous exercise (right) in the gravity-free surroundings seems to help, especially during extended missions.

be able to withstand intense acceleration and the physical effects of short-term weightlessness.

Investigators also knew that spacecraft outside Earth's atmosphere would be bombarded by radiation. Ultraviolet rays from the Sun would pummel the craft with undiminished force, because no air exists to absorb them. Solar-flare eruptions on the Sun's surface send out X rays and electrons into space. X rays are also produced when the free electrons hurling through space strike the metal of a spacecraft's walls. At the same time, spacecraft would encounter high-energy cosmic rays. The discovery of the Earth's radiation belt in 1958 laid bare another source of potential danger.

But studies carried out with unmanned satellites showed that radiation did not offer an insurmountable obstacle to spaceflight. Even very thin sheets of metal could stop most of the ultraviolet rays and the less powerful X rays that shoot from the Sun. Under normal conditions, the walls of the spacecraft would be thick enough to shield its occupants against radiation. It would not be practical to provide shielding against cosmic rays; but normally there would not be enough of this type of radiation to constitute a hazard. And the Earth's radiation belt could be avoided with proper planning.

It was also necessary for engineers to protect manned spacecraft from the tremendous friction-induced heat that would sear the craft as it plunged through the atmosphere on its return from space. The technique finally devised consisted of slowing down the craft with backward-facing braking rockets, called retrorockets. Engineers also fitted the craft with a special shield to absorb the heat produced during the period of reentry.

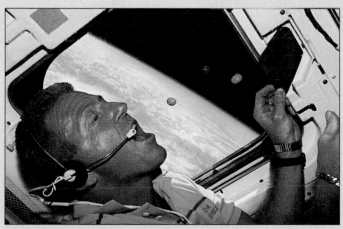

Some skills develop only with practice in the weightless environment of the space shuttle. Not all of these proficiencies are included as part of the training astronauts receive prior to their first mission.

surface, such as the shuttle's cargo-bay doors, where the temperature during reentry will not exceed 1,200° F (649° C).

At liftoff, the space shuttle weighs more than 4.4 million pounds (2 million kilograms). All three engines and both solid-rocket boosters are burning at the moment of launch, producing well over 7 million pounds (3.2 million kilograms) of thrust.

After two minutes of powered flight, at an altitude of about 28 miles (45 kilometers), the solid boosters burn out, separate from the orbiter, and parachute into the ocean for recovery.

Astronauts frequently need to leave their spacecraft to perform various tasks. Equipped with a manned maneuvering unit, a nitrogen jet-propelled device, crew members can now venture some distance from their ships, using a joy-stick mechanism for turns and speed control.

The orbiter and fuel tank continue into space. About 8.5 minutes after launch, at an altitude of 68 miles (109 kilometers), the main engines cut off, and the external tank tumbles into the atmosphere and burns up.

Two maneuvering engines give extra thrust to push the shuttle into orbit and help steer the orbiter in space. They also help it return to Earth. At the end of the mission, the orbiter fires its maneuvering engines, slowing the spacecraft so much that it dives into Earth's atmosphere. The air in the atmosphere has the same effect, acting as a brake. Flying without engine power, the shuttle becomes a glider and makes a sweeping turn to line up with its landing runway. The pilot has only one chance to attempt a landing, but perhaps because the landing is controlled by onboard computers and directional signals sent from ground control, all landings to date have been successful.

Perhaps the most important feature of the orbiter is its payload bay. Stretching 59 feet (18 meters) long and 15 feet (4.5 meters) in diameter, the bay can tote up to 50,000 pounds (22,680 kilograms) into orbit. Unmanned space probes are launched from shuttle payload bays.

At the edge of the payload bay stands a robotic arm, called the remote manipulator system (RMS). Astronauts control this device from the shuttle's aft flight deck, using it to capture and release satellites.

On some missions, astronauts have to leave the shuttle and perform repairs while floating in space—so-called extravehicular activity (EVA). EVAs are sometimes scheduled for satellite-repair tasks. One dramatic satellite "rescue" occurred in 1984 when shuttle astronauts used the RMS to pluck the failing Solar Max satellite from orbit, bring Solar Max into the bay, repair the satellite, and redeploy it into orbit. The experience proved especially valuable late in 1993, when shuttle astronauts used *Endeavour*'s robot arm to snare the faulty Hubble Space Telescope, return it to the payload bay, perform necessary repairs and servicing, and then re-release it into orbit.

During an EVA, the astronaut depends on a special space suit called the extravehicular mobility unit (EMU). This suit has a hard upper torso to which flexible pants are joined, plus gloves and a helmet. A life-support pack connects directly to the torso. (For more details about the space suit, see the article "Dressing for Space.") Before the shuttle first flew, astronauts who ventured into space were always tethered by a lifeline. With the shuttle, the astronaut relies on the manned maneuvering unit (MMU).

The unit snaps onto the back of the EMU and places two joysticks at the astronaut's fingertips for side-to-side motion (left hand) and rotation (right hand). Through a computer, the joysticks command gas thrusters that push the astronaut, untethered, through space.

The Flying Scientists

One of the main objectives of the current space program is to carry out low-gravity-environment experiments that will enhance scientific research and benefit people worldwide. The *Spacelab* module, built by the European Space Agency (ESA), was especially designed for conducting this kind of space research. Containing U-shaped pallets that expose experiments to the vacuum of space, *Spacelab* is a pressurized laboratory designed to fit in a shuttle's payload bay. It can also be linked to the *International Space Station (ISS)*.

The laboratory consists of two segments, each 9 feet (2.7 meters) long and 13.5 feet (4 meters) in diameter. The first segment, the core, contains pressurized modules, pallets, data-processing computers, and some working space. The other segment is a complete laboratory/workshop. The entire module connects to the crew compartment of a shuttle or space station by means of a tunnel.

Packed with scientific instruments, *Spacelab* allows astronauts to perform a wide variety of experiments. The science projects have ranged from physics and astronomy to botany and biology. For example, during one mission, investigators set up a fluid-physics module, in which they studied how fluids spread, change shape, and conduct heat in zero gravity. By studying fluids under these conditions, researchers learned how liquid fuels behave in spacecraft tanks and how lubricants react to being in space.

Spacelab missions often involve crew members who are not professional astronauts, but rather, other scientists specializing in areas such as physics and chemistry. One advantage of the space shuttle over earlier spacecraft is that during liftoff, acceleration is limited to about three times the force of gravity, or 3 G's. Reentry forces are typically less than 1.5 G's. As a result, scientists in good health can travel aboard the shuttle with only a minimum of training, and crews aboard U.S. spacecraft are no longer made up exclusively of highly trained test pilots.

New and Improved

The space-shuttle program got off to a spectacular start with the launching of *Columbia* on April 12, 1981. Five years later, it suffered a tragic setback when the shuttle *Challenger* exploded. A commission appointed by President Reagan to investigate the accident concluded that the explosion had been the result of a faulty sealant ring, called an O-ring, located in the right solid-fuel booster. Hot gases had leaked out of the booster through the faulty seal, burning a hole in the external liquid-fuel tank and setting off an immense explosion.

Following recommendations made by the commission, NASA began redesigning the booster joints and O-rings. The space agency also made a number of management changes and began developing a crew-escape system. The shuttle fleet remained grounded for 32 months until the program resumed with the successful launching of *Discovery* on September 29, 1988.

By 1991, it appeared that the shuttle program had completely regained its momentum. In April of that year, *Atlantis* sent the huge 35,000-pound (15,875-kilogram) Compton Gamma Ray Observatory (CGRO) into low

On January 28, 1986, the shuttle Challenger *and its crew of seven perished when the spacecraft exploded soon after takeoff. In the aftermath of the tragedy, many safety improvements were made to the shuttle.*

The very same technologies that have launched space shuttles, put men on the Moon, and kept such marvels as the *International Space Station (ISS)* in working order have found their way into our industries, our homes, our food, and even our clothing. Off-shoots from space-based technology now appear in just about every city and town.

It may seem strange at first to realize that a young man racking up slam dunks at the gym wears a bit of NASA technology in his athletic shoes, in the form of a shock-absorbing material developed early in the space program for astronauts' Moon boots. But the makings of high-tech athletic shoes, or sunglass lenses that mimic the eye filters of hawks and eagles, or mittens that warm better than wool, represent just a few of thousands of secondary applications of space-based technology that have enriched our lives. Known as "spin-offs," these products and systems have emerged from research conducted at the 10 NASA-managed field centers across the United States.

Two of the most common of those are freeze-dried foods, which were originally created as convenient meals for astronauts in orbit, and cordless tools, developed to make repairs possible during space walks.

But heading the list of successful spin-offs are the medical wonders that daily save and improve the quality of peoples' lives. Take, for example, the excimer-laser technology developed at NASA's Jet Propulsion Laboratory (JPL) in Pasadena, California. This pioneer technology for environmental monitoring—once used solely for remote sensing of Earth's ozone layer—now plays an important role in lifesaving operations on blood vessels. Because this "cool" laser uses ultraviolet-light energy to work at 150° F (65° C), physicians use it to clear fatty deposits that block blood flow in coronary arteries without harming healthy tissue.

Patients who need regular injections rested easier, too, once the Programmable Implantable Medication System (PIMS), a computerized pump, became readily accessible as an automatic drug dispenser. A spin-off that began as a project at NASA's Goddard Space Flight Center in Greenbelt, Maryland, in the 1970s, it took

Much innovative technology developed for space travel has found its way home. The UV-blocking sunglasses above were inspired by the material of space helmet visors; the cushy soles of the athletic shoes below derived from early "Moon boots."

earthly forms as wearable and implantable devices that automatically dispense the right amount of medication to patients.

Computerized tomography, also known as CT or CAT scan, and magnetic resonance imaging (MRI)—designed to computer-enhance images of the Moon—have been incorporated into body-scanning machines that provide diagnoses for millions. Besides scanning the human body, cross-sectioned CT images are able to aid paleontologists in producing highly detailed images of fossils. The technology behind the Advanced Computed Tomography Inspection System (ACTIS), which scans the body for irregularities

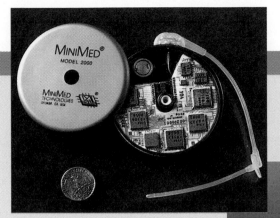

The medical industry has been an important beneficiary of NASA technology. Tiny pumps (left) that supply diabetic patients with on-demand insulin and surgically implantable pacemakers (below) for cardiac patients are space-technology spin-offs that have improved or saved thousands of lives.

such as tumors, made its unglamorous debut as a mechanical sleuth for finding defects in rocket engines.

Often such secondary applications of space technology adapt quite smoothly to unlikely applications. The Hubble Space Telescope (HST), for example, has managed to contribute to protecting our health. Just one of many bits of technology taken from Hubble is its Charged Coupled Device (CCD) chip. For digital biopsies of suspicious breast tissue, these advanced chips can distinguish between a malignant and benign tumor, in many cases eliminating the need for surgical biopsy and saving surgical candidates thousands of dollars.

Space spin-offs have touched all walks of life. The unistix navigational controller, for instance, is a device that allows drivers with physical disabilities to control their automobiles using simple, low-force motions. The device operates with technology initially developed for directing the Lunar Roving Vehicle (LRV) across the Moon's tricky, unfamiliar terrain. One person afflicted with paralysis, who 10 years earlier had watched Apollo astronauts drive the lunar rover with just one hand, using a T-bar, convinced NASA and the U.S. Department of Veterans Affairs to contract with a Colorado firm to transfer transport technology to vehicle systems for the seriously disabled.

On the home front, refrigerator walls become thinner, and their inside space becomes larger, as the result of a new aerogel-based insulation system that is flexible, durable, and easy to use. Potential space applications for the system include insulation for the Reusable Launch Vehicle (RLV), space-shuttle upgrades, interplanetary propulsion, and improved life-support equipment. Markets on Earth include underwater oil pipelines, shipping containers, insulation for automobiles, noise-suppression panels for aircraft, and acoustic-damping insulation for buildings.

To the outdoor adventurer, and for those who just like knowing where they are, NASA has offered an affordable piece of insurance. The agency's satellite-aided tracking and transmitting technology, once restricted for use by seafaring vessels, has been packaged so that hikers, climbers, and travelers can pocket their own personal locator beacon. When activated, the unit emits a 406 MHz distress signal to a constellation of internationally operated satellites orbiting within the Global Positioning System (GPS). Should someone become lost or caught in a life-threatening situation, the National Oceanic and Atmospheric Administration (NOAA) is poised to pick up a distress signal.

Space satellites have also proved to be a huge help to the U.S. Forest Service, providing bird's-eye views of fires blazing across the

(Continued on page 256.)

Space technology has been adapted to hundreds of consumer products. The video camcorder above houses an advanced imaging chip, the same type developed for the Hubble Space Telescope.

coupled a liquid-crystal tunable filter with a CCD camera, they created an extremely sensitive imaging spectrometer.

In one remarkable effort now under way, a Utah firm and NASA are using surplus rocket fuel to save lives in a very unusual way. A relatively recent spin-off, a demining device, uses rocket-propellant-motor waste in its solid form to neutralize land mines in the field. Shaped as a flare, the waste propellant is placed next to an uncovered land mine and ignited; the flare burns a hole in the mine's case and ignites the explosive contents in a controlled way. With the number of active mines estimated to be in the millions, thousands of people are killed or maimed each year. Justifiably, this space spin-off has indeed encountered warm welcomes at international borders.

Help is also on the way for countries that lack an adequate supply of food for their growing populations. Remarkable results have been achieved for cultivating minitubers as seed stock, thanks to a joint effort combining a system from a Wisconsin firm, a technique from China, and a growth chamber from NASA developed as part of a program based at Marshall Space Flight Center in Huntsville, Alabama. The effort succeeded in cutting the process of seed multiplication from seven years to two years. When fully realized, such processes could greatly increase agricultural production.

Considering only this handful of beneficial spin-offs out of thousands that have already dramatically improved peoples' lives, it is nearly impossible to guess what else will come from space research. Today, from the three core technologies considered to be essential to NASA's future success—biotechnology, nanotechnology, and information technology—there should be little doubt that the sky's the limit.

United States. The Terra satellite, for one, beams images each day of fires that occur across the western states. Also gleaned from space research are a number of advancements in the image-processing field. A NASA infrared camera, the Acousto-Optic Imaging Spectrometer (AImS)—originally developed to explore Mars—has assisted Smithsonian Institution scientists in Washington, D.C., in preserving the historic Star-Spangled Banner that flew during the War of 1812. The camera has been able to identify soiled and deteriorating areas of the flag not visible to the human eye. Because the spectrometer measures and analyzes reflected light—and every chemical reflects light differently—it has even been able to determine which stains are authentic Battle of Baltimore dust, which are just harmless dust, and which are from oil and auto fumes that could further decay the flag. Thanks to this helping hand from NASA technology, the conservators expect Old Glory to last for at least another 500 years.

With similar success, in a project for the National Archives during the mid-1980s, text of the ancient Dead Sea Scrolls never before visible became crystal clear through the application of advanced-multispectral-imaging technology developed at JPL. When scientists

orbit. The mission marked the first time in more than five years that astronauts had gone outside the spacecraft for an extravehicular activity. Just days after *Atlantis* landed, *Discovery* streaked into orbit to conduct a series of military experiments for the Department of Defense. That year, a *Discovery* launching marked the 40th shuttle mission. On April 25, 1991, NASA unveiled the *Endeavour*, whose first mission, in May 1992, was a complete success. As of 2003, there have been 111 successful shuttle flights, and two failures.

Other manned space shuttles could soon be orbiting Earth, although they will not belong to the United States. In November 1988, the Soviet Union sent its new shuttle, *Buran*, into orbit for an unmanned test flight. *Buran* was approximate

NASA continues to develop technology that will make longer and longer space travel possible. The focus of attention is on the exploration of the solar system, and NASA hopes to send missions to Mars in the near future. Researchers have found tantalizing evidence that life could once have existed on Mars, including

Since 1965, the Mission Control Center (MCC) in Houston has been the communications hub for all U.S. spaceflight. A specialized team in the Flight Control Room (left) tracks all mission movements, monitoring the expected and ready for the unexpected, from the moment a rocket's boosters ignite, through the course of the mission, and to the second the spacecraft comes to a full stop (above).

ly the same size and shape as the U.S. space shuttles. It rode into space on the powerful new Energia booster, a successor to the ill-fated N-1 Moon rocket. The Soviet space-shuttle program never progressed much further, and collapsed altogether with the dissolution of the Soviet Union. *Buran* never flew again.

Nevertheless, the concept of reusable space vehicles remains appealing to the governments of many nations. China, Japan, and the European Union (EU) all have large or small shuttles in the planning stages.

magnetic material in a 4.5-billion-year-old Martian meteorite that might have been produced by bacteria. The only way to find out for sure if it is possible for life to exist there is to send manned spaceflights to the Red Planet. The *International Space Station* could be the launching point for this mission. Plans are also in the works to use the *ISS* as a way station on return flights to the Moon.

The *International Space Station* itself is an excellent example of collaboration among several countries to achieve these dreams. On our own planet, bitter political conflicts may continue, but in space, at least, men and women are showing that cooperation can bear fruits for the knowledge and benefit of the whole world.

The Boeing Company

The extraordinary pace of innovative space technology makes it clear that the only limits to future space exploration will be the limits of our own imagination.

THE FUTURE OF THE SPACE PROGRAM

by Mark Strauss

How far should we venture into space? Should we build manned stations that orbit our own planet, send pioneers to live on the Moon, explore Mars, even push to the outer reaches of the solar system? The National Aeronautics and Space Administration (NASA), the U.S. space agency, has plans to do all these things, and they have people ready for the adventure. But the price will be steep: space exploration costs money and risks lives. Exactly how fast NASA can carry out its ambitious plans is hard to predict.

The first 25 years of the U.S. space program will probably be remembered as a golden age. From the launching of the first U.S. satellite, to the Mercury program that put our first man in space, to the unforgettable image of the American flag being planted on lunar soil, it seemed that the only limits to space exploration were the limits of our own imagination.

But the 1986 explosion of the space shuttle *Challenger* was a tragic reminder that the road to space will not always be smooth. In the aftermath of the accident, many people raised questions. Should we believe what NASA says it can do? And in what direction is our space program heading? After all, the heady days of the "space race" were apparently over. No longer was the space program driven by a single, all-encompassing goal: President Kennedy's vision to land a man on the Moon before the end of the 1960s. The space shuttle had promised to turn space travel into a routine event. But by the late 1980s, this seemed only a hollow promise.

Following the *Challenger* and *Columbia* disasters, NASA immediately halted shuttle operations while the causes of the failures were found and corrected. Nearly three years passed after the explosion of *Challenger* before engineers felt comfortable launching another shuttle, but eventually the program began to run smoothly once again. At least a year will pass after *Columbia*'s failed 2003 reentry before shuttles will return to orbit.

THE EARTH SCIENCE ENTERPRISE

NASA's Earth Science Enterprise, formerly called Mission to Planet Earth, is an ongoing, in-depth study of the most important planet in our solar system: Earth. It utilizes free-flying satellites, space-shuttle missions, and various airborne and ground-based observations. With this program, scientists are measuring chemicals in the air and oceans, making maps of plant communities, taking Earth's temperature, mapping the planet's magnetic field, and carrying out many other environmental tasks to create a 15-year environmental database from which we can see global changes—both positive and negative.

Why study our planet from space when we live on the ground? One pressing reason: scientists need to answer some troubling questions about Earth as a whole, and observation from space promises to answer many of them: How quickly is human pollution changing the makeup of the planet's atmosphere? What will that mean to the world climate? To what extent do the world's oceans, and the organisms that live in them, control climate? How fast are the rain

forests really disappearing? These problems, and many others, can be answered by space observation.

NASA and other organizations already have orbited satellites to keep an eye on Earth. But the information picked up from the Earth Observing System will make such past observations seem almost insignificant. To process all the new facts, engineers will have to design computers that are bigger and faster than any currently available. Building such massive electronic brains is just as important a part of the project as building the satellites themselves.

PLANETARY EXPLORATION

NASA's second initiative is to continue exploring our solar system. Unmanned probes have already reached some of our neighboring planets. The successful Voyager spacecraft, for instance, have provided us with spectacular close-up pictures of Jupiter, Saturn, Uranus, Neptune, and their moons. In July 1997, the more-sophisticated Mars Pathfinder landed on Mars, where it investigated the planet's geology, atmosphere, and meteorology. The Ga-

To traverse the terrain on other planets, NASA has specially designed a rover vehicle. Its navigation system allows a human operator to plan a general route, while built-in sensors steer it around local obstacles.

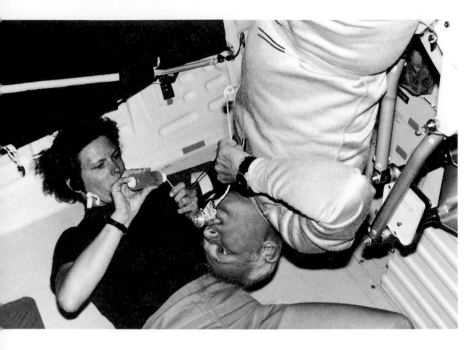

Medical tests conducted on space-shuttle missions measure human adaptability to space travel. The negative physiological effects that astronauts may encounter—and need to overcome—during a lengthy mission are an overriding concern of NASA's medical staff and their research.

lileo probe arrived at Jupiter in late 1995. The Ulysses probe began peeking at the Sun in the summer of 1994.

Still another series of simple, hard-working probes is currently being developed by NASA. Ideally, the little spacecraft that make up NASA's Discovery Program will roll off assembly lines like automobiles, be fitted with the appropriate instruments, and head into space. One such probe is the Near-Earth Asteroid Rendezvous (NEAR-Shoemaker) mission—which, in June 1997, snapped the first close-up photos of the asteroid Mathilde. On February 12, 2001, NEAR-Shoemaker soft-landed on the asteroid 433 Eros after a year-long orbit.

Next will be Cassini, scheduled to arrive at Saturn in 2004 to take a firsthand look at the ringed giant and land a probe on Titan, its large moon. Other probes will target comets, asteroids, moons, Mars, and even the distant world Pluto.

MISSION TO THE MOON

Exploration of our solar system will not be limited to robot probes. Within 30 years, if all goes according to plan, human beings will themselves visit distant worlds.

For starters, NASA envisions a return trip to the Moon. This time, we are not going simply as tourists to take a few photos and then go home. NASA intends to set up a permanently manned lunar base.

The first step to settling the Moon would require scouting its geology and terrain with robot spacecraft. In 1998–99, the Lunar Prospector began that task. In its two-year orbit around our lunar neighbor, the craft mapped its surface and searched for the existence and location of minerals and water ice. In the summer of 1999, the craft was directed to crash into one of the ice-covered crater floors in an attempt to help Earth-bound scientists learn how much water might exist there. Unfortunately, analysis after the impact proved inconclusive.

Once a base is established, astronauts would have to learn to live off the land. Moon pioneers could mine the lunar soil for helium-III, a form of helium that is very rare on Earth, but common on the Moon. Helium-III could be used to power nuclear-fusion reactors and might become a plentiful energy source in the future, perhaps even cheaper than oil.

It is even possible that lunar soil could be used to manufacture construction materials. Volcanic rock on the Moon contains a high concentration of silicon dioxide, which, when heated, melts into glass. By using giant mirrors to focus the Sun's rays, astronauts could melt down the soil, churning out tons of black lunar glass. Robotic machinery could stretch the molten-glass fibers, much like fiberglass. The material could be used for insulation, or it could be poured into molds and shaped into small, igloolike buildings.

An outpost on the Moon would also be a tremendous boon to astronomers. With almost no atmosphere to blur its vision, an optical telescope on the Moon could be 100,000 times more powerful than any telescopes here on Earth.

But perhaps most important, a Moon base would provide astronauts with invaluable experience on how to survive on the surface of a lifeless, alien world. It would be a stepping-stone to the next phase of NASA's solar-system exploration: a manned trip to Mars.

REUSABLE SPACECRAFT

In addition to the space-exploration initiatives outlined by Dr. Fletcher's original task force, NASA officials made plans that were a little closer to Earth.

One of the most frustrating challenges NASA faces is finding an efficient way to get people and payloads into low-Earth orbit. When the space-shuttle program was introduced in the late 1970s, it promised routine access to space. From the very start, however, the space shuttle has suffered de-

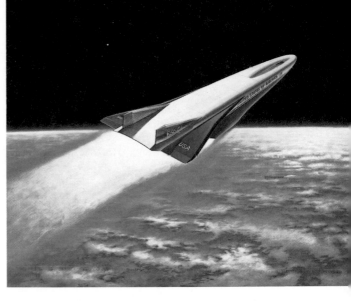

NASA once envisioned the X-33 aerospace plane (a proposed design illustrated above) to replace space shuttles as a more cost-efficient way to launch astronauts and payloads into orbit.

lays, mechanical failures, and constant budget problems. The *Challenger* explosion left the shuttle fleet grounded for nearly three years. And space officials grounded the fleet again after the shuttle *Columbia* disintegrated upon reentry over the western United States on February 1, 2003.

The shuttle was intended to be a low-cost way to launch astronauts into orbit, but, in practice, it costs nearly $300 million per launch. What is more, NASA needs to employ a staff of nearly 12,000 people just to launch the spacecraft!

A future alternative to the shuttle might be something akin to the National Aero-Space Plane, developed jointly by NASA and the U.S. Air Force. Also known as the X-33, it was number 33 in a long line of

To collect astronomical data for use in future space exploration, the Kuiper Observatory, a modified jet equipped with an infrared telescope, flies above the effects of Earth's distorting atmosphere.

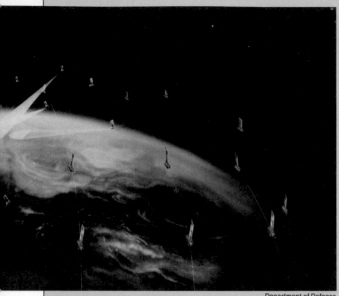

SPACE BASED DEFENSE

The popular press usually referred to it as the "Star Wars" program, but the government called it the Strategic Defense Initiative, or SDI. On March 23, 1983, in a nationally televised address, President Ronald Reagan proposed an audacious new defensive system, which would be based primarily in space. The president envisioned an impenetrable shield that would render Soviet nuclear missiles "impotent and obsolete."

Back then, the proposed SDI arsenal consisted of a variety of high-tech gadgetry, most of which existed only on paper and in scientists' imaginations. One proposed orbiting device was a neutron-particle-beam weapon—a space-based accelerator that would aim atomic particles at a missile to destroy its electronics. Another potential weapon was a chemical laser that could aim intense beams of focused light at a missile's skin, causing its rocket fuel to explode.

In the years following Ronald Reagan's speech, the SDI program attracted many scientists, and much progress was made developing powerful laser beams and miniature rockets. But the technology needed to realize the program remained in the future. Moreover, the collapse of Communism in Eastern Europe and the breakup of the Soviet Union made any scenario of a full-scale nuclear attack seem very unlikely.

Still, some defense experts felt that the possibility of a small-scale missile attack could not be entirely dismissed, especially in light of the rapid proliferation of long-range ballistic missiles in unfriendly countries.

In his 1991 State of the Union message, President George Bush announced

NASA/Air Force experimental aircraft, which also included the X-34, another reusable rocket.

The X-33 would have taken off from a runway like a normal jet, build enough speed to shoot into orbit, and land like a standard airplane.

The spacecraft was being designed to hurl itself faster and higher, until the atmosphere became too thin for its scramjets to function. Then, at a speed of Mach 22 (which is 22 times the speed of sound, or 4 miles—6.4 kilometers—per second), the scramjets would shut down, and a rocket engine would push the space plane to Mach 25, the speed needed to propel it into space.

The X-33 would have cost more than $1 million per launch. Advocates claimed that the craft could be sent back into space a

day and a half after it touched down. (The shuttle requires several months between flights.) And since the aerospace plane would have functioned more like a jet than a rocket, it could have turned around and returned to its point of departure in an emergency, a capability the space shuttle lacks.

During 1996, an important new space technology was successfully tested. Named the McDonnell Douglas *Clipper Graham Single-Stage-to-Orbit* rocket, this craft was designed to follow airline-style operations, enabling a turnaround time of between 72 hours and a week. In its third, and most impressive, test flight, the rocket lifted off its pad, flew to 1,200 feet (366 meters), moved laterally 350 feet (107 meters), and descended vertically, landing within a mere 2 feet (0.6 meter) of its planned touchdown posia refocusing of SDI. The new system would be designated GPALS, for Global Protection Against Limited Strikes. Instead of an impenetrable shield designed to destroy nearly all incoming missiles, the proposed program had been scaled down to stop up to 200 warheads.

The centerpiece of the newly proposed SDI program was "Brilliant Pebbles"—an orbiting fleet of tiny satellites, each 2 feet (0.6 meter) long and weighing about 40 pounds (18 kilograms). Each satellite would fire nonnuclear rockets at an incoming missile, destroying it before impact. The GPALS plan would place between 750 and 1,000 of these weapons in orbit. The satellites would rely on infrared sensors to spot and track the hot exhaust plumes of flying missiles. Other parts of the GPALS picture included small rockets that would leap from the ground.

The defense-from-space concept was abandoned in 1993. In its place, research is focusing on ground-based defenses. In the late 1990s, for example, scientists successfully used ground-based lasers to destroy satellites in orbit above Earth. In 2005, a functioning missile-defense system is once again a priority, with enthusiastic support from President George W. Bush and his administration.

tion. But in March 2001, technical problems, design flaws, rising budgets, and possible flight risks forced NASA to eliminate this program altogether.

In late 2004, *SpaceShipOne*, a small rocket plane funded by Microsoft cofounder Paul G. Allen, soared twice to the edge of space during a two-week span, winning the $10 million "X Prize." The project represents a possible new trend: commercial suborbital flights in a reusable vehicle.

THE NEW MILLENNIUM PROGRAM

As a new millennium begins, NASA plans to accelerate its exploration of space by developing new technology. The New Millennium Program (NMP) will send the first "intelligent" spacecraft into the solar system. These probes will penetrate the surfaces of planets, fly in formation to function as a giant instrument, or touch down on fast-moving comets.

The first test of this technology came with the 1998 launch of Deep Space 1, a spacecraft that successfully utilized a revolutionary ion-propulsion system. In 2001, the U.S. Deep Space 1 mission passed only 1,400 miles (2,200 kilometers) from comet Borrelly, and radioed to Earth the clearest photographs yet of a comet nucleus.

NASA developed technology for a small space-taxi system that would have permitted rapid human access to orbiting space shuttles or space stations. With its wings folded, the craft could have fit within the shuttle's cargo bay.

For many years, the idea of a manned out-post in space was deemed a "castle in the air," a fantasy relegated solely to the arena of science fiction and dreams. Fortunately, some dreams never die; instead, they often can be realized. Today, we stand on the threshold of achieving that dream.

EARLY IDEAS

The concept of a space station is as old as science fiction. In the 19th century, as brilliant-minded advocates were putting aggressive plans for space exploration to paper, the early fabrications of fantasy writers began to take on a new light. The fictional account of a manned naviga-tional satellite for ships at sea in Edward Everett Hale's post–Civil War story "The Brick Moon," for instance, was one flight of fancy that actual-ly proved prophetic. Equally predictive were the life-sustaining methods described for orbiting space stations in the novel *Beyond the Planet Earth*, by Russian rocket scientist Konstantin Tsiolkovsky. From the same book came the idea of building a large, cylindrical space station that would spin along its axis to simulate gravity—a

concept that received serious notice in the scientific community.

In 1923, Romanian Hermann Oberth stirred up some attention when he fused physics with fantasy in his nonfiction work *The Rocket into Interplanetary Space*. He coined the term "space station," and proposed that it be a starting point for flights to the Moon and Mars.

A major breakthrough came with the farmfield launch of the first liquid-fueled rocket by American physicist Robert Goddard in 1926. The event boosted the space-station cause by setting the stage for the powerful rockets it would take to launch sections of a habitable structure into orbit. But even with the release of other nonfiction works, such as Austrian rocket engineer Hermann von Noordung's *The Problems of Space Flying* in 1929—which included a space-station blueprint and proposal that it would be launched by rocket—serious speculation on the subject took a backseat to preparations for a major war. Throughout the 1930s and 1940s, the world as a whole showed virtually no interest in space exploration of any kind.

After World War II, German rocket scientists were coveted by the United States and the Soviet Union for their expertise. One of those engineers, Wernher von Braun, began writing articles and documentaries on spaceflight for *Collier's* magazine and Walt Disney Studios. In one piece, he proposed a wheel-like, nylon-reinforced space station to be accessed by reusable spacecraft. Von Braun envisioned a station in orbit that could serve as an Earth observation post, a laboratory, and, even more exciting, a springboard for flights to the Moon and Mars.

When completed, the International Space Station *(facing page), with its modules, solar arrays, and thousands of other components, will be the ultimate manifestation of technology, a space laboratory once only envisioned in forward-looking works of science fiction, such as the 1968 film* 2001: A Space Odyssey *(above).*

Von Braun was the first to raise wide public attention and bring political savvy to the space-station cause. In a 1952 *Collier's* piece, he set forth his prophecy: "Within the next 10 or 15 years," he said, "Earth will have a new companion in the skies, a man-made satellite that could be either the greatest force for peace ever devised or one of the most terrible weapons of war—depending on who makes and controls it."

THE RACE TO SPACE

As the 1950s approached, von Braun's message resounded eerily across continents. The Cold War deepened, and the space race between the United States and the Soviet Union began to mushroom. Competitive tensions reached a high point on October 4, 1957, with the Soviet launch of the satellite Sputnik 1. In response, the United States promptly established the National Aeronautics and Space Administration (NASA) in 1958, which began working on Project Mercury (1959), the program to send an American into space. In 1961, President John F. Kennedy vowed to put a man on the Moon. In 1969, when astronaut Neil Armstrong met that challenge, the space race had escalated further. Throughout these years, U.S. plans for a space station were on hold.

After the Soviets lost the race to the Moon, they turned their attention toward long-endurance spaceflights and to the development of a space station. Not surprisingly, then, it was the Soviet Union that launched the world's first space station, *Salyut 1*, from Baikonur Cosmodrome in what is now Kazakhstan in April 1971. Its purpose was to study the effects of long-duration spaceflight on the human body and to photograph Earth from space. In the end, the effort had mixed results, with tough lessons learned and valuable lives lost. The missions were plagued from the start with almost endless technical malfunctions. On *Salyut 1*'s final 22-day mission, three cosmonauts perished when air leaked out of the *Soyuz* spacecraft returning them to Earth.

The Soviets launched space-station missions for another 15 years—some highly secretive efforts disguised with *Salyut* names. After 32 missions that involved testing of transport spacecraft and docking of supply ships, the Soviets had laid a substantial foundation for what was to come.

THE *SKYLAB* MISSIONS

In 1972, the Nixon administration approved the reusable space shuttle as a main direction for the U.S. manned space program. The shuttle would ultimately launch and service a space station, the next logical step in NASA's exploration of space.

In 1973, America launched its space station—the rather ordinary-looking *Skylab*—built from a leftover third stage of a Saturn V Moon rocket. The 85-ton structure was never intended to be a permanent home in space, but rather, a workshop to test the long-term effects of weightlessness on the human body. Nonetheless, *Skylab* was sufficiently comfortable for a crew of three, and adequately equipped for studies of the stars, space, and Earth.

Vibrations during liftoff caused *Skylab* to be plagued by technical problems from the start. A critical meteoroid shield was torn loose, taking one of the craft's two solar panels with it. Another piece of the shield had wrapped around the second panel, keeping it from deploying properly. This damage caused temperatures inside the work area to soar to 126° F (52° C). Three crews worked aboard the station (staying for 28, 59, and 84 days, respectively) during the next eight months; it was the first crew's mission to salvage the uninhabitable space station by deploying a parasol sunshade. The scheme worked, and the station's interior cooled to 75° F

Astronaut Owen Garriott takes reading lightly (inset below) while weightless aboard Skylab *(below), the mechanically plagued U.S. space station launched in 1973. Despite difficulties,* Skylab *spent several fruitful years in orbit.*

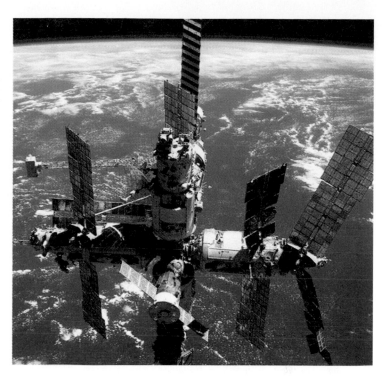

After nearly 15 years of hosting multinational crews in its efficient working areas and comfortable living quarters, the aging Soviet-then-Russian space station Mir was finally brought down in March 2001.

(23.8° C), making *Skylab* once again operational. The rest of the crew's planned activity in space went smoothly. Between them, the three crews brought home thousands of photos of Earth and the Sun, and important data gathered from medical, biological, and technical experiments.

Both the 12,351 man-hours in space (171 days, 13 hours) and the 41 man-hours spent performing extravehicular activities (EVAs) associated with *Skylab* exceeded the combined totals of all of the world's previous spaceflights up to that time. The effectiveness of the *Skylab* astronauts surpassed expectations, especially in their ability to perform complex repair work. The capability to conduct longer manned missions was demonstrated conclusively by *Skylab* crews, and the ferrying of supplies to the station via space vehicles was successfully carried out for the first time. In 1974, after eight months of operation, three manned missions, and multiple engineering tasks by NASA to determine the causes of its failures, *Skylab* was shut down. Five years later, on July 11, 1979, the station fell to Earth, its debris scattering across an area that extended from the southeastern Indian Ocean to a sparsely populated area of Western Australia.

THE COSMONAUTS' SPACE STATION

The Soviet Union meanwhile continued its focus on long-duration missions, and, in 1986, launched the first module of the space station *Mir*. The knowledge the Soviets gained from the Salyut missions paved the way for a space station that would host multinational crews for more than a decade. Russia had more than 20 years experience operating space stations.

Mir orbited high above Earth for 15 years (February 1986 to March 2001), completing more than 86,000 revolutions. Except for two brief periods, it was continuously occupied from March 1986 to August 1999. During this time, cosmonauts and astronauts from dozens of nations lived on the station and performed an array of critical experiments. Crews came and went via Soviet, and then Russian, Soyuz transport modules or U.S. space shuttles.

Originally designed to operate for a minimum of 10 years, *Mir* housed living quarters that included individual crew cabins, a toilet, a shower, kitchen facilities, and a trash-storage area. The station also had a transfer compartment to which modules could be attached; an intermediate compartment that connected the working module to the rear docking ports; and an assembly compartment where fuel tanks and rockets were held.

The breakup of the Soviet Union in 1991 created budgetary problems for the nation's space program, and just at the same time as *Mir* was beginning to feel its age. During its operation, the station had experienced a chemical fire, computer glitches, power-system failures, problems with its critical life-support system, and damage to its solar arrays from an unfortunate collision with a supply vessel. The new Russian government tried to find willing investors, and although some funding was offered by NASA and a few European countries, financial support was inadequate to maintain the mounting expenses of the project.

ISS *crews conduct invaluable experiments, encounter amazing panoramic views, and welcome supply-laden shuttles, as the cosmonaut above is doing.*

In August 1999, the permanent crew abandoned the station, and *Mir* was placed on computer control. In order to prevent tons of burning metal from falling to Earth, a controlled descent was orchestrated, and *Mir* made a final fiery plunge on March 23, 2001, into the southern Pacific Ocean.

AN INTERNATIONAL SPACE STATION

NASA had gained a vast body of knowledge from the many years of space-station successes and disappointments. In 1984, President Ronald Reagan called on Congress to fund a permanently manned space station to be put in orbit by the early 1990s. This task was to be a big one—an effort that would have pleased Werhner von Braun. It would not only launch his vision for Earth's "companion in the skies," it would foster a spirit of peace and cooperation among the major nations of the world.

In 1994, following decades of competition, the new Russian Federation and the United States signed an historic agreement that formed a partnership to develop an international space station. In preparation, the two nations engaged in a series of joint missions involving the space station *Mir*. Under the leadership of President Reagan and his successor, George Bush, U.S. concepts for a grand space station named *Freedom* evolved through several designs, but none ever received congressional approval. Finally, at the direction of President Bill Clinton in 1993, the concept—scaled back and less costly—ultimately emerged as the *International Space Station*, also known as the *ISS*.

The *ISS* is designed to provide scientists and engineers with a world-class, state-of-the-art research center in the microgravity environment of outer space. In-orbit research projects will span such diverse fields as biotechnology and medicine, microgravity sciences, combustion sciences, fluid physics, materials science, Earth science, space science, engineering and technology, and product development. In addition, the station will strive to create excitement and wonder in the field of science education, and to stimulate world peace through an extended term of international cooperation in space.

With a price tag estimated at about $100 billion, the *ISS* will be the largest, most expensive, and most complex multinational scientific project in history. It represents an undertaking of unprecedented scale, and a change in direction away from our home planet and into permanent habitation of space.

The 470-ton station, expected to be fully assembled by the end of this decade, will essentially be a self-contained, modern research building housing a crew of six or seven astronauts in 46,000 cubic feet (1,300 cubic meters) of pressurized volume (the rough equivalent of two Boeing 747 jetliners). Included will be six laboratories, two habitation modules, two logistics modules, a water system, and even parking spaces for visiting spacecraft. With nearly 1 acre (0.4 hectare) of solar panels providing electric power, the *ISS* will ultimately measure 356 feet (109 meters) across and 290 feet (88 meters) long, more than four times larger than *Mir*, its Russian predecessor.

The station will remain high above Earth at an average distance of 250 miles (400 kilometers), with its orbit tipped at 51.6 degrees relative to Earth's equator. This orbit will provide researchers with an excellent platform for Earth observation—some 85 percent of the globe will be visible from its abundance of windows; this location also will allow for accessibility of launch vehicles from a number of other nations.

The assembly of the *ISS* represents a new era of hands-on work in space, involving more space walks than ever before and a new generation of space robotics. It will take some 45 missions—employing the U.S. space shuttle and Russian Soyuz and Progress spacecraft—to haul into space more than 100 elements for the station's construction. These modules, nodes, truss segments, resupply vessels, solar arrays, thermal radiators, and the thousands of other components will be linked in orbit by astronauts during more than 850 hours of space walks.

The *ISS* began taking form in the 1980s, and, in 1993, NASA brought Russia on board to assist in project development. The first segment of the space station, the Russian-built control module *Zarya*, was launched into orbit November 20, 1998. A few weeks later, on December 7, the *ISS* began to grow when the space shuttle *Endeavour* delivered *Unity*—a six sided module to which all U.S. modules will attach—and connected it to *Zarya*. The *Zvezda* module arrived in July 2000, and then, in early 2001, astronauts delivered and connected *Destiny*, the U.S. scientific laboratory, which will store scientific gear and serve as a command-and-control center. Ad-

A key ISS *module*, Zvezda, *began its journey by rail to the Baikonur Cosmodrome, in Kazakhstan. There, it joined with the Proton rocket booster that carried it aloft for hookup with Zarya, the station's first orbiting segment.*

During one of 850 spacewalks planned for the International Space Station, *astronauts Jerry Ross and Jim Newman prepare to unfurl an antenna on* Zarya, *the control module that provided the station with its initial propulsion and power.*

ditional shuttle trips in 2001 and 2002 added a robotic space arm, three pieces of a truss structure, and the Mobile Base System. Following the loss of the space shuttle *Columbia* in 2003, further construction of the station was delayed.

The *ISS* project is so complex and expensive that no individual nation could possibly have tackled it alone. Led by NASA, the project draws on the scientific and technological resources of many nations—including Canada, Japan, Russia, those of the European Space Agency (ESA), and Brazil—in the largest nonmilitary joint effort in history.

When fully functional, the station's eight sets of solar arrays will provide scientists with sufficient energy by converting sunlight to electricity. When all the modules are in place, vast laboratory space will be the site of research aimed at achieving safe, long-term space exploration by human beings. The knowledge gained from these experiments will likely have many earthbound applications as well.

The *ISS* is scheduled for completion sometime between 2006 and 2008. It will be nothing less than a refined city in space, orbiting gracefully at 17,000 miles (27,000 kilometers) per hour above Earth, a place where people from around the world can live and study for long periods of time. And ultimately, the station will serve as a launching point to destinations across the solar system—and the universe.

© Roger Ressmeyer/Starlight

NASA subjects new space-suit designs to rigorous testing for endurance and radiation resistance. The spacewear designated for the space station will have to withstand the most extreme conditions ever faced by astronauts.

DRESSING FOR SPACE

by Lillian D. Kozloski

You're an astronaut in the year 2010, and, you're assigned to work on the *International Space Station* (*ISS*). In addition to testing equipment for a planned lunar outpost, you will be helping to maintain the station itself, performing work that will require long periods of time outside to repair the station's hull. You will need a very special kind of suit to protect you from intense solar radiation, powerful cosmic rays, even micrometeoroids—small, sand-like and rocklike particles that whiz through space at speeds of 60 miles (96 kilometers) per second.

Luckily for you, National Aeronautics and Space Administration (NASA) researchers back in the late 20th century were already testing a new generation of space suits to meet your 21st-century needs. To appreciate their technological wizardry, let's start our story at the very beginning—flipping back to the very first pages in the family album of space suits.

THE NEED FOR PROTECTION

Early in the 19th century, novelists and daredevil pilots were already discovering the need for special suits and equipment for survival in the rarefied regions high above planet Earth. Science-fiction writer Jules Verne correctly predicted in his book *From the Earth to the Moon* that an astronaut would need "an encapsulating type of protection."

Scientists realized early on that an unprotected human would survive just 15 to 30 seconds in the almost-complete vacuum of space. They also knew that without the buffering effect of the atmosphere, a space-walker would be exposed to extremes of cold and heat. In addition, he or she would not have any circulating air to carry off body heat. Other potentially deadly hazards for any unprotected spacewalker would include the occasional bulletlike micrometeoroid, radiation from solar winds and solar flares, and infrared and ultraviolet rays. Scientists, as well as science-fiction writers, correctly suspected that lunar explorers would face much the same hazards, since the Moon's thin atmosphere offers little protection.

PRECURSORS TO THE SPACE SUIT

To protect themselves from the elements, the first high-altitude pilots wore fleece-lined leather jackets, gauntlets, helmets, goggles, breeches, and boots. Due to the thinness of the upper atmosphere, they had difficulty breathing, and some even suffered hallucinations. To compensate, they breathed through tightly fitting face masks attached to oxygen tanks.

Air pressure at high altitudes presented another challenge. While a deep-sea diver experiences greater and greater atmospheric pressure as he or she descends into the ocean, a pilot experiences less and less pressure the higher his or her plane flies. Though the situations are reverse, the lifesaving principles are similar. What is crucial is to buffer the effects of a too-rapid drop in outside pressure. Early high-altitude pressure suits were based on the deep-sea-diving outfits designed to protect divers from too-rapid ascent out of the high pressures found at ocean depths.

In 1907 John Scott Haldane, an English respiratory physiologist, perfected an oxygen pressure suit for deep-sea divers. American balloonist Mark Ridge turned to Haldane for guidance in 1933. Ridge wanted to fly an open balloon gondola into the stratosphere, and knew he would need a pressurized garment to survive.

Haldane and his associate, Sir Robert Davis, did indeed create a suit that could have protected Ridge to an altitude of 50,000 feet (15,240 meters). But the British military ministry refused Ridge permission to flight-test the suit. Given international tensions at the time, officials feared that the balloon and the pressure suit might fall beyond Britain's borders and into the hands of an unfriendly country. So it was not until 1936 that British Flight Lieutenant F. R. D. Swain set a record for the Royal Air Force when he flew to almost 50,000 feet (15,240 meters) wearing a pressure suit based on the Haldane-Davis design.

American aviator Wiley Post was the next significant figure in the story of high-altitude flying. Post had already flown around the world several times. He identified the jet stream, a fast, westerly wind current that circles the Earth at altitudes from 10,000 to 15,000 feet (3,000 to 4,600 meters). Post knew he could not fly in the jet stream without special personal-survival equipment. He approached the B. F. Goodrich Company, which agreed to create the needed suit.

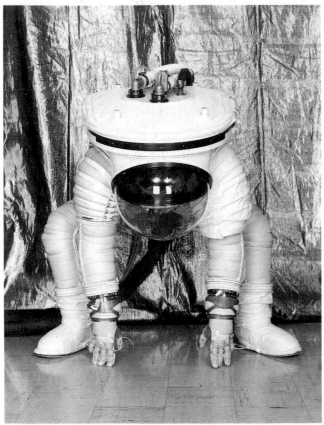
© Roger Ressmeyer/Starlight

Shuttle astronauts have complained that their space suits lack flexibility. Makers of the Mark III suit (above) claim that its "soft" construction will allow space-station astronauts more freedom of movement.

The first B. F. Goodrich suit literally exploded like an overblown balloon the first time it was inflated. Goodrich engineer Russell Colley designed a second suit, but by the time it was completed, Post had gained weight. Post had to be extricated from the overly tight suit while standing in a refrigerated storage room.

Post's third—and finally successful—suit, completed only after careful measurement, produced compressed air from liquid oxygen, which also provided air for breathing. Wearing this suit, Post was able to fly into the upper atmosphere's jet stream in August 1934, upping his record-breaking speed from 180 to 280 miles (290 to 450 kilometers) per hour.

As pilots continued to fly at higher altitudes and faster speeds, they were increasingly plagued by pressure sickness, choking, gas pains, and other physiological problems. In the 1940s and 1950s, the military accelerated the development of pressure suits, the forerunners of today's space suit. During the 1940s pilots survived by forcing extra oxygen into their system, but this would take them no higher than 52,000 feet (15,850 meters). At 65,000 feet (19,800 meters), not even pressurized cabins were enough protection. In 1953 the development of dependable pressure suits enabled pilots to drop the first test hydrogen bomb from the edge of the stratosphere over the Bikini Atoll—an altitude high enough to protect them from the bomb's shock waves.

SUITS GEARED FOR THE MANNED SPACE PROGRAM

Mercury

The United States Manned Space Program began in 1958. Technology from the military pressure-suit program bore rich fruit. The high-altitude suits built by Goodrich soon evolved into the full-pressure space suit used by the Mercury astronauts. It was made of a neoprene-coated, nylon inner layer covered by a high-temperature-resistant aluminized nylon. According to plan, the astronauts would need the suits only if the Mercury spacecraft pressurization system should fail.

Gemini

The space suits that the Air Force developed for the next phase of manned spaceflight, the Gemini program, enabled astronauts to walk outside their spacecraft during extravehicular activities, or EVAs. The spacewalkers were connected to their craft by a life-supporting cord.

The basic Gemini suit was constructed of an inner bladder made from rubberized nylon, which was inflated during pressurization. To prevent this bladder from ballooning, designers used a Dacron fishnet layer, called Link-net. The outer protective layer was made of uncoated Nomex, a tem-

NASA evaluates the comfort and mobility of newly developed space suits in its Weightless Environment Training Facility, a 500,000-gallon water tank in which the water's buoyancy simulates the microgravity of space. Prevailing opinion seems to hold that neither the AX-5 "Michelin Man" all-metal suit (shown at right, about to be dunked) nor the Mark III "soft" suit (below) will be chosen for the job. Most likely, NASA will opt for a hybrid space suit that combines elements of the two main contenders.

Both photos: © Roger Ressmeyer/Starlight

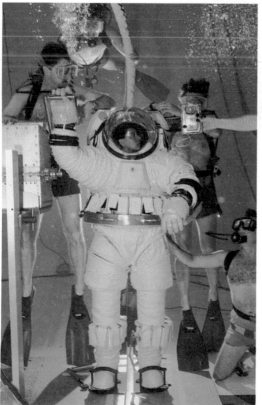

perature-resistant nylon material. During EVAs, astronauts would also don an additional cover, consisting of several layers of uncoated nylon over layers of Mylar and Dacron batten insulation, which in turn was covered with a layer of projectile-resistant nylon that would protect the astronauts from the impact of micrometeoroids.

Gemini astronauts, who were physically active during their EVAs, found several flaws in this suit. Without proper ventilation, they sweated profusely, and their helmet visors fogged. On one occasion in 1966, a small rip in a back zipper of astronaut Eugene Cernan's suit allowed the powerful solar radiation of space to overheat the suit and almost burn him.

Apollo

The Apollo astronauts and Moon walkers were not hampered by the umbilical cord that tethered the Gemini astronauts to their craft. Instead, the Apollo suits used a portable backpack life-support system. Apollo suits were also made to be ex-

THE EVOLUTION OF SPACE SUITS

Space-suit precursor: when pressurized, the outfit worn by aviator Wiley Post (above) during his 1934 high-altitude flights kept him from walking or standing.

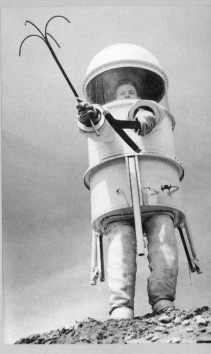

The evolution of space-suit technology has seen its share of reject designs. In the early 1960s, the man-in-a-can approach taken by the "tripod teepee" (above right) lost out, ostensibly because it required excessive space on already cramped spacecraft. In 1978, NASA turned down the "anthropomorphic rescue garment" (above), a space suit designed for the orbital transfer of an astronaut from a disabled shuttle.

NASA ultimately selected a modified version of a U.S. Navy pressurized flight suit as the space suit for the Mercury astronauts. Without its vapor-cover suit, the outfit had a distinctly robotic look (left). What the suit lacked in fashion savvy it made up for in freedom of movement: its flexibility even allowed for a game of baseball on the astronauts' training field.

tremely fire-resistant, in response to the tragic fire in 1967 that killed three astronauts—Virgil Grissom, Edward White, and Roger Chaffee—during ground training aboard *Apollo 1* at Cape Kennedy.

The basic Apollo space suit consisted of a five-layered torso-and-limb suit. It incorporated specially designed joints with convoluted bellows for greater joint mobility. A cable, block, and tackle assembly was needed to keep the suit arms bendable during pressurization while in Earth's atmosphere. The innermost layer resembled a pair of standard long johns, with an interlacing of small tubing stitched on nylon spandex fabric. This in turn was attached to a more comfortable liner made of nylon tricot. The tubed garment circulated cool water over the astronaut's body.

During lift-off and reentry, astronauts wore a three-layer cover for additional fire protection. Astronauts assigned to EVA

Top three photos: National Air & Space Museum; bottom left: Litton Industries; bottom right: UPI/Bettmann Newsphotos

When fully pressurized to five pounds per square inch, the space suit worn by Mercury astronaut M. Scott Carpenter (left) allowed limited mobility.

After years of research and development, the Mercury astronauts emerged in space suits that were aluminized to reflect heat.

Long before any Apollo missions had flown, work had begun on space suits that would protect astronauts on the upcoming lunar landings.

tasks wore a 14-layer protective garment over their basic space suits. This space garment was woven of Teflon-coated glass fibers and Beta cloth, which together resisted both extreme temperatures and the impact of tiny flecks of space debris.

For a workday spent inside the Apollo craft, astronauts changed into lightweight in-flight overalls, much like an automobile mechanic might wear, except that they were woven entirely of fireproof Teflon.

Skylab

Skylab, America's first space station, was launched in 1973. Three crews—all using modified Apollo suits—visited this orbital cluster, and stayed for increasingly longer periods of time. Their duties included extensive repair work on the outer hull of the craft, which had been damaged during launch. They also tended a number of scientific instruments mounted on the outside surface of their indoor workshop.

Top: UPI/Bettmann Newsphotos; lower left: Republic Aviation Corporation; right: National Air & Space Museum

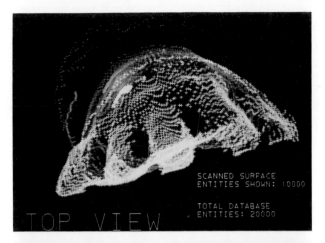

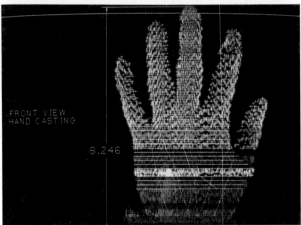

Both photos: ILC Dover

Custom-making an astronaut's gloves presents an engineering challenge to the manufacturers of space suits. At ILC Dover, lasers scan the astronaut's hand, producing accurate models based on 20,000 bits of data. Engineers then fit pieces of fabric to the models. The finished gloves will have ribbed convolutes—ringlike ridges—at the finger joints, and a complex structure of diamonds and squares in the palm.

During one EVA the astronauts installed a parasol over the "roof" of their workshop, thus lowering the inside temperature of the craft to more-bearable limits.

The Space Shuttle

When the space shuttle made its public debut, "shuttlenauts" wore modified U.S. Air Force high-altitude escape suits, similar to those worn by military pilots flying Blackbird reconnaissance aircraft. But shuttle astronauts stopped using such protective clothing after the fleet's first successful test flights.

In 1986 the explosion of the space shuttle *Challenger* forced officials to reassess the fleet's escape and survival systems. After two-and-a-half years of intensive study, the post-*Challenger* space fleet underwent significant modifications. One of the recommendations was to reinstitute emergency-rescue equipment. NASA therefore added to the orbiter a special crew-escape system that jettisons a hatch door if evacuation becomes necessary while airborne. A long telescoping pole would thrust through this open hatchway. Astronauts would hook onto the pole and quickly slide beyond the shuttle, to a point where their parachutes could safely open.

In addition, all crew members must now wear durable, temperature-resistant orange suits during launch and reentry. The new launch-and-entry suits are designed both to counter the low pressures of high altitudes and to protect the astronauts from exposure to temperature extremes. Crew members wearing the suits can survive at or below a 100,000-foot (30,500-meter) altitude for 30 minutes. Inflated bladders inside these suits cushion vital areas of the body. The suit can also be worn with a domed, full-pressure helmet for in-orbit emergency operations.

On some shuttle flights, designated astronauts also need true space suits for EVA assignments. The shuttle fleet's two-piece space suits were a vast improvement over the previous one-piece suits—with their long awkward body zippers. While it took Apollo astronauts, with assistance, close to an hour to suit up, shuttle astronauts can don their space suits in five minutes, unassisted. Shuttle space suits are also computerized to constantly monitor and adjust their own vital life-support systems. Astronauts are alerted when water or oxygen levels drop too low or when any system threatens to malfunction.

While the shuttle suit has proven its worth over the years, astronauts say it has its drawbacks. After several hours of wear, the suits can cause bruises on the shoulders and fingertips from pressure points between the suit and an astronaut's skin. As Kathryn Sullivan, the first American woman to walk in space, has observed, the contours of the shuttle space suit do not correspond exactly to the proportions of an average human being's shoulders and knees.

A SUIT FOR THE SPACE STATION

In looking ahead to its permanently manned space station, NASA is considering space suits with hard bodies. There are many advantages, the most important being that hard suits can maintain higher internal pressures in the vacuum of space than can conventional space suits. This reduces the "prebreathing," or adjustment time, now required before astronauts in soft suits are ready for the low pressures they will encounter during a space walk. At present, astronauts must prepare for low-pressure space walks by prebreathing concentrated oxygen to rid their system of nitrogen. Otherwise, they risk suffering from a potentially fatal condition known to deep-sea divers as "the bends" or caisson disease. This condition occurs when a rapid change in air pressure causes nitrogen dissolved in the body to form bubbles.

Several new space-suit designs are now being developed simultaneously, with modifications being made every step of the way. The top candidates are tested in the weightlessness of nose-diving jets (NASA's famed "Vomit Comets"), as well as at NASA's Weightless Environment Training Facility (WETF). The WETF, one of the world's largest "swimming" pools, is large enough to hold a full-size shuttle replica. It enables suit engineers and astronauts to test a new design's mobility in the micro-gravity of simulated space.

In the early 1990s, two of the hottest space-suit prospects for the space station were the Mark III and the AX-5. Both are modular—that is, they are made of reusable, interchangeable parts that can be mixed and matched to fit different wearers. They are also made of enhanced materials and special layers to better protect astronauts during long periods in open space.

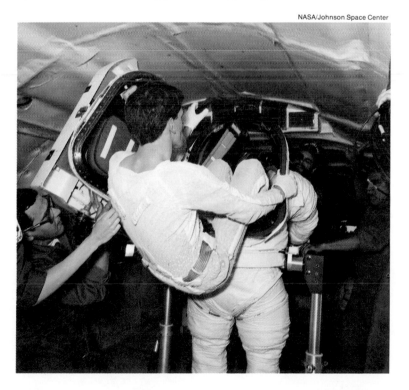

NASA performs many tests to determine the amount of time it takes astronauts to get in and out of a space suit. To properly design the space-station airlocks, NASA also needs to know the volume of space behind and above the suit needed for an astronaut to don or doff the outfit.

SPACESUIT FOR SPACEWALKS

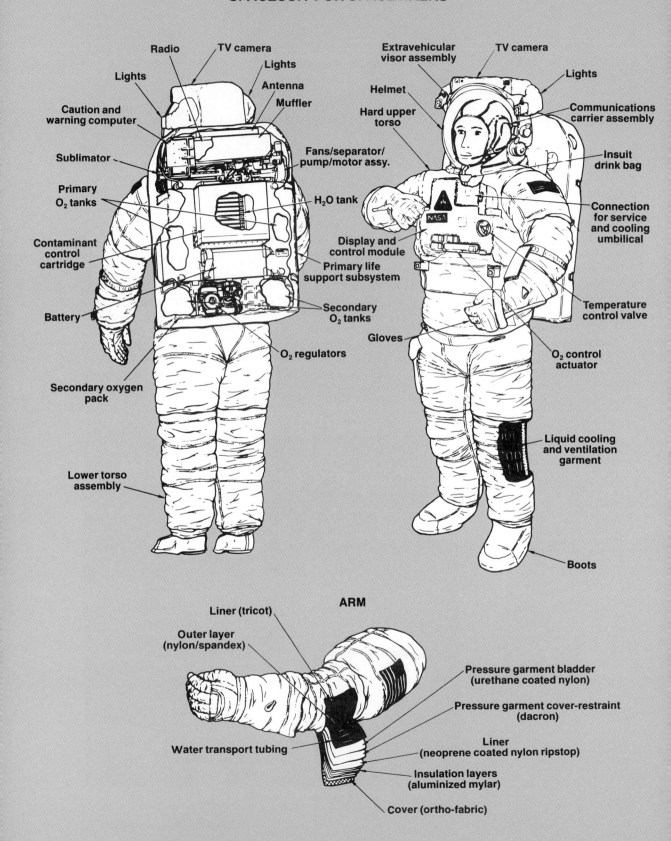

Radio
TV camera
Lights
Lights
Antenna
Muffler
Caution and
warning computer
Fans/separator/
pump/motor assy.
Sublimator
H_2O tank
Primary
O_2 tanks
Contaminant
control
cartridge
Display and
control module
Primary life
support subsystem
Battery
Secondary
O_2 tanks
Secondary oxygen
pack
O_2 regulators
Lower torso
assembly

Extravehicular
visor assembly
TV camera
Helmet
Lights
Hard upper
torso
Communications
carrier assembly
Insuit
drink bag
Connection
for service
and cooling
umbilical
Temperature
control valve
Gloves
O_2 control
actuator
Liquid cooling
and ventilation
garment
Boots

ARM

Liner (tricot)
Outer layer
(nylon/spandex)
Pressure garment bladder
(urethane coated nylon)
Pressure garment cover-restraint
(dacron)
Liner
(neoprene coated nylon ripstop)
Water transport tubing
Insulation layers
(aluminized mylar)
Cover (ortho-fabric)

The Mark III Zero-PreBreathe Suit

Since 1979, NASA has been working on the development of a Zero-PreBreathe space suit (ZPS) for use by space-station astronauts. As its name implies, this suit will enable astronauts to make a quick transition from spacecraft to outer space, without the need to adjust to low pressures with pre-breathing. Normally, it would be pressurized to about 8 psi (pounds per square inch). The current shuttle suits operate at only 4.3 psi; the shuttle cabin is 14.7 psi.

The Mark III ZPS, developed by NASA at the Johnson Space Center in Houston, combines new designs with pieces of the tried-and-true. Space aficionados will recognize the Apollo helmet and glove connectors and the shuttle suit's hard upper torso. However, astronauts "enter" this suit by climbing through a hatch in the upper back. As such, it is even faster to don than the shuttle space suit—an advantage that may prove crucial in the event that emergency repairs to the spacecraft's exterior are needed.

The Mark III is worn with an enhanced thermo-micrometeoroid garment (TMG), an outer cover that provides extra protection from radiation, orbiting space debris, micrometeoroids, and the extreme temperature changes that can occur in the vacuum of space. In its entirety, the Mark III system weighs about 163 pounds (74 kilograms), some 63 pounds (29 kilograms) more than the shuttle suit.

The AX-5

The AX-5, being developed at NASA's Ames Research Center in California, is the brainchild of engineer Vic C. Vykukal. This hard-bodied suit was quickly nicknamed the "Michelin Man" for its rounded, segmented joints and body parts. Its hard body covers not only the torso and limbs, but also the hands and feet. Unlike the Mark III, the aluminum AX-5 has no fabric parts, which may be an advantage in that there is no risk of torn stitches or worn inner bladders. Like the Mark III, the AX-5 is entered from the rear. Its hatch closes much like a refrigerator door, and must be latched shut from the outside by an assistant. It weighs in at about 185 pounds (84 kilograms).

The refinement of space-station suits is likely to continue for many years to come. In all likelihood, the final design will be a hybrid of the best features of the AX-5 and Mark III, truly an apt "business" suit for the 21st century.

The space suits worn by the shuttle astronauts (diagram, facing page) need only withstand the rigors of comparatively brief periods of extravehicular activity (right). For the astronauts building the International Space Station (ISS), the suits will have to endure hundreds of eight-hour days in space.

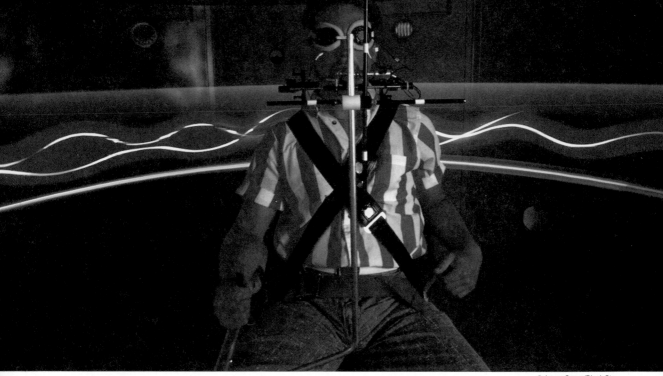

Before being catapulted into space, astronauts must prepare for the rigors of g-forces during lift-off and motion sickness during space travel.

ASTRONAUTS IN TRAINING

by Maura Mackowski

In 1959 no one knew if a human being could survive a flight in space. Could engineers design a vehicle to carry a traveler safely into orbit and back to Earth? Could a human body withstand the heat, vibration, noise, and radiation? Could the mind cope with total isolation in the void of space?

Neither the Soviets nor the Americans, competing to be first in space, knew the answers. Each decided to find out by launching test candidates chosen from the elite ranks of military pilots, proven to be fit, intelligent, adaptable, and able to handle danger.

Hundreds of applicants were screened on paper, and dozens were put through wearying days of medical and physical tests. They were whirled in centrifuges and flipped on tilting tables. They put miles on treadmills and stationary bicycles. They were probed with needles and X rays. Psychologists locked them in isolation rooms, where they couldn't see or hear anything, not even the sound of their own voices. In the end the U.S. chose seven Mercury astronauts, and the U.S.S.R. chose six Vostok cosmonauts as their respective countries' earliest pioneers in space.

U.S. SELECTION AND TRAINING PROGRAM

The centrifuge is gone now, as are most of the grueling tests that made astronaut selection seem like an obstacle course through a torture chamber. Today work experience, college education, and overall physical fitness are used to select America's astronauts.

Every two years the National Aeronautics and Space Administration (NASA) invites people to apply for its pilot and mission-specialist astronaut positions. In 1990–91, for example, 179 people applied as pilots and 2,245 as mission specialists. NASA's minimum requirements include an engineering or science degree and several years of related work experience.

There are no age limitations to being an astronaut, although the average candidate is 32 years old. There is no restriction on size, but weight must be in proportion to height. The current 98 astronauts range in size from 5 feet 1 inch to 6 feet 5 inches (155 to 196 centimeters). A candidate may be disqualified on medical grounds for a chronic condition that would require constant medication and monitoring, such as diabetes or epilepsy.

Of the 1,946 that passed this first hurdle of general good health in 1990–91, 363 were found by a 12-member NASA board to be "highly qualified." A subsequent screening looked at the type of college degree each candidate had, how recently it was earned, how relevant any work experience was to NASA's own programs, and what unique skills each person had to offer. Pilot candidates were also evaluated on their flying experience. The number was whittled to 106, and these candidates were invited to Johnson Space Flight Center in Houston, Texas, for a week of tests and interviews to determine who would fit best with the NASA team. Ultimately 23 people were chosen as astronaut candidates.

Boot Camp

Basic training is the first step for new astronaut candidates. It lasts one year. During this first year, astronaut candidates fly in the backseat of military trainers or ride special private jets modified to handle like the shuttle. The candidates undergo survival training, learning how to cope in any environment should the shuttle make a forced landing. They take scuba lessons and become accustomed to the strange sensation of weightlessness.

There is also plenty of classroom instruction. Astronaut candidates take courses in space physics, geology, meteorology, oceanography, star identification, and medicine. They learn observation techniques that will enable them to orient themselves over the Earth from the shuttle and to interpret what they see in the environment below. In basic training, they also learn how to operate the shuttle systems. They learn enough about electronics and computers so that they can help make repairs in space.

To understand how the shuttle and its experiments work, astronaut candidates travel to the aerospace companies that build them. They also visit many NASA control centers to familiarize themselves with the roles played by ground-support staff—from the crews that clean and repair the shuttle between flights to the mission controllers that monitor each flight. Candidates even take classes in public speaking so they can work with news reporters and give talks to schools, businesses, and other community organizations.

After graduation the candidate is ready to be assigned to a flight. Most crew selections are made a full year before the actual

Astronauts John Young (right) and Robert Crippen (left) are seated at the controls of the space shuttle Columbia *while training for the very first shuttle mission in 1981.*

NASA

Both photos: © Keith Meyers/NYT Pictures

A variety of escape systems have been incorporated into today's space shuttle. To prepare for emergency situations that might occur before lift-off, astronauts rehearse evacuating the shuttle using an aircraft-style inflatable slide (right). An astronaut must grow accustomed to a somewhat unwieldy space suit (left), which is equipped with a parachute, an oxygen supply, and a life raft in case of an emergency evacuation while in flight.

flight, and some may begin preparing for their assignment several years in advance. If the waiting period is long, NASA may assign the new astronauts to ongoing projects, such as a shuttle-orbiter-system upgrade or a long-term research project.

Usually, however, training becomes quite intense once an astronaut is assigned to his or her flight. Any given mission will typically involve a pilot, one or two mission specialists, and several payload specialists. The latter, who are in charge of the experimental equipment and testing procedures on board, may also include engineers and scientists from private industry and other non-NASA astronauts.

Two crew members, usually mission specialists, rehearse for extravehicular activities—EVAs, or "space walks"—in the neutral-buoyancy tank. Dressed in space suits and accompanied by NASA scuba divers, they work some 30 feet (9 meters) underwater, practicing shuttle repairs, satellite retrieval and deployment, and space-station construction.

When working as a team, the crews "fly" shuttle simulators that use the same software found on the real orbiter. They drill in preparation for dozens of anticipated problems, such as landing at emergency airfields, coming down in the water, putting out fires, dealing with pressure leaks, and any other potential emergencies NASA can dream up.

When any one shuttle is in orbit, you'll find the team training for the next flight serving as ground support. Some will work relaying messages from the crew in orbit to NASA officials and back.

And if the actual orbiting crew has to deal with a mechanical problem, the crew-in-waiting will simulate making the necessary repairs on Earth and fax written instructions and diagrams of the procedure

282   **ASTRONAUTS IN TRAINING**

up to the shuttle. If an astronaut in orbit has to take a space walk to make an unexpected repair, an astronaut on Earth will don a pressure suit and practice the task first in the neutral-buoyancy tank.

COSMONAUT TRAINING PROGRAMS

Information about cosmonaut selection and training was very difficult to obtain during the first 30 years of the Soviet program. Since the dissolution of the Soviet Union in 1991, Russia has tried to invigorate its economy by flying foreign experiments and foreign scientists aboard its space missions in exchange for hard cash. Because of this new openness, it is now becoming easier for space historians to learn how the Russian cosmonaut-training program works.

Cosmonaut candidates are usually certified military jet pilots, 35 years old or younger. From time to time, however, civilian scientists, doctors, and engineers have been invited to join the program. A change in the work that goes on in orbit will require more qualified engineers, scientists, and doctors than the military alone can provide.

In an unprecedented event, American financier Dennis Tito paid the Russians $20 million for a comparatively brief round-trip voyage aboard a Soyuz craft destined for the *ISS* in 2001. The 60-year-old California tycoon spent more than seven months in Russia training for his mission. On April 28, 2001, he blasted off with two Russian cosmonauts, and fulfilled a life-long dream.

Selection of cosmonauts is similar to the American process. Candidates must be interviewed, they undergo medical and psychological tests, and their references are checked. Typically, the entire process rules out 99 of every 100 candidates.

Once selected, cosmonauts begin a general education in space sciences, including aerodynamics, navigation, astronomy, computers, ballistics, and medicine. They learn about the systems that run the *Soyuz* capsules, the Progress supply ships, and the space station. New cosmonauts also study the launch complexes and the rockets that boost them into orbit. They observe flight control and tracking operations.

An important part of cosmonaut training, particularly for missions lasting six to 12 months, is exercise. In addition to sports and survival training, the cosmonaut candidates fly jets, make parachute jumps, and undergo weightlessness training.

Basic training lasts roughly two years, but cosmonauts may wait years before being named to a particular team. Once they are assigned, however, they undergo intensive training tailored specifically to their particular mission. Like American astronauts, cosmonauts learn to respond to emergency situations and to conduct the experiments they will tend in flight.

The experiments the cosmonauts will perform come from many different Russian research agencies, including the Academy of Sciences, the Geophysical and Astrophysical institutes, and the State Center of Nature. Cosmonauts train with the scientists and engineers who designed each experiment to learn its purpose and how to operate necessary instruments. They must also learn how to care for any animals, insects, or plants involved in the studies, and how to accurately observe and record test results.

Most cosmonaut training occurs near Moscow, at the Gagarin Cosmonaut Training Center in Star City, where the cosmonauts live full-time. It includes a building with *Soyuz*, *Salyut*, and *ISS* mock-ups and a docking simulator that uses television, models, and realistic lighting under computer control. In the late 1980s, a training simulator was added for the Icarus, the "space motorcycle" that cosmonauts use to maneuver about during their EVAs.

Star City also has pressure chambers for testing spacecraft components, and soundproof rooms for sensory-deprivation tests. There is a planetarium where cosmonauts train to navigate by the stars. Another building contains a water tank, some 75 feet (23 meters) in diameter and 39 feet (12 meters) deep, where cosmonauts practice EVAs. Separate buildings house centrifuges that can simulate blast-off and reentry.

Next door to Star City is Chkalov Air Force Base, where special aircraft take cosmonauts aloft for training flights in which they experience weightlessness.

Space Commerce Corp.

Russia trains its cosmonauts for long stays on manned space stations and the International Space Station. *Cosmonauts hold the record for space endurance—438 days spent in the weightlessness of outer space.*

COMPARISON OF THE AMERICAN AND RUSSIAN PROGRAMS

While there are some similarities, Russian and American training differ in several respects. Cosmonauts spend more time training for weightlessness aboard aircraft, while Americans put in more hours underwater in the neutral-buoyancy tanks.

Both space programs require guest payload specialists from other countries to be completely fluent in the host language, but the Russians offer Russian-language training, while the American guests must already know English.

NASA has extensive written teaching materials, books, and how-to manuals for the various experiments and the shuttle itself. Cosmonaut trainees are given much less printed material and are expected to take copious notes.

The Russian training program also includes extensive testing to match the personalities of its cosmonauts for the most compatible crews possible. To this end, cosmonauts are subjected to ground and in-flight examinations of their pulse rates, brain waves, voice-stress levels, blood-chemistry levels, and even their facial expressions. Good matchups were essential on the program's many long-duration missions. Crew members may have only each other for companionship for months at a time.

Both the United States and Russia stress the importance of team building, but each country has different ways of familiarizing trainees with the philosophy, chain of command, and protocol of their respective space agencies.

Cosmonauts live together in Star City, an enclosed community of 4,000 people, and share after-hours activities. American astronauts usually live in Houston, a city of several million people, and generally team up only during working hours, much like workers at any large corporation.

GUEST CREW MEMBERS

In 1978, the Soviet Union began flying guests from its allied nations in a program known as Intercosmos. French and Indian guests also flew with the Russians, and, in the 1990s, Japan, Austria, Spain, Germany, and the United States signed up to send astronauts to the Russian space station *Mir*. The private Juno project bought training for four British cosmonauts and a flight for one in 1991. Tokyo Broadcasting Corporation purchased a seat for a reporter the same year, and a group of individuals in Texas bought another seat, which they planned to raffle off.

The United States, meanwhile, has flown Russians, Canadians, Europeans, and astronauts of several other nationalities aboard its shuttles.

In all instances, the Russians require that guests pass physical exams and undergo six to 12 months of training. Three months of intensive Russian-language study are followed by general astronautic studies, lessons on how the *ISS* functions, training in performing experiments, and finally, the instructions needed to return safely aboard a Soyuz craft. While shuttle astronauts ride much like airline passengers, guests aboard a tiny Soyuz literally block the reach of the ship's commander and must help by operating the radio, the atmospheric controls for the space suits, a navigational computer, the manual override for cabin oxygen, wastewater routing systems, and a TV system used for docking.

NASA has occasionally flown observers on spaceflights, including Senator Jake Garn of Utah and Saudi Prince Al-Saud. Researchers from private industry have bought seats on a shuttle, including McDonnell Douglas engineer Charles Walker, who has flown three times with an electrophoresis experiment. All these civilians had at least six months of full-time astronaut training. They learned how to eat, dress, wash, and sleep in space, how to operate equipment, and how to respond in an emergency.

A number of countries have flown guest specialists on U.S. space-shuttle and *ISS* missions. These include Canada, Germany, Russia, France, Italy, Japan, Switzerland, Australia, Belgium, Mexico, the Netherlands, and Saudi Arabia. Some of these countries have their own space-science programs, but no launch vehicles. These astronauts are recruited in their own countries according to standards similar to NASA's. They undergo extensive training at home. Once assigned to a flight, they receive further training in the United States.

Russian cosmonauts undergo training in a centrifuge. Its high-speed whirling motion creates punishing forces similar to those encountered during lift-off and reentry operations.

NASA

In 1960, NASA recruited 20 outstanding women pilots to undergo grueling physical and psychological tests to determine their suitability for space travel. Twelve women were selected to continue a second round of training. But in July 1961, NASA abruptly discontinued the female astronaut program. It would be 22 years before the first American woman, Sally Ride (above), would fly in space, serving as a mission specialist on the space shuttle Challenger in 1983.

WOMEN IN SPACE

Tass from Sovfoto

Soviet cosmonaut Valentina Tereshkova was the world's first woman in space. After her historic flight she toured the world, proclaiming, "on Earth, at sea, and in the sky, Soviet women are the equal of men." Some considered the flight a publicity stunt to extol the Soviet system, since it would be almost 20 years before another Soviet woman would fly in space.

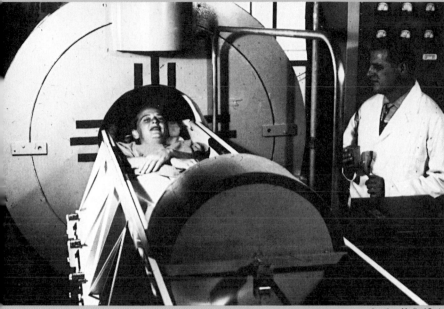

As one of the first female astronaut candidates, Jerrie Cobb (left) underwent extensive medical testing to ascertain that female physiology would be able to withstand the rigors of space travel.

Lovelace Medical Center

Early female astronaut candidates were subjected to ice-water injections in their ears and swallowing 3 feet of rubber tubing. Below, Myrtle Cagle undergoes pulmonary testing.

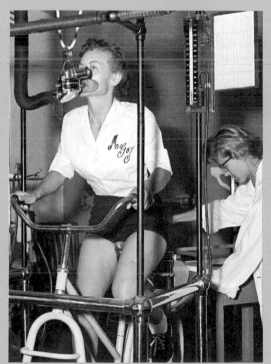

Lovelace Medical Center

NASA

Today NASA's female astronauts undergo the same rigorous preparation for space travel as their male colleagues. Here a female astronaut candidate enters a neutral-buoyancy tank to practice performing simple tasks in a weightless environment.

EUROPEAN SPACE AGENCY'S ASTRONAUT PROGRAM

Sixteen European countries form the European Space Agency (ESA): Austria, Belgium, Denmark, Finland, France, Germany, Greece, Ireland, Italy, Netherlands, Norway, Portugal, Spain, Sweden, Switzerland, and the United Kingdom. Canada, Hungary, and the Czech Republic also participate in certain projects. In 2005, ESA's staff included more than 1,900 scientists, engineers, information-technology specialists, and administrative personnel.

Since 1975, ESA evolved into a major player in international spaceflight and research, and has contributed to a number of major unmanned space missions, including the Hubble Telescope and the Solar and Heliospheric Observatory.

In addition, ESA boasts 15 astronauts from around Europe who train and fly in the U.S. space shuttle, and work side-by-side with Americans and Russians on board the *International Space Station* (*ISS*), positioned in orbit high above Earth.

ESA astronauts are trained at the European Astronaut Centre in Cologne, Germany, where they acquire the necessary knowledge, skills, and proper attitude to perform their duties safely and efficiently aboard the *ISS*. Their training program is organized into three separate phases—each with specific objectives, characteristics, content, and certification.

Basic training gives candidate astronauts knowledge of space technology and science, medical expertise, and skills related to their future operational tasks. It also includes training for special capabilities such as scuba diving. When a candidate completes this one-year training program, he or she is certified as a career astronaut.

Advanced training provides astronauts with the knowledge and skills needed for the operation of *ISS* elements, payloads, and transport vehicles, in addition to the tools necessary to interact effectively with the all-important ground-support crews. Upon successful completion of the one-year advanced-training program, an astronaut is eligible to be assigned to a specific mission.

"Increment-specific training" is the final training program for established ESA astronauts. It is during this period that the astronaut learns the techniques required to accomplish his or her mission successfully. For up to a year prior to launch, astronauts concentrate on working as team members on a number of jobs related to their specific flight. The last few months focus on payload and systems operation, along with on-board training. This final phase typically requires about 18 months to complete.

WOMEN IN SPACE

At the age of 12, Jerrie Cobb had her father fit an old biplane with cushions and blocks so she could learn to fly. By the age of 28, she was a professional pilot and an aircraft-company executive, having already logged over 7,000 flying hours and broken three world speed and altitude records.

To Dr. Randall Lovelace and Brigadier General Donald Flickinger, who had just completed the medical screening and selection of the first seven American astronauts, Cobb looked like a perfect astronaut candidate. It was 1959, the Cold War was on, and word was out that the Soviets were already recruiting female cosmonauts.

Cobb reported to the Lovelace Clinic in Albuquerque, New Mexico, in February 1960 to begin what she hoped would be her trip into space. Over a period of five days, she underwent some 75 tests of health, strength, endurance, and intelligence.

As it became apparent that she was indeed highly qualified, Cobb was sent for a second round of tests in Oklahoma City. She was also asked to recommend other women for the female space corps. She recommended 31 women with the right credentials from among members of "The 99s," an organization founded by pioneer aviator Amelia Earhart and 98 other women fliers.

Twelve candidates passed their medical exams, and two more then reported to Oklahoma City to complete the next phase. In 1961, Cobb passed the third and final battery of tests. Two other women who survived the first cut came to stay with her and continue the grueling tests. Rhae Hurrle Allison

The perils of space travel are painfully underscored when something goes wrong. On January 28, 1986, the crew of the space shuttle Challenger *(left) perished in an explosion seconds after takeoff. On February 1, 2003, the crew of* Columbia *(below) died when their shuttle broke up just moments before its scheduled landing in Florida.*

and Wally Funk both proved highly qualified, with Funk's 10-1/2-hour stay in the isolation tank setting a space-program record.

Then one day, Cobb got the devastating news from Dr. Lovelace. Without any explanation, the Navy had canceled further tests. All the women candidates were sent home. Despite impressive test results, credentials, and the impassioned testimony of Cobb and several other women before Congress, their program was never revived.

It would be 22 years before Sally Ride, in 1983, would become the first American woman in space. In 1984, Kathryn Sullivan became the first American woman to perform an EVA, and in 1995, U.S. Air Force Major Eileen Collins was the first woman to pilot the space shuttle.

Things were not on hold for Soviet women, however. In the early 1960s, several were evaluated, then trained. Ultimately, factory worker and amateur sky diver Valentina Tereshkova won a cosmonaut job. On June 16, 1963, she became the first woman in space. (Space historians agree that Tereshkova's flight was a publicity stunt initiated by Premier Nikita Khrushchev to prove women fared well under Communism.)

In 1982, Soviet engineer Svetlana Savitskaya became the second woman in space, aboard *Soyuz T-7*. With *Soyuz T-12* in 1984, she became the first woman to fly a second mission and the first to make a space walk.

It was the American space shuttle that really opened doors for women astronauts. For the first time, NASA recruited non-pilots—including physicist Sally Ride—to its ranks. Eileen Collins (then a colonel) became the first woman to command a shuttle mission in July 1999, and, in 2005, commanded the first shuttle mission following the *Columbia* disaster more than two years earlier. In July 2001, Janet Kavandi served as mission specialist on the 10th shuttle mission to the space station. Today, nearly 25 percent of NASA's astronauts are women, and that number continues to grow.

Women have also died exploring space: Christa McAuliffe and Judith Resnik during the 1986 launch of *Challenger*, and Laurel Clark and Kalpana Chawla during the 2003 reentry of *Columbia*.

ESA

Astronomers use space probes like the Ulysses (pictured above, nearing Jupiter) to explore the solar system.

SPACE PROBES

by Jeffrey Brune

The *Niña*, *Pinta*, and *Santa Maria* took Columbus and his crew across the Atlantic to the New World. Ships of another sort have taken us across the oceans of space to the next New World. They are called *space probes*, and are unmanned robots that we launch from Earth on missions to explore the Sun and the planets in our solar system. Loaded with instruments designed to add to our knowledge of space, as well as cameras that capture amazing images, these probes are sending home to Earth incredibly exciting data. For example, Voyager 2 sent us shots of the stormy blue world of Neptune. Magellan revealed rock formations on Venus that look like giant pancakes. Voy-

ager 1 flew high enough above our solar system to snap the very first "family portrait" of the Sun, Earth, and just about all of our planetary neighbors.

Although we cannot ride aboard space probes, we may use them as scouts for future human missions. For instance, Moon probes were used to determine the safest places to land on the Moon. The Viking probe, Mars Pathfinder, and Mars Global Surveyor have provided enough preliminary information about the Red Planet to perhaps set the stage for a manned mission in the not-too-distant future.

With each probe we launch, more secrets are revealed about our solar system.

And although we've learned a great deal about the worlds around us, there is still plenty to discover. As the late astronomer Carl Sagan said, "Somewhere, something incredible is waiting to be known." And as our technology has slowly advanced, so too have our unmanned spacecraft become more sophisticated. Let's take a closer look at certain space probes and their fantastic voyages.

PIONEERS

Even with the aid of the biggest and the best telescopes on Earth, the outer planets are just distant points of light. Those glimmers of light slowly began to come into focus in 1972 and 1973, when the United States sent twin probes, Pioneers 10 and 11, toward Jupiter for a close-up view. Scientists were most concerned about the probes' safety while traveling through the asteroid belt found between Mars and Jupiter. They knew there were lots of asteroids in the belt, but they didn't know how many. They also knew that a high-speed collision with a baseball-sized asteroid could easily turn a craft into a tin can. When the probes made it through the asteroid belt without crashing, scientists breathed a collective sigh of relief. That the Pioneer twins both crossed the belt without injury told scientists that there was a great deal of space between the asteroids. Crossing the belt in the future may be easier and safer than once thought.

Pioneer 10 became the first human-made spacecraft to fly by Jupiter and transmit photographic images to Earth. It also charted Jupiter's brutally strong radiation belts, located the planet's magnetic field, and discovered that Jupiter is composed primarily of liquid hydrogen (see also pages 133–138).

After zipping past Jupiter, Pioneer 10 aimed to exit the solar system. On June 13, 1983, it became the first craft to cross the orbit of Neptune, which at the time was farther away than Pluto. Pioneer 10 was officially retired on March 31, 1997, but it still broadcasted a faint signal with a few watts of power (similar to a small flashlight) for almost six more years. On January 23, 2003, from a distance of more than 7.6 billion miles (12.2 billion kilometers), the last signal from Pioneer 10 was detected.

In the early 1970s, NASA began sending space probes to destinations in the outer solar system. The first of these, Pioneer 10 (below, in an artist's conception), took close-up pictures of Jupiter and Neptune before heading out toward interstellar space.

THE MOONS OF VOYAGER

Titania 980 miles

Oberon 945 miles

Triton 1,680 miles

Io 2,255 miles

Rhea 950 miles

Iapet 900 m

Moon 2,160 miles

Europ 1,950 m

Callisto 2,980 miles

Ganymede 3,270 miles

Titan 3,200 miles

Moons visited by Voyager ranged from tiny Iapetus (diameter: 900 miles), moon of Saturn, to Jupiter's giant Ganymede (diameter: 3,270 miles). Ear moon (diameter: 2,160 miles) is considered average size.

Pioneer 11 took a different path than its twin. It screamed past Jupiter toward Saturn at a dizzying 108,000 miles (173,000 kilometers) per hour, the fastest speed ever reached by a human-made object. Despite its velocity, the probe was able to take breathtaking photos of Jupiter's Great Red Spot and observe the planet's polar regions. Reaching Saturn in 1979, it snapped pictures of the moon Titan, two other previously undiscovered small moons, and an additional ring. After leaving Saturn's atmosphere, it flew through space measuring the solar wind. The last transmission of Pioneer 11 was in 1995. Today, it is headed toward the constellation Aquila, and it may pass near one of Aquila's stars in about 4 million years.

Both craft carry a message that intelligent aliens may be able to interpret. The message is a gold-plated plaque showing Earth, a man and a woman, and where our solar system is located in the universe.

VOYAGERS

Two probes, Voyager 1 and 2, proved even more successful than the Pioneer twins. Thanks to the 100,000 or so pictures the Voyagers captured, we now have a more intimate knowledge of the outer planets. Launched in 1977, the Voyager duo embarked on a "grand tour" of the four giant planets—Jupiter, Saturn, Uranus, and Neptune—taking advantage of a rare planetary alignment that occurs about once every 176 years. When the probes reached Jupiter in 1979, they sent back images of the planet's red atmosphere swirling with violent storms and active volcanoes on the moon Io. Using Jupiter's gravity to gain speed, the two probes raced off to Saturn, where they snapped breathtaking pictures of the planet's complex ring system. At this point, the duo took separate paths. Voyager 1 made a close flyby of Saturn's moon Titan, then swung out into interplanetary space. Voyager 2 went on to discover, among many other things, 10 new moons around the planet Uranus and an Earth-sized hurricane on the planet Neptune (see also page 139; page 147; and page 151).

Scientists never expected Voyager 2 to reach Neptune, let alone phone home with such revealing pictures. After all, Neptune was 2.8 billion miles away. And Voyager had become somewhat disabled—its main radio receiver had failed, one of its memory-storing computers had malfunctioned, and a jammed gearbox had made it difficult to swivel its instruments.

But the probe had been traveling for 12 years in space, so it was no wonder it was ailing. Space is no vacation spot. Temperatures can be a bone-chilling –400° F (–240° C). High-speed cosmic dust can create a vicious sort of sandstorm. Then there's the radiation: high-speed protons, electrons, and other particles from the Sun and from exploding stars outside the solar system that can cause onboard computer systems to malfunction or otherwise run amok.

To help the ailing Voyager 2, scientists radioed new computer programs that allowed the probe to work around its health problems. In August 1989, the probe's tele-

vision cameras recorded images of Neptune and radioed the data to Earth. The radio signals were faint whispers across the lonely expanse of space. Back on Earth, scientists tuned in carefully with an array of 38 antennas that spanned four continents. The result was our first glimpse of an astounding world. Neptune appeared as a giant blue slushball with raging storms brewing in its methane atmosphere. On Neptune's largest moon, Triton, there was evidence of volcanoes spewing ice. Voyager 2's "last picture show" was indeed truly spectacular.

Though both Voyager probes ventured past the orbit of Pluto, they never came close enough to that mysterious planet to take pictures. Pluto remains the one member of our solar system still shrouded in almost complete mystery.

In 1992, the Voyagers may have found evidence of the long-sought-after heliopause. Now, the probes are racing toward the stars. Scientists hope to communicate with the Voyagers until about the year 2020. Around that time, their plutonium-based power generators will no longer be able to produce enough electricity to run the onboard computers, radios, and other systems. When the power fades, the Voyagers will con-

NASA

Should the Pioneer probes be intercepted by alien beings, plaques on board would provide the extraterrestrials with information on where the crafts originated and the type of beings that sent them. The Voyager probes visited many of the moons (facing page) in the outer solar system, but detected no trace of life as we know it.

tinue on their journeys, wandering through the Milky Way. Should intelligent aliens encounter either of the Voyager probes, they will find a videodisc aboard the craft, complete with greetings in 60 Earth languages, sounds and pictures from Earth, and even some interstellar music.

GALILEO

When the Pioneer and Voyager probes whisked past the outer planets, they gave us a glorious but brief glance. Scientists have since decided to launch new probes for a more detailed second look at each planet. Jupiter is the subject of the space probe Galileo, named after the Italian scientist who used the first astronomical telescope to discover Jupiter's major moons.

The space probe Galileo was launched by the space shuttle in October 1989 after years of delay and a controversy over its onboard nuclear-power system. Galileo contains a radioisotope thermoelectric gen-

erator (RTG) containing highly radioactive plutonium, which produces electricity for spacecraft instruments. While many spacecraft use solar panels to convert sunlight to electricity, Galileo would be too far from the Sun by the time it reached Jupiter to generate power this way.

The controversy centered around whether the RTG would remain intact if the shuttle were to explode, as the *Challenger* did in 1986. Some scientists were worried that, in such an event, the plutonium in the RTG would shower over parts of Florida, where the shuttle is launched. The U.S. National Aeronautics and Space Administration (NASA) assured the public that the RTGs were rigorously tested and would hold up under explosive conditions. In any case, the shuttle carrying Galileo roared into low-Earth orbit without a glitch and released the probe successfully from its payload bay. A booster rocket then sent the craft from low-Earth orbit on its journey to faraway Jupiter.

© John T. Barr/Gamma-Liaison

Scientists closely track the progress of unmanned space probes as they travel through the solar system. Contact is maintained as long as the electrical power systems on the crafts function normally.

STATION 6
DISPLAY

Originally, Galileo was designed for a 2.5-year direct flight to Jupiter. But changes in the launch system required engineers to devise a longer flight path, one that took six years. Galileo has traveled a course, shaped like a corkscrew, that took it past Venus and back again. As the craft traveled past Earth and Venus, it picked up speed by utilizing some of each planet's gravitational energy to gain added momentum. During this process, Galileo sent back a wealth of data about Venus, Earth, and the Moon.

In 1995, Galileo hurled a probe into Jupiter's violent atmosphere. A parachute slowed its one-hour descent, and it radioed back atmospheric measurements. It found faster winds and drier air than was previously expected—as well as fierce lightning storms. Contact was later lost as the probe was crushed by extreme pressures within the planet's atmosphere.

After the release of the entry probe, Galileo began its multiyear photographic orbital tour of the giant planet and its moons. During its mission, it studied Jupiter's radiation belt, its complex atmospheric weather patterns, the geology and internal dynamics of its moons, and much more. On September 21, 2003, Galileo—nearly out of propellant to steer itself—plunged into the crushing pressure of the Jovian atmosphere, ending its 14-year odyssey.

Cassini

Scientists now have an up-close view of Saturn, thanks to the Cassini probe, launched in 1997. The craft, named for the 17th-century Italian astronomer who discovered four of Saturn's moons, entered the ringed planet's orbit in June 2004 and began its four-year mission. The craft is studying Saturn's 100,000 or so ringlets; its atmosphere and magnetic field; and the planet's 34 known icy moons (two of which Cassini discovered upon its arrival).

The Voyager probes showed that Saturn's largest moon, Titan, has a dense atmosphere. In early 2005, the European Space Agency's (ESA's) Huygens probe disengaged from Cassini and landed on Titan—which has been revealed to be a "flammable world" with a soggy landscape covered in

NASA's Galileo probe, launched from the space shuttle Atlantis, conducted a 14-year photographic survey of Jupiter, including in-depth studies of the planet's radiation belt, weather patterns, and moons.

seas of liquid methane. With temperatures at around −290° F (−180° C), methane gas falls in the form of rain!

Comet/Asteroid Probes

In 1997, the Near Earth Asteroid Rendezvous (NEAR) mission was launched. It flew within 750 miles (1,200 kilometers) of the asteroid 253 Mathilde and photographed its tar-black, heavily cratered terrain. In February 2001, NEAR became the first spacecraft to orbit and land on an asteroid—the potato-shaped 433 Eros.

NASA's Cassini probe, shown in the artist's conception at left, is now conducting a detailed, four-year survey of the planet Saturn. The specially designed Huygens lander disengaged from Cassini in 2005 and embarked on a separate study of Titan, Saturn's largest moon.

Comets, however, rarely come close enough to Earth for study. The passage in 1985 and 1986 of Halley's comet—which swoops by Earth every 76 years—offered unique research opportunities.

Two Vega probes were launched by Soviet Proton rockets. These probes first studied Venus before flying to a rendezvous with Halley's comet in March 1986. The United States did not send a probe to Halley's comet but opted to provide some instruments for the Vega probes, in cooperation with the then–Soviet Union and France. This was the first Soviet mission with an international payload.

There were other Halley probes. The European Space Agency (ESA) launched Giotto with a French Ariane booster in 1985. In March 1986, the probe approached to within 300 miles (480 kilometers) of the comet. Instruments aboard included a mass spectrometer, plasma-ion analyzer, and dust-impact instruments. Japan's Planet A probe also studied the solar wind and included an ultraviolet imaging system.

The United States deployed its International Comet Explorer for rendezvous with the comet Giacobini-Zinner in 1985. In 2001, U.S. Deep Space 1 passed within 1,400 miles (2,200 kilometers) of comet Borrelly, and radioed to Earth the clearest photos yet of a comet nucleus.

In 2004, NASA's Stardust probe penetrated the dust and gas spewing from Comet Wild 2, taking photos and scooping up particles for study when the probe returns to Earth in 2006. ESA's Rosetta spacecraft is scheduled to land on Comet 67P/Churyumov-Gerasimenko in 2014. And NASA's Deep Impact crashed into Comet Tempel 1 on July 4, 2005, providing scientists with new insights into comet composition.

Mars Probes

Of all the planets, Mars most closely mimics the life-sustaining conditions on Earth. That is why scientists believe life once may have evolved on Mars. Our first glimpse of the Red Planet came in 1965, when the NASA spacecraft Mariner 4, one of a series of probes that explored the inner solar system, sent home 21 fuzzy photographs of Mars. Mariners 6 and 7 flew past in 1969 and sent more pictures. Late in 1971, Mariner 9 reached the vicinity of Mars while the planet was being swept by a huge dust storm. Once the dust settled, the craft sent pictures of a great canyon, a towering volcano, and dried-up riverbeds.

Even more exciting were the U.S. Viking missions of 1976, which consisted of two orbiters and two landers. As the orbiters conducted a photographic survey of the planet, the landers, looking for signs of life, scooped up soil samples. Although the landers did not find life, the possibility still exists that some primitive life-form is hiding in a Martian crevice or that life once bloomed and later died out.

The Soviet Union had only partial success with probes to Mars. After many early failures in the 1960s, Mars 5 managed to orbit the planet in 1973 and send back many pictures. That same year, Mars 6 and 7 sent back data from flybys, but their landers missed their targets. In 1988, the Soviets launched two Phobos probes to Mars. Contact with one was lost on its way to Mars. The second came within 100 miles (160 kilometers) of the planet, but then its onboard computer malfunctioned.

NASA launched the Mars Observer in 1992 to orbit the planet for a full Martian year. Unfortunately, in August 1993, just as the Mars Observer was drawing close to the Red Planet, scientists on Earth lost all communication with the probe.

The next successful landing on the Red Planet came on July 4, 1997, 20 years after Viking. Named Pathfinder, this U.S. craft represented an entirely revolutionary and inexpensive way of going into space.

Not only did it enter the Martian atmosphere directly, but it dropped with a parachute and then inflated air bags to cushion its descent to the surface. Once the craft landed, the air bags deflated, and Pathfinder became operational, sending photos of Mars back to Earth within hours. It even deployed a robot rover named Sojourner to roam the surface and measure the chemistry of soil and rock. Together, Sojourner and Pathfinder provided scientists with unprecedented insights regarding Mars.

In 1996, NASA launched the Mars Global Surveyor (MGS), which now orbits Mars and is returning images with finer detail than ever before seen. In early 2004, NASA's twin rovers—"Spirit" and "Opportunity"—arrived on Mars. Scientists later announced some exciting news: the robot geologists had confirmed that the Red Planet once had liquid water on its surface. Orbiting probes, such as NASA's Odyssey and the ESA's Mars Express, have transmitted intriguing images, bolstering the theory that ancient Mars was covered with water.

Earth Probes

While scientists have worked diligently to understand other planets of our solar system, they have not forgotten our home planet. Since the 1960s, satellites have been launched to observe Earth from space and to take measurements of the atmosphere, oceans, and land. But with growing concern for the global environment, there is a pressing need to understand our planet better than we do at present.

In its Earth Science Enterprise, NASA has launched a number of satellites equipped with instruments to monitor such things as temperature, ocean currents, emissions of "greenhouse gases," the extent of pollution, the water cycle, and the pace of rain-forest destruction. This information will allow us to assess the impact we have on the environment. It will also help us make predictions about how, and to what degree, the environment will change in the future.

The program began in the first half of the 1990s (under the name "Mission to Planet Earth"), when NASA launched several satellites called Earth Probes. These orbiting craft were to be followed by a series of massive Earth Observing System (EOS) platforms from which to study our planet. Since then, however, the mission's focus began to shift from data collection to information sharing, and it initiated studies in five major Earth-science disciplines: land surface cover; near-term and long-term climate change; natural hazards research; and atmospheric ozone.

Moon Probes

Exploration of the Moon was hastened by competition between the United States and what was then the Soviet Union. The Soviets scored many early successes with their Luna program, which began in 1959. That year, Luna 1 flew past the Moon, Luna 2 slammed into the lunar surface, and Luna 3 went completely around the Moon. In its lunar orbit, Luna 3 photographed the side not visible from Earth, and transmitted the first photos of this area. Beginning with Luna 9, launched in 1966, several Luna probes soft-landed on the Moon. These probes transmitted pictures, density data, and other information. In 1970, 1972, and 1976, Luna probes scooped up Moon rock and dust samples and sent them to Earth by rocket, a feat the Russians hope someday to repeat on Mars. In 1970 and 1973, Luna probes delivered unmanned wheeled vehicles that roamed the lunar surface, driven by remote control from Earth.

Though the United States got a later start in the race, it was the first—and, as yet, only—country to land humans there. Unmanned probes helped pave the way. Rangers 7, 8, and 9 (1964–1965) took more than 17,000 pictures of the Moon's surface before they crash-landed. A series of Surveyors soft-landed on the Moon and tested its surface. Lunar Orbiters photographed the Moon's surface, revealing suitable landing sites. On July 20, 1969, the *Apollo 11* spacecraft brought the first crew of Americans to the Moon's dusty surface.

In January 1990, Japan became the third nation to launch a probe to the Moon. MUSES-A rocketed from Earth aboard a booster built by Nissan. Once in orbit, the probe's transmission system failed. More Japanese probes will most likely follow.

In January 1994, a new-technology lightweight spacecraft carrying image sensors developed by the Ballistic Missile Defense Organization was launched from Vandenberg Air Force Base in California. During its two-month orbit of the Moon, the Clementine spacecraft captured 1.8 million images of that body's surface. It transmitted back to Earth radar data that led many scientists to believe that there may be water ice in the bottom of a lunar crater near the Moon's south pole.

NASA, too, is looking into the possibility of mining the Moon's resources. In

Space probes also study such heavenly phenomena as comets. In 1986, when Halley's comet made its much-awaited passage by Earth, it was intercepted by the Giotto probe (in the artist's conception below). The probe passed through the dust and gas surrounding the nucleus of the comet and transmitted data back to Earth about comet composition.

ESA

Space probes are manufactured to extremely precise specifications. Engineers assign especially high priority to the systems through which the spacecraft and ground stations will communicate. The Ulysses probe, for instance, has a 5.2-foot-diameter "high gain" antenna that continuously points toward Earth.

1998, NASA launched Lunar Prospector to scout the best places for a human outpost. For two years, the probe mapped the lunar geology and searched for minerals. It found evidence of water ice deep within shadowed craters near the Moon's poles. Metals could be used to construct a lunar base—a potential staging area for human trips to Mars, the asteroids, and beyond. A Moon base would also be ideal for telescopes, as the Moon is largely free of atmosphere, which blurs images, and completely free of the human-made space junk traveling through space, which threatens orbiting telescopes.

Venus Probes

Venus has long been called Earth's "twin," because the two planets have roughly the same size and density. But reports from more than 20 probes to Venus have reported an atmosphere that is more like Earth's worst nightmare.

The world's first robotic flight to another planet, Mariner 2, was launched by the United States in 1962. In a single close flyby of the alien world, the spacecraft reported that Venus has a hellish surface temperature of 896° F (480° C), far too hot for water to exist in liquid form. Venus is victim of a runaway greenhouse effect; its thick cloak of carbon dioxide gas traps solar heat, which mercilessly broils the planet's surface (see also page 99).

In 1967, the United States sent Mariner 5 to Venus. From 1967 to 1970, the Soviets sent four Venera probes, which for the first time in history pierced Venus' clouds and actually landed on the planet itself. From these early missions, we know that the air is so thick and heavy that it exerts a crushing pressure 90 times that felt on Earth's surface. In 1978, the American Pioneer-Venus 1 found swirling clouds of sulfuric acid amid the carbon dioxide cover that enshrouds the planet. En route to Halley's comet in 1985, two Soviet Vega probes released helium-filled balloons into the dense Venusian atmosphere. The balloons were swept great distances by the 155-mile (250-kilometer)-per-hour winds.

Between 1972 and 1981, more Soviet Venera craft soft-landed on Venus, performed soil analysis, and returned striking color photographs of the rock-strewn sur-

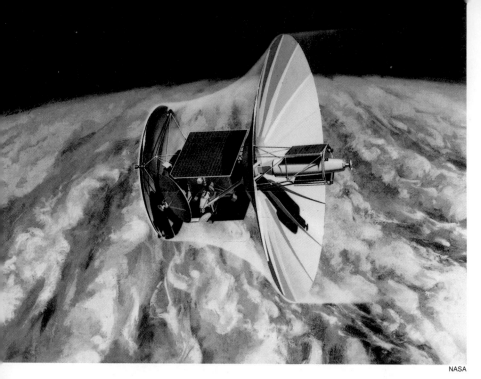

Scientists have developed novel ways to control space probes from bases on Earth. An advanced system called "aerobraking" (illustrated in the artist's conception at left) allows a spacecraft to change its orbit around a planet from elliptical (oval-shaped) to circular.

NASA

rounding the craft. But scientists wanted to have a global picture of Venus' topography. The planet's hazy atmosphere, however, kept the surface shrouded in mystery until the U.S. launched Pioneer-Venus 1 in 1978, and the Soviet Union launched Venera 15 and 16 in 1983. These three probes used radar to pierce the clouds and map many parts of the surface. They revealed, among other things, large craters, continent-sized highland areas, and huge mountains. But the images were fuzzy.

In September 1989, the NASA spacecraft Magellan started radar-mapping the Venusian surface with far better resolution. The craft sent sharp images of a bone-dry world strewn with bizarre patterns of cracks and fissures, channels cut by rivers of lava, mile-high "pancake domes," and giant craters from impacting meteorites. Such a landscape is far different than the plant-covered continents, blue oceans, and polar ice caps of Earth. In October 1994, the Magellan mission ended when scientists allowed the spacecraft to plunge into the thick Venusian atmosphere.

Mercury Probes

NASA's Mariner 10, launched in 1973, remains the only probe to have visited Mercury, the small but swift planet closest to the Sun. Through clever engineering, sci-

entists managed to get *three* flybys of Mercury (and one of Venus) out of the craft. The Sun provided free sunlight, which the craft's solar panels collected to generate power for onboard instruments.

Mariner 10 began its trip with a flyby of Venus. During this time it took the first clear pictures of that planet's swirling atmosphere. Then the craft entered an orbit of the Sun, revolving like a miniplanet every 176 days, exactly twice the time it takes Mercury to orbit the Sun. This trajectory took Mariner 10 past Mercury in March and September 1974 and again on March 16, 1975, when it passed just 200 miles (322 kilometers) above Mercury's surface. After this third and final pass, the attitude-control gas used to stabilize the craft ran out, and the craft slowly tumbled out of control and fell silent.

During its lifetime, Mariner 10 sent thousands of close-up photographs of Mercury, showing what no telescope on Earth could possibly see at the time. The craft revealed a gray planet that looked much like the Moon. Mercury's surface was strewn with impact craters—holes made when space rocks smash into the planet's surface. At first, scientists were going to name these craters after birds or famous cities. But they ended up choosing the names of famous artists, writers, and musicians. If you look at a map of Mercury, you will see craters van Gogh, Mark Twain, and Beethoven, to name a few.

Sun Probes

Since the late 1950s, many craft have been sent to orbit our star, the Sun, including the Soviet Luna 1, the U.S. Pioneers 6 through 9, and the German Helios 1 and 2. These probes studied the Sun itself, its powerful magnetic field, and the solar wind it generates.

But because of the way these probes were launched, they viewed only the Sun's central area, or equator. Most probes, including the early solar probes, are launched in the same direction that Earth orbits the Sun. That is because the probes can receive a natural boost of 18 miles (30 kilometers) per second from Earth's orbital speed. When these probes leave Earth, they travel in the same plane that Earth (and most other planets) travel around the Sun. If this plane, called the *ecliptic*, were solid, it would cut the Sun in half at its equator. Probes traveling on the ecliptic only can study solar activity coming from the Sun's equator; they cannot measure the activity on the solar *poles*, the Sun's top and bottom.

Scientists have long desired a glimpse of the Sun's poles and the space above and below the ecliptic plane. (Imagine how limited our understanding of Earth would be if we knew only the areas around our planet's equator!) To study the Sun's polar regions, scientists would have to send a probe perpendicular (at right angles) to the ecliptic plane. They could not use rockets to achieve this goal, because no rocket is powerful enough to overcome Earth's rapid motion around the Sun. Instead, scientists decided to enlist the help of Jupiter, the largest planet in the solar system. Jupiter's gravity is strong enough to "slingshot" a spacecraft out of the ecliptic plane and into an orbit over the Sun's poles.

In October 1990, NASA and the European Space Agency launched the spacecraft Ulysses toward a rendezvous with Jupiter in February 1992. The Ulysses spacecraft—the first solar probe to explore the Sun's environment at high latitudes—completed the first phase of its primary mission when it passed over the Sun's southern pole in November 1994, and traversed its northern pole in June 1995. In 1991, Japan launched Yohkoh, and in 1995, the European Space Agency launched the Solar Heliospheric Observatory (SOHO). Both are still in operation, teaching us a great deal about the solar wind and the explosive eruptions that radiate from our star.

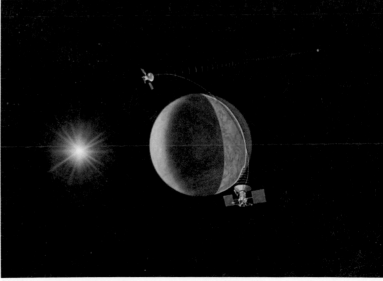

When the Magellan probe (left) reached Venus (below), it used radar waves to produce detailed maps of the planet's surface.

SPACE SATELLITES

by Tom Waters

On October 4, 1957, when the Soviet Union launched the first artificial satellite, Sputnik 1, banner headlines blared around the world. "Russia Launches A Moon," proclaimed page one of the *London Daily Mail*. A *New York Times* editorial called the feat a "concrete symbol of man's coming liberation from the forces which have hitherto bound life to this tiny planet."

Sputnik was a metal sphere 23 inches (58 centimeters) in diameter and 185 pounds (84 kilograms) in mass, carried 560 miles (901 kilometers) above the Earth's surface by an SS-6 rocket. Moving at a speed of 17,896 miles (28,800 kilometers) per hour, Sputnik circled the Earth in 1 hour, 36.2 minutes. It was equipped with two radio transmitters, whose continuous broadcasts were powerful enough to be picked up by amateur radio operators around the world. Its purpose was to test Soviet technological ability and—perhaps more important—to proclaim that ability to

Satellites enhance worldwide communications, conduct scientific research, and provide illuminating photos of atmospheric conditions on Earth and on our neighboring planets.

the world, especially the Soviet Union's great rival, the United States.

U.S. space scientists responded by stepping up their own efforts. On December 6, 1957, the Navy attempted a satellite launch, but it failed. Finally, on February 1, 1958, the Army succeeded in getting Explorer 1, the first U.S. satellite, into orbit. The United States made several more launches in 1958, and the National Aeronautics and Space Administration (NASA) was founded on July 29 of that year.

Since these early stages of the space race, thousands of human-made objects have been placed in orbit by many countries. As the number of artificial satellites in orbit has increased, so has the number of satellite uses. Some satellites are used for radio, television, and telephone communications. Others have cameras used for observing Earth, for weather forecasting, for scientific research, and for military purposes. Still others carry scientific experiments and instruments for observing the universe beyond Earth, such as the Hubble Space Telescope and the Chandra X-ray Observatory. And as the 21st century began, the United States, along with 15 other nations, continued assembly of the orbiting *International Space Station* (*ISS*), although the space shuttle *Columbia* catastrophe in 2003 halted construction for more than two years.

SATELLITE LAUNCHES

For the first 24 years of the space age, satellites were always launched on rockets. Rockets generally carry a single cargo, called a *payload,* into space. The rockets are then discarded and allowed to burn up as they fall back to Earth.

Since 1982, satellites have also been carried into orbit by U.S. space shuttles, reusable spacecraft that are launched by rockets but can glide back to Earth and land on a runway. When the space-shuttle program was first unveiled on September 17, 1976, its primary purpose was to launch most of the United States' satellites. But NASA has not been able to reach the flight-a-week schedule it first envisioned. The actual cost per launch has also proved much

higher than planned. Since the explosion of the space shuttle *Challenger* in 1986, the shuttles have been used only for NASA's own satellites and a select few international scientific satellites.

The business of placing satellites into orbit has become very competitive. For years, the U.S. government launched almost all of the commercial satellites for the non-Communist world. Then, in 1984, the European Space Agency (ESA), a cooperative venture (originally eight countries, now 15) began launching commercial satellites on its own rocket model, Ariane. In 1990, China launched an American-made communications satellite for use by a group of 20 Asian countries. In the late 1990s, Japan was also developing a rocket known as H-2 for commercial use (the project has since been cancelled). And in 1988, NASA began allowing private companies in the United States to perform their own launches on single-use rockets. Today, NASA does not launch any commercial satellites.

ORBITING EARTH

Once a rocket or shuttle has carried a satellite to the correct altitude, it must be placed in an effective orbit. That is, it must begin circling Earth at the correct speed so that it does not immediately tumble back down to the ground. A guidance system turns the satellite so that it is pointing parallel to Earth. Then a rocket engine fires to send it speeding in this new direction. This may be either the same rocket engine that has carried it into space or a different one.

This motion parallel to Earth's surface is what keeps the satellite in the sky. The force of gravity diminishes as one moves away from Earth's surface, but it is still quite strong at typical satellite altitudes. As a result, an orbiting satellite is constantly being tugged back toward Earth. Ideally, however, its motion keeps it from reentering the atmosphere and crashing to the ground because, as the satellite falls toward Earth, it also moves sideways so that it just misses the planet and flies off to the other side.

The most natural orbital path of a moon or satellite revolving around a planet is an el-

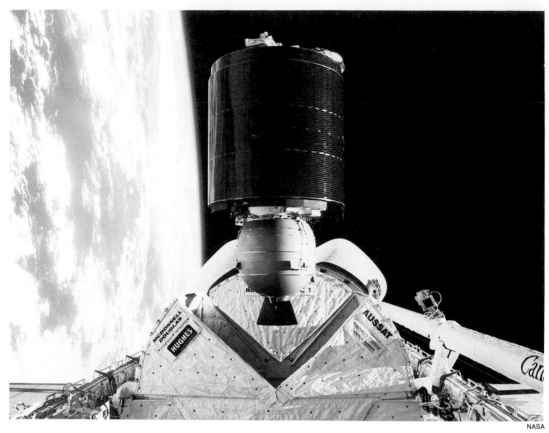

The shuttle era heralded a new means for satellite deployment, formerly achieved by rocket launches. Here Australia's communications satellite, AUSSAT, is released from the shuttle Discovery.

lipse, with the center of that planet at one focus of this ellipse. This is also true of the Earth's orbit around the Sun, as well as the Moon's orbit around the Earth. Although the orbits of artificial satellites are generally elliptical, nearly circular orbits are often used as well.

Every elliptical orbit has an *apogee*, or point farthest from the Earth, and a *perigee*, or point nearest to the Earth. The apogee and the perigee vary widely with different satellites. Sputnik 1 had an apogee of 584 miles (940 kilometers) and a perigee of 145 miles (234 kilometers). The apogee of the U.S. Hubble Space Telescope is 385 miles (619 kilometers), and its perigee is 379 miles (610 kilometers). Sometimes the distance between the apogee and the perigee is very large. For example, the U.S.

craft Explorer 14 had an apogee of 60,835 miles (97,904 kilometers) and a perigee of 173 miles (278 kilometers).

Scientists must decide in advance of a flight what sort of orbit is needed and how high it should be above the Earth. The plane of an artificial satellite's orbit must always include the center of the Earth, but it may be directed in various ways. The actual orbit, worked out in advance, will depend upon the intended mission of the satellite.

The plane of the orbit may pass over both poles as well as the center of the Earth, in which case the orbit is said to be *polar*. An orbit just slightly off the poles can bring a satellite over a different part of the world each time it circles the globe, while eventually returning to pass over

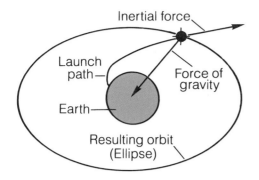

The force of a satellite launched at a speed of 5 to 7 miles per second, combined with the constant tug of Earth's gravity, pull a satellite into an elliptical orbit.

each spot at the same time of day. In this way a single satellite scans the entire planet under constant light conditions. This type of orbit is called *sun synchronous* and is well suited for reconnaissance satellites.

If the plane of a satellite's orbit lies along the equator, the orbit is said to be *equatorial*. The orbit may also be inclined by any number of degrees to the plane of the equator. For example, the inclination of the Explorer 1 was 33.6 degrees. If a satellite has a nearly circular, equatorial orbit 22,282 miles (35,860 kilometers) above the ground, then it has what is known as a *geostationary* orbit. It will take precisely one day to orbit the Earth. Since the Earth is also rotating once a day, the satellite will then remain fixed above one point on the Earth's surface. Geostationary orbits are especially useful for communications and weather satellites.

GUIDANCE IN SPACE

There are many opportunities for error and disaster in spaceflight. The smallest inaccuracy in calculation or the malfunction of a rocket can cause the space vehicle to veer far off target. This is why both rockets and satellites have guidance systems to keep them on course. There are various kinds of systems. For example, in the radio-command guidance system, changes in velocity and direction are broadcast by the spacecraft to a station on the ground.

The data are fed into computers that make the calculations required to keep the craft on course. The necessary adjustments are then broadcast back to the craft, and control motors on the craft carry out the instructions. This procedure may be directed by ground personnel or it may be automatic.

In an inertial-guidance system, the velocity and direction of the satellite are measured by an onboard sensor system. This information is then fed to onboard computers and flight controls. And some spacecraft employ hybrid systems that combine some of the techniques from both radio and inertial systems.

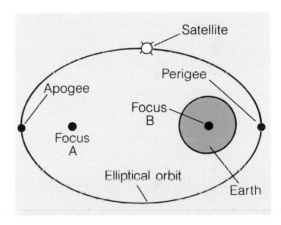

In an elliptical orbit the distance of a satellite's nearest point to Earth (perigee) and its farthest point (apogee) will depend on the satellite's mission.

Most communications satellites are placed in an equatorial orbit, while a polar or inclined orbit is well suited for many reconnaissance satellites.

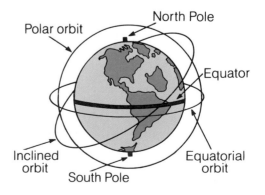

POWER AND COMMUNICATIONS IN SPACE

All spacecraft require a power source to keep their instruments functioning and to provide the necessary radio transmission. Solar cells (waferlike silicon cells) convert sunlight into electric current. These cells must be exposed to the Sun in order to work, so whenever a satellite is in the Earth's shadow, it relies on current stored in a nickel-cadmium battery. This battery is, in turn, recharged by the solar cells. Engineers are now developing more-efficient silicon solar cells, as well as cells made from a gallium arsenide combination to provide lighter and more-durable power sources.

Other power sources are independent of the Sun. The SNAP generator, a device that produces electricity directly from atomic energy, proved successful in the U.S. Navy's Transit satellites in the early 1960s. The Soviet Union has used nuclear reactors to power its satellites since the 1970s. U.S. plans to use nuclear reactors in more satellites have come under criticism due to the danger posed by the radioactive fuel that may eventually fall back to Earth.

Almost all satellites are designed to transmit information to the Earth by means of a telemetering system. In this system, data collected by the scientific instruments on the craft are converted into radio signals, and these are transmitted to ground stations. At these stations, spools of magnetic tape record the signals, and computers decode them. Photographs can also be transmitted in this way, much as they are in television broadcasts.

THE END OF THE FLIGHT

The flight of an orbiting artificial satellite must come to an end eventually. Although the atmosphere is rarefied (much less dense) 124 miles (200 kilometers) from the Earth, no part of space is an absolute vacuum. Some molecules and other particles still exist that far up. When such particles strike an orbiting spacecraft, the individual collisions are insignificant, but the cumulative effect is damaging.

In time the craft will begin to lose velocity. It will not go so high at apogee, and, at its next perigee, it will be closer to the Earth. The spacecraft will eventually fail to balance the pull of gravity and will begin to penetrate deeper into the Earth's atmosphere. Unless special protective measures or devices are provided, a spacecraft reentering the atmosphere is doomed. Just like a meteorite that penetrates the atmosphere, it will be subjected to intense heat as it col-

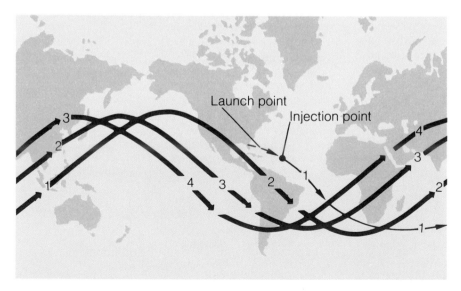

Satellites in polar and inclined orbits pass over different portions of the Earth each time they circle the globe. This is illustrated in these four successive passes of a satellite launched from a point in Florida that went into an inclined orbit at the injection point indicated.

Intelsat V is an advanced communications satellite that simultaneously provides 12,000 two-way telephone circuits and two television channels for communication between the United States and Europe. To keep these instruments functioning, the satellite is powered by solar cells that convert sunlight into electric current.

lides with the increasingly numerous molecules and ions, and it will burst into flames. The chances are very high that the satellite will be completely destroyed. Some fragments, however, may make their way down to Earth. When the Russian space station *Mir* fell out of orbit in March 2001, many large pieces were still intact after reentry. Fortunately, they landed in the Pacific Ocean, without injuring any people or damaging property.

Satellites that escape from Earth's gravitational field may be destroyed by way of collision. For example, they might crash on the Moon. But if they fail to collide with a planet, they may enter orbit around the Sun. After all, everything in our solar system is in the Sun's gravitational field. Once a satellite begins orbiting the Sun, it may continue circling indefinitely.

Today, there are so many satellites roaming space that "space junk" has become a major concern at NASA and the rest of the world's space agencies. Old satellites, often broken into tiny fragments, now threaten to collide with and destroy new ones.

COMMUNICATIONS SATELLITES

Each day, tens of thousands of phone calls are made from the United States to Great Britain. Half of these are carried by a web of undersea fiber-optic cables that stretch across the Atlantic floor, but the other half are transmitted via satellite.

In satellite transatlantic telephone communications, the sound of a speaker's voice is converted to an electrical signal and carried over wires to a transmitting station. There, it is translated into a powerful radio signal and aimed at a small, unmanned spacecraft (or satellite) orbiting 22,282 miles (35,860 kilometers) above Earth's surface. An automated device on board the craft receives the signal, then broadcasts it back down to a receiving station on the other

The InfraRed Astronomical Satellite (IRAS), depicted here as it passes over Western Europe, was launched in January 1983. During its ten months of operation, its instruments collected data on the infrared radiation emitted from over 250,000 sources, including newborn stars, interstellar dust, distant galaxies, and quasars.

side of the Atlantic. The signal is then sent out over wires to the other speaker's home or office. There are now over 75 satellites, operated by more then 20 different companies, national governments, and international organizations, that provide this technologically advanced yet routine service.

Today's satellites are now used to carry all kinds of long-range signals. In addition to transmission of transatlantic calls, satellites direct many calls within the continental United States. Broadcast and cable television programs are relayed by satellite from network headquarters to local stations. Computers use satellites to convey enormous quantities of information to each other.

New uses for satellites are constantly opening up. People who live in remote areas without local TV stations sometimes use dish antennas up to 20 feet (6.1 meters) in diameter to pick up satellite TV signals that are meant primarily for rebroadcast by

local stations. Japan and Germany now have satellites that broadcast TV programming directly to consumers, who need only small dishes to pick up these signals. Several companies are now preparing to offer a similar service in the United States.

Early Communications Satellites

The first satellite to relay messages from one Earth station to another was SCORE (Signal Communicating by Orbiting Relay Equipment), launched December 18, 1958. SCORE received and recorded messages up to four minutes long while flying over one station, then rebroadcast them while flying over another station. The experimental satellite lasted 35 days before its batteries ran down.

Early communications satellites did not amplify radio signals, but merely reflected them, and were thus called *passive* communications satellites. The first true passive communications satellite, Echo 1, was launched by the United States on Au-

308   **SPACE SATELLITES**

gust 12, 1960, less than three years after Sputnik 1 entered orbit. The Echo satellite was actually a plastic balloon 98 feet (30 meters) in diameter, covered with a thin coating of aluminum to reflect radio transmissions. A second, larger Echo began orbiting in 1964.

In Project West Ford in 1963, space scientists spread a thin ring of fine wire needles around Earth. The wires were "tuned" to reflect signals at a certain frequency. Scientists eventually abandoned the program because the ring of wires threatened to disturb astronomical observations. In 1966, researchers tried another novel idea. An Echo-type balloon was covered with precisely spaced wire mesh. The balloon decomposed after a few hours in orbit, leaving a hollow metallic sphere that was five times more reflective than Echo. It was also much less affected by the Sun's radiation and was slowed down less by the atmosphere. These passive satellites were really not practical because of their large size and the powerful equipment required to send and receive messages.

Active Communications Satellites

Bell Telephone tested the commercial value of communications satellites in 1962, when Telstar 1 was placed in orbit. Telstar was an *active* satellite, both amplifying and retransmitting as many as 60 two-way telephone conversations at a time. Like other active satellites, Telstar obtained the electrical power that it needed to receive and transmit signals from banks of solar cells attached to the satellite. Ground stations were established in the United States, Britain, and France. A few months after Telstar 1, Relay 1 was launched for RCA (Radio Corporation of America), adding Italy and Brazil to the countries that received broadcasts from satellites in outer space.

In 1963, Syncom 2 became the first communications satellite to achieve geostationary orbit. It remained over the same position on Earth's surface at all times and was in constant view of almost half the planet. Most communications satellites are now placed in orbits of this type.

From time to time, NASA has participated in programs to test experimental communications systems. NASA's Applications Technology Satellite, ATS-1, was launched on December 6, 1966, to test a variety of instruments, including a 600-channel repeater that could relay color-television programming, as well as radio transmissions between aircraft and ground stations. ATS-1 was also used to develop technology for weather satellites.

In addition to the United States, many countries have developed or purchased their own communications satellites, with numerous others planning to do likewise in the near future. The then Soviet Union began building its orbiting system in 1965, and Russia now has three series of communications satellites (called Molniy, Statsionar, and Gorizont) circling Earth. These satellites bring telephone and television service to remote areas of the country, as well as to parts of Eastern Europe. Since the 1970s, India has used a satellite called SITE to send educational-television programming to thousands of rural villages.

Satellite Networks

By far the most extensive satellite system is that of the International Telecommunications Satellite Consortium, or Intelsat. Since its launch of the world's first commercial communications satellite (Early Bird) in 1965, Intelsat has steadily expanded its communications capability. For example, in 1969, it provided the first live globally televised broadcast of the *Apollo 11* lunar landing and, in 1987, successfully linked 50,000 people in 70 cities across the globe for the world's largest teleconference. As of 2001, Intelsat had 21 satellites in operation, and served the communication needs of more than 200 countries and territories around the world. Intelsat is planning seven more satellite launches by 2003.

Most of the members of Intelsat are national governments, but the American member of the consortium is the Communications Satellite Corporation (COMSAT), a private company established by the U.S. Congress in 1962. COMSAT has been a subsidiary of aerospace giant Lockheed Martin since 1998. It pays Intelsat for the use of its satellites, then sells services to companies

The level of sophistication of reconnaissance satellites has rapidly improved over the past 40 years. In fact, the top-secret military satellites can provide almost instantaneous high-resolution images of objects as small as book titles (photo sequence, right) and the numbers on an automobile license plate. Flexible telescope mirrors compensate for poor weather conditions, and infrared-sensitive cameras permit night photography. In addition to military surveillance, advanced satellite capabilities can provide images of cocaine crops, rain-forest depletion, and hurricane or tornado damage.

such as the American Telephone and Telegraph Corporation (AT&T). COMSAT also operates several of its own satellites. Several other American companies operate satellites, and many other countries have set up public or private satellite systems for domestic communications.

Other international networks operating communications satellites include Intersputnik, which serves Russia and Eastern European countries; Arabsat, which serves 20 Arab nations; Eutelsat, which serves the communication needs of 26 European nations; and Inmarsat, which provides communication services to ships on the high seas. In addition, Indonesia operates a system of three satellites for use by a group of Pacific countries.

Communications Satellite Operation

Until recently, most communications satellites were launched by NASA. But now private companies have taken over most American launches. Europe, Japan, and other countries are also competing in the satellite-launching market. Intelsat has most of its satellites launched by the European Space Agency on Ariane rockets. The consortium also uses the launch services of General Dynamics and other American aerospace companies.

Once in its prescribed position in geosynchronous orbit over the Earth, a satellite is ready to go to work. Its ground station may belong to a country's government, a consortium like Intelsat, or even private individuals. The ground stations usually beam messages to the satellites at one frequency and receive messages at another by using an amplifying device called a transponder. This technology is very efficient because it allows a single ground station to send and receive signals at the same time.

Depending on a satellite's capability, it can be used for telephone service, encoding data, or television transmissions. Its various channels are usually leased to users in the form of half-circuits—two-way connections between the satellite and a ground station. Thus, a pair of half-circuits are required to complete an overseas call. These connections are normally operating round the clock.

Other channels may be used for television transmissions such as news stories and sports events. Finally, a portion of the circuits are held in reserve for emergencies, increased demand within the system, and other special needs.

The Future of Satellite Communications

Ironically, the major obstacles to designing new communications satellites no longer have to do with space technology. Instead, scientists are being stymied by the limited space in the electromagnetic spectrum. Any radio transmission takes place at a particular frequency, and there is a limit to how much can be transmitted on any one frequency. Almost every available frequency that can be used to transmit information is already being used, and the remaining frequencies are being held in reserve for specific purposes.

Engineers are now seeking ways to pack more information into each frequency channel, often by digitally processing signals. This approach has multiplied by five the number of phone calls that can be put through a single Intelsat channel, for example. But engineers believe that signals can be compressed even more in the future. Plans for new satellite-communications services—such as direct television broadcasts from satellites to consumers—depend on continued progress in these digital-signal-compression methods.

© Sipa-Press

Satellite technology is invaluable to military commanders when planning an aerial attack. Here, in satellite photos taken during the Gulf War in 1991, a view of Baghdad, Iraq (above), is magnified many times (left) to capture an image of a bridge that was destroyed by the Allied forces during a bombing raid.

© Orban/SYGMA

OBSERVATION SATELLITES

What better vantage point for observing Earth could there be than a satellite orbiting high above the surface of the planet? For many kinds of observations, apparently, there is none. In the past 40 years, satellite observations of Earth have become routine in a wide range of areas.

Satellite images are used to predict the weather, for example, and to help explain it in televised weather reports. Military-reconnaissance satellites enable countries like the United States and Russia to judge the capabilities of their rivals in peacetime and to monitor the movements of their enemies in combat situations.

As the availability of satellite images increases and the price falls, many more satellite uses keep turning up. An ecologist who wants to study certain tree species can locate large stands of them using commercially available satellite images. Satellites can also monitor large-scale ecological changes, such as the clearing of rain forests in Brazil, Malaysia, and Indonesia. Since much of this tree cutting is done illegally or with little governmental supervision, there is no way to estimate the amount of land being cleared except by the use of satellite-imaging technology.

The United States launched the first Earth-observation satellites: the Tiros 1, a weather satellite launched April 1, 1960, and Corona/Discoverer 14, a military-reconnaissance satellite launched into orbit on August 18, 1960.

Tiros took pictures electronically and transmitted them to Earth on radio waves. But these pictures proved too blurry for military reconnaissance. Corona was developed to capture images with camera film. After exposing the film, the satellite ejected it in a capsule, which an Air Force plane then plucked from the sky. In Corona's pictures, objects as small as 1 foot (0.305 meter) long were clearly visible from space. Viewers could even identify the make of cars in Moscow's Red Square.

The Soviet Union entered the satellite-reconnaissance game in 1962, with its Cosmos 4 satellite, which also used the ejected-capsule method for getting its pictures back to Earth. China followed suit in 1970 with China 1.

Spies in the Sky

The technology of military reconnaissance by satellite has changed considerably over the years. During the 1960s and 1970s, the United States developed satellites that could use their own rocket engines and navigation systems to move from one orbit to another, or to swoop closer to Earth for especially detailed observations.

The U.S. military continued to develop satellites that could relay their information to Earth on radio waves. But film-dropping satellites remained essential for high-resolution pictures until 1976. That year, the first KH-11 went into orbit. KH-11s are U.S. satellites that use very large telescopes and video cameras to observe Earth and continuously transmit pictures to ground stations. Their exact capabilities are a military secret—even their existence is not officially admitted. But it is rumored that KH-11s can pick out objects

6 inches (15.24 centimeters) long, and perhaps as small as 2 inches (5.08 centimeters) long. It may be possible to read automobile license-plate numbers with KH-11 pictures.

The United States stopped using film-return satellites in 1984, and has since developed the Advanced KH-11, with improved nighttime observing ability. While no one will explain how the images are relayed to Earth, the president or military officials can view images from KH-11s within an hour after they are taken.

The Soviet Union launched Cosmos 1426, its own answer to the KH-11, in 1982. But it still uses film-return satellites. It is believed that the Russians do their military spying with less advanced, less expensive observation satellites, but they place more of them in orbit. Meanwhile, at any one time, the United States is said to use two KH-11s, two Advanced KH-11s, and a Lacrosse satellite, which uses radar to make observations at night or through thick cloud cover. All of these satellites are short-lived and must be replaced regularly. The United States and Russia also maintain separate networks of satellites that spy on radio signals around the world, including signals sent from other satellites.

In 1991, the United States, the then Soviet Union, and China were still the only three countries with reconnaissance satellites, but this is rapidly changing. In 1988, Israel launched Offeq 1, an experimental satellite reportedly built with help from South Africa. Israel launched Offeq 2 in 1990. France, Italy, and Spain are collaborating on the development of their own reconnaissance-satellite network. India and Germany each plan to develop military-reconnaissance satellites. Even Japan is reported to be working on a satellite that will make both military and scientific observations. Other countries are likely to undertake satellite-reconnaissance programs in the coming years.

Civilian Observation Satellites

Civilian satellite-observation technology has always lagged behind military capabilities. Civilian organizations lack the lavish funding that is available to the military.

Also, governments try to prevent civilian satellites from gaining capabilities that could affect national security. In 1978 the United States prohibited civilian satellites from producing pictures in which objects smaller than 33 feet (10 meters) can be seen. So civilian satellites had to be made 100 times less sensitive than military ones. In 1987, however, the Soviet Union started selling pictures with 16.5-foot (5-meter) resolution to anyone who could pay, thus rendering the U.S. ban ineffective.

Despite these limitations, civilian satellites are providing valuable information on meteorology, agriculture, forestry, geology, environmental science, and in other areas. The first weather satellite, Tiros, launched in 1960, was primarily an experimental craft, but meteorologists were able to get useful information from its images. More Tiros satellites went up through 1965 for combined experimental and operational use. In 1966 the Environmental Science Services Administration (ESSA) began launching a series of satellites based on the Tiros series to provide routine, daily satellite weather photography. ESSA has since been renamed the National Oceanic and Atmospheric Administration (NOAA), but it is still operating satellites that are advanced versions of Tiros. These satellites, now called NOAAs, fly in near-polar, sun-synchronous orbits, so that they scan the entire planet's surface, always passing over each spot at the same time of day.

NOAA also operates a series of satellites called Geostationary Operational Environmental Satellites (GOES), which fly in geostationary orbits so that they always seem to hover over the same spot on the Earth's surface. They can observe the same part of the Earth continuously, making it possible to see clouds and weather systems in motion. The GOES satellites also measure the heights of the cloud layers they see, making it possible to measure formations in three dimensions. The first GOES was launched on October 16, 1975.

The wavelengths of light reflected from the ocean are directly related to chlorophyll concentrations, which indicate biological activity. An image from the Coastal Zone Color Scanner satellite indicates that the highest concentrations of chlorophyll (red and yellow) hug the shallower coastlines, while the lowest levels (blue) occur in the deeper midocean areas.

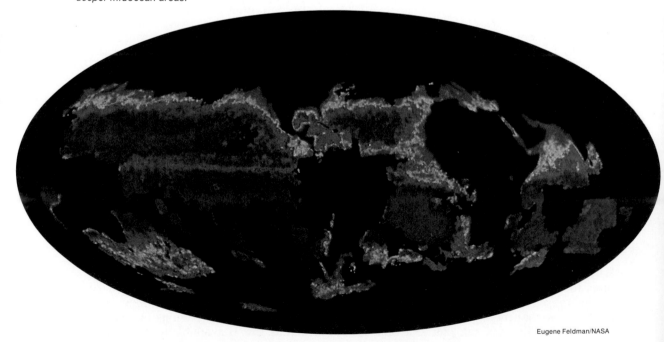

Weather satellites often travel in a geostationary orbit, seeming to hover over the same area of Earth's surface to make continuous observations of clouds and weather systems in motion. The course of a swirling hurricane can then be monitored.

Other countries operate satellites in both sun-synchronous and geostationary orbits. The United States participates in an international joint effort with Japan, Russia, and the European Space Agency to coordinate geostationary satellites that together scan the entire world. The United States launched Landsat 1 on July 23, 1972. It was designed to photograph Earth's surface for geological, biological, and environmental research. Landsat 5, launched on March 1, 1984, could resolve objects as small as 98 feet (30 meters) across and produce black-and-white or color pictures, as well as false-color images that reveal information from different regions of the normally invisible electromagnetic spectrum.

The Landsat program is now part of NASA's Earth Science Enterprise, which allows scientists worldwide to gather images of the planet's oceans, coastal regions, and inland areas as they conduct environmental and climate research. Analysis of satellite data provides scientists with a wealth of information on agriculture, glacier formations, and deforestation. Landsat satellites are also used for other purposes, such as monitoring urban growth.

On April 4, 1999, Landsat 7 was launched from Vandenberg Air Force Base in California aboard a Delta II rocket. It was fitted with three primary instruments: the Multispectral Scanner (MSS); the Thematic Mapper (TM); and the Enhanced Thematic Mapper (ETM+). Both the MSS and TM were installed on previous Landsat models, but the ETM+ was a new component. Combined, these instruments have been able to provide images with clearer resolutions than those from the previous Landsat satellites.

© Steven Hunt/The Image Bank

THE SEARCH FOR EXTRATERRESTRIAL LIFE

by David J. Fishman

To consider the Earth as the only populated world in infinite space is as absurd as to assert that in an entire field of millet, only one grain will grow.
—the Greek philosopher Metrodorus in the 4th century B.C.

Since the beginning of recorded history, people have speculated about humanity's place in the universe: are we alone, or do we share the incredible vastness with other intelligent forms of life? Today, for the first time in history, scientists are armed with knowledge and tools that can begin to answer this fundamental question. On Columbus Day, October 12, 1992, the National Aeronautics and Space Administration (NASA), the U.S. space agency, began sifting the sky for unusual radio signals as part of its 10-year Search for Extraterrestrial Intelligence (SETI) program.

Scientists around the world intend to spend a great deal of time and money searching the heavens for intelligent extraterrestrial (not of this Earth) life. They claim that the conditions that led to the evolution of life on Earth are most certainly not unique in the universe.

EARLY FRUSTRATION

Forty years ago, astronomers were not so optimistic. Scientists agreed it would be extremely unlikely for life to have evolved on or very close to stars themselves, as the high stellar temperatures would prevent the formation of the chemicals needed for life to evolve. Life as we define it, they reasoned, would have to evolve on planets that were far enough away from a star to allow the brewing of life-giving chemicals.

To the disappointment of many, searches of the visible universe during the 1970s and early 1980s yielded no absolute evidence of planets orbiting other stars. Astronomers concluded that planetary solar systems such as our own were extremely rare. And many astronomers concluded that life evolved on our planet and perhaps nowhere else in the universe.

One problem these astronomers faced in their search for hospitable planets, however, was that planets are very difficult to spot directly, even using high-powered telescopes. After all, planets don't emit light or other electromagnetic radiation in the same way that stars do.

Scientists now know that evidence that planets exist is generally indirect. One piece of evidence is derived from the movement of stars. Astronomers can calculate the effect that the gravity of orbiting planets has on a star, and then look to see if this characteristic pattern of movement appears among stars they observe over long periods.

Using recent advances in the tools of astronomy and physics, scientists today can substantiate the existence of other planetary systems. Many astronomers now believe that planets are not rare exceptions, but rather, a part of the star-formation process. Today NASA astronomers estimate that the number of planets in our own Milky Way galaxy alone might number in the hundreds of billions. Surely, they say, the conditions that helped bring about life on Earth must also be duplicated on one or more of these myriad planets.

SETTING THE STAGE FOR LIFE

Many cosmologists (scientists who study the origin and eventual fate of the universe) believe that about 15 billion years ago, all matter and energy were once compressed into a single, tiny point. The theory is that a colossal explosion, often called the Big Bang, ejected seething matter at tremendous speeds in all directions. The universe has been expanding and cooling ever since.

According to this theory, about 5 billion to 10 billion years ago, large clouds of gas began to consolidate under the influence of gravity. As the force of gravity pulled more and more of the mass of gas together, large, ball-like clumps of gas began to form inside these large clouds. When these clumps grew sufficiently large, nuclear fusion ignited them to create the bright, shining stars we see today.

The Big Bang would have produced only hydrogen and helium, the two lightest elements. None of the heavier elements, including those that make up much of our planet and our own bodies—elements such as carbon, oxygen, nitrogen, sulfur, and phosphorus—would have been present in the young universe. But these elements would slowly form by the fusion of lighter particles, a process that takes place inside massive stars.

Before stars run out of the nuclear fuel powering their bright burns, they often explode, creating massive supernovas. The clouds of an expanding supernova are filled with the heavy elements that have been

Scanning the universe for signs of intelligent life might turn up unexpected results. As suggested in the artist's conception at left, life-forms that evolve on planets with conditions dissimilar to those on Earth might appear bizarre to an Earthling's eyes.

ties of such interstellar dust, astronomers have identified many of the molecules needed to start the evolution of life. Scientists call these chemical compounds "biogenic," for their potential ability to produce life.

Astronomers have found evidence of grains of silicate, carbon, ammonia, methane, and even water among the more than 70 types of molecules drifting in space. Some astronomers believe that comets and meteors transport these seeds of life from gas clouds to young planets.

Eventually the molecules making up interstellar gas clouds, including the biogenic compounds, collapse once again to form a new dense cloud of dust and gas, eventually forming a new generation of stars. In the case of our own solar system, one of the random gas clouds in the Milky Way collapsed to form our Sun about 4.6 billion years ago. Our Sun is an unremarkable star, similar in many ways to millions of others in the galaxy. At the time of our Sun's birth, a cooler disk of nearby interstellar material, called a protoplanetary nebula, coalesced and began orbiting the Sun. Ultimately the force of gravity sorted and separated this material into the nine planets we know today.

The Earth-orbiting Hubble Telescope has found evidence of protoplanetary nebulae around several nearby stars. This strongly suggests that planets are continually being formed in our galaxy. No one had ever found one, however, until 1992.

In that year, scientists using the 1,000-foot (305-meter) radio dish at Arecibo, Puerto Rico, found that a pulsar (a rapidly spinning and flashing remnant from a supernova explosion) was accompanied by at least two planets. If planets can exist in the hostile environment near a pulsar, planets might be more plentiful than anyone had ever thought. And where there are planets, many scientists believe, there may be life.

cooked in the interior of the star. This interstellar dust is the potion from which life on Earth—and perhaps on other planets—arose.

Some of this ejected material is constantly undergoing chemical transformations in the cold space between the stars. By examining the light-scattering proper-

Today, scientists believe that many stars are accompanied by their own planetary systems. Finding them, however, was impossible until the mid-1990s, when astronomers were able to develop the technology that can detect if stars wobble—some as little as a few yards per second—as a companion planet tugs on them gravitationally. In 2003, more than 100 planetary systems are known to exist around distant stars.

Life's Chemistry Set

Fossil evidence suggests that Earth was without life for only a small fraction of its existence, perhaps less than 1 billion of its 4.6 billion years. For most of those early years, comets and meteorites fell continuously to Earth, contributing large amounts of biogenic compounds to the young planet. The comets and meteorites, together with volcanoes spewing lava and hot gases, helped create an atmosphere heavy in water vapor, but lacking free oxygen. As Earth cooled, the water vapor eventually condensed and formed the oceans.

For millions of years, ultraviolet radiation from the Sun, cosmic rays from deep space, and frequent lightning brought large amounts of energy to the surface of the young Earth. Eventually, this energy could have resulted in the synthesis of simple organic molecules. After many more millions of years, organic molecules formed more-complex systems. Somehow, organic molecules were able to use surrounding materials to replicate. And that replication was the hallmark of a living system.

Swiftly, the new forms of life began to have an enormous impact on the character of the immature Earth. A billion years after life began, blue-green algae evolved. They survived by tapping the energy of the Sun via photosynthesis. These algae pumped large amounts of oxygen into the atmosphere, setting the stage for more-advanced forms of life to evolve. About 1.7 billion years ago, the first advanced cells appeared. These cells contained a nucleus and primitive structures inside their cell walls. About 1 billion years ago, multicellular organisms appeared, and life, as we know it, began in earnest on this planet.

Using the increased amount of oxygen in the atmosphere and dissolved in the ocean, multicellular organisms proliferated rapidly. Fish appeared about 425 million years ago, and their relatives crawled out onto land about 325 million years ago. Modern humans arrived relatively recently, just 30,000 to 40,000 years ago.

Because humans had evolved appendages that can easily manipulate what we find in our world, our species developed technology—the first example of which was the creation and use of simple tools. Over the course of the past 10,000 years, humans have learned to build shelters, cultivate land for food, and develop written and verbal forms of communication. Over the past 100 years, our species has developed the ability to communicate with each other at the speed of light, using electromagnetic radiation such as radio waves and microwaves.

THE MEANS TO COMMUNICATE

Communicating by electromagnetic radiation, or photons, is the fastest means allowed by the laws of physics. Photons can carry information, are easily generated and detected, are not seriously affected by the magnetic fields pervading outer space, and, at the correct frequencies, have a small probability of being scattered or absorbed. If intelligent life also evolved on other planets, scientists presume that over time, these other beings also would have stumbled upon this ideal method for communicating across the vast heavens.

The Search for Extraterrestrial Intelligence, or SETI, focuses exclusively on stars and planets outside of our own solar system. From observations made here on Earth, and with the many probes sent to investigate our eight neighboring planets, scientists have in effect ruled out the possibility that there are other forms of intelligent life orbiting our Sun. Still, many scientists are convinced that some of our neighboring planets or their moons contain, and are still producing, organic chemicals. They believe it is possible that primitive life-forms now exist or perhaps once existed on other planets or moons in our solar system.

Mercury, the planet nearest the Sun, is somewhat larger than our Moon. Like our Moon, Mercury has little or no atmosphere. Extremely high temperatures, especially on the daylight side of the planet, rule out the possibility that water or organic molecules could exist on Mercury's surface. Venus, the second planet from the Sun, is very similar to Earth in size and density. But it, too, is much hotter than Earth. From a biological point of view, Venus is a grim place. The atmosphere is very unlike Earth's; it consists mostly of carbon dioxide gas, with small amounts of carbon monoxide. Dense clouds of sulfuric acid droplets shroud Venus' surface. Temperatures range from 860° to 1,004° F (460° to 540° C), and atmospheric pressures can be 100 times greater than those at the surface of Earth. The extreme heat and pressure make the existence of water and any accompanying organic compounds extremely unlikely.

Mars, the fourth planet from the Sun, has a diameter half that of Earth. Its atmospheric density is very low, similar to Earth's atmosphere at an altitude of 31 miles (50 kilometers). Mars' atmosphere consists mainly of carbon dioxide with a trace of water. Because the air is so thin, ultraviolet radiation from space, which is harmful to most living things, can easily reach the Martian surface. At the Martian equator, the temperature may reach 50° F (10° C) during the day; at night it may drop to a decidedly uncomfortable –99° F (–73° C).

But Mars does have many features that lead some astronomers to believe it could support life. Its polar ice caps are still composed of frozen water. The 1976 Viking landers examined soil samples that yielded water upon heating. In 2004, twin NASA rovers—"Spirit" and "Opportunity"—found evidence that the Red Planet once had liquid water on its surface. Photographs taken by these small robotic geologists—and images from orbiting space probes—bolster the theory that ancient Mars was covered with water. Could the planet have supported life? Scientists speculate that primitive microorganisms may have existed during Mars' apparently moist history.

In the past, researchers did not consider Jupiter, Saturn, Uranus, and Neptune as suitable homes for alien life-forms. Be-

Judging from Viking 2's vantage point (above), the surface of Mars would seem inhospitable to even the most primitive forms of life. Alien life-forms, if they exist, would likely come from regions of the universe too distant for space probes to visit. Astronomers would, however, be able to pick up electronic messages or signals from faraway civilizations using today's powerful radio telescopes (right).

Top: NASA; above: National Radio Astronomy Observatory

cause of their great distance from the Sun, all are extremely cold. In spite of their immense sizes and masses, the outer planets are less dense than the Earth. Their solid cores are quite small when compared with their large volumes.

Nonetheless, astronomers now know that the ammonia-methane-hydrogen atmospheres typical of these giants can be breeding places for biochemicals. And surprisingly, the outer planets are not always as cold as astronomers once thought: new studies show that some of their cloud layers may be comparatively mild in temperature.

Jupiter is of particular interest to scientists. It may have an internal source of heat, making it warmer than it would be if heated by the Sun alone. And its many-colored cloud coat may contain a large variety of organic compounds.

Laboratory experiments show that organic and biological compounds can evolve in Jupiter-like conditions. The Pioneer and Voyager probes that examined Jupiter's clouds detected violent lightning flashes that might provide the spark of life for a primitive chemical soup. They have detected other hopeful signs that are precur-

EXTRATERRESTRIALS IN THE MOVIES

Science fiction has helped mold our perceptions of how the inhabitants of other planets would appear. Some of the first depictions of extraterrestrial beings appeared in science-fiction magazines of the early 20th century. The film industry's interest in science-fiction topics —including people from outer space—blossomed in the 1950s, perhaps as a result of public interest in rockets, space programs, and a growing number of UFO sightings.

Photos: Photofest

Steven Spielberg's film E.T.: The Extraterrestrial *was the box-office hit of 1982 and the most popular science-fiction movie to date. E.T. (above) caught the hearts of moviegoers as he poignantly sought to return to his home planet.*

Not nearly so lovable were the extraterrestrials portrayed in the 1957 production Invasion of the Saucermen *(left). Though grotesque by Earth standards, any alien who devised a way to travel to Earth would likely have an oversized brain.*

sors of primitive life on the moons of Jupiter and its close neighbor, Saturn.

Although very little is known about Pluto, this outermost planet of our solar system may be of little biological interest. We do know that it is a small, rocky body without an atmosphere. It appears to be too far from the Sun's warming energy for the chemical evolution of life.

WHAT ARE THE ODDS?

Knowing that we have to search outside of our own solar system to find intelligent life, how can we estimate our chances of success? American radio astronomer Frank Drake has developed a way to estimate the number of the universe's intelligent civilizations with which we might be able to communicate. The equation looks like this:

$$N = R_* f_g f_p \, n f_l \, f_i f_c L$$

The number of communicating civilizations is represented by the letter N. For all practical purposes, this number is limited to civilizations living within our own Milky Way. Even at the speed of light, a message would take more than 200,000 years to reach the next major galaxy outside of our Milky Way. Therefore, NASA will not bother trying to listen to other galaxies. The Drake

Television has also gotten aboard the science-fiction band-wagon. In the television show "Alien Nation," the extraterrestrials (as the one depicted at right above) have a distinctly human demeanor, though some obvious differences exist.

Most often, filmmakers allow their extraterrestrials an entirely human appearance; only their intelligence and behavior distinguish them from everyday Earthlings. Such was the case with Nyah (left), the title character in the 1955 sci-fi "classic" Devil-Girl from Mars.

Equation is solved by multiplying a number of factors, beginning with R_*, which stands for the rate of star births within the galaxy.

The fraction of stars suitable for life support is represented by f_g. The next factor is f_p, which represents the portion of stars that might have orbiting planets. The next factor, n, is the estimated percentage of Earth-like planets. All life on Earth is based upon the element carbon, an element that forms readily into complex molecular compounds. Highly complex molecules, such as DNA, incorporate long chains of carbon molecules. Biologists have yet to envision a chemistry for life that doesn't depend on carbon. Therefore, the n factor

assumes that life elsewhere will similarly need carbon-based, Earth-like conditions to evolve.

The next f in the equation, f_l, corresponds to the number of habitable planets that could potentially produce life. The f_i represents the chances of such intelligent forms of life actually evolving. The final f_c is for the number of intelligent civilizations that might develop the ability and desire to communicate with others in the universe. The last factor, L, is the life span of a civilization. This factor is crucial in that scientists fear that any civilization smart enough to make radio contact might also have the ability for mass destruction and self-annihilation. Intelligent societies may evolve all the time, some scientists believe, but because of the limited life spans of civilizations, they may transmit for only a few thousand years. If this is true, the chances of us listening for them at exactly the right time over the many-billion-year history of the universe might be quite small.

In 1961, an international conference on extraterrestrial life worked out the value of N to fall somewhere between 100 and 1 million civilizations. Even if our kind of intelligence is associated with just one star in every 100,000 of the same type as our Sun, there could be at least 400,000 technological civilizations in the Milky Way alone. If the entire universe were taken into account, that number would be considerably larger.

By and large, astronomers approach the concept of extraterrestrial life as an all-or-nothing proposition. Some calculate that in all probability the Earth is the only planet with intelligent life. Others still insist we are surrounded by countless inhabited worlds yet to be discovered.

SEARCHING THE SKY

Since 1960, astronomers have attempted more than six dozen radio searches for what might be interpreted as a "hello-there" signal. Though none of these searches has yielded evidence of extraterrestrial life, together they have covered only a tiny fraction of the space and possible radio frequencies that might contain such a message.

In setting up their detection system, researchers try to think like space aliens. How could we recognize a signal as being of intelligent origin without knowing anything about the civilization sending the message? The first step was to choose a part of the electromagnetic spectrum (similar to a giant galactic radio dial) that would be the least cluttered by background noise such as cosmic static, dust-cloud emissions, and other natural interference. This rationale effectively eliminated the frequencies on the lower end of the dial.

Unfortunately, frequencies on the high end of the dial are absorbed readily by the Earth's atmosphere, making them difficult to detect. This process of elimination led researchers to settle upon a quiet part of the spectrum known as the microwave region.

There are two nice side benefits of using microwave frequencies. First, very little energy is required to make signals at this frequency heard above the natural din of the universe. Second, and more important, hydrogen, the most abundant element in the universe, emits energy at a characteristic frequency of 1,420,405,752 times a second. Translated into radio frequencies (megahertz), this would set the radio dial right smack in the microwave region. Scientists call this the "magic frequency," and expect it would also be the choice of any intelligent, logical alien.

In order to recognize signals produced by technology as opposed to natural sources, scientists again rely on logic. Natural signals tend to spread over a wide range of frequencies, and they are not "in phase," or well-tuned, so to speak. Artificial signals, produced by a transmitter and antenna, are often confined to a narrow range of frequencies and are highly polarized, and the peaks of the waves are "in phase," or "tuned in."

The complexity of these searches is possible only because of recent advances in computer-chip technology that allow data gathering and signal processing to occur at great speed.

MAKING CONTACT

A number of radio searches are presently being carried out, but the most sensitive and comprehensive is called Project Phoenix, the successor to the ambitious NASA SETI program, which was canceled by a budget-conscious Congress in 1993. After losing the government's backing, the SETI program turned to private contributors, such as Microsoft cofounder Paul Allen, for funding. The program's annual budget is an estimated $4 million.

Phoenix began observations in February 1995 using the Parkes 210-foot (64-meter)-diameter radio telescope in New South Wales, Australia. This is the largest radio telescope in the Southern Hemisphere. The project has continued using

The universe could contain thousands of planets with all the conditions necessary to give rise to life. Astronomers hope to detect such planets in the near future. In the meantime, artists continue to create fanciful visions of what such planets might look like.

some of the most powerful instruments on the planet, including the 1,000-foot (300-meter)-diameter radio telescope at Arecibo, Puerto Rico, and the 230-foot (70-meter) and 111-foot (34-meter) dishes that form NASA's Deep Space Network (used to track the Voyager and Pioneer probes).

Phoenix does not scan the whole sky. Rather, it scrutinizes the vicinities of nearby, Sunlike stars. Such stars are most likely to support long-lived planets capable of hosting life. About 1,000 stars are targeted for observation by Project Phoenix—all within 200 light-years of Earth.

Project Phoenix monitors and examines 2 billion radio frequencies for each target star, so most of the "listening" is done by computers, which alert astronomers when-

ever interesting signals are found and need to be analyzed.

By 2004, Project Phoenix had concluded. The study examined more than 700 stars over billions of frequency channels, but found no clearly extraterrestrial transmissions. Scientists are planning newer, even more powerful searches that would make the range and sensitivity of Project Phoenix seem small by comparison.

At present, scientists have no plans to reply if they do indeed receive a message. But officials expect that the nations of Earth would join together to formulate any eventual response. This comprehensive search is certainly only the beginning of what will likely be a very long period of scrutinizing our galaxy.

MATHEMATICS

Every line and shape—be it the arcs and spheres on the facing page, or other figures considerably more simple or vastly more complex—can be expressed through a mathematical equation. Many other concepts beyond geometrical entities can be represented mathematically—the movement of pieces across a chessboard, for example, or the clock that tracks the permissible time for each move, or even the electronic creation of icons and characters on a computer screen.

328–331	Mathematicians and Their Science
332–337	Introduction to Mathematics
338–345	Numerals
346–351	Arithmetic
352–365	Algebra
366–379	Plane Geometry
380–385	Solid Geometry
386–390	Trigonometry
391–400	Analytic Geometry
401–403	Non-Euclidean Geometry
404–413	Statistics
414–423	Probability
424–430	Game Theory
431–437	Calculus
438–445	Set Theory
446–452	Binary Numerals
453–459	Accountants and Their Science

MATHEMATICIANS AND THEIR SCIENCE

Carl Beaird, a mathematician with Rockwell International, writes algorithms that direct the operation of crucial space-shuttle parts. Ruth Gonzalez, a geophysical mathematician with Exxon, deciphers seismic-wave readings to locate valuable reservoirs of oil and gas. Hazel de Burgh, a forensic accountant, uncovers theft and embezzlement by "crunching the numbers" she finds in financial records. The work of these three professionals represents a tiny sampling of the hundreds of ways that mathematicians apply their science today. Mathematics is also a necessary part of all other sciences. In the words of physicist Richard Feynman, "Nature talks to us in the language of mathematics." That is, numbers, mathematical rules, and equations help us make sense of the world around us.

As the "art of logical reasoning," pure mathematics can also be viewed as a search for truth using precise rules of logic. Mathematicians often describe a finely wrought proof as "elegant" or "beautiful," and even amateur mathematicians indulge in number "puzzlers" just for fun. A science, a tool, a language, an art, a game—math is all these things and more.

MATHEMATICS DEFINED

Look up the term *mathematics* in a dozen sources, and you are likely to get as many definitions. It is the study of numbers, the relationships between them, and various operations performed on them. It is the science of quantity, size, and shape. It is also a way to communicate and analyze ideas, a tool for organizing and interpreting data, and—above all, perhaps—a method of logical reasoning unique to humans (at least on this planet).

Despite such broad definitions, many of us still associate mathematics with *arithmetic*, the branch of mathematics that involves counting. But in many ways, arithmetic is to mathematics what penmanship or typing is to writing—a fundamental skill necessary for practicing a greater art. From the earliest calculations performed on fingers, mathematics has developed many useful methods and disciplines.

Arithmetic, the most basic branch of mathematics, involves simple computing (adding, subtracting, multiplying, and dividing, as well as extensions of these operations, such as raising to powers and extracting roots). Arithmetic is also "everyday" mathematics, necessary for everything from sharing items fairly and keeping baseball scores to balancing budgets and estimating costs.

Algebra involves the operations of arithmetic but uses letters and other symbols to represent unknown numbers, as in $x + y2 = 0$. Typically, mathematicians solve algebraic equations for one or more of these "unknowns." *Geometry* is the study of shape, space, and measurement. *Plane geometry* deals with points, lines, and two-dimensional shapes such as squares, circles, and triangles. *Solid geometry* deals with three-dimensional shapes such as cubes, spheres, cones, and cylinders. *Euclidean geometry* follows the laws, or axioms, established by the ancient Greek mathematician Euclid (such as "A straight line can be drawn between any two points."). *Non Euclidean geometry* uses different axioms and new systems of geometric lines and figures.

Trigonometry is the branch of mathematics that uses the relationships between the angles and sides of a triangle to solve measurement problems. *Calculus* is the mathematics of change and motion. *Probability theory* uses formulas to determine the likelihood of specific events occurring. *Statistics* gives us procedures for collecting, organizing, and displaying information about such events.

Number theory is the study of numbers and their properties. A *number theorist* looks at sets of numbers and studies their patterns and relationships. *Set theory* examines the properties of sets (groups of objects, ideas, or numbers) and provides rules for performing operations on them. *Set theorists* often combine sets to determine what elements they have in common.

Logic, the science of reason, ties together all branches of math with formal rules. These rules, often stated by using symbols, enable mathematicians to establish the truth of ideas and draw conclusions from axioms.

HISTORY OF MATHEMATICS

The history of mathematics begins with counting. Cave paintings from the Neolithic period, some 12,000 years ago, show that people were already counting to keep track of the passage of time, distances, and items such as livestock and crops. By 3000 B.C., mathematics was a bona fide science in Sumer (now southern Iraq). Sumerian students used reeds to etch numbers and perform calculations in clay "notebooks." Other Sumerian tablets and monuments show that mathematics was used in business, trade, and government as well.

The earliest known Egyptian use of mathematics appears in the "Rhind Papyrus," a handbook dating from about 1650 B.C. It contains more than 80 mathematical problems, most dealing with practical matters, and the earliest known symbols for mathematical operations. Similar texts appeared in China about the same time.

In each of these early civilizations, mathematics included a system of numbers and simple fractions. Each society had likewise devised methods for multiplying, finding square roots, and measuring area and volume.

In about 600 B.C., the Greeks took mathematics far beyond the realm of basic counting and measuring. They began exploring mathematical ideas with logic, and they developed algebra, geometry, and trigonometry. One of the first great Greek mathematicians was Thales, who, in the 6th century B.C., developed the first geometric proofs, based on step-by-step reasoning. Pythagoras, a contemporary of Thales, developed number theory and many important proofs and discovered irrational numbers (numbers that are not the quotient of two integers). In the 4th century B.C., Euclid set down approximately 500 geometric theorems in *Elements*, a work which would remain the standard "geometry textbook" for the next 2,000 years.

In the 3rd century B.C., Archimedes used math to solve physics problems and to determine the areas of geometric figures. In the 2nd century B.C., the astronomer Hipparchus invented trigonometry to describe the motions of the planets. In the 3rd century A.D., Diophantus, "the father of algebra," developed letter notations to represent unknown quantities.

For the next 1,000 years or so, significant progress was made in India, China, and the Arab world. Among India's most notable contributions were the number zero and our method of writing numbers with the digits 0 through 9. India's mathematicians also introduced negative numbers, as well as various rules for computing irrational numbers, such as the square root of 2.

Mathematical concepts, portrayed on tablets created by ancient peoples thousands of years ago, show how trade, record-keeping, and other prerequisites to civilization depend on mathematics.

The Arab mathematicians advanced the study of algebra, devising rules for solving equations and geometric demonstrations to show why the rules work. The topics they developed in the 9th century compare to those in modern high-school algebra textbooks.

During the Crusades (1100–1300), Europeans translated many important Arabic math books and spread their knowledge throughout the West. The familiar "+" sign for addition and "–" sign for subtraction first appeared in 1489 in German arithmetic books. In 1557, the English mathematician Robert Recorde introduced the equal sign (=); another Englishman, William Oughtred, introduced the multiplication sign (x) in 1631. The division sign (÷) first appeared in a book by German mathematician Johann Heinrich Rahn in 1659.

In the 1500s, great astronomers such as Copernicus, Kepler, and Galileo showed that mathematics could be used to analyze the movements of heavenly bodies. This breakthrough led to many great mathematical advances in the 1600s. One of the most important of these occurred in the 1630s, when French mathematicians René Descartes and Pierre de Fermat discovered how to solve geometric problems with algebra. Today, the combination of algebra and geometry, known as *coordinate geometry*, or *analytic geometry*, involves using algebraic equations to produce lines and curves across a graph. Fermat also introduced probability theory.

Later in the 17th century, two great mathematicians, England's Isaac Newton and Germany's Gottfried Leibniz, independently invented calculus. Over the next century, many European mathematicians applied and extended the ideas of calculus, creating the basis for modern mathematics.

The 1800s have been called the Golden Age of Mathematics because of the many advances developed during this period, including a calculus that uses imaginary numbers, as well as several non-Euclidean geometries. New branches of mathematics included *abstract algebra*, a system that deals with special structures called groups, rings, and fields. These algebraic methods, in turn, gave rise to *transformational geometry*, the study of what happens to figures when they are rotated, flipped, or stretched. Further advances led to the development of *topology*, the study of properties that remain unaltered when a figure or a space is deformed.

Also in the 1800s, England's George Boole and Germany's Gottlob Frege advanced several methods for using algebra to express logical ideas and relationships between such ideas. The structure of "Boolean" and symbolic logic became the basis for modern computer languages.

In the late 1800s, German mathematician Georg Cantor developed the new field of set theory. About the same time, Russia's Sonya Kovalevsky (Sofia Kovalevskaya, the first woman to formally study mathematics in an academic setting) developed partial differential equations, which involve several functions and have important applications in physics and engineering.

Careers in Mathematics

Until the early 20th century, the only career open to a full-time mathematician was a professorship at a university. Today, the picture is very different. Mathematicians are in great demand in many areas of science, technology, and business. Some of the most promising mathematical careers today lie in the booming fields of computer programming, electronic and electrical engineering, actuarial analysis (that is, calculating risks), and accounting. In addition, statisticians work in all areas of science, analyzing and presenting scientific data gathered through field research and experiments.

In general, people who do well in mathematical careers have a natural love of and facility with numbers. They also must be able to organize their work in a logical and precise manner. Verbal and written skills are essential, since mathematicians often need to communicate their findings to people who may be unfamiliar with math concepts.

Training for a career in mathematics begins early, with introductory courses in algebra and geometry in middle school, and intermediate algebra and geometry in high school. More advanced high-school studies can include statistics, precalculus, analytic geometry, trigonometry, probability, and perhaps even calculus. College mathematics usually begins with two years of calculus and advanced algebra. Students may also choose to take courses in computer programming, statistics, probability theory, or engineering.

A four-year college degree in mathematics or a related field such as statistics, computer science, or engineering opens the

The first step on the path to a career in mathematics is to gain a complete understanding of the concepts behind addition, subtraction, multiplication, and division—the four basic operations of arithmetic.

door to many entry-level jobs. But further advancement usually depends on continuing education, whether it be on-the-job training or graduate-level studies.

College-level teaching and research positions generally demand a minimum of six to eight years of study in mathematics or a related field, and the completion of a doctoral thesis. The research behind this thesis may involve "pure" mathematics, such as the resolution of an unsolved mathematical problem, or applied mathematics, such as a significant new application of mathematics in economics, statistics, information science, physical and life sciences, or another chosen field. Teaching mathematics on the elementary to high-school level generally requires a bachelor's or master's degree, with additional teacher training.

MATHEMATICS TODAY AND TOMORROW

Among the most notable mathematical fields today are *chaos theory*, describing the important but unpredictable results of small changes in any kind of system; and *fractal geometry*, dealing with geometric shapes whose details reflect the pattern of the whole. Computers have proved vital to the study and advancement of both of these complex areas. The computer—as well as its simpler cousin, the

calculator—have greatly eased the tedium and increased the accuracy of performing mathematical computations.

Computers operate wholly on the basis of mathematical principles, many of which were set down by the Hungarian-American mathematician John von Neumann in the 1930s. As mathematicians continue to pursue answers to unsolved problems and to open up new fields of study, computers will continue to speed the way.

INTRODUCTION TO MATHEMATICS

The word "mathematics" comes from the Greek *mathemata,* meaning "things that are learned." It may seem odd to apply this phrase to a single field of knowledge, but we should point out that for the ancient Greeks, mathematics included not only the study of numbers and space but also astronomy and music. Nowadays, of course, we do not think of astronomy and music as mathematical subjects; yet the scope of mathematics today is broader than ever.

Modern mathematics is a vast field of knowledge with many subdivisions. There is, first of all, the mathematics of numbers, or quantity. The branch of *arithmetic* deals with particular numbers, such as 3, or $10\frac{1}{2}$, or 12.5. When we add, subtract, multiply, or divide such numbers or get their square roots or squares, we are engaging in arithmetical operations. Sometimes we wish to consider not particular numbers, but relationships that will apply to whole groups of numbers. We study such relationships in *algebra,* another branch of the science of quantity. In algebra, a symbol, such as the letter *a* or *b*, stands for an entire class of numbers. For example, in the formula

$$(a + 2)^2 = a^2 + 4a + 4$$

the letter *a* represents any number. The relationship expressed in the formula remains the same whether *a* stands for 1, or 5, or 10, or any number.

Mathematics also studies shapes occurring in space, which may be thought of as a world of points, surfaces, and solids. We study the properties of different shapes and the relations between them, and we learn how to measure them. This science of spaces is called *geometry. Plane geometry* is concerned with points, lines, and figures occurring in a single plane—a surface with only two dimensions (Figure 1). The study of the three-dimensional world is called *solid geometry* (Figure 2). *Trigonometry* ("triangle measurement") is an offshoot of

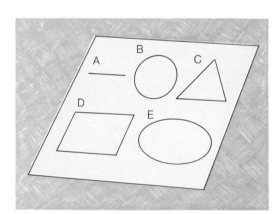

Figure 1. The straight line (A), circle (B), triangle (C), rectangle (D), and ellipse (E) occur in a single plane. Their study is a part of plane geometry.

Figure 2. The cube (A), prism (B), cylinder (C), and cone (D) are not bounded by a single plane. These figures are studied in solid geometry.

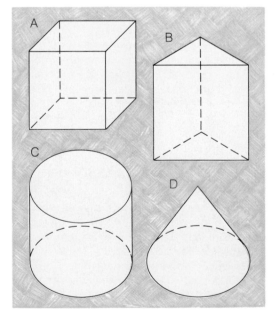

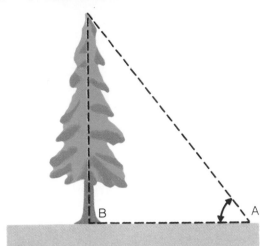

Figure 3. If we know the distance AB and the angle at A, we can calculate how high the tree is by using trigonometry, or triangle measurement, an offshoot of geometry.

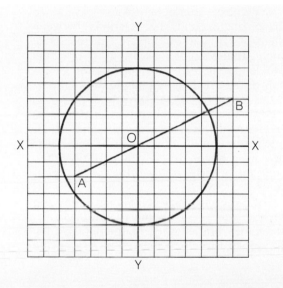

Figure 4. The x axis is at right angles to the y axis. The formula x = 2y indicates the position of AB with respect to the x and y axes. The formula $x^2 + y^2 = 25$ indicates the position of the circle. These relationships are derived from analytic geometry.

geometry. It is based on the fact that when certain parts of triangles are known, one can determine the remaining parts and solve many different problems (Figure 3).

Analytic geometry combines algebra and geometry—generalized numbers and space relationships. It locates geometrical figures in space. It explains circles, ellipses, and other figures in terms of algebraic formulas. In Figure 4, for example, the *x* and *y* axes are at right angles to one

another and meet at the point O. To indicate the position of line AB with respect to the *x* and *y* axes, we use the formula $x = 2y$. To indicate the position of the circle in the diagram, we use the formula $x^2 + y^2 = 25$.

The branch of mathematics called *calculus* is based on the study of functions. If the value of a given quantity depends on the value we assign to a second quantity, we say that the first quantity is a function of the second. For example, we know that the circumference of a circle can always be found by the formula $C = \pi \times d$ (or $C = \pi d$), where C is the circumference, d is the diameter, and π (the Greek letter pi) represents a constant value approximately equal to 3.14159. In this case, C is a function of d since its value will depend on the value we assign to d. In *integral calculus*, we are interested in the limit of the different values of a variable function. In *differential calculus*, we determine the rate of change of a variable function.

Statistics, another branch of mathematics, involves the accumulation and tabulation of data expressed in quantities, and the setting up of general laws based on such data. The theory of *probability* enables one to calculate the chances that certain events will occur—such as the 50 percent chance that a coin toss will produce heads. Probability theory has many applications, such as calculating the number of straights that will be dealt in an evening of poker. In the social sciences, probability can be used to predict the number of boys and girls that will be born in a particular place at a particular time.

These are only a few of the many subdivisions of mathematics. Besides being a most extensive field of knowledge in its own right, it represents a logical approach that can be applied to many different fields. It carefully defines the ideas that are to be discussed and clearly states the assumptions that can be made. Then, on the basis of both the definitions and the assumptions, it forges a chain of proofs, each link in the chain being as strong as any other. Mathematicians have displayed wonderful powers of imagination in determining what can be proved and in constructing ingenious methods of proof.

It might seem rather far-fetched to think of mathematics as a search for beauty. Yet, to many workers in the field, mathematical patterns that are fitted together to form a harmonious whole can produce as pleasing effects as the color combinations of a painter or the word patterns of a poet. Bertrand Russell, an important 20th-century mathematician, wrote in his *Principles of Mathematics,* "Mathematics, rightly viewed, possesses a beauty cold and austere, like that of a sculpture, without any appeal to any part of our weaker nature, without the gorgeous trappings of painting or music, yet sublimely pure, and capable of a stern perfection such as only the greatest art can show."

Mathematics is also an endless source of entertainment. For many generations, mathematicians and others have prepared what are commonly known as mathematical recreations, ranging from simple problems and constructions to brain twisters that can be solved only by experts—and sometimes not even by experts. These recreations are a delightful challenge to one's wits. Sometimes, they bring us into a world of fantasy in which one "proves" that 2 = 1, or constructs a "magic ring" whose outside is its inside (Figure 5).

Mathematics and the Outer World

In the development of the different branches of mathematics, pioneers have often owed much to the observation of the world about them. It has been suggested, for example, that the concepts of "straight line," "circle," "sphere," "cylinder," and "angle," in geometry were derived from nature: "straight line," from a tall reed; "circle," from the disk of the sun or moon; "sphere," from a round solid object like a berry; "cylinder," from a fallen tree trunk; "angle," from the various positions of a bent arm or leg.

Pioneer mathematicians examined these shapes and the relations between them. At first, they applied the results of such studies to the solution of practical problems, such as the construction of canals or the dividing of land into lots for purposes of taxation. Later, they began to study the relationships between various geometrical forms in order to satisfy their intellectual curiosity and not to solve particular problems. In the course of time they built up a series of purely abstract concepts.

As certain mathematicians develop such concepts in geometry and calculus and other branches of mathematics, they are apt to turn their backs entirely on the

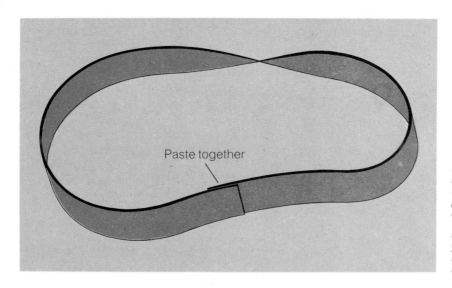

Paste together

Figure 5. This "magic ring" is made by pasting together the two ends of a narrow strip of paper in the form of a ring, after giving one end a twist of 180°. If you then color one side of the ring, you will find that you have colored the whole ring, inside and out. The ring is called a Moebius Strip.

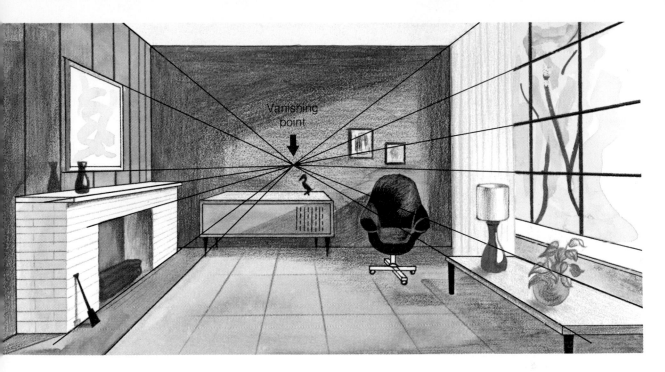

Figure 6. The realistic, three-dimensional effect in this drawing is obtained by having all the horizontal lines that recede from the observer meet at a vanishing point.

world of reality. They have no hesitation in working with equations involving four dimensions, ten dimensions, or any number of dimensions. The German mathematician Bernhard Riemann built up an entire geometry based on the *postulate,* or assumption, that no two lines are ever parallel. Another geometry (recognized independently by three great 19th-century mathematicians: Nikolai Lobachevsky, Karl F. Gauss, and János Bolyai) postulates that through a point not on a given line, there are at least two lines parallel to that line. The German Georg Cantor proposed a "theory of sets" that was highly ingenious and—at least, so it appeared at the time—utterly useless as far as any practical application was concerned.

It has been pointed out that the concern with pure abstraction is not without its dangers. The distinguished mathematician Morris Kline wrote in his *Mathematics and the Physical World,* "Mathematicians may like to rise into the clouds of abstract thought, but they should, and indeed they must, return to earth for . . . food or else die of mental starvation."

Yet even the most abstract speculations of mathematicians may find important applications, sometimes after many years have passed. Thus the Riemannian geometry was to prove invaluable to Albert Einstein when he developed his theory of relativity. Cantor's theory of sets has been applied to various fields, including higher algebra and statistics. As to multiple dimensions, they have been put to work in, of all things, the inspection of industrial products.

Applications

We do not have to give such extreme examples as Riemannian geometry and the theory of sets to show how mathematics has served mankind. Actually, it is deeply rooted in almost every kind of human activity, from the world of everyday affairs to the advanced researches of authorities in many different fields of science.

All of us are mathematicians to some extent. We use arithmetic every day in our lives: when we consult a watch or clock to find out what time it is; when we calculate the cost of purchases and the change that is due us; when we keep score in tennis, baseball, or football.

The accounting operations of business and industry are based on mathematics. Insurance is largely a matter of the compounding of interest and the application of the theory of probability. Certain manufacturers make use of calculus in order to be able to utilize raw materials most effectively. The pilot of a ship or plane uses geometry to plot a course. The surveyor's work is based largely on trigonometry, and the civil engineer uses arithmetic, algebra, calculus, and other branches of mathematics.

Mathematics also serves the branch of learning called the humanities, which includes painting and music. It is the basis of perspective—the system by which the artist represents on a flat surface objects and persons as they actually appear in a three-dimensional world. We may think of perspective as made up of a series of mathematical theorems. One theorem, for example, states that parallel horizontal lines that recede in the same plane from the observer converge at a point called the *vanishing point*. Figure 6 shows how this theorem is applied to the drawing of a room.

In music, too, mathematics plays an important part. The system of scales and the theories of harmony and counterpoint are basically mathematical; so is the analysis of the tonal qualities of different instruments. Mathematics has been essential in the design of pianos, organs, violins, and flutes, and also of such reproducing devices as phonographs and radio receivers.

Mathematics is so important in science and serves in so many of its branches that it has been called the "Queen and Servant of the Sciences" by the noted Scottish-American mathematician, Eric Temple Bell. Here are some examples:

Measurements and other mathematical techniques are vital in the work of the physicist. The physicist uses the mathematical device called the graph to give a clear picture of the relationship between different values—between temperature, for example, and the pressure of saturated water vapor in the atmosphere (Figure 7). The laws of physics are stated in the form of algebraic formulas. Thus to express the idea that the velocity of a body can be determined by dividing the distance covered by the time required to cover this distance, the physicist uses the formula $v = \dfrac{s}{t}$, when v is the velocity, s the space or distance covered, and t the time. The physicist employs geometry and trigonometry in the analysis of forces and in establishing the laws of optics, the science of light.

Like the physicist, the chemist continually uses arithmetical and algebraic operations and graphs. The chemist, too, presents laws in the form of algebraic formulas. The reactions are set down in the form of equations, which from certain viewpoints may be considered as mathematical equations. Chemists also use loga-

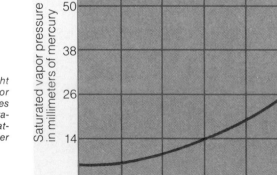

Figure 7. The graph at the right shows how saturated water-vapor pressure in the atmosphere varies with the temperature. The saturation point is reached when the atmosphere can hold no more water vapor at a given temperature.

The scope of mathematics today is broader than ever. Calculations are now performed by huge computers in minute fractions of a second. Sophisticated software is used to formulate and solve mathematical problems.

rithms, a mathematical technique, in calculating the degree of acidity of a substance—the so-called pH value. Plane and solid geometries are used in studying the ways in which atoms or ions (electrically charged atoms) are combined. Thus it can be shown that graphite atoms form a succession of hexagons (six-sided figures) in a series of planes set atop one another, and that the sodium and chloride ions that make up ordinary table salt (sodium chloride) are set at the corners of a series of cubes.

Mathematics has always been closely associated with astronomy. From the earliest days, astronomers measured angles and arcs and made a great many mathematical calculations as they followed the apparent motions of the sun, stars, moon, and planets in the heavens. Today such branches of mathematics as arithmetic, algebra, plane geometry, solid geometry, trigonometry, and calculus are just as useful to the astronomer, as the optical telescope, camera, radio telescope, and other devices that are used in this branch of science.

It would seem difficult to apply the formulas of mathematics to the infinitely varied world of living things. Yet mathematics serves even in biology, the science of life. It plays an extremely important part, for example, in genetics, which is concerned with heredity. To calculate the percentage of individuals with like and unlike traits in succeeding generations, the geneticist makes use of the theory of probability. Mathematics has also been applied to the comparison of related forms of life. Using the method called *dimensional analysis,* researchers have found that the frequency of the beating of a bird's wings can be summed up in a formula. It is rather amazing to see how often this formula applies to species of totally dissimilar birds. Dimensional analysis has also been used to analyze the growth patterns of certain animals, as well as to determine the ratio between the lifetime of a given animal and the time required for the animal to draw a single breath.

Such then, in brief, is the scope of mathematics. In the articles that follow, we shall present some of the more important fields of mathematics, including arithmetic, algebra, plane geometry, solid geometry, trigonometry, analytical geometry, and calculus. We shall tell you what these fields are about and the uses to which they are put by present-day mathematicians.

NUMERALS

The primitive cave man did not have to know much about counting or any other kind of mathematics to keep alive. Home was a cave; food could be gathered from native vegetation or hunted with primitive weapons. However, when people began to collect animals into herds, and particularly when one family entered upon social relations with others, it became necessary to decide how much belonged to each person. It probably sufficed, at the outset, to use such concepts as a little, some, or much. Later, when it became necessary to have a more definite means of determining "how much," people learned to count, and this was the beginning of mathematics.

At first, a person might count the number of animals in a herd by placing a pebble on the ground or tying a knot in a rope for each animal. Each pebble in the growing heap or each knot in the rope would stand for a single animal. Later, a man might use his ten fingers in his calculations. We may surmise that when the ten fingers had been counted, a little stone would be set aside to represent this first ten; the fingers would then be used to count another ten. Another stone would be added to the first one; the fingers would be used to count another ten, and so on. When the stones in the pile would equal the number of fingers, they would represent ten tens. The pile of ten stones would then be taken away, and a larger stone would be put in its place to indicate ten tens or one hundred (Figure 1). Thus three large stones, seven small stones, and eight sticks (standing for eight fingers), would represent three hundreds, seven tens, and eight units—in other words, 378 (Figure 2).

The ten fingers in this case would mark the halting place in a person's calculations; we would call it the *base*. Not all primitive people would use 10, or the number of fingers on both hands, as the base. Some would use only the two hands in counting (and not the fingers of the hands), and their halting place would be two. For others, the fingers of one hand would serve; their halting place would be five. Still others would combine the fingers of both hands and the toes of both feet; twenty would be their halting place.

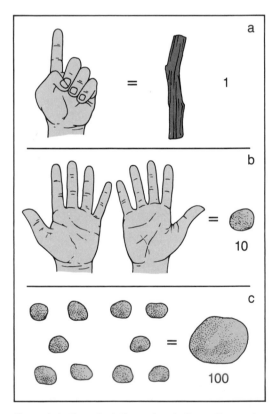

Figure 1. In the calculations of early times, the number 1 might have been represented by a finger or a stick (a). The number 10 could have been represented by the ten fingers of two hands or by a small stone (b). Ten small stones could then be equivalent to one large stone, which would represent 100 (c). In this system, the ten fingers marked the stopping place in counting; in other words, the system was based on 10.

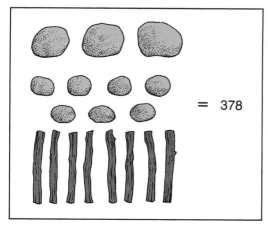

Figure 2. If we were to use the method of calculation illustrated in Figure 1, we would represent the number 378 by three large stones (representing 300), seven small stones (representing 70), and eight sticks (representing 8).

Since stones, pebbles, and sticks are awkward to handle, people created symbols to represent numbers as soon as they learned to write. The symbol that is used to write a number is called a *numeral*. About 5,000 years ago, the Egyptians developed a system for recording numerals on buildings on monuments. This system, called the *hieroglyphic system*, used pictures to represent numerals in the same way that pictures were used to represent words. The

Figure 3. With the hieroglyphic symbols shown below, the ancient Egyptians could write any number.

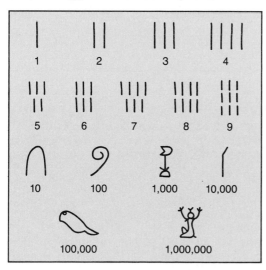

symbol for one was a small vertical stroke that might resemble a small stick. The symbol for 2 was two strokes, the symbol for 3 was 3 strokes, and so on until the symbol for 9 was written as 9 strokes. After the numeral 4, the strokes were grouped in rows of three or four to make the numeral easier to read. See Figure 3.

For the number 10, the base of the decimal system, the Egyptians used a new symbol that resembles an arch. The number 20 was written as two arches and so on until the number 90 which was written as 9 arches. For the number 100, which is 10 times 10, or 10^2, another new symbol resembling a link in a chain, was used. The number 900 was represented by 9 links. For the number 1,000, which is 10 times 100, or 10^3, another new symbol, a stylized lotus flower, was used. For 10,000, or 10^4, the symbol was a bent finger or possibly a bent stick; for 100,000, or 10^5, the symbol was a burbot fish that resembles a tadpole; and for 1,000,000, or 10^6, the symbol was a kneeling figure with arms outstretched.

To write large numbers the Egyptians repeated the symbols as needed. A system such as this is called an *additive system,* because it is necessary to add up the values of all the symbols to find the total number. Numbers of very large size appear in ancient Egyptian records. One record on a 5,000-year-old mace reports that 120,000 prisoners and 1,422,000 goats were captured in a major war. Figure 4 shows how both small and large numbers were written using Egyptian hieroglyphic symbols. The Egyptians wrote their language from right to left and their numbers were also written in this way.

For writing on papyrus, the Egyptians used another system of writing numerals that was not a simple additive system. This system, called the *hieratic system,* used special symbols for numerals instead of repeating the same symbol to show a larger number. The hieratic system of recording numerals is more efficient than the hieroglyphic system and makes it easier to do mathematical calculations. The hieratic numerals for 1 through 9 and for several larger numerals are shown in Figure 5.

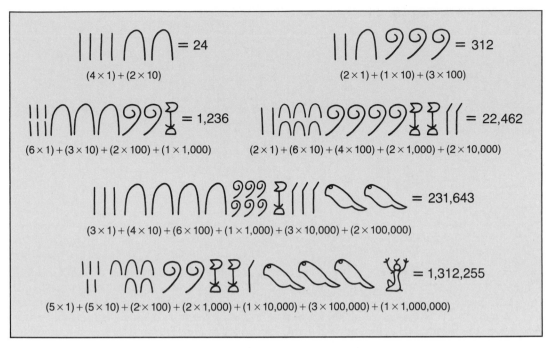

Figure 4. Hieroglyphic numbers were written with the symbols for the numbers of higher value at the right.

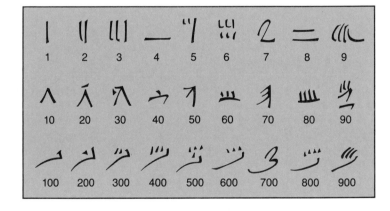

Figure 5. Egyptian hieratic numerals were used for cursive writing numbers on papyrus documents. The form of the numerals varied somewhat with the "handwriting" of each individual scribe.

The Babylonians recorded their language and their numerical records using a wedge-shaped tool to make impressions on wet clay tablets. The characters are called *cuneiform,* a word that means wedge shaped. The soft clay tablets were then baked to become a hard durable record. Many thousands of Babylonian cuneiform records have survived to this day.

The Babylonian numerals for the numbers 1 through 9 were written using groups of vertical wedges. The height of the individual wedges for the numbers 4 through 9 was made less than the height of the wedges for the numbers 1 through 3 in order to form groups of wedges that are easy to read. See Figure 6.

For numbers greater than 60, the Babylonians used positioning to create a numerical system with a base of 60. The position furthest to the right was used to record the number of ones from 1 through

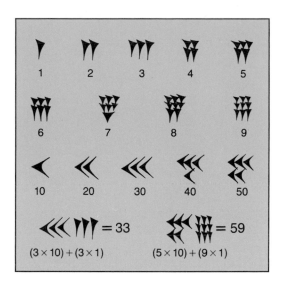

Figure 6. Babylonian cuneiform symbols were used to write numbers on soft clay with a wedge-shaped stick.

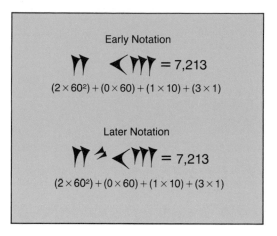

Figure 8. Later Babylonian numerals used a symbol to show an empty place in the middle of a number.

59 (the number of 60^0s). The next position to the left recorded the number of 60s (the number of 60^1s). In this second place the number of 60s was written using the same numerals used to record the number of ones. A small space was left between the symbols in the ones place and the symbols in the 60s place, to clarify the position occupied by a numeral in the second place.

The number 3,599 was written as 59 60s plus 59 ones. Beyond 3,599, numbers were written using the third place from the left to show the number of 60^2s (the number of 3,600s). The fourth space to the left was used to show the number of 60^3s (the number of 216,000s). The fifth space was used

to record the number of 60^4s and so on. Several numbers written with Babylonian cuneiform numerals are shown in Figure 7.

In some numbers, such as 7,213, there are two 3,600s and 13 units but no 60s. In such a case an early system of writing numbers simply left a blank in the place for the 60s. Later a new symbol was added to show clearly that there were no sixties and to avoid confusion as to whether or not a blank had been left. This new symbol, Figure 8, was similar in function to our modern zero when the blank occurred in the middle of a number. However, the Babylonians did not use this symbol to show blank places at the end of a number. Thus the only way to know whether a number was 7,213 or 7,213,000 was from the context in which the number appeared.

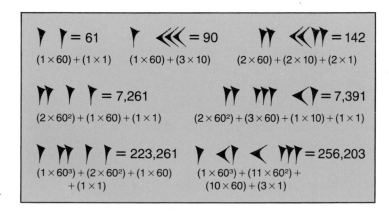

Figure 7. Babylonian numerals greater than 59 made use of positioning to make the writing of large numbers easier. Spaces between groups of symbols helped to identify positions.

Figure 9. The ancient Greeks wrote numbers using the letters of their alphabet. They added three special characters not found in their alphabet for the numbers 6, 90, and 900.

Figure 10. The ancient Hebrews wrote numbers using the letters of their alphabet. In modern Israel, letters are used for numerals only when writing the Hebrew year and for special occasions.

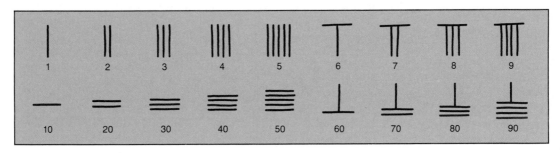

Figure 11. The ancient Chinese developed a system of numerals based on the way sticks were laid out on a table for calculating. This system was also used by early Japanese for writing and calculating.

The ancient Greeks developed several methods of writing numbers. In their most widely adopted version (Figure 9), they used all the letters of their alphabet plus three additional symbols. Each letter stood for a definite value. The first nine symbols represented the units from 1 to 9; the next nine, the tens from 10 to 90; the last nine, the hundreds from 100 to 900. They had no symbol for zero.

To represent thousands, the Greeks added a bar to the left of the first nine letters. Thus **/Γ** stood for 3,000; **/Z** for 7,000.

The total 4,627 was written **/ΔXKZ**, the horizontal base line indicating that these letters formed a numeral. The ancient Hebrews, also, used their alphabet in writing numbers (Figure 10).

A system of rodlike symbols was employed by the ancient Chinese to represent numbers. They had a *place system;* that is, a number symbol took on different values according to the place it occupied in the written number. As shown in Figure 11, the units from 1 through 5 were represented by vertical rods (one rod for each unit). For

I	V	X	L	C	D	M		
1	5	10	50	100	500	1,000		

I	II	III	IV	V	VI	VII	VIII	IX
1	2	3	4	5	6	7	8	9

XII	XIV	XV	XVIII	XIX	XX	XXIV	XXIX
12	14	15	18	19	20	24	29

XXX	XXXIX	XL	LX	LXX	LXXX	XC	XCIX
30	39	40	60	70	80	90	99

CX	CL	CCC	CD	DCCC	CM	MCDL	MCM	MM
110	150	300	400	800	900	1,450	1,900	2,000

Figure 12. Roman numerals are written with 7 letters using both the additive and subtractive principles.

the units from 6 through 9, an upper horizontal rod denoted a value of five units (or 5), to be added to the vertical rods (each equal to 1). The tens from 10 through 50 were written as horizontal rods (one rod for each ten). For the tens from 60 through 90, an upper vertical rod denoted a value of five tens (or 50), to be added to the horizontal rods (each equal to 10).

The hundreds were written in the same way as the units. Thus the symbol II would stand for either 2 or 200, depending upon its position in the number. The thousands were written in the same way as the tens, the ten thousands in the same way as the units, and so on. The number 7,684, therefore, would be written ⊥T≐IIII There was no symbol for zero, and a gap had to be left to indicate it. The number 7,004, for example, would be ⊥ IIII . If the gap were not recognized as such, the number might be read as 74 instead of 7,004.

The Romans probably derived their system of numbers from the Etruscans, earlier inhabitants of Italy. As shown in Figure 12, the Romans used only seven letters of the alphabet to record numbers. We still refer to numerals written with these seven letters as *Roman numerals*.

The early Roman numbers were written in accordance with the *additive principle*. Symbols for larger numbers were written first and followed by symbols for smaller numbers, all to be added together. Thus the number 4 was written IIII, the number 9 was VIIII, the number 90 was LXXXX, and the number 900 as DCCCC. Later the Romans developed the *subtractive principle* to avoid long strings of letters. In accordance with the subtractive principle, if the symbol of a smaller number precedes the symbol for a larger number, the smaller number is subtracted from the larger number. In this way the number 4 came to be written as IV and the number nine as IX, the number 90 as XC, and the number 900 as CM. See Figure 12.

Roman numerals are still used in English and other Western languages for certain specific purposes. They often indicate chapter or volume numbers of books. They are also used on the dials of some clocks as well as on commemorative monuments and tablets. To us, this number system may

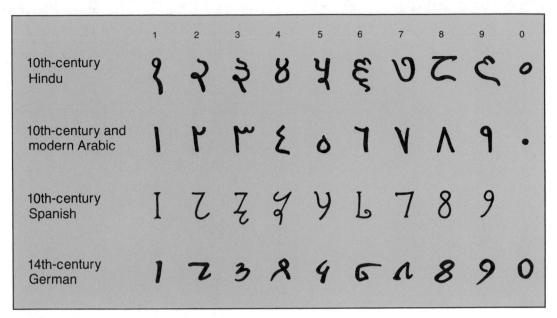

	1	2	3	4	5	6	7	8	9	0
10th-century Hindu										
10th-century and modern Arabic										
10th-century Spanish										
14th-century German										

Figure 13. The evolution of our modern western numerals during the past one thousand years.

seem complicated and cumbersome. For example, in our number system, the year eighteen hundred eighty-eight can be expressed by four symbols: 1888. Written in Roman numerals, the same year is MDCCCLXXXVIII.

Our own system of numerals, the so-called Arabic numerals, should really be called the Hindu-Arabic numerals, since the system originated in India (not long before the Christian era) and was later adopted by the Arabs. The Arabs conquered a large part of Spain in the 8th century and in time introduced the Hindu-Arabic numerals in the conquered land. Figure 13 shows how these numerals looked in the 10th century. The system was gradually adopted by the other peoples of Europe. By the 15th century, the symbols of the system had acquired the form that is so familiar to us.

The base of our system is ten, and so it is called a *decimal system*. (*Decem* means "ten" in Latin.) It is a place system, in which the position of a symbol indicates its particular value. Moving one space to the left increases the value by a multiple of 10, as is shown in the following diagram:

10,000's	1,000's	100's	10's	1's
$(10 \times 1,000)$	(10×100)	(10×10)	(10×1)	1
10^4	10^3	10^2	10^1	10^0

In the number 4,962, the 4 stands for four thousands; the 9, for nine hundreds; the 6, for six tens; the 2, for two units. Therefore, 4,962 is really $4,000 + 900 + 60 + 2$. Consider the number 7,004. The 7 represents seven thousands; the first 0, no hundreds; the second 0, no tens; the 4, four units. Because our number system includes a symbol for zero, there is no possibility of error in reading such a number.

With our ten symbols, we can write any number, no matter how large. Suppose we start with the number 1. If we put a zero to the right of it, the 1 is in the tens column and indicates ten. Continuing to put zeros to the right in this way, we make the value of 1 ten times greater for every zero that we write (10; 100; 1,000; and so on). We can also write extremely small numbers in our system by using a *decimal point*. The first numeral to the right of a decimal point indicates the number of tenths; the second, the number of hundredths; the third, the number of thousandths; and so on.

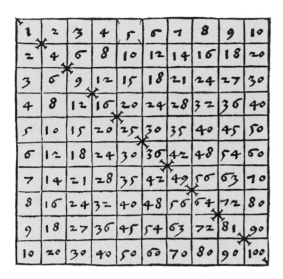

Figure 14. This multiplication table from Arithmetica Boetij *was printed in Germany in 1488. It shows the Hindu-Arabic numerals that were in use then. These numerals are very similar to those used today.*

$$1,000,000.0 = 1 \text{ million, } 10^6$$
$$100,000.0 = 1 \text{ hundred thousand, } 10^5$$
$$10,000.0 = \text{ten thousand, } 10^4$$
$$1,000.0 = 1 \text{ thousand, } 10^3$$
$$100.00 = 1 \text{ hundred, } 10^2$$
$$10.00 = \text{ten, } 10^1$$
$$1.00 = \text{one, } 10^0$$
$$0.1 = \text{one tenth, } 10^{-1}$$
$$0.01 = \text{one hundredth, } 10^{-2}$$
$$0.001 = \text{one thousandth, } 10^{-3}$$
$$0.0001 = \text{one ten-thousandth, } 10^{-4}$$
$$0.00001 = \text{one hundred-thousandth, } 10^{-5}$$
$$0.000001 = \text{one millionth, } 10^{-6}$$

We can make the number even smaller by increasing the number of zeros between the decimal point and the 1. Extremely large or small numbers written in this way are awkward to write and use. In the "Algebra" article we show how to express such numbers conveniently.

Not every place system has ten as its base. The base-two place system is known as the *binary system*. It has only two symbols: 1 and 0. In the binary system, moving one space to the left multiplies the value by 2, the base of the system, as indicated in the following diagram:

32's	16's	8's	4's	2's	1's
(2×16)	(2×8)	(2×4)	(2×2)	(2×1)	1
2^5	2^4	2^3	2^2	2^1	2^0

Let us see how the number 101101 would fit into this scheme:

32's	16's	8's	4's	2's	1's
1	0	1	1	0	1

As the diagram shows, 101101 in the binary system represents: $(1 \times 32) + (0 \times 16) + (1 \times 8) + (1 \times 4) + (0 \times 2) + (1 \times 1) = 32 + 0 + 8 + 4 + 0 + 1 = 45$.

The binary system was ardently advocated by the great 17th-century German philosopher and mathematician Gottfried Wilhelm von Leibniz because of its simplicity and also because he thought that it mirrored creation. Unity (1), he thought, represented God; zero (0) stood for the void from which all things were created.

The binary system has certain practical uses in physics. It also serves in the calculating device called the electronic computer. This device is run by electricity; the current is either off or on. When the current is off, the "0" in the binary system is indicated; when the current is on, the number "1" is indicated. The electronic computer can perform the most intricate calculations with the "0" and "1" of the binary system.

The Duodecimal Society of America has advocated the adoption of the base-twelve system known as the *duodecimal system*. In this, there are twelve symbols: 1, 2, 3, 4, 5, 6, 7, 8, 9, *t* (standing for ten), *e* (standing for eleven), and 0. Moving one space to the left, in the duodecimal system, increases the value twelvefold, as follows:

20,736's	1,728's	144's	12's	1's
$(12 \times 1,728)$	(12×144)	(12×12)	(12×1)	1
12^4	12^3	12^2	12^1	12^0

The numeral 6*et*4 in the duodecimal system represents: $(6 \times 1,728) + (11 \times 144) + (10 \times 12) + (4 \times 1)$. If we perform these multiplications and additions, we see that 6*et*4 is equal to the base-ten numeral 12,076.

For the ordinary purposes of calculation, our decimal system will not be replaced by a system with some other base.

Howard F. Fehr

ARITHMETIC

The computations carried out with the numbers of the decimal system make up the branch of mathematics called *arithmetic*. There are six fundamental operations in arithmetic: addition, subtraction, multiplication, division, involution, and evolution.

Addition

Addition represents the grouping together of numbers. If a primitive man

All addition is based on the addition facts. An addition fact is made up of two numbers from 0 to 9, the addends, and their sum.

TABLE I

ONE HUNDRED ADDITION FACTS

0	0	0	0	0	0	0	0	0	0
+0	+1	+2	+3	+4	+5	+6	+7	+8	+9
0	1	2	3	4	5	6	7	8	9
1	1	1	1	1	1	1	1	1	1
+0	+1	+2	+3	+4	+5	+6	+7	+8	+9
1	2	3	4	5	6	7	8	9	10
2	2	2	2	2	2	2	2	2	2
+0	+1	+2	+3	+4	+5	+6	+7	+8	+9
2	3	4	5	6	7	8	9	10	11
3	3	3	3	3	3	3	3	3	3
+0	+1	+2	+3	+4	+5	+6	+7	+8	+9
3	4	5	6	7	8	9	10	11	12
4	4	4	4	4	4	4	4	4	4
+0	+1	+2	+3	+4	+5	+6	+7	+8	+9
4	5	6	7	8	9	10	11	12	13
5	5	5	5	5	5	5	5	5	5
+0	+1	+2	+3	+4	+5	+6	+7	+8	+9
5	6	7	8	9	10	11	12	13	14
6	6	6	6	6	6	6	6	6	6
+0	+1	+2	+3	+4	+5	+6	+7	+8	+9
6	7	8	9	10	11	12	13	14	15
7	7	7	7	7	7	7	7	7	7
+0	+1	+2	+3	+4	+5	+6	+7	+8	+9
7	8	9	10	11	12	13	14	15	16
8	8	8	8	8	8	8	8	8	8
+0	+1	+2	+3	+4	+5	+6	+7	+8	+9
8	9	10	11	12	13	14	15	16	17
9	9	9	9	9	9	9	9	9	9
+0	+1	+2	+3	+4	+5	+6	+7	+8	+9
9	10	11	12	13	14	15	16	17	18

wanted to find out how many skins he would have if he added three skins to two skins, he would lay three skins on the ground, put down two more, and then count the total number. After he had solved this particular problem again and again, he would no longer have to lay out the skins. He would recall that whenever he added three skins to two skins, the result would always be five skins, and he would do the problem $3 + 2 = 5$ in his head. Similarly, he would learn that $1 + 1 = 2$, $1 + 2 = 3$, $1 + 3 = 4$, and so on.

In the operation of addition, the numbers to be added are called *addends;* the answer is called the *sum:* In the problem $3 + 4 = 7$, 3 and 4 are the addends and 7 is the sum. If one has learned to add all the possible pairs of digits up to $9 + 9$, then one can solve any addition problem. Suppose the problem is $23 + 49$. Remember that 23 stands for 2 tens + 3 units and that 49 stands for 4 tens + 9 units. we can state our problem as follows:

$$2 \text{ tens} + 3 \text{ units}$$
$$+ \ 4 \text{ tens} + 9 \text{ units}$$

First, we would add the units together: $9 + 3 = 12$. (Remember, 12 is really equal to 1 ten + 2 units.) Keeping the 2 in the units column, we would add the 1 to the other numerals in the tens column, giving $1 + 2 + 4$ tens, or 7 tens. The answer then is 7 tens + 2 units, or 72.

Subtraction

In *subtraction,* we take one or more objects from another group of objects. Suppose our primitive mathematician had nine skins and wanted to find out how many skins he would have left if he took five skins away. He would lay out the nine skins on the ground, would take away five skins, and then would count the skins that remained. Later on, he would come to realize that five from nine always leaves four, and he would perform that subtraction in his head. He would then extend this type of calculation to other numbers. He would soon come to know that $9 - 4 = 5$ or that $7 - 6 = 1$. He would need to know only a few such calculations to be able to subtract any number (the *subtrahend*) from any other number (the *minuend*) and get the correct answer (the *remainder*).

Multiplication

Multiplication is really a form of addition. If we did not know how to multiply, we could find the answer to the problem 5×7 by simple addition. For 5×7 means the same thing as five sevens, or $7 + 7 + 7 + 7 + 7$. Adding the five sevens together, we would have 35. Sooner or later we would probably come to realize that when we solve the problem of adding together five sevens, the answer is always 35. We would memorize this particular operation and other similar ones such as three eights (3×8) and seven nines (7×9). These operations up to and including 12×12 are found in the familiar multiplication table. If we could get as far as 9×9, we could do any multiplication problem.

Of course, all this requires a certain amount of memorizing. One multiplication method that avoids the memorizing is called *duplation*, which involves only multiplication by two and addition. This is how duplation works: Suppose we wanted to find out the product of 24 and 18 (24×18). We would perform our calculations thus:

A	B	C	D
1	24		
2	48	2	48
4	96		
8	192		
16	384	16	384
			432

The 432, at the bottom of the last column, is the answer to our problem. All this looks complicated, but it is really quite simple.

As you see, we set up four columns (A, B, C, and D). The first number in column A is always 1, from which we start the process of multiplying by 2: $1 \times 2 = 2$. We write the answer 2 in column A and multiply it by 2: $2 \times 2 = 4$. We write 4 in column A and multiply it by 2: $4 \times 2 = 8$. We continue multiplying by 2 until we reach a

TABLE II

ONE HUNDRED MULTIPLICATION FACTS

0 ×0 ― 0	0 ×1 ― 0	0 ×2 ― 0	0 ×3 ― 0	0 ×4 ― 0	0 ×5 ― 0	0 ×6 ― 0	0 ×7 ― 0	0 ×8 ― 0	0 ×9 ― 0
1 ×0 ― 0	1 ×1 ― 1	1 ×2 ― 2	1 ×3 ― 3	1 ×4 ― 4	1 ×5 ― 5	1 ×6 ― 6	1 ×7 ― 7	1 ×8 ― 8	1 ×9 ― 9
2 ×0 ― 0	2 ×1 ― 2	2 ×2 ― 4	2 ×3 ― 6	2 ×4 ― 8	2 ×5 ― 10	2 ×6 ― 12	2 ×7 ― 14	2 ×8 ― 16	2 ×9 ― 18
3 ×0 ― 0	3 ×1 ― 3	3 ×2 ― 6	3 ×3 ― 9	3 ×4 ― 12	3 ×5 ― 15	3 ×6 ― 18	3 ×7 ― 21	3 ×8 ― 24	3 ×9 ― 27
4 ×0 ― 0	4 ×1 ― 4	4 ×2 ― 8	4 ×3 ― 12	4 ×4 ― 16	4 ×5 ― 20	4 ×6 ― 24	4 ×7 ― 28	4 ×8 ― 32	4 ×9 ― 36
5 ×0 ― 0	5 ×1 ― 5	5 ×2 ― 10	5 ×3 ― 15	5 ×4 ― 20	5 ×5 ― 25	5 ×6 ― 30	5 ×7 ― 35	5 ×8 ― 40	5 ×9 ― 45
6 ×0 ― 0	6 ×1 ― 6	6 ×2 ― 12	6 ×3 ― 18	6 ×4 ― 24	6 ×5 ― 30	6 ×6 ― 36	6 ×7 ― 42	6 ×8 ― 48	6 ×9 ― 54
7 ×0 ― 0	7 ×1 ― 7	7 ×2 ― 14	7 ×3 ― 21	7 ×4 ― 28	7 ×5 ― 35	7 ×6 ― 42	7 ×7 ― 49	7 ×8 ― 56	7 ×9 ― 63
8 ×0 ― 0	8 ×1 ― 8	8 ×2 ― 16	8 ×3 ― 24	8 ×4 ― 32	8 ×5 ― 40	8 ×6 ― 48	8 ×7 ― 56	8 ×8 ― 64	8 ×9 ― 72
9 ×0 ― 0	9 ×1 ― 9	9 ×2 ― 18	9 ×3 ― 27	9 ×4 ― 36	9 ×5 ― 45	9 ×6 ― 54	9 ×7 ― 63	9 ×8 ― 72	9 ×9 ― 81

All multiplication is based on the multiplication facts. A multiplication fact is made up of two numbers from 0 to 9, the multiplier and the multiplicand, and their product.

number that is equal to or just less than the *multiplier* in the original problem. (A multiplier is a number by which another is multiplied.) In the problem 24×18, the multiplier is 18 so in column A we stop at 16. The first number in column B is always the *multiplicand* (a number that is to be multiplied by another), which in this case is 24. Again, we begin multiplying by 2: $24 \times 2 = 48$. We continue the same doubling process, ending when column B has as many numbers as column A. For column C, we select from column A the numbers

© R. Michael Stuckey/Comstock

Arithmetic is essential in every kind of work. In a small business, skill in the basic operations is needed to keep track of inventory, to set prices, and to keep track of the money coming in and going out.

that, added together, will equal the multiplier. Because the multiplier is 18, we take 2 and 16 and write them in column C directly across from their places in column A. In column D we write the numbers from column B that are directly across from those in column C. Finally, we add the numbers in column D for a sum, in this case, of 48 + 384 = 432. Therefore, through duplation, we have determined that the *product* (the answer to a multiplication problem) of 24 × 18 is 432. Of course, anyone knowing the multiplication table could multiply 24 by 18 in much less time than it would take to solve the problem by duplation.

Division

Division is a kind of subtraction. If we divide 12 (the *dividend*) by 4 (the *divisor*) we want to know how many times 4 goes into 12. We perform the following series of subtractions:

$$
\begin{array}{ccc}
12 & 8 & 4 \\
-4 & -4 & -4 \\
\hline
8 & 4 & 0
\end{array}
$$

We have subtracted 4 from 12; then 4 from the remainder 8; then 4 from the remainder 4. Nothing remains. We used 4 as the subtracter three times. Hence the answer (or *quotient*) to the problem 12 divided by 4, or 12 ÷ 4, is 3.

Involution

In the process called *involution,* we raise a number to any desired *power*. The number that is to be raised to the power in question is called the *base*. To raise 2 to the third power, we repeat the base three times as it is multiplied by itself; thus: 2 × 2 × 2. We indicate the power by placing a small figure, called the *exponent,* to the right of the base and above it. For example, 2 to the third power, or 2 × 2 × 2, is written 2^3.

If the exponent is 1, it indicates that the number is not raised to a higher power but remains unchanged. Thus $2^1 = 2$; $5^1 = 5$. When we use the exponent zero, we show that the base is to be divided by itself. Any number with the exponent 0 is always equal to 1. For example, $4^0 = 4 ÷ 4 = 1$; $10^0 = 10 ÷ 10 = 1$. There are also *negative* exponents. (A negative number is one whose value is less than zero, such as −16 or −3.) A base with a negative exponent is equal to the *reciprocal* of the base with the corresponding positive exponent. (A reciprocal of a number is equal to 1 divided by the number; for example, the reciprocal of 4 is $\frac{1}{4}$.) Thus:

$$5^{-1} = \frac{1}{5^1} = \frac{1}{5}$$
$$3^{-2} = \frac{1}{3^2} = \frac{1}{9}$$

Evolution

In the process called *evolution* we are essentially doing the inverse (or opposite) of involution. Given a certain number (for example, 9), we try to find what other number, multiplied by itself a desired number of times (say, two times) will give us the first number. The number we are trying to find is called the *root,* and in this case, because we want a root that will be multiplied by itself two times to equal 9, we call it the *square root* of 9 and express it as $\sqrt{9}$. Because $3 \times 3 = 9$, we would say that the square root of 9 is 3, or $\sqrt{9} = 3$. We could also say that the two 3's are *factors* of 9. (Factors are numbers that can be multiplied together to equal a given product.)

A root that is multiplied by itself three times to give a certain number is called the *cube root* of that number. The cube root of 8, written as $\sqrt[3]{8}$, is 2 because $2 \times 2 \times 2 = 8$.

Fractions

Numbers such as 0, 1, 2, 3, 5, 10, 120, and 3,000 are called *whole numbers,* or *integers.* (Any whole number greater than zero is called a *positive integer.*) When one multiplies one integer by another, the answer is always an integer: $5 \times 6 = 30$; $7 \times 9 = 63$. However, it is not always possible to obtain an integer as an answer when one divides one integer by another. It is true that if we divide 8 apples into 4 equal shares, each share will consist of 2 apples. But if 8 apples are to be divided into 3 equal shares, the answer will not be an integer because $8 \div 3 = \frac{8}{3}$, which is a *fraction,* or "broken number." This does not mean that

we have to divide each of our 8 apples into thirds and give each person 8 thirds. What we need to know is how many whole apples are in $\frac{8}{3}$ apples. By doing simple division we would find that $\frac{6}{3} = 2$, which means that 6 of the 8 thirds is equal to 2 and that 2 thirds will remain. In other words, the fraction $\frac{8}{3}$ can be *reduced* to a whole number and a remaining fraction:

$$\frac{8}{3} = \frac{6}{3} + \frac{2}{3} = 2 + \frac{2}{3} - 2\frac{2}{3}$$

So, to divide 8 apples equally among 3 people, each person would receive 2 whole apples plus $\frac{2}{3}$ apple, for a total of $2\frac{2}{3}$ apples. Because $2\frac{2}{3}$ represents the sum of an integer and a fraction, it is called a *mixed number.*

In a fraction such as $\frac{2}{3}$, the numeral above the line is called the *numerator,* and the numeral below the line is called the *denominator.* Although symbolized with two numerals, the fraction $\frac{2}{3}$ is actually one number. A fraction, like any other number, can be added, subtracted, multiplied, and divided. Operations with fractions follow the basic rules of arithmetic, but there are certain rules about fractions in particular that should be learned. Let us consider the following multiplication problem:

$$\frac{2}{3} \times \frac{4}{5} = \frac{8}{15}$$

Very simply, the product was obtained by multiplying the numerators ($2 \times 4 = 8$) and then multiplying the denominators ($3 \times 5 = 15$). Division by a fraction takes an added step:

$$\frac{2}{5} \div \frac{7}{9} = \frac{2}{5} \times \frac{9}{7} = \frac{18}{35}$$

We notice from the example that the divisor $\left(\frac{7}{9}\right)$ was inverted $\left(\frac{9}{7}\right)$ and was then mul-

© Marcia W. Griffen/Earth Scenes

Fractions are used every day in household weights and measures. If a pie serves 6, each portion is 1/6. This apple pie contains 3/4 cup sugar, 1/4 teaspoon of nutmeg, and 1/8 teaspoon of salt among its ingredients.

tiplied by the dividend $\left(\dfrac{2}{5}\right)$, following the rules for multiplying fractions.

Let us consider the following addition problem:

$$\frac{1}{8} + \frac{1}{8} + \frac{3}{8} = \frac{5}{8}$$

We can see that the three addends, as well as their sum, have the same denominator (8) and that only the numerators were added together ($1 + 1 + 3 = 5$). Adding fractions is very simple when all the denominators are the same, as in the example just shown, but when denominators differ it is necessary to find appropriate equivalents in order to "make" the denominators the same:

$$\frac{1}{8} + \frac{1}{4} = \frac{1}{8} + \left(\frac{2}{2} \times \frac{1}{4}\right) = \frac{1}{8} + \frac{2}{8} = \frac{3}{8}$$

As shown, $\dfrac{1}{4}$ "became" $\dfrac{2}{8}$ when it was multiplied by $\dfrac{2}{2}$. The value of $\dfrac{1}{4}$ did not change because $\dfrac{2}{2} = 1$ and multiplying any number by 1 will not change that number's value. The rule of like-denominators also applies to the subtraction of fractions:

$$\frac{1}{2} - \frac{5}{12} = \left(\frac{6}{6} \times \frac{1}{2}\right) - \frac{5}{12} = \frac{6}{12} - \frac{5}{12} = \frac{1}{12}$$

It is also helpful to remember that a fraction such as $\dfrac{17}{30}$ can be expressed as an operation of division. In other words, $\dfrac{17}{30} = 17 \div 30$, which means that a fraction's numerator is also a dividend and its denominator is also a divisor. The laws of fundamental mathematics prohibit the use of zero as a divisor (because zero multiplied by any number can result only in zero), and therefore, zero can never be the denominator of any fraction.

Negative Integers

If we return now to the integers, we note that when we subtract one positive integer from another, the answer is not always positive. It is true that $7 - 4 = 3$. But suppose we want to subtract 7 from 4. To make the subtraction $4 - 7$ possible, we invent a new kind of number called a *negative integer,* which is represented by an integer with a minus sign in front of it. The answer to the subtraction problem $4 - 7$ is -3.

The mechanics of solving problems such as $12 - 6, 9 - 7, 6 - 13$, and so on is simple enough. We subtract the smaller number from the larger one and we give the result the sign (plus or minus) of the larger number. (Numbers without signs are positive, and therefore "plus" signs are seldom necessary.):

$$12 - 6 = 6 \qquad 4 - 9 = -5$$
$$9 - 7 = 2 \qquad 3 - 7 = -4$$
$$4 - 1 = 3 \qquad 6 - 13 = -7$$

There are as many possible negative integers as there are positive integers. Starting with 0, we can build up a list of negative integers to the left of 0 and a list of positive integers to the right of 0.

$$\ldots -3, -2, -1, 0, +1, +2, +3 \ldots$$

We could extend the list of positive and negative integers in this way indefinitely. There are negative fractions as well as negative integers. Every positive fraction has a negative counterpart, such as $\frac{3}{5}$ and $-\frac{3}{5}$.

The entire set of numbers we have been discussing (positive integers, negative integers, positive fractions, negative fractions, and zero) is called the *rational number system*. We can define a rational number as being zero, an integer (positive or negative), or a fraction (positive or negative) whose numerator and denominator are both integers. Therefore, 5 is a rational number, as are $\frac{1}{2}$ and $-\frac{3}{4}$.

Rules have been devised for the addition, subtraction, multiplication, and division of positive and negative rational numbers so that no illogical results will occur. One of these rules is: "The product of two like-signed numbers is positive." For example, $4 \times 4 = 16$; likewise $-4 \times -4 = 16$. Another of these rules is: "The product of two unlike-signed numbers is negative." For example, $4 \times -4 = -16$; $-7 \times 6 = -42$.

Irrational Numbers

The square root of a number, as we have seen, is one of its two equal factors. Thus $\sqrt{25} = 5$, since $5 \times 5 = 25$. But the square root of 2, or $\sqrt{2}$, cannot be expressed by any rational number. We know that $\sqrt{2}$ must be somewhere between 1.4 and 1.5, since $1.4^2 = 1.96$ and $1.5^2 = 2.25$. We could come closer to the square root of 2 by using more and more decimal places: $1.41^2 = 1.9881$, and $1.414^2 = 1.999396$. But no matter how many decimal places we

add, we will never find a rational number whose square root is 2.

Yet numbers such as $\sqrt{2}$ result from many mathematical calculations, and, because they do not fit into the rational number system, we call them *irrational numbers*. Some examples of irrational numbers are $\sqrt{3}$, $\sqrt{5}$, and $\sqrt[3]{7}$. These are all *real numbers*, just as rational numbers are, even if we cannot express them by integers or fractions.

If we combine all the irrational numbers with all the rational numbers, we get a very large set of numbers called the *real number system*. All the numbers of the system can be represented by points on a straight line. Let one point represent the number 0. Then let points to the right represent positive integers and those to the left, negative integers, as follows:

If the space between the integers is subdivided into as many parts as possible, each of the subdivision points will represent a rational number. No matter how many divisions we may make in this way, however, gaps will always remain. If we fill in the gaps with points representing all possible irrational numbers, such as $\sqrt{2}$, $\sqrt{5}$, and so on, the line will be completely filled. This line is known as the real number *axis*, or *continuum*.

Imaginary Numbers

There are still other numbers besides the real numbers. Let us consider the number $\sqrt{-1}$. This seems to be a contradiction in terms, since a square is always the product of two equal numbers with like signs and is, therefore, always positive. Hence no number multiplied by itself can give a negative real number, and it would seem futile to try to get the square root of such a number. However, mathematicians use the number $\sqrt{-1}$ to form the basis of a number system called *imaginary numbers*, or *complex numbers*. The imaginary number $\sqrt{-1}$ is often indicated by the symbol *i*.

ALGEBRA

In the preceding article, "Arithmetic," we were concerned with particular numbers, which are expressed by symbols. "Sixty-seven" is a particular number. To do arithmetical problems in which sixty-seven plays a part, we use the symbols 6 and 7, combined as 67. We are now going to consider a branch of mathematics in which a symbol, such as the letter a, b, or c, stands not for a particular number, but for a whole class of numbers. This kind of mathematics is called *algebra*.

We can illustrate the difference between arithmetic and algebra by a very simple example:

Take the number 4.   4
Multiply by 5. $4 \times 5 = 20$
Add 4. $20 + 4 = 24$
Multiply by 2. $24 \times 2 = 48$
Subtract 8. $48 - 8 = 40$
Divide by original number (4). $40 \div 4 = 10$

In arriving at the final result, 10, we used the method of arithmetic, involving particular numbers, throughout.

Suppose now that we think of any number. Let us indicate "any number" by the symbol x, and let us go through the same operation as before:

Multiply by 5. $5 \times x = 5x$
Add 4. $5x + 4 = 5x + 4$
Multiply by 2. $2(5x + 4) = 10x + 8$
Subtract 8. $(10x + 8) - 8 = 10x$
Divide by original
     number (x). $10x \div x = 10$

Here we have been using the methods of algebra, because x can be replaced by any number. We could substitute for it 2, or 3, or 15, and the final result would always be 10.

When a generalized number, represented by a letter (such as a), is multiplied by a particular number (such as 5) or by another generalized number (such as b), we do not use multiplication signs, but indicate multiplication by putting these symbols

close to one another. Thus $a \times b = ab$; $5 \times a = 5a$; $5 \times a \times b = 5ab$. We could not indicate the multiplication of two particular numbers in this way; 7×5 could not be given as 75, because 75 really stands for $70 + 5$.

Let us consider another example. In the equation $(2 + 3)^2 = 25$, we are dealing with the particular numbers 2 and 3, and the result is always 25. But suppose that instead of two particular numbers, we used the letters a and b to stand for any two numbers. We would then have the algebraic equation $(a + b)^2 = a^2 + 2ab + b^2$. (The derivation of this equation will be explained later.)

What is significant about $(a + b)^2 = a^2 + 2ab + b^2$ is that it indicates a general relationship that holds true for a great many particular numbers. If we substituted 3 for a and 2 for b, we could have $(3 + 2)^2 = 3^2 + (2 \times 3 \times 2) + 2^2 = 9 + 12 + 4 = 25$. Or we could substitute 5 for a and 6 for b, giving $(5 + 6)^2 = 5^2 + (2 \times 5 \times 6) + 6^2 = 25 + 60 + 36 = 121$.

Algebra, the mathematics of "any numbers," or *variables,* goes to the heart of the relationship between numbers. Generally speaking, it is concerned with particular numbers only insofar as they are applications of general principles. It is also used in the solution of certain specific problems in which we start out with one or more unknown quantities whose values are indicated by algebraic symbols.

An Ancient Discipline

The study of algebra goes back to antiquity. Recent discoveries have shown that the Babylonians solved problems in algebra, although they had no symbols for variables. They used only words to indicate such numbers, and for that reason their algebra has been referred to as *rhetorical algebra*. The Ahmes Papyrus, an Egyptian scroll going back to 1600 B.C., has a number of problems in algebra, in which the unknown is referred to as a *hau,* meaning "a heap."

Little further progress was made in algebra until we come to Diophantus, a 3rd-century A.D. Greek mathematician. He reduced problems to equations, representing the unknown quantity by a symbol suggesting the Greek letter Σ (sigma). He also introduced an interesting system of abbreviations, in which he used only the initial letters of words, after omitting all unnecessary words. If we were to use the method of Diophantus in presenting the problem "An unknown squared minus the unknown will give twenty," we would first state the problem as "Unknown squared minus unknown equals twenty." Then we would use initial letters for all the words except the last, for which we would use the numeral 20, as follows: "USMUE20."

In the 16th century, French mathematician François Viète, (or Victa) used the vowels *a, e, i, o, u* to represent unknown numbers and the consonants *b, c, d, f, g,* and so on to stand for values that remained fixed throughout a given problem. The great 17th-century French philosopher René Descartes proposed the system of algebraic symbols now in use. In this system, *a, b, c,* and other letters near the beginning of the alphabet represent the fixed numbers. The last letters of the alphabet (*x, y, z,* and sometimes *w*) stand for the unknown numbers in a problem. As soon as this symbolism came into general use, algebra grew quite rapidly into a systematic set of rules and theorems that could be applied to all numbers.

The word "algebra" originated from the Arabic title of a work by a 9th-century Persian mathematician, Mohammed ibn Musa Al-Kwarizmi. The work was *Al-Jebr W'al Muqabala,* which means "restoration and reduction." By *al-jebr* or restoration, was meant the transposing of negative terms to the other side of an equation to make them positive. When the Arabs came to Spain, they brought this word with them. In the course of time, *al-jebr* was changed to "algebra," and the word came to be applied not to a single operation, but to all operations involved in modern algebra.

Three Fundamental Laws

Algebra generalizes—that is, expresses in general terms—certain basic laws that govern the addition, subtraction, multiplication, and division of all numbers.

(1) When we add or multiply two integers, the order in which we add or multiply them is immaterial. Thus $2 + 3$ is the same as $3 + 2$, and 4×3 is the same as 3×4. Since this is true for all integers, we set up the following algebraic formulas:

$$a + b = b + a$$
$$ab = ba$$

These are called the *commutative laws* of addition and multiplication.

(2) When more than two numbers are added or multiplied, we can group them in any order we choose, and the answer will always be the same. If 2 is added to $(3 + 6)$, the result is the same as if we added $(2 + 3)$ to 6. Similarly, 2 times the product of 3×6 is the same as 3 times the product of 6×2. These results are indicated in the following formulas:

$$a + (b + c) = (a + b) + c$$
$$a(bc) = (ab)c$$

These are the *associative laws* of addition and multiplication.

(3) If a multiplicand has two or more terms, a multiplier must operate upon each of these terms in turn. Suppose we wish to multiply $(3 + 2)$ by 5, a problem we could set down as $5(3 + 2)$. We would first multiply 3 by 5 and then 2 by 5, giving $15 + 10$, or 25. This rule is called the *distributive law of multiplication* and is given by the following formula:

$$a(b + c) = ab + ac$$

Suppose we want to multiply $a + b$ by $a + b$, which of course would be the same thing as $(a + b)^2$. We would set up the problem as follows:

$$\frac{\begin{array}{r} a + b \\ a + b \end{array}}{}$$

In accordance with the distributive law of multiplication, we (1) multiply the upper $(a + b)$ by the *b* of the lower $(a + b)$, (2) multiply the upper $(a + b)$ by the *a* of the lower $(a + b)$, and (3) add the results:

$$a + b$$
$$a + b$$

$ab + b^2$	(1)
$a^2 + \quad ab$	(2)
$a^2 + 2ab + b^2$	(3)

We use the same distributive law of multiplication in multiplying 25 by 25. Ordinarily, we would present our calculations as follows:

$$\begin{array}{r} 25 \\ \underline{25} \\ 125 \\ \underline{50} \\ 625 \end{array}$$

Because the 2 in 25 is really 20, the same problem can also be expressed by the following:

$$\begin{array}{r} 20 + 5 \\ \underline{20 + 5} \end{array}$$

Using the algebraic formula for the distributive law, having given a and b the values of 20 and 5, respectively, we can carry out the problem as follows:

$$\begin{array}{r} 20 + 5 \\ \underline{20 + 5} \\ 100 + 25 \\ \underline{400 + 100} \\ 400 + 200 + 25 = 625 \end{array}$$

The two methods shown for multiplying 25 by 25 are expressed differently but actually perform the same algebraic operations.

Formulas, Tables, and Graphs

There are different ways of showing how different quantities are related. We can use a formula, set up a table of values, or draw a graph.

Consider the rule: "The area of a square is equal to the square of the length of its side." This is a rather roundabout way of expressing the relationship in question. We could state it much more simply by using the symbol A to represent the number of square units in the area, and the symbol s to represent the number of units in the side. Therefore, the area of any square can be stated as $A = s^2$. This abbreviated rule is called a *formula,* from the Latin word meaning "little form."

If the length of the side of a square is 6, we can get A, the area, by substituting 6 for s in the formula:

$$A = s^2 = 6^2 = 36$$

We can also represent the relationship $A = s^2$ by setting up a *table of values.* Suppose the side of the square is equal to 1; A is then 1^2 or 1. If the side of the square is equal to 2, $A = 2^2$, or 4. Substituting for s the values from 1 through 10, in turn, we obtain the following table of values:

s	1	2	3	4	5	6	7	8	9	10
A	1	4	9	16	25	36	49	64	81	100

This table tells us that if $s = 1$, $A = 1$; if $s = 2$, $A = 4$; if $s = 3$, $A = 9$; and so on.

There is still another way of representing the area of a square. We could construct a *graph,* as in Figure 1. First, we draw two lines, called axes, which are perpendicular to each other. Along the horizontal axis, or base, we mark out a series of numbers at equal intervals, corresponding to the values of s in the table. We mark another series of numbers on the vertical axis that correspond to the values of A.

Within the framework of the axes we create a grid, made of lines perpendicular to both axes and originating from the designated values along those axes. A grid may consist of any number of perpendiculars (such as the ones in Figure 1 that fall between the designated values), which can indicate values not enumerated on the axes. For instance, the vertical line that lies between the s values of 3 and 4 indicates an s value of 3.5. You can see that there is no specific line on the grid for an s value of 3.1, for example, but that value *does* exist on the axis and would simply be estimated by eye to fall just to the right of the 3.

Because the purpose of the graph in Figure 1 is to show the relationship between the values of s and A, we want to translate the values from the table to a series of *points* on the grid. At each value of s (1, 2, 3, 4, and so on) we follow the vertical line upward until we reach the point at which a horizontal perpendicular would meet the corresponding value for A. For instance, the table tells us that when $s = 5$,

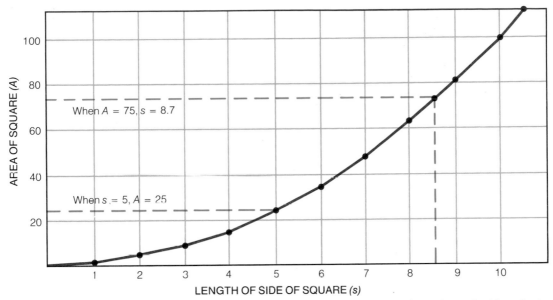

When $A = 75$, $s = 8.7$

When $s = 5$, $A = 25$

AREA OF SQUARE (A)

LENGTH OF SIDE OF SQUARE (s)

Figure 1. The graph of the area of a square, using horizontal and vertical axes, according to the method described in the text. The graph shows how the area of a square increases as the length of the side increases. It is one way of expressing the relation between the length of the side and the area.

$A = 25$. On our grid we find the perpendicular that would indicate $A = 25$ (halfway between the horizontal lines for 20 and 30), and where it meets the vertical line for $s = 5$ we draw, or *map,* a point. When we have mapped the points for each value of s from 1 through 10, we draw a line connecting all ten points, which in this case is an upward curve. This curve is called the graph of the area of a square. It shows how the area increases as the length of the side increases.

We can use the graph to find out the areas of squares with sides not given in the table of values. For example, if $s = 5.5$, we erect a perpendicular at this point, extending it until it meets the graph. From the point of meeting, we erect a perpendicular to the vertical axis. The point where this perpendicular meets the vertical axis will represent the area, which is about 30. (The correct value is 30.25.)

If we know the area of a square, we can find out the approximate length of the side by means of our graph. Suppose the area is 75. From the point corresponding to the number 75 on the vertical axis, we draw a horizontal line to the point where it meets

the graph. From there we drop a perpendicular to meet the s axis, at about 8.7, a very accurate value for s. (The correct value, expressed to five decimal places, is 8.66025.)

Figure 2. Bar graph showing the populations of four countries in the mid-20th century.

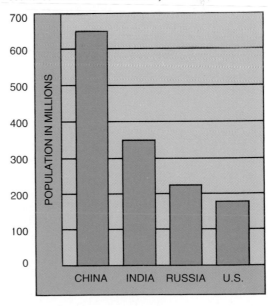

POPULATION IN MILLIONS

CHINA   INDIA   RUSSIA   U.S.

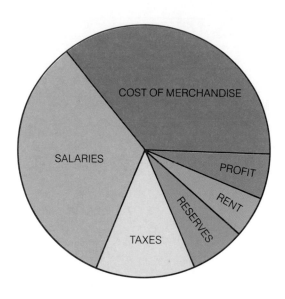

Figure 3. A circle graph indicating how each part of a dollar received by a department store is spent.

COST OF MERCHANDISE

SALARIES

PROFIT

RENT

RESERVES

TAXES

There are many different kinds of graphs. The most common are the *bar graph*, the *circle graph*, and the *line graph*. If, for example, we would like to show how the populations of China, India, Russia, and the United States compare, we could draw four bars (Figure 2). The lengths of the bars would be proportionate to the populations in question.

If we desired to compare parts of a whole quantity, we would use a circle graph. It could serve to indicate how each part of a dollar received in sales in a department store is spent by the store (Figure 3). Each sector of the circle, as compared to the whole circle, would show the proportion given to a particular service.

When a quantity is continuously changing, we would use a line graph. Hospital nurses often make graphs of their patients' temperatures. Figure 4 is an example of one such graph. It covers a 44-hour period, during which the patient's temperature was recorded (with a point on the grid) every 4 hours. As shown, each point is connected to the preceding point by a straight line. The doctor who consults the chart can see at a glance how the patient's temperature has been changing.

To repeat, then, we can show how quantities are related by a formula, a table of values, or a graph. It is the formula that is basic. If a table of values is worked up, a scientist tries to find the formula that will express the relationship in question. After plotting a graph to show the length of a steel cable under increasing tension, an engineer would work out an algebraic formula to sum up his or her findings.

Formulas are extremely important in many branches of pure and applied science. For example, to indicate the speed of a body having uniform rectilinear motion (that is, moving in a straight line at a con-

Figure 4. Nurses sometimes make line graphs of patients' temperatures, taking readings at regular intervals. Readings, in degrees Celsius, taken every four hours may yield a graph like this one.

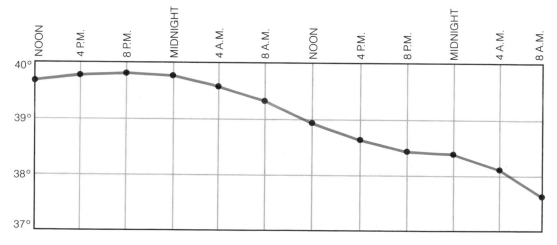

stant speed), the physicist uses the formula $v = \frac{s}{t}$, where v is the average speed of the body, s is the space or distance covered, and t is the time required to travel this distance. We can apply this formula to specific cases by substituting appropriate values for v, s, or t. For example, if a car takes 5 hours to travel 400 kilometers, we could find the average speed by substituting 5 for t and 400 for s. The average speed, then, would be $\frac{400}{5}$ kilometers, or 80 kilometers per hour.

The chemist often has occasion to use the law of J. A. C. Charles and J. L. Gay-Lussac, which states that if the pressure and the mass of a gas are constant, the volume is proportional to the *absolute temperature*. (Absolute temperature is based on the hypothetical lowest possible temperature, *absolute zero*, which is equivalent to $-273.16°$ Celsius.) This law can be stated very concisely by the formula $\frac{V_1}{T_1} = \frac{V_2}{T_2}$, in which V_1 is the volume of a gas at temperature T_1, while V_2 is the volume of a gas at temperature T_2.

Perhaps the most famous formula of all is the Einstein equation, $E = mc^2$. In this equation, E stands for the amount of energy, m for the amount of mass, and c for the speed of light (which is about 300,000 kilometers per second), measured in appropriate units. With this formula the great 20th-century physicist Albert Einstein indicated the amount of energy that appears when matter is transformed into energy.

How Equations are Employed

The equation plays an all-important part in algebra. It may be looked upon as a balance, with equal numerical values on each side of the "equal" sign ($=$). To show how an equation is applied, let us consider the formula for the perimeter (the outside boundary) of a rectangle: $P = 2l + 2w$, where P is the perimeter, l is the length and w is the width. Suppose we have 100 meters of wire with which to make a rectangular enclosure, which is to be 20 meters wide.

We wish to find out the length of this enclosure if we are to use the entire 100 meters of wire. We know that the perimeter will be 100 meters. We also know that the width is to be 20 meters. Substituting 100 for P and 20 for w in the formula, we have $100 = 2l + (2 \times 20) = 2l + 40$. In the equation $100 = 2l + 40$, the 100 on one side of the equal sign is exactly equal to $2l + 40$ on the other side. To find out what l is, we subtract 40 from each side of the equation, resulting in $60 = 2l$. If we divide both sides of the equation by 2, the result is $30 = l$. Therefore, the length of the enclosure will be 30 meters.

In solving the equation, we used the following rule: "If the same operation is performed on each member of an equality, then the results are equal." If we add the same quantity to each side of the equation or subtract the same quantity, the equality will be maintained. It will be maintained, too, if we multiply or divide each side of the equation by the same quantity. Of course, if we multiplied each side of the equation by zero, the result would be $0 = 0$, which would get us nowhere in the task of solving the equation. Division by zero is not permitted.

Equations may be used to solve problems in which no formula is involved but in which certain data are given. Here is a simple problem: "A man is 6 times as old as his son. In 20 years, the father will be only twice as old as his son. How old are the father and son at the present time?"

On the basis of the data, we can write an equation and solve the problem. First, we let x stand for the son's age. Since the father is 6 times as old as his son, his age can be given as 6 times x, or $6x$. In 20 years the son will be $x + 20$ years old. In 20 years, the age of the father will be $6x + 20$ years. At that time, the father's age will be twice that of the son, a relationship that can be expressed by the equation: $6x + 20 = 2(x + 20)$. Applying the distributive law to the right-hand side of the equation, we have $6x + 20 = 2x + 40$. We subtract $2x + 20$ from each side of the equation and get $4x = 20$. If $4x = 20$, $x = 5$. The son's age at the present time, therefore, is 5. Since the father's age at the present time is 6 times that of the son, or $6x$, the father is 30 years old.

Not all problems are as simple as this one, in which the unknown is x. The equation may involve not only an unknown quantity, x, but also higher powers of x. If x^2 is the highest power occurring in an equation, it is called a *quadratic equation*. $x^2 + 6 = 5x$ is an example of such an equation. In various equations, the highest power of x may be x^3 or x^4, or there may be even higher powers.

Identities

When an equation is true for all the replacement values of the variables concerned, it is called an *identity*. A familiar example of an identity is $(a + b)^2 = a^2 + 2ab + b^2$. As we pointed out before, this equation holds true no matter what values we assign to a and b. It can be used as an aid in mental arithmetic. To square 22, we can think of this number as $(20 + 2)^2$, 20 being substituted for a and 2 for b. Mentally we square 20, giving 400; then we double 20×2, giving 80; then we square 2, giving 4. Finally, we have $400 + 80 + 4 = 484$. The answer, then, is 484.

Another identity is $(a - b)^2 = a^2 - 2ab + b^2$. You can verify this by performing the multiplication $(a - b)(a - b)$. We would have:

$$
\begin{array}{r}
a - b \\
a - b \\
\hline
-\ ab + b^2 \\
a^2 -\ ab \\
\hline
a^2 - 2\ ab + b^2
\end{array}
$$

Still another identity is $(a + b)(a - b) = a^2 - b^2$. This also is useful in certain mental-arithmetic problems. If we wish to multiply 34 by 26 in our heads, we can change the problem to $(30 + 4) \times (30 - 4)$. Solving this in accordance with the identity $(a + b)(a - b) = a^2 - b^2$, we have $900 - 16 = 884$. Other well-known identities are:

$(a + b)^3 = (a^3 + 3a^2b + 3ab^2 + b^3)$
$(a - b)^3 = (a^3 - 3a^2b + 3ab^2 - b^3)$
$(a^3 - b^3) = (a - b)(a^2 + ab + b^2)$

Exponents

Exponents simplify the writing of algebraic expressions. Thus $aaabbbcc$, which is really a continuous multiplication (a times a times a times b times b times b times c times c), can be written $a^3b^3c^2$. The mathematician has derived a series of rules for combining exponents. The rules are stated in general terms: a^n stands for the *base a* raised to the *n*th *power*; a^m, for the same base raised to the *m*th power.

(1) $a^na^m = a^{n+m}$. In multiplying powers, we add the exponents of like bases. Thus $2^2 \times 2^3 = 2^{2+3} = 2^5 = 32$.

(2) $a^n \div a^m = a^{n-m}$. In dividing powers, we subtract the exponents of like bases. This means that $2^5 \div 2^2 = 2^{5-2} = 2^3 = 8$.

(3) $(a^n)^m = a^{nm}$. To raise a given power by another power, we multiply the two exponents. For example, $(2^2)^3 = 2^{2\times3} = 2^6 = 64$.

(4) $(ab)^n = a^nb^n$. When a product is raised to a power, each member of the product is raised to that power. Thus $(4 \times 2)^2 = 4^2 \times 2^2 = 16 \times 4 = 64$.

(5) $\left(\dfrac{a}{b}\right)^n = \dfrac{a^n}{b^n}$. When a quotient (as a fraction) is raised to a given power, each member of the quotient must be raised to that power.

$$\left(\frac{2}{3}\right)^3 = \frac{2^3}{3^3} = \frac{8}{27}.$$

It should be noted here that a base with the exponent zero is equivalent to 1. Thus $10^0 = 1$; $3^0 = 1$; $1^0 = 1$. All the rules just stated for exponents apply to zero exponents. For example, $a^na^0 = a^{n+0} = a^n$; $5^3 \times 5^0 = 5^{3+0} = 5^3 = 125$.

A base with a negative exponent is equal to the *reciprocal* of the base $\left(\dfrac{1}{\text{base}}\right)$ with the corresponding positive exponent. Thus $2^{-2} = \left(\dfrac{1}{2^2}\right)$. Negative exponents follow the rules for all exponents. Thus

$$a^{-5}a^3 = a^{-5+3} = a^{-2} = \frac{1}{a^2} \text{ and}$$

$$10^{-7} \times 10^5 = 10^{-7+5} = 10^{-2} = \frac{1}{10^2} = \frac{1}{100}.$$

Exponents can also occur in the form of fractions. Thus we have $a^{1/2}$, $a^{1/3}$, $a^{1/4}$, and so on: $a^{1/2}$ means the square root of a or $\sqrt{a}$; $a^{1/3}$ means the cube root of a, or $\sqrt[3]{a}$; $a^{1/4}$ means the fourth root of a, or $\sqrt[4]{a}$. The numerator in fractional exponents need not necessarily be 1. We frequently deal with exponents such as $\frac{2}{3}$ and $\frac{3}{5}$. In such cases, the numerator stands for the power of a base and the denominator for the root of a base. For example, $10^{2/3}$ is equal to $\sqrt[3]{10^2}$.

All fractional exponents, whether or not the numerator is 1, follow the rule for exponents. For example, $10^2 \times 10^{2/3} = 10^{2+(2/3)} = 10^{8/3} = \sqrt[3]{10^8}$

Expressing Very Large or Very Small Numbers

Exponents provide a convenient way of writing very large or very small numbers. We know that 1,000,000 is 10^6, the exponent 6 representing the number of zeros after 1. We could indicate 5,000,000 as $5 \times 1,000,000$, or 5×10^6. To write 5,270,000, we would multiply 1,000,000, or 10^6, by 5.27. The number would be written as 5.27×10^6. In other words, we can express a large number as the product of two numbers: the first a number between 1 and 10; the second, a power of 10.

The number 5,270,000 is not too formidable, and we can grasp it readily enough. But consider the problems that would arise if, in our calculations, we had to use a number such as 602,000,000,000,-000,000,000,000. It represents the number of molecules in 18 grams of water and is called Avogadro's number, after the early-19th-century Italian scientist Amadeo Avogadro, who worked out the value. It is used in a great many scientific calculations, but practically never in the long form. Instead, it is written as 6.02×10^{23}.

The 20th-century American mathematician Edward Kasner invented a new system of indicating extremely large numbers. He coined the world "googol" to express the number 10^{100}, which would be equivalent to 1 followed by 100 zeros. He invented another term, the "googolplex," to stand for $10^{100^{100}}$, or the figure 1 followed by a googol of zeros, that is, 10,000 zeros.

Exponents can be used just as effectively to express very small numbers. Since a minus exponent indicates how many times the fraction $\frac{1}{\text{base}}$ is repeated as it is multiplied by itself, $10^{-3} = \frac{1}{10} \times \frac{1}{10} \times \frac{1}{10} = 0.001$. Note that the exponent 3, in 10^{-3}, represents the number of digits after the decimal point in the number 0.001. The number 0.005 could be written as 5×0.001, or 5×10^{-3}. Now consider a much smaller number. The wavelength of red light is 0.00000077 meters. We can write this number as 7.7×0.0000001 or 7.7×10^{-7} meters.

Writing a number as the product of a number between 1 and 10 and a power of 10 is called *scientific notation*. It is used widely by scientists and engineers.

Calculations with Logarithms

Exponents have also been put to work to simplify arithmetical calculations. Sup-

TABLE I		
Number	Number expressed as power of 2	Exponent in preceding column
0.25	2^{-2}	-2
0.5	2^{-1}	-1
1	2^0	0
2	2^1	1
4	2^2	2
8	2^3	3
16	2^4	4
32	2^5	5
64	2^6	6
128	2^7	7
256	2^8	8
512	2^9	9
1,024	2^{10}	10

pose that we represent numbers as powers of 2. We know that $2^{-2} = \frac{1}{2^2} = \frac{1}{4}$; $2^{-1} = \frac{1}{2^1} = \frac{1}{2}$; $2^0 = 1$; $2^1 = 2$; $2^2 = 4$; $2^3 = 8$; $2^4 = 16$; and so on. Expressed as a power of 2, therefore, $\frac{1}{4}$, or .25, is 2^{-2}; $\frac{1}{2}$, or .5, is 2^{-1}; 1 is 2^0; 2 is 2^1; 4 is 2^2; 8 is 2^3; 16 is 2^4. Let us now make a table, (Table I), setting down (1) certain numbers, (2) these numbers expressed as powers of 2; (3) the exponents in question.

Consider the problem $0.25 \times 1{,}024$. The table shows that $0.25 = 2^{-2}$ and that $1{,}024 = 2^{10}$. The problem then becomes $2^{-2} \times 2^{10}$. Applying the first given law of exponents, we have $2^{-2} \times 2^{10} = 2^{-2+10} = 2^8$. Consulting the table, we find that $2^8 = 256$, which, then, is the answer to the problem $0.25 \times 1{,}024$. We have changed a problem in multiplication into a simple addition.

Let us take another problem: $1{,}024 \div 32$. Looking at the table, we see that $1{,}024$ is 2^{10} and that 32 is 2^5. Applying the second law of exponents, we have $2^{10} \div 2^5 = 2^{10-5} = 2^5$. We now consult the table and find that 2^5 is equal to 32. This is the answer to $1{,}024 \div 32$. In this case, we have changed a problem in division into a simpler subtraction problem.

Our next problem is to raise 4 to the fifth power. In other words, we want to know what 4^5 would be. The table shows us that 4 is 2^2. From the third law of exponents, we know that $(2^2)^5 = 2^{2 \times 5} = 2^{10}$ which, according to the table, is $1{,}024$. We have solved our problem by a single multiplication instead of multiplying $4 \times 4 \times 4 \times 4 \times 4$.

Suppose we wish to get the square root of $1{,}024$. According to the table, $1{,}024$ is 2^{10}. To get the square root of a given power, we divide the exponent indicating that power by 2. Hence the square root of $2^{10} = 2^{10 \div 2} = 2^5$. Dividing the exponent indicating the power by 2 is really in accordance with the third law of exponents. The square root of a number, as we have seen, is equivalent to the same number with the exponent 1/2. The square root of 2^{10}, therefore, can be expressed as $(2^{10})^{1/2}$. Remember that to multiply a number by 1/2 is the same thing as to divide it by 2. The table shows that $2^5 = 32$. So 32 is the square root of $1{,}024$.

When a number is expressed as a power of a given base (in this case the base two), we call the exponent that indicates the power the *logarithm* of the number. All the exponents in the third column of the table are the logarithms, to the base two, of the numbers in the first column. When the base is two, -2 is the logarithm of 0.25. As a mathematician would put it, $\log_2 0.25 = -2$. Also when the base is two, the logarithm of 4 is 2 and the logarithm of 64 is 6. To multiply numbers, we first add their logarithms. To divide numbers, we first subtract their logarithms. To raise a number to a given power, we first multiply the logarithm of the number by the power in question. To obtain the root of a number, we first divide the logarithm of the number by the desired root. After we have added, subtracted, multiplied, or divided in this way, we find the number that corresponds to the resulting logarithm.

All the logarithms we have mentioned thus far are to the base two. Most tables of logarithms are given to the base ten. Let us now prepare another table (Table II), giving (1) a series of numbers; (2) the numbers expressed as powers of 10; and (3) the logarithms of the numbers, that is, the exponents when the numbers are expressed as powers of 10.

	TABLE II	
Number	Number expressed as power of 10	Logarithm to the base ten (LOG_{10})
0.0001	10^{-4}	-4
0.001	10^{-3}	-3
0.01	10^{-2}	-2
0.1	10^{-1}	-1
1	10^0	0
10	10^1	1
100	10^2	2
1,000	10^3	3
10,000	10^4	4

TABLE III	
Number	Logarithm (base ten)
1	0
2	0.301
3	0.477
4	0.602
5	0.699
6	0.778
7	0.845
8	0.903
9	0.954
10	1

To solve the problem 0.0001×100, we consult the table and find the logarithms of 0.0001 and 100 (-4 and 2, respectively), add the logarithms ($-4 + 2 = -2$), and find the number corresponding to the logarithm -2. This number, as we see from the table, is 0.01. We can also do such problems as $10,000 \div 0.0001$; 10^4; and $\sqrt{10,000}$.

Of course, to be serviceable, a table of logarithms would have to include the logarithms of other numbers besides those in Table II. It would have to give, for example, not only the logarithms of 1 and 10, but also those of 2, 3, 4, 5, 6, 7, 8, and 9. We know that since $1 = 1^0$ and $10 = 10^1$, the logarithm of 2 would be between 0 and 1. Mathematicians have calculated that it is 0.301. This means that, expressed as a power of 10, the number 2 is $10^{0.301}$. The integer part of the logarithm (0 in this case) is called the *characteristic*. The decimal part (.301) is called the *mantissa*.

Here, we give only three decimal places for the sake of simplicity, but logarithms have been calculated to more than twenty places. Depending upon the accuracy desired, one would use a four-place table, or a five-place table, or a seven-place table, and so on.

The logarithms of the numbers from 1 through 10 have been displayed in Table III. Using the table, let us multiply 2 by 4. We add 0.301, the logarithm of 2, and 0.602, the logarithm of 4, and we get the logarithm 0.903. Consulting the table, we

see that 0.903 is the logarithm of 8. A mathematician would say that 8 is the *antilogarithm,* or *antilog,* of 0.903. An antilogarithm is the number that corresponds to a given logarithm. Therefore, 8 is the answer to the problem 2×4. Let us now divide 9 by 3. The logarithm of 9, as we see from the table, is 0.954. The logarithm of 3 is 0.477. Subtracting 0.477 from 0.954, we get 0.477. The table shows that 0.477 is the logarithm of 3. Hence $9 \div 3 = 3$.

Our Table III gives the logarithms for only ten numbers, but mathematicians have prepared tables making it possible to find the logarithm of any number whatsoever. The tables give only the mantissas. We can determine the characteristic in each case by inspection. For example, the logarithm of the number 343 must be between 2 and 3, since $100 = 10^2$ and $1,000 = 10^3$. The logarithm, then, must be 2 and a fraction; so the characteristic must be 2. If we look up a five-place table in order to find the mantissa of 343, we observe that it is .53529. Putting together the characteristic 2 and the mantissa .53529, we have the logarithm 2.53529.

In calculations involving arithmetical problems, we can often save a tremendous amount of time by consulting a table of logarithms. Of course we would not use logarithms to get the answer to 4×5 or $72 \div 9$. But suppose we had to perform the various operations in the following:

$$\frac{-2.953 \times 5.913^5 \times \sqrt{5.973}}{49.743 \times 0.35947^3}$$

If the methods of arithmetic were used, this would be a most laborious task. It could be done in a few minutes if we employed logarithms.

Logarithms to the base ten are called *common logarithms*. In the so-called *natural logarithms,* the base is $2.71828 \ldots$, generally indicated by the letter e. Natural logarithms serve widely in various types of higher analysis because they lead to comparatively simple formulas.

Algebraic Sequences and Series

Many events seem to recur in regular sequences. The sun "rises" every day. The planets revolve in their orbits around the sun so regularly that astronomers can calculate their positions years in advance. People have analyzed periodic happenings by means of algebraic *sequences* and *series*. A sequence is a succession of numbers. A series is a sum of numbers in a sequence. The results of these analyses are sometimes used to predict future happenings.

Arithmetic progression, also called *arithmetic series,* is a sequence in which each term, after the first one, is formed by adding a constant quantity to the preceding term. An example of such a sequence is 1, 3, 5, 7, 9, 11, 13, 15, in which 2 is added to each succeeding number of the sequence. If a stands for the first number, d for the constantly added number, and n for the total number of terms, we can represent the arithmetic sequence algebraically by this formula:

$$a, (a + d), (a + 2d), \ldots, [a + (n - 1)d]$$

Here, $[a + (n - 1)d]$ is the nth term.

If we add n terms together, the sum (s) of the terms is called a series and can be expressed by the following formula:

$$s = \frac{n}{2}[2a + (n - 1)d]$$

Let us apply this formula to the sum of the terms in the sequence 1, 3, 5, 7, 9, 11, 13, 15. There are 8 terms in all. The first term is 1. The quantity that is constantly added is 2. Substituting these values for n, a, and d, we get the following:

$$s = \frac{8}{2}\{(2 \times 1) + [(8 - 1) \times 2]\}$$

If we work out the arithmetic involved, we find that $s = 64$, which can be verified by adding the eight terms of the sequence.

Arithmetic progression is very useful in various types of calculations. It serves, among other things, in finding the total cost of an item bought on an installment plan. Suppose you buy a piano for $1,000. You pay $400 down and agree to pay the other $600 in 20 monthly installments of $30 each, plus the *interest* at 6 percent on the unpaid balance. Let us apply the arithmetic

series to the problem in order to determine the total interest payments that will be required.

The 6 percent interest means "6 percent yearly" and is calculated by a factor of 0.06. The installment period is a month, or 1/12 of a year. The first of these interest payments is $1/12 \times 0.06 \times \$600$ (the unpaid balance), or $3.00. Each month the interest is less than in the preceding month since the unpaid balance is reduced by $30. You would pay $1/12 \times 0.06 \times \$30$, or $0.15 less interest than the month before. The consecutive interest payments, therefore, would be $3.00 (for the first month), $2.85 (for the second month), $2.70 (for the third month), and so on, until the 20 installments would be paid. Going back to the formula for the sum of an arithmetic sequence, we see that n (the number of terms) is 20; a (the first term) is $3.00; d (the constant addend) is $-\$0.15$. Making the appropriate substitutions in the formula, we get the following:

$$s = \frac{20}{2} \times \left\{(2 \times \$3.00) + [(20 - 1) \times -\$0.15]\right\}$$

The answer, representing the total interest paid, is $31.50.

Geometric progression is a sequence in which each term, after the first one, is formed by multiplying the preceding term by a fixed quantity. A typical geometric sequence is 1, 2, 4, 8, 16, in which the fixed multiplier is 2. Algebraically, geometric progression can be represented by

$$a, ar, ar^2, \ldots, ar^{n-1}$$

where a is the first term, r the constant multiplier, and n the number of terms. The sum of n terms of a goemetric sequence—a sum called a *geometric series*—is given by the following formula:

$$s = \frac{ar^n - a}{r - 1}$$

Applying it to the progression 1, 2, 4, 8, 16, the solution is as follows:

$$s = \frac{(1 \times 2^5) - 1}{2 - 1} = 31$$

If you were to add $1 + 2 + 4 + 8 + 16$, you would arrive at the same sum, 31. The formula, therefore, is a simple means by which to add the terms in any geometric sequence.

The geometric series plays an important part in the mathematics of finance. It is used, among other things, in figuring *compound interest*. Suppose that we put $100.00 (the *principal*) in a bank and that the *interest* is 3 percent, compounded annually. Interest is said to be compounded when it applies, not to the principal alone, but to the principal plus the interest that has been periodically added to the principal. To calculate the 3-percent interest on the $100.00 principal for the first year, we can multiply $100.00 by 0.03 to get $3.00. Our total, therefore, at the end of year one is $100.00 + $3.00 = $103.00. The two calculation steps just used are equivalent to this one step: $100.00 × 1.03 − $103.00. That is because "1.03" represents "100 percent + 3 percent."

For the second year we would receive 3-percent interest on our $103.00, which can be expressed as ($100.00 × 1.03) × 1.03, or $100.00 × 1.03^2. Following the same procedure, we would have $100.00 × 1.03^3 at the end of the third year, $100.00 × 1.03^4 at the end of the

fourth year, and so on, representing the following geometric sequence in which 1.03 is the fixed multiplier:

$100.00, $103.00, $106.09, $109.27 . . .

A *binomial sequence* is the expansion of the power of a *binomial*. A binomial consists of two terms connected by a plus or minus sign. The expressions $a + b$, $2x + z$, and $x^2 − y^2$ are binomials. Using our knowledge of exponents, as well as the laws of multiplication, we know that $(a + b)^0 = 1$, $(a + b)^1 = (a + b)$, $(a + b)^2 = a^2 + 2ab + b^2$, and so on. If we continue to expand $(a + b)$ by a power of one, we can arrange the resulting sums in a triangular pattern, as shown in Figure 5.

Figure 6 is a modification of that triangle, and arranged within it are only the *coefficients* of the sums in Figure 5. (The coefficients are the numerals that precede the unknowns a and b as multipliers.) There is a distinct pattern of numerical progression within this arrangement of binomial coefficients. As you will notice, each coefficient is equal to the sum of the two coefficients immediately above it. For example, 15 (of the bottom row) is equal to $10 + 5$ (of the next row up). There is actually no "bottom" to this "binomial triangle"; the power of $(a + b)$ can be

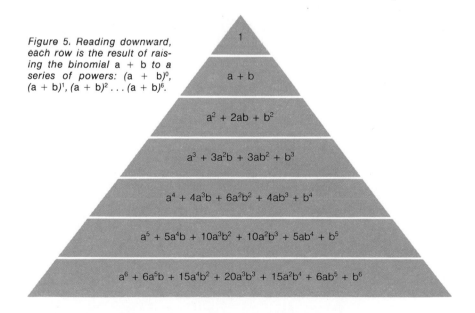

Figure 5. Reading downward, each row is the result of raising the binomial a + b to a series of powers: $(a + b)^0$, $(a + b)^1$, $(a + b)^2$ . . . $(a + b)^6$.

1

a + b

$a^2 + 2ab + b^2$

$a^3 + 3a^2b + 3ab^2 + b^3$

$a^4 + 4a^3b + 6a^2b^2 + 4ab^3 + b^4$

$a^5 + 5a^4b + 10a^3b^2 + 10a^2b^3 + 5ab^4 + b^5$

$a^6 + 6a^5b + 15a^4b^2 + 20a^3b^3 + 15a^2b^4 + 6ab^5 + b^6$

expanded endlessly, as can the progressive pattern of the triangle.

Practical Applications

Let us now refer to Figure 7, where we have put a series of pegs in a shallow box, positioned to imitate the placement of numbers in the binomial triangle (Figure 6). The pegs are just far enough apart so that a small disk will be able to pass between them. We cut out a section of the box's top, as shown; and we built short walls to take the place of the bottom-row pegs, so as to form a series of compartments.

We keep the box in a tilted position so that when a disk is dropped through the gap at the top, it will make its way through the maze of pegs to one of the bottom compartments. Now we drop 64 disks one by one into the box through the gap. We can expect that half of the disks that hit a peg will fall to the left of it and the other half to the right. Hence 32 disks should drop to the left of peg A and 32 to the right of peg A. Of the 32 that fall to the left and strike peg B, 16 should fall to the left of B and should strike peg D; 16 should fall to the right of peg B and should hit peg E. Of the 32 disks that hit peg C, 16 should strike peg E and 16 should strike peg F. That means that 32

disks in all will hit peg E. We can indicate how the disks should fall on their way to the bottom compartments by the diagram in Figure 8.

As we have seen, 32 disks should strike peg B in the second row and 32 should strike peg C. The ratio (comparison of amount) of 32 and 32 is 1-1. In the third row, 16 should strike D; 32 should strike E, and 16 should strike F. The ratio of 16, 32, and 16, is 1-2-1. Going down the rows, the ratios of the disks striking the different pegs would be 1-3-3-1 in the fourth row, 1-4-6-4-1 in the fifth row, and 1-5-10-10-5-1 in the sixth. The disks in the seventh row would follow the distribution 1-6-15-20-15-6-1. Note that these ratios all correspond to the binomial coefficients of Figure 6.

In an actual experiment, the disks will not fall exactly as we have indicated. Some compartments will have one or two more than the number predicted. Others will have one or more less. Yet in every case, the result will be *nearly* that which was forecast. If the experiment is repeated over and over again, in a great number of trials, the number in each compartment will agree more and more closely with the expected number. Thus the coefficients of the binomial sequence provide an effective means for

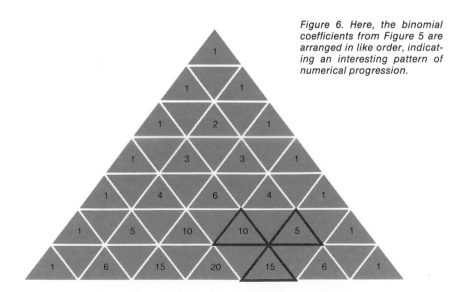

Figure 6. Here, the binomial coefficients from Figure 5 are arranged in like order, indicating an interesting pattern of numerical progression.

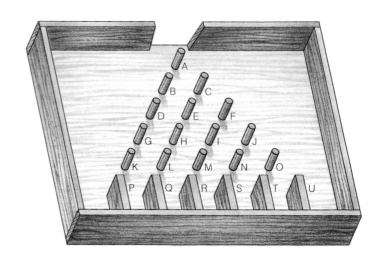

Figure 7. The pegs labeled A, B, C, D, E, and so on are positioned so as to imitate the placement of the numbers in Figure 6. The short walls replace the bottom-row pegs, so as to form compartments.

Figure 8. If we drop 64 disks, one by one, in the box shown in Figure 7, they will make their way down the pegs as indicated here. The ratios of the disks hitting the pegs in each row (right) reproduce the triangle in Figure 6.

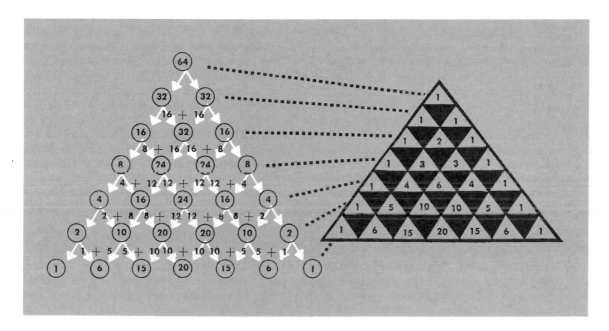

calculating *probabilities* or likelihoods, when the chances of an event occurring are even.

For determining probabilities when the chances are not even, other algebraic analyses have been made. The subject that deals with such analyses is called *statistics,* and its applications are both practical and far-reaching. An insurance company can, for example, use statistics to predict with fair accuracy life expectancies and how much in premiums and interest it will col-

lect during the lifetime of an insured person. To make insurance work, the company must collect enough to be able to pay the insurance when the client dies. Probability and compound interest, as developed by algebra, are therefore the bases on which insurance is built. Thus algebra, which began by examining the relations of arithmetic operations, has become an interpreter of our experience and a guide for the future.

Howard F. Fehr

PLANE GEOMETRY

When we pass from arithmetic and algebra to geometry, we enter a world of shapes occurring in space—a world of points, lines, surfaces, and solids. We study the properties of these shapes and the relations between them. We learn to measure them. At the outset, geometry was used to solve specific problems, but in the course of its development it became a thoroughly abstruse subject. However, this abstruse branch of mathematics can often be put to practical use, as we shall see.

The beginnings of geometry go back far into prehistory. As the population of a given region grew, the natural dwelling places available did not suffice. It became necessary to build shelters, big enough to house families and strong enough to withstand winds, rain, and storms. To make a shelter the proper size, a person had to compare lengths. Thus the roof had to be higher above the ground than the top of the head of the tallest person.

The ancient Babylonians were pioneers in this branch of mathematics. The land between the Tigris and Euphrates rivers, where the Babylonians dwelt, was originally marshland. Canals were built to drain the marshes, and to catch the overflow of the rivers. For the purposes of canal construction, it was necessary to survey the land. In so doing, the Babylonians developed rules for finding areas. These rules were not exact, but the results they gave sufficed for canal construction.

In Egypt, the people who had farms along the banks of the Nile River were taxed according to their holdings. In the rainy season, the river would overflow its banks and spread over the land, washing away all landmarks. It became necessary, therefore, to remeasure the land so that each owner would have his rightful share.

After the floods had subsided, specially trained men, called "rope-stretchers," would establish new landmarks. They would use ropes knotted at equal intervals so that they could measure out desired lengths and divide the land into triangles, rectangles, and trapezoids.

They devised practical rules for the areas of these figures. The rules were of the rough-and-ready variety and were often inexact. We know today, for example, that the area of any triangle is one-half the product of its *altitude* (height) and its base. The Egyptians erroneously gave this area as one-half the product of the base and a side. However, most of the triangles used in their surveying work were long and narrow (Figure 1), and in such triangles there is not too much difference in length between the long side and the altitude. Hence the results of the Egyptians' calculations served as a pretty fair basis for the allotting of land and the taxation of landowners.

Geometry Becomes a Discipline

The Greeks called the early Egyptian surveyors *geometers,* or "earth-measurers" (from the Greek *ge:* "earth," and *metria:* "measurement"). The geometers

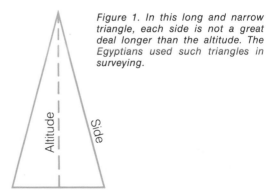

Figure 1. In this long and narrow triangle, each side is not a great deal longer than the altitude. The Egyptians used such triangles in surveying.

found out many facts about triangles, squares, rectangles, and even circles. These facts became a body of knowledge that the Greeks called *geometry,* or "the study of the measurement of the earth." Geometry today involves much more than it did at that early stage; yet it is still concerned with the sizes, shapes, and positions of things.

The Greeks made important advances in the field of geometry. They not only corrected many of the faulty rules of the Egyptians, but also studied the different geometrical figures in order to work out relationships. Thales, a Greek mathematician who lived 2,500 years ago, discovered that no matter what diameter is drawn in a circle, it always *bisects* the circle, that is, cuts it into two halves (Figure 2). He also noticed that if two straight lines cross each other, the opposite angles are always equal, no matter at what angle the lines cross (Figure 3). This was the beginning of the study of figures for the sake of discovering their properties rather than for practical use. The Greeks changed geometry from the study of land measurement to the study of the relations between different parts of the figures existing in space, which is what geometry means today.

After Thales, other Greek mathematicians discovered and proved facts about geometric figures. They also devised various instruments for drawing figures. By custom, the only instruments allowed in the formal study of geometry were an unmarked *straightedge,* (ruler) for drawing straight lines and a *compass* for drawing circles and transferring measurements (Figure 4).

The Greeks proposed various construction problems, to be solved with only the straightedge and the compass. Among these problems were the following: **(1)** *squaring the circle,* or constructing a square whose area exactly equals that of a given circle; **(2)** *duplicating the cube,* or constructing a cube whose volume will be exactly twice the volume of a given cube; and **(3)** *trisecting the angle,* or constructing an angle equal to exactly one-third of a given angle. For over 22 centuries, mathe-

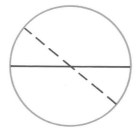

Figure 2. Each of the two diameters shown in the drawing cuts the circle into halves.

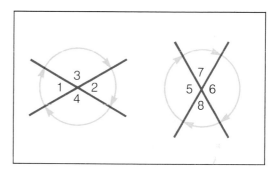

Figure 3. If two lines cross, the opposite angles are always equal. In the examples shown, angle 1 = angle 2; angle 3 = angle 4; angle 5 = angle 6; and angle 7 = angle 8.

Figure 4. By custom, the ancient Greeks used only an unmarked straightedge and compass in presenting and solving geometry problems.

maticians attempted to solve these problems, without success. Finally, in the 19th century, it was proved that it is impossible to square the circle, duplicate the cube, or trisect an angle if one uses only the straightedge and compass. It is possible, however, to make these three constructions with specially designed instruments. Such constructions fall in the domain of higher geometry.

Euclid: The Organizer of Geometry

By the 4th century B.C., there had grown up a vast body of facts concerning geometric figures, but for the most part these facts were unrelated. There were many theorems about triangles and circles, some about similar figures and areas, but no orderly arrangement. The learned Greek mathematician Euclid, who taught at the Museum of Alexandria, in Egypt, about 300 B.C., was the first man to apply a logical development to the mathematical knowledge of his time. He presented this development in his *Elements of Geometry*.

Euclid realized that it is not possible to prove every single thing we say and that we must take certain things for granted. He assumed that everybody knows and uses properly such words as "between," "on," "point," and "line"; hence it is not necessary to define them. He used these undefined terms to give definitions of various figures. Thus he defined a circle as "the set of all points that lie the same distance from a fixed point called the center." Again, Euclid noted that one cannot prove certain statements of relations between geometric figures; for example, "Only one line can be drawn between two points." (In geometry, the term "line" implies a "straight line that extends without end in both directions.") Euclid called such statements "common notions." Today we call them *postulates*.

Euclid used undefined terms, definitions, and postulates to prove *theorems* about geometric figures. A theorem is a statement that gives certain facts about a figure and that concludes from these facts that a certain other fact must be true. A typical theorem is "If two sides of a triangle are equal, the angles opposite these sides must be equal" (Figure 5). This theorem states two facts: There is a triangle and two sides of the triangle are equal. It then draws the conclusion that two of the angles of the triangle are equal. Once a theorem is proved, it can be used to prove other theorems.

Euclid built up a logical chain of theorems that introduced order in what had been a chaos of more or less unrelated facts. Besides organizing a vast body of knowledge about geometric figures, he introduced a method of treatment that became a model for the development of other branches of mathematics and pure science. This method is as valid today as ever.

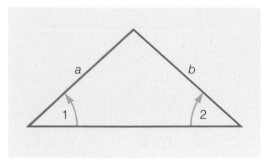

Figure 5. If two sides of a triangle are equal, the angles opposite these sides are equal; that is, if side a = side b, then angle 1 = angle 2.

Two Dimensions

The first branch of geometry we shall consider is *plane geometry*—the study of points, lines, and figures occurring in planes. Just what do we mean by these terms?

A *point* is the simplest element in geometry. It has no length, width, or thickness, which is another way of saying that it has no *dimensions*. We can represent a point by a dot, made with a pencil or a piece of chalk. Such a dot is not a geometric point but a physical point, since it has length, width, and thickness, however small these dimensions may be. In geometric constructions, we have to use physical points, such as pencil dots, to represent geometric points, because it would be impossible for us to set down on paper a point with no dimensions.

A *line*, like a point, is considered an undefined term because it can be represented (as in a drawing) but can be described only in relation to other geometric elements. If we consider a single point and ask how many lines can pass through it, the answer would be "an *infinite* (unlimited) number." But if we ask how many lines can pass through two distinct points, the answer will be, as Euclid determined, "exactly one line." The shortest distance *between* any two points is a *line segment*. A line segment is a portion of a line that is bounded by two points, or *endpoints*; it has only one dimension: *length*. It does not have width and thickness; hence, when we draw a line segment in constructing a geometric figure, we are again giving a physical representation of a geometric element.

If we were confined to a world having only one dimension, such as length, we would have a rather dull time of it. We would be points on a line, being able to move only forward and backward and always bumping into points ahead of us or behind us. In Figure 6, points A and B and segment CD are all parts of the line shown in the figure and must always stay within the line.

Suppose now that we selected a point P outside the line. Line segments drawn from point P to the original line create a series of figures existing in a *plane* (Figure 7). A plane is a surface having the two dimensions of length and width. The surface of a tabletop is a plane. A continuation of the surface would represent part of the same plane. If we were points in a two-dimensional world, we could move freely in any direction, except out of the plane. Our world would have other points like ourselves, and also lines. There would also be a great variety of figures made up of combinations of points and lines—figures such as triangles, squares, circles, and so on.

Angles in Plane Geometry

The name *ray* is given to the part of a line that starts at a given point. A plane figure formed by two rays having the same starting point is called an *angle*. In Figure 8, AB and BC are two rays with the same starting point, B. The angle formed by the two rays is ABC. You will note that in the expression "angle ABC," the "B" is between "A" and "C," indicating that "B" represents the point that the two rays share. That is how angles are always indicated.

If two lines meet so that all the angles formed are equal, the lines are said to be *perpendicular* and the angles are called *right angles*. In Figure 9, line AB is perpendicular to line CD and the four angles (AEC, BEC, AED, and BED) are all equal. If we draw a circle about point E, its length, called its *circumference,* can be divided into 360 equal units, called *degrees* and

Figure 6. Points A and B and segment CD are parts of this line and must always stay within the line.

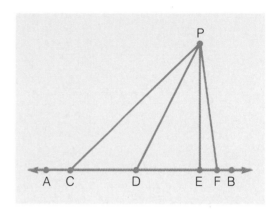

Figure 7. Lines drawn from point P to the line AB create a number of figures (such as PCD) all of which lie in a single plane.

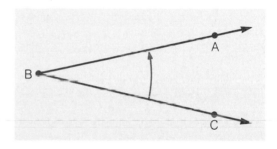

Figure 8. AB and BC are two rays having the same starting point, B. They form angle ABC.

written with the symbol °. The parts of the circle labeled IG, GH, HF, and FI are called *arcs*. (An arc is simply a portion of a circle's circumference.) Each of these arcs has 90° since the circumference of the circle is divided into four equal parts by lines AB and CD. The angle at the center of the circle has the same number of degrees as the arc it cuts off on the circle. Hence each of the four angles here has 90°; in other words, a right angle has a measurement of 90°.

If an angle is less than a right angle (that is, if it has less than 90°) it is called *acute*. It is *obtuse* if it is greater than a right angle (that is, if it has more than 90°). When

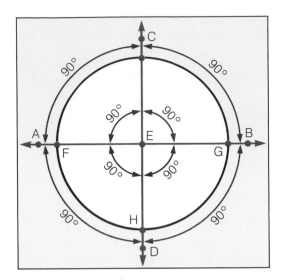

Figure 9. Lines AB and CD are perpendicular to each other; the angles at E are right angles, each having 90°. The arcs cut off on the circle by the intersection of AB and CD each have 90°.

the obtuse angle becomes so large that its sides form a straight line, it is a *straight angle* and has 180°. An angle larger than a straight angle (that is, more than 180°) is called a *reflex angle*. Figure 10 shows these different kinds of angles. Angles can be measured by the instrument called the *protractor*. It consists of a *semicircle* (half a circle) divided into 180 parts, each part representing one degree of angle at the center (Figure 11). As we shall see, angles play an all-important part in the study of geometry.

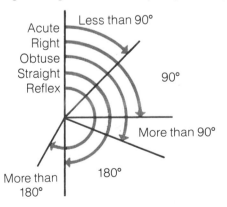

Figure 10. Angles are classified into groups and are named according to size, from acute to reflex.

The Study of Triangles

When three line segments connect three points in a plane, they form a *triangle*. Figure 12 shows examples of the three different kinds of triangles that can be made. There are literally thousands of theorems about the sides, angles, and lines in triangles.

One of the first theorems proved in plane geometry is "If three definite lengths are given, such that the sum of any two

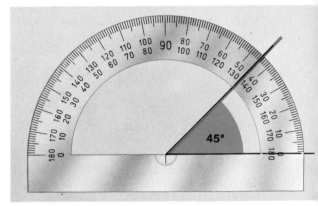

Figure 11. Angles are measured by a protractor.

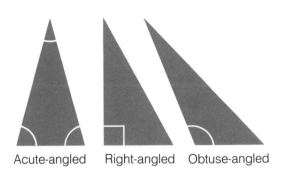

Acute-angled   Right-angled   Obtuse-angled

Figure 12. Three kinds of triangles.

Figure 13. If any two of the line segments 1, 2, and 3 are added, their sum will be greater than the third. Therefore, segments 1, 2, and 3 can be joined to form a distinct triangle.

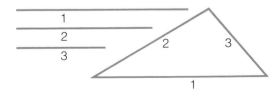

lengths is greater than the third length, it is possible to use the lengths in making a triangle that will have a definite size and shape" (Figure 13). Since the shape never varies, a construction built in the form of a triangle will be rigid and will not "give." Because of this property, interlocking triangles are used in bridge and building designs to prevent structural collapses. A figure of four sides, each of a definite length, could have many different shapes. As shown in Figure 14, such a construction would be collapsible. Hence it cannot be used in rigid construction unless it is braced by a *diagonal* (see Figure 15). Each diagonal makes two triangles of a four-sided figure, and each of these triangles is rigid.

The most famous and perhaps the most important theorem in plane geometry is one dealing with a *right triangle* (a triangle with a right angle). It is called the *Pythagorean theorem*, after its discoverer, the Greek philosopher Pythagoras, who lived in the 6th century B.C. This theorem states that "in a right triangle, the sum of the squares of the *legs* (the two sides that form the right angle) is equal to the square of the *hypotenuse* (the side opposite the right angle)." In right triangle ABC in Figure 16, the sides *a, b,* and *c* are 3, 4, and 5 units, respectively, side *c* being the hypotenuse. According to the Pythagorean theorem, $a^2 + b^2 = c^2$; in this case, $3^2 + 4^2 = 5^2$, or $9 + 16 = 25$. We verify this by constructing, from each side of the triangle, an actual square, the sides of which are equivalent in unit length to the corresponding triangle side. Therefore, as shown in Figure 16, square ABED, for instance, consists of the number of square units represented by a^2. So the sum of square units in square ABED (9) added to those in square BCGF (16) should, and does, equal the number of square units in square ACHI (25).

Figure 17 shows how the squares on the legs of a right triangle can be cut up so as to form the square on the hypotenuse. This is another confirmation of the Pythagorean theorem.

It follows from this theorem that if a triangle has sides such that the sum of the squares of the two shorter sides is equal to

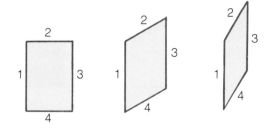

Figure 14. In these four-sided figures, the sides marked 1 are all equal; so are the sides marked 2, those marked 3, and those marked 4.

Figure 15. The four-sided construction is braced with diagonal BD, making two rigid triangles.

Figure 16. A construction such as this proves the Pythagorean theorem.

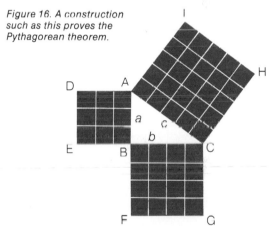

Figure 17. The two squares on the sides of a right triangle can be cut up and rearranged to form the square on the hypotenuse.

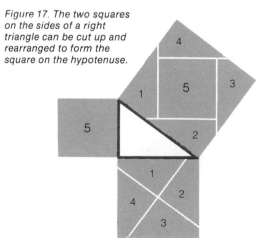

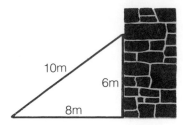

Figure 18. If the wall is perpendicular to the floor, the triangle will fit snugly.

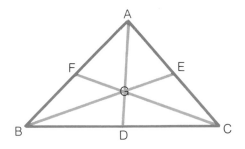

Figure 19. Here, D, E, and F are the midpoints of sides BC, AC, and AB. Note that the three lines CF, BE, and AD meet at G.

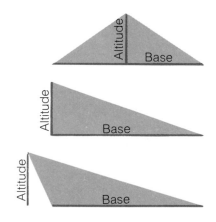

Figure 20. These three triangles have equal bases and altitudes. Hence the areas of the triangles are also equal.

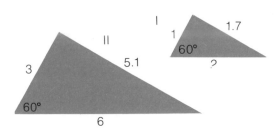

Figure 21. Triangles with equal corresponding angles are similar.

the square of the longest side, the angle opposite the longest side is a right angle. This theorem has various practical applications. The carpenter uses it to see whether a wall is perpendicular to the floor. If, for example, boards of 6, 8, and 10 meters are joined together, as shown in Figure 18, the angle formed by the 6- and 8-meter lengths must be a right angle, since $6^2 + 8^2 = 10^2$, or 36 + 64 = 100. If the wall is truly perpendicular to the floor, the triangle will fit snugly.

The Pythagorean theorem is one of many that reveal an unexpected and important relationship. Here is another instance of such a theorem: In triangle ABC in Figure 19, D, E, and F are the *midpoints* of sides BC, AC, and AB, respectively. Points A, B, and C are the *vertexes* of the triangle. (A vertex is a point at which two sides of a plane figure intersect.) If we connect vertex A to the midpoint, D, of the opposite side, BC, the line segment AD is called a *median*. When we draw the two other medians, CF and BE, we learn that these three medians pass through the same point G, inside the triangle. By measuring, we would also learn that point G, on any of the medians, is two-thirds the distance from the vertex to the opposite side. Plane geometry offers proofs of these statements. Here is another interesting fact about G: If we cut out a triangle of cardboard and draw the three medians, as in Figure 19, we can balance the triangle on the blunt end of a pencil if we put this end directly under G. This point is called the *center of gravity*.

Equal and Similar Triangles

When triangles have the same size, or area, they are called *equal triangles*. All triangles with equal bases and altitudes are equal although they may have many different shapes (Figure 20). Some triangles have the same shape, but are different in size. They are known as *similar triangles*. The corresponding angles of similar triangles are equal and their corresponding sides are always in the same ratio. The two triangles in Figure 21 are similar because the corresponding angles are equal. Each side of triangle II is 3 times as great as the corresponding side of triangle I.

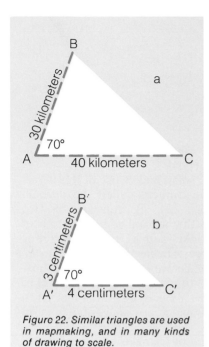

Figure 23. If we double the length of the sides of triangle X, producing triangle Y, the area of Y will be four times as great as the area of X. The area of triangle Z is nine times as great as that of X.

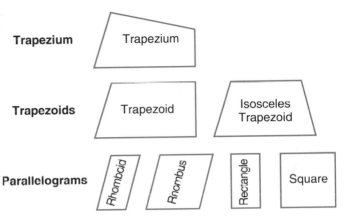

Figure 22. Similar triangles are used in mapmaking, and in many kinds of drawing to scale.

Figure 24. The three basic types of quadrilaterals, or four-sided figures.

Similar triangles are used in drawing to scale. In making a map, for example, we represent a large area of land on a small piece of paper. Suppose site A in Figure 22a is 30 kilometers from site B and 40 kilometers from site C and that the angle CAB is 70°. We are to show these sites on a map, where the scale is to be 1 centimeter = 10 kilometers. First, using a protractor, we draw a 70° angle. To reduce the 40-kilometer distance between A and C to our given scale, we divide 40 kilometers by 10 kilometers/centimeter to get a distance of 4 centimeters, which is the length we draw on our map from point A′, along the corresponding ray of our 70° angle, to endpoint C′. We follow the same procedure for the distance from A to B, which is reduced from 30 kilometers to 3 centimeters and is measured between A′ and B′ along the other ray of the 70° angle. Joining points B′ and C′, we have a proportional representation (Figure 22b) of the triangular area formed by the three sites.

Accurate maps, models, and photographs are similar to the original objects they represent. Hence the angles in such representations are exactly the same as in the originals, and all lines are changed in the same ratio. Their areas also will have a definite ratio, ratios that are the squares of the side-length ratios. For example, if we double each of the sides of a triangle, the area will be 4 times as great. If we triple each of the sides, the area will be 9 times as great. Figure 23 shows that this is so.

If photographic film 1-centimeter square is projected on a screen so that the picture on the screen is 40-centimeters square, the projection is 40^2, or 1,600, times as large as the original. The light used in projecting the film must cover 1,600 times as much area as the film; hence its intensity on the screen is only 1/1,600 as great as the film. This is a striking illustration of the manner in which the geometry of similar figures can be applied to the study of photographic phenomena.

Quadrilaterals

A figure with four sides is called a *quadrilateral*. As shown in Figure 24, there

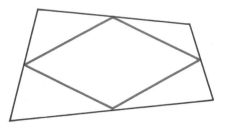

Figure 25. In any quadrilateral, the inner figure formed by joining the midpoints of the sides is a parallelogram.

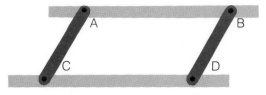

Figure 27. Parallel rulers.

are three basic types of quadrilaterals: the *trapezium,* which has no parallel sides; the *trapezoid,* which has exactly one pair of parallel sides; and the *parallelogram,* with two pairs of parallel sides. The *isosceles trapezoid* is a trapezoid whose two nonparallel sides, or legs, are equal. A *rhomboid* is a parallelogram with no right angles and with only opposite sides equal. A *rhombus* is a parallelogram with four equal sides. A *rectangle* is a parallelogram with four right angles. A *square* is a rectangle with four equal sides (which means a square is also defined as a rhombus with four right angles). In any quadrilateral, the connected midpoints of the sides will create an inner quadrilateral that is a parallelogram (Figure 25).

In a parallelogram, the diagonals bisect each other, no matter how we distort the figure (Figure 26). This is a good example of an *invariant,* a property of a figure that remains true under all distortions. Another invariant is "The opposite sides of a parallelogram are equal."

The draftsman makes use of this invariant in the instrument called the *parallel rulers* (Figure 27). It consists of two straightedges that are joined by two rods of equal length (AC and BD). This device is flexible; hence AB can be at varying distances from CD. However, no matter how AB is moved, it always remains parallel to CD. Using this device, a parallel to a given line can be drawn at any accessible point in a plane.

The study of triangles and quadrilaterals forms much of the subject matter of geometry. All other *polygons* (closed figures having three or more angles and therefore sides) can be divided into triangles and quadrilaterals by drawing diagonals from the vertexes of the polygon. This then means that the basic rules for determining the perimeter and area of triangles and quadrilaterals can be applied to the study of other polygons.

Figure 26. The corresponding sides of these parallelograms are equal. The diagonals of both bisect each other.

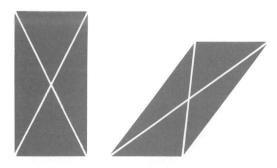

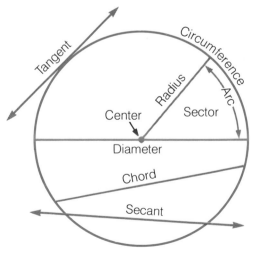

Figure 28. Principal elements related to a circle.

The Circle

A *circle* (see Figure 28) is defined as the set of points in a plane that are a given distance (the *radius*) from a given point (the *center*). A *chord* is a line segment that joins any two points on a circle. A *diameter* is a chord that passes through the circle's center and is actually two radii (the plural of "radius") that form a straight line. A *secant* is a line that *intersects* (or cuts off) a circle at two points. A tangent is a line that intersects a circle at exactly one point. A sector is a region bounded by an arc and the two radii that run to the arc's endpoints. To find the circumference of a circle, we use the formula $c = \pi d$, where c is the circumference, d is the diameter, and π represents a constant number approximately equal to 3.1416. To find a circle's area, we use $A = \pi r^2$, where A is the area and r is the radius.

Any diameter creates two semicircles. A simple and quite surprising theorem involving a semicircle is this: "If any point on a semicircle is joined to the ends of the diameter, an angle of 90° is formed at the point." In Figure 29, AB is the diameter and P is a point anywhere on the semicircle. It is easy to prove that angle APB is 90°: First connect P to the center of the circle (O). Line segments AO, PO, and OB are all radii of the circle and are, therefore, equal. In triangle APO, since AO = PO, the two angles marked $x°$ are equal because "if two sides of a triangle are equal, the opposite angles must also be equal." Likewise, in triangle OPB, PO and OB are equal, and so the angles marked $y°$ must be equal. Ignoring line segment PO, we have triangle APB, whose angles must total 180° because "the sum of the angles of a triangle is 180°." There are two $x°$ angles and two $y°$ angles in triangle APB; hence one $x°$ angle and one $y°$ angle must give half of 180°, or 90°. Since angle APB is composed of an $x°$ angle and a $y°$ angle, it must be equal to 90°; it must be a right angle.

There are various applications of this theorem. For example, a patternmaker can determine if the core box shown in Figure 30 is a true semicircle. He places a device called a "carpenter's square" in the box. If

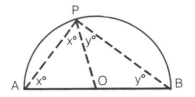

Figure 29. If point P on the semicircle is joined to the diameter at A and B, angle APB will be 90°.

Figure 30. Determining by means of a carpenter's square whether a core box gives a true semicircle.

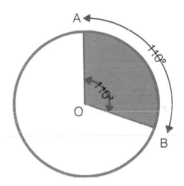

Figure 31. Both the angle at O and the arc that it intercepts (AB) are equal to 110°.

it makes firm contact at three points, as shown, he knows that the pattern will give a true semicircle.

An angle at the center of a circle has as many degrees as the arc that it intercepts on the circle: "A *central angle* is measured by its intercepted arc." In Figure 31, the obtuse angle at center point O is equal to 110°; the arc AB it intercepts is also equal to 110°.

An angle whose vertex is on the circumference of a circle and that intercepts an arc is called an *inscribed angle* (see

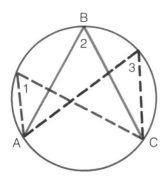

Figure 32. The angles 1, 2, and 3 intercept the same arc (AC) in this circle; therefore they are equal.

angle ABC in Figure 32). No matter where we place the vertex in arc AC's intercepting angle, the angle will remain the same size. In other words, "all inscribed angles intercepting the same arc are equal."

The Path of a Moving Point

It is often necessary in plane geometry to determine the path that a point describes in a plane when it moves according to a fixed rule. If, for example, a moving point must always remain 3 centimeters from a fixed point, it travels in a circle around the fixed point. The mathematician gives the name *locus* (Latin for "position") to the path described by a point. By studying the paths of moving points, we determine how machine parts move and how heavenly bodies appear to move.

We can illustrate the use of the locus by a very simple treasure-hunt problem, as illustrated in Figure 33. A treasure is re-

ported to be buried in a spot *equidistant* (equally distant) from two intersecting roads and also 20 meters west of an oak tree. To find its location in relation to the tree, we think of the tree as the center of a circle with a 20-meter radius; the treasure lies somewhere on that circle's circumference. To find the treasure's location in relation to the two roads, we think of it as a moving point remaining at the same distance from each road. Because the roads intersect, forming an angle, we use the following theorem: "If a point moves so as to be equidistant from the rays of an angle, it will trace a line that bisects that angle." Hence the treasure must be on a line bisecting the angle made by the two roads. This line cuts the circle, as shown, at two places, T and G. The treasure must be at one of these two points. Of the two points, point T is the one west of the tree and must be the location of the treasure.

Machines that are designed to trace moving points are called *linkages* because they consist of linked bars. A compass, which is essentially a movable pair of hinged-together rigid legs, is the simplest linkage; the path it traces is a circle. Another linkage, called Peaucellier's Cell, changes circular motion into straight-line motion (Figure 34). As A in the figure moves around the circle, the point B moves up and down the straight line CD. There are other types of linkages that transform circular motion into linear motion. A study of linkage was necessary to help solve the problem of providing smooth motion in a

Figure 33. To find a treasure 20 meters from a tree and equally distant from two roads, use a locus.

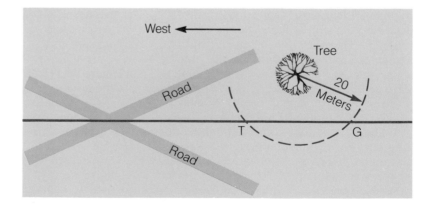

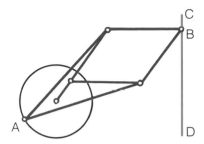

Figure 34. Peaucellier's Cell changes circular motion to straight-line motion. It is a type of linkage.

locomotive, where the straight-line motion of the drive shaft had to be converted into the circular motion of the wheels.

Conic Sections

The circle is the most common type of curve, but there are other kinds. The Greek geometers noticed very early that when a cone was cut by planes at different angles, the intersections gave different kinds of curves: circles, ellipses, parabolas, and hyperbolas collectively known as *conic sections* (Figure 35). The Greek mathematician Apollonius, who lived in the 3rd century B.C., wrote a treatise on the properties of these curves. In more recent times, it was discovered that they could also be defined as paths made in a plane by points moving according to certain rules. Such definitions are particularly meaningful when we put the curves to practical use.

An *ellipse* is the path traced by a point that moves so that the sum of its distances from two fixed points is always the same. The two fixed points are called *focuses,* or *foci.* It is easy to draw an ellipse, using the method illustrated in Figure 36. First we

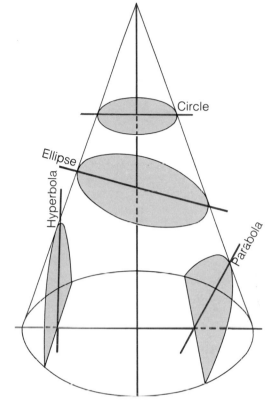

Figure 35. Conic sections—circle, ellipse, parabola, and hyperbola—produced as planes cut a cone.

insert thumbtacks at two fixed points, F_1 and F_2. We then take a piece of string that is larger than twice the distance between F_1 and F_2 and tie the ends together to make a loop. We attach the loop of string to the thumbtack at F_1 and to the thumbtack at F_2 (Figure 36). We draw the string taut with the point of a pencil (Figure 36), and as we move the pencil, its point will trace an

Figure 36. It is easy to draw an ellipse, using two thumbtacks and string, as shown here.

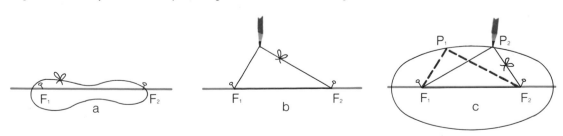

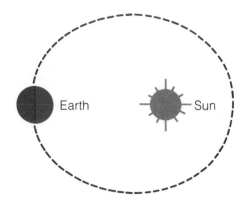

Figure 37. As the Earth travels around the Sun, its orbit is an ellipse, with the Sun at one focus.

ellipse (Figure 36). The sum of the distances from the moving pencil point to the fixed points will remain constant: in Figure 36, $g + h = j + k$.

If a billiard table were elliptical in shape, any ball hit from one focus would rebound through the other focus. In an elliptical room, any sound issuing from one focus will be reflected by the wall to the other focus. This is the principle of the "whispering gallery." The elliptically shaped Mormon tabernacle in Salt Lake City, Utah, is an example. The foci in the tabernacle are clearly marked. A person standing at one focus can distinctly hear a whisper coming from a person at the other focus; those standing nearby hear nothing.

The ellipse has found many practical applications. Power punching machines use elliptical gears. At the narrow ends of the ellipse, the gears move faster, giving a quick return. At the flat parts, the gears move slower, exerting a greater force. Storage tanks and transportation tanks are made elliptical in cross section so as to lower the center of gravity and to lessen the danger of overturning.

The ellipse also serves to explain the movements of various heavenly bodies. All the planets move in elliptical orbits with the Sun at one focus (Figure 37). A planet moves along the orbit so that the radius from the Sun to the planet sweeps through equal areas in the same time. Knowing the elliptical orbit of any planet, astronomers can predict the position of the planet in its orbit at any time.

A *parabola* is the path of a point that moves so that its distance from a fixed line, called the *directrix*, always equals its distance from a fixed point, or focus. Thus, in Figure 38, as a point moves along the parabola, occupying positions P_1, P_2, P_3, and P_4 in turn, $a = b$, $c = d$, $e = f$, and $g = h$. A reflecting searchlight has a parabolic surface with the light source at the focus. All light beams emanating from the focus are reflected from the parabola in parallel rays (Figure 39). Sound detectors have parabolic surfaces. Sound waves are reflected

Figure 38. As a point moves along a parabola, its distance from the directrix equals its distance from the focus.

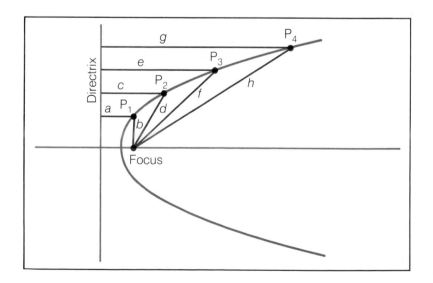

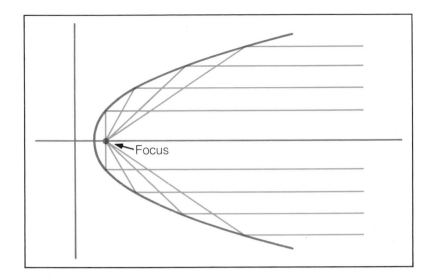

upon striking the surface and are concentrated at the focus. The mirror of a reflecting telescope is in the form of a parabola. Parallel rays of light from a distant heavenly body strike the parabolic surface and, reflected from it, meet at the focus within the telescope tube.

A *hyperbola* is the path of a point moving so that the distance to one fixed point minus the distance to another fixed point is always the same. The diagram in Figure 40 shows a hyperbola in which F_1 and F_2 are the fixed points, or foci, and P_1 and P_2 are

Figure 40. Here, P_1 and P_2 are two positions of a point moving along a hyperbola. The distance to F_1 minus the distance to F_2 always equals the distance between A_1 and A_2.

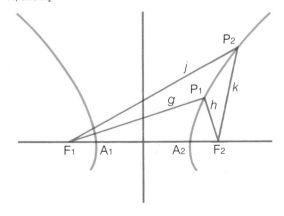

points on the hyperbola. Therefore, $g - h = j - k$, which is equivalent to the distance between A_1 and A_2.

The hyperbola is applied to the Loran (*long range navigation*) system by the use of radar. We can give a general explanation of Loran by referring again to Figure 40: Suppose there are two radar stations, F_1 and F_2, located on land 300 kilometers apart. Electric pulsations are sent out from each station. It takes longer for such pulsations to travel from F_1 to P_1 than from F_2 to P_1, and longer from F_1 to P_2 than from F_2 to P_2. The difference in time is a fixed constant for all points on the hyperbola. If the difference in time is greater or less, we have a different hyperbola.

A ship has a radar device that picks up the differences in time between the pulsations from the two stations. The navigator consults a map upon which are drawn the various hyperbolas corresponding to the various differences in time. He consults the map and locates his own ship on the hyperbola. The hyperbola passing through the "home port" is then picked out, and the difference in the time of the pulsations is noted. The course is changed, until the radar receiver indicates that the ship is on the home-port hyperbola. The difference in pulsations is kept constant and the ship sails home along the hyperbola.

Howard F. Fehr

SOLID GEOMETRY

The two-dimensional world of plane geometry does not suffice to explain the world in which we live—a world of three dimensions. In it, there are many planes, which are boundless and extend in every conceivable direction. There are also many kinds of curved surfaces. We must consider not only north, south, east, and west but also up and down. To explain this three-dimensional world, the branch of mathematics called *solid geometry* has been developed. We use this kind of geometry in building machines, skyscrapers, airplanes, steamships, bridges, and automobiles and also in explaining the phenomena of the universe.

In solid geometry, there are many more possible relationships between geometric elements than in plane geometry. In a single plane, two lines are always either parallel or intersecting. In solid geometry, two lines may be parallel or intersecting, but they may also be *skew lines*. Skew lines are not in the same plane, are never parallel, and never intersect. Only one line, in a plane, can be drawn perpendicular to another line at a given point. In solid geometry, any number of such perpendicular lines can be drawn. For example, the spokes of a wheel are segments of lines, every one of which is perpendicular to the axle at the same point. In a plane, all points at a fixed distance from a fixed point are on a circle. In three-dimensional space, however, they are on a *sphere* containing an infinite number of circles passing through the center.

Angles in Solid Geometry

The simplest angle in solid geometry is called a *dihedral* ("two-faced") *angle*. It is formed by two intersecting planes. The size of this angle is measured by the *plane angle*. This is formed by two lines, one in each face, meeting the edge, or intersection of the two planes, at right angles (Figure 1). When an airplane *banks* (laterally tips), the angle of bank is a dihedral angle between the horizontal and tipped position of the wings (Figure 2). The dihedral angle is measured by an instrument in the airplane, and the size of this angle determines in part the speed with which the airplane will change its direction of travel.

When three planes meet at a point, they form a *trihedral angle* (Figure 3). Each of the angles making up a trihedral angle is called a *face angle*. In Figure 3, ADC, CDB, and ADB are all face angles. If more than three planes meet in a point, the angle is called a *polyhedral* (many-faced) *angle*. The sum of the face angles of a polyhedral angle must be less than 360°. As the sum of the face angles gets closer to 360°, the polyhedral angle becomes less pointed until, at 360°, it becomes a plane (Figure 4). The crystals of minerals show many kinds

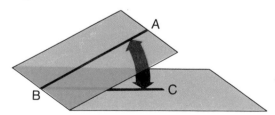

Figure 1. Two intersecting planes form a dihedral angle. Angle ABC, between the planes, is called the plane angle.

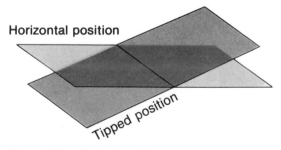

Horizontal position

Tipped position

Figure 2. The dihedral angle between the horizontal and tipped positions of an aircraft's wing is the angle of bank.

of polyhedral angles. An analysis of these angles makes it possible to identify the various minerals.

Five Common Solids

The major part of the study of solid geometry is based on five common solids: the prism, the cylinder, the cone, the pyramid, and the sphere. (Much of the terminology used in solid geometry originates in the study of plane geometry; therefore, it may be helpful to review the article "Plane Geometry" before proceeding.)

The prism. In a prism, the bases, of which there are exactly two, are parallel and equal polygons. The number of sides to a prism's base is equal to the number of its side faces, or *lateral faces,* which are always parallelograms. When the lateral faces of any prism are perpendicular to the bases, that prism is called a *right prism* (Figure 5). A prism is generally named for the shape of its bases. For example, the bases of a *hexagonal prism* are two equal *hexagons* (six-sided figures) and, therefore, intersect with six lateral faces. A *square prism* has two square bases and four lateral faces. When the lateral faces of a square

prism are also square, the prism is called a *cube* and all six faces are equal squares.

To find the area, or surface measure, of a prism, we must first calculate the area of each lateral face. Because any lateral face on a prism is a parallelogram, we use the formula for all parallelograms:

$$A = bh$$

where A is the area, b is the length of any base, and h is the height (or *altitude*) as measured perpendicular to b. The sum of the areas of the lateral faces is called the *lateral area,* and when it is added to the areas of the bases, the result is the *total area* of the prism. The interior of a room is often a rectangular prism. By calculating lateral and total areas, painters, wallpaperers, and remodelers can reasonably estimate the amounts of materials needed for any particular project.

The *volume,* or space-filling measure, of a prism is found by multiplying the area of the base by the altitude of the prism. This calculation is very important in the building of a house. Most builders estimate the construction cost as so much per *cubic unit* (the standard unit of volume). To estimate how much it will cost to build a particular house, we must first find the total volume of the prisms of which the house

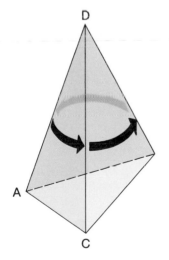

Figure 3. When three planes meet at a point, they form a trihedral angle.

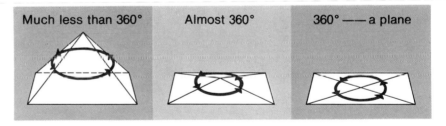

Figure 4. A series of polyhedral angles. As the sum of the face angles becomes greater, the polyhedral angle becomes less and less pointed. At 360° it is a plane.

Figure 5. The prisms shown here are known as right prisms because their bases are at right angles to their sides.

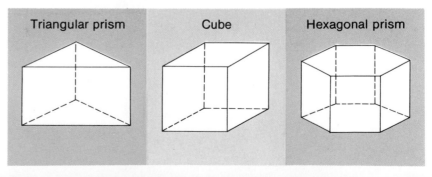

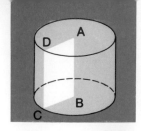

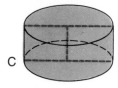

Figure 6. If rectangle ABCD is rotated about side AB, it will mark the boundaries of a cylinder, which will have AB as its axis.

Figure 7. If the height of cylinder A is doubled and the base remains the same, as in B, the volume is doubled. If the height remains the same and the diameter is doubled, as in C, the volume of the cylinder is increased fourfold.

will consist. If the volume in question is 800 cubic meters and the builder gives an estimate of $60 per cubic meter, the cost will be approximately 800 × $60, or $48,000.

The cylinder. If one rotates a rectangle completely about one of its sides, as in Figure 6, it will *define* (mark the boundaries of) the solid called a cylinder. A cylinder is comprised of two flat, circular bases and one curved, lateral surface. The line segment that joins the centers of a cylinder's bases is called the *axis*. An ordinary soup can is a good example of a cylinder; it is specifically a *right cylinder,* in which the axis is perpendicular to the bases. The other classification of cylinders is the *oblique cylinder,* in which the axis is nonperpendicular to the bases.

The lateral area of a right cylinder is $2\pi rh$, in which π (pi) is approximately 3.1416, r is the radius of the base, and h is the height of the cylinder. Suppose that a

canning company needs to know how much metal is required to make a particular size can. In other words, the company wants to know the total surface area of the can, which is determined by adding the lateral area to the areas of the bases (the area of a circle being πr^2).

The volume of a cylinder is found by multiplying the area of the base by the height of the cylinder, or $V = \pi r^2 h$. If the height of a cylinder is doubled and the diameter remains the same, its volume will also be doubled. You can see that this is so by placing one can on top of another just like it. If, however, the height of a cylinder remains the same and the diameter of the base is doubled, its volume will increase fourfold (Figure 7).

It is important to find the volume of a cylinder in computing the capacities of steel cans, gas-storage tanks, water reservoirs, and so on, and also in determining the rate of flow and pressure in pipes containing liquids. To see whether the economy size of a product sold in cans provides a real bargain, calculate the volume of the regular size and that of the economy size and then compare the two. Suppose the regular size can is 12 centimeters tall and has a base with a diameter of 8 centimeters. Suppose the economy-size can is also 12 centimeters tall and has a base with a diameter of 12 centimeters. The regular size costs $1.00, and the economy size $1.50. The problem is this: Will we save money if we buy the economy size? Knowing that $V = \pi r^2 h$, we find the volume of the regu-

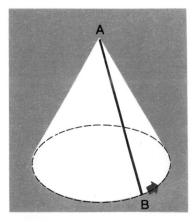

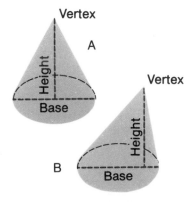

Figure 8. Point A is held fixed while point B follows a circular path. A cone is formed.

Figure 9. Cone A is a right cone. Cone B is an oblique cone.

Figure 10. The frustum of a right cone.

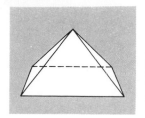

Figure 11. A pyramid with a square base is called a square pyramid.

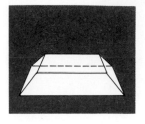

Figure 12. The frustum of a square pyramid.

lar can by substituting 4 for *r* (the radius is half the diameter) and 12 for *h*. Using 3.14 as the value of π, we get 3.14 × 16 square centimeters × 12 centimeters = 602.88 cubic centimeters. The volume of the economy can is 3.14 × 36 square centimeters × 12 centimeters = 1,356.48 cubic centimeters. By dividing 1,356.48 by 602.88 we learn that the economy can holds 2¼ times as much as the regular can. Since the economy can costs only 1½ times as much as the regular, it is, indeed, a bargain.

The cone. A cone is formed by holding one point of a line fixed and rotating the line, following a circular path (Figure 8). The line segment that joins the fixed point to the center of the circular base is the axis of the cone. If the axis is perpendicular to the base, the cone is a *right cone*; a nonperpendicular axis is part of an *oblique cone*. The height of any cone is the perpendicular distance from the vertex to the base. In a right cone, the height is equal to the length of the axis (Figure 9). The formula for the volume of a cone is $V = \frac{1}{3}\pi r^2 h$, where *r* is the radius of the base and *h* is the height of the cone.

When the top of a cone is cut off by a plane parallel to the base, the lower part is called a *frustum* (Figure 10). Many machine parts are in the form of cones or frustums of cones.

The pyramid. In the solid called the pyramid, the lateral faces are triangles whose vertices meet at a common point and whose bases form a polygon. Like a prism, a pyramid is generally named for the shape of its base (Figure 11). The Great Pyramid of Egypt is a *square pyramid.* So is the ancient Egyptian *obelisk* known as "Cleopatra's Needle." The formula for the volume of a pyramid is $V = \frac{1}{3}Bh$, where *B* is the area of the base and *h* is the height of the pyramid.

Like a cone, when the top of a pyramid is cut off by a plane parallel to the base, the lower part is called a frustum (Figure 12). Army squad tents and coal hoppers, among other things, have the shape of the frustum of a pyramid. To calculate the volume of a frustum, a rather complex formula is required. Yet there is evidence that the ancient Egyptians had an exact formula for making such a calculation. They used it in determining the amount of granite required to build sections of their pyramids.

The sphere. If a semicircle is rotated about a diameter (Figure 13), the solid defined is a sphere. When the sphere is cut by a plane, the intersection is a circle. Figure 14 shows various circles formed in this way. If the plane passes through the center of the sphere, the circle of intersection has the same radius as the radius of the sphere. Such a circle is called a *great circle.* All the other circles are *small circles.*

The earth may be considered a sphere in which the north and south poles are the ends of a diameter called the axis (Figure 15). The circles passing through both the north and south poles are great circles. They are known as *circles of longitude.* All the planes (except one) that cut the earth at right angles to the axis form small circles, called *circles of latitude.* There is just one plane that passes through the center of the earth and is at right angles to the axis. It forms the great circle called the *equator.*

Between any two points on the earth (not including the poles) only one great circle can be drawn. All other circles passing through the two points will be small circles. The shortest of all the arcs between the two points is the arc of the great circle (Figure 16). Pilots of aircraft, as far as possible, steer a course determined by the arc of a great circle between their starting points and destinations.

If we think of the earth as a rubber ball and cut this ball along one half of a circle of longitude, we can stretch the ball to form a flat rectangular sheet. The circles of longitude will then become parallel vertical lines and the circles of latitude parallel and equal horizontal lines (Figure 17). This sheet now represents a rectangular map of the world. A map of this type is called a *Mercator projection,* after the 16th-century

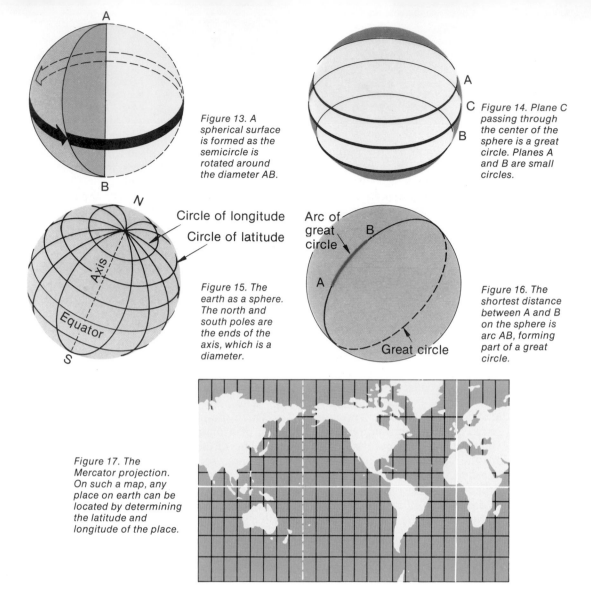

Figure 13. A spherical surface is formed as the semicircle is rotated around the diameter AB.

Figure 14. Plane C passing through the center of the sphere is a great circle. Planes A and B are small circles.

Circle of longitude

Circle of latitude

Figure 15. The earth as a sphere. The north and south poles are the ends of the axis, which is a diameter.

Arc of great circle

Great circle

Figure 16. The shortest distance between A and B on the sphere is arc AB, forming part of a great circle.

Figure 17. The Mercator projection. On such a map, any place on earth can be located by determining the latitude and longitude of the place.

Flemish geographer Gerardus (or Gerhardus) Mercator, who developed it. The great longitudinal circle passing through Greenwich, England, is given the value of 0° longitude. The equator is given the value of 0° latitude. On such a map, any place on earth can be located by determining the longitude and latitude. Also on such a map, the farther we go from the equator, the more we find the original area stretched, so that land areas near the poles seem much larger on the map than they really are on the earth. Users of the map must take such distortions into account.

Figure 18. Three sets of similar solids. Here, the linear dimensions of the larger figures are exactly twice that of the smaller.

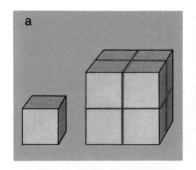

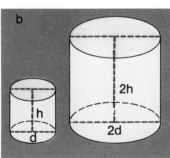

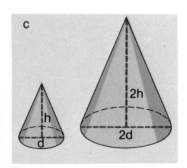

The surface area of a sphere is four times the area of a great circle; the formula is $4\pi r^2$. The earth's radius is approximately 6,380 kilometers; hence the total surface of the earth is $4 \times \pi \times (6{,}380$ kilometers$)^2$, or about 511,000,000 square kilometers.

The volume of a sphere can be expressed by the formula $(4/3)\pi r^3$. The volume of the earth, therefore, is $4/3 \times \pi \times (6{,}380$ kilometers$)^3$, or slightly over 1 trillion cubic kilometers.

Characteristics of Similar Solids

Solids that are of the same shape but of different sizes are said to be *similar*. The corresponding polyhedral angles of similar solids are equal, and the corresponding lines are in proportion.

The areas of similar solids have the same ratio as the squares of the corresponding linear parts. In each of the sets of similar solids in Figure 18, the surface area of the larger figure is 2^2, or 4, times the surface area of the smaller, because the linear parts are 2 times as large. If the linear parts were enlarged 3 times, the area would be 3^2, or 9, times as great.

The volume of similar solids has the same ratio as the cubes of the linear parts. In each of the sets of similar solids in Figure 18, the larger figure has 2^3, or 8, times the capacity of the smaller figure. In the case of the cubes in Figure 18a, you can count 8 small cubes in the larger cube.

The ratio of areas and volumes of similar solids has many practical applications. All spheres are similar. If oranges 8 centimeters in diameter sell for 30 cents a dozen, while oranges 10 centimeters in diameter sell for 50 cents a dozen, which would be the better buy? The volume ratio of a large orange to a small orange is as follows:

$$\left(\frac{10}{8}\right)^3 = \frac{1{,}000}{512} = 1.953$$

The large oranges are a better buy, then, because they have nearly twice the volume for less than twice the cost.

Use in Astronomy

Solid geometry has enabled astronomers to give a useful interpretation of the

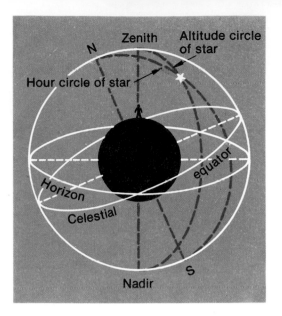

Figure 19. A simplified diagram showing the celestial sphere. Earth is the center of the sphere.

heavens and to calculate the distances and positions of the celestial bodies. The universe is conceived of as a huge *celestial sphere* with an infinitely great radius, which *appears* to revolve around the earth. Figure 19 gives a greatly simplified presentation of such a sphere as seen from the vantage point of a person stationed at latitude 50°. This person stands on a much smaller sphere, which of course is the earth. Directly overhead is the *zenith*; directly below is the *nadir*. The line where the sky seems to meet the earth is called the *horizon*. If the axis of the earth, which passes through the north and south poles, is extended, it will meet the outer bounds of our imaginary celestial sphere at the celestial poles—north and south. The line segment connecting the two celestial poles is the *celestial axis*. The plane of the earth's equator will cut the outer limits of the celestial sphere in a great circle called the *celestial equator*. A great circle passing through the poles and a star is the *hour circle* of the star. The *altitude circle* of the same star is a great circle passing through the zenith and the star.

These are but some of the features of the celestial sphere. They provide a frame of reference that enables the astronomer to trace the motions of celestial objects. This is one of the outstanding contributions of solid geometry to science.

Howard F. Fehr

TRIGONOMETRY

An important offshoot of geometry is *trigonometry,* or triangle measurement. In trigonometry, when certain parts of triangles are known, one can determine the remaining parts and thus solve a great variety of problems.

The founder of trigonometry was the Greek astronomer Hipparchus, who lived in the 2nd century B.C. Hipparchus attempted to measure the size of the Sun and the Moon and their distances from Earth. He felt the need to develop a new type of mathematics that, by applying measurements made on Earth, would enable him to measure objects far out in space. He was thus led to the invention of trigonometry.

Boy and Girl Scouts have occasion to use trigonometry in their field work. A common problem that is put to them is to find the height of a tree. The scout first measures a distance, say 20 meters, from the base of the tree, as shown in Figure 1. This will be the *baseline.* At point A, he or she measures the angle from the ground to the treetop by means of a *protractor.* Let us suppose that this angle is 35°. The scout now knows three facts about the triangle formed when points B (the base of the tree), A (the end point of the line segment drawn from the tree), and C

(the top of the tree) are connected: (1) side AB = 20 meters, (2) angle BAC = 35°, and (3) angle ABC = 90°. (To accurately ascertain angle ABC, we assume that the line segment representing the tree's height, BC, is perpendicular to the ground.)

Then, a smaller triangle similar to the one in the field is drawn. To begin, the scout makes a line segment A´B´ 0.5 meter long, and at A´, draws an angle of 35°— angle B´A´D´—with a protractor. Next, he or she erects a perpendicular to segment A´B´ at B´. This line will intersect A´D´ at C´, and the angle A´B´C´ will be a right angle. The corresponding angles of the large and small triangles are equal: angle CAB = angle C´A´B´; angle ABC = A´B´C´; angle ACB = A´C´B´. Hence, we now have two similar triangles, and the corresponding sides will be proportionate.

The scout now measures side B´C´ and finds that it is 35 centimeters, or 0.35 meter. Since the sides of the similar triangles are proportional, AB is to A´B´ as BC is to B´C´. We know all these quantities except BC, which we can call x. We now have the proportion 20 is to 0.5 as x is to 0.35, which we can write as 20 : 0.5 :: x : 0.35. In any proportion, the product of the *extremes* (the two outer terms) is equal to the product of the *means* (the two inner terms):

$$0.5x = 20 \times 0.35$$
$$0.5x = 7$$
$$x = 14$$

Figure 1. The problem is to find the height of the tree when the angle at A (35°) and the distance AB (20 meters) are known. We show how to solve the problem by means of similar triangles ABC and A´B´C´.

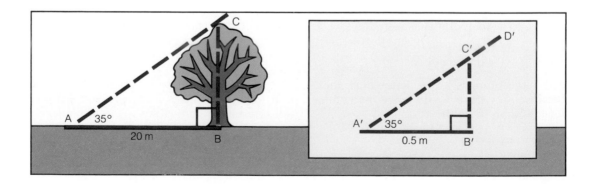

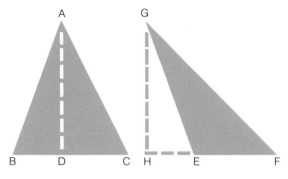

Figure 2. Any triangle can be converted into right triangles by drawing a perpendicular from the vertex to the base.

The height of the tree, then, is 14 meters. By knowing one side and one acute angle of a right triangle, the scout was able to use basic trigonometry to solve the problem.

Trigonometric Functions

Trigonometry is based on the use of the right triangle. It can be applied to any triangle because by drawing an *altitude* (a perpendicular from the vertex to the base) we can always convert it into right triangles. In Figure 2, for example, the altitude AD divides the triangle ABC into the right triangles ADB and ADC; the altitude GH converts the triangle GEF into right triangles GHF and GHE.

Certain basic ratios or relationships between the sides of a right triangle are the very heart of the study of trigonometry. Among these ratios are the sine, cosine, tangent, and cotangent. To understand what these terms mean, let us draw a typical right triangle with angles X, Y, and Z

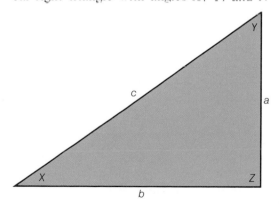

Figure 3. A typical right triangle with the hypotenuse labeled c, and legs a and b.

and sides a, b and c (Figure 3). Angle Z is a right angle; the other two angles are acute angles. Side c, which is opposite the right angle, is the hypotenuse. Sides a and b are called legs. We can now define sine, cosine, tangent, and cotangent as follows:

The *sine* of either of the acute angles is the ratio of the opposite leg to the hypotenuse. The sine of angle X is a/c; the sine of angle Y is b/c.

The *cosine* of either of the acute angles is the ratio of the adjacent leg to the hypotenuse. The cosine of angle X is b/c; the cosine of angle Y is a/c.

The *tangent* of either of the acute angles is the ratio of the opposite leg to the adjacent leg. The tangent of angle X is a/b; the tangent of angle Y is b/a.

The *cotangent* of either of the acute angles is the ratio of the adjacent leg to the opposite leg. The cotangent of angle X is b/a; the cotangent of angle Y is a/b.

A sine, cosine, tangent, or cotangent of an angle is said to be a trigonometric function of that angle because its value depends upon the size of the angle. A given trigonometric function, such as the sine, is always the same for a given acute angle in a right triangle. In Figure 4, for example, angle BAC of right triangle ABC is 30°. This means that angle ABC must be 60° since angle ACB is 90° and the sum of the

Figure 4. Equal angles, such as BAC and B'A'C' shown here, have equal sines.

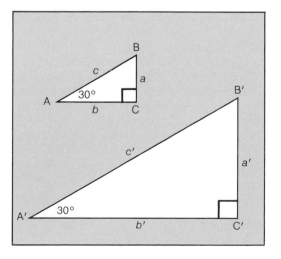

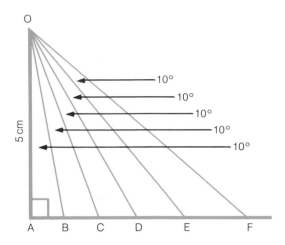

Figure 5. This diagram can be used to determine the tangents of certain angles, as discussed in the text.

interior angles of any triangle is 180°. Angle $B'A'C'$ of right triangle $A'B'C'$ is 30° and Angle $A'B'C'$ must be 60°. Hence the corresponding angles of the two triangles are equal, and the corresponding sides must be in the same ratio. Since this is so, a/c, (the sine of angle BAC) and a'/c' (the sine of angle $B'A'C'$) must be equal. Hence the sine of 30° is always the same no matter how large or how small the right triangle in which it occurs.

Problem Solving

Mathematicians have worked out the values of the trigonometric functions. By way of example, the sine of 40°, to five decimal places, is 0.64279; its cosine, 0.76604; its tangent, 0.83910; its cotangent, 1.1918. To give some idea of how such figures are derived, let us examine the procedure for finding out the tangents of different acute angles. You will recall that the tangent of an acute angle in a right triangle is the ratio of the opposite leg to the adjacent leg.

In Figure 5, side OA is equal to exactly 5 centimeters. Each of the small angles at O is equal to exactly 10°. Angle BOA, therefore, is 10°; angle COA, 20°; angle DOA, 30°; and so on. We now measure AB and find that it is about 0.9 centimeters. Since the tangent of angle BOA is $\dfrac{AB}{OA}$ and since OA = 5, the tangent of the angle is approximately $\dfrac{0.9}{5}$, or 0.18. This is the tan-

gent of the angle 10°, whether the side OA is a centimeter, a meter, or a kilometer. Measuring AC, AD, AE, and so on in turn, we can find the tangents of 20°, 30°, 40°, and so on.

The values of the trigonometric functions can be found in almost any book of mathematical tables and are now one-key operations of many hand-held calculators. Knowing such values, we can work out a variety of measurements with great ease. Let us return to the Boy Scout's problem in Figure 1. We know that AB = 20 meters and that angle CAB = 35°. Because BC (the height of the tree) is our unknown, we will call it x. Therefore, the tangent of angle CAB = $x/20$ meters. Using a table or a calculator, we find that the tangent of 35° = 0.7; so, 0.7 = $x/20$ meters. Multiplying both sides of the equation by 20 meters, we find that x = 14 meters.

In the foregoing problem, the unknown quantity was a part of the tangent ratio. In other trigonometric problems, the cotangent, sine, or cosine might be involved. In still other cases, the unknown quantity might be an angle, as in the following problem.

The cable car in Figure 6 is going up a uniform slope, rising 12 meters in a horizontal distance of 30 meters. What is the angle (x) of the slope? Solving for the tan-

Figure 6. The cable car rises 12 meters in a horizontal distance of 30 meters. What is the angle (x) of the slope?

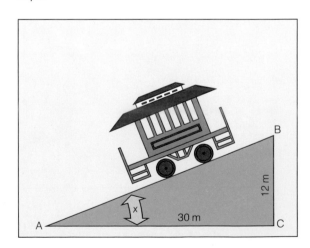

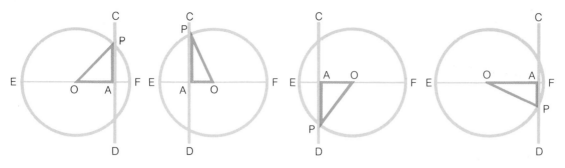

Figure 7. As radius OP goes around the circle in a counterclockwise direction, it makes a series of triangles with the diameter of the circle and with the rod CD kept in a vertical position at the end of the radius.

gent of *x,* we get $\frac{12}{30} = 0.4$. Consulting the table of trigonometric functions, we learn that 0.4 is the tangent of a 22° angle (to the nearest degree); therefore, the angle of the slope is approximately 22°.

The surveyor makes extensive use of trigonometry. First, the surveyor tries to get a fixed line that has no obstruction so that it can be measured fairly accurately. This becomes the baseline, from which numerous calculations can be made. Other measurements, as far as possible, are measurements of angles. Trigonometry is also of vital importance in engineering, navigation, mapping, and astronomy.

Studying Periodic Phenomena

Trigonometry is used in still other ways. For one thing, it serves in the study of various *periodic phenomena.* Any phenomenon that repeats itself in regular intervals of time is called periodic. The tides, for example, are periodic since they rise and fall in regular sequence. The motion of a pendulum bob is also periodic. Let us show how we can describe all periodic phenomena in terms of the sine of an angle.

We know that the spoke of a moving wheel sweeps through 360° as it makes a complete turn. It repeats the same sweep in the second complete turn, in the third complete turn, and so on. Obviously such rotation is periodic. The spoke of a wheel is really the radius of a circle. We can analyze the motion of the radius around the center of the circle by examining the diagrams in Figure 7. We are to suppose that a rod, CD, is kept in a vertical position at the end of the radius as the latter moves around the circle. You will note that a series of right angles is formed as the rod

maintains its vertical position. The line segment AP, joining the points where CD meets the circumference of the circle and the diameter EF, grows longer and then shorter. Angle POA, which is called the *angle of rotation,* also changes as the radius goes around the center of the circle. The hypotenuse of right triangle APO is the radius OP and, therefore, never changes length. If we give OP the value unity (that is, 1), AP will represent the sine of the angle of rotation (POA) since the sine of

$$POA = \frac{AP}{OP}.$$

Let us now analyze the different sine values of the angle of rotation as the radius sweeps around the circle. Sine values above the diameter are expressed as positive values. Values below the diameter are negative values. In Figure 8a, the sine is zero, corresponding to a zero angle of rotation. The sine continues to grow as the radius revolves around the center (b) until it reaches the value 1 in c (when the radius OP forms a 90° angle with the horizontal diameter, the sine = 1). The sine becomes smaller (d) until it reaches zero again in e. The radius continues to rotate below the diameter, where the sines are of negative values. The sine decreases (f) until it reaches the value −1 in g (when the radius OP forms a 270° angle with the horizontal diameter, the sine = −1). The sine becomes greater (h) until, after a complete 360° rotation (i), it becomes zero again.

We can show the variation in the sine by the line graph in Figure 9. Within the circle, we label the different values of the sine (PA) as P_1A_1, P_2A_2, and so on. When the positive and negative sine values are "removed" from the circle and plotted separately, the result is a *sine curve,* which will

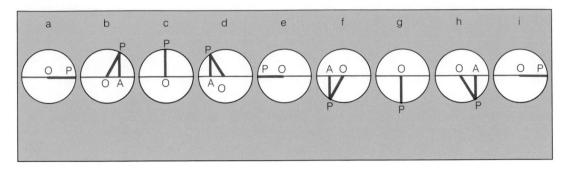

Figure 8. As the radius OP sweeps around the circle, the sine values vary along with the angles of rotation.

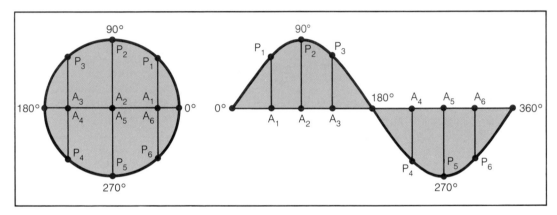

Figure 9. Variations in sine value are shown here by means of a graph. The different values of the sine PA are given here as P_1A_1, P_2A_2, P_3A_3, and so on. The curved line at the right of the circle is known as a sine curve.

repeat itself every 360°. Each fluctuation between the minimum and maximum values of a sine curve is called an *oscillation*.

The sine curve can be applied to, among other things, the periodic phenomena of sound. For example, when a tuning fork is struck, its vibration results in sound waves being sent out. If, immediately after being struck, a tuning fork that gives a tone of middle C is drawn very rapidly over a sheet of paper covered with soot (Figure 10), the vibration will describe a very specific repeating sine curve: In one second, 264 complete oscillations will be produced; middle C always corresponds to 264 vibrations per second, which can also be expressed by saying that middle C has a *frequency* of 264 *hertz*. Suppose we strike a

tuning fork that gives a tone one *octave* (an 8-degree interval between tones) higher than middle C and draw it over the paper as before. In this case, 528 vibrations will occur in one second, which means that the frequency is exactly twice that of middle C.

Sine curves of various amplitudes and frequencies are used to explain phenomena of electricity, light (both polarized and plane), and force, as well as those of sound. Thus trigonometry helps to explain and control our physical environment.

Figure 10. Sine waves made by a vibrating tuning fork as it was passed rapidly over a sheet of paper covered with soot.

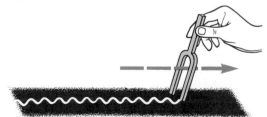

ANALYTIC GEOMETRY

Analytic geometry explains geometric figures in terms of algebraic formulas. From the earliest times, algebra and geometry had been studied as separate subjects. No one had seriously considered before the 11th century that numbers could be used to represent a point or line, or that a geometric figure could serve to represent the value of a number.

One of the first to try to combine algebra and geometry was the 12th-century Persian poet and mathematician Omar Khayyám. He wrote a work on algebra that was clearly influenced by earlier Arab and Greek writings. In this work, Omar showed how to solve algebraic equations by the use of squares, rectangles, and cubes. For example, for a number multiplied by itself, as in $x \times x$, he would use a square, each side of which had a length equal to the value of x. If x were equal to 5, each side of the square would be 5 units long, and the square would be made up of 25 units. If a number were to be a factor three times, as in $x \times x \times x$, Omar would use a cube, each side of which had a length equal to x. See Figure 1.

It was because of this method of solving equations that a number multiplied by itself, or "raised to the second power," came to be known more commonly as the *square of the number*. For the same reason, "x^3" represents "x to the third power" but is read more commonly as "x cubed."

Omar Khayyám made no known effort to solve an equation of the fourth degree—that is, an equation containing a term to the fourth power—by the geometrical method. It is likely that few, if any, mathematicians in his day had even an inkling of a fourth dimension. Today, however, the fourth dimension is an accepted and vital concept in modern physics and mathematics.

The pioneering efforts of Omar Khayyám to break down the barriers between algebra and geometry amounted to very little in his lifetime. Five centuries passed before analytic geometry was developed, through which the mathematical relationship between algebra and geometry finally gained the recognition it deserved.

Cartesian Coordinate System

The fundamental idea of analytic geometry was worked out by the great 17th-century French philosopher and mathematician René Descartes, who claimed that the idea came to him in a dream. He presented this new approach to mathematics in his *Discourse on Method* in 1637. In it he introduced a *system of coordinates* (called the "Cartesian" system, after Descartes),

$5 \times 5 = 25$

$5 \times 5 \times 5 = 125$

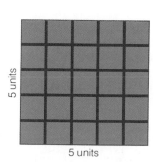

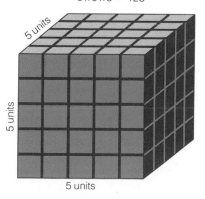

Figure 1. To express a number multiplied by itself, for example 5×5, Omar Khayyám used a square, each side of which was equal to that number of units. To express a number used as a factor three times, as in $5 \times 5 \times 5$, he used a cube.

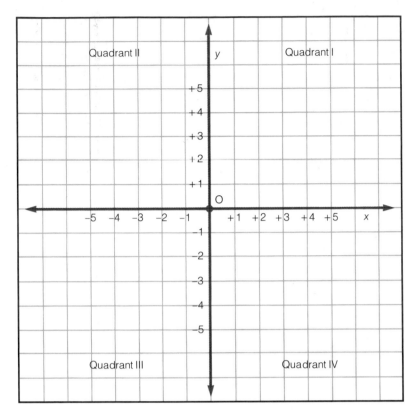

Figure 2. Axes labeled x and y are used to divide a plane into four quadrants. Positive and negative units of distance extend along each axis from the point of intersection, or origin (point O).

by which the location of any point in a plane can be described. Tremendous advances have been made in the study of analytic geometry (also called *coordinate geometry*) since 1637, and the original Cartesian system has been further developed along the way, but the system used

Figure 3. The coordinates of point A are (4, 3) because it is located +4 units along the x-axis and +3 units up, parallel to the y-axis.

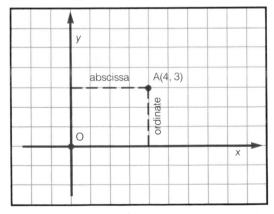

today is essentially that of Descartes. Advancements notwithstanding, the coordinate system is really quite simple and can be explained as follows:

Consider two perpendicular lines, *x* and *y*, as shown in Figure 2. The two lines *x* and *y* are called the *x-axis* and *y-axis*, respectively. The axes divide the plane into four *quadrants*, as labeled in Figure 2. The point of intersection, point O, is called the *origin* and is considered to have a distance value of zero. Units of distance that run along the *x*-axis are positive to the right of the origin and negative to the left of the origin. Units along the *y*-axis are positive above the origin and negative below. Thus, by using this coordinate system, any point in the plane can be described in reference to the *x*- and *y*-axes.

Point A in Figure 3, for instance, is located by counting +4 units along the *x*-axis and +3 units up, parallel to the *y*-axis. The *x*-distance 4 is called the *abscissa* (or *x-coordinate*), and the *y*-distance 3 is called the *ordinate* (or *y-coordinate*). Because the

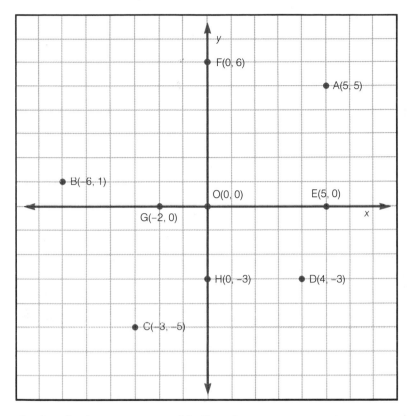

Figure 4. An x and y coordinate in a Cartesian plane can be positive, negative, or zero, depending on its reference to the x- and y-axes.

abscissa is always expressed before the ordinate, point A can be described simply by the ordered pair of numbers, or coordinates, (4, 3).

When Descartes developed his coordinate system, he described points only in the first quadrant. Today we define points in all four quadrants. For any point in a Carte-

Figure 5. For both K and L the value of y is twice that of x. The equation of the line is thus y = 2x.

Figure 6. Any point whose coordinates satisfy the equation y = 2x can be found on line t.

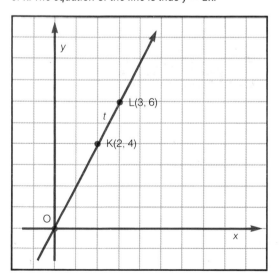

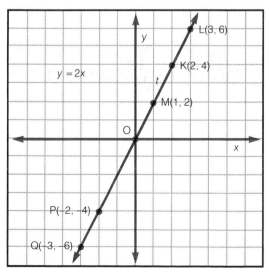

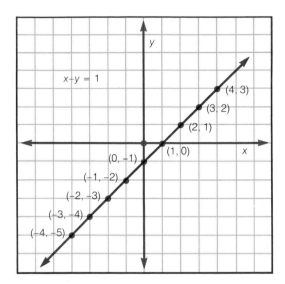

Figure 7. Plotting points from a table based on a line's equation is one way of constructing a graph of the line.

sian plane, the value of each coordinate can be described in exactly one of three ways: positive, negative, and zero. Figure 4 shows examples of each, and from such, certain statements regarding the coordinate system can be made:

1. The abscissa of any point within quadrants I or IV is positive (see points A and D).
2. The abscissa of any point within quadrants II or III is negative (see points B and C).
3. The ordinate of any point within quadrants I or II is positive (see points A and B).
4. The ordinate of any point within quadrants III or IV is negative (see points C and D).
5. The abscissa of any point on the y-axis is zero (see points F, O, and H).
6. The ordinate of any point on the x-axis is zero (see points G, O, and E).
   Note that the origin is always represented by the coordinates (0,0).

The Cartesian coordinate system is particularly valuable because it enables us to analyze a geometric figure described by a *variable* point. ("Variable" here means "able to assume any given value.") If we

think of a point as being able to "move" and thereby "trace out" a figure, we can assign different point coordinates for specific point positions. Under certain conditions, we can write an equation that will hold true for all possible positions of such a point. The equation can then be used in place of the geometric figure that consists of all the positioned points. There are, for example, equations for straight lines, circles, ellipses, parabolas, and hyperbolas.

Graph of a Line

Let us first consider the equation for a straight line, using line t in Figure 5 as an example. To find the equation that defines line t, we determine the coordinates of any two points on the line (excluding any point of intersection with the x- or y-axis). As shown in Figure 5, the coordinates for points K and L are (2, 4) and (3, 6), respectively. You will note that in each instance, the y-coordinate is twice the value of the x-coordinate. Hence the equation of the line t is $y = 2x$.

Knowing this equation, we can use coordinates to locate any point on line t. For example, when $x = 1$ we know that $y = 2 \times 1$, or 2. Translated to coordinates, the point (1, 2) must lie on line t. The values of x and y can be negative as well, as shown in Figure 6. The coordinates of point P, for instance, fit into line t's equation because $2 \times -2 = -4$. Line t, like any line, is a collection of points that continues indefinitely in either direction; the path we draw to represent the line is called its *graph*.

Suppose that the equation of a straight line is given as $x - y = 1$ and that we are required to draw a graph of the line. First, we could set up a table of values for x and y, based on the given equation.

x	4	3	2	1	0	-1	-2	-3	-4
y	3	2	1	0	-1	-2	-3	-4	-5

Once we have set down the x and y values, we can locate the points (4, 3), (3, 2), (2, 1) and so on, as indicated in Figure 7, and we can draw the line connecting the points. This, then, is the straight line indicated by the equation $x - y = 1$.

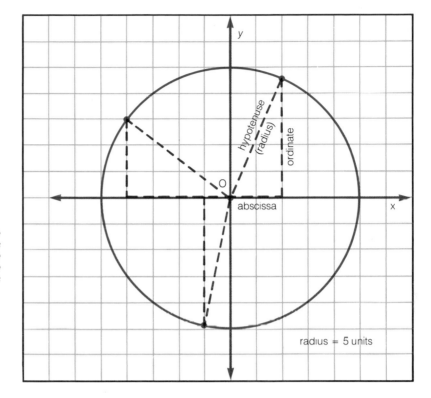

Figure 8. By applying the Pythagorean theorem, as explained in the text, we can determine that the equation of this circle is $x^2 + y^2 = 25$.

hypotenuse (radius)

ordinate

abscissa

radius = 5 units

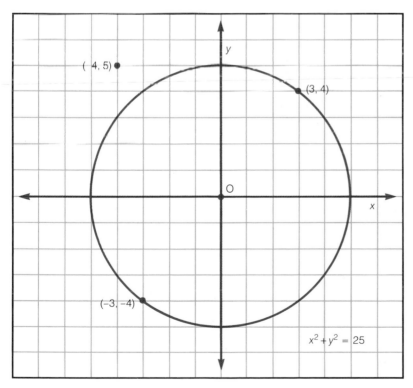

$(-4, 5)$

$(3, 4)$

$(-3, -4)$

$x^2 + y^2 = 25$

Figure 9. Points (3, 4) and $(-3, -4)$ are both on the circle because their co-ordinates satisfy the circle's equation: $x^2 + y^2 = 25$. Point $(-4, 5)$ does not satisfy the equation and is, therefore, not on the circle.

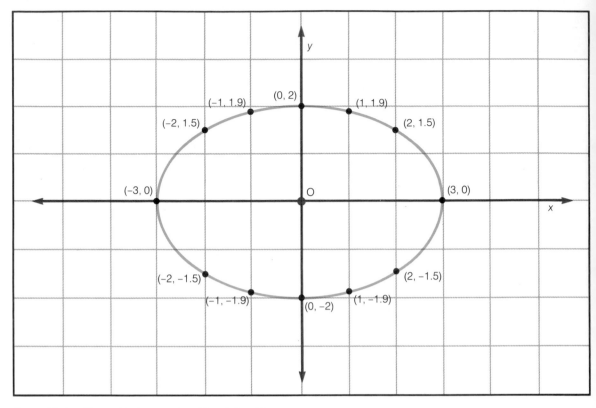

Figure 10. An ellipse with the equation $4x^2 + 9y^2 = 36$.

Graph of a Circle

We can derive the equation of a circle if we apply the Pythagorean theorem (defined in detail in the article "Plane Geometry") to the system of Cartesian coordinates. The Pythagorean theorem states that in a right triangle (a triangle with a right angle), the square of the hypotenuse (the side opposite the right angle) is equal to the sum of the squares of the other two sides.

Let us draw a circle with its center at the origin and with a radius of 5 units (Figure 8). No matter what point on the circle we select, the abscissa along the x-axis, the ordinate, and the radius will form a right triangle, with the radius as the hypotenuse. According to the Pythagorean theorem, in each of the three triangles shown in Figure 8, the square of the abscissa plus the square of the ordinate will be equal to the square of the hypotenuse, that is, 5^2 or 25. In other words, $x^2 + y^2 = 25$ is the equation of the circle in Figure 8.

Suppose we want to see whether a given point is on the circumference of this particular circle. If the sum of the squares of the point's coordinates is equal to 25, the point is on the circle. Consider the point (3, 4), as shown in Figure 9. The sum of 3^2 and 4^2 is $9 + 16 = 25$; hence (3, 4) is on the circumference of the circle. Also on the circumference is $(-3, -4)$, since the sum of -3^2 and -4^2 is also $9 + 16 = 25$. Point $(-4, 5)$, however, is not on the circle, since the sum of -4^2 and 5^2 is $16 + 25 = 41$.

Graph of an Ellipse

Suppose that we are given the information that $4x^2 + 9y^2 = 36$ is the equation of a geometric figure. Let us prepare a graph and see what sort of a figure it is. First, we set up a table of values:

x	0	± 1	± 2	± 3
y	± 2	± 1.9	± 1.5	0

The symbol $\pm$ in the table stands for "plus

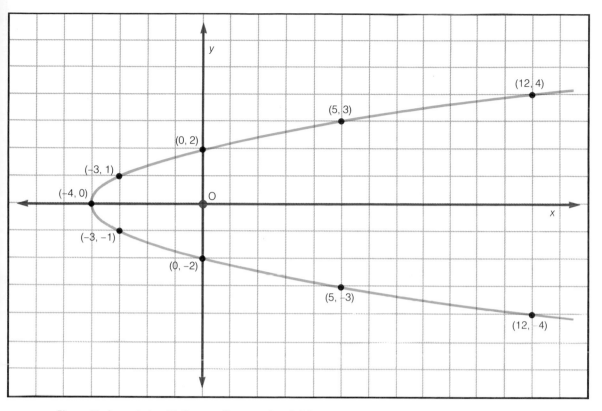

Figure 11. A parabola with the equation $x - y^2 - 4$. It is an open curve.

or minus." For example, 4 is the square of $+2$; it is also the square of -2. Hence a square root of 4 is either $+2$ or -2, or ± 2.

The values in the table are derived as follows. Applying the value $x = 0$ to the equation $4x^2 + 9y^2 = 36$, we have $0 + 9y^2 = 36$; $9y^2 = 36$; $y^2 - 4$; $y = \sqrt{4} - \pm 2$. If x is 1, $4x^2$ in the equation $4x^2 + 9y^2 = 36$ is equal to 4. Then $4 + 9y^2 = 36$; $9y^2 = 32$; $y^2 = 3.6$; $y = \sqrt{3.6} = \pm 1.9$. The other values in the table are derived in the same way.

Let us now locate the points $(0, 2)$, $(0, -2)$, $(1, 1.9)$, $(-1, 1.9)$, $(1, -1.9)$, $(-1, -1.9)$, and the others given in the table, and let us draw a smooth curve to connect these points. As Figure 10 shows, the geometric figure whose equation is $4x^2 + 9y^2 = 36$ turns out to be an ellipse.

Graphs of Open Curves

A typical equation for a parabola is $x = y^2 - 4$, for which we prepare a table of values, as follows:

x	-4	-3	0	5	12
y	0	± 1	± 2	± 3	± 4

If we plot the values $(-4, 0)$, $(-3, 1)$, $(-3, -1)$, $(0, 2)$, $(0, -2)$, and the others given in the table, we have the parabola shown in Figure 11. Since the greater the values of x, the greater the corresponding *absolute values* of y, the parabola is an open curve extending without limit. (An absolute value indicates the magnitude, or "size," of a number without regard for its positive or negative sign.)

A typical hyperbola is $x^2 - y^2 = 4$. To draw a graph of the figure, we first prepare a table of x and y values:

x	± 2	± 3	± 4	± 5	± 6
y	0	± 2.2	± 3.5	± 4.6	± 5.7

When we plot the values given in the table, we obtain a curve with two branches, as shown in Figure 12. The branches extend indefinitely in both directions.

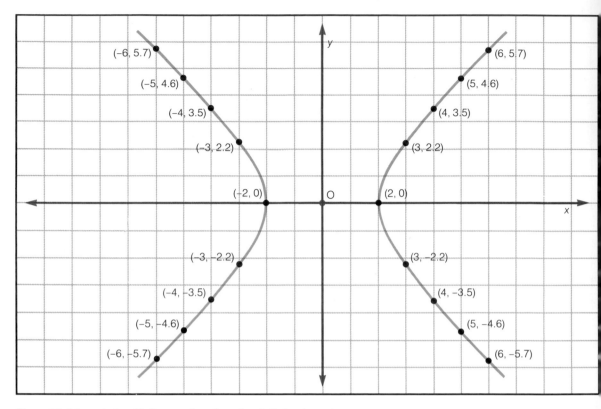

Figure 12. A hyperbola with the equation $x^2 - y^2 = 4$. Its two branches are open curves.

Using the Equations

Equations of geometric figures can be added and subtracted, and many other operations can be performed with them. The equations resulting from such operations can be interpreted by means of graphs drawn up on the basis of x and y values. In this way, algebra can be used to discover geometric relationships. American mathematician Eric T. Bell once said, "Henceforth algebra and analysis [that is to say, analytic geometry] are to be our pilots in the uncharted seas of space and its geometry."

Analytic geometry is often put to practical use. For example, in many towns, gas and water mains can be located by the equations of straight lines using the center of the town as the origin (Figure 13). *Concentric circles* (circles that share the same center) can be used to give zone distances from the center of the town. The intersec-

tions of circles and lines help describe the location of breaks in the mains.

SOLID ANALYTIC GEOMETRY

To locate a point in three-dimensional space, we must give the distance above or below the plane formed by the x- and y-axes. We add a third axis: the *z-axis*, which extends straight up and down (Figure 14). Point A is 6 kilometers east of the origin (x-distance), 8 kilometers south of the origin (y-distance), and 2.5 kilometers up (z-distance). We would locate it by giving the x-, y-, and z-coordinates (6, 8, 2.5). To locate a point in solid analytic geometry, therefore, we need three ordered numbers as our coordinates. In the three-dimensional world, if some point is taken as the origin, any other point in space can be represented by an ordered triplet of numbers and can be definitely located.

In solid analytic geometry, since there are three dimensions, there will be three unknowns to be related in our equations. The equation of a plane is $ax + by + cz = k$, where a, b, c, and k are given numbers. If the coordinates of a point are such that they satisfy the equation of a given plane, the point will be located on the plane. The coordinates of points that are located outside the plane will not satisfy the equation.

The equation of a sphere is $x^2 + y^2 + z^2 = r^2$, r being the radius. It is the extension of the circle equation of plane analytic geometry: $x^2 + y^2 = r^2$. The equation $x^2 + y^2 + z^2 = 25$ represents a sphere whose center is at the origin and whose radius is 5 units long. All the common solids can be represented by an equation or a series of equations with the three unknowns x, y, and z. Solid analytic geometry uses such equations to study the points, lines, surfaces, and solids that exist in space.

HIGHER GEOMETRY

The mathematician is not confined to the analysis of the three-dimensional world, in which an ordered triplet of numbers represents a point. The mathematician

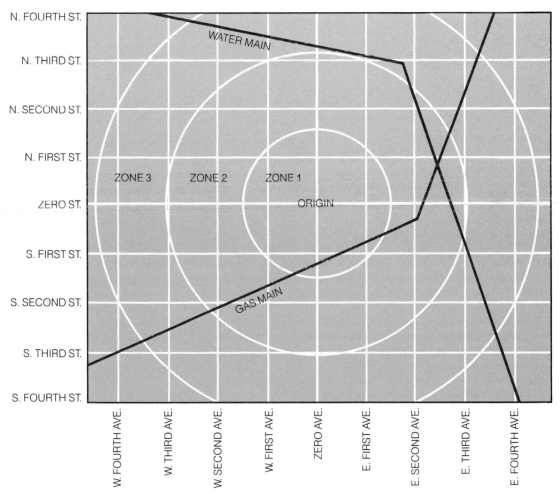

Figure 13. The streets of the town represented here are laid out to form square blocks. Zero St. and Zero Ave. are considered the x- and y-axes; the center of town is the origin. Concentric circles form zones. The geometric relationships between the circles and lines can be used to locate points along the gas and water mains.

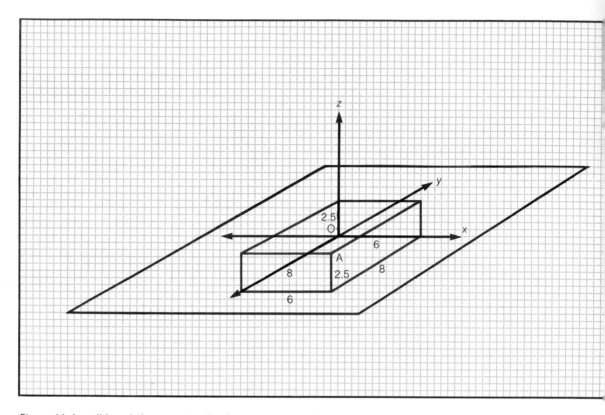

Figure 14. In solid analytic geometry, the three axes x, y, and z, correspond to the three dimensions. Point A, shown here, is 6 kilometers east of the origin, 8 kilometers south, and 2.5 kilometers up.

might ask, "What would an ordered *quadruplet* (foursome) of numbers represent?" One possible answer could be that the coordinates (3, 4, 2, 5), for instance, locate a point in four-dimensional space. The equation $x + y + z + w = 14$ would represent the equation of what our mathematician would call a *hyperplane*; (3, 4, 2, 5) would be a point on this plane. What sort of thing would this hyperplane be? Mathematicians do not know, because they have never seen one. That, however, does not prevent them from working out and using the equation of such a plane and from discovering the properties of the plane by various algebraic operations.

How can one maintain that a four-dimensional world does not exist? Suppose we were two-dimensional creatures living in a two-dimensional world. We would be quite unaware of a three-dimensional world, of which our own limited world would form a part. Yet this three-dimensional world does exist, as we all know. Is it not entirely possible that creatures like ourselves, confined to the best of our knowledge to a world of three dimensions, are really living out our lives in a four-dimensional world, which our senses cannot perceive? It may be, too, that this four-dimensional world is embedded, in turn, in a five-dimensional world, and the five-dimensional world in a six-dimensional world, and so forth. The mathematician finds such speculation fascinating, whether or not it is based on reality.

As a matter of fact, the equations of these higher-dimensional worlds have certain practical applications. For example, the equation of a *hypersphere* (a sphere with more than three dimensions) has been applied in the manufacture of television cathode-ray tubes.

Howard F. Fehr

NON-EUCLIDEAN GEOMETRY

The geometry presented in the articles "Plane Geometry" and "Solid Geometry" and that which is commonly taught in secondary schools is called *Euclidean geometry*. It is so named because it is based on the system established by the Greek mathematician Euclid and taught by him in Alexandria, Egypt, about 300 B.C. He established a logical series of *theorems*, or statements, which were so arranged that each one depended for its proof on (1) the theorems that preceded it and on (2) certain assumptions, or *postulates*. Euclid called these assumptions common notions and he accepted all of them without proof.

In order to prove some of the theorems in the first part of his system, Euclid found it necessary to assume that through a point outside a given line, only one line can be drawn parallel to the given line. He tried hard to prove that this was so, but failed. Finally he had to consider the statement about parallel lines as a common notion, or postulate, which was to be accepted because it was self-evident. The entire system of Euclid depends upon the validity of this particular common notion, which has been called *Euclid's postulate* (Figure 1).

In the centuries that followed, many mathematicians tried to prove that through a point outside a given line, only one line can be drawn parallel to the given line. They were no more successful than Euclid had been. They had to accept Euclid's postulate as self-evident but not proven.

In modern times, not all mathematicians have conceded that the postulate is self-evident. They have felt justified in making different assumptions, and they have built up entire geometries based upon these assumptions. The 19th-century German mathematician Bernhard Riemann based his geometry, called *Riemannian geometry*, on the postulate that no two lines are ever parallel. Another type of geometry was created in the 19th century by the Russian Nikolai Lobachevsky and, independently, by the Hungarian János Bolyai. It was based on the assumption that at least two lines can be drawn through a given point parallel to a given line. The geometries of Riemann and of Lobachevsky-Bolyai are known, therefore, as *non-Euclidean*.

Different Assumptions

To understand the difference between Euclidean and non-Euclidean geometries, let us consider the shortest distance between two points in (1) a *plane*, or flat surface; (2) a *sphere*, or solid circular figure; and (3) a *pseudosphere*, the surface of which suggests two wastepaper baskets joined together at their tops (Figure 2). The shortest distance between two points on any kind of surface is called a *geodesic*.

On a plane, a hemisphere (half of a sphere), and a hemipseudosphere (half of a pseudosphere), we can measure the same distance AB, as shown in Figures 3, 4, and 5. On a plane (Figure 3), the geodesic of

Figure 1. According to Euclid's postulate, one line and only one line, DE, can be drawn parallel to the line AB through point C.

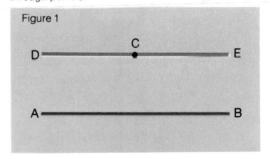

Figure 1

Figure 2. A pseudosphere.

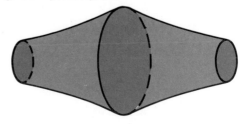

points A and B is a straight line. On a hemisphere (Figure 4), when points A and B lie on the *great circle* (or largest circle of the hemisphere; the center of a great circle is the center of the sphere), the geodesic AB is an arc of the great circle. On a hemipseudosphere (Figure 5), when points A and B lie on the "waist" (also, the largest circle) of the pseudosphere, the geodesic AB is an arc of the waist.

On the plane, hemisphere, and hemipseudosphere (Figures 3, 4, and 5), we draw geodesic AC, perpendicular to AB at A, and geodesic BD, equal to AC in length and perpendicular to AB at B. Finally, we draw the geodesic CD. On the plane, the geodesic CD is a straight line; on the hemi-

sphere, it is an arc of the great circle; on the hemipseudosphere, it is an arc of a lesser circle.

How large are angles 1 and 2 in Figures 3, 4, and 5? The answer to this question will provide an insight into the differences between Euclidean geometry and the non-Euclidean geometries of Riemann and Lobachevsky-Bolyai.

In the case of the plane in Figure 3, it would seem to be obvious that angles 1 and 2 are *right* angles (90°). But we cannot prove this as a geometric theorem unless we first agree that only one line passing through C (that is, the line CD) is parallel to line AB. If we make this assumption, we are accepting Euclid's postulate.

On the hemisphere (Figure 4), angles 1 and 2 are apparently *obtuse* angles (greater than 90°). Can we prove this? Not unless we first assume that every geodesic through C will meet line AB at two points. If we accept this, we can prove that angles 1 and 2 are greater than 90°.

Riemann assumed that even in a plane, any line (such as CD in Figure 3) drawn through an external point (such as C) will meet any other line (AB) at two points. Hence there are no parallel lines in his geometry. He developed a perfectly logical set of theorems based on this assumption.

"But," you will say, "anyone can see that line CD in Figure 3 is parallel to line AB and that the two lines will never meet."

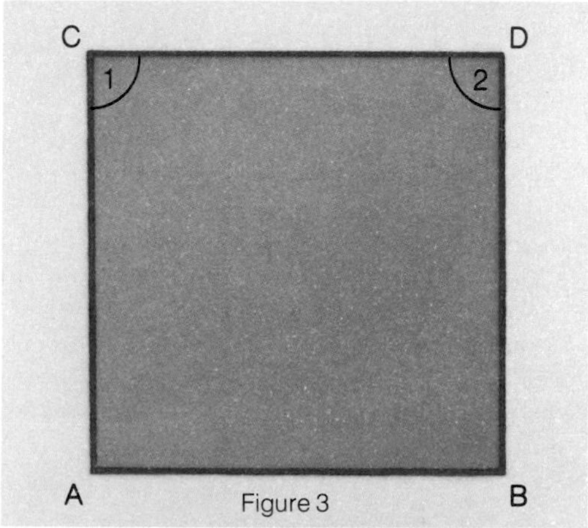

![Figure 3: Square ABCD with C top-left, D top-right, A bottom-left, B bottom-right, angles 1 and 2 marked at C and D]

Figure 3

Figures 3, 4, and 5. The figure ABCD is shown on a plane (Figure 3), a hemisphere (Figure 4), and a hemipseudosphere (Figure 5). In each case, geodesics AC and BD are equal to each other and perpendicular to line AB.

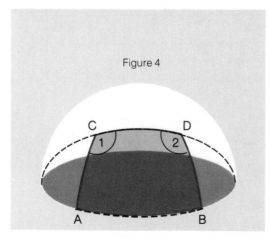

Figure 4

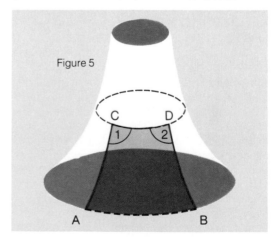

Figure 5

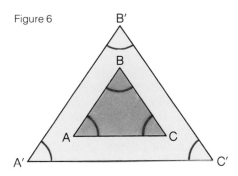

Figure 6

Figure 6. In the geometry of Euclid, the sum of the angles in a triangle, such as ABC, is 180°. If the area of such a triangle is increased so that we have the triangle A'B'C', the sum of the angles is still equal to 180°.

Figure 7. According to the geometry of Riemann, the sum of the angles of a triangle, such as ABC, is always greater than 180°. It increases as the area of the triangle increases, as in triangle A'B'C'.

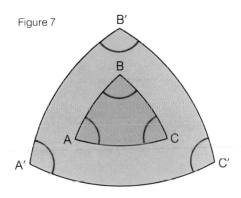

Figure 7

But as long as you cannot prove that this is so, you cannot deny that it is perfectly logical to develop a new kind of geometry based on another assumption.

Let us now examine angles 1 and 2 in the hemipseudosphere (Figure 5). These angles are apparently *acute* (less than 90°). Again, we cannot prove that this is so unless we make an assumption—in this case, that there are two geodesics through C that never meet AB. Lobachevsky and Bolyai made this assumption and applied it to all kinds of surfaces, including those of

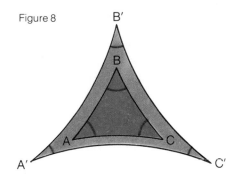

Figure 8

Figure 8. In the geometry of Lobachevsky-Bolyai, the sum of the angles of a triangle, such as ABC, is always less than 180°. It decreases as the area increases, as in triangle A'B'C'.

spheres and planes. Their geometry describes a world quite different from that of Euclid and Riemann—a world in which through every external point there are two lines parallel to a given line.

Of course, three geometries based on such different assumptions are bound to show many striking points of difference. Consider, for example, the sum of the angles of any triangle. In the Euclidean geometry, the sum is 180°. It always remains the same no matter how much the size of a given triangle increases (Figure 6). In the Riemannian geometry, the sum of the angles of a triangle is always greater than 180°. As the area of the triangle increases, the sum of the angles increases (Figure 7). In the geometry of Lobachevsky-Bolyai, the sum of the angles of a triangle is always less than 180° and decreases as the area of the triangle increases (Figure 8).

One cannot say that one of these geometries is correct and that the others are incorrect. Rather, they are different explanations of space, based on different assumptions. We accept the one that offers the most satisfactory interpretation of a particular phenomenon with which we are concerned. For example, the Riemannian geometry has given a better explanation of certain astronomical aspects of Einstein's relativity theory than either the Euclidean or Lobachevsky-Bolyai geometry.

Howard F. Fehr

STATISTICS

Have you ever noticed how much of the information you receive comes to you through numbers? Particularly since the coming of age of electronic computers, more and more kinds of information are being coded, processed, and presented numerically. On any given day, we can expect to see numerical presentations of weather information, the stock market, political polls, business transactions, census data, government operations, and many other types of data.

In most instances, the numerical information in its original form would be difficult to interpret. For this reason, the information is usually organized, summarized, and presented to us in a form that can be more readily interpreted. Frequently this is accomplished by reducing the numerical data to a table or graph or by reporting one number, such as the average, to represent an entire set of numbers. The process by which numerical data are collected and eventually presented in a usable and understandable form is an important part of the mathematical science of *statistics*.

Statistics is important not only for communication; it also provides a basis for decision making. The government makes extensive use of statistics in estimating its budget needs and setting its tax rates. Statistics enables manufacturers to compare production processes when they seek to improve their products or increase their profits. Store managers may rely upon statistical analyses to determine which items they should stock. Scientists employ statistics in comparing the effects of critical variables upon their experiments. Insurance companies rise and fall on the accuracy of their statistical predictions. Engineers base the design of highways and bridges upon statistical studies of materials and traffic. School officials may modify their curricula on the basis of statistical analyses of student achievements and needs. The list of such decision-making uses of statistics is almost endless.

Collection of Data

The science of statistics involves a variety of tasks. Even the seemingly simple business of collecting numerical data requires careful study. Obviously the conclusions of a statistical study can be no more reliable than the figures upon which they are based. The statistician must be sure that the data collected are accurate, relevant to the problem being studied, and representative of the problem. Invalid conclusions drawn from statistical evidence are often due to inadequacies in the data collected. The matter of data collection will not be discussed in detail, but its importance is so great that we should be aware of some of the problems involved.

First, the *population* to be studied must be well defined. What do we mean by "population" here? To the statistician, it may consist of a set of cities, automobiles, books, or even scientific experiments. In fact, the population for a statistical study might be any set of objects having a common characteristic to which a number might be assigned. Of course, the population selected must supply the appropriate numerical data for the problem being studied. If the population of a statistical study is not well defined or is not representative of the problem being studied, the results of the study will be difficult to interpret or apply. For example, surveys of the voting preferences of high-school students would be of questionable value in predicting the results of a national election, since few high-school students can vote.

Once the population has been identified, the particular characteristics to be studied must be represented numerically. Sometimes the numerical data are already available in recorded form. For example, if you wanted to study the rainfall in your city over the past year, you could probably obtain the needed data from your local weather bureau. In this case, the population might be defined as the set of days in the year.

Sometimes the numerical data may be obtained by a simple counting process. You might be interested, for example, in a study of the books in a school library. This project would involve counting the volumes devoted to each of several subjects.

More often, the data for a statistical study are obtained by measuring some common characteristic of the population being studied. If the population were a set of scientific experiments, the scientist might be concerned with such characteristics as time, temperature, volume, and mass. In each case, the scientist would need to use a suitable measuring instrument to assign a number to the characteristic.

In some cases, no measuring instrument is available and the investigator must create a measuring device. A teacher, for example, creates examinations. Each classroom test is an instrument by which student achievement can be measured. Test grades are the numbers assigned to that measurement. As with any other measuring instrument, accuracy is a prime consideration. The investigator would need to know how well the number assigned represents the true value of the characteristic being measured—in this case, student achievement.

The ultimate value of a statistical study depends to a large extent upon the quality of the measuring instrument that is employed. For this reason, the construction and evaluation of such an instrument is often a critical task in a statistical study

Sometimes it is possible to obtain numerical data about each member of a population that is being studied. When this is true, the data are completely representative of the population, and the task of the statistician is to describe the numerical data obtained. This branch of statistics is called *descriptive statistics.*

Sampling a Population

Often it is necessary or practical to collect data only for a *sample* of the population and to make *statistical inferences* about the population itself. An inference is a conclusion about the unknown based upon something that is known. A statistical inference, therefore, is one based upon sta-

tistical data. When data are available only for a sample, the sample represents the known and the population the unknown. Any subject of a population would constitute a sample, but statistical inferences are valid only when the sample is representative of the population. Many techniques are employed by statisticians to insure that the samples they select are representative.

When each member of the population has an equal chance of being chosen, we have what is called a *random sample*. This is usually assumed to be representative of the population. In some special problems, the statistician uses a *stratified sample,* which insures that specific segments of the study population are represented in the sample. The process of identifying a representative sample is a critical task in many statistical studies. In the examples cited in this article, we will assume that the samples used are representative of the populations from which they have been selected.

To summarize the discussion of collecting data, let us consider the following example: Suppose that the population being studied is the set of students in a given grade. If each of these students was assigned to an English class by a random process, the English class would constitute a representative sample of the population. If you were to measure the height, weight, or age of each student in the class, or record each student's score on a particular test, or count the number of people in his or her family, you would obtain a set of numbers. These numbers could then become the data for a statistical study. The data could be used to describe the English class (the sample). They could also be used to make *estimates* or inferences about the total set of students in the grade (the population).

Organizing the Data

Once data have been collected, they must be arranged in some systematic order before a useful interpretation can be made or conclusions drawn. Sometimes a simple table or graph can be quite helpful as a first step toward the statistical analysis of numerical data.

TABLE I

Vocabulary Test Scores in Sixth-Grade Class 6-1

Name	Score	Name	Score
Alex	14	John	16
Barry	19	Joseph	18
Carolyn	16	Karen	14
Catherine	13	Larry	14
Charles	19	Loretta	15
Cynthia	16	Michael	15
David	18	Monica	17
Diane	17	Rebekah	18
Doris	20	Sandra	13
Drew	17	Sean	16
Elaine	16	Seth	17
Elizabeth	16	Sharon	15
Eric	15	Sheila	15
Gabriel	15	Stephanie	14
George	17	Stephen	16
Greg	16	Virginia	13
Janice	12	Zachary	12
Jennifer	16		

TABLE II

Frequency Distribution of Vocabulary Test Scores in Sixth-Grade Class 6-1

Score	Frequency
0	0
1	0
2	0
3	0
4	0
5	0
6	0
7	0
8	0
9	0
10	0
11	0
12	2
13	3
14	4
15	6
16	9
17	5
18	3
19	2
20	1
21	0
22	0
23	0
24	0
25	0

$n = 35$

n = total number of scores

The numerical data presented in Table I are scores obtained by 35 students from one sixth-grade class, Class 6-1, in a vocabulary test. Each score represents the number of test questions that have been answered correctly by a given student. In this case, the word "score" is used in its usual sense. However, regardless of the nature of the numerical data, statisticians often use the term *raw score* to indicate the individual numbers obtained as a basis for a statistical study.

It is difficult to make any useful interpretation of the data in Table I. The simplest way of organizing these data would be to arrange the scores in numerical order. It is common to record only the different raw scores (in this case, 16, 18, 14, and so on) and to note the *frequency* with which each score occurs. Table II is a frequency table prepared from the data in Table I.

Even a cursory examination of Table II permits some elementary interpretation of the data. We can easily observe the highest and lowest scores (20 and 12) and the most frequent scores (15, 16, and 17). We can even begin to have some feeling for the way the scores seem to cluster about a central point—in this case, the score 16.

Further clarification of the data may be obtained by translating Table II into a graphical form. Figure 1 is a common type of *frequency graph* used to present frequency distributions. The numbers below the horizontal line represent scores; the numbers at the left represent the frequency distribution—that is, the number of times each score occurs.

The *frequency polygon* shown in Figure 2 is based on the same idea. In this

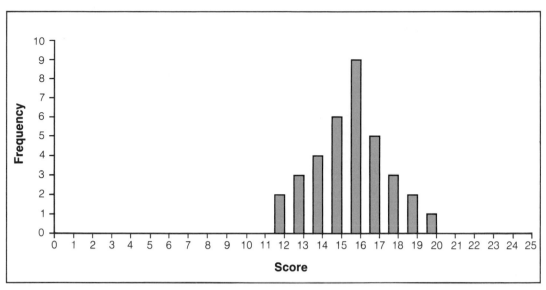

Figure 1. Frequency graph of data in Table II.

case, we imagine lines perpendicular to the scores on the bottom line and lines perpendicular to the frequencies at the left. A point indicates the intersection of a score line and a frequency line. Thus we have a point where the score 12 and the frequency number 2 meet, and a point where the score 16 and the frequency number 9 meet. The points are connected by straight lines. Note that to "complete the appearance" of the polygon, a zero-frequency-point is assigned to the value one unit lower than the lowest score and to the value one unit higher than the highest score.

An examination of these two graphs will reveal exactly the same information

Figure 2. Graphs, such as this frequency polygon, are often easier to interpret than tables.

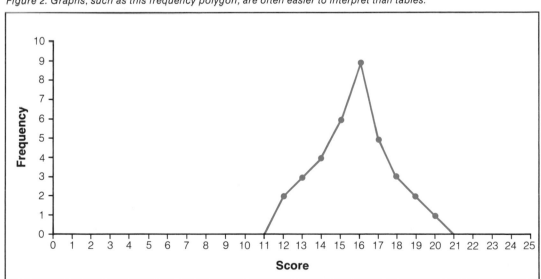

TABLE III

Frequency Distribution of Vocabulary Test Scores In All Sixth-Grade Classes

Score	Frequency
0	0
1	0
2	0
3	1
4	2
5	2
6	3
7	6
8	9
9	7
10	7
11	12
12	20
13	10
14	12
15	24
16	28
17	22
18	13
19	11
20	9
21	5
22	4
23	0
24	0
25	0
	$n = 207$

n = total number of scores

TABLE IV

Grouped Frequency Distribution of Vocabulary Test Scores In All Sixth-Grade Classes

Score	Frequency
2-4	3
5-7	11
8-10	23
11-13	42
14-16	64
17-19	46
20-22	18
	$n = 207$

n = total number of scores

available in Table II. The graphical form often is easier to interpret than the tabular form. In particular, the tendency of scores to cluster around a central point becomes more apparent when the data are presented pictorially.

Grouping Raw Scores

The frequency distribution for raw scores made by all 207 students from all sixth grade classes in the school is shown in Table III. In many statistical studies, particularly when the range of scores is great, it becomes cumbersome to work with all the individual scores. In these cases, it is common to condense the data by grouping the raw scores into class intervals. In studying the scores on the vocabulary test, instead of considering each score individually, we combine a number of adjacent scores to form an interval. Thus we would combine the individual scores 20, 21, and 22 to form the interval 20–22. Intervals are treated in much the same way as we would treat individual raw scores.

A grouped frequency table, based on intervals, is shown in Table IV. It presents scores made by 207 students from all the sixth-grade classes.

When the number of possible individual scores is large, the grouping of data into appropriate intervals enables the investigator to work with a manageable number. However, this grouping method has the disadvantage of obscuring individual scores. Thus all eighteen individual scores in the interval 20–22 might be 22 instead of 9 at 20, 5 at 21, and 4 at 22. We ignore this consideration when working with class intervals. Once the data are compressed by grouping, in all subsequent analysis and computation, we treat individual scores as if they were evenly distributed throughout the interval to which they belong.

Graphical representations of grouped frequency tables are very similar to those presented earlier for ungrouped data. One special kind of graph, the *frequency histogram,* is worthy of note. To construct a histogram from Table IV, as in Figure 3, the frequency of scores in each interval is represented by a rectangle with its center at

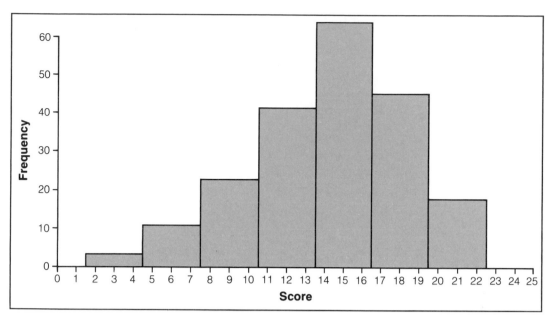

Figure 3. Frequency histogram of data in Table III.

the midpoint of the interval, its height equal to the frequency, and its width equal to the width of the interval's *limits*.

Here it is necessary to define and distinguish between two types of limits. When an interval is identified as 20–22, the limits reported are called *score limits*. They identify the lowest score and highest score that belong to the same interval. For purposes of mathematical treatment and graphical representation, it is common to use the *real limits* 19.5–22.5 to identify this same interval. The interval is represented as extending halfway to the scores immediately preceding and following. Such an interpretation is consistent with the way we usually report measurements. For example, if we were measuring to the nearer meter, any measurement between 19.5 meters and 20.5 meters would be reported as 20 meters.

Calculating Averages

Tables and graphs can help us obtain considerable understanding of a set of scores. However, for many purposes, it is more desirable to try to represent the set of scores by a single number. When selecting a single number to represent a whole set of numbers, the first thing we usually think of is the average. As we have noted earlier, the scores we have been examining seem to cluster around a central point. It is this point of central tendency that statisticians identify when they report an average score. In statistics, there are several types of averages. Three are common in statistical analysis—the *mode,* the *median,* and the *mean.* Each is called a measure of central tendency. For the data with which we have been working in this article, the mode, median, and mean are close in value. This is not always the case. They may be appreciably different.

Mode. The mode is quite easily identified from a frequency table or frequency graph. It is the score that occurs most frequently—in a sense, the most popular score. From the data presented in Table III, we can determine readily that the most frequent score is 16. Thus 16 is the mode of this set of scores. In the grouped data, the *crude mode* would be identified as the midpoint of the interval with the highest frequency. From either Table IV or Figure 3, we can see that the interval of highest frequency is 14–16. Hence 15 would be the crude mode of this distribution since it is the midpoint of the interval. Since individual scores have been obscured, we cannot be sure that it is actually the most frequent individual score, but it is our best estimate of the most frequent score.

Median. The median is the middle score in a set of scores. The data in Table III contains 207 scores. The median is, then, the value of the 104th score. We find that the 104th score is among the 24 scores that all have a value of 15, and the median is therefore 15. If there had been an even number of scores, the median would have been reported as a figure that is halfway between the two middle scores if the two are different.

Since the set of data, presented in Table IV and Figure 3, has been condensed by grouping, we cannot work with individual scores and must find a new procedure for identifying the median. From Table IV, we find that the middle score, the 104th score, must fall in the interval 14–16. Since 79 scores out of the total number of 207 scores fall below this interval, we know that the median will be the 25th score in the interval (79 + 25 = 104). Since for grouped data we must assume even distribution within an interval, we will assume that the median lies 25/64 of the width of the interval above its lowest boundary. We then multiply 26/64 by 3 (the number of scores in the interval) for a product of 25/64 × 3 = 1.2 (rounded to the nearest tenth). We now add 1.2 to the least-value endpoint of the interval 14–16. (We noted previously that this endpoint is 13.5.) Hence we have 13.5 + 1.2 = 15.7. The median, then, as calculated from the grouped data is 15.7.

Mean. The mean is the most commonly used measure of central tendency, and it is the average most of us think of first. It is found by dividing the sum of all the individual scores by the number of scores in the set. The calculation of the sum of the scores can be shortened when a frequency table is available if we multiply each score by its frequency and then find the sum.

The mean for the data in Table III is calculated as follows:

Score		f		
3	×	1	=	3
4	×	2	=	8
5	×	2	=	10
6	×	3	=	18
7	×	6	=	42
8	×	9	=	72
9	×	7	=	63
10	×	7	=	70
11	×	12	=	132
12	×	20	=	240
13	×	10	=	130
14	×	12	=	168
15	×	24	=	360
16	×	28	=	448
17	×	22	=	374
18	×	13	=	234
19	×	11	=	209
20	×	9	=	180
21	×	5	=	105
22	×	4	=	88
		207		2,954

$2,954 \div 207 = 14.27 = 14.3$ = the mean

When computing the mean for grouped data, we assume even distribution of scores within each interval. We multiply the value of the midpoint of each interval by the frequency and divide the sum of the resulting number by the total number of scores.

The mean for the data in Table IV is calculated as follows:

Score		f		
3	×	3	=	9
6	×	11	=	66
9	×	23	=	207
12	×	42	=	504
15	×	64	=	960
18	×	46	=	828
21	×	18	=	378
		207	=	2,952

$2,952 \div 207 = 14.26 = 14.3$, the mean

Selecting Averages

The mode is used less frequently than either the median or the mean. It is useful only when we want to identify the number occurring most frequently in a set of numbers. As a matter of fact, if the mode is to be truly meaningful, one number in a set must occur quite a bit more frequently than any other number in the set. The advantage of the mode is that, like the median, it is easy to identify and understand. But the term "mode" is sometimes ambiguous, because there may be more than one score with the "highest frequency" (see Figure 4). Also, the mode is not reliable as an indication of central tendency, because the most popular score is not always near the center of a given distribution.

The chief advantage of the median is that it is not affected by extreme scores. The "average" income in a community, for example, is often more accurately reflected by the median than the mean, because the value of the median is not influenced by a few very high or very low incomes. The idea of the median is closely related to the concept of *percentiles*—a type of score students receive on certain standard tests in school. The median corresponds to the 50th percentile. Other percentiles can also be used in connection with tests. They are valuable as a basis for comparing individual scores with other scores in a distribution.

For most purposes, the mean is the best measure of central tendency. It is the only one of the three measures that depends upon the numerical value of each score in a distribution. It is a reliable indicator of central tendency because it always identifies the "balancing point" or "center of gravity" in the distribution. Since the mean lends itself better to mathematical computation, it is more suitable for deriving other statistical measures. For example, the means of two sets of data can be used to compute a mean for the combined set of data. This cannot be done with the mode or the median. However, the mean can give us information only about the central point in a distribution. To understand a set of scores more fully, we also need to know how the scores spread out around this central point. For this reason, statisticians develop measures of *dispersion* or *variability.*

The simplest measure of distribution is the *range,* which is defined as the difference between the highest and lowest scores in a distribution. The range of scores reported in Table III is easily identified as being 19. We simply subtract the lowest score (3) from the highest score (22). Since the range is sensitive only to the two extreme scores in a distribution, it is not considered a very satisfactory measure of dispersion. Its weakness is dramatized in the two distributions whose graphs are presented in Figures 4 and 5. In both distributions the mean is 12 and the range of scores is 12. Yet the distributions are obviously different.

As with the median and the mode, the weakness of the range is that it does not take into account the numerical value of each score. A natural measure of dispersion involving every score is the *average difference* between the individual scores and their mean. As we have seen, the mean serves as a "balancing point" for a distribution. Hence we can measure the deviations from the mean in terms of positive and negative differences. Deviations from the mean in one direction would be positive; in the other, negative.

The sum of the deviations from the mean is always zero. This is because the magnitude of negative differences always equals that of the positive differences. To avoid using negatives in the measurement of deviations, we use their *absolute values.* (The absolute value of a number disregards its positive or negative sign; the absolute value of any number x is represented as $|x|$.)

The average of the absolute values of the differences between individual scores and the mean is called the *mean deviation* and is a simple and accurate measure of dispersion. The calculation of the mean deviation for the distribution in Figure 4 is as follows:

$$
\begin{array}{rll}
f & \text{Deviation from mean} & \\
5 \times & |6 - 12| = & 30 \\
10 \times & |9 - 12| = & 30 \\
20 \times & |12 - 12| = & 0 \\
10 \times & |15 - 12| = & 30 \\
\underline{5} \times & |18 - 12| = & \underline{30} \\
50 & & 120
\end{array}
$$

$120 \div 50 = 2.4$, the mean deviation.

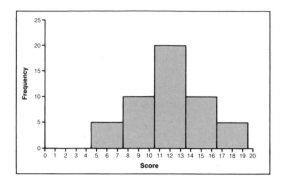

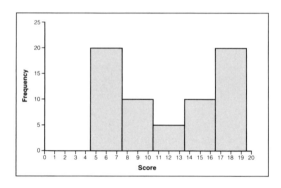

Figure 4, above, and Figure 5, below, show two different distributions of test scores. Both distributions have the same mean, 12, and the same range of scores, 14. In both distributions the lowest score is 5 and the highest is 19. However, the distributions of scores are very different. The mean and range are not sufficient to describe the distributions. A measurement of the deviation of scores from the mean is also needed.

A similar calculation for the distribution of test scores in Figure 5 would yield a mean deviation of 4.6. Therefore greater dispersion is indicated for the distribution in Figure 5.

The use of absolute values presents mathematical difficulties that can be avoided by using another measure. The positive and negative signs that led to the introduction of absolute values could also have been eliminated by squaring the deviations from the mean, since the square of a positive or negative number is always positive. Such a procedure preserves the descriptive qualities of the mean deviation while providing a measure that is easier to handle mathematically. Hence statisticians prefer to use the *standard deviation*, indicated by the symbol "σ", as a measure of

dispersion. The standard deviation is defined as the square root of the average squared deviation from the mean. Thus to calculate the standard deviation, we first find the average of the squares of the deviations. This number is called the *variance*. Suppose we wish to find the variance and standard deviation (σ) for the data in Table II.

Scores in Sixth Grade Class 6-1. The number of scores in this class is 35, and the mean is 15.7. Calculation of the variance and the standard deviation, σ, is as follows:

Frequency	Deviation from Mean Squared		
2 ×	$(12 - 15.7)^2$	=	27.38
3 ×	$(13 - 15.7)^2$	=	21.87
4 ×	$(14 - 15.7)^2$	=	11.56
6 ×	$(15 - 15.7)^2$	=	2.94
9 ×	$(16 - 15.7)^2$	=	0.81
5 ×	$(17 - 15.7)^2$	=	8.45
3 ×	$(18 - 15.7)^2$	=	15.87
2 ×	$(19 - 15.7)^2$	=	21.78
1 ×	$(20 - 15.7)^2$	=	18.49
35			129.15

$129.15 \div 35 = 3.69$, the variance

$\sqrt{3.69} = 1.92$, the standard deviation, σ

Similar calculations would yield a standard deviation of 4.1 for the data in Table IV, Scores in All Sixth-Grade Classes. If we compare these two measures of dispersion, we see that the scores in Table II the scores of Class 6-1, (the sample) are not so "spread out" as the scores in Table IV, the scores of all sixth grade classes (the population).

Interpreting the Data

Together, the mean and the standard deviation give us a reasonably clear picture of a distribution because they describe both its central tendency and its dispersion. Sometimes, if we know the general nature of the distribution, we need only these two numbers to reconstruct the distribution. For example, many sets of measurements have the *normal* distribution shown in Figure 6.

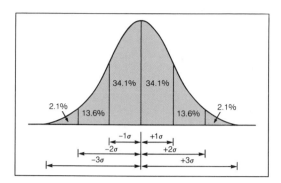

Figure 6. Human intelligence as measured by intelligence tests is believed to be distributed at random. Scores on intelligence tests form a normal distribution. Many other random variables form normal curves.

When a set of numbers "fits" such a standard distribution, we can determine approximately how many of the numbers fall within a given distance of the mean. For the normal distribution, 68.2 percent of the scores fall within one standard deviation of the mean. Thus, given the mean of 14.3 and the standard deviation of 4.1 for the set of scores in Table III, we could "predict" that 68.2 percent of the scores would be between 10.2 and 18.4. Since the distribution is actually given in Table III, we see that 152 of the 207 scores, or 68.1 percent, actually do fall in this interval. The prediction is accurate because the number of scores is relatively large and they do fit the normal distribution.

The knowledge of such general models for distribution coupled with the laws of probability form the basis of *predictive statistics*. Both statistics and probability have to do with distributions, and it is upon this common focus that we capitalize in predictive statistics. In probability, the sample space (population) is known and we predict the composition of a set of outcomes (sample). In statistical inference, the sample (set of outcomes) is known, and we infer the composition of the population (sample space). Thus predictive statistics, also called statistical inference, can be thought of as an application of the laws of probability in reverse.

If we could be certain that the distribution of scores in a sample reflected exactly the distribution of scores in the population from which it was chosen, statistical inferences would be exact and simple to make. But even when a population is known, probability theory tells us that samples will not always be the same. The best we can hope for is that, if the sample is large enough and is carefully chosen, the sample characteristics will closely approximate those of the parent population.

Suppose we had only the data recorded in Table II for Class 6-1 and wished to estimate the mean score for all the English classes. By calculation, we have determined that the scores for Class 6-1 have a mean of 15.7 and a standard deviation of 1.92. Our best estimate of the mean for all classes would be equal to the mean of the sample, Class 6-1. But knowing that samples vary, we would hedge on this estimate. We would give a *confidence interval* within which we would expect the true mean of the population to fall. By assuming the total set of scores to be normally distributed and applying basic laws of probability, we could determine that there is a 95 percent chance that the population mean falls within 1.96 standard deviations or 3.69 score points (1.96 × 1.92). Thus there is a 95 percent chance that the population mean will be 15.7 plus or minus 1.8, or will be between 13.9 and 17.5. The 95 percent is a measure of the confidence or reliability we can place in our estimate. It means that 95 of every 100 populations from which a sample with the given characteristics might be chosen would have a mean within the determined interval. Because of the uncertainties involved in sampling, such an interval estimate, accompanied by a statement of the degree of confidence we can place in the estimate, is preferable to a single number approximation.

The process of establishing confidence intervals permits us to test hypotheses about a population. Modifications of this process permit us to make statistical comparisons of two samples drawn from the same population, to compare a sample to a known population, or to infer other characteristics of an unknown population.

F. Joe Crosswhite

PROBABILITY

How often should we expect all three of the children in a family to be boys?

What are your chances of winning a sweepstakes contest or the door prize at a party?

How likely are you to land on "Boardwalk" in your next turn in a game of Monopoly?

If a baseball player averages 3 hits in 10 times at bat, what are his chances of getting 4 consecutive hits?

Have you ever wondered about the answers to such questions? Scientists often have occasion to study questions of this general type (though much more complicated than the four given above). In seeking the answers, they apply the mathematical theory of *probability*.

Probability is a mathematician's way of describing the *likelihood* that a certain event will take place. It is used to predict the outcome of an experiment when this outcome is governed by the laws of chance. Probability theory enables us to determine probable characteristics of a sample drawn from a population whose characteristics are known. It also provides the basis for part of the related science of *statistics*. Statistical inference is an extension of probability theory. In it, the outcome of an experiment is used to estimate the conditions governing the experiment. We would be drawing a statistical inference if we were to make an educated guess about some population by examining the characteristics of a sample taken from that population.

Let us now consider some examples. Suppose we know that there are 400 boys and 200 girls in a certain school and we conduct the experiment of choosing 1 student from this school at random. In a random selection, each of the 600 students would have exactly the same chance of being chosen. In this experiment, we would say that the probability of choosing a boy is 400 ÷ 600, or ⅔, and the probability of

choosing a girl is 200 ÷ 600, or ⅓. The numbers ⅔ and ⅓ indicate that on the average we should expect to choose a boy "two times out of three" and a girl "one time out of three."

If we repeated this experiment 15 times, our best estimate would be that the sample chosen should contain ⅔ boys and ⅓ girls. This is an example of how probability is used to predict the outcome of an experiment. The probable composition of the sample was determined from the known composition of the population from which it was chosen.

Suppose that in a second school we do not know the proportion of boys and girls but know only that the total number of students is 600. To estimate the ratio of boys to girls, we might conduct an experiment consisting of selecting 20 students at random. If the sample chosen in this experiment contains 10 boys and 10 girls, our best estimate would be that there are equal numbers of boys and girls in the school—that there are 300 boys and 300 girls. In this case, the composition of the sample permits us to make a statistical inference about the composition of the population from which it was drawn.

As you see from these examples, probability and statistical inference are very closely related. The latter may be thought of as an application of probability in which the reasoning process is reversed. Statistical inference is only one aspect of the field of statistics, which also involves the collection, presentation, and analysis of data.

The examples just given illustrate the basic idea of probability and suggest how it may be applied, but they also may be misleading. They were oversimplified in order to avoid some of the more difficult problems that arise in the study of chance phenomena. In the first example, if we repeated the experiment a very large number of times, we might expect to choose a boy at random instead of a girl just about two times out of three. But the chances of selecting exactly 10 boys in a given sample of 15 are really quite small. This would happen only about two times in any ten trials. Most of the samples of 15 would be close to the theoretical ratio of ⅔ (11 boys and 4 girls or 9 boys and 6 girls, for example), but some would not be close at all. We might even choose a random sample of 15 made up entirely of boys. In other words, the "most probable" outcome may not be very probable at all.

In the second example, the fact that our sample contained an equal number of boys and girls could lead us to a very poor estimate of the proportion of boys and girls in the school. We might even have drawn such a sample from the first school, in which there were twice as many boys as girls. In that case, we would have estimated the probability of choosing a boy as ½ when it was actually ⅔.

Many interesting and useful problems in probability are complicated because there are so many *possible* outcomes. If the number of possible outcomes is infinite, we must use calculus in our analysis. In this short introduction to probability theory, we shall deal with simple experiments producing a relatively small number of outcomes. However, the basic principles of probability are the same in simple problems as in more complicated ones. As you read, try to understand these principles, so that you can apply them to more complex situations. It will help you to grasp the subject if you work out all the situations given in the text as well as the special problems.

Probability and Games of Chance

Games of chance involving coins, cards, and dice provide us with simple experiments producing a small number of outcomes. The use of such experiments to illustrate the principles of probability is historically appropriate. Historians tell us that a 17th-century French gambler, the Chevalier de Méré, was interested in the odds involved in a game of chance played with dice. He decided to get in touch with a famous mathematician and scientist, Blaise Pascal, so that the latter might help him with his calculations. Pascal became in-

trigued with the questions that arose in his study of de Méré's problem. He began a correspondence with other mathematicians concerning the matter, and this led to the development of probability theory.

Consider the simple experiment of tossing coins. There are two possible outcomes when we toss a single coin: heads or tails. (We would ignore any toss in which the coin came to rest on its edge.) If the coin is in fair condition and if we toss it vigorously, it seems reasonable to say that heads and tails are equally likely outcomes. A mathematician would say that the probability of heads is ½—that is, that the coin would land heads one time in two on the average.

Suppose we complicate this experiment just a little by tossing the coin twice or, what comes to about the same thing, tossing two coins. We can see that three things might happen in this experiment. We could get two heads, or one head and one tail, or two tails. The diagram in Figure 1 illustrates the possible outcomes in this experiment.

If we examine the diagram carefully, letting H stand for "heads" and T for "tails," we see that there are really four individual outcomes, or elementary events, possible—HH, HT, TH, and TT—when we toss two coins. Note that HT is not considered the same thing as TH. We might, for example, use a nickel and a dime as our two coins.

Since each of the four individual outcomes is equally likely to occur, we would expect to obtain HH one time in four, or, as a mathematician would indicate it, $P(HH) = ¼$. Similarly, we would say $P(HT) = ¼$; $P(TH) = ¼$; $P(TT) = ¼$. Because what happens to the first coin has no effect upon what happens to the second coin, we say that the two tosses are *independent*. When two events are independent, we can use their individual probabilities to compute the probability that both will happen in a single trial of an experiment. In this case, we could have used the probabilities associated with tossing a single coin (that is, $P(H) = ½$; $P(T) = ½$) in order to compute the probabilities

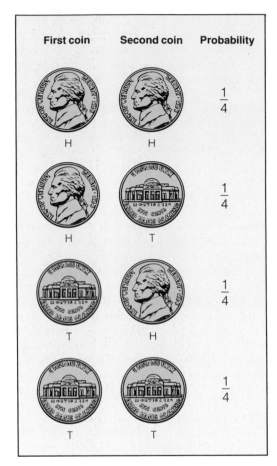

First coin	Second coin	Probability
H	H	$\frac{1}{4}$
H	T	$\frac{1}{4}$
T	H	$\frac{1}{4}$
T	T	$\frac{1}{4}$

Figure 1. Possible outcomes in the tossing of two coins. An analysis of the likelihood of each of the four possible outcomes appears in the text.

associated with tossing two coins. For example, $P(HT) = P(H) \times P(T) = \frac{1}{2} \times \frac{1}{2} = \frac{1}{4}$; $P(HH) = P(H) \times P(H) = \frac{1}{2} \times \frac{1}{2} = \frac{1}{4}$. Since the event "one head and one tail" could occur in two ways, either HT or TH, we would expect to obtain "one head and one tail" two times in four on the average and would assign probability to this event.

We could also use the individual probabilities assigned to the outcomes HT and TH to compute the probability that *either* HT *or* TH will occur. When two events cannot both occur in a single trial of an experiment, the probability that one or the other will occur is the sum of their individual probabilities. Thus $P(HT \text{ or } TH) = P(HT) + P(TH) = \frac{1}{4} + \frac{1}{4} = \frac{1}{2}$. In these examples, we obtain the probability of an event either by counting outcomes of an experiment or by using previously determined probabilities.

We can apply the same principles in other experiments. Consider the question "How often should we expect all three of the children in a family to be boys?" The diagram in Figure 2 illustrates the possible outcomes. If we assumed that equal numbers of boys and girls are born (this is not quite true), we would say that the probability of a boy, $P(B)$, is $\frac{1}{2}$ and that the probability of a girl, $P(G)$, is also $\frac{1}{2}$. The possible outcomes for this experiment would be equal in number to the outcomes for tossing three coins—BBB, BBG, BGB, BGG, GBB, GBG, GGB, and GGG. Since BBB occurs in only one of the eight possible outcomes, we would say $P(BBB) = \frac{1}{8}$. We could also have used the rule for computing the probability that all of several independent events will occur: $P(BBB) = P(B) \times P(B) \times P(B) = \frac{1}{2} \times \frac{1}{2} \times \frac{1}{2} = \frac{1}{8}$. Either way, we would conclude that we should expect all three children in a family to be boys about one time in eight.

Sample Spaces

To determine the probability of a particular outcome of an experiment, we must be able to identify all the possible outcomes. Mathematicians call the set of possible outcomes of an experiment a *sample space* for the experiment. In the simple examples, we shall usually find it convenient to list the sample spaces.

When we considered the experiment of tossing a single coin, our sample space consisted of the two possible outcomes H and T (heads and tails). When we extended the experiment to the tossing of two coins (or one coin twice), we used a sample space of HH, HT, TH, TT. In the experiment of choosing a single student from a known school population, the sample space involved was the set of all students in the school. Since we were concerned only with whether we chose a boy or girl and not with which boy or girl, we could have used a sample space of only two elements—boy and girl. In this case, B could be used to

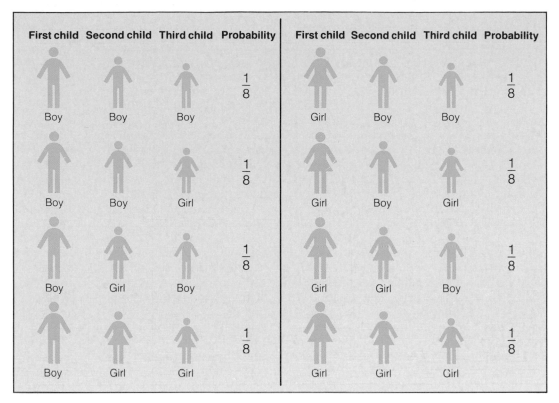

First child	Second child	Third child	Probability	First child	Second child	Third child	Probability
Boy	Boy	Boy	$\frac{1}{8}$	Girl	Boy	Boy	$\frac{1}{8}$
Boy	Boy	Girl	$\frac{1}{8}$	Girl	Boy	Girl	$\frac{1}{8}$
Boy	Girl	Boy	$\frac{1}{8}$	Girl	Girl	Boy	$\frac{1}{8}$
Boy	Girl	Girl	$\frac{1}{8}$	Girl	Girl	Girl	$\frac{1}{8}$

Figure 2. The diagram shows that the probability of having either three girls or three boys in a family of three children is 1/8. The probability of the first child being a boy is 1/2; the probability of the second being a boy is 1/2, and the probability of the third being a boy is 1/2. 1/2 × 1/2 × 1/2 = 1/8.

stand for the set of boys and G for the set of girls. Each individual outcome of a sample space is called a *point* or an *elementary event*.

Although a single experiment will produce only one set of individual outcomes, we may be able to use any one of several different sample spaces, depending on what we are investigating. For example, consider the experiment of drawing one card from a well-shuffled deck of cards. If we are concerned with the individual card drawn, we could use a sample space consisting of 52 elements—every single card in the deck. In the same experiment, we might be concerned only with the face value of the card shown. In that case, our sample space would consist of only 13 elements (2, 3, 4, 5, 6, 7, 8, 9, 10, jack, queen, king, ace). Or we might be interested only in the suit drawn. In that case, we would use the sample space of clubs, diamonds, hearts, spades. If we were concerned only with color, we could use a sample space of only two elements (red, black). In most experi-

ments, we use the sample space identifying the characteristics on which we wish to concentrate in the experiment. We can use the sample space of elementary events to build up other sample spaces by collecting the elementary events with like characteristics.

You have probably played board games, such as Monopoly and Parcheesi, in which your moves were determined by the throw of a die or a pair of dice. A sample space for the experiment of tossing a single die would be the set {1, 2, 3, 4, 5, 6}. It is rather more difficult to generate a sample space for the tossing of a pair of dice. To help us keep things straight, let us suppose that one die is red and the other one green. An outcome of 4 on the red die and 3 on the green die would be different from an outcome of 3 on the red die and 4 on the green die. If we agreed to write the outcome on the red die first and the outcome on the green die second, we could show this difference by setting down the pairs (4,3) and (3,4).

Figure 3 shows the sample space for the experiment of tossing a pair of dice. Suppose that you tossed the dice and that the red die came up 4 and the green die came up 3. Moving horizontally from 4, at the extreme left of the table, until we came to the column headed by 3, we would find the pair (4,3). We shall have occasion to refer to this sample space several times in the course of this article.

See if you can list sample spaces for the following experiments:

1. Toss a coin and a die. [Hint: two points in this sample space could be (H,3) and (T,2).]

2. Toss a nickel, dime, and quarter. If the nickel comes up heads, the dime tails, and the quarter heads, we can indicate this by (H,T,H). You should find 8 points for this sample space.

Probability of an Event

An *event* is by definition any subset of a sample space. In other words, if each member of set A is also a member of set B,

we say that A is a subset of B. If set A = {1, 2, 3} and set B = {1, 2, 3, 4, 5}, then set A is a subset of set B. Thus an event is a set of individual outcomes of an experiment. An elementary event, as we have indicated, is a single individual outcome. In order to assign probabilities to an event— that is, to a set of individual outcomes—we must first be able to assign probabilities to individual outcomes of the experiment.

If we consider, for example, the experiment of drawing a single card from a deck of cards, there are 52 elementary events or individual outcomes possible. If we make a random draw, each card has exactly the same chance of being drawn. Thus to each of the 52 possible outcomes we would assign the same probability: $\frac{1}{52}$. Note that the sum of the probabilities assigned to the elementary events is 1. The probability of an event that is certain is also 1.

The same basic principle may be used to answer the question "What are your chances of winning a sweepstakes contest or the door prize at a party?" In each case,

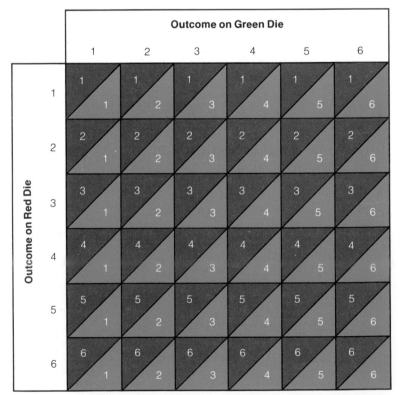

Figure 3. At the right is a sample space for the tossing of a pair of dice. It is assumed that one of the dice is red and the other green; also that the outcome of the red die is given first in each of the pairs shown. Note that in the text the two outcomes, separated by a comma, are given in parentheses. Thus we would refer to (2,5), (4,3), (6,1) and so on.

if the total number of tickets is n and you hold only 1 ticket, then you would have only 1 chance in n of winning. Thus the probability of your winning would be $1/n$.

In the experiment of drawing a card from a deck, we may be concerned only with whether the card is an ace. Then the event with which we are concerned consists of four elementary events: the ace of clubs, the ace of diamonds, the ace of hearts, and the ace of spades. We still would have to draw at random from the entire deck of cards, numbering 52. Since 4 out of the 52 cards belong to the event just described (4 aces), we would say that the probability that the outcome is an ace is $4/52$. We could use the symbols $P(\text{ace}) = 4/52$ to represent this statement.

Suppose that in the preceding experiment, we were concerned only with the color of the card chosen. Do you see why $P(\text{red}) = 26/52$? We can use the probabilities assigned to elementary events to assign probabilities to the points in other sample spaces. For example, if we were using the sample space clubs, diamonds, hearts, spades, we could assign the probability of $\frac{1}{4}$ to each point in the sample space since $P(\text{clubs}) = 13/52 = \frac{1}{4}$.

Rule 1.

If an experiment can result in n different but equally likely outcomes and if m of these outcomes correspond to event X, then the probability of the event is $P(X) = m/n$.

Applying this rule, let us find the probabilities of some events in the experiment of tossing a pair of dice. Figure 3 lists 36 possible outcomes for this experiment. Thus we could assign a probability of $\frac{1}{36}$ to each of the elementary events. Now consider the event "The sum of the numbers shown is 7." If we let r stand for the number on the red die and g for the number on the green die, we can represent the event as $r + g = 7$. How many of the elementary events correspond to this amount? In other words, how many of the pairs in the table add up to 7? Consult the table to find the answer. You will see that $P(r + g = 7) = 6/36$. If we considered the event "The same number appears on both dice," we could call the event "$r = g$" or, as is common in many games played with dice, "double." There are six such pairs: (1,1), (2,2), (3,3), (4,4), (5,5), and (6,6). Thus $P(r = g) = P(\text{double}) = 6/36$. What is $P(r + g > 7)$? (The symbol $>$ stands for "is greater than.") Are you able to find 15 points in the sample space that correspond to this event? You should be able to, for $P(r + g > 7) = 15/36$.

These examples should suggest a way to answer the question "How likely are you to land on 'Boardwalk' in your next turn in a game of Monopoly?" Suppose, for example, that you are located on "Pennsylvania Avenue," which is 5 spaces from "Boardwalk." To determine the probability of your landing on "Boardwalk," carry out the experiment of tossing two dice. You would land on "Boardwalk" if the numbers shown on the dice totaled 5. What is $P(r + g = 5)$?

Try the following problems:

1. If a box contains 4 red marbles and 5 white marbles, what is the probability of drawing a red marble on the first try?
2. What is the probability that you will draw a face card (jack, queen, king) from a deck of cards?
3. What is the probability that you will get a 5 when you toss a single die?
4. What is the probability that you will not get a 5 when you toss a single die?

Complementary Events

There is a relationship that frequently simplifies the computing of a probability. Consider the example pictured in Figure 4. There are 10 points in the sample space S. The event A contains 4 of these points and the remaining 6 points are not in A. The set of points in sample space S that are not in a given set A is called the *complement* of A and is usually indicated by the symbol $\overline{A}$. If the elementary events in the sample space S are equally likely, then $P(A) = 4/10$ and $P(\overline{A}) = 6/10$.

In a sample space of n equally likely events, if an event A occurs in m of the outcomes, then the event $\overline{A}$ will occur in $n-m$ outcomes. Thus if $P(A) = m/n$, then $P(\overline{A}) = (n-m)/n$. Now $(n-m)/n = 1 - m/n$. We obtain this result by dividing both the numerator and the denominator by n, as follows:

$$\frac{\dfrac{n}{n} - \dfrac{m}{n}}{\dfrac{n}{n}} = \frac{1 - \dfrac{m}{n}}{1} = 1 - \frac{m}{n}$$

We now can give the following general rule:

Rule 2.

$$P(\overline{A}) = 1 - P(A)$$

Sometimes it is easier to compute the probability of one of two complementary events than it is to compute the probability of the other. In such cases, we compute the easier probability. We then use the relationship indicated in Rule 2 to derive the probability of the complementary event. For example, in some games played with dice, there is either a premium or a penalty associated with throwing doubles. We could compute the probability of not throwing a double by counting the sample points in Figure 3 that are not doubles. (There are 30 of them.) Or we could compute the probability of throwing a double ($r = g$) and use the relationship in Rule 2 to derive the probability of not throwing a double ($r \neq g$). (The symbol $\neq$ stands for "is not equal to.")

Probability of "A or B"

A situation that often arises is the finding of the probability of an event that might be expressed as "either event A or event B." By the event (A or B) we mean the set of outcomes that correspond to either event A or event B, or possibly both A and B.

Consider the example shown in Figure 5. There are 10 points in the sample space S. In this sample space, $P(A) = 3/10$ and $P(B) = 2/10$. Since the event (A or B) contains the 3 elements of A and the 2 elements

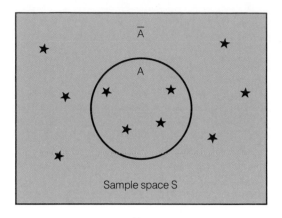

Figure 4. Subsets A and $\overline{A}$ are complementary events in sample space S.

of B, then $P(A \text{ or } B) = P(A) + P(B) = 5/10$. In this instance, there are no elements that are in both A and B; so A and B here are *mutually exclusive* events, meaning that they cannot both occur in a single trial of an experiment. When events A and B are mutually exclusive, we can find the probability of (A or B) simply by adding the probability of A to the probability of B as follows:

Rule 3.

If events A and B are mutually exclusive, then
$$P(A \text{ or } B) = P(A) + P(B).$$

For example, suppose we were required to find the probability of throwing either a 7 or a double in a toss of two dice. Since 7 is an odd number, it is not possible for a single toss of two dice to produce both a 7 and a double. Thus the event (r + g = 7) and the event (r = g) are mutually exclusive. We have already seen that $P(r + g = 7) = 6/36$ and that $P(r = g) = 6/36$. Hence, applying Rule 3, $P(r + g = 7 \text{ or } r = g) = 6/36 + 6/36 = 12/36$. Can you verify this by counting the appropriate points in the sample space shown in Figure 3?

When both events are not mutually exclusive—that is, when they *can* both occur in a single outcome—we cannot use the addition principle of Rule 3. Consider the situation presented in Figure 6. In this example, the sample space S consists of 10 equally likely elementary events; 5 outcomes correspond to event A, and 4 outcomes to event B. Hence $P(A) = \frac{5}{10}$ and $P(B) = \frac{4}{10}$. If we were to apply Rule 3 here, we would have $P(A \text{ or } B) = P(A) + P(B) = \frac{5}{10} + \frac{4}{10} = \frac{9}{10}$. This answer would be incorrect. The reason is that events A and B are not mutually exclusive, since 2 outcomes belong to both A and B. To obtain a correct answer in this case for $P(A \text{ or } B)$, we need to apply the following rule:

Rule 4.

If events A and B are not mutually exclusive, then
$$P(A \text{ or } B) = P(A) + P(B) - P(A \text{ and } B).$$

Therefore, for Figure 6, $P(A \text{ or } B) = \frac{5}{10} + \frac{4}{10} - \frac{2}{10} = \frac{7}{10}$.

Let us consider another example in which this rule could be used. Suppose we wanted to find the probability of drawing either a face card or a spade from a deck of cards. $P(\text{spade}) = \frac{13}{52}$ and $P(\text{face card}) = \frac{12}{52}$. (Remember that each of the 4 suits has 3 face cards: jack, queen, and king.) There are 3 cards that are both face cards and spades. Therefore $P(\text{spade and face card}) = \frac{3}{52}$. Applying Rule 4, we would conclude that $P(\text{spade or face card}) = \frac{13}{52} + \frac{12}{52} - \frac{3}{52} = \frac{22}{52}$. Could you list the 22 cards that would belong to the event (spade or face card)?

Here are two rather simple problems for you to try:

1. What is the probability that you could throw either a 7 or an 11 on a single throw of 2 dice?
2. What is the probability that you would throw either a double or a total of more than 9 on a single toss of 2 dice?

Probability of "A and B"

When two events, A and B, are *independent*, we can compute the probability of the event (A and B) by using the following rule, involving the multiplication principle:

Rule 5.

If events A and B are independent, then
$$P(A \text{ and } B) = P(A) \times P(B).$$

Intuitively, we would expect two events to be independent when they have nothing to do with each other. Although this is usually a reliable rule of thumb, it must be used with care. For example, when two events are mutually exclusive, our first thought might be that they have nothing to do with each other. But when one of two mutually exclusive events occurs, the other cannot possibly occur. Thus the occurrence of one of these events certainly affects the probability that the other also occurs. Mutually exclusive events, therefore, are never independent of one another. For two events to be independent, the occurrence of one must not affect the probability that the other occurs at the same time.

Here is a problem involving two independent events, in which Rule 5 could be applied: Suppose that we toss two dice, one red and one green. What is the probability that the number 1 would come up on the red die and that the number 3 would come up on the green die? In this case, the outcome on the green die has nothing to do with the outcome on the red die. We therefore have two independent events. The probability of any one of the numbers 1, 2,

Figure 5. Subsets A and B are mutually exclusive events in sample space S.

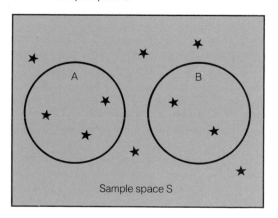

3, 4, 5, and 6 coming up on the toss of a single die is $\frac{1}{6}$. The probability of the outcome (1,3) on a toss of two dice would be calculated as follows, in accordance with Rule 5: $P(1 \text{ and } 3) = P(1) \times P(3) = \frac{1}{6} \times \frac{1}{6} = \frac{1}{36}$.

By using the multiplication principle, we can provide an answer of sorts to the question "If a baseball player averages 3 hits in 10 times at bat, what are his chances of getting 4 consecutive hits?" If we assume that the times at bat are independent trials, and if we let H stand for each hit, we could compute the possibility of 4 consecutive hits in this way: $P(\text{HHHH}) = P(\text{H}) \times P(\text{H}) \times P(\text{H}) \times P(\text{H}) = \frac{3}{10} \times \frac{3}{10} \times \frac{3}{10} \times \frac{3}{10} = \frac{81}{10{,}000}$. We would expect the batter to get 4 hits in a row about 81 times in every 10,000 sequences of 4 times at bat. This probability would hold if we were right in assuming that the 4 times at bat would be independent trials. The assumption might not be a sound one in this case. For one thing, the batter would probably hit better against certain pitchers than against others. Also, getting a hit or not getting a hit might have an effect on his chances the next time at bat.

Consider the event (double and even) in the experiment of tossing two dice. By "double," of course, we mean that the same number would come up on both dice; by "even," that the sum of the two numbers would be an even number. In this case, $P(\text{double}) = \frac{6}{36}$ and $P(\text{even}) = \frac{18}{36}$. If we applied the multiplication principle for independent events, as stated in Rule 5, we would have $P(\text{double and even}) = \frac{6}{36} \times \frac{18}{36} = \frac{108}{1{,}296} = \frac{3}{36}$. But if we examine Figure 3, we will find 6 points that correspond to the event (double and even). Therefore the true value of P(double and even) is $\frac{6}{36}$ and not $\frac{3}{36}$, as our calculation had seemed to indicate. The reason is that in this case the two events are not independent. If we throw a double, we are certain to throw an even number. This means that if we have thrown a double, the probability that we have also thrown an even number is 1. Again, if we know that we have thrown an even number, the probability that we have also thrown a double is $\frac{1}{3}$. This is

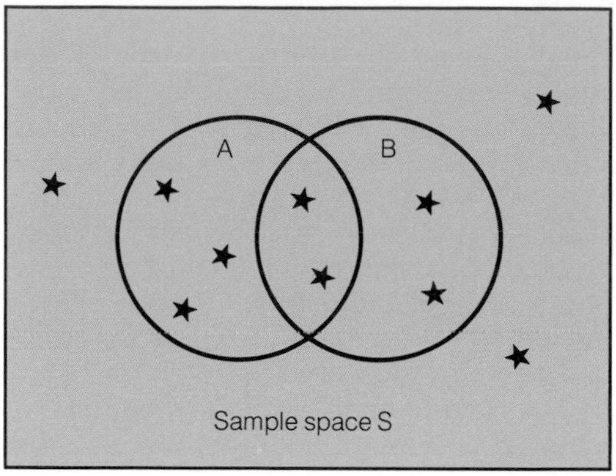

Figure 6. Subsets A and B are nonmutually exclusive events in sample space S.

determined by counting the number of ways an even number can occur (18 in all) and the number of these occurrences that are doubles (6).

In order to calculate P(A and B) when the events are not independent, the multiplication principle for independent events (Rule 5) can be generalized as follows:

Rule 6.

If events A and B are not independent, then
$$P(\text{A and B}) = P(\text{A}) \times P(\text{B/A}).$$

The term "B/A" would be read as "B given A." When we know that the event A occurs, we can compute P(B/A) by thinking of the event A as a reduced sample space. Consider Figure 7. The sample space S consists of 10 equally likely events, of which 5 are in A, 3 are in B, and 2 are in both A and B. Given that A occurs, then any outcome obtained is one of the 5 in A. If we think of these 5 points as a new sample space, then 2 of the equally likely outcomes belong to the event B. Thus $P(\text{B/A}) = \frac{2}{5}$. Applying Rule 6, we can compute $P(\text{A and B}) = P(\text{A}) \times P(\text{B/A}) = \frac{5}{10} \times \frac{2}{5} = \frac{10}{50} = \frac{2}{10}$. This, as you can see, agrees with what we would obtain by a direct count of the points that belong to both A and B in Figure 7.

If events A and B are independent, then the probability that B occurs will not be affected by the fact that A occurs. Thus for independent events, $P(B/A) = P(B)$. Suppose we were to select 1 card from a deck of 52 cards. What is the probability that the card selected will be both a red card (R) and a face card (F)? Since half the cards are red, we know that $P(R) = {}^{26}/_{52}$. Of the 26 red cards, 6 are face cards. Hence $P(F/R) = {}^{6}/_{26}$. Since $P(F) = {}^{12}/_{52} = {}^{6}/_{26}$ and $P(F/R)$ is also ${}^{6}/_{26}$, the events F and R are independent and $P(R \text{ and } F) = P(R) \times P(F)$. Thus the multiplication rule for independent events (Rule 5) is actually just a special case of the more general Rule 6: $P(A \text{ and } B) = P(A) \times P(B/A)$.

Here are some problems involving the probability of event (A and B). (Assume that cards are drawn from a regular 52-card deck.)

1. A coin is tossed and a die is thrown. What is the probability of obtaining heads and a 3?

2. A card is drawn and a die is tossed. What is the probability of getting two 6's?

3. A card is drawn. What is the probability that it is neither a face card nor a red card?

Degree of Confidence

In this brief introduction to probability, we have touched on only a few of the basic principles involved. The scope of probability theory is much broader than our discussion would suggest. For example, we simplified matters a good deal by dealing only with situations in which the individual outcomes of an experiment were equally likely. In many situations this is not the case. Calculations then become more complex, and new dimensions are added to the study of probability.

In our simplified presentation, we merely pointed out that predictions based on probability are uncertain. Scientists accept this but want to know *how* uncertain. They recognize that in trying to predict the outcome of an experiment subject to the laws of chance, they may often be wrong. They need to know how often and how wrong. They want to establish the degree of confidence they can place in their predictions. Probability theory provides the basis for establishing this degree of confidence.

Many Uses

If you go at all deeply into the study of mathematics, you will find occasion to work with some of the more complicated and intriguing aspects of probability theory. You will also obtain a clearer idea of the many ways in which this theory serves humans: it enables scientists to fix a limit within which the deviations from a given physical law must fall if these deviations are not to count against the law. It has been used to calculate the positions and velocities of electrons orbiting around the nuclei of atoms. The fluctuations in density of a given volume of gas have been analyzed by applying probability theory. It has played an important part in genetics; among other things, it has made it possible to calculate the percentage of individuals with like and unlike traits in successive generations. Manufacturers use probability theory to predict the quality of items coming off mass-production lines. Insurance experts make extensive use of the theory; it enables them, for example, to calculate life expectancies so that they may set appropriate life-insurance rates. Finally, because of probability theory, computers can be programmed to predict the outcome of elections on the basis of comparatively few returns and with what is generally a surprising degree of accuracy.

F. Joe Crosswhite

Figure 7. Subsets A and B are nonindependent events in sample space S.

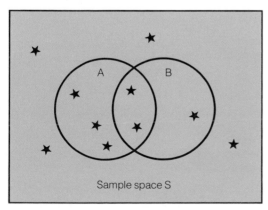

Sample space S

GAME THEORY

Five criminals huddle in a building after committing a crime. Outside waits a lone policeman, determined to capture the leader. The criminals do not know he is out there. Nonetheless, they plan to leave randomly, one at a time, to avoid attracting attention. All the policeman knows is that the leader is the tallest of the criminals. He cannot capture more than one of the men, for he would be overpowered. He has no way of getting help. As the men come out, which should the policeman arrest? The first? The second? The last?

If he made the arrest on a random basis, the policeman would have only a 20 percent chance of getting his man. Game theorists say he can do better by following a certain strategy, or plan of action: Let the first two men go, and arrest the next man to come out who is taller than the first two men. If he does this, the policeman stands a 40 percent chance of capturing the leader.

This is a simple problem in game theory, a branch of mathematics that deals with risk in conflict situations. It gets its name from the fact that so many conflict situations in the real world are similar in basic structure to bridge, poker, checkers, chess, even tic-tac-toe. Both in games and in everyday events, people compete with one another. There are rules by which the game must be played; there are outcomes, or payoffs—such as win, lose, and draw— that result from the opponent's different moves, or strategies; and there is generally some information available to one or more of the players involved.

In game theory it is assumed that the objective of each player is to maximize gains or minimize losses. It is also assumed that the player is faced with a rational opponent whose objective is to do the same. Of course, the cop-and-robbers situation is really a *one-person game*. The robbers

Two boys playing chess, a zero-sum game involving a pair of players following set rules, with a clear objective—simply to win.

Mimi Forsyth, Monkmeyer

Jan Braunle

Mickey Palmer, DPI

The complicated game of football involves two teams pitted against each other to win a game by attaining the higher numerical score. There are rules, but all kinds of strategies and tactics can be worked out. Left, the coach explains a play to members of the team. Right, a play in action.

don't know they are competing with the policeman. If they did, they would try a strategy of their own. They might assume that the policeman is a game theorist and therefore send their leader out first. On the other hand, the policeman might realize that they would think this, and therefore arrest the first man to come out. In short, a game can be complicated.

Aside from one-person games, which are apt to have little value and be easy to solve, perhaps the simplest games are games of two individuals or teams where the losses of one are the gains of the other. This kind of game is called a *two-person zero-sum game*. In a zero-sum game, what one side gains, the other side loses—and vice versa. The total value of the game doesn't increase or decrease.

It is easy to imagine games where this is not the case. Two advertisers competing for a market, for example, might not only increase or decrease their shares of the market through their advertising, but might actually increase the total market. To best illustrate game theory, however, we will stick to the two-person zero-sum game.

Case of the Complicated Collection

Most games are finite. That is, there are only a certain number of strategies, or alternatives, that each player can follow, and the game is "solved" in a certain number of plays, or moves. Some games are also games of *perfect information,* that is, we know, or can see, each move our opponent makes. Checkers, chess, and tic-tac-toe are examples of finite games of perfect information. Chess tends to be interesting because so many different moves are possible. A game such as tic-tac-toe tends to be less interesting because there are so few moves and it can be solved so easily. In fact, in tic-tac-toe the first player can be assured of at least a draw, or tie, if the first mark is put in one of the corner squares. The second player can guarantee a draw by making a mark in the center square.

To illustrate game theory, let's consider a finite, two-person zero-sum game of *imperfect information.* Let's assume that Abe owes you $60 and Bill owes you $40. Abe and Bill get paid on Friday, and the owed money will be available from each only on payday at 5 P.M. at their respective places of employment. Because you cannot be in two places at once, you will be able to collect from either Abe or Bill, not from both. The situation is further complicated by the fact that these two men owe the same amounts of money to a fellow we will call your opponent: Oscar.

Whoever is at Abe's or Bill's place of employment at 5 P.M. gets the money owed there. If both of you show up at one place, you split the money. But if neither of you shows up, Oscar gets the money because he is a special friend of both Abe and Bill. Both you and Oscar have this information. Thus you must determine where you should go to maximize your gain: to Abe's or Bill's?

This is a problem that can be solved by using game theory. It is a conflict situation: You want to get as much money as you can, while Oscar, who could get all the money if you didn't go to either place, wants to minimize his losses. It is a zero-sum game because the total amount to be paid out ($100) stays the same whatever strategies are used.

Choice of Strategies

The game you and Oscar play is called a "2 × 2 game"; there are 2 strategies available to you and 2 available to Oscar: Each of you can go to see either Abe (strategy A) or Bill (strategy B). Some two-person games have many more strategies available to the players. For example, in a 2 × 3 game, your opponent has 3 strategies to choose from while you have only 2. In a 4 × 3 game, you have 4 strategies to your opponent's 3. In a 3 × m game, m means that your opponent has many strategies from which to choose.

Large games can usually be reduced to more manageable proportions because some of the strategies will not make sense in terms of the game. For example, if all the payoffs for a particular strategy are zero, there is no reason to choose this strategy. It may as well be eliminated from consideration.

We can best illustrate a game by a *payoff matrix*. This indicates what happens when players select their different strategies. Figure 1 shows a payoff matrix for the game between you and Oscar. It is conventional to have a matrix show payoffs for the player whose strategies are listed on the left side of the matrix. This is the player who wants to maximize his or her gains. The payoffs shown are gains, in a zero-sum game, for the player whose strategies are listed at the left. The payoffs are losses for

A shopper studying brands of products in a grocery. Manufacturers and advertisers apply game theory to capture a share of the food market.

the person who is named at the top of the matrix.

The matrix in Figure 1 shows that if both you and Oscar choose strategy A (going to see Abe), your payoff will be $30. If you choose A and Oscar chooses B (going to see Bill), your payoff will be $60. If you choose B and Oscar chooses A, your payoff will be $40. If you both choose strategy B, your payoff will be $20.

Some additional figures are shown outside the squares in Figure 1. These help us "solve" the problem following game-theory procedure. The particular theory we will follow was first proposed by the mathematician John Von Neumann in 1929 and extensively developed in a book he wrote with Oskar Morgenstern, published in 1944, titled *Theory of Games and Economic Behavior*.

The figures outside the matrix are called *rim figures*. The column at the right gives the *row minima:* the minimum amount in the row opposite which it appears. The row at the bottom of the matrix gives the *column maxima:* the maximum amount in the column under which it appears. Game theory says that you should choose the strategy that provides the "maximum of your minimum" gains. This is called your *maximin*. Your opponent rationally should choose the strategy that provides the "minimum of his or her maximum" losses. This is called the opponent's *minimax*. In Figure 1, your maximin and Oscar's minimax are circled. By choosing strategy A you guarantee yourself a gain of at least $30; if your opponent should choose strategy B, you will get the entire $60 from Abe. Oscar, however, will likely choose strategy A because it guarantees him a maximum loss of $40. Either one of you could, of course, try to outsmart the other. But then you would be *gambling,* and this is what game theory avoids. It is, instead, a mathematical technique for guaranteeing a minimum gain (or maximum loss) from a conflict situation.

Mixed Strategies and Saddle Points

We assumed that your game with Oscar would be played only once. That is,

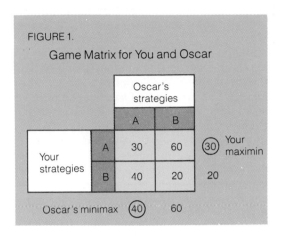

FIGURE 1.

Game Matrix for You and Oscar

each player was to make only one move. But most games, both in real life and among parlor games, involve a number of moves. Matching pennies is a good example. In this game, if you choose a "pure" strategy, such as playing heads all the time, you could wind up losing your shirt (or at least all your pennies). Frequently, such a situation calls for a "mixed" strategy, such as playing heads and tails each 50 percent of the time on a random basis. Tossing the coin before each play would achieve this aim. In fact, even those who know nothing about game theory usually play the game this way.

Now lets look at your game with Oscar again and assume that it is to be played many times. Does a pure strategy then make sense? Not quite. We've determined that Oscar will choose strategy A because, if he doesn't, you might get $60 instead of $30. But let's fool him. Let's choose strategy B, getting $40 instead of $30. How long will Oscar allow this? If you choose B, then he also will choose B, thus reducing your winnings to $20. You can switch back to strategy A and gain $60. But he also will switch back to strategy A. Before long, both of you are employing mixed strategies, trying to best each other. Now the question is what kind of mixed strategy should you employ?

Before we answer this question, let's consider whether or not a mixed strategy should be used in a particular game. Game theory says that a mixed strategy should not be used if the game has a *saddle point.* A game is said to have a saddle point if the maximin equals the minimax; that is, if the maximum of your minimum gains equals the minimum of your opponent's maximum losses. The game with Oscar does not have a saddle point, as you can see by comparing the two circled numbers in Figure 1. Therefore, the game calls for a mixed strategy. If the two circled numbers were equal, then the game would have a saddle point, and each player should choose the pure strategy dictated by his or her maximin or minimax.

To illustrate this, consider Figure 2, in which we have changed the payoffs (or *payouts,* as they are sometimes called) to create a saddle point for the game. Your maximin equals Oscar's minimax. Under these conditions it doesn't make sense for you to choose strategy B. You would only lose. Oscar, who assumes that you are rational, cannot do other than choose strategy A, too. If he chooses strategy B he stands to lose $100 instead of $50. So both of you will continue to choose strategy A. Such a game is said to be *strictly determined.*

Value of the Game

Every game has a certain value. The value of the strictly determined game in Figure 2 is $50. The value of the original game (in Figure 1), played on a one-time basis, is $30. (Both these values are, of course, yours, and we will continue to

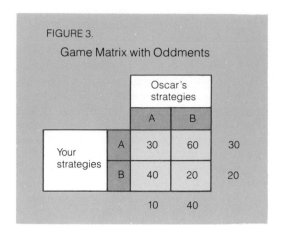

FIGURE 3.

Game Matrix with Oddments

speak of the value of the game in your terms.)

If the original game is to be played on a continuing basis, both you and Oscar will begin mixing your strategies, each trying to get the better of the other. What the two of you are really fighting over is the $10 spread between your guaranteed minimum gain of $30 and his guaranteed maximum loss of $40—if each of you plays a pure strategy. By mixing strategies each of you hopes to get as much of this $10 as possible. This suggests that the value of the game lies somewhere between $30 and $40. How can Oscar assure himself that you get no more than that amount? The answer lies in mixing strategies in a prescribed way.

After determining that the game does not have a saddle point, you may erase the rim figures. Now, determine the absolute differences between the payoffs in each row and column and write these figures in the margins. These figures are called *oddments,* or part of the odds in using each of the strategies. We've done this for you in Figure 3. You can see that the differences in the row payoffs are $30 and $20, while the differences in the column payoffs are $10 and $40. These figures are the ratios with which the different strategies should be played (3 to 2 for you, 4 to 1 for Oscar). Each figure, however, applies to the opposite strategy. In other words, your mixed strategy should be to play strategy B three times and strategy A two times out of every five plays; Oscar's mixed strategy should

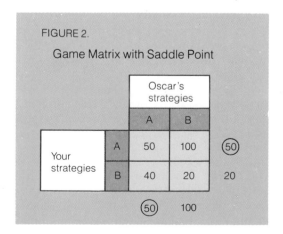

FIGURE 2.

Game Matrix with Saddle Point

be to play strategy A four times and strategy B one time in the same number of plays.

Even though Oscar can easily figure out your overall strategy, it is best to keep him guessing about each individual move. Otherwise he might outfox you. You should choose each move on a random basis. For example, you might throw three red cards, representing strategy B, into a hat together with two black cards representing strategy A. Before each move mix the cards and withdraw one. Let this card determine the strategy you choose. Throw the card back into the hat and repeat the process for the next move. In the long run you will play your strategies in a ratio of 3 to 2, and the probability is high that you will achieve the *value* of the game. The value of the game is easily determined. For each row, multiply the oddment times each payoff in the other row. Add the products together and divide by the sum of the oddments. Average your answers for the rows. This gives the value of the game if you play your prescribed mixed strategy. Do the same for the columns. This gives the value of the game if your opponent plays his prescribed mixed strategy. These two values should be the same. Over the long haul, the value of the game will be achieved if both of you play your prescribed mixed strategies. If one player deviates, chances are that player will not achieve the value of the game.

The arithmetic involved in determining the value of the game is illustrated below:

The value of the game, if both players play rationally (i.e., use their prescribed mixed strategies), is $36.

Non-Zero-Sum and N-Person Games

When we move away from the two-person, zero-sum game, problems become a bit more complicated. For one thing, psychology, negotiation, and communication may become factors in the problems.

A non-zero-sum game, you will recall, is one in which the losses of one player are not necessarily the gains of the other. That is, the total value of the game does not necessarily remain the same throughout the play. An example of a two-person, non-zero-sum game is "the prisoners' dilemma":

Imagine that two criminals suspected of a bank robbery are arrested and placed in separate jail cells so they cannot communicate. If one confesses and turns state's evidence, he will go free. The other will be sentenced to 20 years in prison. If both criminals confess and throw themselves on the mercy of the court, they will each receive a 5-year sentence. If neither confesses, they will each get 1 year for carrying concealed weapons. If you were one of the prisoners, what would you do?

This conflict situation is pictured in Figure 4. The strategies are confession (C) and no confession (NC). Because this is a non-zero-sum game, the payoffs for both players are listed in each square, with player A's payoff to the left of the comma

$$\frac{20 \times 30 + 20 \times 60}{20 + 30} = 36$$

$$\frac{30 \times 40 + 30 \times 20}{20 + 30} = 36$$

$$\text{Value of the game} = \frac{36 + 36}{2} = 36 \quad \text{} \rightarrow \text{rows}$$

$$\frac{40 \times 30 + 40 \times 40}{40 + 10} = 56$$

$$\frac{10 \times 60 + 10 \times 20}{40 + 10} = 16$$

$$\text{Value of the game} = \frac{56 + 16}{2} = 36 \quad \text{} \rightarrow \text{columns}$$

FIGURE 4.

Game Matrix for Prisoners' Dilemma

		Prisoner B	
		C	NC
Prisoner A	C	5,5	0,20
	NC	20,0	1,1

and player B's payoff to the right. Assume you are player A, and study only your own payoff. As a good game theorist, you should choose the strategy that provides your minimax, the minimum of your maximum losses. Thus you should confess. The worst that could happen would be a 5-year sentence.

Your opponent, prisoner B, should choose the same strategy. But this may be oversimplifying the game. Suppose you believe that your opponent is the kind of person who would never confess. What would you do then? It depends on what type of person you are.

Suppose you two were cellmates and could discuss the situation. Would you both agree not to confess? That would make sense. But what about the danger of a double-cross? As you can see, for many (if not most) games, mathematics does not have all the answers.

Games involving more than two people (*n*-person games) can be even more complex. Imagine a situation involving three people: A, B, and C. If A cooperates with B they will split $6. If A cooperates with C they will split $8. If B cooperates with C they will split $10. This is illustrated in the triangle in Figure 5. Who should cooperate with whom to divide the money?

"Look," A says to B, "cooperate with me and I'll give you $4 and keep only $2."

"Don't be silly," says B to A. "I can probably get $5 cooperating with C."

"Nothing doing," says C. "I think I can make a better deal with A. How about it, A? Will you take $2 and leave me $6?"

"Okay," says A.

Then B panics. "Look, A," he says, "I'm willing to split the $6 fifty-fifty."

"Don't lose your head," says C to B. "I'll give you $4."

"But that's what *I* offered you," says A to B.

Round and round it goes. The division of the money will depend on the negotiating talents of those involved. All game theory can tell us is that, by cooperating with one of her opponents, the most A can hope to receive is $2; the most B can hope to get is $4; and the most C can hope for is $6.

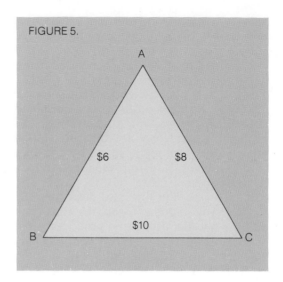

FIGURE 5.

But let us change the rules. Suppose A, B, and C could gain a total of $18 if all three of them cooperated. How should the money be split? Using the previous resolution, we can determine what ratio of the total each player should receive. First we add the maximum amounts receivable by each player, according to the original rules: $2 + $4 + $6 = $12. Player A's ratio, therefore, is $2/12$, or $1/6$; B's is $4/12$, or $1/3$; C's is $6/12$, or $1/2$. If we apply these ratios to the new rules, in which the receivable total is $18, A should receive $1/6$ of $18, or $3; B should receive $1/3$, or $6; C should receive $1/2$, or $9.

As you can see, these simple games give only a hint of the complexity of larger, non-zero-sum games. Game theory has had its greatest success to date with only the most elementary of games, or conflict situations. Undoubtedly it will come to have increasing importance in the future, for so much of life has to do with conflict and competition. As John D. Williams has written in his book *The Compleat Strategyst,* "The concept of a strategy, the distinctions among players, the role of chance events, the notion of matrix representations of the payoffs, the concepts of pure and mixed strategies, and so on give valuable orientation to persons who must think about complicated conflict situations."

Joseph G. Cowley

Calvin Campbell

Nearly rectangular windows fill out the area under the roof of M.I.T.'s Kresge Auditorium. In calculus we use rectangles to find the area under a curve.

CALCULUS

One of the greatest contributions to modern mathematics, science, and engineering was the invention of *calculus* (or as it is sometimes called, *the calculus*) near the end of the 17th century. It is safe to say that without this fundamental branch of mathematics, many technological accomplishments, such as the landing of men on the moon, would have been very difficult, or impossible, to achieve.

The word "calculus" comes from the Latin word for pebble. This name probably originated because pebbles were used thousands of years ago for counting and doing problems in arithmetic. Similar words that we often use are *calculate, calculation,* and *calculator.*

Two people who lived during the 17th century are credited with the invention of the calculus: Sir Isaac Newton of England and Baron Gottfried Wilhelm von Leibniz of Germany. The basic ideas of calculus were developed independently by them within a few years of each other.

Newton, who was one of the greatest physicists of all time, applied the calculus to his theories of motion and gravitation. These theories, often referred to as *Newton's laws,* enabled him to describe mathematically the motion of all objects in the universe—from the tossing of a ball into the air to the revolution of the earth around the sun.

Before Newton and Leibniz, the mathematics used for solving problems was the kind commonly taught in modern secondary schools. This involved subjects such as arithmetic, algebra, geometry, and trigonometry. The basic principles of these subjects were known at least 1,500 years before Newton and Leibniz. Although the mathematical principles studied in these subjects were useful in solving certain kinds of problems, they were not at all suited to solving problems dealing with *changing,* or *varying, quantities*. It was for the purpose of working with such quantities in everyday life that the calculus was invented. We therefore can say that calculus is the "mathematics of change."

Changing, or Varying, Quantities

If a person travels in an automobile at a velocity of 50 kilometers per hour, we know that in 2 hours that person will travel a distance of 100 kilometers. In practice, of course, a driver rarely travels at the same velocity of 50 kilometers per hour for 2 hours. The driver will sometimes stop, sometimes travel at a velocity of 80 kilometers per hour, and sometimes at 40 kilometers per hour.

Scientists use calculus to calculate a rocket's escape velocity as well as its velocity and position at any given time.

NASA

The velocity of the automobile is usually a changing, or varying, quantity. When the velocity is increasing, as when the auto goes from 30 to 40 kilometers per hour, we say that the automobile is being *accelerated,* or that it is undergoing *acceleration*. Similarly, when the velocity is decreasing, as when the auto goes from 40 to 20 kilometers per hour, we say that the automobile is being *decelerated,* or undergoing *deceleration*. If the automobile maintains the same velocity, then we say that it is traveling at a *constant,* or *uniform, velocity*.

Another example of a changing quantity involves a ball that has been dropped or thrown. Suppose we drop a ball from a building. At the instant we drop it, the velocity is zero. Gradually, the velocity increases; that is, the ball accelerates. Finally, when the ball hits the ground, it is traveling at its greatest velocity.

Similarly, if we throw a ball up into the air, it at first travels fast—that is, with a large velocity. Gradually it slows down, or decelerates, until its velocity is zero and it stops for an instant. At this point the ball has reached its maximum height and starts to come down. As it comes down, its velocity increases until the ball hits the ground. The change in the velocity of the ball—or any object that is thrown—is due to the attraction of the earth, which is called the *force of gravity,* or the *gravitational force*.

The same ideas apply to a rocket launched from the earth's surface. By using calculus, it is possible to find the velocity the rocket must have in order to escape the earth's gravity—that is, not return to the earth. This velocity, often called the *escape velocity,* turns out to be about 11 kilometers per second, or about 40,000 kilometers per hour. By means of calculus, we can calculate the time it would take for the rocket to get to the moon and how much fuel would be needed.

There are many other examples of changing, or varying, quantities. When a raindrop or snowflake falls, its size gradually increases. The population of a country changes each year, or even each day. The cost of living changes. The amount of

Tony Duffy

This car's velocity is hardly ever constant. The car accelerates at the start of the race, slows down before each curve, and accelerates again on straightaways.

a radioactive substance, such as radium, changes.

What is a Variable?

Any quantity that is changing, or varying, is referred to in mathematics as a *variable*. In the examples of the automobile, ball, and rocket, the velocity is a variable. Also, the distance of the ball or rocket from the earth's surface is a variable. Even the time, which is changing, is a variable. The population of a country or the cost of living is a variable. When we put air in our tires, the air pressure changes and is a variable. The outdoor temperature and humidity are variables.

In mathematics we often represent variables by symbols, such as letters of the alphabet. Thus we can let v represent velocity, t represent time, p represent pressure in a tire, and so on. These letters stand for numbers. Thus when the velocity is 50 kilometers per hour we can say that $v = 50$. When it is 25 kilometers per hour we can say that $v = 25$, and so on.

In the case of time, we usually measure it from some specific instant, which is often called the *time origin* or *zero time*. For example, the instant at which we drop a ball from a building is zero time, or $t = 0$. After 3 seconds have elapsed, we say that $t = 3$; after 5 seconds, $t = 5$; and so on.

Very often, in practice, we find that one variable depends in some way on another variable. For example, the distance a rocket or ball travels depends on the time of travel. In this instance, we call distance the *dependent variable* and time the *independent variable*.

In general, time is considered as an independent variable, while any variable that depends on it is a dependent variable. Thus the cost of living, which depends on time, is a dependent variable. The outdoor temperature is also a depenent variable.

Many independent variables besides time can occur. For example, the area of a circle depends on the radius. We can call the area A the dependent variable, and the radius r the independent variable.

What is a Function?

If one variable depends on another, mathematicians say that the first variable is a *function* of the second variable. The distance a rocket or ball travels is a function of the time of travel. The area of a circle is a function of the radius of the circle.

Suppose we designate by the letter x any independent variable such as time, radius of a circle, and so on. Suppose further that we designate by the letter y any dependent variable that depends on x, such as the distance traveled by a rocket or the area of a circle. We then can make the statement that "y depends on x" or "y is a function of x," often abbreviated as $y = f(x)$. This is read "y equals f of x."

In terms of this functional notation, we could abbreviate the statement that the cost of living C is a function of the time t by writing $C = f(t)$. Similarly, we could express the fact that the area A of a circle is a function of the radius r by writing $A = f(r)$. A function always indicates that there is a relationship between the dependent and independent variables. One of the important problems in mathematics and its applications to other fields is to determine the nature of these relationships.

In some cases, the relationship between variables is simple. For example, we know from geometry that the area A of a circle is given in terms of its radius r by means of the relationship $A = \pi r^2$, where π is a constant whose value is approximately 3.14159. In other cases, the relationship between variables can be very difficult to obtain. For example, the relationship between the cost of living and time is not known, although we can have some idea about such a relationship based on past experience. However, even though we cannot find such a relationship, it does not mean that there is none.

Rates of Change

Suppose that at 10:00 A.M. an automobile driver is 30 kilometers from a certain town, and at noon the driver is 160 kilometers away from that town. The change in distance in 2 hours, then, is 160 − 30, or 130 kilometers. On dividing this change in distance by the change in time—that is 130 kilometers divided by 2 hours—we obtain 65 kilometers per hour. This is called the driver's *average velocity*. It should be noted that, during the 2 hours, the driver may have been traveling at 80 kilometers per hour some of the time, and 50 kilometers per hour at other times. On the average, however, the driver traveled at 65 kilometers per hour.

We see that the average velocity is the "time rate of change in distance." The actual velocity of the driver at a particular instant is called the *instantaneous velocity*. We can get a good idea of the instantaneous velocity of a driver by finding the average velocity over a very brief interval of time. Thus suppose we know that at 10:00 A.M. the driver is 50 kilometers away from a certain town and that at 10:05 A.M. the driver is 55 kilometers away. The driver, then, has traveled 5 kilometers in 5 minutes, or about 1 kilometer a minute; that is, 60 kilometers per hour. This is the driver's *average velocity,* but it is also a very good approximation to the *instantaneous velocity,* since if the driver did stop during this time or was traveling much slower or faster than 60 kilometers per hour, it certainly couldn't have been for long.

The average velocity is, as we have seen, the time rate of change in distance. The instantaneous velocity is the "instantaneous time rate of change of distance." The problem of finding instantaneous time rates of change of distance, or of other quantities, is one of the most important parts of calculus and has many applications. We shall try to see how such instantaneous rates of change can be found.

Process of Differentiation

Let us consider a ball being dropped from a tall building, such as the Leaning Tower of Pisa, shown in Figure 1. If we let s be the distance (in meters) that the ball falls in a time t (in seconds), then s will depend on t; that is, s will be a function of t, or $s = f(t)$. A formula that reveals the relationship between s and t is

$$s = 4.9t^2 \qquad [1]$$

From this formula we see that at $t = 0$ we have $s = 0$, which is not surprising, since the ball falls zero distance in zero time. After 1 second (that is, $t = 1$) we see from equation [1] that $s = 4.9$, which means that in 1 second the ball has fallen 4.9 meters. Similarly, after 2 seconds (that is, $t = 2$) we see that $s = 19.6$, so that in 2 seconds the ball has fallen 19.6 meters.

Suppose now we want to find the velocity of the ball at the time t (that is, the instantaneous velocity at time t). We increase the time t by a small amount, which we denote by dt. We can think of dt as a "little bit of t."

We now try to find out the distance the ball will travel in the time $t + dt$ (that is, the time t plus the extra bit of time dt). This distance will be the original distance s plus an extra little bit of distance, which we call ds. Since the distance traveled in time $t + dt$ is $s + ds$, we can modify equation [1] to

$$s + ds = 4.9(t + dt)^2 \qquad [2]$$

which can be expanded by multiplication to

$$s + ds = 4.9t^2 + 9.8t(dt) + 4.9(dt)^2 \quad [3]$$

The extra little bit of distance ds that the ball travels can now be obtained by subtracting s from the left side of equation [3] and subtracting its equal value $4.9t^2$ (see equation [1]) from the right side.

$$ds = 9.8t(dt) + 4.9(dt)^2 \qquad [4]$$

Now since dt represents a small number (less than 1), $(dt)^2$ is a very small number. It is so small, in fact, that the last term on the right of equation [4] can for all practical purposes be removed. We thus have

$$ds = 9.8t(dt) \qquad [5]$$

On dividing both sides by dt, we obtain

$$\frac{ds}{dt} = 9.8t \qquad [6]$$

The quantity on the left of equation [6] which is the little bit of distance ds divided by the little bit of time dt, is the instantaneous velocity of the ball at time t. If we let this instantaneous velocity be v, we have

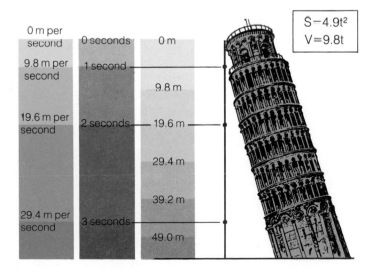

Velocity. Time Distance.

Velocity	Time	Distance
0 m per second	0 seconds	0 m
9.8 m per second	1 second	
		9.8 m
19.6 m per second	2 seconds	19.6 m
		29.4 m
		39.2 m
29.4 m per second	3 seconds	49.0 m

$S = 4.9t^2$
$V = 9.8t$

Figure 1. Suppose a ball is dropped from the top of the Leaning Tower of Pisa. The diagram at left shows the velocity of the ball and the distance it has fallen at given times. Using calculus, one can determine the velocity and distance traveled at any given time.

$$v = 9.8t \qquad [7]$$

If we put $t = 3$ in equation [7] we find $v = 29.4$. This means that, after 3 seconds, the ball is traveling 29.4 meters per second, which is its instantaneous velocity.

The process that we used to obtain the result in equation [6] is known in the calculus as *differentiation*. That part of the calculus that deals with such processes is called *differential calculus*. The quantity ds/dt is called the "*derivative* of s with respect to t," or simply the "derivative of s."

If we like, we can use equation [7] to find the derivative of v with respect to t. To do this, we use exactly the same procedure given for the derivative of s. We increase the time t by dt so that the total time is $t + dt$. Then the velocity v increases by a little bit, which we call dv, so that the new velocity is $v + dv$. From equation [7] we then see that

$$v + dv = 9.8(t + dt) \qquad [8]$$
or $\qquad v + dv = 9.8t + 9.8dt \qquad [9]$

Subtracting v from the left side of equation [9] and subtracting its equal value 9.8t (see equation [7]) from the right side, we have

$$dv = 9.8dt \qquad [10]$$
or
$$\frac{dv}{dt} = 9.8 \qquad [11]$$

The left side of equation [11] is the instantaneous time rate of change of the velocity, which is called the *instantaneous acceleration*. From equation [11] we see that the instantaneous acceleration is a constant. The significance is that when the ball falls toward the earth it increases its velocity by 9.8 meters per second in each second.

Since v is the derivative of s, we see that dv/dt is the derivative of the derivative of s, which is called the *second derivative* of s. It is written as

$$\frac{d^2s}{dt^2} = 9.8 \qquad [12]$$

Minima and Maxima

As we have already mentioned, the process of differentiation—that is, finding derivatives—is studied in that part of cal-

culus known as differential calculus. There are many applications of differential calculus besides those involving velocity and acceleration. One such application is illustrated by the following problem. Let us suppose that we are in the business of making metal cans for a soup company. We are asked by the company to make the cans cylindrical in shape, with the requirement that the cans have a capacity of 1 liter.

We could make the cans tall and narrow or short and wide (Figure 2). How shall we decide what to do? We know that the metal out of which the cans are made will cost money. It is therefore natural to ask ourselves whether we can make the required can by using the least amount—that is, the minimum amount—of metal for the total surface of the can. By the method of differential calculus we can determine the exact measurements (diameter and height) that the can must have in order to contain a given volume and at the same time have the least possible surface area and therefore the least cost. Since we are interested in the least, or minimum, surface area, this is called a problem in finding *minima*.

As another illustration, suppose we have a rectangular piece of cardboard that measures 3 meters by 5 meters. We wish to make an open box from it by cutting out equal squares from the corners and then bending up the sides. The question is, What

Figure 2. A manufacturing company wants to make 1-liter containers. Calculus can be used to determine the minimal surface area needed to contain the required volume.

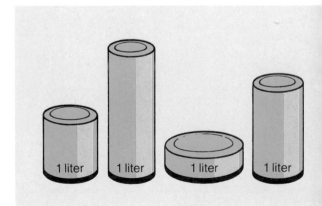

size squares should be cut out so that the box will contain the greatest, or maximum, volume? This problem, which is one in finding *maxima,* can also be solved by differential calculus.

The Process of Integration

We have already seen how, if we are given $s = 4.9t^2$, we can find $ds = 9.8t(dt)$. The process amounts to starting with the total distance s and finding the little bit of distance ds traveled in time dt. We gave the name differentiation to this process.

We now ask, If we are given the equation $ds = 9.8t(dt)$, can we get back to $s = 4.9t^2$? This is the reverse, or inverse, of differentiation. Since ds represents a little bit of distance, it is natural that to find the total distance s we must add up all the little bits of distance ds. The process of such adding is represented mathematically by

$$\int ds = s \qquad [13]$$

The symbol $\int$ is called an *integral* sign, and equation [13] is read "the integral of ds is s." The process of finding integrals is called *integration* and is studied in a part of calculus that is known as *integral calculus.* By methods of integral calculus, we can find, for example, that

$$s = \int ds = \int 9.8t(dt) - 4.9t^2 \qquad [14]$$

so that we have recovered the formula $s = 4.9t^2$. It follows that integration is the reverse, or inverse, of differentiation.

Applications

Just as there are many applications of differential calculus, there are also many applications of integral calculus. One important application is that of finding areas bounded by complicated closed curves or of finding volumes bounded by complicated closed surfaces. Another application is that of finding the total length of a complicated curve or the total area of a complicated surface (Figure 3). The idea involved in such cases is that of *summation,* or addition, of little bits of area or little bits of volume and so involves integration.

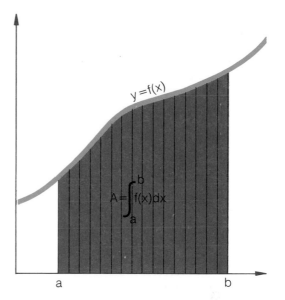

Figure 3. What is the area under y from a to b? We can divide the area into nearly rectangular regions whose areas can be approximated. The sum of these areas is very close to what we want. Integration gives the "best possible approximation," which is the actual area under the curve.

We have seen how the process of integration enables us to go from equation [6] back to equation [1]. Equation [6] involves an instantaneous rate of change. It is a derivative. Equations involving derivatives of quantities that we want to determine are called *differential equations.* Such equations often arise in the mathematical statements of problems in science and engineering, because it is in many cases easier to arrive at a relationship between derivatives of quantities rather than between the quantities themselves. The process of solving differential equations is often also known as "integrating the differential equation."

In the preceding paragraphs we have been able to provide only a glimpse into some of the many important ideas of calculus. In order to appreciate the power of the calculus in solving the many important problems of mathematics, science, and engineering, the student should consult some of the many books on calculus that are available.

Murray Spiegel

SET THEORY

A herd of cows, a flock of birds, a school of fish—each of the words "herd," "flock," and "school" could be replaced by the word "set." A *set* is simply a collection of objects or ideas.

The concept of sets was developed into a new branch of mathematics in the late 19th century by a German mathematician, Georg Cantor. Since the beginning of the 20th century, set theory has developed rapidly, and today it has important applications in nearly every branch of mathematics. In fact, most of our mathematics can be derived from set theory.

Two kinds of notations for sets are in common use. One is the *enumeration notation,* in which, for example, we write {1, 3} for the set consisting of the numbers 1 and 3 and {Roberts, Roye} for the set consisting of the first two presidents of Liberia.

The second notation is the *set-builder notation,* in which we write $\{x|x$ is a whole number} for the set of whole numbers, and $\{y|y$ is one of the first two presidents of Liberia} for the set {Roberts, Roye}. We read $\{x|x \ldots\}$ as "the set of all x such that $x \ldots$." Thus $\{x|x$ is a whole number} is read "the set of all x such that x is a whole number."

Of the two notations, the set-builder notation is the more frequently used in mathematics. Note that the letter, or symbol, used in the set-builder notation is not significant. Thus, for example, $\{x|x$ is a whole number} is the same as $\{y|y$ is a whole number}.

Capital letters are usually used as symbols for sets. We write, for example, A = $\{x|x$ is a whole number}.

The *members,* or *elements,* of a set are simply those things that make up the set. Thus the members of the set {2, 3} are the numbers 2 and 3. The members of the set $\{x|x$ is a United States citizen} are the citizens of the United States. When we say that two sets A and B are equal, we mean that every member of A is a member of B and, conversely, that every member of B is a member of A. For example, {5, 7} = {7, 5}. Note that the order of listing the members is not significant. If x is a member of a set A, we write $x \in$ A. If x is not a member of A, we write $x \notin$ A. Thus $2 \in \{2, 3\}$, but $4 \notin \{2, 3\}$.

Subsets of Sets

Every member of the set {a, b} is a member of the set {a, b, c}. We say that {a, b} is a *subset* of {a, b, c} and write {a, b} $\subseteq$ {a,b, c}. Every member of the set A = $\{x|x$ is an even number} is a member of the set B = $\{x|x$ is a whole number}. We say that A is a subset of B and write A $\subseteq$ B.

Our examples illustrate the "natural" use of the word "subset" to indicate a part of a whole (as, for example, "subtotal" is a part of the total). It is useful, however, to consider that {a, b} $\subseteq$ {a, b}. In general, every set is a subset of itself: A $\subseteq$ A for all sets A.

If A and B are sets, then A $\subseteq$ B means that whenever $x \in$ A, then $x \in$ B. If A is a subset of B but A $\neq$ B, we write A $\subset$ B and say that A is a *proper* subset of B. Thus, for example, {a, b} is a subset of {a, b} but is not a proper subset of {a, b}, whereas {a,b} is both a subset and a proper subset of {a, b, c}.

Union of Sets

Just as two numbers can be combined by addition or multiplication to yield a third number, so can two sets be combined in various ways to yield a third set. In particular, given two sets A and B, we can form their *union,* A $\cup$ B. This is the set whose members are members of A or B (or both). Thus, for example, {a, b} $\cup$ {c, d} = {a, b, c, d} and $\{x|x$ is an odd number} $\cup$ $\{x|x$ is an even number} = $\{x|x$ is a whole number}. In "set-theory language," if A and B are sets, then A $\cup$ B = $\{x|x \in$ A or $x \in$ B (or both)}.

This concept of union is used in many parts of mathematics. In elementary school, for example, the idea of addition of

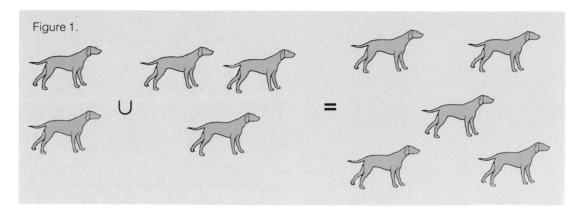

Figure 1.

whole numbers is made real to children by the use of set union. Thus the union of the two sets shown in Figure 1 corresponds to the addition fact $2 + 3 = 5$. In geometry, the concept of union is used to define a triangle as the union of three line segments, each of which has a common end point with each of the other two, as shown in Figure 2.

Suppose we consider

$$\{a, b\} \cup \{a, c\} = \{a, b, c\}.$$

Can we also write

$$\{a, b\} \cup \{a, c\} = \{a, a, b, c\}?$$

Yes, we can. It is true that $\{a, b, c\} = \{a, a, b, c\}$, but we do not "add" to the set $\{a, b\}$ by repeating the symbol "a". For example, consider the set $\{you, reader of this article\} = \{you\} = \{reader of this article\}$. You can't become two persons by naming yourself twice. So we agree, in listing the members of a set, not to list an element more than once.

Intersection of Sets

Similar to the concept of the union of two sets is the concept of the *intersection* of two sets. If A and B are sets, then the intersection of A and B, $A \cap B$, is

$$A \cap B = \{x | x \in A \text{ and } x \in B\}.$$

Thus, for example, $\{a, b, c\} \cap \{a, e, f\} = \{a\}$ and $\{x | x$ is a brown-eyed human being$\} \cap \{x | x$ is a woman$\} = \{x | x$ is a brown-eyed woman$\}$.

Like the concept of union of sets, the concept of intersection of sets finds wide application in mathematics. For example, we can find the set of common divisors of 12 and 18 thus:

$$\{x | x \text{ divides } 12\} \cap \{x \text{ divides } 18\} =$$
$$\{1, 2, 3, 4, 6, 12\} \cap \{1, 2, 3, 6, 9, 18\}$$
$$= \{1, 2, 3, 6\}$$

In geometry, we can symbolize the fact that two lines L_1 and L_2 intersect in a point P:

$$L_1 \cap L_2 = P$$

What about $\{x | x$ is an even number$\} \cap \{x | x$ is an odd number$\}$? Since no number is both even and odd, it may seem as if no answer is possible. To handle this and many similar situations, however, we introduce the concept of the *empty* set. Also called the *null* set, the empty set is symbolized by $\{ \ \}$, or $\varnothing$. Thus, $\{x | x$ is an even number$\} \cap \{x | x$ is an odd number$\} = \varnothing$. Likewise, if the lines L_1 and L_2 are parallel, $L_1 \cap L_2 = \varnothing$.

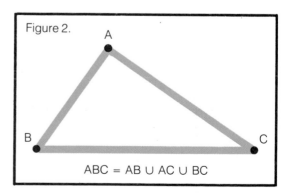

Figure 2.

$$ABC = AB \cup AC \cup BC$$

It is often useful to consider a fixed set, called the *universal* set, such that all the sets under consideration at a particular time are subsets of this universal set. For example, if we are discussing subsets of the whole numbers, such as the set of natural numbers {1, 2, 3, 4, . . .} and the set of even numbers {0, 2, 4, . . .}, we could take our universal set as the set of whole numbers. Similarly, we would take our universal set as the set of all points in the plane if we were discussing subsets of the set of points in a plane, such as the sets of points forming circles and sets of points forming triangles.

Complements of Sets

Suppose our universal set (U) is the set of all students at City High School, and A is the set of all female students at City High. Then the set of all male students at City High is called the *complement* of set A, and is indicated by A'. The complement A' of a set A consists of all elements in the universal set that are not members of A. In symbols, if $A \subseteq U$, then $A' = \{x | x \in U$ and $x \notin A\}$. Thus if our universal set is the set of real numbers and A is the set of rational numbers, then A' is the set of irrational numbers.

Venn Diagrams

It is often helpful to picture sets and set relations by means of what are commonly called *Venn diagrams*. In Figure 3 the region enclosed by each rectangle represents the universal set, and regions inside the rectangle that are enclosed by circles (or other curves) represent subsets of the universal set. Figure 4 shows Venn diagrams that illustrate some concepts of set theory.

Venn diagrams can be used to make plausible—although not actually prove—various statements of equality between sets, such as the two equalities that, in algebra, are called the *distributive properties*:

$$A \cup (B \cap C) = (A \cup B) \cap (A \cup C)$$

and

$$A \cap (B \cup C) = (A \cap B) \cup (A \cap C)$$

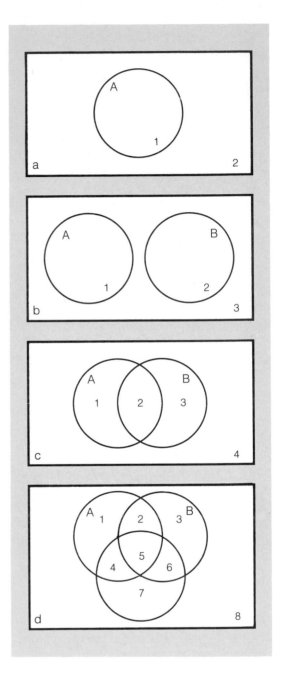

Figure 3. In each Venn diagram, the region enclosed by the rectangle represents the universal set. Subsets are represented by circles (labeled A, B, and C), the placement of which divides the universal sets into distinct regions (labeled 1, 2, 3, . . . , 7). The regions shared by intersecting sets contain the members, or elements, common to both, or all, intersecting sets. Sets A and B in diagram b are called "disjoint" sets because they share no region.

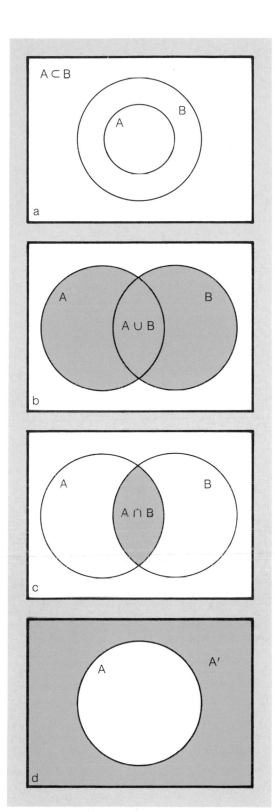

Figure 4. Each Venn diagram represents a particular set relationship: a) a proper subset; b) a union; c) an intersection; d) a complement.

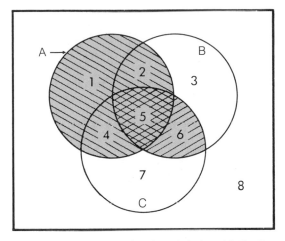

Figure 5. Set A consists of regions 1, 2, 4, and 5. Set B ∩ C consists of regions 5 and 6. Of what regions, then, does set A ∪ (B ∩ C) consist?

[note their similarities to the more familiar algebraic equation a(b + c) = ab + bc]. Thus the entire shaded region in Figure 5 illustrates A ∪ (B ∩ C) while the doubly shaded region in Figure 6 illustrates (A ∪ B) ∩ (A ∪ C). In both cases we obtain the same region. The corresponding situations for A ∩ (B ∪ C) and (A ∩ B) ∪ (A ∩ C) are shown in Figure 7.

Algebra of Sets

There are many analogies between the operations of union and intersection on sets and the operations of addition and multiplication on numbers. It is easy to see, for example, that just as $a + b = b + a$ and $a \times b = b \times a$ for all numbers a and b, it is also true that, for all sets A and B, A ∪ B = B ∪ A and A ∩ B = B ∩ A. Likewise, just as 0 has the property that $a + 0 = a$ and $a \times 0 = 0$ for all numbers a, so does A ∪ ∅ = A and A ∩ ∅ = ∅ for all sets A. Furthermore, just as $a \times 1 = a$ for all numbers a, so A ∩ U = A for all sets A ⊆ U (the universal set).

The analogies are not complete, however. There are properties of our number system for which there are no analogous properties for the algebra of sets, and there are properties of the algebra of sets for which there are no analogous properties for our number system. For example, given a nonzero number a, there exists a number b (the multiplicative inverse of a) such that a

$\times\ b\ =\ 1$. Now U is analogous to 1 in the sense that $A \cap U = A$ for all sets A, and yet, unless $A = U$, there is no set B such that $A \cap B = U$.

On the other hand, the fact that $A \cup A = A \cap A = A$ for all sets A has no analog in arithmetic. We have stated that $A \cap (B \cup C) = (A \cap B) \cup (A \cap C)$ for all sets A, B, and C, and this does have an analog in $a(b + c) = ab + ac$. We have also stated, however, that $A \cup (B \cap C) = (A \cup B) \cap (A \cup C)$ for all sets A, B, and C, and this corresponds to $a + bc = (a + b)(a + c)$ for all numbers a, b, and c. The latter statement, however, is not true. (Try $a = 1$, $b = 2$, and $c = 3$, for example.)

Table I lists a number of identities that hold for all sets A, B, and C that are subsets of some universal set U. Note the parallel-

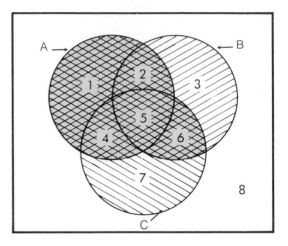

Figure 6. The sets $A \cup B$ and $A \cup C$ are indicated here by slanting lines. Their intersection is the region where the lines crisscross. It is the same set as that in Figure 5.

Table I:	
$A \cup A = A$	$A \cap A = A$
$A \cup B = B \cup A$	$A \cap B = B \cap A$
$A \cup (B \cup C) = (A \cup B) \cup C$	$A \cap (B \cap C) = (A \cap B) \cap C$
$A \cup (B \cap C) = (A \cup B) \cap (A \cup C)$	$A \cap (B \cup C) = (A \cap B) \cup (A \cap C)$
$A \cup \varnothing = A$	$A \cap U = A$
$A \cup A' = U$	$A \cap A' = \varnothing$
$U' = \varnothing$	$\varnothing' = U$
$A \cup U = U$	$A \cap \varnothing = \varnothing$
	$(A')' = A$

Figure 7. The shaded area of diagram a represents the set $A \cap (B \cup C)$, while the shaded area of diagram b represents the set $(A \cap B) \cup (A \cap C)$. Both sets are the same, confirming the identity.

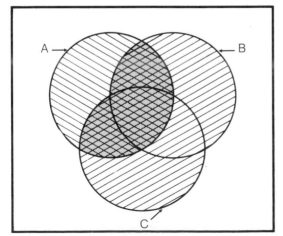

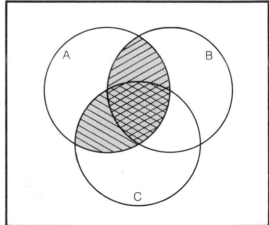

442

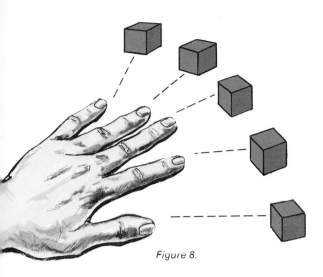

Figure 8.

ism between the corresponding identities in the left- and right-hand columns. All these identities are rather easily seen to hold as a consequence of the definitions of union, intersection, empty set, universal set, and complement, and can be made plausible, as we have seen, by use of Venn diagrams.

Infinite and Finite

What is meant by the word "infinite"? Many people think of infinity as being a very large or incalculable number. When mathematicians speak of an infinite set, however, they do not think of a set with a large number of elements, such as the set of grains of sand on the seashore. Indeed, they find it worthwhile to avoid entirely any direct reference to counting in describing the difference between finite and infinite sets.

To do this, the mathematician first considers the concept of *matching* sets, or, to use more technical language, sets that are in *one-to-one* (1–1) *correspondence*. This is a very natural concept that is used even in the very early stages of instruction in mathematics when a child learns to manually pair off blocks.

A formal definition is as follows: a 1–1 correspondence between two sets A and B is a pairing of the elements of A with the elements of B such that each element of A is paired with precisely one element of B

and each element of B is paired with precisely one element of A. If such a 1–1 correspondence exists between the two nonempty sets A and B, we say that the two sets are *equivalent* and write A ~ B. (We also say that $\varnothing \sim \varnothing$, although we will not use this fact here.)

For finite sets we normally do not bother to attempt a pairing to see if the two sets are equivalent; we simply count the elements in each set. Thus we observe that each of the two sets shown in Figure 8 has five elements, so that we "know" that they are equivalent. Actually, however, the concept of 1–1 correspondence precedes the idea of counting. "Five," for example, is simply the number name that we attach to sets that are in 1–1 correspondence with the fingers of one hand. Primitive man, long before he knew how to count, could keep track of the size of his flock by matching each animal with a pebble. If he dropped a pebble into a container as each animal left the enclosure in the morning, and then removed a pebble as each animal returned in the evening, he would know whether or not the same number of animals returned as had left, without counting.

Now if we have any finite set A, we sense intuitively that no proper subset of A is in 1–1 correspondence with A. Try, for example, matching the set of fingers minus the thumb on one hand with the entire set of fingers on the other hand. But what about infinite sets? Consider the set N = {1, 2, 3, . . .} of natural numbers and the set E = {2, 4, 6, . . .} of even natural numbers. Clearly E is a proper subset of N, and yet E ~ N as shown by the 1–1 correspondence in Figure 9.

We generalize these two examples to make a formal definition: A finite set is a set that has no proper subset equivalent to itself; an infinite set is a set that has at least one proper subset equivalent to itself.

Figure 9.				
Members of N	1	2	3 . . .	n . . .
	$\updownarrow$	$\updownarrow$	$\updownarrow$	$\updownarrow$
Members of E	2	4	6 . . .	2n . . .

Cardinal Number of an Infinite Set

If finite sets are equivalent, they have the same number of elements. That is, they are *equinumerous*. What about infinite sets? For example, is the set E of even numbers equinumerous with the set N of natural numbers? From one point of view it is certainly natural to argue that E and N are not equinumerous, since we take something away from the set N = {1, 2, 3, . . .} to get the set E = {2, 4, 6, . . .}. If we take something away, say 1, from the set {1, 2, 3}, the set we obtain, {2, 3}, is not equinumerous with the set {1, 2, 3}.

Nevertheless, it turns out to be useful to agree that E and N are equinumerous and, in general, to make the following formal definition: Two sets A and B (finite or infinite) are said to be equinumerous, or to have the same *cardinal number* of elements, if and only if A ~ B. We conclude from this definition that the finite sets of Figure 8 have the same cardinal number and that the sets E and N of Figure 9 have the same cardinal number.

Do all infinite sets have the same cardinal number? Consider, for example, the set Q of all positive rational numbers—the set of all natural numbers—together with all the positive fractions: $\frac{1}{2}$, $\frac{17}{19}$, $1\frac{7}{8}$, $\frac{1}{252}$, 0.12, and so on. Are Q and N equinumerous? Again, we may feel intuitively that the answer should be "no," since Q contains many (indeed, an infinite quantity of) numbers not in set N. We can, however, show that Q ~ N, so that, according to our definition, Q and N are equinumerous.

A simple argument that Q ~ N can be based on the diagram shown in Figure 10. It shows the positive rational numbers in an array extending indefinitely to the right and down. (Ignore the arrows for the moment.)

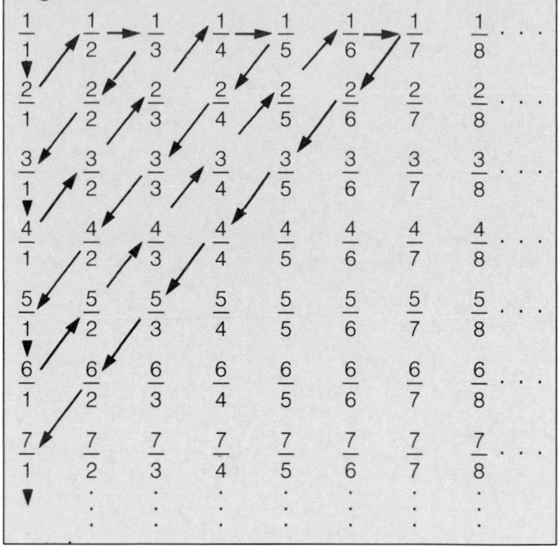

Now suppose we are given a number n ∈ N and wish to describe a rule for associating with n a definite rational number r ∈ Q. We simply follow the arrows in Figure 10, starting with $\frac{1}{1}$ in the top left-hand corner.

As we follow this line we count "one, two, three, . . . , n" as we go through each fraction—except that we don't count repetitions of fractions. For example, suppose

Figure 10.

we have $n = 5$. Then, following the arrows, we count off the five fractions $\frac{1}{1}$, $\frac{2}{1}$, $\frac{1}{2}$, $\frac{1}{3}$, and $\frac{3}{1}$ (omitting $\frac{2}{2} = \frac{1}{1}$) and conclude that corresponding to 5 ∈ N we have $\frac{3}{1}$ ∈ Q. Similarly, if $n = 13$ we obtain $\frac{1}{1}$, $\frac{2}{1}$, $\frac{1}{2}$, $\frac{1}{3}$, $\frac{3}{1}$, $\frac{4}{1}$, $\frac{3}{2}$, $\frac{2}{3}$, $\frac{1}{4}$, $\frac{1}{5}$, $\frac{5}{1}$, $\frac{6}{1}$, and $\frac{5}{2}$ (omitting $\frac{2}{2} = \frac{1}{1}$, $\frac{2}{4} = \frac{1}{2}$, $\frac{3}{3} = \frac{1}{1}$, and $\frac{4}{2} = \frac{2}{1}$). Thus to 13 ∈ N corresponds $\frac{5}{2}$ ∈ Q.

Conversely, given any r ∈ Q, we take its representation as a fraction in lowest terms (such as $\frac{1}{2}$ for $\frac{3}{6}$) and count "how far" it is from $\frac{1}{1}$ along the line (again omitting repetitions). Thus if we have given $\frac{4}{6}$ ∈ Q, we observe that $\frac{4}{6} = \frac{2}{3}$ and count $\frac{1}{1}$, $\frac{2}{1}$, $\frac{1}{2}$, $\frac{1}{3}$, $\frac{3}{1}$, $\frac{4}{1}$, $\frac{3}{2}$, $\frac{2}{3}$; so that corresponding to $\frac{2}{3}$ ∈ Q we have 8 ∈ N.

You may now suppose that all infinite sets have the same cardinal number as N. Certainly this is a plausible conjecture at this point. It turns out, however, that if we add to the set Q of positive rational numbers all the positive irrational numbers, such as $\sqrt{2}$, $\sqrt[3]{2}$, π, $\sqrt[5]{1 + \sqrt{2}}$, and so on, we obtain a set with a cardinal number different from N. Even if we consider only the set Z of rational and irrational numbers between 0 and 1, we obtain, as Georg Cantor showed in 1874, a "larger" set that cannot be matched with N. The union of the set of rational numbers and the set of irrational numbers is the set of real numbers.

The proof that Z is not equinumerous with N rests upon the fact that every real number between 0 and 1 can be written as an infinite decimal. For example, $\frac{1}{2} = 0.5000\ldots$, $\frac{1}{3} = 0.3333\ldots$, $\frac{1}{7} = 0.142857142857\ldots$, $\frac{\sqrt{2}}{2} = 0.7071\ldots$, where the rational numbers (such as $\frac{1}{2}$, $\frac{1}{3}$, and $\frac{1}{7}$) are expressed as repeating decimals, and the irrational numbers (such as $\frac{\sqrt{2}}{2}$) are expressed as nonrepeating decimals.

Now suppose we claim that we have a 1–1 correspondence between the elements of Z and the elements of N, such as:

N		Z	
↓			
1	↔	$0.183478412001\ldots$	$= r_1$
2	↔	$0.369715400000\ldots$	$= r_2$
3	↔	$0.579321715432\ldots$	$= r_3$
4	↔	$0.481762314000\ldots$	$= r_4$
5	↔	$0.673216732167\ldots$	$= r_5$
6	↔	$0.591416789143\ldots$	$= r_6$
7	↔	$0.001326841841\ldots$	$= r_7$
·	↔	$\ldots\ldots\ldots$	$= \ldots$

The digits of r_1, r_2, and so on are chosen arbitrarily so that $r_1 \neq r_2 \neq \ldots$.

Now we form another number in Z as follows: the first digit to the right of the decimal point is chosen as any digit different from the first digit of r_1. The second digit is chosen as any digit different from the second digit of r_2, and so on. Thus the resulting number could be $0.2783254\ldots$ or $0.3723689\ldots$. None of these numbers so chosen, however, can be in our list, since $0.2783254\ldots \neq r_1$ because it differs from r_1 in at least the first decimal place; $0.2783254\ldots \neq r_2$ because it differs from r_2 in at least the second decimal place; and so on. Hence $0.2783254\ldots$ was not present in the (supposedly complete) list, and so our correspondence is not 1–1 as alleged. No matter what listing we propose, the same process will show the listing is incomplete, and we conclude that no 1–1 correspondence between Z and N is possible.

Mathematicians denote the cardinal number of N by $\aleph_0$ (read "aleph-null"— aleph is the first letter of the Hebrew alphabet). They denote the cardinal number of the real numbers by c. A famous question in mathematics is, Does there exist an infinite set of numbers whose cardinal number lies between $\aleph_0$ and c? That is, is there a subset S of the real number R such that the cardinal number of S is neither $\aleph_0$ nor c? The *continuum hypothesis,* as formulated by Cantor, was the conjecture that no such set S exists.

The question of the truth or falsity of the continuum hypothesis claimed the attention of many first-rate mathematicians after it was first formulated by Cantor, but was not settled until 1963. However, it was not settled by a simple "yes" or "no." What was finally shown by the work of Kurt Gödel and Paul Cohen was that within the framework of the set theory accepted by most mathematicians today, either the acceptance of the continuum hypothesis or its rejection yields equally valid systems of mathematics. This still leaves open the question of whether there exists another equally "useful" formulation of set theory in which the continuum hypothesis can be proved true or false. In a sense, then, the continuum hypothesis has been settled in only a relative fashion, and research still continues on this and related problems.

Paradoxes of Set Theory

There are many paradoxes associated with sets that still concern mathematicians today. One very famous one was formulated by the noted mathematician and philosopher Bertrand Russell (1872–1970). It is known as "Russell's paradox." Imagine a barber in a village. The barber, said Russell, shaves only the men who do not shave themselves. The paradox is, Who shaves the barber? The contradictory answer is, If the barber does not shave himself, then he shaves himself; but if he shaves himself, he cannot shave himself. When stated mathematically, in terms of classes of sets, Russell's paradox challenged the very foundations of set theory.

The complete resolution of this and other paradoxes of set theory is still a matter of active concern today. In the meantime, however, most mathematicians continue to use the very useful concept of a set without waiting until all the foundations of set theory are made solid.

Roy Dubisch

BINARY NUMERALS

The *binary numeral system* offers an interesting glimpse into the world of mathematics. It is the simplest numeration system in which addition and multiplication can be performed, for there are only 4 addition facts and 4 multiplication facts to learn. By contrast, in our more familiar *decimal system* there are 100 addition facts and 100 multiplication facts to learn.

The significance and power of the binary system in modern mathematics, however, lie in its practical application in computer technology. Most computers today are binary computers; that is, they use binary numerals in computing and in processing data. With binary numerals, modern computers can perform well over 1 billion computations per second.

Before going into the binary numeral system, we shall take a closer look at the Hindu-Arabic numeral system and the concept of place value in it. An understanding of place value is vital to an understanding of the binary numeral system.

Hindu-Arabic Numeral System

The numeration system most widely used throughout the civilized world today is called the Hindu-Arabic system, probably because it originated with the Hindus and was carried to the Western world by the Arabs. It is a numeration system that fits most of our personal, commercial and technical needs very well.

The Hindu-Arabic system is called a decimal, or *base-ten*, system because it needs only 10 symbols to represent any number. These symbols, which are called *digits*, are 1, 2, 3, 4, 5, 6, 7, 8, 9, and 0.

These 10 symbols stand for the numbers one, two, three, four, five, six, seven, eight, nine, and zero, respectively.

The Hindu-Arabic system is also called a *positional decimal system*, because the number each digit represents depends on its "position," or "place," in the numeral. The far-right place in any numeral (but to the left of a decimal point) is the unit, or one, position. The place value of the next position to the left is ten. In general, the place values from right to left, in any decimal numeral, are ones, tens, hundreds, thousands, and so on. For example, the place values represented by 4,081 are $(4 \times 1,000) + (0 \times 100) + (8 \times 10) + (1 \times 1)$.

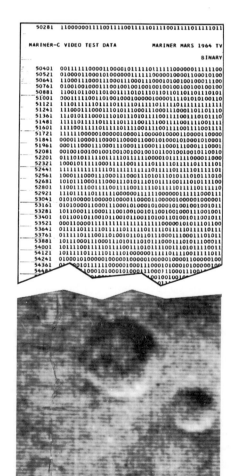

NASA

The binary numeral system is used to transmit photos from space to receiving stations on Earth. The photos are transmitted as radio signals, representing the zeros and ones of the binary system (upper photo right). The binary numbers correspond to different hues and intensities of light in the photographed surface. The digits are then converted by computer to an image consisting of a series of dots. The photo of the Martian surface at right was obtained this way.

Another way of looking at a positional decimal system is through the idea of grouping. Suppose we have a set of 13 dots marked on a sheet of paper. We draw a ring around 10 of these dots. There will be 3 dots remaining. We have 1 set of 10 dots plus 3 remaining single dots. This fact may be expressed as $13 = (1 \times 10) + (3 \times 1)$.

Now suppose we have 37 dots, and that we "ring" them in groups of 10. We will have 3 sets of 10 dots, plus 7 single dots. We could write this as $37 = (3 \times 10) + (7 \times 1)$. Similarly, if we have 128 dots we could have 1 set of 1 hundred or 10 tens, 2 sets of 10, and 8 dots remaining. We could write $128 = (1 \times 100) + (2 \times 10) + (8 \times 1)$. All this emphasis on "tens" seems quite natural to us. After all, we do have 10 fingers and 10 toes. But how do you suppose we would be counting today if our anatomy were not structured as it is?

Binary Numeral System

Imagine all of us with one finger on each of two hands and one toe on each of two feet. Suppose further that all the numbers we use could be expressed with the digits 0 and 1. Since we are going to use only two symbols to write any number, we can call this a binary, or *base-two*, system. In a binary system the value of any place in a numeral is twice as large as the place to its right. Thus the place values—from right to left—in a binary system are ones, twos, fours, eights, and so on.

The number 1 expressed in the binary system would be written as 1_{two}. Thus the number represented by 1_{ten} and 1_{two} is the same. (The subscript *two* indicates that we are expressing numbers in the binary system; the subscript *ten* indicates the decimal system.) How would we indicate 2_{ten} as a binary numeral?

Suppose we have a set of 2 stars. If we draw a ring around them, we have 1 set of 2 stars, and no single stars remaining. We would write $2_{ten} = 10_{two}$, which is read as "1 two plus 0 ones." If we begin with a set of 3 stars and draw a ring around 2 of them, we would have 1 set of 2 stars plus 1 set of 1 star. This would be indicated as $3_{ten} = 11_{two}$, read as "1 two plus 1 one."

How would 4_{ten} be expressed? Notice that we have been making pairs of equivalent sets wherever possible. Thus if we had a set of 4 stars, we could first form 2 sets of 2 stars each. Now draw a ring around these sets. This approach suggests that 4_{ten} may be thought of as 1 four, no twos, and no ones, and written as 100_{two}. In similar fashion, $5_{ten} = 101_{two}$, which is "1 four, no twos, and 1 one.

Note how 6_{ten} would then be treated. We would first have 3 sets of 2 stars in each set. Then we could pair up 2 of these sets, and wind up with 1 set of four, 1 set of two, and no ones. We write 6_{ten} as 110_{two}.

Using the same development, it is clear that $7_{ten} = 111_{two}$, interpreted as 1 set of four, 1 set of two, and 1 one. We can analyze 8_{ten} in the same way. First we have 4 sets of 2 stars in each set. Then we have 2 sets with (2×2) or 4 stars in each. Finally, we have 1 set with $(2 \times 2 \times 2)$ or 8 stars in it. This would be written as 1000_{two} and interpreted to mean 1 eight, 0 fours, 0 twos, and 0 ones. We now summarize what we have learned so far about binary numeration in Table I, and see if we can express our ideas.

TABLE I
Place-Value Chart

8 eights	4 fours	2 twos	1 ones	10 tens	1 ones
			0		0
			1		1
		1	0		2
		1	1		3
	1	0	0		4
	1	0	1		5
	1	1	0		6
	1	1	1		7
1	0	0	0		8
1	0	0	1		9
1	0	1	0	1	0
1	0	1	1	1	1
1	1	0	0	1	2
1	1	0	1	1	3
1	1	1	0	1	4
1	1	1	1	1	5

(Binary | Decimal)

How would we express 106_{ten} as a base-two numeral? Remember, the place values in binary numeration are ones, twos, fours, eights, sixteens, thirty-twos, sixty-fours, one hundred twenty-eights, and so on. The largest place value contained in 106 is sixty-four, so we can figure the binary equivalent as follows:

There is 1 sixty-four in 106.
$$106 - 64 = 42$$

There is 1 thirty-two in 42.
$$42 - 32 = 10$$

There are 0 sixteens in 10.
$$10 - 0 = 10$$

There is 1 eight in 10.
$$10 - 8 = 2$$

There are 0 fours in 2.
$$2 - 0 = 2$$

There is 1 two in 2.
$$2 - 2 = 0$$

There are 0 ones in 0.
$$0 - 0 = 0$$

We conclude that $106_{ten} = 1101010_{two}$. Our answer is correct, but the method used is tedious. There is a simpler process that we could use to derive the same conclusion:

To convert any decimal numeral into its binary form, divide it successively by 2. For example if we divide 106_{ten} successively by 2, we obtain the following seven-step process:

1. $\frac{53}{2)106}$ $\frac{106}{R0}$
2. $\frac{26}{2)53}$ $\frac{52}{R1}$
3. $\frac{13}{2)26}$ $\frac{26}{R0}$
4. $\frac{6}{2)13}$ $\frac{12}{R1}$
5. $\frac{3}{2)6}$ $\frac{6}{R0}$
6. $\frac{1}{2)3}$ $\frac{2}{R1}$
7. $\frac{0}{2)1}$ $\frac{0}{R1}$

The remainders (R), in inverse order, make up the binary equivalent of 106_{ten}. Reading from step 7 back to step 1, the remainders are 1, 1, 0, 1, 0, 1, 0. So $106_{ten} = 1101010_{two}$, which checks with the result we obtained using the longer process.

Binary Addition

Suppose we wish to add 11_{two} and 110_{two}. (In the examples that follow, we shall discard the subscript "two" to avoid cluttering up our notation.) As in base ten, addition in base two is always possible; the sum of any two numbers is unique; addition is commutative and associative; and 0 names the identity element. With these structural properties in mind, it is relatively easy to develop addition in base two.

We begin by expressing the addition facts we know:

$$1 + 0 = 0 + 1 = 1$$

and

$$0 + 0 = 0$$

The only remaining fact we need is $1 + 1$. But we have already found out that $1 + 1 = 10$ in the binary system. We therefore write:

$$1 + 1 = 10$$

We can summarize our addition facts in the form of a matrix for easy reference.

+	0	1
0	0	1
1	1	10

Now let's add $110 + 11$:

$$
\begin{array}{r}
1\leftarrow \boxed{\text{carry over}} \\
110 \\
+ 11 \\
\hline
1001
\end{array}
$$

Discussion: $0 + 1 = 1$, so we write 1 in the ones' place in the sum. Then $1 + 1 = 10$. Write 0 in the twos' place in the sum, and carry over the 1 to the fours column. Again, $1 + 1 = 10$, so write 0 in the sum's fours' place and 1 in the sum's eights' place. (Note: The binary sum $110 + 11 = 1001$ represents the same number values as the decimal sum $6 + 3 = 9$.)

Here are two more examples. See if your sums agree with these.

$$\begin{array}{r} 110101 \\ +\,1100011 \\ \hline 10011000 \end{array} \qquad \begin{array}{r} 1101 \\ +\,1001 \\ \hline 10110 \end{array}$$

Binary Subtraction

Subtraction in the binary system is treated essentially the same as in the decimal system. What is needed is some additional flexibility with binary notation.

From 110 let us subtract 101:

$$\begin{array}{r} 110 \\ -\,101 \\ \hline 1 \end{array}$$

Discussion: We cannot subtract 1 one from 0 ones, so we take 1 unit from the next base position (twos) and think of it as '10' ones. Because, in the binary system, 1 one from 10 ones leaves 1 one, write 1 in the ones' place in the difference. Now, 0 twos subtracted from 0 twos leaves 0 twos, and 1 four subtracted from 1 four leave 0 fours; therefore, 1 is the correct answer.

Here is another example:

$$\begin{array}{r} 1001 \\ -\,11 \\ \hline 110 \end{array}$$

Discussion: Because 1 one from 1 one leaves 0 ones, write 0 in the ones' place in the difference. We can't subtract 1 two from 0 twos. The base position to the left of twos is fours, but there are no fours either. So we go to the eights' place. We change 1 eight to '10' fours. We take one unit from the 10 fours, which leaves 1 four, and change that to '10' twos. Now, 1 two from 10 twos leaves 1 two, so we write 1 in the twos' place in the difference. We still have 1 four remaining, which we show by writing 1 in the fours' place in the difference.

Let us do a more difficult example:

$$\begin{array}{r} 10110 \\ -\,111 \\ \hline 1111 \end{array}$$

Discussion: Because 1 is greater than 0, change 1 two into '10' ones. Now, 1 from 10 is 1. Change 1 four into '10' twos; 1 from 10 is 1. Change the 1 sixteen into '10' eights. Take 1 of these eights, which leaves 1 eight, and change it to '10' fours. Now we complete the subtraction: 1 from 10 is 1; 0 from 1 is 1. The difference is 1111.

Here are two more examples. See if your differences agree with these.

$$\begin{array}{r} 10011100 \\ -\,110101 \\ \hline 1100111 \end{array} \qquad \begin{array}{r} 10101101 \\ -\,1111001 \\ \hline 110100 \end{array}$$

Binary Multiplication

Suppose we wish to multiply 10_{two} and 11_{two}. As in base ten, multiplication in base two is always possible; the product of any two numbers is unique, multiplication is commutative and associative; and 1_{two} names the identity element. Also we assume that the distributive laws hold. That is, multiplication is distributive over addition. Keeping these assumptions in mind, let us develop multiplication in the binary system. We begin by expressing the multiplication facts we know:

$$1 \times 0 = 0 \times 1 = 0$$

and

$$1 \times 1 = 1$$

Our multiplication matrix would then be quite simple.

$\times$	0	1
0	0	0
1	0	1

Now let's multiply 11×10:

$$\begin{array}{r} 10 \\ \times\,11 \\ \hline 10 \\ 10 \\ \hline 110 \end{array}$$

Discussion: Because $1 \times 0 = 0$, write 0 in the product. Because $1 \times 1 = 1$, write 1 to the left of 0 in the first partial product. Now, $1 \times 0 = 0$, so write 0 under 1, in the second partial product; $1 \times 1 = 1$, so write 1 to the left of the 0 just written. Now add.

Now we are ready to examine a more difficult multiplication example.

$$
\begin{array}{r}
1101 \\
\times\ \ 101 \\
\hline
1101 \\
0000 \\
1101 \\
\hline
1000001
\end{array}
$$

Discussion: For the first partial product, $1 \times 1 = 1$, $1 \times 0 = 0$, $1 \times 1 = 1$, and $1 \times 1 = 1$. Every entry in the second partial product is zero. The entries in the third partial product are the same as in the first.

Here are two more examples. See if your products agree with these.

$$
\begin{array}{r}
10111 \\
\times\ \ 1101 \\
\hline
10111 \\
10111 \\
10111 \\
\hline
100101011
\end{array}
\qquad
\begin{array}{r}
11100 \\
\times\ \ \ \ 111 \\
\hline
11100 \\
11100 \\
11100 \\
\hline
11000100
\end{array}
$$

Binary Division

To be able to divide with binary numerals, you must be very familiar with binary multiplication and subtraction. We can use the conventional algorithm to perform division.

Let's divide 11011_{two} by 11_{two}:

$$
\begin{array}{r}
1001 \\
11\overline{)11011} \\
\underline{11} \\
0011 \\
\underline{11} \\
0
\end{array}
$$

Discussion: The divisor 11 is contained in 11 just 1 time; $1 \times 11 = 11$. Subtract and get 0 for the difference; bring down the 0. The 11 is contained 0 times in 0; write 0 in the quotient and bring down the 1. The 11 is contained 0 times in 1; write 0 in the quotient and bring down the 1. The 11 is contained 1 time in 11. The remainder is 0.

Let's look at another example:

$$
\begin{array}{r}
110 \\
101\overline{)11110} \\
\underline{101} \\
101 \\
\underline{101} \\
00
\end{array}
$$

Discussion: The divisor 101 is contained in 111 just 1 time; $1 \times 101 = 101$. Subtract and get 10; bring down the 1. The 101 is contained in 101 also 1 time; $1 \times 101 = 101$. Subtract and get 0; bring down the 0. The 101 is contained 0 times in 0.

Here are two more examples. See if your quotients agree with these. (You may check your work by multiplying the divisor by the quotient to get the dividend.)

$$
\begin{array}{r}
1110 \\
10011\overline{)100001010} \\
\underline{10011} \\
11100 \\
\underline{10011} \\
10011 \\
\underline{10011} \\
0
\end{array}
$$

$$
\begin{array}{r}
1101 \\
1101\overline{)10101001} \\
\underline{1101} \\
10000 \\
\underline{1101} \\
1101 \\
\underline{1101} \\
0
\end{array}
$$

Binary Fractions to Decimals

Converting fractional numbers in binary notation to equivalent decimal numerals is not particularly difficult. The position to the right of the "binary point" has a value of $1/2$; the next position has a value of $1/4$; the next a value of $1/8$; and so on. In each position, the numerator is 1, and the denominator is a power of 2 that depends on the position. For example, the third place to the right of the binary point is $1/2^3$, or $1/8$. The following example illustrates the conversion process.

$$1.1011_{two} = \underline{?}_{ten}$$

NIM: A game based on binary numerals

An interesting game for two persons, called Nim, is based on binary numeration. In this game the players take turns drawing chips from three stacks before them. A player may draw as many chips as he chooses from any stack in a single move. In his next move he may take chips from the same stack or any other stack as he wishes. The player who takes the last chip left from the three stacks is the loser.

If this game is played by an experienced player and a novice, the beginner will rarely win. The secret of the game, as an experienced player will know, is to select the proper number of chips from the correct stack so that your arrangement will be "binary even." This then forces the other player to be "binary odd."

Here is what is meant by "binary even" and "binary odd." Suppose the stacks of chips, designated as A, B, and C, contain nine, eleven, and fifteen chips respectively. Represent nine, eleven, and fifteen in binary form: nine $= 1001_{two}$, eleven $= 1011_{two}$, and fifteen $= 1111_{two}$.

$$
\begin{array}{c|c|c|c|c}
A \to & 1 & 0 & 0 & 1 \\
B \to & 1 & 0 & 1 & 1 \\
C \to & 1 & 1 & 1 & 1
\end{array}
$$

After this is done, focus your attention on the columns of numbers instead of on the original row representations. If the sum (using decimal system addition) of each column is 0 or 2, then your position is "binary even." If not, your position is "binary odd." When it is your turn to move, hope that the position you are in is "odd," because if it is even, any move you make will force you into an odd position and may cause you to lose—if your opponent knows the game.

Suppose you are faced with the illustrated situation of the nine, eleven, and fifteen chips. Your position is clearly "odd," so you must make a move that will leave your position "even." With a little practice you will see that you should remove thirteen of the chips from stack C. If you do, your position will look like this:

$$
\begin{array}{c|c|c|c|c}
A \to & 1 & 0 & 0 & 1 \\
B \to & 1 & 0 & 1 & 1 \\
C \to &   &   & 1 & 0
\end{array}
$$

Quite clearly, the resulting sum of every column is either 2 or 0. In other words, you are binary even. Once you reach a safe (even) position, no matter what your opponent does, you will win, provided you make an "even" move every time.

Solution:

$$1.1011 = (1 \times 1) + (1 \times \frac{1}{2}) + (0 \times \frac{1}{4})$$
$$+ (1 \times \frac{1}{8}) + (1 \times \frac{1}{16})$$
$$= 1 + \frac{1}{2} + 0 + \frac{1}{8} + \frac{1}{16}$$
$$= 1\frac{11}{16}_{ten} \text{ or } 1.6875_{ten}$$

Decimals to Binary Form

To convert a decimal fraction to its binary equivalent, follow these steps: First, write down the fraction. Then, directly below it, write twice the original amount. (In other words, multiply the fraction by 2, using base-ten multiplication.) Then remove the integer to the left of the decimal point and record it to the right (having written the resulting fraction directly below the previous one). For example, if the decimal fraction we wish to convert to binary is 0.721, we write:

```
0.721
1.442      (0.721 × 2)
0.442   1  (the "1" from 1.442)
```

To complete the conversion, we continue by repeating the last two steps (multiplying the most recent amount by 2 and then removing the integer to the left of the decimal point). For 0.721, then, we have (from the beginning):

```
0.721
1.442   1
0.442
0.884   0
0.884
1.768   1
0.768
1.536   1
0.536
1.072   1
0.072
```

The process is repeated until the decimal fraction is reduced to zero, or until the desired number of places in the binary fraction is obtained. The binary equivalent is obtained by reading the recorded digits from top to bottom. Thus, to five places, $0.721_{ten} = 0.10111_{two}$.

Binary Numerals to Octals

A number expressed as a binary numeral is readily expressed as an equivalent in base eight. For a natural number the technique is simple. Since $2^3 = 8$, we begin with the smallest unit and group the "digits" in clusters of three "digits" each.

Example: Convert 10110111_{two} to the equivalent base-eight numeral.

Solution:
$$(10) \quad (110) \quad (111)_{two} = 267_{eight}$$
$$2_{eight} \quad 6_{eight} \quad 7_{eight}$$

Example: Convert 0.1101101_{two} to base eight.

Solution:
$$0.(110) \quad (110) \quad (100)_{two} = 0.664_{eight}$$

Summary

The binary numeral system offers an interesting glimpse into the world of mathematics. Addition and multiplication, at first glance, appear to be very simple operations in the binary system because there are so few facts to learn. A more careful study reveals that numbers of any sizable magnitude require an almost endless sequence of 0's and 1's for their representations. Operations very quickly become bogged down in these long and labored numerals. But computers, because of their tremendous speed, can utilize binary notation to great advantage. Many of the digital computers of earliest design employed decimal notation, but it was soon apparent that binary notation has many advantages over other numeration systems for computer circuit design.

There are many interesting phenomena that lend themselves to binary explanation. If a question can be answered by "yes" or "no"; if a circuit is either "closed" or "open"; if a light bulb is either "on" or "off"; if a choice involves either "male" or "female"—these are the kinds of situations to which mathematicians apply binary notation and find it particularly convenient. The mathematics programs that are currently taught in some elementary and secondary schools treat the subject of binary numeration in some detail.

Irwin K. Feinstein

ACCOUNTANTS AND THEIR SCIENCE

In October 1931, the Chicago gangster Al "Scarface" Capone was sentenced to 11 years in a federal penitentiary and fined $70,000. The Federal Bureau of Investigation (FBI) had long since designated Capone as their "Public Enemy Number One," and for years a special task force had hounded the gangster's criminal organization. But in the end, it was not bootlegging or even murder that sealed Capone's penal fate; instead, the jury that put him away had found the crime boss guilty of tax evasion.

Capone knew that part of the task force investigating him was made up of the Special Intelligence Unit of the Internal Revenue Service (IRS), headed by agent Elmer Irey. But although the gangster never took this threat seriously, it was Irey and his team who found an incriminating Capone ledger and the men with the first-hand knowledge to interpret it: Leslie Shumway and Fred Reis, two Capone bookkeepers who agreed to act as witnesses against their former boss. Between the ledgers and the bookkeepers, the IRS had proof that Capone had received income he had not reported.

WHAT IS ACCOUNTING?

Why were two bookkeepers and their records enough to make a case against the head of one of the most powerful organized-crime syndicates in U.S. history? The answer lies in the nature of the science of accounting. Accounting involves the collection, analysis, and interpretation of the economic data of individu-

In a broad sense, accounting can be defined as a form of numerical analysis—the financial mathematics used by every business and by every individual.

The production line at a factory runs most efficiently when the company's accounting staff knows the status of all supplies and labor, and how they are being allocated.

on within the organization for which they work. They should understand how different departments within a given company interact, where resources such as supplies and labor come from and how they are being allocated, and what realistic courses of action are available to the business in the future. Even in an organization such as Al Capone's—in which financial statements were falsified when presented to the government—it is absolutely necessary for some genuine record of transactions to exist. Without such records being available to the decision makers, the enterprise—legal or illegal—cannot operate effectively. Furthermore, those records, to be useful, must show both the source and the destination of every transaction that takes place.

als or organizations. The information provided by these processes is of many different varieties, depending on who will be using it.

For example, the managers of a company need detailed information that shows the results of past management decisions. By combining this information with a number of other factors, owners and managers can devise new strategies to make the enterprise run as effectively and efficiently as possible. On the other hand, the employees, investors, suppliers, and creditors of a business require more-general information. They need to know how the company is faring so that they can decide whether to continue their relationship with the business. Furthermore, the government requires a different set of information about an organization's financial status so that the authorities can charge the appropriate taxes; also, the government may need to intervene if the company's activities or well-being are connected to the public welfare.

Accountants, by nature of their profession, must have a thorough knowledge of the goings-

THE HISTORY OF ACCOUNTING

Almost as soon as people could write, they began keeping records of what they traded, bought, sold, and owned. Among the first of these record keepers were the civilizations of ancient Mesopotamia—the Sumerians, Assyrians, and Babylonians—who developed an agrarian culture that included bartering and land-ownership, and established governments that levied and collected taxes. Records from this period (c. 3500 B.C.) were imprinted on clay by specially trained scribes. Some artifacts suggest that there was a system for encasing important clay tablets in an outer clay shell, which bore a copy of the record on the inside—an early form of *auditing*, or providing verification of a financial record for another party.

Record making proliferated in ancient Egypt, where pa-

Wherever an economy exists, so too does accounting. Back in 2350 B.C., ancient Sumerian accountants kept records of transactions involving goats and sheep by carving special symbols into stone tablets (above).

pyrus—a primitive form of paper—was far more plentiful and provided a material far easier to work with than clay. The rulers of Egypt possessed great wealth, which they necessarily found the need to reckon carefully. Nevertheless, Egyptian accounting—however thorough it was for its time—did not progress beyond simple list-like inventories.

For the next 2,000 years, the growth of accounting closely mirrored the increasing complexity of economics and banking. The ancient Greeks and Romans used publicly employed accountants to assess taxes and, especially in democratic Greece, to report faithfully to the citizenry on government spending. In the thriving Roman cities, bank loans, currency exchanges, and annual budgets created new types of data and new systems for recording it. Accounting practices had regressed by medieval times, when a largely illiterate population relied on the simple technology of notched sticks to record their tax payments. Nevertheless, the feudal system brought its own accounting challenges, since the owners of manor houses and great estates needed to coordinate the diverse functions within the household and its environs. The English government also maintained a considerable early database in the form of the Domesday Book, a periodically revised property census used to levy taxes on all of the counties in the country.

Accounting methodology remained fairly limited, however, until the Renaissance (14th–16th centuries). It was during this period that an Italian monk named Luca Pacioli wrote a treatise establishing the modern science of accounting. Pacioli was born in Tuscany around 1445. He was educated in a range of disciplines, possessed the highest degree of the time in mathematics, and came along during the period of history in which many aspects of finance were changing to their modern forms. Coined money and the use of Arabic rather than Roman numerals were significant innovations of the period.

Pacioli had learned of a new system of bookkeeping in which transactions were not simply listed, but instead were entered with information on where the resources came from and where they ended up. This system, known

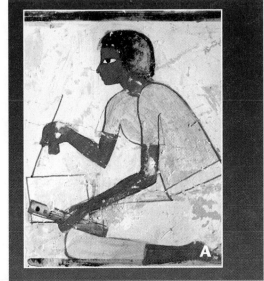

A fresco of an accountant (A) in a royal tomb testifies to the status of the profession in ancient Egypt. The Domesday Book (B), first compiled in 1086, was an important foundation of English accounting. South America's Inca civilization used a complicated system of knots (C), called quipu, for accounting. Luca Pacioli (D, at left) is considered the father of modern accounting.

Tracking the revenue coming into a supermarket (above) or other business falls under the duties of the bookkeeper. Typically, an accountant determines how and what should be done, and the bookkeeper does it. It is often said that accounting begins where bookkeeping leaves off.

as *double-entry bookkeeping*, revolutionized accounting by showing not just the amount of resources exchanged, but their movement and relationships. This in turn allowed accountants to broaden the scope of their functions to an analytical and interpretive level. Moreover, double-entry bookkeeping provided the most effective way to check the accuracy, and quickly view the overall condition, of one's accounts. Pacioli explained the new system—the "Italian method," as it came to be known—in his book *Summa de Arithmetica, Geometria, Proportioni et Proportionalita*. Other fundamental principles and theories of accounting were also contained in the treatise, which was translated into many languages and disseminated throughout Europe in the centuries following its appearance.

As with many disciplines, modern accounting moved toward professionalization and specialization. Nineteenth-century Scotland was home to some of the first accountants' societies, although for many years the job of accountant was intermingled with that of lawyer and merchant. It was in the Edinburgh Society of Accountants that the title "Chartered Accountant" (CA) was first conferred on members. Then, in 1880, the newly formed Institute of Chartered Accountants in England and Wales created accounting standards for its member organiza-

tions, and established an examination for those wishing to become chartered accountants.

With commerce growing exponentially as a result of the Industrial Revolution, the ranks of accountants swelled accordingly. In 1896, New York State was the first to grant the title "Certified Public Accountant" (CPA) to those passing an examination. The United States would have a great need for accountants in the century that followed; the battle over trade monopolies, the growth of labor unions, the birth of the federal income tax, and the Great Depression were economic events that shaped the nation and led to the formation of agencies such as the Departments of Commerce and Labor, the Interstate Commerce Commission (ICC), the Internal Revenue Service (IRS), and the Securities and Exchange Commission (SEC). Accountants became a professional fixture of businesses both large and small, private and public, bankrupt or successful, covert or legitimate.

ACCOUNTING METHODS AND FUNCTIONS

Accountants are said to speak the "language of business," an apt description because they convey economic and financial information in a meaningful way. An accountant can tell an investor if the company in which he or she is interested in buying stock is earning a reasonable profit, can inform a bank if a certain business will likely be able to repay its loan, or can let a manager know whether it has been an historically successful idea to expand operations domestically or overseas.

Accountants work in a wide range of capacities, and their methods vary greatly depending on the function that they serve. Accountants directly employed by businesses are known as private (or corporate) accountants, while certified public accountants (CPAs)—working on their own or as part of accounting firms—have businesses or individuals as clients. Other accountants are employed by local, state, or federal governments; fiduciary accountants work in a

As with any science, and particularly in one so concerned with presenting data in a useful way, every kind of accounting has relied on certain standards, principles, and customs to make its processes as intelligible as possible. Groups such as the Financial Accounting Standards Board (FASB) have established "generally accepted accounting principles" (GAAP) to ensure that the same systems of measurement prevail in most businesses across the country.

For example, in most cases, accountants treat a business as a "going concern" in which assets are viewed in terms of long-term value rather than their value if liquidated. It is also a convention to treat a business as an entity separate from the people who own or operate it. Accountants in the United States use the dollar as a unit of measurement, and assume—despite the fluctuations that affect real currency—that the dollar possesses a stable value.

More-complex standards pertain to the measurement of the value of assets. Sale price—the amount an asset could be sold for on the open market—is not a good measurement for value, because it is assumed that the company is keeping the asset because its use provides more value than it is worth on the market. Rather, economic value is assessed as the amount that the company would be willing to pay for the asset.

With such standards in place, accountants must proceed, as always, by means of a unique combination of mathematical rigor and interpretive artfulness, in service of an organization and with figures and data verifiable by all interested parties.

position such as trustee or as an executor of a deceased person's estate.

Financial Accounting

Accountants working for corporations, either as direct employees or as for-hire CPAs, perform different tasks depending on what data they are being asked by the company to record

and manipulate. Financial accounting, for example, is concerned with the preparation of financial statements for use by owners, investors and creditors, and the general public.

One important type of financial statement is the *balance sheet*. Balance sheets provide an indication of the company's resources at a given moment. The state of these resources is expressed as a relationship of the firm's *assets*, which are valuable possessions including cash, equipment, accounts owed by customers, investments, land, and buildings; of the company's *liabilities*, which include resources such as labor and credit for which future wages or payments are pending; and the corporation's *equity*, which represents funds coming from the owners of the company or from an endowment.

The balance sheet, as its name suggests, must show a balanced rela-

Accounting can be a lucrative profession. Many accountants work for themselves, handling the financial affairs of individuals and small enterprises, and at times lending their expertise to larger corporations.

Careers in Accounting

Accounting is an ever-growing field that can accommodate many interests and ambitions. Financial rewards, professional prestige, an insider's knowledge of the complex business world, and a respected position in the community are among the attractions of the accounting profession.

Virtually all accounting jobs require a bachelor's degree, and many accountants continue their education to obtain a Master of business administration (MBA) in accounting or finance from a business school. Among the top schools are Harvard Business School, Stanford University, and the Wharton School at the University of Pennsylvania.

At these and other colleges and universities, the accounting department is typically one of the larger entities within the school of business. After graduation, many accountants gain practical experience by spending several years employed at a public accounting firm. Some never leave academia, choosing to take an almost philosophical approach to accounting.

At some point, virtually all accountants must pass an examination to become a Certified Public Accountant (CPA) or Certified Management Accountant (CMA). Some may stay on at accounting firms; others may go to work for corporations, start a small private practice, or enter into government service for agencies such as the Internal Revenue Service (IRS), General Accounting Office (GAO), or even the U.S. Department of Defense.

Accounting salaries are competitive, and job opportunities are listed in a variety of journals such as *Accounting Today* and the *CPA Journal*. Information about all aspects of the profession is available from the American Institute of Certified Public Accountants (AICPA), which maintains a helpful Internet site and publishes the *Journal of Accountancy*.

At the college level (below), accounting curricula place a strong emphasis on statistics, economics, and general business practices.

tionship among these resources, in the form of: Total assets = Total liabilities + Total equity. The relationship can also be transformed to: Total assets - Total liabilities = Total equity, in which the equity represents the *net assets* of the company. The balance sheet demonstrates the usefulness of double-entry bookkeeping, because it always shows resources coming from somewhere (expressed as a credit) and going somewhere else (expressed as a debit). If the bookkeeper or accountant has properly kept track of these movements, the statement will be balanced and will provide a complete picture of the company's financial position.

While the balance sheet is much like a "snapshot" of the firm's position at any given moment, the *income statement* is used to show how income has been derived over a certain span of time. An income statement allows an accountant to address the all-important question: Have assets been used profitably in a given period? A *statement of cash flows*, on the other hand, demonstrates the business's available *liquid*, or currently usable, resources.

Managerial Accounting

Most accounting data for a given company are generated for managers, who base their plans and forecasts largely on the successes and failures of past activities. Managerial accountants use past data to create provisional plans known as *budgets*. Budgets predict and control when, how, and by whom resources will be used within a specific time period. There may be separate budgets needed to address cash flow, personnel, the building of infrastructure, or factory production. Although managers ultimately make all of the budgetary decisions, it is the accountants who predict the effects of those decisions, consider whether the manager's plans are viable, and finally compare the initial budgets to the company's actual performance during the given budgetary period.

The Internal Revenue Service employs an enormous number of accountants. Each April, IRS offices receive millions of income tax returns—essentially the accounting summaries of millions of individuals. The IRS accountants and their staffs work feverishly to review the returns and verify their accuracy

Predicting the cost of providing a service, assessing the outcome of a particular course of action, or isolating the source of an unexpected cost are all activities that go beyond simple bookkeeping or "bean counting"; rather, these functions require accountants to approach the information available to them in imaginative and inventive ways. Managerial accounting involves a continual back-and-forth between accountants and managers. Together, they look at the past, make predictions about the future, and then pay attention to what actually happens. Then the whole process repeats itself, as the managers use the accountants' data to refine their operations and make the business as efficient, coordinated, and profitable as possible.

Other Kinds of Accounting

One of the specialized tasks that accountants perform is auditing, or verifying records and procedures to determine their accuracy and efficiency. Most middle- to large-sized companies are required by law to disclose their financial information and to have its accuracy verified by external auditors (frequently chosen by stockholders). Company managers often make use of internal audits to ensure that operations are being conducted properly and appropriately. For example, an accountant might monitor a particular department to discover whether a new telephone system is providing the expected rise in efficiency.

Another chief accounting task is the determination of income for tax purposes. This is an important aspect of business accounting, but many families also hire a CPA every year to provide this service. Tax codes are exceedingly complex and ever-changing, so tax accountants must maintain a working familiarity with the latest regulations and requirements. It is the job of IRS auditors to confirm the accuracy of these income determinations.

In the late 20th century, computer technologies revolutionized the field of accounting. Databases and spreadsheets allowed for the storage of massive amounts of information, which could be easily organized and searched. These tools have allowed businesses to play out different scenarios quickly, and thus determine the most efficient and profitable course of action. As computers have increased in power and speed, more advanced programs have provided accountants with the ability to complete even more complex calculations.

PAST and FUTURE

462–468   Archaeologists and Their Science
469–473   The Early Sky Watchers
474–478   The Calendar
479–483   Paleontologists and Their Science
484–489   Fossils
490–499   Prehistoric Animals
500–506   Science Fiction
507–516   Forensic Science

To a modern visitor, the ruins of ancient buildings, such as those of Tintagel Castle (above, traditionally identified as the birthplace of King Arthur), evoke a certain sense of wonder. What is rarely perceived is the ideal of balanced proportions and symmetry to which the ancient architects strove. Yet this ideal can be realized without symmetry. In the bubbles at left, the presentation of data achieves a sense of balance, as does the spacing between the bubbles themselves.

ARCHAEOLOGISTS AND THEIR SCIENCE

Melodic sounds not heard for more than 50,000 years cast a spell over a recent scientific conference in Washington, D.C. The player—Jelle Atema, a musician and amateur archaeologist from Boston—had in his hands an exact replica of a flute discovered in 1995 in an eastern European cave. Atema had carved his replica from the bone of a prehistoric cave bear, as had the original flute's maker—a Neanderthal man or woman living around the year 50,000 B.C. In learning to play the instrument, Atema discovered it to be far more complex than scientists had originally thought. The flute featured a special "stopper" in the mouthpiece that allowed the player to create a sophisticated range of sounds. Importantly, this complexity told scientists that prehistoric people were probably making simpler instruments far earlier than anyone had previously thought.

Such is the work of archaeology—the study of the human past through the analysis of the material remains that peoples and societies leave behind. From these remnants, archaeologists try to piece together how, and in what kinds of environments, ancient peoples lived. In the process, these scientists have enabled us to glimpse amazing details about humans and human ancestors who walked Earth long before the invention of written records.

AN ANCIENT DISCIPLINE

Archaeology is itself an ancient science, as people have long been curious about their origins. Among the first amateur archaeologists was King Nabonidus, who, in the 6th century B.C., dug into the Babylonian temples of his ancestors. Some 600 years later, the Chinese wrote

At excavation sites known as digs, archaeologists carefully scrape away layers of sediment, hoping to discover artifacts from peoples and societies of long ago.

of their own archaeological past—describing the relics of Asia's Stone Age, Copper Age, and Bronze Age. The Greeks and Romans likewise marveled over ancient artifacts and searched for evidence of a legendary "Golden Age" before their own culture appeared. Then, 1,000 years later, medieval Europeans puzzled over the gigantic stone monuments left by their ancestors in places such as Britain's Stonehenge. During the Renaissance, European royalty began amassing great collections of ancient Greek and Roman statues and other artifacts. For the most part, however, early interest in archaeological objects did not extend beyond the realm of treasure hunters and wealthy collectors. Few showed interest in the science behind their ancient discoveries and collections.

Dr. Jelle Atema plays a flute he made—an exact replica of a Neanderthal instrument.

BIRTH OF A SCIENCE

Science historians generally recognize the German scholar Johann Winckelmann as the "father" of modern archaeology. In 1764, Winckelmann published archaeology's first orderly descriptions of Greek and Roman art, including detailed and historic accounts of objects excavated at Pompeii and Herculaneum. In 1798, the conquering armies of Napoleon brought 40 scholars with them into Egypt to study and describe the contents of the pyramids and temples there. The published accounts caused a popular sensation across Europe and led to the birth of *Egyptology*, a specialized branch of archaeology. Napoleon's soldiers themselves discovered the famous Rosetta Stone. Its inscriptions later enabled the archaeologist Jean-François Champollion to decipher the ancient writings seen in many Egyptian tombs and temples.

The 1800s brought a surge of well-financed, large-scale excavations, or "digs," in the Mediterranean. These included the discovery and excavation of the buried Greek Temple of Artemis at Ephesus, counted among the Seven Wonders of the World. Those archaeologists without the financial backing for such grand projects had to content themselves with uncovering caches of ancient pots, stone tools, and simple weapons in the European countryside. The human bones found among these items provided fossil evidence for possible ancestors to the modern human race. We now know these prehistoric humans as Neanderthals and Cro-Magnons. In the 1920s, Chinese archaeologists located Asia's legendary Shang civilization in northern Asia and unearthed the ruins of its once-spectacular capital.

Johann Winckelmann—Father of Modern Archaeology

Born the son of a cobbler, Johann Joachim Winckelmann studied religion, medicine, and classical languages as a young man. At age 37, he traveled to Rome to become a librarian, and later a curator of antiquities (ancient objects) for the Vatican. Soon after he arrived in Rome, Winckelmann began studying the statues, pottery, and other Greek and Roman relics he saw in many of the city's great private collections. Winckelmann's clear, precise, yet romantic descriptions of Roman and Greek statues proved especially popular in Europe, where they were published in tourist guidebooks.

More important, Winckelmann became the first scholar to go beyond the less-than-illuminating practice of simply trying to identify the gods and other historical figures portrayed in Greek and Roman art. He studied the different artistic styles used by ancient Greek and Roman sculptors. He then used this information to establish historical time periods, or epochs, of Greek and Roman art. In doing so, Winckelmann became the first to sort antiquities by their age, or chronological order. His *History of Ancient Art*, published in 1764, has been widely recognized as archaeology's first modern textbook.

The 1799 discovery of the Rosetta Stone allowed hieroglyphics to be deciphered. The treasures found in 1923 when the tomb of Egypt's pharaoh Tutankhamen was opened caught the public's imagination.

alized that photographs taken from airplanes could reveal many previously unnoticed features such as the outlines of ancient ruins, or even entire systems of buried roads. In the 1930s, archaeologists began studying the diets of prehistoric peoples by teasing apart the fossilized animal bones and seeds found in their fire pits and ancient kitchens. At approximately the same time, Scandinavian scientists realized that the near-microscopic remains of plant pollen could help them study the changing climate of prehistoric times. U.S. researchers, in turn, learned that tree rings could similarly reveal weather patterns of the distant past.

MODERN METHODS

The early 20th century brought the international systemization and application of modern archaeological techniques. These included precise methods for classifying artifacts such as pottery and stone tools. Between 1914 and 1918, archaeologists serving in World War I re-

The most important advance in modern archaeology came in the late 1940s, when U.S. chemist Willard Libby developed a method of dating organic substances such as charcoal, wood, cloth, and fossilized plant and animal remains. He did so by measuring the slow radioactive decay of the element carbon in these

A foremost challenge faced by archaeologists is the determination of an artifact's age. For organic substances, archaeological laboratories apply advanced radiocarbon-dating techniques (below) to conduct age analyses.

materials. Within a few years, archaeologists around the world were using *radiocarbon dating* to determine the age of objects as much as 50,000 years old. Improvements in the technique have since pushed back the reach of radiocarbon dating to 80,000 years. The 20th century also brought laws and international agreements to stop the looting and careless destruction of important archaeological sites.

ARCHAEOLOGICAL ANALYSIS

The digging and discovery of ancient objects represent just the beginning of a modern archaeologist's work. After meticulously photographing, sketching, describing, and labeling their finds, archaeologists carefully wrap a limited number of artifacts for study in the laboratory. There, they gently clean the artifacts and examine them more closely with dissecting microscopes, chemical tests, and other techniques.

Archaeologists also use computers to analyze information such as similarities and differences in the dimensions of various artifacts, and the frequency with which certain types of artifacts occur at different sites. Computers can also help archaeologists to simulate how a site might have originally looked, or even speculate on the likelihood of different kinds of prehistoric human behavior based on the evidence left behind. Computers have even enabled researchers to test ideas about how ancient astronomers might have used gigantic monuments such as Britain's Stonehenge or North America's Moose Mountain to chart the movement of the Sun and stars.

ARCHAEOLOGICAL SPECIALTIES

During the second half of the 20th century, the number of professional archaeologists skyrocketed worldwide from several hundred to many thousand. At the same time, archaeology became a science with a great many specialties. Historical archaeologists, for example, study ancient writings such as 1,500-year-old Chinese textbooks or the daily journals of early American colonists. Underwater archaeologists study sunken artifacts such as ships and flooded ruins. Many archaeologists focus their research on a particular kind of artifact such as pottery, stone tools, or food remains. An ever-

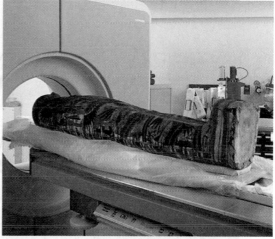

Noninvasive imaging techniques originally developed for humans provide archaeologists with a risk-free method for studying mummies (top) and other irreplaceable artifacts. The counting of tree rings—a time-tested method for dating wooden objects—has become even more reliable, thanks to the magnification supplied by sophisticated microscopes (above).

Careers in Archaeology

In 1860, the Italian archaeologist Giuseppe Fiorelli traveled to the foot of Mount Vesuvius, a volcano on the southwest coast of Italy, to launch a major investigation of a disappeared culture. A century earlier, a farmer digging a well on the site had discovered a buried wall. Treasure hunters followed, uncovering a marketplace, theater,

Sifting sand for artifacts (above) or deciphering ancient inscriptions (right), while perhaps a tedious endeavor for most people, is a labor of love for the archaeologist.

and houses in their frenzied search for buried riches. Now Fiorelli had returned to tease out the details of life in ancient Pompeii, life preserved in a kind of freeze-frame when the sudden and violent eruption of Vesuvius buried the city in A.D. 79.

Fiorelli's excavation of Pompeii marked a dramatic turning point in the history of archaeology, the study of human artifacts. His was the first major archaeological excavation launched not for plunder and profit but for scholarly study. Today's archaeologists follow Fiorelli's tradition. Not treasure hunters but time detectives, these scientists reconstruct the past from clues both large and small, from giant earthen sculptures decipherable only from an airplane to the tiniest of fossil grains from ancient crops.

Like Fiorelli, today's archaeologists still use shovels and trowels as they tunnel down through the layers of time. However, they use much finer tools—from soft brushes to dental picks—in the final stages of an excavation. Modern archaeologists also employ many sophisticated techniques such as computerized carbon dating and thermoluminescence to assign a year to prehistoric materials, infrared photography to reveal the text of faded manuscripts, and spectrometry to analyze organic residues on food utensils.

Most professional archaeologists today receive several years of graduate-level training within a university anthropology department. In addition to class work in such areas as anthropology, history, geology, and laboratory science, their training includes extensive fieldwork. Indeed, every summer, archaeologists, students, and amateur volunteers fan out across North America to work in hundreds of scientifically important "digs." Still others travel to distant continents to assist in ongoing excavations there.

Graduates of such archaeology programs go on to work for colleges and universities, museums, state and federal agencies, and private companies. The U.S. National Park Service and other federal agencies, for example, employ about 800 archaeologists to survey, study, and protect archaeological sites on federal land. In addition, state and local environmental and historical agencies employ archaeologists to guide development around prehistoric and historical sites. Archaeologists fill a similar niche for private engineering and environmental firms that conduct government-required investigations for developers prior to the start of a construction project. Recently, archaeologists have also begun to play an instrumental role in forensic investigations involving buried human remains and related evidence.

increasing number of today's archaeologists combine their archaeological training with degrees in related fields such as anthropology (the study of humans and their cultures) or even geology (the study of rocks and minerals), botany (plants), or zoology (animals).

ARCHAEOLOGICAL CONTROVERSIES AND CHALLENGES

In recent years, most archaeologists have become more sensitive to the rights of the peoples whose artifacts they study. Native Americans and other indigenous peoples have long protested the removal of bones and other sacred items from the sites of their ancient villages. The bones are those of their ancestors, they explain, and deserve the same respect given to bodies buried in European-American graveyards. In recent years, various native groups have begun demanding that museums return their people's ancient sacred objects—such as totem poles, peace pipes, and warrior shields.

The controversy around these issues prompted the U.S. Congress to pass

Archaeological excavation of items from sacred burial sites has led various groups to assert that the graves of their ancestors are being desecrated.

the 1990 Native American Graves Protection and Repatriation Act. The act spells out who owns Native American remains on federal and tribal lands, and sets up strict procedures for their study and return to appropriate tribes. Countries such as Australia and New Zealand have developed similar laws to protect the sacred artifacts of their native peoples. In some cases, native tribes have begun to appoint their own archaeologists to carry out research in a manner that shows respect to their traditions.

Modern archaeology also continues to struggle with the problem of the theft of valuable specimens and the looting of archaeological sites. A worldwide illegal market in antiquities flourishes, and continues to fuel this problem. In response, archaeologists across the globe have urged governments to stop

Archaeologists—always monitoring events in the Middle East, site of some of the world's earliest civilizations— were nevertheless shocked by the magnitude of artifact looting in Baghdad during the Iraq War. Fortunately, most of the items were recovered (left), and security at the museums remains very tight (above).

The Archaeologist Adventurer

Many people today associate archaeology with the swashbuckling adventures of movie characters like "Indiana Jones." This image of the archaeologist-adventurer has a very real basis in fact. Indeed, wealthy and somewhat roguish amateur archaeologists dominated the field through much of the 19th and early 20th centuries, when the colorful accounts of their explorations filled newspapers and popular magazines.

Among the most famous was the rich and cultured German merchant Heinrich Schliemann. In the 1860s, Schliemann scoured classical literature to predict the actual location of legendary Greco-Roman sites. He then financed his own expeditions to uncover them. Among his most spectacular discoveries: the fabled city of Troy.

Following in Schliemann's footprints was the suave British archaeologist and world traveler Sir Arthur Evans. In 1900, Evans uncovered the spectacular palace of Knossos on the island of Crete and then used his vast family fortune to reconstruct the building, including its elaborate frescoes, or painted walls.

Another British nobleman—Sir Mortimer Wheeler—stands out as perhaps the last of archaeology's larger-than-life characters. Described in popular books as "a mixture of military officer, mustachioed dandy, and roguish rake," Wheeler became a high-society celebrity at least as famous for his good looks and romantic life as he was for the remarkable archaeological methods he pioneered in his excavations.

---

or at least slow the illegal trafficking of archaeological objects by better enforcing international antiquity laws.

In 2003, during the Iraq War, these issues gained new prominence after the fall of Baghdad, when thousands of priceless archaeological treasures disappeared from the city's museums. Although most of the artifacts were ultimately recovered, the incident showed how readily the entire archaeological record of a region could have been stolen or destroyed.

On a more promising note, the growing worldwide interest in archaeology has led many governments to better protect their archaeological sites as tourist attractions. In China, for example, tourism helps fund many large, archaeological-research projects. In addition, many countries now require developers and road builders to hire archaeologists to investigate building sites before construction begins. If the archaeologist finds important artifacts, the developer must either change construction plans to avoid destroying them or allow for their safe removal prior to construction.

Such public involvement will only become more important in the future, most experts agree. Much more exploration remains to be done before scientists can hope to answer some of archaeology's most meaningful questions. Why did humans begin farming some 12,000 years ago? Why did they build the first cities, and why did they locate them where they did? Why did so many great societies suddenly vanish, and where did their people ultimately go? Who were the ancestors of modern humans? These and hundreds of other compelling questions stand ready to fuel archaeological research for many centuries to come.

To an underwater archaeologist, a sunken ship is a time capsule of the civilization that produced it. Some shipwrecks have lain undisturbed for centuries.

© Christopher Chippindale

Stonehenge is just one of many ancient monuments thought to be an early astronomical tool.

THE EARLY SKY WATCHERS

by Ray Villard

Simple astronomy played an important role in the cultures of many early peoples. They used the motions of the heavens largely for religious and ceremonial purposes. More practically, celestial motions allowed for the development of the first calendars for planning growing seasons. It was important to know the Sun's rising point on the first day of winter and summer (solstices) as well as the first day of spring and fall (equinoxes). More mathematically sophisticated peoples, such as the Babylonians and the Mayans, plotted the position of the bright planet Venus and even attempted to predict solar and lunar eclipses.

The predawn rising times of selected bright stars were also used to keep track of the seasons. For example, the Egyptians needed to predict when the Nile River would annually flood and thus fertilize the

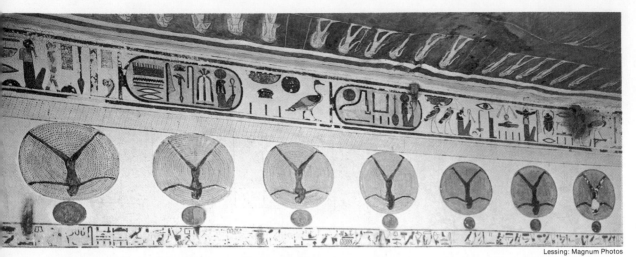

Lessing: Magnum Photos

Many artifacts bear testimony to ancient Egypt's astronomical tradition. The painting above, found on the tomb of Ramses IX, illustrates the death and resurrection of the Sun.

A 16th-century drawing depicts Danish astronomer Tycho Brahe (pointing) and the wall quadrant he used to make the detailed planetary observations that supported a Sun-centered solar system theory.

The Granger Collection

land for crops to be planted. They discovered that when the bright star Sirius first appears in the early-morning sky (called helical rising), flooding soon would follow. This predawn appearance of Sirius happens annually, which allowed the Egyptians to accurately calculate the length of the year to 365 days.

There is abundant evidence that even primitive societies needed to keep track of celestial happenings. Stone patterns arranged on the ground mark the first astronomical ''observatories'' ever built. The most celebrated of these is Stonehenge, a mysterious 100-foot (30.48-meter)-diameter ring of massive, monument-sized (25 tons or 23 metric tons each) stones set on end. Located on the Salisbury Plain in southern England, Stonehenge was built in three distinct phases between 2700 and 1700 B.C. No one knows who built Stonehenge or for what purpose. Certain pairs of stones seem to align to points on the horizon where the Sun would rise and set on special dates. There are a number of other such prehistoric monuments in the British Isles and in Brittany in northwestern France.

At least 50 mysterious, wheel-shaped monuments built by the Native American Indians also have an eerie similarity to Stonehenge. The best example is the Bighorn Medicine Wheel in eastern Wyoming, built around A.D. 1500. Nearly 80 feet (24 meters) across, the wheel has 28 spokes radiating from the center. Besides aligning to the Sun's solstice rising point, the wheel aligns to the rising point of certain key bright stars on selected dates.

An even more fascinating structure, dubbed the "American Woodhenge," can be found in modern-day St. Louis, Missouri. This 410-foot (125-meter)-diameter circle, built around A.D. 1000, has remains of holes dug to anchor 48 large wooden posts. No one knows how high the posts were, but it is believed that one could sight the Sun's solstice from the center of the circle.

Remains of several villages of the Wichita Indians (A.D. 1500) have "council circles," each consisting of a central mound surrounded by a series of depressions arranged in an elliptical pattern. Pairs of ellipses are arranged so that their long axes align with the summer-solstice sunrise and winter-solstice sunset.

The Mayans (A.D. 1000), who inhabited Mexico's Yucatán Peninsula, aligned many features of their cities and buildings to astronomical phenomena. Mayan records show that they were extremely sophisticated at predicting eclipses and the position of Venus. A building called the Caracol, at the ancient city of Chichén Itzá, contains a complex series of windows, walls, and horizontal shafts that seem to point to the location of the Sun and Venus on significant days.

Similar structures are found in the southwestern United States. The Hohokam Indians, who occupied the Casa Grande area near Coolidge, Arizona, from 200 B.C. to A.D. 1475, had a unique building dubbed the "Big House." This three-story structure contains an array of windows and holes that give lines of sight to the horizon. At least half of these openings align to the Sun and Moon on significant dates.

Are many of these alignments coincidence, or did the builders of these monuments have a sophisticated knowledge of

© Comstock

The significance of the Medicine Wheel, in Wyoming's Bighorn Mountains, remains a mystery. One theory suggests that its 28 spokes represent the days of the lunar month; early Indians may have used the wheel as a calendar.

astronomy and the calendar? If some distant future society were to excavate a contemporary airport runway, or even a baseball-park diamond, might they, too, find that it pointed to the Sun's equinox rising and setting points? Nobody knows, of course, but fascinating research continues in this young field of archeoastronomy.

More than any other people, the Chinese kept careful records of major astronomical events. The Chinese recorded sunspots as far back as 800 B.C., and were aware of the Sun's 11-year sunspot cycle fully 2,000 years before modern astronomers "rediscovered" it. At least 20 stellar explosions (supernovas), called "guest stars" by the Chinese, were recorded as far back as A.D. 185. Comets, which were called "broom stars," were duly noted, including every appearance of Halley's comet back to the year 239 B.C.

Driven largely by the superstitions of astrology, which attempted to link celestial alignment to human behavior, Babylonian astronomers kept detailed diaries of celestial events. Unlike the Chinese, the Babylonians were primarily interested in repeatable, cyclical events, so they did not keep records of unpredictable events such as the appearance of a comet or supernova. The Babylonians mapped the apparent path of the Sun across the heavens and established the 12 constellations of the zodiac, which lay along the Sun's path.

In the Chinese and Babylonian civilizations, astronomy and astrology were closely linked. An astronomer was kept in the court of the king or emperor to advise of celestial portents and predict future events. By contrast, in the Western world, the early Greek astronomers were private philosophers, and, in fact, often at odds with established religion. The Greeks were extraordinarily clever and intuitive at conducting purely scientific astronomical observations. They made extraordinary leaps in comprehending the clockwork of the heavens. By 500 B.C., they correctly explained the cause of solar and lunar eclipses. They realized that the Moon reflected sunlight (because of its phases), and that the Sun was much farther away than

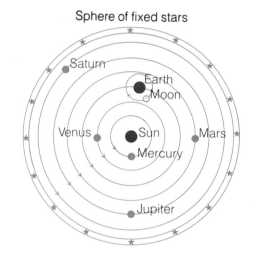

The Greek astronomer Ptolemy believed that Earth was at the center of the universe, with the Sun and planets revolving around it.

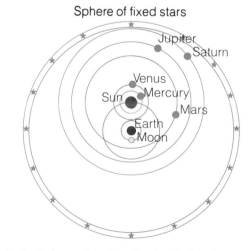

Copernicus challenged Ptolemy's geocentric theory by proposing that Earth, the Moon, and planets all revolve around the Sun.

Tycho Brahe combined the theories of others to propose that the Sun and Moon revolve around Earth, but the other planets revolve around the Sun.

HIGHLIGHTS OF ASTRONOMY HISTORY

1610	Galileo uses telescope for astronomical observations
1665	Newton formulates law of universal gravitation
1695	Edmund Halley predicts the return of a periodic comet
1781	Uranus discovered
1815	Spectrum taken of Sun
1846	Neptune discovered
1905	Albert Einstein develops theory of relativity
1926	Edwin Hubble discovers stars in other galaxies
1930	Pluto discovered
1931	First extraterrestrial radio waves detected
1951	Spiral structure of Milky Way mapped in radio waves
1958–67	Robot spacecraft survey of Moon
1960	First search for artificial interstellar signals
1962	Quasars discovered
1963	Cosmic background radiation detected
1967	First pulsar detected
1969–72	Manned expeditions to Moon
1970	First X-ray detection of a black-hole candidate
1971	First X-ray catalog of sky
1975	First radio message from Earth transmitted to the stars
1976	Experiments for microorganism on Mars (Viking mission)
1977–89	Initial survey of the outer planets via unmanned probes
1987	Nearest supernova in 400 years
1990	Astronomers confirm cosmological nature of the microwave background
1991	First closeup photo taken of asteroid Gaspra
1992	First comprehensive radio Search for Extraterrestrial Intelligence (SETI) begins
1993	Astronomers discover comet broken into 17 pieces
1995	First discovery of extrasolar planet
1998	Water ice confirmed on Moon
2001	The first landing of a space probe on an asteroid (433 Eros)
2003	Most distant extrasolar planet found

the Moon. Through numerous experiments and observations, the Greeks concluded that Earth was a sphere, and they even calculated its diameter. Many philosophers concluded that the Sun, Moon, and planets revolved around Earth, which lay at the center of a huge "celestial sphere." Aristarchus of Samos correctly proposed that, instead, Earth orbited the Sun. However, this idea was far too revolutionary for even the ancient Greek thinkers.

AN ASTRONOMICAL REVOLUTION

The period from the mid-1500s to mid-1600s saw an unprecedented revolution in astronomy. Polish mathematician Nicolaus Copernicus reinvented the notion of a Sun-centered solar system. Detailed planetary observations by Danish astronomer Tycho Brahe provided an invaluable database for supporting Copernicus' theory. Brahe's heir to the astronomical data, Johannes Kepler formulated the laws of planetary motion.

While Kepler was refining his theories, the Italian inventor and scientist Galileo Galilei used the telescope, a recent Dutch invention, to study the heavens. The telescope allowed Galileo to see objects 10 times more clearly than with the unaided human eye. This unveiled a universe that was more complex than sky watchers had dared to imagine, including literally millions of stars in the Milky Way, mountains and valleys on the Moon, shifting phases of Venus as it orbits the Sun, and a tiny moon orbiting the distant planet Jupiter.

Kepler and Galileo assembled evidence that proved the planets orbited the Sun. Neither scientist knew exactly what invisible, all-pervasive force kept the solar system "glued" together. Mathematician Isaac Newton combined Copernicus' theory, Kepler's laws, and Galileo's observations to formulate the law of universal gravitation. This law states that all objects are attracted to other objects, and that the strength of this bond depends on how much matter the objects contain and the distances between them. These laws describe the motion of all bodies in the universe, and remained unchanged until the 20th century.

THE CALENDAR

by Elisabeth Achelis

A calendar page from the medieval manuscript Très Riches Heures *showing the pageantry of celebrations in the month of May.*

Musée Condé, Chantilly, France/Giraudon

The calendar we use today is the product of a great many centuries of patient study and of constant trial and error. When people first looked to heavenly bodies for a way to measure time, they observed that the Sun seemed to make a constantly repeated journey in the heavens, always returning to the same place after many days. (Actually, of course, it is the Earth that makes a yearly revolution around the Sun.) They observed that the Moon also followed a definite cycle.

Most of the earliest calendars were based on Moon cycles. These calendars were made to fit as best they could within the larger framework of the Sun cycle. The year, in these calendars, generally consisted of 12 Moon cycles, or months. Since 12 Moon cycles are not quite equal to a solar year, an extra month—called an *intercalary*, or inserted, month—was added from time to time. A number of ancient peoples—including the Babylonians, Hebrews, Greeks, and Romans—adopted this method of computation.

FIRST SOLAR CALENDAR

The Egyptians were the first to base their calendar on a year of 365 days, approximating the Sun cycle, or solar year. They also made the month a purely arbitrary unit, not corresponding to the actual lunar cycle. The year was divided into 12 months of 30 days each, totaling 360 days, to which were added five extra "feast days.'' The 365-day calendar is believed to have been adopted by the Egyptians in the year 4236 B.C.

In the course of the centuries that followed, it was discovered that the year really consisted of 365¼ days. This additional quarter of a day was causing a gradual shift of the seasons as recorded in the calendar. In 238 B.C., the pharaoh Ptolemy III, also known to history as Euergetes, tried to correct this error in calculation by adding another day to the calendar every four years. It was to be a religious holiday, but unfortunately, the priests were unwilling to accept the extra day. As a result the Egyptian calendar continued to be defective as a measure of the seasons.

THE MAYAN CALENDAR

Another seasonal Sun calendar that was used in antiquity was that of the Mayas of Mexico. Their invention probably goes back to the year 580 B.C., and it was the first seasonal and agricultural calendar produced in America.

The Mayan calendar was arranged differently from that of the Egyptians. The Mayan solar year, called a *tun*, had 18 months of 20 days each. It had a five-day unlucky period at its end to make 365 days. Each month had its own name, and the days were numbered from 0 to 19.

Dovetailed with the Mayan Sun calendar was a religious year, sometimes called a *tzolkin*. The tzolkin contained 13 months of 20 days each. Each day had a name that was combined with the numbers 1 to 13 to count out the 260 days of the tzolkin.

THE JULIAN CALENDAR

The ancient Romans had a moon calendar, which was complicated and most confusing. Originally only 10 months long (March to December), it was soon extended to 12 months by the addition of January and February. A 13th month, called Mercedonius, was occasionally inserted. The 12 months of the Roman year consisted of seven months of 29 days each; four months of 31 days each; and one month,

Februarius (February), with 28 days—making a year of 355 days. The names of the 12 months of the Roman year were as follows:

Name of month	*Origin of name*
Martius	Month of Mars
Aprilis	"Opening" month, when the Earth opens to produce new fruits
Maius	Month of the great god Jupiter
Junius	Month of the Junii, a Roman clan
Quintilis	Fifth month
Sextilis	Sixth month
September	Seventh month
October	Eighth month
November	Ninth month
December	Tenth month
Januarius	Month of the god Janus
Februarius	Month of the Februa, a purification feast

In 153 B.C., January was designated as the first month of the year instead of Martius (our March).

The Romans used a complicated system of reckoning within the month. There were three more-or-less fixed dates—the *calends*, the *ides*, and the *nones*. The cal-

The ancient Maya used several calendars simultaneously, some that rivaled the Julian calendar for precision. This stone tablet is a calendar from Yaxchilán, Mexico, from the 8th century A.D.

© Michael Holford

© John S. Flannery/Bruce Coleman Inc.

This Aztec calendar stone depicts Huitzilopochtli, the Sun god, surrounded by symbols for historic eras, the days of the month, and the stars.

The year 46 B.C. bridged the old and the new calendar. The following year, 45 B.C., was actually the first one using the reformed calendar. Caesar retained the complicated system of calends, nones, and ides within the months. January continued to be the first month of the year. The Roman Senate changed the name of the month Quintilis to Julius (our July) in honor of Caesar. The new calendar was known as the Julian calendar. Later the Roman Senate changed the name of the month Sextilis to Augustus (August) to honor the Emperor Augustus.

THE SEVEN-DAY WEEK

In A.D. 321, the Emperor Constantine issued an edict introducing the seven-day week in the calendar, doing away once and for all with the system of calends, ides, and nones. Constantine established Sunday as the first day of the week, and set it aside as the Christian day of worship.

Although the introduction of the week greatly simplified matters, it brought about a serious defect in the calendar, a defect that is still present today. Both the Egyptian and Julian calendars had been stabilized. That is, every year had been like every other year. Through Constantine's reform the Julian calendar became a shifting one. Now that there were 52 seven-day weeks, totaling 364 days, there was always one day left over in ordinary years, and two days in leap years. This meant that in successive years, the Julian calendar began on different days of the week.

THE GREGORIAN CALENDAR

The true length of the solar year is a trifle less than 365¼ days. It is 365.242199 days, or 365 days, five hours, 48 minutes, and 46 seconds, to be exact. Therefore, the Julian calendar was too long by about 11 minutes. After a number of centuries, the error amounted to several days.

In the year 1582, another momentous calendar reform took place. Pope Gregory XIII determined to adjust the calendar to the seasons. For this purpose, he called

ends always fell on the first of the month. The ides came on the 15th in Martius, Maius, Sextilis, and October and on the 13th in other months. The nones always came on the eighth day before the ides. (The Romans, however, used inclusive numbering and counted the ides themselves, making the nones, meaning ''nine,'' the ninth day before the ides.)

The calendar was entrusted to a council of priests—the College of Pontiffs, presided over by a *pontifex maximus*. The pontiffs were state officials charged with the regulation of certain religious matters, including the fixing of dates for ceremonies.

Julius Caesar was elected pontifex maximus in 63 B.C., but it was not until 47 B.C. that he took the first steps to reform the calendar. Following the suggestions of the famous Greek astronomer Sosigenes, Caesar adopted the solar year for the Roman calendar. He gave it 365 days, plus a quarter-day of six hours. Quarter-days were withheld until a full day had accumulated. The day was then added to the common year as a leap-year day. This happened once every four years.

A manuscript page from an Islamic calendar from Damascus, Syria, circa 1366. The Islamic calendar begins with the first day of Muhammad's journey to Medina, which corresponds to July 15, 622, of the Christian Era.

This Gregorian calendar is the one that we use today.

All Roman Catholic countries adopted the Gregorian reform, but other groups in Christendom were slow in accepting it. The English did not adopt the Gregorian calendar until 1752. France, like the other Catholic countries of Europe, had adopted the Gregorian calendar in 1582; however, for a period beginning in 1792, it was replaced by the "Revolutionary Calendar." In line with other antireligious developments of the time, the days and months of this calendar were given symbolic names, such as "Brumaire" ("month of fog"), denoting the "natural" order of things. In 1806 Napoleon restored the Gregorian calendar as a gesture of reconciliation toward the Church.

Japan adopted the Gregorian calendar in 1873, China in 1912, Greece in 1924, and Turkey in 1927. Russia began to use the

upon the services of mathematician Christopher Clavius and astronomer-physician Aloysius Lilius. They found that the error caused by the excessive length of the Julian calendar amounted to 10 days. To set the year aright, they canceled 10 days from the Julian calendar, so that October 4, 1582, was followed by October 15.

Naturally, this loss of 10 days in the month of October created a certain amount of confusion. To avoid confusion, dates prior to October 15, 1582, were often given thereafter (and are still often given) as O.S. (old style), and dates after as N.S. (new style). If neither O.S. nor N.S. is given after a date, it's assumed to be N.S.

To avoid further error in the calendar, the leap-year rule was changed. In the case of centurial years (those ending in "00"), only the ones that were divisible by 400 were to be leap years. Noncenturial leap years continued to receive an extra day. No attempt was made to equalize the lengths of the months or to stabilize the calendar.

In 45 B.C., Julius Caesar was persuaded by the astronomer Sosigenes to adopt a solar year. The resultant Julian calendar was used extensively for centuries. Below, a Julian calendar from the 5th century.

calendar in 1918, replaced it with another calendar when the Bolsheviks took over the country, and returned to the Gregorian calendar in 1940.

OTHER CALENDARS IN USE

The Gregorian calendar is not the only one used at the present time. For religious purposes, Jews employ the Hebrew calendar, which begins with the year of creation, set at 3,760 years before the beginning of the Christian Era. This calendar is based on the cycles of the Moon. There are 12 months, which are alternately 29 and 30 days in length. An extra month of 29 days is intercalated seven times in every cycle of 19 years. Whenever this is done, one of the 29-day months receives an extra day. The year begins in the autumn.

Another important calendar is the Islamic, or Muslim, calendar. It also is based on the cycles of the Moon. There are 354 days and 12 months, half of which have 29 days, and the other half 30 days. Thirty years form a cycle; 11 times in every cycle, an extra day is added at the end of the year. The Muslim calendar begins with the first day of the year of the Hegira—that is, the

journey of Muhammad to Medina. This date corresponds to July 15, 622, of the Christian Era.

Although the Gregorian calendar is China's official calendar, the Chinese New Year is still calculated by the ancient Chinese lunar calendar. The months of this lunar calendar are known by the names of the 12 animals of the Chinese zodiac: rat, ox, tiger, hare, dragon, serpent, horse, sheep, monkey, rooster, dog, and boar.

MODERN CALENDAR REFORM

The Gregorian calendar has served people well for almost four centuries. Yet some thoughtful people have tried to bring about reforms that would restore stability to the calendar within the framework of the seasonal year.

In 1834 Abbé Marco Mastrofini put forward a plan in which every year would be the same, and the lost stability of the calendar would be restored. In his calendar, there are 364 days in the year—a number easily divisible in various ways. The 365th day and the 366th in leap years were inserted as extra days within the year. Each year would begin on Sunday, January 1. The abbé's idea was so simple that most modern calendar reformers have made it the basis of their own proposals.

Calendar reform lagged until the League of Nations took up the question in 1923. One proposal, the World Calendar, based on the easily divisible number 12, once seemed particularly promising. In this calendar, each equal quarter-year of 91 days, or 13 weeks, or three months, corresponds to a season period. Every year in this calendar is like every other year. The first of every year, for example, falls on a Sunday; Christmas, December 25, falls on a Monday. To provide the necessary 365th day, a day—known as Worldsday—is inserted after December 30 and before January 1. The 366th day in leap years is inserted between June 30 and July 1. The Gregorian 400 centurial leap-year rule is retained. However, the idea was not adopted, and it has met with scant success in the years since.

The beautifully crafted calendar below was created during the Italian Renaissance. It is a unique calendar in that it uses both Sun-based and Moon-based systems to measure time.

G. Tomsich/Photo Researchers

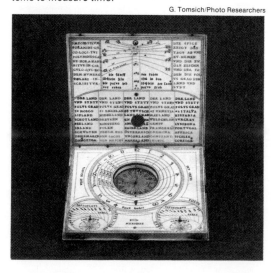

PALEONTOLOGISTS AND THEIR SCIENCE

by Anthony J. Castagno

In 2005, researchers in China discovered fossils of some of the earliest known complex life-forms. The specimens are estimated to be some 550 million years old, which means they date to the Ediacaran period, prior to when animals with bones or shells appeared. The fossils offered numerous insights into early life on Earth. "These fossils provide the key to understand the prelude to the Cambrian explosion, when animals with skeletons and familiar morphologies began to bloom about 540–520 million years ago," said Shuhai Xiao, an assistant professor at Virginia Polytechnic Institute.

An international team of paleontologists and other scientists recently examined ancient human skulls that were found in Ethiopia. The 160,000-year-old remains appear to be those of a new subspecies of *Homo sapiens*, and represent some of the oldest known evidence of modern humans. The finds appear to support the theory that modern *H. sapiens* originated in Africa. Further analysis of these remains and of other artifacts found in the area led scientists to some surprising conclusions: the ancient inhabitants of the region ate hippopotamus meat, fashioned crude stone tools, and may have practiced certain mortuary—or even cannibalistic rituals.

In 2003, in northeastern China, paleontologists discovered the fossils of a small, feathered dinosaur with four wings. Dubbed the "microraptor," the animal lived between 125 million and 145 million years ago, and measured approximately 30 inches (75 centimeters) in length. With two pairs of wings—one set on its forelimbs and the other on its hind legs—the creature may have glided between trees like today's flying squirrel, and swooped down on unsuspecting prey. Many paleontologists believe that birds evolved from some type of small, feathered dinosaur. The microraptor could represent an important part of the puzzle as scientists try to understand how modern birds came into being.

Later in 2003, paleontologists made another amazing find, this time in northern Venezuela. Roughly 6 million years ago, the area was home

Using specialized tools, paleontologists at a dig site (above) scrape away layers of sediment to uncover the fossilized remains of ancient plants and animals.

In the 1920s, Barnum Brown (above, at right) of the American Museum of Natural History in New York did much to advance the study of paleontology in the United States.

The first records of fossils being examined appear in the 1500s. Back then, many people thought that fossils were creations of the devil placed on rocks to lead people astray or freaks of nature. In the 1700s, many believed that fossils were the remains of animals and plants destroyed by the great flood described in the Bible. But by the 1900s, scientists more universally recognized that fossils were the preserved remains, traces, or impressions of organisms from long ago—and that they could reveal enormous amounts of information from past eras, and the discipline of paleontology began to develop.

By the 21st century, paleontologists had used fossils to piece together much of the history and evolution of many types of life. Paleontology is a relatively young science, with discoveries still being made and conclusions about our ancient past still being drawn.

to one of the largest rodents on Earth. A team of paleontologists, led by Marcelo Sanchez-Villagra of Germany's Tübingen University, discovered two fossil skeletons of *Phoberomys pattersoni*, an enormous 1,500-pound (680-kilogram), marsh-dwelling rodent that resembled a giant guinea pig. The fossil skeletons helped paleontologists determine much about the creature, including its size. In addition to its weight, they know the animal was about 9 feet (3 meters) in length, 4 feet (1 meter) tall, and may have used its long tail for balance.

WHAT IS PALEONTOLOGY?

All of the scientists above are indulging their fascination with paleontology: the study of fossils and ancient life-forms, both plant and animal, single-celled and multicellular. It is important, not only because of our curiosity about the plants and animals that lived millions of years ago, but also because paleontology helps to shed light on the evolution and development of modern-day life. Paleontology is the basis for the preparation of geologic maps used by scientists to search for water and mineral sites.

Subdisciplines

Paleontology focuses mainly on the study of fossils found in strata, or layers, of sedimentary rock formed over millions of years. By studying fossils, scientists can identify organisms and better understand the environments they inhabited. There are many subdisciplines in—and sciences related to—paleontology, each of which targets a specific aspect of the field.

Paleobotany. Paleobotany, the study of the history of the Plant Kingdom, is a major branch of paleontology. It encompasses several subdisciplines, including *palynology*, the study of microscopic plant fossils (particularly those of pollen); and *paleoethnobotany*, the study of how prehistoric cultures and peoples used plants.

The noted French botanist and geologist Adolphe-Théodore Brongniart (1801–76), often con-

Paleontology requires attention to detail. Like pieces in a puzzle, fossil fragments must be put together (left) to reveal how an animal or plant once looked.

sidered the "father of paleobotany," is the first to have systematically identified and classified fossil plants. He collected these fossils from scientists worldwide and published his findings in *Histoire des Végétaux Fossiles* (1828–37), in which he drew conclusions about the geologic ages during which the plants lived.

Other significant early contributions to the field were made by the British naturalist William Crawford Williamson (1816–95) and the British botanist D. Henry Scott (1854–1934), who studied the nearly perfect plant fossils found in ancient layers of peat; and by the English botanist Sir Albert Charles Seward (1863–1941), who published a four-volume set titled *Fossil Plants* from 1898 to 1919, and a more general text, *Plant Life through the Ages*, in the year 1931.

In 1965, American paleontologist E. S. Barghoorn published his study of blue-green algae filaments estimated to be approximately 1.9 billion years old, far "younger" than the oldest fossilized remains of life: tiny bacteria that lived 3.6 billion years ago. The study of these and other single-celled organisms—the earliest and most primitive forms of life—is known as *micropaleontology*.

Paleoanthropology. Paleoanthropology is a branch of anthropology that deals with early humans, their origins, evolution, cultures, and way of life. It includes the study of modern humans, *Homo sapiens*, and that of extinct human predecessors, *Homo erectus* and *Homo habilis*.

Paleoanthropology began developing as a science in the early 19th century, when paleontologists realized that some of the shaped stones they had found were actually tools made by early humans. The stone tools gave rise to the expression "Stone Age" to describe these early human times.

Before the discovery of the stone implements, most people applied a literal interpretation to the Bible and assumed that Earth had been created only 6,000 years ago. With in-

Virtually everything we know about dinosaurs was discovered by paleontologists. Museums engage in long negotiations to obtain a dinosaur skeleton; painstaking research is then needed to assemble the skeleton correctly.

creasing evidence that the human race was far older, and additional geologic evidence emerging that Earth was actually many millions of years old, there was, by the end of the 19th century, general scientific acceptance of the theory that humans had descended from a nonhuman, probably apelike ancestor. As early human cultures were studied, paleoanthropologists discovered evidence of metalworking and other signs of emerging technology. Today paleoanthropology is closely allied with such related fields as archaeology in studying tools, buildings, and other remains of early humans to better understand how and where they lived, their social organization, and other factors in their cultures.

Paleobiology. Paleobiology focuses on evolutionary theory—more specifically, on the links that indicate that certain species evolved from others, and on the interrelationships of species and their lifestyles. An example of an evolutionary link is *Archaeopteryx*, a fossil bird that is a link between reptiles and birds; early fossil

Careers in Paleontology

Paleontology is a diverse and endlessly interesting field that involves elements of many other sciences, including geology, biology, chemistry, and physics. As these sciences become more and more specialized, particularly through new technological developments, so, too, does paleontology.

Most career paleontologists have earned a doctoral degree (Ph.D.) in paleontology or one of its specialties, a process that typically takes four to eight years of study beyond the undergraduate level. Preparation for entry into a doctoral program involves studying the sciences in college. Some experts suggest pursuing a double undergraduate major, with degrees in biology and geology; at the very least, it is important to major in one and have completed substantial course work in the other. Other science and liberal-arts courses are important as well.

Various activities sponsored by colleges and museums can provide insight into pale-

ontology and its specialties. Several scholarly journals about paleontology keep readers abreast of the latest findings and enable prospective paleontologists to grow familiar with prominent scientists in the field.

Most paleontologists work for or affiliate with universities or colleges, where they conduct research and teach paleontology and geology. A smaller number of paleontologists work for museums, the government, or private industry. Overall, the job market is tight, but job opportunities exist, especially for highly qualified, well-educated candidates.

whales are considered a transitional link from land-bound mammals to marine mammals such as blue whales.

Because paleontology studies life over great stretches of time, it is possible to trace the evolution of species and to test evolutionary theories against the actual fossil record. Paleobiologists can trace the emergence, flourishing, and disappearance of various species of plants and animals, often discovering important links indicative of evolution.

Taphonomy. Taphonomy is the study of how fossils are formed and preserved. Entire or partial bodies of organisms are called *body fossils*; most are the remains of hard or bony matter such as skeletons, shells, bones, and teeth. Soft organic tissue is less likely to survive the fossilization process, although there are many exceptions. On the shores of Lake Superior, for example, fossils of bacteria and blue-green algae approximately 2 billion years old have been found. In British Columbia, paleontologists discovered well-preserved, fossilized soft-bodied marine worms and crustaceans that are hundreds of millions of years old.

Trace fossils, on the other hand, are marks left in rock by the activities of organisms. *Ichnology*, the study of trace fossils left by burrowing or moving animals, can help reveal information about these organisms and their environment, and also can help us project the speed with which certain ancient animals could move.

Biostratigraphy is the study of the vertical distribution of fossils in rocks, which helps paleontologists ascertain when the fossils were deposited. The exact age of rock can often be determined by radiological analysis, but it also can be estimated by examining the fossils found in various layers, or strata, of the rock—because each geologic stage has distinct fossils. Additionally, rocks from different areas can be compared and conclusions drawn about the environments and organisms that lived there.

Paleoecology. Paleoecologists study fossil organisms in the context of the environment in which they lived, including other species that lived at the same time in the same general area. Much can be determined from the strata in which a fossil is found—not only the fossil's approximate age, but also how the organism lived.

Paleoclimatology studies climates throughout geologic time and strives to determine how

Based on paleontological research, a 19th-century artist named Charles Knight created huge murals of prehistoric animals (above, being restored). The images were so realistic that they ultimately became part of our popular culture.

and why they have changed. Climate itself involves the interrelationships of the atmosphere, the oceans, and the continents; paleoclimatology studies these—including such factors as temperature, precipitation, and barometric pressure—over long periods of time. Much of this information can be gleaned from fossils and their location within certain strata; chemical analyses of glacial ice and other deposits also provide valuable data about ancient climates and weather patterns.

Paleogeography, the study of ancient geography, focuses particularly on the location and configuration of landmasses and oceans, mountains, volcanoes, inland bodies of water, and other ecological features. It is closely related to historical geology, but takes into account many other factors in drawing conclusions about how the world looked millions of years ago.

The subdiscipline of paleogeography called *paleobiogeography* is concerned with the distribution of organisms on the ancient landmasses. For example, the existence of similar fossils in South America and Africa supports the theory that these two continents, now widely separated, were once joined together.

Paleomagnetism. A particularly esoteric subdiscipline of paleontology is paleomagnetism, the study of the history of Earth's magnetic field and how and why it has shifted over the course of thousands to millions of years. Earth's polarity has reversed many times in the past, and currently its magnetic poles are not the same as

its geographic poles. Paleomagnetic studies have shown that the magnetic poles are drifting so that every 10,000 to 20,000 years—a blink of the eye in geologic time—they average out to coincide with the geographic poles.

When rock forms, its minerals line up magnetically along Earth's magnetic poles as they exist at the time. Studying the alignment of the magnetism in rocks has helped confirm the important geologic theories of plate tectonics and continental drift.

THE FUTURE OF PALEONTOLOGY

Paleontology has experienced an enormous increase in public interest over the past several years. As long as people remain fascinated by life in the ancient past, paleontology will continue to be an active, advancing field of science where new and important discoveries are constantly being made. The most common association with paleontology is, of course, the dinosaur, and dinosaurs have never been more popular. The American Museum of Natural History in New York City and the Carnegie Museum in Pittsburgh have permanent dinosaur displays. The ancient reptiles are featured prominently in movies (such as the *Jurassic Park* series), documentaries, books, video games, and Internet sites. This popularity has served to attract a new generation of scientists to the field, who have played a vital role in our future by helping us to understand the past.

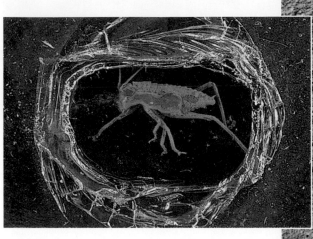

FOSSILS

Fossils are the remains or other evidence of plants or animals that lived at least 10,000 years ago. Fossils can provide a glimpse back to when life first emerged (some 3.8 billion years ago), or to when dinosaurs roamed Earth (some 225 million to 65 million years ago), or to when our modern human ancestors appeared (only about 40,000 years ago). The study of fossils, and the life they represent, is called *paleontology*.

Some fossils are very tiny, having been left by single-celled organisms; others are enormous, such as those of the dinosaurs. Most fossils have been found in sedimentary rock that formed in layers over the ages, but other fossils, such as those of insects, occur in *amber*—the hardened resin of conifers. Fossils also have been discovered in ice and frozen soil, peat bogs and tar pits, and in ancient feces, called *coprolites*, which can give a good indication of what animals ate many millions of years ago.

TYPES OF FOSSILS

Fossils are divided into two types: *body fossils*, the actual bodies or body parts of organisms; and *trace fossils*: burrows, tracks, or other signs of an organism's activities.

Fossils—the remains or other evidence of ancient plants and animals—take many forms. Much has been learned from dinosaur footprints preserved in stone (above), or an ancient grasshopper (inset) held in amber.

Body Fossils

The most-common body fossils are shells, bones, teeth, and other indigestible material that cannot be eaten and, over the years, is buried and preserved.

Shells, whether from microscopic creatures or large clams and snails, are the most frequently found body fossils. Their original calcium carbonate is often preserved chemically intact. Significant chemical change may occur, however, especially if water seeping through the rocks dissolves the shell (leaving only its shape behind), or if the water carries minerals such as silicon dioxide, which eventually replace the original calcium carbonate.

Bones are made primarily of calcium phosphate with spaces for organic material. When this organic material decays, the spaces typically fill with other minerals. This process makes the bone heavier and harder, but usually does not change the chemical composition of the actual bony material. Teeth, also made of calcium phosphate, are harder and have fewer spaces than bone, so they usually undergo little change over the ages.

Plants and soft animals also may be preserved, but usually as imprints in rock that remain when the rock hardens and the organic material decays. When a large amount of plant and animal life is buried and certain pressure and heat conditions exist, it can turn into coal or petroleum, usually without leaving fossils.

Petrified wood is fossilized wood in which the wood has essentially turned to stone. When the wood is buried, the spaces within it start filling up with silica and other minerals. Eventually the wood itself is completely replaced by minerals, leaving behind stone that looks much like the original wood.

Trace Fossils

Types of trace fossils include trails, burrows, tracks, feces, and tools left behind by ancient life-forms. Trace fossils help scientists understand the various life habits of a prehistoric animal, and sometimes even its species and size. In some cases, the only evidence we have of an early organism is scanty chemical traces found in rock. These, too, can be analyzed for clues about ancient life.

Intact dinosaur eggs and eggshell fragments have been discovered, sometimes in or near a nest. Studying these fossils in the context of their location not only can give information about dinosaur reproduction, but also can reveal much about their parenting habits.

FOSSIL-AGE DETERMINATION

The age of fossils can be determined by various methods. One relatively simple method is to compare fossil-rich rock samples in one area with those from another area whose age is known. A more exact method relies on analysis of radioactive materials present in the sample.

This method, known as radiometric dating, is based on what already is known about the rate at which radioactive elements in the rock decay, or give off radioactivity as they transform into other, more-stable elements. A familiar type of radiometric dating is called carbon-14 dating, so named because it is based on the decay of an isotope of radioactive carbon in the sample. This is fairly accurate for determining ages of up to about 35,000 years. Other radioactive elements in the sample can be analyzed to determine the age of rocks that are millions, or even hundreds of millions or billions, of years old.

GEOLOGIC TIME SCALE

In the early 1800s, geologists discovered that there were distinct sequences of strata in sedimentary rock that were similar in different parts of the world. They also found that there were distinct fossils in each of these strata. By studying these fossils and strata sequences, they began to gain a better understanding of what life existed where and when in prehistoric times, and what happened geologically, geograph-

The wood of ancient trees is sometimes preserved as stone through a process called petrification. Petrified wood bears a striking resemblance to the original.

Geologic Timescale

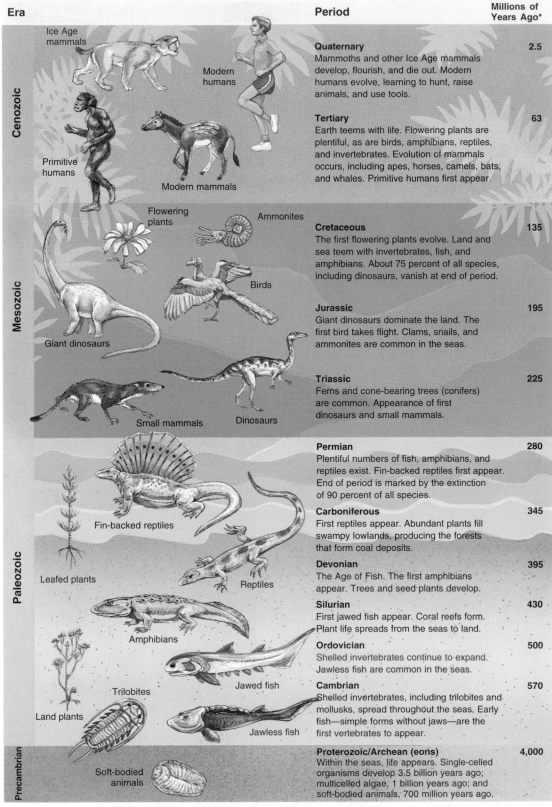

Era		Period	Millions of Years Ago*
Cenozoic	Ice Age mammals / Modern humans / Primitive humans / Modern mammals	**Quaternary** Mammoths and other Ice Age mammals develop, flourish, and die out. Modern humans evolve, learning to hunt, raise animals, and use tools.	2.5
		Tertiary Earth teems with life. Flowering plants are plentiful, as are birds, amphibians, reptiles, and invertebrates. Evolution of mammals occurs, including apes, horses, camels, bats, and whales. Primitive humans first appear.	63
Mesozoic	Flowering plants / Ammonites / Birds / Giant dinosaurs / Small mammals / Dinosaurs	**Cretaceous** The first flowering plants evolve. Land and sea teem with invertebrates, fish, and amphibians. About 75 percent of all species, including dinosaurs, vanish at end of period.	135
		Jurassic Giant dinosaurs dominate the land. The first bird takes flight. Clams, snails, and ammonites are common in the seas.	195
		Triassic Ferns and cone-bearing trees (conifers) are common. Appearance of first dinosaurs and small mammals.	225
Paleozoic	Fin-backed reptiles / Leafed plants / Reptiles / Amphibians / Jawed fish / Trilobites / Land plants / Jawless fish	**Permian** Plentiful numbers of fish, amphibians, and reptiles exist. Fin-backed reptiles first appear. End of period is marked by the extinction of 90 percent of all species.	280
		Carboniferous First reptiles appear. Abundant plants fill swampy lowlands, producing the forests that form coal deposits.	345
		Devonian The Age of Fish. The first amphibians appear. Trees and seed plants develop.	395
		Silurian First jawed fish appear. Coral reefs form. Plant life spreads from the seas to land.	430
		Ordovician Shelled invertebrates continue to expand. Jawless fish are common in the seas.	500
		Cambrian Shelled invertebrates, including trilobites and mollusks, spread throughout the seas. Early fish—simple forms without jaws—are the first vertebrates to appear.	570
Precambrian	Soft-bodied animals	**Proterozoic/Archean (eons)** Within the seas, life appears. Single-celled organisms develop 3.5 billion years ago; multicelled algae, 1 billion years ago; and soft-bodied animals, 700 million years ago.	4,000

*Time in millions of years refers to beginning of periods.

How Fossils Form

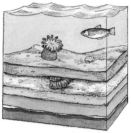

The formation of a fossil begins after an organism, typically a water creature, dies. Gradually, its body sinks through the depths and ultimately settles to the sea bottom.

The soft body parts decay quickly or are eaten by scavengers, leaving behind teeth, bones, and other hard parts. Sand, mud, and other debris settle on these skeletal remains.

Over the centuries, the layers of sediment continue to accumulate, compressing the layers below. Eventually, the uppermost layer might emerge above the water surface.

The compacted sediment is gradually changed into sedimentary rock, and the remains harden into fossils. Eventually, geologic forces may bring the fossil to the surface.

ically, and environmentally to affect this life. These studies also can give information about the evolution and extinction of species, and have provided the basis for many of the current theories on the development of modern life.

The study of fossils led to the development of the *geologic timescale*, which describes the past 570 million years by dividing the time into eras, periods, and epochs. The eras are the largest of the scale divisions, and are separated from each other by geologic events that changed the environment and gave rise to new forms of life. While a true, linear evolution has not been established, the study of fossils and their place on the timescale makes it clear that evolution did take place, and that environmental changes are the driving force in evolution.

Precambrian Time

Precambrian time covers the entire time from the formation of Earth, more than 4 billion years ago, to the start of the Paleozoic era, about 570 million years ago. Life appeared about 3.8 billion years ago in the form of very simple and primitive one-celled organisms. There are few actual fossils from this time, but as chemical and other types of analysis become more sophisticated, scientists can draw conclusions that help provide information about this very long part of Earth's history.

Paleozoic Era

The Paleozoic era lasted about 345 million years, from 570 million years ago to 435 million years ago. Fossils from early in this era indicate that life was limited to the oceans, and animal life was limited to simple invertebrates. By the end of the era, plants and animals had established themselves on land, and vertebrates such as fish and reptiles had evolved.

The Cambrian period. The earliest part of the Paleozoic era lasted about 70 million years and was marked by invertebrate animal life in the seas. Fossils indicate the presence of early mollusks and snails, burrowing worms, and a wide variety of shelled marine animals. There were simple plants in the ocean, and lichens on land. The dominant early chordate, a forerunner of vertebrates, was the trilobite, a small, flat arthropod whose body was divided into three sections, or lobes. There were also many small, clamlike invertebrates and spongelike invertebrates with shell-like structures inside or around their bodies. Most of North America was underwater during this period, and the climate worldwide was warm.

The Ordovician period. The Ordovician period lasted about 70 million years, from 500 million years ago to about 430 million years ago. Landmasses were shifting, and life flourished mainly in the seas. Plant and animal life was

Among the most abundant of fossils are those of trilobites (above), an early and primitive arthropod that may have been the ancestor of modern crabs and spiders.

similar to that at the end of the previous period, but a new group of invertebrates, the graptolites, developed structures suggestive of a spinal cord. Crinoids, or sea lilies, predecessors of the starfish, attached themselves to shells and rocks. The first primitive fish—and the first vertebrates—also appeared during this period.

The Silurian period. The Silurian period lasted about 35 million years, from 430 million years ago to 395 million years ago. The first air-breathing animal, a scorpion, evolved during this period, as did the first vascular plants (land plants with an internal system for transporting water and nutrients). Marine invertebrates were still dominant in the seas, although the trilobites were in decline. Corals were abundant, their remains building large reefs in many areas. Sea lilies and sea scorpions were common.

The Devonian period. This interval lasted about 50 million years, from 395 million years ago to 345 million years ago. Marine vertebrates, such as small sharks, and the lungfish—the first true, or bony, fish—were dominant; these lungfish were capable of gulping air. Land plants, including trees, were widespread. Early amphibians were evolving, and the earliest known insect emerged. The first land vertebrates, amphibians called stegocephalians for the bony armor on their heads, appeared.

The Carboniferous period. This period—from 345 million years ago to 280 million years ago—is sometimes broken into two periods: the Mississippian and the Pennsylvanian. Sharks dominated the seas, and stegocephalians the land. Land plants proliferated, creating dense tropical forests that would later give rise to coal deposits (thus the term "carboniferous"). The first reptiles evolved, joining land animals such as spiders, cockroaches, and scorpions. Also flourishing at this time was the largest insect ever known—a dragonfly with a wingspan of 29 inches (74 centimeters)!

The Permian period. The Permian period lasted from 280 million years ago to 225 million years ago. During this period, the seas retreated, and many marine animals disappeared. As more land appeared, reptiles spread and evolved rapidly. Some were fast and lizardlike; others were sluggish and semiaquatic. The Theriodonts, a small group of carnivorous reptiles with teeth and skulls, would ultimately give rise to the mammals. The trilobites became extinct.

The Permian period—and the Paleozoic era—ended with approximately 1 million years of geologic change called the Appalachian Revolution. During this time, the continents lifted, and huge mountain ranges formed. Seas drained, and deserts appeared, leading to the extinction of many plants and animals that were not able to adapt to their new environments.

The Mesozoic Era

The Mesozoic era lasted about 160 million years, from about 225 million years ago to 65 million years ago; it often is called the *Age of Reptiles* because these animals were dominant throughout the era.

The Triassic period. The Triassic period, from 225 million years ago to 195 million years ago, was when the dinosaurs first appeared. These creatures were large—but not as large as the dinosaurs that would evolve later in the Mesozoic era. The Triassic dinosaurs were slender and rarely reached a length of 15 feet (4.5 meters); they ran on their hind legs. Aquatic reptiles, the ichthyosaurs, were slender, dolphinlike creatures that grew to be 30 feet (9 meters) long. Flying reptiles (the pterosaurs) and the first mammals also developed during this period. The forests were dominated by conifers, although flowering plants, the *angiosperms*, were beginning to evolve.

The Jurassic period. The Jurassic period, from 195 million years ago to 135 million years ago, was a time dominated by dinosaurs. This was the age of *Supersaurus* and *Tyrannosaurus rex*, of *Iguanodon* and *Triceratops*.

Also during the Jurassic period, *Archaeopteryx*—a seagull-sized bird with avian-like feathers, but also a number of reptilian characteristics—appeared. The mammals beginning to emerge during the Jurassic period were very primitive, and mainly smaller than a dog.

The Cretaceous period. The Cretaceous period, from 135 million years to 65 million years ago, began with reptile domination, but ended with most of them—including the dinosaurs—extinct. Snakes and small mammals were evolving. Plant life underwent significant evolution, as flowering plants thrived and became widespread. Poplar and fig trees appeared toward the beginning of the period; by the end, many modern trees and shrubs—including walnut, oak, holly, and maple—were common.

The Cenozoic Era

The Cenozoic era began about 65 million years ago, and is the era in which we now are living. It is divided into two periods: the Tertiary, also known as the *Age of Mammals*, which lasted 63 million years; and the Quaternary, which includes the past 2 million years.

The Tertiary period. When this period began, mammals were small and walked on all fours. Of the seven groups of mammals in existence, three—creodonts, amblypods, and condylarths—predominated; all are now extinct. The other four—primates, marsupials, insectivores, and rodents—still exist today.

As the period progressed, birds and mammals became more advanced; some early relatives of modern animals—including the eagle, horse, monkey, and whale—appeared and rapidly evolved to adapt to cooler and drier conditions. The horse, for example, was evolving a one-toed foot that was better suited to running along plains than was its original five-toed foot. Its body also was becoming larger, evolving from the tiny 12-inch (30-centimeter)-tall *Hyracotherium* (formerly *Eohippus*) toward its current descendant, several times larger.

The first dogs and cats were vicious predators. The dogs would evolve further into their modern relatives such as wolves and bears; the cats evolved into two separate lines. One of these, the true cats, includes the lions and tigers of today; the other, the saber-toothed cats, became extinct. Primates also evolved significantly during the Tertiary period, taking on more characteristics of modern monkeys and apes, including larger brains, and hands with an opposable thumb.

The Quaternary period. The Quaternary period began about 2.5 million years ago with the Pleistocene Ice Age, which lasted until only about 10,000 years ago. During this time, huge glaciers moved southward, covering as much as one-third of Earth's surface. These movements of ice, called *glaciations*, brought about enormous changes in climate and the environment, which, in turn, forced animal and plant life to adapt. Many species became extinct, but new species—including human beings—emerged that were better able to adapt to the changes.

The mammals alive at the start of the Quaternary period were generally larger than their modern relatives. Mammoths and mastodons, similar to the elephant but much larger, were widespread at the start of the period, but extinct by the end of the Pleistocene Ice Age.

The earliest humans emerged near the start of the Quaternary period. By about 250,000 years ago, *Homo sapiens* had emerged, although they did not become identical to modern humans until less than 40,000 years ago. Modern humans have a large brain and undertake higher functions such as planning hunting, developing weapons, and creating paintings and drawings to record activities and ideas.

Sometimes, traces of an organism's soft tissues are preserved, often as a film of carbon. The shadowlike forms below are carbonized fossils of ancient ginkgo leaves.

PREHISTORIC ANIMALS

by Anthony J. Castagno

Long before human beings walked the Earth, an enormously varied array of animals lived in the seas, on the land, and in the air. There were hundreds of thousands of species, including dinosaurs and woolly mammoths, which became extinct and will never be seen again. A few—such as the horseshoe crabs and the coelacanth—survived in forms virtually identical to those of their ancestors of 500 million years ago. For the most part, though, animals living on Earth today evolved to cope with and thrive in their environments, and are thus vastly changed from their ancestors of hundreds of millions of years ago.

THE FIRST SIGNS OF LIFE

It is thought that Earth came into existence about 4.6 billion years ago; the first signs of life are chemical traces found in sediments that date back 3.8 billion years. These chemicals most likely were produced by very simple one-celled plants, and later by blue-green algae. Over the next 3 billion years or so, these primitive cells evolved nuclei and eventually became multicellular. The first signs of fossils on land are from bacteria or fungi that lived 1.2 billion years ago. The first signs of animal life are from soft-bodied invertebrate animals that lived more than 500 million years ago.

Early Fish

The first known fish—which is also the first known vertebrate—was *Anatolepsis*, which appeared about 500 million years ago during the Cambrian period. This scale-covered, jawless creature was part of class Agnatha, to which the present-day lampreys belong. *Anatolepsis* became extinct at the end of the Devonian period, about 350 million years ago.

The first fish with jaws, the acanthodians, were sharklike creatures that arose in the Silurian period, about 410 million years ago; they became extinct about 250 million years ago. Another group of fish with jaws, the plac-

oderms, arose at the beginning of the Devonian period and became extinct about 50 million years later. The cartilaginous fish, class Chondrichthyes, appeared about 370 million years ago and are believed to have evolved from the placoderms.

The modern bony fishes, class Osteichthyes, are believed to have evolved from the acanthodians, and appeared approximately 395 million years ago. The early Osteichthyes

were freshwater dwellers, with marine species appearing about 160 million years later. A group of Osteichthyes, the ray-finned fish, ultimately came to dominate the seas.

By this time, most modern classes of invertebrates had also evolved, as had many marine and freshwater vertebrates. The seas were crowded with invertebrates and fish, but the land was relatively free of all but the most primitive forms of plant life.

Amphibians Emerge

Over the next 100 million to 150 million years, higher plants became more numerous on land, and several animal species developed the systems necessary to live out of the water. The first land vertebrates are thought to have evolved from a class of bony fish called the Choanichthyes, which had fleshy fins and internal nostrils. One of these, a Crossopterygii, was able to gulp air when it rose above the surface of the water. Once these fish ventured onto land, they encountered no predators, of course, and gradually evolved into the first land-based vertebrates—the amphibians.

Early amphibians looked much like fish, except that their fins had evolved into limbs, allowing them to move about on land. Even today, amphibians live most of their lives on land, but must lay their eggs in water. Eventually evolution eliminated this water-dependent stage in some species, and a true land-based animal, the reptile, emerged. Reptiles became the first animals to produce eggs with a protective shell that could survive out of the water—enabling an embryo to develop on dry land.

Early Insects

The oldest known fossil insect is about 390 million years old, although insects probably emerged many millions of years earlier. The first insects likely evolved from a centipede-like, land-inhabiting arthropod. These creatures were probably wingless, somewhat similar to the silverfish of today. Over the next 100 million years, insects diversified greatly, many developing wings and becoming the first animals to fly.

During the Mesozoic era, about 225 million to 65 million years ago, reptiles and insects thrived on the land, while fish—many similar to the sand dollar and sea urchin of today—flourished in the oceans. Insects diversified enormously, adapting to changing conditions. When flowering plants began emerging near the end of the Mesozoic era, there was a huge surge in evolution among insects, producing tens of thousands of species, many of which still exist today.

THE DINOSAURS

The first reptiles emerged about 300 million years ago, and looked much like the lizards of today. During the Mesozoic era, reptiles expanded rapidly and soon dominated the land, seas, and air—giving rise to the other name of this time period: the Age of Reptiles. Prehistoric reptiles, like the reptiles of today, were vertebrates—cold-blooded lung breathers with dry, scaly skin devoid of feathers or hair. They fertilized internally and produced eggs with hard shells to protect the developing embryo and keep it moist. With only a few exceptions, the reptiles became extinct at the end of the Mesozoic era. Before they did, however, one group of reptiles, the dinosaurs, became the largest land animals that ever lived.

Dinosaurs are thought to have evolved from small, crocodile-like reptiles that had

Controversy continues to revolve around claims that Tyrannosaurus rex, Tarbosaurus (above), and other carnivorous dinosaurs were warm-blooded creatures.

small front limbs and larger rear limbs. Some of these reptiles could stand upright and run on their hind legs, using their tails for balance.

The term "dinosaur" is derived from Greek words meaning "terrible lizard," and was proposed in 1842 by the British scientist Sir Richard Owen. Although the taxonomic classification Dinosauria is no longer used formally by scientists, it remains the popular name for describing any of the large lizards of the Mesozoic era. They varied greatly in size—from as little as 4 pounds (2 kilograms) to well over 70 tons—but most weighed more than 1,100 pounds (500 kilograms). Dinosaurs included carnivores (flesh eaters) and herbivores (plant eaters); some walked on four legs; some stood upright and walked on two. Like the reptiles of today, most had dry, scaly skin, but some also had protective bony plates on their heads or bodies.

Approximately 775 genera of dinosaurs have been identified and classified from fossils; there may be 50,000 genera yet to be identified. All told, there were as many as 500,000 individual species during the Mesozoic era. Unfortunately, the vast majority lived in areas whose geology was not conducive to fossil formation, or were so small and fragile that their fossils would be unlikely to be found.

Most paleontologists believe that dinosaurs, like modern reptiles, reproduced by laying eggs. Fossils of dinosaur eggs—including unhatched eggs and egg fragments—have been discovered in many places around the world. Studies of the nests and nearby areas indicate that at least some of the smaller dinosaurs protected and cared for their young in the nests, and that even as they grew larger, the babies tended to remain nearby. Some scientists believe that at least a few dinosaur species may have given birth to living young.

In recent years, controversy has arisen over whether dinosaurs, or at least some dinosaurs, may have been warm-blooded, and thus not true reptiles. Cold-blooded animals cannot regulate their body temperature, and therefore they take on the temperature of their environment. Warm-blooded animals, on the other hand, have internal mechanisms for regulating their body temperature. If some dinosaurs were warm-blooded, they would have had higher rates of metabolism, enabling them to move quickly without waiting for their bodies to warm up, but they also would have required more food for energy. Some of the evidence cited to support the theory of warm-bloodedness includes the upright posture of some dinosaurs; their mammal-like bone structures; and the fact that relatively few dinosaurs were predators, suggesting high food intake.

The first dinosaur fossils probably were discovered in the United States at the end of the 18th century. The first recorded dinosaur fossils, however, are teeth and bones found in 1822 by British physician Gideon Mantell. He called them *Iguanodon* "iguana tooth." Around the same time, Professor William Buckland of Oxford University in Great Britain discovered similar fossils in southern England and named them *Megalosaurus*—"great lizard." Since then, dinosaur bones have been found in almost every country of the world.

Dinosaurs appear to have evolved along two separate lines, with the most-distinct differences being noted in the arrangement of the hipbones. The two lines are formally recognized by these creatures being classified in the orders Saurischia and Ornithischia, within the reptilian subclass Archosauria. In saurischians, meaning "lizard hip," the three bones of the pelvis were arranged in a triangular pattern like that of mod-

Fossils found in South America suggest that the herbivorous Argentinosaurus *(above) may have weighed 100 tons, making it one of the largest creatures ever.*

From fossil remains, scientists have determined that the carnivorous Gigantosaurus carolinii *(above) was 42 feet long, weighed 9 tons, and had 10-inch-long teeth.*

ern lizards. In ornithischians, meaning "bird hip," the bones of the pelvis were usually in a rectangular or tetrahedral pattern, much like the modern bird hip.

Saurischians

The saurischians are divided into two distinct subgroups—the meat-eating, upright theropods, and the predominantly plant-eating sauropods, which walked on all fours.

The theropods. The theropods ("beast feet") had a large (sometimes disproportionately large) head with strong jaws and huge, sharp teeth. Their small front legs were equipped with sharp, curved claws for grasping prey. They walked on large, strong rear legs, typically leaning forward, their long tails providing a stabilizing counterbalance. The hind legs had large feet with three or more toes. These creatures could not walk on four legs.

The smallest theropod was *Compsognathus*, which appeared during the Triassic period at the beginning of the Mesozoic era. The largest theropods developed during the Creta-

ceous period at the end of the Mesozoic era, and included *Tyrannosaurus rex*, which appeared in North America and grew to a height of 20 feet (6 meters) and a length of 50 feet (15 meters).

Another large theropod was the *Gorgosaurus*, which grew to 40 feet (12 meters) in length. This enormous creature had a huge head and jaw and powerful rear legs.

In the mid-1990s, fossils of yet another massive carnivorous dinosaur were discovered in Argentina. Named *Gigantosaurus carolinii*, this beast was nearly 42 feet (12.8 meters) long and weighed about 9 tons. A similar theropod, *Allosaurus*, developed in North America during the Jurassic period, midway through the Mesozoic era. It grew to a length of nearly 33 feet (10 meters). In Africa, paleontologists led by Paul Sereno of the University of Chicago recently discovered remains of a 30-foot (9-meter)-long theropod that also closely resembled the *Allosaurus*. They named it *Afrovenator*, or "African hunter." The presence of three similar dinosaurs—*Gigantosaurus*, *Allosaurus*, and *Afrovenator*—clearly related to a single ancestor, discovered on three separate continents—South America, North America, and Africa—is cited by geologists as evidence that these landmasses were once joined together.

Other theropods include *Struthiomimus*—nicknamed "ostrich" dinosaur for the way in which its toothless jaws are set in a birdlike beak, and *Velociraptor*, a fast-moving predator made famous by the movie *Jurassic Park*.

The sauropods. The sauropods ("lizard feet") had four legs of approximately equal size. These creatures walked on all fours and, al-

though generally considered to have been herbivorous, some may have eaten meat as well.

The sauropods were some of the largest animals that ever lived; indeed, even the smallest sauropods grew to be larger than modern-day elephants. The first sauropod was probably a large dinosaur called *Plateosaurus*. Other sauropods included *Apatosaurus* (formerly known as *Brontosaurus*), which may have weighed as much as 40 tons, and its relative, *Diplodocus*, which weighed about 15 tons but grew to a length of 85 feet (26 meters). Both of these creatures had the typical sauropod body structure: a slender head at the end of a long neck; a stout, elephant-like body supported by sturdy legs; and a long, tapering tail. Because these animals were so huge and had such long necks, scientists once thought they must have lived completely or at least partially in an aquatic environment, depending on the water for buoyancy and using their long necks to keep their heads above the surface for breathing and eating. Recent studies have shown that their legs could have supported their great bulk, and their long necks helped them reach tall plant life. Still, they must have been slow beasts that made relatively easy prey for the theropods.

Other sauropods include *Brachiosaurus*, an East African dinosaur that stood 60 feet (18 meters) tall and weighed 70 tons or more, and *Argentinosaurus*, which, at about 100 tons, was until 1996 considered the largest animal ever to have lived. That year, however, fossils from an even larger dinosaur—aptly named *Supersaurus*—were found. Originally thought to be the remains of two dinosaurs (the other dubbed *Ultrasaurus*), the fossils indicate that *Supersaurus* was at least 134 feet (40 meters) long and weighed well over 100 tons.

Triceratops *(above) lived toward the end of the dinosaur era. These horned creatures traveled in packs and, when threatened, formed circles around the young.*

Ornithischia

The second major group of dinosaurs, the Ornithischians, includes the bipedal herbivorous dinosaurs; the plated dinosaurs; the armored dinosaurs; and the horned dinosaurs.

The ornithopods. The ornithopods ("bird feet") had so many similarities to modern birds that, for years, scientists thought that the two groups were related. This diverse group became the most widespread herbivores, thanks in part to the strong, compact, highly specialized teeth set far back in their mouths. Ornithopods had strong hind legs with a three-toed foot. Although they usually walked upright, they were able to stand on all fours.

The *Iguanodon* (noted earlier as the first dinosaur fossil recorded) was an ornithopod. Interestingly, its hand had four fingers and a primitive thumb. Although an *Iguanodon* has never been found in the United States, a close relative, the duck-billed *Hadrosaurus*, has been. It was about the same size as the *Iguanodon*, about 30 feet (9 meters) long, standing about 14 feet (4 meters) tall, and weighing about 4 tons. It is called "duck-billed" because—as might be expected—its head ends in what looks like the bill of a duck. Its teeth are highly compacted, and its hand has four fingers but no thumb. Some hadrosaurs, such as *Corythosaurus*, had a bony crest on the head that may have served as protection or as part of its sensory system.

The stegosaurs. The small-headed and small-toothed "plated dinosaurs" moved very slowly on all fours. The best known of these

If, as some claim, Supersaurus *(left) had indeed exceeded a length of 134 feet, the dinosaur would have been more than five times as long as an elephant.*

creatures—*Stegosaurus*—had one or two rows of upright bony plates along its back; it grew to a length of 30 feet (9 meters). Originally, the bony plates were thought to have a protective function only; recent analysis, however, has shown that they actually had many spaces through which blood could have flowed. If this is so, the plates could have played a role in a cooling system for the creature's blood, which would add further support to the theory that some dinosaurs were warm-blooded.

The ankylosaurs. These "armored dinosaurs," with bodies covered with bony plates and spikes, were broad, low-to-the-ground creatures with short, stocky legs. One notable example, *Scolosaurus*, had an armored skull and a body covered with plates separated by strips of

Fossil specimens of Archaeopteryx *(above)—the earliest known feathered creature—suggest that it may have been the evolutionary link between reptiles and birds.*

skin from which the armor derived some flexibility. Other genera of armored dinosaurs included *Nodosaurus*, *Edmontonia*, *Dyoplosaurus*, *Palaeoscincus*, and *Ankylosaurus*.

The ceratopians. These "horned dinosaurs" were the last of the major dinosaurs to appear and the most successful of the armored dinosaurs. The earliest known ceratopian, *Protoceratops*, lived in the region of Asia that is now Mongolia; it was small and short, only about 6 feet (2 meters) long, with an unarmored body and small horns. So far, *Protoceratops* is the only ceratopian discovered outside of North America. The best known ceratopian is *Triceratops*, which had a horn on its nose and another

large horn projecting out from above each eye. It grew to be about 30 feet (9 meters) long. *Triceratops* and its relative, *Torosaurus*, were among the last dinosaurs to become extinct, some 65 million years ago.

PREHISTORIC FLIERS

There is much scientific discussion about the nature of the prehistoric animals that flew through ancient skies. Some believe they were dinosaurs or closely related to dinosaurs; others look to an entirely different origin. Some notable differences distinguish the flying reptiles that became extinct from the birds of that time that survived through to modern days, but there also are similarities. To this day, the paleontological community is divided about the origin of modern birds, and no clear evolutionary line has yet been established.

The flying reptiles were called pterosaurs. They had a large breastbone and long wings made of a thin membrane of skin, indicating that they were indeed capable of flight. They also had long, thin bodies with skeletons made of thin, hollow bones—another adaptation for flight, but one that made them poor specimens for fossilization. There are about 121 known species of pterosaurs, many of which are believed to have lived on or near the water, although it appears they were capable of walking on land as well. Some had a hairlike covering, perhaps for insulation and warmth, supporting the theory of warm-bloodedness. Warm-bloodedness also is indicated by their lifestyle: flying requires a great deal of energy.

The first pterosaur fossils were found in 1784 by Italian scientist Cosimo Collini, who thought they belonged to an amphibian. Throughout the 1800s, other pterosaur fossils were misidentified as those of prehistoric bats or other types of flying animals. The largest of these, the pterodactyls, reached a wingspan of 50 feet (15.5 meters). *Tupuxuara*, the remains of which have been found in Brazil, had a wingspan of about 18 feet (5.5 meters).

The earliest known bird, *Archaeopteryx*, was a crow-sized creature that weighed about 1 pound (0.5 kilogram) and had feathers. Nevertheless, many scientists still consider it to have been a dinosaur. It had a furcula (wishbone), like a modern bird, but also had a tail and

What Happened to the Dinosaurs?

There are a number of theories about why the dinosaurs, a large group of animals that had thrived for more than 140 million years, suddenly died out over a relatively short period of time. These theories range from an asteroid impacting Earth, to changes in climate and geography, to increases in cosmic radiation.

The asteroid theory was proposed in 1980 by American physicist Luis Alvarez and his son, Walter. They suggested that an asteroid had struck Earth at the end of the Cretaceous period of the Mesozoic era. They based this theory on higher-than-normal amounts of the element iridium in sedimentary layers from that period, claiming that the iridium came from space. The impact threw up an enormous cloud of dust that blanketed Earth and killed much of the planet's plant life, which, in turn, interrupted the food chain. A crater has been found in Mexico that supports this theory. Skeptics, however, say that the iridium could have come from volcanic eruptions over a longer period of time, and that widespread dust from these eruptions caused the climate changes.

Another theory suggests that as landmasses began moving apart as part of continental drift, this process would have changed the geography and other environmental conditions to which the dinosaurs had become accustomed.

Other theories suggest that a supernova may have blanketed Earth with radiation that killed off the dinosaurs, or that there may have been an as-yet-unexplained gravitational disturbance that caused comets and asteroids to crash into Earth.

In any event, when the dinosaurs died out, it gave other animals—particularly terrestrial mammals and, ultimately, humans—an opportunity to flourish.

---

clawed fingers like a reptile. *Archaeopteryx* also had a long, thin finger on each hand that appears to have framed or supported a wing.

Fossils of a birdlike animal, *Protoavis*, discovered in 1986, are believed to be 225 million years old, 75 million years older than *Archaeopteryx*. *Protoavis* appears to have had reptilian characteristics, but, like *Archaeopteryx*, it had well-developed wings. It also had a keel, allowing it to fly; *Archaeopteryx* lacked this structure, meaning it could glide but probably not fly. Other fossilized bird remains date to the end of the Mesozoic era, and include the *Hesperornis regalis*, a flightless diving bird that was about 6 feet (1.8 meters) long.

The number of species of pterosaurs began decreasing about 88 million years ago; by 65 million years ago, they, like the dinosaurs, were extinct. Birds, however, thrived. By the end of the Mesozoic era, more than 35 species of birds had evolved, becoming strong fliers and adapting to many different environments. Some scientists think that birds replaced pterosaurs as part of the process of natural selection: when birds competed with pterosaurs for the same niche, the birds won.

PREHISTORIC MAMMALS

The earliest mammals emerged during the Triassic period of the Mesozoic era, more than 190 million years ago, evolving from mammal-like reptiles that lived about 100 million years earlier. Like mammals of today, these creatures were warm-blooded; gave birth to live young that were nourished by milk; had hair; had lower jaws made of a single bone on each side; and had three bones in the middle ear.

Most early mammals were small and nocturnal. Compared to the enormous dinosaurs, they were relatively inconspicuous, but they survived and evolved to exploit a wide variety of niches; when dinosaurs became extinct, mammals were ready to step in and fill the void.

Mammals evolved into several forms to optimize their presence in virtually all environments: marine mammals such as whales, dolphins, and seals; subterranean digging mammals such as the mole and groundhog; flying and gliding mammals such as bats and some squirrels; and running mammals such as the horse and dog. Mammals were very adaptable, quickly evolving structures that enabled them to better cope with their environments. For example, the limbs of land mammals evolved into the flippers of marine mammals or the wings of a bat.

There were four orders of mammals during the Jurassic period, three of which (Pantotheria, Symmetrodonta, and Triconodonta) survived into the Cretaceous period, and one of which (Multituberculata) continued into the Cenozoic.

Primitive pantothere mammals were the direct ancestors of the marsupials (oppossums, kangaroos, etc.) and the placentals (cats, horses, humans, etc.). Modern egg-laying mammals—monotremes, such as the duck-billed platypus—are descended from an unknown line that also dates back to this time.

The era in which we are living now, the Cenozoic era, which began about 65 million years ago, has been called the Age of Mammals. Climates and environments have changed greatly over the past 65 million years, and mammals have adapted to accommodate these changes.

At the beginning of the Cenozoic era, much of Earth was warm and moist. In North America, where forests dominated, early primates such as the lemurs, a predecessor of humans, developed. Large, rhinoceros-like animals called *Titanotheres*, which stood about 8 feet (2.4 meters) high at the shoulder and had a pair of horns jutting out from their skull, shared the forests with primitive horses, dogs, and cats. Unlike the domesticated pets of today, however, these animals were vicious predators, armed with razor-sharp teeth, strong jaws, and great speed. Bats and rodents, nearly identical to their modern relatives, were widespread.

About 35 million years ago, as the climate began cooling and drying slightly, some areas became savannas, plains, and deserts, and new plant life began to evolve. These plants, including many new grasses, led to further evolution among the mammals. For example, the foot of the horse evolved from three-toed to essentially one-toed, enabling the creature to run faster and farther to escape predators or to find food. The first Bovidae, early ancestors of sheep and bison, appeared in Europe and later in North America. In Africa, some primates moved from the trees to live on the ground, giving rise to the animals that would evolve into humans.

A pivotal event in the history of mammals—the Pleistocene Ice Age—occurred from about 2.5 million to about 10,000 years ago. It was once thought that there were four or five major moves, or advances, of glaciers during this time. Recent studies, however, have shown that there actually were many advances of glaciers in which huge sheets of ice, often hundreds of feet thick, moved down from the polar region and covered much of North America and Europe. During at least one of these, ice reached as far south as Mexico and covered about one-third of Earth's surface. When the ice moved southward, plants and animals that had evolved in the relatively temperate climates were displaced by Arctic species. Some mammals and other animals that were relatively mobile moved southward in advance of the ice. When the glaciers receded, giving way to a warmer period known as an "interglacial," many of the animals returned to northerly regions and reestablished themselves.

Glaciation also affected the level of the oceans. As Earth's water froze under the huge glaciers, the oceans receded and continental shelves and other land that had been underwater appeared. In some cases, this created a bridge from one continent to another, such as the one that connected North America and Asia across the Bering Sea. The changing climate and sudden appearance of new land where oceans had been undoubtedly affected the evolution of mammals, including humans.

Many of the mammals alive at that time were much larger than their modern descendants. Enormous elephants were widespread in North America, and huge rhinoceroses roamed

Soon after the bones of birdlike Mononychus *(above) were discovered in Mongolia, scientists began debating whether or not the animal was an avian ancestor.*

Mammoth
Mammuthus

Woolly rhinoceros
Coelodonta antiquitatus

Brontotherium

Eohippus
Hyracotherium

Tritomnodon

Triconodon

Saber-toothed cat
Smilodon

Prehistoric mammals ranged from the tiny and primitive Triconodon *that lived more than 135 million years ago to the mammoth, woolly rhinoceros, and saber-toothed cat, all of which became extinct before historical times.*

much of what is now the European continent. In Southern California, remains of an exotic array of Pleistocene mammals have been preserved in the La Brea tar pits.

The mammoths, and in particular the woolly mammoths, were common throughout Europe, Asia, and North America during the Pleistocene Ice Age, at least in part because of their ability to handle the cold. They are ancestors of the elephant, but with a high-crowned head and ridged teeth. They had thick skin and a reddish woolly coat mixed with coarse black hair. The largest mammoth, the imperial mammoth (*Mammuthus imperator*), was about 15 feet (4.6 meters) high at the shoulders.

Several well-preserved mammoth specimens have been found in the permafrost of Alaska and Siberia. The first of these was found around the year 1400, and at least 5 of the 40 found since then have been in nearly perfect condition; indeed, their meat was still fresh! The two most-famous woolly mammoths, discovered in Russia, are estimated to be 33,000 and 39,000 years old, respectively; they are now displayed at museums in St. Petersburg.

Another group of now-extinct prehistoric mammals is the ground sloths, animals related to today's tree sloths. They appeared in South America approximately 26 million years ago and gradually spread into North America. Some of these creatures were as small as squirrels; others, such as the giant ground sloth, *Megatherium*, were larger than modern-day elephants. Some relatives of the ground sloth, such as the *Glyptodon*, had armor somewhat akin to that of the modern armadillo.

During the final 100,000 years of the Pleistocene Ice Age, many of the large mammals became extinct: North America lost 73 percent of its large mammals, South America 80 percent, Australia 94 percent, and Europe 30 percent. It is uncertain whether these extinctions occurred because these large animals were unable to adapt to the changing climates or whether they were killed by the ancestors of modern humans. At this point, the study of prehistoric animals becomes the study of early hominids, discussed in the articles "The Human Species" and "Human Evolution" in Volume 5 of THE NEW BOOK OF POPULAR SCIENCE.

SCIENCE FICTION

Science fiction—a literary genre, or category, sometimes paired with fantasy under the broader field of speculative fiction—originated during the rise of scientific inquiry and Romantic literature in the late 18th and 19th centuries. Sci-fi came of age as a genre in the first four decades of the 20th century, and by mid- to late century, it had become hugely popular—especially as cinematic entertainment. From the beginning, science fiction has dealt with the effects of imagined science on society, the potential impacts of actual science, and speculations about worlds other than our own. A refusal to be limited by the laws of cosmology (the doctrines that describe the natural order of the universe) has infused the genre with energy and has contributed to its longevity and popular appeal.

Authors of science fiction have written about such subjects as space travel, time travel, lost and newly discovered worlds, extraterrestrial cultures, artificial life and intelligence, post-apocalyptic societies, parallel and alternative universes, and lost ages of history.

IN THE BEGINNING

Arguably, the first significant science-fiction novel is Mary Shelley's *Frankenstein* (1818), the story of an obsessed scientist who dares to believe he can create life and is ultimately destroyed by his creation. Some of the works of Edgar Allan Poe, especially *The Narrative of Arthur Gordon Pym of Nantucket* (1838) and the short story "The Unparalleled Adventure of One Hans Pfaall" (1835), are other early examples of the genre, written long before the term "science fiction" was coined.

Many scholars consider French novelist Jules Verne to be the father of modern science fiction, citing as examples his classic novels *A Journey to the Center of the Earth* (1864) and *20,000 Leagues Under the Sea* (1870). Soon after came Robert Louis Stevenson's *The Strange Case of Dr. Jekyll and Mr. Hyde* (1886) and the immensely influential novels and stories of the British writer H.G. Wells. Wells's *The Time Machine* (1895), *The Invisible Man*

In less than 200 years, science fiction has evolved from a little-known category of novel-writing to a highly creative literary genre and the focus of state-of-the-art filmmaking (left).

(1897), and *The War of the Worlds* (1898) inspired hundreds of authors to experiment with the possibilities of the genre. Among them was Edgar Rice Burroughs, who, though best remembered for his Tarzan stories, wrote more than a dozen books about space exploration and alien life-forms on Mars and Venus.

Science fiction as a distinct genre took a bold step forward in 1826, when writer and editor Hugo Gernsback founded *Amazing Stories*, the first magazine devoted entirely to speculative fiction based on ideas from the realm of science. Gernsback referred to the stories he published as "scientifiction," but the more graceful term "science fiction" appeared often in his magazine and soon gained widespread usage. Today, Hugo Gernsback's legacy is acknowledged through the annual Hugo Award, the principal literary honor bestowed on writers of science fiction.

Gernsback's magazine generated many imitators, including *Weird Tales*, *Astounding Stories*, *The Magazine of Fantasy & Science Fiction*, and *Galaxy*. These so-called pulp magazines of the 1930s and 1940s—often called the Golden Age of science fiction—were especially popular with young readers. Some of the avid fans of the sci-fi pulps grew up to become the great science-fiction writers of the next generation.

A BRAVE NEW WORLD

Social upheavals across the globe beginning in the 1930s engendered science fiction of a more serious kind. The stories published in pulp magazines typically centered around space and time travel, with stock characters encountering fantastic creatures from other worlds. By the mid-20th century, science fiction was mov-

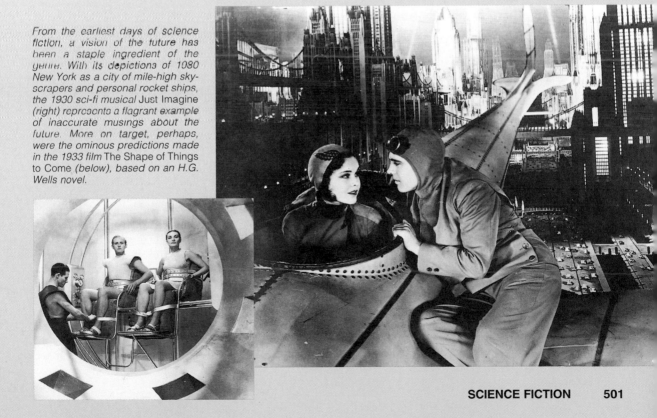

From the earliest days of science fiction, a vision of the future has been a staple ingredient of the genre. With its depictions of 1980 New York as a city of mile-high skyscrapers and personal rocket ships, the 1930 sci-fi musical Just Imagine (right) represents a flagrant example of inaccurate musings about the future. More on target, perhaps, were the ominous predictions made in the 1933 film The Shape of Things to Come (below), based on an H.G. Wells novel.

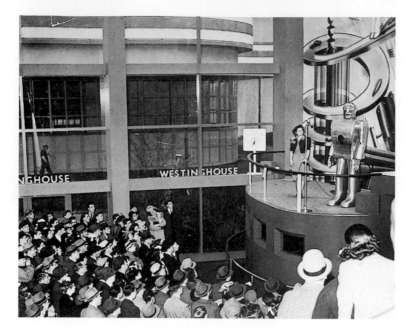

The 1939 World's Fair in New York played an important role in bringing the forward-looking concepts of science fiction to the general public. Its exhibits of robots, television, and other technological innovations had, up until then, been almost exclusively the province of sci-fi writers and their readers.

ing away from the traditional subjects of those older "space operas" to more-sophisticated explorations into ways that the future might affect society on our own planet. Speculations about the possibilities of utopian (ideal) societies and their dystopian opposites date back as early as Plato's *Republic* in the 4th century B.C., but acquired new urgency in the 20th century. Novels such as Aldous Huxley's *Brave New World* (1932) and George Orwell's *1984* (1949) examined challenges that had been facing society since the Industrial Revolution, challenges that became even more urgent with the Great Depression, World War II, the Cold War with the Soviet Union, the dominance of technology, and threats of nuclear and environmental destruction. This marked a significant turning point in popular speculative fiction. Increasingly, the genre would examine threats to society and offer templates for change.

Many authors who grew up reading the pulp magazines in the 1930s and 1940s would become associated with a "New Wave" of more-sophisticated science fiction in the 1950s and 1960s. Among the notable works of the period are Ray Bradbury's *The Martian Chronicles* (1950) and *Fahrenheit 451* (1953); Isaac Asimov's *The Foundation Trilogy* (1951–53) and *I, Robot* (1950); Walter Miller, Jr.'s *A Canticle for Leibowitz* (1959); Robert Heinlein's *Stranger in a Strange Land* (1961), *The Puppet Masters* (1951), and *Starship Troopers* (1959); Arthur C. Clarke's *2001: A Space Odyssey* (1968); Frank

Herbert's *Dune* series (1965–85); and Ursula Le Guin's *The Left Hand of Darkness* (1969) and *The Dispossessed* (1974). In addition to the authors above, any list of influential science-fiction writers of the past 40 or 50 years would have to include Anne McCaffrey, Harlan Ellison, Philip K. Dick, Stanislaw Lem, and H.P. Lovecraft. A number of literary novelists who rose to prominence in the 1960s and 1970s preferred not to be labeled as science-fiction writers, though their works contain many elements associated with the genre. The best known of them is Kurt Vonnegut, Jr., whose *Slaughterhouse-Five* (1969), *The Sirens of Titan* (1959), *Cat's Cradle* (1963), and other novels and stories contain imaginative, witty, and brilliantly evoked visions of time travel and extraterrestrial cultures.

As the literary form became more sophisticated, two distinct types of science fiction became apparent. Stories and novels based on actual science, sometimes referred to as "hard" science fiction, explored technological developments within the limits of what was theoretically possible. Often these explorations placed more emphasis on ideas or arguments than on character development, prose style, and other literary qualities. The amazingly prolific Isaac Asimov is often cited as a model of this type of author. In his fiction, he has speculated on a broad range of "possible tomorrows," featuring robots, supercomputers, nuclear energy, and other technological advancements that already (or are someday likely to) exist. Significantly, Asimov was trained as a scientist, earning a doctorate degree in biochemistry and teaching for several years in a medical school. Many of his more than 425 books are serious nonfiction studies of various scientific subjects.

Whereas the emphasis of hard science fiction is on real science, "soft" science fiction re-

Outer space (top) is a favorite science-fiction venue. The seemingly sophisticated computer technology envisioned in Stanley Kubrick's 1968 film 2001: A Space Odyssey (above) had been far surpassed by definitive technological advancements by the time the turn of the millennium actually rolled around.

laxes the rules considerably. Here, the author's ideas may originate from any number of other sources, including anthropology, sociology, mythology, history, theology, philosophy, psychology, and politics. More emphasis is typically placed on character, setting, emotions, and human behavior than on technological realism. Ray Bradbury helped define this category of science fiction, with stories that begin with typical themes, such as rocket travel and life on other planets, but emphasize the thoughts and feelings that such themes evoke in human beings. Much of the New Wave science fiction of the 1970s, with its focus on existential dilemmas, human emotion, and character motivation, can be classified as "soft."

A more recent development in the genre is the "cyberpunk" novels of the 1980s and 1990s, with their emphasis on computer networks, hacking, and individuals in conflict with all-powerful corporations. Notable examples include William Gibson's *Neuromancer* (1984), Bruce Sterling's *Islands in the Net* (1988) and

Heavy Weather (1994), Richard Powers's *Galatea 2.2* (1995), and Neal Stephenson's *Snow Crash* (1992). Other acclaimed contemporary authors who are stretching the boundaries of science fiction include Orson Scott Card, Greg Bear, Kim Stanley Robinson, Robert J. Sawyer, and Octavia Butler.

APOCALYPSE POW!

Science fiction has always translated well into radio, film, and television. Radio "serials" were as popular in the 1930s and 1940s as the pulp magazines upon which many of their stories were originally based. As television gained widespread acceptance in the 1950s, producers were quick to recognize the possibilities for science-fiction series.

From early silent films, such as *A Trip to the Moon* (1902) and *Metropolis* (1927), to the final installments of the *Star Wars* saga, Hollywood has been eager to bring science fic-

tion to the big screen. Films such as *King Kong* (1933) and *The War of the Worlds* (1953) were notable for their imaginative departure from conventional methods of filmmaking, especially in their innovative use of special effects.

The low-budget "B" movies of the 1950s and 1960s often capitalized on the "Red Scare." Communism and the terrors of nuclear war became fodder for many inexpensive films featuring alien invasions, postnuclear scenarios, and pseudoscientific portrayals of monsters mutated from nuclear fallout. Japan offered an influential contribution in the form of giant-monster movies, most notably *Godzilla, King of the Monsters!* (1956), which was followed by countless mutations.

The escalation of the "space race" following the Soviet launching of the Sputnik satellite in 1957 fueled decades of intense public interest in science-fiction television programs, books, and films. The television series *Star Trek*, which premiered in 1966 and ran for three seasons, produced the fan phenomenon of "Trekkies" (satirized in the 1999 film *Galaxy Quest*), and is notable for its enduring mainstream

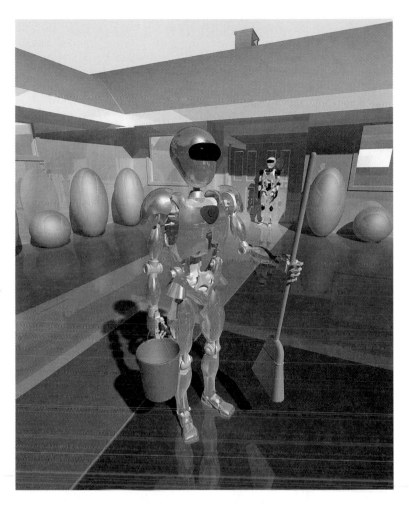

Robots have gone from being little more than a science-fiction fantasy to playing an essential role in industry. Nevertheless, even the most astute sci-fi visionary declines to predict on the record when robots will begin to engage in mundane household tasks.

popularity. Films such as *Planet of the Apes* (1968) examined evolution and racial equality, while *Soylent Green* (1973) addressed the crisis of overpopulation (and offered a practical, though distasteful, solution).

SOMETHING SPECIAL

In 1968, the release of *2001: A Space Odyssey* marked the beginning of a new era in Hollywood science fiction. This landmark film, directed by Stanley Kubrick and based on the Arthur C. Clarke novel, broke new cinematic ground with its high production values. Never before had so much care been given to a science-fiction movie's sets, costumes, or music. It was especially revolutionary in its use of special effects. Ironically, this highly speculative film was made with a greater emphasis on "realism" than were most realistic films of the era.

In 1977, Hollywood history was made yet again with the release of George Lucas's *Star Wars*, the first of a series of linked sequels and prequels that would influence popular culture to a degree never seen before. The box-office smash would have a profound effect on film-making for generations to come. Within a few years, various visions of contact with extraterrestrial cultures produced such blockbusters as *Close Encounters of the Third Kind* (1977), *Superman* (1978), *Alien* (1979), and *E.T.—The Extraterrestrial* (1982).

Director Ridley Scott's *Blade Runner* (1982), long a cult favorite, gradually became recognized as another groundbreaking film, this time one that exhibited a cyberpunk influence.

Based on the novel *Do Androids Dream of Electric Sheep?* (1968) by Philip K. Dick (whose works would continue to be made into films long after his death), *Blade Runner* was set in a bleak, futuristic Los Angeles. Although it featured innovative special effects, the movie was at heart an existential inquiry into what it means to be human. The yearning for life manifested by the film's "replicants" (cyborgs) raised dark and deeply philosophical questions about morality and the human condition.

Director James Cameron's *The Terminator* (1984) was a time-travel thriller that explored a darker side to this science-fiction concept: android assassins traveling back in time to eliminate the ancestors of future enemies. Like dozens of early sci-fi novels and stories, it addressed the possibility that robots and other technological advances might someday turn against their human inventors.

The 1980s brought additional innovations in contemporary science-fiction films. Just as movies such as *Star Wars, The Return of the Jedi* (1983), and *E.T.* were pioneering sophisticated new possibilities for puppetry and animatronics, other films, such as 1982's *Tron*, were exploring the uses of computer-generated imagery (CGI). Fairly innocuous early CGI characters—such as the stained-glass knight in 1985's *Young Sherlock Holmes*—quickly led to a menagerie of monsters more convincing and terrifying than any previously seen, from the wrathful superman of *The Lawnmower Man* (1992), to the ruthless assassin-clones of *The Matrix* (1999) and its sequels.

TODAY AND TOMORROW

Science fiction is as deeply integrated into 21st-century popular culture as the Hollywood Western was half a century ago. New books and films continue to address social issues and current events, from global warming (2004's *The Day After Tomorrow*), to bigotry and intolerance (the *X-Men* movies), to biotechnology and genetic engineering (the *Jurassic Park* films). Today's sophisticated audiences demand a level of veracity, or at least feasibility, that earlier writers and filmmakers did not need to address. The original *Star Trek* television series could take for granted its audience's willing suspension of disbelief. The franchise's more-recent incarnations—such as *Star Trek: The Next Generation*, *Deep Space Nine*, or *Enterprise*—would require full-time scientists to be employed as script-checkers to verify the plausibility of their plot lines.

Not surprisingly, science fiction is a staple of the enormously popular video-game world. Such games as *Half-Life*, *Halo*, *Resident Evil*, *StarCraft*, *Space Quest*, and dozens of others—including many based upon *Star Wars*, *Blade Runner*, and other science-fiction films—rely on futuristic or otherworldly settings to bring their story lines alive with a simple touch of the control pad. It surprised many observers (though not the millions of enthusiasts who play the games), when, in the early 21st century, the video-game industry surpassed the film industry in terms of total revenue generated.

The influence of science fiction on the real world has sometimes taken surprising turns. Many prominent scientists credit the genre for influencing the course of their own careers. The Hungarian-born American nuclear physicist Leo Szilard, who helped develop the first nuclear reactor and made significant contributions to the development of the first atomic bomb, has written that an H.G. Wells novel about atomic energy, titled *The World Set Free* (1914), inspired his insights into how nuclear fission might release enormous amounts of surplus energy. When German scientist Wernher von Braun was pioneering the use of rocketry during World War II, he maintained a subscription to what he described as his favorite magazine, *Astounding Science Fiction*. Stephen Hawking, the brilliant Cambridge physicist, admits that during his first few years as a college student, he spent more time reading science fiction than studying his science textbooks.

Many ideas first presented as science fiction have later emerged as scientific reality. Jules Verne's novels were remarkably prescient, anticipating a great number of the 20th century's achievements in science and technology. Rockets, robots, radar, television, artificial intelligence, personal computers, cellular telephones, the Internet, and countless other commonplace facets of contemporary life were all first conceived in the pages of science fiction.

Sometimes reality, rather than imitating art, bows to it, as when thousands of people listening to Orson Welles's 1938 radio broadcast of *The War of the Worlds* went running into the streets in panic, believing that the United States was under attack by alien invaders from Mars. Apollo astronauts christened one of the craters of the Moon "Dandelion Crater," in honor of the novel *Dandelion Wine* (1957) by Ray Bradbury. In a similar gesture, the U.S. National Aeronautics and Space Administration (NASA) named the first space shuttle *Enterprise*, in tribute to the starship featured on the beloved TV series *Star Trek*.

As for the future, the only limits are what can be imagined. As times continue to change, they will undoubtedly inspire new and provocative speculations that explore the shadow region between reality and possibility. In the world of science fiction, after all, there is little difference between the two.

FORENSIC SCIENCE

Forensic science—the use of scientific tools and methods for the purposes of the law—has long captured the public imagination. The popular character Sherlock Holmes, for example, uses his acute powers of observation to reach penetrating insights that in turn allow him to solve London's most baffling mysteries. Clarice Starling, the Federal Bureau of Investigation (FBI) agent in the film *The Silence of the Lambs*, seeks a psychological profile of a serial killer based

largely on the physical evidence he has left behind. And on the hit television show *CSI*, crime scene investigators use neat gadgetry and ingenious procedures to track down criminals—and manage to look quite stylish while doing so.

In the real world, forensic science may not be quite as glamorous or dramatic—although more than a few famous cases have hinged on forensic testimony—but it is extremely important and no less interesting. The intellectual curiosity, careful method, creative application of technology, and devotion to the truth that characterize fictional forensic scientists are also the hallmarks of the actual scientists, technicians, and law-enforcement agents who concern themselves with the physical evidence of a crime.

Forensic science applies scientific tools and methods to the law. Most forensic investigations begin with the gathering of evidence at a crime scene—a process best carried out with scientific precision.

WHAT IS FORENSICS?

Forensic science, or forensics, encompasses a range of specialties, each applying the techniques and procedures of some branch of the sciences for legal ends. There are dedicated forensics agents in the various law-enforcement communities, but because of the scope of sciences involved, much forensic science takes place in private or university laboratories.

Some types of physical evidence are commonly associated with crime scenes: fingerprints, dental records, blood, bodies, and bullets, to name a few. Just analyzing these types of evidence can require the expertise of fingerprint analysts, forensic odontologists, serologists, forensic pathologists, and ballistics experts. But there is a field of forensics for analysis of bones and other remains (forensic anthropology), buildings and vehicles (forensic engineering), chemicals (forensic toxicology), genetic evidence (DNA analysis), insects (forensic entomology), computer-related crime (computer forensics), financial records (forensic accounting), and more. The branch of forensics concerned with gathering and analyzing evidence from a crime scene is known as *criminalistics*.

New technologies and specializations have continually added to the wide range of forensic expertise available. But this level of expertise is also a fairly recent phenomenon in the history of law and law enforcement. In fact, the idea that scientific procedure has as much to offer the law as eyewitness testimony or the use of informants has been a fairly late development.

Forensic science is a growing field with a range of possibilities for employment. Almost any job in forensics requires at least a bachelor's degree in science, especially chemistry or biology; several universities offer a master's degree in forensic science. No less important is that a prospective forensic scientist be methodical, patient, and detail oriented.

Many forensic scientists work in some law-enforcement capacity, for police departments, or for any number of other government agencies. But law enforcement is hardly the only option. There are many jobs in forensics at private laboratories, consulting firms, legal-defense firms, medical examiners' offices, hospitals, or in university research labs.

The wide variety of agencies and labs all have varying requirements for their agents, assistants, and technicians. But many foren-

Although part of the education of an aspiring forensic scientist is certain to include the occasional field trip to a crime scene (above), most of the student's time will be spent in classrooms and laboratories.

sic scientists tend to be highly specialized, and carry advanced degrees in their particular field. And because the field is constantly changing, with new techniques and technologies, most forensic scientists update their credentials with continuing education throughout their careers.

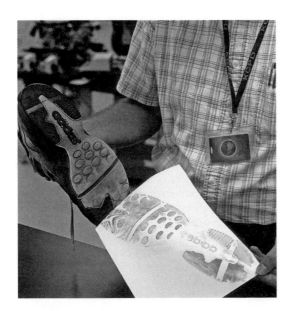

Impressions of footsteps (left) and tire tracks must be obtained immediately after their discovery to avoid contamination by onlookers and others who might inadvertently walk through the evidence field.

Forensics does have a history, however. One of the oldest examples on record appears in a 13th-century Chinese text, which relates the story of a man murdered with a sickle. The local detective had all the sickles in the village brought to one place, and though all were clean, flies were drawn to the tool still marked with invisible traces of blood. Faced with the proof, the owner of the tainted sickle was compelled to confess to his crime.

More-systematic developments in forensic sciences accompanied the growth of medical knowledge in Europe, where, by the 16th and 17th centuries, physicians studied cadavers and

began to recognize and record the effects of various causes of death on the body. This meant that an investigator could examine the internal organs and know, for example, whether a victim had died from a violent attack. By the early 19th century, chemists could detect traces of arsenic in a corpse. Meanwhile, several notable criminal cases were solved by the application of logic and procedure. Among these cases was the 1784 trial of John Toms, who was convicted of shooting and killing a man named Edward Culshaw. Toms had used a flintlock pistol, a device loaded with gunpowder and a ball of lead packed down with a wad of paper. Police recovered the wad of paper from the fatal shot, and discovered that it was a bit of newspaper—one that fit together perfectly with a piece of torn paper found in Toms' pocket when he was arrested. This kind of proof would later be designated a *fracture match*, meaning that one part of a piece of evidence is matched to its other part.

In 1880, a Scottish physician, Dr. Henry Faulds, published a paper describing the uniqueness of fingerprints and their possible use as a means of identification (although the recognition of fingerprints as an identifying characteristic has been a part of human lore for centuries). By 1892, the Englishman Sir Francis Galton published a book, *Finger Prints*, offering a system of fingerprint analysis. These initial discoveries and systems led to a revolution in the ability of law-enforcement agents to identify both victims and suspects of a crime—an ability augmented considerably a century later, with the development of DNA analysis by Sir Alec Jeffreys in 1985.

The rise of forensics in modern times has coincided with its increased tools and effectiveness. But its ever-growing use has served an important social benefit as well. Forensic scientists pride themselves on the objectivity called for by scientific procedures and methodologies. That objectivity has meant that forensics is a powerful tool for both prosecution and defense, conviction and exoneration. The principles of forensics are such that its practitioners serve the truth above all else.

Fingerprints are considered primary evidence. When "dusting" for fingerprints (above), investigators use a special powder that makes the prints visible. Some hard-to-find fingerprints can be revealed through advanced laboratory techniques (left). Law-enforcement databases compare fingerprints (far left) from a crime scene to those of thousands of other known criminals.

AT THE CRIME SCENE

Homicide, assault, kidnapping, burglary, arson, fraud—whatever the crime, there will virtually always be some evidence left at the scene. This is a scientific principle, in fact, first expressed in the early 1900s by the criminologist Edmond Locard. Locard said that when an individual comes into contact with another person and/or with a place, that individual will both leave something behind and take something away. The job of crime-scene investigators is to identify and protect the area where this exchange took place, and then gather evidence in order to establish both what transpired and who is responsible.

Consider a murder scene. Investigators arrive to discover paramedics, police officers, and television reporters, all wanting to help or curiously looking on. Anyone entering the scene has the potential to contaminate the evidence: they might step on a footprint in the carpet, for example, or leave a hair of their own behind. So the investigators' first job is to survey and secure the crime scene. The first questions are: Is the scene safe? Is the criminal still there? Is there a gas leak? Once they are satisfied that there is no apparent danger, investigators must make an educated guess as to how far the scene extends—the murder might have occurred inside a residence, but the key piece of evidence might be tire tracks on the street out front. Investigators would rather err on the side of sealing off too much area than starting too small and finding they had left an important clue exposed to contamination outside the boundary.

Once the area is marked and sealed off to further entry, investigators will enter and begin their search for clues. This process is painstaking; investigators move slowly and systematically, because they, too, run the risk of disturbing evidence as they go, and a piece of evidence, once disturbed, cannot be put back into place. And the important physical detail could be almost anything: investigators note the position of light switches and drapes and doors and windows, the condition of the furniture, the weather, distinctive smells, whether the heating or air-conditioning is on, how much mail there is, what's in the ashtrays or the medicine cabinet, the contents of the trash. They look for signs of a struggle, and look for tool marks that might indicate a forced entry. They even look for what is *not* there—a wallet, car keys, a briefcase.

An important part of the investigators' approach is documentation. Crime scenes are photographed thoroughly and methodically. The scene itself, the victim, the individual pieces of evidence, even the crowd looking on (where key witnesses or even the criminal himself might be standing) are all photographed. Film is still the preferred medium, since it is considered more difficult to alter than digital images, and thus more reliable for presentation in court. Investigators also take extensive notes and sketch out the crime scene, noting the position and relationships of all the evidence.

Though anything might be a crucial clue, investigators pay special attention to the victim's body, of course, and some particular types of *trace evidence*:

Fingerprints

The ridges on the pads of human fingers are unique to each individual—not even identical twins share the same pattern. Furthermore, these patterns are resilient and consistent, staying much the same through aging and injury. In more than a century of identifying fingerprints, investigators have become more sophisticated at classifying the so-called arches, loops, and whorls that characterize each print, and the number of fingerprints kept on record has also increased considerably. Nevertheless, the basic principle has remained the same.

There are several kinds of prints that might appear at a crime scene. *Visible prints* are those left behind when an individual has dust, grease, or some other substance on his or her finger. When that individual touches a clean surface, the substance is left behind in the shape of the print. *Molded prints*, on the other hand, are left when an individual leaves an impression in some soft surface such as wax, or in a viscous substance such as blood. Finally, *latent prints* are the usually invisible marks left on regular surfaces as a result of the natural oils on an individual's skin.

Specialized laboratory procedures have been developed that can detect the presence of even microscopic amounts of blood and other bodily fluids on the clothing worn by a crime victim or the perpetrator.

Crime-scene investigators still "dust" for fingerprints—meaning that they spread powder over an area, and the powder sticks to the prints, making them visible. Such prints are photographed, but can then also be "lifted" by transferring the powder—now in the shape of the print—to a piece of tape. Investigators also use cyanoacrylate fumes or ninhydrin spray, two means of spreading particles that will stick to a latent print. Improved technology means that prints can be lifted from ever-more-irregular surfaces, including the skin of a victim's body.

Blood

Because struggles and violence often result in bloodshed, investigators are particularly alert to the presence of blood at a crime scene. They describe blood as being wet or dry; in stains, spatters, or pools; left in plain sight or hidden by an attempt to clean and conceal it. Liquid blood is lifted with gauze, on which it is allowed to dry, while investigators will leave dried blood that has been found on a carpet, bedsheet, or other item, and simply transport the item or the bloodstained portion of it to the laboratory. Blood samples are quickly refrigerated and processed at a lab, along with samples found on clothing, and samples from an autopsy if there is a body.

The pattern of blood drops or spatters can tell the story of what happened at a crime scene. Investigators pay attention to the size and shape of droplets to determine how much blood was being shed, and from where. Spatters often indicate violent blows, and their direction—which tends to follow the swing of a weapon back away from a blow given—can be used to reconstruct how many blows occurred and where the parties involved were located.

When a person dies under suspicious or unnatural circumstances, a medical examiner (right) performs an autopsy to determine the time and cause of death. When the victim has been deceased for some time, the degree of decomposition makes dental records (below) especially important for establishing an identity. Facial-reconstruction experts are able to create amazingly accurate models (bottom) of the victim's face using data supplied by forensic anthropologists.

a crime scene. There is a fixed order, in any given location, in which insects will inhabit a corpse, and by identifying the insects present—and thus what stage of the order is occurring—an investigator can determine with great accuracy the time elapsed since the victim's death (officially called the postmortem interval) and also the location in which the body decomposed.

The first insects to arrive on a corpse are necrophagous, or corpse-eating, species. In many instances, flies dominate for the first three days, laying eggs in the body that hatch as maggots. Maggots will eat the still-moist flesh for the following few days. Species of beetles will join the maggots or follow to eat the increasingly dried-out flesh, while other insects—ants and wasps, for example—arrive to feed on the species eating the flesh.

Forensics entomologists continually do research to add to their knowledge of insect behavior, perhaps most famously at a Tennessee research facility known as the Body Farm. There, dozens of bodies at a time are allowed to decompose in a variety of situations—in direct sunlight, underwater, in shallow graves—to allow researchers to gather valuable data about putrefaction, insect colonization, and also the decay of skeletons.

Hair, fibers, and other evidence

Other common examples of trace evidence are human hair and clothing fibers, both of which tend to be left behind—especially in the event of a struggle—and both of which carry distinctive markings. At the crime scene, inves-

Blood remains may be minute, concealed against dark surfaces, or may have been cleaned up. Even with strong cleansers, however, it is difficult to remove all traces. Investigators use a high-intensity ultraviolet light, held at different angles, to see hidden bloodstains. And they also use a chemical compound called luminol to reveal stains made invisible by cleaning. Luminol is $C_8H_7N_3O_2$, mixed with liquid so that it may be sprayed from a bottle onto the surfaces at the scene. Luminol reacts with hemoglobin—a blood protein—in a chemical reaction that produces energy. This energy is given off in the form of glowing light. Investigators photograph this light before it fades, thus making a record of the hidden bloodstain.

Insects

The field of forensic entomology arose because insects can yield important information at

tigators carefully collect such evidence for transport to the laboratory, where it can be examined. They place evidence in bags, lift it with tape, even use so-called forensic vacuums to gather and keep track of what they collect. Other small but distinctive and identifiable types of evidence may include paint chips, pieces of glass (for example, glass from a broken headlight at the scene of a hit-and-run), pollen, soil, and bullets and spent cartridge casings.

Investigators always seek to strike a balance between gathering too much from a scene or not enough, between working carefully and working quickly enough to stop a trail from going cold. When they are satisfied that the pertinent evidence has been documented and/or collected, the crime scene is released.

EXAMINING THE VICTIM

When a person is a victim of a crime, law-enforcement officers may have that person's body examined using the techniques of forensic pathology. Such examinations are routinely carried out in the case of assault or rape. When a person dies under suspicious or unnatural circumstances, or as the result of violence, the victim is brought to a medical examiner (M.E.), who often subjects the body to an *autopsy*, or postmortem. The autopsy process involves looking closely at the outside and inside of a corpse to determine the cause, manner, and time of death.

A victim arrives at the medical examiner's office in a sterile body bag. The body is photographed, and the condition and placement of the clothes are noted before they are removed. It is important, as at the crime scene, that every step in the process be documented. Any external evidence, such as gunpowder residue or bloodstains, is examined; wounds are recorded; a rape kit may be administered. The M.E. looks under the fingernails for tissue that may have come from fending off an assailant.

The body is cleaned, measured, weighed, and its distinguishing features described. It is placed on an autopsy table, with a body block underneath its back to push the chest upward. This is to aid in opening the chest for the internal exam. The M.E. makes a large, Y-shaped incision, with a cut from each shoulder to the breastbone, and then another long cut down to

A ballistics expert fires a handgun into a water tank (below), retrieves the bullet, and then compares it to bullets from the crime scene. Telltale marks (left) can link the bullet to a firearm used in another crime.

the groin. The skin and muscle are pulled away, revealing the rib cage, which in turn is opened to expose the internal organs. These organs are removed and examined, with samples taken of each. The contents of the stomach are recorded. Later, the scalp is removed and the skull opened with a saw, allowing the brain to be removed and also examined (often to look for a hemorrhage that would indicate a blow to the head). Throughout the exam, the M.E. may use X-rays as a guide, especially if he or she is attempting to preserve the pathway of bullets or other foreign materials for further study.

From an autopsy, the M.E. can ascertain the cause of death, since cardiac arrest, for example, and blood loss will leave the organs in two different conditions. There will also be information concerning the manner of death; for example, are the gunshots consistent with self-inflicted wounds, pointing to suicide, or were bullets fired from a distance, suggesting a homicide? Finally, the M.E. can evaluate the time of death. Body temperature, the stiffening of the corpse, the color of the skin, the pooling of blood in the body, and the contents of the stomach and intestines may all indicate the elapsed time since the death.

Forensics experts are often called upon to identify a victim as well. If the body is intact, fingerprints are an option, as are DNA and hair samples—especially if there is some basis for comparison. But when highly decayed remains are found, or a body is severely damaged (as in a building collapse, for example), other forensic tools may be called upon. Forensic odontology deals with the evaluation of dental evidence. Teeth are particularly durable and likely to survive events that much of the body cannot; they are also unique to each person. Forensic odontologists compare teeth to dental records, which include X-rays and the particular pattern of root canals, fillings, and so on, for a given patient. These scientists may also be called on to determine whether bite marks on a suspect were made by a particular victim trying to defend himself or herself.

When only skeletal remains are found, investigators turn to forensic anthropologists, who apply the science of bones to the identification of victims. From a collection of bone remains, a forensic anthropologist may be able to tell how many victims are represented, their genders (from the pelvic bone and the skull), and their size, age, and health at the time of death. It is also possible to determine how long the victim or victims have been deceased, and perhaps the manner of their deaths—especially if there are bones showing the effects of sharp or blunt weapons, or gunshots. Forensic anthropology

How Does DNA Analysis Work?

Any two human beings have about 99.9 percent of their DNA in common. The genetic blueprint is overwhelmingly identical across our species. But within each cell, the genes—the parts of DNA that contain the code for producing proteins—are separated by long strings of noncoding DNA that hold them together. These noncoding strings are full of repetitive sequences, and it is in the number of these repetitions that an individual differs from every other (except identical twins, who are genetically the same).

By a method called restriction fragment length polymorphism (RFLP) analysis, the individualized sequences of DNA can be isolated for analysis. Alternatively, in the case of polymerase chain reaction (PCR) analysis, the sequences needed for testing can be replicated from a very small portion of DNA, allowing researchers to operate from a much smaller initial sample. In either case, the resulting fragments are placed in a gel, where, by a process called electrophoresis, pieces of the DNA sequence separate out according to size. The relative positions of these pieces are then recorded as a pattern that looks some-

Every person's DNA sequence can be represented as a pattern of bands not unlike a bar code—a "fingerprint" of sorts that can be used as evidence if matched to a DNA sample from another source.

thing like a bar code—and which represents an individual's unique genetic "fingerprint," suitable for comparison to a sample from a suspect, victim, or database.

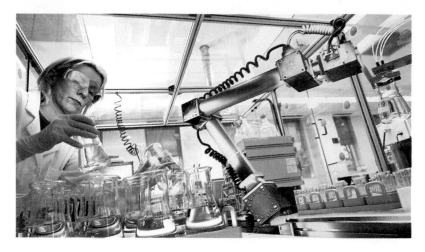

also includes the art of facial reconstruction, in which experts can build up facial bones with clay to form an approximate model of the living person's face. This model, or a photo of it, can be shown to witnesses or family members to help discover or verify the identity of a victim.

AT THE LABORATORY

Whether in a police crime lab or at a private or university laboratory that offers forensic analysis, there are specialties and procedures that allow investigators to glean information from a wide array of evidence.

Forensic toxicology is used to evaluate chemicals from the body. Was a victim intoxicated, drugged, or poisoned? Toxicologists attempt to ascertain what toxins are present and to what degree. This can be a straightforward process—blood-alcohol content, for example, is relatively easy to measure in a sample—but some chemicals can change their form or concentration in the body or become difficult to detect. Toxicologists use urine, hair, stomach contents, and blood to obtain samples. They look around a body, asking what chemicals might have been left behind at the scene, or even taking samples from insects that fed on a body. Once samples have been obtained, they can be analyzed using gas chromatography, emission spectroscopy, or other procedures.

Ballistics is the science concerned with the behavior and effects of projectiles—in most cases, bullets. Firearms, of course, tend to be mass-produced, and one firearm of a given make and model shares certain properties with all the others of the same make and model. But, luckily for forensics, every firearm (and any object,

in fact) is in certain ways unique. This is important because each gun leaves a different and unique set of markings on a bullet that travels through its barrel. These markings can be observed on the bullet, and then compared to other bullets to see if they were fired from the same weapon. If researchers have a bullet and then find a suspicious firearm, they can test-fire another bullet in the lab, and then compare the test bullet with the one recovered from a crime scene or body. If the test bullet matches the recovered bullet, the same firearm was used—and the owner of the weapon will likely find him- or herself a suspect in the crime.

Document examination, or diplomatics, concerns the verification and identification of documents, often in cases of fraud and forgery. Document examiners might compare signatures or handwriting samples to determine authenticity, checking, for example, under an angled light for the indentations that would reveal that a signature had been traced. These researchers also examine everything from diaries to wills, counterfeit currency, and fine art. By the same principles that make individual firearms unique, so, too, inks and papers—and the stamps, typewriters, printers, and copiers that process them—all leave signs that can be identified—sometimes by the application of that very specialized instrument, the naked eye.

DNA analysis is among the highest-profile forensic techniques, thanks especially to its controversial role in sensational cases such as the O.J. Simpson trial, in which its reliability was successfully called into question by the defense. Nevertheless, since its introduction in the mid-1980s, DNA analysis has become steadily more accepted in courtrooms—leading to convictions, but also to the exoneration of long-incarcerated individuals cleared after the fact by the application of this new method to old evidence.

Polygraph tests (below) are used by investigators to evaluate alibis, but their results are not always admissible as evidence in court. Federal, state, and local law-enforcement agencies now have access to extensive databases (right) with which to correlate certain types of crime to known criminals.

viding a profile outlining the suspect's likely personality and behavior. Such profiles are often compiled with the help of convicted criminals.

Other powerful tools for locating suspects are the increasingly complex and sizable databases now available to law enforcement. Major databases include the FBI's Integrated Automated Fingerprint Identification System (IAFIS), the National Integrated Ballistic Information Network (NIBIN), and the Combined DNA Index System (CODIS). These databases allow law enforcement to compare, with speed and accuracy, any fingerprints, firearms, and DNA, respectively, to up to several million samples on file.

When a case finally reaches the courtroom, forensics experts are often called to testify for either side. It is the job of the expert to provide convincing credentials and to make his or her scientific methods and conclusions clear to a jury of ordinary citizens. Witnesses for both sides may be questioned as to the accuracy of their findings and their own expertise. In any trial involving forensic evidence, it may become crucial for either side to be able to show that the *chain of custody* has remained intact. The chain of custody refers to the passage of evidence from the crime scene to the lab, into and out of storage, and to the courtroom. Either side may be called upon to produce documentation about who handled what evidence and when, between or at any point along the chain and anywhere in between. If the chain of custody is not documented at even one point, the evidence can be considered contaminated and will not be admissible in court.

The realities of forensic science do not quite match their portrayal on television. Real forensic analysis is slow and expensive, the result of a collaboration among many experts, not always ending in success. Stunning finds are few and far between. But realistic or not, forensic science makes a compelling story. Its very existence argues that method and objectivity have an enduring place in the world of justice.

Because it shows that some percentage of convicts are innocent, DNA analysis has raised serious new questions about the death penalty.

DNA is a powerful forensic tool, enabling investigators to identify victim or suspect from increasingly small samples of blood, hair, semen, saliva, or other tissue. And with the actual testing procedures increasingly standardized and automated, the chance of erroneous results has climbed to one in many billions.

MAKING A CASE

Whatever happened at the scene, it is usually afterward—with the photographs developed, the autopsy report completed, and the data from the various labs compiled—that investigators determine the true nature of a crime, and who is responsible. Here, other aspects of forensic science may come into play. Suspects may be subjected to polygraph or electroencephalograph tests—lie detectors—to evaluate their alibis. They may also be examined by a forensic psychiatrist, who can determine whether a suspect is mentally ill or debilitated.

Forensic psychiatrists may also help investigators still searching for a perpetrator, by pro-

SELECTED READINGS

WHAT IS SCIENCE?

Bobick, James, Naomi E. Balaban, and Science and Technology Department, Carnegie Library of Pittsburgh. *The Handy Science Answer Book.* Detroit, Mich.: Visible Ink Press, 3d ed., 2003; 680 pp.—Tackles questions in all realms of science for the insatiably curious.

Cobb, Vicky, and Kathy Darling. *You Gotta Try This: Absolutely Irresistible Science.* New York: Morrow, 1999; 144 pp., illus.—An easy-to-read book about experimentation and the application of the scientific method to solving problems.

Highfield, Roger. *The Science of Harry Potter: How Magic Really Works.* New York: Viking, 2002; repr. 2003; 256 pp.—Uses elements of the Harry Potter books as a springboard to discuss real scientific issues.

Silver, Brian L. *The Ascent of Science.* New York: Oxford University Press, 1998; repr. 2000; 552 pp., illus.—A detailed and insightful history of science and the people involved.

Taylor, Charles, and Stephen Pople. *The Oxford Children's Book of Science.* New York: Oxford University Press, 1996; 192 pp., illus.—A lavishly illustrated, engaging, and readable introduction to scientific disciplines from physics to molecular biology; for younger readers.

Teresi, Dick. *Lost Discoveries: The Ancient Roots of Modern Science—From the Babylonians to the Maya.* New York: Simon & Schuster, 2003; 453 pp.—How the roots of Western science often go back to India, Egypt, Mesopotamia, China, and other ancient civilizations.

Trefil, James, et al., eds. *The Encyclopedia of Science and Technology.* New York: Routledge, 2001; 560 pp., illus.—Broad general coverage of science, profusely illustrated.

Wolke, Robert L. *What Einstein Didn't Know: Scientific Answers to Everyday Questions.* Secaucus, N.J.: Carol Publishing, 1997; repr. 1999; 256 pp., illus.—The science behind everyday things, from why soap bubbles are round to how nonstick cooking spray works.

ASTRONOMY & SPACE SCIENCE

GENERAL WORKS

Begelman, Mitchell. *Turn Right at Orion: Travels through the Cosmos.* Reading, Mass.: Perseus Books, 2000; 264 pp.—An epic journey across millions of years of time, skillfully disguising astronomy as a science-fiction adventure.

Burnham, Robert. *The Reader's Digest Children's Atlas of the Universe.* Pleasantville, N.Y.: Reader's Digest Children's Books, 2000; 128 pp., illus.—An eye catching and fact-filled reference.

Hawking, Stephen W. *The Universe in a Nutshell.* New York: Bantam Doubleday Dell, 2001; 216 pp., illus.—Complex concepts are wonderfully explained by the famed cosmologist; beautifully illustrated.

Kirshner, Robert P. *The Extravagant Universe: Exploring Stars, Dark Energy, and the Accelerating Cosmos.* Princeton, N.J.: Princeton University Press, 2002; 282 pp.—Describes astrophysicists at work unraveling the secrets of the accelerating universe; for advanced readers.

Levy, David, ed. *The Scientific American Book of the Cosmos.* New York: St. Martin's Press, 2000; 416 pp., illus.—A guide by eminent authorities to what we know about the size, age, and nature of our universe.

Melia, Fulvio. *The Black Hole at the Center of Our Galaxy.* Princeton, N.J.: Princeton University Press, 2003; 189 pp.—A lucid look at black holes, through an examination of the black hole at the heart of the Milky Way.

Moore, Sir Patrick, and Lief Robinson, eds. *Astronomy Encyclopedia: An A–Z Guide to the Universe, rev. ed.* New York: Oxford University Press, 2002; 464 pp., illus.—More than 3,000 articles—accompanied by beautiful photographs, maps, and diagrams—describe our amazing cosmos, astronomers, and space programs.

Nemiroff, Robert J., and Jerry T. Bonnell. *The Universe: 365 Days.* New York: Harry N. Abrams, 2003; 740 pp., illus.—Photographs of outer space compiled by the astrophysicists who created the popular science website *Astronomy Picture of the Day (APoD).*

Redfern, Martin. *The Kingfisher Young People's Book of Space.* Greenville, S.C.: Kingfisher Books, 1998; 96 pp., illus.—An engaging look at space observation and exploration and our place in space and time in the universe.

Seife, Charles. *Alpha and Omega: The Search for the Beginning and End of the Universe.* New York: Viking, 2003; 294 pp., illus.—A science writer discusses the history of, and exciting current developments in, cosmology.

Wiese, Jim. *Cosmic Science: Over 40 Gravity-Defying, Earth-Orbiting, Space-Cruising Activities for Kids.* New York: John Wiley, 1997; 128 pp., illus.—An engaging look at astronomy and space technology through a series of down-to-earth projects by the author of *Rocket Science* (1995).

ASTRONOMERS AND THEIR SCIENCE

Andronik, Catherine M. *Copernicus: Founder of Modern Astronomy.* Minneapolis: Enslow, 2002; 112 pp., illus.—A biography of the 15th-century scientist who recognized the idea of a moving earth; for younger readers.

Bishop, Nic. *Looking for Life in the Universe.* Boston: Houghton Mifflin, 2002; 80 pp., illus.—Follows the work of astrophysicist Jill Tatar of the Search for Extraterrestrial Intelligence (SETI) Institute; for younger readers.

Gormley, Beatrice. *Maria Mitchell: The Soul of an Astronomer.* Grand Rapids, Mich.: Eerdmans, 2004; 149 pp., illus.—For younger readers, an extraordinary biography of a groundbreaking mid-19th-century female astronomer.

Lord, M. G. *Astro Turf: The Private Life of Rocket Science.* New York: Walker, 2005; 259 pp.—An exploration of the wild early days at the Jet Propulsion Laboratory at the California Institute of Technology by the daughter of an engineer who worked on the Mariner Mars 69 mission when most people considered rocket science to be a science-fiction fantasy.

Tyson, Neil de Grasse. *The Sky Is Not the Limit: Adventures of an Urban Astrophysicist.* New York: Doubleday, 2000; 208 pp.—The memoirs of the director of the American Museum of Natural History's Hayden Planetarium range from a look at the universe to the problems faced by black scientists.

STUDYING THE SKY

Dickinson, Terence. *Summer Stargazing: A Practical Guide for Recreational Astronomers.* Buffalo, N.Y.: Firefly Books, 1996; 64 pp., illus.—An informative handbook for recreational stargazers; does not require a telescope.

Ferris, Timothy. *Seeing in the Dark: How Backyard Stargazers Are Probing Deep Space and Guarding Earth from Interplanetary Peril.* New York: Simon & Schuster, 2002; 379 pp.—The noted astronomer tells what the novice observer can see in the sky, and profiles some of the best-known amateur and professional stargazers.

Goldsmith, Donald. *Connecting with the Cosmos: Nine Ways to Experience the Wonder of the Universe.* Naperville, Ill.: Sourcebooks, 2002; 208 pp.—A collection of fascinating sky-watching activities that can be done virtually anywhere.

Graun, Ken. *Touring the Universe: A Practical Guide to Exploring the Cosmos Through 2017.* Tucson, Ariz.: Ken Press, 2002; 128 pp., illus.—A fascinating armchair tour of the universe written especially for beginners; includes photos, star charts, and worldwide eclipses through 2017.

Kerrod, R. *Hubble: Mirror on the Universe.* Toronto: Firefly Books, 2003; 192 pp., illus.—A breathtaking look at images from the Hubble Telescope with a clearly written text explaining various concepts in astronomy.

Kidger, Mark. *The Star of Bethlehem: An Astronomer's View.* Princeton, N.J.: Princeton University Press, 1999; 306 pp.—The science behind the Christmas star.

Moore, Patrick. *Atlas of the Universe.* Skokie, Ill.: Rand McNally, rev. ed., 1998; 288 pp., illus.—A comprehensive tour of astronomy and the universe.

Panek, Richard. *Seeing and Believing: How the Telescope Opened Our Eyes and Minds to the Heavens.* New York: Viking Penguin, 1998; repr. 1999; 192 pp.—A fascinating account of the technical progress of the telescope and the ways in which it advanced human knowledge.

Schaaf, Fred. *Seeing the Sky: One Hundred Projects, Activities, and Explorations with Astronomy.* New York: John Wiley, 1991; 224 pp.—Experiments for amateur astronomers.

Sesti, Giuseppe Maria. *The Glorious Constellations: History and Mythology.* New York: Harry N. Abrams, 1991; 496 pp., illus.—A look at how people have viewed the stars.

Stott, Carole. *The New Astronomer.* New York: DK Publishing, 1999; 144 pp., illus.—A comprehensive, practical, and passionate guide for the would-be stargazer.

THE SOLAR SYSTEM

Croswell, Ken. *The Alchemy of the Heavens: Searching for Meaning in the Milky Way.* Garden City, N.Y.: Anchor/Doubleday, 1995; repr. 1996; 352 pp., illus.—A look at the confluence of chemicals and events that led to the formation of our galaxy.

———. *Magnificent Universe.* New York: Simon & Schuster, 1999; 192 pp., illus.—An illustrated tour of our universe.

Facaros, Dana, and Michael Pauls. *The Travellers' Guide to Mars: Don't Leave Home without It.* Old Saybrook, Conn.: Cadogan Books, 1997; 108 pp.—A lighthearted and informative look at what you might find if you could travel to Mars.

Harrington, Philip S. *Eclipse! The What, Where, When, Why, and How Guide to Watching Solar and Lunar Eclipses.* New York: John Wiley, 1997; 272 pp.—Includes information about types of eclipses, how to photograph and videotape an eclipse, and upcoming events through the year 2017.

Heath, Robin. *Sun, Moon & Earth.* New York: Walker, 2001; 64 pp., illus.—An incredible compendium of information in a small format.

Johnston, Andrew K. *Earth from Space.* Washington, D.C.: Smithsonian, 2005; 272 pp., illus.—Spectacular images of our planet from the latest generation of satellites.

Koppes, Steven N. *Killer Rocks from Outer Space: Asteroids, Comets, and Meteorites.* Minneapolis: Lerner Publications, 2003; 112 pp., illus.—An award-winning look at the sometimes catastrophic effects of meteor and comet impacts on the history of Earth.

Levy, David H. *Comets: Creators and Destroyers.* New York: Simon & Schuster, 1998; 256 pp., illus.—One of the world's most famous discoverers of comets draws liberally on his own experiences in this readable account of how comets and asteroids have affected our lives.

McNab, David, and James Younger. *The Planets.* New Haven, Conn.: Yale University Press, 1999; 240 pp., illus.—The illustrated companion text to the BBC series.

Ride, Sally, and Tam O'Shaughnessy. *Exploring Our Solar System.* New York: Crown, 2003; 112 pp., illus.—A beautifully illustrated overview of our solar system for younger readers; includes a list of space flights.

Schaaf, Fred. *Planetology: Comparing Other Worlds to Our Own.* New York: Franklin Watts, 1996; 128 pp., illus.—Fascinating comparisons; for younger readers.

Standage, Tom. *The Neptune File.* New York: Walker, 2000; 256 pp.—How 19th-century scientists discovered the existence of an unseen planet by studying the effects of its gravity on the orbit of Uranus.

Sussman, Art. *Dr. Art's Guide to Planet Earth: For Earthlings Ages 12 to 120.* White River Junction, Vt.: Chelsea Green Publishing, 2000; 128 pp., illus.—Clear explanations of how our planet works, with colorful illustrations.

BEYOND THE SOLAR SYSTEM

Boss, Alan. *Looking for Earths: The Race to Find New Solar Systems.* New York: John Wiley, 1998; 240 pp.—A fascinating account of the long search for planets outside our solar system, the first of which was not found until mid-1995.

Couper, Heather, and Nigel Henbest. *Big Bang: The Story of the Universe.* New York: DK Publishing, 1997; 48 pp., illus.—For younger readers; the amazing story of the origin and evolution of our universe.

———. *Black Holes.* New York: DK Publishing, 1996; 48 pp., illus.—Describes the role that black holes play in our universe; for younger readers.

Gribbin, John. *Unveiling the Edge of Time: Black Holes, White Holes, Wormholes.* New York: Crown, 1992; repr. 1994; 248 pp., illus.—Demystifies the subject for nonscientists.

Nemiroff, Robert J., and Jerry T. Bonnell. *The Universe: 365 Days.* New York: Harry N. Abrams, 2003; 740 pp., illus.—Two astrophysicists present a breathtaking look at the universe via 365 high-resolution images from NASA.

Simon, Seymour. *Galaxies.* New York: Morrow, 1988; repr. 1991; 32 pp., illus.—Clear, beautifully illustrated explanation of the origin and existence of galaxies; for grades 3 to 6.

Skurzynski, Gloria. *Zero Gravity*. New York: Simon & Schuster, 1994; 32 pp., illus.—Explains gravity and what life would be like without it; especially useful for younger readers.

Tyson, Neil de Grasse, Charles Liu, and Robert Irion. *One Universe: At Home in the Cosmos*. Washington, D.C.: Joseph Henry Press/National Academies Press, 2000; 224 pp., illus.—An overview of the current state of knowledge of the universe, from its tiniest particles to its grandest theories, with many useful illustrations.

SPACE EXPLORATION

Branley, Franklyn M. *The International Space Station*. New York: HarperCollins, 2000; 36 pp., illus.—A guide to the construction and operation of the space station; for younger readers.

Burrows, William E. *This New Ocean: The Story of the First Space Age*. New York: Random House, 1998; repr. 1999; 912 pp., illus.—A history of spaceflight from the first Sputnik in 1957 to the end of the Cold War in 1991.

Clary, David. *Rocket Man*. New York: Hyperion, 2003; 324 pp.—An engaging biography of one of the pioneers of space travel, Robert H. Goddard (1882–1945).

Goldsmith, Donald. *Voyage to the Milky Way: The Future of Space Exploration*. New York: TV Books, 1999; 320 pp.—A well-written overview of the subject.

Kevles, Bettyann Holtzmann. *Almost Heaven: The Story of Women in Space*. New York: Basic Books, 2003; 274 pp., illus.—The long struggle and ultimate success of women trying to enter a formerly all-male industry.

Kraft, Chris. *Flight: My Life in Mission Control*. New York: Dutton, 2001; 372 pp.—The autobiography of the former NASA flight-control director in the pioneering days of human space travel.

Kranz, Gene. *Failure Is Not an Option: Mission Control from Mercury*. New York: Simon & Schuster, 2000; 415 pp., illus.—A former NASA flight director recalls the earliest days of space exploration.

Levinson, Paul. *Realspace: The Fate of Physical Presence in the Digital Age, On and Off Planet*. New York: Routledge, 2003; 176 pp.—A fascinating discussion of why space exploration is necessary.

Ride, Sally. *Voyager: An Adventure to the Edge of the Solar System*. New York: Crown, 1992; 36 pp., illus.—The story of the Voyager 1 and 2 space probes; diagrams and color photographs add to the easy-to-read text.

Vaughan, Diane. *The* Challenger *Launch Decision: Risky Technology, Culture, and Deviance at NASA*. Chicago: University of Chicago Press, 1995; repr. 1997; 592 pp., illus.—An in-depth look at how the culture of the National Aeronautics and Space Administration (NASA) may have sent the space shuttle *Challenger* and its crew to their fate.

LIFE BEYOND EARTH

Aczel, Amir D. *Probability 1: Why There Must Be Intelligent Life in the Universe*. New York: Harcourt Brace, 1998; 240 pp.—A mathematician argues convincingly that the number of planets suitable for life is extremely large, although his theory of the probability of life actually appearing is unconvincing.

Shapiro, Robert. *Planetary Dreams: The Quest to Discover Life beyond Earth*. New York: John Wiley, 1999; 320 pp.—A bio-

chemist presents a solid and readable overview of the case for space exploration.

Skurzynski, Gloria. *Are We Alone? Scientists Search for Life in Space*. Washington, D.C.: National Geographic Society, 2004; 96 pp., illus.—An overview of the subject, including scientists describing their lives and work; for younger readers.

MATHEMATICS

GENERAL WORKS

Benjamin, Arthur, and Michael B. Shermer. *Mathemagics: How to Look Like a Genius without Really Trying*. Los Angeles: Lowell House, 2d rev. ed., 1998; 240 pp.—Everyday mathematics made easy.

Berlinski, David. *The Advent of the Algorithm: The Idea That Rules the World*. San Francisco: Harcourt Brace, 2000; 368 pp.—Reveals how the algorithm made the modern world possible; by the author of *A Tour of the Calculus* (1996).

Best, Joel. *More Damned Lies and Statistics: How Numbers Confuse Public Issues*. Berkeley: University of California Press, 2005; 217 pp.—In this sequel to *Damned Lies and Statistics* (2001), the author further explains how numbers can be manipulated and how to evaluate the validity of statistics.

Devlin, Keith. *The Millennium Problems: The Seven Greatest Unsolved Mathematical Puzzles of Our Time*. New York: Basic Books, 2003; 237 pp.—Explaining modern math to the popular reader by discussing its greatest puzzles.

du Sautoy, Marcus. *The Music of the Primes: Searching to Solve the Greatest Mystery in Mathematics*. New York: HarperCollins, 2003; 352 pp.—A detailed account of Riemann's hypothesis, the oldest and most difficult of unsolved mathematical problems; for advanced students.

Farmelo, Graham, ed. *It Must Be Beautiful: Great Equations of Science*. New York: Granta Books, 2002; repr. 2003; 308 pp.—An engaging collection of essays by notable scientists and historians showing how powerful equations have sparked almost magical transformations in science and history.

Gardner, Martin. *The Colossal Book of Mathematics: Classic Puzzles, Paradoxes, and Problems*. New York: Norton, 2001; 704 pp., illus.—Explores a wide range of abstract mathematical concepts in a populist style, ranging from using geometry to dissect the world of artist M. C. Escher to making visual music with fractals.

Gardner, Robert. *Science Projects about Methods of Measuring*. Springfield, N.J.: Enslow, 2000; 128 pp.—Activities for upper-middle-school students involving the art and science of measurement.

Heilbron, J. L. *Geometry Civilized: History, Culture, and Technique*. New York: Oxford University Press, 1998; repr. 2000; 328 pp., illus.—An engaging and beautifully designed exploration of the history of geometry and a discussion of its innumerable applications, ranging from cathedral architecture to cloverleaf traffic patterns.

Ifrah, Georges. *The Universal History of Numbers: From Prehistory to the Invention of the Computer*. New York: John Wiley, 1999; repr. 2000; 663 pp., illus.—A brilliant look at the worldwide naming, recording, and manipulating of numbers throughout history.

Kaplan, Robert, and Ellen Kaplan. *The Art of the Infinite: The Pleasures of Mathematics*. New York: Oxford University Press, 2003; repr. 2004; 336 pp., illus.—A serious and illuminating introduction to the magic of mathematics by the authors of *Nothing That Is: A Natural History of Zero* (1999).

Linklater, Andro. *Measuring America: How an Untamed Wilderness Shaped the United States and Fulfilled the Promise of Democracy.* New York: Walker, 2002; 310 pp., illus.—The history of American measurement, and how it contributed to the staying power of inches and ounces in a world of meters and grams.

Lundy, Miranda. *Sacred Geometry.* New York: Walker, 2001; 64 pp., illus.—A fun look at plane geometry and the influence it had on the ancient world.

Mazur, Barry. *Imagining Numbers (Particularly the square root of minus fifteen).* New York: Farrar, Straus & Giroux, 2003; 268 pp.—A lucid exploration of the history of imaginary numbers.

Niederman, Derrick, and David Boyum. *What the Numbers Say: A Field Guide to Mastering Our Numerical World.* New York: Broadway Books, 2003; repr. 2004; 288 pp., illus.—An accessible look at numeric data in relation to everyday contexts.

Ryan, Mark. *Everyday Math for Everyday Life: A Handbook for When It Just Doesn't Add Up.* New York: Warner Books, 2002; 320 pp.—Demystifies such things as converting a recipe or foreign currency, calculating gas mileage, and computing a tip.

Stewart, Ian. *Flatterland.* Reading, Mass.: Perseus Books, 2001; 320 pp.—A satirical and savvy guide through modern mathematical speculation by the author of *Nature's Numbers: The Unreal Reality of Mathematical Imagination* (1995), which explores numbers at work in such things as a snowflake and a horse's gallop.

Wallace, David Foster. *Everything and More: A Compact History of* ∞. New York: Atlas Books/Norton, 2003; 319 pp., illus.—An energetic and insightful look at the nature of infinity; for advanced readers.

Watkins, Matthew. *Useful Formulae.* New York: Walker, 2001; 64 pp., illus.—A practical compendium of mathematical and physical formulas.

Woods, Michael, and Mary B. Woods. *Ancient Computing: From Counting to Calendars.* Minneapolis: Lerner Publications, 2000; 88 pp., illus.—A look at computing development from the Stone Age through the Roman Empire.

MATHEMATICIANS AND THEIR SCIENCE

Aczel, Amir D. *Chance: A Guide to Gambling, Love, the Stock Market, and Just About Everything Else.* New York: Avalon/Thunder's Mouth Press, 2004; 161 pp., illus.—In tracing the stages of thought devoted to solving a mathematical puzzle, the author of *Fermat's Last Theorem* (1996) explains how probability theory can help you in Las Vegas and everyday life.

Alder, Ken. *The Measure of All Things: The Seven-Year Odyssey and Hidden Error That Transformed the World.* New York: Free Press, 2002; repr. 2003; 422 pp., illus.—How two French astronomers spent seven years, beginning in 1792, creating a new standard unit of measurement, the meter, that was supposed to equal exactly one ten-millionth of the distance from the North Pole to the Equator.

Sabbagh, Karl. *The Riemann Hypothesis: The Greatest Unsolved Problem in Mathematics.* New York: Farrar, Straus & Giroux, 2003; 340 pp.—Mathematicians talk about the problem—and about themselves and their colleagues.

Watson, Richard. *Cogito, Ergo Sum: The Life of René Descartes.* Boston: David R. Godine, 2002; 375 pp.—An idiosyncratic biography of the inventor of analytic geometry.

Young, Robin V., and Zoran Minderovic, eds. *Notable Mathematicians: From Ancient Times to the Present.* Detroit: Gale, 1998; 612 pp., illus.—A comprehensive look at 300 mathematicians, from ancient times to the present; includes a list of milestones in mathematics.

PAST & FUTURE

ARCHAEOLOGISTS, ANTHROPOLOGISTS, AND PALEONTOLOGISTS

Batten, Mary. *Anthropologist: Scientist of the People.* Boston: Houghton Mifflin, 2001; 64 pp., illus.—Describes fieldwork by anthropologists examining the complex world of an Amazonian hunter-gatherer tribe to convey the science and art of anthropology.

Kerley, Barbara. *The Dinosaurs of Waterhouse Hawkins.* New York: Scholastic, 2001; unpaged, illus.—For younger readers, the biography of one of the dinosaur-study pioneers who built full-sized models of the creatures based on scientific speculation.

Koppel, Tom. *Lost World: Rewriting Prehistory, How New Science Is Tracing America's Ice Age Mariners.* New York: Atria Books, 2003; 288 pp.—Field archaeology in action, tracing the arrival of the earliest Americans and overturning long-held theories.

Marrin, Albert. *Secrets from the Rocks: Dinosaur Hunting with Roy Chapman Andrews.* New York: Dutton, 2002; 64 pp., illus.—A fascinating look at what it means to be an explorer; for younger readers.

Novacek, Michael. *Time Traveler: In Search of Dinosaurs and Ancient Mammals from Montana to Mongolia.* New York: Farrar, Straus & Giroux, 2002; 368 pp., illus.—The curator of paleontology at the American Museum of Natural History writes about the working life of a modern paleontologist, including fieldwork.

Robinson, Andrew. *Lost Languages: The Enigma of the World's Undeciphered Scripts.* New York: McGraw-Hill, 2002; 352 pp., illus.—The author investigates ongoing efforts to code-break several of the "lost languages" that puzzle archaeologists and linguists.

Romer, John and Elizabeth. *The History of Archaeology: Great Excavations of the World.* New York: Facts on File, 2001; 216 pp., illus.—A guide to famous, often eccentric archaeologists and the techniques they used in excavating sites ranging from Pompeii to Oaxaca.

Sis, Peter. *The Tree of Life: Charles Darwin.* New York: Farrar, Straus & Giroux, 2003; 44 pp., illus.—Mingles maps, diary entries, and lively quotes to redefine what a picture book can be; for young readers.

Wallace, David Rains. *Beasts of Eden: Walking Whales, Dawn Horses, and Other Enigmas of Mammal Evolution.* Berkeley: University of California Press, 2004; repr. 2005; 340 pp., illus.—A richly detailed and lively look at the efforts of paleontologists to shed light on the development of mammals in geologic time.

PALEONTOLOGY AND PREHISTORIC ANIMALS

Barrett, Paul. *National Geographic Dinosaurs.* Washington, D.C.: National Geographic Society, 2001; 192 pp., illus.—A beautifully illustrated guide to the life and times of the dinosaurs.

Benton, Michael J. *When Life Nearly Died: The Greatest Mass Extinction of All Time.* New York: Thames & Hudson, 2003; 336 pp., illus.—Vividly describes and explores the causes of the extinction of 95 percent of all life on Earth 251 million years ago.

Chorlton, Windsor. *Woolly Mammoth: Life, Death, and Rediscovery.* New York: Scholastic, 2001; 40 pp., illus.—Highlights the knowledge and expertise needed to excavate and remove a frozen woolly mammoth; for younger readers.

Ellis, Richard. *Sea Dragons: Predators of the Prehistoric Oceans.* Lawrence: University Press of Kansas, 2003; 314 pp., illus.—A detailed look at the fiercest predators in the prehistoric oceans.

Fortey, Richard. *Life: A Natural History of the First Four Billion Years of Life on Earth.* New York: Knopf, 1998; 346 pp., illus.—A British paleontologist, whose other works include *Trilobite! Eyewitness to Evolution* (2000), describes the biological history of Earth, including extraordinary and extinct organisms and the latest paleontological controversies.

Gee, Henry. *A Field Guide to Dinosaurs: The Essential Handbook for Travelers in the Mesozoic.* New York: Barron's Educational Series, 2003; 192 pp., illus.—A well-illustrated guide to more than 50 species.

Nothdurft, William, et al. *The Lost Dinosaurs of Egypt.* New York: Random House, 2002; 256 pp.—First-rate popular science, mixing history and desert drama in the tale of the rediscovery of the bones of the second-largest dinosaur on record.

Parker, Steve. *Dinosaurus: The Complete Guide to Dinosaurs.* Westport, Conn.: Firefly Books, 2003; 448 pp., illus.—Organizes the major dinosaur families and identifies 500 species, with illustrations, written descriptions, and traits.

Sloan, Christopher. *SuperCroc and the Origins of Crocodiles.* Washington, D.C.: National Geographic Society, 2002; 64 pp., illus.—Ancient crocodiles from the Mesozoic era brought to life through incredible illustrations and descriptive text.

Tanaka, Shelley. *New Dinos: The Latest Finds! The Coolest Dinosaur Discoveries!* New York: Atheneum, 2003; 48 pp., illus.—How electron microscopes, CT scans, and computer models have revised notions about dinosaurs, and how much remains to be discovered; for young readers.

Walker, Sally M. *Fossil Fish Found Alive: Discovering the Coelacanth.* Minneapolis: Carolrhoda, 2002; 64 pp., illus.—The discovery of a fish that existed millions of years before dinosaurs walked the earth; for younger readers.

Wallace, David Rains. *Beasts of Eden: Walking Whales, Dawn Horses, and Other Enigmas of Mammal Evolution.* Berkeley: University of California Press, 2004; 327 pp., illus.—A history of efforts to shed light on mammal development in geological time.

Zoehfeld, Kathleen Weidner. *Dinosaur Parents, Dinosaur Young: Uncovering the Mystery of Dinosaur Families.* New York: Clarion Books, 2001; 64 pp., illus.—How some dinosaurs tended their eggs and cared for their young; for younger readers; beautifully illustrated.

EARLY SKYWATCHERS AND CALENDARS

Duncan, David Ewing. *Calendar: Humanity's Epic Struggle to Determine a True and Accurate Year.* New York: Avon Books, 1998; repr. 1999; 240 pp., illus.—The fascinating history of humanity's struggle with dates.

Krupp, Edwin C. *Echoes of the Ancient Skies: The Astronomy of Lost Civilizations.* New York: Oxford University Press, rev. ed., 1994; 386 pp., illus.—A world tour of ancient temples, tombs, and observatories, illustrating how the skies were used by people to create religion and calendars.

FUTURISM AND SCIENCE FICTION

Brockman, John, ed. *The Next Fifty Years: Science in the First Half of the 21st Century.* New York: Viking, 2002; 320 pp.—A fascinating collection of essays by some of the world's most visionary scientists.

Brooks, Rodney A. *Flesh and Machines: How Robots Will Change Us.* New York: Pantheon Books, 2002; 260 pp., illus.—The director of the MIT Artificial Intelligence Laboratory says that robots will have feelings and consciousness in another 20 years, and speculates about the ways in which this will affect future humans; for advanced readers.

Dixon, Dougal, and John Adams. *The Future is Wild.* New York: Firefly Books, 2002; 160 pp., illus.—The companion volume to the Animal Planet television series looks millions of years into the future of Earth, long after humans have become extinct.

Fukuyama, Francis. *Our Posthuman Future: Consequences of the Biotechnology Revolution.* New York: Farrar, Straus & Giroux, 2002; 256 pp.—A bioethicist looks at the technological developments that allow scientists to directly intervene in the genetic process, and the ethical problems these pose as we struggle with the issue of how to regulate the biotechnology industry of the future; for advanced readers.

Gifford, Clive. *How the Future Began: Machines.* New York: Kingfisher Books, 1999; 63 pp., illus.—A basic look at cutting-edge, machine-based technology and its potential applications for the future.

McKibben, Bill. *Enough: Staying Human in an Engineered Age.* New York: Henry Holt, 2003; repr. 2004; 288 pp.—The best-selling science writer discusses the benefits and dangers inherent in a range of technology that threatens our very humanness.

Perkowitz, Sidney. *Digital People: From Bionic Humans to Androids.* Washington, D.C.: Joseph Henry Press, 2004; 238 pp.—A comprehensive and compact survey of robotics and bionics, organized by function; raises questions about distinctions between living and nonliving objects.

Rees, Martin. *Our Final Hour: A Scientist's Warning: How Terror, Error, and Environmental Disaster Threaten Humankind's Future in This Century—on Earth and Beyond.* New York: Basic Books, 2003; 228 pp.—The author of *Our Cosmic Habitat* (2001) describes how the choices we make in the next few decades might decide the fate of life on Earth and beyond.

Illustration Credits

222 Yerkes Observatory
223 © SRW
224 The University of Utah Physics Department
225 Michael W. Friedlander, Washington University, St. Louis
226 Collection of California Institute of Technology; University of California Radiation Laboratory
230 Big Bear Solar Observatory, photo courtesy of R.L. Moore
232 © Roger Ressmeyer/Corbis
233 Corbis Images
234 © David Nance; NASA; © Roger Ressmeyer/Corbis
235 AP/Wide World Photos
236 © David Young-Wolff/PhotoEdit
237 Photo: © Roger Ressmeyer/Corbis; inset: © Corbis
238– NASA
240
241 © Sovfoto/Eastfoto
242 NASA
244– NASA
245
246 Top left: NASA; bottom right: Hulton/Archive by Getty Images
248– NASA
252
253 The Associated Press
254 SW Production/Index Stock Imagery/Picture Quest; © Nick Ut/AP/Wide World Photos
255 Photo courtesy of Minimed Technologies, Sylmar, CA; © Max Aguilera-Hellweg/TimePix
256 PRNews Photo/Sony Electronics Inc./AP/Wide World Photos
257 NASA
258 The Boeing Company
259 NASA
260 NASA
261 Both illustrations: NASA
262 Department of Defense
263 NASA
264 NASA
265 The Everett Collection
266– NASA
269
270 © Roger Ressmeyer/Starlight
272 © Roger Ressmeyer/Starlight
273 Both photos: © Roger Ressmeyer/Starlight
274 Top three photos: National Air & Space Museum; bottom left: Litton Industries; bottom right: UPI/Bettmann Newsphotos
275 Top: UPI/Bettmann Newsphotos; lower left: Republic Aviation Corporation; right: National Air & Space Museum
276 Both photos: ILC Dover
277 NASA/Johnson Space Center
278 Hamilton Standard/Courtesy of the National Air & Space Museum
279 NASA
280 © James Sugar/Black Star
281 NASA
282 Both photos: © Keith Meyers/NYT Pictures
284 Space Commerce Corp.
285 Novosti/Sovfoto
286 NASA; inset: Tass from Sovfoto
287 Top and bottom left: Lovelace Medical Center; bottom right: NASA
289 Both photos: NASA
290 ESA
291 NASA
293 NASA
294 © John T. Barr/Gamma-Liaison
295 NASA
296 NASA
299 ESA
300 NASA
301 Both images: NASA/JPL
302 NASA
304 NASA
307 COMSAT
308 JPL/NASA
310– Photos: © Charles & Ray Eames/The Eames Office
311
312 © Sipa-Press; inset: © Orban/SYGMA
314 Eugene Feldman/NASA
315 NASA
316 © Steven Hunt/The Image Bank
318 © Kevin A. Ward and Alan Clark
319 © Kevin A. Ward and Alan Clark
321 NASA; National Radio Astronomy Observatory
322– Photos: Photofest
323
325 © Kevin A. Ward
326 © Shinobu Hirai/Photonica
327 © Adam Nadel/AP/Wide World Photos
328 © Michael Newman/PhotoEdit
329 The Granger Collection; Brown Brothers
330 Corbis/Bettmann
331 © Bob Daemmrich Photography, Inc./Uniphoto Picture Agency
337 © Shambroom/Photo Researchers

348 © R. Michael Stuckey/Comstock
350 © Marcia W. Griffen/Earth Scenes
424 Mimi Forsyth/Monkmeyer
425 Jan Braunle; Mickey Palmer/DPI
426 Paul Conklin/Monkmeyer
431 Calvin Campbell
432 NASA
433 Tony Duffy
446 NASA
453 © Steve Niedorf Photography/The Image Bank/Getty Images
454 © Andy Sacks/Stone/Getty Images; © Dagli Orti/Musée du Louvre Paris/The Art Archive
455 © Dagli Orti/The Art Archive; Public Record Office London/The Art Archive; The Granger Collection; © Erich Lessing/Art Resource, NY
456 © Monika Graff/The Image Works
457 © Spencer Grant/PhotoEdit
458 © Spencer Grant/PhotoEdit
459 © David Kohl/AP/Wide World Photos
460 © Larry Grant/Taxi/Getty Images
461 © Wilfried Krecichwost/Stone/Getty Images
462 © Israel Talby/ASAP/Woodfin Camp & Associates
463 Photo by Lisa Strong, © 2000 Exploratorium; background image: Dover Publications, Inc.
464 Top two photos: Art Resource, NY; bottom: © James King-Holmes/Science Photo Library/Photo Researchers
465 © Alexander Tsiaras/Stock, Boston Inc./PictureQuest; © Adam Hart-Davis/Science Photo Library/Photo Researchers; background image: Dover Publications, Inc.
466 © Bill Aron/PhotoEdit; The J. Paul Getty Trust
467 © Terrence Moore; © James Hill/Getty Images; © Scott Peterson/Getty Images
468 © Jonathan Blair/Woodfin Camp & Associates; background image: Dover Publications, Inc.
469 © Christopher Chippindale
470 Lessing/Magnum Photos; The Granger Collection
471 © Comstock
474 Musée Condé, Chantilly, France/Giraudon
475 © Michael Holford
476 © John S. Flannery/Bruce Coleman Inc.
477 Both illustrations: Art Resource
478 G. Tomsich/Photo Researchers
479 © Phil Degginger/Color Pic
480 Denver Museum of Natural History; © François Gohier/Photo Researchers
481 © James Joern
482 Michael Newman/PhotoEdit
483 © James Joern
484 © Dr. Paul A. Zahl/Photo Researchers; © François Gohier/Photo Researchers
485 © John Lythgoe/Planet Earth Pictures
488 © Ken Lucas/Planet Earth Pictures
489 © Martin Land/Science Photo Library/Photo Researchers
490– © Steven Kirk/© 1994 The Walt Disney Company. Reprinted with permission of
491 Discover Magazine.
493 © Bill Parsons/© 1996 The Walt Disney Company. Reprinted with permission of Discover Magazine.
494– Top left: Bill Parsons/© 1996 The Walt Disney Company. Reprinted with permis-
495 sion of Discover Magazine; crossover photo: Carl Buell/© 1997 The Walt Disney Company. Reprinted with permission of Discover Magazine.
496 © James L. Amos/Photo Researchers
497 © Steven Kirk/© 1994 The Walt Disney Company. Reprinted with permission of Discover Magazine.
498 Carl Buell/© 1994 The Walt Disney Company. Reprinted with permission of Discover Magazine.
500 Lucasfilm/20th Century Fox/Kobal Collection
501 Kobal Collection; Archive by Getty Images
502 Archive by Getty Images
503 Lucasfilm/20th Century Fox/Kobal Collection; The Everett Collection
504 © Ethan Miller/Getty Images; © Rommel Pecson/The Image Works
505 Digital Art/Corbis
507 © Jim Cole/AP/Wide World Photos
508 © Sangjib Min/Daily Press/AP/Wide World Photos; © Mikael Karlsson/Arresting Images
509 © Ashley Cooper/Corbis; © Michael Schumacher/Amarillo Globe News/AP/Wide World Photos
510 © Don Ryan/AP/Wide World Photos; © Paul Cunningham/The Times Record/AP/Wide World Photos; SNL/DOE/Photo Researchers
511 © Norm Rowan/The Image Works
512 © Ken Kaminesky/Take 2 Productions/Corbis; © Susan Meiselas/Magnum Photos; © Paul Sancya/AP/Wide World Photos
513 © Mikael Karlsson/Arresting Images
514 © Andrew Brookes/Corbis
515 Bayer AG/AP/Wide World Photos
516 © Mikael Karlsson/Arresting Images; © John Richmeier/The Leavenworth Times/AP/Wide World Photos

Cover credits, front: NASA and E. Karkoschka (University of Arizona); clouds background: Digital Stock. Spine: Masterfile. Back: NASA and E. Karkoschka (University of Arizona)

INDEX

ALPHABETICAL INDEX

The index that follows is a complete set index: it covers all the articles found in each of the six volumes of *The New Book of Popular Science*. This index is repeated in its totality in the back of each volume.

Throughout this index, a subject heading that is covered by an entire article is printed in boldface capital letters and is followed by the volume and page numbers, indicating where the article appears in *The New Book of Popular Science*. For example, the entry:

ACCOUNTING 1:453–59

indicates that an article on accounting can be found in volume 1, pages 453 to 459 inclusive. A subject that is covered within an article is printed in boldface capital and lowercase letters, and the volume and specific pages are noted. For example, the entry:

Acetic acid 3:94, 99, 114

indicates that information on acetic acid can be found on pages 94, 99, and 114 of volume 3. In all text references throughout the index, volume numbers are printed in boldface type. Page numbers referring to the entire article about the subject heading are in boldface; other page numbers are in lightface type. Multiple volume and page references to one subject are filed in numerical order.

Illustrations are identified by the abbreviation *illus*. References to the illustrations, as well as to the charts, tables, and diagrams, are filed after all references to the text.

Subjects in this index may be subdivided to make information on specific aspects of the topic readily accessible. These subentries are indented and listed alphabetically below the main entry. The example below has two subentries.

Aerospace engineering 6:20
    aeronautical engineering **3:**192
    composite materials **6:**230–31

Some entries include a brief identification of the subject. The identification, enclosed in parentheses, may note the scientific field in which the term is commonly used, define the subject in a few words, or describe a person's nationality and profession.

Absorption (in physics)
Ada (computer language) **6:**378
Adams, John Couch (English astronomer) **1:**79, 152; **3:**182
American Woodhenge (archaeological site, Missouri) **1:**471

The index includes *see* and *see also* references. *See* references guide the reader from one term to another. They are used for abbreviations, for synonyms, for inverted headings, and for alternative spellings.

Accelerators, Particle *see* Particle accelerators
ALU *see* Arithmetic/logic unit
Amebas *see* Amoebas
Ascorbic acid *see* Vitamin C

See also references direct the reader to related subject entries.

Accidents *see also* Safety
Air *see also* Atmosphere
Astronauts *see also* Cosmonauts
Atomic theory 3:3–4, 304–5 *see also* Atoms

Subjects are filed alphabetically, letter by letter. When a subject heading is made up of more than one word, it is still arranged alphabetically, letter by letter.

Air *see also* Atmosphere
Air-conditioning systems 3:236
    illus. **2:**479
Airglow 2:151–52
Air masses 2:186–88
Airplanes 6:153–60, 164
    air pollution **2:**468
    engines **6:**162–64
Air-traffic-control radar 6:259

A

A380 (aircraft) 6:164
A0620-00 (binary star) 1:212
Aa *see* Block lava
Aardvarks 5:13
illus. 5:12
Aardwolves 5:102
A-arms 6:146
Abalones 4:241
Abdomen
  insects 4:274
  muscles of the body 5:192
  pregnancy 5:300–301
  spiders 4:257
Abductor muscles 5:189
Abell 2256 (galaxy)
  illus. 1:59
Abherents 6:208
AbioCor (artificial heart) 5:504
Abnormal psychology 5:340–41
Aborigines, Australian 2:86
Abscesses 5:207, 236
Abscissas 1:392–93
Abscission 4:72
Absolute magnitude 1:191
  table(s) 1:192
Absolute temperature scale *see*
  Kelvin temperature scale
Absolute values (of numbers)
  1:411–12
Absolute zero 3:89, 136, 190,
  358–59
Absorption (in physics)
  color 3:297–98
  light 3:283
  sound 3:205, 208
Absorption lines 1:87 88
Absorption spectra 3:296
Abstract algebra 1:330
Abstract thinking 5:353
Abyssal plains 2:270
Abyssinian cats
  illus. 5:90
AC *see* Alternating current
Acacias 4:118
Academy of Science (Chicago,
  Illinois) 1:66
Acadian Orogeny 2:73
Acanthocephala 4:202
Acanthodians 1:490; 4:316, 329
Acceleration 3:141, 151
  falling objects 3:153–54
  gravity 3:179
  manned spaceflight 1:250
  Newton's second law 3:156–57
  illus.
    due to gravity 3:151
Accelerator nerves 5:198
Accelerators, Particle *see* Par-
  ticle accelerators
Accelerometers 6:173
Accessory factors *see* Vitamins
Accessory fruits 4:103
Access time (of computers)
  6:363

Accidents *see also* Safety
  Belgian ferry (1987) 6:112
  coal mining 2:353–55
  emergency rooms 5:481
  industrial pollution 2:455
  lightning 2:179
  nuclear reactors 2:372–75
  oil tankers 2:328
ACCOUNTING 1:453–59
Accretion disks 1:212; 2:12–13
ACE inhibitors 5:467
Acela Express (train) 6:130
Acetabulum 5:180
Acetaminophen 5:292
Acetic acid 3:94, 99, 114
Acetone 3:114
Acetylcholine 5:225–26
  myasthenia gravis 5:194
Acetyl coenzyme A (Acetyl
  CoA) 3:437–38
Acetylene 3:110; 6:207
  diagram(s) 3:66
Acetylsalicylic acid *see* Aspirin
Achernar (star) 1:27
Achilles' tendon 5:190
Achlorhydric anemia 5:211
Achromatic lenses 3:291
ACID RAIN 2:124, 172, 463,
  472–76
  coal burning 2:358
  forestry 4:131
  taiga 4:165
  temperate forests 4:148
Acid Rain Program (U.S.) 2:471,
  474, 476
ACIDS 3:94–99, 114
Acid sulfate salt 3:97
Acne 5:267
Acorn cycle 4:147
Acorn worms 4:308–9, 311
  illus. 4:311
Acoustical engineering 3:208
Acoustics *see* Sound
Acousto-Optic Imaging Spec-
  trometer 1:256
Acquired characteristics 3:502
Acromegaly 5:243
Acromion process 5:179
Acrylic resins 5:501
Actin 5:186
Actinides 3:25, 30
Actinium 3:34
Actinobacteria 4:29
Actinomycin A 5:463
ACTIS *see* Advanced Computed
  Tomography Inspection
Activated charcoal *see* Char-
  coal, Activated
Activating system (of nerve net-
  work) 5:406
Activation analysis 3:320
Activation energy 3:58, 60
Active galaxies *see* Galaxies,
  Energetic
Active immunity 5:238
Active transport 3:437
  diagram(s) 3:436

Acupuncture 5:292, 510–11
  veterinary science 4:465
Acute angles 1:369–70
Acute rheumatic fever 5:429
ACVs *see* Air-cushioned vehicles
Ada (computer language) 6:378
ADA (enzyme) *see* Adenosine
  deaminase
Adams, Charles (American
  ecologist) 3:473
Adams, John Couch (English
  astronomer) 1:79, 152;
  3:182
Adam's apple 5:177
Adaptation (in biology)
  animal behavior 4:189–90
  antelopes 5:127
  camels 5:116–17
  cartilaginous fish 4:324
  desert animals 4:169
  desert plants 4:167
  endangered species 2:495
  flowering plants 4:107
  insectivores 5:25
  life characteristics 3:377–78
  lizards 4:357–61
  pinnipeds 5:64
  plants 4:10
  populations and communities
    3:481–82
  wetland plants 4:152
  whales 5:47
Adaptation (in psychology)
  5:358–59
Adaptive optics 1:44, 52
Adaptive radiation
  illus. 3:507
ADD *see* Attention deficit disorder
Addaxes 2:86; 5:129
Addend 1:346
Adder's-tongue ferns 4:81
Addiction, Drug *see* Substance
  abuse
Addison's disease 5:246
Addition 1:346, 353
  binary numerals 1:446, 448–49
  table(s) 1:346
Addition reaction (in chemistry)
  3:110
Additive color mixing 3:298
Additives, Food 6:81–84
  algae 4:50, 53
Additives, Plastic 6:214
Adductor muscles 5:189
Adenine 3:123, 411; 5:309–10
  illus. 3:409
Adenomas 5:244
Adenosine deaminase 5:422
Adenosine triphosphate *see*
  ATP
Adenoviruses 3:392
Adequate Intakes (AIs) 5:390
Adequate Yearly Progress
  (AYP) number 6:327–28
Adhesion 3:76
Adipose capsule (of kidney)
  5:259
Adirondack Mountains 2:472

Adler, Alfred (Austrian psychologist)
illus. **5:**340
Adler Planetarium (Chicago, Illinois) **1:**67
illus. **1:**70, 72
Adobe (building material) **6:**26
Adobe Photoshop 6:274
Adolescence 5:330–32
alcohol use **5:**377
marijuana use **5:**372
tobacco use **5:**377
Adolescent medicine 5:413
Adrenal glands 5:246
illus. **5:**170
Adrenaline (Epinephrine) 3:115; **4:**190; **5:**199, 246
Advanced Camera for Surveys (ACS) 1:49
Advanced Computed Tomography Inspection (ACTIS) 1:254–55
Advanced Coronal Explorer (ACE) 2:158
Advanced Gas Turbine engine 6:219
Advanced materials 6:228–30
Advanced Research Projects Agency (ARPA) 6:303
Advanced X-Ray Astrophysics Facility *see* Chandra X-Ray Observatory
Advection 2:161, 163
Adventitious roots 4:68, 80
Advertising 6:308
Aeolipile 6:96
illus. **6:**97
Aeration (water purification) **2:**444, 448; **6:**56
illus. **2:**443, 462
Aeration, Zone of 2:115
Aerial photography 1:464
Aerobic bacteria 2:487; **4:**30
Aerobic exercise 5:398, 401, 404
Aerobic system (energy use) **5:**400
illus. **3:**434
Aerobraking
illus. **1:**300
Aerodynamics *see* Fluid dynamics
Aerogel-based insulation 1:255
Aerolites *see* Stone meteorites
Aeronautics *see* Aviation
Aerosol spray cans 3:13
Aerospace engineering 6:20
aeronautical engineering **3:**192
composite materials **6:**230–31
Aerospace planes 1:261–62
illus. **1:**261
Affective disorders 5:351, 466
Afferent fibers 5:224
Afferent limbs 5:227
Afforestation 4:129
Afghanistan 2:52, 211

Africa
AIDS **5:**441, 444, 446
forests **4:**126, 128
grasslands **4:**140–43
human fossils **1:**479
plateaus **2:**80
wilderness areas **2:**513
wind erosion **2:**427
illus. **2:**76; **4:**141
African-Americans *see* Blacks
African buffalo 5:134
African civets 5:100
African crested porcupines 5:42–43
African elephants 5:103, 105–6
African hunting dogs 5:82
illus. **5:**81
African linsangs 5:101
African pygmy squirrels 5:41
African rock pythons 4:370
African sand foxes 5:83
African sleeping sickness *see* Sleeping sickness
African wild asses 5:110
Afrovenator **1:**494
Afterbirth 5:304
Afterburners 6:106, 163
Afterdamp 2:354
Agar 4:53
Agassiz, Louis (Swiss-American naturalist) **4:**313
Agave (Century plant) 4:298
Aged *see* Old age
Agene (Nitrogen trichloride) 6:83
Agent Orange 2:463
Agglutinin 5:209
Agglutinogen 5:209
Aggregate fruits 4:103
Aggression 5:155
Aging 3:466–68; **5:**333–34 *see also* Old age
cancer **5:**433
exercise benefits **5:**402
gray hair **5:**266
infertility **5:**306
osteoarthritis **5:**427–28
Agoutis 5:45
Agranulocytosis 5:212
Agribusiness 6:58, 60
Agricultural-research stations 4:268
Agriculture
acid rain **2:**476
antibiotics **3:**506
beekeeping **4:**287
biofuels **2:**396–97
botany **4:**7
butterflies and moths **4:**305
climates of the world **2:**209
conservation **2:**408–9, 411–12
ecosystems **2:**454
endangered species **2:**502
engineering today **6:**20
entomology **4:**270
erosion **2:**123–24, 431–32
fish farming and **6:**90

genetics **6:**67–75
genetic technology **3:**420–21, 423
grasslands **4:**139, 142–43
horticulture and agronomy **4:**170–75
insect pests **4:**268
microbiology **3:**449
modern farms **6:**57–66
natural gas uses **2:**345
New Stone Age **6:**4–5
plant pathology **4:**5
radioisotopes **3:**320–21
rain forests **4:**159–61
silviculture **4:**86, 128–30
space technology **1:**256
veterinary science **4:**465
water pollution **2:**458
zoological research **4:**182
illus.
reclaimed desert **2:**408
space science **1:**234
Agriculture, U.S. Department of 5:388–89
Agroforestry 4:131
AGRONOMY 4:170–75
Agulhas Current 2:240
AI *see* Airborne interception radar; Artificial intelligence
AIDS (Acquired Immune Deficiency Syndrome) 5:239, 441–46
blood diseases **5:**212
diseases that "jump" from animals to humans **4:**468
infectious diseases **5:**430–31
substance abuse **5:**375
Ailanthus moths 4:307
Ailerons 6:159
illus. **6:**160
Air *see also* Atmosphere
circulation **2:**181–88
gases and their properties **3:**68
insulating properties **3:**233–34
pollution *see* Air pollution
solution **3:**79
water vapor **3:**69
weight of **3:**183
Air bags 6:134–35
illus. **3:**139
Airborne interception radar 6:258
Airbus Industrie 6:164
Air-conditioning systems 3:236
illus. **2:**479
Air-cooled engines 6:143
Aircraft, Human-powered 6:94–95
illus. **6:**91
Aircraft carriers
illus. **6:**254
Air-cushioned vehicles (ACVs) 6:116
Airfoils 6:95
Airglow 2:151–52
Air Jordans
illus. **1:**254
Airlift pumps 2:441

Airliners *see* Airplanes
Air masses 2:186–88
Airplane condensation trails
  2:163–64
Airplanes 6:153–60, 164
  aerospace engineering 6:20
  AeroSpace Plane 1:261–62
  air pollution 2:468
  engines 6:162–64
  human-powered 6:94–95
  jet engines 6:105–6
  pressurized cabins 2:149–50
  wing lift 3:184
  illus.
    airplane factory 6:185
    basic parts 6:159
    crop dusting 2:461
    early commercial airliner 6:9
    jet propulsion 6:105
    wing lift 3:185
Air plants *see* Epiphytes
AIR POLLUTION 2:451, 466–71
  automobiles 6:134
  carbon cycle 4:21
  climate change 2:220, 477–82
  coal burning 2:358
  fossil fuels 2:306
  gases and their properties 3:73
  global warming 2:480
  mosses' sensitivity to 4:60
  respiratory diseases 5:222
  waste disposal 2:397, 484
  weather modification 2:145–46
Airports 2:145; 6:128
Air pressure *see* Atmospheric
  pressure
Air pump 3:189
  illus. 3:190
Air resistance *see* Drag
Air roots 4:153
Air sacs *see* Alveoli
Airships *see* Dirigibles
Air-traffic-control radar 6:259
Akashi Kaikyo (bridge, Japan)
  6:50
Akron (airship) 6:151
Aksum (Ethiopia) 6:18
Alaska
  earthquake (1964) 2:52
  Exxon Valdez 2:328, 465
  glaciers 2:96–97
  oil drilling 2:307; 4:165
  pipelines 2:329
  seismic warning center 2:259
  Tongass National Forest 4:158,
    160
  volcanoes 2:433
  illus.
    glaciers 2:418
    natural gas drilling 2:338
    pipelines 2:330, 343
    Valdez 2:331
Alaska Current 2:241
Alaska Lands Act (U.S., 1980)
  2:515
Alaska Pipeline *see* Trans-
  Alaska Pipeline

Albatrosses 4:396, 446
  illus. 4:445
Albedo 1:115, 126
Albert (prince of Monaco) 2:236
Albert 1 (monkey sent into
  space) 1:246
Alberta
  Athabasca tar sands 2:325
  Banff Springs 2:64
  Wood Buffalo National Park
    5:133
Albinism 3:503
Alcantara Bridge (Spain) 6:50
Alchemy 3:2–3
Alcock, John (English aviator)
  6:155
Alcohol (in beverages)
  cancer 5:436
  excretory system 5:260–61
  fermentation 4:40
  fetal alcohol syndrome 5:301
  laws 5:377
  stroke-risk reduction 5:234
  substance abuse 5:369, 371,
    375–76
Alcoholics Anonymous 5:376
Alcohols (in chemistry) 3:113
Aldebaran (star) 1:32, 192
Aldehydes 2:467; 3:114
Alderflies 4:280
Alderney, Race of 2:248
Aldosterone 5:246
Aldosteronism 5:246
Aldrin, Edwin E., Jr. (American
  astronaut) 1:245
Aleppo pines 4:90
Aleutian Islands 2:59, 281
Aleutian Trench 2:269
Alexander the Great 6:117–18
Alfvén, Hannes (Swedish scientist) 1:22
ALGAE 4:46–53
  coral reefs 2:285, 287
  early classification of 4:183
  energy source 2:398
  eutrophication 2:414, 460–61;
    4:124
  geysers 2:65
  lichens 4:43
  photosynthesis 4:18
  plant evolution 4:12
  sandy-shore flora 4:137
  sloths covered with 5:34
  water supply problems 2:412,
    442–43
  illus. 2:440
ALGEBRA 1:329–30, 332,
  352–65
  analytic geometry 1:391–400
  set theory 1:441–43
Algenib (star) 1:30
Algin 4:53
Algol (star) 1:30, 32
Algorithms (in computer programming) 6:379
Algor mortis 3:469
Alien Nation (TV program)
  illus. 1:323

Alimentary canal 5:248
Alkali metals 3:29–30
Alkaline-earth metals 3:30
Alkalis *see* Bases
Alkanes 3:111
Alkenes 3:111–12
Al-Kwarizmi, Mohammed ibn
  Musa (Persian mathemati-
  cian) 1:353
Alkylation 2:332
Alkynes 3:112
Allagash Wilderness Waterway
  (Maine) 2:511
  illus. 2:510
Allan Hills meteorite 4:31
Alleghenian Orogeny 2:74
Alleles 3:409, 500–501
Allen, Paul G. (American entre-
  preneur) 1:263, 324
Allende meteorite 1:171–72
Allergens 5:241, 447–49
ALLERGIES 5:447–49
  antivenins 4:367
  genetically engineered foods
    6:75
  immune system 5:241
  sulfites 6:83
Alligator lizards 4:358–59
Alligators 2:505; 4:380, 382–84
  life span 5:324
  illus. 4:381–82
Alligator snappers 4:378–79
Alligator weed 4:269
Allison, Rhae Hurrle (American
  aviator) 1:288–89
All-or-none response (in physiol-
  ogy) 5:226
Allosaurus 1:494
ALLOYS 3:79; 6:174–84
Alluvial aprons 2:424
Alluvial fans 2:85, 104, 424
Alluvial plains 2:76, 103
Alluvium 2:103
Alpacas 5:117
Alpenhorn
  illus. 3:203
Alpha blockers 5:467
Alpha Centauri (star) 1:27
Alpha Cephei (star) 1:112
Alpha-linolenic acid 5:382
Alpha particles 3:126, 317
  cosmic rays 1:228
  particle detectors 6:359
  illus. 3:318
Alpha radiation 2:363; 3:126–28
Alpha submarines 6:122
Alphecca (star) 1:29
Alpheratz (star) 1:30
Alpide belt 2:47
Alpine club moss 4:77
Alpine glaciers 2:93, 96–99
  illus. 2:95
Alpine habitat 3:498; 4:162
  illus. 4:165
Alpine pennycress 3:129
Alps 2:70, 282
  glacial erosion 2:123

Alps (cont.)
glaciers **2:**96, 98
railroad tunnels **6:**48
resort development **2:**456
wind **2:**186
illus. **2:**67
Altair (star) **1:**30, 192
**ALTERNATE ENERGY
SOURCES 2:**305–7, 332,
395–99
Alternate leaves 4:73
Alternating current 3:254–55;
6:247
generator **2:**311–12, 317
high-speed trains **6:**130
illus.
generator **3:**253
**Alternation of generations
3:**455; **4:**9, 15
aphids **4:**276
bryophytes **4:**59–61, 63
coelenterates **4:**218
conifers **4:**87
ferns **4:**80–81
horsetails **4:**75–76
Alternative medicine *see*
Complementary and alter-
native medicine
Altimeters 6:258–59
Altiplano (plateau, Bolivia) **2:**80
Altitude
atmospheric pressure **2:**149–50
mammals' adaptations to **5:**6–7
precipitation **2:**170
Altocumulus clouds 2:165
illus. **2:**164
Altostratus clouds 2:165
illus. **2:**164
Altricial birds 4:396
ALU *see* Arithmetic/logic unit
Alum 2:444
Alumina *see* Aluminum oxide
Aluminum 3:31, 34
density **3:**11
heat of fusion **3:**228
metals and alloys **6:**183
Nd:YAG laser **5:**488
**Aluminum oxide (Alumina)
6:**183, 218
Aluminum sulfate 2:436, 444
Alvarez, Luis (American physi-
cist) **1:**497; **6:**355
illus. **1:**173
Alvarez, Walter (American scien-
tist) **1:**497
illus. **1:**173
Alveoli (singular **Alveolus**)
5:202, 217, 219, 261
illus. **5:**216
Alvin (submersible) **2:**224, 276–
79; **4:**314; **6:**123–24
illus. **6:**123
Alzheimer's disease 5:233, 334,
353–54, 384
AM *see* Amplitude modulation
Amalgamation 6:177
Amanitas 4:44
Amateur astronomy 1:14–15

Amazing Stories (magazine)
1:501
Amazon Basin (Brazil) **2:**75, 77
rain forests **4:**161
Amazon dolphins 5:60
Amazonian manatees *see* Brazil-
ian manatees
Amazon River
tidal bore **2:**247
Amber 3:244
fossils **1:**484; **2:**139
illus. **2:**138
Ambergris 5:52
Ambivalence 5:350
Amblypods 1:489
Ambrosia beetles 4:299
Amebas *see* Amoebas
American alligators 4:384
**American Association for the
Advancement of Science
(AAAS) 3:**371; **6:**321
American badgers 5:96–97
American bison 5:132–33
American black bears 5:74
American Cancer Society 5:432
American chestnut trees 4:5,
148
American crocodiles 4:384
**American Dietetic Association
(ADA) 5:**390
American elk 5:120–21
American flycatchers 4:448–49
American golden plovers 4:437
**American Heart Association
(AHA) 5:**403
American kestrels 4:418
American larches *see* Tama-
racks
**American Museum of Natural
History** (New York City)
1:483
American nightingales *see* Her-
mit thrushes
American pine martens 5:95
American Revolution
submarines **6:**118–19
American robins 4:454
illus. **4:**447
**American Society for Engineer-
ing Education (ASEE)
6:**15, 19
**American Standard Code for
Information Interchange**
see ASCII
**American Standards Associa-
tion numbers** *see* ASA
numbers
**Americans with Disabilities Act
(ADA) 5:**368
American toads 4:348
**American whooping cranes
2:**502; **4:**438
American Woodhenge (archaeo-
logical site, Missouri) **1:**471
Americium 3:34
Amides 3:115
Amines 3:114–15

Amino acids 3:121–22
DNA and RNA **3:**412, 415
life, origin of **3:**381
meteorites **1:**173
organic acids **3:**114
proteins **5:**379
pyridoxine **5:**384
Amino group 3:114, 121
Amiodarone 5:467
Ammeters 3:257–58
Ammonia 3:69, 83, 94
atmosphere **2:**148
chemical bonding **3:**52, 65
chemical industry **6:**205, 208
comets **1:**161
excretory system **5:**258
Jupiter **1:**136
laboratory preparation **3:**137
life, origin of **3:**380
molecules in space **1:**318
nitrogen cycle **3:**491
outer planets **1:**321
production **3:**241
Saturn **1:**140
water purification **2:**446
diagram(s) **3:**52, 66–67
illus.
laboratory preparation **3:**136
Ammonium chloride 3:67, 87,
105
Ammonium hydroxide 3:99
Ammonium ion 3:67
Ammonium sulfate 2:360, 473;
3:67
Amnesia 5:352, 362
Amniocentesis 5:303
sonography used with **5:**454
illus. **5:**302, 418
Amnion 5:297, 304
illus. **5:**296
Amniotic cavity 5:297
Amniotic fluid 4:381
Amobarbital 5:373
Amoebas 3:451; **4:**209–11
illus. **4:**206–7, 210; **5:**217
Amoebic dysentery 4:209
Amorphous solids 3:12, 89
Amperage 2:317
Ampere (unit of measurement)
3:256
Ampère, André Marie (French
physicist) **3:**256, 264
illus. **2:**313
Amphetamines 5:373
AMPHIBIANS 4:205, 340–42
acid rain **2:**476
extinct species **2:**496–97
frogs **4:**343–48
genetic variation **3:**505
herpetology **4:**336–39
metamorphosis **4:**187
ozone layer depletion **2:**482
pets **4:**490
prehistoric animals **1:**488, 492
reproduction **3:**457
salamanders **4:**349–51
wetlands **4:**154
zoo exhibits **4:**476

Amphibious vehicles 6:116
Amphipods 4:254
Amphotericin B 5:474
Ampicillin 5:463
Amplifiers 6:248, 290
Amplitude (of waves) 3:196
  light waves 3:324
  ocean waves 2:251
  pendulum motion 3:161
  sound waves 3:199
Amplitude modulation (AM)
    6:248, 288–89
  illus. 6:289
Amtrak trains 6:130
  illus. 6:129
Amylase 5:252
Amyloid precursor protein
    5:233
Amyotrophic lateral sclerosis
    5:233, 320
Anabaena 4:33
  illus. 4:30
Anacondas 4:355, 370
  illus. 4:368
Anaerobic bacteria 4:27, 30, 34
  methane 2:478
  sewage purification 2:488
Anaerobic system (energy use)
    3:435–36, 438; 5:400–401
  see also Fermentation
  illus. 3:434
Analgesics 5:291–92
Analog computers 6:362
Analog to digital (A/D) conver-
    sion 6:284
Anal sphincter 5:255
ANALYTICAL CHEMISTRY 3:7,
    129–33
  forensic science 1:515
  spectroscopy 3:327–28
  titration 3:98–99
ANALYTIC GEOMETRY 1:330,
    333, 391–400
Anaphase 3:442, 445
Anaphylaxis 5:410
Anasazi (Native American cul-
    ture) 2:436
Anatolepsis 1:490
Anatomy 4:179
ANATOMY, Human 5:153–54,
    161–72
  blood and lymphatic system
    5:205–14
  bones 5:173–84
  brain and nervous system
    5:223–34
  digestive system 5:248–56
  ears 5:274–77
  endocrine system 5:242–47
  excretory system 5:257–62
  eyes 5:268–73
  heart and circulatory system
    5:195–204
  muscular system 5:185–94
  respiratory system 5:215–22
  skin 5:263–67
  teeth 5:278–82
Anchovies 2:237; 4:332; 6:89

Andean condors 4:416
Andean highland cats 5:92
Anderson, Carl D. (American
    physicist) 1:228–29
  illus. 1:226
Andes Mountains 2:43, 68, 70,
    214
  volcanoes 2:59
Andrew (hurricane, 1992) 2:199
Androgen 5:246
Andromeda (constellation) 1:30
  see also Great Nebula in
    Andromeda
Androsterone 5:467
Anechoic chambers
  illus. 3:198
Anemia 5:210–11, 386
Anemometers 2:188
Anemonefish
  illus. 4:176
Aneroid barometers 3:70, 187
  illus. 3:186
Anesthesia 5:412, 465–66,
    477–78
  dentistry 5:469
  pain relief 5:291–92
  illus. 5:478
Angel dust (drug) see PCP
Angel Falls (Venezuela) 2:422
Angina pectoris 5:439
  transdermal skin patches 5:470
Anglograms 5:439
Angiographs
  illus. 5:450
Angioplasty 5:439, 490–91
  drug delivery technology 5:473
  illus. 5:491
Angiosperms see Flowering
    plants
Angiotensin-converting enzyme
    inhibitors see ACE inhibi-
    tors
Angle of incidence 3:284
Angle of reflection 3:284
Angle of refraction 3:284
Anglerfish 4:194, 333–34
  illus. 4:332
Angles (in geometry) 1:369–70,
    380–81
  non-Euclidean geometry
    1:402–3
  trigonometry 1:387–89
Angular momentum 3:308
Anhingas 4:446
ANIMAL BEHAVIOR 4:182,
    188–97
  ants 4:283–84
  arachnids 4:258–63
  birds 4:386, 396
  dolphins 5:57–59
  earthquake precursors 2:54
  social life of mammals 5:10
  zoo activities 4:472–74
Animal communication 4:191
  ants 4:283
  bees 4:288
  dolphins 5:56, 58–59

  frogs 4:343, 345–46
  primates 5:147, 149
  whales 5:47
Animal curators 4:475
Animal experimentation 4:338
  dissection 3:514–15
  genetic technology 5:475
  space travel 1:246–47
Animal migration 4:189, 191
  biorhythms 3:380
  birds 4:154, 394
  Canada geese 4:441
  cranes 4:438–39
  fish 4:333
  hydropower dams 2:380
  magnetic field of Earth 3:267
  monarch butterflies 4:306
  plovers 4:437
  sandpipers 4:436
  terns 4:435
  illus. 3:266
Animal proteins see Complete
    proteins
Animal psychology see Animal
    behavior
Animal rescue 4:473, 490
Animal research 4:338–39, 468
ANIMALS 4:183–87 see also
    specific animals and animal
    groups
  breeding 6:75
  classification 3:397–98; 4:198–
    205
  climates of the past 2:215–16
  consumers in ecosystems
    2:453
  deep-sea animals 2:222, 271–
    72, 278
  defenses see Defense mecha-
    nisms
  desert life 2:86; 4:169
  embryology 3:460–62
  endangered species 2:493–505
  fastest runner 5:89
  fossils 1:484–89
  geologic record 2:19, 21
  grasslands 4:140
  pain 5:292
  pets 4:480–90
  plant compared with animal
    4:187
  polar regions 2:90, 92
  prehistoric animals 1:490–99
  rain forest 4:158
  reproduction 3:456–57
  seed dispersal 4:99
  tundra and taiga 4:164
  veterinary science 4:464–68
  zoology 3:372–73; 4:178–82
  zoos 4:469–79
  diagram(s)
    cell structure 3:427
Animal shelters 4:490
Animal welfare 4:468
  zoos 4:470–72, 474
Animism 5:156
Anions 3:31, 50, 63, 97, 102
Anis (birds) 4:402

Ankles 5:181
Ankylosaurs 1:496
Annapolis Basin tidal-power
    plant (Canada) 2:399
Annealing 6:182
ANNELIDS 4:202, **242–45**, 249
Annuals (plants) 3:466; 4:10,
    107, 136, 168
Annular eclipses 1:118, 178
Anodes 3:102; 6:247–48
    illus. 6:249–50
Anole lizards 4:195–96, 358–59,
    361–62
Anomalies (in seismology) 2:54
Anorexia nervosa 5:355
Anoxygenic photosynthesis
    4:28
Anseriformes 4:398, 433,
    440–43
Answering machines 6:244
Antabuse 5:376
Antagonistic muscles 5:189
Antarctic Drift see West Wind
    Drift
Antarctic Peninsula 2:91
Antarctic regions 2:88, 91–92
    climates of the past 2:217–18
    climatology 2:146
    deserts 2:81
    global warming 2:480
    icebergs 2:261–62
    ice pack 2:263
    ice sheet 2:93–94, 97, 218
    meteorites 1:173; 4:31
    ocean currents 2:237, 239
    ozone hole 2:153–54, 482
    illus. 2:96, 480
Antarctic Treaty 2:92
Antares (star) 1:30, 192
Anteaters 5:15, 33–35
    illus. 5:12, 15
ANTELOPE 5:126–31
Antelopine wallaroos 5:18
Antennae 4:274
    beetles 4:291
    butterflies and moths 4:303,
        306
    crustaceans 4:248
Antenna pigments 4:22
Antennas, Microwave
    illus. 2:389
Antennas, Radar 6:254, 256
Antennas, Radio 6:289–90
Antennas, Television 6:294–95
    illus. 6:295
Antheridia 4:61, 63, 76, 81
Anthers 4:101
Anthocyanin 4:18
Anthodites 2:128, 131
Anthozoa 4:200
Anthracite 2:347–48, 356–57,
    360, 445
Anthrax 3:447; 5:424
    illus. 3:451
Anthropology 1:481, 514–15
Antibiotics 5:460, 463–64
    bacteria 3:453; 4:34

cells 3:426–27
ears 5:277
fungi 4:38
infectious diseases 5:431
microbiology 3:447–48
organ transplant recipients
    5:241
resistance of bacteria to 3:506
Antibodies 5:237–38
    agglutinins 5:209
    AIDS 5:442–44
    allergies 5:447–49
    blood plasma 5:206
    B lymphocytes 5:207
    lymphatic system 5:214
    mother to fetus 5:300
    organ transplants 5:497
    resistance to infection 5:426
    virus infection 3:393
Anticlines 2:324
    illus. 2:37
Anticoagulants 5:234, 467
Anticonvulsants 5:466–67
Antidepressants 5:356, 376, 466
    pain relief 5:292
Antidiuretic hormones 5:243–44
Antielectrons see Positrons
Antifreeze 3:229; 6:142
Antigens 5:236–37, 241, 442,
    471
    agglutinogens 5:209
    organ transplants 5:497
Antihistamine drugs 5:449
Antihydrogen 3:21
Anti-inflammatory drugs 5:449
Antilles Current 2:240
Antilogarithms 1:361
Antimatter 3:21, 308
Antimony 3:29, 31–32, 34
Antineutrinos 3:309, 338
Antineutrons 3:21
Antioxidants
    food additives 6:81
    Vitamin C 5:387
    Vitamin E 5:384
Antiparticles 3:21, 307–8
Antiperistalsis 5:252
Antiprotons 3:21
Antipsychotic drugs 5:356, 466
Antiquarks 3:311
Antiquities trafficking 1:467–68
Antiretroviral drugs 5:239, 465
Antiroll (Antisway) bars 6:146
Antiseptics 5:477
Antisocial personality 5:353
Antitrade winds 2:184
Antivenin 4:367
Antiviral drugs 5:445, 465
Antivirus software 6:3977
Antlers 5:119–23
Ant lions 4:280
Antoinette IV (airplane) 6:153
Ants 4:280–85
    anteaters' diet 5:34
    communication 4:191
    defense mechanisms 4:194
    feeding behavior 4:194

    illus.
        leaf-cutter ants 4:284
        milking aphids 4:283
        queen and slaves 4:283
        replete 4:284
        worker ant 4:282
Antshrikes
    illus. 4:450
Anus 5:254
Anvil (in the ear) 5:275, 509
    illus. 3:205; 5:276
Anxiety disorders 5:350–51, 356
Aorta 5:195, 202
    illus. 5:168–69
Aortic valve 5:198–99
Apatosaurus 1:495
Apertures
    cameras 6:265–66
    telescopes 1:44
Apes 5:138, 143–45, 147
    compared to humans 5:153,
        155
Apgar, Virginia (American physi-
    cian)
    illus. 5:326
Aphanites 2:134
Aphelion 1:110
Aphids 3:456–57; 4:194, 269,
    276, 284
    illus. 4:283
Aphragmabacteria 4:29
Aphrodite Terra (feature on
    Venus) 1:100
Apical meristems 3:463; 4:15,
    66, 69, 71, 88
Apicomplexa 4:211–12
Apnea 5:409
Apocrine glands 5:265
Apodiformes 4:399–400
Apogamy 4:83
Apogee 1:304
Apoidea 4:285
Apollonius of Perga (Greek
    mathematician) 1:377
Apollo program 1:239, 244–47
    fatal fire 1:239, 274
    Moon 1:123–24, 298
    space suits 1:273–75
    illus.
        command module 1:244
        lunar landing 1:121, 245
        space suits 1:275
Apollo-Soyuz Test Project
    (1975) 1:247–48
Apoptosis 3:470
Appalachian Mountains 2:44,
    70, 72–74, 282
    streams and valleys 2:425
Appalachian Plateau 2:73, 80
Appalachian Revolution (geol-
    ogy) 1:488
Apparent focus see Virtual focus
Apparent images see Virtual
    images
Apparent magnitude see Magni-
    tude
Apparent motion (illusion) 5:339
Appendicular skeleton 5:174

Appendix *see* Vermiform appendix

Appert, Nicolas (French scientist) 6:79

Appetite 5:255

Appian Way (road, Italy)
illus. 6:43

Apple-blossom weevils 4:299

Apples 6:84
illus. 4:170, 172

Appliances, Household *see* Household appliances

Application programs 6:372

Applications Technology Satellite 1:309

Applied entomology 4:268, 270

Apprenticeships 6:12

Apterygota 4:278

Aquaculture 2:407; 4:314; 6:89–90
oyster farming 4:236, 238
veterinary science 4:465

Aqua-Lung 2:224

Aquariums 4:314, 470, 472, 474, 476
illus. 4:467, 473

Aquarius (constellation) 1:32

Aquatic food chain
illus. 3:490

Aquatic genets 5:100

Aquatic plants 4:137

Aquatic rats 5:43

Aqueducts 2:442; 6:7
Rome, ancient 2:436; 6:17, 52–53
illus. 2:435; 6:17, 34

Aqueous humor 5:271

Aqueous solutions 3:55

Aquicludes 2:114

Aquifers 2:86, 114, 117–19, 409–10, 440–41

Aquila (constellation) 1:30, 292

Arabian baboons *see* Hamadryas baboons

Arabian Desert 2:83

Arabian oryx 4:477; 5:129–30
illus. 4:477

Arabian Sea 2:196, 199, 234

Arabic numeral system *see* Hindu-Arabic numeral system

Arabic science and invention
algebra 1:330, 353
geography 2:298
numerals 1:344

Arabsat 1:310

ARACHNIDS 4:203, 247–48, 256–63

Arachnoid 5:231

Aragonite 2:127–28

Aral Sea 2:108, 451–52

Aramids 6:229

Araucaria 4:159

Arborvitae 4:89

Arcella 4:210

Archaea 4:29, 34–35

Archaebacteria 3:383; 4:27, 34–35
cell dynamics 3:434
cell structure 3:426
classification 3:399
illus. 3:376, 433

Archaeoastronomy 1:472

Archaeognatha 4:278

ARCHAEOLOGY 1:462–68
deep-sea exploration 2:277, 279
illus. 6:2

Archaeopteryx 1:481–82, 489, 496–97; 4:390–91, 398
illus. 1:496

Arch bridges 6:50
illus. 6:49

Arch dams 6:52
illus. 6:55

Archegonia 4:61, 63, 76, 81, 87

Archerfish
illus. 4:193

Arches (in architecture) 6:33
illus. 6:34

Arches (of the feet) 5:182

Arches (rock formations) 2:85, 120, 418

Arches National Park (Utah) 2:85

Archimedes (Greek mathematician) 1:66, 330; 2:381
illus. 1:329

Archimedes' principle 3:190
illus. 3:191

Architectural engineering 6:20

Archosaurians 4:380

Arc lamps 2:320

Arcs (parts of circles) 1:369, 402

Arctic foxes 5:5, 83

Arctic gyrfalcons 4:419

Arctic hares 5:38

Arctic National Wildlife Refuge (Alaska) 4:164–65
energy 2:307
petroleum 2:329
wilderness 2:515

Arctic Ocean 2:88, 229, 235, 241, 260–61

Arctic regions 2:88–90
climates of the past 2:219
global warming 2:480
groundwater 2:116
ice pack 2:262–63
jet streams 2:150
lichens 4:43
ozone depletion 2:482
soil management 2:412
tundra 4:162–64
illus. 2:211

Arctic right whales *see* Bowhead whales

Arctic terns 4:394, 435

Arcturus (star) 1:29, 192

Ardipithecus ramidus 5:160

Area
circle 1:375
cylinder 1:382
prism 1:381
similar solid 1:385
sphere 1:385
table(s) 6:425

Arecibo Observatory (Puerto Rico) 1:13, 42–44, 56, 325
pulsar found with planets 1:318
illus. 1:55; 6:261

Arenal (volcano, Costa Rica)
illus. 2:70

Areola 5:294, 299

Arêtes 2:98

Argentavis magnificens 4:391

Argentina
genetic identification of missing children 3:400
pampa 2:78; 4:140–41
Patagonian desert 2:83
illus. 2:76, 82

Argentinosaurus 1:495
illus. 1:493

Argo (underwater sled) 2:277, 279

Argon 2:149; 3:33–34, 68
insulating properties 3:234
lasers 5:488; 6:351

Argonauts *see* Paper nautiluses

Argus pheasant 4:425

Ariane (rocket) 1:311

Arid climates 2:214

Ariel (moon of Uranus) 1:150

Aries (constellation) 1:32

Aristarchus (Moon crater) 1:120–21

Aristarchus of Samos (Greek astronomer) 1:473

Aristolochia plants 4:158

Aristotle (Greek philosopher)
animal behavior 4:188
astronomy, history of 1:11–12
atmospheric science 2:142
biology, history of 3:367, 369
classification of living things 3:395; 4:199
dolphins 5:55
early underwater craft 6:117
earthquakes 2:7, 47
fish, study of 4:312–13
herpetology 4:337
life, characteristics of 3:375
ornithology 4:386
physics, history of 3:141
psychology, history of 5:336
zoology 4:179
illus. 1:11; 4:200

ARITHMETIC 1:328–29, 332, 346–51
binary numerals 1:446–50
computers 6:362
logarithms 1:360

Arithmetic/logic unit 6:365, 370

Arithmetic progression 1:362

Arizona
Glen Canyon Dam 6:56
Lake Saguaro 2:439
Meteor Crater 1:121; 2:110
sand dunes 2:429

Arizona (cont.)
wilderness areas **2:**511–12
illus.
Barringer Crater **1:**171
Grand Canyon **2:**15, 135
plant communities **4:**132
Arizona-Sonora Desert Museum
4:477
Arkansas
climate **2:**211
Hot Springs National Park **2:**64
Arkwright, Richard (English
inventor) **6:**189
Arlandes, François Laurent d'
(French aviator) **6:**149–50
Armadillos 4:194; **5:**33, 35
illus. **5:**9
Armatures 3:254
Armenia
earthquakes **2:**52
Armillaria gallica **4:**37
Armillaria ostoyae **4:**37
Armillary spheres 1:66
Arms (of the body) **5:**179
artificial *see* Artificial arms
muscles of the body **5:**192
reattaching severed limbs
5:410, 479
illus. **5:**178
Arms, Robot 6:198–99
Armstrong, Neil A. (American
astronaut) **1:**245
Army ants *see* Driver ants
Armyworms 4:305, 307
Aromatic compounds 3:112–13
ARPANET (computer network)
6:303, 385
illus. **6:**305
Arrhythmias 5:440, 467, 505
Arsenic 3:29, 31–32, 34
photovoltaic cells **2:**388
radioisotope tracers **3:**319
water pollution **2:**463–64
ART *see* Assisted reproductive
technology
Art 1:3
Artemis, Temple of (Ephesus,
Greece) **1:**463
Arteries 5:195–96, 202, 204
aging **3:**468
illus. **5:**169, 196
Arterioles 5:202
Artesian wells 2:117
ARTHRITIS 5:183, **427–29**
illus. **5:**288
ARTHROPODS 4:203–4, **246–49**
arachnids **4:**256–63
crustaceans **4:**250–55
infectious diseases **5:**428
insects **4:**272–76
myriapods **4:**264–65
Arthroscopy 5:480
Artificial arms 5:502–3
illus. **5:**500, 502
Artificial blood *see* Synthetic
blood
ARTIFICIAL BODY PARTS
5:500–509

Artificial bone 5:459
Artificial ears 5:507–8
Artificial elements 3:17
Artificial eyes 5:507–8
Artificial hands 5:502–3
illus. **5:**501; **6:**21
Artificial hearts 5:504–5
illus. **5:**504
Artificial hips 5:503–4
illus. **5:**183, 503
Artificial insemination 5:306
veterinary science **4:**467–68
Artificial intelligence (AI) 6:202,
301, 373–74
Artificial joints 5:428, 501,
503–4
Artificial kidney machines
5:262, 506
illus. **5:**499, 507
Artificial knees 5:503
Artificial legs 5:501, 503
Artificial reefs 2:287
Artificial respiration 5:222
illus. **5:**219
Artificial satellites *see* Satellites,
Artificial
Artificial teeth 5:282, 509
Artiodactyls 5:13
bison, buffalo, and oxen
5:132–35
camels and llamas **5:**116–17
deer family **5:**118–23
giraffes and okapis **5:**124–25
pigs and hippopotamuses
5:114–15
ASA numbers 6:271
Asbestos 2:469; **5:**436
Asbestosis 2:469
Ascending colon 5:254
Ascension Island (Atlantic
Ocean) **2:**283
Asch, Solomon (American psychologist) **5:**340
Aschelminthes 4:201
ASCII (American Standard Code
for Information Inter-
change) 6:364
Ascocarps 4:40
Ascorbic acid *see* Vitamin C
Ascospores 3:455; **4:**42
Aseptic technique (in surgery)
5:477
Asexual reproduction 3:452
algae **4:**48–49
bacteria **4:**31–32
coelenterates **4:**217–19
cyanobacteria **4:**33
fungi **4:**38, 40–42
insects **4:**276
plants **4:**15
sponges **4:**215–16
spores **4:**62
vertebrates **3:**457
Ash (residue)
acid rain **2:**475
air pollution **2:**466–67
coal **2:**346
volcanic *see* Volcanic ash

Asia
AIDS **5:**441, 444, 446
grasslands **4:**140–41
monsoons **2:**183
waste disposal **2:**486
Asian elephants 5:103, 105–6
life span **5:**324
Asian water buffalo *see* Water
buffalo
Asian wild asses *see* Kulans;
Onagers
Asiatic black bears 5:74
Asiatic linsangs 5:101
Asimov, Isaac (American writer)
5:156
Aspdin, Joseph (English building
contractor) **6:**25
Aspect ratio 6:297
Asperger syndrome 5:354
Aspergillus **4:**44
Asphalt 2:330, 333
fossils **2:**139
paving material **6:**43–44
roofing material **6:**36
Aspirin 5:277
arthritis treatment **5:**428–29
chemistry **3:**94
clot prevention **5:**234, 439
drugs **5:**461–62
pain relief **5:**291
Assemblers (computer programs)
6:378
Assembly language 6:377–78
illus. **6:**376
Assembly line 6:192
illus. **6:**9, 21, 191, 198
Asses 5:110
Assets 1:457–58
Assisted reproductive technol-
ogy 3:456
Association (in psychology)
5:336
Association areas (of the brain)
5:229
Associative laws
algebra **1:**353
Assumptions (in psychology)
5:344
Astatine 3:29, 32, 34–35
ASTEROIDS 1:75, **167–69**
dinosaur extinction **1:**497
space probes **1:**291, 295
Asthenosphere 2:8, 25, 68
Asthma 2:468–69; **5:**222
allergies **5:**241, 447–49
inhalers **5:**469
Astigmatism
eye disorders **5:**273
laser surgery **5:**489
lenses **3:**291; **6:**331
Astraea (asteroid) **1:**168
Astrochemistry 3:9
Astrogeology 2:4
Astrolabes 6:168
illus. **6:**169
Astrology 1:472

Astronauts *see also* Cosmonauts
auroras, view of **2:**156
careers in space science **1:**236
health monitoring **5:**492
oceanographic training
2:226–27
space station **1:**264–69
space suits **1:**270–79
training **1:**250–51, 280–89
illus.
original seven **1:**240
on space shuttle **1:**251
women **1:**286–87
ASTRONAUT TRAINING
1:280–89
illus. **1:**237
Astronomical observatories *see*
Observatories, Astronomical
cal
Astronomical units 1:110, 164
ASTRONOMY 1:3–4, 10–17
asteroids **1:**167–69
black holes **1:**204–14
calendar **1:**474–78
collapsed and failed stars
1:197–203
comets **1:**158–66
constellations **1:**24–36
cosmic rays **1:**224–31
cosmology **1:**18–23
eclipses **1:**175–80
history *see* Astronomy, History
of
infrared and ultraviolet
astronomy **1:**60–64
interstellar space **1:**218–23
invisible astronomy **1:**53–54
mathematics **1:**330, 337
meteors and meteorites
1:170–74
Milky Way **1:**181–89
Moon **1:**113–26
navigation **6:**165
night sky **1:**24–36
planetarium **1:**65–72
planets *see* names of specific
planets
quasars and energetic galaxies
1:215–17
radar astronomy **6:**261
radio astronomy **1:**55–57
solar system **1:**73–79
solid geometry's use in **1:**385
space science and **1:**233
spectroscopy **3:**302
stars **1:**190–96
Sun **1:**80–93
telescopes **1:**37–44
telescopes in space **1:**45–52
X-ray astronomy **1:**58–59
ASTRONOMY, History of 1:11–
12, 469–73
list of highlights **1:**473
Astro Observatory 1:51
Astrophysics 3:145
Aswan High Dam (Egypt) **2:**379
illus. **6:**54

Asynchronous transfer mode
(ATM) 6:386, 390
Atabrine 2:360
Atacama Desert 2:83, 416
AT&T 6:245, 309
Atarax *see* Dephenylmethanes
Atari (video game company)
6:298–99
Athabasca tar sands (Canada)
2:325
Atherosclerosis 5:439, 490–91;
6:351
Athlete's foot 3:451; **4:**43; **5:**428
Athletic shoes 1:254
Atkins Diet 5:394
Atlantic bay scallops 4:239
Atlantic Ocean 2:229, 231–32,
234
average depth **2:**271
continental drift **2:**38
currents **2:**236–37, 239–41
hurricanes **2:**196, 199
icebergs **2:**260–61
ocean basin **2:**270
ocean-floor dynamics **2:**270
plate tectonics **2:**43
pollution **2:**464
ridge **2:**40
seabed boulders **2:**276
tides **2:**246
volcanic islands **2:**283
volcanoes **2:**59
map(s) **2:**266
plate tectonics **2:**41
Atlantis (space shuttle) **1:**253,
257
illus. **1:**251
deploying Atlas 3 **2:**153
deploying space probe **1:**295
lift off **1:**238
ATLAS *see* Atmospheric Laboratory for Applications and
Science
Atlas (cervical vertebra) **5:**175
illus. **5:**176
Atlas cedars 4:92
Atlas moths 4:306
ATMOSPHERE 2:14, 147–54
air circulation **2:**182
Antarctic research **2:**92
atmospheric science **2:**141–46
auroras **2:**155–58
buoyancy **3:**188
carbon cycle **4:**21
climate change **2:**477–82
climates of the world **2:**209–10,
216
clouds and fog **2:**159–65
cosmic rays **1:**224
Earth **1:**105
heat transfer **3:**238–39
invisible astronomy **1:**54
Jupiter **1:**135
life, origin of **3:**380–81
magnetic storms **3:**271
Mars **1:**131–32
meteors and meteorites **1:**170

photochemical reactions **3:**8
photosynthesis **4:**12, 19
planets **1:**320–22
Pluto **1:**157
pollution *see* Air pollution
resolving power of telescopes
1:44–45
sciences of **1:**5
spaceflight **1:**306–7
Sun **1:**82–83
Titan **1:**144–45
Venus **1:**101–2
water contains gases from
2:172
water vapor in **2:**171
weather forecasting **2:**203–4
Atmosphere (unit of measurement) **3:**70, 72
Atmospheric Laboratory for
Applications and Science
illus. **2:**153
Atmospheric pressure 2:149–
50; **3:**72, 186–87
barometers **3:**70
boiling point **3:**78, 230
compared to Earth's interior
2:26
high-altitude aviation **1:**271
hurricanes and typhoons
2:199–200
tornadoes **2:**192
wind **2:**182–83
ATMOSPHERIC SCIENCE
2:141–46
Atmospheric water cycle 2:145
Atolls 2:283, 286
illus. **2:**283
Atomic Age 6:9, 11
Atomic bombs 3:15
Atomic energy *see* Nuclear
energy
Atomic mass (Atomic weight)
3:4, 20
carbon family **3:**31
chemical elements, list of
3:34–46
periodic table **3:**24
Atomic models 3:17–19
Atomic nucleus *see* Nucleus,
Atomic
Atomic number 3:19–20
chemical elements, list of
3:34–46
periodic table **3:**24
Atomic orbitals 3:332
Atomic reactors *see* Nuclear
reactors
Atomic Resolution Microscope
(Lawrence Berkeley Laboratory, California) **6:**335
Atomic theory 3:3–4, 304–5 *see*
also Atoms
Atomic weight *see* Atomic mass
Atomizers 3:183
diagram(s) **3:**184
ATOMS 3:3–4, 16–21
Bohr's theory **3:**328

ATOMS (cont.)
  chemical bonding **3:**47–52
  electrochemistry **3:**100–101
  elementary particles **3:**304–11
  entropy **3:**242
  interstellar space **1:**219
  ions, molecules, and compounds **3:**63–67
  laser study **6:**350–51
  nanotechnology **6:**340
  nuclear chemistry **3:**124–28
  physics, history of **3:**142
  quarks **3:**312
  size **3:**21
  standing wave **3:**331
  structure **2:**362; **3:**47–48
  illus. **3:**16, 242
Atom smashers *see* Particle accelerators
Atovaquone 5:445
ATP 3:434–35, 437–39
  exercise **5:**188
  photosynthesis **4:**24
Atria (Auricles) 5:198, 200–201
  illus. **5:**169
Atrial natriuretic factor 5:201
Atrioventricular node 5:201
Attention deficit disorder (ADD) 5:363, 366, 368
Attractive forces *see* Binding forces
Atwood, Wallace (American scientist) **1:**66
A.U. *see* Astronomical Units
Audion piano 3:218
Audio recording *see* Sound recording
Auditing 1:454, 459
Auditory canal 5:274
  illus. **5:**276
Auditory hallucinations 5:349
Auditory nerve 5:276
Audubon, John James (American naturalist) **4:**387, 404, 431
Audubon Aquarium of the Americas' Caribbean Reef (New Orleans)
  illus. **4:**473
Audubon Society 4:387–89
Auger mining 2:350
Augustus (Roman emperor)
  calendar **1:**476
Auks 4:438
Auricle (in the ear) **5:**274
Auricles (in the heart) *see* Atria
Auriga (constellation) **1:**32
Aurochs 5:134
Aurora australis 1:89; **2:**155; **3:**269
Aurora borealis 1:89; **2:**155; **3:**269
AURORAS 2:88, 151–52, **155–58**
  magnetism **3:**269
  illus. **2:**151; **3:**269
Ausable Chasm (New York)
  illus. **2:**421

AUSSAT (communications satellite)
  illus. **1:**304
Australia
  air pollution **2:**468
  archaeology **1:**467
  Christmas-tree plants **4:**118–19
  dingoes **5:**80–81
  endangered species **2:**496
  extinct mammals **1:**499
  Eyre, Lake **2:**111
  grasslands **4:**140–41
  Great Barrier Reef **2:**286
  Great Basin **2:**108
  marsupials **5:**16–22
  monotremes **5:**14–15
  rabbits **5:**38
  rail transportation **6:**127
  sand dunes **2:**429
  Snowy River Project **2:**410
  tornadoes **2:**193
  illus.
    Sydney Opera House **6:**40
Australopithecus **5:**159–60
Autism 5:350, 354
  illus. **5:**367
Autism Spectrum Disorders (ASDs) 5:354
Autoclaves 5:477
Autografts 5:496
Autoimmune diseases 5:240–41
Autologous transfusions 5:210, 477
Autologous transplantation (of bone marrow) **5:**212
Automated rail service 6:128
Automatic period (in human growth) **5:**325
Automatic pilot 6:196
Automatic tide gauges 2:248–49
AUTOMATION 6:194–202
  factories **6:**193
  illus.
    egg industry **6:**58
Automatons 6:195
AUTOMOBILES 6:133–48
  abandoned automobiles **2:**451
  acid rain **2:**474, 476
  air pollution **2:**467–68
  ceramic engine parts **6:**219
  electric **2:**321
  engine **6:**99–102
  engineering plastics **6:**212
  gasoline use **2:**332
  gas turbines **6:**104–5
  hydrogen powered **2:**399
  mass production **6:**192–93
  modern materials **6:**229
  natural gas as fuel **2:**345
  radar speed detector **6:**260
  road construction **6:**43
  simple machines **3:**175
  stopping distance **3:**166
  synthetic fuels **2:**397
  illus.
    assembly line **6:**21, 191, 194
    ceramic parts **6:**220

  crash test **3:**157
  development **6:**136–37
  heavy traffic **2:**453
  junkyard **2:**486
  plastic engine **6:**215
  recycled parts **2:**415
  solar-powered race car **2:**387
  streamlined design **3:**157
Autonomic nervous system 5:232
Autopsy 3:469
  forensic science **1:**513–14
  illus. **1:**512
Autotrophs 4:11
Autumn
  constellations **1:**30, 32
  deciduous trees **4:**18, 72, 145
  illus. **2:**207; **4:**148
  map(s)
    constellations **1:**33
Auxins 4:114–15, 172
Avalanches 2:96, 173, 456
Avastin 5:437
Average deviation (in statistics) **3:**511
Averages (in statistics) **1:**409–12; **3:**511
Aversion therapy 5:338, 357
Avery, Oswald (Canadian-American bacteriologist) **3:**117, 370, 411
Avian flu 3:393
Aviaries *see* Birds
AVIATION 6:149–64
  aeronautical engineering **3:**192
  airplane condensation trails **2:**163–64
  atmospheric science **2:**143, 145
  human-powered **6:**94–95
  jet streams **2:**186
  navigation **6:**165
  radar **6:**255, 258–59
  space suit precursors **1:**271–72
  supersonic flight **3:**206
  wind shear **2:**188
Avicenna (Persian scholar) **2:**7
Aviculture 4:387
Avidin 5:385
Aviette (human-powered aircraft) **6:**94
AV node *see* Atrioventricular node
Avocets 4:438
Avogadro, Amadeo (Italian scientist) **1:**359; **3:**4, 56
  illus. **3:**54
Avogadro's number 1:359; **3:**56
Ax
  illus. **3:**172
AX-5 (space suit) **1:**277, 279
  illus. **1:**273
Axial skeleton 5:174
Axis (cervical vertebra) **5:**175
  illus. **5:**176
Axis (of rotation)
  illus. **1:**74
Axis deer 5:120
Axolotls 4:338, 342, 351

Axons 5:171, 224
   illus. 5:227
Aye-ayes 2:501–2; 5:137
Azaspirodecanediones 5:356
Azathioprine 5:240–41, 428
Azidothymidine *see* AZT
Azimuthal quantum number *see*
      Subsidiary quantum num-
      ber
Azlocillin 5:463
Azores (islands, Atlantic Ocean)
      2:45, 283
AZT (drug) 3:393; 5:445, 465
Aztecs 4:337, 470
   illus. 1:476

B

B. F. Goodrich Company
      1:271–72
Babesia bigemina 4:212
Babies 5:304–5
   AIDS 5:443, 445
   of alcoholic mothers 5:375
   breathing cycle 5:220
   chlamydia 5:430
   cigarette smoke 5:374–75
   diarrhea 5:429
   of drug-abusing mothers 5:301
   fontanels 5:176
   heart rate 5:197
   physical growth 5:325–30
   illus. 5:326–27
      fetal alcohol syndrome 5:301
      premature 5:304
Babirusas 5:115
Baboons 4:195; 5:142, 146–48
   illus. 4:196; 5:136, 141, 146
Babylonian civilization
   algebra 1:352
   archaeology 1:462
   astronomy 1:11, 469, 472
   canals 6:45
   numerals 1:340–41
   plane geometry 1:366
Bacillus 4:28; 5:427
   illus. 3:448
Backbone 5:153, 174–76
   babies 5:328
   chiropractic 5:512
   frogs 4:344, 347
   turtles 4:375
   illus. 5:165, 174
Back pain 5:287
Backshore (of a beach) 2:293
Back swamps 2:104
Back-up files (computer) 6:371–
      72, 386
Backwash marks (on beaches)
      2:295
Bacteria 3:448–50; 4:27–32
   botany 4:6
   carbon cycle 4:21
   cell division 3:440–41
   classification 3:396, 399; 4:55,
      183
   decomposition 3:470

digestion 5:253
food poisoning 6:77
fossils 1:490
fungi toxins 4:38
gene swapping 3:389
genetic engineering 3:108, 118,
      402–3, 420; 6:73–75
groundwater 2:119
hydrothermal vents 2:272, 278
infectious diseases 5:424,
      426–27
methane production 2:397
mitochondria 3:428
nitrogen cycle 3:491
photosynthetic organisms, evo-
      lution of 4:20
reproduction 3:452–53
resistance to antibiotics 3:506;
      5:464
sewage purification 2:487–88
ultraviolet lamps 3:281
   illus. 3:376; 5:423
      cell structure 3:427; 4:26
Bacterial myositis 5:194
Bacterial vaccines 5:238
Bacteriochlorophyll 4:31
Bacteriophages 3:388, 391, 448;
      4:32
   illus. 3:386
Bactrian camels 5:117
   illus. 5:116
Badgers 4:169; 5:10, 96–97
Badlands 2:417–18
Baekeland, Leo (Belgian chem-
      ist) 6:215
Baer, Karl von (Estonian zoolo-
      gist) 4:180
Bagworms 4:307
Bahamas 2:283
Bailey, Jacob (American geolo-
      gist) 2:273
Baily's beads 1:178
Bain, Alexander (Scottish inven-
      tor) 6:244
Bakelite 6:215
Baker's yeast 4:40
Baku oil fields (Azerbaijan)
      2:322
Balance (Equilibrium) 4:253;
      5:275, 286
Balance sheets 1:457–58
Bald cypresses 4:85, 152–53
Bald eagles 2:502, 505; 4:158,
      417
   DDT in body tissues 3:489
   illus. 2:500; 4:417
      hologram 6:275
Bald-faced hornets
   illus. 4:288
Baldness 5:319, 421
Baleen 5:8, 49
Baleen whales 5:12, 48–52
Balkhash, Lake (Kazakhstan)
      2:111
Ball-and-socket joints 5:178–80
Ballard, Robert (American
      oceanographer)
   illus. 2:224; 6:124

Ballistic missiles *see* Missiles
Ballistics (forensics) 1:515–16
Ball lightning 2:178
   illus. 2:177
Balloon angioplasty 5:439, 491
Balloons
   aircraft 6:149–50
   atmospheric research 2:153,
      188
   buoyancy 3:188
   weather balloons 2:204, 206
   illus. 2:147
      atmospheric research 2:401,
      480
      radiosonde 2:152
      space astronomy 1:46
Balloon valvuloplasty 5:440
Ball pythons 4:370
Balsam firs 4:86, 91
Baltica 2:70, 73
Baltic Sea 2:229, 232
Baltimore orioles 4:461
   illus. 4:459
Banded anteaters 5:21
Banded palm civets 5:101
   illus. 5:100
Banded sand snakes 4:371
Bandicoots 5:20
Banding of birds 4:389
Band-tailed pigeons 4:429
Banff National Park (Canada)
      2:512–13
Banff Springs (Canada) 2:64
Banking, Electronic 6:309
Banks (of continental shelves)
      2:265, 268
Baobabs 4:142
Barasinghs *see* Indian baras-
      inghs
Barbary apes 5:142
Barberries 4:45
Barbiturates 5:356, 358, 373–74,
      466
Barchans (sand dunes) 2:84,
      428, 430
Bar codes
   illus. 6:363
Bardeen, John (American physi-
      cist) 3:359
Barghoorn, E. S. (American
      paleontologist) 1:481
Barium 2:364; 3:30, 35
Barium-lanthanum 140 3:319
Bark (of trees) 4:87, 89, 165
Bark beetles 4:298–99
Barking deer *see* Muntjacs
Bark lice 4:279
Bar magnet 3:262
   illus.
      field lines 3:263
Barnacles 4:247, 250, 252,
      254–55
   illus. 4:255; 5:46
Barnard, Christiaan N. (South
      African surgeon) 5:498
   illus. 5:411
Barnard, Edward E. (American
      astronomer) 1:166, 183

Barn owls **4:**421
Barometers **2:**142, 149; **3:**70, 187
Barracudas **4:**335
Barred antshrikes
illus. **4:**450
Barred owls **4:**421
Barrel vaults
illus. **6:**35
Barrier bars **2:**280
Barrier islands **2:**289, 292; **4:**152
Barrier reefs **2:**285–86
Barringer Crater (Canyon Diablo) (Arizona) **1:**174
illus. **1:**171
Barton, Otis (American scientist)
illus. **6:**123
Bartram, William (American naturalist) **4:**386
BART subway system **6:**48
illus. **6:**128
Baryon numbers **3:**309
Baryons **3:**307, 310–11, 313
Basal-cell cancer **5:**267, 436
Basal cells **5:**263
Basal metabolic rate **5:**396, 401
Basal slip (of glaciers) **2:**95
Basalt **1:**126; **2:**31, 34, 129, 134
Bascule bridges **6:**50
Baseball stadium
illus. **2:**308
Base-eight numeral system *see* Octal numeral system
Basements **6:**34
BASES (Alkalis) (in chemistry) **3:**29, 94–99; **6:**203
Bases (in mathematics) **1:**348
Base-ten numeral system *see* Decimal system
Base-twelve numeral system *see* Duodecimal system
Base-two numeral system *see* Binary numeral system
BASIC (computer language) **6:**375–76, 378–80
Basidiospores **4:**44
Basilar membrane **5:**275–76
Basilisks (lizards) **4:**354, 358
illus. **4:**356
Basking sharks **4:**328
Basophils **5:**207–8, 241
Bass (fish) **6:**89
Bassoons **3:**216
Bates, Marston (American zoologist) **4:**182
Batholiths **2:**33
Bathymetry **2:**264
Bathyscaphes **2:**276
Bathyspheres **6:**122
illus. **6:**123
Bathythermographs **2:**242
illus. **2:**236
Batocera **4:**297
Batrachotoxin **4:**347
BATS **5:**9, 11, **29–32**
echolocation **4:**192

humidity requirements **5:**6
life span **5:**324
plant eaters **5:**8
plant pollination **4:**158
illus. **3:**203; **4:**115
Batteries
electric **2:**310; **3:**104–5
electrolysis **3:**102
rechargeable **1:**306
storage *see* Secondary batteries
diagram(s) **2:**309
Battleships **6:**110
Bauer, David L. V. **6:**317
Bauersfeld, Walter (German scientist) **1:**67
Bauxite **6:**183
Bay Area Rapid Transit *see* BART subway system
Bay Bridge *see* San Francisco-Oakland Bay Bridge
Bayeux tapestry
illus. **1:**160
Bay lynx *see* Bobcats
Bay of Fundy (North America) *see* Fundy, Bay of
B cells **5:**237, 442
BCS theory of superconductivity **3:**359–61
Beach cusps **2:**295
Beaches **2:**289–90, 292–95
Beaded lizards **4:**360, 362
Beagle (British ship)
illus. **3:**504
Beaked whales **5:**53–54
Beaks **4:**395
birds of prey **4:**414
perching birds **4:**447–48
illus. **4:**393
Beam bridges **6:**49–50
Beam pipes **6:**357
Beams (in construction) **6:**30–31
Beam splitters **5:**495
Beans **3:**463
Bear cats *see* Binturongs
Beard moss **4:**60
BEARS **5:**69–75
brown bears **4:**158
life span **5:**324
polar bears **2:**90, 500, 503
social life **5:**10
winter sleep **5:**5
illus.
polar bear **2:**87
Beat patterns (in acoustics) **3:**208
Beaufort, Sir Francis (English admiral) **2:**188
Beaufort wind scale **2:**188
illus. **2:**187
Beauty quarks *see* Bottom quarks
Beavers **5:**42
dam building **2:**110
extinct giant beaver **5:**39
social life **5:**10
illus. **2:**109; **4:**191; **5:**43

Becquerel, Antoine (French physicist) **3:**6, 124
Bednorz, Johannes Georg (Swiss physicist) **3:**360; **6:**221
Bedouin (people) **2:**86
Bedrock **2:**30, 133
Beds (of streams) *see* Channels
Beebe, William (American scientist) **6:**122
illus. **6:**123
Beef tapeworms **4:**226
Beehive cluster *see* Praesepe
Beehive ovens **2:**358
Beehives **4:**286–87
Bee hummingbirds **4:**404
Beekeeping **4:**287
illus. **4:**281
Bees **4:**280, 285–88
allergic reaction to sting **5:**448
animal behavior **4:**192
life span of queen **5:**324
plant pollination **4:**158
pollen brushes **4:**274
reproduction **3:**457; **4:**276
diagram(s) **4:**285
illus. **3:**452
dancing **4:**286
Beeswax **4:**287
BEETLES **4:**158, 280, **291–99**
illus.
bombardier beetle **4:**294
diving beetle **4:**293
firefly **4:**295
Goliath beetle **4:**297
Japanese beetle **4:**297
lady beetle **4:**291
leaf beetle **4:**298
snout beetle **4:**299
target tortoise beetle **4:**298
tiger beetle **4:**291
Beets **4:**171
Behavior, Animal *see* Animal behavior
Behavior, Human *see* Psychology
Behavior, Plant *see* Plant behavior
Behaviorism *see* Experimental psychology
Behavior modification **5:**338, 349, 357, 368
Behring, Emil von (German bacteriologist) **5:**424
Beijerinck, Martinus W. (Dutch botanist) **3:**370
Belgian draft horse **5:**109
Belgium
ferry accident (1987) **6:**112
Bell, Alexander Graham (Scottish-American inventor) **6:**237
Bell, Jocelyn (British astronomer) **1:**201, 209
Bell frogs **4:**344
Bells **3:**217
Bell X-1 rocket plane **6:**157
Belted kingfishers **4:**407

Belts (of Jupiter) 1:135
Beluga whales 5:53
Benazepril 5:467
Bends (Caisson disease) 1:277; 5:221; 6:48
Bengal, Bay of 2:196, 199, 234
Bengal tigers 2:513
Benguela Current 2:239
Benhaim, Martin (German cartographer) 2:298
Benign tumors 5:434
Benthic zone 3:499
Bentonite 2:433
Bents (in construction) 6:41
Benz (automobile)
 illus. 6:136
Benz, Karl (German engineer) 6:99, 133
Benzene 2:467; 3:112; 5:436
Benzodiazepines 5:356, 358, 373, 466–67
Bergedorfer Spectral Catalog 1:184–85
Bergius hydrogenation process 2:359–60
Bergschrunds 2:97
Beriberi 5:384
Bering Glacier (Alaska) 2:96
Bering Sea 2:230–31
Berkelium 3:35
Berlin (Germany) 2:118
Berm 2:293
Bermuda petrels see Cahows
Berners-Lee, Tim (English researcher) 6:307
Bernoulli's principle 3:183–84, 193
 illus. 3:192
Berylliosis 2:469
Beryllium 3:30, 35; 6:184
 illus.
  atomic structure 3:245
Berzelius, Jöns Jakob (Swedish chemist) 3:4
Bessemer process 6:30, 178
 illus. 6:181
Best Friend of Charleston (locomotive) 6:125
Beta-agonist bronchodilators 5:449
Beta blockers 5:467
Beta cloth 1:275
Betacyanin 4:18
Betamax 6:281–82
Beta particles 3:126–27, 317, 338
 illus.
  penetrating power 3:318
Beta Pictoris (star)
 illus. 2:13
Beta radiation 2:363; 3:126–28
Beta-thalassemia see Thalassemia
Betelgeuse (star) 1:32, 192
Bethe, Hans (German-American physicist) 1:89
Betsiboka River
 illus. 2:419

Bevatron 6:358
Bewick's wrens 4:452
Beyond the Planet Earth (book, Tsiolkovsky) 1:264
Bhopal chemical accident (India) 2:455
Bialowieza Forest (Poland–Belarus) 5:133
Bible
 creation, description of 3:501
 petroleum, references to 2:322
 water, references to 2:436
Biceps jerk 5:227
Biceps muscle 5:189–90
 illus. 5:166
Bichirs 4:331
Bicuspids (teeth) 5:279
Bicuspid valve see Mitral valve
Bicycles 5:398; 6:92, 94
 gears 3:172
 illus. 5:395; 6:93
Biela's comet 1:161
Biennials (plants) 4:107
Big Bang theory 1:18–21, 48, 62, 317; 3:144
 illus. 1:18; 2:9
Big Bend (area, Texas–Mexico) 2:513
Big Crunch theory 1:23
"Big Dig" (Boston, Massachusetts) 6:22, 48
Big Dipper (constellation) 1:25, 29
Big Horn Medicine Wheel (Wyoming) 1:470–71
Big Inch (pipeline) 2:338
Big Moose Lake (New York) 2:472
Bikini Island (Pacific Ocean) 2:286
Bile 5:252
Bilirubin 5:262
Billiard balls 3:166–67
Bills (of birds) see Beaks
Bimetallic strips see Compound bars
Binary fission 3:440–41, 452–53; 4:31–32
 illus. 3:441
BINARY NUMERAL SYSTEM 1:345, 446–52; 6:375
 computers 6:363–64, 370
Binary stars 1:58, 192, 197–98, 211–12
 illus. 1:195, 205
Binding forces (Attractive forces) 3:76
Binge eating 5:355
Binnig, Gerd (German physicist) 6:337
Binocular microscopes 6:331–32
Binoculars 3:288
Binocular vision 5:272
 human evolution 5:158
 robots 6:201
Binomial nomenclature 3:395–97; 4:4, 179, 199, 267

Binomial sequences 1:363–64
Binturongs 5:101
BIOCHEMISTRY 3:7–8, 116–23
 cell dynamics 3:432–39
 drug addiction 5:370
 genes 3:411–15
 life 3:375–76, 381–83
 life, origin of 1:319–20
 mental health 5:356
 microbiology 3:449
 nutrition 5:378–90
 ornithology 4:389
 radioisotope studies 3:319
 viruses 3:385–86
 zoology 4:179
Biodegradable plastics 6:85, 215
Biodiesel 2:397
Biodiversity 4:146, 160–61
Bioelectricity 3:377
 fish 4:320, 328, 333
 heart 5:200–201
 plant behavior 4:117
 platypus 5:15
Bioengineering see Bionics
Biofeedback 5:357, 511–12
 illus. 5:355
Biofuels 2:332, 396–97
Biogenic compounds 1:318–19
Biogeochemical cycles see Nutrient cycles
Biogeography 2:300
Biological clocks
 biorhythms 3:380
 bird migration 4:394
 light 5:268
 plant movements 4:115
Biological control of insects 2:411; 4:175
Biological extinction (of lakes) 2:111
Biological magnification 3:489
Biological oxidation 2:487
BIOLOGY 1:6–7; 3:366–73 see also Biochemistry; Botany; Evolutionary biology; Life; Marine biology; Microbiology; Zoology
 experimental biology 3:508–15
BIOLUMINESCENCE 3:62, 377; 4:295, 316
 illus. 3:60, 377; 4:218, 332
Biomass 2:396, 398, 407
Biomass Production Chamber
 illus. 1:234
Biomedical engineering see Bionics
BIOMES 3:492–99; 4:182
 ecology 3:472
 grasslands and savannas 4:138–43
 plant communities 4:132–37
 rain forests 4:156–61
 temperate forests 4:144–49
 tundra and taiga 4:162–65
 wetlands 4:150–55
 map(s)
  major biomes of world 3:495

Bionics 5:500–509; 6:21
Biophysics 3:145, 376–77
Biopsies 1:255; 5:436
BIORHYTHMS 3:380–81
BIOSPHERE 3:484, 492–99
  environmental pollution 2:454
Biosphere reserves 2:513
Biostratigraphy 1:482
Biotechnology 4:468; 5:309
  botany 4:7
Biotin 5:385
Biotite 2:34
Bipedalism 4:380; 5:159–60
Bipinnately compound leaves
  4:73
Bipolar affective disorder 5:351,
  466
Bipolar cells 5:270
BIRD CLASSIFICATION
  4:397–99
Bird guides (books) 4:386–88
Birding (Bird-watching)
  4:387–89
BIRDS 4:205, 390–96
  acid rain's effects 2:476
  acorn cycle 4:147
  Antarctica 2:92
  aviaries in zoos 4:476
  biorhythms 3:380
  birds of prey 4:414–21
  classification 4:397–99
  eggs affected by DDT 2:411
  endangered species 2:496,
    502–3
  evolution 1:479
  flightless 4:409–13
  fossils 1:481–82, 489
  grasslands 4:140
  mating behavior 4:195
  migration 4:191
  nests 4:197
  nonperching birds 4:400–408
  ornithology 4:385–89
  perching birds 4:447–63
  pets 4:481–82, 485–86
  pigeons 4:428–31
  plant pollination 4:158
  prehistoric animals 1:496–97
  savannas 4:140–41
  seeds scattered by 4:158
  senses 4:192
  tapeworms 4:226–27
  tundra and taiga 4:164
  waterbirds and shorebirds
    4:432–46
  wetlands 4:154
  wildfowl 4:422–27
  illus.
    aviaries 4:474
    body structures 4:391
Bird's-nest fungi 4:45
Birds of paradise 4:462
  illus. 4:462
BIRDS OF PREY 4:395, 414–21
  DDT in body tissues 3:489
BirdSource (Web site) 4:389
Bird-watching see Birding
Bird-wing butterflies 4:304

Birth see Childbirth
Birth defects 5:421
  dioxins 2:463
  environmental influences
    5:301–2
  folate protects against 5:386
  genetic diseases 5:418
Birthmarks 6:351
Birth weight, Low 5:301
Biscay right whales see Right
  whales
Bishop pines 3:507
Bismarck (ship) 6:124
Bismuth 3:31–32, 35
BISON 2:509; 4:140; 5:132–33
  illus. 2:403
Biting lice 4:279
Bits 6:364
Bitterns 4:444
Bitumen 2:396; 6:26
Bituminous coal 2:347, 356–58,
  360
Bivalves 4:203, 235–39
Black, Joseph (Scottish chemist)
  3:3
Black-and-white photography
  6:270–73
Black-backed jackals 5:80
Black bears 5:74
  illus. 5:70
Blackbirds 4:455, 460–61
Blackbody radiation 3:322–25
Blackbucks 5:131
Black caimans 4:383
Black-capped chickadees
  illus. 4:455
Blackett, Patrick M. S. (British
  scientist) 2:29
Black-faced cuckoo-shrikes
  4:450
Blackfish see Pilot whales
Black-footed cats 5:92
Black-footed ferrets 2:501
Black grouse 4:426
BLACK HOLES 1:59, 187,
  201–2, 204–14
  active galaxies 1:216
  relativity theory 3:351–52
Black honey ants 4:285
Black light
  illus. 3:275
Black-lung disease 2:355, 469
Blackpoll warblers 4:459
Black rails 4:440
Black rhinoceroses 5:113
  illus. 5:112
Black right whales see Right
  whales
Blacks
  AIDS 5:444
  sickle-cell disease 5:321
Black skimmers 4:436
Blacksmithing
  illus. 6:175
Black smokers see Hydrothermal
  vents
Blacksnakes 4:371, 374
Black spruces 4:90–91

Black swans 4:441
Black-tailed prairie dogs 2:501
Black-tailed rattlesnakes
  illus. 4:363
Black vultures 4:169
Blackwater (wastewater)
  2:486–87
Black water beetles 4:293
Black widow spiders 4:261, 263
  illus. 4:260
Black-winged stilts 4:438
Bladder, Urinary 5:260–61, 299
  illus. 5:167–68, 258, 295
Bladderworts 4:109, 111–12
Blade Runner (film) 1:505
Blades (of leaves) 4:71
Blanc, Mont (France)
  illus. 2:67
Blast furnaces 6:177–78
  illus. 6:179, 181, 184
Blastula 3:460; 5:296
Blending (in genetics) 3:408
Blepharisma 4:213
Blepharitis 5:273
Blériot, Louis (French aviator)
  6:153
Bleuler, Eugen (Swiss physician)
  5:349
Blights see Plant blights
Blimps 6:151
Blind mole rats 5:43
Blindness
  Vitamin A deficiency 5:383
Blind snakes 4:369
Blind spot 5:271
Blinking 5:269
Blips 6:257
Blister beetles 4:299
Blister copper 6:183
Blizzards 2:169
Block and tackle 3:174
  illus. 3:175
Block faulting 2:71
Block Island (Rhode Island)
  2:281
Block lava 2:61
Blogs (Web logs) 6:309
BLOOD 4:186; 5:164, 172,
  205–13
  bats' diet 5:32
  circulation 5:195–204
  circulation during sleep 5:405,
    408
  filtration by kidneys 5:259–60
  flow to infected areas 5:236
  forensic science 1:511–12
  LDL-phoresis 5:493–94
  pH values 3:98
  radioisotope tracers 3:319
  surgery 5:476–77
  synthetic blood 5:210, 506;
    6:208
  tests 5:212–13, 449
Blood cells 5:325
Blood clotting 5:208
  anticoagulants 5:467
  blood plasma 5:206

disorders 5:212
heart attack 5:439
heart disease 5:440
polycythemia 5:211
Protein C 5:475
Vitamin K 5:384
illus. 5:208–9
Blood groups 5:209
chart(s) 5:210
Blood plasma 5:164, 205–6
antibodies 5:471
LDL-phoresis 5:494
transfusion 5:210
Blood pressure 5:203–4
sleep 5:407–8
chart(s) 5:203
Blood transfusions 5:209–10,
444, 477
Blood vessels
angioplasty 5:490–91
artificial body parts 5:505
diagnostic imaging 5:454
pain 5:288
illus. 5:216
Blooms, Algal 4:47–48
Blowfish *see* Puffer fish
Blowholes (whale nostrils) 5:47,
49, 52, 56
Blow molding 6:213–14
Blowouts (sand formations)
2:429–30
Blubber (whale fat) 5:47–48, 56
Bluebirds 4:454
Bluebuck *see* Nilgais
Blue crabs 4:251
Blue-footed boobies
illus. 4:433
Blue foxes 5:83
Blue gas *see* Water gas
Blue-green algae *see* Cyanobacteria
Blue Grotto (cave, Italy) 2:129
Blue jays
illus. 4:463
Blue jets (lightning) 2:141
Blue-ray (DVD format) 6:287
Blue Ridge Mountains 2:72
Blue Ridge Province 2:72–73
Blue-spotted stingrays
illus. 4:327
Blue-striped snappers
illus. 4:315
Blue whales 2:500–501; 5:2, 46,
49, 54
illus. 5:50
B lymphocytes 5:207, 426
Boas (snakes) 4:369–70
illus. 4:368
Boats 6:107 *see also* Ships and
shipping
fishing vessels 6:88
human-powered 6:91–92
speedboat collisions 3:193
whirlpool danger 2:248
illus.
speedboat collision 3:192
Bobcats 5:91
Bobolinks 4:460

Bobwhites 4:424
Bock hand *see* MyoBock hand
Bode, Johann Elert (German
astronomer) 1:148, 167–68
Bode's law 1:167
illus. 1:77
Bodo 4:208
Body, Human *see also* Anatomy,
Human; Diseases; Health;
Physiology
artificial body parts 5:500–509
homeostasis 3:378
human sciences 1:7
water content 2:435
Body Farm (research facility,
Tennessee) 1:512
Body fossils 1:482, 484–85
Body Mass Index (BMI) 5:393
Body of the stomach 5:249
Body temperature 5:395 *see
also* Ectotherms; Homeotherms
birds 4:394
death 3:469
desert animals 4:169
exercise 5:399
mammals 5:4
muscle-produced heat 5:189
perspiration 5:265
regulation by skin 5:267
sleep 5:408
thermography 5:458
whales 5:47–48
Body weight *see* Weight, body
Boeing 747 (airplane) 6:157
Boeing 777 (airplane) 6:157
Boeing 787 Dreamliner (aircraft)
6:164
Boeing *Clipper* (airplane) 6:156
illus. 6:155
Boeing V-22 Osprey (aircraft)
6:161
Bog lemmings 4:154
Bogoslof Island (Bering Sea)
2:58
Bogs 2:347; 4:137, 153–54, 163,
165
eutrophication 2:461
Bohemian waxwings 4:452
Bohr, Niels (Danish physicist)
3:6, 19, 143, 327–28, 332,
333
diagram(s)
atomic model 3:17
illus. 3:323
Bohrium 3:35
Boiling 3:229–31
Boiling point 3:77–78, 229
covalent molecules 3:52
water 3:84–85
illus. 3:79
Boiling-water nuclear reactors
2:367
diagram(s) 2:367
Bola spiders 4:260
Boll weevils *see* Cotton-boll weevils
Bolometers 3:274

Bolyái, János (Hungarian mathematician) 1:335, 401–3
Bombardier beetles
illus. 4:294
Bombing radar 6:258
Bond energy (chemistry) 3:58
Bonding, Chemical *see* Chemical bonding
Bonefish 4:332
Bone marrow 5:207
anemias 5:211
osteomyelitis 5:184
red blood cells 5:174, 206
transplants 5:212, 241, 436,
499
white blood cells 5:207
BONES 5:173–84
arthritis 5:427
babies 5:327–28
bone china 6:217
bony fish 4:329
CAT scan images 5:459
changes with age 5:332–33
connective tissue 5:164
density measurement 5:453–54
forensic anthropology 1:514–15
fossils 1:485
stem-cell technology 3:423
vitamin D 5:384
Bongo 5:128
Bonneville, Lake (extinct lake,
Utah) 2:86
Bonneville Dam (Oregon–
Washington) 6:53
BONY FISH 4:205, 315, 317–18,
320, **329–35**
prehistoric animals 1:488, 490,
492
Bonytongues 4:332–33
Boobies 4:446
illus. 4:400
Bookkeeping 1:456
Book lice 4:279
Book lungs 4:247, 258
Boole, George (English mathematician) 1:300
Boom-and-bust cycles (of populations) 3:478–79
Boomslangs 4:372
Boötes (constellation) 1:29
Booting programs 6:368–69
Bopp, Thomas (American amateur astronomer) 1:15
Bora 2:186
Boreal forests 2:480; 4:164–65
Bores, Tidal *see* Tidal bores
Boric acid 2:370; 3:31
Boring sponges 4:216
Borlaug, Norman (American scientist) 4:170–71
Born, Max (German physicist)
3:331
illus. 3:323
Bornean Bay cats 5:92
Boron 2:388; 3:29, 31, 35, 48
Boron family of elements 3:31
Borrelly, Comet 1:263, 296
Bose-Einstein statistics 3:307

Bosons 3:21, 307, 311
Boston (Massachusetts)
  "Big Dig" project 6:22, 48
  drumlin islands 2:289
  water supply 2:442; 6:53
  illus. 6:20
BOTANICAL CLASSIFICATION
  4:54–57
BOTANY 1:7; 3:366, 372; 4:2–7
  see also Plants
  paleobotany 1:480–81
Bothe, Walther (German physicist) 1:226
Botrychium **(Southern grape fern)** 4:81
Bottle-nosed dolphins 5:60
  illus. 5:59
Bottle-nosed whales 5:53
Bottom quarks 3:20, 314
Botulism 5:430; 6:77
Bouguer, Pierre (French scientist) 1:104
Boulders 2:99
Boulton, Matthew (English manufacturer) 6:190
Bourdon spring gauges 3:187
Boutos *see* Amazon dolphins
Bouvard, Alexis (French astronomer) 1:152
Bovids 1:498 *see also* Cattle
  antelope 5:126–31
  bison, buffalo, and oxen 5:132–35
Bowerbirds
  illus. 4:195, 458
Bowfins 4:331–32
Bowhead whales 5:51–52, 54
Bowman's capsule 5:259
Box-elder trees 4:141
Box fish *see* Trunkfish
Box turtles 4:379; 5:324
  diagram(s)
    shells 4:377
  illus. 4:378
Boyle, Robert (English chemist) 3:3, 72, 141
  illus. 3:4
Boyle's law 3:72, 74, 187, 189, 223
  illus. 3:71
B-quarks *see* Bottom quarks
Braces, Orthodontic 5:281
Brachial plexus 5:232
Brachiopods 4:202
Brachioradialis
  illus. 5:166
Brachiosaurus 1:495
Bracken ferns 4:78–79
Bracket fungi (Shelf fungi) 4:39, 44–45
Brackish water 2:232; 4:152
Bradbury, Ray (American writer) 1:503, 506
Brahe, Tycho (Danish astronomer) 1:78, 473
  comets 1:165
  supernova 1:198

illus. 1:470
  solar system theory 1:472
Braided streams 2:103
Brain
  arachnids 4:258
  crustaceans 4:253
  dolphins 5:58
  human *see* Brain, Human
  insects 4:274
  mammals 5:4
  primates 5:137
  prion diseases 3:390–91
  reptiles 4:353
  sperm whales 5:52
BRAIN, Human 5:154, **223–34**
  aging 5:334
  alcohol's effect on 5:371
  babies 5:328–29
  cell damage 5:239
  cells 5:325
  diagnostic imaging 5:457, 459
  human evolution 5:158–60
  laser surgery 5:489
  learning disabilities 5:363
  memory 5:361–62
  mental health 5:353–54, 356
  nicotine's effect on 5:371
  pain 5:288, 290, 292
  physiological psychology 5:339
  sleep 5:405
  substance abuse 5:373–75
  tumor surgery 5:479
  vision 5:272
  illus. 5:228, 450
    formation of memory 5:362
    PET scans 5:351, 456
    schizophrenia 5:350
    sensory map 5:231
Brain death 3:468
Brain stem 5:228, 230, 288, 406
Brain waves 5:406
  illus. 5:408
Brakes 6:134, 147–48
Branchiostomas see Lancelets
Brand, Vance D. (American astronaut) 2:221
Brash (sea ice fragments) 2:262
Brass 3:79; 6:175
Brass instruments 3:217
Brave New World (novel, Huxley) 1:502
Braxton-Hicks contractions
  5:301
Brazil
  alcohol-fuel production 2:396
  Amazon tidal bore 2:247
  Itaipu Dam 2:380; 6:56
  rain forests 4:156, 161
  space station 1:269
  wilderness areas 2:515
  illus.
    burning forest 2:404; 4:160
    Butantan Institute 4:337
    Itaipu Dam 2:379
Brazil Current 2:240
Brazilian manatees 2:499; 5:62
Breaching (of whales) 5:50

Bread mold 4:39
  illus. 3:375
Breaker points
  illus. 6:142
Breakers (ocean waves) 2:254–55, 291
Breakwaters 2:124
Breastbone *see* Sternum
Breast-feeding
  illus. 5:305
Breasts 5:294
  cancer 5:402, 433
  implants 5:506
  mammography 5:459
  pregnancy 5:299–300
  illus.
    thermographic image 5:457
"Breathalyzer" test 5:261
  illus. 5:260
Breathing *see* Respiration
Breccia 2:33, 35, 134
Breech births 5:305
Breeder reactors 2:307, 368
Breeding *see* Genetics; Genetic technology; Plant breeding; Reproduction
Breeding Bird Census 4:388
Breeding Bird Survey, North American 4:388–89
Breeds of dogs 4:481, 486
Brenthidae 4:299
Brick 6:23–24, 26–27
  building techniques 6:37–38
  world's longest brick bridge 6:50
"Brick Moon" (story, Hale) 1:264
Bridalveil Falls (California)
  illus. 2:97
Bridges (in computer networking) 6:389
Bridges (in dentistry) 5:282
Bridges (in transportation) 6:49–50
  Brooklyn Bridge 6:15
  caissons 3:185
  cast iron 6:29–30
  reinforced concrete 6:31
Bright-line spectra *see* Emission spectra
Brightness (of color) 3:301
Brilliant Pebbles (defense system) 1:263
Brine shrimp 4:255
Briquet's syndrome *see* Somatoform disorder
Briquettes 2:357, 360
Bristlecone pines 4:85, 90
  illus. 3:464
Bristle ferns 4:83
Bristletails 4:277–78
Bristle worms 4:245
British Columbia 2:158, 171; 4:143
British Nautical Almanac 6:170
British Thermal Units *see* BTUs
Brittle stars (animals) 4:223
Broadband fluorescence 3:382
Broad-faced potoroos 5:19

Broad-winged hawks 4:416–17
Brocket deer 5:122
Broglie, Louis V. de (French physicist) 3:143, 330
  illus. 3:323
Bromide 5:466
Bromine 2:154, 482; 3:32, 35, 69–70
Bromo group 3:110
Bronchi (singular Bronchus) 5:217
  illus. 5:168, 216
Bronchial rami (singular ramus) 5:217
  illus. 5:168
Bronchioles 5:217
  illus. 5:216
Bronchiolitis 5:429
Bronchitis 2:468
Bronchodilators 5:241
Brongniart, Adolphe-Théodore (French botanist) 1:480–81
Brontosaurus see Apatosaurus
Brontotherium
  illus. 1:499
Bronx High School of Science (NYC) 6:327
Bronze 3:31; 6:174
Bronze Age 6:5–6, 10
Brooding patch 4:396
Brooke, John Mercer (American scientist) 2:273
Brooklyn Bridge (New York) 6:15, 50
  illus. 6:16
Brooks, W. R. (American astronomer) 1:166
Brooks Range (Alaska) 2:89
Broom plants 4:119
Broomrape 4:112
Broomsedge 4:125
Brown, Arthur (English aviator) 6:155
Brown, Barnum (American paleontologist)
  illus. 1:480
Brown, Louise (first "test-tube baby") 3:456
Brown, Robert (Scottish botanist) 3:71
Brown algae 4:50, 53
  illus. 4:48
Brown bears 4:158; 5:70, 73–74, 324
Brown coal 2:347
Brown creepers *see* Tree creepers
Brown dwarf stars 1:202–3
Brownian movement 3:71, 340
Brown pelicans 2:503; 4:446
Brown-rot fungi 4:42
Brown-Séquard, Charles Édouard (French physiologist) 5:467
Brown thrashers 4:453
Browsers (computer programs) 6:307–8, 391
Bruangs *see* Malayan sun bears

Bruises 5:212
Brush-footed butterflies 4:305
Brush turkeys 4:423, 427
Brush wallabies 5:18
Bryde's whales 5:50
BRYOPHYTES 4:12, 55–56, 58–63
Bryozoa 4:202
BTUs (British Thermal Units) 3:225
Bubble chambers 1:226; 6:359
  illus. 6:360
Bubble memory 6:371
Bucherer, A. H. (German physicist) 3:347
Buckland, William (British scientist) 1:493
Buckyballs *see* Fullerenes
Budding (in biology)
  asexual reproduction 3:456
  coelenterates 4:217–18
  plants 4:69
  sponges 4:215–16
  tunicates 4:309
  virus infection 3:392
  yeasts 4:40
  illus. 3:453
Budgets 1:459
Buds, Flower 4:101
Bud scales 4:145
BUFFALO 5:133–34
Buffalo grass 4:139
Buffers, Chemical 3:98; 5:206
Buffon, Comte de (French naturalist) 2:11; 3:473
Bugatti Type 41 Royale (automobile)
  illus. 6:136
Bugs, True 4:279
BUILDING, Techniques of 6:32–41
  archaeological sites 1:466, 468
  construction materials 6:23–31
  earthquake precautions 2:50
  insulation 3:234
  International Space Station 1:269
  solar heating and cooling 2:381–83, 386
  illus.
    demolition 3:57
    flying buttress 6:7
    solar panels 2:381
Bulimia 5:355
Bullard, Sir Edward (British geophysicist) 2:29
Bullen, Keith E. (Australian scientist) 1:107; 2:26–27
Bullets 1:515
Bullet Train
  illus. 6:129
Bullfrogs 4:345–46, 348
Bull sharks 4:327
Bull snakes 4:371
Bumblebees 4:288
Buntings 4:457–58
  illus. 4:457

Buoyancy
  fluid dynamics 3:188, 190–91
  ships 6:112
  submersibles 6:123
Buoys 2:242, 275
Buprestidae *see* Metallic wood borers
Bupropion hydrochloride (Zyban) 5:377
Buran (space shuttle) 1:257, 283
Burchell's zebras 5:109–10
Burettes 3:133
  illus. 3:135
Burros *see* Donkeys
Burroughs, Edgar Rice (American writer) 1:501
Burrowing animals 4:140, 169
Burrowing lizards 4:358
Burrowing owls 4:419
Burrowing pythons 4:370
Burrowing snakes 4:369–70
Burrs 4:104
Bursas 5:183, 193
Bursitis 5:183, 193
Burying beetles 4:294
Busch, Andreas (German astronomer) 1:66
Buses (electrical conductors) 2:317–18
Buses (vehicles) 2:345; 6:128
  illus.
    methane-operated 2:396
Bush, George W. (American president) 1:263; 2:307, 515
Bush, Vannevar (American engineer) 6:302–3
Bushmasters (snakes) 4:374
Bushnell, David (American inventor) 6:119
Bush pigs 5:114
Bush vipers 4:374
Business *see also* Industry
  accountants 1:453–59
  Internet growth 6:308–9
Bus networks (of computers) 6:387
  illus. 6:386
Buspirone 5:356
Bustards 4:438
Butadiene 2:334, 345
Butane 2:332; 3:111
Butcher birds *see* Shrikes
BUTTERFLIES 3:366; 4:280, 300–306
  animal behavior 4:192, 196
  defense mechanisms 4:194, 276
  endangered species 2:505
  monarch butterflies 6:75
  diagram(s) 4:301
  illus. 4:177
    development 4:275
    European skipper 4:306
    fritillary 4:305
    monarch 4:190, 302
    morpho 4:304

BUTTERFLIES (cont.)
  Palos Verde blue **4:**304
  swallowtail **4:**303
Butterfly fish 4:333, 335
  illus. **4:**334
Buttes 2:80, 85, 418
  illus. **2:**79
Buttock pads 5:141–43
Buttocks
  muscles of the body **5:**192
Buttress dams 6:52
  illus. **6:**54
Buttresses 6:33
Butyl group 3:110
Butyric acid 3:114; **4:**259
Butyrophenones 5:466
Bykovsky, Valery F. (Soviet cosmonaut) **1:**241
Bypass surgery 5:439
By-product ovens 2:358
  illus. **2:**357
Byssinosis 2:469
Bytes 6:364

C

C (computer language) **6:**375–76, 381
C++ (computer language) **6:**378
Cabbage butterflies 4:304
Cabbage webworms 4:305
Cables, Electric 2:317–18
  computer networks **6:**388
  submarine **2:**264, 269
Cable television 6:295
  computer modems **6:**366
  high-definition television **6:**297
  interactive TV **6:**304
  Internet **6:**390
Cable-tool drilling 2:326
Cactus plants
  adaptations **4:**136, 167
  desert life **2:**86
  plant behavior **4:**115
  threatened species **2:**497
  illus.
    first-light cactus **4:**115
    pollinated by bat **4:**115
    saguaro **4:**166
    showy mound cactus **2:**86
Cactus wrens 4:452–53
CAD/CAM (Computer-Aided Design/Manufacturing)
  6:193, 197
  illus. **5:**503; **6:**197, 390
Caddis flies 4:280
Cadillac (automobile)
  illus. **6:**137
Cadmium 2:463–64; **3:**35
Cadmium poisoning 2:469
Caecilians 4:337, 340–42, 349
Caesarean sections *see* Cesarean sections
Caffeine 5:260, 373
Cagle, Myrtle (American aviator)
  illus. **1:**287

CAH *see* Congenital adrenal hyperplasia
Cahows 2:503–4
Caiman lizards 4:360
Caimans 4:380, 383
Caisson disease *see* Bends
Caissons 3:185; **6:**15
Calamites 4:74–75
Calcaneus 5:181–82
  illus. **5:**175
Calcarea 4:200
Calcite *see* Calcium carbonate
Calcitonin 5:247
Calcium 3:30, 35
  bone diseases **5:**184
  nutrition **5:**387
  radioisotope tracers **3:**319
  salts in ocean **2:**229
  thyroid and parathyroid glands
    5:247
  tooth development **5:**282
  Vitamin D **5:**384
  illus.
    spectrum **3:**327
Calcium carbide 6:207
Calcium carbonate (Calcite)
    2:36, 133, 135, 138; **3:**30
  carbon cycle **3:**489–90
  caves **2:**125, 127–28
  coral reefs **2:**284–86
  crustaceans' shells **4:**246
  fossils **1:**484
  water hardness **2:**446–47
Calcium channel blockers 5:467
Calcium hydroxide *see* Hydrated lime
Calcium oxide *see* Lime
Calcium phosphate 5:173
Calcium sulfate *see* Gypsum
CALCULUS 1:329–30, 333, **431–37; 3:**147
Calderas (craters) **2:**58, 108
Caledonian Mountains 2:73
CALENDAR 1:469, **474–78**
  Stone Age **6:**4
California *see also* Los Angeles
  alternative fuels **2:**332
  beach erosion **2:**294
  climate **2:**211
  coast formation **2:**120, 291–92
  dams **6:**53, 56
  earthquakes **2:**52–54
  geothermal energy **2:**391
  La Brea Tar Pits **2:**139
  ocean waves **2:**254
  Owens River Valley **2:**5–7
  sand dunes **2:**429
  Santa Ana wind **2:**186
  sea caves **2:**129
  Sierra Nevada **2:**33
  water desalination **2:**448
  water pollution **2:**459
  Yosemite National Park **2:**98
  illus.
    air pollution **2:**466
    Bridalveil Falls **2:**97
    earthquake (1989) **2:**50

    Golden Gate Bridge in fog
      2:162
    hot springs **2:**64
    Owens River Valley **2:**4
    San Andreas Fault **2:**49
    sequoias **4:**1
    Shasta Lake **2:**107
California, University of 2:376
California boas *see* Rosy boas
California condors 2:505; **4:**416
  illus. **2:**503
California Current 2:210, 241
California Desert Protection Act
    (1994) **2:**509
California gnatcatchers
  illus. **2:**499
California gray whales *see* Gray whales
California quails 4:424–25
  illus. **4:**423
California red firs 4:91
California sea lions 5:66
  illus. **5:**63
Californium 3:35
Caller ID 6:241
Callisto (moon of Jupiter) **1:**138
Call-waiting 6:241
Calomel (Mercurous chloride)
    3:99
Caloric theory 3:220
Calories 3:58, 224–25; **5:**400–401
  burned by walking **5:**403
  carbohydrates **5:**381–82
  fats **3:**120; **5:**383
  measurement **3:**61
  proteins **5:**379–80
  weight control **5:**391, 393
Calorimeters 3:61
  illus. **3:**61, 221, 225
Calorimetry 3:225
Calvin cycle 4:24
Calving (of glaciers) **2:**260
Cambium 3:463; **4:**15, 69
Cambrian period 1:487
  crustaceans **4:**250
  prehistoric animals **1:**490
  trilobites **4:**249
  map(s) **2:**40
  table(s) **1:**486; **2:**18–19
Camcorders 6:282–83, 287
  illus. **1:**256
CAMELS 2:86; **4:**169; **5:**116–17
  illus. **2:**85
Cameras 6:262–63
  color television **6:**292
  digital photography **6:**273–74
  eyes compared with **5:**271–72
  Hubble Space Telescope **1:**49
  lenses **3:**290
  ROSAT **1:**64
  television cameras **6:**290–94
  diagram(s)
    television camera **6:**293
Cameroon
  Lake Nios eruption **2:**61, 109
Camille (hurricane, 1969) **2:**200

Camouflage
  deer 5:120
  fish 4:334–35
  insects 4:276
  sloths 5:34
  zebras 5:109
  illus. 3:503
Camshafts 6:100, 139
Canada
  Athabasca tar sands 2:325
  British Columbia precipitation 2:171
  climate 2:242
  conifer forests 4:87
  dams in Quebec 6:52, 56
  fireball impact (1999) 1:169
  Fundy, Bay of 2:246
  geomagnetic storms 2:158
  glacial lakes 2:108
  grasslands 4:143
  hot springs 2:64
  hydroelectric power 2:380
  ice ages 2:218
  oil pipelines 2:329
  petroleum 2:335
  space station 1:269
  taiga 4:165
  tidal energy 2:249, 399
  tundra 2:77
  wilderness areas 2:512–13
  Wood Buffalo National Park 5:133
  illus.
    Fundy, Bay of 2:245, 248
    Niagara Falls 2:102
    Nova Scotia shore 2:293
Canada geese 4:441
  illus. 4:440
Canada hemlocks *see* Eastern hemlocks
Canadian Shield 2:89
Canals (Martian features) 1:127–28
Canals (water transportation) 6:45–46
  illus. 2:438
Canards (of aircraft) 6:95
Canaries 4:461
Canaries Current 2:241
Canary Islands (Atlantic Ocean) 2:71
Cancellous bone 5:174
Cancer (constellation) 1:29
CANCER (disease) 5:432–37
  aging 3:467
  AIDS 5:441, 443
  air pollution 2:468
  bones 5:184
  cell division 3:444
  cervical 5:443
  diagnostic imaging 5:459
  dioxins 2:463
  drug delivery technology 5:473
  exercise benefits 5:402
  fiber, dietary 5:381
  genetic diseases 5:421
  lung *see* Lung cancer

lymphatic system 5:214
nanotechnology therapies 6:342
nursing 5:485–86
oncology 5:413
pain relief 5:470–71
radiation exposure 2:372; 3:127
radioisotopes 3:319–20
skin 5:267
smoking 5:374
surgery 5:479
vagina 5:302
viruses 3:389
X-ray exposure 5:452
illus.
  chest X-ray 5:221
Candelabra trees 4:142
Candida albicans 3:451; 4:40–41
Cane toads
  illus. 4:345
Canidae *see* Dog family
Canine teeth *see* Cuspids
Canis Major (constellation) 1:32
Canis Minor (constellation) 1:32
Canker sores 5:281
Cankerworms 4:305, 307
Cannibalism
  chimpanzees 5:144
Canning of food 6:79
Cannon-boring devices 3:189–90
Canoeing
  illus. 2:510
Canopus (star) 1:27
Canopy (of a rain forest) 4:156–57
Cantilever bridges 6:50
  illus. 6:49
Cantor, Georg (German mathematician) 1:330, 335, 438
Canvasback ducks 4:443
Canyon Diablo (Arizona) *see* Barringer Crater
Canyons 2:419
Canyons, Submarine *see* Submarine canyons
Capacitors 6:248
Cape Bareen geese 4:432
Cape Cod (Massachusetts)
  Cape Cod Canal 2:247–48
  wind turbines 2:387, 399
Cape hunting dogs *see* African hunting dogs
Capek, Karel (Czech author) 6:197
Capella (star) 1:32, 192
Cape Wind (wind farm) 2:387, 399
Capillaries 5:195–96, 202–3
  lungs 5:218–19
  illus. 5:169
Capillary action 3:76
Capillary fringes (of water tables) 2:115
Capone, Al (American gangster) 1:453
Capricornus (constellation) 1:30

Caprimulgiformes 4:399–400, 402–4
Caprock 2:324, 336
Capsids 3:386
Capsomeres 3:387
Captive-breeding programs 4:472–73, 477
Capuchin monkeys 5:140, 146
Capybaras 5:39, 45
Caracals 5:91
  illus. 5:92
Caracaras 4:418
Caracol (building, Chichén Itzá) 1:471
Carapace 4:257, 375
Carbamazepine 5:356
Carbohydrates 5:380–82
  biochemistry 3:118–19, 121
  calories 3:61
  life, characteristics of 3:376
  photosynthesis 4:17–18
  weight control 5:394
Carbon 3:31, 36 *see also* Diamond; Graphite
  activated *see* Charcoal, Activated
  atomic size 3:21
  carbon cycle 4:21
  coal 2:346–47
  color of graphite 3:28
  Drake's Equation 1:323
  fossils 2:139
  isotopes 3:20
  life, origin of 3:380
  molecules in space 1:318
  nonmetals 3:27
  organic chemistry 3:106–8
  peat 4:155
  primary batteries 3:105
  Sun 1:89
  diagram(s)
    atom 2:362; 3:18–19
Carbon 14 3:128, 321 *see also* Radiocarbon dating
Carbon 15 3:128
Carbonate hardness 2:446
Carbonates 2:138
Carbon black 2:334, 345
Carbon-carbon composites 6:231
Carbon cycle (in biology) 3:488–90; 4:21
Carbon cycle (in physics) 1:89
Carbon dating 1:485; 2:16–17
Carbon dioxide 3:69
  air pollution 2:470
  atmosphere 2:147–50, 154; 4:155
  breathing 4:185; 5:215, 218–20
  carbon cycle 3:488–89; 4:21
  carbonic acid 3:87
  cave formation 2:126–27
  chemical bonding 3:52
  coal combustion 2:358
  coal mines 2:354
  excretory system 5:258, 261
  fuel gases 2:359

Carbon dioxide (cont.)
greenhouse effect **3**:238–39
greenhouse gases **2**:478
lasers **5**:488; **6**:351
life, origin of **3**:380
Mars **1**:132
nanotechnology **6**:343
natural gas **2**:345
photosynthesis **4**:17, 24
rain water **2**:172
savanna grasses absorb **4**:143
Venus **1**:101
volcanoes **2**:7
water softening **2**:447
water solution **3**:84
diagram(s)
Lewis structure **3**:67
Carbon family of elements 3:31
Carbon fiber 6:148
Carbon fixation 4:24
Carbonic acid 2:126, 172; **3**:87, 94
Carboniferous period
coal **2**:347
ferns **4**:78
fossils **1**:488
plants **4**:74
table(s) **1**:486; **2**:18–21
Carbon monoxide
air pollution **2**:467–68, 471; **3**:73
atmosphere **2**:147
coal mines **2**:354
comet **1**:160
electricity, generation of **2**:358
fuel gases **2**:359
radioactive tracers **5**:456
Carbonyl group 3:114
Carbureted water gas 2:359
illus. **2**:358
Carburetors 6:100, 139
Carcajous *see* Wolverines
Carcinogens 5:434–37
Cardiac catheterization *see* Angiograms
Cardiac muscle 5:164, 172, 187, 200
illus. **5**:186, 189
Cardiac output 5:198
Cardiac skeleton 5:198, 200
Cardinals (birds) **4**:447, 458
illus. **4**:390
Cardiology 5:413
Cardiopulmonary resuscitation (CPR) 5:222
Cardiovascular disease *see* Heart disease
Cardiovascular physiology 3:373
Careers
accounting **1**:458
acoustics **3**:202
aeronautical engineering **3**:192
agronomy **4**:173
archaeology **1**:466
astronomy **1**:13
biology **3**:371

botany **4**:6
chemistry **3**:5
ecology **3**:474
engineering **6**:19
entomology **4**:270
forensic science **1**:508
forestry **4**:129
genetics **3**:404
geography **2**:300
herpetology **4**:338
horticulture **4**:173
ichthyology **4**:314
mathematics **1**:331
medicine **5**:414
microbiology **3**:449
nursing **5**:486
oceanography **2**:225
optical engineering **3**:287
ornithology **4**:387
paleontology **1**:482
pharmacy **5**:462–63
physics **3**:143
psychology **5**:342–47
science education **6**:328
scientific research **1**:4
space science **1**:236
technical trades **6**:12
veterinary science **4**:466
zoology **4**:180
zoos **4**:475
CargoLifter airship 6:151
Cargo ships 6:112–14
Carhart, Arthur G. (American public official) **2**:510
Caribbean Sea 2:229, 234, 240
hurricanes **2**:196
illus.
Tobago Cays **2**:280
Caribou 4:164; **5**:119, 123
Caries *see* Dental caries
Carina (constellation) **1**:27
Carlsbad Caverns (New Mexico) **2**:125–26, 131
illus. **2**:126
Carnassial teeth 5:9, 69, 77, 85, 99
Carnegie Museum (Pittsburgh, Pennsylvania) **1**:483
Carnivorous animals 3:485; **5**:8–9, 13
bats **5**:32
bears **5**:69–75
cat family **5**:84–92
dog family **5**:77–83
mustelids **5**:93–98
pinnipeds **5**:63
viverrids **5**:99–102
CARNIVOROUS PLANTS 4:108–12, 113, 117–18, 154
Carolina parakeets 2:496
Caroline Islands (Pacific Ocean) **2**:283
Carotene 4:18
Carotenoids 4:49–50, 72
Carothers, Wallace Hume (American chemist) **6**:215
Carp 4:333; **6**:89–90

Carpal bones 5:179
illus. **5**:174, 178–79
Carpal tunnel syndrome 5:182
Carpels 4:99–102
Carpenter, M. Scott (American astronaut) **1**:240–41
illus. **1**:275
Carpenter ants 4:284
Carpet beetles 4:291, 294
Carpet pythons 4:370
Carrageenan 4:53
Carrier current 2:320
Carrier frequency 6:288–90, 295
Carrion beetles *see* Burying beetles
Carrots
illus. **6**:68
Carrying capacity (of habitats) **3**:479, 482
graph(s) **3**:480
Cars *see* Automobiles
Carson, Rachel (American biologist) **3**:472, 474
Cartesian coordinates 1:392–94; **3**:336
Cartier-Bresson, Henri (French photographer)
illus. **6**:271
Cartilage 5:174–75, 177
arthritis **5**:183, 427, 429
bone development **5**:327
cartilaginous fish **4**:324
transformed into bone **5**:328
CARTILAGINOUS FISH 1:490; **4**:205, 315, **323**, **323–28**
Cartography *see* Maps
Cartwright, Edmund (English inventor) **6**:190
Carvel construction (of ships) **6**:109
Cascade process 3:354
Cascade Range 2:43, 59, 67
Case hardening 6:182
Cash-flow statements 1:458
Caspian Sea 2:107–8, 219, 452
Casques (of birds) **4**:407, 412
Cassegrain focus 1:38
illus. **1**:39
Cassini, Giovanni Domenico (Italian-French astronomer) **1**:142
Cassini division 1:142–44
Cassini spacecraft 1:145, 260, 295; **3**:382
illus. **1**:296
Cassiopeia (constellation) **1**:26
Cassiopeia A (supernova remnant)
illus. **1**:58; **3**:280
Cassowaries 4:412
illus. **4**:411
Caste system
ants **4**:281–82
bees **4**:286
termites **4**:290
Cast iron 6:29–30, 175, 178, 187–88
Cast-iron pipes 2:449

Castor (star) **1:**32
Casuariiformes 4:398
Catalysts 3:55, 62; **6:**206
Catalytic converters 2:468;
    3:73; **6:**140–41
    chemistry **3:**62
    negative effects **6:**134
Catalytic cracking 2:331
Catamounts see Cougars
Cataracts (in the eyes) **5:**271,
    508
Catbirds 4:453
Catenary curves 6:33
Caterpillars 4:301–2, 304–5, 307
    illus.
        monarch butterfly **4:**302
        spicebush swallowtail **4:**301
        woolly-bear **4:**306
CAT FAMILY 5:84–92 see also
    Cats, Domestic
    endangered species **2:**500
    evolution **1:**489
Catfish 4:333; **6:**90
    illus. **6:**87
Cathedrals 6:7, 25, 33
    illus. **6:**36
Catheters
    angiogram **5:**439
    angioplasty **5:**439, 490–91
    balloon valvuloplasty **5:**440
    post-surgery monitoring **5:**480
Cathode-ray tubes (CRTs)
    6:249–50
    television **3:**300; **6:**295–96
    illus. **6:**249
Cathodes 3:102; **6:**247–48
    illus. **6:**247, 249–50
Cations 3:31, 50, 63, 97, 102
Catopril 5:467
Cats, Domestic 4:190; **5:**324
    pets **4:**480–82, 484–86, 490
    illus. **5:**85, 90
CAT scans 5:234, 452–53,
    458–59
Catskill Mountains 2:80
    illus. **2:**68
Cattails
    illus. **4:**150
Cattle 5:134
    beef tapeworm **4:**226
    dairy farming **6:**64–66
    evolution **5:**127
    feedlots **6:**60
    grasslands **4:**140
    methane production **2:**146, 478
    milking machines **3:**186
    rain forests, dangers to **4:**160
    selective breeding **6:**71
    illus. **2:**76; **6:**58
Caudata see Salamanders
Caustic soda see Sodium
    hydroxide
Cavendish, Henry (English sci-
    entist) **3:**178
    illus.
        gravity experiment **3:**177
Cave of the Winds (Niagara
    Falls, New York) **2:**129

Cave painting
    illus. **6:**4
Cave pearls 2:128
CAVES AND CAVERNS
    2:125–31
    carbon dioxide–water solution
        3:84
    coastal formation **2:**291–92
    lake formation **2:**110
    water changes the land **2:**418
    illus. **2:**1; **3:**87
        cutaway view of limestone
            cave **2:**127
        wind caves **2:**431
Caviar 4:331
Cavies 5:45
Cayley, Sir George (British sci-
    entist) **6:**152
Caymans see Caimans
CBT see Computer Based Train-
    ing
CCDs see Charge-coupled
    devices
CD-4 cells (Helper T cells;
    T-helper lymphocytes)
    5:236–37, 442–43, 445
    AIDS **5:**212, 239
CDMA (cellular standard) **6:**245
CDPD (cellular standard) **6:**245
CD-ROMs 6:299–300
CDs (Compact discs) 6:285–87,
    299
    data storage **6:**372
    illus.
        CD player **6:**286
Cecropia moths 4:306
    diagram(s) **4:**301
    illus. **4:**307
Cecum 5:8, 254
Cedars 4:85–87, 92
    wood construction **6:**28
Cedars of Lebanon 4:92
Cedar waxwings 4:452
Cedros Island mule deer 5:122
Ceilometers 2:164
Celera Genomics 3:420
Célerifères
    illus. **6:**93
Celestial equator 1:36
Celestial globes 1:66
    illus. **1:**9
Celestial navigation 6:165–66
Celestial sphere 1:32, 36, 385
Cell biology (Cytology) 3:366;
    4:181
Cell body 5:171
CELL DIVISION 3:440–45, 459–
    60, 467
CELL DYNAMICS 3:432–39
Cell membranes 3:428–29 see
    also Plasma membrane
Cell phones see Cellular technol-
    ogy
Cell plate 3:442–43
Cells (in air pressure) **2:**210

Cells (in biology) **5:**161–63 see
    also Cell division; Cell
    dynamics; Cell structure
    aging **3:**467–68; **5:**334
    algae **4:**47–48
    animals **4:**185
    biology, history of **3:**369
    cancer **5:**433–34
    death **3:**468, 470
    early life **4:**184
    glossary **3:**430
    human growth **5:**325
    life, characteristics of **3:**376,
        378
    life, origin of **1:**319
    malignant **5:**434
    membranes see Cell mem-
        branes
    osmosis **3:**80
    plant cytology **4:**4
    plants **4:**9, 14, 65
    prokaryotes **4:**26–27
    types of **3:**432–33
    viral infection **3:**391–93
    illus. **5:**162
        human cheek cells **6:**333
        malignant **5:**433
        muscle cells **3:**439
        plants **4:**10
        potato **6:**74
CELL STRUCTURE 3:424–31
    glossary **3:**430
    illus. **5:**162
Cellular Digital Packet Data see
    CDPD
Cellular One (company) **6:**243
Cellular respiration 3:436–38
Cellular response 5:237
Cellular slime molds 4:51–52
CELLULAR TECHNOLOGY
    6:242–45
    digital photography **6:**274
    health and cell phones **3:**277
    illus.
        phone displays e-mail **6:**243
Cellulose 3:118–19
    algae **4:**48, 51
    commercial plastics **6:**214–15
    plant cells **4:**9, 14
    portland cement mixture **6:**26
    ruminants' digestion **4:**35
Cellulose acetate 6:215
Cell walls 3:426, 430–31; **4:**14,
    28–29
    microbiology **3:**448, 451
Celsius, Anders (Swedish
    astronomer) **3:**191
Celsius temperature scale
    3:135, 191, 223
    table(s) **6:**421
Cement 6:24–26, 218
Cementum 5:278
    illus. **5:**280
Cenozoic era 1:489, 498; **2:**19
    table(s) **1:**486; **2:**20–21
Center of gravity 3:181–82
    human body **5:**153

Center of gravity (cont.)
  ships 6:112
  triangle 1:372
  illus. 3:179–80
Centigrade scale *see* Celsius temperature scale
Centipedes 4:197, 249, 264–65
  illus. 4:247
Central alpha agonists 5:467
Central America 2:52, 515
Central Artery/Tunnel Project (Boston, Massachusetts) *see* "Big Dig"
Central cells (in botany) 4:103
Central nervous system 5:224, 227–31
  medications 5:465–67
Central Park Zoo (New York City) 4:470
  illus. 4:469
Central plateaus 2:79
Central processing unit (CPU) 6:365, 369–70, 376
Central tendency 3:511
Centrifugal force 3:158, 160–61
  mirror casting 1:41
Centrifugal pumps 2:441, 449–50
Centrifuges 3:133
  astronaut training 1:280
  blood tests 5:213
  centrifugal force 3:160
  medical technology 5:493–94
  illus. 1:285; 3:160
Centrioles 3:430–31, 442
  illus. 5:162
Centripetal force 3:158–60
Centromeres 3:441–42
Centruroides scorpions 4:263
Century plant *see* Agave
Cephalochordates 4:205, 309
Cephalopods 4:203, 232–35
Cephalosporin antibiotics 4:38
Cephalothorax 4:248, 256–57
Cepheus (constellation) 1:26
CERAMICS 6:216–21
  artificial body parts 5:501, 503
  engineering today 6:21
  modern materials 6:229
  superconductivity 3:360
Ceratopians 1:496
Cerci 4:274
Cereal rust 4:45
Cerebellar cortex 5:230
Cerebellar hemisphere 5:230
Cerebellum 5:229–30
Cerebral-anemia theory of sleep 5:405
Cerebral arteriosclerosis 5:234
Cerebral cortex 5:4, 228–29, 362
Cerebral hemispheres *see* Cerebrum
Cerebral hemorrhage *see* Stroke
Cerebral thrombosis 5:234
Cerebrospinal fluid 5:228, 231

Cerebrospinal nervous system *see* Central nervous system
Cerebrum 5:158–59, 228–29
Ceres (asteroid) 1:75, 168
Cerium 3:36
CERN *see* European Center for Particle Physics
Cernan, Eugene A. (American astronaut) 1:273
  illus. 1:245
Certified Management Accountant (CMA) 1:458
Certified Public Accountant (CPA) 1:456, 458
Cervical plexus 5:232
Cervical vertebrae 5:175
  illus. 5:175–76
Cervix, Uterine 5:294, 299, 304
  cancer 5:443
  illus. 5:295
Cesarean sections 5:305
Cesium 3:29, 36
Cesium 137 2:372; 3:319
Cessna *Citation* S/2 (airplane)
  illus. 6:163
Cetacea 5:12, 46, 55
Cetus (constellation) 1:32
CFCs *see* Chlorofluorocarbons
Chachalacas 4:423, 427
Chacma baboons 5:142
Chadwick, Sir James (English physicist) 3:7
Chaetognatha 4:202
Chaffee, Roger (American astronaut) 1:274
Chagas' disease 4:208; 5:428
Chain of custody (forensics) 1:516
Chain reactions 2:364–67; 3:124
  diagram(s) 2:365
Chalazion 5:273
Chalk 2:120, 135
  illus.
    cliffs of Dover 2:35; 4:210
Challenger (space shuttle)
  explosion 1:239, 253, 258–59, 261, 276
  illus.
    crew 1:289
    explosion 1:253
Challenger expedition 2:223, 273
  illus. 2:272
Challis, James (British astronomer) 1:152
Chambered nautiluses 4:234
  illus. 4:233
Chamberlin, Thomas C. (American astronomer) 2:11
Chameleons 4:195, 358–59
  illus. 4:193
Champollion, Jean-François (French archaeologist) 1:463
Chandra X-ray Observatory 1:47, 52, 59; 3:280

CHANGES OF STATE (Phase changes) 3:13–14, 75–78, 226–31
Chang Heng (Chinese scientist) 2:7
Channels (of streams) 2:419, 422, 424
Chaos (amoeba) 4:209
Chaos theory 1:331
Chaparral bushes 4:167
Chaparrals 3:495; 4:135
Chapman, Frank (American ornithologist) 4:387
Characteristic (part of logarithm) 1:361
Charadriiformes 4:399, 432–38
Charcoal, Activated 2:444–45
Charcot, Jean Martin (French physician) 5:336
Charge conjugation 3:310
Charge-coupled devices (CCDs) 6:291–92
  digital photography 6:273
  imaging, diagnostic 1:255
  telescopes 1:38
Charges, Electrical *see* Electrical charges
Chariots (wheeled vehicles)
  illus. 6:6
Charles, Jacques-Alexandre-César (French scientist) 3:74; 6:150
Charles' law 1:357; 3:74, 222
  illus. 3:72
Charm quarks 3:20, 314
Charnley, Sir John (English scientist) 5:503
Charon (moon of Pluto) 1:79, 156–57
Chartered Accountant (CA) 1:456
Chassis 6:135, 145–46
Chawla, Kalpana (American astronaut) 1:289
Cheese 4:35, 43–44
  illus. 6:81
Cheetahs 2:500; 5:88–89
  illus. 5:89
Chelicerae 4:257
Chelicerates 4:247–48
Chemical analysis *see* Analytical chemistry
Chemical Bond, The (book, Pauling) 3:9
CHEMICAL BONDING 3:47–52, 88–89
  chemical reactions 3:57–58
  organic chemistry 3:108–10
Chemical changes *see* Chemical reactions
Chemical defenses (of plants) 4:117–18
Chemical elements *see* Elements
Chemical engineering 6:20
Chemical geology 2:3

CHEMICAL INDUSTRY 6:203–8
  acids, bases, and salts **3:**99
  air pollution **2:**467
  catalysts **3:**62
  coal-derived chemicals **2:**360
  industrial pollution **2:**462–63
  microbiology **3:**449
  natural gas **2:**345
  petroleum **2:**334
  plastics and polymers **6:**209–15
  illus.
    plastics production **3:**113
Chemical lasers 6:346
Chemical oceanography 2:223
CHEMICAL REACTIONS
    3:57–62
  chemical industry **6:**206
  equations **3:**54–56
  matter, study of **3:**14
  organic chemistry **3:**110–11
  radioisotopes **3:**319
Chemical sedimentary rocks
    2:135–36
Chemical symbols 3:4, 53
  list **3:**34–46
CHEMISTRY 1:6; **3:**2–9
  acids, bases, salts **3:**94–99
  analytical chemistry **3:**129–33
  atoms **3:**16–21
  biochemistry **3:**116–23
  ceramics **6:**216–21
  chemical bonding **3:**47–52
  chemical industry **6:**203–8
  drugs **5:**460, 462
  electrochemistry **3:**252–53
  elements **3:**34–46
  elements, families of **3:**26–33
  entropy **3:**240–43
  forensic science **1:**509, 515
  formulas and equations
    3:53–56
  gases **3:**68–74
  life, origin of **1:**319–20
  mathematics **1:**336–37
  matter, study of **3:**10–15
  measurement **3:**134–37
  metals and alloys **6:**174
  modern materials **6:**226–33
  Nobel Prize winners **6:**407–17
  nuclear chemistry **3:**124–28
  organic chemistry **3:**106–15
  periodic table **3:**22–25
  photosynthesis **4:**17–18
  plastics and polymers **6:**209–15
  reactions *see* Chemical reac-
    tions
  soil chemistry **4:**175
  techniques **3:**134–37
  water **3:**82–87
  table(s)
    constants of measurement
      6:409
Chemolithotrophic bacteria
    4:31, 35
Chemosynthesis 3:376, 434
Chemotactic bacteria 4:29
Chemotherapy 3:117; **5:**437
  leukemia **5:**211–12

Cheney, Dick 5:505
Chernobyl nuclear accident
    (Ukraine) **2:**373–74
  carcinogenic effects **5:**435
  environmental pollution **2:**455
  illus.
    aftermath **2:**373
Chernozemic soil 2:77;
    4:134–35
Cherokee salamanders 4:350
Cherry trees 4:452
Chest 5:175
  mechanics of breathing **5:**218
  muscles of the body **5:**192
  ribs **5:**177–78
Chestnut blight 4:5, 42, 148
Chestnut trees 4:5, 148
Chevrolet Corvette
  illus. **6:**138
Chichén Itzá (ancient city,
    Mexico) **1:**471
Chickadees 4:456
  illus. **4:**392, 455
Chickens 4:195, 212 *see also*
    Poultry farming
  illus. **4:**386
Childbirth 5:304–5, 485
**Childhood disintegrative disor-
    der 5:**354
Children
  acute rheumatic fever **5:**429
  air pollution **2:**469
  allergies **5:**447
  developmental psychology
    5:342
  immunization schedule **5:**238
  language use **5:**155
  learning disabilities **5:**363–68
  pain **5:**287, 291
  parasitic diseases **5:**420
  pets **4:**486, 490
  physical growth **5:**325–32
  pituitary gland disorders **5:**243
  rickets **5:**184
  sleep disorders **5:**409
  teeth **5:**278–79
  vaccination **5:**237
  illus.
    obesity **5:**393
    pediatric ward **5:**479
Chile
  Atacama Desert **2:**416
  earthquakes **2:**46
  evaporite deposits **2:**36
Chilopoda 4:203
Chimaeras (fish) **4:**323–25
  illus. **4:**325
Chimney swifts 4:405
Chimpanzees 5:144, 146–47
  heart transplanted into human
    5:496
  learning **5:**148–49
  life span **5:**324
  reproduction **5:**146
  symbolic behavior **5:**149
  tools, use of **4:**192–93
  illus. **4:**470; **5:**143, 148–49

China
  acupuncture **5:**510
  archaeology **1:**462–63, 468
  astronomy, history of **1:**472
  canals **6:**45–46
  cast iron construction **6:**29
  ceramics **6:**217
  coal **2:**348
  deserts **2:**83
  earthquakes **2:**47, 52, 54
  fish farming **6:**89–90
  fossils **1:**479; **4:**98
  geology, history of **2:**7
  grasslands **4:**140–41
  hot-air balloons **6:**149
  hydroelectric power **2:**380
  loess deposits **2:**432–33
  maglev trains **3:**267; **6:**131
  metallurgy **6:**175
  natural gas, early use of **2:**337
  nuclear energy **2:**376
  numerals **1:**342–43
  oil spills **2:**328, 465
  Qiantang River tidal bore **2:**247
  smallpox vaccination **5:**430
  solar power **2:**381
  technology and society **6:**7
  Three Gorges Dam **2:**410;
    6:22, 56
  wilderness areas **2:**513
  zoos **4:**470
China Sea 2:246
China white (drug) **5:**374
Chinchillas 5:45
  illus. **5:**44
Chinese alligators 4:384
Chinese lunar calendar 1:478
Chinese ring-necked pheasant
    4:425
Chinese water deer 5:121
Chinook (wind) **2:**100
Chipmunks 4:147; **5:**10, 41
Chips, Computer *see* Micropro-
    cessors
Chiropractic 5:512
  illus. **5:**513
Chital *see* Spotted deer
Chitin 4:246, 251, 291
  algae **4:**48
  chytrids **4:**51
  fungi **3:**431; **4:**37, 41
  insects **4:**246
Chitons 4:241
Chitosan 5:507
Chkalov Air Force Base (Rus-
    sia) **1:**283
Chladni, Ernst F. F. (German
    physicist) **3:**216–17
Chlamydia **4:**30–31; **5:**430, 472
Chlamydomonas **4:**48–49
Chloracne 2:462–63
Chloralkali industry 6:208
Chloramphenicol 5:464
Chlorella **3:**428
Chloride
  nutrition **5:**387
Chlorination 2:444, 487
  water purification **2:**446

Chlorine 3:32, 36
  atomic structure 3:69
  chemical industry 3:99;
    6:207–8
  covalence 3:51
  ionic bonding 3:49–50, 63–64
  ozone layer 2:154, 482
Chlorine bleach 3:95
Chlorine fluoride 3:51
Chlorine gas 3:104
Chlorobia 4:29
Chloroflexa 4:29
Chlorofluorocarbons (CFCs)
  chemical industry 6:208
  global warming 2:479
  ozone layer damage 1:109;
    2:154, 482; 3:73
Chloroform 5:465
Chloro group 3:110
Chlorophyll 3:431; 4:18
  absorption of light 3:297
  algae 4:49–50
  cyanobacteria 4:19
  early life 4:28
  leaves 4:145
  photosynthesis 3:433; 4:9,
    23–24
  illus. 4:10
    ocean concentrations 1:314
Chloroplasts 3:430–31; 4:14, 20,
    22–23, 34, 66, 68, 71
  cyanobacteria 3:428
  illus. 3:429; 4:10, 20
Chlorosomes 4:31
Chlorpromazine 5:466
Choanichthyes 1:492
Choanocytes (Collar cells)
    4:208, 215
Choanoflagellates 4:215
Chokedamp 2:354
Cholera 2:457
Cholesterol 5:383
  dietary fiber 5:381
  fats 3:120–21
  hypercholesterolemia 5:420
  LDLs 5:494
Chollas
  illus. 4:168
Chondrostei 4:331
CHORDATES 1:487; 4:205,
    308–11
Chorion 5:296
Chorionic villus sampling (CVS)
    5:303
Choroid coat (in the eye) 5:269
  illus. 5:271
Chousinghas 5:128–29
Christmas Bird Count 4:388–89
Christmas tree (capping device)
    2:340
  illus. 2:325
Christmas-tree plants 4:118–19
Christy, James W. (American
    astronomer) 1:157
Chromatic aberration 1:39;
    3:291; 6:331
Chromaticity diagrams 3:302
Chromatids 3:441–42, 444–45

Chromatin 3:410, 427
Chromatograms 3:130
Chromatographs 3:136
Chromatography 3:130–32
  illus. 3:1, 131
Chromatophores 4:232, 364
Chrominance 6:293–94
Chromium 3:36
  artificial body parts 5:501
  electroplating 3:103–4
  malleability, lack of 3:27
  trace mineral 5:388
Chromoplasts 3:431
Chromosomes 3:123, 410; 4:181
  amphibians 4:338
  biology, history of 3:370
  cell division 3:441–45
  cell structure 3:427
  genetic diseases 5:419–21
  genetics 3:401–2
  human 3:416; 5:161–62, 293,
    310–13, 318, 323
  McClintock, Barbara 3:412–13
  organism with most 4:81
  illus. 5:162
    Down syndrome 5:419
Chromosphere 1:82–83
Chronic pain 5:287–88
Chronometers 6:170
Chroococeus
  illus. 4:30
Chrysalises 4:302
Chrysanthemums 4:116
Chrysler Airflow (automobile)
  illus. 6:136
Chu, Paul C. W. (American
    physicist) 3:361; 6:221
  illus. 6:220
Chubb Crater (Canada) 1:121
Chuck will's widows 4:403
Chunnel (England–France) 6:48
  illus. 6:46
Churyumov-Gerasimenko,
    Comet (67P) 1:296
Chyme 5:251–53
Chymotrypsin 5:252
Chytrids 4:51–52, 348
Cicindelidae 4:292–93
Ciconiiformes 4:398, 433,
    444–46
Cigarettes see Smoking (of
    tobacco)
Ciguatera 4:53
Cilia 3:430–31; 4:225; 5:163,
    216–17, 236
  protozoans 4:212–13
Ciliary body
  illus. 5:271
Ciliates (Ciliophora) 3:451;
    4:211–13
CIM see Computer integrated
    manufacturing
Cincinnati Zoo (Ohio) 4:476
Cinder cones (volcanoes) 2:57
Cine 360 (film format) 1:72
Cingular (company) 6:245
Cinnamon bears 5:74
Ciprofloxacin 5:464

Circadian rhythms 4:115–17
Circles 1:369, 375–77, 383
  graph(s) 1:395–96
  illus. 1:374
Circuit boards 6:340
  illus. 6:1
Circuit breakers 2:317, 319;
    3:259
  illus. 2:321
Circuits, Electrical see Electrical
    circuits
Circular accelerators 6:353,
    355–59
CIRCULATORY SYSTEM 4:186;
    5:172, 195–204
  angioplasty 5:490–91
  arachnids 4:258
  artificial body parts 5:504–6
  birds 4:394
  crustaceans 4:253–54
  development in babies
    5:326–27
  diagnostic imaging 5:454, 459
  dolphins 5:56
  evolution in mammals 5:4
  exercise 5:397
  fish 4:319–20
  human, before birth 5:296–97
  insects 4:274
  medications 5:467
  whales 5:47
  illus. 5:169
Circumference of a circle 1:369,
    375
  illus. 1:374
Cirques 2:98
Cirrhosis of the liver 5:375
Cirri 4:213
Cirrocumulus clouds 2:165
  illus. 2:164
Cirrostratus clouds 2:165
  illus. 2:164
Cirrus clouds 2:165
  illus. 2:164, 185
Cistus flowered sundews 4:111
Cities see Urban areas
Civets 5:100
Civil engineering 6:20, 22
Civil War, U.S.
  rail transportation 6:126
  submarines 6:119
Clams 4:238
  hydrothermal vents 2:278
  life span 5:324
  shells as defense 4:254
  illus. 4:232
Clam worms 4:245
Clapboard 6:28
Clarinets 3:216
Clark, Laurel (American astro-
    naut) 1:289
Clark, Ronald W. (author) 6:16,
    20
Classes (in biological classifica-
    tion) 3:397
Classical conditioning 5:338,
    359
Classical physics 3:144–45

CLASSIFICATION OF LIVING THINGS 3:394–99
animal-like protists 4:211
arachnids 4:262–63
birds 4:397–400
botany 4:3–4, 54–57
butterflies and moths 4:303
cartilaginous fish 4:324–25
crustaceans 4:254
early classifications 4:183–84
fish 4:319
fungi 4:41
insectivores 5:24
insects 4:277–80
mammals 5:11–13
monerans 4:29
plantlike protists 4:52–53
turtles 4:377–79
zoological 4:179, 198–205
Clastic rocks see Fragmental rocks
Clavicle 5:178
  illus. 5:165, 174
Clavius (lunar crater) 1:113
Clavius, Christopher (Bavarian mathematician) 1:477
Clawed African toads 4:346
Clay 2:35
  caves 2:126–27, 129
  ceramics 6:217
  climate analysis 2:216
  groundwater 2:113–14, 119
  tablets for writing 1:454
Clay, Jacob (Dutch scientist) 1:226
Clean Air Acts (U.S.) 2:471
  1963 2:471
  1970 6:134
  1990 2:172, 358, 474
Clean Water Act (U.S., 1970) 2:458
Clear-cutting of timber 4:129, 146, 149
Clear Skies Act (U.S., 2003) 2:476
Clearwing moths 4:307
Cleavage (in biology) 3:460; 5:162
Cleavage (in minerals) 2:137; 3:64
Clementine spacecraft 1:114, 298
Clermont (steamboat) 6:110
  illus. 6:111
Click beetles 4:294–95
Cliffs 2:418, 422
CLIMATES OF THE PAST 2:215–20
  archaeology 1:464
  geological studies 2:8
  geologic record 2:19, 21
  paleoecology 1:482–83
CLIMATES OF THE WORLD 2:207–14
  air pollution 2:8, 469–70, 477–82
  Arctic Ocean's effects on 2:235

biomes 3:492–93, 498
climatology 2:146
climax communities 4:125
convection currents 3:235
erosion, factor in 2:121–22
greenhouse effect 2:154
ocean currents 2:242
ocean's effects on 2:222
past ages 2:215–20
polar regions 2:87–92
precipitation 2:170–72
rain forests' role 4:161
seawater's salt content 2:229
volcanoes' effect 2:62
water diversions 2:410
wetlands' role 4:155
  map(s) 2:208
Climatology 2:142, 146, 209, 300
Climax communities 3:483; 4:122, 125
Clinical genetics 3:404
Clinical psychology 5:345–46
Clinker construction (of ships) 6:109
Clipper Graham Single-Stage-to-Orbit rocket 1:262–63
Clipper ships 6:110
Clitoris
  illus. 5:295
Cloaca 4:395; 5:14
Clock genes 3:380
Clock paradox 3:347
Clocks and watches
  quartz crystals 3:91
Clock speed (of computers) 6:363, 370
Clonidine 5:470
CLONING 6:14
  genetic technology 3:422–23
  Lincoln's genes 5:318
  mitosis 3:443
  monoclonal antibodies 5:471–72
  organ transplants 5:479
  sheep 6:75
  stem-cell research 5:422
  veterinary science 4:468
Closed control systems (in automation) 6:195
Cloth see Textile industry
Clothing, Protective
  coal miners 2:355
  illus.
    nuclear-power plant workers 2:371
Clothoid loops 3:159
Clotting see Blood clotting
Cloud chambers 6:359
  cosmic rays 1:225, 227–28
  illus. 1:226
Clouded leopards 5:88
  illus. 5:1
Cloud Garden (book, Dyke) 4:2
CLOUDS 2:159–65
  hurricanes 2:197–99
  precipitation 2:166–67
  thunderclouds 2:175–76

Cloud seeding 2:145
Cloud streets 2:163
Clown fish
  illus. 4:219
Clozapine 5:356
Club fungi 3:455; 4:41, 44–45
  parasol ants 4:284–85
CLUB MOSSES 4:13, 56, 60, 74–75, 76–77
Clumber spaniels
  illus. 5:3
Clumped populations 3:479
Cluster (spacecraft) 2:158
Cluster galaxies see Galactic clusters
Clutches 6:144
Clydesdale horses
  illus. 5:108
CMOS see Complimentary metal oxide semiconductor
Cnidaria see Coelenterates
Coagulation (in physiology) see Blood clotting
Coagulation (water treatment) 2:444–45
COAL 1:90; **2:**35–36, **346–60**
  acid rain 2:473
  alternative-fuel source 2:395–96
  chemical reaction 3:62
  combustion 3:62
  composition 2:133
  conservation 2:415
  energy 2:305, 398
  environmental pollution 2:306–7
  formation 3:188
  fossils 1:485; 4:74
  gasification see Coal gasification
  heat energy 3:219
  hydrogen production 2:399
  liquefaction see Coal liquefaction
  minerals 2:136
  organic chemistry 3:108
  peat 4:62
  strip mining 2:456
  illus.
    mining 2:306
    steelmaking 6:180
Coal dust 2:354–55; 3:62
Coalescence (of clouds) 2:167
Coal gasification 2:359, 395
  illus. 2:342, 358
Coal liquefaction 2:359–60, 395
Coal oil see Kerosene
Coalsack (dark nebula) 1:27, 183, 186, 219
  illus. 1:182
Coal tar 2:360
Coastal drift 3:319
Coastal plains 2:76
Coastal redwoods 4:92–93
COASTS 2:288–95
  deserts 2:83
  environmental pollution 2:456
  erosion 2:124, 255

COASTS (cont.)
groundwater contamination
2:118
hurricanes 2:200
plant communities 4:137
precipitation 2:170
tsunamis 2:257–58
urban-wastewater runoff 2:486
wind-turbine locations 2:387
Coatis
illus. 5:75
Cobalt 3:36
artificial body parts 5:501
atomic number 3:20, 24
isotopes 3:317, 319–20
meteorites 1:172
Cobb, Jerrie (American aviator)
1:288–89
illus. 1:287
COBE *see* Cosmic Background
Explorer
COBOL (computer language)
6:378
Cobras 4:355, 365, 372–73;
5:101
illus. 4:371
Cocaine 5:373, 375–76, 462
Coccidiosis 4:212
Coccus 4:28; 5:426–27
illus. 3:448
Coccyx 5:175–76
Cochlea 5:275
illus. 5:276
Cochlear implants 5:509
illus. 5:508
Cockatoos 4:396, 401
illus. 4:401
Cockcroft, John D. (English
physicist) 6:353–54
Cockerall, Christopher (British
inventor) 6:116
Cockroaches 3:500; 4:278, 293
illus. 4:278
Cocks-of-the-rock 4:449
Coconut palm trees
illus. 4:102
Coconuts 4:103–4
Cocoons 4:276, 286
illus.
spider eggs 4:256
Cod 2:407; 4:333
Code Division Multiple Access
see CDMA
Codeine 5:292, 373
Code Red worm 6:394–95
Codes (in communications) 6:317
CODIS *see* Combined DNA Index
System
Codling moths 4:305
Codons 3:123, 412; 5:310
Codosiga 4:208
Coefficient of cubical expan-
sion 3:222
Coefficient of friction 3:165
Coefficient of heat conduction
3:233
Coefficient of linear expansion
3:221–22

Coelacanths 4:330–31
illus. 4:330
COELENTERATES 4:200, 214,
216, **217–19**
Coenzyme A 3:437
Coevolution 3:506
Cognitive psychology 5:343–44
Cognitive therapy 5:357
Coherent light 3:292; 6:275, 345
Cohesion 3:76
Coil loading 6:239
Coke (coal residue) 2:346, 358;
6:175
by-products 2:360
cast iron 6:188
illus. 2:357; 6:180
Colchicine 5:429
Cold, Common 5:429, 431
Eustachian tubes 5:275
viruses 3:388
vitamin C 3:9
zinc lozenges 5:387
Cold-blooded animals *see* Ecto-
therms
Cold fronts 2:187
Cold seeps 2:278
Cold seeps 2:278
Cold sores 3:392–93
Coleco (company) 6:298
Coleoptera 4:280, 292
Colic 5:449
Colic valve *see* Ileocecal valve
Coliform bacteria 2:442
Coliiformes 4:399–400
Colima (volcano, Mexico) 2:62
Collagen 3:468; 4:184; 5:173,
386–87, 507
Collagenous fibers 5:264
Collarbone *see* Clavicle
Collar cells *see* Choanocytes
Collar clouds *see* Rotating wall
clouds
Collared peccaries 5:115
Collections, Scientific 6:313
insects 4:271
rocks, minerals, and fossils
2:139–40
Collective farms 6:59
Collenchyma cells 4:66
Collimators 3:294
Collini, Cosimo (Italian scientist)
1:496
Collins, Eileen (American astro-
naut) 1:289
Collins, Michael (American
astronaut) 1:245
Collision theory 2:11
illus. 2:10
Colloids 3:425
Colobus monkeys 5:141
Colombia 2:58
Colon (in anatomy) 5:254–55
Colon cancer 3:418; 5:402
COLOR 3:293–303 *see also* Pro-
tective coloration
auroras 2:157
autumn leaves 4:72
butterflies 4:300–301

clouds 2:162
desert animals 4:169
feathers 4:392
fish 4:316
heat absorption 3:238
hummingbirds 4:404
light waves 3:273
lizards 4:359–60
minerals 2:138
snakes 4:364
tundra plants 4:163–64
wavelengths 3:323–24
Colorado
Denver air pollution 2:470
Colorado Plateau 2:79
Colorado potato beetles 4:298
Colorado River 2:85, 120, 122,
438
illus.
canals 2:438
Colorado spruces 4:91
Colorado squawfish
illus. 2:501
Color blindness 3:301; 5:319–
20, 421
Color changes
lizards 4:359–60
Color dispersion *see* Refraction
of light
Color enhancement (in diagnostic imaging) 5:458–59
illus. 5:450
Color gamuts 3:302
Colorimetry 3:302
Color photography 6:270–73
Colors (in particle physics)
3:315–16
Color television 6:292, 296
illus.
camera 6:293
Color vision 3:300–301; 4:342
see also Color blindness
Color wheel 3:298
illus. 3:298
Colossal squid 4:233
Colostrum 5:301
Colt, Samuel (American manu-
facturer) 6:191
Colter, John (American explorer)
2:65
Colubridae 4:370–72
Colugos 5:11
Columbia (space shuttle) 1:239,
259, 261
first mission 1:253
illus.
astronauts at controls 1:281
crew of last mission 1:289
Columbia black-tailed deer
5:121
Columbia Plateau 2:34, 79–80
Columbidae 4:428
Columbiformes 4:399
Columbus, Christopher (Italian
navigator)
illus.
lunar eclipse 1:180

Column and beam construction
see Post and lintel construction
Column chromatography 3:132
Columns (cave formations) 2:128
Columns (in architecture)
6:30–31
Coma, Diabetic 5:245
Coma Berenices (constellation)
1:29, 186
Comas (of comets) 1:77, 159
Comb-footed spiders 4:260–61,
263
Combined DNA Index System
(CODIS) 1:516
Comb jellies (Ctenophora)
4:201
Combustion 3:58, 62
rocket thrust 1:242–43
COMETS 1:76–77, **158–66**
amateur astronomy 1:14–15
Chinese astronomy 1:472
IRAS 1:61
Jupiter's collision with 1:138
life, origin of 1:318–19
meteor showers 1:171
solar eclipses 1:180
space probes 1:296
Commensalism 3:483
Common bile duct 5:252
illus. 5:167
Common cold *see* Cold, Common
Common dolphins 5:56–57,
59–60
Common kingfishers 4:407
Common loons 4:433–34
Common porpoises 5:60
illus. 5:56
Common rorquals *see* Fin
whales
Communication
animals *see* Animal communication
cellular technology 6:242–45
computer modems 6:366
computer networking 6:384–91
electronics 2:321
geomagnetic storms 2:158
Internet 6:302–11
interplanetary 1:320
photonics 6:224–25
plant behavior 4:118
radio and television 6:288–97
radio waves 3:281
recording, sound and video
6:278–87
technology and society 6:8–9
telegraph and telephone
6:234–41
Communications Decency Act
(U.S., 1996) 6:311
Communications Satellite Corporation 1:309–10
Communications satellites
1:307–11
passive 1:307–8

photovoltaic cells 2:386
telephone 6:240
COMMUNITIES (in ecology)
3:472, **476–83**
definition 3:477
plant communities 4:132–37
succession 4:120–25
Commutative laws 1:353
Commutators (electrical) 3:255
Compact bone 5:173–74
Compact discs *see* CDs
Compaction 2:50
Companion animals *see* Pets
Comparative biology 3:367
Compasses, Gyroscopic 3:270;
6:173
Compasses, Magnetic 3:267–68,
270; 6:166
illus. 3:271
Competition (in ecological communities) 3:480–81, 506
Competitive exclusion 3:480–81
Compilers (computer programs)
6:380
COMPLEMENTARY AND
ALTERNATIVE MEDICINE
5:510–14
gnetophytes 4:96
horsetails 4:76
veterinary science 4:465
Complementary colors 3:298
Complements (in biochemistry)
5:237
Complete flowers 4:101
Complete proteins 5:379–80
Complex numbers *see* Imaginary numbers
Complimentary metal oxide
semiconductor (CMOS)
6:273
Composite materials 6:23, 148,
230–31
Composites (plants) 4:142
Composite volcanoes 2:57
Compost 2:192; 4:245
Compound bars 3:222, 224
Compound fractures 5:182, 184
Compound leaves 4:71, 73
Compound light microscopes
3:450
Compound optical systems
6:331
COMPOUNDS, Chemical 3:17,
53–54, **63–67**
ionic compounds 3:50
life 3:375–76, 380
water, reaction with 3:87
Compressed air 3:190
illus.
paint sprayer 3:189
Compressed-air disease *see*
Bends
Compressed natural gas 2:345
Compression
construction 6:25, 27, 30–31
gases 3:13, 72
wave motion 3:195, 198

diagram(s)
sound waves 3:199
Compressional waves *see* P
waves
Compression molding 6:214
Compressor stations (natural
gas industry) 2:342–43
Compsognathus 1:494; 4:390
Compton, Arthur H. (American
physicist) 1:227; 3:124
Compton Gamma Ray Observatory 1:59, 231, 236
cosmic rays 1:231
electromagnetic spectrum 3:280
telescopes in space 1:47, 52
illus. 1:51
Compulsions 5:350–51
Compulsive personality 5:353
Computer Based Training 6:383
Computer chips *see* Microprocessors
Computer engineering 6:21
Computer graphics
planetariums 1:72
science-fiction films 1:506
video games 6:299, 301
illus. 6:376
experimental biology 3:515
video games 6:300
Computer integrated manufacturing (CIM) 6:193
Computerized axial tomography
see CAT scans
Computerized numerical control (CNC) machines
6:197
Computer memory *see* Memory
(computer)
COMPUTER NETWORKING
6:373, **384–91**
Internet 6:302–11
security systems 6:395–96
video games 6:301
illus. 6:366, 373
COMPUTER PROGRAMMING
6:375–83
accounting 1:459
downloadable applications
6:309
Internet 6:304–11
robots 6:194, 199–200
software 6:372
COMPUTERS 6:13, **361–74**
accounting 1:459
atmospheric science 2:143, 146
automation 6:197
automobile design 6:148
binary system 1:345, 446
cellular technology 6:243–45
computer networking 6:384–91
diagnostic imaging 5:452–54
DNA computers 3:405, 419
Earth Observing System 1:259
engineering today 6:21
experimental biology 3:515
factories 6:193
farms, modern 6:61–62, 64

COMPUTERS (cont.)
fax modems **6:**244
holography **6:**277
integrated circuits **6:**253
Internet **6:**302–11
mathematics **1:**331
medical technology **5:**493
nanotechnology **6:**340–41, 343
oceanic research **2:**224, 226
photonic computers **6:**225
programming *see* Computer
programming
robots **6:**201–2
satellite communication **1:**308
security *see* Computer security
space guidance **1:**305
weather forecasting **2:**200,
204–6
zoological research **4:**182
illus.
cattle feeding control **6:**58
digital music creation **6:**285
farm productivity **4:**175
library patrons **6:**1
vacuum tubes in 1950's computer **6:**250
weather forecasting **2:**201
zoological research **4:**181
Computer screens *see* Monitors
COMPUTER SECURITY
6:392–97
Comsat *see* Communications
Satellite Corporation
Concave lenses 5:272
Concave mirrors 3:286–87
Concentrated solutions 3:79–80
Concentrates (of ores) **6:**175–77
Concentration (chemistry) **3:**61
Conception *see* Fertilization
Concert halls 3:208
Conches 4:241
Concorde (airplane) **6:**157
illus. **6:**163
Concrete 6:24, 26, 218
building techniques **6:**40–41
concrete gravity dams **6:**52
house construction **6:**34
paving material **6:**43–44
prestressed concrete **6:**31
reinforced concrete **6:**30–31
illus.
concrete gravity dams **6:**55
Concussions 5:234
Condensation 2:163–64; **3:**77,
231
cloud formation **2:**166–67
Condensers (electrical) **3:**248
Conditioning (in psychology)
5:227, 338
Condors 2:505; **4:**414, 416;
5:324
illus. **2:**503; **4:**416
Conduction, Electrical 2:309–
10; **3:**358–62
Conduction of heat 3:232–34
illus. **3:**233

Conductors, Electrical 3:246,
254, 256, 258
ionic compounds **3:**64
metals **3:**26–27
nonmetals **3:**28
polymers **6:**215
salts in water **3:**87
Condylarths 1:489
Condyles 5:181
Cone-bearing plants *see* Gym-
nosperms
Cones (in the eyes) **5:**270–71
Cones (in geology) **2:**56–58
Cones (in geometry) **1:**383
illus. **1:**332, 382
Cones (of trees) **4:**86–88, 164
cycads **4:**97
illus. **4:**56
Congenital adrenal hyperplasia
5:246
Congenital defects *see* Birth
defects
Congestive heart failure
5:439–40
Conglomerate (rock) **2:**35, 135
Congo eels (salamanders) **4:**351
Conic sections 1:162, 377–79
Conidia 4:38, 41–42
CONIFERS 4:10, 57, **84–93**
biomes **3:**496–97
fossils **1:**488
leaf shape **4:**72
plant communities **4:**134–35
rain forests **4:**159
taiga **4:**164
illus.
seed cone **4:**56
sexual reproduction **4:**86
Conjugated allergens 5:449
Conjugation (in biology) **3:**453–
54; **4:**32
illus. **4:**213
Conjunctivitis 5:273
Connecticut 2:378
illus. **2:**379
Connective tissue 5:163–64,
174
arthritis **5:**427–29
breast-implant problems **5:**506
cardiac skeleton **5:**198
lungs **5:**218
muscle repair **5:**193
tendons and ligaments **5:**190–
91, 193
Conscious memory 5:362
Consciousness (in psychology)
5:156
CONSERVATION 2:402–15
ecology **3:**474
endangered species **2:**503–5
energy **2:**304; **3:**142
fish **4:**312
forestry **4:**126–31
grasslands **4:**143
rain forests **4:**161
songbird habitat **4:**451
wetlands **4:**155

wilderness **2:**506–15
zoos **4:**473, 477
Conservation of electrical
charge 3:308
Conservation of matter and
energy 3:3, 308
chemical reactions **3:**54
continuous-creation theory **1:**21
heat energy **3:**219
mechanical energy **3:**164–67
Conservation of momentum,
Law of 3:141, 308
Earth, origin of **2:**9–10
Consonance (in music) **3:**212–14
Constance, Lake (Europe) **2:**461
Constant acceleration, Law of
3:141
Constantine (Roman emperor)
calendar **1:**476
CONSTELLATIONS 1:24–36
Babylonian astronomy **1:**472
map(s) **1:**26–28, 31, 33–34
Constipation 5:255
Construction *see* Building, Tech-
niques of
CONSTRUCTION, Materials of
2:469; **6:23–31**
Construction engineering 6:20
Constructive interference 3:197
Consumers (in ecosystems)
2:453; **3:**485
Consumptive demands on for-
ests 4:126–27, 131
Contact allergens 5:448
Contact lenses 4:468; **5:**508
illus. **5:**270
Contact prints 6:273
Contact process (in chemistry)
illus. **6:**204
Containerships 6:113
Containment buildings (of
nuclear reactors) **2:**371
Contamination, Food 6:76–77
Continental crust 2:30–31
Continental Divide 2:101
CONTINENTAL DRIFT 2:38–41,
220, **231, 272**
satellite studies **2:**2–3
Continental glaciers 2:94, 97–99
Antarctica **2:**91–92, 261
illus.
Antarctica **2:**96
Continental-humid climates
2:213
Continental islands 2:280–81
Continental margin 2:265
Continental plates 2:281
Continental rise 2:269–70
Continental shelves 2:265, 268
Arctic Ocean **2:**235
coastal formation **2:**288–89
islands **2:**281
Pacific Ocean **2:**230
Continental shields 2:89
Continental slopes 2:268–69
Continents
animal life **4:**141

origin **2:**14
map(s)
  in 50 million years **2:**45
  previous positions **2:**40
Continuous-creation theory *see* Steady state theories
Continuous emission spectra 3:295
Continuous miners 2:351, 353
illus. **2:**354
Continuous-path programming 6:200
Continuous-wave radar *see* Doppler radar
Contour currents 2:238
Contour feathers 4:392
Contour plowing
illus. **6:**59
Contractile vacuoles 4:209, 213
Controlled forest fires 4:130–31
Control rods (of nuclear reactors) **2:**366–67
Controls (in experiments) **3:**510–11
Control units (of computers) **6:**365, 370
Convection 2:29, 160–61, 163; **3:**234–37
illus. **3:**233
  Earth's interior **2:**27
Convection theory of continental drift 2:39, 44
Convention on International Trade in Endangered Species (CITES) 2:500, 505
Convergence (of technologies) **6:**309
Convergent evolution 3:502
Convergent thinking 5:344
Converging lenses 3:290
illus. **3:**289
Convex lenses 1:37; **5:**272
Convex mirrors 3:288–89
Conveyor belts
illus. **2:**351
Convulsions 5:466–67
Coolants 2:367
Cooley, Denton A. (American surgeon) **5:**504
Cooling *see* Heat transfer
Cooling systems (of automobiles) **6:**142–43
Cooper, L. Gordon, Jr. (American astronaut) **1:**240–41
Cooper, Leon N. (American physicist) **3:**359–60
Cooper's hawks 4:417
Coordinate geometry *see* Analytic geometry
Coordinates *see* Cartesian coordinates
Coordination *see* Motor skills
Coots 4:439–40
Cope, Edward (American herpetologist) **4:**338
Copepods 4:251, 254–55

Copernican system 1:78, 473; **3:**141
illus. **1:**66, 472
Copernicus (artificial satellite) **1:**63
Copernicus (Moon crater) **1:**122
Copernicus, Nicolaus (Polish astronomer) **1:**12; **3:**141
illus.
  manuscript **1:**78
Copper 3:36
  early use of **6:**5
  heat conduction **3:**232
  heat of fusion **3:**198
  metals and alloys **6:**174, 182–83
  noble metals **3:**27, 30
  nutrition **5:**388
  radioisotope tracers **3:**319
  secondary batteries **3:**105
  smelting **6:**177
  specific heat **3:**225
illus.
  smelting **6:**182
Copperheads (snakes) **4:**366, 374
illus. **4:**372
Copper sulfate 2:443; **3:**87
Coprolites 1:484
Copyright laws 6:310
Coraciiformes 4:399–400, 406–7
Coral fungi 4:44
Coral reefs 2:36, 283–87, 291
illus. **3:**477
  ocean waves **2:**253
Corals 2:284–85; **4:**184, 219
  atolls **2:**283
  climate analysis **2:**216
  feeding behavior **4:**193
  fossils **1:**488
illus. **2:**284–85
Coral snakes 4:372–73
illus. **4:**371
Corcovado Volcano (Chile) **2:**59
Cord 812 (automobile)
illus. **6:**136
Cordelia (shepherding moon of Uranus) **1:**150
Cordgrass *see* Spartina
Cordilleran System 2:67
Core (of a nuclear reactor) **2:**365, 371
Core (of Earth) **1:**107; **2:**14, 22, 25–28
  rotation **2:**29
  wave motion **3:**195
illus. **2:**24
Coriolis effect 2:182, 237–38
Cork 4:72
Cork cambium 4:89
Cormorants 3:489; **4:**409, 446
Corn (Maize) 6:69–70
  alcohol fuel **2:**396
  food preservation and processing **6:**84
  genetically engineered **6:**74–75

  horticulture and agronomy **4:**171
  McClintock, Barbara **3:**413
  per-acre yields **4:**172
illus.
  insecticide spray **6:**63
Corn Belt 6:58
Cornea 5:269
  surgical reshaping **5:**272, 489
  transplants **5:**498–99
illus. **5:**271
Cornell University (Ithaca, New York) **4:**388–89
Corn poppies
illus. **4:**57
Corn smut 4:45
Corona 1:82, 85–86
  auroras **2:**156
illus. **1:**82, 88–89
Corona Borealis (constellation) **1:**29
Corona/Discoverer 14 (artificial satellite) **1:**313
Coronagraphs 1:82, 92
Coronal mass ejections (CMEs) 3:271
Coronary arteries 5:202
Coronary-artery disease 5:401, 439, 472
Coronaviruses 5:429
Corpuscular theory of light 3:329
Corrective Optics Space Telescope Axial Replacement 1:50
Correlation (in statistics) **3:**511
Corrosion 3:101, 103
  acid rain **2:**476
  steel, weakness of **6:**30
Corsica 2:281
Cort, Henry (English inventor) **6:**188
Cortex (of the brain) *see* Cerebral cortex
Cortex (plant tissue) **4:**67, 69
Corti, Organ of *see* Organ of Corti
Corticosteroids *see* Steroids
Corticotropin *see* Thyroid-stimulating hormone
Cortisol *see* Hydrocortisone
Cortisone 5:449
Corvidae 4:462–63
Corvus (constellation) **1:**29
Corythosaurus **1:**495
Cosines 1:387–88
Cosmetics 5:448
illus. **2:**335
Cosmic Background Explorer (COBE) 1:48, 62
Cosmic background radiation 1:20, 23
COSMIC RAYS 1:224–31
  atmosphere **2:**151
  effects on astronauts **1:**251
  life, origin of **1:**319
  relativity theory **3:**346
Cosmic-ray showers 1:227–28

Cosmic year **1:**189
Cosmological principle 1:21
Cosmology 1:18–23; **3:**144–45
  relativity theory **3:**352
Cosmonauts 1:239, 241
  non-Russian **1:**285
  training programs **1:**283–84
  illus.
    women **1:**286
Cosmos (TV series) **6:**321
Cosmos 4 (artificial satellite)
  1:313
Cosmotron 6:357–58
COSTAR *see* Corrective Optics
  Space Telescope Axial
  Replacement
Costa Rica 4:78, 126
  illus.
    volcano **2:**70
Cotangents 1:387–88
Cotingas 4:449
Cotopaxi (volcano, Ecuador)
  2:59, 62
Cottage industry 6:188
Cotton-boll weevils 4:299
Cotton crops 6:74
Cotton sedge 4:163
Cottontail rabbits 5:38
  illus. **5:**37
Cotyledons 3:463; **4:**88, 104–6
Cotylosaurs 5:2–3
Coudé focus 1:38
  illus. **1:**39
Cougars 5:89, 91
Coulomb (unit of measurement)
  3:256
Coulomb, Charles Augustin de
  (French physicist) **3:**256
Coulomb attraction *see* Electro-
  static attraction
Counselors 5:346
Countercurrents (in the ocean)
  2:241
Courtship of animals 3:457;
  4:189, 195–96
  arachnids **4:**261
  birds **4:**396
  grouse **4:**426
  insects **4:**276
  lizards **4:**362
  lyrebirds **4:**449
  reptiles **4:**354
  salamanders **4:**351
  snakes **4:**366, 369
  turtles **4:**376
  illus.
    display **3:**503
Cousteau, Jacques-Yves
  (French diver) **2:**224
  illus. **2:**225
Covalence 3:50–52, 64–65, 101
  carbon family **3:**31, 109
  ceramics **6:**219
  nitrogen family **3:**31
  oxygen family **3:**32
  water molecule **3:**82–83
Covered bridges 6:49
Cowbirds 3:483; **4:**396, 460

Cow insects 4:284
Cowpox 3:393; **5:**430
Cows *see* Cattle
COX-2 inhibitors 5:292
Coyotes 3:396, 507; **5:**79
  illus. **5:**80
Coypus *see* Nutrias
CPR *see* Cardiopulmonary resus-
  citation
**CPT (Charge, parity, time-rever-
  sal) symmetry 3:**310
CPU *see* Central processing unit
C-quarks *see* Charm quarks
Crab-eating macaques 5:142
Crabgrass 4:124
Crab Nebula 1:198, 206, 231
  illus. **1:**202
Crabs 4:248, 250–51, 254–55
  beach markings **2:**295
  hydrothermal vents **2:**278
  illus. **4:**247, 250
    sponge crab **4:**253
Crack (drug) **5:**373, 376
Cracking (in chemistry) **2:**331
Cracks (in bones) *see* Stress
  fractures
Cramp 5:289
Cranberry bogs
  illus. **4:**153
Cranes (birds) **4:**438–39
Cranial nerves 5:229, 231–32
Craniopharyngioma tumors
  5:244
Cranium 5:176–77, 328
Crankcases 6:141
Crankshafts 6:99–100
Crash test
  illus. **3:**157
Crater Lake (Oregon) **1:**121;
  2:58, 106, 108
  illus. **2:**106
Craters
  astrogeology **2:**4
  Mars **1:**130
  Mercury **1:**97–98, 300–301
  meteorites **1:**171, 174
  Moon **1:**113, 120–21, 126
  Venus **1:**100
  volcano **2:**56, 58, 61
  illus. **1:**171
    Mercury **1:**95
    Moon **1:**116, 121
Crayfish 4:254
  diagram(s) **4:**252
Cray supercomputer
  illus. **6:**364
Cream of tartar 3:99
Creatine 5:439
Creativity 5:155–56
Credit (in accounting) **1:**458
Creeping junipers 4:90
Creep strength 6:184
Crenarchaeota 4:29
Crenulate leaves 4:73
Creodonts 1:489; **5:**63
Creosote bushes 4:136
Crepuscular animals 4:169
Crescendo sleep pattern 5:407

Crested auklets
  illus. **4:**436
Crested newts
  illus. **4:**351
Crests (of floods) **2:**420
Crests (of waves) **2:**250
Cretaceous period
  birds **4:**391
  cartilaginous fish **4:**323
  dinosaurs **1:**494
  flowering plants **4:**13
  fossils **1:**489
  mammals **5:**5
  map(s) **2:**41
  table(s) **1:**486; **2:**20–21
Creutzfeldt-Jacob disease 3:390
Crevasses 2:96–98
Crib death *see* Sudden infant
  death syndrome
Crick, Francis H. C. (British biophysicist) **3:**6, 91, 117,
  411–12; **5:**309
  biology, history of **3:**370, 372
  genetics **3:**402
  illus. **3:**401; **5:**314
Crickets (insects) **4:**83, 279
Crime
  computer crime **6:**393, 395, 397
  forensic science **1:**507–16
Crime scene 1:510–11
Criminalistics 1:507
Crinoidea 1:488; **4:**204, 224
Crippen, Robert J. (American
  astronaut)
  illus. **1:**281
Criss-crosses *see* Common dol-
  phins
Cristae 3:431
Critical mass 2:365
Crocodiles 4:353–55, 380, 384,
  437–38
  illus. **4:**355, 380, 382
    tagging with radio transmit-
    ters **4:**339
CROCODILIANS 2:505;
  4:380–84
Crocuses 2:497
Crohn's disease 5:240, 256
Cromolyn sodium 5:449
Crookes tubes 5:451–52
Crop (in bird's digestive system)
  4:394
Crop management 4:174
Crop milk 4:197, 429
Crop rotation 4:174
Crops *see* Agriculture
Crossing over (in genetics)
  3:444; **5:**311, 313
Crossopterygii 1:492
Cross-pollination 4:102
Cross-training 5:404
Crowbars 3:169
Crown (of a tooth) **5:**282
  illus. **5:**280
Crowned pigeons 4:429
Crows 4:463
CRTs *see* Cathode-ray tubes

Cruise ships 6:114
  illus. 6:116
Cruising, Timber 4:128
Crushing (of ores) 6:176
CRUSTACEANS 4:203, 247–48, 250–55
CRUST OF EARTH 1:107; 2:14, 30–37
  continental drift 2:38–41
  earthquakes 2:46–54
  gravity 3:179–81
  minerals 2:138
  nonmetals 3:27
  nutrient cycles 3:491
  ocean floor 2:270, 276
  plate tectonics 2:41–45, 68–74
  pregeologic period 2:17–18
  Illus. 2:24, 268–69
Crux (constellation) 1:27
Cryolite 6:183
Cryophilic algae 4:47
Cryosurgery 5:437, 479
Cryptodira 4:377
Cryptosporidiosis 5:443
Crystal lattices *see* Lattices, Crystal
Crystalline solids *see* Crystals
Crystallography 3:91
Crystal Palace (London, England) 6:38–39
Crystals 3:89–93
  ceramics 6:219
  electron diffraction by 3:331
  Identification by refraction 3:285
  igneous rocks 2:134
  interstellar space 1:223
  Ionic compounds 3:50
  metals, structure of 3:27
  minerals 1:380–81; 2:136–37
  snow 2:168–69
  solids 3:12
  structure 3:241–42
  illus. 3:88
    effect on electromagnetic waves and electrons 3:330
    quartz 3:240
    snow 2:169
C-sections *see* Cesarean sections
CSMA (computer protocol) 6:387
CT scans *see* CAT scans
Cube root 1:349
Cubes (geometric shapes) 1:381
  illus. 1:332
Cubical expansion, Coefficient of *see* Coefficient of cubical expansion
Cubic crystals 3:90
Cuckoos 4:401–2
Cuckoo-shrikes 4:450
Cuculiformes 4:399–402
Cucumber beetles 4:298
Cud 4:194; 5:8, 118–19
Cugnot, Nicolas (French engineer) 6:98, 133
Culshaw, Edward (English murder victim) 1:509
Cultivars 4:174–75

Cultural geography 2:301
Cultured pearls 4:235
Cultures (in microbiology) 3:514
  illus.
    laboratory dishes 3:446, 515
Cumulative genes 5:319
Cumulonimbus clouds 2:165, 175
  illus. 2:161, 164
Cumulus clouds 2:163, 165
  illus. 2:159, 161, 164
Cuneiform
  illus. 1:341
Cup fungi 4:42
Curassows 4:423, 427
Curculionidae 4:299
Cured wood 6:29
Curie (unit of measurement) 3:318
Curie, Marie (French physicist) 2:16; 3:6, 15, 32, 124
  illus. 3:125
Curie, Pierre (French physicist) 3:124
Curie point 3:265
Curing (of plastics) 6:211
Curium 3:37
Curlews 4:436
Current, Electric *see* Electric current
Current density 6:221
Current meters 2:242
Currents, Ocean *see* Ocean currents
Cursors 6:367
Curtain wall 6:25
Curtis, Heber D. (American astronomer) 1:189
Curveball 3:185
Curves (in geometry) 1:377
  graph(s) 1:397
Curvilinear motion 3:149, 158–61
Cuscuses 5:19
Cushing's syndrome 5:246
Cusimanses 5:101
Cuspids (Canine teeth) 5:279
Cuticle
  bryophytes 4:58–59
  cacti 4:167
  earthworms 4:242
  ferns 4:79
  flowering plants 4:99
  hair 5:266
  leaves of plants 4:70, 85
  plants 4:12, 65, 67
  stems of plants 4:69
Cuttlebone 4:234
Cuttlefish 4:233–34
Cutworms 4:305, 307
Cuyahoga River
  illus. 2:455
Cuzco (Peru)
  illus. 6:24
CVS *see* Chorionic villus sampling
Cyanide process 6:177

Cyanobacteria (Blue-green algae) 3:450; 4:26–27, 29, 32–35, 50
  chloroplasts 3:428
  life, origin of 1:319, 490
  paleontology 1:481
  photosynthesis 4:18–19
  graph(s)
    population cycles 3:479
  illus. 3:448; 4:30
Cyanogen 1:160
Cybercafés
  illus. 6:311
Cybernetics 6:196
Cyberpunk fiction 1:503–5
Cyberspace 6:303 *see also* Virtual reality
Cyborgs 1:505
CYCADS 4:57, 94–95, 97
Cyclamates 6:83
Cycles (in electricity) 2:311
Cyclones 2:203
  hurricanes and typhoons 2:195–200
  Indian Ocean 2:234
  tornadoes 2:189–94
Cyclosporine 4:36; 5:241, 479, 497
Cyclostomes 4:321–22
Cyclotrons 1:231; 3:338; 6:355–57
  illus. 6:356
Cygnus (constellation) 1:30
Cygnus A (radio star)
  illus. 1:57
Cygnus X-1 (binary star system) 1:212
  illus. 1:207
Cylert *see* Pemoline
Cylinder blocks 6:138–39
Cylinders (geometric shapes) 1:382–83
  illus. 1:332
Cylinders (of gasoline engines) 6:99, 101, 138
Cynodictis 5:77
Cypresses 4:85, 89, 92 *see also* Bald cypresses
  illus. 2:511; 4:91
Cyprian cedars 4:92
Cystic fibrosis 5:418, 420
  gene therapy 3:421
Cytochromes 3:437
Cytokinesis 3:442–43
Cytokinins 4:68
Cytology *see* Cell biology; Cells
Cytoplasm 5:161–62, 171
  bacteria 4:29
  cell structure 3:428
  human egg cell 5:311
  plant cells 4:14, 66–67
  illus. 5:162
Cytosine 3:123, 411; 5:309–10
  illus. 3:409
Cytoskeleton 3:430–31
Czech Republic 2:469

D

Dacron 1:272–73
  artificial body parts 5:504–5
Daddy longlegs 4:248, 258,
    261–62
  illus. 4:262
Daedalus (in Greek mythology)
    6:91
Daedalus 88 (human-powered
    aircraft) 6:95, 157
Daimler, Gottlieb (German inven-
    tor) 6:133
Dairy farming 6:64–66
Dall's porpoises 5:60
Dalton, John (English chemist
    and physicist) 3:3–4, 305
  illus. 3:4
Damars 4:89
DAMS 6:51–56
  beaver dams 5:42
  China 6:22
  conservation 2:410
  geological effect 2:48, 124
  hydroelectric power 2:377,
    379–80
  lakes 2:110
  water pressure 3:185
  diagram(s) 2:378
  illus. 2:437
    construction in Montana 6:18
    gravity dam 3:185
    Itaipu Dam 2:263
  table(s) 2:446
Damselflies 4:154, 278
Dancing of bees 4:288
  illus. 4:286
Dandelion Crater (Moon) 1:506
Dander (scales from animal skin)
    5:448
Daniel Johnson Dam (Canada)
    6:52
  illus. 6:55
Daphnia see Water fleas
Daraprim see Pyrimethamine
Darby, Abraham (English metal-
    lurgist) 6:175, 188
Darcy's law (water supply) 2:116
Dark-field microscopes 3:450;
    6:333
Darkling beetles 4:296
Dark matter (Missing mass)
    1:52, 189, 203, 234
Dark nebulas 1:183, 186
  illus. 1:182
Dark reactions (in photosynthe-
    sis) see Light-independent
    reactions
Darmstadtium 3:46
Darwin, Charles (English natural-
    ist) 3:502–4
  biology, history of 3:370
  botany 4:4
  carnivorous plants 4:110–11
  earthworms 4:243
  human evolution 5:157
  reef evolution, theory of 2:286

zoology 4:180–81
  illus. 3:368; 4:203; 5:158
Darwin's finches
  illus. 3:507
Darwin's rheas 4:412
Databases 5:493
Data compression 1:311
Data deficient (IUCN category)
    2:499
Datagrams 6:305
Data processing
  accounting 1:459
Dating methods (in geology)
    1:107–8; 2:16–17
  fossils 1:485
  plate tectonics 2:43
Daughter isotopes 2:16
da Vinci, Leonardo see
    Leonardo da Vinci
Davis, Sir Robert (English scien-
    tist) 1:271
Davisson, Clinton J. (American
    physicist) 3:331
  illus. 3:323
Davy, Sir Humphrey (English
    chemist) 2:354
Dawn redwoods 4:85, 93
Day After Tomorrow (film) 1:506
Day-care centers 5:429
DBS see Direct Broadcast Satel-
    lites
DC-3 (airplane) see Douglas
    DC-3
DDI (Didanosine, Dideoxyi-
    nosine) 5:445
DDT 2:411, 502–3; 3:472, 489
Dead dunes 2:430
Dead reckoning 6:165–67
Dead Sea 2:107, 422
Dead Sea Scrolls 1:256
Deafness 5:276–77
  artificial body parts 5:508–9
Death 3:464, 468–70
  human awareness of 5:156
Death adders (snakes) 4:374
Death feigning 5:22, 26
Death Valley (California) 2:83, 86
  illus.
    National Park 2:508
Deathwatch beetles 4:295–96
DeBakey, Michael (American sur-
    geon) 5:411
Debit 1:458
De Broglie waves 3:330–31
  illus. 3:329
Debugging 6:380–81
Decapods 4:250, 253, 255
Decay, Organic see Decomposi-
    tion
Decay, Radioactive see Radioac-
    tive decay
Decay chains 2:363
Decibel 3:201, 211
Decidua 5:294, 296
Deciduous teeth (Milk teeth)
    5:278–79, 326

Deciduous trees
  plant communities 4:133–34,
    136
  taiga 4:165
  temperate forests 3:495–96;
    4:144
  tropical biomes 3:494
Decimal system 1:344–45,
    446–47
  converting to binary form 1:452
Declination (star position) 1:36
Declination of the compass
    3:269
Décollement 2:70
Decomposition
  bacteria 4:35
  carbon cycle 4:21
  death 3:470
  ecosystems 3:487, 489, 491
  environmental pollution
    2:453–54
  fungi 4:36, 38–39
  greenhouse gases 2:478
  temperate forests 4:145
  waste disposal 4:392
  water pollution 2:460–61
  wetlands 4:151
Decomposition of water 3:104
Decompression sickness see
    Bends
Deep Impact (space probe)
    1:161, 296
Deep Rover (submersible) 6:124
  illus. 6:117
Deep Sea Drilling Project 2:276
DEEP-SEA EXPLORATION
    2:223–24, 271–79
Deep-sea vents see Hydrother-
    mal vents
Deep Space 1 (space probe)
    1:131, 263, 296
Deep Space 2 (space probe)
    1:131
Deep Space Network 1:325
Deepwater waves 2:251
Deep-well injection (for hazard-
    ous waste disposal) 2:491
DEER FAMILY 5:118–23
  acorn cycle 4:147
  animal behavior 4:195
  range 5:10
  reproduction 5:6
  white-tailed deer 2:504
Deer ticks 4:147, 259, 263
Defecation 5:257
Defense, Military
  Strategic Defense Initiative
    1:262–63
Defense, U.S. Department of
    3:321; 6:303
Defense mechanisms (of ani-
    mals and plants)
  allergies 5:447–49
  animal behavior 4:194–95
  frogs 4:347–48
  golden moles 5:26
  hedgehogs 5:26

insects **4:**276
lizards **4:**362
mammals **5:**9
opossums **5:**22
plant behavior **4:**117–18
polecats **5:**94
porcupines **5:**42
sea cucumbers **4:**224
skunks **5:**97
sponges **4:**215
turtles **4:**376
Defibrillators 5:440, 505
Deflation (wind erosion) **2:**122
De Forest, Lee (American inventor) **6:**248
Deforestation 2:124, 172–73, 214
extinction of species **2:**497
De Havilland Comet (airplane) **6:**156–57
Dehydration 3:470; **5:**429
Deimos (moon of Mars) **1:**75, 132
Deinococci 4:29
De Kay's snakes 4:371
Delambre, Jean Baptiste (French astronomer) **1:**151–52
Delavan, Comet 1:165
Delayed implantation 5:31, 05, 97
Delirium 5:353, 356
Delirium tremens 5:375
Delphinus (constellation) **1:**30
Delta (star) **1:**32
Delta-H *see* Heat of reaction
Delta map turtles
illus. **4:**378
Delta plains 2:76, 424
Deltas (of rivers) **2:**104–5, 290, 292, 424
illus. **2:**424
Deltoid muscles 5:166, 190
Delusions 5:349
Dementia 5:353, 356
Alzheimer's disease **5:**334
nervous system **5:**233
Democritus (Greek philosopher) **3:**16, 304; **6:**338
Demonstrations, Scientific 6:313
Demospongiae 4:200, 216
Denatured proteins 3:122
Dendrites 5:171, 224
illus. **5:**227
Dendrochronology 4:88
illus. **2:**216
Deneb (star) **1:**30, 192
Denebola (star) **1:**29
Denial of service attacks 6:394
Denitrification 2:479
Denominator 1:349–50
Density 3:11
Earth **1:**104; **2:**25–26
fluids **3:**183–84
gases **3:**69–70
ice **3:**86

ocean water **2:**229–30, 238
Sun **1:**81
wave motion, effect on **3:**196
Dental arch 5:279
Dental caries 5:280, 282
Dentate leaves 4:73
Denticles 4:315, 324–25, 328
Dentifrices 5:281
Dentin 5:278
illus. **5:**280
Dentistry 5:279
dentists' X-ray exposure **5:**452
forensic science **1:**514
lasers in medicine **5:**489
ultrasonic drill **5:**491
illus. **5:**466
forensic science **1:**512
X-rays **3:**126
Dentures 5:282, 509
Denver (Colorado) **2:**470
Deoxyribonucleic acid *see* DNA
Deoxyribose
illus. **3:**415
Dependence on drugs 5:370, 374, 461
Dependent personality 5:352
Depersonalization disorder 5:352
Dephenylmethanes 5:373
Deposition (in clouds) **2:**167
Deposition (of gases) **3:**231
Deposits, Natural
coastal formation **2:**289–93
rivers **2:**103
stream deposits **2:**420, 423–24
Deprenyl 5:233
Depressant substances 5:371, 373–74, 466
Depression 5:351, 356 *see also* Antidepressants
chronic pain **5:**287
substance abuse **5:**375
Depth of field 6:265–66, 268
Dermagraft 5:507
Dermal fibers 5:264
Dermal tissue 4:65, 67–68
Dermis 5:264–65, 267
Dermocarpa
illus. **4:**30
Dermoptera *see* Colugos
Derricks 2:326–27, 340
illus. **2:**328
DES *see* Diethylstilbestrol
Desalination of seawater 2:448–49; **3:**137
Descartes, René (French philosopher and mathematician) **1:**330, 353, 391–92; **3:**141
Descending colon 5:254
Descriptive statistics 1:405
Desensitization (in psychology) **5:**357
Desert animals 2:86; **3:**494–95; **4:**169
lizards **4:**358
snakes **4:**364
Desert cats 5:92

Desertification 2:84; **4:**143, 169
Desert pavement 2:122
DESERT PLANTS 2:86; **3:**494; **4:**135–36, **166–69**
leaves **4:**70
DESERTS 2:81–86; **3:**494, 497
climate **2:**214, 216, 218
dust storms **2:**432
groundwater **2:**113, 116
human-caused erosion **2:**124, 404
Iceland's lava desert **2:**58
plant communities **4:**135–36
plants **4:**166–69
sand dunes **2:**429
water erosion **2:**417, 419
wind erosion **2:**122–23, 426–27
illus.
nomads **2:**212
reclaimed desert **2:**408
map(s)
main deserts of the world **2:**82
Desert tortoises
illus. **2:**509
Designer drugs 5:374
Desipramine 5:376
Desktop computers *see* Personal computers
Desmans *see* Water moles
Des Moines (Iowa) **2:**441
Destiny (space-station module) **1:**269
Destroying angel (mushroom) **4:**44
Destructive distillation (of oil shale) **2:**324
Destructive interference
wave behavior **3:**197
Detached retina 5:273, 589
Detectors, Particle *see* Particle detectors
Detergents
petroleum products **2:**334
phosphates **2:**414
water pollution **2:**461
illus.
basic solutions **3:**95–96
Detoxification 5:375–77, 384
Detrital sedimentary rocks 2:135
Deuterium 2:362, 376; **3:**20
Deuterium oxide *see* Heavy water
Deuteromycetes *see* Imperfect fungi
Developing (in photography) **6:**272
Developmental biology *see* Embryology
Developmental psychology 5:342–43, 347
Deveron River 2:103
Devilfish (octopuses) **4:**233
Devilfish (whales) *see* Gray whales
Devil-Girl from Mars (film)
illus. **1:**323

Devil's Tower National Monument (Wyoming) **2:**418
Devonian period 1:488, 490; **4:**74
map(s) **2:**40
table(s) **1:**486; **2:**18–19
De Vries, Hugo (Dutch biologist) **3:**370, 401
Dewlaps (skin flaps) **5:**123, 128
Dew point 2:159, 166
DEXA (Dual-energy X-ray absorptiometry) 5:453–54
Dexedrine *see* Dextroamphetamine
Dextroamphetamine 5:368
Dextrostat *see* Dextroamphetamine
Dholes 5:81–82
Diabetes 5:244–45
biochemistry **3:**119
genetic diseases **5:**421
insulin pump **5:**470
pancreas transplantation **5:**499
vision disorder **5:**489; **6:**351
illus.
insulin administration **3:**117
Diabetes insipidus 5:244
DIAGNOSIS, Medical 5:450–59
antibodies **5:**471
blood tests **5:**212–13
cancer **5:**436
heart disease **5:**438–39
learning disabilities **5:**364, 367
monoclonal antibodies **5:**472
radioisotopes **3:**319
space program **1:**254–55
substance abuse **5:**369–70
illus.
computer-equipped laboratory **6:**374
Diagnostic and Statistical Manual of Mental Disorders (DSM) **5:**340, 349
Dialysis, Kidney *see* Artificial kidney machines
Diamagnetic substances 3:263
Diameter of a circle 1:375
illus. **1:**374
Diamond beetles 4:299
Diamond pythons 4:370
Diamonds 2:136
electron structure **3:**28
graphite **3:**241
identification by refraction **3:**285
meteorites **1:**173
Diana (hurricane, 1990) **2:**199
Diane (hurricane, 1955) **2:**199
Diaper rash 5:449
Diaphragm (in anatomy) **5:**178, 190, 218
Diarrhea 5:255, 429
Diastole 5:199–200
Diastolic pressure 5:204
chart(s) **5:**203
Diatomic molecules 3:53, 69
Diatoms 4:47, 51
illus. **4:**50; **6:**333

Diatonic scale (in music) **3:**213
table(s) **3:**213
Diazepam 5:356
Dibatags 5:131
Dichloroethane 3:110
Dichroism 3:292
Dick, Philip K. (American writer) **1:**505
Dickerson, Mary (American herpetologist) **4:**338
Dicotyledons 4:57, 106–7
Didanosine *see* DDI
Didinium **4:**213
Didoxyinosine *see* DDI
Dieffenbachia **4:**158
Dielectric heating 2:320
Dielectrics 3:248
Diesel, Rudolf (German inventor) **6:**102
Diesel-electric locomotives *see* Locomotives—diesel-electric
Diesel engines 6:102–3
automobiles **6:**139, 141
electricity, generation of **2:**314–15
ships **6:**111–12
Diesel fuels 2:332, 397
Diet *see also* Nutrition
cancer **5:**436
crocodilians **4:**382
dental health **5:**282
human development **5:**160
owls **4:**420
prehistoric people **1:**464
sharks **4:**326
weight control **5:**391–94
Dietary fiber *see* Fiber, Dietary
Dietary Guidelines for Americans 2005 **5:**389
Dietary Reference Intakes (DRIs) 5:390
Dietetic technicians 5:390
Diethyl ether 3:114
Diethylstilbestrol (DES) 5:301–2
Differential calculus 1:333, 436
Differential equations 1:437
Differential polarization microscopes 6:333–34
Differentials 6:144
Differential white-cell count 5:213
Differentiation of cells 3:459–60; **4:**184
Difflugia **4:**210
Diffraction
color **3:**294
optics **3:**292
wave behavior **3:**197
Diffraction, Electron *see* Electron diffraction
Diffraction grating 3:294
illus. **3:**295
Diffuse reflection 3:284
Diffusion 3:69–70
capillaries **5:**202–3
nuclear fuel enrichment **2:**366

respiration **5:**218–19
diagram(s)
cells **3:**436
Digestion *see also* Digestive system
animal **4:**186
arachnids **4:**258
bacteria's role in **4:**35
carnivorous plants **4:**108–10
human **5:**239, 248–56
sharks **4:**326
DIGESTIVE SYSTEM 4:186; **5:**172, **248–56** *see also* Digestion
babies **5:**326
birds **4:**394–95
changes with age **5:**332–33
epithelium **5:**163
insects **4:**274
lagomorphs **5:**36
mammals **5:**8
microbiology **3:**449
muscle **5:**171
illus. **5:**167
Digistar (computer graphics imaging device) **1:**72
Digital cameras 6:245, 273–74, 287
Digital computers *see* Computers
Digital8 camcorders 6:287
Digital light processing (DLP) *see* Rear-projection televisions
Digital Subscriber Lines (DSL) 6:390
Digital subtraction angiography *see* DSA scans
Digital technology *see also* Computers
cellular communication **6:**243–44
data compression **1:**311
hearing aids **5:**277
photography **6:**273–74
radio **6:**290
recording, sound and video **6:**283–87
synthesizers **3:**218
telephone **6:**241
television **6:**296–97
Digital television 6:296–97
Digital to analog (D/A) conversion 6:285
illus. **6:**284
Digital versatile discs *see* DVDs
Digital videodiscs *see* DVDs
Digital video recorder *see* DVR
Digit span *see* Memory-span limit
Dihedral angles 1:380
Dik-diks 5:131
Dikes (in geology) **2:**32
Dilute solutions 3:79
Dimensional analysis 1:337
Dimorphism 4:300–301, 304
Dingoes 5:80–81

Dinoflagellates (Pyrrophyta) 4:47, 51, 53, 200
illus. 4:50
Dinosaurs 1:483, 492–96
extinction 1:169, 174, 497
feathers and wings 1:479
fossils 1:485, 488
reptiles 4:352
illus.
Argentinosaurus 1:493
footprints 1:484
Gigantosaurus 1:494
Supersaurus 1:494
Tarbosaurus 1:492
Triceratops 1:495
Diodes 6:247–48, 251
Dioecious plants 4:101
Dione (moon of Saturn) 1:145–46
Diophantus (Greek mathematician) 1:330, 353
Dioxins 2:462–63; 3:489
Diphtheria 5:429–30
Diplodocus 1:495
Diploid cells 3:410, 443, 504
Diploid phase (of plants) 4:15
Diplomatics *see* Document examination
Diplopoda 4:203
Dipoles 3:262
Dipping needle *see* Inclination of the compass
Direct Broadcast Satellites (DBS) 6:295
Direct current 3:254–55; 6:130
Directional selection 3:506
Direct thrombin inhibitors (DTIs) 5:467
Direct-view televisions *see* Rear-projection televisions
Dirigibles 3:188; 6:150–51
Dirty-snowball theory 1:161
Disaccharides 3:119; 5:380
Disc brakes 6:147
diagram(s) 6:148
Discharge (flow of a stream) 2:419
Disclimax communities 4:125, 135
Discourse on Method (treatise, Descartes) 1:391
Discovery (space shuttle) 1:253, 257
oceanography 2:221
illus. 1:304
Discovery Program (NASA) 1:260
DISEASES
air pollution 2:468–69
allergies 5:447–49
arthritis 5:427–29
bacteria 4:30–31, 34
blood diseases 5:210–12
bones 5:182–84
cancer 5:432–37
digestive system 5:255–56
genetic *see* Genetic diseases
global warming 2:480–81

heart *see* Heart disease
immune system 5:239–41
infectious *see* Infectious diseases
insect carriers 4:268–69
microbiology 3:451
muscular system 5:194
nervous system 5:232–34
pain 5:289–91
plants *see* Plant diseases
prions 3:390–91
respiratory diseases 5:222
skin diseases 5:267
substance abuse 5:374–75
tick-borne diseases 4:259, 263
urinary tract 5:262
Dish antennas 1:308; 6:294–95
illus. 6:295
Disinfectants 5:423
Disks (in the vertebral column) 5:174–75
Disneyland
illus.
monorail 6:128
Disney World
Animal Kingdom 4:477
illus.
Animal Kingdom 4:471
Disorders, Body *see* Diseases
Dispersion of light 3:294
Displacement (in physics) 3:149–50, 274
Displacement (ship measurement) *see* Tonnage
Displacement (size of automobile engine) 6:138
Dissection 3:514–15
Dissociative disorders 5:351–52
Dissociative identity disorder 5:352
Dissonance (in music) 3:212
Distillation 3:137
chemical industry 6:206
petroleum 2:329–30
water desalting 2:448
illus. 3:137
Distribution systems, Electric 2:318–19
Distributive law of multiplication 1:353–54
Distributors (of automobiles) 6:141
Diuretics 4:76; 5:467
Diurnal animals and plants 3:380
Diurnal inequalities (of tides) 2:245
Diurnal tides 2:246
Divergent evolution 3:502
Diverging lenses 3:290
Diverticular disease 5:256
Dividend (in mathematics) 1:348
Divides (in geology) *see* Watersheds
Diving beetles 4:293
illus. 4:293

Division (in mathematics) 1:348
binary numerals 1:450
fractions 1:349–50
logarithms 1:360
Divisor 1:348
D layer (of the atmosphere) 2:151
DLP (Digital light processing) *see* Rear-projection televisions
DNA 3:411–12
aging 3:467
AIDS 5:442–43
anatomy, human 5:162
bacteria 4:32
biology, history of 3:370, 372
cell division 3:440–41
cloning 3:423
coded messages 6:317
Franklin, Rosalind 3:6, 91
genetic diseases 5:418–19, 421
genetic engineering 6:74–75
genetics 3:402
heredity, human 5:309–10
Human Genome Project 5:321
Neanderthals 5:160
nucleotides 3:123
plant breeding 6:70
prokaryotes 3:427
radiation damage 3:127
viruses 3:389, 392
illus. 3:116, 365, 409–11
replication 3:441
simplified structure 5:309
DNA computers 3:405, 419
DNA fingerprinting 3:400, 403–4, 418–19; 5:322
forensic science 1:514–16
illus. 5:320–21
DNA helicase 3:440
DNA ligase 3:440
DNA polymerase 3:440
Dobsonflies 4:280
Doctors *see* Physicians
Document examination (forensics) 1:515
Dodge Durango (automobile)
illus. 6:137
Dodos 4:409, 428–29
DOG FAMILY 5:77–83
evolution 1:489
teeth 5:70
Dogfish 4:327
illus. 4:324
Dogs, Domestic 5:78
animal behavior 4:191–92, 195
classification 3:396
heartworms 4:230
life span 5:324
pets 4:481, 484–86, 490
tapeworms 4:226
illus. 5:3
Clumber spaniels 5:3
heart with heartworms 4:229
veterinary care 4:464
Dog Star *see* Sirius
Dogwood anthracnose
illus. 4:44

Dogwood trees
illus. **4:**100
Doldrums (winds) **2:**184, 196
Dollar as unit of measure 1:457
"Dolly" (cloned sheep) **3:**422;
6:14, 75
Dolly Sods Wilderness (West
Virginia) **2:**512
Dolomite 2:111
Dolomites (mountains, Italy)
illus. **2:**124
DOLPHINS 5:55–60
killer whales **5:**53
limits on taking **2:**413
pilot whales **5:**53
Domain names 6:305
Domes (in architecture) **6:**26, 33,
41
illus. **6:**35
Domesday Book 1:455
Domestication of animals 6:4
camels and llamas **5:**117
cattle **5:**134
cheetahs **5:**89
dogs **5:**78
falconry **4:**419
pets **4:**481
river otters **5:**98
water buffalo **5:**133–34
yaks **5:**135
Dominance hierarchies 5:10,
147
Dominant genes 3:407–8;
5:315–16, 318, 420; **6:**70
diagram(s) **3:**407
Dominican Republic 2:52
Donacia **4:**298
Donkeys 3:396; **5:**110
Donora (Pennsylvania) **2:**468
Donor organs for transplants
5:497–99
Doolittle, Jimmy (American pilot)
6:155
Doorbells
illus. **3:**265
Dopamine 5:233, 334, 356, 499
Doping (in electronics) **2:**389;
6:232
Doppler color flow imaging
5:454, 459
Doppler effect 1:19
navigation **6:**171
sound **3:**207
Sun's spectrum **1:**87
illus.
sound **3:**207
Doppler radar 2:205–6;
6:255–56
electromagnetic spectrum **3:**279
tornadoes **2:**194
weather forecasting **6:**261
illus.
tornado tracking **2:**191
Doppler ultrasound 5:303
Dormancy
bryophytes **4:**59
desert animals' eggs **4:**169

desert plants **4:**168
fern spores **4:**79, 82
fungi **4:**38–40, 42
grasses **4:**139
perennials **4:**107
seeds **4:**104–5
Dormice 5:44
Dot-matrix printers 6:368
Double bonds (in chemistry)
3:109, 111–13
Double covalent bonds 3:52
Double-entry bookkeeping
1:456
Double helix (form of DNA
chains) **3:**91, 123
illus. **3:**116
Double-star theory 2:11–12
Double-wattled cassowaries
4:412
Douglas, David (Scottish bota-
nist) **4:**92
Douglas DC-3 (airplane) **6:**156
Douglas firs 4:86, 91–92
illus. **4:**84
Doves 4:430–31
Downers *see* Depressant sub-
stances
Down feathers 4:392
Downloading (of data files)
6:305, 386
Down quarks 3:20, 313
Down syndrome 3:416; **5:**421
illus. **5:**419
Downwelling, Oceanic 2:236–38
Downy mildew 3:451
Doxirubicin 5:474
Draco (constellation) **1:**26
Drafting (in bicycling) **6:**94
Drag (Resistance) 3:192–93
air **6:**94
aviation **6:**158
falling objects **3:**154, 155
water **6:**91–92
Dragonflies 4:154, 276, 278
fossils **1:**488
illus. **4:**184, 246, 272
Drainage basins (of rivers) **2:**419
Drais de Sauerbrun, Baron Karl
von (German inventor)
6:92
Drake, Edwin L. (American oil
producer) **2:**323
Drake, Frank (American scientist)
1:322
Drake Equation 1:322–23
Drakes 4:443
Drawing, Scientific 3:515
Drawing pads (of computers)
6:366
Dreamcast (video-game system)
6:301
Dreams 5:342, 407
Dredging 2:290, 294
deep-sea exploration **2:**273
fishing **6:**87
Drela, Mark (American aircraft
designer) **6:**95

Drexler, K. Eric (American scientist) **6:**339
Drift-bottle method 2:236, 242
Drift mines 2:350, 354
illus. **2:**350
Drift nets 6:87
Drift tubes 6:353
Drilling
deep-sea exploration **2:**275–76
geothermal energy **2:**394
lasers in manufacturing **6:**347
natural gas **2:**340–41
oil wells **2:**326–27
tunnels **6:**47–48
water wells **2:**439–40
illus.
natural gas **2:**338
oil wells **2:**324–25, 327
water wells **2:**116
Drills (animals) **5:**143
Drills, Dental 5:491
Drinker-Collins respirator *see*
Iron lung
Dripstones 2:127
Driven wells 2:441
Driver ants 4:285
Drivetrains 6:135, 138
illus. **6:**135
Drizzle 2:167
Drogues 1:241
illus. **1:**257
Dromaeosaurs 4:390
Dromedaries 5:117
illus. **5:**116
Drones (bees) **3:**457; **4:**286–88
Drongos 4:447–48
Drosophila **4:**181
Droughts 2:172
Dust Bowl **2:**123
hydrometeorology **2:**145
irrigation **2:**409
water conservation **2:**409
wells **2:**117
Drug abuse *see* Substance
abuse
DRUG DELIVERY TECHNOL-
OGY 5:468–75
implantable pumps **1:**254
illus.
implantable pumps **1:**255
DRUGS (Medications) 5:460–67
AIDS research **5:**445
allergic reactions **5:**448
allergy treatment **5:**241, 449
anesthesia **5:**477–78
arthritis **5:**428
biochemistry **3:**117
cancer treatment **5:**437
careers in pharmacy **5:**462–63
computer programs **5:**493
delivery methods **5:**468–75
fertility drugs **5:**307
frog-skin secretions **4:**348
immunosuppressants **5:**479
learning disabilities **5:**368
mental illness treatment **5:**356
microbiology **3:**449

organic chemistry **3:**107
pain relief **5:**291–92
plant-derived **2:**497
rain-forest products **4:**161
resistance of bacteria to **3:**506
substance abuse **5:**369–70
substance abuse treatment
   5:376–77
veterinary science **4:**465, 468
viruses **3:**393
weight-loss drugs **5:**393
Drug-seeking behavior 5:370
Drum brakes 6:147
  diagram(s) **6:**148
Drumlins 2:99, 289
Drums (in architecture)
  illus. **6:**35
Drums (musical instruments)
  3:216
  illus. **3:**216
Dry-bulk ships 6:113–14
Dry-cask storage (of radioactive
  waste) **2:**370
Dry cells *see* Primary batteries
Dry cleaning
  illus. **3:**96
Dry ice 3:93, 231
  illus.
    sublimation **3:**226
Drying (food preservation) **4:**34;
  6:77–78
  illus. **6:**76
Dry-wall construction 6:37
DSA scans 5:453, 458
DSL (Digital subscriber lines)
  6:304
DSR scans 5:453, 458
DTs *see* Delirium tremens
**Dual-energy X-ray absorptiom-
etry** *see* DEXA
Dubnium 3:37
Duchenne muscular dystrophy
  5:194, 319, 421
Duck-billed platypuses *see*
  Platypuses, Duck-billed
Ducks 4:154, 392, 395, 442–43
  illus. **4:**441–42
    wood duck **4:**154
Ductility 3:27–28
Ductus epididymis *see* Vas epi-
  didymis
Duesenberg SSJ (automobile)
  illus. **6:**136
Du Fay, Charles (French scien-
  tist) **3:**250
Dugongs 5:8, 12–13, 61–62
Dugout canoes
  illus. **6:**3, 92
Duikers 5:130–31
Dulbecco, Renato 3:405, 420
Dulles Airport Terminal (Wash-
  ington, D.C.)
  illus. **6:**31
Dulse 4:50
Dumbbell Nebula in Vulpecula
  illus. **1:**184
Dumps (computer printouts)
  6:364–65

Dunes, Sand *see* Sand dunes
Dung beetles 4:296–97
Duodecimal system 1:345
Duodenal ulcers 5:256
Duodenum 5:251
  illus. **5:**167, 250
Duplation 1:347–48
Duplexers 6:256
Duplicating the cube 1:367
Duragesic *see* Fentanyl
Durand, Peter (English inventor)
  6:79
Duryea, Charles and Franklin
  (American inventors) **6:**133
Dusky salamanders 4:351
Dust 5:447
  air pollution **2:**466
  allergies **5:**448
  atmospheric **2:**153, 159, 466
  climate analysis **2:**217
  wind erosion **2:**426
Dust Bowl 2:123, 409; **4:**143
  illus. **2:**122
Dust clouds 2:164
Dust devils 2:85, 190
Dusting (in agriculture) *see*
  Spraying and dusting
Dust mites 4:263
Dust storms 2:430–32; **4:**143
  Mars **1:**132
  illus.
    Mars **1:**129
Dutch elm disease 4:42
DVDs (Digital versatile discs)
  6:287, 372
DVR (Digital video recorder)
  6:207, 304
Dwarf antelopes 5:131
Dwarf fruit trees
  illus. **4:**1
Dwarfism 5:243
Dwarf lemurs 5:137
Dwarf mistletoe 4:119
Dwarf mongooses 5:101
  illus. **5:**99
Dwarf sharks 4:327
Dwarf squirrels 5:40
Dye lasers 6:346
Dyes 6:203–4
Dyke, Tom Hart (British botanist)
  4:2
Dynamic range (of sound) **6:**285
**Dynamic spatial reconstruc-
tions** *see* DSR scans
Dynamos
  illus. **2:**310
Dynamo theory 2:29
Dyscalculia 5:366
  illus. **5:**367
Dysgraphia 5:366
Dyslexia 5:365–66
  illus. **5:**421
Dyspnea 5:222
Dyspraxia 5:366
Dysprosium 3:37
Dystopian societies 1:502
Dytiscidae *see* Diving beetles

E

E = mc² *see* Mass-energy equation
E. coli *see* Escherichia coli
Eagle (spacecraft)
  illus. **1:**245
Eagle owls 5:324
Eagles 2:502, 505; **4:**158,
  415–17
  illus. **2:**500; **4:**392
    bald eagle **4:**417
    beak **4:**393
Eardrum 3:205; **5:**274–75
  illus. **5:**276
Early Bird (spacecraft) **1:**309
EARS 5:274–77
  artificial *see* Artificial ears
  balance **5:**286
  moles **5:**25
  owls **4:**420
  sound **3:**199
  whales **5:**47
  illus.
    cochlear implant **5:**508
Ear shells *see* Abalones
EARTH 1:74, **103–12** *see also*
  Core (of Earth); Crust of
  Earth; Interior of Earth;
  Mantle of Earth
  age *see* Earth, Age of
  atmosphere **1:**60, 306–7;
    2:147–54
  atmospheric science **2:**141–42
  climates of the world **2:**207–14
  conservation **2:**402–15
  eclipses **1:**175–79
  ecosystem cycles **3:**484–91
  erosion **2:**120–24
  geography **2:**296–301
  geology **2:**2–8
  gravity **3:**177–78
  interior **2:**22–29
  life, origin of **1:**319–20;
    3:379–83
  magnetic field **2:**59, **3:**266–67,
    270–71
  origin *see* Earth, Origin of
  polar regions **2:**87–92
  satellites, artificial **1:**259, 297,
    312
  seen from the Moon **1:**126
  sphere, Earth as a **1:**383, 385
  Sun's effect on Earth **1:**80–81,
    86, 90, 234
  illus. **1:**76
    attraction of the Moon **3:**177
    inner planets **1:**73
    seen from the Moon **1:**125
    sunlight distribution **3:**493
  map(s)
    biomes **4:**134
    climatic zones **2:**208
    continents **2:**40, 45
    crustal plates **2:**38
    deserts **4:**167
    grasslands **4:**139

EARTH (cont.)
  ocean currents **2:**238
  ocean depths **2:**231
  ocean floors **2:**266–67
  ocean topography **2:**241
  precipitation **2:**170
  rain forests **4:**157
  temperate forests **4:**145
EARTH, Age of 2:15–21
  radiometric age-dating **2:**13–14
EARTH, Origin of 2:9–14, 31
Earth dams 2:437
Earth Observing System (EOS)
  1:259, 297
Earth pillars 2:173, 418
Earth Probes 1:297
EARTHQUAKES 2:23, 25, **46–54**
  Himalayas **2:**72
  laser monitoring **6:**351
  measuring **2:**50–51
  oceans **2:**269
  plate tectonics **2:**40–41, 43, 45
  seismology **2:**4
  streams dammed by **2:**423
  tsunamis **2:**256–57, 259
  volcano warnings **2:**60
  illus.
    laser monitoring **6:**349
    notable quakes **6:**427–28
    wave motion **3:**196
    zones **2:**48
  table(s) **2:**52
Earth science education 6:325
Earth Science Enterprise
  1:108–9, 259, 297
  atmosphere **2:**154
Earth sciences 1:5
Earthstar fungus
  illus. **3:**454
Earthstars 4:45
Earthworms 3:457; **4:**242–44;
  5:324
  diagram(s) **4:**243
  illus. **4:**242; **5:**217
Earwax 5:277
Earwigs 4:279
East Africa Rift Zone 2:71
Eastern hemlocks 4:93
Eastern larches *see* Tamaracks
Eastern moles 5:24
Eastern red cedars 4:90
Eastern white pines 4:72, 90
Eastern Wilderness Act (U.S.,
  1974) **2:**515
East Greenland Current 2:241
East Indian tree swifts 4:405
Eating disorders 5:355
Ebb currents 2:247
Ebbinghaus, Hermann (German
  psychologist) **5:**360–61
Ebb tides 2:244
Ebola virus
  illus. **3:**385, 451
Eccrine glands 5:265
ECHINODERMS 4:204, **220–24**
Echinoidea 4:204, 224
Echo (artificial satellite) **1:**308–9
Echocardiograms 5:438–39

Echolocation 3:203
  bats **5:**30, 32
  dolphins **5:**56
  whales **5:**47
  illus. **5:**57
Echo planar MR scanners 5:455
Echo sounding *see* Sonar
Eclampsia 5:301
Eclipse feathering 4:443
ECLIPSES 1:118–19, **175–80**
  amateur astronomy **1:**15
  Earth eclipse seen from Moon
    1:126
  Greek astronomy **1:**472
  Mayan astronomy **1:**471
  solar atmospheres **1:**82
  illus. **1:**86
Ecological succession *see* Suc-
  cession, Plant
ECOLOGY 3:373, **471–75;**
  4:181–82
  animal ecology **3:**373
  Aristotle **3:**367
  botany **4:**5–6
  paleoecology **1:**482–83
  plants **3:**372
  satellite monitoring **1:**312–13
e-commerce 6:308–9
Economic botany 4:7
Economic data 1:453–59
Economic geography 2:301
Economic geology 2:4
Economic value 1:457
**Economo, Baron Constantin
  von** (Austrian physiologist)
  5:405
ECO-O.K. 4:161
ECOSYSTEMS 2:453–56; **3:**373,
  484–91
  climax classification **4:**125
  conservation **2:**402–15
  death, role of **3:**464
  ecology **3:**471–75
  forestry **4:**126, 128
  genetic engineering **6:**75
  geography **2:**300–301
  plant communities **4:**132–37
  plant succession **4:**120–25
  populations and communities
    3:476–83
Ecotones 4:132
Ecstasy (drug) **5:**374
Ectoderm 3:461; **5:**297
Ectopic pregnancy 5:301
**Ectotherms (Cold-blooded ani-
  mals)**
  amphibians **4:**342
  desert animals **4:**169
  fish **4:**320
  lizards **4:**360–61
  reptiles **4:**352
  snakes **4:**365
  turtles **4:**375–76
Eczema 2:469
Eddy currents 6:92
Eden Project
  illus. **3:**492
EDENTATES 5:11, **33–35**

Edge-tone instruments
  3:215–16
Ediacaran period 1:479
Edison, Thomas A. (American
  inventor) **2:**308
  illus. **2:**318
  dynamo **2:**310
Edmonton–Great Lakes pipeline
  2:329
Education
  learning disabilities **5:**367–68
  science education **6:**320–29
Educational psychology 5:346
Eels 4:317, 332; **6:**124
Eelworms 4:230
  illus. **4:**228
Efferent fibers 5:224
Efferent limbs 5:227
Effort arm (of levers) **3:**169
Effusion 3:70–71
Efts 4:351
Egg-eating snakes 4:372–73
Egg-laying mammals *see*
  Monotremes
Eggs 3:455, 457; **5:**311
  birds **4:**396
  cell division **3:**443
  crocodilians **4:**381
  dinosaur eggs **1:**485
  farms, modern **6:**60
  fish **4:**320
  human embryology **5:**293–96
  infertility **5:**306–7
  insects **4:**275
  kiwi eggs, size of **4:**413
  marsupials **5:**16
  monotremes **5:**14–15
  mutations **5:**419
  ostrich eggs, size of **4:**411
  raw white contains avidin **5:**385
  reptiles **4:**352, 354–55
  snakes **4:**366, 368
  illus. **5:**306
    modern farm production **6:**60
Egg sacs 4:262
Egg tooth 4:362, 368, 381, 396
Ego 5:342
Egrets 4:445
  illus. **4:**437
Egypt
  Aswan High Dam **2:**379
Egypt, Ancient
  accounting **1:**454–55
  agriculture **4:**171
  algebra **1:**352–53
  archaeology **1:**463
  astronomy **1:**11, 469–70
  building techniques **6:**32
  calendar **1:**474–75
  canals **6:**45
  cats **4:**481
  construction materials **6:**24–26
  crocodile worship **4:**384
  dams **2:**124; **6:**52
  drugs, history of **5:**462
  fish farming **6:**89–90
  mathematics, history of **1:**329

metallurgy **6:**174–75
numerals **1:**339
plane geometry **1:**366
pyramids **1:**383; **6:**18
scarab beetle **4:**296–97
ships **6:**107
snakes **4:**337
water supply **2:**435–36; **6:**17
zoology **4:**179
zoos **4:**470
illus.
numerals **1:**340
pottery making **6:**5
pyramids **6:**17
tomb painting **1:**464, 470
Egyptology 1:463
Ehrlich, Paul (German bacteriologist) **3:**447; **5:**431
Eider ducks 4:443
8-millimeter videocassettes 6:282
Eigler, Don (American physicist) **3:**16
Eimeria **4:**212
EINSTEIN, Albert (German-American physicist) **3:**339–41
mass-energy equation **1:**357; **3:**15
quantum theory **3:**326–27
relativity, theory of **3:**142, 344–45, 349–52
stimulated emission **6:**344
illus. **3:**142, 323
Einstein equation 1:357; **3:**15
Einsteinium 3:37
Einstein X-Ray Observatory (HERO-2) 1:51, 58–59
Eland 5:126, 128
Elasticity
Earth's interior **2:**26–27, 48
wave motion, effect on **3:**196
Elastin 3:468
Elastomers 5:501; **6:**211
Elaters (liverwort cells) **4:**63
E layer (of the atmosphere) **2:**151
Elbow 5:179, 189–90
Elderly *see* Old age
Electrical charges 3:244–50, 308
ionic bonding **3:**49–50
subatomic particles **3:**47, 306
water molecule **3:**83
Electrical circuits 3:252, 258–59
Electrical conduction *see* Conduction, Electrical; Conductors, Electrical
Electrical engineering 6:20
Electrical resistance *see* Resistance, Electrical
Electrical stimulation
pain relief **5:**292
Electrical systems (of automobiles) **6:**141
Electric batteries *see* Batteries
Electric cars 2:321; **6:**148
Electric catfish 4:320

Electric current 2:309–11; **3:**244, 250–60 *see also* Electricity
conductivity **3:**358
current density **6:**221
magnetism **3:**261, 264
Electric doorbells 3:260
Electric eels 4:320, 333
Electric eyes *see* Photoelectric cells
Electric fields 2:388–89
Electric generators *see* Generators, Electric
Electric heating 2:320
ELECTRICITY 2:308–21; **3:**244–60
atmosphere **2:**151–52
atoms **3:**18
auroras **2:**158
automobiles powered by **6:**148
bioelectricity *see* Bioelectricity
coal-fueled power plants **2:**307, 358
electrochemistry **3:**100–105
energy demands **2:**305
geothermal energy **2:**66, 390–92
hydroelectric power **2:**377–80
lightning **2:**174–80
nuclear energy **2:**368–69
physics, history of **3:**142
quarks **3:**20
radioisotopes **3:**321
solar power **2:**384–89
superconducting transmission wires **3:**362; **6:**220
superconductors **3:**353–63
tidal energy **2:**249
illus.
generating facility **2:**312
Electric lighting 2:308–9, 319–20
Electric locomotives *see* Locomotives—electric
Electric meters 2:319; **3:**257–58
Electric motors 2:308, 320–21
factory, history of the **6:**191–92
illus. **3:**255
Electric potential *see* Potential, Electric
Electric power *see* Electricity
Electric power plants *see* Power plants
Electric rays (fish) **4:**328
Electric transformers *see* Transformers, Electric
Electric trolleys 6:127
Electric wiring *see* Wiring, Electric
Electrocardiograms 5:438
Electrocardiographs 2:321; **5:**201, 480
Electrochemistry 2:321; **3:**8, 101
Electroconvulsive therapy 5:356–57
Electrocortical spectral analysis 5:361
Electrodes 3:102, 252
Electrodialysis 2:448–49

Electroencephalographs 1:516; **2:**321
Electrojet 2:152
Electrolysis 2:321; **3:**101–4
copper refining **6:**183
Hall-Héroult process **6:**183
hydrogen production **2:**399
metallic separation **6:**178
salt, chemicals from **6:**207
zinc extraction **6:**184
illus.
Hall-Héroult process **6:**183
Electrolytes 3:8, 101, 252
Electrolytic cells 3:102
diagram(s) **3:**101
Electromagnetic fields 3:254
Electromagnetic radiation *see* Electromagnetic spectrum
ELECTROMAGNETIC SPECTRUM 1:53–54; **3:**272–81
see also Light; Radio waves
atomic spectra **3:**327–28
carcinogenic effects **5:**435–36
extraterrestrial life **1:**324
heat transfer **3:**237–39
nebulas **1:**219
Sun **1:**87–89
X-rays **5:**452
illus. **1:**220
calcium vapor **3:**327
neon gas **3:**327
Sun **1:**91
white light **3:**294, 326
Electromagnetic waves *see* Electromagnetic spectrum
Electromagnetism 3:63, 142, 144, 254, 311
Electromagnets 3:255, 266
maglev systems **6:**131–32
superconductivity **3:**362–63
illus. **3:**268
Electrometallurgy 2:321
Electrometers 6:337
Electromotive force 3:252
Electromyographs 5:511
Electron acceptor molecules 4:24
Electron affinity 3:49, 51–52
Electron diffraction 3:331–32
Electronegativity 3:28, 32, 65, 83, 100, 104
Electron guns
television **6:**291, 296
transmission electron microscopes **6:**335
diagram(s) **6:**292
Electronic Age 6:11, 13
Electronic mail *see* E-mail
Electronic musical instruments 3:217–18
ELECTRONICS 6:246–53
computers **6:**361–74
deep-sea exploration **2:**279
electricity **2:**321
engineering **6:**20
Internet **6:**302–11

ELECTRONICS (cont.)
 liquid crystals 3:92
 medical technology 5:492–93
 radar 6:254–61
 radio and television 6:288–97
 telegraph and telephone
  6:234–41
 video games 6:298–301
Electron jump 3:278
 illus. 3:276
Electron microscopes 3:450;
  6:334–36
 viruses 5:427
 illus. 3:7, 388; 6:330, 334, 336
Electrons 2:362–63; 3:6, 18–19,
  305–7
 atmosphere 2:151
 chemical bonding 3:47–52, 63
 conduction, electrical 3:358
 conductivity 3:26–27
 cosmic rays 1:228–29
 diffraction 3:331
 electricity 3:245–48
 electrochemistry 3:100–101
 electromagnetic radiation
  3:278–79
 electronics 6:246–47
 electron microscopes 6:334–36
 lightning 2:175
 magnetism 3:263–64
 noble gases 3:33
 nonmetals 3:28
 nuclear changes 3:15
 photosynthesis 4:23–24
 photovoltaic cells 2:386–88
 plasma 3:353
 quantum theory 3:143, 328,
  330–34
 stability 3:310
 superconductivity 3:359–60
 water molecule 3:83
Electron shells see Shells,
 Atomic
Electron-transport chains
  3:100, 437–38; 4:24
Electron volt 1:228; 6:354
Electrophoresis 3:133
Electroplating 2:321; 3:102–4
Electroscopes 1:225; 3:247–48
Electrostatic accelerators 6:354
Electrostatic attraction 3:47
Electrostatic precipitators 2:471
Electrostatic separation (of min-
 erals) 6:176
Elemental gold see Native gold
Elementary events (in probabil-
 ity) 1:417
Elementary particles see Par-
 ticles, Elementary
ELEMENTS 2:362; 3:3–5, 17,
  19–20, 34–46
 Big Bang theory 1:317
 chemical bonding 3:47–52
 families of 3:26–33
 nuclear chemistry 3:124
 periodic table 3:22–25, 333–34
Elephant beetles 4:297
Elephant birds 4:391

Elephant fish 4:325, 332–33
Elephant hawkmoths
 illus. 4:307
Elephantiasis 4:230
ELEPHANTS 5:13, 103–6
 ancestor 1:498; 5:61
 animal behavior 4:195
 illus. 2:76; 3:478; 4:183, 471
Elevated railroads 6:128
Elevators (airplane control sur-
 faces) 6:159
 illus. 6:160
Elf owls
 illus. 4:420
ELISA test see Enzyme-linked
 immunosorbent assay test
Elk 5:120–23
Ellipses 1:110, 377–78
 orbits of comets 1:162
 orbits of satellites 1:303–4
 illus. 1:396–97
Elliptical galaxies 1:221–22
Ellsworth, Lincoln (American
 explorer) 2:87
El Nath (star) 1:32
El Niño (ocean current) 2:188,
  225; 6:89
 illus. 2:186
El Salvador 2:52
Elsasser, Walter M. (German-
 American physicist) 2:29
Elytra 4:291–92
E-mail 6:305, 311, 391
 computer security 6:394, 397
Embankment dams 6:52
 illus. 6:54
Emboli (singular Embolus) 5:212
Embryo lavage 5:307
EMBRYOLOGY 3:372, 458–63;
  4:179–80
 Aristotle 3:367
 humans 5:296–99
 life, characteristics of 3:376
Embryonic diapause 5:18
Embryonic shield 5:297
Embryos
 cell division 3:443
 cloning 6:14
 gastrulation 3:461
 human kidneys 5:259
 human reproduction 5:296–97,
  299
 seed 4:88
 stem cells 5:422
 illus. 5:296, 298
Emergency medicine 5:416,
  481, 485
Emergent layer (of a rain forest)
  4:157
Emergent properties
 Gestalt psychology 5:339
 plant communities 4:132
Emergent wetlands see Marshes
Emission-control systems (of
 automobiles) 6:140–41
Emission spectra 3:295
 illus. 3:296

Emotions
 allergies 5:449
 complementary and alternative
  medicine 5:511
 diarrhea 5:255
 pain 5:288–89
Empedocles (Greek philosopher)
  3:312
Emperor penguins 4:396, 413
 illus. 4:197
Emphysema 2:468; 5:222
Empires (in biological classification) 3:399
Empire State Building (New
 York City) 2:180; 6:40
Emus 4:412–13
 illus. 4:411
Enamel (of teeth) 5:278, 280
 illus. 5:280
Enceladus (moon of Saturn)
  1:145–46; 3:382
Encephalartas
 illus. 4:97
Encephalitis 5:426
Encke, Johann Franz (German
 astronomer) 1:142–43
Encke division 1:143
Encke's comet 1:164
Encryption programs 6:397
ENDANGERED SPECIES 2:493–
  505
 antelopes 5:129–30
 apes 5:144
 asses 5:110
 California condors 4:416
 chinchillas 5:45
 crocodiles 4:384
 cycads 4:97
 deer family 5:119, 121–22
 desert life 2:86
 dingoes 5:81
 dugongs 5:62
 elephants 5:103
 environmental pollution 2:456
 grasslands 4:140
 green turtle 4:377
 guemals 5:122
 IUCN definition 2:498
 jaguars 5:88
 lemurs 5:137
 manatees 5:62
 monkeys 5:142
 northern spotted owl 4:421
 ocelots 5:91
 panda 5:75
 pink fairy armadillos 5:35
 rain-forest destruction 1:109
 reptiles 4:355
 rhinoceroses 5:111–13
 seals 5:65
 terns 4:435
 tigers 5:87
 veterinary science 4:468
 water buffalo 5:133
 whales 5:49–52, 54
 wolverines 5:96
 wolves 5:78–79

yaks **5**:135
zebras **5**:109
zoos **4**:473, 477
Endangered Species Act (U.S., 1973) **2**:498, 504–5
Endeavour (space shuttle) **1**:50, 257, 269
Endocarditis 5:440
Endocardium 5:199
ENDOCRINE SYSTEM 3:462; **5**:172, **242–47,** 467
illus. **5**:170
Endocrinology 3:117–18
Endocytosis 3:437
Endoderm 3:461; **5**:297
Endodermis 4:67
Endolymph 5:275
Endometrium 5:294
Endoplasmic reticulum 3:429–30; **4**:14
Endoprocta *see* Kamptozoa
Endorphins 5:289, 292, 514
Endoscopes 5:480, 490
illus. **6**:224
Endosperm 3:463; **4**:103, 106
Endospora 4:29
Endosymbiosis 3:428
Endothermic reactions 3:58–59
diagram(s) **3**:59
Endotherms *see* Homeotherms
End-tidal capnographs 5:478
Energetic galaxies *see* Galaxies, Energetic
Energetic Gamma Ray Experiment Telescope (EGRET) 1:231
ENERGY 1:5–6; **2**:302–99
alternate sources **2**:395–99
bird flight **4**:394–95
calories **5**:401
cell dynamics **3**:433–39
changes of state **3**:14
chemical reactions **3**:14, 57–62
conservation, law of **3**:15, 142, 308
ecosystem dynamics **3**:485–86
electricity **2**:308–21
engines **6**:96–106
entropy **3**:240
gases **3**:68
geothermal energy **2**:390–94
heat energy **3**:219–25
hydroelectric power **2**:377–80
kinetic theory **3**:141–42
laser fusion **6**:348–49
life, characteristics of **3**:376–77
light **3**:283
mass-energy equation **3**:15, 341, 348–49
metabolic rate **5**:395–96
muscle action **5**:187–88
nuclear energy **2**:361–76
particle accelerators **6**:352–59
photosynthesis **4**:18–19, 22–24
plant succession **4**:121
protein **5**:379
quantum theory **3**:322–34

radiochemical reactions **3**:125
simple machines **3**:168
solar power **2**:381–89
stars **1**:192–93
tidal energy **2**:249
work **3**:163–67
table(s)
metabolic rate **5**:396
Energy, U.S. Department of 2:392, 396, 398; **3**:321
nuclear-waste disposal **2**:370
Energy medicine 5:514
Energy pyramid (in ecosystems) **3**:486
Engelmann spruces 4:91
ENGINEERING 6:7, 15–22
careers in acoustics **3**:202
careers in optics **3**:287
science education **6**:329
Engineering geology 2:6
Engineering plastics 6:212, 228–29
Engineering psychology 5:347
ENGINES 6:96–106
airplanes **6**:162–64
automobiles **6**:135, 138–39
ceramic **6**:219
jet aircraft **6**:163–64
solar-powered **2**:381
illus.
automobiles **6**:215, 220
England *see also* Great Britain
brick construction **6**:27
coastal erosion **2**:294
early weather forecasting **2**:142–43
London air pollution **2**:468
Severn River tidal bore **2**:247
tides **2**:245
water pollution **2**:457–58
white cliffs of Dover **2**:120
zoos **4**:470
chart(s)
pollen stratigraphy **2**:217
illus.
chalk cliffs **2**:35; **4**:210
English Channel 2:281; **6**:48
illus.
Chunnel **6**:46
English sparrows *see* House sparrows
English yews 4:93
Enkephalins 5:288–89
Enlargers (in photography) **6**:273
Enos (chimpanzee sent into space) **1**:247
Entamoeba histolytica **4**:209
Enterogastrone 5:251
Enterprise (space shuttle) **1**:506
Enterprise servers *see* Mainframe computers
Entertainment Software Rating Board 6:300
Enthalpy *see* Heat of reaction
Entire leaves 4:73
Entognatha 4:278
ENTOMOLOGY 3:367; **4**:266–71
see also Insects

ENTROPY 3:240–43
Enveloped viruses 3:387, 392
Environment
Aristotle's thoughts on **3**:367
chemical industry **6**:206
child development **5**:329–30
dams' impact **2**:380; **6**:56
deserts and people **4**:168–69
ecology **3**:471–75
engineering today **6**:21
forest protection **4**:148–49
geography **2**:300–301
geological careers **2**:6
geothermal energy plant **2**:394
heredity and environment **3**:415; **5**:308
horticulture and agronomy **4**:175
observations from space **1**:259, 297, 312
oil pipelines **2**:329
plant communities **4**:132–37
plant succession **4**:120–25
pollution *see* Environmental pollution
taiga **4**:165
tidal energy plant **2**:249
waste disposal **2**:483–92
wetlands **4**:150–55
zebra mussels in Great Lakes **4**:237
Environmental biology 3:372–73
Environmental chemistry 3:8–9
Environmental engineering 6:21
ENVIRONMENTAL POLLUTION 2:451–56 *see also* Air pollution; Thermal pollution; Water pollution
acid rain **2**:472–76
amphibians **4**:339
analytical chemistry **3**:129
biological magnification **3**:489
carcinogens **5**:437
coal burning **2**:358
endangered species **2**:502–3
energy systems **2**:306–7
forestry **4**:131
frogs, effects on **4**:348
ginkgo's tolerance of **4**:94, 96
nanotechnology **6**:343
rain water **2**:172
temperate forests **4**:148
illus.
gull caught in six-pack ring **4**:434
Environmental pollution 2:394
Environmental Protection, Protocol on (1996) **2**:92
Environmental Protection Agency 2:458
acid rain **2**:172, 476
Environmental resistance 3:477–78
Environmental sciences 1:6
Enzyme-linked immunosorbent assay test (ELISA) 5:213, 444

Enzymes
  carnivorous plants **4**:108, 110
  cell dynamics **3**:439
  chemical reactions **3**:62
  digestive **4**:35, 186
  DNA **3**:440
  fat-storing **5**:392–93
  food spoilage **6**:77
  fungi **4**:37–38
  on-off switching **3**:117
  prokaryotes **3**:427
  protein **3**:121
  restriction enzymes **6**:72
Eocene epoch
  butterflies and moths **4**:301
  horses **5**:107
  rhinoceroses **5**:111
  viverrids **5**:99
  table(s) **2**:20
Eohippus *see* Hyracotherium
Eosinophils 5:208
Eosuchians 4:356
***Ephedra* 4**:96
Ephemerides 1:163–64
Epicardium 5:199
Epicenter 2:48
Epicotyl 3:463; **4**:88, 104, 106
Epidemics 2:457–58; **5**:429, 431
Epidemiologists 5:430
Epidermis (layer of the skin)
  5:263–64, 266–67
Epidermis (of a plant) *see* Dermal tissue
Epididymis *see* Vas epididymis
***Epidinium* 4**:213
Epiglottis 5:217
Epigynous flowers 4:102
Epilepsy 5:459, 466–67
Epinephrine *see* Adrenaline
Epiphyses 5:327
Epiphytes (Air plants) 4:60,
  76–77, 153, 157
  ferns **4**:78, 80
  leaves **4**:70
  whisk ferns **4**:82
Epiphytic algae 4:47
Epitaxial growth 6:232
Epithelioma 5:267
Epithelium 5:163–64, 171, 250
Epizoic algae 4:47
Epochs 2:20
Epoxy 6:212
EPROM (computers) **6**:369
Epsilon Lyrae (star) **1**:30
Epsomite 2:128
Epsom salts *see* Magnesium sulfate
Equalization (in sound recording)
  6:285
Equal triangles 1:372
Equanil *see* Propanediols
EQUATIONS (in chemistry) **3**:54–
  56, 60
Equations (in mathematics)
  algebra **1**:352, 357–58
  analytic geometry **1**:394–400
  differential equations **1**:437
Equations, Nuclear 3:127–28

Equator 1:383–84
  climates of the world **2**:209
  wind **2**:182, 184
Equatorial Countercurrent
  2:241
Equatorial orbits 1:305
Equids *see* Horse family
Equilibrium (in chemistry) **3**:56
  solutions **3**:77, 80
Equilibrium (in physics)
  entropy **3**:241, 243
  gravity **3**:181–82
  motion **3**:155
Equilibrium (in physiology) *see*
  Balance
Equilibrium constant 3:241
Equity 1:457–58
Eras (in geology) **1**:487; **2**:19
Erasable Programmable-Only
  Memory *see* EPROM
Eratosthenes (Greek astronomer) **1**:66
Erbium 3:37
Ergonomics 5:347
Eridanus (constellation) **1**:27, 32
Erie, Lake 2:459, 461
  illus. **2**:465
Erikson, Erik (American psychologist) **5**:342–43
  illus. **5**:339
Ermine weasels 5:93
  illus. **5**:95
Eros (asteroid) **1**:168, 260, 295
EROSION 2:120–24
  agronomy **4**:175
  Appalachians **2**:72, 74
  coastal formation **2**:255, 290–
    92, 294
  deserts **2**:84–85; **4**:169
  dust storms **2**:431
  glaciers **2**:97–99
  grasslands **4**:143
  lake formation **2**:109–10
  mineral formation **2**:137
  modern farms **6**:63–64
  mosses prevent **4**:60
  mountain formation **2**:71
  plain formation **2**:76
  plants prevent **4**:10
  plateaus **2**:80
  rain **2**:173
  rain forests **4**:160
  rivers **2**:102
  submarine canyons **2**:269
  temperate forests **4**:149
  volcanoes **2**:60
  water **2**:416–25
  wetlands **4**:154–55
  winds **2**:426–33
  illus. **2**:103
    mountain formation **2**:68
    rock outcroppings **2**:1
Erosion bases (of streams)
  2:422
Erosion terraces 2:424–25
Erythroblastosis fetalis 5:209
Erythrocytes *see* Red blood cells

Escape velocity (in rocketry)
  1:432; **3**:351
***Escherichia coli* 3**:449; **4**:32
  water contamination **2**:442
  illus. **4**:29
Escorial (palace, Spain)
  illus. **6**:35
Esophageal sphincter 5:249,
  255
Esophagus 5:216, 249
  illus. **5**:167–68, 250
ESPN (sports channel) **6**:304
Essential amino acids 5:379
  table(s) **3**:122
Essential fatty acids 3:120;
  5:382–83
Essential nutrients 5:378
Esters 3:114
  experiment to produce **3**:115
Estivation 4:169, 344–45
Estrogen 5:184, 246–47, 470
Estuary plant communities
  4:137
E.T.: The Extra–Terrestrial (film)
  illus. **1**:322
Eta Carinae Nebula
  illus. **1**:184
Ethane 3:68, 110
Ethanol *see* Ethyl alcohol
Ether (in physics) **3**:341, 343–44
Ethernet 6:388
Ethers (in chemistry) **3**:113–14;
  5:465
Ethics
  accounting standards **1**:457
  genetics **3**:405
  genetic technology **3**:423
  pain in animals **5**:292
  science fiction **1**:505
Ethiopia
  ancient construction **6**:18
  human fossils **1**:479
Ethnobotany 4:7
Ethology 3:367, 372; **4**:182, 188,
  386; **5**:347 *see also* Animal
  behavior
Ethosuximide (Zarontin)
  5:466–67
Ethyl alcohol (Ethanol) 2:396;
  3:111
  diagram(s)
    fermentation **3**:435
Ethyl chloride 3:76
Ethylene 3:109–10; **6**:208, 210
Ethyl group 3:110
Etna, Mount (volcano, Sicily)
  2:58, 62
Etruscans 1:343
Eubacteria *see* Bacteria
Eucalyptus trees 2:398; **4**:159
Eucaryotes *see* Eukaryotes
Euclid (Greek mathematician)
  1:330, 368, 401
Euclidean geometry 1:329, 401,
  403 *see also* Plane geometry; Solid geometry
Euclid's postulate 1:401

Euergetes I (Egyptian pharaoh)
    see Ptolemy III
Eugenics 3:423
Euglena 4:47–48, 51, 53, 200
Eukaryotes 4:19–20, 184, 206
    cell division 3:441–45
    cell structure 3:427–31
    classification of living things
        3:399
Eurasia 2:77
Eurasian badgers see Old World
    badgers
Eurasian cuckoos 4:402
Europa (moon of Jupiter) 1:138,
    236–37; 3:382
    illus. 1:137
Europe
    air pollution 2:469
    archaeology 1:463
    climates of the past 2:218
    continental drift 2:38
    continental islands 2:281
    environmental pollution
        2:451–52
    extinct mammals 1:499
    forestry 1:127
    ocean currents and climate
        2:242
European bison 5:133
European blackbirds 4:455
European bullfinches 4:461
European Center for Particle
    Physics (CERN) (formerly
    European Center for
    Nuclear Research) 3:311,
    357; 6:307, 358
    illus. 3:305
European elk see Moose
European hares 5:38
    illus. 5:37
European larches 4:92
European musk beetles 4:297
European pine martens 5:95
European polecats 5:94
European red deer 5:120
European robins 4:454
European skippers (butterflies)
    illus. 4:306
European Space Agency 1:253,
    296, 303
    astronauts 1:288
    auroral research 2:158
    solar probes 1:301
    space station 1:269
European sparrow hawks 4:415,
    419
Europium 3:31, 37
Eurostar (high-speed train) 6:130
Euryarcheota 4:29
Eustachian tube 5:221, 275
Eutelsat 1:310
Euthanization of pets 4:483,
    490
Eutrophication 2:111, 412, 414,
    460–62
    dams 2:380; 6:56
    freshwater biomes 3:499

plant succession 4:124
    illus. 4:124
EV1 (electric car) 6:148
EVA see Extravehicular activity
Evans, Sir Arthur (British
    archaeologist) 1:468
Evaporation (Vaporization)
    3:75–76
    changes of state 3:228–29
    mineral formation 2:137
    reservoirs 2:439
    water desalting 2:448
    illus. 3:77
Evaporites 2:36, 136
Evening stars 1:94, 99
Even parity 3:337
Event horizon 1:206
Everest, Mount (Asia) 2:72, 230
    illus. 2:74
Everglade kites 4:417
Everglades National Park
    (Florida) 4:154–55
    illus. 4:155
Evergreens 4:85, 156
Evidence collection (forensics)
    1:510, 513, 516
Evolution (in mathematics) 1:349
EVOLUTION, Human 5:157–60
EVOLUTIONARY BIOLOGY
    3:500–507
    amphibians 4:340–41
    animals, origin of 4:184
    antelopes 5:126–27
    arthropods 4:249
    bats 5:29
    birds 4:390–91
    bison, buffalo, and oxen 5:132
    camels and llamas 5:116
    carnivores 5:69–70
    carnivorous plants 4:110–11
    cartilaginous fish 4:323
    cat family 5:84–85
    classification of living things
        3:397, 399
    coelenterates 4:216
    death, role of 3:464
    deer 5:118
    DNA fingerprinting 3:419
    dog family 5:77–78
    dolphins 5:55–56
    edentates 5:33
    elephants 5:103–4
    endangered species 2:493–94
    eukaryotes 3:428
    fish 4:316
    fossils 1:487; 2:16
    frogs 4:343
    fungi 4:39
    giraffes and okapis 5:124
    horse family 5:107–8
    human see Evolution, Human
    hyenas 5:101–2
    insectivores 5:23
    jawless fish 4:321
    kidneys 5:259
    life, characteristics of 3:778
    lizards 4:356–57

mammals 1:497–98; 5:2–5
mammals, egg-laying 5:14
marsupials 5:17
mutations 5:320
paleobiology 1:481–82
photosynthetic organisms
    4:19–20
pinnipeds 5:63–64
plants 4:11–12
primates 5:136–37
reptiles 4:352
rhinoceroses 5:111
rodents 5:39
salamanders 4:350
sirenia 5:61
snakes 4:363–64
viruses 3:389
viverrids 5:99
whales 5:46–47
zoology 4:180–81
Evolutionary zoology 3:373
Ewing, Maurice (American geo-
    physicist) 2:40
Excimer lasers 1:254; 5:489–91
Exclusion principle (in physics)
    3:315, 333
Exclusive Economic Zones
    2:413
EXCRETORY SYSTEM 5:257–
    62, 467
    drug elimination 5:461
    illus. 5:168
EXERCISE 5:395–404
    arthritis treatment 5:428
    cosmonaut training 1:283
    oxygen debt 3:438
    weight control 5:392, 394
Exercise stress test 5:439
Exhaling (Exhalation; Expira-
    tion) 5:215, 218
Exhaust gas recirculation 6:140
Exhaust systems (of automo-
    biles) 6:140
Exobacteria 4:31
Exoskeleton 4:246–47, 249
    crustaceans 4:248, 251
    insects 4:272–73
Exosphere 1:105; 2:152–53
    illus. 2:150
Exothermic reactions 3:58
    diagram(s) 3:59
Exotic material 1:214
Expanding-universe theory
    1:17, 19–20, 23
Expansion of materials 3:221
Experimental psychology
    5:337–38, 346
EXPERIMENTS, Scientific 1:2;
    3:508–15
    ammonia preparation 3:137
    buoyancy of salt water 3:191
    crystal growing 3:93
    distillation of a pure liquid 3:137
    ester production 3:115
    fats, testing saturation of 3:123
    heat-conductivity of water 3:233
    lift on an airplane wing 3:193

EXPERIMENTS, Scientific
(cont.)
magnetizing an iron nail **3:**264
oxygen preparation **3:**137
paper chromatography **3:**130
rate of fall of objects of different
weights **3:**153–54
science fairs and projects
6:314, 317–19
water distillation **3:**137
water filtration **2:**445
waves, ocean **2:**250–51
illus.
heat-conductivity of water
3:234
preparation and collection of
gases **3:**136
Expert systems 6:374
Expert witness 1:516
Expiration (in physiology) *see*
Exhaling
Exploration *see also* Space
exploration
deep-sea exploration **2:**271–79
geography **2:**298
sailing ships **6:**109–10
Explorer (artificial satellite)
1:303–4
Explosions
chemical reactions **3:**58, 62
illus. **3:**57
Explosives
coal mining **2:**352–53
firedamp **2:**354
petroleum prospecting **2:**326
tunnel construction **6:**47
Exponential growth 3:478
Exponents 1:348, 358–59
logarithms **1:**360
Exposure (in photography)
6:266, 268, 270
Expression, Muscles of 5:190
Expressive disorders 5:365
Extensor muscles 5:189
External combustion engines
6:96, 102
Extinct in the wild (IUCN definition) **2:**498
Extinct species 2:493–97
aurochs **5:**134
Cretaceous period **1:**489
dodos **4:**428–29
ferns **4:**78
fish ancestors **4:**316
flightless birds **4:**409
grasslands **4:**140
heath hen **4:**426
horsetails and club mosses
4:74–75
hunted by humans **2:**403–4
IUCN definition **2:**498
marsupial species **5:**17
Miss Waldron's red colobus
5:141
passenger pigeons **4:**428, 431
Permian period **1:**488
prehistoric animals **1:**490–99

Quaternary period **1:**489
rain forests **1:**109; **4:**161
Steller's sea cow **5:**61
Tasmanian wolf **5:**22
trilobites **4:**249
Extrasensory perception (ESP)
5:347
Extrasolar planets 1:10, 44
Extraterrestrial life *see* Life,
Extraterrestrial
Extratropical lows (storms)
2:197
Extravehicular activity (Space
walks) 1:244, 252–53
astronaut training **1:**282
space stations **1:**267, 269
space suits **1:**272–76
illus. **1:**252, 279; **6:**13
gravity in space **3:**181
Extreme Ultraviolet Explorer
(EUVE) 1:51, 64
Extremophiles *see* Archaebacteria
Extrusion molding 6:212
illus. **6:**213
Extrusive masses (of rock)
2:32–33
***Exxon Valdez* oil spill 2:**328,
465
Eyed elaters 4:294–95
Eyeglasses 5:508
Eyelids 4:342; **5:**269
EYES 5:268–73
aging **5:**332–33
algae eyespots **4:**48–49, 51
artificial *see* Artificial eyes
artificial lens **5:**499, 508
babies **5:**329
birds **4:**395
birds of prey **4:**415
color inheritance **5:**316, 318–
19, 420
color of iris **5:**325
cornea transplants **5:**498–99
crustaceans **4:**248, 252
eclipse protection **1:**178
frogs **4:**348
human evolution **5:**158
inflammation **5:**447
insects **4:**248, 274
lasers in medicine **5:**480, 489;
6:351
lizards **4:**360
muscles **5:**190
owls **4:**419–20
snakes **4:**364
spiders **4:**258
Vitamin A **5:**383
illus.
artificial lens **5:**508
fruit fly **6:**336
lasers in medicine **6:**351
pupil size **5:**188
Eyes (of hurricanes) **2:**196–200
Eyeteeth *see* Cuspids
Eye walls (of hurricanes) **2:**198
Eyre, Lake (Australia) **2:**111

F

Fabrics *see* Fibers, Synthetic;
Textile industry
Facial bones 5:177
Facial reconstruction (forensics)
illus. **1:**512, 515
Facial vibrissae *see* Whiskers
Facilitated diffusion *see* Active
transport
Facing, Stone 6:25
Facsimile transmission *see* Fax
machines
FACTORIES 6:185–93
automation **6:**196
chemical industry **6:**205–6
lasers **6:**346–48
manufacturing engineering **6:**22
nanotechnology **6:**341
illus. **1:**454; **6:**203
Factors (in mathematics) **1:**349
Factory ships 5:54; **6:**88
Faculae 1:83
Facultative anaerobes 4:30
FADH$_2$ (energy-carrier molecule)
3:437–38
Fahrenheit, Gabriel Daniel (Ger-
man physicist) **3:**191
Fahrenheit temperature scale
3:223
table(s) **6:**421
Faint-Object Spectrograph
1:138
Fairings 6:94
Fairy rings 4:44
Fairy terns 4:435
Falconiformes 4:398
Falconry 4:419, 482
Falcons 2:502; **4:**414–15, 418
Falkland Current 2:240
Fallopian tubes 5:294–96, 301,
306–7
Fall overturn (lake water cycle)
2:111
Fallow deer 5:119–20
False-color scanning electron
microscopes
illus. **6:**336
False coral snakes 4:370
False ribs 5:177
illus. **5:**174
False scorpions *see* Pseudo-
scorpions
Families (in biological classifica-
tion) **3:**399
Families (of elements on the
periodic table) **3:**24
Family (in sociology)
farms, modern **6:**59
humanistic psychology **5:**344
Family practice (in medicine)
5:415
Fangs 4:365, 372–74
Fan-jet engines *see* Turbofan
engines
Fantail pigeons 4:430

Faraday, Michael (English physicist) **3:**101, 249, 254
illus. **2:**315
Farming, Fish *see* Fishing and fish farming
FARMS, Modern 6:57–66
Farsightedness 5:272, 489
illus. **5:**271
Far Ultraviolet Spectroscopic Explorer (FUSE) 1:64
Fast-attack submarines 6:122
Fast Auroral Snapshot (FAST) satellite 2:157–58
Fasting 5:255, 393
Fatigue, Metal 6:229
Fatigue, Muscle 5:188–89
Fats 5:382–83
  biochemistry **3:**120–21
  biodiesel fuel **2:**397
  calories **3:**61
  chemical industry **3:**62
  digestion **5:**252
  energy for muscle action **5:**187
  energy source **5:**381
  nonpolar substances **3:**81
  organic chemistry **3:**111, 114
  saturation levels **3:**123
  weight control **5:**391–94
Fat-soluble vitamins 5:383–84
Fatty acids 3:120; **5:**382, 494
  energy storage **3:**438
Faulds, Henry (Scottish physician) **1:**509
Faults (geology) **2:**47–48
  mountain formation **2:**68–70
  oil deposits **2:**324
  plate tectonics **2:**11–12
Fax machines 6:244
Featherbacks (fish) **4:**332–33
Feathers 4:390–93
  cassowaries and emus **4:**412
  owls **4:**420
  ptarmigans **4:**425–26
Feather stars (animals) **4:**224
Feces 5:254–55
  cancer screening test **5:**436
  desert animals **4:**169
  drug elimination **5:**461
  lagomorphs **5:**36
Federal Bureau of Investigation (FBI) 1:516
Federal Communications Commission (FCC) 6:243
Feedback 6:194–95, 197
Feeder bands (of hurricanes) **2:**198
Feeding frenzy (of sharks) **4:**326
Feeding levels *see* Trophic levels
Feedlots 6:60
illus. **6:**58
Feet (anatomy)
  birds **4:**395
  bones **5:**181–82
  human bipedalism **5:**160
  lizards **4:**358
  mollusks **4:**231, 235
  muscles of the body **5:**192

owls **4:**420
perching birds **4:**447
plantigrade **5:**70
illus.
  birds **4:**392
  bones **5:**181
Feldspar 2:33–34, 122, 137, 216
Feline leukemia 4:465
Felix (cat sent into space) **1:**247
Femur 5:181, 504
illus. **5:**165, 174–75, 180, 451
Fenestra ovalis *see* Oval window
Fenfluramine 5:393
Fennecs 5:83
Fen-phen 5:393
Fentanyl 5:374, 470
Fer-de-lance (snakes) **4:**374
Fermat, Pierre de (French mathematician) **1:**330
Fermentation 3:435–36
  Aspergillus **4:**44
  bacteria **4:**34–35
  biomass **2:**396
  food preservation **6:**78
  microbiology **3:**447
  yeast **4:**40
  diagram(s) **3:**435
Fermentors
illus. **4:**28
Fermi, Enrico (Italian-American physicist) **3:**124
illus. **3:**125
Fermi-Dirac statistics 3:307
Fermi National Accelerator Laboratory (Batavia, Illinois) **3:**311, 314; **6:**358–59
Fermions 3:307
Fermium 3:37
Fern mosses 4:61
FERNS 4:13, 56, **78–83,** 119
  reproduction **3:**455
  illus. **3:**453; **4:**56
Ferrari Testarossa (automobile)
illus. **6:**138
Ferrets 2:501; **5:**6, 94
Ferromagnetic materials 3:263
Ferryboats 6:112, 116
Fertility drugs 5:307, 312
Fertilization (in reproduction) **3:**457; **5:**295–96, 311
  conifers **4:**88
  embryology **3:**460
  plants **3:**455–56; **4:**102–3
  salamanders **4:**351
  illus. **5:**296
  laboratory methods **6:**14
Fertilizers 4:174
  anthracite ash **2:**360
  chemical industry **6:**205
  global warming **2:**479
  nitrogen cycle **3:**491
  phosphate **2:**414
  sewage **2:**486–87
  uptake studies **3:**320
  water pollution **2:**411–12, 461
Fetal alcohol syndrome 5:301, 375
Fetal-cell transplants 5:233

Fetch (wind action) **2:**254
FETs *see* Field-effect transistors
Fetuses 5:296, 299–302
  birth **5:**304
  illus. **5:**171, 297–99, 302
  amniocentesis **5:**418
  stem-cell injection **5:**303
Feynman, Richard (American physicist) **1:**328; **3:**140; **6:**339
F factor plasmids 4:32
Fiber, Dietary 5:380–81
Fiberglass 6:41, 212
FIBER OPTICS 6:222–25
  computer network cables **6:**388, 390–91
  medical technology **5:**489–90
  planetariums **1:**72
  telephone **6:**240
  total internal reflection **3:**285
  illus. **3:**286
Fibers, Muscle *see* Muscle fibers
Fibers, Nerve *see* Nerve fibers
Fibers, Synthetic 6:211–12, 215
  modern materials **6:**229–30
  natural gas **2:**345
  petroleum **2:**334
  illus. **3:**32
Fiberscopes 3:288; **6:**223–24
Fibonacci series 6:381–82
  illus. **6:**383
Fibrin 5:208
Fibrinogen 5:206, 208, 212, 472
Fibrous-root systems 4:68
Fibula 5:181
  illus. **5:**165, 174–75, 180
Fiddleheads (fern fronds) **4:**79, 81, 83
Fiddler crabs 3:380
Fiedler, Ralph (American astronomer) **1:**220–21
Field-effect transistors (FETs) 6:252
Field studies (in psychology) **5:**340
Field studies (of wildlife) **3:**473; **4:**339
  ichthyology **4:**313–14
Fight or flight response 3:377
Filaments (of flowers) **4:**101
Filarial worms 4:230
Filariasis 4:230, 268
File servers *see* Servers
File-sharing services 6:310
File Transfer Protocol (FTP) 6:305
Film, Photographic 6:262–63, 271–72
  developing **6:**272
  military satellites **1:**313
  illus.
    developing **3:**95
Filmy water ferns 4:78
Filoplumes 4:392
Filterable viruses *see* Viruses
Filters (in photography) **6:**270

Filters (water treatment)
 sand **2:**436, 443, 445–46
 illus. **2:**442, 450
Filtration 6:206, 215
Filtration, Water 2:119, 443
 diagram(s) **2:**440–41
Fimbriae 4:29
Financial statements 1:457
Finbacks *see* Fin whales
Finches 3:481; **4:**461
 illus. **3:**507; **4:**460
Fine Guidance Sensors 1:49
Fingal's Cave (Scotland)
 2:129–30
Finger Lakes (New York) **2:**98,
 108
Fingerprints 5:264
 forensic science **1:**509, 511,
 516
 illus. **1:**510
Fingers 5:180
 nails **5:**266
 pain receptors **5:**288
 tendons **5:**193
 touch, sense of **5:**286
 illus.
 polydactyl inheritance **5:**311
Fins 4:317–18, 330
 cartilaginous fish **4:**323, 325–
 26, 328
Fin whales 5:49–50
Fiords *see* Fjords
Fiorelli, Giuseppe (Italian
 archaeologist) **1:**466
Fir club moss 4:77
 illus. **4:**76
Fire
 clearing land **2:**404
 early use of **5:**160; **6:**4
 forests *see* Forest fires
 grasslands **4:**139, 142
 plant succession **4:**122
 steel, weakness of **6:**30
 illus.
 campfire **3:**58
 Kuwait oil-well fires **2:**334
 San Jacinto River **2:**459
Fire algae *see* Dinoflagellates
Firearms 1:515
Fire bosses (mining supervisors)
 2:355
Fire-control radar 6:258
Firedamp 2:354
**Fire danger rating and burning
 index 4:**131
Fired brick 6:26–27
Firefighting 2:450; **4:**130–31
 illus. **2:**449
Fireflies 4:196, 295
 illus. **3:**60, 377; **4:**295
Fire hydrants 2:450
 illus. **2:**449
Fireplaces 3:237
Fireproofing 6:30
**Fire-protection engineering
 6:**21
Firewalls, Computer 6:395, 397
Fireweed 4:163

Firn 2:95–97
Firs 4:86–87, 91; **6:**28–29
First law of motion 3:155–56
First-light cacti
 illus. **4:**115
**Fischer-Tropsch water-gas pro-
 cess 2:**360
FISH 4:315–20
 acid rain's effects **2:**475–76
 aquariums **4:**474, 476
 bats' diet **5:**32
 bony fish **4:**329–35
 conservation **2:**407
 courtship **4:**196
 dams and reservoirs **2:**410–11
 dams' effect on **2:**380; **6:**56
 endangered species **2:**503
 extinct species **2:**496–97
 fishing and fish farming
 6:86–90
 fossils **1:**488
 genetic variation **3:**505
 harvesting **2:**407, 412–13
 ichthyology **4:**312–14
 jawless fish **4:**321–22
 perception **4:**192
 pets **4:**481, 484, 486
 prehistoric animals **1:**490, 492
 reproduction **3:**457
 swimming **4:**317–18
 diagram(s) **4:**317
 body structures **4:**316
 marine biomes **2:**233
**Fish and Wildlife Service, U.S.
 2:**504; **4:**388–89
Fishers (mammals) **5:**95
Fish hawks *see* Ospreys
**FISHING AND FISH FARMING
 6:**86–90 *see also* Whaling
 Atlantic Ocean **2:**232
 cod **4:**333
 conservation **2:**412–13
 dolphin deaths **5:**56–57
 fishery management **4:**312
 Indian Ocean **2:**234
 Pacific Ocean **2:**230
 pearl fisheries **4:**235
 sharks, overfishing of **4:**326
 illus.
 artificial insemination **2:**406
Fishing cats 5:92
Fish ladders 2:380, 410
Fish oils 6:86
Fission (in biology) **4:**31–32 *see
 also* Meiosis; Mitosis
 illus. **4:**213
Fission, Nuclear *see* Nuclear
 fission
Fissionable materials 2:364,
 368
Fission products 2:364
Fissure eruptions (volcanoes)
 2:58
Fissures (in the brain) **5:**229
Fitzgerald, G. F. (Irish physicist)
 3:346
**Fitzgerald-Lorentz contraction
 3:**346

Fitzroy, Robert (English meteorologist) **2:**142–43
Fixation (in psychology)
 5:343–44
Fjords 2:123, 265, 288
 illus. **2:**289, 418
Flagella 3:427, 430–31
 bacteria **4:**29
 coelenterates **4:**217
 protozoans **4:**207
 sperm **5:**295
 sponges **4:**215
Flagellates 3:451; **4:**207–9
Flamingos 4:445
 illus. **4:**393, 444
Flanges (of the leg bones) **5:**181
Flash (programming language)
 6:309
Flashbacks (from LSD use)
 5:372
Flash floods 2:202, 417
Flash guns 6:268, 270
Flashlights 3:253
 illus. **3:**252
Flatfeet 5:182
Flatfish 4:335
Flat-headed cats 5:92
Flat-screen television 6:297
Flat-slab construction 6:31
FLATWORMS 4:201, **225–28**
Flavin adenine dinucleotide *see*
 FADH$_2$
Flavorings 6:81–82
Flavors (of quarks) **3:**314
FlavrSavr tomato 6:74
F layers (of the atmosphere)
 2:151–52
Flea beetles 4:269
Fleas 4:280
Fleming, Sir Alexander (Scottish
 physician and bacteriolo-
 gist) **3:**447; **5:**431, 463
 illus. **4:**33
Fleming, John (English physicist)
 6:247–48
Flemming, Walther (German
 cytologist) **3:**410
Flesh-eating disease 5:425
Fletcher, James (American
 space administrator) **1:**259
Flexible light guides 6:224
Flexor muscles 5:189
Flexure lines (in the skin) **5:**264
Flickers 4:408
 illus. **3:**500
Flies 3:375; **4:**273, 280
 decomposition **3:**470
 plant pollination **4:**158
Flight
 airplanes **6:**158–60
 bats **5:**29–30
 birds **4:**393–94
 human-powered **6:**94–95
 prehistoric animals **1:**496–97
FLIGHTLESS BIRDS 4:409–13
 Galápagos cormorants **4:**446

FLIP (Floating Instrument Platform)
  illus. **2:**278
Flip-flops 6:370
Floating Instrument Platform
  see FLIP
Floating ribs 5:177
  illus. **5:**174
Floc (Flocculence) 2:444–45;
  6:212
Floebergs 2:262
Floes 2:262
Flood control 2:105; **4:**154
Flood currents 2:247
Floodplains 2:103–4, 423–25
Floods 2:103, 105
  deserts **2:**85
  hurricanes **2:**200
  land change **2:**416–18, 423,
    425
  Netherlands (1953) **2:**294
  watches and warnings **2:**202
Flood tides 2:244
Floppy disks 6:372
Floriculture 4:173–74
Florida
  alligators **2:**505
  artificial reefs **2:**287
  Everglades **4:**154–55
  fringing reefs **2:**285
  manatee protection efforts **5:**62
  mangrove swamps **2:**290
  Okeechobee, Lake **2:**108
  sinkholes **2:**126
  tornadoes **2:**193
  water desalination **2:**448
  wilderness areas **2:**511–12
  illus.
    Everglades **4:**155
    mangrove swamp **2:**291
    solid-waste disposal **2:**485
Florida arrowroots 4:97
Florida Current 2:240
Florida panthers
  illus. **2:**498
Flossing (of teeth) 5:281
Flotation 3:191
Flounder 4:335
Flour 3:463
Flowcharts 6:382
  illus. **6:**383
FLOWERING PLANTS 4:10, 13,
  57, **98–107**
  embryology **3:**463
  flower clocks **3:**381
  fossils **1:**488–89
  reproduction **3:**455–56
  illus. **3:**481
Flowers 4:100–104
  bats' diet **5:**32
  floriculture **4:**173–74
  monocots and dicots **4:**107
  diagram(s) **3:**455
Flow imaging *see* Doppler color
  flow imaging
Flowstone 2:128

FLUID DYNAMICS 3:183–93 *see
  also* Gases; Liquids
  heat transfer **3:**233–34
Fluidity 3:12
Flukes (flatworms) 4:201, 227–28
  illus. **4:**227
FluMist 5:474
Flunitrazepam (Rohypnol) 5:374
Fluorescence 3:275, 296
Fluorescence microscopes
  3:450; **6:**334
Fluorescent lighting 2:320;
  3:281, 296
Fluoridation 2:446; **5:**280; **6:**208
Fluoride 3:33; **5:**388
Fluorine 3:32–33, 37
  chemical industry **6:**208
  covalence **3:**51
  water supply **3:**87
Fluorite 2:137–38
Fluorocarbons *see* Chlorofluoro-
  carbons
Fluoro group 3:110
Fluoroquinoines 5:464
Fluoxetine (Prozac) 5:466
Flupentixol 5:376
Flutes 3:216, 462
  illus. **3:**463; **6:**4
Fly ash 2:475, 484
Flycatchers 4:448–49, 455
  illus. **4:**448
Flyer **(airplane) 6:**153
  illus. **6:**152
Flying boats 6:156
  illus. **6:**155
Flying buttress
  illus. **6:**7
Flying Cloud **(clipper ship)**
  illus. **6:**110
Flying fish 4:318, 333–34
Flying foxes 5:32
Flying lemurs *see* Colugos
Flying lizards 4:358
Flying shuttles 6:189
Flying snakes 4:372
Flying squid 4:233
Flying squirrels 5:41
Flyspeck formulas *see* Lewis
  structures
Flywheels 6:99
  illus. **6:**98
FM *see* Frequency modulation
F-numbers (in photography)
  6:265
Foam, Plastic 6:214
Focal length 3:286; **6:**264–66
Focus (in optics) 3:286, 290
  photography **6:**263–64, 266
Focus (in seismology) 2:23, 48
Foehn 2:186
FOG 2:159–60
  illus. **2:**162
Folate (Folic acid) 5:386
Folds (in geology) 2:68–70
  illus. **2:**37
Folic acid *see* Folate

Folklore *see* Legends and folklore
Folk medicine *see* Complementary and alternative medicine
Follicles *see* Graafian follicles;
  Hair follicles
Follicle-stimulating hormone
  5:243
Fomalhaut (star) 1:32
Fontanels (Fontanelles) 5:176,
  328
Fontinalis **4:**61
Food *see also* Genetically engineered foods; Nutrition
  algae **4:**53
  allergies **5:**448
  animals' feeding behavior
    4:193–95
  bacteria **4:**34–35
  calories **3:**61; **5:**401
  cellular energy **3:**434
  energy for muscle action **5:**187
  fish as human food **4:**320
  fishing and fish farming
    6:86–90
  genetics and production
    6:67–75
  irradiation process **3:**201
  modern farms **6:**57–66
  nutrition **5:**378–90
  population, limits to growth of
    3:482
  preservation *see* Food preser-
    vation and processing
  rain-forest products **4:**159
  safety **4:**468
  space technology **1:**256
Food and Drug Administration
  5:504, 506
  homeopathy **5:**513
Food chain 3:486
  carbon cycle **4:**21
  copepods **4:**251
  environmental pollution **2:**111,
    452, 502
  lichens **4:**43
  plants **4:**10
  illus. **3:**490
Food Guide Pyramid 5:388
Food poisoning 4:34; **6:**77
**FOOD PRESERVATION AND
  PROCESSING 4:34;
  6:76–85**
  freeze-drying **3:**93
  natural gas cooking **2:**344–45
  radioisotopes **3:**320
Food pyramid (ecology) 4:249
Food pyramid (nutrition) *see*
  Food Guide Pyramid
Food web 3:486; **4:**52
Foot (anatomy) *see* Feet
Footings (in construction) 6:34
Foramen magnum 5:153, 177
Foramina 5:176
Foraminifers 4:210–11
**Forbidden lines (in the nebular
  spectrum) 1:**220

Forbush, Scott E. (American physicist) 1:227
Forbush effect 1:227
Force
    gravity 3:176
    magnetism 3:261–71
    motion 3:154–55
    simple machines 3:169
    work 3:162–63
Forced vibrations (in acoustics) 3:200
Forceps 5:305
Ford, Henry (American automobile manufacturer) 6:192
Ford, Model T (automobile) see Model T Ford
Ford Motor Company 6:193
Ford Mustang (automobile)
    illus. 6:137
Ford Taurus (automobile)
    illus. 6:137, 228
Ford Thunderbird (automobile)
    illus. 6:137
Foredeep 2:71, 73
FORENSIC SCIENCE 1:507–16
    archaeology 1:466
    autopsy 3:469
    crystallography 3:91
    entomology 4:266, 270–71
    genetic technology 3:418–19
    psychology 5:346
    illus. 3:418
Foreshocks 2:54
Foreshore (of a beach) 2:293
Forest certification 4:149
Forest fires 2:180, 408; 4:130–31
    climate change 2:220
    conifers can withstand 4:87
    plant succession 4:122
    satellite monitoring 1:255–56
    taiga 4:165
    temperate forests 4:146–47
    thinning growth to prevent 4:149
    illus. 3:475; 4:120, 130, 160
Forest rangers 4:128
Forest reserves 2:509; 4:127
FORESTRY 4:126–31
Forests see also Deforestation
    acid rain 2:476
    carbon cycle 4:21
    climate analysis 2:216
    conservation 2:408
    fires see Forest fires
    forestry 4:126–31
    global warming 2:480
    high-latitude biomes 3:496–97
    multiple use 2:509
    northern spotted owl 4:421
    plant communities 4:133–36
    plant succession 4:123–25
    rain forests 4:156–61
    songbird populations 4:451
    temperate forests 4:144–49
    tropical biomes 3:493–94
    illus. 2:402
        regeneration after fire 2:400

Forest Service, U.S. 2:509–11; 4:127, 143, 149, 160
Forest Stewardship Council 4:149, 161
Forgery 1:515
Forget-me-nots 4:164
Forgetting 5:358, 360–61
Forked venation 4:73
Formaldehyde 2:467; 3:114
    diagram(s) 3:67
Formant theory 3:212
Formic acid 3:114
Formosan rock macaques 5:142
Formulas (in algebra) 1:354, 356–57
FORMULAS (in chemistry) 3:53–54
FORTRAN (Formula Translator) (computer language) 6:378, 381
Fossett, Steve (American aviator) 6:150, 164
Fossil fuels 2:398, 414–15; 4:17
    see also Coal; Natural gas; Petroleum
    acid rain 2:473
    air pollution 3:73
    algae 4:53
    carbon cycle 3:490; 4:21
    chemical energy 3:62
    energy systems 2:305
    greenhouse effect 2:154, 478
    heat energy 3:219–20
FOSSILS 1:484–89; 2:132, 138–39, 215 see also Paleontology
    arthropods 4:249
    birds 4:390
    climate analysis 2:216–18
    collecting 2:139–40
    cyanobacteria 4:33
    dinosaurs 1:493–94
    Earth, age of 2:15–17
    evolutionary biology 3:501
    fish 4:316
    flowering plants 4:98
    geologic record 2:19–21
    ginkgoes 4:94–95
    hedgehog 5:23, 27
    how fossils form 1:487
    human evolution 5:156, 159–60
    insects 1:492
    life, origin of 3:379–80
    liverworts 4:62
    lizards 4:356
    microbes 4:27
    mountains 2:73
    paleobotany 4:7
    paleontology 1:479–83
    peat bogs 4:154
    plant evolution 4:11–12
    prehistoric animals 1:490
    pterosaurs 1:496–97
    rays 4:328
    seal-like mammal 5:63–64
    sedimentary rocks 2:36
    snakes 4:363

illus.
    Koonwarra plant 4:99
    rock studies 2:32
Fossil water 2:86
Foucault, Jean-Bernard-Léon (French physicist) 1:109–10
Foucault pendulum 1:109–10
    illus. 1:111
Foundation Seamounts (extinct undersea volcanoes) 2:124
Four-cycle engines 6:99–101, 103
Four-dimensional continuum 3:345
Four-horned antelopes see Chousinghas
Four-stroke engines see Four-cycle engines
Four-wheel drive
    illus. 6:135
Fovea centralis 5:271
Foveola (robotic vision system) 6:201
Foxes 5:5, 82–83
Fox squirrels 5:40
    illus. 5:41
Fractal geometry 1:331
Fractional distillation 3:137
Fractionating towers 2:330
    illus. 2:333
Fractions 1:349–50
    binary numerals 1:450
Fracture (in minerals) 2:137
Fracture lines 3:91
Fracture match (forensics) 1:509
Fractures, Bone 5:182
Fracture zone (of glaciers) 2:95–96
Fragile-X syndrome 5:319, 421
Fragilitas ossium 5:182
Fragmental rocks 2:35
Frames (in data transfer) 6:388
France
    environmental pollution 2:456
    high-speed trains 6:130
    natural bridges 2:423
    oyster farming 4:238
    plains 2:77
    Race of Alderney 2:248
    Roman aqueducts 6:17
    solar-power plant 2:384
    tidal energy 2:249, 399
    wind 2:186
    illus.
        early sewers in Paris 2:435
        Mont St. Michel 2:246
        Pic du Midi Observatory 1:41
        solar-power plant 2:384
Francis reaction turbines 2:316
    diagram(s) 2:313, 378
Francium 3:29, 37
Frankenstein (book, Shelley) 1:500

Franklin, Benjamin (American scientist and patriot) **2:**178, 180
electricity **3:**142
kite experiment **3:**250
weather observations **2:**203
Franklin, Rosalind (British chemist) **3:**6
crystallography **3:**91
DNA **3:**117, 402, 411
Frasch process 6:206
Fraternal twins 5:295–96, 311–12
Fraud 1:515
Fraunhofer lines *see* Absorption lines
Frederick II (Holy Roman Emperor) **4:**386
Fredonia (New York) **2:**337
Free association 5:342, 357
Freedom (space station) *see* International Space Station
Freedom of the Seas (ship) **6:**114
Freedom Tower (New York City) **6:**22
Free fall 3:153 54
Free radicals 3:467–68; **5:**233
Free speech 6:311
"Free spirit" atoms 1:227
Free-tailed bats 5:32
Free vibrations (in acoustics) **3:**200
Freeze (drug) *see* Methamphetamine
Freeze-drying 3:93; **6:**80
Freezing
food preservation **6:**80
plants resistant to **6:**73
water desalting **2:**449
Freezing point 3:78, 88, 92
changes of state **3:**227
water **3:**84–85
Freezing rain (Glaze) 2:167
Frege, Gottlob (German mathematician) **1:**330
Freighters (ships) **6:**113
Frequency (of waves) **1:**311; **6:**288
cellular technology **6:**243
Doppler effect **1:**19
electromagnetic spectrum **3:**272–73, 278
light **3:**293, 324
musical instruments **3:**214
sound **1:**390; **3:**199
television transmission **6:**294
illus.
electromagnetic spectrum **3:**274
sound spectrum **3:**200
Frequency modulation (FM) 6:288–90
illus. **6:**289
Frequency multiplexing 6:240–41
Freshwater biomes 3:499

Freud, Sigmund (Austrian psychoanalyst) **5:**155, 341–42, 357
illus. **5:**338
Friction
airplane's drag **6:**158
energy to overcome **5:**396
fluid dynamics **3:**192
human-powered transportation **6:**91–92, 94
motion **3:**154–55
tsunamis **2:**257
wind **2:**183
work **3:**165–66
Friendship 7 (spacecraft)
illus. **1:**239
Frigate birds 4:393, 446
Frilled lizards 4:362
illus. **4:**360
Fringe-toed lizards 4:358
Fringing reefs 2:285, 291
Frisch, Karl von (Austrian zoologist) **4:**288
Fritillaries (butterflies) **4:**305
illus. **4:**305
Frog-eating bats 5:32
Frogmouths *see* Owlet nightjars
FROGS 4:340–42, **343–48**
courtship **4:**196
Galvani's experiments **3:**250–51
life span **5:**324
Opalina **4:**213
illus. **4:**184, 340
child holding frog **5:**286
embryology **3:**462
glass frog **4:**343
life cycle **4:**344
pygmy marsupial frog **4:**346
spring peeper **4:**343
From the Earth to the Moon (book, Verne) **1:**271
Fronds 4:79, 81
Frontal bone 5:176
illus. **5:**174–75
Frontal clouds 2:161
Frontal lobe (of the brain) **5:**228–29
Fronts 2:187–88, 190
Front-wheel drive 6:135, 138
illus. **6:**135
Frosch, Paul (German bacteriologist) **5:**424
Frostbite
illus. **3:**467
Frost wedging (by glaciers) **2:**97
Fructose 3:119; **5:**380
Fructose biphosphate 3:435
Fruit bats 5:29, 32
Fruit flies 4:181
illus. **6:**336
Fruiting bodies 4:37, 39, 42, 44–45
Fruits 4:103–4
compared to cones **4:**86
nutrition **5:**381
pomology **4:**172
weight control **5:**394

Fruit trees
illus. **4:**1
Frustums 1:383
illus. **1:**382
F-stops 6:265, 270
illus. **6:**266
table(s) **6:**268
Fucoxanthin 4:50
Fuel-cell technology 2:399
coal gasification **2:**358
engines **6:**148
Fuel efficiency 6:134
Fuel gas
manufactured gas **2:**344, 359
natural gas **2:**336–45
illus. **2:**358
Fuel injection 6:102–3, 139
Fuel rods (of nuclear reactors) **2:**366, 375, 490
illus. **2:**369
Fuels *see also* Fossil fuels
alternate sources **2:**395–99
automobiles **6:**148
coal **2:**346–60
electricity, generation of **2:**312
natural gas **2:**336–45
nuclear reactors **2:**365–66, 369–70
peat **4:**62
petroleum **2:**322–35
rockets **1:**243, 249
solar power **1:**90
wood **4:**146
Fuel system
automobile engines **6:**139
diesel engines **6:**102–3
gasoline engines **6:**100
Fugue state 5:352
Fujita Scale
table(s) **2:**194
Fulcrum 3:169
Fulgurites 2:180
Fullerenes 6:343
Fulling (of cloth) **6:**187
Fulmars 4:446
Fulton, Robert (American engineer) **6:**110
Functional groups (in chemistry) **3:**111
table(s) **3:**110
Functional stage (in human growth) **5:**325
Functions (in mathematics) **1:**333, 434
Fundus 5:249–50
Fundy, Bay of 2:246, 249, 399
illus. **2:**245, 248
FUNGI 4:36–45, **54–55**
carbon cycle **4:**21
cell walls **3:**431
classification **3:**398–99; **4:**183
early classification of **4:**184
fossils **1:**490
infectious diseases **5:**428, 474
microbiology **3:**451
movement **4:**185
mycorrhiza **4:**68, 112

FUNGI (cont.)
    radioisotope tracer studies
        3:320
    reproduction **3:**454–55
Funiculi (singular **Funiculus**)
    5:230
Funk, Wally (American aviator)
    1:289
Funnel-web spiders 4:261, 263
Funny bone 5:179
Fur see also Wool
    allergenic materials **5:**448
    badgers **5:**97
    beavers **5:**42
    chinchillas **5:**45
    foxes **5:**82–83
    minks **5:**94
    moles **5:**25
    muskrats **5:**44
    rodents' cheek fur **5:**40
    sea otters **5:**98
**Fur-bearing animals, Endan-
    gered 2:**500, 505
Furnaces see also Blast fur-
        naces; Open hearth fur-
        naces; Solar furnaces
    blackbody **3:**323
    electric furnaces **6:**179
    mirror casting **1:**41–42
Furnas County stone (meteorite)
    1:171
Fuse boxes 3:259
Fuses 2:319; **3:**259
Fusible alloys 3:228
Fusion, Heat of see Heat of
    fusion
Fusion, Nuclear see Nuclear
    fusion
Fusion inhibitors (AIDS drugs)
    5:445
Fusion point see Melting point

G

g (acceleration due to gravity)
        3:179–81
    free fall **3:**153–54
    illus. **3:**151
    table(s) **3:**179
Gabbros 1:126
Gaboon vipers 4:374
Gabor, Denis (British scientist)
    6:276
Gadolinium 3:31, 37
Gagarin, Yuri A. (Soviet cosmo-
    naut) **1:**241
Gajdusek, Carleton (American
    scientist) **3:**391
Galactic clusters 1:186
    illus. **1:**59
Galactorrhea 5:244
Galactose 5:380
Galagos 5:137–38
Galápagos cormorants 4:446
Galápagos Islands 2:282–83
    Darwin's visit **3:**502, 504
    finches **3:**481

marine iguanas **4:**358
    turtles **4:**379
Galápagos turtles 4:379
    illus. **4:**379, 465
Galaxies 1:195–96, 215
    cosmology **1:**19–21
    energetic galaxies **1:**215–17
    infrared astronomy **1:**61
    interstellar space **1:**218–19,
        221–22
    invisible astronomy **1:**54
    Milky Way **1:**24–25, 181–89
    Plasma Universe theory
        1:22–23
    X-ray **1:**59
    illus.
        galactic cluster **1:**59
        merging **1:**216
        NGC 4565 **1:**60
GALAXIES, Energetic 1:215–17
Gale-force winds 2:196
Galen (Greek physician) **5:**412,
        432
    illus. **5:**411
Galeras 6:109
Galilee, Sea of (Israel) **2:**461
Galileo (Italian scientist) **1:**12, 37,
        78, 134, 473
    falling objects **3:**153
    Moon **1:**113
    physics, history of **3:**141
    Saturn **1:**141
    Sun **1:**83
    thermometers **2:**142; **3:**223–24
    illus. **1:**11
        records of Jupiter **1:**79
        replica of his telescope **1:**40
Galileo (space probe) **1:**259–60,
        294–95
    asteroids **1:**168
    Jupiter's atmosphere **1:**135
    Jupiter's collision with comet
        1:138
    Jupiter's moons **1:**138, 236
    Moon **1:**124
Gall, Franz Joseph (German
    phrenologist) **5:**336
Gallbladder 5:252, 256
    illus. **5:**167, 249
Galle, Johann Gottfried (Ger-
    man astronomer) **1:**79,
        142, 153; **3:**182
Galleons 6:109
Galleys (warships) **6:**107–8
Galliformes 4:398, 423
Gallinules 4:439–40
Gallium 3:31, 37
Gallium arsenide 6:233
Gallstones 5:256
Gall wasps (Gallflies) 4:290
Galton, Sir Francis (English sci-
    entist) **1:**509
Galvani, Luigi (Italian anatomist)
    3:250–51
Galvanizing 3:103; **6:**182
Galvanometers 3:257
    illus. **3:**256
Game birds see Wildfowl

Game Boy 6:299, 301
GameCube 6:301
GameGear 6:299
Game management 2:407
Games of chance 1:415–23
**Gamete intra-fallopian transfer
    5:**307
Gametes (Sex cells) 3:410;
        5:293
    algae **4:**48
    human heredity **5:**311
    meiosis **3:**443–45
GAME THEORY 1:424–30
Gametophytes 3:455; **4:**15
    conifers **4:**87–88
    ferns **4:**81, 83
    flowering plants **4:**102–3
    ginkgo **4:**96
    horsetails **4:**75–76
    mosses **4:**59–63
Gamma globulins see Immuno-
    globulin G
**Gamma hydroxybutric acid
    (GHB) 5:**374
Gamma-ray astronomy 1:52, 54,
        59, 187, 231
Gamma rays 1:58; **3:**317, 319
    antimatter **3:**21
    black hole **1:**213
    cosmic rays **1:**228
    electromagnetic spectrum
        3:277–78
    nuclear chemistry **3:**126–28
    nuclear energy **2:**363
    illus.
        penetrating power **3:**318
        scan of liposomal uptake
            sites **5:**474
Ganglia 5:232, 270
Gangrene 5:211–12
Gangue 6:175
Gannets 4:446
    illus. **3:**476
Ganymede (moon of Jupiter)
        1:138; **2:**155, 157
    illus. **1:**137
Garbage compactors 2:492
Garden pea plants 4:115
Garden spiders 4:261
Garn, Jake (American senator
    and astronaut) **1:**285
Garnets 2:37
    computer memory **6:**371
    Nd:YAG laser **5:**488
    illus. **2:**36
Garofalo (whirlpool) **2:**248
Garriott, Owen K. (American
    astronaut)
    illus. **1:**266
Gars 4:331–32
Garter snakes 4:366, 371
    illus. **4:**369
Garwin, K. (American physicist)
    3:338
Gas, Fuel see Fuel gas
Gas, Natural see Natural gas
Gas chromatography 3:132

Gas-cooled nuclear reactors 2:367–68
diagram(s) 2:368
Gas-driven oil wells 2:324
GASES 3:3–4, 12–13, **68–74,** 226
air pollution 2:467, 471
atmosphere 2:147, 149, 152
chemical reactions 3:61–62
entropy 3:242
fluid dynamics 3:183–93
greenhouse gases 2:478–79
interstellar space 1:219–20
laboratory preparation 3:137
lakes 2:111
liquids, differences from 3:184
matter, study of 3:14
plasma 3:353–54
rain's chemical nature 2:172
solubility 3:81
spectra 3:295
sublimation 3:92–93
vapors 3:76
volcanoes 2:61
water solutions 3:84, 87
Gas lasers 6:346
Gasohol 2:396
Gasoline 2:330, 332, 476
chemical energy 3:62
composition 3:111
energy demands 2:305
lead emission 2:468
solutions 3:75
unleaded 6:141
Gasoline engines 6:99–102
airplanes 6:162–63
automobile 6:138–39
Gaspra (asteroid) 1:168
Gastric juice 5:250–51
Gastric ulcers 5:256
Gastrin 5:246
Gastrinomas 5:245–46
Gastrocnemius
illus. 5:166
Gastroenterology 5:413
Gastroesophageal reflux *see* Heartburn
Gastrointestinal tract 5:248
alcohol's effect on 5:375
infectious diseases 5:429
medications 5:467
surgery for obesity 5:393
Gastropods 4:203, 239–41
Gastroscopes 6:223
Gastrotricha 4:201
Gastrulation 3:461
illus. 3:462
Gas turbines 2:315; 6:104–5
diagram(s) 2:311
Gas vesicles 4:33
Gates (in electronics) 6:341
Gaur 5:134–35
Gause, G.F. (Russian microbiologist) 3:480
Gauss, Karl Friedrich (German mathematician) 1:168, 335
Gaussberg, Mount (volcano, Antarctica) 2:92

Gavials 4:380, 382, 384
illus. 4:383
Gaviiformes 4:398, 432–34
Gay-Lussac, Joseph-Louis (French scientist) 3:74
Gay-Lussac's law 3:74, 223
Gazelles 4:194; 5:131
GCI *see* Ground-controlled interception radar
Gear ratio 3:172; 6:143
Gears 3:172; 6:143–44
illus.
silicon nanogears 6:343
Geckos 4:353, 356–62
illus. 4:352, 358, 360
Geese 4:441; 5:324
illus. 4:440
Gegenschein *see* Zodiacal light
Geiger-Mueller counter 1:226–27
Gell-Mann, Murray (American physicist) 3:313
Gemini (constellation) 1:32
Gemini spacecraft 1:244
space suits 1:272–73
Gemma (star) *see* Alphecca
Gemma cups 4:63
Gemmae 4:83
Gemmules 4:216
Gemsboks 5:129–30
Gemstones 2:136
illus. 2:137
Gene amplification 4:182
Gene flow 3:505
Gene mapping 3:404–5, 420
Genera (singular Genus) 3:395
General anesthesia 5:477–78
General Land Office 2:508
General Sherman tree (giant sequoia) 4:93
General theory of relativity 3:349–52
Generators, Electric 2:180, 310–16; 3:253–55
wind-driven turbines 2:387
illus. 3:251
Genes
aging, causes of 5:333–34
biology, history of 3:370, 372
body structure 5:161–62
cloning 5:318
discovery of 4:181
evolution 3:500
genetic diseases 5:418–20
genetics 3:402
heredity 3:407–10, 412; 5:310
Human Genome Project 5:321
human heredity 5:308, 315–20, 323, 325
human reproduction 5:293
McClintock, Barbara 3:412–13
naming of 3:401, 406
nucleotides 3:123
plant genetics 6:70
Genesis (video-game system) 6:299
Gene splicing
illus. 3:417

Gene therapy 5:309
AIDS vaccine research 5:446
Alzheimer's disease 5:334
genetic technology 3:421–22
muscular dystrophy 5:194
treatments and dangers 5:422
Genetically engineered foods 6:74–75
agronomy 4:173
drug delivery technology 5:474
ethical concerns 6:75
Genetically modified organisms *see* Transgenic organisms
Genetic code 3:419
Genetic counseling 3:403–4; 5:422
GENETIC DISEASES 5:418–22
genetic technology 3:418
human heredity 5:309, 319–20
Huntington's chorea 5:354
malocclusions of teeth 5:281
rheumatoid arthritis 5:428
transposable elements 3:413
Genetic drift 3:505
Genetic engineering *see* Genetic technology
Genetic markers 3:418, 423; 6:321
Genetic profiling *see* DNA fingerprinting
GENETICS 3:400–405 *see also* Heredity; Heredity, Human
agriculture 6:67–75
bacteria 4:32
biology, history of 3:370, 372
biorhythms 3:380
body weight 5:392
bone density 5:184
botany, history of 4:4
cancer 5:435
drug abuse 5:370
embryology 3:459
evolutionary biology 3:500–501, 503–5
genetic diseases 5:418–22
genetic technology 3:416–23
heredity 3:406–15
human knowledge 5:156
mathematics 1:337
Neurospora 4:42
viruses 3:389
zoology 4:181
GENETIC TECHNOLOGY 3:118, 372, 401, **416–23;** 6:22
agriculture 6:71–75
bacteria 4:6, 35
botany 4:7
drug delivery technology 5:474–75
food production 6:72, 74–75
genetics 3:402–3
microbiology 3:448, 451
organic chemistry 3:108
plant breeding 4:173
technology and society 6:14
veterinary science 4:468
viruses 3:389

GENETIC TECHNOLOGY (cont.)
  illus. **3:**417
    gene splicing **3:**417
Genets 5:100
Genome 3:405; **5:**309, 321, 418
  embryology **3:**459
  rice **6:**14
Genotypes 3:408; **5:**315, 420
  bacteria **4:**32
  evolutionary biology **3:**504, 506
Genus *see* Genera
Geochemistry 3:8
Geodes 2:137, 140
Geodesics 1:401–2; **3:**350–51;
    6:41
Geodesy 2:5; **3:**145
Geoelectricity 2:54
Geoffroy's cats 5:92
**Geographic information sys-
    tems (GIS) 2:**299
Geographic poles *see* Poles,
    Geographic
GEOGRAPHY 2:296–301
  careers **2:**300
  marine **2:**265–70
  paleogeography **1:**483
Geological Survey, U.S. 2:202
Geologic column *see* Stratigra-
    phy
Geologic time scale 1:485–87;
    2:18–21
GEOLOGY 1:5; **2:**2–8
  careers **2:**6
  caves **2:**125–31
  climates of the past **2:**215–20
  coasts **2:**288–95
  continental drift **2:**38–41
  deserts **2:**81–86
  Earth's age **2:**15–21
  Earth's crust **2:**30–37
  ecosystems **3:**487–88
  erosion **2:**120–24
  geography **2:**301
  groundwater **2:**112–19
  islands **2:**280–83
  lakes **2:**106–11
  mountains **2:**67–74
  oceanography **2:**222–23
  plains and plateaus **2:**75–80
  plate tectonics **2:**41–45
  reef research **2:**286
  rocks, minerals, and fossils
    2:132–40
  water erosion **2:**416–25
  wind erosion **2:**426–33
Geomagnetic storms 2:158
Geomagnetism (field of study)
    3:145 *see also* Earth; Mag-
    netic fields; Magnetism
Geometer moths 4:307
**Geometric progression
    1:**362–63
Geometric spiders *see* Orb
    weavers
Geometry 1:329–30, 332–33
  analytic geometry **1:**391–400
  chemistry, use in **1:**337

non-Euclidean geometry
    1:401–3
  plane geometry **1:**366–79
  solid geometry **1:**380–85
Geomorphology 2:4, 300
Geophysical exploration
  geothermal resources **2:**393–94
  natural gas **2:**338–39
  petroleum **2:**325–26
  plate tectonics **2:**45
Geophysics 2:5, 22–23; **3:**145
    see also Earthquakes
  plate tectonics **2:**39, 42–43
Georges Bank 2:265, 268
George Washington (nuclear
    submarine) **6:**121
Geostationary orbits 1:305
Geotail (spacecraft) **2:**158
GEOTHERMAL ENERGY 2:66,
    390–94
Geotropism 4:114
Gerbils 5:44
Gerenuks 5:131
Geriatrics 5:413
Germanium 3:29, 31, 37; **6:**250
German measles *see* Rubella
Germany
  forestry **4:**129
  high-speed trains **6:**131
  plateaus **2:**80
Germer, Lester H. (American
    physicist) **3:**331
    illus. **3:**323
Germination 3:463; **4:**104, 168
  flowering plants **4:**105–6
"Germ theory of disease" 3:447
Gernsback, Hugo (American
    writer, editor) **1:**501
Gesner, Abraham (Canadian sci-
    entist) **2:**323
Gestalt psychology 5:339
GEYSERS 2:63–66, 117
  on Triton **1:**155
    illus. **3:**8
Geysers, The (steam field, Cali-
    fornia) **2:**66, 391
    illus. **2:**392
Ghana 2:110
Gharials *see* Gavials
GHB *see* Gamma hydroxybutric
    acid
Ghost bats 5:32
Giacobini-Zinner, Comet 1:296
    illus. **1:**164
Giant burrowing frogs 4:345
Giant clams 4:238
Giant earthworms 4:242
Giant forest hogs 5:115
Giant Geyser (Yellowstone
    National Park) **2:**65
Giant horsetails 4:76
Giant hummingbirds 4:404
Giant muntjacs 5:119
Giant pandas 2:513; **5:**75
    illus. **2:**494; **5:**69
Giant salamanders 4:350
Giant sequoias 4:85, 93

Giant silk-spinning moths
    4:306–7
Giant skippers (butterflies) **4:**303
Giant squid 4:233
Giant squirrels 5:41
Giant stars 1:192
Giant tortoises
    illus. **3:**465; **4:**354
Gibbons 5:7, 143, 145, 147–48
Gibbs, Josiah Willard (American
    physicist) **3:**359
GIFT *see* Gamete intra-fallopian
    transfer
Gigabit Testbed Initiative 6:390
Gigantism 5:243
    illus. **5:**244
Gigantosaurus carolinii **1:**494
    illus. **1:**494
Gila monsters 4:360, 362; **5:**324
    illus. **4:**360
Gila National Forest 2:510
Gilbert (hurricane, 1988) **2:**199
Gilbert, Sir William (English phy-
    sician) **1:**104; **2:**29
  electricity **3:**250
  magnetism **3:**268
Gilbert Islands (Pacific Ocean)
    2:283
Gilbert's potoroos 5:19
Gill fungi 4:44
Gill nets 6:87
    illus. **6:**88
Gills 4:186
  amphibians **4:**342
  crustaceans **4:**254
  fish **4:**318–19, 329
  salamanders **4:**349–50
Gill slits 4:309
Gill spiracles 4:322
Gingivitis 5:280–81
GINKGOES 4:57, 73, **94–97**
  reproduction **3:**456
    illus. **1:**489; **4:**94–95
Giotto (space probe) **1:**161, 296
    illus. **1:**298
GIRAFFES 4:140; **5:**124–25
    illus. **3:**501; **4:**472
Girder bridges 6:49–50
Girders 6:34
Gir National Park (India) **5:**85
GIS *see* Geographic information
    systems
Giza, Great Pyramid of *see*
    Great Pyramid of Khufu
Gizzard 4:395
Glacial deposits 2:216
Glacial erratics 2:99
Glacial periods *see* Ice ages
Glacial striae 2:99, 123
Glacier National Park (Montana)
    2:108
Glacier plucking 2:97
GLACIERS 2:93–99
  climates of the past **1:**489;
    2:217–19
  coasts **2:**288–89
  continental shelves **2:**265

dust storms **2**:432
erosion **2**:123
icebergs **2**:260–61
island formation **2**:280–81
lake formation **2**:107–8
polar regions **2**:89, 91–92
waterfalls **2**:422–23
illus. **2**:218, 418
Glands 5:242–47
Glaser, Donald (American physicist) **1**:226; **6**:359
Glass
amorphous solid **3**:89
building construction **6**:41
expansion of solids **3**:222
heat conduction **3**:232–33
index of refraction **3**:285
Middle Ages **6**:7
Moon manufacture **1**:261
natural glass **2**:133–34
photonic crystals **6**:225
transmission of light **6**:223
illus.
blowing glass **3**:232
Glass (drug) *see* Methamphetamine
Glass fibers 1:275
Glass frogs
illus. **4**:343
Glass sponges 4:216
Glaucoma 5:273, 489
illus.
test **5**:270
Glaze *see* Freezing rain
Glen Canyon Dam (Arizona) **6**:56
Glenn, John H., Jr. (American astronaut) **1**:241
illus. **1**:239–40
Gliders 6:152–53
Gliding (by birds) **4**:393
Gliese 229B (brown dwarf) **1**:202
GlobalFlyer (airplane) **6**:164
Global Positioning System (GPS) 1:255, **2**:2–3; **6**:172
cellular communication **6**:243
geomagnetic storms **2**:158
illus. **2**:299
Global Protection Against Limited Strikes 1:263
Global Surveyor (spacecraft) *see* Mars Global Surveyor
Global Systems for Mobile (GSM) Communications *see* GSM
GLOBAL WARMING 1:109; **2**:477–81
Antarctic ice shelf melting **2**:91
Arctic, effect on **2**:88–89
climate changes **2**:219
climates of the world **2**:214
coral reef damage **2**:287
endangered species **2**:500
environmental pollution **2**:453
geological studies **2**:8
greenhouse effect **2**:154
methane **2**:146
savanna grasses **4**:143

Globes (maps) **2**:298
illus. **2**:296
Globigerina **4**:211
Globular clusters 1:187
Gloeocapsa **4**:33
Glomar Challenger (ship) **2**:276
illus. **2**:274
Glomerulonephritis 5:262
Glomerulus 5:259
GLORIA (sonar device) **2**:275
Glossary
cell structures **3**:430
Glossy ibises 4:446
Glow plugs 6:141
Glowworms 4:295
Glucagon 5:244–46
Glucagonoma 5:246
Glucose 3:119; **5**:380
cell dynamics **3**:434–35, 437
crystals **3**:90
diabetes **5**:244–45
photosynthesis **4**:24
illus.
blood-sugar levels **5**:380–81
intravenous infusion **3**:118
Gluons 3:21, 311, 316
illus. **3**:312
Gluttons (animals) *see* Wolverines
Glyceraldehyde phosphate 3:435
Glycerol (Glycerin) 3:121; **5**:382
Glycine 3:121–22
Glycogen 5:187–88, 381, 400–401
calorie storage **3**:121
cellular energy **3**:438
Glycolipids 5:474
Glycolysis 3:434–36, 438
Glyptodon **1**:499
Gnatcatchers
illus. **2**:499
Gnawing mammals *see* Rodents
Gneiss 2:37, 136
illus. **2**:136
Gnetophytes 4:15, 96
Gnetum **4**:96
Gnus *see* Wildebeests
Goats
animal behavior **4**:195
reproduction **5**:6
vegetation destroyed by **2**:497
illus. **5**:7, 10
Goatsuckers 4:402–3
Gobi Desert 2:83, 214; **4**:166
Gobies 4:320, 335
Goddard, Robert H. (American rocket pioneer) **1**:235, 239, 265
illus. **1**:235
Godwits 4:436
GOES (weather satellite) **1**:314
Goethe, Johann Wolfgang von (German writer and scientist)
illus. **4**:202
Goiters 5:247

Gold 3:38
amalgamation **6**:177
cyanide process **6**:177
ductility **3**:27
electroplating **3**:104
malleability **3**:27
metals **6**:174
minerals **2**:137
noble metals **3**:27, 30
specific gravity **2**:138
specific heat **3**:225
illus.
bullion **6**:177
hammering **3**:47
panning for **6**:176
Golden algae (Chrysophyta) 4:47, 50–52, 200
Golden bamboo lemurs 2:501
Golden cats 5:92
Golden eagles 4:417
Goldeneyes
illus. **4**:392
Golden Gate Bridge (San Francisco, California)
illus. **2**:162; **6**:49
Golden jackals 5:80
Golden mice 5:43
Golden moles 5:26
Golden plovers 4:437
Golden retrievers
illus. **5**:77
Goldfinches
illus. **4**:460
Goldfish 4:333
Gold salts 5:428
Golgi apparatus 3:429–30, 442; **4**:14
illus. **5**:162
Goliath beetles 4:297
illus. **4**:297
Gomphotherium **5**:103
Gonads 5:247, 293
Gonarezhou Park (Zimbabwe) **2**:513
Gondwanaland 2:72, 74
map(s) **2**:40–41
Gonorrhea 5:429, 472
Gonyaulax **4**:53
Goodall, Jane (British ethnologist) **5**:144
illus. **5**:149
Goode, George Brown (American ichthyologist) **4**:313
Google (computer search engine) **6**:308
Googol 1:359
Googolplex 1:359
Goose *see* Geese
Gophers (animals) **5**:42
Gophers (computer programs) **6**:305
Gopher snakes 4:371
Gorges 2:102
Gorgosaurus **1**:494
Gorillas 5:144, 148
mountain gorilla **2**:502
illus. **2**:499; **5**:13, 143
Gorizont (artificial satellite) **1**:309

Goshawks **4:**415, 417, 419
Gossamer Albatross (human-powered aircraft) **6:**95, 157
Gossamer Condor (human-powered aircraft) **6:**94–95
illus. **6:**91
Gothic arches **6:**33
illus. **6:**36
Gotthard railway tunnel (Switzerland) **6:**48
Gould, Stephen Jay (American biologist) **3:**501; **6:**321
Gourds **4:**115
Gout **5:**429
Governors (automatic speed controls) **2:**313–14; **6:**195–96
Gowen cypresses **4:**85
GPALS *see* Global Protection Against Limited Strikes
GPS *see* Global Positioning System
Graafian follicles **5:**294
Gracilis
illus. **5:**166
Grackles **4:**460
Graded coal **2:**356
Graduated cylinders
illus. **3:**135
Grafting (plant propagation) **4:**172
Graf Zeppelin (airship) **6:**150
Grain dust combustion **3:**62
Grain mills **6:**186
Grains **6:**69–70
Grain weevils **4:**299
Gram (unit of measurement) **3:**135
Gram-negative bacteria **4:**29
Gram-positive bacteria **4:**29
Grana **4:**22–24
Grand Banks (Newfoundland, Canada) **2:**265, 269
Grand Canyon (Arizona) **2:**18–19, 79–80, 85, 120, 418–19
illus. **2:**15, 135, 416
Grand Coulee Dam (Washington) **6:**53, 56
illus. **6:**55
Grand Unification Theory *see* Unified force theory
Grand Viaduc du Millau (bridge, France) **6:**50
Granisetron (Kytril) **5:**467
Granite **2:**34, 134, 172–73
illus. **2:**134
Granite mosses **4:**163
Grapes **4:**172
Graphene **6:**341
Graphics, Computer *see* Computer graphics
Graphite **1:**337; **2:**136; **3:**28, 105
diamonds **3:**241
nuclear reactors **2:**366–68
illus.
micrograph **6:**337

Graphs
algebra **1:**354–56
analytic geometry **1:**394, 396–97
statistics **1:**406–8
illus. **1:**407, 409, 412–13
Graptolites **1:**488
Grasses **4:**123–24, 138–43
Grasshopper mice **5:**43
Grasshoppers **4:**279
diagram(s) **4:**273–74
illus. **1:**484; **3:**487; **4:**247, 275
GRASSLANDS **3:**494–95; **4:**135, 138–43
songbird populations **4:**451
Graupel **2:**169
Gravel **2:**35, 113
Gravel-packed wells **2:**440
Graves' disease **5:**247
Gravitational collapse **1:**204–6
Gravitons **3:**21, 311
GRAVITY **3:**176–82 *see also* Weightlessness
black hole **1:**204–6
bosons **3:**21
comets, orbits of **1:**162
Earth **1:**104
elementary particles **3:**311
falling objects **3:**154
geotropism **4:**114
human-powered transportation **6:**91
low-gravity science **1:**253, 268
Moon **1:**125
mountain building **2:**69–70
muscles **5:**190
Newton's law **1:**473; **3:**141, 147
relativity theory **3:**350
roller-coaster rides **3:**159
satellites of planets **1:**144
solar system **1:**78–79
Sun **1:**81
tides **2:**243–44
weight **3:**11
Gravity concentration (in mineral separation) **6:**176
illus. **6:**178
Gravity maps (of ocean floor) **2:**265
Gravity meters **2:**325–26
Gravity Probe B *see* Relativity Mission
Gray, Stephen (English scientist) **3:**250
Gray foxes **5:**83
Gray grampuses *see* Risso's dolphins
Gray kangaroos **5:**18
Graylags *see* Greylags
Gray matter **5:**224, 228–30
Gray seals **5:**64
Gray squirrels **5:**40, 324
Graywater (wastewater) **2:**486–87
Gray whales **5:**52
Gray wolves **5:**10, 78–79
illus. **2:**505
Grazing animals **4:**140

Greases **2:**333
Great Backyard Bird Count **4:**389
Great Barrier Reef (Australia) **2:**286
Great Basin (Australia) **2:**108
Great Basin (United States) **2:**83; **4:**166
Great Britain (island) **2:**281
ice ages **2:**218
wilderness areas **2:**514
Great circles **1:**383, 385
non-Euclidean geometry **1:**402
illus. **1:**384
Great Dark Spot (feature of Neptune) **1:**151, 154
Great Divide *see* Continental Divide
Great Eastern (ship)
illus. **6:**112
Greater Bear (constellation) *see* Ursa Major
Greater bulldog bats **5:**32
Greater Dog (constellation) *see* Canis Major
Greater flamingos **4:**445
Greater Indian rhinoceroses **5:**112–13
Greater rheas **4:**412
Great Falls (Yellowstone River) **2:**422
Great Geysir (geyser, Iceland) **2:**65
Great gray owls **4:**421
Greathead shields **6:**48
Great horned owls **4:**420–21
Great Karroo (plateau, South Africa) **2:**162
Great Lakes **2:**99, 106, 108, 111
glacial erosion **2:**123
lampreys **4:**322
water pollution **2:**462
zebra mussels **4:**237
Great Nebula in Andromeda **1:**30, 221
illus. **1:**53
Great Nebula in Orion (M42) **1:**32, 218–20
illus. **1:**221; **2:**12
Great northern divers *see* Common loons
Great Observatories Program **1:**47, 59, 62
Great Plains (U.S.)
dust storms **2:**75, 430–32; **4:**143
sand dunes **2:**429
illus. **4:**142
Great Plains toads **4:**348
Great Pyramid of Khufu (Giza, Egypt) **6:**18, 25
Great Red Spot (feature of Jupiter) **1:**137
illus. **1:**133, 136
Great Salt Lake (Utah) **2:**86, 107
Great Smoky Mountains **2:**72
variety of trees **3:**496
Great Victoria Desert **2:**83

Great white herons 4:444
Great white sharks 4:327
 illus. 4:323
Great White Spot (feature of Saturn) 1:140
 illus. 1:141
Grebes 4:433–34
Greece 2:52
Greece, Ancient
 accounting 1:455
 aeolipile 6:96
 agriculture 4:171
 algebra 1:353
 archaeology 1:463
 astronomy, history of 1:11–12
 atmospheric science 2:142
 atomic theory 3:304
 biology 3:367
 botany 4:3
 building techniques 6:33
 coal, use of 2:348
 construction materials 6:26
 geography 2:297–98
 "Ladder of Nature" 3:501
 mathematics, history of 1:329–30
 matter, theories of 3:16
 medicine 5:412
 numerals 1:342
 plane geometry 1:366–68, 371, 377
 planetariums 1:66
 psychology 5:335–36
 submarines and submersibles 6:117–18
 technology and society 6:7
 trigonometry 1:386
 universe, theories of 1:77, 472–73
 warships and galleys 6:107–8
 zoology 4:179
Green algae 4:12, 48–49, 53, 60
Green bacteria 4:31
Green Belt Movement (Africa) 4:126
Greenhouse effect 2:154, 477–79 see also Global warming
 carbon cycle 4:21
 climates of the world 2:214
 heat transfer 3:238–39
 hydropower reservoirs 2:380
 solar power 2:382
 Venus 1:101, 299
 illus. 3:239
Greenhouse frogs 4:346–47
Green jays 4:463
Greenland
 climates of the past 2:217, 219
 coastal erosion 2:292
 continental drift 2:38–39
 fireball impact (1997) 1:169
 glaciers 2:89, 260–61
 ice sheet 2:94, 97, 218
Greenland right whales see Bowhead whales
Green Mountains 2:72–73

Greenpeace (environmental group)
 illus. 5:51
Green Revolution 4:170, 172; 6:71
Green snakes 4:371
Greenstick fractures 5:182
Green turtles 4:377
Greenwich Observatory (England)
 illus. 6:170
Green wood 6:29
Gregorian calendar 1:476–78
Gregory XIII (pope) 1:476–77
Grévy's zebras 5:109
Greylags 4:441
Grey plovers 4:437
Gribbles 4:251, 255
Griffith, A. A. (British scientist) 6:106
Grippe see Influenza
Grisons 5:96
Grissom, Virgil I. (American astronaut) 1:241, 274
 illus. 1:240
Grist mills see Grain mills
Grizzly bears 5:73
 illus. 5:72
Groin vaults
 illus. 6:35
Grokster 6:310
Grooming (animal behavior) 5:147
 illus. 5:146
Grosbeaks 4:458
 illus. 4:457
Ground beetles 4:269, 293
Ground cedar 4:77
Ground-control approach (GCA) radar system 6:259
Ground-controlled interception (GCI) radar 6:258
Groundhogs see Woodchucks
Ground lines 2:318
Ground sloths 1:489
Ground squirrels 5:41–42
Ground tissue 4:65–66
GROUNDWATER 2:112–19
 cave formation 2:126
 coal mines 2:354–55
 dissolved minerals 3:84
 earthquakes 2:54
 environmental pollution 2:456
 hot springs and geysers 2:63–66
 purification 2:446–48; 3:87
 waste contamination 2:483, 491
 wells 2:439–41
 wetlands 4:150–51
Ground Wave Radar 2:263
Group therapy
 illus. 5:347
Groupthink 5:340
Grouse 4:395, 422–23, 425–26
Growlers (small icebergs) 2:260
Growth
 animals 4:187

conifers 4:88–89
 fungi 4:37
 hair 5:266
 humans 5:323–34
 insects 4:275–76
 plants 4:15, 69–70, 113–15
 plants 3:463
 populations 3:478–79
 snakes 4:368
GROWTH, Human 5:323–34
 pituitary gland 5:243
Growth hormones 5:243
 bacteria, uses of 4:35
 plants 4:114–15
Grubs 4:292
Gruiformes 4:399, 433, 438–40
Grunions 4:334
Grysbok 5:131
GSM (cellular standard) 6:245
Guacharos see Oilbirds
Guanacos 5:117
Guanine 3:123, 411; 5:309–10
 illus. 3:409
Guans 4:423
Guard cells 4:13, 67–68, 70
Guemals 5:122
Guenons 5:143
Guerezas 5:8, 141
Guericke, Otto von (German physicist) 3:250
Guerin, Pierre (French astronomer) 1:143
Guidance in space 1:305; 6:258
 Hubble Space Telescope 1:49
Guided missiles see Missiles
Guinea fowl 4:423, 427
Guinea pigs 5:45, 324
 illus. 4:179
Guinea worms 4:230
Guitarfish 4:328
 illus. 4:327
Gulf Stream 2:210, 229, 232, 239–42
Gulf War (1991) see Persian Gulf War
Gullies 2:417
Gulls 4:189, 434–35
 illus.
  caught in six-pack ring 4:434
Gum, Nicotine 5:376
Gums (of the mouth) 5:280–82
Gunpowder 3:96; 6:8
Guns see Firearms
Guppies 5:324
Gutenberg, Beno (German-American geophysicist) 2:25
Gutenberg line 2:25
Guyots 2:270
Gymnomycota 4:200
Gymnophiona see Caecilians
Gymnosperms (Cone-bearing plants) 4:84–85, 88
 gingko and cycads 4:94–97
Gynecology 5:415

Gypsum (Calcium sulfate) 2:36, 136, 138, 446–47; **3:**87
  caves **2:**128
  desert **2:**216
  hydration of anhydrite **2:**173
  lakes **2:**111
  wallboard **6:**37
Gypsy moths 4:117–18, 147–48, 269, 305
Gyres 2:239, 241; **3:**493
Gyri (singular **Gyrus**) **5:**228–29
Gyroscopes 6:173

H

Haber process 6:205
Habitats
  area needs of species **3:**486
  destruction of **2:**456
  fish **6:**89
  mammals **5:**7–8
  zoo exhibits **4:**474, 476–77
  graph(s)
    carrying capacity **3:**480
Habituation (to drugs) **5:**461
Hackers 6:393
Hadrons 3:307, 311, 313
Hadrosaurus **1:**495
Haeckel, Ernst (German biologist) **3:**399, 473; **4:**25–26
Hafnium 3:38
Hagenbeck, Carl (German animal dealer) **4:**471
Hagfish 4:315–17, 321–22
  illus. **4:**322
Hahnemann, Samuel (German physician) **5:**513
Hail 2:145, 170–71, 175–76
Hair, Animal *see* Fur; Wool
Hair, Human 5:265–66, 333
  illus. **3:**467
Hair cells 5:275–76
Hair follicles 5:265–66
  illus. **5:**264
Hairy-eared dwarf lemurs 5:137
Hairy-nosed wombats 5:20
Hairy rhinoceroses *see* Sumatran rhinoceroses
Hairy-tailed moles 5:24
  illus. **5:**25
Haldane, John Scott (English physiologist) **1:**271
Hale, Alan (American amateur astronomer) **1:**15
Hale, Edward Everett (American writer) **1:**264
Hale, George Ellery (American astronomer) **1:**40–41
Hale-Bopp, Comet 1:166
Hales, Stephen (English physiologist) **3:**369; **4:**3
Hale Telescope 1:41
  illus. **1:**40
Half-life 2:363–64, 372; **3:**128, 318
  radioactive dating **2:**16–17
  graph(s) **3:**321

Halides 2:138; **3:**33
Hall, Asaph (American astronomer) **1:**132, 140
Halley, Edmund (English astronomer) **1:**162; **3:**148
Halley's comet 1:160–64
  apparent brightness **1:**165
  Chinese astronomy **1:**472
  life, origin of **3:**382
  space probes **1:**296
  illus. **1:**158, 165, 298
Hall-Héroult process 6:183
Hallucinations 5:349, 409
Hallucinogens 5:371–72
Halocarbons 2:479, 482; **3:**111, 115
Halogenation 3:111
Halogen headlights 6:141
Halogens 3:32–33
Halons 2:482
Ham (chimpanzee sent into space) **1:**247
  illus. **1:**246
Hamadryas baboons 5:142
  illus. **4:**196; **5:**141
Hammer (in the ear) **5:**275, 509
  illus. **3:**205; **5:**276
Hammerheads (insect larvae) **4:**295
Hammerhead sharks 4:317, 327
  illus. **4:**326
Hamsters 5:44
  illus. **4:**484
Hamstring muscles 5:194
Handheld video games 6:299
Hands 5:153–54 *see also* Fingers
  artificial *see* Artificial hands
  bone formation **5:**327
  bones, names of **5:**179–80
  carpal tunnel syndrome **5:**182–83
  human evolution **5:**160
  muscles of the body **5:**192
  skin **5:**264
  tendons **5:**193
  transplants **5:**499
  illus.
    arthritis **5:**288
    bones **5:**179
    X-ray image **5:**427, 451
Handwriting 1:515
Hanging valleys 2:98, 422–23
Hanuman langurs 5:141
Haploid cells 3:410, 443, 445
Harbor porpoises *see* Common porpoises
Hard disk drives 3:265; **6:**372, 388
Hardness (of minerals) **2:**137
Hardness, Scale of *see* Mohs' hardness scale
Hard palate 5:177
Hard-shell clams 4:238
Hardware (computer) **6:**365–72
Hard water 2:446–48; **3:**30
Hardwoods 6:28
  plant succession **4:**123, 125
  temperate forests **4:**144

Hardy, James D. (American surgeon) **5:**498
Hares 5:6, 37–38
Hare wallabies 5:18
Hargreaves, James (English inventor) **6:**189
Harmattan 2:186
Harmony (in music) **3:**212–13
Harpoon guns 5:54
Harrier military jet 6:161
Harris, Thaddeus (American physician) **4:**268
Harrison, John (English inventor) **6:**170
Harrison, Ross (American zoologist) **4:**182
Hartebeests 5:130
Harvard Observatory (Massachusetts) **1:**163
Harvard pyramid (food guide) **5:**389
Harvestmen *see* Daddy longlegs
Harvey, William (English physician) **5:**412
Hashish 5:371
Hassium 3:38
Hatcheries, Fish 6:89
Hatchet fish 4:333
Haustoria 4:37, 112
Haversian canals 5:174
Haversian systems 5:173–74
Hawaiian honeycreepers
  illus. **4:**456
Hawaiian Islands 2:44, 69, 282
  botany **4:**2
  endangered species **2:**497–98
  eucalyptus plantation **2:**398
  lava caves **2:**129
  precipitation **2:**171, 416
  tsunamis **2:**258
  underwater volcano **2:**279
  volcanoes **2:**55, 57–59
  illus.
    plate tectonics **2:**44
Hawking, Stephen W. (English physicist) **1:**212–13, 506
  science education **6:**320
  illus. **3:**141
Hawkmoths 4:276, 306
Hawks 4:415–18
Hayden Planetarium (New York)
  illus. **1:**68
Hay fever 5:241, 448
Hazardous wastes 2:484, 488–92 *see also* Radioactive wastes
  bacteria used to clean up **4:**6
  water pollution **3:**85
  well contamination **2:**119
  illus.
    disposal **2:**454
Haze 2:160
HCG *see* Human chorionic gonadotropin
HD DVD (DVD format) **6:**287
HDTV *see* High definition television

Head (in anatomy)
  injuries 5:234
  insect 4:274
  muscles of the body 5:192
Headaches 5:290
Head fish see Ocean sunfish
Healing see Injuries
Health see also Diseases; Indus-
    trial health; Medicine
  antibiotic resistance 3:506
  climates of the world 2:209
  electromagnetic radiation 3:277
  exercise and fitness 5:395–404
  fish 4:320
  insects 4:268–69
  medical ecologists 3:475
  mental health 5:348–57
  nuclear energy 2:372
  nutrition 5:378–90
  ozone layer depletion 2:482
  pets 4:482, 487, 490
  substance abuse 5:369–77
Health and Human Services,
    U.S. Department of 5:389,
    499
Healthy Forest Initiative 4:149
Healthy Forests Restoration Act
    (U.S., 2003) 4:149
Heard sound 3:199
Hearing
  birds 4:395
  brain 5:229
  cats 5:85
  crustaceans 4:253
  ears 5:274–77
  fish 4:333
  humans 3:199, 205
  learning disabilities 5:365
  whales 5:47
  table(s).
    harmful sound levels 3:201
Hearing aids 5:277, 508
HEART 4:186; 5:164, 172, 195–
    204
  artificial see Artificial hearts
  babies 5:326–27
  birds 4:394
  cardiac muscle 5:187
  disease see Heart disease
  exercise benefits 5:401
  fish 4:319–20
  mammals 5:4
  medications 5:467
  reptiles 4:354
  snakes 4:364
  surgery 5:479
  target heart rate 5:402
  transplants 5:496, 498
  diagram(s) 5:197
  illus. 3:439; 5:169
    cardiac muscle 5:186, 189
    heartworms in dog 4:229
    larger-than-life model 1:7
Heart attacks 5:290, 439
  cocaine 5:375
  diagnosis of risk 5:472
Heartburn 5:255

HEART DISEASE 5:438–40
  air pollution 2:468
  diagnostic imaging 5:454, 459
  fat in diet 5:382–83
  smoking and health 5:374
Heart-lung machines 5:504
Heart murmurs 5:440
Heart urchins 4:224
Heartworms 4:230
  illus. 4:229
Heat capacity 3:326–27
Heat conduction see Conduction
    of heat
HEAT ENERGY 3:219–25
  cancer treatment 5:437
  changes of state 3:226–27
  chemical industries 6:206
  chemical reactions 3:58–60, 62
  clouds conserve heat 2:162
  energy 3:141
  friction 3:166
  gaseous state 3:68–69, 72
  geothermal energy 2:390–94
  heat transfer 3:232–39
  lizards need for 4:360–61
  outflow from Earth 2:28
  radioisotopes 3:318, 321
  solids, effect on 3:89, 91–92
  thermal pollution 2:464
  thermodynamics 3:144
Heat engines 6:96
  illus. 2:382
Heat exchangers (of nuclear
    reactors) 2:367
Heath hens 4:426
Heating systems
  electric heating 2:320
  geothermal hot-water heat
    2:66, 392–93
  heat transfer 3:236–37, 239
  incineration by-product 2:484
  radioisotope decay 3:321
  solar power 2:382–83
Heat lightning 2:178
Heat of fusion 3:228
Heat of reaction 3:59–60
Heat of vaporization 3:231
Heat pumps 2:320
Heat shields (on spacecraft)
    1:240, 249
Heat therapy 2:321
HEAT TRANSFER 3:232–39
  cooling effect of evaporation
    3:229
  infrared radiation 3:281
Heavy lasers 6:346
Heavy metals see Metal poison-
    ing
Heavy water 2:366–67
Hebrew numerals
  illus. 1:342
Hedgehogs 5:26–27
  fossil 5:23
Heels (of the feet) 5:182
Hefner, Lake (Oklahoma) 2:439
Heisenberg, Werner (German
    physicist) 3:332
  illus. 3:323

Heisenberg uncertainty prin-
    ciple see Uncertainty prin-
    ciple
Helical scan 6:281
Helicobacter pylori 5:256
Helicopters 6:160–61
Helictites 2:128
Heliocentric system see Coper-
    nican system
Heliopause 1:293
Helios (solar-powered aircraft)
    6:157
Helios (space probe) 1:301
Helioseismology 1:190
Heliosphere 1:234
Heliozoans 4:211
Helium 3:33, 38
  airships 6:151
  atomic structure 3:48, 63
  balloons 3:188
  discovery of 3:5
  Jupiter 1:136
  Mercury (planet) 1:98
  Moon 1:260
  stars 1:192–93, 195, 197
  Sun 1:86, 88–89, 191
  weight of 3:184
Hell Gate (New York City)
  tidal current 2:248
Helmet quails see California
    quails
Helmets
  illus. 2:355
Helminths 5:428
Helmont, Jan Baptista van
    (Flemish biochemist) 3:369
Helper T cells see CD-4 cells
Hematocrit reading 5:213
Hematologic system 5:196
Hematomas 5:234
Hemichordates 4:204, 308–9,
    311
Hemipseudospheres 1:401–2
Hemiptera see Bugs, True
Hemispheres (in geometry)
    1:401–2
Hemlocks 4:87, 93
Hemoglobin 5:203, 206, 211,
    213
  adaptation to high altitude 5:7
  anemia 5:210
  genetics 3:402
  genetic technology 5:475
Hemolymph 4:274
Hemolytic anemia 5:211
Hemophilia 5:212, 319, 421
  AIDS acquired through transfu-
    sions 5:443
  illus.
    Queen Victoria's descendants
      5:317
Hen harriers see Marsh hawks
Henry III (English king) 4:470
Henry of Portugal (Portuguese
    prince) 6:167–68
Heparin 5:207–8, 467
Hepatitis 3:393; 5:375

Hepatitis B (Serum hepatitis) **5:**210, 475

Heptane 3:75, 111

Herald of Free Enterprise (ferry-boat) **6:**112

Herbals (books) **4:**3

Herbicides 2:462, 502

Herbivores 3:485; **5:**8
  bison, buffalo, and oxen **5:**132–35
  camels and llamas **5:**116–17
  deer family **5:**118–23
  giraffes and okapis **5:**124–25
  marsupials **5:**17–20

Hercules (constellation) **1:**30

Hercules beetles 4:297

Hereditary diseases *see* Genetic diseases

HEREDITY 3:395, **406–15** *see also* Evolution; Genes; Genetic technology; Heredity, Human
  genetics **3:**400–405

HEREDITY, Human 5:308–22, 323, 325
  allergies **5:**447
  body weight **5:**392
  cancer **5:**435
  genetic diseases **5:**418–22

Hermaphrodites 3:457; **4:**187, 244, 320

Hermes (asteroid) **1:**169

Hermetic systems 6:360

Hermit crabs 4:216

Hermit thrushes 4:455
  illus. **4:**453

HERO-2 *see* Einstein X-Ray Observatory

Herodotus (Greek historian) **2:**322

Heroin 5:373–74, 376

Herons 4:444
  illus.
  beak **4:**393

Hero of Alexandria (Greek mathematician and physicist) **6:**96

Herpes viruses 3:388, 392–93
  illus. **3:**385, 451

HERPETOLOGY 4:336–39 *see also* Amphibians; Reptiles

Herrick, Richard (American kidney transplant recipient) **5:**496

Herring 4:332

Herschel, Sir William (German-English astronomer)
  infrared radiation **1:**60; **3:**274
  Saturn **1:**140
  star survey **1:**184
  Uranus **1:**147

Hertz (unit of measurement) **6:**288

Hertz, Heinrich R. (German scientist) **3:**276; **6:**255

Herzsprung-Russell diagram
  illus. **1:**193

Hesperornis regalis **1:**497

Hess, Harry (American geologist) **2:**41

Hess, Victor F. (Austrian physicist) **1:**225

HETE-2 *see* High Energy Transient Explorer

Heterocysts 4:35
  illus. **3:**448

Heterodyning 3:218

Heterografts 5:496

Heterotrophs 4:11, 30

Hewish, Antony (British astronomer) **1:**209

Hexactinellida 4:200, 216

Hexadecanol 2:439

Hexadecimal numeral system 6:364–65

Hexagonal crystals 3:90

Hexane 3:75

Heyerdahl, Thor (Norwegian explorer) **2:**235, 464

Hibernacula 4:111–12

Hibernation 5:5
  bats **5:**30–31
  bears **5:**71, 74
  dormice **5:**44
  frogs **4:**344
  poorwills **4:**403
  snakes **4:**365–66

Hibiscus 4:158

Hidalgo (asteroid) **1:**168

Hieroglyphic system 1:339
  illus. **1:**340

High blood pressure *see* Hypertension

High-definition television (HDTV) 6:293, 297

High Energy Astrophysical Observatory-2 *see* Einstein X-Ray Observatory

High Energy Transient Explorer (HETE-2) 1:59

Highland climates 2:214

High-latitude biomes 3:496–98

High-level wastes 2:370

Highly active antiretroviral therapy (HAART) 5:239, 445

High-quality proteins *see* Complete proteins

High species richness and diversity 4:132

High-speed trains 6:130–32
  illus. **6:**129

High-sulfur fuel oil 2:473

High tides *see* Flood tides

High-voltage lines *see* Transmission lines, Electric

High-water interval (of tides) **2:**246

Highways *see* Roads and highways

Highwheelers 6:92, 94

Hijacked computers *see* Zombie computers

Hilus (of kidney) **5:**259

Himalayan bears
  illus. **5:**72

Himalayan cats
  illus. **5:**90

Himalayan deodars 4:92

Himalayas 2:72, 80, 173
  illus. **2:**73; **4:**135

Hindenburg (airship) **3:**188; **6:**150
  illus. **6:**151

Hindu-Arabic numeral system 1:344–45, 446

Hinnies 5:110

Hip *see* Hips

Hipparchus (Greek astronomer) **1:**330, 386

Hippocampus 5:361–62

Hippocrates (Greek physician) **2:**463; **3:**367; **5:**412, 432
  illus. **5:**411

Hippopotamuses 5:115
  illus. **5:**9, 114

Hips 5:180–81 *see also* Artificial hips

Hirohito (Japanese emperor)
  illus. **4:**204

Hirudinea 4:202

His-Purkinje system 5:201

Histamines 5:241, 448

Histology 3:366

Histoplasmosis 5:428

Historical geography 2:301

Historic archaeology 1:465

Historic geology 2:4

Histrionic personality 5:352

Hittites 6:175

HIV *see* Human immunodeficiency virus

Hives 5:447

HLA genes *see* Human lymphocyte antigen genes

Hoary marmots 5:42

Hoatzins 4:423, 427
  illus. **4:**427

Hoba meteorite 1:171

Hog deer 5:120

Hog-nosed skunks 5:97

Hog-nosed snakes 4:371
  illus. **4:**370

Hogs *see* Pigs

Hohokam Indians 1:471

Holland, John P. (Irish-American submarine designer) **6:**119

Holland VI (submarine) **6:**119–20

Holly ferns 4:81, 83

Holmium 3:38

Holocene maximum *see* Postglacial optimum

Holocephali *see* Chimaeras

HOLOGRAPHY 6:275–77

Holosteans 4:331

Holothuroidea 4:204, 224

Home-care programs, Medical 5:481

Home-health aides 5:484, 486

Home Insurance Building (Chicago, Illinois) **6:**30, 39

Homeopathy 5:512–13

Homeostasis 3:378**

Homeotherms (Warm-blooded animals) 5:47
dinosaurs 1:493
fish such as tuna 4:320
pterosaurs 1:496
Homestead Act (U.S., 1862) 2:509
Homing pigeons 4:428–30
Hominids 5:156, 159–60
Homo erectus 5:160
Homo floresiensis 5:156
Homografts 5:496
Homo habilis 5:160
Homologous pairs (chromosomes) 3:444–45
Homologous structures (in anatomy) 3:502
Homo sapiens see Human species
Homosexuality 5:441, 444
Homozygosity 3:504–5
Honda Civic
illus. 6:137
Honda Insight 6:148
Honey 4:286–88
Honey badgers see Ratels
Honeybees 4:285–88
illus. 3:452; 4:285–86
Honeycreepers
illus. 4:456
Honeydew (aphid secretion) 4:284
Hong Kong Island
illus. 2:281
Hood, Mount (Oregon) 2:60
Hooded pitohuis
illus. 4:448
Hooke, Robert (English scientist) 3:148, 369, 424, 446; 4:3
Hook-nosed snakes 4:371
Hookworms 4:229–30
illus. 4:225
Hoover Dam (Arizona–Nevada) 2:48; 6:52–53
illus. 2:312; 6:55
Hormones
aging 3:468
animal behavior 4:190–91
biochemistry 3:117–18, 121
cell dynamics 3:439
embryology 3:462
endocrine system 5:242–47
infertility treatments 5:306–7
Hornbills 4:407
Hornblende 2:33–34
Horned larks 4:449–50
Horned liverworts see Hornworts
Horner, Jack (American paleontologist) 2:132
Hornets 4:289
illus. 4:288
Horns (in geology) 2:98
Horns (of animals)
antelopes 5:126
rhinoceroses 5:111–13
Hornworts 4:56, 58, 63
Horse cars see Trolleys

HORSE FAMILY 5:107–10
prehistoric animals 1:498
Horse latitudes 2:184
Horsepower (unit of measurement) 3:167
Horses, Domestic 5:107–9
antivenin production 4:367
classification 3:396
evolution 1:489
life span 5:324
pets 4:487
veterinary medicine 4:467
illus.
dressage competition 5:109
pets 4:484
Horseshoe bats 5:324
Horseshoe crabs 4:203, 248, 257
illus. 4:249
Horseshoe magnets 3:262
illus. 3:261
field lines 3:263
HORSETAILS 4:13, 56, 74, 75–76
Horseweed 4:124–25
HORTICULTURE 4:170–75
photoperiodism 4:116
Hospitals 5:480–81
Hot-air balloons 3:188; 6:149–50
Hot spots (in geology) 2:44–45, 59
HOT SPRINGS 2:63–66, 117 see also Hydrothermal vents
lake beds 2:109
life in 3:376
ocean floor 2:45, 222, 224, 272, 278
volcano warnings 2:60
illus. 2:64, 66, 80; 3:8
Hot Springs National Park (Arkansas) 2:64
Hot-water heaters 3:235, 239
House finches
illus. 4:460
Houseflies 4:273
Household appliances 2:308–9, 320, 344
House mice 5:43
Houseplants 4:78, 158
Houses
construction 6:23–31, 34, 36–37
House sparrows 4:461–62
illus. 4:461
House spiders 4:260
House wrens 4:452
Hovercraft see Air-cushioned vehicles
Howard, Luke (English chemist) 2:163
Howler monkeys 5:8, 10, 139–40, 146–48
Hoyle, Fred (British astronomer) 1:21
HTML (Hypertext markup language) 6:307, 378

Hubble, Edwin (American astronomer) 1:19; 3:144
illus. 1:12
Hubble's law 1:20
Hubble Space Telescope 1:16, 47, 49–50, 237, 303
apogee and perigee 1:304
auroras 2:157
black holes 1:212
Charon 1:157
electromagnetic spectrum 3:280
interstellar space 1:223
Jupiter's collision with comet 1:138
Kuiper Belt 1:159
Pluto 1:157
repair 1:252
star and planet formation 1:318
supernovas 1:201
ultraviolet astronomy 1:64
illus. 1:12, 47
Hudson Bay (Canada) 2:218
Hudson River
Palisades 2:33
illus. 2:413
Hue (of color) 3:300
Huemuls see Guemals
Hugo (hurricane, 1989) 2:199
Hugo Award 1:501
Hülsmeyer, Christian (German physicist) 6:255
Human chorionic gonadotropin (HCG) 5:299
Human Genome Project 3:405, 420; 5:156, 321
illus. 5:313
Human geography 2:301
Human granulocytic ehrlichiosis (HGE) 4:259
Human immunodeficiency virus (HIV) 5:239, 430, 441–46
blood diseases 5:212
blood tests 5:213
blood transfusions 5:210, 477
cancer 5:436
drug treatment 5:465
viruses 3:387–88, 393
illus. 3:364, 392; 5:240
Humanistic psychology 5:344
Human lymphocyte antigen genes 5:428
HUMAN-POWERED TRANSPORTATION 6:91–95
aircraft 6:157
early underwater craft 6:118
HUMAN REPRODUCTION AND BIRTH 3:461; 5:293–307
illus.
embryo development 3:461
life cycle 3:457
Humans and the environment 3:372
carbon cycle 4:21
desertification 2:84
deserts 4:168–69
ecology 3:471–75
grasslands 4:142–43

Humans and the environment (cont.)
  pollution **2:**454
  population growth **3:**482
  rain forests **4:**159–61
  temperate forests **4:**146–48
  wetlands **4:**155
Human sciences 1:7
HUMAN SPECIES 5:152–56 *see also* Anatomy, Human; Body, Human; Heredity, Human; Psychology
  cloning **3:**423; **6:**14
  environment, effects on *see* Humans and the environment
  evolution **5:**157–60
  extinction of other species caused by **2:**495, 497, 500–502
  fossils **1:**479, 489
  genetic technology **3:**423
  Human Genome Project **3:**405, 420
  human sciences **1:**7
  life span **5:**324
  paleoanthropology **1:**481
  population growth **3:**482
  science fiction **1:**505
Humboldt, Alexander von (German geographer and naturalist) **2:**299; **3:**473
Humboldt Current *see* Peru Current
Humerus 5:179
  illus. **5:**165, 174–75, 178
  fracture **5:**182
Humidity
  groundwater level **2:**113
  mammals' requirements **5:**6
  wetlands' effect on **4:**155
Hummingbird moths 4:306
Hummingbirds 4:158, 395–96, 404; **5:**197
  illus. **4:**397, 404
Humoral response 5:237
Humpback whales 5:50–51
Hunger 5:255, 392, 394
Hunley, H.L. (Confederate submarine) **6:**119
Hunting *see also* Whaling
  endangered species **2:**500–501, 504
  falconry **4:**419
  sealing **5:**68
Huntington's disease 5:320, 354, 418–20
HURRICANES AND TYPHOONS 2:195–200
  Atlantic Ocean **2:**232
  cloud seeding **2:**145
  Pacific Ocean **2:**230
  radar tracking **2:**204; **6:**260–61
  weather forecasting **2:**206
  illus.
    satellite picture **1:**315
Hurricane surges 2:200

Hutton, James (Scottish geologist) **2:**7–8
Huxley, Aldous (English writer) **1:**502
Huygens (space probe lander) **1:**145, 295
Huygens, Christiaan (Dutch physicist) **1:**142; **3:**273, 329
Hyades (star cluster) **1:**32, 186
Hyakutake, Comet 1:166
Hyatt, John Wesley (American inventor) **6:**214
Hybrid cars 6:102, 148
Hybridomas 5:471–72
  illus. **5:**473
Hybrids 5:315–16, 318, 420
  evolutionary biology **3:**505, 507
  mules and hinnies **5:**110
  plants **4:**173
Hycanthone 5:465
Hydantoins 5:467
Hydra (constellation) **1:**29
Hydrarch succession 4:124
Hydras (coelenterates) **4:**218
  illus. **3:**454
Hydrated lime (Calcium hydroxide) 3:87, 99; **6:**207
Hydrates 3:87
  diagram(s) **3:**86
Hydration
  cement **6:**26
  chemical action of rain **2:**173
Hydraulic action (of a river) **2:**421
Hydraulic brakes 6:147–48
Hydraulic head (height of dam) **2:**377
Hydraulic mining 2:353
Hydraulic systems 3:186
  illus. **3:**186
Hydrocarbons 3:111–13
  air pollution **2:**467, 471
  gasoline **3:**75
  natural gas **2:**341
  petroleum **2:**323, 330
Hydrochloric acid 3:96
  achlorhydric anemia **5:**211
  uses **3:**99
  water solution **3:**79, 95
Hydrocortisone 5:246, 449
HYDROELECTRIC POWER 2:312, 316, **377–80**
  energy **2:**305
  solar power **1:**90
  tides **2:**249
  diagram(s) **2:**313
Hydrofluoric acid 3:99
Hydrofoils 6:114–16
Hydrogen 3:19, 38, 332
  atmosphere **2:**152
  atomic structure **3:**47–48, 69
  balloons **3:**188; **6:**150
  bond energy **3:**58
  chemical industry **6:**207
  coal conversion **2:**358, 396
  comets **1:**161

  covalence **3:**51–52
  fuel **2:**398–99
  interstellar space **1:**63, 219–21
  isotopes **2:**362; **3:**20
  Jupiter **1:**136
  life, origin of **3:**380
  magnetic resonance imaging **3:**270
  metal and nonmetal **3:**29
  nonmetals **3:**27
  nuclear reactor **2:**371, 374
  outer planets **1:**321
  photosynthesis **4:**17
  radio frequency **1:**55–56, 324
  stars **1:**192–93, 197
  Steady State theory **1:**21
  Stirling engines **6:**102
  Sun **1:**86, 88–90, 191, 195
  valence **3:**49, 63
  water molecule **3:**82–83
  illus. **2:**362; **3:**332
Hydrogenation
  petroleum **2:**331–32
Hydrogen bombs 2:376; **3:**15, 128
Hydrogen bonds 3:52, 65, 83–86
Hydrogen cyanide 1:144; **3:**66
Hydrogen fluoride 3:83; **6:**208
Hydrogen fuel cells *see* Fuel-cell technology
Hydrogen gas 3:104
Hydrogen ions 3:95–96
Hydrogen peroxide 3:55
Hydrogen phosphide 4:151
Hydrogen recombiners 2:371
Hydrogen sulfide 1:136; **3:**32
  diagram(s) **3:**66
Hydrogen sulfite 3:103
Hydroids 4:217–18
Hydrologic cycle *see* Water cycle
Hydrometeorology 2:145, 166
Hydronium ions 3:95, 104
Hydrophilidae *see* Water scavengers
Hydrophones 2:264, 274, 279
Hydroponics *see* Soilless agriculture
Hydro-Quebec 6:56
Hydrosphere 1:106; **3:**499
Hydrothermal vents 2:224, 270, 272, 278 *see also* Hot springs
  archaebacteria **4:**34
  life, extraterrestrial **3:**382
  life in **3:**376, 383
  illus. **2:**275; **3:**376, 433
Hydroxychloroquine 5:428
Hydroxyl group 3:111
Hydroxyl ions 3:95–96, 104
Hydrozoa 4:200
Hyena dogs *see* African hunting dogs
Hyenas 5:101–2
Hygiene, Dental 5:281–82
Hygrometers 2:142
Hymenoptera *see* Social insects

Hyoid bone 5:177
Hyperactivity disorder 5:366, 368
Hyperbolas 1:379
    illus. 1:398
Hyperbolic radio navigation systems 6:171
Hypercholesterolemia 5:420
Hypergonadism 5:247
Hyperion (moon of Saturn) 1:146
Hyperons 3:310–11
Hyperopia see Farsightedness
Hyperparathyroidism 5:247
Hyperplanes 1:400
Hypersonic flight 6:106
Hyperspheres 1:400
Hypertension 5:204
    aldosteronism 5:246
    exercise benefits 5:401–2
    medications 5:467, 470
    stroke 5:234
    toxemia 5:301
    chart(s) 5:203
Hypertext 6:306–7
Hypertext transfer protocol (http) 6:307
Hyperthermia
    cancer treatment 5:437
Hyperthyroidism 5:247
Hyperventilation 5:220
Hyper X program 6:106
Hyphae 3:455; 4:37–38, 41, 285
Hypnagogic sleep 5:407
Hypnosis 5:330, 400
    illus. 5:346
Hypocenter see Focus (in optics)
Hypochondriacal depression 5:351
Hypocotyl 3:463; 4:104–6
Hypoglycemia 5:245
Hypogonadism 5:247
Hypogynous flowers 4:101
Hypoparathyroidism 5:247
Hypophysis see Pituitary gland
Hypopituitarism 5:244
Hyposensitization 5:449
Hypotension 5:204
Hypothalamus 5:405–6, 408
    pituitary gland 5:243
Hypotheses, Scientific 1:1; 3:510; 6:317–18
    Aristotle 3:367
    psychological research 5:337
Hypothyroidism 5:247
Hypoxia
    illus. 5:222
Hyracoidea 5:13
Hyracotherium (Eohippus) 1:489; 5:107–8
    illus. 1:499
Hyraxes 5:13
Hysteria 5:342, 355

I

IAFIS see Integrated Automated Fingerprint Identification System
Iapetus (moon of Saturn) 1:146
    illus. 1:142
I-beams 6:30
Ibises 4:445–46
Ibuprofen 5:428
ICAM see CAD/CAM
Icarus (asteroid) 1:169
Icarus (Greek mythology) 6:91
Icarus (spacecraft) 1:283
ICD see Implantable cardioverter defibrillator
Ice (drug) see Methamphetamine
Ice (frozen water) 3:85–86, 89
    clouds 2:167
    coastal formation 2:292
    expansion 3:229
    glaciers 2:93–99
    heat of fusion 3:228
    Moon 1:114
    thundercloud 2:175–76
    illus.
        insulating properties 3:233
ICE (high-speed train)
    illus. 6:129
Ice ages 2:218
    coastlines 2:288
    glaciers 2:93
    prehistoric animals 1:498–99
ICEBERGS AND SEA ICE 2:91, 235, 260–63
    boulders carried by 2:276
    global warming 2:88, 91, 480
    Titanic 2:277
Icebreakers (ships) 2:263
Ice-cap climates 2:213–14
Ice caps see Continental glaciers
Ice climbing
    illus. 2:99
Ice Hotel (Quebec, Canada)
    illus. 3:233
Ice islands 2:235, 260
Iceland
    climates of the past 2:219
    geothermal energy 2:392
    geysers 2:65–66
    part of Mid-Atlantic Ridge 2:270
    plate tectonics 2:44
    volcanic island 2:283
    volcanoes 2:57–59
    whaling 2:413
    illus. 2:390, 393
Iceland moss 4:43
"Ice-minus" bacteria 6:73
Ice pack see Icebergs and sea ice
Ice pellets 2:170
Ice sheets see Continental glaciers
Ice storms 2:167
Ichneumon flies 4:290
Ichneumon wasps 4:269
Ichnology 1:482

ICHTHYOLOGY 3:373; 4:312–14
    see also Fish
Ichthyosaurs 1:488
Ichthyostega 4:341
ICs see Integrated circuits
Icy-conglomerate theory see Dirty-snowball theory
Icy dwarfs 1:74
Id 5:342
Ida (asteroid) 1:168
Idaho 2:511
Ideal-gas laws 3:72, 74, 222–23
    illus.
        Boyle's law 3:71
        Charles' law 3:72
Identical twins 5:295, 312
    body weight 5:392
Identities (in algebra) 1:358
Identity crises 5:342
Identity theft 6:382
Ides (Roman dates) 1:475–76
Ig E see Immunoglobulin E
Igneous rocks 2:31–34, 133–34
    Earth 1:106
    fossils 2:138
    mountains 2:69
    volcanic islands 2:282
Ignis fatuus 4:151
Ignition systems (of automobiles) 6:141
    illus. 6:142
Iguanas 4:355–56, 358, 360–62
    illus. 3:505; 4:357
Iguanodon 1:493, 495
Ikeya, K. (Japanese astronomer) 1:166
Ikeya-Seki, Comet 1:165–66
Ikonos (artificial satellite)
    illus. 2:296, 298
Ileocecal valve 5:253
Ileum 5:251
Iliac artery
    illus. 5:169
Ilium 5:180–81
    illus. 5:174
Illinois
    coal 2:360
Illusions 5:339
    ocean waves 2:250
    illus. 5:344–45
Image file (digital technology) 6:273–74
Image orthicon tubes 6:290–91
Image processing (digital technology) 6:274
Imaginary numbers 1:351
IMAGING, Diagnostic 5:450–59
    cancer 5:436
    electricity 2:321
    heart disease 5:438–39
    illus.
        archaeological uses 1:465
        cancer 5:432
IMAX (film format) 1:72
Imbrium, Mare (lunar feature) 1:120
Immune-deficiency diseases 5:241

IMMUNE SYSTEM 5:235–41
AIDS **5:**441–46
alcohol's effect on **5:**375
allergies **5:**447–49
arthritis **5:**183, 428–29
cancer prevention **5:**435
cancer treatment **5:**437
diabetes (type I) **5:**245
gene therapy **5:**422
infectious diseases **5:**425–26
lymphatic system **5:**214
monoclonal antibodies **5:**472
organ transplants **5:**479, 497
silicone, effects of **5:**506
virus infection **3:**393
illus.
cancer research **5:**434
Immunity to disease 5:237–38
Immunization 5:412, 430–31
schedule for children's immunizations **5:**238
Immunogens 5:446
Immunoglobulin A (Ig A) 5:237, 241
Immunoglobulin E (Ig E) 5:241, 447–49
Immunoglobulin G (Ig G) 5:206, 237–38, 241, 449
Immunology 3:372
Immunosuppressant drugs 5:241, 479, 497
Immunotherapy 5:241, 437
Impalas 5:131
Imperfect flowers 4:101
Imperfect fungi 4:42–44
Imperial mammoths 1:499
Impetigo 5:425, 428
Implantable cardioverter defibrillator (ICD) 5:505
Implantable infusion pump 5:470–71
Implantation (of an embryo) **5:**296
Implants, Breast *see* Breasts—implants
Implants, Dental 5:282
Implants, Sensory *see* Sensory implants
Impoundments *see* Reservoirs
Imprinting (in psychology) **4:**188–89; **5:**359
Impulse turbines 2:316
illus. **2:**313
Impurities (in crystals) **3:**91; **6:**250–51
Inca civilization 1:455
Inca doves 4:431
Incandescent lamps 2:319
Inchworms 4:307
Incident rays (of light) **3:**283–84
Incinerators 2:484, 492
illus. **2:**485
Incisors 5:279
Inclination of the compass 3:269
Inclined planes 3:171
Inclusion bodies 4:30
Income statement 1:458

Incomplete dominance (in genetics) *see* Blending
Incomplete flowers 4:101
Incomplete proteins 5:379–80
Incubation period
AIDS **5:**443
Incus *see* Anvil
Independent assortment of genes 3:409, 445; **5:**316
diagram(s) **3:**408
Index of refraction 3:285
fiber optics **6:**223
India
Bhopal chemical accident **2:**455
crocodile veneration **4:**384
earthquakes **2:**47, 52
mathematics, history of **1:**330
mountain formation **2:**72
sand dunes **2:**429
snakebite deaths **4:**367
tornadoes **2:**193
volcanoes **2:**58
wilderness preservation **2:**513
illus.
separation from Antarctica **2:**42
Indian barasinghs 5:121
Indian cobras 4:373
Indian elephants *see* Asian elephants
Indian foxes 5:83
Indian Ocean 2:229, 234
atolls **2:**283
currents **2:**237, 239–40
ocean basin **2:**270
ridge **2:**40
tides **2:**246
tropical cyclones **2:**196
tsunamis (2004) **2:**50, 256–57, 259
Indian pipe 4:112
Indian rhinoceroses *see* Greater Indian rhinoceroses
Indian rock pythons 4:370
Indians, American *see* Native Americans
Indicators (in chemistry) **3:**98
Indicators (in electronics) **6:**256–57
Indigo 6:203
Indigo snakes 4:371
Indinavir 5:445
Indium 3:31, 38
Individualized Educational Program (IEP) 5:367–68
illus. **5:**365
Individuals with Disabilities Education Act (IDEA) (U.S., 1990) **5:**368
Indomethacin 5:429
Indonesia
earthquakes **2:**50, 52
island arcs **2:**281
Java rain forests **4:**160
tsunamis **2:**50, 256–57
volcanoes **2:**61–62, 433
wilderness areas **2:**515

Indo-Pacific ridley turtles
illus. **4:**375
Indricotherium **5:**111
Indris 5:137
Induction (in embryology) **3:**459–60
Induction, Electromagnetic 3:247–49
Induction heating 2:320
Indusia 4:81
Industrial chemistry 3:9
Industrial engineering 6:20
Industrial health
air pollution **2:**468–69
cancer **5:**432, 436
Industrial pollution 2:455; **3:**489
Industrial psychology 5:347
Industrial Revolution 6:8–9, 11
carbon cycle **4:**21
forests **4:**127
Industrial wastes 2:488–89, 491
biological magnification **3:**489
water pollution **2:**458, 462–64
illus.
water pollution **2:**405, 452
Industry *see also* Business
air pollution **2:**471
bacteria, uses of **4:**35
chemical industry **6:**203–8
environmental pollution **2:**451
factories **6:**185–93
fiber optics **6:**223–24
human-caused erosion **2:**124
Internet growth **6:**308–9
lasers **6:**346–48
modern materials **6:**226–33
natural gas use **2:**345
radioisotopes **3:**320
Industry & Business Library (NYC) **6:**326
Inert gases *see* Noble gases
Inertia 3:10–11, 141
human-powered transportation **6:**91
Newton's first law **3:**155–56
roller-coaster rides **3:**159
work **3:**167
Inertial-confinement fusion 3:356–57
Inertial-guidance systems 1:305; **6:**172–73
Infantile paralysis *see* Poliomyelitis
Infants *see* Babies
Infections 5:236, 238–39
ears **5:**277
fungi **3:**451
problems of surgery **5:**477
Infectious arthritis 5:429
INFECTIOUS DISEASES 5:413, 423–31 *see also* names of diseases
Inferior vena cava 5:200
illus. **5:**169
Infertility 5:305–7
assisted reproduction **3:**456
gonorrhea **5:**429

hypogonadism 5:247
microsurgery 5:479
Infiltration galleries 2:441
Inflammation 6:425–26
arthritis 5:428–29
immune system 5:237
infection 5:236
pain 5:290
Inflammatory bowel disease
5:240–41, 255–56
Influenza virus 3:388–89
vaccine 5:474
illus. 3:385
**Information storage and
retrieval** *see* Data processing
**Infrared Astronomical Satellite
(IRAS)** 1:49, 61–62, 187
starburst galaxies 1:217
illus. 1:308
INFRARED ASTRONOMY 1:54,
60–62
galactic core 1:187
high-altitude aircraft 1:46
interstellar space 1:223
optical telescopes 1:38–39
telescopes in space 1:48–49
Infrared cameras 1:256
Infrared cirrus 1:61
Infrared radiation 3:274, 281
see also Infrared
astronomy
atmosphere 2:150
heat transfer 3:238
hurricane structure study 2:198
weather forecasting 2:204
Infrasonic sound 3:199
illus. 3:200
Ingenhousz, Jan (Dutch-Austrian
physician) 3:369; 4:17
Inguinal nodes
illus. 5:170
Inhalants (allergens) 5:448
Inhaler (drug-delivery device)
5:469
Inhaling (Inhalation; Inspiration)
5:215, 218
Inheritance *see* Genetics
Inherited diseases *see* Genetic
diseases
Injection (of drugs) 5:375,
469–70
Injection molding 6:212–13
Injuries
bones 5:182–83
brain and nervous system
5:234
ears 5:277
emergency rooms 5:481
healing process 5:239
muscles 5:194
pain 5:289–90
Inkjet printers 6:367–68
Inks 1:515
Ink sacs (of mollusks) 4:232
Inland seas 2:107
Inmarsat 1:310

Inner ear 5:275
illus. 5:276
Inorganic chemistry 3:7–8, 106
Input (to computers) 6:365–67
Inscribed angles 1:375–76
INSECT CLASSIFICATION
4:267, 277–80
Insect-eating animals *see* Insectivores
Insecticides
conservation of wildlife 2:411
entomology 4:268
insects' resistance to 4:273
pollution 2:502
INSECTIVORES 5:9, 11, 23–28
anteaters 5:34–35
bats 5:31–32
marsupials 5:20–21
INSECTS 4:204, 246–49, 272–76
allergies 5:448
animal behavior 4:192, 197
beetles 4:291–99
biological control 2:410
butterflies and moths 4:300–
307
carnivorous plants 4:109
classification 4:277–80
decomposition 3:470
desert animals 4:169
endangered species 2:505
entomology 4:266–71
flowering plants 4:13, 98–99
forensic science 1:512
forestry 4:131
fossils 1:488
grasslands 4:140
pest management 6:62–63
pets 4:490
population cycles 3:478–79
prehistoric animals 1:492
radioisotope tracer studies
3:320
reproduction 3:456–357
respiration 4:186
social insects 4:281–90
temperate forests 4:147–48
tundra and taiga 4:164
wetlands 4:154
zoo exhibits 4:476
illus.
breathing mechanism 5:217
pest management 2:409
Inselbergs 2:84
Insomnia 5:409
Inspiration (in physiology) *see*
Inhaling
Instant messaging (IM) 6:391
Instinct 4:188–89
Instruments, Aircraft 6:154–55
Instruments, Scientific 3:136
see also Laboratory methods; specific instruments
Insulation, Electrical 2:316–17,
319; 3:246, 358
Insulation, Thermal 1:255;
3:233–34
spacecraft 1:240, 249

Insulin 5:244–45
genetic engineering 3:402–3,
420; 4:35; 5:475
insulin pump 5:470
organic chemistry 3:115
illus.
administration 3:117;
5:470–71
Insulinomas 5:245
Integers 1:349–51
Integra 5:507
Integral calculus 1:333, 437
**Integrated Automated Finger-
print Identification Sys-
tem (IAFIS)** 1:516
Integrated circuits 6:13, 253,
371
electronic musical instruments
3:250
metalloids 3:29
modern materials 6:232
illus. 3:362; 6:233, 246
**Integrated computer-assisted
manufacture** *see* CAD
/CAM
**Integrated pest management
(IPM)** 6:62–63
**Integrated Services Digital Net-
work (ISDN)** 6:390
Integumentary system 5:172
see also Skin
Intel Corp. 6:304
Intelligence
animal behavior 4:193
artificial intelligence 6:202
dolphins 5:56–58
elephants 5:106
primates 5:148–49
puberty and adolescence 5:332
Intelligence testing 5:347
Intelsat 1:309, 311
illus. 1:307
Intel Science Talent Search
6:317
Intensity (of sound) 3:200–201,
206
Intensive-care units (ICUs)
5:480
Interaction of drugs 5:461, 493
Interactive languages 6:383
Interactive TV 6:304
Intercalary month 1:474
Intercalated disks 5:187, 200
Intercast 6:304
Interception radar 6:258
Interchangeable parts 6:191
Intercosmos (Soviet space pro-
gram) 1:285
Interdigestive secretion 5:250
Interference (in physics)
color 3:294
holography 6:275–76
light 3:292, 329
sound 3:208
wave motion 3:197
Interference (in psychology)
5:360–61
Interference microscopes 6:332

Interferometers 3:292
Interferometry
   holography 6:277
   radio astronomy 1:56–57
   telescopes 1:52
Interferons 3:393; 5:465, 475
Interglacial period 1:498
INTERIOR OF EARTH 2:22–29
   see also Core (of Earth);
      Mantle of Earth
Interleukin 2 5:437, 445
Intermediate frequency (IF)
   6:289–90
Intermediates (chemicals) 6:204
Intermolecular forces 3:81
Internal-combustion engines
   6:96, 99–102
   air pollution 2:467
   automobile 6:138–39
   electricity, generation of 2:314
Internal medicine 5:412–13
Internal Revenue Service 1:459
Internal waves (in the ocean)
   2:251
International Astronomical
   Union 1:79, 98, 122
International Classification of
   Diseases (ICD) 5:349
International Comet Explorer
   (space probe) 1:296
International Science and Engi-
   neering Fair 6:312, 314
International Space Station (ISS)
   1:257, 268–69; 6:13
   astronaut training 1:288
   engineering in the future 6:22
   space suits 1:270–71, 277
   illus. 1:250, 264
International System of Units
   see SI units
International Thermonuclear
   Experimental Reactor
   (ITER) 2:376
International Ultraviolet
   Explorer (IUE) 1:50–51,
   63–64
International Union for the Conservation of Nature and
   Natural Resources (IUCN)
   2:498–99, 504, 514
International Whaling Commission 5:53–54
INTERNET 6:302–11, 391, 393
   airline-ticket purchases 1:460
   cable television 6:390
   computer security 6:392, 397
   science education 6:321
   Web pages 6:378
   wide area networks 6:384–85
   illus. 6:389
   table(s)
      country codes 6:445–46
Internship, Medical see Residency
Interpersonal therapy 5:357
Interspecific competition 3:480
Intersputnik 1:310
Interstellar dust 1:61, 318

INTERSTELLAR SPACE
   1:218–23
Intertidal zone 3:499
Intertropical convergence zone
   2:184, 196
Intervals (in music) 3:212–13
Intervertebral disks 5:175
Intestinal juice 5:252
Intestines 5:251–55
   babies 5:326
   inflammatory bowel disease
      5:240–41
   pain 5:290
   illus. 5:167
Intoxication see Alcohol—sub-
   stance abuse
Intranets 6:308
Intravenous infusion of glucose
   illus. 3:118
Intrinsic factor 5:386
"Introduction to Outer Space"
   (pamphlet) 1:233
Introspection 5:338, 343
Intrusion-detection systems (on
   computers) 6:395–96
Intrusive masses (of rock)
   2:32–33
Inuit (people) 2:90, 155
Inundation zones (of tsunamis)
   2:258
Invariance principles (in physics) 3:309–10
Invariants (in geometry) 1:374
Invasion of the Saucermen (film)
   illus. 1:322
Invasive species 3:478
Inventions
   agriculture 4:171
   technology and society 6:2–14
   tools of science 1:3
Inverse barometric effect 2:200
Invertebrates
   movement 4:185
   pain 5:292
   prehistoric animals 1:490, 492
   reproduction 3:456–57; 4:187
INVISIBLE ASTRONOMY
   1:53–54
   infrared astronomy 1:60–62
   radio astronomy 1:55–57
   telescopes in space 1:47–52
   ultraviolet astronomy 1:62–64
   X-ray astronomy 1:58–59
In vitro fertilization (IVF) 3:456;
   5:307
   illus. 5:306
Involuntary muscles see
   Smooth muscles
Involution (in mathematics)
   1:348–49
Io (moon of Jupiter) 1:137–38,
   292; 2:155, 157
   illus. 1:135
Iodine 3:32, 38
   hyperthyroidism 5:247
   radioisotopes 3:319–20; 5:459
   salamanders' maturity 4:351
   trace mineral 5:388

Iodine 131 2:372
Iodo group 3:110
Ion-exchange process (water
   treatment) 2:447–48
Ionic bonding 3:49–50, 63, 101
   ceramics 6:219
Ionic compounds 3:50, 63–64,
   81
Ionization
   acids, bases, salts 3:95
   ceramics 6:218–19
   plasma 3:353–54
Ionization chambers 1:225
Ionosphere 1:89, 105; 2:151
   pulse-echo radio 6:255
Ions
   atmosphere 2:151–52
   chemical bonding 3:50, 63–64
   electrochemistry 3:101
   geologic dating 2:17
   nervous system 5:224–25
   particle accelerators 6:353
   solutions 3:75
IPM see Integrated pest management
Iran
   earthquakes 2:47, 52
   water conservation 2:410
Iraq 1:467–68
IRAS see Infrared Astronomical
   Satellite
IRAS-Araki-Alcock comet
   illus. 1:61
Ireland 2:281; 4:4
   illus. 2:348
Iridescence 3:294, 296
Iridium 3:39
   dinosaur extinction 1:174, 497
   radioisotopes 3:319
Iris (of the eye) 5:270, 272
   illus. 5:271
Irish elk 5:118
Irish moss 4:60
   illus. 4:49
Irminger Current 2:241
Iron 3:39
   cast iron 6:29–30, 175
   chemical symbol 3:53
   Curie point 3:265
   density 3:11
   Earth's interior 2:28–29
   factory, history of the 6:187–88
   liver 5:206
   Mars 1:131
   metallurgy 6:174–75, 177–82
   meteorites 1:172
   radioisotope tracer 3:319
   rust 3:14, 103
   specific heat 3:225
   stars 1:199
   trace mineral 5:387
   water-supply impurity 2:448
   illus.
      cast iron 6:29
      factory, history of the 6:187
      metallurgy 6:179–80
      wrought iron 6:175
Iron Age 6:7, 10

Iron lung **5:**222
Iron meteorites **1:**171–72; **2:**28
Iron oxide **2:**36, 135; **6:**218
  magnetism **3:**267
Irradiation of food **3:**281; **6:**80
Irrational numbers **1:**351
Irregular galaxies **1:**221
Irrigation **2:**118, 409; **6:**64
  agronomy **4:**174
  canals **6:**45
  deserts and people **4:**168–69
  early civilizations **2:**436; **6:**17
  illus. **2:**117; **6:**61
Irritable-bowel syndrome **5:**255
Irritation hypothesis (for cancerous cell growth)
  illus. **5:**435
Ischemia **5:**234
Ischium **5:**180–81
  illus. **5:**174
ISDN *see* Integrated Services Digital Network
Ishihara color disk
  illus. **3:**301
Islamic calendar **1:**478
  illus **1:**477
Island arcs **2:**45, 69–70, 280–82
  plate tectonics **2:**42
ISLANDS **2:**280–83
  erosion **2:**124
  extinct species **2:**495–97
  plate tectonics **2:**42, 44–45
  volcanic islands **2:**58
  illus.
    volcanic islands **2:**44
  table(s)
    largest islands **2:**282
Islets of Langerhans **5:**245–46
Isoclinic regions **3:**270
Isogonic regions **3:**270
Isoleucine **3:**122
Isomagnetic charts **3:**270
Isomerization **2:**331
Isoniazid **5:**464
Isoprene **3:**112
Isopropyl acetate **3:**115
Isosceles trapezoids **1:**374
Isostasy **2:**69, 72
Isotope dating *see* Radiometric age-dating
Isotopes **2:**362; **3:**20, 125–26, 317 *see also* Radioisotopes
Israel
  illus. **2:**389, 408
Itaipu Dam (Brazil–Paraguay) **2:**380; **6:**56
  illus. **2:**379
Italy
  Blue Grotto **2:**129
  Garofalo whirlpool **2:**248
  geothermal energy **2:**390–91
  Vaiont Dam **6:**53
  illus. **2:**124
iTunes **6:**310
IUCN *see* International Union for the Conservation of Nature and Natural Resources

Ivanovsky, Dmitry (Russian scientist) **3:**384–85; **5:**424
Ives, H. E. (American physicist) **3:**347
IVF *see* In vitro fertilization
Ivory **5:**53, 103
Ivory-billed woodpeckers **2:**501

J-K

Jābir ibn Hayyān (Arabian alchemist) **3:**2–3
Jacanas **4:**438
Jackals **5:**79–80
Jackfruit
  illus. **4:**12
Jackrabbits **5:**38
  illus. **5:**37
Jackscrews **3:**173
  illus. **3:**174
Jacobsen, Stephen C. (American scientist) **5:**503
  illus. **5:**500
Jacobson's organ **4:**354, 360
Jacob's staffs **6:**169
Jacquard looms **6:**195
Jaguars **2:**500; **5:**88
  illus. **4:**158; **5:**87
Jaguarundis **5:**92
Jakobshavn Glacier (Greenland) **2:**260
James, William (American philosopher) **5:**337
James Bay (Canada) **2:**249, 380
Janis, Irving (American psychologist) **5:**340
Jansky, Karl G. (American engineer) **1:**55
Janssen, Zacharias (Dutch lens maker) **6:**331
Janzen, Daniel (American forester) **4:**126
Japan
  artificial reefs **2:**287
  atomic-bomb survivors **5:**435
  cultured-pearl industry **4:**235
  earthquakes **2:**52, 54
  geothermal energy **2:**393
  high-speed trains **6:**130–32
  island arcs **2:**69, 281
  oyster farming **4:**238
  solar observatory **1:**93, 301
  space probes **1:**296, 298
  space station **1:**269
  Tokyo air pollution **2:**468–69
  volcanoes **2:**59
  whaling **2:**413
  illus. **3:**244
Japan, Sea of **2:**231
Japan Current *see* Kuroshio
Japanese beetles **4:**297
  illus. **4:**297
Japanese black pines **4:**90
Japanese hemlocks **4:**93
Japanese larches **4:**92
Japanese martens **5:**95
Japanese waxwings **4:**451–52

Japanese yews **4:**93
Japan Victor Company **6:**281
Jarmo (archaeological site, Mesopotamia) **6:**26
Jarvik-7 (artificial heart) **5:**504
  illus. **5:**504
Jarvik 2000 (left-ventricular assist device) **5:**504
Jason (robot) **2:**279
Jason Jr. (robot) **2:**277
Java (Indonesia) **4:**160
Java (programming language) **6:**309, 378
Javan rhinoceroses **5:**112–13
JAWLESS FISH **4:**205, 315–16, 321–22
  prehistoric animals **1:**490
Jaws **5:**176–77
  bone from stem cells **3:**423
  cartilaginous fish **4:**323
  insects **4:**274
  reptiles **4:**353
  snakes **4:**363–65
  illus. **5:**280
Jays **4:**463
  illus. **4:**463
Jeans, Sir James (British astronomer and mathematician) **2:**10–11
Jeep (automobile)
  illus. **6:**136
Jefferson, Thomas (American president)
  insect pests, study of **4:**268
Jeffreys, Sir Alec (British geneticist) **1:**509; **3:**418
Jeffreys, Sir Harold (British scientist) **2:**11
Jejunum **5:**251
Jellyfish **4:**214, 219
  illus. **4:**217–18
Jenner, Edward (English physician) **3:**393; **5:**237, 412, 423
  illus. **5:**424
Jenny Craig **5:**394
Jersey cattle
  illus. **5:**134
Jerusalem pines *see* Aleppo pines
Jesus Christ lizards *see* Basilisks
Jet aircraft **6:**156–57
  air pollution **2:**468
  engines **6:**105–6, 163–64, 229
  V/STOL aircraft **6:**161
  illus. **6:**469
    commercial jetliner **6:**149
    engine **6:**230
    Harrier **6:**161
Jetfoil (ship) **6:**116
Jet lag **3:**380
Jet Propulsion Laboratory **1:**232
Jet pump **3:**193

Jet streams 1:105; **2:**150–51, 185–86
  clouds **2:**163
  Post, Wiley **1:**271–72
  tornadoes **2:**192
Jetties 2:124, 294
Jewel beetles 4:295
Jewish calendar 1:478
Jock itch 5:428
Johannsen, Wilhelm (Danish botanist) **3:**401, 406
Johrei 5:514
Joint firs 4:96
Joint Global Ocean Flux Study 2:225
Joint Oceanographic Institution for Deep Earth Sampling (JOIDES) 2:276
Joints (in anatomy)
  aging **3:**468
  arthritis **5:**427, 429
  artificial *see* Artificial joints
  chiropractic **5:**512
  pain **5:**289
Joists 6:34
Joliot-Curie, Frédéric and Irène (French physicists) **3:**124
Jones, Brian (British balloonist) **6:**150
Jordan, David Starr (American ichthyologist) **4:**313
Jordan River 2:422
Josephson junctions 6:371
Joshua Tree National Park (California)
  illus. **2:**508
Joule (unit of measurement) **3:**162, 225
Joule, James Prescott (English physicist) **3:**220
Joyner-Kersee, Jackie (American athlete)
  illus. **5:**219
Joysticks 6:159, 300
JPEG (Joint Photographic Experts Group) 6:274
J/psi particles 3:314
  illus. **3:**312
Jugular vein
  illus. **5:**169
Julian calendar 1:475–77
Jumping spiders 4:258, 260
June bugs *see* May beetles
Jung, Carl (Swiss psychologist)
  illus. **5:**343
Jungles 4:156
Junipers 4:85–87, 89–90
  illus. **4:**124
Junkers, Hugo (German inventor) **6:**154
Juno (asteroid) **1:**168
Juno project (Soviet space program) **1:**285
JUPITER 1:74, **133–38**
  asteroids, origin of **1:**169
  auroras **2:**155, 157

  brown dwarf, compared with **1:**202
  comets, influence on **1:**164
  Comet Shoemaker-Levy **1:**165
  Galileo probe **1:**294–95
  gravity assist for spacecraft **1:**301
  infrared astronomy **1:**60–61
  life, possibility of **1:**320–22
  Pioneer probe **1:**291
  Voyager probes **1:**292
  illus. **1:**75–76, 203, 290
Jupiter's family of comets 1:164
Jurassic Park (film) **1:**483, 506
Jurassic period 1:494
  fossils **1:**488–89
  table(s) **1:**486; **2:**20–21
Just Imagine (film)
  illus. **1:**501
Kaifeng pagoda (China)
  illus. **6:**29
Kakapos 4:401, 409
  illus. **2:**497
Kalahari Desert 2:83
Kamerlingh-Onnes, Heike (Dutch physicist) **3:**359; **6:**220
Kamptozoa 4:202
Kanellopoulos, Kanellos (Greek bicyclist) **6:**95, 157
Kangaroos 4:140; **5:**8, 17–19
  illus. **5:**7, 16
Kansas City, Missouri
  tornadoes (2003) **2:**201
Kant, Immanuel (German philosopher) **2:**9
Kaolin 6:217
Kaolinite 2:122
Kaons (K-mesons) 3:20, 310
Kaplan reaction turbines 2:316
  diagram(s) **2:**378
Kaposi's sarcoma 5:239, 441, 443
Kapteyn, J. C. (Dutch astronomer) **1:**184
Karst region (Slovenia–Croatia) **2:**126, 172
Kasner, Edward (American mathematician) **1:**359
Katmai (volcano, Alaska) **2:**433
Katrina (hurricane, 2005) **2:**199–200
Kauris 4:87
Kavandi, Janet (American astronaut) **1:**289
Kay, John (English inventor) **6:**189
Kayaks 6:92
Keck Observatory (Hawaii) **1:**13, 41, 179
  galactic core **1:**187
  illus. **1:**43
Keels 6:109
Keller, Horst Uwe (German astronomer) **1:**161
Keloids 5:239

Kelp 2:397–98; **3:**476; **4:**47, 50
  illus. **4:**7, 46, 48
Kelvin, William Thomson, Baron (British physicist) **2:**27
Kelvin temperature scale 3:74, 135–36, 223, 358–59
  table(s) **6:**421
Kennedy, John F. (American president) **1:**240
Kentucky
  Mammoth Cave **2:**131
Kenya
  wilderness preservation **2:**514
Kepler, Johannes (German astronomer)
  Copernican system **1:**473
  planetary motion **1:**12, 78; **3:**141, 161
  supernovas **1:**198
Keratin 4:391; **5:**112, 263, 507
Kermode's bears 5:74
Kerogen 2:395–96
Kerosene 2:323, 330, 332
Kestrels 4:418
Ketones 2:467; **3:**114; **5:**245, 381
Ketosis 5:394
Kettledrums 3:216
  illus. **3:**217
Kevlar fiber 6:229
Keyboards (of computers) **6:**366
Key deer 5:121–22
Keyhole surgery *see* Minimally invasive surgery
KH-11 (artificial satellite) **1:**313
Kiangs 5:110
Kidneys
  babies **5:**327
  cancer **5:**437
  drug elimination **5:**461
  excretory system **5:**258–60, 262
  mammals **5:**4
  pain **5:**290
  primate kidneys transplanted **5:**496
  scarlet fever **5:**238–39
  transplants **5:**496, 498–99
  illus. **5:**168
Kidney stones 5:262, 491–92
Kilauea (volcano, Hawaii) **2:**55, 58, 61
Kilby, Jack (American scientist) **6:**253
Kilimanjaro, Mount (Tanzania) **2:**67, 71
Killer T cells 5:237
Killer whales 3:476; **5:**53, 67
  illus. **5:**3, 56
Kilns
  ceramics **6:**218
  construction materials **6:**26–27, 29
Kilocalories 3:58, 61, 225
Kilowatt-hours 2:319; **3:**258
Kilowatts 2:319
Kinescopes *see* Picture tubes
Kinesthesia 5:286

Kinetic energy 3:71, 75–76, 78, 190
  radioactive decay 3:349
  work 3:164
Kinetic theory 3:71–72, 141
  heat energy 3:221
King, Mary-Claire 3:400
Kingbirds 4:449
King cobras 4:373
King crabs see Horseshoe crabs
Kingdoms (in biological classification) 3:396, 398–99
Kingfishers 4:406–7
Kinglets 4:455
King rails 4:439
King snakes 4:371
Kinkajous
  illus. 5:75
Kirchhoff, Gustav (German physicist) 3:5
Kismet (robot) 6:202
Kiss II (holographic movie)
  illus. 6:276
Kitasato, Shibasaburo (Japanese bacteriologist) 5:424
Kites (birds) 4:415, 417
Kitti's hog-nosed bats 5:32
"Kitty Hawk" (Apollo command module)
  illus. 1:244
Kiwis (birds) 4:398, 413
  illus. 4:412
Klinefelter's syndrome 5:314
Klipspringers 5:131
Klystrons 6:249
K-mesons see Kaons
Kneecap see Patella
Knee jerk 5:227, 408
Knees (of cypress trees) 4:153
Knees (of the body)
  artificial see Artificial knees
Knife fish 4:320
Knight, Charles (Amer. artist)
  illus. 1:483
Knot (unit of speed) 2:236; 6:167
Knuckles 5:179
Koalas 5:20
Kobe (Japan) 2:52, 54
Kobs 5:130
Koch, Robert (German physician) 3:447; 4:25; 5:424
Kodiak bears 5:73
Köhler, Georges (German physiologist) 5:472
Köhler, Wolfgang (German-American psychologist) 4:193
Kokia kookei (plant)
  illus. 2:496
Koko (gorilla) 5:149
Kolhörster, Werner (German physicist) 1:225–26
Kolyma Range (Siberia) 2:89
Komarov, Vladimir M. (Soviet cosmonaut) 1:247
Komodo dragons 4:353, 357, 361
  illus. 2:495

Kookaburras 4:407
Koonwarra plants
  illus. 4:99
Köppen, Vladimir (German meteorologist) 2:211
Korn, Arthur (German inventor) 6:244
Kovalevskaya, Sofia (Russian mathematician) 1:330
Kraits 4:373
Krakatau (volcano, Indonesia) 2:433
Krebs citric acid cycle 3:437
  diagram(s) 3:435
Kremer Prizes 6:94–95
Krikalev, Sergei (Soviet cosmonaut)
  illus. 1:268
Krill 5:49
Kristall (space module) 1:283
Kruger National Park (South Africa) 2:513
Krypton 2:364; 3:33, 39, 68
Krypton 85 2:372
Kudus 5:128
  illus. 5:127
Kudzu vines 4:113
Kuiper, Gerard P. (Dutch-American astronomer) 1:159
Kuiper Belt 1:76, 157, 159
Kuiper Observatory
  illus. 1:261
Kulans 5:110
Kurchatovium see Rutherfordium
Kurds (people) 2:86
Kuroshio (Japan Current) 2:210, 229, 241
Kuru 3:390
Kuwait
  illus.
    oil-well fires 2:334
Kvant (space module) 1:283
Kwajalein (atoll, Marshall Islands) 2:283
Kwashiorkor 3:122; 5:379
Kyoto Protocol (1997) 2:482
Kytril see Granisetron

L

Labeling of food 6:84
  illus. 5:388
Laboratory methods 1:3
  archaeology 1:465
  biology 3:514–15
  chemistry 3:134–37
  gene transfer 6:74–75
  illus. 1:4
    fertilization 6:14
    microbiology 3:446
    safety hoods 3:513
Laboratory reports 3:512 see also Research papers, Scientific
Labor pains 5:304
Labrador Current 2:229, 241–42, 261

La Brea Tar Pits (California) 1:499; 2:139
Labyrinthomorpha 4:211
Laccadives (islands, Indian Ocean) 2:283
Laccoliths 2:33
Lacertid lizards 4:353
Lacewings 4:280
Lachrymal ducts 5:269
Lachrymal glands 5:269
Lacrosse (artificial satellite) 1:313
Lactic acid (Lactate) 3:435, 438; 5:187–88, 401
  diagram(s)
    fermentation 3:435
Lactobacillus 3:449; 4:34
Lactose 3:119; 5:380
"Ladder of Nature" 3:501–2
Ladybird beetles (Ladybugs) 4:194, 269, 291–92, 294
  illus. 4:291
Lady ferns 4:83
LAGOMORPHS 5:12, 36–38
Lagoons 2:283, 286, 289–90
La Grande Complex (hydro-power facility, Quebec, Canada) 2:380
Laika (dog sent into space) 1:235, 246–47
  illus. 2:246
La Jolla (California)
  coast 2:120, 291–92
  ocean waves 2:254
  sea caves 2:129
Lake Nicaragua sharks see Bull sharks
Lake plains 2:76
LAKES 2:106–11
  acid rain 2:472, 476
  biomes 3:499
  eutrophication 2:412, 460–61
  glaciers 2:99
  largest underground lake 2:131
  oxbow lakes 2:104, 422
  plant communities 4:137
  playa lakes 2:85–86
  sediment 2:216–17
  graph(s)
    cyanobacteria cycle 3:479
  table(s)
    world's largest lakes 2:109
Lamarck, Jean Baptiste (French naturalist) 3:502
  illus. 3:501
Lamb, Sir Harold (British scientist) 2:29
Lambert crazyweed 4:141
Lamellae 4:22, 358; 5:173
Laminarin 4:50
Laminates 6:214
Lampreys 3:483; 4:315–17, 321–22
  illus. 4:321
Lancelets 4:310–11
  illus. 4:310
Lanceolate leaves 4:73

Land
air circulation affected by water temperature **2:**182–83
conservation **2:**402–15
geography **2:**297, 300–301
surface mining, effects of **2:**307
terrestrial ecologists **2:**475
water changes the land **2:**416–25
Land breezes 2:183
Land crabs 4:248, 254
Landes (European plains) **2:**77
Landfills
hazardous wastes **2:**489, 491; **3:**85
waste disposal **2:**397, 484–85
illus. **2:**487
Land mines 1:256
Landry, Bridget (American space scientist) **1:**232
Landsat (satellite) **1:**315
Landscape Arch (Utah) **2:**85
Landslides 2:109, 173, 423
Langford, John S. (American aircraft designer) **6:**95
Langford, Nathaniel (American park superintendent) **2:**65
Langley, Samuel Pierpont (American scientist) **3:**274
Language
chimpanzees' use of **5:**149
computer programming languages **6:**375–78
confusion of wildfowl names **4:**423
development **5:**160
dolphins **5:**58–59
hearing problems **5:**276
human species **5:**154–55
learning disabilities **5:**365–66
schizophrenia **5:**350
Langurs 5:141
Lanthanides 3:25, 30–31
Lanthanum 3:39
Laparoscopes 5:256, 480
Laplace, Pierre-Simon de (French mathematician and astronomer) **2:**9
Lapse rate of the air 2:161, 214
Laptop computers 6:363
illus. **6:**368
Larches 4:85, 87, 92
Large Binocular Telescope (LBT) (Arizona) **1:**42
Large Hadron Collider 3:311, 357; **6:**359
Large intestine 5:253–55
illus. **5:**167, 249
Large Magellanic Cloud 1:201
Larks 4:449–50
Larvae 4:276
acorn worms **4:**311
ants **4:**282–84
bees **4:**286–87
beetles **4:**292–93, 295, 298
butterflies and moths **4:**301–2, 305, 307

echinoderms **4:**221–22
honeybees **4:**286
salamanders **4:**349
wasps **4:**289
Larynx 5:155, 177, 216–17
illus. **5:**168, 170, 216
Laser printers 6:368
LASERS 3:341; **6:**344–51
angioplasty **5:**490–91
automobile-part treatment **6:**228
cloud studies **2:**164
coherent light **3:**292
dentistry **5:**282
holography **6:**275–77
light shows **1:**71; **2:**131; **6:**349–50
medical technology **5:**488–90
military defense **1:**263
photochemistry **3:**8
photodynamic therapy **5:**437
photonics **6:**225
planetariums **1:**72
recording, sound and video **6:**286–87
Strategic Defense Initiative **1:**262
transphasors **6:**371
illus.
cutting metal **3:**290
eye surgery **5:**416
light shows **1:**65
matter, study of **3:**10
medical technology **5:**491
LASH (Lighter Aboard Ship) vessels 6:113
illus. **6:**114
Lassen Volcanic National Park (California) **2:**58
Las Vegas
illus. **2:**304
Lateral buds 4:69–70
Lateral line system (of fish) **4:**320
Lateral meristem *see* Cambium
Laterite 4:160
Latin America 4:156; **5:**441
Latissimus dorsi 5:185
Latitude 1:383–84; **6:**167–69
climates of the world **2:**210–11
planetarium simulation **1:**69–70
Latosolic soil 4:133, 135–36
Lattices, Crystal 3:64, 90, 358
superlattice **6:**232
Laughing gas *see* Nitrous oxide
Laurasia
map(s) **2:**40–41
Lava 2:33, 56–58, 60–62
cave formation **2:**129
hot spots **2:**44
magnetization **2:**39, 43
Moon **1:**120
illus. **4:**121
Laval, Carl G. P. de (Swedish inventor) **6:**103

Lavoisier, Antoine-Laurent (French chemist) **3:**3, 369; **4:**179
illus. **3:**4
Law
archaeological finds **1:**467
endangered species **2:**504–5
forensic science **1:**507–16
forest protection **4:**148–49
genetic technology **3:**423
Internet **6:**310–11
pollution controls **2:**235, 452, 471
substance abuse **5:**377
water rights **2:**438
wilderness areas **2:**507, 510
Lawn mowers
illus.
solar-powered **2:**386
Law of the Sea 2:413
Lawrence, Ernest O. (American physicist) **6:**355, 358
Lawrence Berkeley Laboratory (California) **6:**335, 358
Lawrence Livermore Laboratory (California) **2:**392
illus.
linear accelerator **6:**354
Lawrencium 3:39
Lawson criterion 2:376
Laxatives 5:355
LCDs *see* Liquid-crystal displays
L class submarines
illus. **6:**121
LDL-pheresis 5:493–94
L-dopa *see* Levodopa
LD process *see* Oxygen process
Lead 3:31, 39
air pollution **2:**468, 471
catalytic converters **6:**141
environmental pollution **2:**455, 463
freezing point **3:**88
geologic dating **2:**16
heat of fusion **3:**228
metals **6:**182–84
Lead-acid batteries 3:105, 253
Leaf beetles 4:298
illus. **4:**298
Leaf-cutter ants *see* Parasol ants
Leaf insects 4:276, 279
Leaf monkeys *see* Langurs
Leaf-nosed bats 5:30
Leaf-nosed snakes 4:371
Leaf primordia 4:69, 71
Leafy sea dragons
illus. **4:**333
Leakey, Richard (American anthropologist) **5:**156
Leap year 1:476–77
Learned helplessness 5:344
Learning
aging affects speed of **5:**334
animal behavior **4:**192
birds **4:**396
child development **5:**342

dementia **5:**353
disabilities **5:**363–68
memory **5:**358–62
primates **5:**148–49
programmed instruction **6:**383
**LEARNING DISABILITIES
5:363–68**
Least bitterns 4:444
Least sandpipers 4:436
Least weasels 5:93
Leatherbacks (turtles) **4:**353,
377–78
illus. **4:**377
Leather fungi *see* Bracket fungi
Leather tanning 4:35
Leaves 4:10
carnivorous plants **4:**108–10
conifers **4:**85
cycads **4:**97
deciduous trees **4:**144–45
desert plants **4:**167
ferns **4:**79–80
ginkgoes **4:**95
monocots and dicots **4:**107
plant behavior **4:**117
vascular plants **4:**12, 64, 70–73
diagram(s) **4:**70
illus.
autumn colors **2:**207
fossil **2:**139
LeBlanc, Nicolas (French chemist) **6:**203
LeBlanc process 6:203
Le Bris, Jean-Marie (French
aviator) **6:**152
Lechuguilla (cavern, New
Mexico)
illus. **2:**130, 420
Lechwes 5:130
Lederer, L. (American physicist)
3:338
Lee, T. D. (American physicist)
3:338
Leeches 4:244
illus. **4:**244
Leeuwenhoek, Anton van
(Dutch biologist) **3:**369,
424, 446; **4:**25; **5:**412, 423
**Left-ventricular assist devices
(LVADs) 5:**504
Legends and folklore
air travel **6:**149
Alexander the Great **6:**117–18
auroras **2:**155
bats, superstitions about **5:**31
crocodilians **4:**384
Daedalus and Icarus **6:**91
dolphins **5:**57–58
geologic phenomena **2:**7
hippopotamuses "sweat blood"
5:115
lemmings **5:**44
nocturnal lights over wetlands
4:151
tides **2:**243
unicorns **5:**53, 130

Legs
artificial *see* Artificial legs
bones **5:**180–81
insects **4:**274
lizards **4:**357–58
mammal evolution **5:**3
muscles of the body **5:**192
reattaching severed limbs
5:479
Legumes 4:141–42
nitrogen fixation **3:**491; **4:**35;
6:73
nutrition **5:**380
roots **4:**68
Leibniz, Gottfried Wilhelm von
(German philosopher and
mathematician) **1:**330, 345,
431
Leibniz Mountains (lunar feature) **1:**122
Leith, Emmet (American scientist) **6:**276
Lejeune, Jerome (French geneticist) **3:**416
Lemmings 3:478; **4:**164, 191;
5:44
graph(s)
population cycles **3:**479
Lemurs 2:501; **5:**137
Lenoir, Étienne (French engineer) **6:**99
Lens (of the eye) **5:**271–72
aging **5:**332
artificial lens **5:**508
focus **3:**290
organ transplants **5:**499
Lenses (in optics) **3:**289–91
microscopes **6:**330–33, 335
photography **6:**262–65
telescopes **1:**37, 39
Leo (constellation) **1:**29
Leonardo da Vinci (Italian artist
and engineer)
fossils **2:**7
plans for flying machine **6:**152
Leonids (meteor showers) **1:**161,
171
Leonov, Aleksei A. (Soviet cosmonaut) **1:**244
Leopard cats 5:92
Leopard geckos 4:362
Leopards 2:499–500; **5:**87–88
illus. **2:**504
Leopold, Aldo (American naturalist) **2:**510; **3:**474
Lepidodendrons 4:74
Lepidoptera *see* Butterflies;
Moths
Leptocephalus larvae 4:332
Lepton numbers 3:309
Leptons 3:20–21, 307, 311, 313
Lesseps, Ferdinand de (French
businessman) **6:**46
Lesser anteaters 5:35
Lettuce
illus. **6:**68
Leucine 3:122
Leucoplasts 3:431; **4:**14

Leukemia 5:211–12
bone-marrow transplants **5:**436,
499
Leukocytes *see* White blood
cells
Leukocytosis 5:207
Levavasseur, Léon (French
inventor) **6:**153
Levees, Natural 2:103–4, 110,
424
Leverrier, Urbain-Jean-Joseph
(French astronomer) **1:**79,
153; **3:**182
Levers 3:169–71
bones act as levers **5:**190
oars **6:**92
Levitation 3:363
illus. **3:**353
Levodopa 5:233
Lewis, Gilbert (American chemist) **3:**51
**Lewis and Clark expedition
2:**299
Lewis structures 3:51, 65–67,
109
Leyden jars 3:248
Liabilities 1:457–58
Libby, Walter (American chemist)
1:464
Liberty, Statue of
illus. **3:**100
Liberty ships
illus. **6:**113
Libido 5:342
Libra (constellation) **1:**30
Libraries
science libraries **6:**326
illus. **6:**1, 363
Librations 1:118
Librium *see* Diazepam
**Libyan (Egyptian) wild cats
5:**92
Lice 4:272, 279
illus. **4:**275
**Licensed practice nurses
(LPNs) 5:**483–84
Lichens 4:43, 49, 60, 163
fossils **1:**487
plant succession **4:**122–23
Lick granuloma 4:465
Lie detectors 1:516
LIFE 3:374–83
aging, death, and decomposition **3:**464–70
biology **3:**366–73
chemistry of *see* Biochemistry
climates of the past **2:**215–16
energy flow in ecosystems
3:485–86
first signs of **1:**487, 490; **4:**11
interstellar space study **1:**223
origin of **1:**318–20; **4:**27
reproduction **3:**452–57
requirements for survival **3:**492
water content of living things
3:488

LIFE, Search for Extraterrestrial 1:316–25
  bacteria theory **4:**31
  Mars **1:**131, 297; **3:**321
  science fiction **1:**501, 505
  space science **1:**233–34; **3:**382
Life expectancy 5:334
Life science education 6:325
Life span 3:465–66
  birds **4:**396
  pets **4:**485
  table(s)
    longevity records **3:**466
    various animals **5:**324
Lift (in aviation) **3:**193; **6:**158
  diagram(s) **3:**193
Lift pump 2:441; **3:**187–88
Lift-slab construction 6:40
Ligaments 5:174, 190–91
  artificial body parts **5:**504
Light *see also* Sunlight
  auroras **2:**155–58
  biorhythms **3:**380
  black holes **1:**204
  color **3:**293–303
  Doppler effect **1:**19
  Einstein's equation **3:**341
  electromagnetic spectrum **3:**273–75
  ether concept **3:**343
  fiber optics **6:**222–25
  holography **6:**275–77
  invisible astronomy **1:**53–54
  lasers **6:**344–51
  Newton's studies **3:**147–48
  nocturnal lights over wetlands **4:**151
  optical microscopes **6:**330–34
  optics **3:**144
  photography **6:**262
  phototropism **4:**114
  physics, history of **3:**142
  quantum theory **3:**323–24, 328–30
  speed of **3:**348
Light fuel oils 2:332
Light-independent reactions (in photosynthesis) **4:**23–24
Lighting
  automobile systems **6:**141
  electric lighting **2:**319–20
  gases, uses of **3:**68
  photography **6:**268, 270
  illus.
    baseball stadium **2:**308
    fluorescent lighting **3:**33
    halogen lamps **3:**33
    photography **6:**269
    urban areas **2:**304
Light lasers 6:346
LIGHTNING 2:174–80; **3:**248–49
  atmospheric carbon dioxide **2:**149
  electrical transmission lines **2:**318
  Jupiter **1:**321
  life, origin of **1:**319; **3:**380
  red sprites and blue jets **2:**141
  volcanoes **2:**61
Lightning bugs *see* Fireflies
Lightning rods 2:178, 180
Light pens 6:366
Light quanta *see* Photons
Light ray 3:282–83
Light reactions (in photosynthesis) **4:**23–24
Light therapy 5:514
Light-water nuclear reactors 2:367
Lignite 2:347, 357
Lilienthal, Otto (German inventor) **6:**152
Lilies 4:168
Lilius, Aloysius (Italian astronomer and physician) **1:**477
Lilly, John C. (American scientist) **5:**59
Limbic system 5:288
Limbs (of the body) *see* Arms; Legs
Lime (Calcium oxide) (chemical compound) **3:**87
  chemical industry **6:**207
  construction materials **6:**25
  countering acid rain **2:**476
Lime-soda ash process (water treatment) **2:**447
Limestone 2:36–37, 133, 135–36, 172
  acid rain **2:**476
  carbon cycle **3:**490
  caves **2:**125–29
  chemical industry **6:**207
  construction materials **6:**25
  erosion **2:**121
  fossils **2:**140
  groundwater **2:**113, 117, 119
  lake formation **2:**110
  illus.
    steelmaking **6:**180
    wind caves **2:**431
Limnetic zone 3:499
Limnology 2:107
Limonite 2:128
Limpets 4:240–41
Linacs *see* Linear accelerators
Lincoln, Abraham (American president) **5:**318
Lincoln Continental (automobile)
  illus. **6:**136–37
Lincoln Park Zoo (Chicago, Illinois) **4:**470
Linda Hall Library (Kansas City, Missouri) **6:**326
Lindbergh, Charles (American aviator) **6:**155
Lindow man 4:154
Line (in geometry) **1:**368–69
  graph(s) **1:**394
Linear accelerators 6:353–55
Linear expansion, Coefficient of *see* Coefficient of linear expansion
Linear leaves 4:73
Linear momentum 3:308
Linkages (machines to trace moving points) **1:**376–77
Linked genes 3:410
Linnaeus, Carolus (Swedish naturalist) **3:**191, 395, 397; **4:**3–4, 54, 179, 199, 267, 277, 397; **5:**136
  biology, history of **3:**369
  flower clocks **3:**381
  illus. **4:**201
Linoleic acid 3:120; **5:**382
Linolenic acid 3:120
Linsangs 5:100–101
Lintels *see* Post and lintel construction
Lions 5:84–86, 324
Lion's-mane jellyfish 4:214
Lipase 5:252–53
Lipids 3:121; **5:**382
  energy storage **3:**438
  life, characteristics of **3:**376
Lipoproteins 3:121; **5:**493–94
Liposomes 5:473–74
  illus. **5:**474
Lippmann, Gabriel (French photographer) **6:**276
Lip-reading 5:276
Liquefaction (of soils) **2:**50
Liquefaction point *see* Condensation
Liquefied natural gas 2:343
Liquefied petroleum gas 2:334
Liquid-borne wastes 2:485–89
Liquid-crystal displays (LCDs) 3:92; **6:**297
  color **3:**300
Liquid crystals 3:92; **6:**228–29
Liquid diets 5:394
Liquid-fuel rockets 1:243
Liquid lasers 6:345–46
Liquid-metal-cooled breeder reactors
  diagram(s) **2:**369
Liquid resources (in accounting) **1:**458
LIQUIDS 3:12, **75–81**, 226
  entropy **3:**242
  expansion with heat **3:**222
  fluid dynamics **3:**183–93
  gases, differences from **3:**184
  heat conduction **3:**233
  matter, study of **3:**14
Lister, Joseph (British physician) **3:**447
Liter (unit of measurement) **3:**135
Lithification 2:135
Lithium 3:29, 39
  mental illness treatment **5:**356, 466
Lithosphere 1:106–7; **2:**8, 25
  earthquakes **2:**47
  plate tectonics **2:**68
Lithotripsy 5:256, 491–92
Litmus paper 3:98
  illus.
    pH testing **3:**97
Little Bang theory 1:23

Little Big Inch (pipeline) 2:329, 338
Little blue penguins 4:413
Little brown bats 5:32
Little Dipper (constellation) 1:26
Little Ice Age 2:219–20
Littleneck clams see Hard-shell clams
Little Red Spot (feature of Jupiter) 1:137
Littoral zone 3:499
Liver 5:252
    alcohol-caused damage 5:375
    babies 5:326
    cancer 5:479
    cells 5:325
    cirrhosis 5:375
    excretory system 5:262
    iron storage 5:206
    metabolizing drugs 5:461
    transplants 5:498
    illus. 5:167, 249
Liver flukes 4:227–28
Liverworts 4:55, 58, 62–63
Livestock see also Cattle; Pigs; Sheep
    genetics 6:70–71, 75
    genetic technology 3:420–21, 423
    pets 4:481
    veterinary medicine 4:467–68
Living dunes 2:430
Livingstone, David (Scottish explorer) 4:384
Livor mortis 3:469
LIZARDS 4:353–55, 356–62
    courtship 4:195–96
    research 4:338
    illus. 4:356
        basilisk 4:356
        eating grasshopper 3:487
        fossil in amber 2:138
        frilled lizard 4:360
        gecko 4:358, 360
        Gila monster 4:360
        iguana 4:357
        skeleton 4:357
LLAMAS 5:6–7, 116–17
Llanos 2:78; 4:141
LNG see Liquefied natural gas
Load (material carried by stream) 2:420
Load arm (of levers) 3:169
Loadstone see Lodestone
Lobachevsky, Nikolai Ivanovich (Polish-Russian mathematician) 1:335, 401–3
Lobe-finned fish 4:317, 330–31
Lobsters 4:248, 250–54; 6:87–88
    illus. 4:253
Local anesthesia 5:477–78
Local area networks 6:373, 386–89
Local Group of galaxies 1:16
    illus. 1:187
Locard, Edmond (French criminologist) 1:510

Loci (singular Locus) (in geometry) 1:376
Lockjaw see Tetanus
Locks (on waterways) 6:46
    illus. 6:45
Locomotion of animals 4:185
    brain control of 5:159
    fish 4:317–18
    lizards 4:357
    snakes 4:364
    worm lizards 4:359
Locomotives
    diesel-electric 6:127
    electric 6:127
    steam 6:97, 125, 127
    illus. 6:9, 126
Locus see Loci
Lodestone (Magnetite) 2:34; 3:268
    illus. 3:268
Lodgepole pines 4:122
Loess 2:432–33
Loetschberg railway tunnel (Switzerland) 6:48
Löffler, Friedrich (German bacteriologist) 5:424
Logarithms 1:336–37, 360–61
    Richter scale 2:51
Logging see Lumber
Logic 1:329–30; 6:370
Logs, Ship's 6:167
Loihi (underwater volcano) 2:279
London (England)
    brick construction 6:27
    environmental pollution 2:468
    water pollution 2:457–58
Long-billed marsh wrens 4:452
Long-day plants and animals 4:116
Long-distance navigation see Loran
Long-eared owls 4:421
Longevity see Life span
Long-footed potoroos 5:19
Long-horned beetles 4:276, 291–92, 297–98
Long Island (New York) 2:281
    glacial-moraine shoreline 2:289
    water supply 2:118
Longitude 1:383–84; 6:167, 169–70
    illus. 1:384; 6:168
Longitudinal dunes 2:428–29
Longitudinal waves 3:195
Longleaf pines 4:148
Longline fishing 6:87
    illus. 6:89
Long-necked clams see Soft-shell clams
Long-nosed armadillos 5:33
Long-nosed chimaeras 4:325
Long-period comets 1:76
Longshore currents 2:289–90
Long-tailed tenrecs 5:28
Long-tailed weasels 5:93
Long-term care nursing 5:487
Long-term memory 5:360–61
Long-term potentiation 5:361

Long Valley Caldera (California) 2:5
Longwall mining 2:351–52, 355
Loons 4:432–34
Loopers (caterpillars) 4:307
Loops (in computer programs) 6:382
Loosestrife
    illus. 4:118
Lopez-Alegria, Michael (American astronaut)
    illus. 6:13
Loran 1:379; 6:171
Lorentz, Hendrik (Dutch physicist) 3:346
Lorenz, Konrad (Austrian biologist) 4:188–89
Lories 4:401
Lorises 5:138
Los Angeles (California)
    air pollution 2:467–68
    San Andreas Fault 2:54
    water supply 2:442
    illus. 2:333, 466; 3:73
Lost Sea, The (Tennessee) 2:131
Lotuses 4:105
Loudness of sound 3:206
    musical sound 3:211
Lou Gehrig's disease see Amyotrophic lateral sclerosis
Louisiana
    artificial reefs 2:287
Louisiana Purchase 2:508
Louse see Lice
Lovebirds 4:401
    illus. 4:400
Love Canal (New York) 2:489
Love (L) waves 2:49
Low-carb diets 5:394
Low-density lipoproteins 3:120; 5:401, 493–94
Low-e (Low-emission) glass 3:234
Lowell, Francis Cabot (American manufacturer) 6:190
Lowell, Percival (American astronomer) 1:156; 3:182
Lowland gorillas 5:144
Low temperature scanning electron microscopes 6:336
Low tides see Ebb tides
LPG see Liquefied petroleum gas
LRV (Lunar roving vehicle) 1:124
    illus. 1:245
LSD 5:372
Lubricants
    petroleum 2:330, 332–33
Lubrication systems (of automobiles) 6:141–42
Lucy (Australopithecus fossil) 5:160
Lumbar vertebrae 5:175
    illus. 5:175–76
Lumber 6:28–29 see also Trees
    conifers 4:86

Lumber (cont.)
  logging can lead to drought
    2:172
  silviculture **4:**128–30
  taiga **4:**165
  temperate-forest management
    4:146, 149
  uses of forests **4:**131
  wilderness **4:**160–61
Lumbosacral plexus 5:232
Luminance 6:293
Luminol 1:512
Luna (spacecraft) **1:**123, 298
  Sun probes **1:**301
Luna moths 4:306–7
  illus. **4:**300
Lunar bases 1:126
Lunar day 2:244, 246
Lunar exploration *see* Moon—
    exploration
Lunar module 1:245
  illus. **1:**119
Lunar Orbiters 1:123, 298
Lunar Prospector 1:114, 124,
    236, 260, 299
Lunar roving vehicle *see* LRV
Lunar vehicles *see* LRV;
    Lunokhods
Lunation *see* Synodic month
Lung cancer 5:433, 436–37
  air pollution **2:**469
  radon **5:**435
  smoking **5:**374
Lungfish 1:488; **4:**318, 331
Lungs 4:186; **5:**215, 217–19
  aging **5:**333
  air pollution **2:**468–69
  blood flow **5:**196, 212
  cancer *see* Lung cancer
  epithelium **5:**163
  excretory system **5:**261
  fetus **5:**300
  fungus infections **5:**428
  respiratory diseases **5:**222
  smoking-related illness **5:**374
  snakes **4:**364
  transplants **5:**498
  illus. **5:**167–69, 216
Luniks (spacecraft) **1:**123
Lunokhods (moon cars) **1:**123
Lunules 5:266
Lupines 4:105
Lupu Bridge (China) **6:**50
Lupus *see* Systemic lupus
    erythematosus
Lusitania (ship)
  illus. **6:**115
Luster 2:138; **3:**27
Luteinizing hormone 5:243
Lutetium 3:39
LVADs *see* Left-ventricular assist
    devices
Lycopods 4:56, 60
Lye *see* Sodium hydroxide
Lyme disease 4:147, 259, 263,
    269; **5:**118, 429
  ecological research **3:**471
Lymph 5:214

LYMPHATIC SYSTEM 5:172,
    214, 442
  immune system **5:**236–37
  white blood cells **5:**207
  illus. **5:**170, 214
Lymph nodes 5:207, 214, 236
Lymphocytes 5:207, 214, 236,
    442
  multiple sclerosis **5:**233
  organ transplants **5:**497
  resistance to infection **5:**426
Lymphoma 5:436
Lymph vessels 5:214
Lynx (animals) **2:**493; **5:**91
  graph(s)
    populations of lynx and hares
      3:480
Lynx (video game system) **6:**299
Lyra (constellation) **1:**30
Lyre (musical instrument)
  illus. **6:**6
Lyrebirds 4:447, 449
Lysine 3:122
Lysosomes 3:430–31
  illus. **5:**162
Lyttleton, Raymond (British
    astronomer) **2:**12

M

M1A2 tanks 6:105
M 31 (galaxy) *see* Great Nebula
    in Andromeda
M 42 (nebula) *see* Great Nebula
    in Orion
M87 (galaxy) **1:**212
Maathai, Wangari (Kenyan envi-
    ronmentalist) **4:**126
Macadam 6:43
Macaques 5:142
  illus. **5:**140
MacArthur, R. (American ecolo-
    gist) **3:**481
Macaws 4:401
  illus. **4:**401–2
MacCready, Paul M., Jr. (Ameri-
    can aircraft designer) **6:**95
Macerals 2:133
Machine language 6:375–78
Machines
  automation **6:**194–202
  nanotechnology **6:**340
  simple machines **3:**168–75
Machines, Law of 3:169
Machine tools 6:191
Macintosh (computer) **6:**308
Mackerel 4:318
Macmillan, Kirkpatrick (Scottish
    inventor) **6:**92
Macon (airship) **6:**151
MacPherson struts 6:146
Macquarie Island (Pacific
    Ocean) **2:**45
**Macrocytic megaloblastic ane-
    mia 5:**386
Macrometeorology 2:143
Macromolecules 3:65; **6:**210

Macronutrients 3:487; **5:**378–83
Macrophages 5:236, 426
  illus. **5:**235
Macular degeneration 5:273,
    489
Madagascar 2:281
  endangered species **2:**501–2
  lemurs **5:**137
  illus. **2:**419
Mad-cow disease 3:390
Maelstrom (whirlpool) **2:**248
Magazines, Science 6:320
Magellan (spacecraft)
  Venus **1:**100–101, 290, 300
  illus. **1:**101, 301
Magellan, Ferdinand (Portu-
    guese navigator) **2:**223,
    230, 264, 272
Magellanic Clouds 1:27, 189
Maggots 3:375, 470
Maglevs (trains) **3:**267, 362–63;
    6:130–32
  illus. **3:**145, 357; **6:**129
Magma 2:31–34, 37, 57, 59–60,
    62, 69, 71
  Earth **1:**106
  earthquakes **2:**48
  geothermal energy **2:**394
  minerals **2:**137
  plateau formation **2:**78–79
  rocks **2:**133–34
Magnavox Company 6:298
Magnesium 3:30, 40
  alloys **6:**184
  atomic structure **3:**48
  chlorophyll **4:**18
  meteorites **1:**172
  nutrition **5:**387
Magnesium carbonate 2:446–47
Magnesium chloride 2:229; **3:**87
**Magnesium sulfate (Epsom
    salts) 2:**136; **3:**30, 97, 99
  ocean **3:**87
  water hardness **2:**446–47
Magnet *see* Magnetism
Magnetars 1:201
Magnetically levitated trains *see*
    Maglevs
Magnetic axis 3:262
Magnetic bottles 2:376;
    3:354–56
Magnetic compasses *see* Com-
    passes, Magnetic
Magnetic fields 3:262–63
  atmosphere's effect on **2:**152
  auroras **2:**156–58; **3:**269
  bird migration **4:**394
  circular accelerators **6:**353
  cosmic rays **1:**226–27
  Earth **2:**29; **3:**266–67, 270–71
  electrical energy **2:**309, 317
  electric generators **3:**254
  interstellar space **1:**223
  Mercury **1:**98
  Neptune **1:**154
  neutron stars **1:**201
  ocean **2:**270, 272

paleomagnetism 1:483
plasma confinement 3:354–56
plate tectonics 2:39, 42–43
Sun 1:84–85, 93
illus. 1:228; 3:262
Magnetic moment 3:306
Magnetic poles *see* Poles, Magnetic
Magnetic quantum number 3:333
Magnetic recording 3:265; 6:279–83
Magnetic resonance imaging (MRI) 5:454–55, 458–59
heart disease 5:439
magnetism 3:270
memory and learning studies 5:361
spectroscopy 3:133
illus. 3:129; 5:416, 455
Magnetic separation (of ores) 6:176
Magnetic storms 3:271
Magnetic tape 6:368, 371–72
recording sight and sound 6:279–80
Magnetic therapy 5:514
MAGNETISM 3:261–71
ceramic superconductors 6:221
Earth 1:104–5; 2:29
maglev system 6:130–32
plate tectonics 2:39, 42–43
Sun 1:85
Magnetite *see* Lodestone
Magneto-hydrodynamic (MHD) generators 2:398
Magnetometers 2:60; 3:271
natural gas prospecting 2:339
petroleum prospecting 2:325–26
Magnetosphere 1:93; 2:156; 3:266
Magnetotail 2:157
Magnetrons 6:249
Magnets *see* Magnetism
Magnet schools 6:327
Magnification
microscopes 6:330–31
Magnifying glasses 6:330–31
Magnitude 1:25, 165
Magnus effect 3:185
Magoun, H. W. (American physiologist) 5:406
Magpies 4:463
Mahuang plants 4:96
Maidenhair ferns 4:83
Maidenhair trees *see* Ginkgoes
Mail, Electronic *see* E-mail
Maiman, T. H. (American physicist) 6:345
Maine
wilderness areas 2:511
illus. 2:510
Mainframe computers 6:362–63, 384, 386
Main-sequence stars 1:192–93, 195

Maintained vibrations (in acoustics) 3:200
Maize *see* Corn
Majority carriers 6:251
Major minerals (in nutrition) 5:387
Malachite 2:138
Malagasy mongooses 5:101
Malaria 4:212, 268–69
antimalarial drugs 5:464–65
sickle-cell disease 3:505; 5:321
worldwide infection 5:428
illus.
infected red blood cells 5:213
patients 4:212
Malayan sun bears 5:74
illus. 5:73
Maldives (islands, Indian Ocean) 2:283
Malignant tumors 5:434
Mallard ducks 4:443
illus. 4:442
Malleability 3:27–28
Mallee fowl 4:423
Malleus *see* Hammer (in the ear)
Malocclusion 5:281
Maltose 5:380
Mambas (snakes) 4:373
illus. 4:366
MAMMALS 4:205; 5:2–13
antelopes 5:126–31
bats 5:29–32
bears, pandas, and raccoons 5:69–76
camels and llamas 5:116–17
cat family 5:84–92
classification 3:397
deer family 5:118–23
dog family 5:77–83
dolphins 5:55–60
edentates 5:33–35
elephants 5:103–6
endangered species 2:495–96
fossils 1:488–89
genetic variation 3:505
giraffes 5:124–25
horse family 5:107–10
humans 5:152–56
insectivores 5:23–28
lagomorphs 5:36–38
marsupials 5:16–22
monotremes 5:14–15
mustelids 5:93–98
pigs and hippopotamuses 5:114–15
pinnipeds 5:63–68
prehistoric animals 1:497–99
primates 5:136–49
rarest mammal 5:113
rhinoceroses 5:111–13
rodents 5:39–45
sirenia 5:61–62
whales 5:46–54
Mammary glands 5:2, 4
human *see* Breasts
Mammography 5:459, 506
Mammoth Cave (Kentucky) 2:125–26, 131

Mammoths 1:489, 499; 5:103–4
bones used as construction materials 6:24
illus. 1:499
bones used as construction materials 2:215
Man (Homo sapiens) *see* Human species
Man (in biology) *see* Men
Man, Prehistoric *see* Prehistoric people
Manatees 2:499; 5:8, 12–13, 61–62
illus. 5:4
Manay cloudrunners 5:40
Mandibles 5:176–77
crustaceans 4:248, 251
insects 4:274
illus. 5:174, 176
Mandrills 5:142–43
illus. 5:142
Maned marmoset
illus. 5:139
Maneuvering rockets 1:240, 251–52
Mangabeys 5:142
Manganese 3:40
ocean floor 2:45, 222–24
trace mineral 5:388
water supply impurity 2:448
Manganese dioxide 3:55, 105
Manganese oxide 6:343
Mangrove trees 2:290; 4:152–53
illus. 2:291; 4:152
Manhattan (ship)
illus. 6:113
Manhattan Project 3:124
Mania 5:351, 356
Manic-depressive disorder *see* Bipolar affective disorder
Manned maneuvering unit (MMU) 1:252–53
MANNED SPACE PROGRAMS 1:238–57
astronaut training 1:280–89
space stations 1:264–69
table(s)
spaceflights 6:431–44
Manometers 3:187; 5:204
Manson, Patrick (British physician) 4:268
Mantell, Gideon (British physician) 1:493
Mantids 4:279
Mantis flies 4:280
Mantissa 1:361
Mantis shrimp 4:254
Mantle (of mollusks) 4:231, 234
Mantle of Earth 1:107; 2:14, 25–28
deep-sea exploration 2:276
hot spots 2:44–45
illus. 2:24
Mantodea *see* Mantids
Manufactured gas 2:337, 344, 359
Manufacturing *see* Factories
Manufacturing engineering 6:22

Manure 2:397
Manx cats
  illus. **5:**90
Maple trees **4:**104–5
  illus. **4:**18, 71
    drawing sap **4:**146
Maps
  Earth's outer core **2:**25
  geography **2:**297–98
  geologic maps **1:**480; **2:**140
  global weather maps **2:**143–44
  Mercator projection **1:**383–84
  navigation **6:**167
  ocean floor **2:**264–65, 273–75
  prehistoric map inscribed on
    bone **6:**4
  similar triangles used in map-
    making **1:**373
Maracaibo, Lake (Venezuela)
  illus. **2:**328–29
Marasmus **5:**379
Marble **2:**37, 136
  illus. **2:**136; **3:**30
Marbled cats **5:**92
Marbled polecats **5:**94
Marchantia **4:**63
Marconi, Guglielmo (Italian engineer) **3:**281
Marfan's syndrome **5:**420
Margays **2:**500; **5:**92
Margulis, Lynn (American biolo-
  gist) **3:**428
Maria (lunar features) **1:**113, 120,
  122, 126
Maria (Martian features) **1:**127
Mariana Trench (Pacific Ocean)
  2:230, 269, 271, 276
Marijuana **5:**371–72, 375, 377
Marine biology **2:**222; **3:**373
  biomes **3:**499
  fossils **2:**138–39
  hydrothermal vents **3:**376
  oxygen in water **3:**87
  water pollution **2:**503
  illus. **2:**247
Marine iguanas **4:**358, 362
Marineland of the Pacific **4:**314
Marine Mammal Protection Act
  (U.S., 1972) **2:**413; **5:**57,
  72
Mariner (spacecraft) **1:**296–97,
  299
  Mars **1:**129, 132
  Mercury **1:**97–98, 300
Marine resources, Conservation
  of **2:**412–13
Marine-west-coast climates
  2:213
Marine World (Vallejo, California)
  4:472
Marion's tortoises **5:**324
Mariotte, Edmé (French scientist)
  3:222–23
Mark III space suit **1:**277, 279
  illus. **1:**272–73
Marlins **4:**335
Marmosets **5:**139, 146
Marmots **5:**41–42

Marquesas Islands **2:**282
Marrow *see* Bone marrow
MARS **1:**74, **127–32**
  life **1:**320; **3:**321, 382; **4:**31
  meteorites **1:**173; **3:**130
  mission plans **1:**257
  satellites **1:**75
  space probes **1:**232–33, 236–
    37, 290, 296–97
  illus. **1:**73, 76, 321, 446
Mars (space probe) **1:**297
Mars Climate Orbiter **1:**131
Mars Express (space probe)
  1:297
Mars Global Surveyor (space-
  craft) **1:**131, 236–37, 290,
  297
Marshall, Robert (founder of Wil-
  derness Society) **2:**510
Marshall Islands (Pacific Ocean)
  2:283
Marsh birds **4:**438–40
Marsh deer **5:**122
Marshes **2:**290, 292; **4:**136–37,
  151–52
Marsh gas *see* Methane
Marsh hawks **4:**415, 417–18
Marsh mongooses **5:**101
Mars Microprobe Mission *see*
  Deep Space 2
Mars Observer (space probe)
  1:297
Mars Odyssey (space probe)
  1:131
Mars Pathfinder (space probe)
  1:131, 232, 290, 297
Marsupial moles **5:**20–21
MARSUPIALS **5:**5, 11, **16–22**
Martens **5:**95
  illus. **5:**94
Martha's Vineyard (island, Mas-
  sachusetts) **2:**281
Masked boobies
  illus. **3:**505
Maslow, Abraham (American
  psychologist) **5:**344
Mason Act (New York, 1970)
  2:505
Masonry construction **6:**24
Mass **3:**10–11, 341, 349
  conservation, laws of **3:**308
  Earth **1:**104
  elementary particles **3:**305–6
  falling objects **3:**154
  Fitzgerald-Lorentz contraction
    3:346
  Milky Way **1:**203
  stars **1:**192, 195
  universe, end of the **1:**23
  weight, comparison with **3:**21,
    178, 180
  table(s)
    elementary particles **3:**315
Massachusetts *see also* Boston
  refuse-burning power plant
    2:397
  tidal currents **2:**247–48
  illus. **4:**153

Massachusetts Institute of
  Technology (MIT) (Cam-
  bridge, Massachusetts)
  6:202
  illus. **6:**19
Massage therapy **5:**514
Mass-energy equation ($E = mc^2$)
  3:15, 128, 341, 348–49
Mass-luminosity law **1:**193
Mass peristalsis **5:**254–55
Mass production **6:**191–92
  automobiles **6:**134
Mass spectrometers **2:**17; **3:**133
  illus. **2:**16
Mast cells **5:**241, 448
Mastigophora **4:**207
Mastigures **4:**362
Mastodons **1:**489; **5:**103
  illus. **5:**104
Mastrofini, Marco (Italian priest)
  1:478
Masts **6:**109
Mata matas (turtles)
  illus. **4:**378
MATERIALS SCIENCE **6:**22,
  226–33
  magnetic materials **3:**263–64
  nanotechnology **6:**340–41, 343
  phase-change materials **3:**230
MATHEMATICS **1:**5, **328–31,**
  332–37
  algebra **1:**352–65
  analytic geometry **1:**391–400
  arithmetic **1:**346–51
  binary numerals **1:**446–52
  calculus **1:**431–37
  game theory **1:**424–30
  learning disabilities **5:**366
  non-Euclidean geometry
    1:401–3
  numerals **1:**338–45
  plane geometry **1:**366–79
  probability **1:**414–23
  science education **6:**329
  science fairs and projects
    6:313–14
  set theory **1:**438–45
  solid geometry **1:**380–85
  statistics **1:**404–13
  trigonometry **1:**386–90
  table(s)
    physical constants **6:**420
    symbols **6:**426
Mathilde (253) (asteroid) **1:**168,
  236, 260, 295
Matrix (in anatomy) **5:**164
Matrix (in chemistry) **6:**230
Matte **6:**182–83
MATTER **3:**3, **10–15**
  atoms **3:**16–21
  changes of state **3:**226–31
  chemical bonding **3:**47–52
  comet **1:**160
  conservation, laws of **3:**14–15,
    308
  continuous-creation theory **1:**21
  distribution in the universe **1:**20

gases **3:**68–74
interstellar space **1:**218–23
kinetic theory of *see* Kinetic theory
solids **3:**88–93
states of **3:**57–58
water, states of **3:**82
Matter waves *see* De Broglie waves
Matthews, Drummond H. (British oceanographer) **2:**42–43
Mauna Kea (volcano, Hawaii)
illus. **1:**43
Mauna Loa (volcano, Hawaii) **2:**44, 58
Maxillae 4:274
Maxima (in calculus) **1:**436–37
Maximin (in game theory) **1:**427
Maximum sustained yield (in ocology) **2:**406–7
Maxwell, James Clerk (Scottish physicist) **2:**10; **3:**142, 275–76
Maxwell Montes (feature on Venus) **1:**100
Mayan civilization
astronomy **1:**469, 471
calendar **1:**475
May beetles 4:297
May flies 3:466; **4:**276, 278; **5:**324
Mayor, Michel (Swiss astronomer) **1:**10
Mayr, Ernst (American biologist) **3:**507
Mazda Miata MX-5 (automobile)
illus. **6:**138
McAdam, John (Scottish businessman) **6:**43
McAuliffe, Christa (American teacher) **1:**289
McCaughey, Bobbi (American mother of septuplets) **5:**307
McClintock, Barbara (American scientist) **3:**412–13
McMillan, Edwin (American physicist) **6:**355, 357
McMurdo Station (Antarctica) **2:**92
MDMA (drug) *see* Ecstasy
Mead, Lake (Arizona–Nevada) **2:**48
Meadowlarks
illus. **4:**392
Meadow mice 4:420
Meal worms 4:296
Mean (type of average) **1:**410–11; **3:**511
Mean calorie 3:225
Meanders 2:103, 421, 424–25
Mean deviation (in statistics) **1:**411–12
Measles 5:238, 431
Measurement *see also* names of measuring devices
laboratory methods **3:**134–37, 511–13

mensuration of forests **4:**128
table(s) **6:**419–24
Measuring worms 4:307
Mechanical advantage 3:169–70
Mechanical energy 3:164–67
Mechanical proteins 3:439
MECHANICAL WAVES 3:194–97
ocean waves **2:**250–55
sound **3:**198–99
Mechanics (in physics) **3:**141
fluid dynamics **3:**183–93
motion **3:**149–61
work **3:**162–67
Median (type of average) **1:**410–11; **3:**511
Median nerve 5:182
Mediators (in biochemistry) **5:**448
Medical botany 4:7
Medical entomology 4:268–70
Medical geography 2:301
Medical herpetology 4:339
Medical history (of a patient) **5:**449, 493
Medical technicians 5:411
MEDICAL TECHNOLOGY 5:488–95
space program **1:**254–55
Medical waste 2:491
illus. **2:**489
Medications *see* Drugs
MEDICINE 5:410–17 *see also* Diagnosis, Medical; Diseases; Health
artificial body parts **5:**500–509
autopsy **3:**469
botany in the future **4:**7
careers **5:**414
coal-tar chemicals **2:**360
complementary and alternative medicine **5:**510–14
drug delivery **5:**468–75
drugs **5:**460–67
electricity, medical uses of **2:**321
fiber optics **6:**223
forensic science **1:**508–9
frog toxins **4:**347
gene therapy **3:**421–22
genetics **3:**404
ginkgo **4:**95
hot springs **2:**64
Human Genome Project **3:**420
human sciences **1:**7
lasers **6:**351
leech therapy **4:**244
lichens **4:**43
medical entomology **4:**268–69
medical technology **5:**488–95
mental health **5:**348–57
microbiology **3:**449
nanotechnology **6:**341–42
Nobel Prize winners **6:**407–17
nuclear chemistry **3:**125
nursing **5:**482–87
organ transplants **5:**496–99
pain relief **5:**291–92
petroleum, early uses of **2:**323

radioisotopes **3:**319–20
rain-forest products **4:**161
snakebite treatment **4:**367
space medicine *see* Space medicine
surgery and hospitalization **5:**476–81
technology and society **6:**9
veterinary science **4:**464–68
zoological research **4:**182
Mediterranean climates 2:212–13
Mediterranean Sea 2:229, 232
pollution **2:**451
volcanoes **2:**58
Medulla (of the kidney) **5:**259
Medulla oblongata 5:198, 230, 304
Medusae 4:217–19
Meerkats 5:101
Megalopolis 2:460
Megaloptera 4:280
Megalosaurus 1:493
Megapixels 6:273
Megaspores 4:15, 87
Megatherium 1:499
Meiosis 3:410, 443–45; **5:**311, 313
conjugation **3:**454
illus. **3:**445
Meitner, Lise (Austrian physicist) **3:**128
Meitnerium 3:40
Melanin 5:264, 267
hair **5:**265–66
Melanoma 5:267, 436–37
Melanophores 4:360
Molindjo trees 4:96
Melody 3:212
Meloidae 4:299
Meltdown (of a nuclear reactor) **2:**371
Melting point 3:78, 227–28
covalent molecules **3:**52
crystals **3:**91–92
ionic compounds **3:**50, 64
Membranes, Cell *see* Cell membranes
MEMORY 5:358–62
alcohol's effects on **5:**375
amnesia **5:**352
dementia **5:**353–54
learning disabilities **5:**365
Memory (computer) **6:**363, 365, 368–69, 376
digital photography **6:**274
external devices **6:**366, 371–72
Memory cells 5:237
Memory-span limit 5:360
Men (in biology)
age and reproduction **5:**333
chromosomal defects **5:**314
hearing problems **5:**277
infertility **5:**305–6
learning disabilities **5:**367
prostate cancer **5:**433
puberty in boys **5:**332

Men (cont.)
  sex-linked inheritance **5:**319, 421
  sex organs **5:**294–95
Menarche 5:332
Mendel, Gregor Johann (Austrian botanist) **3:**403; **4:**4; **5:**309, 315; **6:**70–71
  biology, history of **3:**369
  genetics **3:**401
  heredity **3:**407–9
  illus. **3:**368; **5:**310
Mendelevium 3:40
Mendeleyev, Dmitry (Russian chemist) **3:**4, 23
Mendel's laws 5:315–16
Menderes River 2:421
Mengele, Josef (German Nazi) **5:**322
Meninges (singular **Meninx**) **5:**227, 231
Meningitis 5:233
Meniscus 3:76
  illus. **3:**135
Menopause 3:468; **5:**294, 333
  osteoporosis **5:**184
Menstruation 5:294, 297, 306, 331–32
Mensuration 4:128
MENTAL HEALTH 5:348–57
  abnormal psychology **5:**340–41
  aging **5:**334
  substance abuse **5:**375
Mental illness *see* Mental health
Mental retardation 5:301
Mental set 5:344
Mepacrine 5:465
Meprobamate 5:356
Mercalli Intensity Scale 2:51
  table(s) **2:**53
Mercator, Gerardus (Flemish geographer) **1:**384; **2:**298
Mercator projection 1:383–84; **2:**298; **6:**167
  illus. **2:**297
Mercedes-Benz (automobile)
  illus. **6:**136–37
Mercuric oxide 3:54–56
Mercurous chloride *see* Calomel
Mercury (element) **3:**40
  barometers **3:**70
  chemical symbol **3:**53
  density **3:**183
  dry cell **3:**105
  manometers **3:**187
  melting point **3:**27
  specific gravity **3:**183
  specific heat **3:**225
  superconductivity **3:**359
  thermometers **3:**191–92
  water pollution **2:**463, 503
  illus. **3:**12
MERCURY (planet) **1:**74, **94–98**
  life, possibility of **1:**320
  perihelion **3:**351
  solar eclipses **1:**180
  space probes **1:**300–301
  illus. **1:**73, 76

Mercury (space program) **1:**240–41, 272
  illus.
    astronauts **1:**240
    space suits **1:**275
Mercury-arc lamps 2:320
Mercury oxide 3:105
Mergansers 4:441–42
Meridians 1:25, 29
Meristems 3:463, 467; **4:**9, 69
Mermaid purses 4:328
Merz, Patricia (American scientist) **3:**391
Mesarch succession 4:122–23
Mesas 2:80, 85, 418
Mesenchyme 4:215–17
Mesentery 5:251
Meseta (plateau, Spain) **2:**80
Mesmer, Franz (Austrian physician) **5:**336
Mesoderm 3:461; **5:**297
Mesometeorology 2:144
Mesons 3:307, 311, 315–16
  cosmic rays **1:**229–30
  parity **3:**337–38
  quarks **3:**313
  strangeness **3:**310
Mesonychids 5:47
Mesophyll 4:70
Mesopotamia
  accounting **1:**454
  construction materials **6:**26
  water supply **2:**435; **6:**17
  writing systems **6:**5–6
Mesosphere 1:105; **2:**151
  illus. **2:**150
Mesothermal climates *see* Subtropical climates
Mesozoa 4:201
Mesozoic era 1:492–94, 497; **2:**19
  fossils **1:**488–89
  ginkgoes **4:**94
  table(s) **1:**486; **2:**20–21
Mesquite trees 4:136, 167
Messenger RNA 3:414
Messerschmitt Me 163 Komet (airplane) **6:**156
Messier 31 (galaxy) *see* Great Nebula in Andromeda
Messina, Strait of 2:248
Metabolic pathways 3:439
Metabolism 3:396, 402
  bacteria **4:**30–31
  cell dynamics **3:**432–39
  drugs **5:**460–61
  gout **5:**429
  life, characteristics of **3:**376
  sleep **5:**407
  thyroid gland **5:**246
  waste products **5:**257
Metacarpal bones 5:179–80
  illus. **5:**165, 174, 178–79
Metallic ions 3:96–97
Metallic oxide 3:360
Metallic wood borers 4:295
Metalloids 3:25, 29
Metallurgy *see* Alloys; Metals

Metal poisoning 2:463–64
METALS 6:174–84
  air pollution **2:**467–69
  alkali metals **3:**29–30
  alkaline-earth metals **3:**30
  artificial body parts **5:**501
  boron family **3:**31
  chemical bonding **3:**52
  construction materials **6:**29–30
  corrosion **3:**103
  elements **3:**26–27
  engineering today **6:**22
  expansion with heat **3:**222
  heat conduction **3:**233
  modern materials **6:**229–30
  periodic table **3:**25
  salts **3:**33
  transition metals **3:**30–31
  water, reactions with **3:**86–87
  water pollution **2:**463–64
  illus.
    bonding **3:**52
    chemical analysis **3:**1
Metamorphic foliation 2:37
Metamorphic rocks 2:31, 36–37, 133–34, 136
  Earth **1:**106
  fossils **2:**138
  mountains **2:**69, 72
Metamorphism (in geology) **2:**37, 136
Metamorphosis 4:187
  amphibians **4:**342
  ants **4:**282
  butterflies and moths **4:**301–3
  frogs **4:**346
  insects **4:**249, 275–76
  salamanders **4:**349
  wasps **4:**289
  illus.
    frog **4:**344
    monarch butterfly **4:**302
    salamanders **4:**350
Metaphase 3:442, 444
Metastasis 5:434
Metastatic tumors 5:184
Metatarsal bones 5:182
  illus. **5:**165, 174, 180–81
Meteor Crater (Arizona) **1:**121; **2:**110
METEORITES 1:77, **170–74**; **2:**28
  Antarctica **2:**92
  atmosphere of Earth **2:**148–49
  Canada (1999) **1:**169
  life, origin of **1:**319; **4:**31
  lunar crater formation **1:**121
  Martian rock **1:**131; **3:**130
  illus. **1:**172
Meteorological tides 2:237
Meteorology *see also* Weather
  atmosphere **2:**147–54
  atmospheric science **2:**141–43
  careers **2:**144
  clouds and fog **2:**159–65
  thunder and lightning **2:**174–80

METEORS 1:77, 170–74
atmosphere **2:**151
comets **1:**161
lake formation **2:**110
life, origin of **1:**318
Perseids **1:**30
radar astronomy **6:**261
Meteor showers 1:171
Meter (unit of measurement)
3:135
Meters, Electric *see* Electric
meters
Methadone 5:376
Methamphetamine 5:373
illus. **5:**374
Methane 3:109
atmospheric increase **2:**146
coal mines **2:**354–55
comets **1:**161
energy uses **3:**68
greenhouse gases **2:**478–79
Jupiter **1:**136
life **3:**376, 380
molecules in space **1:**318
natural gas **2:**341
Neptune **1:**153
nocturnal lights over wetlands
4:151
outer planets **1:**321
Pluto **1:**157
Saturn **1:**140
Titan's atmosphere **1:**145, 295
waste conversion **2:**397, 487
wetlands **4:**155
illus. **3:**67, 108
Methanol (Methyl alcohol)
2:332, 395, 397; **3:**113
Methanometers 2:355
Methionine 3:122
Methotrexate 5:240, 428
Methyl bromide 2:479
Methyl butyrate 3:114
Methyl chloride 2:479; **3:**111
**Methylenedioxymethamphet-
amine** *see* Ecstasy
Methyl group 3:110
Methylphenidate (Ritalin) 5:368
Metoclopramide 5:467
Metoprolol 5:467
Metric system 3:135, 512–13
table(s) **6:**422
Metrodorus (Greek philosopher)
1:316
Mexican bean beetles 4:294
Mexico
air pollution **2:**468
axolotls **4:**351
beetle larvae as food **4:**298
earthquakes **2:**52
geothermal energy **2:**392
Green Revolution **4:**170; **6:**71
Paricutín **2:**62
wilderness areas **2:**513
illus. **2:**61, 453
Mexico, Gulf of
artificial reefs **2:**287
hurricanes **2:**196

natural-gas deposits **2:**341–42
tides **2:**246
Meyer, Lothar (German chemist)
3:24
Miacids 5:69–70, 84, 93, 99
Miami Seaquarium 4:314
Micas 2:33–34, 37, 137
beach sands **2:**293, 295
Mice 5:43
acorn cycle **4:**147
life span **5:**324
owls prey upon **4:**420
transgenic **6:**72
illus. **5:**39
cloned animals **6:**14
hairless **5:**433
Michaud, Pierre (French inventor) **6:**92
Michell, John (English astronomer) **1:**204
Michelson, Albert A. (American
physicist) **3:**343
Michigan 2:429; **4:**37
Michigan State University 6:202
MICROBIOLOGY 3:366, 373,
446–51
ecology **3:**474
infectious diseases **5:**423–31
thermophilic proteins **3:**2
Microbursts 2:145, 188
Microcells 6:243–44
Microcomputers *see* Personal
computers
Microelectronics 5:492–93
Microgravity *see* Gravity—low-
gravity science; Weight-
lessness
Microinjection (fertility technique)
5:306
Micrometeorology 2:145
Micromonas 4:47
Micronutrients 3:487; **5:**383–88
Microorganisms *see* Microbiology
Micropaleontology 1:481
Microphones 6:238, 248
**Microprocessors (Computer
chips) 6:**253, 370–71
DNA computers **3:**419
nanotechnology **6:**340
pacemakers **5:**505
photonic computers **6:**225
video games **6:**298–99
illus. **3:**362; **6:**253
Microraptor 1:479
MICROSCOPES 3:514; **6:**330–37
entomology **4:**267
medical technology **5:**495
microbiology **3:**450
microorganisms **3:**369; **5:**423
optics **3:**288
taxonomy **4:**179
illus.
Hooke's microscope **3:**425
Microsoft Corp. 6:301, 307–9
Microspora 3:451; **4:**211
Microspores 4:15

Microstraining (water purification) **2:**443
Microstructures (of materials)
6:227
Microsurgery 5:479, 494–95
Microthermal climates *see* Temperate zone—climates of
the world
Microwave ovens 3:281
superheated water **3:**231
illus. **3:**275
Microwaves 3:275
communications **1:**324
telephone **6:**239–40
Microwhip scorpions 4:263
Mid-Atlantic Ridge 2:47, 59,
231, 264, 270
illus.
fit of continents around **2:**40
map(s) **2:**41, 266
Midbrain 5:230
Middle Ages 6:7–8, 10
medicine **5:**412
Middle ear 5:274–75
illus. **3:**205; **5:**276
Mid-oceanic ridge 2:71, 270,
274
crust formation **2:**31
earthquakes **2:**47
Indian Ocean **2:**234
plate tectonics **2:**39–40, 42–45,
68–69
map(s) **2:**41
Midwives 5:485
Migraine headaches 5:290
Migration of animals *see* Animal
migration
**Milankovich theory of climate
change 2:**219
Mildews 4:41–42
Military aircraft 6:151, 161
Military radar 6:258
illus. **6:**257
**Military reconnaissance satel-
lites 1:**312–13
**Military training of engineers
6:**19
Milk
fermentation **4:**34–35
galactorrhea **5:**244
pasteurization **6:**79–80
powdered **6:**76
Milking machines 3:186
**Milkweed longhorn beetles
4:**298
MILKY WAY 1:16, 30, **181–89,**
195–96, 221
black hole **1:**212
interstellar space **1:**218–20
invisible astronomy **1:**54
IRAS view **1:**61
night sky **1:**24–25
radio noise **1:**55
Sun **1:**81
illus. **1:**53, 181, 188, 222–23
infrared image **1:**183

Miller, Stanley (American chemist) **3:**372, 381
illus. **3:**383
Millikan, Robert A. (American physicist) **1:**225
Milliliter (unit of measurement) **3:**135
Millipedes 4:249, 264–65
Mills 6:7, 185–87
Milstein, César (Argentine-British physiologist) **5:**472
Miltown *see* Propanediols
Milwaukee (Wisconsin)
water pollution **2:**459
Mimas (moon of Saturn) **1:**145–46
Mimicry 4:276, 297–98
Mimosas *see* Sensitive plants
Mineralization (fossil formation) **2:**139
Mineralogy 2:3
MINERALS (in geology) **2:136–38**
beach sands **2:**293
collecting **2:**139–40
conservation **2:**413–15
crystals **1:**380–81
deserts **2:**85–86
economic geology **2:**4
geologic record **2:**19, 21
identification by refraction **3:**285
igneous rocks **2:**33–34
metal compounds **3:**27
Moon search for **1:**298–99
nutrient cycles **3:**491
ocean **2:**229–30
ocean floor **2:**45, 222–24, 268
ores **6:**175–77
soil depletion **2:**409
water solutions **3:**84
Minerals (in nutrition) **5:**387–88
excretory system **5:**258–59
Mineral water 2:117
Miniature clovers 4:79
MiniDV camcorders 6:287
Minima (in calculus) **1:**436
Minimally invasive surgery 5:479–80
Mining
coal **2:**349–56
dust diseases **2:**469
engineering today **6:**22
environment **2:**307, 456
Moon, possibility on **1:**298–99
rain forests, dangers to **4:**160
illus. **2:**306
coal mining **2:**346
Minivets 4:450
Mink 2:496; **5:**94
Minke whales 5:50
Minkowski, Hermann (German physicist) **3:**345
Minnows 4:333
Minority carriers 6:251
Minuend 1:347
Miocene epoch 5:101
table(s) **2:**20

Mir (space station) **1:**248, 267–68, 283
guest crew members **1:**285
illus. **1:**267, 284
Mir (submersible) **2:**277; **6:**124
Mira (star) **1:**32
Mirach (star) **1:**30
Mirages 3:291
Miranda (moon of Uranus) **1:**150
illus. **1:**150
Mirror Fusion Test Facility 3:356
Mirrors 3:285–89
cameras **6:**263
Hubble Space Telescope **1:**49–50
lasers **6:**345
solar reflectors **2:**384–85
telescopes **1:**38–42, 44
illus.
solar-power plant **2:**384
Miscarriage 5:302
Missile-carrying submarines (SSBNs) 6:121–22
Missiles (weapons) **6:**121–22
radar control **6:**258
space-based defense against **1:**262–63
Missing mass *see* Dark matter
Mission Control Center (Houston, Texas)
illus. **1:**257
Mission to Planet Earth *see* Earth Science Enterprise
Mississippian period 1:488
table(s) **2:**18–19
Mississippi River 2:419–21
delta plain **2:**76, 105
flood control **2:**105
meanders and oxbows **2:**103–4
Mississippi Valley 2:77
Missouri
New Madrid earthquake **2:**51
Times Beach **2:**463
Miss Waldron's red colobus 5:141
Mist 2:160, 167
Mistletoe 3:483; **4:**104, 112, 119
Mistral 2:186
Mitch (hurricane, 2004) **2:**200
Mites 4:248, 257–58, 262–63
Mitnick, Kevin (American hacker) **6:**397
Mitochondria 3:430–31; **4:**14
aging **3:**467–68
bacteria **3:**428
cell dynamics **3:**437
genetics **3:**400
diagram(s) **3:**429; **5:**162
Mitosis 3:441–43; **5:**162–63, 310
illus. **3:**442
Mitral (Bicuspid) valve 5:198–99
Mnemonic devices 5:362
Moa plants 4:82
Mobitex 6:245
Mockingbirds 4:192, 396, 453
Mode (type of average) **1:**409–11

Model T Ford (automobile) **6:**192
illus. **6:**136, 191
Modems 6:304, 366, 389–90
faxes **6:**244
Moderators (of nuclear reactors) **2:**366
Modern physics 3:145
Modulation 6:289
Modulators 6:256
Moebius Strip
illus. **1:**334
Moeritherium **5:**103
illus. **5:**104
Mohole Project *see* Project Mohole
Mohorovičić, Andrija (Croatian seismologist) **2:**25
Mohorovičić discontinuity 2:25
illus. **2:**24
Mohs' hardness scale 2:137
Mojave Desert 4:166
Molarity 3:80
Molar mass 3:56
Molars (teeth) **5:**279–80
Molasse 2:71–73
Molding (of plastics) **6:**212–14
Molds (fungi) **3:**375, 451; **4:**38, 41
antibiotics **5:**463
decomposition **3:**470
reproduction **3:**455
illus. **3:**375; **4:**38
Mole (unit of measurement) **3:**56, 58, 80
Molecular beam epitaxy 6:232
Molecular biology 3:373
Molecular compounds 3:65
Molecular orbitals 3:332
Molecules 3:17, 53–54, 64–67
aromatic compounds **3:**112
chemical bonding **3:**47
covalence **3:**50–52
liquids **3:**75–78
smell **5:**283–84
water **3:**82–83, 85
illus. **3:**84, 242
Mole rats 5:43
Moles (animals) **5:**6, 24–26
Moles, Mechanical 6:48
Mole vipers 4:374
MOLLUSKS 4:202–3, 231–41
carbon cycle **3:**489–90
fishing **6:**87
fossils **1:**487
Molniya (communications satellite) **1:**309
Molting 5:6
arthropods **4:**247
beetles **4:**292
birds **4:**392
butterflies and moths **4:**301–3
crustaceans **4:**251
reptiles **4:**355
snakes **4:**368
illus. **4:**366
Molybdenum 3:40
Momentum 3:141, 156, 308
Newton's third law **3:**158

Monadnock, Mount (New Hampshire) 2:425
Monadnocks 2:425
Monarch B (human-powered aircraft) 6:95
Monarch butterflies 4:276, 305–6; 6:75
illus. 4:190, 302
MONERANS 4:25–35, 54–55, 184
classification of living things 3:398–99
illus. 3:448; 4:55
Mongolian asses *see* Kulans
Mongolian wild horses *see* Przhevalski's wild horses
Mongooses 5:100–101
illus. 5:99
Monier, Joseph (French gardener) 6:31
Monitors (lizards) 4:356–57
Monitors (of computers) 3:300; 6:367
Monkey-puzzle trees 4:85
illus. 4:87
Monkeys 5:7–8, 10, 138–43, 146–48
Monkey's dinner-bell trees 4:119
Monk parakeets 4:197
Monoamine oxidase inhibitors 5:356, 466
Monoclimax theory 4:125
Monoclinic crystals
illus. 3:90
Monoclonal antibodies 5:471–73
Monocoque fuselages 6:153–54
Monocots 4:57, 100–7
Monoculture 2:412
Monocytes 5:208
Monoecious plants 4:101
Monomers 6:210
Mononucleosis 3:392
Mononychus
illus. 1:498
Monophonic recording 6:279
Monoplanes 6:153
Monopoles 3:262
Monorails 6:128, 130
illus. 6:128–29
Monosaccharides 3:118; 5:380
Monosodium glutamate 6:84
Monosodium urate 5:429
MONOTREMES (Egg-laying mammals) 1:498; 5:5, 11, 14–15
Monounsaturated fats 3:120; 5:382–83
Monsoon Drift (ocean current) 2:240
Monsoons 2:183, 230
climates of the world 2:212
ocean currents 2:234, 237
Monsters (science fiction) 1:504
Montana
coal 2:360

farmland 6:64
Glacier National Park 2:108
wilderness areas 2:511
illus. 6:18
Montane squirrels 5:40
Monterey Canyon (submarine canyon, California) 2:269
Monterey cypresses 4:92
Monterey pines 3:507
Montezuma cypresses
illus. 4:91
Montgolfier, Joseph-Michel and Jacques-Étienne (French inventors) 6:149
Month (time period) 1:474–75, 478
Montreal Protocol (1987) 2:482
Mont St. Michel (France)
illus. 2:246
Monuments (rock formations) 2:418
Monument Valley (Arizona) 2:123
Mood disorders *see* Affective disorders
Moog, Robert (American composer) 3:218
MOON (of Earth) 1:25, **113–26**
Apollo 11 landing 1:239
calendar 1:474
eclipses 1:175–80
exploration 1:245–47, 260–61, 298–99; 6:13
gravitational force 3:177–78, 181
meteorites 1:173
motion 3:160–61
origin 2:13
space probes 1:236, 290, 298–99
tides 2:243–46
illus. 1:175
Apollo 11 landing 1:245
Apollo photograph 1:113
eclipse 1:178
gravitational attraction of Earth 3:177
planetarium exhibit 1:68
Mooneyes 4:332–33
Moon rats 5:27
Moon rocks 1:74, 123, 126, 247, 298
analytical chemistry 3:130
Moose 5:118, 122–23
Moraines 2:99, 108, 289
Moray eels 4:332
Morels 4:40, 42
illus. 4:45
Morgan, Thomas Hunt (American zoologist) 4:181
Morley, Edward W. (American physicist) 3:343
Morley, Lawrence W. (Canadian scientist) 2:42–43
Mormon Tabernacle (Salt Lake City, Utah) 1:378
Morning sickness 5:299
Morning stars 1:94, 99

Morphine 5:292, 373, 468–69
Morphology 3:372; 4:4
Morphos (butterflies) 4:304–5
illus. 4:304
Morris, Robert Jr. (American hacker) 6:394
Morse, Samuel F. B. (American inventor) 6:234–35
Morse Code
illus. 6:236
Mortar 6:24–26
Morula 3:460; 5:296
Moseley, Henry (British physicist) 3:6
MOSFET transistors 6:252–53
Mosquitoes
bats' diet 5:32
disease carriers 4:182, 268–69
encephalitis 5:425–26
malaria 4:212; 5:428
illus. 4:212
Mosquito ferns 4:79
Mosses 4:56, 58–62, 123, 163–64
reproduction 3:455
Mother-of-pearl (Nacre) 4:234–35, 241
MOTHS 4:280, 300–303, 306–7
courtship 4:196
illus.
cecropia 4:307
elephant hawkmoth 4:307
luna moth 4:300
owlet moth 4:275
yucca moth 4:169
Motility (of the intestines) 5:255
MOTION 3:149–61 *see also* Newton's laws of motion
cell structure 3:431
fluid dynamics 3:191–93
physics, history of 3:141
planets 1:78–79
relativity theory 3:342–52
solids, particles in 3:89
waves 2:250–51
Motion pictures
digital recording 6:287
holography 6:277
Internet and copyright 6:310
planetarium uses 1:72
science fiction 1:504–6
sound sources 5:277
Motion sickness 5:470
Motivation 5:344
Motmots 4:407
Motor area (of the brain) 5:229
illus. 5:231
Motor fibers *see* Efferent fibers
Motor learning 5:359
Motor neurons 3:462
Motors, Electric *see* Electric motors
Motor skills 5:365–66
Mouchot, Augustin (French inventor) 2:381
Moulton, Forest Ray (American astronomer) 2:10–11

Mountain gorillas 2:502; 5:144
  illus. 2:499; 5:143
Mountain lions *see* Cougars
Mountain passes 2:98
Mountain ranges 2:67
MOUNTAINS 2:67–74
  biomes 3:498
  climates of the world 2:210, 214
  clouds 2:161, 163
  continental drift 2:39
  deserts 4:166
  formation 2:43–44
  glaciers *see* Alpine glaciers
  island arcs' similarities 2:282
  Moon 1:122
  plate tectonics 2:42
  precipitation 2:170–71
  volcanoes 2:55–62
  water storage 2:100–101
  wind 2:186
  map(s)
    notable mountain peaks 2:71
Mountains, Submarine 2:230, 270, 274
  Arctic Ocean 2:235
  Indian Ocean 2:234
Mountain zebras 5:109
Mount St. Helens (volcano, Washington) *see* Saint Helens, Mount
Mount Wilson Catalog (star survey) 1:184
Mourning doves 4:430
Mouse (animal) *see* Mice
Mouse (computer) 6:366
  illus. 6:367
Mousebirds 4:405
Mouse lemurs 5:137
Mouth 5:216
  insects 4:272, 274
  rodents 5:39–40
Movement, Plant *see* Plants—movement
Movies *see* Motion pictures
Moxibustion 5:510
Mozambique 2:513
Mozilla (Web browser) 6:308
MP3 (online coding system) 6:310
MRI scans *see* Magnetic resonance imaging
MSG *see* Monosodium glutamate
MSN TV (formerly WebTV) 6:309, 391
Mucous membranes 5:236
  excretory system 5:260
  nose 5:216, 283
  uterus 5:294
  illus. 5:285
Mucus 5:236, 250–51
  frogs 4:348
  hagfish 4:322
  snails 4:240
Mud 2:35–36
  streams 2:423
  volcanic ash 2:62
  illus. 2:173; 3:78

Mud puppies 4:351
Mudskippers 4:335
  illus. 4:334
Mud snakes 4:371
Mud volcanoes 2:58
Mufflers 6:140
Mufli (human-powered aircraft) 6:94
Muir, John (American naturalist) 2:509
  illus. 2:508
Mule deer 5:121
  illus. 5:122
Mules 5:110
Muller, Johannes (German anatomist) 4:337
Müller, Karl Alex (Swiss physicist) 3:360; 6:221
Mullis, Kary (American scientist) 3:419
Multiple births 5:307 *see also* Twins
Multiple-personality disorder *see* Dissociative identity disorder
Multiple sclerosis 5:233, 320
Multiple use (of forests) 4:131
Multiple Use and Sustained Yield Law (U.S., 1960) 2:511
Multiplexing 6:290
Multiplicand 1:347
Multiplication 1:347–48
  algebra 1:353–54
  binary numerals 1:446, 449–50
  logarithms 1:360–61
  table(s) 1:347
Multiplier 1:347–48
Multiprocessing systems 6:373
Multispectral imaging technology 1:256
Mu-mesons *see* Muons
Mummification 3:470
  illus. 1:465; 3:468
Munsell color standard 3:302
  illus. 3:299
Muntjacs 5:119
Muons (Mu-mesons) 1:230; 3:21, 338, 346–47
Muridae 5:43–44
Musci *see* Mosses
Muscle fibers 5:186, 191, 194
  illus. 3:439
Muscles *see* Muscular system
Muscle sense *see* Kinesthesia
Muscle tone *see* Tonus
Muscular dystrophy 5:194
MUSCULAR SYSTEM 5:163–64, 172, 185–94
  aging 3:468
  animals 4:185
  babies and children 5:328
  cells 5:325
  changes with age 5:332
  exercise 5:396–97, 399–401
  heart *see* Cardiac muscle
  insects 4:275

kinesthesia 5:286
massage therapy 5:514
oxygen debt 3:438
pain 5:288–89
relaxation 5:406
chart(s) 5:192
illus. 5:166, 191; 6:332
MUSES-A (space probe) 1:298
Museums and science centers 6:322–23
Mushrooms 3:455; 4:37, 39, 44
  illus. 4:55
Music
  careers in acoustics 3:202
Musical instruments 1:462; 3:214–18; 6:4
  illus.
    lyre 6:6
    orchestra 3:210–11
    prehistoric 6:4
MUSICAL SOUNDS 3:209–18
  mathematics 1:336
Musk 5:24
  civets 5:100
  deer 5:119
  muskrats 5:44
Musk deer 5:119
Musk oxen 4:164; 5:135
Muskrats 4:154; 5:44
Mussels 4:237, 239
  illus. 4:221
Mussuranas 4:372
MUSTELIDS 5:93–98
Musth 5:106
Mutations 3:415; 5:320–21
  aging, causes of 5:334
  bacteria 3:453; 4:32
  biology, history of 3:370, 372
  cancer 3:444; 5:434–35
  De Vries, Hugo 3:401
  evolutionary biology 3:503
  genetic diseases 5:418–19
  nucleotides 3:123
  illus. 3:415
    hypothesis for cancerous cell growth 5:435
Mutualism 3:483
Myasthenia gravis 5:194
Mycelium 4:37, 41
MYCIN (database) 6:374
Mycobacteriosis 5:443
Mycobacterium 4:34
Mycology 3:372; 4:36 *see also* Fungi
Mycoplasmas 3:425; 4:28–29
Mycorrhizae 4:68, 77, 112
  fungi 4:36, 39, 42
  temperate forests 4:145
Mycoses 5:428
Myelin sheath 5:224, 229–30, 233
  Vitamin B$_{12}$ 5:386
  illus. 5:227
Mylar 1:273
Mynahs 4:486
MyoBock hand 5:503
  illus. 5:501
Myocardial disease 5:439–40

Myocardial infarctions *see* Heart attacks
Myocarditis 5:440
Myocardium 5:199
Myoelectric prostheses 5:502–3
Myofibrils 5:164, 186
Myopia *see* Nearsightedness
Myosin 4:52; 5:186
Myositis 5:194
Myotonic dystrophy 5:194
MyPyramid (food guide) 5:389
MYRIAPODS 4:248, **264–65**
Myrtle warblers 4:459
Myxomycota *see* Plasmodial slime molds
Myxozoa 4:211

N

Nabonidus (Babylonian king) 1:462
Nacre *see* Mother-of-pearl
Nacreous clouds 2:150
NADH (energy-carrier molecule) 3:435, 437–38
NAEP *see* National Assessment of educational Progress
Naiads (young insects) 4:276
Nails, Human 5:266, 333
Nail-tailed wallabies 5:18
Naked viruses 3:387
Naltrexone 5:376
Namib Desert 2:83
Naming *see* Nomenclature
Nanobacteria 4:31
Nanometer 3:21
Nanoseconds 6:377
Nanoshells 6:342
NANOTECHNOLOGY 6:22, **338–43**
Nanotubes 6:340
  Illus. 6:339, 340
Nansen bottles 2:275
  illus. 2:273
Nantucket (island, Massachusetts) 2:281
Naphthalene 3:112
Napoleon I 1:477
Napster 6:310
Narcissistic personality 5:352
Narcolepsy 5:409
Narcotics 5:292
Narcotics Anonymous 5:376
Narwhals 5:53
NASA *see* National Aeronautics and Space Administration
Nasal cavities 5:177
Nasal sprays 5:449, 474
Nashville warblers 4:459
Nasser, Lake (Egypt) 2:379
Nastic movements 4:117
Natchez (steamboat) *illus.* 6:111
National Academies 6:329
National Academy of Sciences (NAS) 2:154, 465; 5:390

National Aeronautics and Space Administration (NASA) 1:233, 303
astronauts 1:280–84
aurora research 2:158
Earth Science Enterprise 1:108–9, 259, 297
extraterrestrial life 1:317
Great Observatories Program 1:47; 3:280
guest crew members 1:285
infrared astronomy 1:62
life, extraterrestrial 3:382
science education 6:321
SP-100 project 3:321
space program plans 1:257–63
space shuttles 1:248–49, 253
space stations 1:265, 269
space suits 1:271–77, 279
X-ray astronomy 1:59
National Aerospace Plane *see* Aerospace planes
National Aquarium (Washington, D.C.) 4:470
National Assessment of Educational Progress (NAEP) 6:328
National Center for Atmospheric Research (NCAR) 2:146, 226
National Center for Complementary and Alternative Medicine 5:510
National Centers for Environmental Prediction 2:143, 202
National Commission on Mathematics and Science Teaching for the 21st Century 6:326–27
National Consortium for Specialized Schools of Mathematics, Science, and Technology 6:327
National Environmental Policy Act (U.S., 1970) 6:56
National forests 2:509, 511; 4:160
National Geographic Society 2:299
National Grasslands (U.S.) 4:143
National Hurricane Center (Miami, Florida) 2:200, 206
National Institutes of Health
complementary and alternative medicine 5:510
science libraries 6:326
National Integrated Ballistic Information Network (NIBIN) 1:516
National Library of Medicine 6:326
National Meteorological Center 2:206
National Museum of Natural History (Washington, D.C.) *illus.* 4:205

National Oceanic and Atmospheric Administration
deep-sea exploration 2:279
ocean-current study 2:242
ocean-research satellites 2:224
vocational training 2:144
weather satellites 1:314
National Ocean Service 2:248–49
tsunami warning 2:259
National parks 2:405; 4:127–28, 131
archaeology 1:466
National Parks Branch (Canada) 2:513
National Science Education Standards (NSES) 6:324
National Weather Service 2:143, 201–3, 206
tornadoes 2:190, 193–94
National Wilderness Preservation System 2:507
Nation at Risk (report, National Commission on Excellence in Education) 6:326
Native American Graves Protection and Repatriation Act (U.S., 1990) 1:467
Native Americans
archaeology 1:467
astronomy 1:198, 470–71
bison 5:132
caribou 4:164
hot springs 2:64
irrigation projects 2:436
mollusks 4:236, 238
petroleum 2:323
tidal energy plant 2:249
Native gold 6:174
Natu, W. J. H. (Dutch physiologist) 5:405
Natural bridges 2:423
NATURAL GAS 2:305, 323–24, 328, **336–45**
conservation 2:415
continental shelves 2:232
Natural immunity 5:237
Natural selection 3:502, 505–7; 5:157–58
Darwin, Charles 3:370
insects 4:273
Naturopathy 5:513–14
Nausea 5:299
acupuncture treatment 5:511
Nautile (submersible) 2:277; 6:124
Nautilus (nuclear submarine) 6:120–21
Nautiluses 4:234–35
Naval engineering 6:22
NAVIGATION 6:165–73
bird migration 4:394
geometry's use in 1:379
ocean currents 2:242
radar 6:258–59, 261
space technology 1:255
Navios (ship) 6:109

NAVSAT program (Project TRANSIT) 1:306; 6:171–72
NAVSTAR program *see* Global Positioning System
Neanderthals 5:160
Neap tides 1:117; 2:245
illus. 2:244
Near-Infrared Camera and Multi-Object Spectrometer (NICMOS) 1:49
Near-infrared radiation 1:60
NEAR-Shoemaker (Near-Earth Asteroid Rendezvous) 1:168, 236, 260, 295
Nearsightedness 5:272, 489
illus. 5:271
Near threatened species (IUCN definition) 2:498–99
Nebraska
giant hailstone 2:171
Nebular hypothesis 2:9–10
Nebulas *see also* Dark nebulas
interstellar space 1:218–20
illus. 1:21, 57, 184–86, 221
Neck
muscles of the body 5:192
Neckbones *see* Cervical vertebrae
Necropsy 3:469
Nectar 4:102
Nectaries 4:101–2
Neddermeyer, S. H. (American physicist) 1:229
Needle-exchange programs
illus. 5:375
Needlefish 4:334
Needles (leaves of conifers) 4:85
Negative electrical charges 3:245–46
Negative integers 1:350–51
Negative phototropism 4:114
Negatives (in photography) 6:271–73
Negative umbra 1:176, 178
Nematocysts 4:217, 219
Nematodes *see* Roundworms
Nematomorpha 4:201
Nemertea 4:201
Nenets (people)
illus. 2:88
Neodymium 3:40; 5:488
Neolithic Age *see* New Stone Age
Neon 3:33, 40
electric lighting 2:320
electron movement 3:19
signs 3:186
illus.
artwork of neon tubes 3:68
neon sign 3:12
spectrum of neon gas 3:327
Neoplasms 3:444
Neoteny 4:351
Neotropical Migratory Bird Conservation Act (U.S., 2000) 4:451
Neotropical squirrels 5:40

Nepal
illus. 2:213
Nephritis *see* Glomerulonephritis; Pyelonephritis
Nephrons 5:259
NEPTUNE 1:74, **151–55**
auroras 2:157
discovery 1:79; 3:182
life, possibility of 1:320–21
Pluto's discovery and 1:79
space probes 1:290–91, 293
illus. 1:148
Neptunium 3:41
Nereid (moon of Neptune) 1:155
Nerve cells (Neurons) 4:185; 5:154, 171, 224
damage 5:239
embryology 3:462
sleep-wakefulness cycle 5:405
illus. 5:227
Nerve centers *see* Ganglia
Nerve fibers 5:224
pain 5:288
skin 5:267
spinal cord 5:230–31
Nerves *see* Nervous system
NERVOUS SYSTEM 4:185; 5:172, **223–34**
babies 5:328–29
crustaceans 4:253
insects 4:274
lancelets 4:311
learning disabilities 5:364
microsurgery 5:1463
muscle activity, control of 5:189
nicotine's effect on 5:370–71
pain 5:288, 290, 292
sleep-wakefulness cycle 5:405–6
touch, sense of 5:285–86
Nests 4:197
ants 4:282
birds 4:396
bird's-nest soup 4:405
birds of prey 4:415
daddy longlegs 4:262
moles 5:25
termites 4:290
wasps 4:289
illus.
weaverbirds 4:461
Net assets 1:458
Netherlands
land reclamation 2:294
plains 2:77
water pollution 2:459, 464
illus. 2:339
Nets
fishing 6:87
insect collecting 4:271
Netscape 6:307
Net venation 4:72
Networking, Computer *see* Computer networking
Neural arches 5:176
Neural network systems 6:374
Neural tube 5:299, 386
Neurilemma 5:224

Neurobiology 3:372
Neuroglia 5:228
Neurology 5:232, 417
Neurons *see* Nerve cells
Neurophysiology 3:373
Neuroptera 4:280
Neuroses 5:341
Neurospora 4:42
Neurotransmitters 5:356
pain 5:288–89
plants 4:114
Neustonic algae 4:47
Neutral equilibrium 3:182
illus. 3:181
Neutralization 3:96
Neutrinos 1:86; 3:21, 306
Neutron activation analysis 3:320
Neutron capture 1:231
Neutron-deficient isotopes 3:318
Neutron-excess isotopes 3:318
Neutrons 2:362–64, 366; 3:7, 18, 47, 245, 305–7
atomic mass 3:20
isotopes 3:125
quarks 3:20, 313, 316
radioisotopes 3:317–18
illus. 3:312
Neutron stars 1:59, 201, 205, 209–10 *see also* Pulsars
plasma 3:13
Neutrophils 5:207, 426
Nevada
radioactive-waste depository 2:307, 371, 490
Nevado del Ruiz (volcano, Colombia) 2:58
Nevirapine 5:445
Newcomen, Thomas (English inventor) 6:97, 190
Newell, Homer E. (NASA historian) 1:233
New England warblers 3:481
Newlands, John (English chemist) 3:23
New Madrid earthquake (Missouri) 2:51
New Mexico
Carlsbad Caverns 2:131
illus. 2:130, 134, 420
New Millennium Program (NMP) (NASA) 1:263
New Orleans (Louisiana) 2:76, 104–5
Newsgroups (on the Internet) 6:306
New Stone (Neolithic) Age 6:4–5, 10, 24, 26
mathematics, history of 1:329
Newton (unit of measurement) 3:155, 162, 169

NEWTON, Sir Isaac (English scientist) **1:**431, 473; **3:146–48** see also Newton's law of universal gravitation; Newton's laws of motion
  calculus **1:**330
  color **3:**293
  corpuscular theory of light **3:**329
  light, experiments with **3:**142, 329
  light spectrum **3:**273
  mechanics, laws of **3:**324
  Newtonian universe **3:**341
  static machine **3:**250
  telescopes **1:**38
  illus. **3:**142
Newtonian focus 1:38
  illus. **1:**39
Newtonian mechanics 3:144
Newton's law of universal gravitation 1:78, 473; **2:**243–44; **3:**176–77
Newton's laws of motion 1:242, 401; **3:**141, 144, 147–48, 155–58
Newts 4:341, 351
New World monkeys 5:139–40, 146–47
New York
  acid rain **2:**472
  Finger Lakes **2:**98, 108
  Long Island shoreline **2:**289
  Love Canal pollution **2:**489
  Mason Act **2:**505
  natural gas **2:**337
  illus. **2:**68, 413, 421
New York City
  Blizzard of 1888 **2:**169
  subways **6:**128
  tidal currents **2:**247–48
  water supply **2:**442
  World Trade Center **2:**455
  World Trade Center site **6:**22
New Zealand
  archaeology **1:**467
  geothermal energy **2:**393
  geysers **2:**66
  illus. **2:**65, 392
Nextel 6:245
Next Generation Internet (NGI) 6:390–91
Next Generation Space Telescope (NGST) 1:237
Nexuses (in anatomy) **5:**187
NGC 224 (galaxy) see Great Nebula in Andromeda
NGC 4395 (galaxy) **1:**212
NGC 4565 (galaxy)
  illus. **1:**60
NGC 6521 (galaxy) **1:**212
Niacin 5:384
Niagara Falls 2:129, 422–23
  illus. **2:**102
Niagara River 2:104

NIBIN see National Integrated Ballistic Information Network
Nicaragua 2:52
Niches (in ecosystems) **2:**454; **3:**477
Nickajack Lake (exhibit, Tennessee Aquarium) **4:**476
Nickel 3:41
  atomic number **3:**20
  Earth's interior **2:**28
  electroplating **3:**103
  meteorites **1:**172
Nickel-cadmium batteries 1:306
Nicotinamide see Niacin
Nicotine 5:370–71, 376–77
  nasal sprays **5:**474
  transdermal skin patches **5:**470
Nicotinic acid see Niacin
Nielsbohrium see Bohrium
Night blindness 5:270, 383
Night-blooming cacti 4:115
Night crawlers 4:243
Nighthawks 4:403
Nightingale, Florence (English nurse) **5:**482–83
Nightjars see Goatsuckers
NIGHT SKY 1:24 36; 2:155–58
Night terrors 5:409
Night-vision goggles
  illus. **3:**273
Nikolayev, Andrian G. (Soviet cosmonaut) **1:**241
Nile crocodiles 4:437–38
  illus. **4:**382
Nile plovers 4:437–38
Nile River
  flooding **2:**105
  meanders **2:**103
  sediment **2:**419
  water supply **2:**435–36
Nilgais 5:128
Nim (game) **1:**451
Nimbostratus clouds 2:165
  illus. **2:**164
1984 (novel, Orwell) **1:**502
99s, The (women's aviation organization) **1:**288
Niño, El see El Niño
Nintendo (video game company) **6:**298–301
Niobium 3:41
Nios, Lake (Cameroon) **2:**61, 109
Nipples 5:294
Nipride see Sodium nitroprusside
Nissan (company)
  space probes **1:**298
Nitrates 2:411–12
  nitrogen cycle **3:**491
Nitric acid 2:473–74, 476; **3:**96, 99
Nitric oxide 2:154
Nitrile 3:110
Nitrogen 3:31–32, 41
  atmosphere **1:**105; **2:**149, 151–52
  atomic structure **3:**69

  auroras **2:**157
  blood **5:**221
  ceramic superconductors **6:**221
  covalence **3:**52
  cryosurgery **5:**479
  fertilizers **6:**205
  fuel gases **2:**359
  geysers on Triton **1:**155
  life, origin of **3:**380
  lightning's production of nitrates for plants **2:**179
  microbiology **3:**450
  organic compounds **3:**114–15
  plants **4:**68; **6:**75
  protein **5:**378
  transformations due to bacteria **4:**31
  illus.
    liquid nitrogen **3:**26
Nitrogen cycle 3:490–91
Nitrogen dioxide 3:69
Nitrogen engines 6:148
Nitrogen family of elements 3:31–32
Nitrogen fixation 3:491; **4:**35, 122–23; **6:**73
Nitrogen oxides 2:467, 471, 473–76; **3:**73
Nitrogen trichloride see Agene
Nitroglycerin patches 5:470
Nitro group 3:110
Nitrous oxide (Laughing gas) 2:479; **5:**465
Nixon, Richard (American president) **1:**239, 248
NMR scans see Magnetic resonance imaging
NOAA (weather satellite) **1:**314
Nobelium 3:41
Nobel Prize winners in science 6:407–17
Noble firs 4:91
Noble gases 3:28–29, 33, 48, 63, 69
Noble metals 3:27, 30
No Child Left Behind (NCLB) Act (U.S. 2001) **6:**327
Nociceptors 5:288
Noctilucent (Night-shining) clouds 2:151, 162
Nocturnal animals and plants 3:380; **5:**6
  owls **4:**418–21
  zoo exhibits **4:**474
  illus.
    animals **4:**472
Nodes (in computer networking) **6:**385
Nodes (in ocean basins) **2:**246
Nodes (of the Moon's orbit) **1:**118, 176
Nodes of Ranvier 5:224–25
Noise
  careers in acoustics **3:**202
  hearing damage **5:**277
  tornadoes **2:**191
  illus.
    damaging levels **3:**201

Noise pollution 2:451
Noise-reduction headphones
3:208
Nomads 2:86
illus. 2:212
Nomenclature
biology 3:369
chemical elements 3:3
comets 1:162–63
hurricanes 2:199
lunar features 1:122
Mercury's craters 1:98, 300–
301
wildfowl 4:423
Nomex fiber 6:229
No More War! (book, Pauling)
3:9
Noncarbonate hardness 2:447
Nonconsumptive demands on
forests 4:127, 131
Nonelectrolytes 3:101–2
Nones (Roman dates) 1:476
NON-EUCLIDEAN GEOMETRY
1:329, 401–3
Non-ionizing radiation 5:436
Nonliving environment 2:453
Nonmetals 3:25–29
halides 3:33
Nonnucleoside reverse tran-
scriptase inhibitors
(NNRTIs) 5:445
NONPERCHING BIRDS 4:400–
408
Nonrenewable resources
2:413–15
Nonsense syllables experiment
5:359–60
Nonspecific defense mecha-
nisms 5:236
Nonsteroidal anti-inflammatory
drugs (NSAIDS) 5:240,
291–92
Nonvascular plants *see* Bryo-
phytes
Nonverbal learning disabilities
5:366
Non-zero-sum game 1:429–30
Noordung, Hermann von (Austrian rocket engineer)
1:265
Noradrenaline (Norepinephrine)
5:246, 356
Norfolk island pines 4:84
Nori 4:50
Normalizing (of steel) 6:182
Normal sulfate salt 3:97
Normandie (ship) 6:114
North America
acid rain 2:474
continental islands 2:281
extinct birds 2:496
extinct mammals 1:498–99;
2:495–96
grasslands 4:140
ice ages 2:218
rain forests 4:159
North Atlantic Current 2:241–42

North Atlantic right whales *see*
Right whales
North Carolina
coast 2:292
wilderness areas 2:512
illus. 2:292
North celestial pole 1:36
Northeasterlies 2:185
Northeast trade winds 2:184
North Equatorial Current
2:240–41
Northern bobwhites 4:424
Northern Cross (constellation)
see Cygnus
Northern Crown (constellation)
see Corona Borealis
Northern Hemisphere
climates of the past 2:219
constellations 1:25–26
jet streams 2:150–51
ocean currents 2:238, 240–41
seasons 1:110–12
winds 2:182, 184–85, 188
illus. 1:24; 2:184–85
Northern lights *see* Aurora
borealis
Northern mockingbirds 4:453
Northern (Steller) sea lions 5:66
Northern spotted owls 4:421
illus. 4:421
North Pacific Current 2:241
North Pole 1:26
North Sea 2:232, 464
North Star 1:26, 112; 6:167–68
Norway
acid rain 2:473
coastal formation 2:289
fjords 2:123
hydroelectric power 2:379
Maelstrom whirlpool 2:248
salmon farming 6:90
whaling 2:413
illus. 2:289, 418
Norway rats 5:43
Norway spruces 4:91
Norwegian Current 2:241
Nose 5:177, 215–16, 283–84
human evolution 5:158
proboscis monkeys 5:141
Nosema bombycis 4:212
Nothofagus 4:159
Notochord 4:308–9
jawless fish 4:322
lancelet 4:311
Nova (TV series) 6:321
Nova Aquilae 1918 (star) 1:200
illus. 1:201
Novas (stars) 1:197–98
Nova Scotia
tidal-power plant 2:399
illus. 2:245, 248, 293
Novaya Zemlya 2:281
N-p-n bipolar transistors
6:251–52
NR-1 (submersible) 6:124
NSAIDs *see* Nonsteroidal anti-
inflammatory drugs
NSFnet 6:385

n-type semiconductor 6:232,
250, 346
Nubium, Mare (lunar feature)
1:122
Nuclear and particle physics
3:145
Nuclear changes 3:15
NUCLEAR CHEMISTRY 3:6, 9,
124–28
NUCLEAR ENERGY 2:361–76,
415; 3:15
electricity, generation of 2:312,
314
energy 2:305, 307
engineering today 6:22
history 2:374–75; 3:7
nuclear chemistry 3:125
particle accelerators 6:352–59
radioisotopes 3:317–21
stars 1:192–93
submarines 6:120–22
submersibles 6:124
Sun 1:81, 86, 89–90
Nuclear engineering 6:22
Nuclear envelope 3:428–29
Nuclear fission 2:364–65; 3:15,
128, 318–19
Nuclear fusion 2:375–76; 3:15,
128
laser fusion 6:348–49
plasma 3:354
room-temperature experiments
2:376
stars 1:197
Sun 1:74, 89
diagram(s) 2:375
Nuclear magnetic resonance
imaging *see* Magnetic
resonance imaging
Nuclear membrane 5:161
Nuclear-power plants 2:314,
368–75; 6:9
accidents 2:372–75, 455
waste disposal 2:307
illus. 2:361; 3:15; 6:13
Nuclear reactors 2:365–68, 371;
3:128
accidents 2:372–75
artificial satellites 1:306
electrical energy 2:314
Moon, future uses of 1:126
space program 3:321
illus. 2:366–69
Nuclear Security Infrastructure
Act (U.S., 2005) 2:375
Nuclear submarines 6:120–22
Nuclear wastes *see* Radioactive
wastes
Nuclear weapons 2:361, 365,
368; 3:15
nuclear chemistry 3:128
Pauling's protests against 3:9
science fiction 1:504
test explosions 2:23
Nucleic acids 3:122–23, 411
life, characteristics of 3:376
viruses 3:386, 392
Nucleoids 3:427; 4:26

Nucleoli (singular **Nucleolus**) 3:427–28, 430; 5:161
illus. 5:162
Nucleons 3:145
Nucleoside reverse transcriptase inhibitors 5:230, 445
Nucleotides 3:123
illus. 3:409
Nucleus, Atomic 3:9, 18, 47, 245, 305
cosmic rays 1:224, 228
nuclear chemistry 3:124–28
nuclear energy 2:361–65, 375–76
particle accelerator 6:354
quarks 3:312
Nucleus, Cell 3:427, 430; 4:184; 5:161
cell division 3:441–45
plants 4:14
skeletal muscle cells 5:186
illus. 5:162
Nucleus of a comet 1:159
Nuclides 3:126
Nullipores 2:283
Numbats *see* Banded anteaters
Number theory 1:329
NUMERALS 1:330, 338–45
binary numerals 1:446–52
Numerator 1:349–50
Numerically controlled (NC) machines 6:196–97
Nuptial flights (of insects) 4:282
Nursery-web spiders 4:260, 262
Nurses 5:411
NURSING 5:482–87
Nursing assistants 5:484, 486
Nutcrackers 3:170
Nuthatches 4:456–57
Nutmeg trees 4:158
Nutrias 5:44–45
Nutrient cycles (in ecosystems) 3:487–91
NutriSystem 5:394
NUTRITION 5:378–90
bacteria 4:30–31
biochemistry 3:117
cancer prevention 5:437
disease reduction 5:431
fats 3:120
food 5:378–90
lagomorphs 5:36
naturopathy 5:514
plants' life processes 4:13
plants of the wetlands 4:151
proteins 3:122
weight control 5:391–94
illus.
food guides 5:389
Nutritional anemia 5:211
Nylon 6:210, 212
space suits 1:272–74
Nymphs (young insects) 4:276

O

Oakmoss 4:60
Oaks
acorn cycle 4:147
gypsy moths 4:117–18
mycorrhizal associations 4:112
wood construction 6:28
Oars, Rowboat 6:92
Oases 2:86, 116
winds 2:426
illus. 2:114
Oats
illus. 4:105
Obelisks 6:18
Oberon (moon of Uranus) 1:150
Oberth, Hermann (Romanian scientist) 1:265
Obesity
cancer 5:436
exercise benefits 5:402
fat in diet 5:383
population 5:388
severe (morbid) 5:363
weight control 5:393
Objectives (optical lenses)
microscopes 6:331
telescopes 1:37–38
Objectivity (in experimentation) 1:2; 3:509
Obligate anaerobes 4:30
Obliquus externus abdominis
illus. 5:166
Obliquus internus abdominis
illus. 5:166
Oboes 3:216
Observation, Scientific 1:1–2
Observatories, Astronomical
astronomy, history of 1:470
electromagnetic radiation 3:280
Moon as an observing station 1:126
Observer (space probe) *see* Mars Observer
Obsessive-compulsive disorder 5:350–51
Obsidian 2:34, 134
illus. 2:134
Obstetrics 5:415
Obtuse angles 1:369–70
Occipital bone 5:176
illus. 5:175
Occipital lobe (of the brain) 5:228–29
Occluded fronts 2:188
Occultations 1:14, 119
OCEAN 2:228–35, 264–70
biomes 3:499
carbon dioxide absorption 2:478
cave formation 2:129–30
climates of the world 2:210
coasts 2:288–95
currents 2:236–42
deep-sea exploration 2:271–79
earthquakes 2:50
Earth's available water 3:488

engineering today 6:22
fossils 1:487–88
hot springs 2:64
hurricane formation 2:199
icebergs and sea ice 2:260–63
life, origin of 3:383
marine resources, conservation of 2:412–13
oceanography 1:5; 2:221–27
origin 2:14, 228
plant communities 4:137
plate tectonics 2:40–43, 45
pollution 2:464–65, 503
radioisotope studies 3:319
reefs 2:284–87
rift and ridge 2:40, 42
solar collector 2:385
springs 2:116–17
submarines and submersibles 6:117–24
tides 2:243–49
tsunamis 2:256–59
volcanoes 2:58, 69, 71
waves 2:250–55
winds 2:182–83, 188
illus.
chlorophyll 1:314
map(s)
depths 2:231
OCEAN CURRENTS 2:229–30, 236–42; 3:493
Arctic Ocean 2:235
climates of the world 2:210
coastal formation 2:289–90, 292
Indian Ocean 2:234
merchant shipping lines 6:110
physical oceanography 2:223
seawater, study of 2:275
tracking methods 3:319
Ocean Drilling Program 2:225–26, 276
Ocean Dumping Ban Act (U.S., 1988) 2:464
Ocean engineering 6:22
Ocean glitter 2:227
Oceanic crust 2:31
Oceanic islands 2:280
coral atolls 2:283
volcanic islands 2:282–83
Ocean liners 6:114
illus. 6:115
OCEANOGRAPHY 2:221–27
careers 2:225
Ocean-power plants 2:382
Ocean sunfish 4:335
Ocean Topographic Experiment *see* TOPEX/Poseidon
Ocellated turkeys 4:427
Ocelli 4:248, 274
Ocelots 2:500; 5:91
illus. 5:89
Ocotillo plants 4:168
Octadecanol 2:439
Octal numeral system 1:452
Octane 3:62, 75, 111
Octane number
illus. 3:107

Octave 3:212–13
Octet rule 3:49, 63
Octopuses 4:233
    illus. 4:231
Ocular lenses 6:331
Odd parity 3:337
Odonata 4:278
Odontoceti see Toothed whales
Odors
    allergies 5:448
    animals 4:191
    beetles 4:297
    halogens 3:33
    hydrogen sulfide 3:32
    natural gas 2:341
Odyssey (space probe) 1:297
Odyssey (video-game system)
    6:298
Oersted, Hans Christian (Danish
    physicist) 3:254, 264;
    6:235
Offeq 1 (artificial satellite) 1:313
Office of Space Science 1:233
Offset rocks 2:48–49
Offshore natural gas deposits
    drilling operations 2:341
    pipelines 2:342
    illus. 2:340–41
Offshore oil deposits 2:232, 413
    illus. 2:327–29
Ofloxacin 5:464
Ohio
    illus. 2:455
Ohio River 2:420; 3:85
Ohm (unit of measurement)
    3:256
Ohm, Georg Simon (German
    physicist) 3:256
Oil see Petroleum
Oilbirds 4:403–4
Oil glands see Sebaceous
    glands
Oils, Fish see Fish oils
Oils, Vegetable see Vegetable
    oils
Oil shale 2:324–25, 395–96
Oil spills 2:306, 465
    coral reef damage 2:287
    Indian Ocean 2:234
    tanker accidents 2:328
    illus. 2:331; 3:81; 5:98
Okapis 5:125
Okeechobee, Lake (Florida)
    2:108
Okefenokee National Wildlife
    Refuge (Georgia) 2:512
    illus. 2:511
Oklahoma
    Lake Hefner 2:439
    tornado (1948) 2:193
Old age 5:333–34 see also Aging
    air pollution 2:468
    bone injuries 5:182
    geriatrics 5:413
    osteoporosis 5:184
    pain 5:287
Old Faithful (geyser) 2:63, 65

Old Red Sandstone Continent
    2:73
Old Stone (Paleolithic) Age
    6:3–4, 10
Old World badgers 5:97
    illus. 5:96
Old World monkeys 5:140–43,
    147–48
Olericulture 4:172–73
Olfactory cells 5:283
    illus. 5:285
Olfactory nerve 5:283–84
Oligocene epoch
    butterflies and moths 4:301
    table(s) 2:20
Oligochaeta 4:202, 242–44
Oligotrophic lakes 3:499
Olive baboons 5:142
Olivine 2:28, 34
Olms 4:351
Olympus Mons (Martian moun-
    tain) 1:130
Omar Khayyám (Persian poet
    and mathematician) 1:391
Omega Navigation System
    6:171
Omega particles
    illus. 3:312
Ommatidia 4:252
Omnimax projectors 1:72
Omnivores 3:486
Onagers 5:110
Oncillas 5:92
Oncogenes 5:434
Oncology 5:413, 485–86
Online services 6:306
Ontario
    illus. 2:102
On the Origin of Species (book,
    Darwin) 3:370, 502, 504
Onychophora 4:203
Oort, Jan Hendrik (Dutch
    astronomer) 1:159
Oort cloud 1:76
Ooze, Oceanic 2:270, 273;
    4:211–12
Opalina 4:213
Open clusters see Galactic clus-
    ters
Open fractures see Compound
    fractures
Open hearth furnaces 6:178–79,
    183–84
    illus. 6:180
Open-pit mining see Strip mining
Open Systems Interconnection
    (OSI) 6:388–89
    illus. 6:387
Operant conditioning 5:338,
    357, 359
    illus. 5:341
Operating systems (of comput-
    ers) 6:372
Operation Site Down 6:310
Operculum 4:61, 315, 325,
    329–30
Ophelia (shepherding moon of
    Uranus) 1:150

Ophioglossum see Adder's-
    tongue ferns
Ophiuchus (constellation) 1:29
Ophiuroidea 4:223–24
Ophthalmologists 5:270
Opiates 5:373–74
Opik, E. (Estonian astronomer)
    1:165
Opium 5:373
Opossums 5:10, 19, 22
Oppenheimer, J. Robert (Ameri-
    can physicist) 1:204, 206
Oppolzer, Theodor (Austrian
    astronomer) 1:179
Opportunistic infections 5:239,
    241, 441, 443
Opportunity (planetary rover)
    1:131, 297; 3:382
Opposable feet 4:358
Opposite leaves 4:73
Opthalmology 5:416
Opthalmoscopes
    illus. 5:269
Optical fibers see Fiber optics
Optical illusions 3:292
Optical instruments 3:288.
    microscopes 6:330–37
    telescopes 1:37–42, 44
Optical microscopes 6:330–34
Optical switches 6:371
Optic disk (of the eye) 5:271
Opticians 5:270
Opticks (book, Newton) 3:148
Optic nerve 5:270
OPTICS 3:144, 282–92 see also
    Light
    fiber optics 6:222–25
    holography 6:275–77
    microscopes 6:330–37
    photography 6:262–74
    resolving power of telescopes
        1:44, 52
Optometrists 5:270
Orange trees
    illus. 4:19
Orangutans 2:502; 5:144–46
Orbitals, Atomic and molecular
    3:19, 332
Orbiters (of space shuttles)
    1:249, 252
Orbiting Solar Observatory
    illus. 1:89
Orbits (in astronomy) 1:78–79
    comet 1:76, 162–64
    Earth 1:110–12; 2:220
    gravitation 3:177, 182
    Mercury 1:96–97
    Moon 1:118
    motion, laws of 3:160–61
    Pluto 1:157
    satellites, artificial 1:303–5
    Uranus 1:147
Orb weavers (spiders) 4:261
Orcas see Killer whales
Orchestra
    illus.
        arrangement of instruments
        3:210–11

Orchids 2:497; 4:105, 158
Orders (in biological classification) 3:396
Ordinates 1:392–93
Ordovician period
  fossils 1:487–88
  chart(s) 1:486
  table(s) 2:18–19
Oregon
  Crater Lake 2:108
  fungal mats 4:37
  illus. 2:106
Oregon Coast Aquarium (Newport, Oregon) 4:473
Ores 2:136; 6:175–77
  copper ores 6:182
  lead ores 6:183
  zinc ores 6:184
Organelles 3:427; 4:207; 5:162
  illus. 3:425
Organic acids 3:114
ORGANIC CHEMISTRY 3:4, 7, 106–15
  life 3:375–76, 381–83
Organization for Economic Co-operation and Development (OECD) 6:329
Organ of Corti 5:275
Organogenesis 3:461–62
Organotrophic bacteria 4:30, 35
Organ-pipe corals 4:219
Organs (musical instruments) 3:215–16
Organs (of the body) 4:185; 5:171–72
  damage and healing 5:239
  embryology 3:461–62
  life, characteristics of 3:376
ORGAN TRANSPLANTS 5:479, 496–99
  drug delivery technology 5:473
  genetic engineering 3:421
  heart 5:440
  immune system 5:241
  zoological research 4:182
Oribis 5:131
Orioles 4:460–61
  illus. 4:185, 459
Orion (constellation) 1:32
  Great Nebula in Orion 1:218–20
  illus. 1:221; 2:12
Orlistat 5:393
Ornamental horticulture 4:174
Ornithischians 1:493, 495–96
ORNITHOLOGY 3:373; 4:385–89
  see also Birds
  illus. 4:397
Ornithopods 1:495
Ornithopters 6:152
Orogeny 2:68–74
Orographic clouds 2:163
Orographic rainfall 2:171
Oroville Dam (California) 6:53, 56
Orreries 1:66
Orthodontists 5:281
Orthopedics 5:415, 480, 501–4

Orthoptera 4:279
Orthorhombic crystals 3:90
Orwell, George (English writer) 1:502
Oryx 4:477; 5:129–30
Oscillation, Period of (of tides) 2:245–46
Oscillatoria 4:33
  illus. 4:30
Oscillators 6:248–49, 289–90
Oscilloscopes 6:250
  illus. 3:250
Oscines see Songbirds
Osculum 4:215
Osmium 3:41
Osmosis 2:449; 3:80; 4:66–67
Osmotic pressure 3:80
OSO see Orbiting Solar Observatory
Ospreys 2:502; 4:415, 418
Osseointegration 5:509
Ossicles 4:221; 5:274–75
Osteichthyes see Bony fish
Osteoarthritis 5:183, 427–28
Osteomalacia 5:184, 384
Osteomyelitis 5:182, 184
Osteopenia 5:184
Osteophytes see Spurs
Osteoporosis 5:182, 184, 453–54
Osteosclerosis 5:184
Ostracoderms 4:316
Ostriches 4:396, 398, 410–11
  illus. 4:392, 398
Ostrich ferns 4:83
Otolaryngology 5:416
Otosclerosis 5:500–9
Otter civets 5:101
Otters 5:98
  illus. 2:452
Otto, Nikolaus (German engineer) 6:99
Otto Bock hand see MyoBock hand
Ouachita Mountains 2:74
Oughtred, William (English mathematician) 1:330
Outer planets 1:74, 292–93; 2:13
Outlet streams 2:101
Outpatient surgery 5:480–81
Output (in data processing) 6:365, 367–68
Ova see Eggs
Oval window (in the ear) 5:275–76
Ovaries (female sex organs) 5:247, 294, 306
  cancer 5:402
  flowering plants 3:455
  illus. 5:295
Ovaries (of plants) 4:100–101, 103–4
Ovate leaves 4:73
Ovenbirds 4:448
Overbank stage (of streams) 2:420
Overdose (of drugs) 5:374

Overeaters Anonymous 5:393
Overgrazing 2:214, 404, 456; 4:143
Overtones 3:207
Ovipositors 4:274, 276, 285–86
Ovulation 5:294
Ovules 3:463; 4:87–88, 103
Owen, Sir Richard (British scientist) 1:493
Owens Fall Dam (Uganda) 6:56
Owens River Valley 2:5–7
  illus. 2:4
Owl butterflies 4:306
Owlet moths 4:272, 307
  illus. 4:275
Owlet nightjars 4:404
Owls 4:399, 415, 418–21
  life span 5:324
  senses 4:395
  illus. 4:386
    eating lizard 3:487
    elf owl 4:420
    hunting rodent 4:414
    northern spotted owl 4:421
    saw-whet owls 4:420
Owston's palm civets 5:101
Oxbow lakes 2:104, 110, 422
OXEN 5:134–35
Oxidation
  electrochemistry 3:100–101
  electron transport 3:437–38
  food spoilage 6:77
  life, origin of 3:383
  metals 3:27
OXIDATION-REDUCTION REACTION 3:100–101, 102
  corrosion 3:103
Oxides
  alkaline-earth metals 3:30
  boron family 3:31
  copper oxides 6:182
  minerals 2:138
Oxidizing agents 3:100
Oxygen 3:32, 41 see also Oxidation
  algal photosynthesis 4:53
  atmosphere 1:105, 319; 2:148–49, 151
  atomic structure 3:47, 69
  auroras 2:157
  bond energy 3:58
  circulatory system 5:196, 200, 203
  corrosion 3:103
  covalence 3:51–52
  diatomic molecules 3:53
  Earth's crust 2:138
  exercise 5:397, 400–401
  freezing point 3:88
  geologic thermometers 2:217
  high-altitude aviation 1:271–72
  laboratory preparation 3:137
  lakes 2:111
  lasers in manufacturing 6:347
  life, origin of 3:380, 383
  Mars 1:131
  meteorites 1:172

Oxygen (cont.)
  molar mass **3:**56
  nonmetals **3:**27
  photosynthesis **4:**10, 12, 16, 19, 24, 28, 145
  plant respiration **4:**13
  respiratory system **4:**185; **5:**215, 218–21
  wastes, purification of **2:**487
  water molecule **3:**51–52, 82–83
  water solution **3:**84
  illus.
    laboratory preparation **3:**136
Oxygen cycle 3:490
Oxygen debt 3:438; **5:**400–401
Oxygen family of elements 3:32
Oxygenic photosynthesis 4:28
Oxygen (LD) process 6:179
Oxyhemoglobin 5:206
Oxytocin 5:243
Oyans *see* African linsangs
Oyashio Current 2:241
Oysters 2:291; **4:**234, 236, 238
Ozone 2:149–50, 469; **4:**12, 19
  air pollution **2:**154, 471
  molecule **3:**65
Ozone layer 2:92, 149, 153–54
  chlorofluorocarbons **6:**208
  climate change **2:**481–82
  environmental pollution **2:**453; **3:**73
  geomagnetic storms **2:**158
  photosynthesis **4:**28
  skin cancer **5:**436
  studies **1:**108–9

P

Pacas 5:45
Pacemaker (of the heart) **5:**164, 187, 200
Pacemakers (electric devices) **5:**440, 492, 505
  illus. **1:**255
Pacific moles 5:24
Pacific Ocean 2:229
  average depth **2:**271
  climate analysis **2:**217
  coral reefs **2:**283
  currents **2:**188, 237, 239–41
  earthquakes **2:**47
  hurricanes and typhoons **2:**196, 199
  ocean basin **2:**270
  ocean-floor dynamics **2:**270
  tides **2:**246
  tsunamis **2:**256
  volcanic islands **2:**282–83
  volcanoes **2:**59, 275
  map(s) **2:**267
Pacific silver firs 4:91
Pacific Tsunami Warning Center 2:259
Pacinian capsules 5:286
Pacioli, Luca (Italian mathematician) **1:**455–56

Packaging, Food 2:333; **6:**85
  plastics **6:**211
Packet switching 6:305, 385–86
  diagram(s) **6:**306
Pack ice *see* Icebergs and sea ice
Paddle controllers (of video games) **6:**300
Paddlefish 4:331
Paddle wheels 6:110
Page, Robert M. (American physicist) **6:**255
Pagers 6:244
Pagodas 6:29
Pahoehoe 2:61
PAIN 5:287–92
  acupuncture treatment **5:**511
  cancer pain relief **5:**469–71
  chiropractic treatment **5:**512
  touch **5:**285–86
  illus.
    rating scales **5:**291
Pain-management centers 5:292
Painted buntings
  illus. **4:**457
Painter, Theophilus (American zoologist) **4:**181
Painters (cats) *see* Cougars
Paints
  allergies **5:**448
  color mixing **3:**299
  corrosion prevention **3:**103
Pair-production theory of cosmic-ray showers 1:228
  illus. **1:**229
Pakistan
  Tarbela Dam **6:**56
Palate 5:177
Paleoanthropology 1:481
Paleobiogeography 1:483
Paleobiology 1:481–82
Paleobotany 1:480–81; **3:**372; **4:**7
Paleocene epoch
  table(s) **2:**20
Paleoclimatology *see* Climates of the past
Paleoecology 1:482–83
Paleoethnobotany 1:480
Paleogeography 1:483
Paleolithic Age *see* Old Stone Age
Paleomagnetism 1:483; **2:**39, 42–43
Paleomastodon **5:**103
PALEONTOLOGY 1:479–83; **2:**4
  see also Fossils
  fossils **1:**484–89
  herpetology **4:**337
Paleozoic era 1:487–88; **2:**19, 21
  table(s) **1:**486; **2:**18–21
Paleozoology 3:373
Palisade parenchyma 4:70
Palisades (bluffs, New Jersey) **2:**33
Palisades (cave formations) **2:**128
Palladium 3:41–42

Pallas (asteroid) **1:**168
Pallas' cats 5:92
Palma (extinct volcano, Canary Islands) **2:**60
Palmate leaves 4:72
Palmate lobed leaves 4:73
Palmately compound leaves 4:73
Palm civets 5:101
  illus. **5:**100
Palmer, Daniel David (American chiropractor) **5:**512
Palm trees 2:119
  illus. **4:**102
Palomar Observatory (California) **1:**41
Palos Verde blue butterflies
  illus. **4:**304
Paloverde trees 4:168
Palps 4:274
Palynology 1:480
Pamaquine 5:464–65
Pamir Plateau (Asia) **2:**80
Pampas 2:75, 78; **4:**140
  illus. **2:**76
Pampas cats 5:92
Pampas deer 5:122
Pan (sea ice fragments) **2:**262
Panama Canal 6:46
Pancake ice 2:262
Pancake turtles 4:378
Pancreas 5:244–46, 252
  alcohol's effect on **5:**375
  babies **5:**326
  transplants **5:**499
  illus. **5:**167–68, 170, 249
Pancreatic juice 5:252
Pancreozymin 5:252
Pandaka pygmaea **4:**320
Pandas 2:513; **5:**75–76
  illus. **2:**494; **4:**470; **5:**69
Pangaea 2:70, 73–74
  map(s) **2:**40
Pangolins 5:11–12
Panic disorder 5:350
Panpipes
  illus. **3:**209
Pantheon (Rome, Italy) **6:**26, 33
Panthers 5:88
  illus. **2:**498
Pantothenic acid 5:385
Pantotheres 1:498; **5:**5
Paper 1:515
Paper chromatography 3:130–31
Paper industry
  conifers **4:**86
  pollution from mills **2:**462, 470
  rain-forest products **4:**159
Paper nautiluses 4:235
Papilloma viruses 3:388
Papin, Denis (French inventor) **6:**96–97
Papua New Guinea
  earthquakes and tsunamis **2:**52, 256
Parabolas 1:378–79
  illus. **1:**397

Parabolic dish antennas 6:294
Parabolic mirrors 1:38
Paracelsus (Swiss physician)
  3:3; 5:462
Paracrystals see Liquid crystals
Paraguay
  Itaipu Dam 2:380; 6:56
  illus. 2:379
Parakeets 2:496; 4:197
Parallax 1:191
Parallel electric circuits 3:259
  illus. 3:258
Parallelograms 1:374
  illus. 1:373
Parallel rulers 1:374
Parallel venation 4:72–73
Paralysis 5:230, 234
Paramagnetic substances 3:263
Paramecium 3:428, 454; 4:213
  illus. 4:213
Parameters (in programming)
  6:196
Paranal Observatory (Chile)
  1:37
Paranoia 5:349, 373
Parapsychology 5:347
Parasites
  bacteria 4:30–31
  infectious diseases 5:428, 431
  microbiology 3:451
  populations and communities
    3:482–83
  protists 4:51
  protozoans 4:207–9
  viruses 3:379, 390–93
  water pollution 2:450
  illus. 3:447
Parasitic animals
  ants 4:284
  cowbirds 4:396, 460
  cuckoos 4:402
  flatworms 4:225–28
  jawless fish 4:321–22
  leeches 4:244
  roundworms 4:228–30
  ticks 4:259
Parasitic fungi 4:37–39, 42, 45
Parasitic plants 3:485; 4:112
Parasol (Leaf-cutter) ants
  4:284–85
  illus. 4:284
Parasympathetic nervous system 5:232
Parathyroid gland 5:247
  illus. 5:170
Parazynski, Scott (American
  astronaut)
  illus. 1:250
Parchment worms 4:245
Parenchyma cells 4:65–66,
  68–70
Paricutín (volcano, Mexico) 2:57,
  62
  illus. 2:61
Parietal bones 5:176
  illus. 5:174
Parietal lobe (of the brain)
  5:228–29

Paris (France)
  illus. 2:435
PARITY (in physics) 3:306, 310,
  335–38
Parkes radio telescope (New
  South Wales, Australia)
  1:324
Parkinson's disease 5:233, 334,
  354, 499
Parrots 4:401, 482, 486
  illus. 4:401, 484
Parsons, Charles A. (English
  inventor) 6:103
Parthenon (Athens, Greece) 6:33
Partial zona drilling (fertility
  technique) 5:306
PARTICLE ACCELERATORS
  1:231; 3:143–44; 6:352–59
  particle speeds 3:348
  radioisotopes 3:318
  superconductivity 3:357
  illus. 3:305, 314
PARTICLE DETECTORS
  6:359–60
PARTICLES, Elementary 2:362,
  364–65; 3:20, 304–11
  auroras 2:155–58
  black hole 1:212
  cosmic rays 1:226–29
  parity 3:335–38
  particle accelerators and detec-
    tors 6:352–60
  quarks 3:144, 312–16
  solids 3:12
  Sun 1:86, 88–89
  wave mechanics 3:279
  tablo(s) 3:315
Particulate matter (air pollutant)
  2:358, 467, 469–71; 3:73
Particulate radiation 5:435
Partridge 4:423
Pascal (computer language)
  6:378
Pascal, Blaise (French mathematician) 1:415
Pascal's law 3:186
Passenger pigeons 2:496;
  4:428, 431
Passenger ships 6:114
  illus. 6:115
Passeriformes see Perching
  birds
Passive-aggressive personality
  5:353
Passive immunity 5:238
Passive smoking 5:374, 437
Passwords, Computer 6:396
Pasteur, Louis (French biochem-
  ist) 4:25; 5:412, 424
  microbiology 3:447
  spontaneous generation 3:369–
    70, 375
  illus. 3:368; 5:411
Pasteurization 3:447; 6:79–80
Patagium 5:8
Patagonian cavies 5:45
Patagonian desert 2:83
  illus. 2:82

Patches, Transdermal see trans-
  dermal skin patches
Patch-nosed snakes 4:371
Patella 5:181
  illus. 5:165, 174–75, 180
Patellar reflex see Knee jerk
Pathfinder (space probe) see
  Mars Pathfinder
Pathogens 4:34; 5:427, 442
Pathology 3:469; 4:4–5; 5:417
Patina
  illus. 3:100
Pattern-recognition systems
  6:201, 374
Pauli, Wolfgang (Austrian physi-
  cist) 3:333
  illus. 3:323
Pauli exclusion principle see
  Exclusion principle
Pauling, Linus (American chem-
  ist) 3:6, 9, 117
Pauropoda 4:204
Pavlov, Ivan (Russian physiolo-
  gist) 5:338, 357, 359
Payloads (of rockets) 1:303
Payload specialists 1:249, 253
Pay-per-view television 6:295
PCBs see Polychlorinated biphe-
  nyls
P-channel JFET transistors
  illus. 6:252
PCM see Pulse code modulation
PCP (Phencyclidine) 5:372, 374
PCR see Polymerase chain reac-
  tion
PCS see Personal communica-
  tions services
PCTVs 6:309
PDAs (Personal digital assis-
  tants) 6:309
  illus. 6:370
Peaches
  illus. 4:103
Peacocks 4:195, 423
  illus. 4:422
Pearl River (China) 2:328, 465
Pearls 4:234–35
Pearly nautiluses see Cham-
  bered nautiluses
Pears
  illus. 4:103
Peary, Robert (American
  explorer) 1:171
Peas 6:68
  illus. 4:103
Peat 2:347; 4:62, 153, 155, 163
  illus. 2:348
Peat moss 4:61–62, 137, 153,
  163, 165
Peaucellier's Cell 1:376
  illus. 1:377
Pebrine 4:212
Peccaries 5:115
  illus. 5:12
Pectoralis major 5:190
  illus. 5:166
Pectoralis minor
  illus. 5:166

Pediatrics 5:413, 485
Pediments (eroded mountains) 2:84
Pedipalps 4:248, 257
Pegasus (constellation) 1:30
Pegmatite 2:34
Pei, I. M. (American architect) 6:41
Pekans see Fishers
Pelage 5:6
Pelagic sealing 5:68
Pelagic zone 3:499
Pelecaniformes 4:398, 433
Pelée, Mount (volcano, West Indies) 2:58, 61
Pelican Island Wilderness (Florida) 2:511
Pelicans 2:503; 4:446
  illus. 4:445
Pellagra 5:384
Pelton waterwheels see Impulse turbines
Pelvis 5:3, 181
  muscles of the body 5:192
  illus. 5:165
Pemoline (Cylert) 5:368
Pendentives
  illus. 6:35
Pendulums
  energy, law of conservation of 3:164–66
  Foucault pendulum 1:109–10
  measurement of g 3:180
  periodic motion 3:161
  illus. 3:161, 165, 178
Peneplains 2:71, 76, 425
Penguins 2:92, 503; 4:396, 398, 413
  illus. 4:197
Penicillin 4:38, 43; 5:431, 463; 6:9
  microbiology 3:447
  strep infection treatment 5:429
  illus. 4:33
Penicillium 3:455; 4:38, 43–44
Penis 3:457; 5:293–95
Pennsylvania
  Donora air pollution 2:468
  natural gas 2:337–38
  petroleum industry 2:323
  Three Mile Island accident 2:373
Pennsylvanian period 2:21
  Alleghenian Orogeny 2:74
  coal 2:347
  fossils 1:488
  table(s) 2:20–21
Penstocks 2:377
Pentamidine 5:445
Pentaquarks 3:311, 316
Pentastomida 4:204
Penteconters 6:107–8
Penumbra 1:175–78
Penzias, Arno (American scientist) 1:20
People-moving systems 6:128
Pep pills see Stimulant drugs
Peptic ulcers see Ulcers, Peptic

Peptide linkage 3:122
Peptidoglycan 3:426, 448; 4:26
Percentiles 1:411
Perception 5:334, 339, 364–65
  color 3:301–3
  illus. 5:344–45
Perch (fish)
  diagram(s) 4:316–17
  illus. 4:330, 335
Perched water table 2:115–16
  illus. 2:115
PERCHING BIRDS 4:397, 399, 447–63
  feet 4:395
  populations 4:451
Percussion instruments 3:216–17
Père David's deer 5:121
Peregrine falcons 2:502; 4:419
Perennials (plants) 4:10, 107, 136, 167
Perfect cosmological principle 1:21
Perfect flowers 4:101
Perfumes
  illus. 3:115
Pericardial disease 5:440
Pericardium 5:199–200
Pericycle 4:67, 69
Perigee 1:304
Perigynous flowers 4:101–2
Perihelion
  comets 1:164
  Earth 1:110
  Mercury 3:351
Perilymph 5:275
Period (in physics) 3:161, 195
Periodic motion 3:161
Periodic springs 2:117
PERIODIC TABLE 3:4, 19–20, 22–25
  elements, families of 3:26–33
  quantum theory 3:332–34
  illus. 3:22–25, 28–29
Periodontal diseases 5:280–81
Periodontal membrane 5:278
Periodontitis see Pyorrhea
Periods (in astronomy) 1:164–65
Periods (in geology) 2:20
Periods (of elements on the periodic table) 3:24–25
Periods (of ocean waves) 2:251–53
Periods, Menstrual see Menstruation
Peripheral nervous system 5:231–32
Periscopes 3:288
Perissodactyla 5:13
  horse family 5:107–10
  rhinoceroses 5:111–13
Peristalsis 5:252
Peritoncum 5:250–51
Peritrichida 4:213
Periwinkles (mollusks) 4:240
Perkin, William Henry (English chemist) 6:204

Perlman, Steve (American botanist) 4:2
Permafrost 2:89, 412; 4:135, 162, 164
Permanent magnets 3:265
Permanent teeth 5:279–80
Permeable rock 2:114
Permian period 1:488; 2:21; 4:94
  chart(s) 1:486
  map(s) 2:40
  table(s) 2:20–21
Permit (nuclear submarine)
  illus. 6:122
Pernicious anemia 5:211, 386
Perseids (meteor showers) 1:30, 161
Perseus (constellation) 1:30
Persian asses see Onagers
Persian Empire
  petroleum 2:322
Persian Gulf 2:234
  oil spills 2:465
  water temperature 2:229
Persian Gulf War (1991)
  oil spills 2:465
  telemedicine 5:493
  illus. 2:334
Personal area network (PAN) 6:245
Personal communications services (PCS) 6:243–44
Personal computers (Microcomputers) 6:362–63, 371
  artificial arm 5:503
  computer networking 6:386, 388
  computer security 6:397
  Internet 6:306, 309
  video games 6:299
  illus. 6:361
Personal digital assistants see PDAs
Personality 5:342–43
  drug addiction 5:370
Personality disorders 5:352–53
Perspective (in art) 1:336
  illus. 1:335
Perspiration 5:164
  body temperature control 5:267
  content of 5:261–62
  evaporation 3:76
  exercise 5:399
  mammals 5:4
  sleep 5:408
  sweat glands 5:265
Peru
  anchovy fishing 6:89
  earthquakes 2:52
  ocean upwelling 2:237
Peru Current 2:239
Pervasive Development Disorders (PDDs) see Autism Spectrum Disorders

Pesticides **2:**410, 452; **4:**131, 269; **6:**62 *see also* Herbicides; Insecticides
  biological magnification **3:**489
  Carson, Rachel **3:**472
Pests and pest control *see also* Herbicides; Insecticides; Pesticides
  agronomy **4:**175
  ants **4:**284
  beetles **4:**291, 294, 298–99
  caterpillars **4:**305, 307
  crustaceans **4:**251, 254–55
  entomology **4:**267–70
  forestry **4:**131
  rusts and smuts **4:**45
  temperate forests **4:**147–48
PET *see* Polyethylene terephthalate
PET (Positron emission tomography) 5:361, 456–59
  illus. **5:**351, 456
Petals 4:101, 103
Petechiae 5:212
Peterson, Roger Tory (American ornithologist) **4:**388
Petioles 4:71, 79
Petrels 2:503; **4:**446
Petri dishes
  illus. **3:**446, 515
Petrification *see* Mineralization
Petrified wood 1:485
Petrochemicals 2:334, 452; **6:**208
PETROLEUM 2:305, **322–35**
  algae **4:**53
  Arctic **2:**90, 307
  conservation **2:**415
  continental shelves **2:**232, 268
  Earth's supply **2:**335
  environmental pollution **2:**455
  fossils **1:**485
  high-sulfur fuel **2:**473
  Indian Ocean **2:**234
  oil spills *see* Oil spills
  organic chemistry **3:**108
  organic compounds **3:**7
  petrochemicals **6:**208
  plastics converted into **5:**492
  plate tectonics **2:**45
  refining *see* Refining of petroleum
  stratigraphy **2:**4
  taiga **4:**165
  tankers **6:**113
  water pollution **2:**306
  illus.
    derricks **2:**328–29
    drilling **2:**306
Petroleum coke 2:334
Petrology 2:3
PETS 4:480–90 *see also* Cats, Domestic; Dogs, Domestic
  veterinary science **4:**466–68
Petterman Glacier (Greenland) **2:**260–61
Petuntse 6:217
Pewees 4:449

Pewter 6:175
pH 3:97–98; **5:**258–59
  illus. **2:**473; **3:**97
Phages *see* Bacteriophages
Phagocytes 5:214, 236
Phagocytosis 5:237
Phalanges 5:180, 182
  illus. **5:**165, 174, 178–81
Phalaropes 4:438
Phanerites 2:134
Phantom-limb pain 5:289
Pharaoh ants 4:284
Pharmacy *see* Drugs
Pharynx 5:177, 216, 249
  illus. **5:**167–68, 216
Phase (in electricity) **2:**311–12
Phase-change materials 3:230
Phase changes *see* Changes of state
Phase-contrast microscopes 3:450; **6:**332
Phases of the Moon 1:115–16
  illus. **1:**114, 177
Phasmida 4:279
Pheasants 4:195, 422–25
  illus. **4:**424
Phencyclidine *see* PCP
Phenobarbital 5:356, 466
Phenol-formaldehyde
  illus. **6:**210
Phenolic resins 6:212
Phenotypes 3:408; **5:**316
  evolutionary biology **3:**504, 506
Phentermine 5:393
Phenylalanine 3:122
Phenyl group 3:110
Phenylketonuria 5:420
Pheochromocytoma 5:246
Pheromones 4:191, 196, 283
  pest control **4:**269–70
  reproduction **3:**457
  illus.
    traps **4:**271
Philippines
  coral reefs **2:**207
  illus. **2:**433
Philippine sambars 5:121
Philosopher's stone (mythical substance) **3:**3
Philosophy 1:3
Phiomia **5:**103
Phloem 4:12, 65–67, 69, 89, 99
  leaves **4:**70–71
Phobias 5:350
Phobos (moon of Mars) **1:**75, 132
  illus. **1:**128
Phobos (space probe) **1:**297
Phoebe (moon of Saturn) **1:**146
Phoebes (birds) **4:**449
Phoenicians
  navigation **6:**167
Phoenix Project (radio scan of space) *see* Project Phoenix
Phonographs 6:278–79
  illus.
    stereo cartridge **6:**279
Phoronida 4:202

Phosphates
  conservation **2:**414
  polyatomic ions **3:**67
  water pollution **2:**411–12, 461
Phosphene 3:66
Phosphocreatine 5:188
Phospholipids 3:436–37; **5:**473
Phosphorescence 3:296; **4:**151
Phosphorus 3:31–32, 42
  fertilizers **6:**205
  meteorites **1:**172
  nutrient cycles **3:**491
  nutrition **5:**387
  radioisotope tracers **3:**320
  water pollution **2:**461–62; **4:**155
Phosphorus cycle 2:414
Photoautotrophs 4:31, 33
Photochemical smog 2:467–68
Photochemistry 3:8
Photoconductive materials 6:233
Photodynamic therapy 5:437
Photoelectric cells 2:310–11
Photoelectric effect 2:385–86; **3:**142, 326, 340
  light energy **3:**283
Photoemissive cells *see* Phototubes
Photographic film *see* Film, Photographic
PHOTOGRAPHY
  asteroids, discovery of **1:**168
  diagnostic imaging **5:**451–52
  forensic science **1:**511
  holography **6:**275–77
  ultraviolet radiation **3:**275
  illus. **1:**509; **3:**95
Photolysis 4:24
Photonic computers 6:225
Photonic crystals 6:225
Photonics 6:224–25
  illus.
    circuits **6:**341
Photons 1:207–8; **3:**21, 306–7, 311
  communication **1:**320
  cosmic rays **1:**229
  electron jump **3:**19, 278
  photoelectric effect **3:**142
  stimulated emission **6:**344
  illus.
    electron jump **3:**276
Photoperiodism 4:115–16
Photosphere 1:82–83, 86
Photospheric granulation 1:83
PHOTOSYNTHESIS 4:9–10, 13, **16–24,** 99, 106
  algae **2:**285; **4:**46, 49, 53
  bacteria **4:**31, 33
  biology, history of **3:**369
  carbon dioxide **2:**148–49, 478
  carnivorous plants **4:**108
  cell dynamics **3:**433–34
  cell structure **3:**427, 431
  chemical reactions **3:**59
  early life **4:**28
  energy transformation **3:**376

PHOTOSYNTHESIS (cont.)
leaves 4:71
nutrient cycles 3:488, 490
plant evolution 4:11–12
trees 4:145
whisk ferns 4:82
Photosystems 4:22–23
Phototracking see Solar tracking
Phototronic cells see Photovoltaic cells
Phototropism 4:114
Phototubes 6:250
Photovoltaic cells (Solar cells) 1:306, 309
heat transfer 3:239
solar power 2:385–89
Phreatophytes 2:119
Phrenology 5:336
Phycobilins 4:18, 50
Phycocyanin 4:33
Phycoerythrin 4:33
Phycology 3:372
Phyla (singular Phylum) 3:399
Phyllite 2:37
Physical changes
illus.
cold, effects of 3:139
Physical chemistry 3:4–8, 145
Physical dependence (on drugs) 5:370
Physical geography 2:300–301
Physical map (of the genome) 5:321
Physical oceanography 2:223
Physical science education 6:325
Physical therapy 5:234, 486, 501
PHYSICIANS 5:410–17, 487
Physicians' assistants 5:411
PHYSICS 1:6; 3:140–45
atoms 3:16–21
changes of state 3:226–31
electricity 3:244–60
electromagnetic spectrum 3:272–81
elementary particles 3:304–11
entropy 3:240–43
geophysics 2:5
lasers 6:344–51
magnetism 3:261–71
mathematics 1:336
motion 3:149–61
Nobel Prize winners 6:407–17
nuclear energy 2:361–76
parity 3:335–38
particle accelerators and detectors 6:352–60
periodic table 3:22–25
quantum theory 3:322–34
radioisotopes 3:317–21
relativity theory 3:342–52
simple machines 3:168–75
space physics 1:234
superconductors 3:353–63
table(s)
constants of measurement 6:409

Physiological psychology 5:338–39, 345–46
Physiology 3:366; 4:179
aging 5:333–34
animals 3:373
blood and lymphatic system 5:205–14
brain and nervous system 5:223–34
digestive system 5:248–56
endocrine system 5:242–47
excretory system 5:257–62
exercise and fitness 5:395–404
growth and development 5:323–34
hearing 5:274–77
heart and circulatory system 5:195–204
human reproduction and birth 5:293–307
immune system 5:235–41
insect 4:274–76
muscular system 5:185–94
Nobel Prize winners 6:407–17
pain 5:288–89
plant physiology 3:372; 4:4–5
respiratory system 5:215–22
skin 5:263–67
sleep 5:405–9
smell, taste, and touch 5:283–86
vision 5:268–73
illus.
growth and development 5:331
Phytochrome 4:116–17
Phytogeography 2:300
Phytoplankton see Plankton
Pi (p) 1:375
Piaget, Jean (Swiss psychologist) 5:342
illus. 5:343
Pia mater 5:231
Pianos 3:214–15
Piazzi, Giuseppe (Italian astronomer) 1:75, 167–68
Piccard, Auguste (Swiss scientist and inventor) 2:276; 6:123
Piccard, Bertrand (Swiss balloonist) 6:150
Piccard, Jacques (Swiss scientist) 2:276; 6:123
Piccolos 3:216
Pic du Midi Observatory (France)
illus. 1:41
Pices V (submersible) 6:124
Piciformes 4:399–400, 407–8
Pickling 6:78
Picoseconds 6:377
Picture tubes see Cathode-ray tubes
Piculets 4:408
Pied-billed grebes 4:434
Piedmont glaciers 2:96–97
Piedmont Plateau 2:80
Piedmont plateaus 2:79

Piedmont Province 2:72–73
Piers (in construction) 6:39
Piezoelectricity 6:229, 337
Pigeon milk see Crop milk
PIGEONS 4:197, 428–31
Pig iron 6:178
Pigments 3:413
color mixing 3:299
genetics 3:402
hair 5:265–66
leaves 4:145
photosynthesis 3:433; 4:18–19, 22
pregnancy 5:300
skin 5:264, 266–67
PIGS 5:114–15
methane gas 2:397
pork tapeworm 4:226
selective breeding 6:71
trichinosis 4:228–29
illus. 4:32
Pig-tailed langurs 5:141
Pikas 5:38
Piked whales see Minke whales
Pilâtre de Rozier, Jean François (French aeronaut) 6:149–50
Pili 3:427; 4:29
Pillars, Earth see Earth pillars
Pill bugs 4:248, 251, 254
illus. 4:258
Pilot blacksnakes 4:366, 371
Piloting (in navigation) 6:165
Pilot lights 2:344
Pilot whales 5:53
illus. 5:56
Pi-mesons see Pions
PIMS see Programmable Implantable Medication System
Pinatubo, Mount (volcano, Philippines) 2:62
illus. 2:433
Pinching bugs see Stag beetles
Pinchot, Gifford (American forester and public official) 2:509; 4:127
Pine grosbeaks
illus. 4:457
Pinel, Philippe (French physician) 5:349
Pine martens 5:95
illus. 5:94
Pine nuts 4:90
Pines 4:86–87, 89–90, 148
mycorrhizal associations 4:112
needles 4:72
plant succession 4:123, 125
reproduction 4:87–88
species 3:507
wood construction 6:28
illus. 4:88
Pine snakes 4:371
Pinhole camera
illus. 3:283
Pink fairy armadillos 5:35
Pinna see Auricle (in the ear)
Pinnacles (coral formations) 2:283

Pinnae (in botany) **4:**79
Pinnate leaves 4:72
Pinnately compound leaves
4:73
Pinnately lobed leaves 4:73
PINNIPEDS 5:13, **63–68**
Pinnules 4:79
Piñons *see* Pine nuts
Pinophyta *see* Gymnosperms
Pintail ducks 4:443
Pioneer (space probes) **1:**291–
92, 300
auroras **2:**157
Jupiter **1:**134, 137
Saturn **1:**140
Sun probes **1:**301
Venus probe **1:**100, 102, 299
illus. **1:**291
information about Earth **1:**293
Pioneer communities (of plants)
3:483; **4:**121
Pions (Pi-mesons) 1:230; **3:**338
Pipefish 4:334–35
Pipelines
coal slurry **2:**357
natural gas **2:**337–38, 341–42
penstocks **2:**377
petroleum **2:**328–29
illus.
natural gas **2:**336, 339, 343
Trans-Alaska Pipeline **2:**330
Pipettes
illus. **3:**135
Piranhas 4:333
Pirellae 4:29
Pisces (constellation) **1:**32
Pisces V (submarine) **2:**279
Piscis Austrinus (constellation)
1:32
Pisé blocks 6:26
Pistils *see* Carpels
Pistons
automobile engines **6:**138
diesel engines **6:**103
gasoline engines **6:**99–100
steam engines **6:**99
illus. **6:**98
Piston-type pumps 2:449
Pitch (of sound) **3:**205–6, 210;
5:277
Pitch (viscous substance) **2:**360
Pitchblende 3:124
Pitcher plants 4:108–11
Pitching (in aeronautics)
illus. **6:**159–60
Pith 4:69
Pitman arms 6:145
Pituitary gland 5:243–44
illus. **5:**170
Pit vipers 4:372, 374; **5:**97
Pixels 3:300; **6:**273, 297
illus. **3:**300
Placebos 3:511
Placenta 3:462; **5:**296–97, 304
Placental mammals 5:5
Place system of numerals
1:340–45, 446–47

Placoderms 1:490; **4:**316, 323,
329
Plages 1:83
PLAINS 2:75–78, 183
Plains Indians 5:132
Planaria **4:**228
Planck, Max (German physicist)
3:142, 324–26, 341
illus. **3:**323
Planck's blackbody radiation
law 3:325
Planck's constant 3:325
PLANE GEOMETRY 1:329, 332,
366–79
Planes (in geometry) **1:**369,
401–2
Planet A (space probe) **1:**296
PLANETARIUMS 1:65–72
Planetary science 1:16
Planetesimal hypothesis 2:11
Planetesimals 2:11
Planet of the Apes (film) **1:**505
Planetoids *see* Asteroids
Planets 1:74 *see also* names of
specific planets
Drake's Equation **1:**323
extrasolar **1:**10, 44
extraterrestrial life **1:**317–22
formation **2:**13
gravitation **3:**182
motion **1:**78–79
night sky **1:**25
weight on **3:**181
illus.
outside solar system **1:**9
tilt of axes **1:**74
Plankton
algae **4:**46–47, 50, 52
carbon cycle **4:**21
copepods **4:**251
echo sounding location **2:**274
freshwater biomes **3:**499
microbiology **3:**451
oxygen cycle **3:**490
ozone layer depletion **2:**482
Plan-position indicators 6:257
Plantation system 6:59
PLANT BEHAVIOR 4:113–19
Plant blights 4:42
PLANT BREEDING 4:10, 170–
75; **6:**67–75
genetic technology **3:**420, 423
Plant diseases 4:5
chestnut blight **4:**148
forestry **4:**131
fungi **4:**41–42, 45
radioisotope tracers **3:**320
Plant lice *see* Aphids
Plant pests 4:269
Plant proteins *see* Incomplete
proteins
PLANTS 4:8–15
and acid rain **2:**476
aging **3:**466–67
and air pollution **2:**469
animals compared with **4:**183,
187

atolls, vegetation of **2:**283
behavior **4:**113–19
biology, history of **3:**369
botany **3:**372; **4:**2–7
bryophytes **4:**58–63
carnivorous plants **4:**108–12
cell division **3:**442–43
cell structure **3:**431
classification **3:**398; **4:**54–57
climates of the past **2:**216
coal formation **2:**346–47
communities **4:**132–37
deserts **2:**84, 86; **4:**166–69
diseases *see* Plant diseases
ecology **3:**475
electron-transport chain **3:**100
embryology **3:**462–363
endangered species **2:**493, 497
energy storage **3:**438
erosion prevented by **2:**417
ferns **4:**78–83
flowering plants **4:**98–107
fossils **1:**484–89
genetics and food production
6:67–75
genetic variation **3:**504–5
geologic record **2:**19, 21
groundwater level **2:**113
horsetails and club mosses
4:74–77
minerals in groundwater **3:**84
movement **4:**9, 113, 116–17,
185
mutations from radiation
3:320–21
nitrogen cycle **3:**491
ozone layer depletion **2:**482
paleobotany **1:**480–81
parasitism **3:**483
photosynthesis **4:**16–24
phreatophytes **2:**119
polar regions **2:**90, 92
population distribution **3:**479–80
producers in ecosystems **2:**453
rain forest **4:**158
reproduction **3:**455–56
seed dispersal **4:**104
spores **4:**62
succession **4:**120–25
tundra and taiga **4:**163–65
vascular plants **4:**64–73
virus infection **3:**391–92
wetlands **4:**150–55
illus.
cell structure **3:**427
clusters of wildflowers **3:**481
coal formation **2:**348
endangered species **2:**496
Plaques (in atherosclerosis)
5:234, 439, 490–91
Plasma (ionized gas) **3:**13, 145,
353–54
changes of state **3:**231
confinement **2:**376; **3:**354–57
Plasma Universe theory
1:22–23
Sun **1:**88
Plasma, Blood *see* Blood plasma

Plasma display panels 3:300; **6:**297
Plasma membrane (Cell membrane) 3:430, 436–37
  cell structure **3:**425
  life, characteristics of **3:**376
  plants **4:**14, 26
  diagram(s) **5:**162
Plasma physics 3:145
Plasma Universe theory 1:22–23
Plasmids 3:420, 427; **4:**32; **6:**74–75
  antibiotic resistance **3:**506
  bacteria **3:**453
  microbiology **3:**448
Plasmodesmata 4:14
Plasmodial slime molds 4:51–52
Plasmodium **3:**454; **4:**212; **5:**428
Plasmoquine 5:464
Plastic and reconstructive surgery 5:416
Plastic flow (of glaciers) **2:**95
PLASTICS 6:209–15
  allergies **5:**448
  amorphous solids **3:**89
  artificial body parts **5:**501, 507
  dentistry **5:**280
  food packaging **6:**85
  modern materials **6:**228
  ocean pollution **2:**464–65
  petroleum products **2:**334
  illus.
    petroleum derivatives **2:**335
    production **3:**113
Plastids 3:430–31; **4:**14, 20
Plastron 4:375
Plateau flows *see* Fissure eruptions
PLATEAUS 2:75, **78–80,** 210
Platelets 5:208, 212, 473
Plateosaurus **1:**495
Plates (in geology) **2:**32, 68
  plate tectonics **2:**41–45
  map(s) **2:**38
PLATE TECTONICS 2:8, **41–45**
  earthquakes **2:**47
  lakes **2:**108
  laser measurement **6:**351
  mountains **2:**68–74
  ocean floor **2:**270
  satellite studies **2:**2–3
  volcanoes **2:**59
Platinum 3:27, 30, 42; **5:**501
Plato (Greek philosopher) **3:**141; **5:**335–36
Platypuses, Duck-billed 5:15
  illus. **5:**14
Playa lakes 2:85–86
PlayStation (video-game system) **6:**298–99, 301
Pleiades (star cluster) **1:**32, 186, 219
  illus. **1:**186
Pleistocene epoch 1:498–99; **2:**20; **5:**108
  table(s) **2:**20

Pleurodira 4:377, 379
Plexuses 5:232
Plies (of tires) **6:**146
Pliny the Elder (Roman scholar)
  dolphin-human friendship **5:**57–58
  ferrets used for rabbit-hunting **5:**94
Pliocene epoch 5:84
Plovers 4:437–38
Plug domes 2:58
Plumage *see* Feathers
Plum curculios 4:299
"Plum pudding" atomic model 3:18
Plunge pools 2:102
Plutarch (Roman writer) **5:**57
PLUTO 1:74, 79, **156–57**
  discovery **3:**182
  life, unsuitability for **1:**322
  mission plans **1:**237
  origin **2:**13
Plutonium 1:294; **2:**368, 370; **3:**42, 321
Plutons 2:69
Ply (of tires) *see* Plies
Plymouth Voyager (automobile)
  illus. **6:**137
Plywood 6:29
  illus. **6:**28
Pneumatic caissons 5:221; **6:**15
Pneumatic drills 6:47–48
Pneumocystis carinii **5:**441, 443, 445
Pneumonia 5:429
  AIDS **5:**239, 443
  transplant recipients **5:**497
P-n junctions 2:389; **6:**251–52
Poaching (illegal hunting) **2:**500, 513
Pocket gophers 5:42
Podicipediformes 4:398, 432–34
Podocarpus 4:87, 89
Podsolic soil 4:134
Poe, Edgar Allan (American writer) **1:**500
Point (in geometry) **1:**368, 376
Point-and-shoot cameras *see* Viewfinder cameras
Point-source pollution 2:458
Point-to-point programming 6:199–200
Poison-dart frogs 4:347
Poisoning 3:470 *see also* Toxins
  food poisoning **6:**77
  metal poisoning **2:**463–64
Poison ivy 4:117; **5:**448
  illus. **4:**116–17
Poisonous algae 4:53
Poisonous animals
  amphibians **4:**337, 339, 342
  arachnids **4:**263
  centipedes **4:**264–65
  coelenterates **4:**217
  frogs **4:**347–48
  jellyfish **4:**214
  lizards **4:**360, 362

  reptiles **4:**337
  scorpion fish **4:**335
  shrews **5:**28
  snakes **4:**339, 363, 365, 367, 372–74
  stingrays **4:**328
  illus.
    hooded pitohuis **4:**448
Poisonous mushrooms 4:44
Poisonous plants 4:117–18
Pokemon 6:299
Polar (satellite) **2:**158
Polar bears 2:90, 500, 503; **4:**164; **5:**71–72
  locomotion **5:**70–71
  illus. **2:**87; **4:**469
Polar bonds 3:52
Polar charges 3:50
Polar continental air masses 2:187
Polar covalence 3:65, 83
Polar easterlies
  diagram(s) **3:**494
Polar-front theory 2:203
Polaris (star) **1:**26, 112
Polarity (in embryology) *see* Differentiation of cells
Polarity (in embryonic cells) **3:**460
Polarized light 3:292; **6:**333
  Crab Nebula **1:**231
  from distant stars **1:**223
  visible to some animals **4:**192
Polarizing microscopes 6:333
Polar maritime air masses 2:187
Polar molecules 3:81
Polar nuclei (in plants) **3:**463
Polaroid film 6:272
Polar orbits 1:304
POLAR REGIONS 2:87–92 *see also* Antarctic regions; Arctic regions
  air masses **2:**187
  auroras **2:**155–58
  climates of the world **2:**209–11, 213–14
  greenhouse effect **2:**154
  jet streams **2:**150–51
Polar winds 2:185
Polecats 5:94
  illus. **5:**93
Poles, Geographic 1:104–5; **3:**268–69
  Sun **1:**301
Poles, Magnetic 1:104–5; **3:**262
  auroras **2:**156
  magnetism **3:**262, 268–69
  paleomagnetism **1:**483
  Sun **1:**85
Poliomyelitis 5:233, 431
  iron lung **5:**222
  virus **3:**387–88
  illus. **5:**427
Political geography 2:301
Pollen 3:455–56
  air pollutant **2:**466

allergies **5**:448
archaeology **1**:464
bees **4**:286
conifers **4**:84, 86–88
paleontology **1**:480
peat bogs **4**:154
chart(s)
  climate study **2**:217
illus.
  fossilized pollen studies **2**:8
Pollination 3:456; **4**:102
beekeeping **4**:287
rain-forest plants **4**:158
illus.
  hand-pollination of hybrids **3**:402
Polling (computer protocol) **6**:387
Pollution, Environmental *see* Environmental pollution
Pollux (star) **1**:32
Polo, Marco (Venetian traveler) **2**:322
Polonium 3:6, 29, 32, 42
Polyacrylamide 6:212
Polyakov, Valeri (Russian cosmonaut) **1**:248
Polyatomic ions 3:67
Polycarbonates 6:212, 228
Polychaeta 4:202
Polychlorinated biphenyls (PCBs) 2:462, 503; **3**:489
Polyclimax theory 4:125
Polycythemia 5:211
Polydactyly
illus.
  heredity **5**:311
Polyesters 6:211–12
Polyethylene 6:210–11, 215
artificial body parts **5**:501
Polyethylene terephthalate (PET) 6:211–12
Polygenic characteristics 3:408
Polygenic inheritance 5:319
Polygonal nets (of polar soil) **2**:89
Polygons 1:374
Polygraph tests 1:516
Polyhedral angles 1:380–81
Polymerase chain reaction (PCR) 3:419; **5**:322, 444
forensic science **1**:514
Polymerization 2:332; **3**:320
POLYMERS 3:7; **6**:209–15
artificial body parts **5**:501
modern materials **6**:228–29
organic chemistry **3**:110, 112
Polyplacophora 4:203
Polyps (coelenterates) **4**:217–19
Polysaccharides 3:119
algae cells **4**:48
cellular energy **3**:438
synthetic skin **5**:507
Polystyrenes 6:211
Polytrichum **mosses 4**:61
Polyunsaturated fats 3:120; **5**:382–83
Polyurethanes 6:211
Polyvinyl alcohol 6:212

Polyvinyl chloride (PVC) 3:112; **5**:436; **6**:211, 215
Pomology 4:172
Pompeii (Italy) **1**:466
Ponderators 3:348
Ponderosa pines 4:72, 90
illus. **4**:88
Ponds
eutrophication **4**:124
plant communities **4**:137
Pondweed
illus. **4**:21
"Pong" (video game) **6**:298
illus. **6**:299
Ponies 5:109
Pons (of the brain) **5**:230
Pons, Jean-Louis (French amateur astronomer) **1**:166
Pons-Brooks, Comet 1:164
Pont d'Arc (natural bridge, France) **2**:423
Pont de Quebec (bridge, Canada) **6**:50
Pont du Gard (aqueduct, France) **6**:17
Poorwills 4:403
Popocatepetl (volcano, Mexico) **2**:4
Popovich, Pavel R. (Soviet cosmonaut) **1**:241
Population biology 3:366–67
Population geography 2:301
POPULATIONS 3:476–83
definition **3**:476–77
ecology **3**:472
environmental pollution **2**:406, 452, 455–56
Porcelain 6:217–18
Porcupine fish 4:194, 335
Porcupines 5:42–43
illus. **5**:42
Pork tapeworms 4:226
Porous rocks 2:113
Porphyritic rocks 2:34, 134
Porpoises 5:55, 60
Porsche 944 (automobile)
illus. **6**:138
Portland cement 6:25–26
Portolano charts 6:167
illus. **6**:166
Portugal
tsunamis **2**:258
Portuguese man-of-war 4:218
illus. **4**:215
Port-wine stains 5:489
Poseidon (artificial satellite) *see* TOPEX/Poseidon
Position-line navigation 6:170
Positive crankcase ventilation (PCV) 6:141
illus. **6**:140
Positive electrical charges 3:245–46
Positron emission tomography *see* PET
Positrons 3:21, 308, 317
cosmic rays **1**:228–29

induced radioactivity **3**:128
PET scans **5**:456–57
radioisotopes **3**:318
Possums *see* Opossums
Post, Wiley (American aviator) **1**:271–72
illus. **1**:274
Post and lintel construction 6:32–33
Postclimax communities 4:125
Postglacial climatic revertance 2:219
Postglacial optimum 2:218
Postulates 1:368, 401
Posture
bipedalism **5**:159–60
humans compared to other primates **5**:153
muscle tone **5**:193
Potash 2:345
Potassium 3:29, 42
nutrition **5**:387
ocean salts **2**:229
salts **3**:99
water, reaction with **3**:86
Potassium bromide 3:99
Potassium carbonate 3:99
Potassium-channel blocking drugs 5:467
Potassium chloride 3:30, 99
Potassium hydroxide 3:96
Potassium iodide
illus. **3**:65
Potassium nitrate 3:96, 99
Potassium sulfate 3:99, 105
Potassium thiocyanate 5:467
Potatoes 4:4; **6**:84–85
illus.
  cells **6**:74
Potential, Electric 2:309–10; **3**:252
Potential energy 3:164
Potoos 4:403
Potoroos 5:19
Pott, Percival (British physician) **5**:432
Pottery
illus. **6**:5
Pottos 5:138
Pouched mammals *see* Marsupials
Pouched mice 5:21
Poultry farming 6:58, 60, 66, 71
illus. **6**:65
Pouter pigeons 4:430
Powdery mildews 4:41–42
Power (in physics) **3**:167
Power brakes 6:148
Power lines *see* Transmission lines, Electric
Power plants *see also* Nuclear-power plants; Nuclear reactors
acid rain **2**:473–76
environmental pollution **2**:307
refuse-burning **2**:396–97
solar-power plants **2**:386

Power plants (cont.)
Space Solar Power Stations
2:389
tidal energy **2:**249
illus. **2:**310
hydroelectricity **2:**378–79
hydroelectric steam **2:**377
solar power **2:**384
thermal power **2:**248, 392
tidal power **2:**248
Powers (in mathematics) **1:**348
magnification **6:**330–31
Power steering 6:145
Pox viruses 3:388
PPIs *see* Plan-position indicators
Praesepe (star cluster) **1:**29, 186
Prairie chickens 4:195, 426
Prairie dogs 2:501; **5:**42
illus. **5:**41
Prairies 2:77; **3:**482, 495; **4:**140–
41, 143
Praseodymium 3:42
Praying mantises 4:276
illus. **4:**279
Precambrian time 1:479, 487
table(s) **1:**486; **2:**18–19
Precast concrete 6:41
Precession 1:70, 112; **2:**220
Precious corals 4:219
PRECIPITATION (meteorology)
2:166–73
acid rain **2:**472–76
clouds **2:**162
deserts **2:**81, 85; **4:**166
groundwater **2:**112–13
hydrometeorology **2:**145
polar regions **2:**88
rain forests **4:**156
savannas **4:**141
taiga **4:**164
temperate forests **4:**144
tundra **4:**163
water cycle **3:**86
Preclimax communities 4:125
Precocial birds 4:396
Precursors (in seismology) **2:**54
Predators 2:493 *see also* Birds
of prey
animal behavior **4:**192, 194–95
arachnids **4:**258–61
cartilaginous fish **4:**323
natural selection **3:**506
populations and communities
3:481–82
shrikes **4:**450–51
snakes **4:**364–65
water's importance to **5:**6
Predictive statistics *see* Statistical inference
Preeclampsia *see* Toxemia
Preening 4:392
Pregnancy, Human 5:296–303
folate consumption **5:**386
nurse-midwives **5:**485
Rh factor **5:**209
sonography **5:**454
substance abuse **5:**374
substance abuse during **5:**375

PREHISTORIC ANIMALS
1:490–99
birds **4:**391
fossils **1:**484–89
Prehistoric people
archaeology **1:**462–64
coal, use of **2:**348
conservation **2:**403–4
fossils **1:**489
illus. **2:**215
Premature babies
illus. **5:**304
Premature closure 5:340
Premolars
human *see* Bicuspids
Prenatal testing 5:303
genetic technology **3:**417, 423
illus. **5:**302
Presbyopia 5:272
Presenile dementia 5:353
Preservation, Food *see* Food
preservation and processing
Presidents, U.S.
pet animals **4:**488–89
Pressure (in physics) *see also*
Atmospheric pressure
chemical reactions **3:**61–62
Earth's interior **2:**26
gases **3:**72
gas measurement **3:**187
ideal-gas laws **3:**72, 74
liquids **3:**184–85
oceanic **2:**224, 271
solubility **3:**81
Sun **1:**190
Pressure (sensation) **5:**286
Pressure suits 1:272
Pressure waves *see* P waves
Pressurized-water nuclear reactors 2:367
diagram(s) **2:**366
Prestige (oil tanker) **2:**465
illus.
oil spill **2:**331
Prestressed concrete 6:31
Prevailing winds 2:184–85;
3:493
diagram(s) **3:**494
Preventive medicine
cancer **5:**437
exercise **5:**401–2
veterinary science **4:**465
Pribilof Islands (Bering Sea)
5:68
Prides (groups of lions) **5:**84–86
Priestley, Joseph (English chemist) **3:**3; **4:**17
Primary batteries (Dry cells)
3:105, 252–53
illus. **2:**309; **3:**104
Primary-care centers 5:481
Primary colors 3:298
Primary endosperm cell 3:463
Primary succession 4:121
Primary waves (in physics) *see*
P waves

PRIMATES 5:13, **136–49**
ancestors of modern humans
5:157–60
classification **3:**396–97
fossils **1:**489
humans **5:**152–56
parental care **4:**197
prehistoric animals **1:**498
Primatology 3:373
Prime focus 1:38
illus. **1:**39
Prime meridian
illus. **6:**170
Primordial soup 3:372, 381
Princeton Large Torus 3:356
**Princeton Plasma Physics
Laboratory 2:**376
Prince William Sound 2:465
Principal focus 3:286
**Principal quantum number
3:**333
Principia (book, Newton) **3:**141,
148
Printers, Computer 6:367–68
digital photography **6:**274
Printing 6:273
color **3:**299–300
illus.
color **3:**298
Printing press 6:8
Printouts, Computer 6:364
Prions 3:379, 390–91
Prionus imbricornis **4:**298
Prisms (geometric shapes)
1:381–82
illus. **1:**332
Prisms (in optics) **3:**327
color **3:**294
corrective lenses **5:**272–73
illus. **3:**273, 294, 326
PROBABILITY 1:329–30, 333,
414–23
algebra **1:**365
sex determination **5:**314–15
statistics **1:**413
Problems of Space Flying (book,
Noordung) **1:**265
Problem solving 5:343–44
animal behavior **4:**193
Proboscidea 5:13, 103
Proboscis monkeys 5:141
illus. **5:**140
Procamelus **5:**116
Procellariiformes 4:398, 433,
446
Processing, Food *see* Food
preservation and processing
Processing speed (of computers) **6:**363
Prochloron 4:34
Procyon (star) **1:**32, 192
Producer gas 2:359
illus. **2:**358
Producers (in ecosystems)
2:453; **3:**485
Product (in mathematics) **1:**348
Products, Chemical 3:54, 56

Profiling (forensics) 1:516
Profiling software (computer security) 6:396
Profundal zone 3:499
Progesterone 5:247, 294, 306
Program for International Student Assessment (PISA) 6:329
Programmable Implantable Medication System (PIMS) 1:254
Programmable Read-Only Memory see PROM
Programming see Computer programming
Progress (spacecraft) 1:269, 283
Project 2061 6:321, 324
Project FeederWatch 4:389
Projection (in photography) 6:273
Projection microscopes 6:334
Project Mohole 2:275–76
Projectors, Planetarium 1:67, 69
    illus. 1:65, 67
Project Phoenix 1:324–25
Project TRANSIT see Navsat program
Project West Ford 1.309
Prokaryotes 4:19, 26–27
    cell structure 3:426–27, 430
    classification 3:399
    illus. 3:441
Prolactin 4:190; 5:243
    galactorrhea 5:244
Prolegs (of caterpillars) 4:302
PROM (computer memory) 6:369
Promethium 3:31, 42
Prominences, Solar 1:82
    illus. 1:87, 179
Pronator muscles 5:189
Pronghorns 5:127
Pronuclei (singular Pronucleus) 5:295
Propane 2:332; 3:111
Propanediols 5:356, 373
Propellers
    airplanes 6:162–63
    ships 6:110–11
Properties (in chemistry) 6:227
Prophase 3:442–44
Propionic acid 3:114
Propolis 4:286
Propranolol 5:467
Proprietorial sense (in canids) 5:78
Prop roots 4:68, 153
Propylene 3:111
Propyl group 3:110
Prospecting see Geophysical exploration
Prostaglandins 5:292
Prostate gland 5:295, 433
Prostheses see Artificial body parts
Protactinium 3:42
Protactinium 234 2:363; 3:127–28

Protease inhibitors 3:393; 5:239, 445, 465
Protective coloration 4:194; 5:9
    insects 4:276
    light's effects on mammals 5:6
    owls 4:419
    weasels 5:94
    illus. 5:95
Protective mechanisms (of animals) see Defense mechanisms
Protein C 5:475
Protein channels 3:437
    diagram(s) 3:436
Protein pumps 3:437
    diagram(s) 3:436
Proteins 5:378–80
    aging, causes of 5:333–34
    Alzheimer's disease 5:233, 334, 353–54
    biochemistry 3:7, 121–22
    blood 5:206
    calories 3:61
    cancer, role in 5:434
    cell dynamics 3:439
    digestion 5:250
    genes 3:402
    life, characteristics of 3:376
    muscle cells 5:186
    prions 3:391
    spared by carbohydrates 5:381
    synthesis in cells 3:412–15
    thermophilic 3:2
    viruses 3:386
    diagram(s)
        protein synthesis 3:414
Proteobacteria 4:29
Proteus mirabilis
    illus. 4:26
Prothrombin 5:206, 208, 212
Protists 4:54–55, 184–85, 199–200
    algae 4:46–53
    cell structure 3:427, 431
    classification 3:398–99
    microbiology 3:450–51
    monerans once classified with 4:25–26
    protozoans 4:206–13
    reproduction 3:453–54
Protoavis 1:497
Protoceratops 1:496
Protochordates 4:221, 308–11
Protocols (in computer networking) 6:387–88
Protogalaxies 1:217
Proton accelerators 6:357–58
Protonema 4:60
Proton-proton reaction 1:89–90
Protons 2:362–63; 3:6, 18, 47, 245, 305–7, 309–10
    acids 3:95
    atomic number 3:19–20
    cosmic rays 1:228
    quarks 3:20, 313, 316
    stability 3:310
    illus. 3:312
Proto-oncogenes 5:434

Protoplanetary disks
    illus. 2:12
Protoplanetary nebulas 1:318
Protoplasm 3:425, 430; 4:52; 5:161
Protospongia 4:208
Protostars 1:193, 223
    illus. 1:190, 218
Protosun 2:12
PROTOZOANS 4:200, 206–13
    early classification of 4:183
    infectious diseases 5:428
    microbiology 3:451
    illus. 3:447
Protractors 1:370
Proturans 4:277–78
Proxima Centauri (star) 1:27, 81
Prozac see Fluoxetine
Prusiner, Stanley (American biochemist) 3:391
Przhevalski's wild horses 5:108
    illus. 5:109
Pseudomonas 5:463
Pseudopods 4:207, 209, 212
Pseudoscorpions 4:263
Pseudospheres 1:401
    illus. 1:402
Psilotophyta 4:56
Psittaciformes 4:399–401
Psocoptera 4:279
Psoriasis 5:267
Psychiatric medicine 5:417
    forensic science 1:516
    medications 5:466
    nursing 5:486–87
    treatments 5:356–57
Psychic secretion 5:250
Psychoanalysis 5:341–42
PSYCHOLOGY 5:335–47
    adolescence 5:332
    careers 5:342–47
    color perception 3:303
    exercise benefits 5:402–3
    mental health 5:348–57
    pain sensitivity 5:289, 291
    substance abuse 5:370, 376
    veterinary science 4:465
    weight-control habits 5:392, 394
Psychometry 5:347
Psychoses 5:341
    antipsychotic drugs 5:466
    major depression 5:351
    PCP 5:372
Psychosomatic disorders 5:354
Psychosurgery 5:357
Psychotherapy 5:341–42, 357
    learning disabilities 5:368
    pain relief 5:292
PT-109 (torpedo boat) 6:124
Ptarmigan 4:423, 425–26
    illus. 4:425
Pterobranchia 4:311
Pterodactyls 1:496
Pterosaurs 1:488, 496; 4:352
Pterygota 4:278
Ptilidae 4:299

Ptolemaic system
illus. 1:472
Ptolemy III (Egyptian pharaoh)
1:475
Ptyalin 5:249
p-type silicon 6:232, 251, 346
Puberty 5:330–32
Pubis 5:180–81
illus. 5:165, 175
Public health
ecology 3:475
entomology 4:269
environmental pollution 2:457–58, 467–69
veterinary science 4:464–65
Public utilities
electricity 2:320
natural gas 2:343–44
water supply 2:449–50
Puck (moon of Uranus) 1:150
Pudus 5:122
Puerperal period 5:305
Puff adders 4:374
Puffballs 4:39, 45
illus. 4:42
Puffer fish (Blowfish) 4:317–18, 335
illus. 4:329
Puffins 4:438
illus. 4:435
Pulleys 3:174
illus. 3:175
Pulmonary arteries 5:196
illus. 5:169
Pulmonary veins 5:196
illus. 5:169
Pulmonic valve 5:198–99
Pulp (of teeth) 5:278
illus. 5:280
Pulsars 1:201, 209
Crab Nebula 1:231
planets 1:318
radio astronomy 1:56
illus. 1:202–3; 2:12
Pulse (in physiology) 5:204
monitoring heart rate 5:402
sleep 5:407
Pulse code modulation 6:284
illus. 6:284
Pulsed electrical fields 6:81
Pulsed radar 6:256–57
Pulse-echo radio 6:255
Pulse oximeters 5:478
Pumas *see* Cougars
Pumice 2:6–7
Pumped-storage hydroelectric plants 2:378
Pumping stations
illus. 2:439
Pumps
fluid dynamics 3:187–88
heat pumps 2:320
medication dosage 5:470–71
vacuum pump 3:185–86
water supply 2:441, 449–50
illus.
air pump 3:185

insulin pump 5:244, 471
vacuum pump 3:186
Pupae 4:276
ants 4:282
bees 4:286–87
beetles 4:292
butterflies and moths 4:302
illus. 4:302
Pupil (of the eye) 5:270, 272
illus. 5:188, 271
Pupin, Michael I. (American physicist) 6:239
Purification of water *see* Water purification
Purkinje system *see* His-Purkinje system
Purple bacteria 4:18, 31
Purple dyes 6:204
Purple loosestrife
illus. 4:118
Purse-seine nets 6:87
illus. 6:89
Purse-web spiders 4:260
Pus 5:207, 236, 426
Putrefaction 3:470
PVC *see* Polyvinyl chloride
P waves 3:194–95
earthquakes 2:49, 51, 54
seismic waves 2:23–25
illus. 2:50
Pycnogonida 4:204
Pyelonephritis 5:262
Pyemia 5:212
Pygmy beetles 4:297
Pygmy chimpanzees 5:144
Pygmy falcons 4:414
Pygmy hippopotamuses 5:115
Pygmy marmoset 5:139
Pygmy marsupial frogs
illus. 4:346
Pygmy rattlers 4:374
Pygmy squirrels 5:40–41
Pyloric sphincter 5:251
Pylorus 5:249
Pyorrhea 4:209; 5:281
Pyramids (geometric figures)
1:383
Pyramids (of the kidneys)
illus. 5:168
Pyramids, Egyptian 6:18, 24–25
illus. 6:17
Pyridoxine (Vitamin B$_6$) 5:384
Pyrimethamine (Daraprim)
5:465
Pyrites 3:383
Pyroclastic flows 2:62
Pyroclastic rocks 2:33, 134
Pyroxene 2:33–34
Pyruvate (Pyruvic acid)
3:435–37
Pythagoras (Greek philosopher)
1:94, 329–30, 371; 3:141
illus. 1:329; 3:142
Pythagorean theorem 1:371–72, 395
Pythons 4:353, 355, 368, 370

Q-R

Qiantang River 2:247
Qi gong 5:514
Quadrants 6:168–69
Quadrilaterals 1:373–74
Quagga mussels 4:237
Quahogs *see* Hard-shell clams
Quails 4:422–25
QUALCOM 6:245
Qualitative analysis
analytic chemistry 3:130
spectroscopy 3:327–28
Quality of sound *see* Timbre
Quantitative analysis
analytical chemistry 3:130
titration 3:98–99
Quantum-cascade lasers 6:346
Quantum chromodynamics
3:316
Quantum dots 6:342
"Quantum jump" 3:143
Quantum mechanics 3:143, 145
laws of 3:330–31
Schrödinger's "fuzzy" atomic model 3:19
Quantum numbers 3:307, 333–34
Quantum physics 3:143
QUANTUM THEORY 3:142, 322–34, 341
predictions 3:307–8
radiant energy 3:278
Quarantines (in agriculture) 6:63
Quark confinement 3:315
QUARKS 3:7, 20, 144, 311, 312–16
Quartz 2:33–34, 37, 137–38
beach sands 2:293
pure crystals 3:91
illus. 3:240
Quartzite 2:37, 136
Quasars 1:217, 220
radio astronomy 1:56
Steady State theory 1:22
X-ray astronomy 1:59
illus. 1:23, 215
Quasi-stellar objects *see* Quasars
Quaternary period 1:489; 2:20
map(s) 2:41
table(s) 1:486; 2:20–21
Quebec
dams 6:52, 56
geomagnetic storms 2:158
hydroelectric power 2:380
tidal energy 2:249
Queen bees 3:457
illus. 3:452
Queen Elizabeth (ship) 6:114
Queen Elizabeth 2 (ship)
illus. 6:115
Queen Mary (ship) 6:114
illus. 6:115
Queen Mary 2 (ship) 6:114
illus. 6:115

Queens (in social insects)
ants **4**:282–84
bees **4**:286–88; **5**:324
termites **4**:290
wasps **4**:289
illus.
ants **4**:283
termites **4**:290
Queloz, Didier (Swiss astronomer) **1**:10
Quenching 6:182
Questioning 1:3
Quetzals 4:406
illus. **4**:406
Quicklime *see* Lime
Quillworts 4:56
Quinidine 5:467
Quinine 3:114; **5**:462, 464–65
Quinolines 5:464–65
Quipu
illus. **1**:455
Quotient 1:348
Rabbit fish 4:325
Rabbits 5:37–38
color adaptation **3**:378
dingoes **5**:81
grasslands **4**:140
life span **5**:324
teeth **5**:8
Rabies 5:424
diagnosis **5**:472
raccoons **5**:76
vaccinations **3**:447; **4**:467
virus **3**:388
Raccoons 5:70, 76
illus. **5**:11
Racers (snakes) **4**:371
Race runners (lizards) *see* Whiptail lizards
Races (tidal currents) **2**:248
Rack-and-pinion steering system 6:145
RADAR 6:254–61
atmospheric research **2**:188
bird tracking **4**:389
cloud studies **2**:164
electromagnetic spectrum **3**:279
geomagnetic storms **2**:158
hurricane-structure study **2**:198
iceberg detection **2**:263
Loran **1**:379
military satellites **1**:313
navigation **6**:172
oceanographic studies **2**:265
radio astronomy **1**:42, 55
weather observations **2**:204
illus. **1**:55; **6**:173
Radar altimeters 6:258–59
Radial artery 5:204
Radial dunes 2:84
Radial keratotomy 5:272
Radial symmetry 4:220–21
Radial wells 2:441
Radiant-heating systems 3:239

Radiation 3:340 *see also* Electromagnetic spectrum; Solar radiation
alpha, beta, and gamma emissions **3**:126–27
astronomy **1**:60–64
Big Bang theory **1**:20
black holes **1**:212–13
cancer, cause of **5**:435–36
cosmic rays **1**:224–31
DNA damage **3**:467
environmental pollution **2**:455
heat transmission **3**:237–39
irradiation of food **6**:80
nuclear energy **2**:362–64, 372
organ transplants **5**:497
radioisotopes **3**:317–21
spacecraft **1**:251
stimulated emission **3**:341
X-rays **1**:58–59
illus. **3**:233
Radiation belt *see* Van Allen radiation belt
Radiation therapy 3:319; **5**:437
Radiators (of automobiles) **6**:142
Radicle 3:463; **4**:68, 88, 104–5
RADIO 6:9, **288–90**
atmospheric research **2**:153
bird tracking **4**:389
cellular technology **6**:242–43
navigation **6**:170–71
Radioactive dating *see* Radiometric age-dating
Radioactive decay 3:126–27, 307, 317–18
dating methods **1**:107
Earth's interior **2**:28
meson **1**:230
nuclear energy **2**:362–64
illus. **2**:26
Radioactive isotopes *see* Radioisotopes
Radioactive series *see* Decay chains
Radioactive wastes
disposal **2**:307, 370–71, 490
illus. **2**:490
Radioactivity 2:16–17; **3**:6, 15, 124, 126, 128
life, origin of **3**:381
radioisotopes **3**:317
Radioallergosorbent test (RAST) 5:449
Radio altimeters *see* Radar altimeters
RADIO ASTRONOMY 1:47–48, 54, **55–57** *see also* Infrared astronomy
extraterrestrial life **1**:324–25
galactic core **1**:187
radar **6**:261
radio telescopes **1**:42–43
Radiocarbon dating 1:485; **2**:16–17; **3**:127
archaeology **1**:464–65
illus. **1**:464
Radiochemistry 3:9, 124

Radio-command guidance systems 1:305
Radiography 3:317, 319
Radioheliographs 1:92
RADIOISOTOPES 3:126–28, **317–21**
dating methods **2**:16–17, 107
nuclear energy **2**:362–64, 372
Radioisotope thermoelectric generators 1:294; **3**:321
Radioisotope tracers 3:317–20
diagnostic imaging **5**:456, 459
zoological research **4**:182
Radiolarians 4:212
Radiology 5:416
Radiometers 2:242
Radiometric age-dating 2:16–17; **3**:127
Earth, origin of **2**:13–14
fossils **1**:485
meteorites **1**:170
minerals and rocks **1**:107–8
Radionuclides *see* Radioisotopes
Radio relay systems 6:239–40
Radiosondes 2:153
illus. **2**:152
Radiosurgery 5:479
Radio telescopes 1:42–43, 55–56
Arecibo Observatory **1**:13
extraterrestrial life **1**:324–25
interstellar space **1**:219, 223
radioheliographs **1**:92
illus. **1**:10, 55–56, 321; **6**:261
Radiotherapy *see* Radiation therapy
Radio waves 1:55–56
atmosphere's effect on **2**:152
earthquakes **2**:54
electromagnetic spectrum **3**:275–76
electronics **6**:248
extraterrestrial life **1**:324
health effects **3**:277
Jupiter **1**:136
magnetic resonance imaging **3**:270
MRI imaging **5**:455
quasar **1**:220
radar **3**:279; **6**:254–61
radio **6**:288–89
Radium 3:6, 30, 42–43, 124
illus. **2**:363
Radium 226 2:364; **3**:128
Radius (arm bone) **5**:179
illus. **5**:165, 174–75, 178
Radius of a circle 1:375
illus. **1**:374
Radon 3:33, 43, 128
carcinogen **5**:435
earthquake prediction **2**:54
well contamination **2**:119
illus. **2**:363
***Rafflesia arnoldi* 4**:112
Ragweed 4:125
Rahn, Johann Heinrich (German mathematician) **1**:330

Rails (birds) 4:439–40
RAIL TRANSPORTATION
    6:125–32
  coal, use of 2:348, 357
  steam locomotive 6:97
  tunnels 6:47–48
  illus.
    Chunnel 6:46–47
    electric train 2:321
    maglev train 3:145
Rain 2:167, 170–71, 409
  air pollution 2:467
  atmospheric dust 2:466, 470
  biomes 3:493
  chemical nature of 2:172
  climates of the world 2:212–14
  coastal formation 2:290
  deserts 4:166
  hurricanes 2:200
  water changes the land
    2:416–17
Rainbow Bridge (Utah) 2:423
Rainbow holograms 6:277
  illus. 6:276
Rainbows
  illus. 3:299
Rainbow snakes 4:370–71
Rainfall *see* Rain
RAIN FORESTS 4:156–61
  biomes 3:493–94, 496
  climates of the world 2:212
  destruction 1:109
  entomology 4:270
  extinct species 2:497
  ferns 4:78
  forestry 4:126, 128
  plant communities 4:133, 135
  water erosion 2:417
  wilderness conservation 2:515
  illus. 4:64, 128, 131, 156
    burning forest 2:404; 4:160
    cleared for agriculture 2:493
    temperate biomes 3:497
    tropical biomes 3:496
Rain-forest selaginella
  illus. 4:77
Rainier, Mount (Washington)
    2:60, 96
Rain-shadow effect 2:83, 214;
    4:138, 142, 166
  biomes 3:493, 498
Raisins 6:76
RAM *see* Random-access
    memory
Ramapithecus 5:159
Rami 5:177
Ramjet engines 6:106, 164
  illus. 6:105
Ramsey, W. H. (British scientist)
    2:28
Rance Tidal Works (France)
    2:249, 399
Rand McNally Building (Chi-
    cago, Illinois) 6:30, 39
Random-access memory (RAM)
    6:368, 370–71
Random populations 3:479–80

Range (animals' territory)
  bears 5:73
  cats 5:84
  mammals 5:10
  viverrids 5:99–100
Range (in statistics) 3:511
Range markers (on radar
    screen) 6:257
Ranger (spacecraft) 1:123, 298
Ranvier, Nodes of *see* Nodes of
    Ranvier
Rapamune *see* Sirolimus
Rapid eye movement (REM)
    sleep 5:407
  illus. 5:408
Rapids 2:102, 422
  illus. 2:100
Raptors *see* Birds of prey
Rare and Endangered Species
    Act (U.S., 1966) 2:515
Rare-earth elements *see* Lan-
    thanides
Rarefaction
  wave motion 3:195, 198
  diagram(s) 3:199
Ras Algethi (star) 1:30
Ras Alhague (star) 1:30
Raspberries
  illus. 4:103
RAST *see* Radioallergosorbent
    test
Ratels 5:96
Ratfish *see* Chimaeras
Rating systems
  video games 6:300
Rational number system 1:351
Rat kangaroos 5:19
Rats 4:192; 5:5, 43
  illus. 5:341
Rat snakes 4:371
Rattlesnakes 4:364, 366, 372,
    374
  desert adaptations 4:169
  senses 4:192
  illus. 4:189, 354, 363
Ravens 4:463
Ray, John (British scientist)
    3:395
Ray-finned fish 1:492; 4:330–35
Rayleigh (R) waves 2:49
Raynaud's disease
  illus. 5:512
Rayon 6:215
Rays (fish) 4:315, 317–18, 320,
    323–25, 328
  illus. 4:327
Rays (in geometry) 1:369
Rays (lunar features) 1:114,
    121–22
RCA Corporation 1:309
RDAs *see* Recommended Dietary
    Allowances
Reactants, Chemical 3:54–56
  alkali metals 3:29–30
  halogens 3:32–33
  nitrogen group 3:32
Reaction centers (in photosyn-
    thesis) 4:22

Reactions, Chemical *see* Chemi-
    cal reactions
Reaction turbines 2:316
Reactivity (of atoms) 3:48
Reactors (electric cables) 2:317
Reactors, Nuclear *see* Nuclear
    reactors
Reactor vessels (of nuclear
    reactors) 2:365
Read, A. C. (American aviator)
    6:155
Reading disorders *see* Dyslexia
Read-only memory (ROM)
    6:368–69, 371
Reagan, Ronald (American presi-
    dent) 1:262
Real images 3:286
Real number system 1:351
Real-time ultrasound 5:303
Rear-projection televisions
    6:297
Rear-wheel drive
  illus. 6:135
Réaumur, René (French scien-
    tist) 3:473
Réaumur temperature scale
  table(s) 6:421
Rebar (reinforced concrete) 6:30
  illus. 6:31
Reber, Grote (American radio
    amateur) 1:55
Recent epoch
  table(s) 2:20
Receptacles (of flowers) 4:101
Reception, Radio 6:248, 289–90
  diagram(s) 6:289
Reception, Television 6:295–96
Receptive disorders 5:365
Receptor cells 5:284
Recessive genes 3:408–9;
    5:315–16, 318–20, 420;
    6:70
  diagram(s) 3:407
Reciprocals (of numbers)
    1:348–49
Reciprocating engines
  diesel 2:314
  steam 6:97–99
Reclaimed wastewater 6:64
Reclamation Act (U.S., 1902)
    6:53
Reclosers (circuit breakers)
    2:319
Recombinant DNA 5:474–75
Recombination (in genetics)
    3:505; 4:32
Recommended Dietary Allow-
    ances (RDAs) 5:389–90
Reconstructive surgery *see*
    Plastic and reconstructive
    surgery
Recorde, Robert (English math-
    ematician) 1:330
Recorders, Videocassette *see*
    Videocassette recorders
Recording *see* Sound recording;
    Video recording
Records, Phonograph 6:278–79

Recreation, Wilderness 2:509, 515
Rectangles 1:374
Rectification 6:247
Rectifiers 3:255
Rectilinear motion 3:149
Rectilinear propagation of light 3:283
Rectum 5:254
  illus. 5:167–68, 249
Rectus abdominis
  illus. 5:166
Rectus femoris
  illus. 5:166
Recycling of waste 2:483, 492
  industrial chemistry 3:9
  illus. 2:483, 491
Red algae 4:18, 48, 50, 53
Red-bellied snakes 4:371
Red blood cells 3:319; 5:162–64, 206, 212–13
  bone marrow 5:174
  broken down in liver 5:262
  folate 5:386
  mammals' adaptation to altitude 5:6
  no nucleus or chromosomes 5:311, 419
  polycythemia 5:211
  substitutes for 5:506
  illus. 5:205, 208
    malaria-infected 5:213
Redbud trees 4:141
Red cedars
  illus. 4:124
Red-cockaded woodpeckers
  illus. 4:408
Red corals see Precious corals
Red Data Book (endangered species information) 2:499, 504
Red deer 5:120–21
Red-eyed vireos 4:460
  illus. 4:458
Red foxes 5:82–83
Red giant stars 1:192, 195, 197
Red grouse 4:426
Red Hills salamanders
  illus. 2:501
Redi, Francesco (Italian biologist) 3:375, 509
  illus. 3:510
Red kangaroos 5:18
Redox processes see Oxidation-reduction reaction
Redpolls
  illus. 4:393
Red raspberry slime mold
  illus. 4:51
Red Sea
  cyanobacteria 4:33
  salinity 2:229
Redshift 1:19, 208
Red-shouldered hawks 4:416–17
Red sprites (lightning) 2:141
Red squirrels 5:40
Red-tailed hawks 4:417

Red tide 4:47
Reducing agents 3:100
Reduction (in arithmetic) 1:349
Reduction (in chemistry) 3:27, 100
Red-winged blackbirds 4:460
Red wolves 2:505; 5:78
  illus. 5:79
Redwoods 4:10, 85, 87, 92–93
  rain forests 4:159
  wood construction 6:28
Red worms 4:245
Reed, Walter (U.S. Army doctor) 4:268–69
Reedbucks 5:130
  illus. 5:131
Reed fish 4:331
Reed instruments 3:216
REEFS 2:284–87, 290–91
  coral atolls 2:283
  fossils 1:488
  illus. 2:253
Reef scraps 2:286
Reentry maneuvers (of spacecraft) 1:240–41, 244, 251
Reeve, Christopher (American actor) 5:234
Refining of petroleum 2:329–32
  acid rain 2:474
  illus. 2:333
Reflecting telescopes 1:38
  illus. 1:43
Reflection (in physics)
  light 3:283–84; 6:222
  mechanical waves 3:197
  sound 3:203
  illus. 3:283–84
Reflectors see Reflecting telescopes
Reflectors, Solar see Solar reflectors
Reflex actions 5:226–27, 230
  babies 5:329
  pain response 5:288
  sleep 5:408
  startle response 3:377
  illus.
    nerve pathways 5:289
Reflex angles 1:370
Reflex arc 5:227
Reflex center 5:227
Reflux, Gastroesophageal see Heartburn
Reforestation 2:408; 4:126–27
Refracting telescopes 1:37–39
  illus. 1:38, 40
Refraction (of waves) see also Refraction of light
  mechanical waves 3:197
  sound 3:204
Refraction of light 3:284–85
  color 3:293–94
  fiber optics 6:222
  telescopes 1:37–38
  illus. 3:285, 294
Refractories 6:218
Refractors see Refracting telescopes

Refrigeration
  food preservation 6:80
Refrigeration of foods 6:79
Refuse see Solid wastes
Regal pythons see Reticulated pythons
Regeneration 3:456; 4:187
  crustaceans 4:248, 251
  earthworms 4:243–44
  lizards 4:338, 358
  Planaria 4:228
  salamanders 4:338, 349
  sea cucumbers 4:224
  starfish 4:223
  illus. 4:222
Regional geography 2:297
Registered dietitians 5:390
Registered nurses 5:483, 486
Registers (of computers) 6:370
Regulator proteins 3:459
Regulator stations (natural gas industry) 2:344
Regulus (star) 1:29
Regurgitation 5:440
Rehabilitation Act (U.S., 1973) 5:368
Rehabilitation medicine 5:486, 501
Reid, John B., Jr. (American geologist) 2:5–7
Reiki 5:514
Reindeer see Caribou
Reindeer moss 4:60, 163
Reinforced concrete 6:30–31
  building techniques 6:40
  road construction 6:44
  water pipes 2:449
Reinforced plastics 6:214
Reinforcement (in psychology) 5:338
Rejuvenated streams 2:425
Relativistic particles 3:348
RELATIVITY, Theory of 3:142, 342–52
  black holes 1:204, 208
  elementary particles 3:306
  space science 1:237
  wormholes 1:214
Relativity Mission (Gravity Probe B) 1:237
Relaxation techniques 5:289, 357
Relay (communications satellite) 1:309
Relay systems, Microwave 6:239–40
Reliability (in statistics) 3:511, 513
Religion 1:3
Rem (radiation unit) 2:372
Remainder 1:347
Remotely operated vehicles 6:200–201
  illus. 6:200
Remote manipulator system 1:252
REM sleep see Rapid eye movement sleep

Renaissance 6:8, 10
  medicine 5:412
  menageries 4:470
Renal anatomy *see* Kidneys
Renewable resources 2:406–13
Renin (hormone) 5:246
Rennin 5:250
Rensselaer Polytechnic Institute (RPI) (Troy, New York) 6:19
ReplayTV 6:287
Repletes (honey ants) 4:285
  illus. 4:284
Report Program Generator *see* RPG
Reports, Laboratory *see* Laboratory reports
Reprocessing of nuclear fuel 2:370
Reproducibility (in experiments) 3:513
REPRODUCTION 3:452–57 *see also* Alternation of generations; Asexual reproduction; Sexual reproduction
  acorn worms 4:311
  alligators 4:384
  animals 4:185–86
  bacteria 4:31–32
  bats 5:31
  birds 4:396
  bryophytes 4:59–61
  cartilaginous fish 4:324
  cell division 3:440–45
  cloning 3:422–23
  conifers 4:87–88
  crocodiles 4:381
  crustaceans 4:255
  dinosaurs 1:493
  dolphins 5:59
  egg-laying mammals 5:14–15
  elephants 5:106
  embryology 3:458–63
  ferns 4:80–83
  fish 4:320
  flowering plants 4:102–4
  frogs and toads 4:345–47
  fungi 4:38–39
  ginkgo and cycads 4:95
  humans *see* Human reproduction and birth
  insects 4:273, 275–76
  lancelets 4:311
  life, characteristics of 3:375
  life span 3:465–66
  light's effects on mammals 5:6
  lions 5:86
  livestock breeding 4:467–68
  lizards 4:361–62
  marsupials 5:16–17
  myriapods 4:265
  owls 4:420–21
  plants 4:9, 12–13, 15
  primates 5:145–46
  rabbits and hares 5:37–38
  reptiles 4:354–55
  salamanders and newts 4:351
  sponges 4:215–16
  tigers 5:87
  tunicates 4:309–10
  whales 5:48
  zoos 4:471–72, 477
Reproductive potential (of populations) 3:477–78
Reproductive system 4:185–86
  human 5:293–95
REPTILES 4:205, 352–55
  crocodilians 4:380–84
  dinosaurs 1:492–96
  extinct species 2:496–97
  fossils 1:488–89
  genetic variation 3:505
  herpetology 4:336–39
  lizards 4:356–62
  mammals' ancestors 5:2–3
  monotremes resemble 5:14–15
  pets 4:481, 490
  prehistoric animals 1:492
  pterosaurs 1:496
  snakes 4:363–74
  turtles 4:375–79
  zoo exhibits 4:476
Reptiles, Age of *see* Mesozoic era
Research papers, Scientific 3:512; 6:313, 319
RESERVOIRS 2:110, 410, 437–39, 450; 6:51–56
  geological effect 2:48
  hydroelectric power 2:377–80
  table(s)
    largest 2:438
Residency (in medicine) 5:414
Residual fuel oils 2:332
Resin 4:89
Resistance (in physics) *see* Drag
Resistance (of microbes to drugs) 5:445, 464–65
  bacteria 4:34
  evolutionary biology 3:506
Resistance (of the immune system to infection) 5:425–26
Resistance, Electrical 2:320; 3:256–58, 358; 6:220
Resistance, Environmental *see* Environmental resistance
Resistance heating 2:320
Resnik, Judith (American astronaut) 1:289
Resolution (Resolving power) 1:43–44
  microscopes 3:450; 6:330
  radio telescopes 1:56
Resolution (research ship) 2:276
Resonance 3:200
Resonance acceleration 6:353
Resonant particles 3:311
Resource Conservation and Recovery Act (U.S.) 2:491
Resource partitioning (in ecology) 3:481
Resources, Conservation of *see* Conservation
Respiration
  amphibians 4:342
  animal 4:185–86
  arachnids 4:258
  arthropods 4:247
  atmosphere 2:149
  babies 5:326
  baby's first breath 5:304
  bacteria 4:30
  birds 4:394
  carbon cycle 4:21
  cell dynamics 3:436–38
  crocodilians 4:381–82
  crustaceans 4:254
  excretory system 5:261
  exercise 5:397, 399
  fish 4:318–19, 329–30
  frogs 4:348
  humans 5:215–22
  insects 4:274
  mammals 5:4
  plants 4:13
  sleep 5:408
  turtles 4:375
  water cycle 3:488, 490
  diagram(s) 4:318
Respirators 5:222
Respiratory nerve center 5:220
RESPIRATORY SYSTEM 4:185–86; 5:172, 215–22
  air pollution 2:468
  allergies 5:448
  circulatory system 5:196
  diseases and pollution 2:469
  dolphins 5:56
  drug delivery technology 5:474
  infectious diseases 5:429
  inhaled illicit drugs 5:375
  ribs and 5:177–78
  virus infection 3:392
  whales 5:47
  illus. 5:168
Responsiveness (in biology) 3:377–78
Rest mass 3:306
Restriction enzymes 3:417; 5:322; 6:72
Restriction fragment length polymorphism (RFLP) analysis 1:514
Resurrection ferns
  illus. 4:82
Resurrection plants 4:77
Retailing, Online *see* e-commerce
Retardation, Mental *see* Mental retardation
Reticulated pythons 4:370
Reticuloendothelial system 5:207
Retina 5:270–72
  color vision 3:301–3
  laser surgery 5:480, 489
  illus. 5:271
Retinene 5:270
Retrograde motion (of planets) 1:77; 3:141
Retro-rockets 1:240, 251

Retroviruses 5:441
Rett syndrome 5:354
Réunion Island (Indian Ocean) 2:56
Reverberation 3:203, 208
Reverberatory furnaces
  illus. 6:182
Reversal of Earth's magnetic field 3:271
Reverse osmosis 2:449
Reverse transcriptase 5:441–42
Reversible reactions 3:55–56
Revolutionary Calendar (France) 1:477
Revolutionary War see American Revolution
Revolutions (in geology) 2:20
Reward system (in the brain) 5:371
Rhea (moon of Saturn) 1:145–46
Rheas (birds) 4:398, 412
Rheboks 5:130
Rheiformes see Rheas
Rhenium 3:43
Rhesus monkeys 5:142, 147
Rheumatic fever 5:429, 440
Rheumatoid arthritis 5:183, 240, 473
Rheumatoid factor 5:428
Rheumatoid nodules 5:428
Rh factor 5:209
"Rhind Papyrus" 1:329
Rhine River 2:459
RHINOCEROSES 1:498–99; 5:111–13
  illus. 1:499; 4:465
Rhinoceros vipers 4:374
Rhinoviruses 3:388, 393; 5:429
Rhipidistians 4:330
Rhizobium 4:68
Rhizoids 4:37, 61, 81–82
Rhizomes 3:456; 4:79, 81, 139
Rhizopoda see Cellular slime molds
Rhodium 3:43
Rhodophyta see Red algae
Rhodopsin see Visual purple
Rhodospirillum
  illus. 4:27
Rhomboids 1:374
Rhombuses 1:374
Rhône Glacier (Europe) 2:96
Rhumb lines 6:167
Rhyolite 2:34, 134
Rib cartilages 5:177
Riboflavin (Vitamin B$_2$) 5:384
Ribonucleic acid see RNA
Ribose
  illus. 3:415
Ribosomal RNA 3:415
Ribosomes 3:123, 414, 430
  bacteria 4:29–30
  cell structure 3:428–29
  cellular energy 3:439
  prokaryotes 3:427
Ribs 5:177–78
  turtles 4:375
  illus. 5:165, 174

Rice 3:423; 4:460
  genome 6:14
Rice rats 5:43
Rice tenrecs 5:28
Rice weevils 4:299
Richard I (king of England) 6:16
Richards, Linda (American nurse) 5:482
Richardson Mountains 2:89
Richter, Burton (American physicist) 3:314
  illus. 3:316
Richter Magnitude Scale 2:50–51
Ricinuleids 4:262–63
Rickets 5:184, 384
Rickettsia 4:30–31; 5:428
Ride, Sally K. (American astronaut) 1:289
  illus. 1:286
Ridge, Mark (American balloonist) 1:271
Ridge, Mid-oceanic see Mid-oceanic ridge
Riemann, George Friedrich Bernhard (German mathematician) 1:335, 401
Riemannian geometry 1:335, 401–3
Rift valleys, Submarine 2:40, 270
  diagram(s) 2:42
Rigel (star) 1:32, 192
Right angles 1:369–70
Right ascension (star position) 1:36
Right triangles 1:371, 387–88
Right whales 5:51–52, 54
Rigor mortis 3:469
Rill marks (on beaches) 2:295
Rills (lunar features) 1:114, 122
Rimstone 2:128
Rimus 4:87
Ring compounds 3:112–13
Ringhals 4:373
Ring-necked snakes 4:371
Ring networks (of computers) 6:386
  illus. 6:386
Ring of Fire (volcanoes around Pacific Ocean) 2:59, 256
Rings (around planets)
  Neptune 1:154–55
  Saturn 1:140–44
  Uranus 1:149–50
  illus. 1:139, 145
Rings, Tree see Tree rings
Ringworm 3:451; 4:43; 5:428
Rio Grande 2:459
Rip currents 2:239, 292
Ripple marks (on beaches) 2:293, 295
Riptides see Rip currents
Risca, Viviana 6:317
Risso's dolphins 5:60
Rita (hurricane, 2005) 2:200
Ritalin see Methylphenidate

Rittenberg, David (American chemist) 3:117
Ritter, Carl (German geographer) 2:299
Ritter, Johann Wilhelm (German physicist) 3:275
Riverbanks Zoo and Garden (Columbia, South Carolina) 4:476
RIVERS 2:100–105
  acid rain 2:475–76
  biomes 3:499
  coastal formation 2:290, 292
  deltas 2:424
  erosion 2:120, 122, 418–25
  groundwater 2:115
  lake formation 2:109–10
  plant communities 4:137
  pollution 2:406, 460–61
  sediment flow 3:319
  table(s)
    great rivers of world 2:105
Rivularia
  illus. 4:30
RMS see Remote manipulator system
RNA 3:6, 413–15
  AIDS 5:442
  nucleotides 3:123
  virus 3:392
Roadrunners 4:402
  illus. 4:403
Roads and highways 6:42–44
  human-caused erosion 2:124
  illus.
    construction 6:20
Roan antelopes 5:129
Roaring forties 2:185
Robert E. Lee (steamboat)
  illus. 6:111
Robins 4:395, 454
  illus. 4:447
Robosurgery 5:480
Robot manipulator arm see Remote manipulator system
ROBOTS
  deep-sea exploration 2:222, 277, 279
  factories 6:192
  nanotechnology 6:339
  science fiction 1:505–6
  spacecraft 1:232–33, 236
  space probes 1:290
  telesurgery 6:391
  illus. 1:6
    assembly lines 6:21
    nanorobot 6:338
    science fiction 1:505
    trash collection 2:484
Roche, Edouard (French astronomer) 1:144
Roche's limit 1:144
Roches moutonnées 2:99
Rock cavies 5:45
Rock cycle 2:37, 133–34
Rock doves 4:429
Rocket (locomotive) 6:125

Rocket boosters *see* Solid-rocket boosters
Rocket fuel 1:243, 249
Rocket into Interplanetary Space (book, Oberth) **1:**265
Rockets 1:239–40, 242–43
  airplanes **6:**156
  atmospheric research **2:**153
  cosmic-ray research **1:**227
  engines **6:**105–6, 164
  escape velocity **1:**432
  National Aerospace Plane **1:**262
  rocket science **1:**235, 265
  satellite launches **1:**303
Rocket science 1:235
Rock-filled dams
  illus. **6:**54
ROCKS 2:3, **132–36**
  biostratigraphy **1:**482
  climate's effect on **2:**216
  coastal formation **2:**291
  collecting **2:**139–40
  deserts **2:**84–85
  Earth **1:**106; **2:**30–37
  Earth, age of **2:**15–21
  erosion **2:**120–24
  geothermal energy **2:**393
  glacier plucking **2:**97
  groundwater **2:**113–19
  magnetization **2:**39
  minerals in ecosystems **3:**491
  moon rocks *see* Moon rocks
  mountains **2:**69–70, 73
  plant succession **4:**122–23
  streams **2:**420
  volcanic ash **2:**433
  volcanic rock **2:**61–62, 134
  weathering **2:**121
  wind erosion **2:**427
Rock salt *see* Sodium chloride
Rock selaginella 4:77
Rockville Bridge (Pennsylvania) **6:**50
Rock wallabies 5:18
Rocky Mountains 2:67, 171, 186
  illus. **4:**165
Rocky Mountain spotted fever 4:263; **5:**428
Rocky River hydroelectric project (Connecticut) **2:**378
  illus. **2:**379
RODENTS 5:12, **39–45**
  acorn cycle **4:**147
  desert life **2:**86; **4:**169
  fossils **1:**480
  grasslands **4:**140
  hibernation **5:**5
  pets **4:**481, 487
  teeth **5:**8
Rodger, Calbraith (American aviator) **6:**153
Rods (in the eyes) **5:**270–71
Roebling, John Augustus (American engineer) **6:**15, 50

Roebling, Washington Augustus (American engineer) **6:**15
  illus. **6:**16
Roe deer 5:122
Roentgen, Wilhelm Konrad (German physicist) **3:**276; **5:**451
Roentgenium 3:46
Roentgen rays *see* X-rays
Roentgen Satellite *see* ROSAT
Rogers, Carl (American psychologist) **5:**344
Rogun Dam (Tajikistan) **6:**53
Rohrer, Heinrich (Swiss physicist) **6:**337
Rohypnol *see* Flunitrazepam
Roller coasters 3:159
Rolling (aircraft movement)
  illus. **6:**159–60
Rolling (in steelmaking)
  illus. **6:**30
Roll-on, roll-off ships 6:113
Rolls Royce Phantom IV (automobile)
  illus. **6:**136
ROM *see* Read-only memory
Roman numerals 1:343–44
Romanov family (Russian royalty) **5:**322
Rome, Ancient
  accounting **1:**455
  agriculture **4:**171
  aqueducts **2:**436; **6:**17, 52–53
  archaeology **1:**463
  bridges **6:**50
  building techniques **6:**33
  calendar **1:**475–76
  ceramics **6:**217–18
  construction materials **6:**26
  dams **6:**52
  geography **2:**298
  maps **6:**167
  medicine **5:**412
  metallurgy **6:**175
  numerals **1:**343
  roads **6:**42–43
  technology and society **6:**7
  tunnels **6:**47
  illus.
    aqueducts **2:**435; **6:**17
    building techniques **6:**33–34
"Roofies" *see* Flunitrazepam
Roof membrane (in the ear) **5:**276
Room-and-pillar mining 2:351–52, 355
  illus. **2:**352
Roosevelt, Theodore (American president) **2:**405, 509; **4:**127
  illus. **2:**508
Root (in mathematics) **1:**349
Root canal 5:280
Root caps 4:66
Root fungi *see* Mycorrhizae
Root hairs 4:66

Roots (of plants)
  desert plants **4:**167
  erosion prevented by **2:**417
  ferns **4:**80
  geotropism **4:**114
  grasses **4:**139
  mangrove trees **4:**153
  monocots and dicots **4:**107
  vascular plants **4:**12, 64–68
  diagram(s) **4:**67
Roots (of teeth)
  illus. **5:**280
Rorqual whales 5:49–51, 54
Rorschach Inkblot Test
  illus. **5:**337
Rosa, Emily 6:317
ROSAT (artificial satellite) **1:**51, 59, 64
Roseate spoonbills 4:446
  illus. **4:**444
Roses 4:174
Rosetta (spacecraft) **1:**296
Rosetta Stone 1:463
  illus. **1:**464
Rosette Nebula in Monoceros
  illus. **1:**185
Rose weevils 4:299
Rossi, Bruno (Italian physicist) **1:**227
Rossi X-ray Timing Explorer (RXTE) 1:52, 59
Ross Sea 2:91
Rosy boas 4:370
Rotary drilling 2:326–27
  illus. **2:**324
Rotary engines 6:102
  illus. **6:**101
Rotating wall clouds 2:192
Rotation
  Earth **1:**109–10; **2:**25–26, 29, 182, 209–10, 220, 247
  Mercury **1:**97
  Milky Way **1:**187, 189
  Pluto-Charon system **1:**157
  telescopes in motion **1:**44
  Uranus **1:**149
  illus.
    tilt of axes of planets **1:**74
Rotifera 4:201
Roughage *see* Fiber, Dietary
Rough endoplasmic reticulum 3:429
Round window (in the ear) **5:**275–76
ROUNDWORMS 4:202, **225–30**
Routers 6:304, 389
Rover vehicles
  illus. **1:**259
ROVs *see* Remotely operated vehicles
Royal antelopes 5:126, 131
Royal cells 4:286
Royal jelly 4:286
RPG (computer language) **6:**378
Rubber 3:112; **4:**159
  synthetics **2:**334; **6:**211, 215
Rubber boas 4:370**

Rubella (German measles) 5:302
Rubidium 3:29, 43
Ruby Falls (Tennessee) 2:131
Ruby lasers 6:345
Rudders 6:109, 159–60
Ruffed grouse 4:426
Rugae 5:250
Rumford, Count (Benjamin Thompson) (American-born British physicist) 3:220
Ruminants 5:8, 13, 118–23
  antelopes 5:126–31
  bacteria in digestion 4:35
  bison, buffalo, and oxen 5:132–35
  camels and llamas 5:116–17
  feeding behavior 4:193–94
  giraffes and okapis 5:124–25
Runcorn, Stanley K. (British scientist) 2:29
Runners (on plants) 3:456
Running (sport) 5:398, 400–401
  illus. 5:215
Running pine 4:77
Runoff (of water) 2:416, 458
Run-of-river hydroelectric plants 2:378
Ruppel's foxes 5:83
Rush tyrants 4:449
Ruska, Ernst (German physicist) 6:334, 337
Russell, Bertrand (British mathematician and philosopher) 1:334, 445
Russell's paradox 1:445
Russell's vipers 4:374
Russia see also Union of Soviet Socialist Republics
  Arctic's natural resources 2:90
  geothermal energy 2:392–93
  mammoth specimens 1:499
  manned space programs 1:285
  natural gas 2:330
  space station 1:267–69
  steppes 2:77; 4:140–41
  submarines 6:122
  triticale 6:71
Rust (iron corrosion) 2:172; 3:14, 101, 103, 375; 6:30
  illus. 3:375; 6:227
Rusts (fungi) 3:451; 4:45
Rusty-spotted cats 5:92
Ruthenium 3:43
Rutherford, Ernest (British scientist) 3:6, 18, 126, 328; 6:359
  diagram(s)
    atomic model 3:17
  illus. 3:323
Rutherfordium 3:37, 43

S

SAARDs see Slow-acting anti-rheumatic drugs

Saber-toothed cats 5:84
  illus. 1:499
Sabine, Wallace C. (American physicist) 3:208
Sable antelopes 5:127–29
  illus. 5:128
Saccharides see Carbohydrates
Sac fungi 4:40–44
Sacral vertebrae 5:175–76
Sacred lotus plants 4:105
Sacroiliac joint 5:176
Sacrum 5:175–76, 180–81
  illus. 5:174, 176
Saddlebacks see Common dolphins
Saddle points (in game theory) 1:428
Safety
  automotive safety 6:134–35
  chemical industry 6:206
  coal mining 2:353–55
  electric-power transmission 2:316–17
  genetically engineered foods 6:75
  laboratory methods 3:513
  laser shows 6:350
  marine safety radar 6:258
  nuclear reactors 2:314, 368, 371–72, 376
  sharks 4:326
  spelunking 2:130
  thunderstorms 2:178–79
  ticks, protection against 4:259
  tornadoes 2:194
Safety belts see Seat belts
Safety lamps 2:354
Safety rods (of nuclear reactors) 2:371
Sagan, Carl (American astronomer) 1:08, 291; 6:321
Sagebrush 2:7; 4:167
Sagitta (constellation) 1:30
Sagittarius (constellation) 1:30, 183
Sagittarius A (possible black hole) 1:187
Sago palms 4:97
Saguaro, Lake (Arizona) 2:439
Saguaro cacti 2:86
  illus. 3:497; 4:166
Sahara 2:77, 81, 83, 86, 404; 4:166
  dust storms 2:432
  sand dunes 2:429
  temperature swings 2:82
  wind 2:186
  illus. 2:85
Sailing ships 6:109–11
Sails 6:107, 109
Saint Elmo's fire 2:178
  illus. 2:177
Saint Helens, Mount (volcano, Washington) 2:55, 57, 59, 62
  illus. 2:60
Saint Lawrence, Gulf of 2:265
Saint Lawrence Seaway 6:45

Saint Peter's Basilica (Rome, Italy)
  illus. 6:35
Saker falcons 4:419
SALAMANDERS 4:336–37, 340–42, 349–51
  animal behavior 4:190
  research 4:338
  illus. 2:128, 501; 4:340
Salicylic acid 5:462
Saline breast implants 5:506
Salinity 2:229, 275; 6:64
Saliva 5:236, 248–49
Salmon 4:333
  aging 3:466
  dams 2:380, 410; 6:56
  fish farming 6:90
  illus. 3:465; 4:185, 318, 331
Salmonella 4:30, 339; 5:424–25; 6:77
  pets that carry bacteria 4:490
  illus. 4:27
Salt (Common salt; Table salt) see Sodium chloride
Saltatory propagation 5:225
Salt bridges 3:105
Salt domes 2:324
Salting (food preservation) 6:78
Salt lakes 2:107
Salt marshes 4:152
Salt pans 2:86
SALTS (in chemistry) 3:94–99
  see also Sodium chloride
  blood 5:206
  halide salts 2:138
  halogens 3:33
  ionic compounds 3:50
  lakes 2:111
  ocean 1:106; 2:229–30; 3:87
  polar substances 3:81
  sedimentary deposits 2:36
  sedimentary rocks 2:136
  water, reaction with 3:87
  water solutions 3:84
Saltwater see Seawater
Saluki 4:481
Salvadori monitors 4:357
Salvarsan 3:447
Salyut (space station) 1:248, 265–66
Samarium 3:43
Sambars 5:121
Samoa 2:282
Sample-and-hold process (digital recording) 6:284
Sample spaces (probability) 1:416–18
Sampling (in statistics) 1:405
San (people) 2:86
San Andreas Fault (California) 2:40–41, 47, 53–54
  illus. 2:49
Sanchez-Villagra, Marcelo (Venezuelan paleontologist) 1:480
Sand 2:35
  beach sands 2:290, 293, 295

Sand (cont.)
caves **2:**129
climate's effect on **2:**216
coastal drift **3:**319
deserts **2:**81, 84, 122–23
fulgurite **2:**179–80
groundwater **2:**113–14
wind erosion **2:**426–27
illus. **1:**4; **2:**123
Sandbars 2:289, 423–24
Sandblasting (wind erosion)
2:427
Sand boas 4:370
Sandbox trees 4:119
Sand Country Almanac (book,
Leopold) **3:**474
Sand dollars 4:224
illus. **4:**223
Sand dunes 2:84, 290, 426–30
plant succession **4:**123–24
illus. **2:**83, 121; **4:**123
Sand foxes 5:83
San Diego Wild Animal Park
(California) **4:**472, 477
San Diego Zoo (California)
4:476–77
Sandpipers 4:436–37
Sandstone 2:35, 37, 135
cave formation **2:**129
construction materials **6:**25
groundwater **2:**118
illus. **2:**135
Sandstorms 2:85, 427
San Francisco (California)
San Andreas Fault **2:**54
illus.
earthquake (1989) **2:**50
Golden Gate Bridge **2:**162
San Francisco-Oakland Bay
Bridge 6:22
Sanger, Frederick (British bio-
chemist) **3:**417
Sanitary landfills *see* Landfills
Sanitation 2:119; **5:**431
San Jacinto River
illus.
fire **2:**459
San Joaquin Valley (California)
2:459
San Juan (nuclear submarine)
illus. **6:**121
San Juan River
illus. **2:**103
SA node *see* Sinoatrial node
Santa Ana wind 2:186
Santos-Dumont, Alberto (Brazil-
ian aviator) **6:**150
Saolas 5:134
Sap 4:89
Saprophytes 4:37–38
Saprospirae 4:29
Sapsuckers 4:408
illus. **4:**393
Sarcodines 3:454; **4:**209–12
Sarcolemma 5:200
Sarcomastigophora 4:211
Sardines 4:332
Sargasso Sea 2:241

Saroses 1:179
SARS *see* Severe acute respira-
tory syndrome
SARSAT *see* Satellite-aided
tracking
Sartorius
illus. **5:**166
Sastrugi 2:98
Satcoms *see* Communications
satellites
Satellite-aided tracking 1:255
Satellite Laser Ranging 6:351
Satellite radio 6:290
Satellites (moons) **1:**25, 74–75
Jupiter's moons **1:**134, 137–38
Mars' moons **1:**132
Moon **1:**106
Neptune's moons **1:**155
Saturn's moons **1:**144–46
Uranus' moons **1:**150
SATELLITES, Artificial 1:302–15
atmospheric research **2:**153
aurora research **2:**158
cosmic-ray research **1:**227
defense, military **1:**263
Earth studies **1:**259, 297;
2:2–3, 5, 41
geography **2:**296
navigation **6:**171–72
ocean-current study **2:**242
oceanic exploration **2:**224
SeaSat **2:**265
solar instruments **1:**93
solar power station **2:**389
space station **1:**264–69
television **6:**294–95
TOPEX/Poseidon **2:**242, 255
weather **2:**164, 200, 204–6
X-ray astronomy **1:**58–59
Satellite TV *see* Direct Broadcast
Satellites
Saturated fats 3:111, 120;
5:382–83
Saturated hydrocarbons 3:111
Saturated solutions 3:80
Saturation (of color) **3:**300–301
Saturation, Zone of (ground-
water) **2:**115, 117, 119
illus. **2:**113
Saturn (automobile) **6:**148
SATURN (planet) **1:**74, 139–46
auroras **2:**155, 157
Cassini spacecraft **1:**295; **3:**382
life, possibility of **1:**320–22
satellites **1:**75
space probe **1:**292
illus. **1:**75–76
Saturn (rocket) **1:**244, 266
illus. **1:**243
Saturn (video-game system)
6:299
Saturn's family of comets 1:164
Saud, Al- (Saudi prince) **1:**285
Saudi Arabia 2:335
illus. **2:**448
Saurischians 1:493–95
Sauropods 1:494–95

Saussure, Nicholas Theodore
de (Swiss botanist) **4:**17
Savannah (steamship) **6:**111
Savannas 2:77–78, 212; **3:**494;
4:136, 140–43
illus. **2:**76; **3:**496
Savery, Thomas (English inven-
tor) **6:**190
Savitskaya, Svetlana (Soviet
cosmonaut) **1:**289
Sawdust 3:62
Sawflies 4:280
Saw grass 4:155
Saw-whet owls
illus. **4:**420
Saxifrage 4:164
Saxitoxin 4:53
Saxophones 3:216
Say, Thomas (American natural-
ist) **4:**267
Scalar quantities 3:151–52
Scala structures (of the ear) *see*
Stairways (of the ear)
Scaled quails 4:425
Scale insects 4:269
Scales (in music) **3:**212
Scales (of animals)
butterflies and moths **4:**300
crocodilians **4:**381
lizards **4:**358–59
reptiles **4:**352–53
snakes **4:**364
illus. **4:**318
Scallops 4:238–39
Scaly anteaters *see* Pangolins
Scandium 3:43
Scanners (computer-input
devices) **6:**366
illus. **6:**363
Scanners (in medical diagnosis)
3:319
Scanning (of television pictures)
6:292–94
diagram(s) **6:**294
Scanning electron microscopes
3:450
illus. **6:**330, 336
Scanning emission micro-
scopes 6:335–36
Scanning tunneling micro-
scopes 3:16; **6:**337, 340
Scaphopods 4:203, 241
Scapula 5:178–79
illus. **5:**165, 174–75
Scarab beetles 4:296–97
Scarlet cups (fungi) **4:**40
Scarlet fever 5:238–39
Scarlet flamingos *see* Greater
flamingos
Scarlet macaws 4:401
illus. **4:**402
Scarlet tanagers 4:458
Scarps (cliffs on Mercury)
1:97–98
Scars 5:239
Scattering of light 2:162

Scavengers 3:486–87
  birds of prey 4:415–16
  scarab beetles 4:296–97
Scents (of flowers) 4:102
Schaus swallowtail butterflies
  illus. 4:303
Schawlow, A. H. (American
  physicist) 6:345
Schirra, Walter M., Jr. (American
  astronaut) 1:241
  illus. 1:240
Schist 2:37, 136
Schistosomiasis 4:227
Schizoid personality 5:353
Schizophrenia 5:349–50, 356
  medications 5:466
  substance abuse 5:375
  illus.
    PET scan of brain 5:456
Schleiden, Matthias Jakob (German physiologist) 3:369,
  424
  illus. 3:426
Schliemann, Heinrich (German
  archaeologist) 1:468
Schmidt, Karl Patterson (American herpetologist) 4:372
Schoenheimer, Rudolf (American chemist) 3:117
School nursing 5:487
Schools (of fish)
  illus. 4:190, 315
Schott's pygmy cedars 4:168
Schrieffer, J. Robert (American
  physicist) 3:359–60
Schrödinger, Erwin (German
  physicist) 3:19, 331
  illus. 3:323
Schrödinger wave equation
  3:331, 333
Schroeder, William (artificial
  heart recipient) 5:504
Schwann, Theodor (German
  physiologist) 3:369, 424
  illus. 3:426
Schwarzschild radius *see* Event
  horizon
Schwassmann-Wachmann,
  Comet 1:164
SCI *see* Ship-controlled intercep-
  tion radar
Science centers *see* Museums
  and science centers
SCIENCE EDUCATION 6:320–29
SCIENCE FAIRS AND
  PROJECTS 6:312–19
SCIENCE FICTION 1:500–506
Science projects *see* Science
  fairs and projects
Scientific method 1:1–3; 3:367,
  509–10
  Aristotle 3:367
  ecology 3:473
  experiments 3:509–10
  science education 6:324
  science fairs and projects
  6:317–19
Scientific notation 1:359

Scientific Revolution 6:18
Scimitar oryx 5:129–30
Scintillation counters 6:359
Scintillators 1:52
Scissorbills *see* Skimmers
Scissors 3:170
Sclera 5:269
  illus. 5:271
Scureids 4:66
Sclerenchyma cells 4:66
Scolosaurus 1:496
Scolytidae 4:299
Scopolamine 5:470
SCORE (communications satel-
  lite) 1:308
Scorpion fish 4:335
Scorpion flies 4:280
Scorpions 4:248–49, 257–59,
  261–63
  fossils 1:488
  illus. 4:258
Scorpius (constellation) 1:30, 58
Scotch pines 4:72, 90
Scotland 2:129–30, 465
Scott, D. Henry (British botanist)
  1:481
Scouring rushes *see* Horsetails
Scours (animal disease) 6:73
Sco X-1 (binary star) 1:58
Scramjet engines 1:262;
  6:105–6
Scrapie 3:390
Screech owls 4:420–21
Screening tests (in medicine)
  5:436
Screw propellers 6:110–11
Screws 3:172–73
Screwworm flies 3:320, 4:270
  illus. 6:63
Scripps Canyon (California)
  2:268–69
Scripps Institution of Oceanog-
  raphy 2:224; 4:314
Scrotum 5:294
Scrub biomes 3:494
Scrub wallabies 5:18
Scuba diving 2:224; 4:313
Sculling 6:92
Scurvy 5:387
Scyphozoa 4:200
SDI *see* Strategic Defense Initia-
  tive
Sea *see* Ocean
Sea anemones 3:456; 4:219
  illus. 4:176
Sea Around Us (book, Carson)
  3:472
Seabeam 2:265, 274–75
  illus. 2:272
Seabirds 4:446
Seaborgium 3:43
Sea breezes 2:170, 183
Sea caves 2:129–30
Sea Cliff (submersible) 6:124
Sea cows *see* Sirenians
Sea cucumbers 4:224
  illus. 4:223

Sea dragons
  illus. 3:478; 4:333
Seafloor spreading 2:40–41, 47
Seafloor vents *see* Hydrothermal
  vents
Seagulls *see* Gulls
Sea horses 4:318, 334–35
Sea ice *see* Icebergs and sea ice
Sealants, Dental 5:280
Sea lettuce *see* Ulva
Sea level
  coastlines 2:288
  glacial melting 2:88–89, 93
  glaciation 1:498
  global warming 2:154
Sea lilies 4:224
Sea lions 2:503; 5:10, 63, 66
  illus. 5:1
Seals (animals) 5:63–64, 66–67
  endangered species 2:498, 503
  illus. 4:467
Sea mice 4:245
Sea minks 2:496
Seamounts 2:71, 234, 270
Sea of Galilee *see* Galilee, Sea
  of
Sea otters 3:476; 5:98
  illus. 2:452
Sea pens
  illus. 4:216
Seaplanes 6:153
  illus. 6:162
Search for Extraterrestrial Intelligence program (SETI)
  1:317, 320, 324
Sea robins (fish) 4:335
SeaSat (artificial satellite) 1:315;
  2:265
Seashores *see* Coasts
Sea snakes 4:372, 374
Seasonal dimorphism 4:301
Seasons of the year 1:110–12
  astronomy, history of 1:469–70
  calendar 1:478
  climates of the world 2:209
  jet streams 2:150–51
  lake temperatures 2:111
  Mars 1:129
  sleep depth variations 5:407
  Uranus 1:149
  wet and dry seasons 2:171
Sea spiders 4:248
Sea squirts (Tunicates) 4:205,
  309–10
  illus. 4:308
Sea stars *see* Starfish
Sea swallows *see* Terns
Seat belts 6:134
Sea tortoises 3:465–66
Sea turtles 4:377–78
  illus. 3:266
Sea urchins 3:476; 4:197, 224
  illus. 3:477; 4:222
Sea vases
  illus. 4:309
Seawalls 2:294

Seawater 2:229–30
  aquifer contamination 2:118
  chemical oceanography 2:223
  corrosion 3:103
  decomposition 3:104
  deep-sea exploration 2:275
  desalting *see* Desalination of
    seawater
  dissolved elements in 3:82, 84,
    87
  nuclear fusion 2:376
  oxygen content 2:217
  salt content 2:228
  sea ice 2:262–63
  solutions 3:75
  illus. 3:83
Seaweeds 2:397–98; 4:46, 48,
  53
Seawolf (nuclear submarine)
  6:121
Sea World (San Diego, California) 4:472
  illus. 4:471
Sebaceous glands 5:265–67
Sebum 5:265
Secobarbital 5:373
Second (unit of measurement)
  3:136
Secondary batteries (Storage
  batteries; Wet cells)
  3:105, 253; 6:141
  illus. 3:102, 104
Secondary climatic optimum
  2:219
Secondary colors 3:298
Secondary growth (of plants)
  4:70
Secondary succession 3:483;
  4:121–22, 124–25
Secondary waves (in physics)
  see S waves
Secondhand smoking *see* Passive smoking
Second law of motion 3:156–57
Secretary birds 4:416
Secretin 5:252
Secular variations of Earth's
  magnetic field 3:270–71
Sedative-hypnotic drugs 5:374
Sedatives 5:373
Sedges 4:117, 153
Sedillot, Charles (French physician) 3:446
Sediment
  alluvial fans 2:104
  coasts 2:289–90, 292
  continental slopes 2:268
  delta formation 2:104
  floodplains 2:104
  mountains 2:69, 71, 74
  plateau formation 2:79
  reservoirs 2:380
  rivers 2:103, 122; 3:319
  water changes the land 2:417,
    419–20, 422–25
  water supply, removal from
    2:444–45
Sedimentary reefs 2:284

Sedimentary rocks 1:106; 2:4,
  31, 34–36, 133, 135–36
  fossils 1:480, 484–85; 2:138
  mountains 2:71, 73
  ocean floor 2:276
  volcanic ash 2:433
Sedimentation rate of red blood
  cells 5:213
Seebeck effect 3:224
Seed banks 2:497
  illus. 2:496
Seed coat 3:463
Seeding (of crystals) 3:93
Seed plants 3:455; 4:13
  illus. 3:463
Seeds 3:456, 462–63 *see also*
  Seed plants
  conifers 4:84, 86, 88
  dispersal 4:99, 104, 119, 158
  flowering plants 4:103–4
  germination 4:104–6
  illus.
    dispersal 4:119
Seed-tree cutting 4:129, 146
Seepage springs 2:116
Sega (video game company)
  6:299, 301
Segmented worms *see* Annelids
Segregation (in genetics)
  3:408–9; 5:316, 318
Seiche (ocean waves) *see* Stand-
  ing waves (Seiche)
Seifs 2:84
Seismic gaps 2:54
Seismic sea waves *see* Tsuna-
  mis
Seismic tomography 2:25
Seismic waves 2:22–25
  earthquakes 2:49
  wave behavior 3:195–97
  illus. 2:50
Seismographs 2:23, 49, 51, 53
  natural gas prospecting 2:339
  petroleum prospecting
    2:325–26
Seismology 2:4; 3:145 *see also*
  Earthquakes
Seismometers 2:5, 51, 60
  early China 2:7
Sei whales 5:50
Sejnowski, Terrence J. (Ameri-
  can computer scientist)
  6:374
Seki, T. (Japanese astronomer)
  1:166
Seladangs *see* Gaur
Selandia (ship) 6:112
Selection cutting of timber
  4:129, 146
Selective absorption of light
  3:297–98
Selective reabsorption (in the
  kidney) 5:260
Selective serotonin receptor
  antagonists 5:466
Selenium 3:29, 32, 43; 5:388
Self-pollination 4:102

Self-replication (in technology)
  6:339, 343
Selway-Bitterroot wilderness
  (Idaho-Montana) 2:511
Semen 5:295
Semicircles 1:375
Semicircular canal (in the ear)
  5:275
  illus. 5:276
Semiconductor lasers 6:346
Semiconductors 2:310, 321;
  6:246–47, 250–51
  genetically engineered materi-
    als 3:108
  metalloids 3:29
  photovoltaic-power systems
    2:385
  production 6:231–33
  silicon 3:91
Semidiurnal tides 2:246
Seminal vesicles 5:295
Semipermeable membranes
  3:80
Semiplumes 4:392
Semmelweis, Ignaz Philipp
  (Hungarian physician)
  5:423
Senescence *see* Aging
Senile dementia 5:353
Senile plaques 5:353–54
Senior citizens *see* Old age
Sense organs *see* Senses and
  sensation
Senses and sensation *see also*
  Nervous system
  animal behavior 4:191–92
  arachnids 4:257–58
  Aristotle's classification 5:336
  birds 4:395
  butterflies and moths 4:301
  cartilaginous fish 4:324, 326
  crustaceans 4:252–53
  fish 4:320
  insects 4:273–74
  learning disabilities 5:364–65,
    368
  lizards 4:360
  nervous tissue 5:164
  pain 5:287–92
  skin 5:267
  smell, taste, and touch
    5:283–86
  snakes 4:364
Sensitive plants 4:9, 117
Sensors (in electronics) 6:201–2
Sensory areas (of the brain)
  5:229
  illus. 5:231
Sensory fibers *see* Afferent
  fibers
Sensory implants 5:507–9
Sepals 4:101
Sepia 4:234
September 11, 2001 2:455
Septic embolus 5:212
Septic tanks 2:488
Septum 5:177, 198
Septuplets 5:307

Sequence (in DNA) 5:309
Sequences (in mathematics)
    1:361–62
Sequoias 4:85, 93
    illus. 3:466; 4:1, 85
Seral stages 4:121
Serengeti Plain (Africa) 4:140,
    142
    illus. 3:496; 4:141
Seres 4:121
Series (in mathematics) 1:362–63
Series electric circuits 3:259
    illus. 3:258
Serotonin 3:115; 5:356
    pain 5:292
Serotonin reuptake inhibitors
    5:356
Serpens (constellation) 1:29–30
Serpent stars 4:223
Serpulid reefs 2:290–91
Serrate leaves 4:73
Sertraline (Zoloft) 5:466
Serum 5:208
Serum albumin 5:206
Servals 5:91–92
Servers (computers) 6:307, 362,
    386, 388
Service dogs 4:487
Service module (of spacecraft)
    1:245
Servomechanisms 6:196, 199
Servo robots 6:199
SESs see Surface effect ships
Sessile leaves 4:71, 73
SETI see Search for Extraterres-
    trial Intelligence program
SET THEORY 1:329–30, 335,
    438–45
Settling basins 2:445
Severe acute respiratory syn-
    drome (SARS) 3:393
Severe combined immunodefi-
    ciency disease (SCID)
    3:422; 5:241, 422
Severn River 2:247
Sewage 2:485–88
    bacterial decomposition 4:35
    eutrophication 2:460–61
    methane source 2:397
    water pollution 2:457–60
    well contamination 2:119
Seward, Sir Albert Charles
    (English botanist) 1:481
Sewers 2:485–87
Sex cells see Gametes
Sex chromosomes 5:313–14,
    419–21
Sex determination 5:313–15
    lizard eggs 4:362
    illus. 5:312
Sex hormones 3:121; 5:246–47,
    467
Sex-linked inheritance 5:319–
    20, 420–21
Sex organs
    aging 5:333
    female 5:294

male 5:294–95
    puberty 5:330
    illus.
        female 5:295
        male 5:295
Sextants 6:169
Sexual behavior 3:457
    AIDS 5:444
Sexual dimorphism
    butterflies and moths 4:301
    crustaceans 4:255
Sexual intercourse 5:294–95
Sexually transmitted diseases
    (STDs) 5:429–30, 472
Sexual reproduction 3:452
    algae 4:46, 48–49
    animals 4:185–86
    coelenterates 4:218–19
    embryology 3:458–63
    fungi 4:38–39, 42
    human heredity 5:311–12
    human reproduction 5:293–307
    plants 4:12, 15
    sponges 4:215
    diagram(s) 4:86
Sexual selection 3:506–7
Shad 4:332
Shadow zone (in Earth's interior)
    2:25
Shaft mines 2:350–51, 354
    illus. 2:350
Shaking tables 6:176
    illus. 6:178
Shale 2:35, 37, 135–36
    fossils 2:140
    oil shale 2:324–25
    illus. 2:135
Shallow-water waves 2:251
Shamrock spiders 4:261
Shang civilization 1:463
Shape of Things to Come, The
    (film)
    illus. 1:501
Shapley, Harlow (American
    astronomer) 1:187, 189
Sharks 4:315, 317–18, 320,
    323–28
    fossils 1:488
    illus.
        great white shark 4:323
        hammerhead shark 4:326
Sharp-shinned hawks 4:417
Shasta, Mount (California) 2:60
Shasta Dam (California) 6:56
Shasta Lake (California)
    illus. 2:107
Shearwaters 4:446
Shear waves see S waves
Sheep
    adaptation to high altitude 5:6
    cloning 6:75
    liver fluke 4:227–28
    methane production 2:478
    selective breeding 6:71
    illus.
        sheared by a robot 6:201
Sheet floods 2:417–18
Shelf fungi see Bracket fungi

Shelford, Victor (American
    ecologist) 3:473
Shelford, Victor (American
    zoologist) 4:181–82
Shelley, Mary (English writer)
    1:500
Shells (of animals)
    crustaceans 4:251
    foraminiferans 4:210–11
    fossils 1:484–85
    mollusks 4:235–36, 238–41
    turtles 4:375
Shells (racing boats) 6:92
Shells (Whirlers) (bones in nasal
    cavities) 5:177
Shells, Atomic 3:19, 48–49
    diagram(s) 3:18, 48
Shelters, Animal see Animal
    shelters
Shelterwood cutting 4:129, 146
Shenandoah (airship) 6:150
Shepard, Alan B., Jr. (American
    astronaut) 1:241
    illus. 1:240
Shetland Islands
    oil spills 2:465
Shetland ponies 5:108
SHF see Super High Frequency
Shield-tailed snakes 4:370
Shield volcanoes 2:57
Shifting cultivation 4:159–60
Shingles (in construction) 6:28
Shining Rock (North Carolina)
    2:512
Shinkai 6500 (submersible) 6:124
Shinkansen system (Japanese
    trains) 6:130
Shin splints 5:194
Ship-controlled interception
    (SCI) radar 6:258
Ship Rock Peak (New Mexico)
    2:418
    illus. 2:134
SHIPS AND SHIPPING 6:107–16
    see also Boats
    Bronze Age 6:6
    iceberg collisions 2:260, 263
    navigation 6:165–73
    oil tankers 2:328
    radar 6:254, 258
    Titanic 2:277
Shipworms see Teredos
Shipwrecks 2:279; 6:124
    illus. 1:468; 2:227, 264
Shire draft horses 5:108–9
Shivering 5:189
Shock absorbers 6:146
Shock waves
    lithotripsy 5:492
Shoemaker-Levy 9, Comet
    1:138, 165
Shooting stars see Meteors
Shorebirds see Waterbirds and
    shorebirds
Shore pines 4:85
Short circuits 2:316; 3:259
Short-day plants and animals
    4:116

Short-eared owls **4**:419–21
Shorthair cats
illus. **5**:90
Short-period comets 1:76
Short-tailed bats 5:31
Short-tailed whip scorpions
4:263
Short-term memory 5:360–61
Shortwall mining 2:351
Shortwave radio 6:288
Short-winged hawks 4:415, 417,
419
Shotgun fungi 4:39
Shoulder blade *see* Scapula
Shrew moles 5:26
Shrews 5:2, 11, 27–28
illus. **5**:23, 27
Shrikes 4:450–51
Shrimp 4:248, 250, 254–55
SHRIMP (Sensitive High Reso-
lution Ion MicroProbe)
2:17–18
Shutters (of cameras) **6**:266
Shutter speeds 6:266
illus. **6**:267
table(s) **6**:268
Shuttles (for weaving) **6**:189
Siamangs 5:145
Siberian tigers 5:86
illus. **2**:493
Sibutramine 5:393
Sickle-cell anemia 5:211, 321,
419–20
genetic variation **3**:505
Pauling, Linus **3**:9
Side-blotched lizards 4:362
Side effects (of medications)
5:461
Side-necked turtles 4:379
Sidereal month 1:117
Sidereal year 1:110
Siderites *see* Iron meteorites
Siderolites *see* Stony iron mete-
orites
Side-scan sonar 2:275, 277
Side-striped jackals 5:80
Sidewinding (of snakes) **4**:364
Siding (for houses) **6**:26
SIDS *see* Sudden infant death
syndrome
Sierra Nevada range (California)
2:33, 67
Sieve elements 4:66–67
Sieve plates 4:67, 100
Sieve-tube members 4:100
Sigmoid colon 5:254
Signals, Television 6:293–94
Sign language 5:149, 276
Sika deer 5:121
Sikorsky, Igor (Russian inventor)
6:154
Sildenafil (Viagra) 5:467
Silent Spring (book, Carson)
3:472, 474
Silent zone *see* Zone of silence

Silica (Silicon dioxide) 2:135;
3:31
diatoms **4**:47, 51
fossils **1**:485
geysers **2**:65
horsetails **4**:76
hot springs **2**:64
silicosis, cause of **2**:469
Silicates 2:138
Earth's interior **2**:28
igneous rocks **2**:134
outer space **1**:318
Silicon 3:29, 31, 44 *see also*
Silica
Earth's crust **2**:138
integrated circuits **6**:232, 253
meteorites **1**:172
photovoltaic cells **2**:386–87,
389
semiconductors **3**:91; **6**:250
illus.
integrated circuits **6**:233
Silicon dioxide *see* Silica
Silicone-gel breast implants
5:506
Silicone rubber 5:501
Silicon tetrachloride 3:66
Silicosis 2:469
Silkworms 4:191, 212, 270, 302
Silky anteaters 5:34–35
Silliman, Benjamin (American
scientist) **2**:323
Sills (in geology) **2**:32–33
Silt 2:35–36; **4**:151–52
water supply **2**:438–39
Silting basins 2:439
Silurian period
fossils **1**:488
table(s) **1**:486; **2**:18–19
Silver 3:44
electroplating **3**:102–3
film, photographic **6**:271
noble metals **3**:27, 30
Silver cyanide 3:102–3
Silver firs 4:91
Silverfish (insects)
illus. **4**:278
Silver foxes 5:83
Silver maples 4:141
Silversides 4:334
Silviculture 4:128–30
Simien jackals 5:80
Similar solids 1:385
illus. **1**:384
Similar triangles 1:372–73
Simoom (Simoon) 2:186
Simple fractures 5:182
Simple fruits 4:103
Simple leaves 4:71, 73
SIMPLE MACHINES 3:168–75
Simple sugars *see* Monosaccha-
rides
Simplon Tunnel (Italy–
Switzerland) **6**:48
Simpson, James (English engi-
neer) **2**:436
Sine curves 1:389–90
Sines 1:387–89

Singapore
noise pollution **2**:451
Single-electron transistor scan-
ning electrometers 6:337
Single-lens reflex cameras
6:263, 268
Single photon emission com-
puted tomography
(SPECT) 5:457
Singularity (a point in space hav-
ing no dimension) **1**:206,
213
Sinkholes 2:126
Sinoatrial node 5:200
Sinuses 5:177
Siphons (of mollusks) **4**:235
Siphons (tubes for moving liq-
uids) **3**:188–89
SIRENIANS 5:12–13, **61–62**
Sirens (amphibians) **4**:351
Sirius (satellite radio) **6**:290
Sirius (star) **1**:25, 32, 192, 470
Sirocco 2:186
Sirolimus (Rapamune) 5:497
Sitka spruces 4:159
illus. **4**:89
SI units 3:135–36
Sjögren's syndrome 5:240
Skates (fish) **4**:318, 328
Skeletal muscles 5:164, 185–86
illus. **5**:186
Skeleton *see also* Exoskeleton
babies and children **5**:327–28
bipedalism **5**:160
birds **4**:393
bony fish **4**:329
human anatomy **5**:172–82
illus. **5**:165, 174–75
arthritis sites **5**:428
Skew lines 1:380
Skidding (of automobiles) **3**:158,
160, 166
illus. **3**:158
Skill memory 5:362
Skimmers 4:435–36
SKIN 5:263–67
aging, effects of **3**:468; **5**:333
allergies **5**:448
amphibians **4**:342
cancer **2**:154; **5**:433, 436–37
cartilaginous fish **4**:324
cells **5**:325
color inheritance **5**:319
epithelium **5**:163–64
essential fatty acids **5**:383
excretory system **5**:261
frogs **4**:348
fungus infections **5**:428
immune system **5**:235
infectious diseases **5**:428–29
laser treatments **5**:489
lizards **4**:358–60
salamanders **4**:349
sense and sensation **5**:285–86
synthetic skin **5**:507
transdermal skin patches
5:469–70
Skinks 4:356, 360

Skinner, B. F. (American psychologist) 5:338, 357
    illus. 5:341
Skin tests 5:449
    illus. 5:448
Skipjacks *see* Click beetles
Skippers (butterflies) 4:303, 306
Skjellerup, Comet 1:165
Skobeltsyn, D. V. (Russian physicist) 1:225
Skull 5:176–77
    babies 5:328
    mammal 5:4
    illus. 5:165, 176
        human evolution 5:157
Skunks 4:169; 5:97
Sky
    color 3:296
    night sky 1:24–36
    planetarium 1:65–67, 69–70
Skydiving
    illus. 3:154
Skylab (space station) 1:248, 266–67
    fall to Earth 1:307
    solar investigations 1:93
    space suits 1:275–76
    illus. 1:266
Skyscrapers 6:27, 30–31, 39–40
    illus. 6:15
Slack currents 2:247
Slag 6:182–83
Slag wool 2:360
Slaked lime *see* Hydrated lime
Slash pines 4:90, 148
Slate 2:37, 136
    illus. 2:136
Slater, Samuel (American manufacturer) 6:190
Slayton, Donald K. (American astronaut)
    illus. 1:240
SLE *see* Systemic lupus erythematosus
Sleds, Underwater 2:277, 279
SLEEP 5:405–9
    biorhythms 3:380
Sleeping sickness 4:208; 5:428
Sleep talking *see* Somniloquism
Sleepwalking 5:409
Sleet 2:167
Slender lorises 5:138
Slides, Color 6:272–73
Slime eels *see* Hagfish
Slime mat (water filtration) 2:443
Slime molds 3:454; 4:51
Slim flower scurf pea 4:139
Slit-faced bats 5:32
Slit lamps
    illus. 5:269
Slope mines 2:350, 354
    illus. 2:350
Sloth bears 5:75
Sloths 1:499; 5:8, 33–34
Slow-acting antirheumatic drugs 5:240
Slow lorises 5:138
Sludge 2:447, 486–88

Slugs (mollusks) 4:240
Sluice gates 2:439
Slurry, Coal 2:357
Small Astronomy Satellite-1 *see* Uhuru
Small circles 1:383
    illus. 1:384
Small intestine 5:251–53
    transplants 5:499
    illus. 5:167, 249
Smallpox 3:393; 5:237, 423, 430–31
    virus 3:387–88
SMELL, Sense of 5:283–84, 285
    see also Odors; Scents
    butterflies 4:305
    changes with age 5:333
    crustaceans 4:253
    elephants 5:106
    primates' senses 5:158
    sharks 4:324
    snakes 4:364
Smelting 6:177–78
    acid rain 2:473–74
    copper 6:182–83
    lead 6:183–84
Smilodon *see* Saber-toothed cats
Smithsonian Institution
    weather reporting 2:203
Smog 2:452, 467
Smoke
    acid rain 2:475
    air pollution 2:466–67
Smoking (food preservation) 6:78
Smoking (of tobacco)
    air pollution 2:467; 3:73
    antismoking treatments 5:376–77
    cancer 5:436–37
    cocaine users 5:375
    legal restrictions 5:377
    low birth weight 5:301
    lung cancer 5:433
    nicotine supplements 5:376, 470, 474
    respiratory diseases 5:222
    substance abuse 5:370–71, 374
Smooth endoplasmic reticulum 3:429
Smooth-fronted caimans 4:383
Smooth muscles 5:164, 186–87
    illus. 5:186
Smuts 3:451; 4:45
Snails 4:239–40
    fossils 1:487
    hosts for flukes 4:227
    reproduction 3:457
Snakebites 4:367
Snakeflies 4:280
Snake-necked turtles 4:379
SNAKES 4:353–55, 363–74 *see also* Sea snakes
    compared to lizards 4:356–57, 362
    desert life 2:86
    herpetology 4:337

life span 5:324
mongooses 5:101
    illus. 3:503; 4:337, 365
SNAP generators 1:306; 3:321
Snappers (fish)
    illus. 4:315
Snapping beetles *see* Click beetles
Snapping turtles 4:378
    illus. 2:511
Sneezing 5:447
Snellen chart 5:273
Snipes
    illus. 4:393
Snoring 5:489
Snorkels 6:120
Snout beetles *see* Weevils
Snow 2:168–69, 173
    atmospheric dust 2:466
    climates of the past 2:217
    color 3:297
    glacial formation 2:93–97
    hydrogen bonding 3:83
    measurement 3:319
    illus. 2:169; 3:82
Snow geese 4:441
Snow leopards 2:499; 5:88
    illus. 2:504; 4:470
Snowshoe rabbits 2:493; 5:6, 38, 91
    graph(s)
        populations of lynx and hares 3:480
    illus. 5:36
Snowy owls 4:419–21
Snowy River Project (Australia) 2:410
Snub-nosed langurs 5:141
Snyder, Hartland S. (American physicist) 1:204, 206
Soap 3:78, 121
Social bees 4:286
SOCIAL INSECTS 4:191, 197, 280, 281–90
Social organization
    early humans 5:100
    humans and aggression 5:155
    primates 5:146–47
    wolves 5:78–79
Social psychology 5:339–40
Social skills 5:366
Social wasps 4:288–89
Society and technology *see* Technology and society
Sockets, Eye 5:268
Sockeye salmon
    illus. 3:465
Soda ash *see* Sodium carbonate
Soda straws (cave formations) 2:128
Soddy, Frederick (British scientist) 3:126
Sodium 3:29, 44
    electrochemistry 3:101
    ionic bonding 3:49–50, 63–64
    Io's sodium cloud 1:138
    nutrition 5:387

Sodium (cont.)
  water, reaction with **3**:86
  diagram(s) **3**:18
Sodium bicarbonate 3:99
Sodium carbonate (Soda ash)
  3:87; **6**:203, 208
Sodium chloride 1:337; **2**:36;
  3:30, 33, 87, 96, 99
  chemical bonding **3**:47, 50
  chemical industry **6**:207
  electrochemistry **3**:101
  excretory system **5**:260
  ionic bonding **3**:49–50, 63–64
  ocean **2**:229; **3**:87
  solution **3**:78, 80
  water solution **3**:83
  zeolite renewed by **2**:447
  diagram(s) **3**:64
Sodium hydroxide 3:94–96, 99,
  104; **6**:207–8
Sodium nitrate 2:36
Sodium nitrite 6:83–84
Sodium nitroprusside (Nipride)
  5:467
Sodium pump (in physiology)
  5:225
Sodium stearate 3:121
Sodium sulfate 3:81
Soft coal *see* Bituminous coal
Soft palate 5:177
Soft-shell clams 4:238
Soft-shelled turtles 4:378
Software, Computer *see* Computer programming
Softwood 4:86; **6**:28
Soil 1:106
  acid rain neutralization **2**:475
  agronomy **4**:175
  antibiotic production **5**:463–64
  atolls **2**:283
  bacteria **4**:35
  bryophytes help form **4**:60, 62
  climate analysis **2**:216
  conservation **2**:408–9, 412
  earthquakes **2**:50
  earthworms **4**:243, 245
  erosion *see* Erosion
  floodplains **2**:104
  grasslands **4**:139
  loess **2**:432–33
  Mars **1**:131
  microbiology **3**:450
  moles **5**:25
  nutrient cycles **3**:491
  plant communities **4**:133–35
  plant succession **4**:123–24
  polar regions **2**:89
  rain forests **4**:159–60
  tundra **4**:162–63
  volcanic ash **2**:433
  wetlands **4**:152
Soil geography 2:300
Soilless agriculture
  illus. **6**:68
Soil-water belt 2:114
Sojourner (Martian surface rover)
  1:131, 232, 297
  illus. **1**:131

Solar and Heliospheric Obser-
  vatory (SOHO) 1:93, 236,
  301; **2**:158
Solar atmosphere *see* Atmo-
  sphere—Sun
Solar batteries 1:90
Solar cells *see* Photovoltaic cells
Solar collectors 1:90; **2**:382–83,
  385
  illus. **2**:303, 306, 383, 388;
  3:188, 190, 220
Solar constant 1:90
Solar-cooking stove
  illus. **3**:239
Solar cycle 1:84–86; **2**:157–58
Solar disk *see* Photosphere
Solar energy *see* Solar power
Solar engines 1:90
Solar evaporators 2:448
Solar flares 1:80–81, 83, 85, 88
  atmospheric ionization **2**:152
  Earth's climate **2**:220
  illus. **1**:83–84, 230
Solar furnaces
  illus. **2**:384
Solar-heating systems 3:239
Solar Mass Ejection Imager
  (SMEI) 2:158
Solar maximum 1:80–81, 85, 88,
  93
Solar Maximum Mission Satel-
  lite (SMMS) 1:81, 252
  illus. **1**:249
Solar nebulas 2:12
Solar panels 2:382
Solar polar caps 1:85–86
Solar ponds
  illus. **2**:389
SOLAR POWER 1:89–90;
  2:381–89
  aviation **6**:157
  electricity, generation of **2**:312
  space station **1**:268
Solar radiation 1:88–89, 93;
  2:149, 152, 382
  global warming **2**:477–78
  heat transfer **3**:237–39
  life, origin of **3**:381
  ozone layer **2**:481–82
  planets' formation **2**:13
  wind **2**:181–82
Solar reflectors 2:384–85
SOLAR SYSTEM 1:25, 73–79
  see also Asteroids; Comets; Meteors; Planets; Satellites; Sun
  exploration **1**:259–60
  Milky Way **1**:189
  origin **1**:318; **2**:9–14
  space science **1**:233–34
Solar telescopes 1:90, 92
Solar-thermal-electricity con-
  version 2:385
Solar thermospheric tides 2:152
Solar tracking (by plants)
  4:116–17

Solar wind 1:89, 93
  auroras **2**:156–58
  cosmic rays **1**:227
  Jupiter **1**:134
  magnetic field of Earth **3**:266–
    67, 271
  particles **1**:247
  space probes **1**:301
  illus. **1**:85
Solar year 1:476
Soldier ants 4:281–83
Soldier termites 4:290
Solenodons 5:28
Solenoids 3:264
Soles (fish) **4**:335
Soleus
  illus. **5**:166
Solid analytic geometry
  1:398–99
Solid-fuel rockets 1:243
SOLID GEOMETRY 1:329, 332,
  380–85
Solid-rocket boosters 1:243,
  249, 252
  Challenger explosion **1**:253
SOLIDS 3:11–12, 88–93, 226
  entropy **3**:242
  heat conduction **3**:233
  materials science **6**:227
  matter, study of **3**:14
Solid-state lasers 6:345, 351
Solid-state physics 3:91
Solid wastes 2:484–85
Solifluction 2:89
Solitary sandpipers 4:436
Soliton waves 2:221
  illus. **2**:226
Solubility 3:80–81
Solutes 3:79
SOLUTIONS (in chemistry)
  2:421; **3**:78–81, 105
Solvay process 6:203, 208
Solvents 3:79, 82–87
Somalia 2:257
Somatic cells 3:443; **5**:419
Somatoform disorder 5:355
Somatostatin 5:475
Somnambulism *see* Sleepwalk-
  ing
Somniloquism 5:409
Sonar (Echo sounding) 3:203–4
  fishing **6**:88
  iceberg detection **2**:263
  navigation **6**:172
  oceanographic studies **2**:264,
    273–75
  illus. **2**:223
Songbirds (Oscines) 4:449–63
  population **4**:451
Sonic booms 3:206
Sonic sounding *see* Sonar
Sonography 5:454, 459
Sony Corporation
  Trinitron tube **6**:296
  video games **6**:298–99, 301
  video recording **6**:281
Soot 2:467
Sooty shearwaters 4:446

Sooty terns 4:432
Sori (of ferns) 4:81
Sosigenes (Greek astronomer)
   1:476
Sotalol 5:467
SOUND 3:198–208; 5:277
   acoustics 3:144
   careers in acoustics 3:202
   musical sound 3:209–18
Sound energy (medicine) 5:514
Sounding (of whales) 5:47
Sounding poles 6:166
Soundings, Nautical 2:264–65,
   272–73 see also Sonar
Soundproofing materials 3:205
   illus. 3:198
SOUND RECORDING 6:278–87
   Internet 6:310
Sound waves 3:198–99
   Doppler effect 1:19
   medical technology 5:491–92
   sonography 5:454
Source zones (of rivers) 2:102
South Africa
   Great Karroo 2:162
   wilderness areas 2:513
South America
   extinct mammals 1:499
   forestry 4:128
   grasslands 4:140, 142
   plains and plateaus 2:78, 80
   volcanoes 2:59
South Beach Diet 5:394
South Carolina Railroad 6:125
South celestial pole 1:36
South China Sea 2:328
South Crillon Glacier (Alaska)
   2:96
Southeasterlies 2:185
Southeast trade winds 2:184
South Equatorial Current 2:240
Southern Cross (constellation)
   see Crux
Southern grape ferns see Botrychium
Southern Hemisphere
   climates of the past 2:219
   constellations 1:26–27
   ocean currents 2:238–40
   seasons 1:110–12
   wind 2:182, 184–85, 188
Southern lights see Aurora aus-
   tralis
Southern right whales see Right
   whales
Southern sea lions 5:66
Sow bugs see Pill bugs
Soybeans 2:482; 4:44; 6:90
   genetically engineered 4:7;
   6:74
Soylent Green (film) 1:505
Soyuz spacecraft 1:247–48
   astronauts 1:283, 289
   guest crew members 1:285
   solar investigations 1:93
   space stations 1:266, 269
SP-100 project 3:321

Space
   gas molecules 3:74
   relativity theory 3:344–46
   uniformity, principle of 3:509
Spacecraft see also Space
   shuttles
   aerospace engineering 6:20
   reusable spacecraft 1:261–63
   robot spacecraft 1:232–33, 236
   satellites, artificial 1:302–15
   space probes 1:290–301
Space docking 1:240, 244
Space exploration
   astronaut training 1:280–89
   electromagnetic radiation 3:280
   extraterrestrial life 1:317, 320,
   324–25
   future programs 1:258–63
   manned flights 1:238–53, 257
   Mars 1:129–31
   Mercury 1:97–98
   Moon 1:123–26
   navigation 6:173
   photovoltaic-cell use 2:386
   planetarium simulation 1:71
   radar 6:261
   satellites, artificial 1:302–15
   science fiction 1:501
   space probes 1:290–301
   space stations 1:264–69
   space suits 1:270–79
   technology and society 6:9, 13
   Venus 1:100–102
   table(s) 6:402–42
Space frames (in construction)
   illus. 6:41
Space Infrared Telescope Facility (SIRTF) see Spitzer
   Space Telescope
Spacelab (space laboratory module) 1:253
Space maintainers (in dentistry)
   5:279, 281
Space medicine
   illus.
     experiments 1:260
Space oceanography 2:226–27
Space physics 1:234
SPACE PROBES 1:290–301
   astronomy 1:17
   New Millennium Program 1:263
   radioisotope thermoelectric
     generators 3:321
   remotely operated vehicles
     6:201
   space shuttles 1:252
   Sun 1:93
SPACE PROGRAM, Future of
   1:258–63
SPACE SCIENCE 1:4–5, 232–37
   life, origin of 3:382
SpaceShipOne (rocket plane)
   1:263

Space shuttles 1:238–39, 248–
   49, 252–53, 257; 6:13 see
   also Atlantis; Buran; Challenger; Columbia; Discovery; Endeavour; Hermes
   astronaut training 1:281
   Hubble Space Telescope, ser-
     vicing of 1:50
   oceanic research 2:227
   problems 1:261
   rockets 1:243
   satellite launches 1:303
   space stations 1:269
   space suits 1:276–77
   telescopes in space 1:51
   women astronauts 1:289
   illus. 1:295
     astronaut training 1:282
     launch 1:248
     space suits 1:278
     telescopes 1:51
   table(s)
     spaceflights 6:439–43
Space Solar Power Stations
   2:389
SPACE STATIONS 1:248,
   264–69
   space suits 1:270–71, 277, 279
SPACE SUITS 1:270–79
   extravehicular activity 1:252
   Mercury program 1:240
   illus. 1:234, 274–75, 282
Space taxis
   illus. 1:263
Space Telescope, Hubble see
   Hubble Space Telescope
Space Telescope Imaging Spec-
   trograph (STIS) 1:49
Space-time concept 3:345–46
Space vehicles see Spacecraft
Space walks see Extravehicular
   activity
Spadefoot toads 4:344, 346
Spain
   oil spill 2:465
Spam (unsolicited e-mail) 6:311
Spandex 6:210–11
Spanish moss 4:60
Spanworms 4:307
Spark plugs 6:139, 141
   illus. 6:142
Sparrow hawks see American
   kestrels
Sparrows 4:461
   illus. 4:461
Spartina 4:152
Spatial abilities 5:366
Spats (young oysters) 4:236
Species 3:395–96
   evolution 3:507
   new discoveries 5:38
Specific gravity 3:183
   Earth's interior 2:25–26
   mineral properties 2:137–38
   ocean water 2:229–30
Specific heat 3:84, 225
SPECT see Single photon emis-
   sion computed tomography

Spectacled bears **5**:75
Spectacled caimans **4**:383
Spectacled cobras *see* Indian cobras
Spectacled eiders
illus. **4**:443
Spectral distribution curves **3**:324
illus. **3**:325
Spectral lines **3**:5, 351
Spectrograms **3**:295
Spectrographic analysis **1**:52
Spectrographs **3**:295
astronomy **1**:13, 15
telescopes in space **1**:49
illus. **1**:234
Spectrometers *see* Spectrophotometers
Spectrophotometers **3**:132–33, 136
blood analysis **5**:213
illus. **3**:131, 295
Spectroscopes **1**:219; **3**:5
color **3**:294–95
illus. **1**:91
Spectroscopic analysis **3**:132
space technology **1**:256
Spectroscopy **3**:132–33, 327–28
stars **3**:302
Sun's composition **1**:191
ultraviolet astronomy **1**:64
Spectrum, Electromagnetic *see* Electromagnetic spectrum
Speculum (nickel compound) **1**:39
Speech *see* Language
Speech formation, Computerized **6**:367
Speech recognition devices **6**:366–67
Speed (drug) *see* Amphetamines
Speed (in physics) **3**:150
insects' defense mechanisms **4**:276
swifts **4**:405
Speed detectors **6**:260
Speed of light **3**:201, 282, 348
Speed of sound **3**:201, 206
Speleology *see* Caves
Spelunking **2**:125, 130–31
Sperm **3**:455, 457; **5**:293–95, 311
cell division **3**:443
infertility **5**:305–6
mutations **5**:419
Spermaceti **5**:52–53
Spermatazoa (singular **Spermatozoon**) *see* Sperm
Sperm whales **5**:52–54, 58
Sperry, Elmer (American inventor) **6**:155
Sphagnum *see* Peat moss
Sphenisciformes *see* Penguins
Sphenoid bones **5**:176
Sphenophyta **4**:56, 75
Sphere fungi **4**:42
Spheres (geometric figures) **1**:383–85, 399, 401

Spherical aberration **1**:50; **3**:291; **6**:331
illus. **3**:290
Spherical mirrors **3**:286, 288
illus. **3**:287
Sphincter muscles **5**:190, 260–61
Sphinx moths **4**:306
Sphygmomanometers **5**:204
Spica (star) **1**:29
Spicebush silkworms **4**:306
Spicebush swallowtail butterflies
diagram(s) **4**:301
Spicules (of sponges' skeletons) **4**:215–16, 219
Spicules (of the Sun) **1**:83
Spider crabs **4**:250
Spider monkeys **5**:7–8, 139, 146, 148
Spiders **4**:248, 257–58, 260–63
courtship **4**:196
digestion **4**:186
diagram(s) **4**:257
illus. **4**:247, 256
black widow spider **4**:260
trap-door spider **4**:258
wolf spider **4**:261
Spiders (computer programs) **6**:308
Spider silk **4**:260, 262
genetic engineering **6**:14
illus. **4**:256
Spider webs **4**:260–61
illus. **4**:260
Spike mosses **4**:56, 76–77
Spillways **2**:437; **6**:51
Spin (in physics) **3**:306–7, 313, 315
Spina bifida **5**:320
Spinal column *see* Backbone
Spinal cord **5**:176, 223, 230–31
injuries **5**:234
pain **5**:288
primitive chordates **4**:309
illus. **5**:232
Spinal nerves **5**:232
Spindle fibers (in cells) **3**:442, 444–45
Spine (in anatomy) *see* Backbone
Spine-cheek anemonefish
illus. **4**:176
Spines (of plants) **4**:167
Spinner dolphins **5**:56–57
Spinning jennies **6**:189
Spin quantum number **3**:333
Spiny anteaters **5**:15
illus. **5**:15
Spiny dogfish **4**:327
illus. **4**:324
Spiny puffer fish
illus. **4**:329
Spiracles **4**:264, 273–74, 328
Spiral eddies **2**:227
Spiral galaxies **1**:185–86, 221
Spiral-horned antelopes **5**:128–29
Spiral valves (of sharks) **4**:326

Spirillum **4**:28; **5**:427
illus. **3**:448
Spirit (planetary rover) **1**:131, 297, 320; **3**:382
Spirit of Freedom (balloon) **6**:150
Spirit of St. Louis (airplane)
illus. **6**:155
Spirochaetae **4**:29
Spirogyra **4**:49
Spirometers **5**:218
Spirostomum **4**:213
Spitting cobras **4**:373
Spitting spiders **4**:260
Spitz, Armand (American astronomer) **1**:67
Spitzer, Lyman (American physicist) **3**:355
Spitzer Space Telescope **1**:47, 49, 62, 237; **3**:280
Spix's macaws
illus. **4**:402
Splat cooling **6**:230
Spleen **5**:206
white blood cells **5**:207
illus. **5**:167–68
Spoilage, Food **6**:76–77
Sponge crabs
illus. **4**:253
SPONGES (Porifera) **4**:184, 200, 214–16
digestion **4**:186
feeding behavior **4**:193
reproduction **3**:456
illus. **3**:453
Spongiform encephalopathy **3**:390
Spongin **4**:215–16
Spongy parenchyma **4**:70
Spontaneous generation **3**:367, 369–70, 372, 375
microbiology **3**:447
Redi, Francesco **3**:509–10
Spoonbills **4**:445–46
illus. **4**:444
Sporangia **4**:37, 81–82
illus. **4**:56, 81
Spores **3**:443, 454–55; **4**:62
bacteria **4**:30
bryophytes **4**:63
ferns **4**:81–82
fungi **4**:38–39, 42, 44–45
moss **4**:60–61
protozoans **4**:212
illus. **3**:453
Sporophores **4**:39
Sporophytes **3**:455; **4**:15
conifers **4**:87–88
ferns **4**:81
horsetails **4**:75–76
liverworts **4**:63
mosses **4**:59, 61
Sporozoans **4**:212
Sporozoites **4**:212
Sports cars
illus. **6**:138
Sports medicine **5**:514
SPOT (artificial satellites) **1**:315

Spotted-breasted orioles
  illus. **4:**459
Spotted deer 5:120
Spotted dolphins 5:56–57
  illus. **5:**59
Spotted flycatchers 4:455
Spotted hyenas 5:102
Spotted sandpipers 4:437
Sprains 5:194
Spray bottles 3:188
Spraying and dusting (of crops)
  illus. **6:**63
Spring (season)
  constellations **1:**29
  jet streams **2:**150–51
  map(s)
    constellations **1:**28
Springbok 5:131
  illus. **5:**126
Spring force 3:155
Spring peepers
  illus. **4:**343
Springs (of water) **2:**116–17, 119
  desert oases **2:**86
  hot springs **2:**63–64
  submarine cold seeps **2:**278
  Illus. **2:**118
Springtails 4:277–78
Spring thermometers 3:224
Spring tides 1:117; **2:**245
  illus. **2:**244
Sprint PCS 6:245
Spruces 4:86–87, 90–91
  illus. **4:**89
Spurs (bony growths) **5:**183, 427
Spur-thigh tortoises
  illus. **4:**376
Sputnik (spacecraft) **1:**46, 233,
    235, 240, 302, 304; **6:**13
  illus. **1:**233
Squall bands (of hurricanes)
  2:197–99
Squamous-cell cancer 5:267,
    436
Square-lipped rhinoceroses *see*
    White rhinoceroses
Square root 1:349, 351, 360
Squares (geometric figures)
  1:374
Squaring the circle 1:367
Squash beetles 4:294
Squashes (vegetables) **6:**74
Squawfish
  illus. **2:**501
Squids 4:232–33
Squirrels 3:396; **5:**8, 40–42, 324
Squirting cucumbers 4:119
Sri Lanka
  water conservation **2:**410
SSBNs *see* Missile-carrying sub-
    marines
SSNs *see* Fast-attack submarines
Stabbing cats 5:84
Stabilizing selection 3:506
Stable equilibrium 3:182
  illus. **3:**180
Stag beetles 4:296

Stag's-horn moss *see* Running
    pine
Stairways (of the ear) **5:**275
Stalactites 2:128
Stalagmites 2:128
Stamens 4:101, 103
Standard deviation (in statistics)
  1:412; **3:**511
Standing waves (in physics)
  3:197, 331
  illus. **3:**329
Standing waves (Seiche) (water)
  2:111, 251
Stands (of trees) **4:**128
Stapes *see* Stirrup
Staphylococcus **4:**34; **5:**184,
    194, 428
Staphylothermus marinus
  illus. **3:**432
Starburst galaxies 1:216–17
Star catalogs 1:184–85
Starch
  biochemistry **3:**119
  cellular energy **3:**438
  food source **5:**380
Star City (Russia) **1:**283–84
Star clusters 1:186–87
Stardust (space probe) **1:**161,
    296
Starfish 4:186, 204, 222–24
  illus. **3:**477; **4:**220–22; **6:**117
Stargazers 4:320
Starlings 4:462
  illus. **4:**462
Star networks (of computers)
  6:386
  illus. **6:**386
Star-nosed moles 5:24–25
STARS 1:16, **190–96**
  black holes **1:**204–6
  collapsed and failed stars
    1:197–203
  color **3:**302
  constellations **1:**24–35
  cosmic rays, origin of **1:**231
  defined **1:**202
  Drake's Equation **1:**323
  extraterrestrial life **1:**317–18
  interstellar space **1:**218–20,
    223
  IRAS telescope **1:**62
  Milky Way **1:**181–87, 189
  plasma **3:**13
  Sun **1:**80–93
  X-ray astronomy **1:**58–59
  illus.
    dying **1:**17
    formation **1:**22, 196
    life cycle **1:**197
  map(s) **1:**26–28, 31, 33–34
STARS, Collapsed and failed
  1:135, **197–203,** 204–6
Star Spangled Banner 1:256
Starters (of automobiles) **6:**141
Startle response 3:377
Star Trek (TV series) **1:**504–6
  illus. **1:**504
Starvation 3:470

Star Wars (film) **1:**505; **6:**321
"Star Wars" defense plan *see*
    Strategic Defense Initiative
Starzl, Thomas (American sur-
    geon) **5:**498
State, Changes of *see* Changes
    of state
Static electricity 3:244, 246–47
  von Guericke's machine for
    producing **3:**250
Stationary fronts 2:188
Stationary waves *see* Standing
    waves (Seiche)
Statistical inference 1:413–14
STATISTICS 1:404–13
  algebra **1:**365
  laboratory data **3:**511, 513
  mathematics **1:**329, 333
Statocysts 4:253
Statsionar (communications sat-
    ellite) **1:**309
Staudinger, Herman (German
    chemist) **6:**215
STDs *see* Sexually transmitted
    diseases
Steady state theories 1:21–23
Steam
  geothermal energy **2:**390–91
  geysers **2:**64–65
  metal compounds **3:**86–87
  mineral formation **2:**137
  volcanoes **2:**58, 61–62
  volume **3:**69
Steamboat Geyser (Yellowstone
    National Park) **2:**65
Steam engines 6:96–99 *see also*
    Steam turbines; Steam
    vehicles
  factory, history of the **6:**190–91
  Industrial Revolution **6:**8
  Watt's governor **6:**195–96
Steam locomotives *see* Locomo-
    tives—steam
Steamships 6:110–11
Steam stations 2:312–14
  diagram(s) **2:**316
Steam turbines 2:312–14;
    6:103–4
  steamships **6:**111
Steam vehicles 6:98, 133
Steel
  artificial body parts **5:**501
  coal, uses of **2:**358
  construction materials **6:**29–31,
    39–40
  expansion **3:**221
  factory, history of the **6:**187–88
  metallurgy **6:**175, 178–82
  Titanic (ship) **2:**277
  water in manufacture of **2:**435
  illus.
    molten steel **3:**219
Steel pipes 2:327, 449
Steenboks 5:131
Steering systems 6:144–45
Stegocephalians 1:488
Stegosaurs 1:495–96
Stegosaurus **1:**496

Steinmetz, Charles Proteus (German-American engineer) 2:180
Steinmetz generator 2:180
Stele 4:67, 69
Stellarators 3:355–56
Stellar nurseries 1:62, 223
Steller sea lions see Northern sea lions
Steller's jays
  illus. 4:463
Steller's sea cows 5:61
Stem cells 3:423; 5:422
  illus.
    prenatal therapy 5:303
Stems 4:64, 68–71
  whisk ferns 4:82
  diagram(s) 4:69
Steno, Nicolaus (Danish scientist) 2:7
Stenosis 5:440
Stents 5:491
Stephen Island wrens 4:409
Stephenson, George (English inventor) 6:125
Steppe polecats 5:94
Steppes 2:75, 77, 214; 4:140
Stereo phonograph records 6:278–79
  illus. 6:279
Stereo radio 6:290
Stereoscopic binocular microscopes 6:332
Stereoscopic vision see Binocular vision
Sterility, Reproductive see Infertility
Sterilization (in microbiology) 5:477
Sterilization, Reproductive
  screwworm fly 3:320
  veterinary medicine 4:467
Sternomastoid
  illus. 5:166
Sternum 4:393; 5:177
  illus. 5:165, 174–75
Steroids 3:121
  adrenal glands 5:246
  allergies 5:449
  arthritis 5:240, 428–29
  immune system 5:241
  spinal-cord injury 5:234
  transplant recipients 5:497
Stethoscopes 5:204
Stevenson, E. C. (American physicist) 1:229
Stick-and-slip vibrations (in acoustics) 3:200
Stick construction see Wood frame construction
Stick insects 4:276, 279
Sticklebacks 4:196, 334
Stigmas (of plants) 4:100–101
Stilts (birds) 4:438
Stimulant drugs 5:373
Stimulated emission 6:344
Stingrays 4:328
  illus. 4:327

Stings, Insect 4:285–86
Stinkhorns 4:45
Stirling Energy Systems (SES) 2:388
Stirling engines 6:102
Stirrup (in the ear) 5:275–76, 508–9
  illus. 3:205
STIS see Space Telescope Imaging Spectrograph
Stoats see Ermine weasels
Stocks (rock masses) 2:33
Stockton & Darlington Railway 6:125
Stoichiometry 3:56
Stokes, George (English physicist) 3:275
Stoma see Stomata
Stomach 5:239, 249–51
  babies 5:326
  human body 5:171
  muscle 5:171
  pain 5:290
  pH of stomach juices 3:98
  ruminants 5:8
  secretions 5:236
  surgery to limit obesity 5:393
  illus. 5:167, 250
Stomach worms 4:230
Stomata 4:12–13
  conifers 4:85
  desert plants 4:167
  flowering plants 4:99, 107
  photosynthesis 4:24
  vascular plants 4:67, 70–71
  illus. 4:68
Stone 6:23–26
  building techniques 6:32–33
  longest stone bridge 6:50
Stone Age 1:481; 6:3–5, 10
  ceramics 6:217
Stonefish
  illus. 4:194
Stone flies 4:276, 279
Stonehenge (archaeological site, England) 1:470
  illus. 1:469
Stone martens 5:95
Stone meteorites 1:172; 2:28
Stony corals 4:219
Stony Gorge Dam (California)
  illus. 6:54
Stony iron meteorites 1:172–73; 2:28
Stool see Feces
Stopping distance 3:166
Storage batteries see Secondary batteries
Storage units (of computers) see Memory (computer)
Storks
  illus. 4:443
Storm petrels 4:446
Storm Prediction Center (SPC) (Norman, Oklahoma) 2:193–94, 206

Storms
  hurricanes and typhoons 2:195–200
  lightning and thunder 2:174–80
  ocean waves 2:251–52, 254
  tornadoes 2:189–94
  weather forecasting 2:202–4
Storm windows 3:234
Stoves, Gas 2:344
Straight angles 1:370
Straight Wall (lunar feature) 1:122
Strain gauges 6:201
Strainmeters 2:5
Strains (muscle injuries) 5:194
Strangeness (in physics) 3:310–11, 313
  table(s) 3:315
Strange quarks 3:20, 313
Strangling figs 4:157
Strategic Defense Initiative (SDI) 1:262–63, 303
Stratified-charge engines 6:102
Stratigraphy 1:482; 2:4, 36
  illus.
    pollen 2:217
Stratocumulus clouds 2:165
  illus. 2:161, 164
Stratosphere 1:105; 2:150–51, 153–54
  illus. 2:150
Stratus clouds 2:163, 165
  illus. 2:164
StreamCast Networks 6:310
Streamlining 3:193; 6:92
  illus.
    race car 3:157
Streams see Rivers
Street, J. C. (American physicist) 1:229
Streetcars see Trolleys
Streptococcus 5:425, 428–29
  illus. 4:27
Streptomycin 5:464
Stress (in physics) 6:25, 27, 30
Stress (in physiology, psychology) 5:246, 356
Stress fractures 5:182
Stress test see Exercise stress test
Striated muscles see Skeletal muscles
Stridulating organs 4:291, 297
Stringed instruments 3:214–15
Striped hyenas 5:102
Striped muscles see Skeletal muscles
Striped palm squirrels 5:41
Striped skunks 5:97
Strip mining 2:307, 349–50, 456
  illus. 2:350
Strobili 4:76–77
Stroke 5:233–34
  aging 5:334
  diagnosis of risk 5:472
  MRI diagnosis 5:455
Strokkr (geyser, Iceland) 2:66
Stroma 4:22–23; 5:206

Stromboli (volcano, Italy) **2:**59–60
Strong force 1:205–6; **3:**18, 21, 307, 311, 316
Strontium 3:30, 44, 319
Strontium 90 2:363, 372
Structural color 3:296–97; **4:**300
Structural formulas (in chemistry) *see* Lewis structures
Structural geology 2:3–4
Structuralism (psychology) **5:**339
Structures (of materials) **6:**227
Struthiomimus **1:**494
Strychnine 5:462
Studebaker (automobile) *illus.* **6:**137
Studs (in construction) **6:**36
Sturgeons 4:331
Styles (parts of plants) **4:**100–101
Stylonychia **4:**213
Styrene 2:334
Styrofoam 6:211
Subaqueous tunnels 6:48
Subarctic climates 2:213; **4:**164
Subatomic particles *see* Particles, Elementary
Subbituminous coal 2:347, 357
Subclimax communities 4:125
Subduction 2:47, 69–70, 72
Subdural hemorrhages 5:234
Sublimation 3:14, 69, 78, 92–93
    changes of state **3:**231
    freeze-drying **6:**80
    illus.
        dry ice **3:**226
Subluxation 5:512
Submarine canyons 2:234, 265, 268–69
Submarine mountains *see* Mountains, Submarine
SUBMARINES 6:117–22
    compressed air **3:**185
    deep-sea exploration **2:**222, 276, 278–79
    fluid dynamics **3:**185, 191
    ichthyology **4:**313–14
    nuclear fuel **2:**366
    illus. **3:**183; **6:**165
Submarine volcanoes *see* Volcanoes, Submarine
SUBMERSIBLES 2:276–78; **6:**122–24
    ichthyology **4:**313–14
    illus. **2:**271
Submissive behavior 4:195
Submucous coat (of the stomach) **5:**250
Suboscines 4:448–49
Subsidiary (Azimuthal) quantum number 3:333
Subsistence farming 2:454; **6:**59
SUBSTANCE ABUSE 5:369–77
    AIDS **5:**444
    birth defects **5:**301
    prescription drugs **5:**461
Substations, Electrical 2:318

Substitution reaction (in chemistry) **3:**110–11
Subsurface water *see* Groundwater
Subtraction 1:346–47, 449
Subtractive color mixing 3:298–300
Subtrahend 1:347
Subtropical climates 2:212–13
Subtropical-humid climates 2:213
Subways 6:128
SUCCESSION, Plant 4:120–25, 163
    populations and communities **3:**483
Succulents 4:136, 167
Sucking lice 4:279
Sucrose 3:119; **5:**380
Suction pump *see* Lift pump
Suctorians 4:213
Sudden infant death syndrome 5:375
Suez Canal (Egypt) **6:**45–46, 111
Sugar 5:380, 382 *see also* Glucose
    biochemistry **3:**118–19
    crystals **3:**90
    dental caries **5:**280, 282
    food preservation **6:**78
    fuel production **2:**396
    photosynthesis **4:**17–18
    solution **3:**78
Sugar-beet eelworms 4:230
Sugar maples 4:105
    illus. **4:**146
Sugar pines 4:90
Sulci (singular **Sulcus**) **5:**229
Sulfadithiazole 5:464
Sulfa drugs 2:360; **5:**445
Sulfanilamide 5:464
Sulfates 2:36, 138; **3:**97
Sulfathiazole 5:464
Sulfides, Copper 6:182
Sulfites 3:67; **6:**83
Sulfur 3:32, 44
    chemical industry **6:**206–7
    chemosynthesis **3:**376
    cloud pollution **2:**164
    color **2:**138; **3:**28
    hot springs **2:**64
    nutrition **5:**387
    radioisotope tracers **3:**320
Sulfur bacteria 4:18
Sulfur butterflies 4:302, 304
Sulfur dioxide
    acid rain **2:**172, 473, 475–76
    air pollution **2:**469, 471; **3:**73
    corrosion **3:**103
    volcanoes **2:**61
Sulfur hexafluoride 6:208
Sulfuric acid 3:94, 97, 99
    acid rain **2:**473–76
    chemical industry **6:**205–7
    Venus **1:**320
    illus.
        contact process **6:**204

Sullivan, Harry Stack (American psychologist) **5:**350
    illus. **5:**342
Sullivan, Kathryn (American astronaut) **1:**277, 289
Sulphur-bottom whales *see* Blue whales
Sulu Sea 2:251
Sum 1:346
Sumatra 2:256, 257
Sumatran rhinoceroses 5:112
Sumer
    mathematics, history of **1:**329
Summer 1:110, 112
    constellations **1:**29–30
    jet streams **2:**150–51, 185
    polar regions **2:**87–88
    illus.
        wind patterns **2:**185
    map(s)
        constellations **1:**31
Summer monsoons 2:183
Sumner, Thomas (American ship captain) **6:**170
SUN 1:25, 73–74, 78, **80–93** *see also* individual headings beginning with Solar
    air, circulation of **2:**181–83
    amateur astronomy **1:**15
    atoms **1:**222
    auroras **2:**156
    biomes **3:**492–93
    calendar **1:**474–75
    climates of the world **2:**209
    color **3:**297
    comets **1:**76–77
    Earth's climate **2:**220
    eclipses **1:**118–19, 175–80
    ecosystems **3:**484–85, 487
    heat **3:**219
    life, origin of **1:**318
    navigation **1:**168
    nuclear fusion **3:**354
    power source *see* Solar power
    radiation **1:**60
    space probes **1:**236, 301
    space science **1:**234
    stars **1:**190–91
    temperature and dimensions **1:**192
    tides **2:**243, 245–46
    water cycle **2:**100
    illus.
        eclipse **1:**175, 179
        energy reaching Earth **3:**493
Sunbirds 4:457
Sunblocks 5:437
Sunburn 5:267
Sunday (day of week) **1:**476
Sundews 4:109–13, 115
Sun dune cats 5:92
Sun ferns 4:79
Sunflowers 4:113, 141
    illus. **3:**374, 402; **4:**142
Sunglasses 1:254
Sunis 5:131

Sunlight
 color **3**:297
 mammals, effects on **5**:6
 photosynthesis **4**:16–24
 polar regions **2**:87–88
 skin cancer **5**:436–37
 vitamin D **5**:384
Sunrise 2:162
Sunset 2:162, 433; **3**:297
Sun spiders *see* Wind scorpions
Sunspot cycle *see* Solar cycle
Sunspots 1:80–81, 83–85, 88
 atmospheric ionization **2**:152
 Chinese astronomy **1**:472
 cosmic rays **1**:227
 Earth's climate **2**:220
Sun synchronous orbits 1:305
Superchargers 6:140
Supercomputers 6:362–63
 illus. **6**:364
Superconducting tape 3:363
SUPERCONDUCTORS 3:353–63
 ceramics **6**:220–21
 maglev systems **6**:132
 Tevatron **6**:358–59
Supercooled liquids 2:175
 water **3**:93, 231
Superego 5:342
Superfetation 5:38
Superfund sites 5:492
Supergiant stars 1:192
Supergranulation 1:83
Superheated liquids
 water **3**:231
Super High Frequency 6:294
Superior vena cava 5:200
 illus. **5**:169
Super NES (video-game system)
 6:299
Supernovas 1:195, 197–201,
 206
 Chinese astronomy **1**:472
 cosmic rays, origin of **1**:231
 dinosaur extinction **1**:497
 life, origin of **1**:317
 solar system, origin of **2**:12
 X-ray **1**:59
 illus. **1**:49–50, 58, 198–99; **2**:11
Superoxide dismutase 5:233
Superposition (in geology) **2**:7
Super Proton Synchrotron
 (SPS) 6:358
Supersaturated solutions 3:80
Supersaurus **1**:495
 illus. **1**:494
Supersonic flight 3:206; **6**:105,
 157
Superstition Wilderness (Ari-
 zona) **2**:511–12
Supertankers (ships) **2**:328
Supinator muscles 5:189
Supportive proteins 3:439
Suppressor genes 5:434
Suppressor T cells 5:237
Surface effect ships (SESs)
 6:116
Surface friction 6:92

Surface impoundments (for
 waste disposal) **2**:491
Surface mining *see* Strip mining
Surface tension 3:76
Surface washing (of sand filters)
 2:446
Surface waves (in physics) **2**:49;
 3:194–95
Surfing
 illus. **2**:254
Surf zone 2:254
SURGERY 5:476–81
 angioplasty **5**:490–91
 arthritis treatment **5**:428
 artificial body parts **5**:500–509
 bypass surgery **5**:439
 cancer **5**:436
 Cesarean section **5**:305
 laser operations **5**:489
 medical specialties **5**:415
 nurses **5**:485
 organ transplants **5**:496–99
 pain-receptor destruction **5**:292
 prenatal surgery **5**:418
 spinal-cord injuries **5**:234
 telesurgery **6**:391
 valvular disease **5**:440
 veterinary science **4**:468
 weight reduction **5**:393
Surinam toads 4:347
Surrogate motherhood 5:307
Surtsey (volcanic island, Iceland)
 2:58
 illus. **2**:282
Surveying
 mensuration of forests **4**:128
 plane geometry **1**:366
 trigonometry **1**:389
 illus. **2**:301
Surveyors (spacecraft) **1**:123,
 298
Survival of the fittest *see* Natural selection
Survival Service (conservation
 agency) **2**:498, 504
Suspension bridges 6:15, 50
 illus. **6**:49
Suspension systems (of auto-
 mobiles) **6**:145–46
 illus. **6**:147
Sustained-yield forestry 4:130
Sutton, Walter (American cytolo-
 gist) **3**:401–2, 410
Sutures (in the skull) **5**:176
Swain, F. R. D. (British aviator)
 1:271
Swains Island (American Samoa)
 2:283
Swainson warblers 4:459
Swallowing 5:216–17, 249, 275
Swallows (birds) **4**:450
Swallow-tailed kites 4:417
Swallowtails (butterflies) **4**:302–4
 illus. **4**:301, 303
Swammerdam, Jan (Dutch natu-
 ralist) **4**:267
Swamp deer *see* Indian baras-
 inghs

Swamps 4:137, 152–53
Swans 4:441
 illus. **4**:439
Swarming of bees 4:287
Swash marks (on beaches)
 2:295
SWATH ships 6:114
S waves 3:195
 earthquakes **2**:49, 51, 54
 seismic waves **2**:23–25
 illus. **2**:50
Sweat *see* Perspiration
Sweat glands 5:164, 265
 illus. **5**:264
Sweden
 illus. **4**:130
Swelling 5:300
Swells (ocean waves)
 illus. **2**:250
Swifts 4:405
Swim bladder (of fish) **4**:318,
 330–33
Swimming 5:398
 illus. **5**:399
Swing bridges 6:50
Swiss cheese plants 4:114
Switching, Telephone 6:238
 illus. **6**:238–39
Sword ferns
 illus. **4**:78
Swordfish 4:318, 335
Sydney (Australia)
 air pollution **2**:468
 illus. **6**:40
Sydney funnel-web weavers
 4:263
Symbiosis
 algae in coral reefs **2**:285, 287
 fungi **4**:37
 hermit crab and sponge **4**:216
 humans and microbes **5**:425
 lichens **4**:43
 plovers and crocodiles
 4:437–38
 populations and communities
 3:482–83
 illus. **4**:169
Symbolic behavior 5:149
Symbols, Chemical *see* Chemi-
 cal symbols
Symbols, Mathematical 1:330,
 352–53
Symmetry (in physics) **3**:336
Sympathetic nervous system
 5:232
Sympathetic resonance 5:276
Symphyla 4:204
Synapses 5:224, 288, 361
Synaptic clefts 5:226
Synaptic vesicles 5:225
Synchrocyclotrons 6:355, 357
Synchronizers 6:256
Synchrotron radiation 1:231
Synchrotrons 1:231
Synclines
 illus. **2**:37
Syncom (communications satel-
 lite) **1**:309

Synergistic muscles **5:**189
Synfuels *see* Synthetic fuels
Synodic month **1:**116
Synoptic meteorology **2:**143
Synovial membrane (Synovium)
    5:183, 240, 428
Synthesizers, Electronic **3:**218
Synthetic blood **5:**210, 506;
    6:208
Synthetic fibers *see* Fibers, Syn-
    thetic
Synthetic fuels **2:**395–98
Synthetic rubber *see* Rubber—
    synthetic
Syphilis **3:**447; **5:**233, 429
Syringes
    illus. **3:**135
Systemic lupus erythematosus
    5:240
Systems, Geologic **2:**20
Systems analysis and design
    1:460
Systole **5:**199–200
Systolic pressure **5:**204
    chart(s) **5:**203
Szilard, Leo (American physicist)
    1:506

T

Tablecloth (cloud over Table
    Mountain) **2:**163
Tablelands *see* Plateaus
Table Mountain (South Africa)
    2:163
Table of values (in mathomatics)
    1:354
Tachyons **3:**311
Taconic Orogeny (Disturbance)
    2:73
Tadpoles **4:**338, 342, 346
    illus. **4:**344
Tagging of animals **4:**339
Tahiti
    tides **2:**246
TAIGA **3:**496–97; **4:**134–35
Tailless whip scorpions **4:**263
Tails (of animals)
    lizards **4:**358
    lyrebirds **4:**449
    monkeys **5:**139–43
    prehensile **4:**358; **5:**8, 19, 35,
        101
    salamanders **4:**350
Tails (of comets) **1:**77, 159
Tajikistan
    earthquakes **2:**52
    Rogun Dam **6:**53
Takahes **4:**409
    illus. **4:**410
Takeuchi, H. (Japanese scientist)
    2:27
Taklamakan (desert, China) **2:**83
Talking in sleep *see* Somnilo-
    quism
Talons **4:**414–15

Talus (of the foot) **5:**181–82
    illus. **5:**180
Talus slopes (of mountains)
    illus. **2:**425
Tamanduas *see* Lesser anteaters
Tamaracks (American larches)
    4:92, 164
Tamarins **5:**139
Tamarisk trees
    illus. **4:**118
Tambora (volcano, Indonesia)
    2:60–62
Tanagers **4:**458
    illus. **4:**458
Tangents **1:**387–89
Taniguchi, Norio (Japanese sci-
    entist) **6:**339
Tankers (ships) **6:**113
    petroleum **2:**328
    illus. **2:**332, 339
Tank farms (oil storage) **2:**328
Tanks, Water **2:**450
    illus. **2:**447
Tanning booths
    illus. **3:**274
Tantalum **3:**44–45
Tape gauges **2:**248
Tape recorders **6:**280–81
    diagram(s) **6:**280
Tapeworms **3:**457; **4:**201,
    225–27
    illus. **4:**227
Taphonomy **1:**482
Taproot systems **4:**68
Tar **2:**139
Tarbela Dam (Pakistan) **6:**52, 56
    illus. **6:**54
Tarbosaurus
    illus. **1:**492
Tardigrada **4:**204
Target heart rate **5:**402
Target tortoise beetles
    illus. **4:**298
Tarpon **4:**332
Tarsal bones **5:**182
    illus. **5:**174–75, 180–81
Tar sands **2:**325, 396
Tarsiers **5:**138
Tasmanian devils **5:**21–22
Tasmanian wolves **5:**22
TASTE, Sense of **5:**284–85
    crustaceans **4:**253
Taste buds **5:**284, 333
    illus. **5:**285
Tattoos **6:**351
Tau particles (in physics) **3:**21
Tau protein **5:**233
Taurus (constellation) **1:**32
Taxation **1:**453, 455, 459
Taxonomy *see* Classification of
    living things
Taylor, A. H. (American physicist)
    6:255
Tayras **5:**96
T cells **5:**236–37, 442
TCP/IP **6:**305
TD-1 (artificial satellite) **1:**63
Teachers **6:**327, 328

Tear glands *see* Lachrymal
    glands
Technetium **3:**45, 360
TECHNOLOGY AND SOCIETY
    1:7; **6:**2–14
    artificial body parts **5:**500–509
    careers in technical trades **6:**12
    conservation movement as
        reaction to **2:**404–5
    environmental pollution
        2:454–56
    genetic technology **3:**416–23
    geography **2:**299
    Internet **6:**302–11
    modern farms **6:**60–62
    science education **6:**325
    science fiction **1:**502, 505–6
    space program **1:**254–56
Tectonic processes *see* Plate
    tectonics
Teenagers *see* Adolescence
Teeter tails *see* Spotted sandpip-
    ers
TEETH **5:**278–82
    artificial *see* Artificial teeth
    bears **5:**70
    carnivores **5:**9, 69
    cartilaginous fish **4:**324
    cats **5:**85
    dogs **5:**70, 77
    evolution in mammals **5:**3
    fossils **1:**485
    grazing animals **4:**140
    herbivores **5:**8
    insectivores **5:**24
    kangaroos **5:**17
    lizards **4:**360
    manatees and dugongs **6:**52
    milk teeth **5:**326
    raccoons **5:**70
    reptiles **4:**353
    rodents **5:**39–40
    snakes **4:**364
    walruses' tusks **5:**67–68
    illus. **5:**167
Teflon **6:**208, 215
    artificial body parts **5:**501, 505
    space suits **1:**275
Teisserenc de Bort, Léon Phi-
    lippe (French meteorolo-
    gist) **2:**143
Tektites **2:**4
Telecommunications *see* Com-
    munication
TELEGRAPH **6:**8, 234–36
    early weather forecasting
        2:142, 203
Telemedicine **5:**492–93
Telemetry **1:**306; **5:**492
Teleost fish **4:**331–35
TELEPHONE **6:**8–9, 237–41
    artificial satellites **1:**307–9
    cellular technology **6:**242–43
    computerized speech **6:**367
    computer modems **6:**366
    computer networking **6:**389–91
    Internet access **6:**309

TELEPHONE (cont.)
photonics 6:224
illus.
e-mail on cell phone 6:243
Telephoto lenses 6:264–65
Teleprinters 6:236
TELESCOPES 1:12–13, 17,
37–44 *see also* Radio telescopes
amateur astronomy 1:15
astronomy, history of 1:473
coronagraph 1:82
ground-based advantages over
in-space 1:52
IRAS 1:61–62
optics 3:288
solar telescopes 1:90, 92
in space *see* Telescopes in
space
thermocouples 1:60
illus.
Galileo's telescope 1:11, 40
TELESCOPES IN SPACE 1:15–
16, 45–52
infrared astronomy 1:61–62
Moon base 1:126, 261, 299
radio astronomy 1:57
ultraviolet astronomy 1:63–64
Telesurgery 5:480; 6:391
Teletypewriters 6:236
TELEVISION 6:290–97
artificial satellites 1:308–9, 311
interactive TV 6:304
microsurgery viewing 5:495
MSN TV 6:309, 391
science education 6:321
screens 3:300; 6:295–97
UltimateTV 6:287
video games 6:298
video recording 6:282, 287
illus.
8-mm videocassettes 6:283
Television microscopes 6:334
Telharmonium 3:217
Telluric lines 1:88
Tellurium 3:29, 32, 45
Telnet 6:305
Telomeres 3:412
Telophase 3:442, 445
Telstar (communications satellite)
1:309; 6:240, 295
illus. 6:241
Tempel 1, Comet 1:161, 296
TEMPERATE FORESTS 3:495–
396; 4:133–34, 144–49
illus. 3:497
Temperate rain forests *see* Rain
forests
Temperate zone
biomes 3:493, 495–96
climates of the world 2:213
jet streams 2:150
precipitation 2:171
Temperature 3:221
atmosphere 2:148, 150–52
body *see* Body temperature
chemical reactions 3:60–61

climates of the world 2:212–14
clouds 2:167–68
deciduous trees' leaves 4:145
deep seawater 2:271, 275
deserts 2:82; 4:166
Earth's interior 2:22, 27
gases 3:70, 72
global warming 1:109;
2:477–81
greenhouse effect 2:154
groundwater 2:116
ideal-gas laws 3:74
kinetic energy 3:75
lakes 2:111
mammals' environment 5:5
ocean water 2:229, 238
plasma state 3:13
polar regions 2:88
precipitation 2:170–72
saturation 3:80
skin sense 5:286
solubility 3:80–81
stars 1:191, 202
Sun 1:74, 81, 190
superconductors 3:354, 360
taiga 4:164
tundra 4:162
vapor pressure 3:77
volume of solids 3:12
table(s)
comparison of scales 6:421
Temperature inversions 2:470;
3:73
Tempered scale (in music) 3:213
Tempering 6:182
Temple of Artemis *see* Artemis,
Temple of
Temporal bones 5:176
Temporal lobe (of the brain)
5:228–29
Tendinitis 5:193
Tendons 5:164, 190–91, 193
artificial body parts 5:504
Tendon sheaths 5:193
Tendrils 4:115
Tennessee
aquariums 4:314
caves 2:131
Tennessee Aquarium 4:476
Tennessee River 6:56
Tennessee Valley Authority
(TVA) 6:53
"Ten-percent law" (of energy
loss) 3:486
Tenrecs 5:28
Tensile strain 6:27, 30–31
Tensional force 3:155
Tension headaches 5:289–90
Tensor fasciae latae
illus. 5:166
Tentacles 4:217, 219, 232
Terbium 3:45
Teredos (Shipworms) 4:239
Tereshkova, Valentina (Soviet
cosmonaut) 1:241, 289
illus. 1:286
Terminal buds *see* Apical mer-
istems

Terminal fibrils 5:225
Terminals, Computer 6:372–73,
384, 386
Terminator, The (film) 1:505
Termites 4:276, 278, 290
anteaters' diet 5:34
Trichonympha 4:209
illus. 4:209
Terns 4:394, 396, 435
Terrapins 4:375
Terra satellite 1:256
Terrestrial Planet Finder (TPF)
1:237
Terrestrial planets 1:74
Territories (in biology) 3:479;
4:191
Terrorism 2:455, 456; 5:430
computer security 6:397
nuclear reactors 2:375
Tertiary period
fossils 1:489
table(s) 1:486; 2:20–21
Tesla, Nikola (Serbian-American
engineer)
illus. 2:320
Testes 5:247, 293–94
illus. 5:170, 295
Testing, Educational 5:362
learning disabilities 5:364
science education 6:327–29
illus. 5:363
Testosterone 5:246–47, 313, 467
Tetanus 5:194, 424, 430
Tethys (moon of Saturn)
1:145–46
Tethys Sea
map(s) 2:40–41
Tetracyclines 5:464
Tetragonal crystals 3:90
Tetrahydrocannibol *see* THC
Tevatron 3:311; 6:358–59
Texas 2:292
illus. 2:459
Texas cattle fever 4:212
Texas horned toads
illus. 4:345
Textile industry
automation 6:195
bacteria, uses of 4:35
factory, history of the 6:187–90
natural gas, use of 2:345
illus. 6:193
TGV (high-speed train) 6:130
illus. 6:129
Thailand
illus. 2:256
Thalamus 5:288
Thalassemia 5:420
Thales of Miletus (Greek phi-
losopher) 1:329; 3:244
astronomy, history of 1:11
geometry 1:367
lodestone 3:261
Thalidomide 5:301
Thallium 3:31, 45
Thallus 4:37, 42, 44, 62
Thames River 2:457–58
THC (Tetrahydrocannibol) 5:371

T-helper lymphocytes *see* CD-4 cells
Theodolites 2:5
Theophrastus (Greek naturalist) 3:473; 4:3
Theorems 1:368, 401
Theramin 3:218
Therapeutic cloning 5:422
Therapeutic touch 6:317
Therapy animals 4:487
Theriodonts 1:488
Thermal conductivity *see* Coefficient of heat conduction
Thermal cracking 2:331
Thermal energy 2:382, 390–94
Thermal gradient 2:382, 385
Thermal insulation *see* Insulation, Thermal
Thermal ionization 3:354
Thermal pollution 2:307, 455, 464
Thermal springs *see* Hot springs
Thermal vents *see* Hydrothermal vents
Thermionic emission 6:247
Thermistors *see* Thermoresistors
Thermochemistry *see* Heat of reaction
Thermocouples (Thermopiles) 1:60; 3:224
Thermodynamics 3:144
  chemical reactions 3:59–60
  energy transfer in ecosystems 3:486
  entropy 3:240–43
  heat transfer 3:232–39
Thermoelectric couples 2:311
Thermoelectric hypothesis 2:29
Thermoelectricity 2:29
Thermoelectric systems, Solar
  illus. 2:388
Thermography 3:281; 5:458
  illus. 3:238; 5:457
Thermometers 2:142; 3:223–24
  fusible alloys 3:228
  liquids, expansion of 3:12
  illus.
    clinical 3:192
    liquid-crystal 3:92
    maximum-minimum 3:193
    pop-up timers 3:228
    scales of temperature 3:223
Thermonuclear explosions
  cosmic rays, origin of 1:231
Thermophilic algae 4:47
Thermophilic microbes 3:2; 4:27
Thermopiles *see* Thermocouples
Thermoplastic polyester 6:212
Thermoplastics 6:210–11
Thermoresistors (Thermistors) 3:224
Thermoscopes 3:223–24
Thermoset plastics 6:210–12, 214
Thermoset polyester 6:212

Thermosphere 1:105; 2:151–52
  illus. 2:150
Thermostats 6:195
  illus. 6:196
Thermotogae 4:29
Theropods 1:494
"The Wave" (stadium cheer)
  illus. 3:194
Thiamine (Vitamin B_1) 5:384
Thighbone *see* Femur
Thigmomorphogenesis 4:115
Thigmotropism 4:114–15
Thin-client computers 6:309
Thinking 5:343
Third law of motion 3:158
35mm single-lens reflex cameras 6:263, 268
Thistles 4:104
Thomas Jefferson High School for Science and Technology (Alexandria, Virginia) 6:327
Thompson, Benjamin (American-born British physicist) *see* Rumford, Count
Thomson, Elihu (American inventor) 3:276
Thomson, Joseph John (English physicist) 3:18; 6:246
  diagram(s)
    atomic model 3:17
Thoracic vertebrae 5:175, 177
  illus. 5:175–76
Thorax (of insects) 4:274
Thorium 2:28; 3:45
Thorium 231 2:364
Thorium 234 2:363; 3:127
Thorne, Kip (American physicist) 1:213–14
Thorold's deer 5:121
Thought disturbances 5:349–50
Thrashers 4:453–54
Threadworms *see* Roundworms
Three-dimensional video games 6:301
Three-dimensional vision *see* Binocular vision
3DO Company 6:299
Three Gorges Dam (China) 2:380, 410; 6:22, 56
Three Mile Island nuclear-power plant (Pennsylvania) 2:373
Three-phase generators 2:311–12
Three-toed sloths 5:34
Threonine 3:122
Thresher (submarine) 2:221
Thresher sharks 4:328
Thrips 4:279
Thrombi (singular Thrombus) 5:212
Thrombin 5:208
Thrombocytopenia 5:212
Thrombokinase (Thromboplastin) 5:208
Thrombolytic drugs 5:467
Thrush (disease) 4:40–41

Thrushes (birds) 4:454
  illus. 4:453
Thrust 1:242; 6:106
Thrust faults 2:69
Thrust vectoring 6:161
Thulium 3:45, 319
Thumbs 5:153, 180
THUNDER 2:178–79
  sound waves 3:201, 203
Thunderclouds 2:175–76
  tornadoes 2:191–92
Thunderstorms 2:174–80
  lightning 3:248–49
  study 2:141
  tornadoes 2:189–92
  watches and warnings 2:202
  weather forecasting 2:206
Thylacines *see* Tasmanian wolves
Thylakoids 3:431; 4:22
Thymine 3:123, 411; 5:309–10
  illus. 3:409, 415
Thymus glands 5:207, 237, 332
  illus. 5:170
Thyroid cartilage *see* Adam's apple
Thyroid gland 5:246–47
  illus. 5:170
Thyroid-stimulating hormone 5:243
Thyroxine 5:246–47
Thysanura 4:278
Tibetan Plateau 2:72, 80, 210
  illus. 2:78
Tibetan sand foxes 5:83
Tibia 5:181
  illus. 5:165, 174–75, 180
Tibialis anterior
  illus. 5:166
Ticarcillin 5:463
Tice, George (American photographer)
  illus. 6:270
Ticks (arachnids) 4:248, 258–59, 262
  disease carriers 4:212, 259, 263
  Lyme disease 4:269; 5:118
  Rocky Mountain spotted fever 5:428
Tic-tac-toe 1:425
Tidal bores 2:247
Tidal currents 2:247–48
Tidal energy 2:249, 312, 399
  illus. 2:248
Tidal islands 2:280
Tidal marshes *see* Salt marshes
Tidal resonance 2:246
Tidal theory 2:11
Tidal waves *see* Tsunamis
TIDES 1:117; 2:243–49
  biorhythms 3:380
  coastal formation 2:292–93
  physical oceanography 2:223
  tidal currents 2:247–48
  tsunami warning 2:259
  illus.
    research 2:222

Tide staffs 2:248
Tide Tables 2:249
TIFF (Tagged Image File Format) 6:274
Tiger beetles 4:292–93
illus. 4:291–92
Tiger moths (Woolly bears) 4:302, 307
illus. 4:306
Tigers 2:500, 514; **5:**86–87
Bengal tigers 2:513
Chinese tigers 2:513
dholes 5:81
illus. 2:493, 513; 5:2, 87
Tiger salamanders 4:351
Tiger sharks 4:327
Tiger snakes 4:374
Tilapia 6:90
Tiltmeters 2:5, 60
Tiltrotor XV-15 (aircraft) **6:**161
Timber *see* Trees
Timberline 3:498
Timber wolves *see* Gray wolves
Timbre (Quality of sound) **3:**207
Time
calendar 1:474–78
entropy 3:243
geologic record 2:18–21
period motion 3:161
relativity theory 3:344–47
uniformity, principle of 3:509
Timed-release medications 5:469
illus. 5:468
Time Lines
biology 3:368
technology 6:10–11
Time Machine, The (book, Wells) 1:213
Time reversal invariance 3:309–10
Times Beach (Missouri) **2:**463
Time-sharing systems (in data processing) **6:**372–73, 383
Time travel 1:213–14, 501
Timpani *see* Kettledrums
Tin 3:31, 45, 53
Tinamous 4:396, 398, 413
Tinea *see* Ringworm
Ting, Samuel (American physicist) **3:**314
illus. 3:306
Tinnitus 5:277
Tip-ups *see* Spotted sandpipers
Tire pump *see* Air pump
Tires
automobiles 6:134, 146–47
bicycles 6:94
lunar vehicles 1:124
Tirol (region, Europe) **2:**173
Tiros (artificial satellite) **1:**313–14
Tissues 4:185; **5:**163–64, 171
damage and healing 5:239
life, characteristics of 3:376
plant 4:15, 65–68
stem-cell technology 3:423
Tissue typing 5:497

Titan (moon of Saturn) **1:**75, 144–46, 292, 295
illus. 1:142
Titan arum
illus. 4:112
Titania (moon of Uranus) **1:**150
illus. 1:149
Titanic (ship) **2:**260, 277; **6:**124
illus. 2:263; 6:115
Titanium 3:45
alloys 6:184
artificial body parts 5:501
submarine hulls 6:122
Titanotheres **1:**498
Titov, Gherman S. (Soviet cosmonaut) **1:**241
Titration 3:98–99, 133
illus. 3:98, 132
Tits (Titmice) **4:**455–56
illus. 4:455
Titusville (Pennsylvania)
oil well 2:323, 337
TiVo 6:287, 304
T lymphocytes 5:207, 212, 426
Toadfish 4:333–34
Toads 4:345, 348
illus. 4:345–46
Tobacco
smokeless tobacco 5:436
smoking *see* Smoking (of tobacco)
illus.
plant with firefly genes 3:389
Tobacco mosaic virus 3:6, 384–85, 387–88; **5:**424
Tobacco worms 4:305
Tobago Cays (islands, Caribbean Sea)
illus. 2:280
Toes 5:182
birds of prey 4:414, 420
gout 5:429
lizards 4:358
Toilet claws 5:137
Tokamaks 2:376; **3:**356
illus. 2:375
Token-passing (computer protocol) **6:**387–88
Tokyo (Japan)
air pollution 2:468–69
illus. 3:244
Tolerable Upper Intake Levels (ULs) 5:390
Tolerance (to drugs) **5:**370–71
Tollund man 4:154
Tolman, Edward (American psychologist) **5:**343
Toluene 3:112
Tomatoes
genetically engineered 4:7; 6:74
per-acre yields 4:172
plant breeding 6:67–68
Tombaugh, Clyde W. (American astronomer) **1:**157; **3:**182
Tomography *see* CAT scans; PET; Seismic tomography

Toms, John (English murderer) **1:**509
Tone quality (in music) **3:**211–12
Tones (sounds) **5:**277
Tongass National Forest (Alaska) **4:**158, 160
Tongs 3:170–71
Tongue 5:284
frogs 4:348
snakes 4:364
touch pressure 5:286
illus. 5:167, 285
lymphatics 5:170
Tonnage (Displacement) **6:**107, 112
Tonus (Muscle tone) **5:**193, 227
Tools (implements)
animals' use of 4:193; 5:106, 144, 148–49
human development 1:481; 5:152, 158, 160
nanotechnology 6:339
rock collecting 2:139–40
illus.
early hand tools 6:4–5
Tooth *see* Teeth
Tooth buds 5:300
Toothed whales 5:12, 48–49, 52–54
Tooth shells 4:241
TOPEX/Poseidon (artificial satellite) **2:**242, 255
Topical geography 2:297
Topknot pigeons 4:429
Topology (in computer networking) **6:**386–87
Topology (in mathematics) **1:**330
Top quarks 3:20, 314
TOPS (Take Off Pounds Sensibly) 5:394
Tori (singular **Torus**) (doughnut-shaped containers) **3:**355–56
TORNADOES 2:164, **189–94,** 202
hurricanes 2:200
hurricanes compared to 2:195
Kansas City (2003) 2:201
radar tracking 6:261
watches and warnings 2:194, 202
weather forecasting 2:206
illus. 2:141, 206
Torosaurus **1:**496
Torpedoes (fish) **4:**328
Torpedoes (weapons) **6:**119
Torpor 5:30
Torque 6:143
Torque converters 6:144
Torr (unit of measurement) **3:**70, 72
Torricelli, Evangelista (Italian scientist) **2:**142; **3:**70, 186–87
Torsion balance 1:104
Tortoises *see* Turtles
Torus *see* Tori
Total internal reflection 3:285

Total Ozone Mapping Spec-
trometers (TOMS) 2:154
illus. **2:**481
Toucans 4:408
illus. **4:**407
TOUCH, Sense of 5:285–86
plants **4:**114–15
robots **6:**201–2
Tovdal River 2:472–73
Tower telescopes 1:92
Townes, Charles H. (American
physicist) **6:**345
Toxemia 5:301
Toxic wastes *see* Hazardous
wastes
Toxins
bacteria **4:**34; **5:**424, 427
drugs, effects of **5:**461
excess fat-soluble vitamins
5:383
forensic science **1:**515
immunization **5:**430
infectious diseases **5:**425
nervous system **5:**234
Toxoids 5:238
Toxoplasmosis 5:239, 302
Toyota Corona (automobile)
illus. **6:**137
Toyota Prius (automobile) **6:**148
illus. **6:**137
T-quarks *see* Top quarks
Trace evidence (forensics)
1:511–12
Trace fossils 1:482, 484–85
Trace minerals 5:387–88
Tracers, Radioisotope *see*
Radioisotope tracers
Trachea (Windpipe) 5:163, 178,
217
illus. **5:**167–68, 170, 216
Tracheae 4:246–47, 274
Tracheids 4:66, 88, 100
Tracks (in magnetic recording)
6:280
Trades, Technical 6:12
Trade winds 2:184, 237
diagram(s) **3:**494
Trains, Railroad *see* Rail trans-
portation
Trance 5:409
Tranquilizers 5:373
Trans-Alaska Pipeline System
(TAPS) 2:329, 335
illus. **2:**330
Trans-Amazon Highway (Brazil)
2:515
Transatmospheric vehicles *see*
Aerospace planes
Transcervical balloon tubo-
plasty 5:307
TransCyte 5:507
Transdermal skin patches
5:376, 469–70
Transfer molding 6:214
Transfer of mechanical energy
3:166–67
Transfer RNA 3:415

Transformation (in genetics)
4:32
Transformational geometry
1:330
Transformers, Electric 2:317;
3:259–60
magnets **6:**230
illus. **2:**315; **3:**260
Transfusions, Blood *see* Blood
transfusions
Transgenic organisms 3:389,
403; **6:**14
genetic technology **3:**420, 423
Transistors 6:13, 250–53, 340
TRANSIT, Project *see* NAVSAT
program
Transitional zones (of rivers)
2:102–3
Transition metals 3:30–31
Transits (in astronomy) **1:**98, 102
Translocations (chromosome
disorders) **5:**421
Transmission, Radio 6:288–89
Transmission, Television 6:289,
294–95
Transmission electron micro-
scopes 3:450; **6:**335
illus. **6:**334
Transmission lines, Electric
2:307, 317–18
lightning safeguards **2:**178
radiation and health **3:**277
superconductivity **3:**362; **6:**220
illus. **2:**319
Transmission mains *see* Aqueducts
Transmissions, Automobile
6:143–44
Transmutation 2:371
Transphasors 6:371
Transpiration 2:171; **4:**71
Transplants, Organ and tissue
see Organ transplants
Transponders 1:311; **6:**295
TRANSPORTATION 6:42–50
animals shipped to zoos **4:**473
automobiles **6:**133–48
aviation **6:**149–64
disabled drivers, controls for
1:255
energy demands **2:**305, 332
engineering today **6:**22
human-powered **6:**91–95
Moon travel problems **1:**124
navigation **6:**165–73
oil transportation **2:**328–29,
334–35
rail transportation **6:**125–32
ships and shipping **6:**107–16
underground coal mines **2:**351,
353–54
Transport proteins 3:439
Transposable elements (in
genetics) **3:**413
Transrapid electromagnetic
system 6:131
Transuranium elements 3:7, 46
Transverse colon 5:254

Transverse dunes 2:428
Transverse waves 3:195
Trap-door spiders 4:260
illus. **4:**258
Trapeziums 1:374
illus. **1:**373
Trapezius
illus. **5:**166
Trapezoids 1:374
illus. **1:**373
Trauma *see* Emergency medi-
cine; Injuries
Travel industry 6:373
Travertine 2:64, 135–36, 139
Trawlers 6:88
Trawl nets 6:87
illus. **6:**88
Treadmills 5:439
Tree creepers 4:457
illus. **4:**456
Tree ferns 4:78–79, 83
Tree frogs 4:347–48
Tree kangaroos 5:19
illus. **5:**18
Tree kingfishers 4:406
Tree line *see* Timberline
Tree rings 4:15, 69, 88
archaeology **1:**464
illus. **1:**465; **2:**216
Trees *see also* Forests
aging **3:**466–68
capillary action **3:**76
conifers **4:**84–93
construction materials **6:**28
flowering plants **4:**99
forestry **4:**126–31
fossils **1:**488
ginkgo and cycads **4:**94–97
grasslands **4:**141–42
mammal habitats **5:**7–8
rainfall, effect on **2:**171
rain forests **4:**150–50
temperate forests **4:**144–45
Tree snakes 4:371–72
illus. **4:**369
Tree squirrels 5:8, 40–41
Trenches, Deep-sea 2:42, 45,
264, 269–70
Trench mouth *see* Vincent's
infection
Trends in International Mathe-
matics and Science
Study (TIMSS) 6:329
Très Riches Heures (illuminated
calendar)
illus. **1:**474
Trevithick, Richard (English
engineer) **6:**98, 125
illus. **6:**126
Triadobatrachus **4:**343
Trial-and-error learning *see*
Operant conditioning
Triangles (geometric figures)
1:370–73
non-Euclidean geometry **1:**403
trigonometry **1:**386–90
truss **6:**33–34
illus. **1:**387, 403

Triangles (musical instruments) 3:216
Triangulation 1:191
Triassic period
  conifers 4:84
  dinosaurs 1:494
  fossils 1:488
  mammals 1:497; 5:3
  map(s) 2:41
  table(s) 1:486; 2:20–21
Tributaries 2:423
Tributary valleys 2:422
Triceps muscle 5:189–90
  illus. 5:166
Triceratops 1:496
  illus. 1:495
Trichina worms 4:228–29
Trichinosis 4:228–29
Trichomes 4:33
Trichomonas 4:208–9
Trichonympha 4:209
  illus. 4:209
Triclinic crystals 3:90
Triconodon
  illus. 1:499
Tricuspid valve 5:198–99
Tricyclic antidepressants 5:356, 466
Trieste (bathyscaphe) 2:276; 6:123
Triggerfish 4:318, 335
Triglycerides 3:121; 5:382
TRIGONOMETRY 1:329–30, 332–33, 386–90
Trihedral angles 1:380
  illus. 1:381
Trilobites 1:487–88; 4:247, 249–50, 257
  illus. 1:488; 4:252
Trimethoprim 5:445
Trinocular microscopes 6:331
Triodes 6:248–49
Triple-beam balance
  illus. 3:134
Triple bonds (in chemistry) 3:110, 112
Triple covalent bonds 3:52
Triple X syndrome 5:314
Triremes 6:107
  illus. 6:108
Trisecting the angle 1:367
Trisomy 5:421
Tristan da Cunha (islands, Atlantic Ocean) 2:44–45
Tritemnodon
  illus. 1:499
Triticale 4:175; 6:71
Tritium 2:362, 376; 3:20
Triton (moon of Neptune) 1:151, 155
  Voyager probe 1:293
  illus. 1:153
Triton (nuclear submarine) 6:121
Trochlea 5:179
Trogoniformes 4:399–400, 405–6
Trogons 4:405–6
  illus. 4:405

Trolleys (Streetcars) 6:127–28
Trombones 3:217
Trona 6:208
Trophallaxis 4:283
Trophic (feeding) levels 3:485
Tropical continental air masses 2:187
Tropical cyclones 2:196
Tropical depressions 2:197
Tropical diseases 2:480–81
Tropical fish 3:457
Tropical maritime air masses 2:187
Tropical rain forests see Rain forests
Tropical storms 2:197
Tropical wave (low-pressure zone) 2:196
Tropic birds 4:446
Tropics
  biomes 3:493–94
  climates of the world 2:210–12
  lake temperatures 2:111
  plant communities 4:133, 136
  precipitation 2:167, 170–71
  rain forests 4:156–59
  soil management 2:412
  wind 2:187
Tropisms 4:114–15
Tropopause 1:105; 2:149
Troposphere 1:105; 2:143, 149–50, 153, 209
  illus. 2:150
Tropospheric-scatter communication systems 6:240
Troughs (of waves) 2:250
Trout 4:322, 333; 6:89
Troxidone 5:466
True ribs 5:177
  illus. 5:174
Truffles 4:42
Trumpeter swans 4:432, 441
Trunkfish 4:335
Trunk lines 6:238
Trusses (in architecture) 6:33–34, 38–39, 49
  illus. 6:36
Truth quarks see Top quarks
Trypanosoma 3:447; 4:208; 5:428
  illus. 4:208
Trypsin 5:252
Tryptophan 3:122; 5:384
Tsangpo Valley (Tibetan Plateau)
  illus. 2:78
Tsetse flies 4:208
  illus. 4:208
Tsiolkovsky, Konstantin E. (Russian scientist) 1:264
TSUNAMIS (Seismic sea waves; Tidal waves) 2:50, 247, 251, 256–59
Tuamotu Islands (Pacific Ocean) 2:283
Tuataras 4:353, 355
  illus. 4:353
Tubal ovum transfer 5:307
Tube-nosed birds 4:446

Tubercles 5:236
Tuberculosis 3:447; 5:236
  AIDS 5:443
  drug treatment 5:464
  Koch, Robert 5:424
  illus.
    bacteria 3:451
Tube sponges
  illus. 4:214
Tubulidentata 5:13
Tuff 2:33, 134, 433
Tufted titmice 4:456
Tug-barges 6:113
Tugboats 6:113
Tuke, William (English philanthropist) 5:349
Tumors
  bone 5:184
  brain 5:234
  drug delivery technology 5:473
  islet cells 5:245–46
  laser treatment 5:489
  pain 5:290
  pituitary gland 5:244
  radioisotope tracers 3:319
  illus. 3:444
Tuna 4:318, 320, 335
  nets catch dolphins 5:56–57
TUNDRA 2:77, 88–90; 4:162–64
  biomes 3:497
  climates of the world 2:213
  plant communities 4:135
Tundra lupines 4:105
Tungsten 3:45
  automobile headlights 6:141
  freezing point 3:88
  genetic engineering 6:75
  melting point 3:27
  scanning tunneling microscopes 6:337
Tunguska meteorite 1:174
Tuning forks 1:390; 3:212, 216
Tunnels (of moles) 5:25
Tunnels (transportation) 6:47–48
  compressed air 3:185
  illus. 6:46
Tupuxuara 1:496
Turbellarians 4:201, 228
Turbidity currents 2:269
Turbines 6:103–5
  electricity, generation of 2:312–16, 377–78, 399
  wind power 2:387
Turbochargers 6:139–40
Turbofan (Fan-jet) engines 6:106, 163
TurboGrafx-16 (video game system) 6:299
Turbojet engines 6:106, 163
  illus. 6:105
Turbojet Ferry (Hong Kong–Macau) 6:114
Turboprop engines 6:106, 164
  illus. 6:105
Turbulence 2:183
  fluid dynamics 3:192–94
  water 6:92
Turgor movement 4:185

Turions 4:112
Turkey (country)
earthquakes 2:47, 52
Turkeys (birds) 4:422–23,
426–27 see also Poultry
farming
illus. 4:426
Turkey vultures 4:169, 416
Turner's syndrome 5:314
Turtle (submarine) 6:118–19
Turtledoves 4:430–31
TURTLES 4:353–55, 375–79
extinct 2:497
life span 3:465–66; 5:324
marine species 2:413
diagram(s) 4:377
illus.
desert tortoise 2:509
Galápagos turtles 4:465
giant tortoise 3:465; 4:354
Tusks
elephants 5:103–4
musk deer 5:119
narwhals 5:53
walruses 5:9, 67–68
Tussocks 4:141
Tweezers 3:170–71
Twilight 3:297
Twin-hull ships 6:114
Twin-lens reflex cameras 6:263
Twin paradox 1:214
Twins 5:295–96, 311–12, 392
genetics 3:403
Twin Towers (New York City) see
World Trade Center
Twisted-winged parasites 4:280
Twisters see Tornadoes
Two-cycle engines 6:101
Two-person zero-sum games
1:425–26
Two-point threshold (of percep-
tion) 5:280
Two-stroke engines see Two-
cycle engines
2001: A Space Odyssey (film)
1:505; 6:373–74
illus. 1:265, 503
Two-toed sloths 5:34
illus. 5:33
Tycho (Moon crater) 1:121–22
Tycho Brahe (Danish astrono-
mer) see Brahe, Tycho
Tympanum (in the ear) see Ear-
drum
Typhoid fever 5:430
Typhoons see Hurricanes and
typhoons
Tyrannosaurus rex 1:494
Tyrant flycatchers see American
flycatchers
Tyrosine 3:122
Tzolkin (Mayan religious year)
1:475

U-V

U-boats 6:120
illus. 6:121
UCLA (University of California
at Los Angeles) see Cali-
fornia, University of
Uganda
Owens Fall Dam 6:56
UHF see Ultra High Frequency
Uhuru (artificial satellite) 1:51,
58, 212
illus. 1:207
Ukraine
Chernobyl nuclear accident
2:373–74, 455
triticale 6:71
illus. 2:373
Ulcerative colitis 5:240, 255
Ulcers, Peptic 5:256
Ulna 5:179
illus. 5:165, 174–75, 178
ULs see Tolerable upper intake
levels
UltimateTV 6:287
Ultra High Frequency 6:243,
294
Ultralight airplanes
illus. 6:162
Ultramicroscopes 6:333
Ultrasonics 3:199
medical technology 5:491–92
prenatal testing 5:303
sonography 5:454
illus.
ocean-current tracking 2:240
prenatal testing 5:302
sound spectrum 3:200
veterinary use 4:464
Ultrasound see Sonography
ULTRAVIOLET ASTRONOMY
1:54, 62–64
astronomy, history of 1:46
telescopes in space 1:50–51
Ultraviolet light 3:275, 281 see
also Ultraviolet astronomy
atmosphere 2:150–54
camera lens filters 6:270
forensic science 1:512
health effects 3:277
life, origin of 1:319; 3:381
ozone layer 2:481–82
skin cancer 5:436–37
spacecraft 1:251
sunglass lenses 1:254
vitamin D 5:384
illus.
tanning booth 3:274
Ultraviolet microscopes 6:334
Ulva 4:12, 49
Ulysses spacecraft 1:93, 260,
301
illus. 1:92, 290, 299
U-Matic 6:281
Umbilical cord 3:462; 5:296, 304
illus. 5:297
Umbra 1:175–78

Umbriel (moon of Uranus) 1:150
illus. 1:149
Uncertainty principle (in phys-
ics) 3:332, 334
Uncompahgre fritillary butterflies
illus. 4:305
Unconscious mind 5:342
Underground gasification of
coal 2:359
Underground houses 6:37
illus. 6:38
Underground rivers 2:126
Underground water see Groundwater
Undersea sleds see Sleds,
Underwater
Understory (of a rain forest)
4:157–58
Undertows see Rip currents
Underwater acoustics 3:202
Underwater archaeology 1:465;
2:279
illus. 1:468
Underwater tunnels see Sub-
aqueous tunnels
Ungulates 5:13
bison, buffalo, and oxen
5:132–35
deer family 5:118–23
elephants 5:103–6
giraffes and okapis 5:124–25
grassland animals 4:140
horse family 5:107–10
rhinoceroses 5:111–13
Unheard sound 3:199
Unicorns 5:53, 130
Unified force theory 3:144, 340,
352
Uniformitarianism (in geology)
2:8
Uniformity of space and time,
Principle of 3:509
Uniform populations 3:479
Uniform resource locators see
URLs
Unifying concepts and processes (science education)
6:324
Union of Soviet Socialist
Republics (1921–1991)
see also Russia; Ukraine
communications satellites 1:309
cosmonauts 1:283–85, 289
manned space flights 1:240,
241, 244, 247–48, 257
Mars probes 1:297
military satellites 1:313
Moon exploration 1:123
satellites, artificial 1:233, 235,
302–3, 306, 310
space probes 1:296, 298–300
space station 1:265–67
Unipolar affective disorder
5:351
Uniramia 4:247–49
Unistix navigational controller
1:255

Unit cells **3:**90
United Nations **4:**128; **5:**444, 446
United Nations Educational, Scientific, and Cultural Organization (UNESCO) **2:**513
United Nations Environment Program (UNEP) **2:**514
United Network for Organ Sharing (UNOS) **5:**499
United States
  agriculture **4:**171–72
  AIDS **5:**441, 444, 446
  earthquakes **2:**52
  energy consumption **2:**305
  grasslands **4:**139, 142
  National Highway System **6:**43
  natural gas **2:**338
  nuclear energy **2:**369–70
  obesity **5:**388
  pet ownership **4:**480–81, 488–89
  petroleum **2:**335
  temperate forests **4:**144, 146, 148–49
  tornadoes **2:**190, 192–93
  water supply **2:**435
  wilderness **2:**506–12, 515
  zoos **4:**470
  map(s)
    tornadoes **2:**190
United States (ship)
  illus. **6:**115
Unity (space-station module) **1:**269
Universe **1:**16–17, 189
  astrochemistry **3:**9
  cosmology and theory of relativity **3:**352
  cosmology relativity **3:**145
  structure and evolution **1:**234, 236
UNIVERSE, Origin of the **1:**18–23, 234
UNOS *see* United Network for Organ Sharing
Unsaturated hydrocarbons **3:**111
Unstable equilibrium **3:**182
  illus. **3:**180
Ununbium **3:**46
Ununhexium **3:**46
Ununoctium **3:**46
Ununquadium **3:**46
Upatnieks, Juris (American scientist) **6:**276
Uploading (of data files) **6:**386
Uppers *see* Stimulant drugs
Up quarks **3:**20, 313
Upsilon particles
  illus. **3:**312
Upwelling, Oceanic **2:**236–38
Uracil **3:**123, 413
  illus. **3:**415
Ural Mountains **2:**43, 70

Uranium **3:**45–46
  atomic structure **3:**48
  isotopes **2:**362; **3:**125
  nuclear energy **2:**364–66, 368, 370; **3:**6
  radioactive decay **2:**28; **3:**127
Uranium 234 **3:**128
Uranium 235 **2:**368
  nuclear energy **2:**363–66
  radioactive dating **2:**16
Uranium 238
  nuclear energy **2:**362, 366, 368
  radioactive dating **2:**16–17
Uranium hexafluorides **2:**366; **6:**208
Uranium oxide **2:**366, 370
URANUS **1:**74, 79, **147–50**
  auroras **2:**157
  life, possibility of **1:**320–21
  Neptune, discovery of **3:**182
  space probes **1:**293
  illus. **1:**75, 148
Urban areas
  air pollution **2:**467–68
  climates of the world **2:**214
  construction materials **6:**24, 26–27
  environmental pollution **2:**454–56
  groundwater depletion **2:**118
  mass transportation **6:**128
  sewage crisis **2:**460
  waste disposal **2:**484–88
  water pollution **2:**457–58
  illus.
    electric lighting **2:**304
Urban forestry **4:**131
Urban geography **2:**301
Urea **3:**107; **5:**258–59
"U" Regulations (wilderness laws) **2:**510
Ureters **5:**259–61, 498
  illus. **5:**168, 258
Urethra **5:**261, 295
  illus. **5:**258
Urey, Harold (American chemist) **3:**381
  illus. **3:**383
Uric acid **5:**258–59, 429
Urinary tract **5:**257, 262
  illus. **5:**258
Urination **4:**169; **5:**261, 299
Urine **5:**203, 260–61
  desert animals **4:**169
  drugs eliminated in **5:**461
  nitrogen cycle **3:**491
URLs (Uniform resource locators) **6:**307
Urochordates **4:**309
Urogenital system **5:**172
Urohydrosis **4:**169
Urology **5:**415
Ursa Major (constellation) **1:**25, 29
Ursa Minor (constellation) **1:**26
U.S. RDAs *see* Recommended Dietary Allowances

USDA (United States Department of Agriculture) **5:**388
U-shaped dunes **2:**429
Ussuri meteorite **1:**171
Utah
  Arches National Park **2:**85
  Rainbow Bridge **2:**423
  illus. **2:**103
Utah arm (artificial limb) **5:**503
  illus. **5:**500, 502
Uterine milk (of marsupials) **5:**16
Uterus **5:**293–94, 299, 305
  birth **5:**304
  illus. **5:**295–96
Utilities, Public *see* Public utilities
Utopian societies **1:**502
V-1 (rocket) **6:**156
V-22 Osprey (aircraft) **6:**161
Vaccines and vaccination **5:**237–38
  AIDS research **5:**446
  allergies **5:**449
  Alzheimer's disease **5:**334
  bacteria **4:**34
  cancer immunotherapy **5:**437
  drug delivery **5:**474
  Malaria Vaccine Initiative **5:**428
  medicine, history of **5:**423–24
  microbiology **3:**447
  rabies **5:**424
  recombinant DNA **5:**475
  smallpox **5:**430
  veterinary science **4:**465, 467–68
  viruses **3:**393
  illus. **5:**427
Vacuoles **3:**430–31; **4:**14, 208
Vacuum **3:**185–86
Vacuum cleaners **3:**190
Vacuum evaporation **3:**230–31
Vacuum processing (of steel) **6:**179
Vacuum pumps **3:**186, 190
Vacuum tubes **6:**247–50
  image orthicon **6:**290–91
  musical instruments **3:**218
  telephone **6:**239
Vacuum tunneling **6:**337
Vadose circulation **2:**115
Vagina **5:**294–95, 299, 302, 304
Vaginal ultrasound **5:**303
Vagus nerves **5:**198
Vaiont Dam (Italy) **6:**53
Valence **3:**24, 48–49
Valence electrons **3:**19, 33, 48–49, 100, 109
Valhalla (feature on Callisto) **1:**138
Valine **3:**122
Valium *see* Diazepam
Vallarta, Manuel S. (Mexican mathematician) **1:**227
Valley and Ridge Province **2:**73
Valley glaciers *see* Alpine glaciers

Valleys 2:102, 419, 421–22, 424–25
glacial erosion 2:98, 123
mechanical action of rain 2:173
Valves (of engines) 6:139
Valves (of the heart) 5:198–99, 204
artificial heart valve 5:505
balloon angioplasty 5:491
heart disease 5:440
rheumatic fever 5:429
illus.
artificial heart valve 5:504
Vampire bats 5:32
Vanadium 3:46
Van Allen radiation belt 1:89, 105; 3:267
illus. 3:266
Van de Graaff, Robert (American physicist) 6:354
Van de Graaff accelerators 6:354
Van der Waals, Johannes Diderik (Dutch chemist) 3:74
Van der Waals forces 3:74
Van Drebbel, Cornelius (Dutch inventor) 6:118
Vaporization see Evaporation
Vaporization, Heat of see Heat of vaporization
Vapor pressure 3:77–78
graph(s)
pressure-temperature relationship 1:336
Vapors 3:69, 76–77
Vapor-turbine cycle 2:391–92
Variable condensers see Condensers
Variables (in experiments) 3:510
Variables (in mathematics) 1:352, 433–34
Variable stars 1:14
Varro, Marcus Terentius (Roman scholar) 3:446
Varves 2:216 17
Varying hares see Snowshoe rabbits
Vascular bundles see Veins (Vascular bundles)
Vascular cambium 4:70, 88
VASCULAR PLANTS 4:12, 64–73, 99–100
fossils 1:488
Vascular rays 4:69
Vascular tissue 4:65–67, 107
Vas deferens 5:295
Vas epididymis 5:295
Vaterland (steamship) 6:111
Vaults (in architecture) 6:33
illus. 6:35
vBNS (very-high-performance Backbone Network Service) 6:385
VCRs see Videocassette recorders
Vector quantities 3:151–53
illus. 3:150

Vectors (in genetic engineering) 6:74–75
Vega (space probes) 1:296, 299
Halley's comet 1:161
Venus probe 1:102
Vega (star) 1:30, 61–62, 112
Vegetable oils 3:120–21
biodiesel fuel 2:397
Vegetables
complex carbohydrates 5:382
olericulture 4:172–73
weight control 5:394
Vegetative reproduction 3:456; 4:9, 82
Veins (in anatomy) 5:195, 202–3
illus. 5:169, 196
Veins (Vascular bundles) (in botany) 4:67, 70–73
Veins (in geology) 2:137
Veksler, Vladimir (Soviet physicist) 6:355
Vela (constellation)
illus. 1:203
Veld 4:142
Veligers 4:237
Velocipedes 6:92
illus. 6:93
Velociraptor 1:494
Velocity 3:150, 348–49
Venae cavae 5:204
illus. 5:168
Venera (spacecraft) 1:100, 299–300
Venereal diseases see Sexually transmitted diseases
Venezuela
Angel Falls 2:422
giant rodent fossils 1:479–80
petroleum 2:325
savannas 4:141
illus. 2:328–29
Venice (Italy)
illus. 2:298
Venn diagrams 1:440–41
Venom
arachnids 4:263
centipedes 4:265
platypuses 5:15
shrews 5:28
snakes 4:339, 365, 367, 372–73
Ventifacts (sandblasted rocks) 2:427
Ventilation
coal mining 2:355
Ventouses 5:305
Ventricles 5:198, 200–201, 203
illus. 5:169
Vents, Hydrothermal see Hydrothermal vents
Vents, Volcanic 2:32–33, 56, 58, 61
lake beds 2:109
Venules 5:202–3
VENUS 1:74, 99–102
astronomy, history of 1:469
gravity-assisted flight 1:295

life, possibility of 1:320
Mayan astronomy 1:471
space probes 1:290, 299–300
illus. 1:15, 73, 76, 301
Venusian Eye (storm on Venus) 1:102
Venus's-flytraps 4:9, 109, 111
plant behavior 4:117
illus. 4:108
Verbal learning 5:359
Verizon 6:245
Vermiform appendix 5:254
illus. 5:167
Vermilion flycatchers
illus. 4:448
Vermis (of the brain) 5:230
Vernal equinox 1:36
Verne, Jules (French author) 1:271, 500, 506
Vernix caseosa 5:305
Vertebrae 5:33, 174–76
Vertebral column see Backbone
Vertebrates 4:205
digestive system 4:186
first known vertebrate 1:490
first land vertebrate 1:492
fossils 1:488
mammals 5:2
pain 5:292
reproduction 3:457
illus.
similarity of embryos 3:458
Vertical lift bridges 6:50
illus. 6:49
Vertical turbine pumps 2:441
Very High Frequency 6:294
Very Large Array (radio telescope, New Mexico) 1:43, 57
illus. 1:42, 56
Very Large Telescope (VLT) 1:37
Very Long Baseline Array (radio telescopes) 1:43, 57
Very Long Baseline Interferometry 1:48, 57
Vesalius, Andreas (Flemish physician) 5:451
Vesicles (cell structures) 3:429, 431, 437, 442
Vespa 4:289
Vesper rats 5:43
Vessel cells 4:66
Vessel elements 4:100
Vesta (asteroid) 1:168
Vestibule (of the ear) 5:275–76
Vesuvius, Mount (volcano, Italy) 2:57, 59, 61–62
excavation of Pompeii 1:466
illus.
plaster cast of victim 2:62
Veterinary entomology 4:269–70
VETERINARY SCIENCE 4:464–68
careers 4:466
ornithology 4:386–87
zoos 4:471, 475
Veterinary technicians 4:475

VHF *see* Very High Frequency
VHS format 6:281–82
Viagra *see* Sildenafil
Vibrations 3:199–200, 214
Vibrato (in music) 3:210–11, 217
Viceroy butterflies 4:276
Victoria (English queen)
   illus. 5:316
   hemophilia inheritance 5:317
Victoria, Lake (Africa)
   illus. 2:460
Vicuñas 5:6–7, 117
Videocassette recorders (VCRs)
   3:265; 6:281–83
   diagram(s) 6:282
VIDEO GAMES 6:298–301
   science fiction 1:506
   illus. 1:504
VIDEO RECORDING 6:278–87
   digital cameras 6:274
   magnetism 3:265
Vidicon tubes 6:291
   diagram(s) 6:292
Vienna Convention for the Pro-
   tection of the Ozone
   Layer (1985) 2:482
Vieraella 4:343
Viète, François (French math-
   ematician) 1:353
View cameras 6:262–63
Viewfinder cameras 6:262
   illus. 6:263
Viking (spacecraft) 1:297
   extraterrestrial life 1:320; 3:321
   Mars 1:129–31, 290
Vikings (people) 2:155
Viking ships 6:108–9
Villi
   chorionic villus sampling 5:303
   human embryo 5:296
   intestine 5:253
   illus. 5:252
Vincent's infection 5:281
Vinci, Leonardo da *see*
   Leonardo da Vinci
Vine, Allyn (American scientist)
   2:276
Vine, Frederick J. (British ocean-
   ographer) 2:42–43
Vinegar 3:94
Vines 4:157
Vinson Massif (peak, Antarctica)
   2:91
Vinyl chloride *see* Polyvinyl chlo-
   ride
Violence in video games 6:300
Violets
   illus. 4:116
Violins 3:215
Vioxx 5:292
Vipers 4:353, 372, 374
Virchow, Rudolf (German biolo-
   gist) 3:425; 4:181
   illus. 3:426
Vireos 4:459–60
   illus. 4:458
Virgin forest 4:128

Virginia 2:378
   illus. 4:152
Virginia clappers 4:439
Virginia deer 5:121
Virgo (constellation) 1:29
Virions 3:388
Virtual Boy (video-game system)
   6:301
Virtual focus 3:288
Virtual images 3:286
Virtual reality 6:301
Virulence 5:424–25
VIRUSES 3:379, 384–93
   AIDS 5:441–46
   antiviral drugs 5:465
   bacteriophages 4:32
   biology, history of 3:370
   cancer 5:436
   cold, common 5:429
   gene therapy 3:421
   genetic engineering 3:420; 6:74
   immune system 5:236
   infectious diseases 5:424,
      427–28
   microbiology 3:447, 451
   illus. 5:423
      hypothesis for cancerous cell
       growth 5:435
Viruses, Computer 6:393–94,
   397
Virus vaccines 5:238
Viscachas 5:6–7
Visceral muscles *see* Smooth
   muscles
Visceral pain 5:290
Visible light 3:273, 282
Vision 5:268–73
   aging 5:332–33
   bats 5:31
   birds 4:395
   brain 5:229
   color vision 3:301–3
   laser correction 5:489
   learning disabilities 5:364–65
   primates 5:137
   robots 6:201
   snakes 4:364
Vistaril *see* Dephenylmethanes
Visual acuity 5:273
Visual BASIC (computer lan-
   guage) 6:378
Visual purple 5:270
Vital capacity 5:218
Vitamin A 5:270, 383
Vitamin B_1 *see* Thiamine
Vitamin B_2 *see* Riboflavin
Vitamin B_6 *see* Pyridoxine
Vitamin B_{12} 5:211, 386
Vitamin B complex 5:384–86
Vitamin C 3:9; 5:282, 386–87
Vitamin D 5:184, 384
Vitamin E 5:384
Vitamin H *see* Biotin
Vitamin K 5:212, 384
Vitamin M *see* Folate
Vitamins 4:35; 5:383–87; 6:82
Viticulture 4:172
Vitreous humor 5:271

VIVERRIDS 5:84, 99–102
Viviparous lizards 4:362
Vocal cords 3:217; 5:217
Voice, Singing 3:210, 217
Voice chips 6:244
Voice mail 6:241
Volatile liquids 3:77
Volatile organic compounds
   3:73
Volcanic ash 2:56–57, 62, 220,
   433
Volcanic islands 2:282–83
Volcanic neck (Volcanic plug;
   Plug dome) 2:33, 56
Volcanic rock *see* Rocks—volca-
   nic rock
Volcanic vents *see* Vents, Volcanic
VOLCANOES 2:55–62
   Antarctica 2:92
   ash 2:433
   atmosphere, formation of 2:147
   climate changes 2:220
   earthquakes 2:47–48
   hot springs 2:64
   Io 1:138
   islands 2:281, 289
   lakes 2:108–9
   life, origin of 1:319; 3:380
   Mars 1:130
   Moon 1:121, 126
   mountains 2:67–68, 70–71
   oceans 2:279
   Owens River 2:5–7
   plateau formation 2:79
   plate tectonics 2:41, 43–44
   reef formation 2:286
   tsunamis 2:256
   Venus 1:101
   waterfalls 2:423
   illus. 1:135; 2:69–70, 148
   map(s) 2:57
   table(s) 6:429–30
Volcanoes, Submarine 2:58, 71,
   264, 270
   Indian Ocean 2:234
   oceans 2:69
   Pacific Ocean 2:275
   volcanic island 2:282–83
Volcanology 2:4
   illus. 2:3
Volkswagen (automobile)
   illus. 6:136
Volt 3:257
Volta, Alessandro (Italian physicist) 3:142, 251, 257
   illus. 2:311
Volta, Lake (Ghana) 2:110
Voltage 2:310–11, 317–20
   X-rays 3:277
Voltage multiplier 6:353–54
Voltaic cells 3:104–5, 252
Voltaic pile 3:251
Voltmeters 3:258
Volume
   cone 1:383
   cylinder 1:382–83

frustum **1**:383
ideal-gas laws **3**:72, 74
matter **3**:10
prism **1**:381–82
pyramid **1**:383
similar solid **1**:385
sphere **1**:385
table(s) **6**:425
Volumetric flask
illus. **3**:135
Voluntary muscles *see* Skeletal
muscles
Volvox **4**:49
illus. **4**:46
Vomiting 5:251, 355
Von Braun, Wernher (German-
American engineer) **1**:235,
265, 506
Vonnegut, Kurt, Jr. (American
writer) **1**:502
Von Neumann, John (Hungarian-
American mathematician)
1:331, 427
Von Ohain, Hans (German engi-
neer) **6**:106
Vortex machines
illus. **2**:193
Vorticella **4**:213
Voskhod spacecraft 1:244
Vostok spacecraft 1:241
Voyager (aircraft) **6**:230
Voyager (space probes) **1**:259,
292–94
auroras **2**:157
Jupiter **1**:134, 137–38
Neptune **1**:151, 154–55, 290
Saturn **1**:139–40, 143–44, 146
Uranus **1**:148–50
illus. **1**:242
V/STOL aircraft 6:161
Vulnerable species (IUCN defini-
tion) **2**:498
Vulpecula (constellation)
illus. **1**:184
Vultures 4:169, 391, 415–16, 418
illus. **3**:465; **4**:415
Vykukal, Vic C. (American engi-
neer) **1**:279

W

Wadis 2:85
Waialeale, Mount (Hawaii) **2**:171,
416
Waimangu Geyser (New
Zealand) **2**:66
Wairoa Geyser (New Zealand)
2:66
Waksman, Selman (American
biochemist) **5**:463
Waldeyer, Heinrich Wilhelm
(German scientist) **5**:310
Waldseemüller, Martin (German
cartographer) **2**:298
Walker, Charles (American engi-
neer) **1**:285
Walking (as exercise) **5**:398, 403

Walking ferns 4:82
Walking fish 4:335
Wallabies 4:140; **5**:18
Wallace, Alfred Russel (English
explorer-naturalist) **3**:502
Wallaroos 5:18
Wall creepers 4:457
Walruses 5:9, 63–64, 67–68
illus. **4**:186
Walsh, Donald (American naval
officer) **2**:276; **6**:123
Walt Disney Concert Hall (Los
Angeles, California) **3**:208
Walt Disney World *see* Disney
World
Walton, Ernest T. S. (English
physicist) **6**:353–54
Wandering albatrosses 4:446
Wankel, Felix (German engineer)
6:102
Wankel rotary engines 6:102
illus. **6**:101
Wapiti *see* American elk
Warblers 3:481; **4**:455
illus. **4**:454
Warfare
aviation **6**:154, 156
ships **6**:107–10
submarines **6**:118–22
Warfarin 5:467
Warm-blooded animals *see*
Homeotherms
Warm fronts 2:187
War of the Worlds, The (novel,
H. G. Wells) **1**:506
Warrigals *see* Dingoes
Warships 6:107–10
Warthogs 5:114
Warts 3:388
Washington (state, U.S.)
earthquakes **2**:52
fungal mats **4**:37
Mount St. Helens **2**:55
illus. **2**:60, 370
Wasps 4:280, 288–90
allergic reaction to sting **5**:448
asexual reproduction **4**:276
plant pollination **4**:158
diagram(s) **4**:289
WASTE DISPOSAL 2:483–92
energy **2**:307, 396–97
industrial chemistry **3**:9
microbiology **3**:449
oceans **2**:223, 230, 234–35,
464–65
plastics **6**:215
radioactive waste **2**:370–71
toxic waste sites **2**:489
water pollution **2**:457–62; **3**:85
illus.
radioactive waste **2**:370
Wastewater 2:485–89; **6**:64
Wasting syndrome 5:443
Watches *see* Clocks and watches

WATER 3:82–87 *see also* Ice,
Steam; Water (Hydrologic)
cycle
air circulation **2**:182–83
aquariums **4**:474, 476
camels' requirements **5**:117
chemical bonding **3**:47, 52, 57,
65
color **3**:296
conservation **2**:409–11
dams and reservoirs **6**:51–56
decomposition **3**:104
density **3**:183
desert animals **4**:169
under deserts **2**:86
distillation **3**:137
Earth **1**:106
entropy **3**:243
erosion **2**:416–25
excretory system **5**:258–59,
261–62
expands when frozen **3**:89
freezing **3**:88, 229
geothermal wells **2**:391
groundwater **2**:112–19
hard water **3**:30
heat conduction **3**:233
hot springs and geysers
2:63–66
hydroelectric power **2**:377–80
index of refraction **3**:285
ionic-compound solutions **3**:64
ionization **3**:97
lakes **2**:106–11
life, extraterrestrial **3**:382
mammals' requirements **5**:6
Mars **1**:130–31, 297, 320
molecule **3**:81
Moon **1**:114, 298–99
neutralization reactions **3**:96
nuclear reactors **2**:366–67
ocean **2**:228–35
oxygen isotopes' use in analysis of climates **2**:217
plant communities **4**:137
pollution *see* Water pollution
precipitation **2**:166–73
purification *see* Water purification
redox reaction **3**:101
rivers **2**:100–105
specific heat **3**:225
thermochemical equation **3**:59
vascular plants **4**:70–71
water supply **2**:434–50
weathering **2**:122
wetlands **4**:136–37, 150–55
diagram(s)
covalent bond **3**:50
Lewis structure **3**:65, 67
molecules in phase changes
3:227
Water beetles 4:293
**WATERBIRDS AND SHORE-
BIRDS 4**:432–46
Waterbucks 5:130
Water buffalo 5:133–34

Water bugs
  illus. **4:**196
Water bug traps (plants) **4:**111
Water cobras 4:373
Water (Hydrologic) cycle 2:100–
  101, 436–37; **3:**86
  atmospheric science **2:**145
  ecosystems **3:**488, 490
  rain forests' role **4:**161
  wetlands' role **4:**155
  diagram(s) **2:**436
Water debt 5:399
Water deer 5:121
Water-driven oil wells 2:324
WATER EROSION 2:416–25
Waterfalls 2:98, 102, 422–23
  cave formation **2:**129
  lake formation **2:**109
  illus. **2:**97, 102
Water ferns 4:79
Water filtration *see* Filtration,
  Water
Water fleas *(Daphnia)* **4:**250–51,
  255
Waterfowl 2:407–8; **4:**440–43
Water frames 6:189
Water gas 2:359
  illus. **2:**358
Water hyacinths
  illus. **4:**150
Water-jet technology 3:186
Water kingfishers 4:406–7
Water lilies
  illus. **4:**57, 110, 113
Water mains 2:450
Watermelons 6:68
Water mice 5:43
Water mills 6:7, 186
Water moccasins (snakes) **4:**374
  illus. **4:**373
Water molds 3:451, 455;
  4:51–52
Water moles 5:26
Water mosses 4:61
WATER POLLUTION 2:306–7,
  410, 457–65; **3:**85
  acid rain **2:**475–76
  agricultural runoff **6:**63–64
  algae **4:**47
  biological magnification **3:**489
  coral reef damage **2:**287
  eutrophication **2:**460–61; **4:**124
  fertilizers **2:**411–12
  geological careers **2:**6
  groundwater **2:**119
  industrial wastes **2:**462–64
  lakes **2:**111
  Mediterranean **2:**451
  ocean **2:**230, 234–35
  pesticides **2:**502
  rain water **2:**172
  rivers **2:**406
  sewage **2:**457–61
  wastewater **2:**486–87
  wetlands protect against **4:**155
  illus.
    industrial wastes **2:**452

Water power *see* Hydroelectric
  power
Water pressure 3:184
Water purification 2:442–48;
  3:87
**Water Resources Development
  Act** (U.S., 2000) **4:**155
Water scavengers 4:293
Watersheds (Divides) 2:101, 425
Water snakes 4:366, 371–73
**Water-soluble vitamins
  5:**384–87
Water spangles 4:79
Waterspouts (tornadoes) **2:**190
  illus. **2:**192
WATER SUPPLY 2:434–50
  engineering in the past **6:**17
  pollution *see* Water pollution
  purification **3:**87
  use per person **2:**409
  water cycle **3:**86
Water table 2:115
  wetlands **4:**150–51, 155
  illus. **2:**113, 115
Water turbines 2:316, 377
  diagram(s) **2:**313, 378
Water vapor 3:69
  atmosphere **2:**148–50, 171
  clouds and fog **2:**159–60, 164,
    167
  hurricane formation **2:**197
  graph(s)
    pressure-temperature rela-
      tionship **1:**336
Waterworts 4:73
Watson, James D. (American
  biochemist) **3:**6, 91, 117,
  411–12; **5:**309
  biology, history of **3:**370, 372
  genetics **3:**402
  illus. **3:**401; **5:**314
Watson, John B. (American psychologist) **5:**338
Watson, Thomas A. (American
  engineer) **6:**237
Watson-Watt, Robert A. (British
  physicist) **6:**255
Watt (unit of measurement)
  3:167, 257
Watt, James (Scottish inventor
  and engineer) **6:**97, 190,
  195
Watt-hour 3:258
**Watt-hour meters (Wattmeters)
  2:**319; **3:**258
Wave cycle 3:195
Wave function (in physics) **3:**337
Wavelength 3:195, 272
  sound waves **3:**198–99
  telescopes **1:**43–44
  visible light **3:**282, 293
  X-rays **1:**58
Wave mechanics 3:278–79
  electron behavior **3:**19
  light **3:**291–92
Wave-particle duality *see* Wave
  mechanics

Waves *see* Electromagnetic spectrum; Mechanical waves
WAVES, Ocean 2:250–55
  cave formation **2:**129
  coastal formation **2:**291–92
  coasts **2:**289
  earthquakes **2:**50
  erosion **2:**120, 124
  hurricanes **2:**200
  lakes **2:**106, 111
  physical oceanography **2:**223
  solitons **2:**221
  tsunamis **2:**256–59
  illus. **2:**123
    solitons **2:**226
Wave speed 3:196
Wave tanks
  illus. **2:**255
Wax
  beeswax **4:**287
  earwax **5:**277
  petroleum products **2:**333
  rain-forest products **4:**159
Waxwings 4:451–52
W-bosons (W particles) 3:21,
  311; **6:**358
Weak force 3:21
Weak interactions 3:307, 310–
  11, 338
Weasels 5:6, 93–94
  illus. **5:**95
Weather
  air pollution **2:**469–70
  archaeology **1:**464
  atmosphere **2:**149
  climates of the world **2:**207–14
  coastal formation **2:**290, 292
  convection currents **3:**235
  hurricanes and typhoons
    2:195–200
  precipitation **2:**166–73
  tornadoes **2:**189–94
  water's specific heat **3:**84
  weather forecasting **2:**201–6
  wind **2:**181–88
Weather balloons *see* Balloons
**WEATHER FORECASTING
  2:**142–44, 146, **201–6**
  atmospheric study **2:**153
  cloud patterns **2:**164
  computer modeling **2:**226
  hurricanes and typhoons **2:**200
  radar **6:**260–61
  tornadoes **2:**193–94
  waves, ocean **2:**255
Weathering 2:120–22
Weather modification 2:145–46
Weather satellites 1:312–14;
  2:164
Weaverbirds 4:396
  illus.
    nests **4:**461
Weavers (birds) **4:**461–62
Webcam images
  illus. **6:**391
Weberian apparatus 4:333
Web-footed tenrecs 5:28
Web pages 6:378

Webs, Spider see Spider webs
Web spinners 4:279
WebTV see MSN TV
Weddell Sea 2:91
Wedges 3:171–72
  illus. 3:173
Weeds 4:174
Week (time period) 1:476
Weevils 4:298–99
  illus. 4:299
Wegener, Alfred (German scientist) 2:38–39
Weight (in physics) 1:104
  gravity 3:178–81
  mass, compared to 3:11, 21
  Moon 1:125
Weight, Body
  AIDS 5:443
  low birth weight 5:301
  weight control 5:391–94
  table(s)
    healthy weights 5:392
WEIGHT CONTROL 5:391–94
  calories 3:61
  exercise benefits 5:402
Weightless Environment Training Facility 1:277
  illus. 1:273
Weightlessness 1:250, 253
Weight lifting 5:404
  illus. 5:397
Weight Watchers 5:394
Weinrich, M. (American physicist) 3:338
Welding
  lasers 6:348
Welles, Orson (American actor) 1:506
Wells (water supply) 2:116–17, 439–41
  contamination 2:119
  earthquake prediction 2:54
  geological effect 2:48
  hot water wells 2:391
Wells, H. G. (English author) 1:213, 500 501; 6:302
Welwitschia 4:96
Wertheimer, Max (Czech psychologist) 5:339
West African manatees 5:62
West Australia Current 2:239
Westerlies 2:184–85, 237
  diagram(s) 3:494
Western blot test 5:213, 444
Western ground snakes 4:371
Western larches 4:92
Western tanagers
  illus. 4:458
Western toads 4:348
Western yellow pines see Ponderosa pines
West Indian manatees 5:62
West Indies 2:281, 283
Westinghouse, George (American inventor)
  illus. 2:317
West Nile virus 2:481
  illus. 3:393

West Virginia
  wilderness areas 2:512
West Wind Drift 2:239–40
Wet cells see Secondary batteries
WETLANDS 2:407–8; 4:136–37, 150–55 see also Bogs; Marshes; Swamps
  illus. 3:496
Whale (nuclear submarine)
  illus. 6:122
Whalebone see Baleen
Whaler sharks see Bull sharks
WHALES 2:500–501; 5:8–9, 46–54 see also Dolphins
  blue whales 5:2
  classification 5:12
  fossils 1:482
  heart rate 5:197
  life span 5:324
Whale sharks 4:320, 327
Whale songs 5:47, 51, 56
Whaling 2:413; 5:54
Wheat 4:170, 172; 6:71
  illus. 4:19, 23
Wheat-barberry rust see Cereal rust
Wheel and axle 3:173
  automobiles 6:146
  Bronze Age 6:6
  illus. 3:174
Wheeler, John (American scientist) 1:204, 214
Wheeler, Sir Mortimer (British archaeologist) 1:468
Whelks 4:240
Whipple, Fred L. (American astronomer) 1:161
Whippoorwills 4:403
Whip scorpions 4:261–63
Whip snakes 4:366, 371
Whip spiders see Tailless whip scorpions
Whiptail lizards 3:457; 4:357
Whirlers see Shells (Whirlers)
Whirligig beetles 4:293
Whirlpools 2:248
Whiskers (of cats) 5:85
Whisk ferns 4:56, 82
Whispering galleries 1:378
Whistling hares see Pikas
Whistling swans 4:441
Whistling thorns 4:142
White, Edward H. (American astronaut) 1:244, 274
Whitebellies see Common dolphins
White blood cells 5:164, 207–8, 213
  blood diseases 5:211–12
  resistance to infection 5:426
  illus. 6:335
White dwarf stars 1:93, 192, 195, 205
  nova 1:197, 199
  plasma 3:13
  spectral lines 3:351
White firs 4:91

White-handed gibbons
  illus. 5:145
Whitehead, Robert (English inventor) 6:119
White House pets 4:488–89
White ibises 4:446
White light 3:295, 327
White-lipped peccaries 5:115
White matter 5:229–30
White mica 2:34
White pelicans 4:446
White pines 4:90
White rats 5:5
White rhinoceroses 5:113
  illus. 5:111
White Sea 2:229
White spruces 4:91
White-tailed deer 2:504; 5:121
  illus. 5:118
White whales see Beluga whales
Whitney, Eli (American inventor) 6:191
Whittaker, R. H. (American biologist) 3:399; 4:26
Whittle, Frank (British pilot) 6:106
Whole numbers see Integers
Whooping cough 5:430
Whooping cranes 2:502; 4:438
  illus. 4:438
Whorled leaves 4:70
Whorled pogonias
  illus. 2:496
Whydahs
  illus. 4:449
Wichita Indians 1:471
Wide-angle lenses 6:264
  illus. 6:267
Wide area networks 6:384–86
Wide Field/Planetary Camera 2 (WF/PC2) 1:49, 64, 138
Wideroe, Robert (Norwegian engineer) 6:354
Wien, Wilhelm (German physicist) 3:274
Wiener, Norbert (American mathematician) 6:196
Wild 2, Comet 1:161, 296
Wild and Scenic Rivers Act (U.S., 1968) 2:515
Wild-animal pets 4:490
Wild asses see African wild asses; Kulans; Onagers
Wild asters 4:125
Wild boars 5:114
Wild cats 5:92
Wildebeests 4:194; 5:130
WILDERNESS 2:506–15; 4:160
Wilderness Act of 1964 (U.S.) 2:507, 511, 515
Wildflowers
  illus. 3:481
WILDFOWL 4:422–27, 423
Wild goats
  illus. 5:10
Wildlife conservation 2:406–8; 4:468, 473, 477
  zoology, careers in 4:180

Wildlife Conservation Society (New York City) **4**:473, 477
Wildlife parks 4:472, 477
Wilkins, Maurice (British biophysicist) **3**:6, 412
Wilkinson, John (English inventor) **6**:191
Williamson, William Crawford (British naturalist) **1**:481
William the Conqueror (English king)
illus.
ship used by **6**:109
Will-o'-the-wisp 4:151
Willow bark 5:291
Wilmut, Ian (Scottish scientist) **3**:422; **6**:75
Wilson, Alexander (Scottish ornithologist) **4**:386
Wilson, Charles (Scottish physicist) **6**:359
Wilson, Christine (American astronomer) **1**:166
Wilson, Comet 1:166
Wilson, Robert (American scientist) **1**:20
Wilson, Volney (American scientist) **1**:229
Wilson cloud chamber 1:225, 227–28; **6**:359
Wilson's phalaropes 4:438
Winckelmann, Johann (German archaeologist) **1**:463
WIND 2:181–88
air pollution **2**:470
biomes **3**:493
cave formation **2**:129
climates of the world **2**:209–10
coastal formation **2**:290, 292
convection currents **3**:235
desert formation **2**:82–83
erosion *see* Wind erosion
human-caused changes **2**:146
hurricanes **2**:195–97, 199–200
iceberg movement **2**:261
jet streams **1**:105
lake formation **2**:110
ocean currents **2**:236–37
ocean waves **2**:250, 252, 254
pollination **4**:102
precipitation **2**:170
tornadoes **2**:190–92, 194
wind as power source **2**:387, 399
illus.
prevailing winds **3**:494
wind as power source **2**:302
Wind (research satellite) **2**:158
Wind-driven ocean currents 2:236–37
WIND EROSION 2:122–23, 426–33
Wind farms 2:387
illus. **2**:302, 399
Wind instruments 3:215–16
Windlass 3:173
illus. **3**:174

Windmills 6:186
illus. **3**:175
Windpipe *see* Trachea
Wind scorpions 4:261, 263
Wind shear 2:188
Wings (in aeronautics) **6**:158
Wings (in aviation) **3**:193
Wings (of animals)
bats **5**:29
beetles **4**:291–92
birds **4**:393
evolution **3**:502
insects **4**:272, 274
social insects **4**:281
Winter 1:110–12
clouds **2**:161
constellations **1**:32
jet streams **2**:150–51, 185
polar regions **2**:87
illus.
wind patterns **2**:184
map(s)
constellations **1**:34
Winter monsoons 2:183
Wireless communication 6:242–45
Wireworms 4:295
Wiring, Electric 2:319
Wisconsin 2:459
Wisdom teeth 5:280
Wisents *see* European bison
Withdrawal from drugs 5:375–77
nicotine **5**:371, 376–77
symptoms **5**:370
Wöhler, Friedrich (German chemist) **3**:107
Wolf, Max (German scientist) **1**:67, 168
Wolf herring 4:332
Wolf spiders 4:260, 262
illus. **4**:261
Wolverines 5:95–96
Wolves 2:505; **3**:396; **5**:78–79
domestication **4**:481
dominance **5**:10
evolutionary biology **3**:507
illus. **3**:481; **5**:5, 79
gray wolves **2**:505
Womb *see* Uterus
Wombats 5:20
illus. **5**:12, 21
Women (in biology)
aging **3**:468
AIDS **5**:444
breast cancer **5**:433
chromosomal defects **5**:314
infertility **5**:306–7
menopause **5**:333
osteoporosis **5**:184
pregnancy and birth **5**:297, 299–301, 304–5
puberty in girls **5**:331–32
sex organs **5**:294
illus.
sex organs **5**:295
Women astronauts 1:288–89
illus. **1**:286–87

Wood *see also* Lumber
breakdown by burning **3**:13–14
building techniques **6**:33–34
conifers **4**:90–93
construction materials **6**:23–24, 27–29
energy source **2**:398; **4**:146
petrified **1**:485
polymerization **3**:320
Wood, Ken (American botanist) **4**:2
Wood-boring beetles *see* Longhorned beetles
Wood Buffalo National Park (Alberta, Canada) **5**:133
Wood-chip oil 2:398
Woodchucks 5:41
Woodcocks 4:438
Woodcreepers 4:448
Wood ducks
illus. **4**:154
Wood frame construction 6:34, 36–37
Wood frogs 4:344
Woodland bison 5:133
Woodland Park Zoo (Seattle, Washington) **4**:474
Woodpeckers 2:501; **4**:194, 407–8
feet **4**:395
illus. **4**:392, 408
Wood-plastics 3:320
Woods Hole Oceanographic Institution 2:224, 242, 276, 278; **4**:314
Wood ticks 4:263
Wood warblers 4:458–59
Wool, Llama 5:117
Woolly bears (insects) *see* Tiger moths
Woolly daisies
illus. **4**:168
Woolly mammoths 1:499
Woolly monkeys 5:139
Woolly rhinoceroses
illus. **1**:499
Woolly spider monkeys 5:139
WORK (in physics) **3**:162–67, 168
Worker ants 4:281–85
Worker bees 3:457; **4**:286–87
Worker termites 4:290
Workstations, Computer 6:363, 386
World Calendar 1:478
World maps *see* Earth—*map(s)*
World Ocean Circulation Experiment (WOCE) 2:225
World's Fair (1939)
illus. **1**:502
World Trade Center (New York City) **2**:455
design for twin-towers' site **6**:22
World War I
aviation **6**:150–51, 154
sonar **2**:264, 273
submarines **6**:120

World War II
aviation **6:**151, 156
radar **6:**255
submarines **6:**120
World Wide Web 6:306–11, 378
World Wildlife Fund 2:514
Worm-eating warblers 4:459
Worm gears 6:145
Wormholes (hypothetical tunnels)
1:213–14
illus. **1:**210–11
Worm lizards 4:356–57, 359
Worms
annelids **4:**242–45
coast formation **2:**290–91
deep-sea worms **2:**278
fossils **1:**487
illus.
deep-sea worms **2:**275
Worms, Computer 6:392, 394
Worm snakes 4:371
W particles *see* W-bosons
Wrens 4:447, 452
Wright, Orville and Wilbur
(American aviators and
inventors) **6:**152
Wrinkles (in skin) **5:**264
illus. **3:**467
Wrists 5:179
Writing, Early history of 6:5–7
archaeology **1:**463
Writing disorders *see* Dys-
graphia
Wrought iron 6:178
illus. **6:**175
Wu, C. S. (American physicist)
3:338
Wundt, Wilhelm (German phi-
losopher) **5:**337
Wyoming 2:360

X-Y-Z

X.25 (computer packet switching
procedures) **6:**385
X-33 (aerospace plane) **1:**261–62
illus. **1:**261
X-43A (aircraft) **6:**106
Xanthophyll 4:18
Xbox (video-game system) **6:**301
X chromosomes 5:313–14, 319,
420–21
Xenarthra *see* Edentates
Xenon 3:33, 46, 319
Xenoy 6:228
Xerarch succession 4:123–24
Xerophthalmia 5:383
Xerophytes 2:214
Xerox Corporation 6:244
Xihoumen Bridge (China) **6:**50
XM (digital radio service) **6:**290
X-Men (film) **1:**506
Xochimilco, Lake (Mexico) **4:**351
X Prize 1:263
X-RAY ASTRONOMY 1:54,
58–59
black holes **1:**187, 212

telescopes in space **1:**51–52
X-ray diffraction 3:91, 281
analytical chemistry **3:**133, 136
biophysics **3:**145
illus. **3:**132
X-rays 5:412
astronomy *see* X-ray astronomy
CAT scans **5:**452–53
chromosome damage **5:**302
DEXA **5:**453–54
diagnostic imaging **5:**451–52
DSR and DSA scans **5:**453
electromagnetic spectrum
3:276–77
mammography **5:**459
organ transplants **5:**497
spacecraft **1:**251
stellar sources **1:**212
illus. **5:**450–51, 458
arthritic hands **5:**427
chest X-ray **5:**221
dentistry **3:**126
implanted pacemaker **5:**505
X-ray tomography 3:382
XV-15 (aircraft) *see* Tiltrotor
XV-15
Xylem 4:12, 65, 67, 88, 99
aging **3:**468
leaves **4:**70–71
stems **4:**69
Xylophones 3:216
illus. **3:**216
Yahoo! (Internet search engine)
6:308
Yaks 5:135
illus. **5:**6, 132
Yang, C. N. (American physicist)
3:338
Yangtze River 2:380, 410; **6:**22,
56
Yawing
illus. **6:**159–60
Yazoo tributaries 2:104
Y chromosomes 5:313–14, 319,
420
illus. **5:**322
Yeager, Charles (American avia-
tor) **6:**157
Year (time period) **1:**110–12,
474–78
Yeasts 3:455; **4:**37, 40–41
illus. **4:**39
Yellow baboons 5:142
Yellow-bellied sea snakes 4:374
Yellow fever 4:182, 269; **5:**431
Yellow jackets (insects) **5:**448
diagram(s) **4:**289
Yellow pines *see* Ponderosa
pines
Yellow River 2:105
Yellowstone National Park
(Idaho–Montana–Wyoming)
2:44, 63, 65, 509, 512
bison **5:**133
cyanobacteria in water **4:**33
microorganisms in water **3:**2
obsidian **2:**34

telemedicine **5:**493
illus. **2:**66
hot springs and geysers **2:**80;
3:8
mud pots **3:**78
sequoias **4:**1
Yellowstone Plateau 2:79
Yellowtail 6:90
Yellow-throated martens 5:95
Yellow warblers
illus. **4:**454
Yerkes Observatory (Wisconsin)
1:39
Yews 4:86, 89, 93
Yoga 5:404
illus. **5:**399
Yohkoh satellite 1:93, 301
Yolk 3:462
Yolk sac 5:297
Yorktown (ship) **6:**124
Yosemite National Park (Califor-
nia) **2:**509
Bridalveil Falls **2:**98
glacial erosion **2:**123
Young, John W. (American astro-
naut)
illus. **1:**281
Young, Leo C. (American physi-
cist) **6:**255
Young, Thomas (English physi-
cian and physicist) **3:**329
Yo-yo dieting 5:393–94
Ytterbium 3:46
Yttrium 3:46; **5:**488
Yttrium-barium-copper oxide
illus. **3:**359
Yucca moths
illus. **4:**169
Yucca Mountain (Nevada) **2:**307,
371, 490
Yuccas
illus. **4:**169
Yukawa, Hideki (Japanese physi-
cist) **1:**229
Zahniser, Howard (American wil-
derness advocate) **2:**510
Zambezi sharks *see* Bull sharks
Zarontin *see* Ethosuximide
Zarya (space-station module)
1:269
Z-bosons (Z particles) 3:21,
311; **6:**358
Zebra mussels 4:237, 239
Zebras 5:109–10
illus. **4:**141; **5:**5, 89
Zebus 5:134
Zeiss planetariums 1:67, 69
illus. **1:**67–68
Zeolite 2:447–48
Zephyr (train)
illus. **6:**127
Zeppelin, Count Ferdinand von
(German aeronaut) **6:**150
Zeppelin, Wolfgang von (Ger-
man aeronaut) **6:**151
Zeppelins 6:150
Zero 1:330

Zero-sum games 1:425–26
Zidovudine *see* AZT
ZIFT *see* Zygote intra-fallopian
 transfer
Zimbabwe 2:513
Zinc 3:46
 corrosion 3:103
 metals and alloys 6:182, 184
 secondary batteries 3:105
 soil pollution 3:129
 trace mineral 5:387
Zinc chloride 3:105
Zinc oxide 2:399; 3:103
Zircon 2:18
Zirconium 3:46
 artificial joints 5:503
 nuclear energy 2:366, 370–71,
 374
Z number *see* Atomic number
Zodiac
 Babylonian astronomy 1:472
 Chinese 1:478
 constellations 1:29–30, 32

Zodiacal light 2:153
Zollinger-Ellison syndrome
 5:246
Zoloft *see* Sertraline
Zombie computers 6:394
Zona pellucida 5:306
Zone of audibility
 illus. 3:204
Zone of silence 3:204
Zoogeography 2:300; 3:475
ZOOLOGICAL CLASSIFICATION
 4:198–205
ZOOLOGY 1:7; 4:178–82 *see
 also* Animals; names of ani-
 mals and groups of ani-
 mals
 biology 3:366, 372–73
 ecology 3:475
Zoom lenses 6:265
Zoom-lens microscopes
 5:494–95

Zoonoses 4:464–65
ZOOS 4:180, 338–39, **469–79**
Zoospores 4:48
Zooxanthellae 2:285, 287
Zoropterans 4:279
Z particles *see* Z-bosons
Zvezda (space-station module)
 1:269
Zweig, George (American physi-
 cist) 3:313
Zyban *see* Bupropion hydrochlo-
 ride
Zygomycetes 4:39, 41
Zygosporangia 4:39
Zygospores 4:48
Zygote intra-fallopian transfer
 (ZIFT) 5:307
Zygotes 3:445; 5:295
 algae 4:48
 embryology 3:459–60